To the Student:

This text was created to provide you with a high-quality educational resource. As a publisher specializing in college texts for business and economics, our goal is to provide you with learning materials that will serve you well in your college studies and throughout your career.

The educational process involves learning, retention, and the application of concepts and principles. You can accelerate your learning efforts utilizing the study guide that accompanies this text:

- Student Workbook and Study Guide, Second Edition.

This learning aid is designed to improve your performance in the course by highlighting key points in the text and providing you with assistance in mastering the basic concepts.

Check your local bookstore, or ask the manager to place an order for you today.

We at Irwin sincerely hope that the text and the accompanying Student Workbook and Study Guide will assist you in reaching your goals both now and in the future.

FOUNDATIONS OF BUSINESS LAW

Foundations of Business Law

SECOND EDITION

PHILLIP J. SCALETTA, JR.
Krannert School of Management
Purdue University

GEORGE D. CAMERON III
Graduate School of Business Administration
The University of Michigan

BPI
IRWIN

Homewood, IL 60430
Boston, MA 02116

Cover illustration: Barbara Maslen

© RICHARD D. IRWIN, INC., 1986 and 1990

Sponsoring editor: Craig S. Beytien
Project editor: Waivah Clement
Production manager: Irene H. Sotiroff
Designer: Diane Beasley
Artist: Mark Swindle
Compositor: Arcata Graphics/Kingsport
Typeface: 10/12 Galliard
Printer: Von Hoffmann Press, Inc.

Library of Congress Cataloging-in-Publication Data

Scaletta, Phillip J.
    Foundations of business law / Phillip J. Scaletta, Jr., George D.
Cameron III. — [2nd ed.]
        p.   cm.
    ISBN 0-256-08266-g
        1. Commercial law—United States—Cases.   2. Commercial law—
United States.   I. Cameron, George Dana, 1935–   .   II. Title.
    KF888.S32   1990
    346.73′07—dc20
    [347.3067]   89–18055
                                                                    CIP

Printed in the United States of America
1 2 3 4 5 6 7 8 9 0 VH 7 6 5 4 3 2 1 0

To our families, reviewers, adopters,
colleagues, and friends, for their suggestions,
support and understanding during the
years this book was in process.

Preface

The job of a Business Law author is a daunting one. Law schools have the luxury of three years in which to train lawyers. Even then, many law school students do not take courses on all the topics covered in the typical Business Law text. Every year, the body of the Law grows massively, with thousands of new cases, statutes, and regulations. In some areas, such as international trade, computers, and reproductive medicine, the Law is barely able to keep up with science and technology. (As examples, see the *Katsafanas* case in Chapter 6 and the *Whitehead-Gould* case in Chapter 50.)

In constructing a Business Law text, the author must first select the topics to be included. The choice is no longer as obvious as it once was (or seemed to be). Thirty years' worth of discussion has not improved our understanding of the phrase "legal environment," which is part of the AACSB standards for the Business School core curriculum. To some, it means that our students need study only the philosophy of Law, the structure of our legal system, and court procedures. Each of those topics is worthy, of course, and is covered in one or more semesters in Law School. But these do not seem to be the "core" topics for a business manager. A business manager is presumably engaging in business transactions—in other words, making contracts (or at least trying to). What's the "core" for that manager? What's the "bottom line"? What should a future manager find in the Business Law course which will help understand the process of running a business? One might readily agree that more undergraduates ought to study Jurisprudence, Legal Process, and Constitutional Law. The point is that those fine courses are not a substitute for the *core* Law course for business managers.

This book is premised on the idea that future business managers need to be made aware of the legal rules which most directly have an impact on their day-to-day business operations. Doing business *is* engaging in commercial transactions—by definition! What does the Law have to say about that process? *That's* the "core" for future business managers. Our major focus is therefore on these topics—Contract Law, Sales of Goods, Secured Transactions, Commercial Paper, Property Law, Agency, Partnerships, and Corporations. If doing business means making deals, future managers need to know how to do that; also, whether or not the deal is enforceable. (As examples of this focus, see the *Texaco* case in Chapter 9 and the *Carl Wagner* case in Chapter 39.)

We do not ignore the structure of our legal system and its procedures, but they are treated as introductory and supplementary topics, not as the core of the text. Chapter 1, for instance, contains an excellent discussion of how our case law system works, and how the various components—cases, statutes, and regulations—relate to each other. Similarly, Chapter 2 covers the structures of the national and state court systems, and civil procedure. Chapter 3 presents the major constitutional provisions which have an impact on business operations; and Chapter 4 shows how International Law is applied by our courts.

What about the major regulatory topics—Antitrust Law, Labor Law, Securities Law, Land Use Law—as parts of the "legal environment"? Since government does place significant restraints on transactions in each of these areas, we have included a separate chapter on each of these four topics. In each case, however, we have tried to place the chapter with the business activity being regulated. Land use regulation is part of the section dealing with ownership of property. Labor Law follows our discussion of agency and employment. Securities Law is found in the corporation section. Antitrust Law is part of the introductory section, both because it has important international effects and because it is a significant area of criminal liability.

The second key decision which the Business Law author must make relates to the format of our most important teaching tool, the court cases, and how they should be presented. Here again, there are a number of different approaches, but for this text, we wanted to use real cases. To us, that means that there must be a substantial section quoted from the court's actual opinion—to give the student a better sense of why the court felt its outcome was correct. We believe, the court cases are the best way to involve the students in the material, since they are real-life examples of the kinds of problems which confront business managers every day. We have used a combination of in-chapter "briefed" cases, with Facts-Issue-Decision-Reasons, and end-of-chapter discussion cases, which are divided into Facts and Opinion. The briefed format is easier to understand, since we identify the Issue and specify the Decision/result. The somewhat longer discussion case found at the end of most chapters can be used as a review of the chapter materials, and as a means of testing the students' understanding. We do not believe that the same level of student involvement can be achieved with cases which are nothing more than editorial summaries by the author.

Case selection is also important. Cases should be relevant to the point being made, but should also be interesting on the facts. Other factors being equal, a more recent case is probably preferable to an earlier one. We have tried to retain the best cases from the first edition, and have added nearly 100 new ones. Almost all of the cases in the three new chapters—Accountants' Liability, Decedents' Estates, and Insurance—are new to this edition. Many of the cases displaced from the first edition appear in this edition as end-of-chapter problems, so they can still be used for class discussion. (There are about 150 new problems in this edition.)

A new edition also involves updating of materials, and improving the text presentation of topics. In addition to the three new chapters noted above, we have made important revisions in Chapters 1, 2, 7, 9, 19, 23, 27, 31, 42, and 44. We have added notes on the important international developments in the areas of International Sales of Goods (Chapter 4) and European Products Liability (Chapter 20). We have resequenced the chapters on Commercial Paper.

Other, more subtle polishing has occurred as well, either on our own initiative or at the suggestion of our reviewers or adopters.

Finally, we needed to make decisions on how to present the material, particularly the types of learning guides which would be included in the chapters. Each Part commences with an Overview of what is contained in the chapters to follow. Each chapter then commences with a list of Objectives, to provide an outline and a focus. Important Terms are highlighted as mentioned in the chapter. Margin Notes emphasize major points being presented. There is a Lead-in for each briefed case in the chapter. Many chapters contain Exhibits to illustrate relationships between concepts, or to outline a series of points, or to show actual sample documents. Each chapter text concludes with a Significance paragraph, to explain why the chapter concepts are important, and how they fit into the larger topic. A list of Terms and Concepts appears at the end of each chapter, for review purposes. Also at the end of each chapter are four review Questions, to check understanding of major topics, and four review Problems, to test the students' ability to apply the materials to new fact situations. Appendixes include the U.S. Constitution, most of the Uniform Commercial Code, a Glossary, a Table of Cases, and an Index. Supplementary materials include a Student Workbook/Study Guide, an Instructor's Manual, Transparency Masters, and a Test Bank.

Our previous four texts have benefited greatly from the suggestions of our reviewers, adopters, and colleagues. We have been privileged to have had some of "the best and brightest" read and comment on our work. Again for this edition, the book has been strengthened by an outstanding team of reviewers: Denise A. Bartles, of Missouri Western State College; Ted Dinges, of Longview Community College; Jenelle M. Kurtz, of St. Cloud State University; Gene A. Marsh, of the University of Alabama; Dennis Pappas, of Columbus State Community College; and Clark Wheeler, of Santa Fe Community College. We especially want to thank them for their many thoughtful and perceptive comments and suggestions.

We also give special thanks and express our sincere appreciation to our wives and families for their encouragement and support.

Phillip J. Scaletta, Jr.
George D. Cameron III

Brief Contents

Contents

FOUNDATIONS OF BUSINESS LAW

PART ONE

Introduction to Law and the Legal System

Part One is designed to introduce you to the law and provide a basic foundation on which to build as you continue through the various specialized parts of this text. For example, Part Two, Contract Law, is a study of contracts and presumes the student has acquired the foundation of Part One.

Part One might be termed an introduction to the legal environment of business. It covers the definition of law and a comparison of law in the United States to that of foreign countries; the civil procedure followed in national and state court systems; the regulation of business by administrative agencies and the constitutional limitations on such regulation; the international legal implications the businessperson must be aware of when involved in trade outside of the United States; the problems of antitrust and trade regulation; criminal law and tort law; and accountants' liability.

All of these general areas comprise an important part of the environment in which a business operates on a day-to-day basis.

1

Legal Systems and Legal Sources

CHAPTER OBJECTIVES

THIS CHAPTER WILL:

- Define the term *law*.
- Discuss the sources of law in the United States.
- Outline the classifications of law.
- Explain the use of uniform laws in our legal system.
- Introduce the *Restatements of the Law* and their role in the legal system.
- Introduce the doctrine of precedent.
- Compare our legal system with other major types.

Today, in our modern society, the Law is everywhere. For better or worse, courts are deciding disputes arising out of all types of relationships and transactions. In New York, a court decides that New Zealand, rather than the San Diego entry, won the Americas' Cup yacht race. Meanwhile, the United States Supreme Court, and the U.S. court system as a whole, struggles to define the boundary between the rights of the fetus and the rights of the mother seeking an abortion.

Our focus in this book is on the Law as it relates to Business, but even with this limitation, the range of issues still staggers the imagination. The transactions we will consider cover the broadest possible spectrum, from the trivial, to the most intimate, to the very complex, to the international. Mr. Lefkowitz reads ads in his daily paper and goes to the store on two occasions to buy the advertised merchandise. When he leaves the store empty-handed and unhappy both times, he sues. What are his rights? (See the *Lefkowitz* case in Chapter 10.) Are contracts for so-called surrogate motherhood, by which a woman agrees to bear a child for someone else, legally enforceable? (See the *Whitehead-Gould* case in Chapter 50.) To what extent can computer programs be protected by patent or copyright? (See the *Apple Computer* case in Chapter 32.) Can a Japanese corporation be forced to defend a lawsuit in Illinois if one of its products causes injury there? (See the *Wiles* case in Chapter 2.) As you can see from just these few examples, we are going to be concerned with some interesting—and difficult—economic and social problems.

■ DEFINITIONS AND SOURCES

Blackstone's definition

In the broadest sense, *law* is a rough synonym for the noun *rule*. A law is a rule of conduct. In the physical sciences, one studies the "law of gravity" and other similar rules regarding the behavior of physical objects. We are concerned here with the rules for human and organizational conduct for which governmental sanctions are provided. As defined by the famous English jurist, William Blackstone, law is the expression of the country's sovereign, "commanding what is right and prohibiting what is wrong." In the United States, law is promulgated by the sovereign people, acting through their constitutionally selected representatives. The people as a whole, through our representatives, prescribe the rules of conduct for individuals and organizations.

Holmes' definition

Writing just before the turn of the century, Oliver Wendell Holmes, Jr., provided another famous definition of law: "The prophecies of what the courts will do in fact, and nothing more pretentious, are what I mean by the law." At the time, the courts were clearly the dominant legal institution in this country. Congress and the state legislatures were generally not inclined to interfere in individuals' private conduct or business affairs. There were very few regulatory agencies. Today, by contrast, the legal scene is much changed. Our legislatures have created hundreds of national, state, and local regulatory agencies that have the power to issue regulations, to decide matters under their jurisdiction, or to do both. These legislatures continue to pass more laws to tax and to regulate businesses and individuals. Clearly, today, the courts are only one source of law, although they do still set the ground rules for the operation of our legal system as a whole.

Hierarchy of sources

Constitutions, Statutes, and Cases. An organization's constitution contains its basic governing rules and the distribution of rights, powers, and duties. It is the "supreme law" for that organization. The United States Constitution expressly declares itself to be just that—"the *Supreme Law of the Land.*" Legal rules from any other source—national, state, or local governing bodies—can be challenged in court, and declared invalid, if they conflict with the provisions of the U.S. *Constitution.* Similarly, within each of our 50 states, that state's constitution is the supreme law (so long as it does not conflict with the U.S. Constitution). All actions by governmental (and other) organizations within that state must also conform to the legal rules contained in the state's constitution.

Statutes = legislative enactments

Statutes are Acts of Congress, and enactments by the state legislatures. Statutes are passed when the legislature perceives that some public problem has arisen and is not being solved properly (or at all) under the existing legal rule. The national Clean Air and Clean Water Acts of the 1970s are examples of this kind of legal rules.

Much of the Law is still found in the reported decisions of the national and state courts. Our system requires that judges give reasons for their decisions, that they explain where they found the legal rule they used, and how the rule applies to the facts of that case. These explanations then become the source of the rules for future cases that involve the same (or very similar) problems. This system of using prior cases is discussed in more detail later in the chapter, as the *"Doctrine of Precedent."*

Case law from prior court decisions

Treaties. Article II, Section 2, of the Constitution gives the President the power to make treaties; however, all treaties must be made with the advice and consent of the Senate of the United States. This source of law is increasingly important in our relationships with foreign nations, as treaties affect both military matters and our trade relationships with the other nations of the world. With today's satellite communication and computer networks interwoven across the globe, we need new international legal agreement on rules for conducting international business. Treaty power is an important way to meet those needs.

Internal effect of treaties

The treaty power of the United States is a source of law not only for international affairs but also for internal affairs. A treaty, once approved by the Senate, has the same force and effect as laws enacted by the U.S. Congress. Thus, a treaty concerning U.S. internal affairs is superior to any state law or any state constitution. Note that the State Supreme Court in the *LeBlanc* case recognizes and applies this rule to invalidate the State's "fishing license" requirement.

PEOPLE OF THE STATE OF MICHIGAN v. LEBLANC

248 N.W.2d 199 (Michigan, 1976)

FACTS Albert B. LeBlanc, a Chippewa Indian, was convicted for fishing without a license and for fishing with a gill net in violation of Michigan state law. He appealed on the basis that an 1836 treaty with the Chippewas granted them perpetual fishing rights, without restriction.

ISSUE   Is the treaty of 1836 granting fishing rights superior to Michigan law?

DECISION   Yes. The conviction for fishing without a license is reversed. The conviction for gill net fishing is remanded to the lower court to determine whether the statute outlawing the use of such nets is necessary to prevent a substantial depletion of fish supply. If the outlawing of such nets is necessary from a conservation standpoint, then that conviction will stand.

REASONS   The state claimed that language in an 1855 treaty with the Chippewas meant that they had surrendered their fishing rights. The Court of Appeals, however, disagreed with the state and the decision of the lower courts.

Justice Williams spoke for the State Supreme Court:
"Defendant's appeal of these convictions presents complex issues involving, on the one hand, the existence and continued vitality of fishing rights for Chippewa Indians under the Treaty of 1836 and the Treaty of 1855, and, on the other hand, the authority of the State of Michigan in the conservation of natural resources to regulate the exercise of whatever fishing rights remain reserved by the Chippewas under those treaties.

"Specifically, three central issues require resolution:

1. Did the Chippewa Indians, pursuant to the Treaty of 1836, in ceding their title to the territory involved, reserve the right to fish in the waters where defendant was arrested?

2. If such fishing rights were reserved by the Chippewas in the Treaty of 1836, were these rights relinquished by the Treaty of 1855?

3. If the Chippewas continue to possess reserved fishing rights, may the State of Michigan regulate the exercise of those rights, and if so, to what extent?

"We hold that the Chippewa Indians did reserve fishing rights in the waters where defendant was arrested pursuant to the Treaty of 1836, that these fishing rights were not relinquished by the Treaty of 1855, and that the State of Michigan has limited authority to regulate those rights, as described below.

"Specifically, with regard to the State's authority to regulate off-reservation fishing rights, the state regulation is valid only if:

1. it is necessary for the preservation of the fish protected by the regulation;

2. the application of the regulation to the Indians holding the off-reservation fishing right is necessary for the preservation of the fish protected; and

3. the regulation does not discriminate against the treaty Indians. . . .

"The United States Supreme Court [has] held as follows:

> [T]he right to fish at those respective places is not an exclusive one. Rather, it is one "in common with all citizens of the Territory." Certainly the right of the latter may be regulated. And we see no reason why the right of the Indians may not also be regulated by an appropriate exercise of the police power of the State. The right to fish "at all usual and accustomed" places may, of course, not be qualified by the State, even though all Indians born in the United States are now citizens of the United States. . . . But the manner of fishing, the size of the take, the restriction of commercial fishing, and the like may be regulated by the State in the interest of conservation, provided the regulation meets appropriate standards and does not discriminate against the Indians. . . .

"We affirm the Court of Appeals reversal of defendant LeBlanc's conviction for fishing without a commercial license. We also affirm the Court of Appeals remand to the District Court on the charge of fishing with an illegal device. The determination on remand of whether the application of the state prohibition against gill nets to the Chippewas is valid should be made in accordance with the standards set out in this opinion."

Administrative Agencies.   Another large body of law is created by the various regulations and pronouncements of administrative agencies, both national and state. On the national level we have agencies such as the National Labor Relations Board (NLRB), the Federal Trade Commission (FTC), and the Equal Employment Opportunity Commission (EEOC). On the state level we have agencies such as the Public Utilities Commission (PUC), the Workers' Compensation Board, and various consumer commissions.

Agency regulations as law

Administrative agencies are created by national or state legislatures, which delegate specific tasks and functions to the agency. The legislature may later limit the agency's authority or dispose of the agency entirely. We will discuss constitutional law and administrative agencies in more detail in Chapter 3.

State Legal Systems.   The Tenth Amendment to the Constitution provides that the powers not delegated to the United States by the Constitution or prohibited by it to the states are reserved to the states, respectively, or to the people. This amendment is often called the *states' rights amendment*. It allows the states to govern themselves in all areas where the Constitution does not specify national regulation. States may not enter into treaties, but other than that, their governments generate laws in much the same way as the national government. The state constitution provides the basic rules, the state legislature adopts statutes, the state courts decide specific cases, and the state administrative agencies adopt regulations to deal with problems in their assigned areas.

States' reserved powers

Public Law and Private Law

Rules for individual transactions

Most legal systems recognize two broad categories of legal rules: public law and private law. *Private law* is concerned with the legal relationships between individuals. The role of the government is limited to setting and enforcing the ground rules of the game; the decision on whether to "play" or not, with whom, about what, and on what terms is left to the individuals and organizations involved. For example, no one (as yet) orders you to buy a new TV. If you think you might want one, you decide on the make and model and then negotiate with one or more retailers to try to get the best price and terms. The role of the government in this private law transaction is limited to specifying the requirements for an enforceable contract and the remedies available in the event of a breach by one of the parties.

Government as a player

Public law areas, by contrast, involve the government acting in its sovereign capacity in some way—either as a contending party, or by forcing action or inaction, or by specifying the terms of a relationship. Criminal law, constitutional law, and administrative law are major public law areas. *Criminal law* involves the government as the prosecutor, claiming that a wrong has been done against society as a whole. *Constitutional law* provides the basic framework for the functioning of the government, as well as guarantees of rights and prohibitions against certain government actions. *Administrative law* covers all the areas of governmental regulation through administrative agencies. In the field of labor law, for example, the National Labor Relations Board (NLRB) polices union-management relations and the Equal Employment Opportunity Commission (EEOC) tries to prevent discrimination in employment. Although commercial law was (and perhaps still is) primarily a private law topic, there are now many important public law aspects in this field. We will examine most of these, as well as the more traditional public law areas such as labor law, antitrust

■ EXHIBIT 1–1
Relationships among Major
Areas of Substantive Law

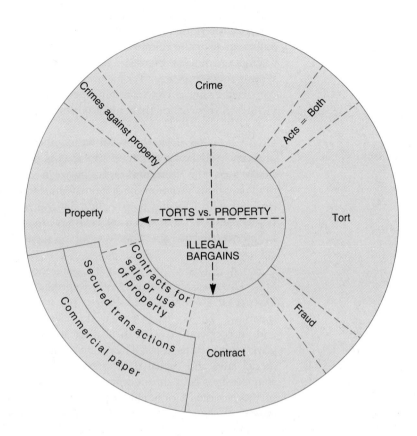

law, and securities law. These public law rules are sometimes called the "legal environment" of business.

Substantive and Procedural Law. Law is also classified as substantive law and procedural law. *Substantive law* defines the rights and duties of individuals and institutions in their mutual relationships. In a jury trial, for example, after the jurors have heard the evidence, the judge instructs them on "the law." The judge is giving them the substantive law of the case. In the same trial, *procedural law* governs the admission of evidence, the sequence of the lawsuit, and possible appeal. Procedural law can be defined as the law that governs the enforcement of substantive law. It is essentially concerned with the rules of the game, not necessarily the outcome. Procedural law will be discussed further in Chapter 2 when we review the court system and its procedure.

Substantive law can be further subdivided into criminal law and civil law.

Legal rights versus rules for enforcement

Criminal Law. Criminal law encompasses national and state statutes that make the commission or omission of certain acts punishable by fine or imprisonment. In criminal cases, the state or national government prosecutes the person who disobeyed the criminal law.

For example, Harry Horrible mugged a woman, took her pocketbook, and ran. The police arrested him and he was prosecuted for assault and battery and theft, found guilty, and sentenced to jail. The woman lost her purse and several dollars, missed several days of work at her job, and still has unpaid

Wrongs against society and wrongs against individuals

doctor and hospital bills because of her injuries. The criminal law does not give her the right to have her bills paid, to be compensated for her pain and suffering, or to be reimbursed for the cost of a new purse. Criminal law only attempts to fine or imprison the wrongdoer. The wrong being punished is a wrong against society. Today, some states do impose a requirement that the convicted criminal restore any property to the victim. Some states also permit victims to recover for their injuries from a state fund.

Civil Law.   Civil law provides for compensation for personal injury, loss of property, and breach of contract. This is the body of statutory and case law that sets out the rights and duties between individuals in society. For example, in the previous situation the state may put Harry Horrible in jail under criminal law, but who is going to pay the bills and reimburse the victim for her loss? Under civil law, more specifically tort law, the woman could sue Harry Horrible for monetary damages. This would be a separate lawsuit.

Uniform Laws.   The National Conference of Commissioners on Uniform State Laws was created in 1891. Representatives from each of the states, the District of Columbia, and Puerto Rico gathered to promote uniformity in state laws. The conferees reviewed the various state laws and judicial decisions and, in cooperation with the American Law Institute, drafted model statutes governing various areas. They then suggested that the states adopt these new model laws and repeal their previous laws. The ultimate goal was uniform state business laws throughout the country. The most notable accomplishment of the National Conference of Commissioners on Uniform State Law is the *Uniform Commercial Code,* which has been adopted in 49 states. Louisiana is the only state that has not adopted the entire Uniform Commercial Code. Other uniform laws deal with such topics as partnerships and decedents' estates.

UCC adopted

Restatements of the Law.   The American Law Institute has published treatises called *Restatements of the Law* covering many business related areas, such as torts, property, trusts, and agency. The American Law Institute's writers have attempted to review the vast volume of case law and to set out in organized, encyclopedia-like form the generally accepted rules of law on specific topics. These *Restatements* are not like the statutes of a state. They are only for reference and are periodically revised and updated. They serve a very useful purpose by allowing lawyers and judges to quickly see what the generally accepted rule of law is on a specific legal point. Judges often adopt the rules set out in the *Restatements,* thus making those rules part of the actual law. As of May 1989, for example, the Restatement of Torts had been cited by 7,410 U.S. courts and 16,029 state courts.

A.L.I. Restatements

■ **COMPARATIVE LEGAL SYSTEMS**

Historically, the two major types of legal systems that developed in Western civilization were the English common law and the continental European civil law. Within each of these groups there are, of course, variations from country to country—sometimes significant variations. England, for example, does not recognize the power of judges to declare legislative acts unconstitutional, but the United States does give its judges such power. In addition to these two major groups, the Communist legal systems constitute a third distinct type. Religious and customary legal systems still have considerable importance in many countries, particularly in Asia and Africa. There are also several countries whose legal systems are a blend of two or more types.

From country to country, the way the courts are structured, the method used for selecting judges, and the organization of attorneys vary. The legal rules may be very different: for example, in some Moslem countries the loss of a hand is the penalty for theft. Generally, however, for purposes of categorization, legal scholars rely on the differences in the structure of the law itself—specifically, differences in the *source* of the law. Who makes the law—judge, legislator, or administrator? What is the relationship of these three types of governmental power to each other? The answers to these two questions will usually place a particular country within one of the major categories.

■ ANGLO-AMERICAN LEGAL SYSTEMS

Although the terms are not precisely interchangeable since a few countries have a case-law system yet are clearly not "Anglo-American," most writers mean to identify the English common law when they speak of a common-law system. The key to a common-law system is the courts' decisions in actual cases that have been litigated in the past. Current cases are decided on the basis of the rules announced in prior ones. To produce fairness and predictability, the rule used yesterday to decide the case between Jones and Smith should also be used to decide the similar case which is now before the court between Green and Harris. The working presumption of the system is summed up in the Latin phrase *stare decisis:* "Let the decision stand."

Stare decisis

Doctrine of Precedent

Once a particular rule has been announced for a particular kind of case, that rule should generally be followed in future cases involving the same problem, unless there are compelling reasons for changing the rule. Confronted with a new problem that demands a solution, the judges try to reason by analogy from the older rules to develop the new rule for the new situation.

The *doctrine of precedent* operates in three different ways, or at three different levels: the effect of the decisions of a higher court on lower courts within the same system, the effect of prior decisions of the same court on a current case, and the effect of prior decisions in other states or countries on a current case. Where there is a clearly applicable precedent case, a lower court in the same jurisdiction should follow the precedent and apply the rule it establishes—100 percent of the time. In practice, the rule is not quite that simple because trial judges may try to avoid the precedent if they disagree with the result it produces in the case at hand. When that happens, the trial court will, of course, be reversed on appeal, unless the higher court wishes to change its mind and reverse or modify its own precedent.

Lower courts' use of appellate court precedents

Prior decisions of same appellate court

Typically, when judges, lawyers, and commentators speak of the doctrine of precedent they are referring to its second level of operation; that is, the relationship between prior decisions of the same court and the case which is to be decided now. What impact should these prior decisions in similar cases

■ **EXHIBIT 1–2**
Operation of the
Doctrine of
Precedent

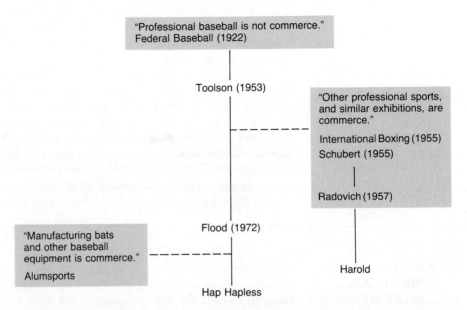

OPERATION OF THE DOCTRINE OF PRECEDENT

have on the case at hand? Most courts will follow their established precedent cases most of the time, particularly in the commercial law areas emphasized in this book. Societal changes since the precedent-setting decision may determine whether or not the court will follow a particular precedent. The U.S. Supreme Court was unanimous in overruling the clearly incorrect precedent established in the 1896 *Plessy* case.

BROWN v. BOARD OF EDUCATION OF TOPEKA

347 U.S. 483 (1954)

FACTS
This decision covers separate cases filed in Kansas, South Carolina, Virginia, and Delaware. In each of the cases black children seek the aid of the courts in obtaining admission to public schools of their community on a nonsegregated basis. The plaintiffs contend that segregated schools are not "equal," and cannot be made "equal." This segregation is alleged to deprive the plaintiffs of the equal protection of laws under the Fourteenth Amendment. The U.S. Supreme Court in the case of *Plessy* v. *Ferguson*, 163 U.S. 537 (1896), had found that equality of treatment is accorded when the races are provided substantially equal facilities even though these facilities are separate. This was the so-called separate but equal doctrine.

ISSUE
Was the Fourteenth Amendment right to equality under the law violated by segregated school systems? Should the precedent of *Plessy* v. *Ferguson* be followed or overruled?

DECISION
Yes. *Plessy* v. *Ferguson* is overruled as precedent.

REASONS
Chief Justice Warren said:
"Today, education is perhaps the most important function of state and local governments. Compulsory school attendance laws and the great expenditures for education

both demonstrate our recognition of the importance of education to our democratic society. It is required in the performance of our most basic public responsibilities, even service in the armed forces. It is the very foundation of good citizenship. Today it is a principal instrument in awakening the child to cultural values, in preparing him for later professional training, and in helping him adjust normally to his environment. In these days, it is doubtful that any child may reasonably be expected to succeed in life if he is denied the opportunity of an education. Such an opportunity, where the state has undertaken to provide it, is a right which must be made available to all on equal terms. . . .

"We conclude that in the field of public education the doctrine of 'separate but equal' has no place. Separate educational facilities are inherently unequal. Therefore, we hold that the plaintiffs and others similarly situated for whom the actions have been brought are, by reason of the segregation complained of, deprived of equal protection of the laws guaranteed by the 14th Amendment."

[This decision made segregation of public school systems illegal.]

Different facts = Different result

Courts are generally more willing to reexamine points of constitutional, criminal, and tort law than they are to upset established rules in contract and commercial law where parties have based business relationships on existing rules. In many cases, a court may not want to reverse its previous decision (as in the *Brown* case) because doing so might upset many other contracts and relationships; however, the court still may not want to follow its precedent. In such cases a court may use one of several devices to avoid the precedent. Occasionally, a court will simply ignore one of its own precedents, although this is hard to do if one of the lawyers has cited the precedent case in his or her legal brief or argument. The most common avoidance tactic is called ***distinguishing the precedent on the facts,*** meaning that the court shows how the precedent case really involved facts which were sufficiently different to justify a different decision. That process was used by the U.S. Supreme Court to distinguish baseball—which had been exempted from regulation by Congress as a result of a 1922 precedent—from all other professional sports.

All of court's opinion / The law

Another mechanism for avoiding an undesirable precedent is to ***distinguish the precedent on the law.*** The precedent is a precedent only for the rule of law that was actually necessary to the decision in the case. The judge writing the opinion of the court may have said a lot of things, but not everything in the opinion is necessarily a binding rule for future cases. These nonbinding "extra" statements in opinions are called *obiter dicta,* or just *dicta,* meaning that the court is saying things that are not actually necessary to decide the case. Perhaps the most famous example of such *dicta* is Chief Justice Marshall's opinion in *Marbury* v. *Madison,* reported later in this chapter. After commenting at length on the validity of Marbury's claim, Marshall said the Supreme Court was not in fact empowered to hear the case! Obviously, nothing in that opinion having to do with the merits of the case is "the Law" for future similar cases.

A brand new type of case

Finally, the doctrine of precedent operates in a third way. Suppose that the case which has to be decided today is unprecedented, that is, no decided cases in the state have ever dealt with the problem. The court can respond in two ways. One approach is simply to dismiss the complaint for failure to state a cause of action; this usually occurs where the plaintiff wants the court to recognize a new right or a new theory of liability. Where the underlying theory of liability has been recognized, but there is simply no case applying it to the given situation, the courts will use precedents in a third way—by borrowing some precedent from other states, or even from other countries, particularly from countries with similar legal systems. However, it is important to note that one state's decisions are not binding rules in a second state unless and until courts in the second state accept them as precedents in cases decided there.

The New York judge in the *Cohen* case was faced with an "unprecedented" problem.

COHEN v. BAYSIDE FEDERAL SAVINGS AND LOAN ASSOCIATION

309 N.Y.S.2d 980 (New York, 1970)

FACTS   Richard Alan Rothchild became engaged to be married to Carol Sue Cohen, the plaintiff in this action. Both were over 21 years of age. Richard gave Carol a diamond "engagement" ring which was valued at $1,000. Shortly before the wedding date, Richard was killed in an automobile accident. Carol began this action to establish her right to the ring.

ISSUE   Can an engagement ring, given in contemplation of marriage, be recovered from a "donee," by the estate of the "donor," when the contemplated marriage fails to occur because of the death of the "donor"?

DECISION   Judgment for Carol, the donee.

REASONS   **Justice Tessler recognized he was going to have to make his own decision.**
"[R]eference to [the] common law rules formulated prior to 1935 is of little help in the present instance since this case appears to be one of first impression in this State. In the absence of any controlling authority, this court has sought help by looking to applicable decisional law in other jurisdictions, the general principles underlying engagement ring cases in general, and, finally, to what justice requires in this situation.

"An examination of the relevant authorities in other states indicates that they are split. . . .

"Nor does an examination of the principles underlying the gift of engagement ring cases in general clearly point the way to a particular result. . . .

"Thus, a confusing body of law has grown up around the engagement ring and, after careful consideration of these principles, this court has decided that Carol should keep the ring because that result is equitable and because 'justice so requires' for the following reasons: While the engagement ring to some people in the mod world of today is just another material possession, and while it has not been unknown in some circles for recipients of these rings to flaunt them, to compare their luster, number of carats, etc., with the rings of their friends, for the vast majority the ring still remains a hallowed symbol of the love and devotion that a prospective husband and wife bear for each other. In my judgment, no gift given during a lifetime can approach the meaningfulness and significance of the engagement ring. When Richard gave the ring to Carol, he obviously intended that she have it and keep it unless she affirmatively did something to prevent the marriage of the parties. While it is improbable that at the time of the gift either gave a thought to the consequences that would arise in the event of the death of one of the parties, I firmly believe that had Richard thought of these consequences he would have intended that in the event of his untimely death Carol should keep the ring as a symbol of this love and affection. There appears to be no reason, in logic or morals, to prevent such a result.

"This court frankly acknowledges that implicit in this determination is a recognition that the gift of an engagement ring is a special occasion interwoven with romance and mutual love. It is a meaningful act symbolic of much more than the ordinary and usual business transaction. . . .

"I cannot believe that the age-old ritual of giving an engagement ring to bind the mutual premarital vows can be or is intended to be treated as an exchange of consideration as practiced in the everyday marketplace. Can it be seriously urged that the giving of this ring by the decedent 'groom' to his loved one and bride-to-be can be treated as the ordinary commercial or business transaction requiring the ultimate in consideration and payment? I think not. To treat this special and usually once in a lifetime occasion as one requiring quid pro quo, is a mistake and unrealistic."

Distinction between Law and Equity

In addition to the doctrine of precedent, a second distinguishing characteristic of an Anglo-American legal system is the distinction between "law" and "equity." This distinction occurs only in civil cases, not in criminal law. It is the result of a special combination of historical circumstances in England, during the formative years of the common law. There is no logical reason for the existence of the two separate types of cases; indeed, the distinction was abolished in England by Act of Parliament in 1873, after 500-some years of existence. However, this dualism was frozen into American law by the adoption of the Seventh Amendment to the U.S. Constitution and similar provisions in state constitutions.

Trial by jury—A constitutional distinction

The distinction arose because the king's common-law courts had not been authorized to hear all types of cases and to grant all types of remedies. The common-law courts acquired their subject-matter jurisdiction grudgingly from the older feudal courts, sometimes only after a considerable political struggle. For many litigants, however, the common-law courts were a more desirable forum for the resolution of disputes. Tenants might not feel that they could get a fair hearing in a manorial court presided over by their landlord, the local earl or baron. Common people almost certainly preferred the trial by jury used in the common-law courts to the trial by combat or trial by ordeal used in the older courts. Thus, litigants wished to use the common-law courts.

Need for equity

To have a case heard by the common-law courts, however, the prospective litigant had to fit his or her claim into one of the recognized "writs," or forms of action. The litigant had to show, in other words, that the case was one of the kinds which the common-law courts had been authorized to hear. Since at one time there were numerous different writs, sometimes differing from each other only in seemingly insignificant details, this was not always an easy process. Use of the wrong writ was usually fatal to the plaintiff's case. If no writ was available that described the plaintiff's fact situation and granted the desired relief, the plaintiff was out of luck—at least as far as the common law courts were concerned.

■ **EXHIBIT 1–3**
English Legal System
(1350–1873)

Criminal Law	Civil Law				
	Common law writs (forms of action)				Equity
	Assumpsit	Trespass	Replevin	Ejectment	
	contract dollar damages	tort dollar damages	return of personal property	return of real property	
JURY	JURY				NO JURY

At some point in the early to middle 1300s, dissatisfied or potential litigants discovered an alternative avenue for resolving their grievances. Since the king was the "fountain of Justice," why not petition the king directly and ask him to solve the problem? The king, acting through his chief legal official, the chancellor, did in fact recognize such petitions, or at least some of them. In time, additional judges were hired to staff this new court, which became known as the Chancery Court or the **_Equity Court._** The basic idea justifying the new court was that it heard only those cases for which the common-law courts provided no remedy at all or only an inadequate one. In such cases, the Chancery Court was empowered in the king's name to hear the dispute and to issue whatever orders were necessary to resolve it. This alternate court thus provided the needed flexibility in a system that had grown extremely rigid and had failed to develop new remedies to meet new problems.

Equitable remedies

The two major new remedies developed by the equity court were the **_injunction,_** by which the court orders a person to do something or to stop doing something, and **_specific performance,_** by which the court forces a party to do what he or she has contractually promised to do. Neither of these special types of court orders were given by the old common-law courts. The equity courts also developed many other special remedies, many of which will be noted in later chapters.

While court procedure was generally less formal in the equity courts, the major procedural distinction, and the one that got frozen into the constitutions in the United States, was that no jury was used by the equity courts. The equity judge could use an individual fact finder, or "master," and was authorized to empanel an *advisory* jury if he wished to do so. In contrast to the common-law courts, however, the equity judge was in no way bound by the jury's determination. The equity judge was still free to enter his own decision on the facts of the case.

Merger of law and equity

Although, as indicated previously, England has no more separate equity court, the distinction is alive and well in the United States. While Congress and the state legislatures have the power to combine the courts and the judges organizationally, and to provide for a unified system of civil procedure, a legislative body in this country cannot unilaterally amend a constitution. Thus, without a constitutional amendment, there is no way to overcome the requirement in the Seventh Amendment that cases "at common law" and involving $20 or more, be tried to a jury. State civil procedure systems are bound by similar provisions in state constitutions. Thus, if at least one of the litigants in a civil case demands a trial by jury, the trial judge must make an initial determination as to whether the case is of a type that was heard "at common law" under the old law-equity dual system. If it is, the trial court judge has no discretion; the case must be tried to a jury. If the case is one that would have been heard in an equity court, or one involving a newly created statutory right that was unknown at common law, the Constitution does not require a trial by jury. For these non-common law cases, the legislature is free to specify whatever method of trial they wish.

Trial by Jury

The trial by jury is a third distinguishing feature of an Anglo-American legal system. While early Greek law used a vote of all assembled freemen to decide some trials (you may recall that Socrates was condemned to drink poisonous hemlock), and while other systems have used and do use some form of the jury, it has a very special place in the historical development and the current operation of the Anglo-American legal system.

Historically, the jury developed as an important check against the arbitrary exercise of governmental power, both in England and in the United States. Particularly in criminal cases, this function continues to be exercised by the jury today. In civil cases, the jury injects into the legal system the "conscience of the community" on such matters as the standard of care expected of an ordinary reasonable person.

Jury's power

In no other legal system does the jury have the power to hear such a wide range of cases. All but the most minor criminal violations are triable to a jury. Many violations of agency regulations are also subject to trial by jury. It is true that a litigant seeking a special equitable remedy will not have the right to a jury in most states, but that exception still leaves most ordinary civil cases subject to a trial by jury. The ordinary civil lawsuit for money damages for tort or for breach of contract is required to be tried to a jury if either litigant demands one. (Many states, however, do not use a jury in their small claims courts, where only a limited dollar recovery is permitted, usually $1,000 or less.)

Likewise, in no other system is the jury given as much discretion in arriving at its verdict, or is the verdict given the same finality, as in an Anglo-American system. If the plaintiff alleges facts which state a valid legal claim, and then at the trial introduces some minimal evidence in support of those allegations, the result in that civil case is up to the jury. The trial judge will instruct jurors as to what the law is and what their options are, and in some states may even comment on the weight of the evidence presented, but the jury will decide the outcome. There are some procedural safeguards against obviously incorrect verdicts, but in the vast majority of cases the judgment will be entered based on the verdict of the trial jury.

Judicial Review

There are, of course, differences from country to country within the Anglo-American legal family. Again, England no longer uses the distinction between law and equity. It also rarely uses the trial by jury for civil cases, in contrast to the United States. Perhaps the most significant difference, however, is that Great Britain does not recognize *judicial review:* the power of the courts to declare legislative acts unconstitutional. As in most parlimentary systems, the

Court review of statutes

legislature is the final source of political power (other than the people as a whole); the courts are subordinate to the legislature.

Under the separation of powers doctrine, U.S. courts have the power to invalidate legislative as well as administrative acts, found to be in conflict with the Constitution. State courts have similar power under their state constitutions. Moreover, the issue of constitutionality may be raised by any litigant in any sort of case. A debtor whose car is repossessed because monthly payments were not being made may ask a state or national court to declare that the repossession procedure provided by state law violates the due process clause of the U.S. Constitution, for example. While a few countries have so-called constitutional courts, their jurisdiction can be invoked only in a special, limited procedure. Judicial review as it is practiced in the United States is still a unique institution.

The *Marbury* case was the first use of this unique power by the U.S. Supreme Court.

MARBURY v. MADISON

5 U.S. (1 Cranch) 137 (1803)

FACTS   Thomas Jefferson, a Democratic-Republican, was elected President of the United States in the election in 1800. He defeated John Adams the incumbent President who was a Federalist. After the election, the Federalist-dominated Congress, to assure Federalist control of the judiciary, created 58 new judgeships in early 1801. Departing President John Adams was still signing the commissions to be delivered to the new judges on March 3, the eve of the inauguration of President Jefferson. The commission of William Marbury and three others had been signed by Adams but not yet delivered. James Madison, the new Secretary of State under Jefferson, discovered these signed but undelivered commissions, and President Jefferson told him not to deliver them. Mr. Marbury then sued Secretary of State Madison under a provision of the Judiciary Act of 1789, which authorized the U.S. Supreme Court to issue a writ of *mandamus* to order a public official to do his official duty, namely deliver the commissions to the appointed judges. This action was brought as an original action in the Supreme Court.

ISSUE   Does the U.S. Supreme Court have jurisdiction to issue writs of mandamus in original proceedings?

DECISION   No. Case dismissed.

 REASONS   Chief Justice Marshall (who had also been acting as secretary of state and had caused the problem by not delivering the commissions in the first place) first used the opinion to chastise Madison and Jefferson for their wrongdoing. He reviewed the applicability of the writ of mandamus to Executive officers. He then dismissed the case because the Supreme Court could only exercise original jurisdiction given by the Constitution. Therefore, the section of the 1789 Judiciary Act that purported to give the Court the power of mandamus was unconstitutional. Only his reasons for dismissing the case are "the Law" in the *Marbury* decision.

"If an Act of the Legislature, repugnant to the Constitution, is void, does it, notwithstanding its invalidity, bind the courts, and oblige them to give it effect? Or, in other words, though it be not law, does it constitute a rule as operative as if it was a law? This would seem . . . an absurdity too gross to be insisted on. . . .

"It is emphatically the province and duty of the judicial department to say what the law is. Those who apply the rule to particular cases, must of necessity expound and interpret that rule. If two laws conflict with each other, the courts must decide on the operation of each.

"So if a law be in opposition to the Constitution; if both the law and the Constitution apply to a particular case, so that the court must either decide that case conformably to the law, disregarding the Constitution; or conformably to the Constitution, disregarding the law, the court must determine which of these conflicting rules governs the case. This is of the very essence of judicial duty.

"If, then, the courts are to regard the Constitution, and the Constitution is superior to any ordinary Act of the Legislature, the Constitution, and not such ordinary Act, must govern the case to which they both apply."

■ OTHER LEGAL SYSTEMS

Codes of law

Court cases in a civil-law system

Civil-Law Systems. The other major type of legal system that developed under Western civilization is called the civil-law system, or the code-law system. There is some ambiguity in either term. All legal systems hear and decide civil-law cases, in the sense of disputes between individuals, and many countries refer to their statutes dealing with particular topics as "codes." A civil-law or code-law *system,* however, is one in which the body of the legal rules is contained in one or a few comprehensive legislative enactments. All the law is brought together at one time, in a systematized statement of the applicable legal rules. In France, for example, the process occurred in the early 1800s, under Napoleon's reign. National legal codes for the whole of France were adopted, covering civil law, civil procedure, criminal law, criminal procedure, and commercial law. The civil code is still the basic law in France today; the same rules would be applied to work out much the same results in ordinary cases of tort and contract. (See Exhibit 1–4.)

Court cases in such a system are not considered to be an authoritative source of the legal rules, as they are in an Anglo-American system. The fact that a particular court interpreted a particular provision of the civil code in a particular way does not mean that future courts are bound to interpret that provision in the same way. They may or may not do so. The law is in the code, not in the cases. Where *several* cases all have interpreted a provision in a particular way, the French courts may feel bound to reach the same result in future cases, under the doctrine of *jurisprudence constante.* The major agency for growth and change, however, is the legislature, not the courts.

Civil-law systems are used by most of the countries of Western Europe, and Central and South America. Many of the countries of Asia and Africa adopted civil and commercial codes patterned on those of Western Europe to facilitate business transactions and commercial development. Japan and Thailand adopted most of the German Civil Code. So did pre-communist China. Turkey used the Swiss Codes and later added a commercial code based on the German

■ EXHIBIT 1–4
Other Legal Systems

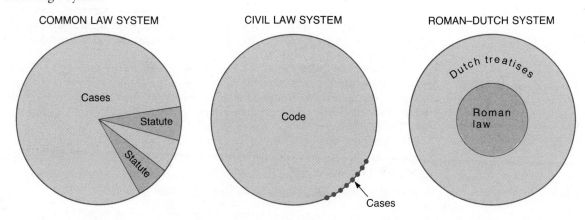

one. Many countries which were colonies have residues of the codes that were imposed on them during their colonial period.

Roman-Dutch Systems. As the result of another historical combination of circumstances, a very few countries today operate under what is called a Roman-Dutch System. These are former Dutch colonies, which were under Dutch rule at a time when the Netherlands had not yet adopted its modern civil code. (It did so in 1823.) The Dutch system at the time was based on the Roman law, as explained and developed by Dutch commentators. Several centuries of Roman legal developments had been summarized and systematized under the Emperor Justinian in the *Corpus Juris Civilis,* published from 529 to 534 A.D. The Dutch scholars then wrote comments explaining how the various Roman law rules applied in their country. Under this system, the "law-giver" is the professor, not the judge and not the legislator. The judges should be guided by the authoritative textbook statements as to what the law is and how it is to be applied. The legislature of course has the power to change the law by enacting statutes, but until it does so, the law is in the textbooks.

This rather strange system exists, at least in residual form, in the former Dutch colonies of South Africa and Sri Lanka (Ceylon) and, perhaps, in Guyana.

Soviet Legal Systems. While Communist theory initially emphasized a future society in which there would be no need for Law and the other organs of state power, the reality of governing a large and diverse empire has forced some rather dramatic doctrinal and operational changes. Prior to the Bolshevik Revolution in 1917, Russia had been slowly developing as a civil-law system. Tsarist Russia was an autocracy of the most extreme sort for most of its history, but some substantial progress toward the development of an independent Bench and Bar had been made with the reforms of 1861 and 1864. Presumably, further progress along these lines would have been made under the non-Bolshevik revolutionaries.

During most of its history, the Bolshevik regime has wavered between the

Roman law, plus Dutch texts

Socialist law

ideological purity expressed in the idea that the law would "wither away" after the Revolution, and the practical necessities involved in ruling the Soviet Union. Stalin decided in the 1930s that he needed a stronger state apparatus, rather than a "withered" one, and the concept of "socialist legality" was emphasized. Socialist law was to be developed as law of a "new type," not based on the exploitation of one class by another, as were all "bourgeois" legal systems. This new legal system was to function in the interim period between the Revolution and the achievement of the stage of full Communism. Officially, the law is still supposed to "wither away" at some future date, but the time frame is rather indefinite. For the present, the practicalities of governance have prevailed over ideological purity.

How, then, does Soviet/Socialist law differ from other systems? First, of course, its theoretical underpinnings are quite different. Justice is a bourgeois abstraction; Soviet judges should be guided instead by their revolutionary legal consciousness. Second, all governmental agencies and institutions are really sources of legal rules; the decree or order of a lower level agency stands as the rule to be obeyed, unless and until it is superseded by a rule from a higher authority. Third, and perhaps most significant, the government and the party are above the law, rather than the other way around. One would find it hard to imagine, for instance, that any Soviet court could order Gorbachev to produce documents that he wished to keep secret, as happened to President Nixon. Fourth, as a corollary, the Bench and Bar in the USSR are not fully independent of governmental and political control. While Soviet lawyers have some considerable latitude in handling ordinary contract, tort, and property cases, they cannot function as the fearless champions of civil rights. As a result, there is a fifth dissimilarity from Western systems: civil rights are granted or withheld by the Soviet regime to suit its own political and economic purposes; they may be exercised only in accordance with the wishes of the regime.

The Soviet system does have codes which have been adopted by the legislative bodies (although they may not be organized in quite so comprehensive a fashion as those in most civil-law countries). It does have courts, judges, and lawyers. In recent years, the regime has seemed to give the legal experts more freedom to operate. None of these surface similarities, however, should be allowed to obscure the fundamental differences that remain.

Religious and Customary Systems.   For hundreds of millions of people, a religious or customary legal system provides the rules for their personal rights and behavior. Such topics as parent-child and husband-wife relationships, inheritance and other property rights, charitable transfers, and an individual's relationship with a religious organization are likely to be covered under these systems. A religious or customary system typically does not cover the legal topics involved in modern commerce and industry—business organizations, commercial contracts, patents and copyrights, and the like.

Customary or tribal law still governs the personal lives of many Africans. In the Moslem countries of North Africa, the Middle East, and the rest of Asia, the *Koran* provides an authoritative source of legal rules for the topics which it covers. In India, Hindu law applies to the vast majority of the population. Jewish law contains provisions for marriage, divorce, and charitable giving which many of that faith feel are binding legal rules. Tribal law is still applied in many cases involving the personal or property rights of American Indians.

Mixed Systems.   Because of the worldwide dispersal of legal, political, economic, and social ideas, many countries today have what might be best described as a "mixed" legal system. After the Dutch had imposed their Roman-Dutch legal system on the island of Ceylon, for example, the island became an English colony. English commercial statutes like the sales of goods act were adopted for Ceylon by the new colonial power. Both of these colonial legal systems continued to coexist with several early customary systems that predated the Dutch. The English commercial statutes were also adopted for India during its colonial period; since independence, India has patterned many of its constitutional law concepts on those of the U.S. Supreme Court. Iraq patterned its commercial code after that of France. And so it goes.

India and Ceylon

As a result, any U.S. business engaging in international commercial transactions needs to be aware of exactly what set of rules will apply to the particular activity involved. U.S. personnel traveling to, or stationed in, a particular country need to be carefully briefed on what behavior pattern is expected and acceptable. Competent counsel needs to be engaged prior to the undertaking of any such international business activity.

In the following case the defendant is attempting to introduce Jewish law as the controlling law concerning the transaction between the parties.

CONGREGATION B'NAI SHOLOM
v. MARTIN

173 N.W.2d 504 (Michigan, 1969)

FACTS

In January of 1959, defendant Morris Martin became chairman of the Synagogue Building Committee. On April 22, 1959, plaintiff contracted Ira J. Miller, a professional fund raiser, to assist in raising funds to build a new synagogue. On or about June 1, 1959, Morris Martin delivered to plaintiff's campaign office four pledge cards. The first three were signed, respectively, by Irving Martin, Jack Martin, and Morris Martin. The fourth was signed by Morris Martin in the name of Bessie Martin Steinberg. The four pledge cards were not filled out as to amount. Morris Martin wrote the words, "Total Donation $25,000.00" on an attached scrap of paper. Later in the year 1959, disputes arose between Morris Martin, chairman of the Synagogue Building committee, and other members of the Congregation. On October 29, 1959, and again on November 8, 1959, Morris Martin attempted to withdraw the pledge.

On December 20, 1962, plaintiff, a nonprofit corporation brought suit against Morris Martin, Irving Martin, Jack Martin, and Bessie Martin Steinberg. On November 17, 1965, the defendants filed a motion to amend their answer, which the trial judge denied. On August 24, 1966, the trial judge issued an opinion in which he granted judgment in favor of plaintiff against defendant Morris Martin for the sum of $25,000, plus interest at 5 percent from June 30, 1964; Morris Martin was granted the right within 30 days to introduce a third party action for contribution from defendants Jack Martin and Irving Martin. Appeal was taken from the judgment in favor of plaintiff and against Morris Martin to the Court of Appeals, which affirmed the trial judge. The case was then appealed to the Michigan Supreme Court.

ISSUE   Should the defendants have been permitted to amend their answer so as to raise the application of Jewish Law as a defense?

DECISION   Yes. Judgment reversed, and case remanded for further proceedings.

REASONS   **Justice Adams was convinced that the lower courts had made a mistake.**
"The trial judge erred in denying defendants' motions for leave to amend for the reason that the affidavit of Dr. Rabbi Bernard B. Perlow raised a question of fact as to Jewish custom which may be controlling upon the parties. . . .

"The defendants' motions to amend were supported by the affidavit of a Dr. Rabbi Bernard D. Perlow, a rabbi and a scholar. After stating his qualifications as an expert witness, he included the following points in his opinion:

> 5. That the religious customs, practices, and laws binding on all Jews are codified in the work known as the *Shulchan Aruch;* that this code is generally regarded as binding as a matter of religious faith by both Orthodox and Conservative Jews . . .
> 6. That in the opinion of this deponent, the *Shulchan Aruch,* as well as the custom and tradition for more than a thousand years, prohibits the bringing of a suit in the civil courts of any state by a synagogue against any of its members or vice versa and is contrary to Jewish law and is prohibited; that any such civil controversy must be first brought before the Jewish religion court known as the Beth Din (a Jewish rabbinical court); that under Jewish law, matters of charity to the synagogue go to the heart of the Jewish religion; that a charitable contribution to a synagogue is considered a religious matter by and between the synagogue and the member; that for a synagogue to file a suit against one of its members upon an alleged charitable contribution without submitting it to a Beth Din is what is known in Jewish law as a "Chillul Hashem" which is a profanation of God's name and such action is such a grave sin in Jewish law, that it warrants excommunication. . . .
> 7. That it is expressly stated in Hyman E. Goldin's translation of Rabbi Solomon Ganzfried's *Code of Jewish Law, Kidzur Schulchan Aruch* published in New York City by the Hebrew Publishing Company in 1961, volume 4, page 67, that it is forbidden to bring a suit in the civil courts even if their decision would be in accordance with the law of Israel; that even if the two litigants are willing to try the case before such a court, it is forbidden; that even if they make an oral or a written agreement to that effect, it is of no avail; that whoever takes a case against another Jew involving religious matters, is a Godless person and he has violated and defiled the law of Moses. . . .

"Nothing appears in the record before us in this case to warrant the trial judge's denial of the motion. When the rights of the parties are being tested on motions for summary judgment filed, not at the election of the parties themselves but at the behest of the trial judge, a defendant should most certainly be allowed to amend to assert any defense he may have before the court has ruled. . . ."

■ **SIGNIFICANCE OF THIS CHAPTER**   Before beginning to study and learn specific rules of law, a student must first establish a general foundation upon which to build further blocks of knowledge. In establishing such a foundation it is necessary for the student to be able to define law, to understand the need for law in our society, to know the sources of our law, and to have a general understanding of how our legal system operates.

DISCUSSION CASE

FLOOD v. KUHN
407 U.S. 258 (1972)

FACTS: Curtis C. Flood began his major league career in 1956 when he signed a contract with the Cincinnati Reds. He had no attorney or agent to advise him on that occasion. He was traded to the St. Louis Cardinals before the 1958 season. Flood rose to fame as a center fielder with the Cardinals during the years 1958–1969.

In October 1969, Flood was traded to the Philadelphia Phillies of the National League in a multiplayer transaction. He was not consulted about the trade. He was informed by telephone and received formal notice only after the deal had been consummated. In December his request to the commissioner of baseball to be made a free agent was denied.

Flood then instituted his antitrust suit in U.S. District Court. The complaint charged violations of the U.S. antitrust laws and civil rights statutes, violation of state statutes and the common law, and the imposition of a form of peonage and involuntary service contrary to the 13th Amendment. Flood sought declaratory and injunctive relief and treble damages.

The District Court judge denied the request for an injunction. Trial was held in 1970. The District Court judge held that the cases of *Federal Baseball Club* v. *National League,* 259 U.S. 200 (1922), and *Toolson* v. *New York Yankees, Inc.* 346 U.S. 356 (1953), were controlling. Judgment was entered for the defendants.

On appeal, the U.S. Second Circuit Court of Appeals affirmed the District Court opinion. The case was accepted for review by the U.S. Supreme Court.

■

Justice Blackmun gave the opinion for the court:
For the third time in 50 years the Court is asked specifically to rule that professional baseball's reserve system is within the reach of the federal antitrust laws. Collateral issues of state law and of federal labor policy are also advanced.

The Legal Background

A. *Federal Baseball Club* v. *National League* . . . was a suit for treble damages instituted by a member of the Federal League (Baltimore) against the National and American Leagues and others. . . .

Mr. Justice Holmes, in speaking succinctly for a unanimous Court, said:

The business is giving exhibitions of baseball, which are purely state affairs. . . . But the fact that in order to give the exhibitions the Leagues must induce free persons to cross state lines and must arrange and pay for their doing so is not enough to change the character of the business. . . . [T]he transport is a mere incident, not the essential thing. That to which it is incident, the exhibition, although made for money would not be called a trade or commerce in the commonly accepted use of those words. As it is put by the defendant, personal effort, not related to production, is not a subject of commerce. That which in its consummation is not commerce does not become commerce among the states because the transportation that we have mentioned takes place. . . .

In the years that followed, baseball continued to be subject to intermittent antitrust attack. The courts, however, rejected these challenges on the authority of *Federal Baseball.* In some cases stress was laid, although unsuccessfully, on new factors such as the development of radio and television with their substantial additional revenues to baseball. For the most part, however, the Holmes opinion was generally and necessarily accepted as controlling authority. . . .

C. The Court granted certiorari . . . in the *Toolson, Kowalski,* and *Corbett* cases . . . and affirmed the judgments of the respective courts of appeals in those three cases . . . *Federal Baseball* was cited as holding "that the business of providing public baseball games for profit between clubs of professional baseball players was not within the scope of the federal antitrust laws," and:

Congress has had the ruling under consideration but has not seen fit to bring such business under these laws by legislation having prospective effect. The business has thus been left for 30 years to develop, on the understanding that it was not subject to existing antitrust legislation. The present cases ask us to overrule the prior decision and, with retrospective effect, hold the legislation applicable. We think that if there are evils in this field which now warrant application to it of the antitrust laws it should be by legislation. Without reexamination of the underlying issues, the judgments below are affirmed on the authority of *Federal Baseball Club of Baltimore* v. *National League of Professional Baseball Clubs,* supra, so far as that decision determines that Congress had no intention of including the business of baseball within the scope of the federal antitrust laws. . . .

H. This series of decisions understandably spawned extensive commentary, some of it mildly critical and much of it not; nearly all of it looked to Congress for any remedy that might be deemed essential.

I. Legislative proposals have been numerous and persistent. Since *Toolson* more than 50 bills have been introduced in Congress relative to the applicability or nonapplicability of the antitrust laws to baseball. . . .

In view of all this, it seems appropriate now to say that:

1. Professional baseball is a business and it is engaged in interstate commerce.

2. With its reserve system enjoying exemption from the federal antitrust laws, baseball is, in a very distinct sense, an exception and an anomaly. *Federal Baseball* and *Toolson* have become an aberration confined to baseball.

3. Even though others might regard this as "unrealistic, inconsistent, or illogical," see *Radovich,* . . . the aberration is an established one, and one that has been recognized not only in *Federal Baseball* and *Toolson* but in *Shubert, International Boxing,* and *Radovich,* as well, a total of five consecutive cases in this Court. It is an aberration that has been with us now for half a century, one heretofore deemed fully entitled to the benefit of *stare decisis,* and one that has survived the Court's expanding concept of interstate commerce. It rests on a recognition and an acceptance of baseball's unique characteristics and needs.

4. Other professional sports operating interstate—football, boxing, basketball, and presumably, hockey and golf—are not so exempt.

5. The advent of radio and television, with their consequent increased coverage and additional revenues, has not occasioned an overruling of *Federal Baseball* and *Toolson.*

6. The Court has emphasized that since 1922 baseball, with full and continuing congressional awareness, has been allowed to develop and to expand unhindered by federal legislative action. Remedial legislation has been introduced repeatedly in Congress, but none has ever been enacted. The Court, accordingly, has concluded that Congress as yet has had no intention to subject baseball's reserve system to the reach of the antitrust statutes. This, obviously, has been deemed to be something other than mere congressional silence and passivity. . . .

7. The Court has expressed concern about the confusion and the retroactivity problems that inevitably would result with a judicial overturning of *Federal Baseball.* It has voiced a preference that if any change is made, it come by legislative action that, by its nature, is only prospective in operation. . . .

This emphasis and this concern are still with us. We continue to be loath, 50 years after *Federal Baseball* and almost two decades after *Toolson,* to overturn those cases judicially when Congress, by its positive inaction, has allowed those decisions to stand for so long and, far beyond mere inference and implication, has clearly evinced a desire not to disapprove them legislatively.

Accordingly, we adhere once again to *Federal Baseball* and *Toolson* and to their application to professional baseball. We adhere also to *International Boxing* and *Radovich* and to their respective applications to professional boxing and professional football. If there is any inconsistency or illogic in all this, it is an inconsistency and illogic of long standing that is to be remedied by the Congress and not by this Court. If we were to act otherwise, we would be withdrawing from the conclusion as to congressional intent made in *Toolson* and from the concerns as to retrospectivity therein expressed. Under these circumstances, there is merit in consistency even though some might claim that beneath that consistency is a layer of inconsistency. . . .

[W]hat the Court said in *Federal Baseball* in 1922 and what is said in *Toolson* in 1953, we say again here in 1972; the remedy, if any is indicated, is for congressional, and not judicial, action.

The judgment of the Court of Appeals is affirmed. . . .

■ IMPORTANT TERMS AND CONCEPTS

Supreme law of the land	uniform laws
Constitution	Restatements
statute	distinguish on the facts
case law	distinguish on the law
doctrine of precedent	equity
treaty	injunction
administrative agency	specific performance
public law	trial by jury
private law	judicial review
substantive law	Civil-Law System
procedural law	Roman-Dutch System
criminal law	Soviet System
civil law	

■ QUESTIONS AND PROBLEMS FOR DISCUSSION

1. What is the difference between a common-law system and a civil-law system?
2. What is the difference between substantive law and procedural law? Give an example of each.
3. How does a court distinguish a precedent case on the facts?
4. Why was the court of equity developed?
5. Harold owns and operates a traveling dog and pony show. He gives exhibitions in several states. The U.S. secretary of agriculture attempted to impose regulations on Harold as to the care and feeding of his animals, pursuant to authority granted under the Ani-

mal Welfare Act. Harold says that his exhibitions are not interstate commerce and that he is, therefore, not subject to congressional regulation under the authority of the *Federal Baseball* case. How should the court rule, and why? Would there be a different result if Harold had a permanent location and gave exhibitions only in that one place?

6. Bropp was convicted of possession of burglar tools after police had stopped his car, searched it without a warrant, and found the burglar tools. He was convicted in 1960. At that time, a state could permit the use of improperly seized evidence in a criminal trial if it wished to do so. In 1961, the U.S. Supreme Court reversed its earlier precedent case, and held that a state could not use any illegally seized evidence in a criminal trial. Bropp now appeals his conviction, on the basis of the new ruling by the U.S. Supreme Court. How should the state appeals court rule? Explain.

7. Alumsports, Inc., a manufacturer of baseball bats, sued Batoff Company for alleged patent infringement. Alumsports said that it had the patent on a certain design for aluminum baseball bats and that Batoff was making the same product. Batoff argues that the patent is invalid since baseball is not commerce and Congress lacks the power to regulate it. Thus the congressionally established patent system cannot be applied to baseball equipment. What result, and why?

8. Hap Hapless, the former owner of a now-bankrupt minor league baseball team, sues the commissioner of major league baseball and all the major league club owners for damages sustained to his franchise when a major league team moved into the same geographic area. Hap alleges that the fans went to see the major league games, rather than coming to see his minor league team play. He says that the loss in revenues which resulted forced him to go out of business. He claims damages for unfair competition under the appropriate sections of the antitrust laws. The commissioner and the owners argue that the case should be dismissed, under the authority of *Federal Baseball*. How should the court rule, and why?

2

Courts and Civil Procedure

CHAPTER OBJECTIVES
THIS CHAPTER WILL:

- Introduce the courts and levels of appeal in our state and national court systems.
- Discuss the jurisdiction of state and national courts.
- Explain the general rules that apply when conflicts of law arise.
- Introduce the procedure followed in civil lawsuits.
- Examine methods of enforcing court judgments.
- Explain class action suits.
- Compare arbitration and mediation as means of resolving disputes.

Legal principles are meaningless without effective procedures for resolving disputes concerning the law and for enforcing the law.

In Chapter 1 we referred to the two major classifications of law: procedural and substantive. This chapter deals primarily with ***procedural law,*** the law that governs the resolution and enforcement of substantive law.

In the United States we do not have a single system for resolving disputes and enforcing the law; we have several. We have the national judicial system, 50 different state judicial systems, the quasi-judicial systems of the various national and state administrative agencies, and nonjudicial dispute-resolving systems called ***arbitration*** and mediation.

In this chapter we will look at these systems and review their procedures. Our purpose is not the make a lawyer of you, but rather to familiarize you with the procedures that a lawyer must pursue in handling your case or claim.

■ NATIONAL COURT SYSTEM

In Article III, the U.S. Constitution specifies only a Supreme Court, and gives Congress the power to create such lower courts as it wishes. The national court system now consists of three main levels of courts—District Courts, Courts of Appeal, and the Supreme Court—plus several specialty courts and many administrative agencies.

The U.S. District Courts are the main trial courts in the national court system. There is at least one U.S. District Court in each state; states with larger populations may have more. Each court may have several judges, and meet in several different locations, depending on where the lawsuits are arising within the district.

U.S. District Courts have both criminal and civil jurisdiction. Their jurisdiction over criminal lawsuits applies only in cases involving violations of national laws. For example, if someone stole a car in New York, the theft would be a crime in the state of New York and would be prosecuted in the New York State court system. If the thief drove the car across a New York State border into New Jersey, then a national crime would be committed, since transporting stolen goods across state lines is a violation of national law.

U.S. District Court—federal question jurisdiction

The U.S. District Court also has jurisdiction in civil cases, in two general categories. First, the court has jurisdiction when the suit involves a "federal question" regardless of the dollar amount of the controversy. Such cases include claims under national laws on patents, copyrights, antitrust, admiralty, securities, and other such topics. Any case in which the United States is being sued as party defendant also involves a "federal question" and would be brought in a U.S. District Court.

U.S District Court-diversity of citizenship jurisdiction

The second category of the U.S. District Court's civil jurisdiction encompasses cases where no federal question is involved. Ordinary tort and contract cases may be brought in U.S. District Court if there is diversity of citizenship between the parties, ***and*** if at least $50,000 is at issue. ***Diversity of citizenship*** means that all plaintiffs must be citizens of a state different from the state of residence of any of the defendants. The claims of the plaintiffs may not be aggregated to meet the minimum of $50,000 unless this is specifically allowed by the statutory law involved.

When there is complete diversity and each plaintiff has a claim of at least

■ **EXHIBIT 2–1**

United States Courts of Appeal and United States District Courts

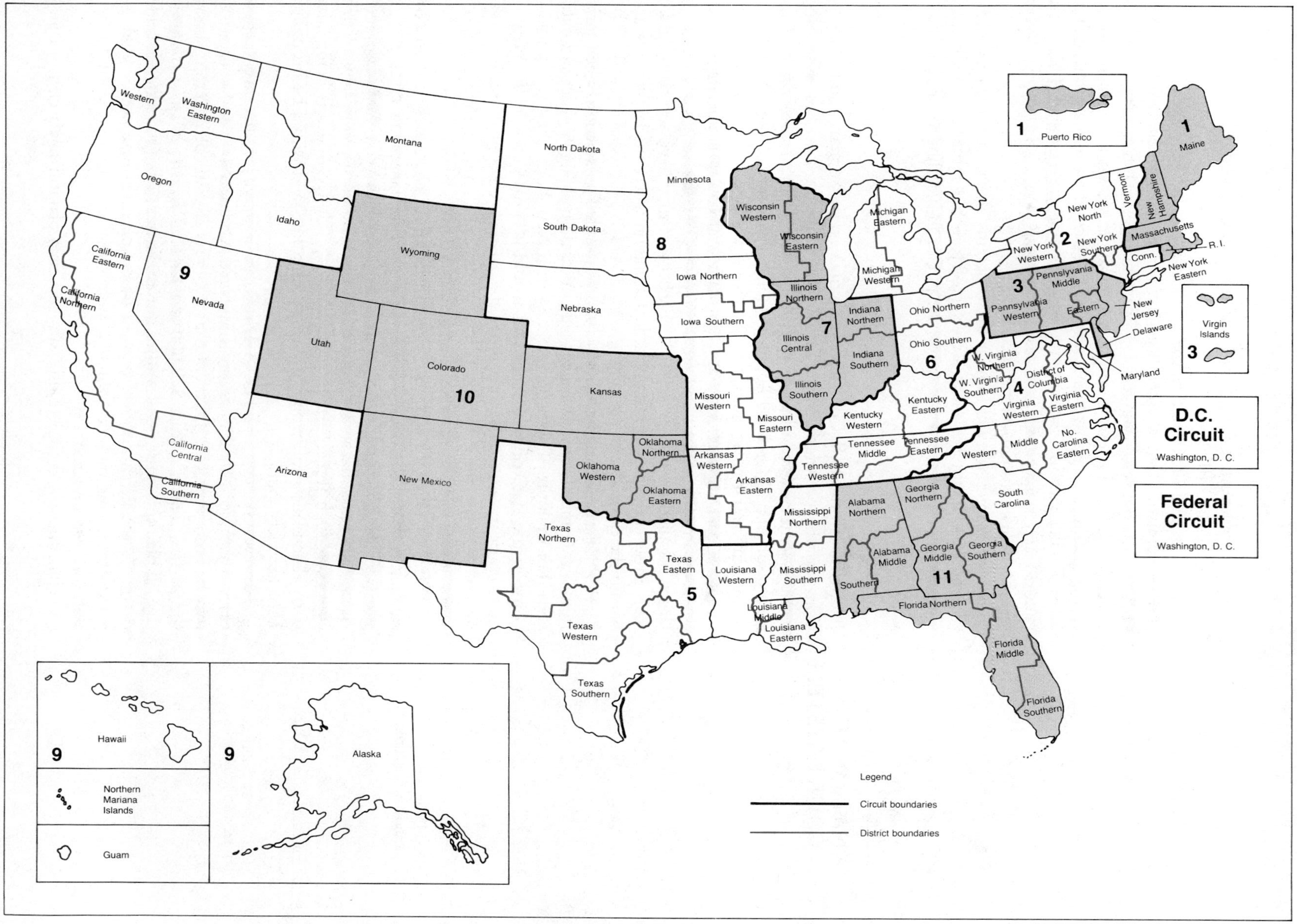

$50,000, plaintiffs have a choice of where to file their lawsuit. A national court could hear the case, but a state court also would have jurisdiction over the persons and the subject matter. This is called *concurrent jurisdiction,* since both national and state courts would have jurisdiction. If the plaintiff files in a state court which has proper jurisdiction over the parties and the subject matter, but there is complete diversity and the plaintiff's claim is $50,000 or more, then the defendant may have the case removed from the state court to the U.S. District Court. Once the plaintiff properly files in the U.S. District Court, the case must stay in the national court system. In other words, a transfer can be requested from a state court to the U.S. District Court, but not from a U.S. District Court to a state court.

U.S. Courts of Appeals

The *U.S. Courts of Appeals* are also called U.S. Circuit Courts of Appeals. There are 12 circuits throughout the country. Basically these are reviewing courts similar to the state appellate courts; no new evidence may be submitted to them. Their hearing is not a trial; it is simply a review. The review is based on the trial record, written arguments (briefs) filed by the attorneys, and oral arguments by the attorneys.

In addition to these 12 Circuit Courts of Appeals we now have a 13th Court of Appeals, the new U.S. Court of Appeals for the Federal Circuit, previously mentioned. The primary difference between this new court and the other 12 Courts of Appeals is that the jurisidiction of the new Court of Appeals for the Federal Circuit is stated in terms of subject matter (appeals from the specialty courts) rather than by geography. The new court will hear all the appeals on cases which involve the subject matter within its jurisdiction regardless of the region of the country where the claim or action originated.

U.S. Supreme Court

The *Supreme Court of the United States* is the court of final resort for appeal for any case. The U.S. Supreme Court is primarily a reviewing court; however, the U.S. Constitution, Article III, Section 2, empowers the Supreme Court of the United States, in certain cases, to be a trial court. In cases affecting ambassadors, other public ministers, and consuls, and cases in which a state is a party, the Supreme Court has original jurisdiction and may act as a trial court. The Constitution says *may,* however, and not *must.* The Supreme Court decides whether or not to hear such cases.

Limited review of state cases by U.S. Supreme Court

Federal question review

The highest state courts' decisions may be reviewed by the Supreme Court where the validity of a U.S. treaty or statute is in question or where a state statute may be in conflict with the U.S. Constitution or national laws. The U.S. Supreme Court may also be requested to review cases where a *federal question* is involved. The party requesting the review must usually submit a petition for a *writ of certiorari,* a formal request for review. This petition is then circulated among the nine justices of the U.S. Supreme Court, who decide whether a federal question is involved; that is, does the legal question involve rights claimed under the U.S. Constitution or any U.S. laws or treaties, and is this federal question important enough to warrant a full hearing before the Supreme Court? Several thousand cases are submitted to the U.S. Supreme Court for review each year; however, the Court hears only a few hundred cases. At least four of the nine justices must vote in favor of a review before the writ of certiorari is granted. If a writ of certiorari is granted, the case is then scheduled for a formal hearing. Prior to the formal hearing the Court reviews transcripts of testimony and the decisions of the lower courts, together

■ **EXHIBIT 2–2**
The National Court System

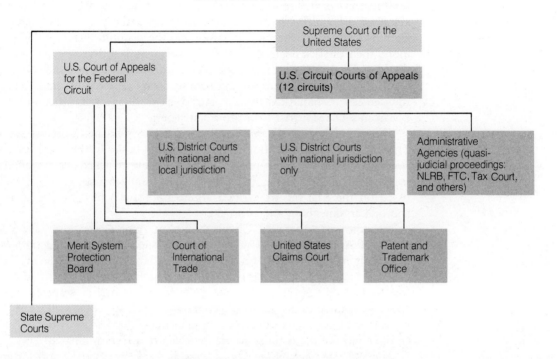

THE NATIONAL COURT SYSTEM

with briefs of the law prepared by the attorneys for both sides. In the hearing, attorneys argue before the Court. The Justices then discuss the case, and one of the Justices voting with the majority writes the opinion for the Court.

In addition to the appeals which come from the various state courts of last resort, the U.S. Supreme Court also reviews cases decided by the 13 U.S. Courts of Appeals. Also, in a few special cases, appeals can be taken directly from a U.S. District Court to the Supreme Court.

U.S. Specialty Courts

Specialty courts, such as the Court of International Trade, the U.S. Claims Court, the Patent and Trademark Office, the Merit System Protection Board, and some other national agencies, hear only a particular category of cases, such as "claims" against the national government. Appeals from these courts are now made to a newly created U.S. Court of Appeal for the Federal Circuit. This new court was established by the Federal Courts Improvement Act of 1982.

U.S. Bankruptcy Courts

The newest specialty courts are the Bankruptcy Courts, created by the Bankruptcy Act of 1978 and its amendments of 1984. One of these new courts is attached to each U.S. District Court, to hear and decide all bankruptcy cases within that District. Appeals from a Bankruptcy Court go first to its District Court, then to the appropriate U.S. Court of Appeals.

**Administrative
Agencies**

Also having specialized jurisdiction are such agencies as the Federal Trade Commission, the Securities and Exchange Commission, the National Labor Relations Board, and the Equal Employment Opportunity Commission. The jurisdiction of such administrative quasi-judicial agencies is limited to cases involving their specialty area. The agencies' power to enforce their decisions is usually also limited. Generally, a party to an agency action, who does not want to voluntarily comply with the agency's decision, may appeal for review by the U.S. Court of Appeals. Conversely, the agency may have to request the U.S. Court of Appeals to approve and enforce its decision by court order. (See Exhibit 2–2).

The following case discusses the relationship between national and state courts.

PENNZOIL CO. v. TEXACO, INC.

107 S.Ct. 1519 (1987)

FACTS
Getty Oil Co. and appellant Pennzoil Co. negotiated an agreement under which Pennzoil was to purchase about three sevenths of Getty's outstanding shares for $110 a share. Appellee Texaco, Inc. eventually purchased the shares for $128 share. On February 8, 1984, Pennzoil filed a complaint against Texaco in the Harris County District Court, a state court located in Houston, Texas, the site of Pennzoil's corporate headquarters. The complaint alleged that Texaco tortiously had induced Getty to breach a contract to sell its shares to Pennzoil; Pennzoil sought actual damages of $7.53 billion and punitive damages in the same amount. On November 19, 1985, a jury returned a verdict in favor of Pennzoil, finding actual damages of $7.53 billion and punitive damages of $3 billion. The parties anticipated that the judgment, including prejudgment interest, would exceed $11 billion.

Texaco did not argue to the trial court that the judgment, or execution of the judgment, conflicted with federal law. Rather, on December 10, 1985—before the Texas court entered judgment—Texaco filed this action in the United States District Court for the Southern District of New York in White Plains, New York, the site of Texaco's corporate headquarters. Texaco alleged that the Texas proceedings violated rights secured to Texaco by the Constitution and various federal statutes. It asked the District Court to enjoin Pennzoil from taking any action to enforce the judgment. Pennzoil's response, and basic position, was that the District Court could not hear the case. First, it argued that the Anti-Injunction Act, 28 U.S.C. § 2283, barred issuance of an injunction. It further contended that the court should abstain under the doctrine of *Younger* v. *Harris,* 401 U.S. 37 (1971). Third, it argued that the suit was in effect an appeal from the Texas trial court and that the District Court had no jurisdiction.

The District Court rejected all of these arguments. On appeal, the Court of Appeals for the Second Circuit affirmed. Pennzoil appealed to the U.S. Supreme Court.

ISSUE
Can a U.S. District Court enjoin enforcement of a state court judgment, pending an appeal in the state courts?

DECISION
No. Judgment reversed, and case remanded to the U.S. District Court, with instructions to dismiss the complaint.

▥ REASONS Justice Powell spoke for the U.S. Supreme Court.

"Both the District Court and the Court of Appeals failed to recognize the significant interests harmed by their unprecedented intrusion into the Texas judicial system. Similarly, neither of those courts applied the appropriate standard in determining whether adequate relief was available in the Texas courts. . . .

"Another important reason for abstention is to avoid unwarranted determination of federal constitutional questions. When federal courts interpret state statutes in a way that raises federal constitutional questions, 'a constitutional determination is predicated at any time—thus essentially rendering the federal-court decision advisory and the litigation underlying it meaningless. . . .' This concern has special significance in this case. Because Texaco chose not to present to the Texas courts the constitutional claims asserted in this case, it is impossible to be certain that the governing Texas statutes and procedural rules actually raise these claims. Moreover, the Texas constitution contains an 'open courts' provision, Art. I, § 13, that appears to address Texaco's claims more specifically than the due process clause of the Fourteenth Amendment. Thus, when this case was filed in Federal Court, it was entirely possible that the Texas courts would have resolved this case on state statutory or constitutional grounds, without reaching the federal constitutional questions Texaco raises in this case. As we have noted, . . . abstention in situations like this 'offers the opportunity for narrowing constructions that might obviate the constitutional problem and intelligently mediate federal constitutional concerns and state interests. . . .

"In sum, the lower courts should have deferred on principles of comity to the pending state proceedings. They erred in accepting Texaco's assertions as to the inadequacies of Texas procedure to provide effective relief. It is true that this case presents an unusual fact situation, never before addressed by the Texas courts, and that Texaco urgently desired prompt relief. But we cannot say that those courts, when this suit was filed, would have been any less inclined than a federal court to address and decide the federal constitutional claims. Because Texaco apparently did not give the Texas courts an opportunity to adjudicate its constitutional claims, and because Texaco cannot demonstrate that the Texas courts were not then open to adjudicate its claims, there is no basis for concluding that the Texas law and procedures were so deficient that *Younger* abstention is inappropriate. Accordingly, we conclude that the District Court should have abstained."

▪ STATE COURT SYSTEMS

Each state has designed its own state court system to fit its own needs. No uniform pattern applies to all states; however, most follow a general pattern with a four-tier judicial system.

The first tier, or lowest level of the typical state judicial system, consists of *specialty courts of limited jurisdiction.* The *justice of the peace court* was perhaps the oldest of these specialty courts. Normally, this court had jurisdiction over civil cases involving small amounts of money, nonfelony criminal matters, and traffic cases in which the accused person is willing to plead guilty. Usually, there was no provision for a jury trial in this court. The judge in most instances served part-time and was often not a lawyer. Court was often held in the judge's home or place of business.

State trial courts with limited jurisdiction

Many states have now replaced their J.P. courts with county courts or district courts. Typically, these newer courts will hear minor criminal cases and civil

■ **EXHIBIT 2–3**
State Court System

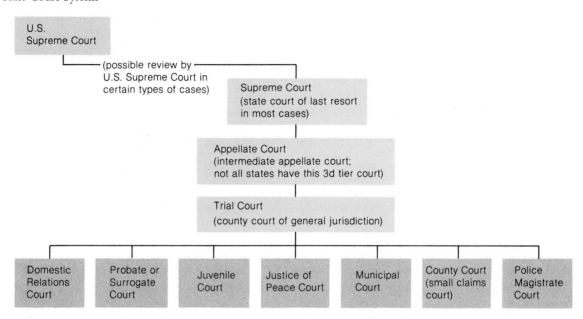

cases where a small amount of money is involved. Many states also have a specific small claims court for civil cases where a very small amount is involved, for example, $1,000 or less. While there usually is no trial by jury in a small claims court, it generally is available in a county court or district court. These juries may have only 6 members, rather than 12. The judges in these newer courts are normally required to be lawyers. Appeals may go to the trial court of general jurisdiction, or directly to the state's intermediate appellate court.

Also found in the first tier of state judicial systems are *domestic relations courts.* These courts generally handle cases involving marital relations and child custody. *Probate courts,* also known as *surrogate courts,* generally administer decedents' estates, the guardianship of minor children and persons declared incompetent to handle their own affairs, and matters involving juveniles. Some states use a separate court to hear juvenile cases. Typically there is no provision for trial by jury in domestic relations, probate, and juvenile cases. These courts usually answer to the trial court of general jurisdiction, but again some states permit appeals directly to an appellate court.

State trial courts with general jurisdiction

In the second of four tiers of the typical state court system we find the ***trial court with general jurisdiction.*** This court may be called a circuit court, a superior court, a common pleas court, or (in New York) the supreme court. In most states, each county has one or more trial courts with general jurisdiction. In all states, these are courts of record, meaning proceedings are recorded. Usually there is no limit on the monetary amounts involved in cases in these courts. They handle criminal, civil, and equity matters.

The third tier in this four-tier structure in an *intermediate appellate court.* This court hears appeals from the courts below it. The ***appellate court*** is a reviewing court; no new evidence is presented to it. The court reviews the trial transcript, the testimony, and the decision of the lower court. The attorneys for each side submit written briefs of the law which they contend applies, and the court, in some cases, listens to oral arguments of the attorneys of each side. Then this court renders one of three types of decisions: to affirm the lower court's decision, to reverse the lower court's decision and give judgment to the appealing party, or to reverse the lower court's decision and send the case back for a new trial or other proceedings in accordance with the court's opinion.

State appellate courts

The party wishing to appeal a lower court's judgment (called the ***appellant***) must allege error in the trial. For example, perhaps the trial judge allowed the jury to hear inadmissible evidence or gave the jury incorrect instructions on the law.

In some states the title of the appellate case may be reversed from the title of the case in the lower court. For example, Smith sued Jones in the lower court. The case is titled *Smith* v. *Jones*. Smith won; Jones appeals. Some states now list the case as *Jones* v. *Smith*.

This third tier, the intermediate appellate court, is not found in all states. It is usually needed in states with large populations and a large volume of cases.

State supreme courts

The fourth tier of state judicial systems is the state's *court of last resort*. This court may be called the supreme court of errors and appeals, the supreme judicial court, the court of appeals, or simply the ***supreme court***. Like the intermediate appellate court, this is a reviewing court; it holds no new trials. The procedure for review in this court is similar to the procedure for review at the intermediate appellate court level. This court, however, is the party's last resort for appeal in the great majority of the cases that originate in the state court system.

▪ CIVIL PROCEDURE

Jurisdiction over Persons. Thus far, we have been talking about ***subject-matter jurisdiction,*** that is, which courts have power to hear which kinds of cases. To hold a lawsuit, however, it is not enough just to find a court which can hear that kind of case. It is also necessary to find one which can assert its power over the parties to the dispute. In order to have this ***jurisdiction over the persons,*** there must be some sufficient relationship between the parties and the state where the court is located. The plaintiff nearly always establishes this relationship by filing the complaint with the court; by doing so, the plaintiff is consenting to have the dispute heard by that court. The real problem arises from having to get jurisdiction over the defendant.

Jurisdiction over Defendant

If the defendant also consented to have the case heard in a particular court, there would be no problem. Usually, in the real world, defendants are not that cooperative. As a second alternative, the plaintiff can always go to the defendant's ***domicile*** state, and bring the lawsuit there. For example, a Delaware corporation can always be sued in Delaware—by anyone, from anywhere, for anything, regardless of where the claim arose. (However, even though there would be *jurisdiction* to hear the case, a Delaware court might decline to do so, on the grounds that another location might be more convenient for the parties and the witnesses.) Our legal system also recognizes jurisdiction over a person anywhere he or she is personally served with process from a court in that location. A person on vacation in Hawaii, for instance, could be sued in Hawaii (state or national courts) if personally served with a summons from the Hawaii court while physically present in Hawaii.

Limited Personal Jurisdiction.   In many cases, none of these three alternatives is workable. The defendant will not give the plaintiff the advantage of consenting to have the lawsuit in the plaintiff's state. The defendant's home state may be far away, and/or inconvenient for the plaintiff. And the defendant will not be dumb enough to come to the plaintiff's state so that personal service of process can occur there. In this sort of situation, most states are willing to apply so-called *long-arm jurisdiction* statutes, if the defendant has had some minimum contact with the state.

A state is willing to reach out the long arm of its Law, and to force an out-of-stater to appear in its courts, when the dispute or claim arises out of something which that person has done in the state. If the out-of-stater has come into the state and committed a wrong, it's only fair that a lawsuit arising out of that wrong be heard where the wrong was done.

Similarly, if the nonresident made a contract in this state, or agreed to perform a contract in this state, claims for breach of those contracts should be heard here—and the nonresident should have to appear and defend the lawsuit. The nonresident who owns land or other tangible property (such as a car or boat) should be subject to suit, on claims that relate to ownership of that property, in the state where the property is physically located. Today, most states recognize that, at least in this group of cases, it is fair to force the out-of-stater to defend a lawsuit in the state where the injury occurred. Some states extend this long-arm principle to other transactions. The U.S. Supreme Court is the final judge as to which long-arm rules are "fundamentally fair" under the Due Process clause of the Fourteenth Amendment, and which are not (and thus cannot be used).

In the long-arm cases, service of process is usually made by sending certified copies of the complaint and summons by registered mail, to the defendant's out-of-state address. If the plaintiff has no such address available, a notice of the lawsuit must be placed in the classified section of a newspaper, usually once a week for several weeks.

Choice of Law.   Applying these long-arm principles, a plaintiff might have a choice of several states in which to file. And if there is diversity of citizenship and at least $50,000 involved, the U.S. District Courts in those same states would also be available. For example, an Idaho customer makes a contract with a Delaware corporation whose home office is in New York City, to have a $10 million condominium built in Arizona. The contract is negotiated and signed in Chicago, by representatives of the two companies. If the Idaho customer alleges damages have been caused due to improper construction, a lawsuit could almost certainly be filed in Delaware, New York, Illinois, or Arizona. (But *not* in Idaho, where the defendant has done nothing.)

Choice of law rules on procedure

How does the plaintiff decide where to sue, if there is a choice? Of course, cost and convenience are part of the plaintiff's decision. Perhaps even more important, however, are the differences in the Law which will be applied, since each court will use its own procedural rules in processing the case. Differences could occur in whether a jury trial is available, whether the verdict must be unanimous, whether certain evidence is admissible, whether there are limits on the damages recoverable, and similar procedural matters.

Choice of law rules on substance

Which state's substantive law should be used? The answer here may not be quite as clear, but there are some generally accepted rules. In the hypothetical lawsuit case above, if there was a question as to the validity of the contract, Illinois law should probably be used to decide that issue, since that is where the contract was made. If there is a question as to whether the contract was

■ EXHIBIT 2–4

Procedure in a Civil Lawsuit

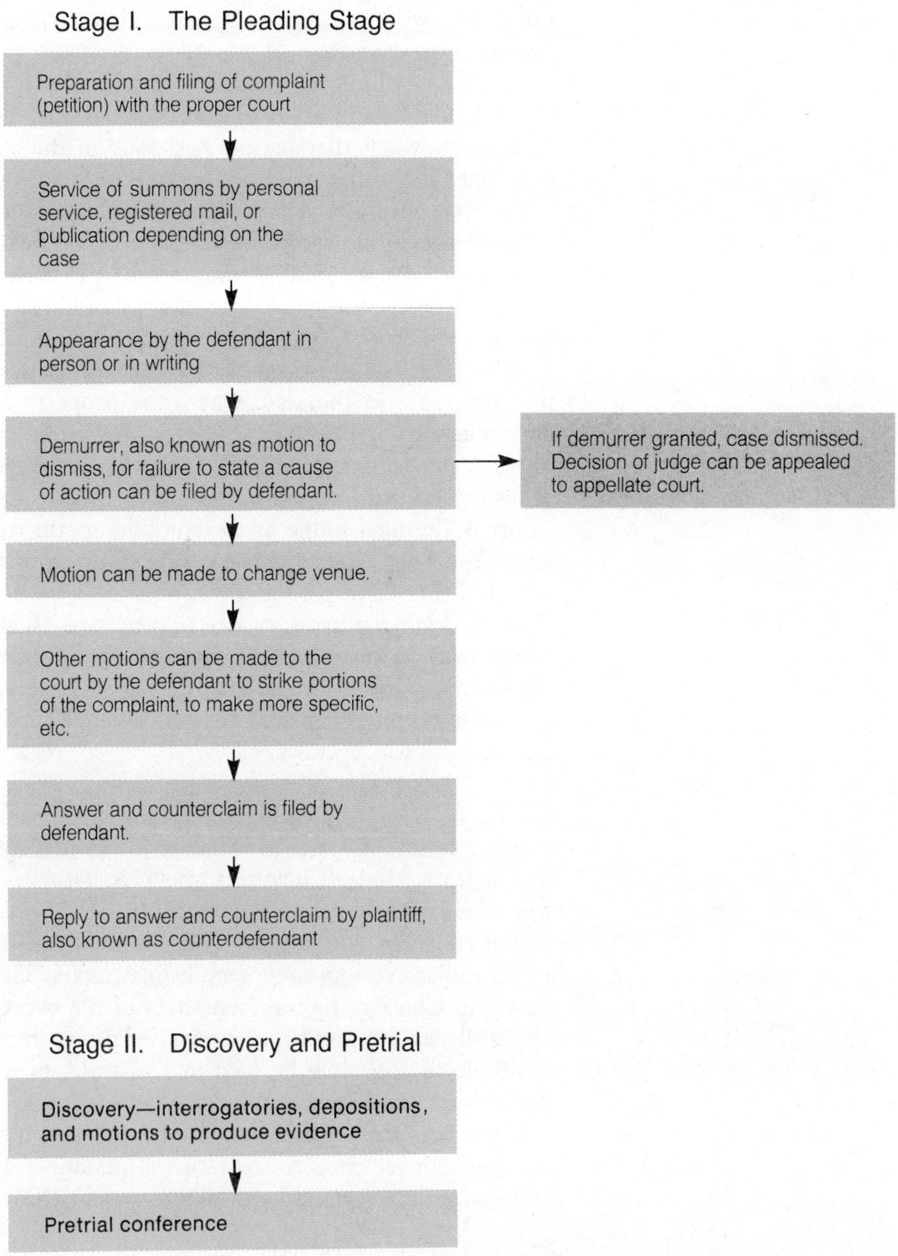

Stage I.   The Pleading Stage

Preparation and filing of complaint (petition) with the proper court

↓

Service of summons by personal service, registered mail, or publication depending on the case

↓

Appearance by the defendant in person or in writing

↓

Demurrer, also known as motion to dismiss, for failure to state a cause of action can be filed by defendant. → If demurrer granted, case dismissed. Decision of judge can be appealed to appellate court.

↓

Motion can be made to change venue.

↓

Other motions can be made to the court by the defendant to strike portions of the complaint, to make more specific, etc.

↓

Answer and counterclaim is filed by defendant.

↓

Reply to answer and counterclaim by plaintiff, also known as counterdefendant

Stage II.   Discovery and Pretrial

Discovery—interrogatories, depositions, and motions to produce evidence

↓

Pretrial conference

■ **EXHIBIT 2–4**
(concluded)

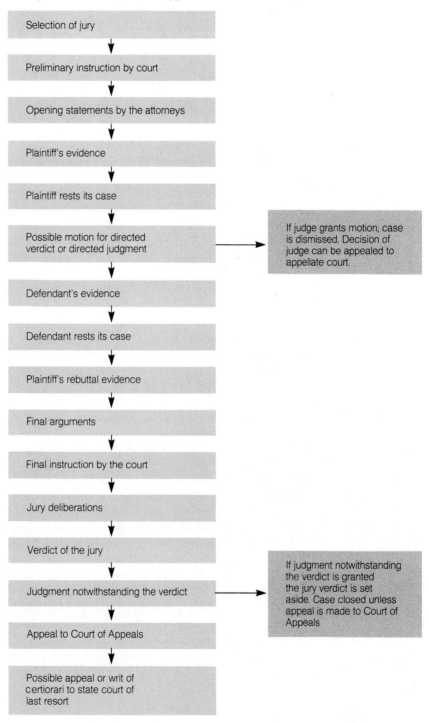

Stage III. The Trial and Appeals

Selection of jury

Preliminary instruction by court

Opening statements by the attorneys

Plaintiff's evidence

Plaintiff rests its case

Possible motion for directed verdict or directed judgment

If judge grants motion, case is dismissed. Decision of judge can be appealed to appellate court.

Defendant's evidence

Defendant rests its case

Plaintiff's rebuttal evidence

Final arguments

Final instruction by the court

Jury deliberations

Verdict of the jury

Judgment notwithstanding the verdict

If judgment notwithstanding the verdict is granted the jury verdict is set aside. Case closed unless appeal is made to Court of Appeals

Appeal to Court of Appeals

Possible appeal or writ of certiorari to state court of last resort properly performed by the builder, Arizona law should probably be used to decide that issue, since that is where the builder was doing the work. Where a tort (civil injury) case is involved, some states use the law of the state where the injury occurred. Other states use an analysis which tries to decide which state has the most significant contacts with the occurrence, and then use that state's substantive law. U.S. District Courts, in diversity cases, use the choice-of-law rules of the state in which they are located. A U.S. District Court in Illinois, for example, hearing the hypothetical builder case noted above, would use the same choice of law rules as the state courts in Illinois use.

Venue.   Jurisdiction, as defined above, means the authority or power to hear a case. Technically, all courts of general jurisdiction in a state might have jurisdiction to hear a specific type of case. The question then arises, which one of those many courts which had jurisdiction *should* hear the case? *Venue* rules decide that question. Most state venue statutes provide that a lawsuit against a defendant be commenced in the defendant's county of residence or in the county in which the cause of action arose. For example, if a plaintiff in an automobile accident case filed suit in a county other than the county where the accident occurred or where the defendant resided, then the defendant could have the venue changed to one of those locations.

Venue-proper location of trial within a state

Venue also may be changed when the possibility of selecting a fair and impartial jury in the county where the lawsuit was filed is in question. In that case, the defendant could request a change of venue to an adjoining county. This might occur in a case involving local residents who assume that all college students drink beer and drive at high rates of speed. In that case, it would be better to change the venue to an adjoining county where the residents are not in constant contact with college students and might not be prejudiced against students.

Pleading Stage
Plaintiff's complaint

The first step in filing a lawsuit is preparing a ***complaint,*** sometimes called a *petition* or a *declaration*. The complaint will state the names of the parties: the party bringing the action is called the ***plaintiff,*** and the party being sued is called the ***defendant.*** The complaint will state the plaintiff's version of what happened, where, when, how, and why it happened, and that it happened because of the defendant's wrongful acts. Then it will state what the injuries or damages were, and it will usually conclude with a request for an amount of money.

Court summons to defendant

The attorney for the plaintiff will file this complaint with the clerk of an appropriate court. The clerk will issue a ***summons,*** that is, a written notice of the lawsuit which informs the defendant when and where to appear to defend the case. The summons is ***served*** on, that is, physically presented to, the defendant. Usually a copy of the complaint is served along with the summons so that the defendant will know the particulars of the lawsuit.

Service of Process.   The rules for serving a summons vary for different types of lawsuits and from state to state. The most common method is service to the defendant in person by a sheriff or another authorized official. Service may also be made by registered or certified mail with a return receipt. In some jurisdictions, a summons may be legally served if it is handed to a member of the defendant's household; however, there are restrictions as to the age of the party receiving the summons. Handing the summons to the defendant's husband or wife would be proper service, but handing it to the defendant's eight-year-old child would not.

Service by registered mail, or by publication, is permitted in some cases—for instance, the long-arm cases noted above.

Default judgment

Once the complaint has been filed and the summons has been properly served on the defendant, the defendant must appear in court within a specified time, such as 20 days within receipt of the summons. Failure to appear either in person or by an attorney within that time will be treated as an admission of guilt, and the court will enter a ***default judgment*** against the defendant. Under certain circumstances, the defendant may have this default judgment set aside. An example would be when the defendant can prove service of the summons was improper.

Defendant's motion to dismiss

The defendant may challenge the sufficiency of the complaint by filing a ***demurrer,*** or ***motion to dismiss,*** or attack the complaint with motions concerning jurisdiction or venue. To be legally sufficient, a complaint must state a ***cause of action.*** That is, the complaint filed by the plaintiff must state that the plaintiff had a specific legal right, that the defendant had a legal duty and breached it, and that the plaintiff was injured as a proximate result of the breach. This is the first of several safety valves in the trial of a civil lawsuit. If the judge finds the plaintiff has not stated a case, the demurrer will be granted and the lawsuit is dismissed. The plaintiff is still free to file a new complaint.

Defendant's answer

The next important pleading is the ***answer,*** in which the defendant must affirm or deny the allegations the plaintiff made in the complaint. The defendant may very well admit some facts, such as the time and place of the occurrence. The defendant would, however, deny allegations regarding his or her negligence. In addition to answering the plaintiff's claims, the defendant may make a claim for damages by filing a ***counterclaim.*** This is also called a ***cross complaint*** in some states. In this pleading the defendant will allege that the plaintiff was negligent and will state a claim for damages. The plaintiff may now answer the cross complaint or counterclaim in a pleading called a ***reply.*** The plaintiff is given this second turn at bat to respond to new matters which the defendant may have raised for the first time.

At this point, both parties—and the court—have been told what facts are in dispute, and what legal theories and arguments each side may use during the trial. Many states have another safety valve here—the ***motion for summary judgment,*** or judgment on the pleadings. This motion asks the trial court judge to rule that there is no real dispute on the facts, and that one side is entitled to judgment as a matter of law. If the motion is granted, one side wins, on the merits, and the case is over.

Pretrial Stage

During the ***pretrial stage,*** the parties and their lawyers prepare the case for trial. Most major metropolitan areas have a long backlog of cases, so a case filed today may not come to trial for several years. This presents several problems. Witnesses tend to forget facts about the case as time goes by. They may die or move out of the jurisdiction, which means they cannot legally be brought back for trial.

Interrogatories-Questions to parties

Three general methods of *discovery* are used. First, each party may file interrogatories to be answered by the other. *Interrogatories* are lists of questions that probe for information about the person, the incident, and the damages. The questions must be relevant to the case, but interrogatories tend to be "fishing expeditions." They are usually not admissible as evidence in court, but state rules vary.

Depositions-Written testimony

Interrogatories normally are followed by depositions. A *deposition* is sworn testimony that is subject to cross-examination, and is admissible as evidence. Depositions may be taken from the parties and from witnesses, both witnesses to the incident and expert witnesses such as doctors, engineers, and economists.

Depositions basically serve two purposes. First, they discover the testimony. A party who has testified under oath will be guilty of perjury if he or she materially changes the testimony later. Second, depositions preserve the testimony in case the witness dies or moves and cannot be located. Doctors and other experts testifying in a case may not be able to appear at the trial, but their depositions can be used.

Production of physical evidence

A third discovery procedure is a motion by one party to have the other party produce certain items of evidence for review. For example, the defendant may ask the plaintiff for copies of medical reports, bills, photographs, and other material that the plaintiff intends to submit at the trial.

Privilege against disclosure

Courts may not compel testimony, or production of documents, in violation of a recognized *privilege* of confidentiality. Such privileges may exist under a state's general common-law rules of evidence or under a specific statute. As will be more fully discussed in Chapter 6, persons cannot be required to testify as to matters which might subject them to criminal prosecution. Attorneys cannot testify about matters their clients communicated to them in confidence. Other widely recognized privileges exist for communications to the clergy, physicians, and spouses. In some states, statutes may provide privileges against disclosure for the records of teachers, newspaper reporters, accountants, and others. Generally, a privilege against disclosure can be waived by the person in whose favor it operates. A client, for instance, could waive his or her privilege and permit an attorney to testify as to matters which otherwise could not be disclosed. In the following case, the U.S. Supreme Court decides on the existence and extent of an accountant's privilege.

U.S. v. ARTHUR YOUNG & CO.

465 U.S. 805 (1984)

FACTS

Arthur Young & Co., auditor for Amerada Hess Corp., reviews Amerada's financial statements in compliance with the U.S. securities laws. In making this review, Young & Co. prepared tax accrual work papers to verify Amerada's statement of its contingent tax liabilities. In these work papers Young evaluated Amerada's reserves for such taxes. In 1975 the Internal Revenue Service audited Amerada's tax returns for 1972–74 and discovered a questionable payment of $7,830 from a "special disbursement account." The IRS began a criminal investigation, as authorized by IRC § 7602, and asked Young for all its Amerada files, including the tax accrual work papers. Amerada told Young not to turn over this material. The U.S. District Court ordered Young to produce the documents, but the U.S. Court of Appeals reversed.

ISSUE   Are these documents protected by a CPA-client privilege?

DECISION   No. Judgment reversed (although the U.S. Supreme Court did agree that the work papers were relevant to the IRS investigation).

REASONS   **Chief Justice Burger delivered the opinion for a unanimous Court:**

"We now turn to consider whether tax accrual work papers prepared by an independent auditor in the course of a routine review of corporate financial statements should be protected by some form of work-product immunity from disclosure under § 7602. Based upon its evaluation of the competing policies of the federal tax and securities laws, the Court of Appeals found it necessary to create a so-called privilege for the independent auditor's work papers. . . . The purpose of [§ 7602] is not to accuse, but to inquire. Although such investigations unquestionably involve some invasion of privacy, they are essential to our self-reporting system, and the alternatives could well involve far less agreeable invasions of house, business, and records. . . .

"While § 7602 is 'subject to the traditional privileges and limitations' . . . any other restrictions upon the IRS summons power should be avoided 'absent unambiguous directions from Congress.'. . . We are unable to discern the sort of 'unambiguous directions from Congress' that would justify a judicially created work-product immunity for tax accrual work papers summoned under § 7602. Indeed, the very language of § 7602 reflects precisely the opposite: a congressional policy choice *in favor of disclosure* of all information relevant to a legitimate IRS inquiry. . . . If the broad latitude granted to the IRS by § 7602 is to be circumscribed, that is a choice for Congress and not this Court, to make. . . ."

Pretrial conference

After both sides have completed discovery, the court will schedule a ***pretrial conference.*** The purpose of the pretrial hearing is twofold. First, it enables the judge to get the attorneys representing the plaintiff and the defendant together and to determine whether or not there can be an amicable settlement. Here the judge acts more as a meditator than as a judge. When possible, the judge will encourage the parties to negotiate a settlement so the case can be dismissed before trial. If, on the other hand, a settlement appears impossible, the judge will try to determine whether any items of evidence can be admitted without objection to save time at the trial. In some jurisdictions, the judge will have the parties exchange lists of the witnesses they are going to have testify. The theory is that the trial should present no surprises and that each party should have an opportunity to know the other party's evidence. If it appears that the case will have to be tried, a trial date will be set.

Trial Stage
Jury selection

Unless the judge is to hear a case without a jury, the first step in a trial is the selection of a jury. (Generally, there is no right to trial by jury in equity cases. Even if the parties have the right to a jury trial, they may waive it.) Traditionally, a jury was composed of 12 persons but many jurisdictions have reduced that number to 6 for some cases. ***Jury selection*** is a very important phase of the trial. To have a fair trial, jurors must be unbiased, fair, and impartial.

Voir dire examination

A list of prospective jurors is selected at random from the eligible voters in the county where a state court lawsuit is to be tried or in the court district where a U.S. District Court suit is to be tried. Prospective jurors are called to the courtroom where attorneys for the plaintiff and the defendant question them to uncover biases or other reasons they could not serve as fair and impartial jurors. For example, the prospective jurors may be asked whether they are related to any of the parties in the lawsuit or any of the attorneys, whether they have had business dealings with the parties, or whether they know the parties socially. They may also be asked whether they have read about the cause of action in the newspapers and whether they have already formed an opinion about the guilt or innocence of the parties. This examination is called *voir dire*. In some states, the judge asks these questions.

Challenges to jurors

If a prospective juror admits prejudice, or if a prejudice is implied by a relationship to someone associated with the case, the prospective juror will be *challenged for cause*. If the court agrees that the prospective juror is prejudiced or cannot be a fair and impartial juror, the prospective juror will be dismissed. In addition to the challenges for cause, each side in the lawsuit will be given a certain number of *peremptory challenges.* No cause need be stated for making a peremptory challenge. The purpose of the peremptory challenge is to give each side an opportunity to dismiss certain jurors who, for one reason or another, the attorney feels may be prejudiced against his or her client. Peremptory challenges may or may not be used.

Court's preliminary instructions to jury

After the jury has been selected and seated in the jury box, the judge will give jurors *preliminary instructions* concerning the trial. The judge will outline the issue for trial and explain the burden of proof, the credibility of witnesses, and the manner in which the jurors should weigh the testimony they are about to hear.

Attorney's opening statements to jury

The *opening statement* is not evidence; it is only a preview of coming attractions. As the complaining party, the plaintiff has the burden of proof, thus has first opening statement. In the opening statement the plaintiff's attorney tells jurors what type of case they are to hear and briefly explains what the plaintiff intends to prove. The defendant's attorney then makes an opening statement, telling the jury what the defendant expects to prove. Now the jury has an overview of the case and is ready to hear the evidence.

Examination of witnesses for plaintiff

The plaintiff, having the burden of proof, is first to present evidence. The plaintiff's attorney calls a *witness* to the stand and asks this person questions; this is called *direct examination.* After this questioning, the defendant's attorney can *cross-examine* the witness to test the accuracy of the witness's statements. After the cross-examination, the plaintiff's attorney can conduct *redirect examination* to try to reestablish points challenged on cross-examination. Exhibits such as photographs, charts, documents, and articles of clothing may be submitted as evidence. This process continues until all of the plaintiff's witnesses have testified.

Motion for directed verdict

The defendant may now make a *motion for a directed verdict* if there is a jury. If the judge feels that no issue of fact is to be decided by the jury, then the judge will direct a verdict in favor of the defendant. If there is no jury, a motion can be made for a directed judgment in favor of the defendant. If an issue of fact has been raised for the jury to decide, then the trial must go on.

Defendant's evidence

The defendant's attorney will now call the defense witnesses, and the same process of questioning will occur. The defendant's attorney will ask questions under direct examination; the plaintiff's attorney will cross-examine; and the defendant's attorney will have an opportunity for redirect examination of the witnesses. The defendant may submit exhibits of evidentiary material for the defense. Then the defendant rests. The plaintiff has the right to recall witnesses or to call additional witnesses for the sole purposes of rebutting the defendant's evidence.

Attorney's final arguments

Since the plaintiff has the burden of proving the case against the defendant, the plaintiff is entitled to present the first closing argument. This is also called a *summation.* Here, the plaintiff's attorney reviews all the testimony and tries to convince the jurors that the plaintiff's evidence is stronger than the defendant's evidence and that the plaintiff should win. In a civil case the jury decides not only who is right but also the amount of the verdict. Thus, the plaintiff's attorney also argues the value of the plaintiff's claim. The defendant's attorney then argues the opposite side of the case. Then the plaintiff is entitled to a final rebuttal or closing argument.

Judge's instructions to the jury

The jurors now need to know what substantive law applies to the case. The judge reads prepared instructions on the law to the jury. In most jurisdictions, the attorneys for each side prepare proposed instructions, and the judge selects those appropriate for the case. The judge may also add instructions not submitted by either attorney. After hearing the *judge's instructions* on the law, jurors are taken to the jury room. Their first order of business is to select a foreman, then they commence deliberations.

Jury's verdict

When the jurors have reached agreement they return to the courtroom and the foreman reads their *verdict.* The verdict must be unanimous in most jurisdictions, although some states require agreement of only 10 of 12, or 5 of 6 jurors. Since civil juries decide both questions of fact and the dollar amount of the verdict, they seldom become a *hung jury,* which is a jury that has become deadlocked in trying to reach a unanimous verdict.

Judgment N.O.V.

Judgment notwithstanding the verdict (N.O.V.) is another safety valve in the system. The judge has veto power over the jury in the rare situations where the jury has obviously failed to follow the instructions on the law. At such times the judge can disregard the verdict and enter a judgment contrary to it. In the vast majority of cases, however, the judge enters a judgment on the basis of the jury's verdict.

In the following case the trial court judge granted a motion for judgment not withstanding the verdict, but the appellate court reversed and reinstated the verdict of the trial court jury.

MORAN v. FABERGÉ, INC.

332 A.2d 11 (Maryland, 1975)

FACTS

On June 8, 1969, Nancy Moran, then 17 years old, visited the home of Mr. and Mrs. Grigsby to meet with a number of friends, including Randy Williams, a young lady of 15 years, who was residing with Grigsbys at the time. The group congregated in the basement, which was being used as a family room and laundry room.

Everyone left the basement, except Nancy and Randy. Apparently these two girls were at a loss for entertainment as eventually they centered their attention on a lit Christmas-tree-shaped candle on a shelf behind the couch. The girls began to discuss whether the candle was scented. After agreeing that it was not, Randy, while remarking "Well, let's make it scented," impulsively grabbed a "drip bottle" of Fabergé's Tigress cologne, which had been placed by Mrs. Grigsby in the basement for use as a laundry deodorant, and began to pour its contents onto the lower portion of the candle somewhat below the flame. Instantaneously, a burst of fire sprang out and burned Nancy's neck and breasts as she stood nearby watching but not fully aware of what her friend was doing.

Ms. Moran brought suit against Fabergé, Inc. The jury gave a verdict in favor of Ms. Moran. However, the judge granted judgment notwithstanding the verdict in favor of defendant, Fabergé, Inc. Plaintiff appealed.

ISSUE   Were there questions of fact in this case, so that it was one for a jury decision?

DECISION   Yes. Trial court judge overruled, and jury verdict reinstated.

REASONS   **Judge Digges thought that the case was one for the jury to decide.**
"[W]e think that in the products liability domain a duty to warn is imposed on a manufacturer if the item it produces has an inherent and hidden danger about which the producer knows or should know, [and which] could be a substantial factor in bringing injury to an individual or his property when the manufacturer's product comes near to or in contact with the elements which are present normally in the environment where the product can reasonably be expected to be brought or used. . . . Under this analysis the unusual and bizarre details of accidents, which human experience shows are far from unlikely, are only significant as background facts to the individual case; it is not necessary that the manufacturer foresee the exact manner in which accidents occur. Thus, in the context of this case, it was not necessary for a cologne manufacturer to foresee that someone would be hurt when a friend poured its product near the flame of a lit candle; it was only necessary that it be foreseeable to the producer that its product, while in its normal environment, may be brought near a catalyst, likely to be found in that environment, which can untie the chattel's inherent danger. For example while seated at a dressing table, a woman might strike a match to light a cigarette close enough to the top of the open cologne bottle so as to cause an explosion, or that while seated in a similar manner she might turn suddenly and accidentally bump the bottle of cologne with her elbow, splashing some cologne on a burning candle placed on the vanity. So, in the words of the Supreme Court of Missouri: 'If there is some probability of harm sufficiently serious that ordinary men would take precautions to avoid it, then failure so to do is negligence. . . .'

"It is our opinion then, that the totality of the evidence presented in this case, viewed most favorably toward the petitioner, was legally sufficient to enable the jury to find that Fabergé's failure to place a warning on its Tigress cologne 'drip bottle' constituted actionable negligence. We say this because there was evidence presented at trial which, if accepted as true, tends to show that Fabergé's Tigress cologne possessed a latent danger of flammability; that Fabergé, through its officials, knew or should have known of this danger; that it is normal to find in the home environment both flame and cologne; that it was reasonably foreseeable to Fabergé that the flame and the cologne may well come in contact, one with the other, so as to cause an explosion which injures a person who happens to be standing nearby—Nancy; and that a reasonably prudent manufacturer, knowing of its product's characteristics and propensities, should have warned consumers of this latent flammability danger."

Civil Appeals

After the judgment has been entered, the losing party has a right to an *appeal.* Notice of intent to appeal must be given within a specified time after the judgment is rendered. The procedure before the appellate court has been discussed earlier in this chapter. After all appeal procedures have been exhausted, a final judgment will be rendered, provided the court judgment has been affirmed. Of course, if there was a reversal, then we are faced with a new trial or other action in accordance with the appellate court's instructions. In the great majority of cases, no appeal is filed, and at the end of the time allotted for filing an appeal, the judgment becomes final.

■ ENFORCEMENT OF JUDGMENTS

Execution against property

Garnishment

Lien against property

A judgment rendered against a party is worthless without a procedure to enforce and collect it. In years past, persons were put in debtor's prison for failing to pay their bills, but no such procedure exists today. Now, a person who obtains a judgment for money against another person has basically three ways to collect that judgment. The party on whose behalf the judgment was rendered can ask for court *execution against the debtor's property.* This means the debtor's property may be sold at a public sale, and the proceeds may be applied against the judgment. State and national laws, however, exempt some types of property from execution.

A second way to collect is *garnishment,* a court order to third parties to turn over money or property belonging to the debtor. State and national garnishment laws do not allow the judgment creditor to secure the debtor's total wages. Bank accounts may also be garnished.

The third way to collect is to secure a *lien,* or charge, against property owned by the debtor. For example, a lien may be placed against real estate owned by the debtor. The debtor cannot sell and give clear title to the real estate without first paying the lien. In some cases, the property may be sold through a court process to enforce the lien.

■ FULL FAITH AND CREDIT

Enforcement of judgments from other states

The property the judgment debtor owns in the state that issued the judgment may not be enough to satisfy it. If the debtor owns property in other states, the judgment creditor may ask the courts in one of those other states to enforce the judgment there. When this happens, the "Full Faith and Credit Clause" in Article IV of the U.S. Constitution comes into play. This clause requires each state to give *full faith and credit* to the public acts, records, and judicial proceedings of other states. The successful judgment creditor cannot be forced to relitigate the whole case in other states to enforce the claim. Other states can, however, examine the judgment to make sure that the court that issued it had jurisdiction. If the court in the state where the judgment was rendered had jurisdiction, the other states have no choice; they must enforce the judgment just as they would one of their own. The ultimate decision as to what are adequate jurisdictional bases is made by the U.S. Supreme Court, since a matter of constitutional interpretation is at issue. In the following case, the Illinois courts are being asked to recognize a Nevada divorce decree.

KECK v. KECK

309 N.E. 2d 217 (Illinois, 1974)

FACTS
James E. Keck filed a divorce petition in Cook County, Illinois, in December 1967. Dolores Keck answered the complaint and asked for separate maintenance. In October 1968, while the Illinois case was still pending, James moved to Nevada and received a divorce through the Nevada courts. He then moved back to Illinois. The trial court upheld Dolores's claim that the Nevada decree was invalid, but the appeals court reversed, saying that the Nevada decree must be given full faith and credit.

ISSUE
Did the Nevada courts have jurisdiction to issue the divorce decree?

DECISION
No. Trial court judgment for Dolores affirmed; appeals court reversed.

REASONS
Justice Davis acknowledged that divorce proceedings are a special case, in that a decree is valid if the issuing court has jurisdiction over *one* spouse (the plaintiff), at least as to the termination of the marriage, and that jurisdiction over the defendant spouse is not necessary.

The issue was thus narrowed to whether the Nevada courts had jurisdiction over James, and that depended in turn on whether he had established domicile there.

"[T]he evidence presented . . . overcame the presumption of such domicile created by the introduction into evidence of the Nevada divorce decree. It is well established that the question of domicile is largely one of intention and that to establish a new domicile a person must physically go to a new home and live there with the intention of making it his permanent home. . . . Here plaintiff lived in Nevada only two months, he returned immediately upon obtaining his decree, he retained his apartment in Chicago and returned there, he retained his job in Chicago and returned to it, he retained his Chicago bank accounts and his Illinois driver's license. Within one or two days after arriving in Nevada, he contacted a lawyer about getting a divorce. The evidence presented to the trial court clearly supports the conclusion that the plaintiff went to Nevada for the purpose of obtaining a divorce and with the intent of returning to Illinois. The plaintiff did not establish a *bona fide* domicile in Nevada, and the trial court was warranted in concluding that the Nevada decree was invalid and in denying it full faith and credit."

▪ CLASS ACTIONS

Traditionally, plaintiffs have pursued their claims on an individual basis. However, courts have occasionally permitted plaintiffs to represent a large class of claimants where the claims of all the parties are similar and arise out of the same occurrence. This is called a *class action*. The most common example of a class action is one shareholder bringing an action against a corporation for some alleged mismanagement and resulting loss. That one shareholder represents all other similar stockholders who allege similar damage. Obviously, the court can hear one case more expeditiously and at less expense than hundreds or thousands of similar cases. Class actions also help overcome inequality of means. The big corporation can afford litigation more than a single plaintiff can. However, if many plaintiffs join forces, the expense is far less for each individual.

Under the current Federal Rules of Civil Procedure, four prerequisites must be met before a class action may be maintained in the U.S. District Court:

Requirements for a class action in U.S. District Court

1. The class is so numerous that joinder of all its members is impractical.
2. The class members' claims have common questions of law or fact.
3. The claim or defense of the class representative is typical of that of the absent class members.
4. The representative will fairly and adequately protect the interests of the class.

The rules also provide that *one* of the following conditions must exist:

1. The prosecution of separate actions might result in inconsistent or varying judgments.
2. The prosecution of separate actions might in practice dispose of the interests of other members or impede their ability to protect those interests.
3. The defendant has acted or refused to act on grounds generally applicable to all members of the class, so that injunctive or declaratory relief for the whole class is appropriate.
4. The court finds that a class action is the best method to adjudicate the controversy.

If a class action is filed in U.S. District Court, the amount per claim must be at least $50,000. This prevents the U.S. District Courts from being flooded with class actions. The individual states also have rules for class actions, many of which are similar to the federal rules, with one notable exception. State courts require no minimum amount per claim. Also many states have passed specific environmental and consumer laws authorizing class actions under certain circumstances.

Alternate Dispute Resolution Arbitration

One normally associates *arbitration,* or binding private dispute settlement, with labor law and the arbitration of grievances under labor contracts. Arbitration, of course, is used extensively in labor-management relations; however, it has also been utilized in settling other types of disputes.

In government, public employees are often not allowed to strike. Instead, agreements between labor and management often are reached by submitting both parties' offers to one or more arbitrators for a final decision about contract terms. This procedure is being used more extensively as union membership spreads among public employees.

Reasons for arbitration of a dispute

Another type of arbitration that is gaining popularity is the commercial arbitration of business disputes that would normally be handled in civil lawsuits. If a breach of contract case were filed in a civil court, for example, court costs and legal fees would cost both parties a considerable amount and, usually, considerable time would elapse before the case came to trial. Arbitration can be a cheaper, faster solution than litigation. For example, suppose the parties are disputing their obligations under a contract to build a multimillion dollar building. Time is of the essence. The parties cannot wait six or seven years for this case to come to trial. If the case is submitted to arbitration, they can get a decision quickly and proceed in accordance with the arbitrator's decision.

Technical expertise can be another benefit of arbitration. The typical judge does not have expertise in all fields, but parties can select a commercial arbitrator with knowledge about the subject area of their dispute.

Arbitration requires no set procedure, such as one would find in a court of law or even in an administrative agency. Both parties, however, must meet one prerequisite: they must agree to submit the dispute to arbitration. This can be done by inserting an arbitration clause into the original document, such as a contract. Even without such a clause, the parties may agree later to submit a dispute to arbitration.

The American Arbitration Association was formed as a national not-for-profit association to encourage the use of arbitration in resolving disputes. It has a panel of recommended arbitrators who will hear commercial arbitration disputes, and panels of recommended arbitrators who will hear labor disputes.

The Federal Mediation and Conciliation Service, a government agency, also has a panel of recommended arbitrators for labor disputes. Both the American Arbitration Association and the Federal Mediation and Conciliation Service offer to supply the names of recommended arbitrators; the parties select the arbitrator they want and pay the arbitrator directly. Usually the two sides share the arbitrator's fee equally.

The main objections to the use of arbitration for resolving disputes are that there is no direct right of appeal and no direct power or procedure for enforcement of the arbitrator's decision.

Finality of arbitrator's decision

By agreeing to submit a dispute to arbitration, a party also agrees to abide by the arbitrator's ruling. The only exceptions would be if someone could prove that the arbitrator had a financial or personal interest in the matter which prejudiced the decision, or that fraud or perjury was involved in the testimony, or that the arbitrator mistakenly failed to follow the law on a material issue. Otherwise, the arbitrator's decision is final. If one of these exceptions can be proved, a court will set aside the arbitrator's decision.

There is only one solution to the problem of enforcement. If the loser refuses to abide by the arbitrator's decision, the winner's only recourse is to go to court to have the arbitrator's decision enforced.

Arbitration is a fast, inexpensive method for resolving commercial disputes. However, its effectiveness depends greatly on the attitude of the parties. Most businesses today want their legal disputes settled out of court and as cheaply and quickly as possible. Arbitration can be the answer.

Mediation-assisting negotiations

Mediation.   A mediator does not decide the dispute between the parties, but rather tries to help them reach a negotiated settlement. The mediator can suggest compromises and trade-offs to the parties. Having a neutral third party be the first to suggest a compromise can be very useful in solving the dispute, especially when neither side wants to be the first to "give in." The mediation process is totally under the control of the parties, and the solution can be whatever they agree to.

Private Judges.   A newer procedure which holds great promise for solving business disputes involves the hiring of a private judge, with the parties paying a fee for this service. These persons are usually retired judges who are expert in a particular area of the Law. Their decisions are binding on the parties, and they are bound to follow the normal court rules on evidence. Unlike a regular court, however, the trial can be held in private, at the parties' convenience. In many states, no official transcript is required, although the decision can be appealed to the regular appellate courts. The advantages to this procedure are speed, convenience, privacy, and expertise.

Mini-Trials.   Another very promising new procedure is the mini-trial. Each side prepares a presentation of the essential parts of its side of the dispute. The presentation is made before a neutral advisor, who has no power to decide the dispute. The presentation is brief, no more than one or two days—in contrast to weeks or months for a complex case in the regular courts. The presenter for each side does have the authority to settle the dispute on the spot. If they fail to settle, the neutral advisor—an expert in the area—may indicate which way the case would probably be decided in court. The parties may then negotiate further. This system is similar to mediation in that any settlement must be accepted by both sides. It otherwise has the same advantages as the private judge system.

■ SIGNIFICANCE OF THIS CHAPTER

Every executive in business must realize the possibility of legal disputes and involvement in the legal process. This chapter introduced both the state and national court systems. It described the procedure of a civil lawsuit from the filing of the suit to the final appeal and enforcement of the judgment, including a discussion of the formal legal system. This chapter also reviewed dispute resolution by private arbitration, which saves time and legal expenses and is used in a large number of commercial contracts.

A basic understanding of these processes is useful in working with a lawyer to prepare a case, and in deciding whether to settle or to litigate.

DISCUSSION CASE

WILES v. MORITA IRON WORKS CO.
530 N.E.2d 1382 (Illinois, 1988)

FACTS: Plaintiff Floyd Wiles, a resident of Cook County, Illinois, sued defendant Morita Iron Works Co. Ltd., a Japanese corporation which designed and manufactured the machine that allegedly caused plaintiff's injuries. Plaintiff's employer, Astro Packaging Co., is a corporation that operates plants in Hawthorne, New Jersey and Alsip, Illinois. Astro purchased four machines from defendant. Two were shipped to the New Jersey plant, and two were shipped to the Illinois plant. Plaintiff was employed at Astro's Alsip, Illinois plant. One of the machines allegedly caused personal injuries to plaintiff, for which plaintiff seeks damages from defendant. The cause of action sounds in strict liability and negligence.

Defendant filed a special and limited appearance and

a motion to dismiss, challenging the in personam jurisdic-tion of the court, pursuant to the Illinois Long Arm Stat-ute. The motion was supported by the affidavit of Motoo Morita, defendant's president. The trial court quashed the service of process on the defendant and dismissed defendant from this action "due to lack of personal jurisdic-tion." Plaintiff appealed, and the Appellate Court reversed the Trial Court. Now MIW appeals.

■

Justice Clark delivered the opinion of the Illinois Su-preme Court:

The sole issue presented in this appeal is whether the defendant's contacts with the State of Illinois are sufficient to subject the defendant to the *in personam* jurisdiction of the Illinois courts. . . .

By "purposefully availing" itself of opportunities in the forum State, such as by purposefully directing itself to forum residents, a defendant subjects itself to the possi-ble exercise of that forum's jurisdiction. Satisfaction of this "purposeful availment" requirement ensures that an alien defendant will not be forced to litigate in a distant or inconvenient forum solely as a result of "random," "fortuitous," or "attenuated" contacts, or the unilateral act of a consumer or some other third person. Jurisdiction will only be proper where the contacts proximately result from actions by the *defendant himself* that create a "substan-tial connection" with the forum State. Only in situations "where the defendant 'deliberately' has engaged in signifi-cant activities within a State or has created 'continuing obligations' between himself and residents of the forum [has] he manifestly . . . availed himself of the privilege of conducting business there, and . . . it is not presump-tively unreasonable to require him to submit to . . . litiga-tion in that forum."

Applying these principles to the facts before us, we hold that MIW did not have the requisite minimum con-tacts with the State of Illinois to subject it to the personal jurisdiction of the circuit court.

The thrust of the plaintiff's due process argument here is that MIW should have reasonably anticipated being sued in Illinois because it directly sold its products to a New Jersey corporation that had an industrial plant in Illinois. Specifically, the plaintiff alleges that MIW must have had either "actual or constructive knowledge" that Astro had a plant in Illinois and therefore should have anticipated that the product may find its way into Illinois. According to the plaintiff, MIW's intentional act of placing its products into the stream of commerce by delivering the air cell formers to Astro in Japan, coupled with MIW's "actual or constructive" knowledge that some of these products would eventually find their way to Illinois, is sufficient to form the basis for State court jurisdiction under the due process clause.

[W]e believe that even under the broader version of the stream of commerce theory there were no minimum contacts between defendant Morita and the State of Illi-nois. Under the facts presented in the instant case, an exertion of personal jurisdiction over this defendant by the Illinois courts would still be inconsistent with due process. Under either interpretation of the stream of com-merce theory, it is clear that purposeful availment of the forum's market requires, at a *minimum,* that the alien defendant is "*aware* that the final product is being marketed in the forum State." The record in this case is totally devoid of any evidence that the defendant was aware either during contract negotiations or at the time of delivery of the products to Astro in Japan that Astro intended to transport two of the air cell formers to Illinois, or that Astro even had a plant in Illinois. Without any evi-dence of such knowledge on the part of the defendant, on this basis alone we would have to conclude, under either theory, that [MIW] made no effort, directly or indirectly, to serve the market for its product in Illinois and that the air cell formers were, therefore, brought into Illinois solely by the unilateral act of Astro. "The unilateral activity of those who claim some relationship with a nonresident defendant cannot satisfy the require-ment of contact with the forum State." The fact that the defendant now knows the machines were sent to Illi-nois, as revealed in the defendant's affidavit, is of no conse-quence in the determination of whether this defendant has purposefully availed itself of the privilege of conduct-ing activities within Illinois.

For the foregoing reasons the judgment of the appellate court is reversed and the judgment of the circuit court is affirmed.

■ IMPORTANT TERMS AND CONCEPTS

procedural law
arbitration
mediation
U.S. District Court
U.S. Court of Appeals

U.S. Supreme Court
diversity of citizenship
concurrent jurisdiction
federal question
writ of certiorari

U.S. Bankruptcy Court
state specialty court
state trial court
state appellate court
state supreme court
jurisdiction over subject-
    matter

jurisdiction over person
domicile
limited personal
    jurisdiction
long-arm jurisdiction
choice of law
venue

pleadings
complaint
summons
service of process
default judgment
motion to dismiss
answer
reply
counter-claim
cross-complaint
motion for summary
    judgment
pretrial
discovery
interrogatories
deposition
privilege
pretrial conference
trial
jury selection
voir dire examination
challenge for cause

peremptory challenge
preliminary instructions
opening statements
direct examination
witness
cross-examination
redirect examination
motion for directed verdict
summation
judge's instruction
verdict
judgment notwithstanding
    the verdict
appeal
execution against property
garnishment
lien
full faith and credit
class action
private judge
mini-trial

■ QUESTIONS AND PROBLEMS FOR DISCUSSION

1. What are long arm statutes, and what purposes do they serve? Give an example where a long arm statute would be used.

2. What substantive law must a U.S. District Court apply in a trial of a tort case? What procedural law will the court follow?

3. How does jurisdiction differ from venue? Define and discuss each term.

4. What is a demurrer? Where in the trial stage could it be used?

5. One of the statutes setting up the U.S. Veterans Administration provides that all records under its jurisdiction shall be "confidential and privileged." Sanchez, who had been treated in a VA hospital in New Mexico for certain service-related injuries, was involved in a car accident. Sanchez sued Knoze, the other driver, alleging that Knoze was at fault and that Sanchez

was permanently disabled. Knoze's lawyer thinks that Sanchez may be using the accident to try to recover for his war injuries and asks for a discovery order against Sanchez's VA hospital records. How should the court rule, and why?

6. Mrs. Franc was walking across a railroad bridge owned by the Pennsylvania Railroad. She slipped and fell through a gap in the planking on the bridge. She did not see the gap as it was covered with snow. She was seriously injured. The bridge was not constructed for pedestrian traffic and was private property. However, many townspeople had used this bridge to cross the creek for several years. The railroad was aware of that fact. Mrs. Franc sued the railroad for damages for her injuries, and the jury gave her a verdict. The judge then entered a judgment notwithstanding the verdict in favor of the railroad.

   Was the trial judge correct? Why or why not?

7. Cuthbert filed a $250,000 medical malpractice action against Dr. Jillian Peabody in U.S. District Court in Minisoda. Cuthbert was a resident of North Pagoda; he had gone to Minisoda, where Dr. Peabody had her offices, for treatment. Cuthbert's lawsuit was filed more than two years, but less than three years, after the negligent treatment by Dr. Peabody. Her lawyer says that the lawsuit should be dismissed because Minisoda's statute of limitations for such claims is two years. Cuthbert's lawyer says that North Pagoda's three-year statute of limitations period should be applied. Which lawyer is correct, and why?

8. Little Company sued the Biggie Corporation, alleging that Biggie had committed several antitrust violations which injured Little Co. Little Co. asked the trial court for a discovery order to produce certain Biggie's books and records which related to Biggie's marketing practices and market shares. Sam Slick, who was vice president for finance at Biggie, said that the company did not have such records available. When the court ordered production, Slick swore under oath that he was unable to comply. It has now been learned that Slick did have such records available. What sorts of remedial action might the court take now? Discuss.

3

Constitutional Law and Administrative Regulation

CHAPTER OBJECTIVES

THIS CHAPTER WILL:

- Explore constitutional limitations on government regulation of business.
- Examine the protections found in the First Amendment.
- Explain the power the commerce clause gives Congress.
- Describe how the contract clause limits state regulation of business.
- Introduce the privileges and immunities clause and the equal protection clause found in the Fourteenth Amendment.
- Discuss administrative agencies and their power to adjudicate disputes.

The *U.S. Constitution* provides the framework within which our governmental agencies and our society must operate. It provides the basic rules for deciding disputes between the agencies themselves, and among agencies and businesses and individuals. We have already noted, in both Chapter 1 and Chapter 2, the constitutional limits to courts' power to hear cases. Other constitutional rules will be discussed as they apply to specific topics in later chapters.

In this chapter we will discuss the primary constitutional limitations on the regulation of business. Protections exist against actions by both national and state governments. Similar protections are found in state constitutions against arbitrary or unfair actions by the states and their agencies. A business affected by such arbitrary state action may thus challenge such action under applicable provisions of that state's constitution, as well as under the appropriate clauses of the U.S. Constitution.

Since much business regulation results from action taken by national and state administrative agencies, this chapter also outlines their origin, functions, and procedures.

■ CONSTITU-TIONAL LIMITATIONS

Fifth Amendment due process procedural limitations

Substantive limitations

Limits on National Government Regulations. The general prohibition against unfair or arbitrary action by the national government and its agencies is the *due process clause* contained in the *Fifth Amendment:* "nor shall any person . . . be deprived of life, liberty, or property, without due process of law."

This clause is one of the greatest legal statements ever made, an important step in the development of Anglo-American common law. The clause has both procedural and substantive content. Procedurally, it means that actions of the national government which affect specific individuals can only be taken by following certain required steps, and that, overall, the government's decision must be reached through a process that is "fundamentally fair" to those affected. Fairness in the constitutional sense usually requires a hearing before an impartial decision maker, adequate notice of the proposed action, the right to be represented by counsel, the right to confront and cross-examine adverse witnesses, the right to present one's own witnesses and arguments, and the right to court review of the initial decision.

Substantively, the due process clause means the government simply may not do some things, even if it follows an established procedure. This clause is thus an important protection against tyranny of a majority. Even after Congress passes a bill and the President signs it, the constitutionality of the statute may be challenged. A law may be ruled unconstitutional because it violates one of the specific provisions of the Constitution, such as freedom of speech, or because it violates the division of power established between national and state governments or among the three branches of the national government.

Statutes may also be invalidated if they attempt to regulate matters that are none of the government's concern. In 1970, for example, the U.S. Supreme Court overturned a state law prohibiting the distribution of birth control information to married adults (*Griswold* v. *Connecticut*). Presumably, a similar national statute would also be unconstitutional. There is a constitutional "right to privacy" even though it is not expressly stated anywhere in the Constitution. The Ninth

Amendment specifically states that the list in the other amendments is not exclusive.

Bill of Rights limitations

Violations of Specific Bill of Rights Sections. Even though proper legislative procedure was followed in passing a statute, and even though the enforcement agency is proceeding in accordance with the statute's provisions, such action by the government cannot violate any of the specific protections found in the *Bill of Rights.* These include all the specific criminal procedure requirements we will discuss in Chapter 6; the *First Amendment* freedoms of speech, press, assembly, and religion; the prohibition against taking private property unless just compensation is paid; and others. Not all of these provisions have always been vigorously enforced, especially when businesses are being affected rather than individuals. The privilege against being forced to testify against oneself in a criminal case is generally not applicable to corporations, for example. As indicated in the *Metromedia* case at the end of this chapter, several justices feel that commercial speech is not entitled to the same constitutional protection as individual speech.

Fourth Amendment

In the following case, the majority of the Court felt that a business's rights had not been violated by the Environmental Protection Agency.

DOW CHEMICAL CO. v. UNITED STATES

476 U.S. 227 (1986)

FACTS

Petitioner Dow Chemical Co. operates a 2,000-acre facility manufacturing chemicals at Midland, Michigan. The facility consists of numerous covered buildings, with manufacturing equipment and piping conduits located between the various buildings exposed to visual observation from the air. At all times, Dow has maintained elaborate security around the perimeter of the complex, barring ground-level public views of these areas. It also investigates any low-level flights by aircraft over the facility. Dow has not undertaken, however, to conceal all manufacturing equipment within the complex from aerial views. Dow maintains that the cost of covering its exposed equipment would be prohibitive.

In early 1978, enforcement officials of EPA, with Dow's consent, made an on-site inspection of two power plants in this complex. A subsequent EPA request for a second inspection, however, was denied, and EPA did not thereafter seek an administrative search warrant. Instead, EPA employed a commercial aerial photographer, using a standard floor-mounted, precision aerial mapping camera, to take photographs of the facility from altitudes of 12,000, 3,000, and 1,200 feet. At all times the aircraft was lawfully within navigable airspace.

EPA did not inform Dow of this aerial photography, but when Dow became aware of it, Dow brought suit in the District Court, alleging that EPA's action violated the Fourth Amendment and was beyond EPA's statutory investigative authority. The District Court granted Dow's motion for summary judgment on the ground that EPA had no authority to take aerial photographs and that doing so was a search violating the Fourth Amendment. EPA was permanently enjoined from taking aerial photographs of Dow's premises and from disseminating, releasing, or copying the photographs already taken.

The Court of Appeals reversed, and the case was appealed to the U.S. Supreme Court.

ISSUE

Does this aerial photography by the EPA violate the Fourth Amendment?

DECISION   No. Judgment of the Court of Appeals affirmed.

REASONS   **Chief Justice Burger found no constitutional violation.**

"Dow plainly has a reasonable, legitimate, and objective expectation of privacy within the interior of its covered buildings, and it is equally clear that expectation is one society is prepared to observe. . . . Moreover, it could hardly be expected that Dow would erect a huge cover over a 2,000-acre tract. In contending that its entire enclosed plant complex is an 'industrial curtilage,' Dow argues that its exposed manufacturing facilities are analogous to the curtilage surrounding a home because it has taken every possible step to bar access from ground level. . . .

"Dow's inner manufacturing areas are elaborately secured to ensure they are not open or exposed to the public from the ground. Any actual physical entry by EPA into any enclosed area would raise significantly different questions, because '[t]he business-man, like the occupant of a residence, has a constitutional right to go about his business free from unreasonable official entries upon his private commerical property.' . . . The narrow issue raised by Dow's claim of search and seizure, however, concerns aerial observation of a 2,000-acre outdoor manufacturing facility *without* physical entry. . . .

"[T]he Government has 'greater latitude to conduct warrantless inspections of commercial property' because 'the expectation of privacy that the owner of commercial property enjoys in such property differs significantly from the sanctity accorded an individual's home.' . . .

"[U]nlike a homeowner's interest in his dwelling, '[t]he interest of the owner of commercial property is not one in being free from any inspections.' And with regard to regulatory inspections we have held that '[w]hat is observable by the public is observable without a warrant, by the Government inspector as well.' . . .

"It may well be, as the Government concedes, that surveillance of private property by using highly sophisticated surveillance equipment not generally available to the public, such as satellite technology, might be constitutionally proscribed absent a warrant. But the photographs here are not so revealing of intimate details as to raise constitutional concerns. Although they undoubtedly give EPA more detailed information than naked-eye views, they remain limited to an outline of the facility's buildings and equipment. The mere fact that human vision is enhanced somewhat, at least to the degree here, does not give rise to constitutional problems. An electronic device to penetrate walls or windows so as to hear and record confidential discussions of chemical formulae or other trade secrets would raise very different and far more serious questions; other protections such as trade secret laws are available to protect commercial activities from private surveillance by competitors.

"We conclude that the open areas of an industrial plant complex with numerous plant structures spread over an area of 2,000 acres are not analogous to the 'curtilage' of a dwelling for purposes of aerial surveillance; such an industrial complex is more comparable to an open field and as such it is open to the view and observation of persons in aircraft lawfully in the public airspace immediately above or sufficiently near the area for the reach of cameras.

"We hold that the taking of aerial photographs of an industrial plant complex from navigable space is not a search prohibited by the Fourth Amendment."

Congress's power under the commerce clause

Outer Limits of the Commerce Clause.   Under Article I, Section 8 of the Constitution, Congress is given full power to regulate interstate commerce, foreign trade, and commerce with the Indian tribes. On these topics, the Supreme Court has said several times that the power of Congress is as complete as if there were only a national government, and is subject only to the restrictions contained in other sections of the Constitution. Congress clearly has the power under the *commerce clause* to pass the Occupational Safety and Health Act (OSHA), for example, but it could not provide for warrantless searches of private property.

So long as it acts within constitutional limits, Congress has a free hand regarding the extent and type of regulation it places in interstate commerce. It may outlaw practices that are harmful to the public, and it may restrict or prohibit interstate shipments of dangerous products. It may itself specify illegalities in some detail, or it may choose to legislate only broad guidelines and to delegate to an administrative agency the power to make the detailed rules of practice. It may adopt national legislation which preempts state laws, or it may delegate most of its power to regulate a particular area to the states.

If it wishes, Congress may also regulate intrastate commerce that has an impact on interstate commerce. The rationale for this auxiliary power is that it is necessary, or may be necessary, to effectively regulate interstate commerce. In the famous case of *Wickard* v. *Filburn,* (1942), the Supreme Court upheld, under the commerce clause, regulations of agricultural production which reached all the way to a farmer who was growing grain for use on his own farm. The Court said his use of his own grain did affect interstate commerce, since he would not be buying grain in the interstate grain market. If everyone grew and used their own grain, there would be no market. If that analysis is valid, it's hard to imagine many activities that could not be subjected to the commerce power if Congress wished to do so. Of course, if a particular statute says that it applies only to those activities "in" commerce, rather than to any which "affect" commerce, Congress is indicating that the statute is not to apply to purely intrastate matters.

The following case is an example of the broad authority of Congress to regulate business under the commerce clause of the U.S. Constitution. The court found that even though the activities were local in character, they still substantially affected interstate commerce and thus were subject to regulation by Congress.

Regulation of local commerce which affects interstate commerce

McLAIN v. REAL ESTATE BOARD OF NEW ORLEANS, INC.

444 U.S. 232 (1980)

FACTS

Plaintiff filed a civil antitrust action, seeking an injunction and treble damages, on behalf of himself and all other purchasers of residential real estate in the prior four years in the Greater New Orleans area who had used the services of one of the defendant real estate brokers. Plaintiff alleged a conspiracy to fix commission rates and real estate prices. Defendants moved to dismiss alleging: (1) that their activities were only local in nature; (2) that there was no legal requirement that a broker be employed in the sale of real estate; and (3) that they did not usually procure financing or insurance, nor did they examine the validity of the sellers' titles. The U.S. District Court dismissed the complaint, and the Court of Appeals affirmed.

ISSUE

Are the brokers subject to the Sherman Act?

DECISION   Yes. Judgment reversed, and case remanded for trial.

REASONS   Chief Justice Burger held the brokers' activities did affect interstate commerce in several ways.

"The broad authority of Congress under the Commerce Clause has, of course, long been interpreted to extend beyond activities actually *in* interstate commerce to reach other activities that, while wholly local in nature, nevertheless substantially *affect* interstate commerce. . . . This Court has often noted the correspondingly broad reach of the Sherman Act. . . . During the near century of Sherman Act experience, forms and modes of business and commerce have changed along with changes in communication and travel, and innovations in methods of conducting particular businesses have altered relationships in commerce. Application of the Act reflects an adaptation to these changing circumstances. . . .

"The conceptual distinction between activities 'in' interstate commerce and those which 'affect' interstate commerce has been preserved in the cases, for Congress has seen fit to preserve that distinction in the antitrust and related laws by limiting the applicability of certain provisions to activities demonstrably 'in commerce.' . . . It can no longer be doubted, however, that the jurisdictional requirement of the Sherman Act may be satisfied under either the 'in commerce' or the 'effect on commerce' theory. . . .

"On the record thus far made, it cannot be said that there is an insufficient basis for petitioners to proceed at trial to establish Sherman Act jurisdiction. It is clear that an appreciable amount of commerce is involved in the financing of residential property in the Greater New Orleans area and in the insuring of titles to such property. The presidents of two of the many lending institutions in the area stated in their deposition testimony that those institutions committed hundreds of millions of dollars to residential financing during the period covered by the complaint. The testimony further demonstrates that this appreciable commercial activity has occurred in interstate commerce. Funds were raised from out-of-state investors and from interbank loans obtained from interstate financial institutions. Multistate lending institutions took mortgages insured under federal programs which entailed interstate transfers of premiums and settlements. Mortgage obligations physically and constructively were traded as financial instruments in the interstate secondary mortgage market. Before making a mortgage loan in the Greater New Orleans area, lending institutions usually, if not always, required title insurance, which was furnished by interstate corporations. Reading the pleadings, as supplemented, most favorably to petitioners, for present purposes we take these facts as established.

"At trial, respondents will have the opportunity, if they so choose, to make their own case contradicting this factual showing. On the other hand, it may be possible for petitioners to establish that, apart from the commerce in title insurance and real estate financing, an appreciable amount of interstate commerce is involved with the local residential real estate market arising out of the interstate movement of people, or otherwise."

Limits on State Government Regulation. As units of government which are sovereign within their own area, the states retain, under the U.S. Constitution, their "police power." The *police power* of a government is its power to regulate activities under its jurisdiction to promote the public health, safety, and welfare. The **states' police powers** in this regard are limited, however, by general and specific provisions in the Constitution. Some of these limitations

States' Police Power

are prohibitions against particular types of state action, such as the **Contracts Clause.** Article I, Section 10 reads in part as follows: "No State shall pass . . . any . . . Law impairing the Obligation of Contracts. . . ." Originally, the provision was intended to prevent state legislatures from passing laws that would prevent the enforcement of valid contracts and the collection of debts. For a period of some 50 years after the Civil War, the contracts clause was one of the major legal arguments used to invalidate government regulations of business. Rejected as an argument in 1934 in the *Blaisdell* case, the Contracts Clause fell into disuse until 1978, when it was revived in the *Allied Structural* case. It now appears that only the most arbitrary interferences with contract rights will be invalidated under this clause.

Privileges and Immunities. A corporation is not considered a "citizen" for the purposes of the privileges and immunities clause of the Fourteenth Amendment. Therefore, the corporation need not be given any of the privileges and immunities of citizenship. Individual citizens conducting their businesses, however, would be protected by that clause. Even corporations might benefit indirectly, if a state's regulation of individual employees were held unconstitutional. When Alaska passed a statute requiring that its residents be hired in preference to new arrivals for work on oil and gas projects, employer corporations could not challenge the statute on this basis. The act was, however, ruled unconstitutional when it was challenged by five newly arrived workers who had been denied jobs in favor of Alaska residents (*Hicklin* v. *Orbeck,* 1978). The corporations operating these projects in Alaska were thus free to hire anyone who applied for the job and was qualified, Alaska resident or not.

Fourteenth Amendment privileges and immunities

Equal Protection. Since the word used in this section of the Fourteenth Amendment is "person," and corporations are persons, neither they nor individuals can be denied "equal protection" by a state. This clause does not mean that a state cannot draw distinctions and treat different persons differently. It does mean, however, that any distinctions must be based on reasonable and rational criteria. There can be no arbitrary or invidious discrimination.

Two tests are used by the courts when violations of this clause are alleged. The **strict scrutiny test** is used where the regulation impacts on a fundamental right, such as freedom of speech, or where it adversely affects a "suspect class" of persons. A suspect class is one which has been subjected to past acts of discrimination, or which may have special disadvantages. Such groups might include racial, religious, or nationality minorities. Such state regulations will pass the test only if necessary to achieve a "compelling state interest," and if drawn as narrowly as possible to achieve it.

The alternative, and easier, test is the **rational basis** requirement. With no fundamental rights or suspect classes involved, a state classification would be presumed valid if there were any rational basis for it. The state's differential treatment must be related to the regulatory objective sought by the state, but if it is, it is presumed valid. The fact that other methods might be used to achieve the same result is not enough to invalidate a state's choice under this test. Many state regulations would be invalid under the first test; very few would be under this one. Most business regulations will probably be tested under this second, more generous standard.

Fourteenth Amendment equal protection

Strict scrutiny test

Rational basis test

Due Process.   As was true under the Fifth Amendment, due process has both a substantive and a procedural content. Procedurally, no state can deny any person (including corporate persons) life, liberty, or property, without following a fair procedure. Since the Fourteenth Amendment does not itself spell out all the details of required criminal procedure found in the Bill of Rights, the courts have allowed some flexibility to the states in that area. For example, the Fifth Amendment requires indictment by a grand jury in serious crimes, but the states are permitted to use an alternate procedure called an *information*. The information drafted by the prosecutor/district attorney serves the same function as an indictment in informing the court and the defendant what the charges are, what facts are alleged, and what possible penalties are involved. While the details may vary from state to state and from regulation to regulation, the overall procedure must be basically fair to the affected parties.

Fourteenth Amendment due process—procedural limitations

The substantive meaning of the ***Fourteenth Amendment due process*** clause is similar to that of the Fifth Amendment. Even if a fair procedure is provided, the courts may rule that the content of the regulation makes it invalid. Such invalidity may be found because the regulation violates a specific prohibition of the Constitution or because it infringes on one of the protected rights.

Substantive limitations

Since the 1930s most of the Justices have been more willing to defer to the state legislatures' judgments as to regulations of property and contract rights than to those which infringe on personal freedoms such as speech, press, and assembly. Some Justices and textwriters continue to believe that commercial speech is less deserving of protection than noncommercial speech, and may use that distinction to validate one regulation while invalidating another. Not all Justices make these distinctions or apply them in the same way, so that the court is badly divided in many such cases. A majority may agree on the result in a case, but for quite different reasons, and there may be one or more dissenting opinions. As a result, it is often difficult to extract any rules or guidelines for future business conduct.

Commerce Clause.   Another very significant limitation on the regulatory power of state governments stems from the power granted to Congress under the commerce clause. Since one of the major purposes of the Constitution was to create a national marketplace for our people's goods and services, the states cannot unduly or unfairly interfere with interstate commerce. Similarly, the commerce clause limits the states' power to tax interstate business.

Commerce clause limitations on states

To be valid, state regulations cannot discriminate against interstate commerce in favor of local businesses. Interstate businesses must be given a fair chance of competition in local markets. Second, a state regulation cannot unduly burden interstate commerce. In one famous case, an Illinois statute required curved mud-flaps over the rear tires of all large trucks. The flat mud-flaps which were used to comply with the laws of all other states would not comply with the Illinois law. Nor would the curved mud-flaps comply with the other states' laws. As a result, an interstate trucker would have to drive around Illinois, or stop at the state borders to change mud-flaps, or drive through and risk a ticket. The U.S. Supreme Court decided that this state law unduly burdened the interstate truckers and held it unconstitutional. A similar question is raised about Minnesota's milk-container law in the next case.

MINNESOTA v. CLOVER LEAF CREAMERY CO.

419 U.S. 456 (1981)

FACTS In 1977, the Minnesota Legislature enacted a statute banning the retail sale of milk in plastic nonreturnable, nonrefillable containers, but permitting such sale in other nonreturnable, nonrefillable containers, such as paperboard milk cartons. Clover Leaf Creamery Co. brought this action challenging the statute and contends that the statute violates the Equal Protection and Commerce Clauses of the Constitution.

The parties agree that the standard of review applicable to this case under the Equal Protection Clause is the familiar "rational basis" test. Moreover, they agree that the purposes of the Act cited by the legislature—promoting resource conservation, easing solid waste disposal problems, and conserving energy—are legitimate state purposes. Thus, the controversy in this case centers on the narrow issue of whether the legislative classification between plastic and nonplastic nonreturnable milk containers is rationally related to achievement of the statutory purposes. The Minnesota District Court, the trial court, found the statute invalid. The Minnesota Supreme Court also found the statute invalid, and the State of Minnesota appealed to the U.S. Supreme Court.

ISSUE Does the statute unduly burden interstate commerce?

DECISION No. Judgment reversed.

REASONS **Justice Brennan thought the Minnesota statute was a permissible use of the state's power.**

"Although parties challenging legislation under the Equal Protection Clause may introduce evidence supporting their claim that it is irrational, . . . they cannot prevail so long as 'it is evident from all the considerations presented to [the legislature], and those of which we may take judicial notice, that the question is at least debatable.' . . . Where there was evidence before the legislature reasonably supporting the classification, litigants may not procure invalidation of the legislation merely by tendering evidence in court that the legislature was mistaken. . . .

"The state identified four reasons why the classification between plastic and nonplastic nonreturnables is rationally related to the articulated statutory purposes. If any one of the four substantiates the state's claim, we must reverse the Minnesota Supreme Court and sustain the Act. . . .

"The Minnesota Supreme Court found that plastic milk jugs in fact take up less space in landfills and present fewer solid waste disposal problems than do paperboard containers. . . . But its ruling on this point must be rejected for the same reason we rejected its ruling concerning energy conservation: it is not the function of the courts to substitute their evaluation of legislative facts for that of the legislature.

"We therefore conclude that the ban on plastic nonreturnable milk containers bears a rational relation to the state's objectives, and must be sustained under the Equal Protection Clause.

"The District Court also held that the Minnesota statute is unconstitutional under the Commerce Clause because it imposes an unreasonable burden on interstate commerce. We cannot agree.

"When legislating in areas of legitimate local concern, such as environmental protection and resource conservation, states are nonetheless limited by the Commerce Clause. . . . Even if a statute regulates 'even-handedly,' and imposes only 'incidental' burdens on interstate commerce, the courts must nevertheless strike it down if 'the burden imposed on such commerce is clearly excessive in relation to the putative local benefits.' . . . Moreover, 'the extent of the burden that will be tolerated will of course depend on the nature of the local interest involved, and on whether it could be promoted as well with a lesser impact on interstate activities.' . . .

"Since the statute does not discriminate between interstate and intrastate commerce, the controlling question is whether the incidental burden imposed on interstate commerce by the Minnesota Act is 'clearly excessive in relation to the putative local benefits. . . . We conclude that it is not. . . .

"A nondiscriminatory regulation serving substantial state purposes is not invalid simply because it causes some business to shift from a predominantly out-of-state industry to a predominantly in-state industry. Only if the burden on interstate commerce clearly outweighs the state's legitimate purposes does such a regulation violate the Commerce Clause."

Congressional preemption of state action

Finally, a state regulation is not valid where Congress, under the commerce clause, has preempted the particular subject area. The *Flood* case at the end of Chapter 1 is one such example; Congress has preempted the regulation of professional sports. Frequently, Congress does not specify whether it wishes to preclude state action on a particular subject, so the courts are forced to imply a congressional intent from the legislative history of the national statute and from the degree of comprehensiveness of the national regulations.

■ ADMINISTRA-TIVE AGENCIES

Origins and Functions. Often referred to as the "headless fourth branch of government," *administrative agencies* originated as a means to deal with the complex problems of a modern urban society. Judges and juries lack the technical expertise to solve problems in such areas as telecommunications, transportation, investment securities, and labor relations. Furthermore, court procedures tend to be technical and subject to lengthy delays.

Reasons for establishment of agencies

The original idea of the independent regulatory agency was to provide a body of technical experts who could render faster decisions, based on the realities of the field, and free of the legal technicalities of the courtroom. Congress also wanted these agencies free of direct control by the President, so that they would be better able to implement the policy standards established by Congress in the statutes creating the agencies and defining their powers. The idea was for Congress to set out the basic objectives and standards, and the agencies then to implement those policies with detailed rules and individual decisions.

Originally, there was considerable concern over the extent to which Congress could lawfully delegate the legislative power given to it in Article I to these other bodies. One of the centerpieces of Franklin D. Roosevelt's New Deal, the National Industrial Recovery Act of 1933, was invalidated on these grounds in the famous "sick chicken" case, *Schechter Poultry Corp.* v. *United States*, 295 U.S. 495 (1935). The NIRA authorized industry groups to draw up "codes of fair competition" which could then be approved by the President. Schechter had been prosecuted for violating such a code. The Supreme Court said that

Congress could not lawfully give such groups a blank check for whatever regulations they thought wise. The NIRA was declared unconstitutional. Subsequently, grants of discretion almost as broad to administrative agencies have been upheld, so that the Schechter rule is of little value today.

Problems. Gradually, as administrative agencies' procedures became more formalized, they were subject to many of the same criticisms that had earlier been leveled against the courts. Delays and technicalities existed in agency proceedings, too. Not all agency members were experts; some were political cronies, lacking experience in the areas they were supposed to be regulating. Many staffers drifted back and forth between agencies and private employment, creating the appearance at least of serious conflicts of interest. Questions were raised by scholars and affected parties about the fairness of a hearing where the same body was investigator, prosecutor, and judge, *and* was charged by Congress with implementing specific policy results.

New Deal agencies

Our national economy is strong and vibrant enough to tolerate some tinkering of this sort, but there are limits. The New Deal created agencies like a computer doing permutations of the alphabet. The 1960s and 1970s were almost as bad, and in some ways, even worse. Entire industries were subjected to bureaucratic controls—banking, transportation, communication, power. Key aspects of nearly all industries were subjected to agency control—labor relations, issuance of securities, trade practices, mergers. Nearly all businesses are subject to environmental and safety controls. Such controls are not totally evil or counterproductive; in many cases they were adopted because of gross abuses. The total impact of such regulations, however, can be devastating. At some point, a straw breaks the camel's back; one additional regulation becomes a cost that makes the business unprofitable. The real miracle of American business is that it has persevered, and prospered, despite these massive additional costs.

Reform and Deregulation. In the late 1970s people finally began to talk seriously about deregulating significant sectors of the economy. In part, this discussion was due to a resurgence of free market economics, but it also occurred because the regulated economy was not performing satisfactorily.

Costs versus benefits

Innovation was occurring, and new jobs were being created in white-collar, unregulated industries such as computers. Steel, autos, and transportation—burdened with stifling regulations and conflict-oriented labor relations—were in trouble. The Japanese model of labor-management cooperation was promoted as the wave of the future. Administrative rules were seen as barriers to new methods and new relationships. The nuclear power industry, for example, has been prevented from expanding in the United States, while it flourishes in such countries as France and Japan.

Significant deregulation has already occurred in the power, banking, and transportation industries. In other areas, agencies such as the Occupational Safety and Health Administration have a more realistic view of their function. Instead of requiring the rehanging of fire extinguishers that were an inch or two out of line with the OSHA standards, the agency has now concentrated on more serious health hazards in the workplace. At the state level, "sunset" laws are being considered, which would terminate an agency after a certain number of years unless specific legislative renewal of the agency was enacted.

No one wants to return to the days of robber barons and polluted air and water. The challenge for both business and government, as we move toward the 21st century, is to develop administrative regulations only where necessary and to make them rational and cost-effective.

■ ADMINISTRATIVE PROCEDURE

The following discussion focuses on the constitutional and statutory requirements for administrative action. The general rules for most national agencies are set out in the Administrative Procedure Act.

Requirement of a Hearing. When an agency is acting in its legislative capacity, adopting rules, it need not hold a trial-type hearing. If it does hold hearings prior to the adoption of such a rule, it is not bound by the evidence produced at the hearing, any more than Congress is in its legislative capacity. When an agency acts as a court, however, and adjudicates an individual matter, it usually can do so only after a trial-type hearing. In this capacity, it is bound by the evidence in the record, just as a court would be. Its decision must be based on that evidence and stem from that evidence. While the agency is given considerable discretion in setting the details of that hearing, it must be basically fair to those affected.

Rule-making versus adjudication

Requirement of Notice. If there is to be a trial-type hearing, the party affected must be given adequate notice to prepare for it. In practice, however, the courts have interpreted this requirement quite loosely. The evidence introduced may vary from the charges alleged, unless the variation would be unfair to the affected party.

Notice usually is sent through the mail to directly affected parties. Where a general agency decision is involved, notice is usually given through the *Federal Register,* the official bulletin for agency action.

Requirement of Confrontation. Our legal system does not favor secret accusers. Personal prejudice and envy may be motivating factors in the accusation. We want the accusers to come forward and to be available for cross-examination. We feel that truth and justice can only be served when the accusers and the accused confront each other. Otherwise, as Justice Douglas once stated, "So far as we or the Board know, the accusers may be psychopaths or venal people, . . . who revel in being informers. They may bear old grudges. Under cross-examination their stories might disappear like bubbles. Their whispered confidences might turn out to be yarns conceived by twisted minds or by people who, though sincere, have poor faculties of observation and memory."

Right to confront and cross-examine witnesses

Once again, however, these general rules requiring confrontation are subject to modification under particular circumstances, through the agency's administrative discretion. The U.S. Supreme Court ruled in 1960 that the persons who had accused state voter registrars of violations of national voting laws did not have to appear and confront the registrars. The Court felt that anonymity had to be preserved in that situation. This case (*Hannah* v. *Larche,* 363 U.S. 420) is clearly an exception to the general rule.

Right to Counsel.   As is true in criminal proceedings, the person accused in an administrative proceeding is entitled to be represented by counsel. This requirement is also a deeply imbedded element of our common-law heritage. The right to counsel may be limited, however, where the agency is conducting an investigation, rather than adjudicating a disputed matter. In one famous case, *In re Groban,* 352 U.S. 330 (1957), the U.S. Supreme Court decided that a state fire marshal conducting an arson investigation did not have to give witnesses the right to counsel, even though they had been compelled to appear and to testify. The witnesses were not directly accused—yet. The court felt that this sort of investigation was analogous to a grand jury investigation of possible crimes, where the right to counsel has traditionally been limited.

Right to an Impartial Hearing Officer.   One of the traditional concerns with administrative agencies is their alleged lack of impartiality, since they are charged with the enforcement of the statutes so as to produce the desired policy results. Part of this concern is also due to the fact that staff members may move back and forth between an agency and the industry it is trying to regulate; the fear is that such persons may become promoters rather than regulators. Legislative directions to the agency are sometimes not clear: Congress directed the original Atomic Energy Commission to promote *and* regulate the atomic power industry. These sorts of problems are an inevitable part of the agency regulatory process and are tolerated as part of the price of using the agency method.

Decider with a personal stake in outcome = unfair proceeding

Where the administrator has a direct, personal share in the outcome of a proceeding, however, the possibility of bias is so great that the procedure, or the administrator, or both, must be changed. In one classic example, the mayors of Ohio cities were given the power to hear alleged violations of the prohibition laws. The mayor would be paid court costs only if the accused was found guilty. In *Tumey* v. *Ohio,* 273 U.S. 510 (1927), the U.S. Supreme Court held that this procedural arrangement violated the accused person's right to an impartial decision on the charges.

To try to separate their investigation/prosecution functions from their trial/adjudication functions, many agencies have a separate staff of hearing examiners, now called *administrative law judges* (ALJs). The prosecuting staff decide whether to issue a complaint. If they do, there is a hearing before an ALJ, who must render a decision on the facts presented during the hearing.

Right to Review.   Part of the agreement on using the administrative agency system, with all its ambiguities and conflicting loyalties, was an understanding that court review of these decisions would be available. Some possibility of unfairness could be tolerated, if court review were available to correct the most obvious abuses.

Record review versus *de novo* review

In many of the important agencies, such as the NLRB, the FCC, and the FTC, the agency itself—the board or commission—may review the findings and order of its ALJ prior to a court appeal. This internal agency review procedure varies somewhat from agency to agency. In some instances, the review is a limited one, "on the record": Did the ALJ follow the statute, and is his or her order supported by evidence in the trial record? If so, the agency affirms the decision, much as an appellate court would. In other agencies, the board or commission may itself use the hearing record for making *its own* decision in the matter, just as if it had heard the case itself—a **de novo review.**

Limited court review

While courts are quite willing to reverse an agency's interpretation of its statute, they generally defer to the agency's findings of fact and its orders, if based on evidence in the hearing record. The agency is the expert, and its policy decisions should stand, unless they are arbitrary or biased. For the most part, courts are not an effective check on agency decisions, since few decisions will be unsupported in the hearing record.

SCHWEIKER v. GRAY PANTHERS

453 U.S. 34 (1981)

FACTS

The Gray Panthers is an organization formed to promote the rights of the elderly. The national Medicaid program provides funds to states that pay for medical treatment for the poor. An individual's benefits depend on the financial resources "available" to him or her. Some states assume ("deem") that part of a spouse's income is available to an applicant for Medicaid. As a result, some persons do not qualify for benefits at all, or qualify for reduced benefits. The Gray Panthers challenged the U.S. regulations that permit the states to deem a spouse's income to the Medicaid applicant without examining the facts of the individual case. Both the U.S. District Court and the Court of Appeals for the District of Columbia held the regulations invalid.

ISSUE

Are the administrative regulations permitting "deeming" arbitrary, capricious, or otherwise unlawful?

DECISION

No. Judgment reversed and case remanded.

REASONS

Writing for the majority, Justice Powell said that Secretary Schweiker had properly exercised the authority delegated by Congress in adopting these regulations. With millions of applicants, a requirement for an individual hearing in each case could potentially use up most of the agency's resources. None of the dollars spent on holding hearings would be available to pay medical bills.

"Congress explicitly delegated to the Secretary broad authority to promulgate regulations defining eligibility requirements for Medicaid. We find that the regulations at issue in this case are consistent with the statutory scheme and also are reasonable exercises of the delegated power. . . .

"The Social Security Act is among the most intricate ever drafted by Congress. Its Byzantine construction, as Judge Friendly has observed, makes the Act 'almost unintelligible to uninitiated.' Perhaps appreciating the complexity of what it had wrought, Congress conferred on the Secretary exceptionally broad authority to prescribe standards for applying certain sections of the Act. . . . Participating States must grant benefits to eligible persons 'taking into account only such income and resources as are, *as determined in accordance with standards prescribed by the Secretary,* available to the applicant.' . . .

"In view of this explicit delegation of substantive authority, the Secretary's definition of the term 'available' is 'entitled to more than mere deference or weight.' . . . Rather, the Secretary's definition is entitled to 'legislative effect' because, 'i[n] a situation of this kind, Congress entrusts to the Secretary, rather than to the courts, the primary responsibility for interpreting the statutory term.' . . . Although we do not abdicate review in these circumstances, our task is the limited one of ensuring that the Secretary did not 'excee[d] his statutory authority' and that the regulation is not arbitrary or capricious."

■ QUASI-JUDICIAL PROCEDURES IN ADMINISTRATIVE AGENCIES

The National Labor Relations Board, the Federal Trade Commission, the Environmental Protection Agency, the Occupational Safety and Health Administration, and many other national and state administrative agencies daily hear disputes concerning violations of their rules and regulations. Typically the businessperson will have more contact with administrative agencies than with the court system. The procedure for the determination of disputes in the administrative agency system is termed *quasi-judicial* because it does not have the full authority of a court and because the party being tried does not have the right to trial by jury. Nearly all decisions of administrative bodies are subject to judicial review by an appellate court.

To give the student an understanding of a typical administrative agency quasi-judicial procedure, we will follow a National Labor Relations Board case from beginning to end.

NLRB Procedure in Unfair Labor Practices Cases

Charge.   An NLRB regional office is notified that an employer or a union is engaged in one or more unfair labor practices. This means that the employer or the union has violated the statutory rules by which both labor unions and management must conduct themselves. The complaining party is then asked to complete a charge, which is simply a form specifying what unfair labor practice has been committed and by whom. Once a charge is filed, a field examiner conducts an investigation. This is done to determine whether there is sufficient evidence of a violation to proceed to a formal hearing. If the field examiner does not find evidence sufficient to support further activity in the case, then the charge will be dismissed.

Formal Complaint.   If the evidence found was sufficient to justify pursuing the case, then a formal complaint will be filed by the NLRB's office of General Counsel. This complaint contains the specific allegations of wrongdoing. The employer or the labor union alleged to be in violation will be given a copy, as well as an opportunity to answer the charges.

Answer.   The answer filed in this case is similar to the answer filed in a civil case. The answer may deny some allegations and admit others. Typically, allegations concerning violation of the National Labor Relations Act will be denied, and allegations concerning time and place will be admitted.

Hearing.   A hearing is then scheduled at which an administrative law judge hears testimony. Witnesses are presented by both parties in a manner similar to the procedure followed in a trial of a civil lawsuit. At the end of the testimony, the parties are allowed to make summarization statements.

■ **EXHIBIT 3–1**
Quasi-Judicial Procedure in
an Administrative Agency—
the NLRB

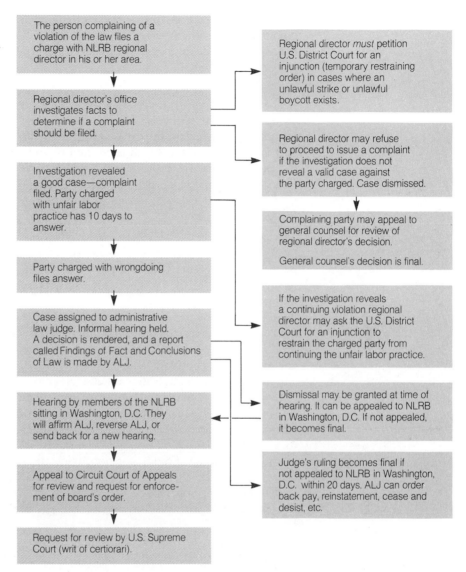

Findings of Fact and Conclusions of Law. The administrative law judge (ALJ) will prepare a written decision entitled "Findings of Fact and Conclusions of Law." After the ALJ has rendered a decision, either of the parties may request an appeal. This must be done within 20 days after the decision. If an appeal is not requested, the decision of the ALJ becomes final. If a request for an appeal is made, then the parties will file legal briefs to support their positions. They may request oral arguments before the five-member National Labor Relations Board in Washington, D.C.

Board Review. The Board will review the briefs of the parties, hear oral arguments, and render a decision and order. The NLRB itself has no legal power to enforce its order. If the finding is against the employer or the union and that party refuses to comply with the Board's order, then the Board must ask the U.S. Court of Appeals for a judgment to enforce its order. Or, if the employer or the union feels that the NLRB decision is incorrect or unfair, it may appeal the decision to the U.S. Court of Appeals.

Review by the U.S. Court of Appeals. The U.S. Court of Appeals will review the decision of the NLRB upon the petition of any interested party, or upon request of the NLRB if enforcement of an order of the Board is requested. The review by the court is concerned with two questions: first, was the decision of the Board supported by substantial evidence? and second, did the Board follow the correct substantive law? If the court agrees with the Board's decision, it will order compliance. If the court disagrees with the Board, it can reverse the Board's decision and dismiss the case, or send the case back for a rehearing.

Review by the Supreme Court of the United States. Either party may petition the Supreme Court of the United States for a writ of certiorari to review the decision of the U.S. Court of Appeals. If the writ of certiorari is granted, a review will be had, and the parties will have to comply with the final judgment of the U.S. Supreme Court. If the Supreme Court refuses to issue a writ of certiorari, then the judgment of the U.S. Court of Appeals is final. The failure of a party to obey a court order can be punishable as either civil or criminal contempt of court.

The procedure of the National Labor Relations Board is typical of the procedure used by most of the administrative agencies that have quasi-judicial authority. In other words, an investigation will be conducted and an initial hearing will be held before an administrative law judge, with the right of an appeal to a quasi-judicial board, and with the right of a later appeal to an appellate court. The legal justification for not giving the right to trial by jury in these cases is that they are not legal trials and that the decision rendered is not a civil judgment for money. They are more like an *equity injunction*—an order to comply with the law, an order to pay back wages, or an order to re-hire.

The flowchart on the preceding page shows the procedures for an unfair labor practice case before the NLRB.

■ **SIGNIFICANCE OF THIS CHAPTER**

Government regulation of business is one of the most important legal areas for the modern business manager. Many business decisions are subject to detailed, and often confusing, regulations. Likewise, entire industries may operate under an administrative agency as the watchdog of the public interest. In this context, it is important to remember that even the government must play by the rules, and that court review is available where an agency oversteps its boundaries or acts in an arbitrary and unfair manner.

This chapter outlined the basic framework for government regulation of business. Other specific constitutional issues will be raised in Chapters 4, 6, 13, and 49. Questions about the constitutionality of a particular government action may be raised by the affected party, so each of us needs to know the basic rules.

METROMEDIA, INC. v. CITY OF SAN DIEGO

453 U.S. 490 (1981)

FACTS: Metromedia Inc. owns a large number of outdoor advertising signs and billboards (in San Diego). San Diego passed an ordinance that restricted the use of billboards and some other outdoor advertising in the city. The alleged purpose was "to eliminate hazards to pedestrians and motorists brought about by distracting sign displays" and "to improve the appearance of the city." Metromedia sued to enjoin the enforcement of the ordinance. The trial court ruled that the ordinance was an unconstitutional exercise of the city's police power and a violation of plaintiff's First Amendment rights. The California Court of Appeals affirmed, but the California Supreme Court reversed. The case was appealed to the U.S. Supreme Court.

■

Justice White gave the opinion for the court:

This Court has often faced the problem of applying the broad principles of the First Amendment to unique forums of expression. . . . Each method of communicating ideas is "a law unto itself" and that law must reflect the "differing natures, values, abuses and dangers" of each method. We deal here with the law of billboards. Billboards are a well-established medium of communication, used to convey a broad range of different kinds of messages. . . .

But, whatever its communicative function, the billboard remains a "large, immobile, and permanent structure which like other structures is subject to . . . regulation.". . . Moreover, because it is designed to stand out and apart from its surroundings, the billboard creates a unique set of problems for land-use planning and development.

Billboards, then, like other media of communication, combine communicative and noncommunicative aspects. As with other media, the government has legitimate interests in controlling the noncommunicative aspects of the medium . . ., but the 1st and 14th Amendments foreclose a similar interest in controlling the communicative aspects. Because regulation of the noncommunicative aspects of a medium often impinges to some degree on the communicative aspects, it has been necessary for the courts to reconcile the government's regulatory interests with the individual's right to expression. . . .

Appellant's principal submission is that enforcement of the ordinance will eliminate the outdoor advertising business in San Diego and that the 1st and 14th Amendments prohibit the elimination of this medium of communication. . . . Because our cases have consistently distinguished between the constitutional protection afforded commercial as opposed to non-commercial speech, in evaluating appellants' contention we consider separately the effect of the ordinance on commercial and noncommercial speech.

The extension of First Amendment protections to purely commercial speech is a relatively recent development in First Amendment jurisprudence. Prior to 1975, purely commercial advertisements of services or goods for sale were considered to be outside the protection of the First Amendment. . . .

Although the protection extended to commercial speech has continued to develop, commercial and noncommercial communications, in the context of the First Amendment have been treated differently. . . .

The constitutional problem in this area requires resolution of the conflict between the city's land-use interests and the commercial interests of those seeking to purvey goods and services within the city. In light of the above analysis, we cannot conclude that the city has drawn an ordinance broader than is necessary to meet its interests, or that it fails directly to advance substantial government interests. In sum, insofar as it regulates commercial speech the San Diego ordinance meets the constitutional requirements. . . .

It does not follow, however, that San Diego's general ban on signs carrying noncommercial advertising is also valid under the 1st and 14th Amendments. The fact that the city may value commercial messages relating to onsite goods and services more than it values commercial communications relating to off-site goods and services does not justify prohibiting an occupant from displaying its own ideas or those of others.

As indicated above, our recent commercial speech cases have consistently accorded noncommercial speech a greater degree of protection than commercial speech. San Diego effectively inverts this judgment, by affording a greater degree of protection to commercial than to noncommercial speech. There is a broad exception for onsite commercial advertisements, but there is no similar exception for noncommercial speech. The use of on-site billboards to carry commercial messages related to the commercial use of the premises is freely permitted, but the use of otherwise identical billboards to carry noncommercial messages is generally prohibited. The city does not explain how or why noncommercial billboards located in places where commercial billboards are permitted would be more threatening to safe driving or would detract more from the beauty of the city. Insofar as the city tolerates billboards at all, it cannot choose to limit their content to commercial messages; the city may not conclude that the communication of commercial information concerning goods and services connected with a particular site is of greater value than the communication of noncommercial messages. . . .

Despite the rhetorical hyperbole of The Chief Justice's dissent, there is a considerable amount of common ground between the approach taken in this opinion and that suggested by his dissent. Both recognize that each medium of communication creates a unique set of First Amendment problems, both recognize that the city has a legitimate interest in regulating the noncommunicative aspects of a medium of expression, and both recognize that the proper judicial role is to conduct "a careful inquiry into the competing concerns of the State and the interests protected by the guarantee of free expression.". . . Our principal difference with his dissent is that it gives so little weight to the latter half of this inquiry. . . .

Because the San Diego ordinance reaches too far into the realm of protected speech, we conclude that it is unconstitutional on its face. The judgment of the California Supreme Court is reversed and the case remanded to that court.

■ IMPORTANT TERMS AND CONCEPTS

U.S. Constitution
Fifth Amendment due process of law
Bill of Rights
First Amendment
Fourth Amendment
Commerce Clause
states' police power
Contracts Clause
Fourteenth Amendment privileges and immunities
Fourteenth Amendment equal protection of the law
strict scrutiny test
rational basis test
Fourteenth Amendment due process of law
preemption
administrative agency
hearing
notice
confrontation
right to counsel
administrative law judge (ALJ)
de novo review
charge
formal complaint

■ QUESTIONS AND PROBLEMS FOR DISCUSSION

1. What is the purpose of the "equal protection" clause of the U.S. Constitution? Who is it meant to protect? Must a state always treat all persons and corporations equally? Explain.
2. What is the purpose of the supremacy clause of the Constitution?
3. What is the *Federal Register*? What purpose does it serve?
4. Is there a constitutional right of privacy? If so, where is it stated in the Constitution? Discuss.
5. An Oklahoma statute prohibits opticians from selling eyeglass lenses without a prescription from a licensed optometrist or ophthalmologist. It also prohibits retail stores from providing space for any person who purports to perform eye examinations. These provisions were challenged by an optician as violations of his 14th Amendment rights to due process and equal protection. What is the result in this litigation, and why?
6. The State of Arizona passed a law that prohibits railroad trains crossing through the state of Arizona to have more than 70 freight cars, or 14 passenger cars. The Southern Pacific Railroad violated this law by having more cars than allowed and was prosecuted for violation of the law. Their defense was that the law was unconstitutional. How should the court rule? Is this law constitutional? Why?
7. Acme Company sues for an injunction to prevent picketing outside its plant. Union members were carrying signs that read: "The men on this job are not 100 percent affiliated with the A.F.L." Several truckers refused to cross the picket line to make deliveries to Acme. The union says its signs are a form of free speech, protected by the Fourteenth Amendment, which incorporates the rights listed in the First Amendment. Who's right here, and why?
8. The deeds to real estate located in an expensive subdivision prohibit the sale of the property to blacks or Orientals. These deed restrictions were challenged by both current owners and prospective buyers as denying persons their rights under the Fourteenth Amendment. Some current owners claim that the restrictions cannot be challenged under the Fourteenth Amendment since no state action is involved, only private agreements. Who is right, and why?

4

International Law

CHAPTER OBJECTIVES

THIS CHAPTER WILL:

- Introduce international law and identify its sources.
- Describe the International Court of Justice and its purpose.
- Explain why U.S. courts have jurisdiction to hear international law disputes in some cases.
- Discuss why international arbitration is preferable to going to court in many international law cases.
- Introduce letters of credit and the ways they are used in international trade.

Modern international trade

The **U.S. Constitution** is the **supreme law of the land** in the United States, but its supremacy stops at our national borders. This has not deterred most large U.S. companies and many smaller ones from engaging in international trade. U.S. firms may execute contracts with foreign governments, set up foreign subsidiaries, or sell directly to foreign customers by sending U.S. sales personnel abroad, by hiring agents in the foreign country, or by shipping goods directly to the foreign customer.

Huge **multinationals,** corporations operating in many countries, have been called the "new world order" and the "successor to the nation-state." Examples include Mobil, Gulf, Shell, Hoover, IBM, and Xerox. Each of these companies derives 50 percent or more of its income from foreign operations.

International business involves high stakes. Ninety percent of all U.S. corporations with sales of over $1 billion are multinationals. Although international trade represents only 17 percent of the U.S. gross national product, it dominates the economies of many other countries. The importance of international commerce is growing, especially as U.S. firms commence trade with the communist countries of Eastern Europe and Asia. Students, therefore, must couple their knowledge of the U.S. legal system with an understanding of international law.

■ INTERNA-TIONAL LAW: AN INTRO-DUCTION

International trade is nothing new. Neither are international relations and treaties between sovereign states. Almost from earliest recorded history, societies developed customs for handling international affairs. Much early international law concerned rules for foreign diplomats and the law of the sea—freedom of passage, rights of ships in foreign ports, salvage and fishing rights, and the like.

Ancient international codes

City-states and nations that were important commercial centers often published collections of the customs which governed international trade. Evidence indicates that the Egyptians had such international law practices by 1400 B.C. Rhodes, the largest of the Dodecanese Islands, in the Aegean Sea, had a "code" of international law by 700 B.C. The Greek city-states also developed customs for dealing with diplomatic personnel and international trade. The Roman Empire's **ius gentium,** the law that dealt with noncitizens, eventually came to dominate the Roman legal system, overshadowing the **ius civile,** which covered Roman citizens.

An important collection of international legal practices was published by Visby, Sweden, one of the most important members of the Hanseatic League in the 11th century. Other trade customs were recorded when Louis IX of France published the Code of Oléron in the mid-13th century. Legal historians generally date modern international law from the adoption of the Treaty of Westphalia in 1648.

■ SOURCES OF INTERNA-TIONAL LAW

International law is drawn from the widest variety of sources; customs, treaties, judicial precedents, and textbooks have all contributed to its development. Hugo Grotius, a Dutch lawyer, is usually called "the father of international law" because of his great work, *De Jure Bellis ac Pacis,* published in 1625. In it he wrote that international law is based on the **natural law** common to all

■ **EXHIBIT 4–1**
International Law

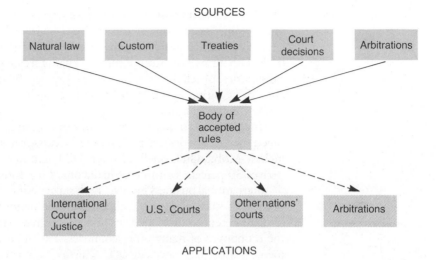

SOURCES

Natural law · Custom · Treaties · Court decisions · Arbitrations

Body of accepted rules

International Court of Justice · U.S. Courts · Other nations' courts · Arbitrations

APPLICATIONS

Grotius and natural law

nations—the "dictate of right reason." This was in marked contrast to the "positivists," who derived international law from the *customs* of nations in their dealings with each other. In fact, both of these elements have played a part, along with specific *treaties* governing the international relations of two or more countries, and decisions of arbitrators and national and international courts.

Justice Story uses the "natural law" approach in the following case. It shows that International Law is more than just the average of the laws of the various nations.

U.S. v. THE SCHOONER LA JEUNE EUGÉNIE

2 Mason 409 (U.S. Circuit Court, 1822)

FACTS   An American warship, commanded by one Lieutenant Stockton, seized the schooner *La Jeune Eugénie* off the coast of Africa while it was being employed in the slave trade. The schooner was owned by French citizens who objected to the jurisdiction of the U.S. court in this forfeiture action. They contended that even though the slave trade was prohibited by French law, that was a matter which only French courts can decide. The United States contended that the slave trade also violated the law of nations.

ISSUE   Does the slave trade violate international law?

DECISION   Yes. Schooner confiscated from its owner but "delivered over to the consular agent of the King of France, to be dealt with according to his own sense of duty and right."

REASONS   **Justice Story did not think himself bound by the fact that slavery was still in force in the United States and that it had been and was recognized in other countries.**

"[T]he first question naturally arising out of the asserted facts is, whether the African slave trade be prohibited by the law of nations; for, if it be so, it will not, I presume, be denied, that confiscation of the property ought to follow, for that is the proper penalty denounced by that law for any violation of its precepts. . . .

"I shall take up no time in the examination of the history of slavery, or of the question, how far it is consistent with the natural rights of mankind. . . . That it has existed in all ages of the world, and has been tolerated by some, encouraged by others, and sanctioned by most, of the enlightened and civilized nations of the earth in former ages, admits of no reasonable question. That it has interwoven itself into the municipal institutions of some countries, and forms the foundation of large masses of property in a portion of our own country, is known to all of us. Sitting, therefore, in an American court of judicature, I am not permitted to deny, that under some circumstances it may have a lawful existence; and that the practice may be justified by the condition, or wants, of society, or may form a part of the domestic policy of a nation. . . .

"But this concession carries us but a very short distance towards the decision of this cause. It is not, as the learned counsel for the government have justly stated, on account of the simple fact that the traffic necessarily involves the enslavement of human beings, that it stands reprehended by the present sense of nations; but that it necessarily carries with it a breach of all the moral duties, of all the maxims of justice, mercy, and humanity, and of the admitted rights, which independent Christian nations now hold sacred. . . .

"Now the law of nations may be deduced, first, from the general principles of right and justice, applied to the concerns of individuals, and thence to the relations and duties of nations; or, secondly, in things indifferent or questionable, from the customary observances and recognitions of civilized nations; or, lastly, from the conventional or positive law, that regulates the intercourse between states. . . .

"[N]o practice . . . can obliterate the fundamental distinction between right and wrong. . . .

"[T]he African slave trade . . . is repugnant to the great principles of Christian duty, the dictates of natural religion, the obligations of good faith and morality, and the eternal maxims of social justice."

■ INTERNA-TIONAL COURT OF JUSTICE

UN elects ICJ judges

Chapter XIV of the Charter of the United Nations set up the International Court of Justice, in accordance with an annexed statute. This statute is a comprehensive code which governs the organization of the court, the jurisdiction of the court, and the procedure to be followed by the court.

The statute provides that the International Court of Justice shall consist of 15 judges and that no more than 2 judges may be from the same country. These judges must be persons of high moral character, and they must have the same qualifications as would be required in their respective countries for appointment to the highest judicial offices there, or they must be *jurisconsults* of recognized competence in international law. The judges are elected by the General Assembly and by the Security Council of the United Nations from a list of nominations submitted by nominating bodies from the various member nations. Their term of office is nine years, with five members of the court being reelected or replaced every three years.

Only for disputes between nations

The International Court of Justice was not set up to hear disputes between private citizens concerning international contract or property disputes. Since only nations may be parties in cases brought before the International Court of Justice, that court's decision are of less significance to international business operations than are the decisions of national courts which apply international law.

■ INTERNATIONAL LAW IN U.S. COURTS

International law has generally been recognized in U.S. courts, either as a part of the common law or as a body of practice and doctrines that the common-law courts would have recognized and enforced. Two very important constitutional provisions relate to international law. Article III, Section 2 extends the jurisdiction of the national courts to "all cases affecting ambassadors, other public ministers, and consuls" and to "all cases of admiralty and maritime jurisdiction." In addition, a citizen of a foreign nation could have a case tried in a U.S. District Court under *diversity of citizenship* rules. It thus appears that most international cases heard in this country will be tried in a U.S. District Court.

U.S. Constitution supremacy clause

The second important constitutional provision relating to international law produces more controversial results. Article VI, Section 2 provides: "This Constitution, and the laws of the United States which shall be made in pursuance thereof; and all treaties made or which shall be made, under the authority of the United States, shall be the supreme law of the land; and the judges in every state shall be bound thereby, anything in the constitution or laws of any state to the contrary notwithstanding."

On its face, this is a logical and commonsense provision: the laws of the whole prevail over those of the parts. The problem arises because of the words used. To be "supreme," national "laws" (acts of Congress) must be made "in pursuance" of the Constitution, that is, subject to its protections and the powers delegated to Congress. Treaties, however, need only have been made "under the authority of the United States," that is, negotiated by the President and *ratified* by two thirds of the Senate.

Senate ratification of treaties

Since the President, by the terms of Article II, Section 2, must get the "advice and consent" of two thirds of the Senate before a treaty becomes the "supreme law of the land," an important check still remains on arbitrary action by the executive which might violate provisions of the Constitution. Presumably, two thirds of the Senate would not vote to ratify a treaty which was blatantly unconstitutional. That protection was removed by a series of cases in the 1930s and 1940s, which dealt with the internal effect of international agreements that had not been submitted to the Senate for ratification as treaties.

While several later cases have indicated that the executive could not enforce an agreement which violated specific provisions of the Bill of Rights, the basic "supremacy" problem remains. From a business standpoint, the danger is that such political settlements may have drastic consequences for the private ownership of property in the foreign country and for the enforceability of contracts. The meaning and effect of treaties is determined by the courts, just as is true for statutes, as seen in the following case.

SUMITOMO SHOJI AMERICA, INC. v. AVAGLIANO

457 U.S. 176 (1982)

FACTS Sumitomo Shoji America, Inc. is a New York corporation and wholly owned subsidiary of Sumitomo Shoji Kabushiki Kaisha, a Japanese general trading company. Respondents are past and present female secretarial employees of Sumitomo. All but one of the respondents are U.S. citizens; that one exception is a Japanese citizen living in the United States. Respondents brought this suit as a class action claiming that Sumitomo's alleged practice of hiring only male Japanese citizens to fill executive, managerial, and sales positions violated Title VII of the Civil Rights Act of 1964. Respondents sought both injunctive relief and damages.

Sumitomo asked the court to dismiss the complaint as it was exempt from coverage of the civil rights laws as a result of the Friendship, Commerce, and Navigation Treaty between the United States and Japan. The District Court refused to dismiss. The Court of Appeals reversed, saying Sumitomo was exempt under the provisions of the Treaty.

ISSUE Does Article VIII(1) of the Friendship, Commerce, and Navigation Treaty between the United States and Japan provide a defense to a Title VII employment discrimination suit against an American subsidiary of a Japanese company?

DECISION No. Judgment reversed, and case remanded.

REASONS Chief Justice Burger saw no exemption in the treaty.

"Interpretation of the Friendship, Commerce, and Navigation Treaty between Japan and the United States must, of course, begin with the language of the Treaty itself.

"Article VIII(1) of the Treaty provides in pertinent part:

> [C]*ompanies of either Party* shall be permitted to engage, within the territories of the other Party, accountants and other technical experts, executive personnel, attorneys, agents, and other specialists of their choice. . . .

"Clearly Article VIII(1) only applies to companies of one of the Treaty countries operating in the other country. Sumitomo contends that it is a company of Japan, and that Article VIII(1) of the Treaty grants it very broad discretion to fill its executive, managerial, and sales positions exclusively with male Japanese citizens. . . .

"Sumitomo is 'constituted under the applicable laws and regulations' of New York; based on Article XXII(3), it is a company of the United States, not a company of Japan. As a company of the United States operating in the United States, under the literal language of Article XXII(3) of the Treaty, Sumitomo cannot invoke the rights provided in Article VIII(1), which are available only to companies of Japan operating in the United States and to companies of the United States operating in Japan."

▪ INTERNATIONAL ARBITRATION

Reasons for international arbitration

It is very common for international business contracts to contain an arbitration clause whereby the parties agree to submit any controversy relating to the contract to an arbitrator or an arbitration panel, rather than to go to court. In any business contract dispute, arbitration will almost certainly save time and legal expense, and the parties can select an arbitrator with expertise in the substantive area involved. These same advantages hold at the international level, but there are additional procedural reasons for including such a clause in the international contract. With an international dispute, there are always potential questions as to which court in what country would have jurisdiction, how service of process can be effected across international boundaries, and which country's law applies. These problems can be minimized with an arbitration clause in business contracts that specifies the law to be applied, the method of selecting the arbitrator, the procedures to be followed, and the allocation of expenses between the parties. While it is true that arbitrator's awards are sometimes not paid voluntarily, they will generally be enforced by the courts of most nations if a lawsuit is necessary.

■ INTERNA-TIONAL TAXATION

U.S. Constitutional limits on taxation of international firms

Doing business across international boundaries may also involve complex taxation questions. As a rule, businesses can be required to pay different types of taxes by the countries in which they are doing business, in accordance with principles similar to those used by U.S. courts in determining the validity of taxes imposed on out-of-state businesses. The U.S. Supreme Court has ruled that multinational firms cannot be required to pay state or local taxes which duplicate taxes they are already paying in their home country.

■ THE ACT OF STATE DOCTRINE AND THE SOVEREIGN IMMUNITY DOCTRINE

The *act of state doctrine* is an international law doctrine that provides that the courts in one country shall not adjudicate a politically sensitive dispute which would require the court to sit in judgment on the legality of acts of a foreign country, when those acts were committed in that foreign country and not in the country where the court is sitting. This doctrine may be invoked by private foreign litigants as well as foreign governments. Therefore this doctrine differs from the doctrine of *sovereign immunity,* as sovereign immunity applies only to a foreign country, not to private foreign litigants. The sovereign immunity doctrine of international law provided that a foreign country was immune from being sued in another country as a result of its sovereign or public acts. Since many foreign governments actually own and operate commercial ventures, the question arose as to whether sovereign immunity applies when it is the foreign country which is operating a commercial venture. In 1976 the U.S. Congress passed the Foreign Sovereign Immunities Act (FSIA), which provides that a foreign country engaged in commercial matters in the United States will not be immune from suit in the U.S. courts for its commercial acts.

In the following case the International Association of Machinists and Aerospace Workers Union sued the Organization of Petroleum Exporting Countries (OPEC), alleging that OPEC was guilty of violation of U.S. antitrust laws. Their price fixing allegedly caused high prices for oil in the United States. The court reviewed the sovereign immunity doctrine and the act of state doctrine and found they could not adjudicate this case because of the act of state doctrine.

INTERNATIONAL ASSOCIATION OF MACHINISTS v. OPEC

649 F.2d 1354 (U.S. Ninth Circuit, 1981)

FACTS   The IAM was disturbed by the high price of oil and petroleum-derived products in the United States. They believed the actions of the Organization of the Petroleum Exporting Countries, popularly known as OPEC, were the cause of this burden on the American public. Accordingly, IAM sued OPEC and its member nations in December of 1978, alleging that their price-setting activities violated United States antitrust laws. IAM sought injunctive relief and damages. The District Court entered a final judgment in favor of the defendants, holding that it lacked jurisdiction and that IAM had no valid antitrust claim.

The OPEC nations produce and export oil either through government-owned companies or through government participation in private companies. Prior to the formation of OPEC, these diverse and sometimes antagonistic countries were plagued with fluctuating oil prices. Without coordination among them, oil was often in oversupply on the world market, resulting in low prices.

OPEC achieves its goals by a system of production limits and royalties which its members unanimously adopt. There is no enforcement arm of OPEC. The force behind OPEC decrees is the collective self-interest of the 13 nations.

After formation of OPEC, it is alleged, the price of crude oil increased tenfold and more.

ISSUE   Can a U.S. District Court hear an antitrust suit against foreign governments?

DECISION   No. Judgment affirmed.

REASONS   **Circuit Judge Choy discussed the international problems such a suit would create.** "In the international sphere each state is viewed as an independent sovereign, equal in sovereignty to all other states. It is said that an equal holds no power of sovereignty over an equal. Thus the doctrine of sovereign immunity: the courts of one state generally have no jurisdiction to entertain suits against another state. This rule of international law developed by custom among nations. Also by custom, an exception developed for the commercial activities of a state. The former concept of absolute sovereign immunity gave way to a restrictive view. Under the restrictive theory of sovereign immunity, immunity did not exist for commercial activities since they were seen as non-sovereign. . . .

"The District Court was understandably troubled by the broader implications of an antitrust action against the OPEC nations. The importance of the alleged price-fixing activity to the OPEC nations cannot be ignored. Oil revenues represent their only significant source of income. Consideration of their sovereignty cannot be separated from their near total dependence upon oil. We find that these concerns are appropriately addressed by application of the act of state doctrine. While we do not apply the doctrine of sovereign immunity, its elements remain relevant to our discussion of the act of state doctrine. . . .

"The remedy IAM seeks is an injunction against the OPEC nations. The possibility of insult to the OPEC states and of intereference with the efforts of the political branches to seek favorable relations with them is apparent from the very nature of this action and the remedy sought. While the case is formulated as an anti-trust action, the granting of any relief would in effect amount to an order from a domestic court instructing a foreign sovereign to alter its chosen means of allocating and profiting from its own valuable natural resources. On the other hand, should the court hold that OPEC's actions are legal, this 'would greatly strengthen the bargaining hand' of the OPEC nations in the event that Congress or the executive chooses to condemn OPEC's actions. . . .

"While conspiracies in restraint of trade are clearly illegal under domestic law, the record reveals no international consensus condemning cartels, royalties, and production agreements. The United States and other nations have supported the principle of supreme state sovereignty over natural resources. The OPEC nations themselves obviously will not agree that their actions are illegal. We are reluctant to allow judicial interference in an area so void of international consensus. An injunction against OPEC's alleged price-fixing activity would require condemnation of a cartel system which the community of nations has thus far been unwilling to denounce. The admonition . . . that the courts should consider the degree of codification and consensus in the area of law is another indication that judicial action is inappropriate here. . . .

"The act of state doctrine is applicable in this case. The courts should not enter at the will of litigants into a delicate area of foreign policy which the executive and legislative branches have chosen to approach with restraint. The issue of whether the FSIA allows jurisdiction in this case need not be decided, since a judicial remedy is inappropriate regardless of whether jurisdiction exists. Similarly, we need not reach the issues regarding the indirect-purchaser rule, the extraterritorial application of the Sherman Act, the definition of 'person' under the Sherman Act, and the propriety of injunctive relief."

■ U.S. ANTITRUST LAW AND INTERNATIONAL TRADE

The *Sherman Antitrust Act* was passed by the U.S. Congress in 1890 to deter anticompetitive acts such as price fixing, a division of markets between competitors, a conspiracy to restrain trade, and other monopolization activities that unlawfully restrain trade. The law contains criminal provisions and also provides that the persons who were injured by the anticompetitive actions can sue for treble damages. The Clayton Act was passed in 1914 to amend and clarify the 1890 Sherman Antitrust Act. The antitrust law as amended not only applies to activities and transactions by persons and corporations within the boundaries of the United States, but also applies to trade beyond the borders of the United States. If a U.S. citizen or corporation trades with a foreign citizen, a foreign business entity, or a foreign government, it is still subject to the antitrust law of the United States. The injured party, whether such party is a foreign citizen, business entity or a foreign government, has the right to file an action for treble damages in the United States courts against the party or parties who have committed illegal trade practices in violation of the U.S. antitrust laws. The U.S. Supreme Court so held in *Pfizer, Inc.* v. *Government of India,* the discussion case at the end of this chapter.

■ FOREIGN CORRUPT PRACTICES ACT

In 1977 the Congress passed the *Foreign Corrupt Practices Act.* Investigations by the Securities and Exchange Commission prior to 1977 revealed that a large number of U.S. firms were making illegal bribes and payments to foreign officials to get special treatment regarding the awarding of contracts, and to waive regulations. Congress felt that our firms when doing business internationally should adhere to the same standards of business ethics they would be legally obligated to adhere to if the transactions were made in the United States. The FCPA amends the 1934 Securities Exchange Act in three main areas: a U.S. firm, whether or not subject to the 1934 Act's registration and disclosure requirements, is prohibited from bribing foreign officials to misuse their official position to benefit the firm; a firm subject to the 1934 Act must maintain books and records which, in reasonable detail, accurately and fairly reflect the firm's transactions and must also maintain a system of internal accounting controls which reasonably ensure that transactions are properly executed and recorded and that corporate assets are protected; new criminal penalties of up to $1 million for the firm and of up to $10,000 and five years' imprisonment for the individuals involved may be imposed for willful violations.

■ INTERNATIONAL SALES OF GOODS

A recent major addition to International Law has tremendous importance for U.S. businesses. In 1980, representatives of 62 nations, meeting in Vienna, unanimously approved a new treaty—the United Nations Convention on *Contracts for the International Sale of Goods (CISG)*. CISG was ratified by the U.S. Senate in 1986. Our ratification, along with those of China and Italy, was deposited with the UN on December 11, 1987, making a total of 11 ratifications. According to its terms, CISG takes effect one year after the deposit of the 10th country's ratification. It thus became legally effective on January 1, 1988.

CISG applies only to commercial transactions, not to consumer sales. It applies only if the sale of goods occurs between parties whose places of business are in two different countries, both of which have ratified CISG. It does not cover such controversial topics as liability for product-related deaths or injuries, or questions such as fraud or illegality, or the rights of third parties. Such issues remain subject to the national laws of the various countries.

CISG contains important changes from the UCC rules which might otherwise be applicable if a U.S. business was one of the parties to the international sale of goods transaction. Unlike the UCC, CISG does not require a writing for enforcement of the contract. However, an offeror may insist on a written acceptance of the offer, and the parties may agree that only a written modification of their contract is valid. CISG does permit an adopting nation to override this rule by continuing to require a signed writing for sales contracts. Hungary, for one, has already done so.

CISG also modifies the UCC rules on "open" price terms, the "mirror image" rule, and the use of custom to supply missing details. U.S. firms buying or selling internationally need to be aware of these important changes. You should keep them in mind as you study Part Two on Contracts.

■ LETTERS OF CREDIT

The letter of credit is a very common, and very useful, financial arrangement in international trade. Of course, it may also be used for business transactions occurring wholly within one country or even as a means of establishing one's credit for nonbusiness purposes, but its main use is in international business transactions.

UCC definition

The basic idea of a letter of credit is simple enough. As defined in UCC 5–103, a *letter of credit* means "an engagement by a bank or other person made at the request of a customer . . . that the issuer will honor drafts or other demands for payment upon compliance with the condition specified in the credit." A letter of credit may be either revocable or irrevocable. In many cases the draft or demand for payment must be accompanied by the presentation of certain required documents, such as a bill of lading indicating that goods have been shipped. Typically the "customer" referred to in the above definition is a foreign buyer of goods. The letter of credit is being used as the payment mechanism for the goods. The buyer goes to its bank, where it has established credit, and requests that the bank issue a letter of credit in favor of the overseas seller, which is the "beneficiary" of the credit. The credit will indicate the maximum amount of money that the seller is authorized to draw and will specify what documents the seller will have to present to the bank in order to get the money. Quite frequently, the arrangment will provide for the buyer's bank to transmit the letter to a bank in the seller's country, for convenience. When the seller ships goods according to the terms of the sales contract, it presents the shipping documents to the bank and gets the contract price for them.

Conflict of laws

Within the United States, *Article 5 of the Uniform Commercial Code* governs letters of credit. In international transactions, the parties should specify which country's law controls. In the absence of such a provision in the parties' contract, the general rules of private international law (choice of law rules) would determine which country's law should be applied to the dispute. As to disputes between the customer and its bank relating to the issuance and validity of the letter of credit, the law of the country of issuance would probably be applied. As to the responsibilities of the correspondent bank in the seller's country for handling the credit and verifying the documents presented, that country's law should be applied. Once again, it's best to anticipate such problems and make provisions in the contract for handling them when and if they arise.

AMERICAN BELL INTERNATIONAL, INC. v. ISLAMIC REPUBLIC OF IRAN

474 F. Supp. 420 (New York, 1979)

FACTS

Bell sued for an injunction to prevent Manufacturers Hanover Trust Company from making any payments under its Letter of Credit to defendants Iran or Bank Iranshahr or their successors. Bell, a wholly owned subsidiary of AT&T, made a contract in 1978 with the Imperial Government of Iran to provide consulting services and equipment to improve Iran's international communications system. The contract provided a complex mechanism of payment to Bell of some $280 million, including a $38 million down payment. Iran could demand return of the down payment at any time, but the amount so refundable would be reduced by 20 percent of the invoices filed by Bell to which Iran did not object. In other words, as satisfactory performance on both sides occurred, Bell got to retain more of the advance guarantee. About $30 million was still refundable at the time of trial. Iran required a guarantee that it would get the money refunded if it asked for it, so Bell had Bank Iranshahr sign an irrevocable letter of guaranty in favor of the Iranian government. To protect Bank Iranshahr in the event that it was forced to honor the guaranty, Bell obtained a letter of credit from Manufacturers in favor of Bank Iranshahr. If Manufacturers received confirmation from Bank Iranshahr that it had been forced to pay the Iranian government, Manufacturers had to reimburse Bank Iranshahr. Bell in turn promised to reimburse Manufacturers for any such amounts paid out under the letter of credit. After the Iranian revolution Bell was left with substantial unpaid invoices and claims, and it terminated its performance under the contract in January 1979. In July 1979 Manufacturers received a demand from Bank Iranshahr for $30,220,724; this demand was refused on the ground that it did not conform to the terms of the letter of credit. Bell then brought this action. A conforming demand for payment had now been received from Bank Iranshahr.

ISSUE   Should an injunction issue against payment of the letter of credit?

DECISION   No. Motion denied, but a payment delay ordered to permit appeal.

REASONS   **Judge MacMahon felt that Bell had failed to make out a case for a preliminary injunction.**

"There is credible evidence that the Islamic Republic is xenophobic and anti-American and that it has no regard for consulting service contracts such as the one here. Although Bell has made no effort to invoke the aid of the Iranian courts, we think the current situation in Iran, as shown by the evidence, warrants the conclusion that an attempt by Bell to resort to those courts would be futile. . . . However, Bell has not demonstrated that it is without adequate remedy in this court against the Iranian defendants under the Sovereign Immunity Act which it invokes in this very case. . . .

"In order to succeed on the merits, Bell must prove, by a preponderance of the evidence, that either (1) demand for payment of the Manufacturers Letter of Credit conforming to the terms of the Letter has not yet been made . . . or (2) a demand, even though in conformity, should not be honored because of fraud in the transaction. . . .

"[T]he United States now recognizes the present Government of Iran as the legal successor to the Imperial Government of Iran. That recognition is binding on American courts. . . . Though we may decide for ourselves the consequences of such recognition upon the litigants in this case . . . , we point out that American courts have traditionally viewed contract rights as vesting not in any particular government but in the state of which that government is an agent. . . .

"Plaintiff's argument requires us to presume bad faith on the part of the Iranian government. . . . On the evidence before us, fraud is not more inferable than an economically rational decision by the government to recoup its down payment, as it is entitled to do under the consulting contract, and still dispute its liabilities under that Contract."

■ **SIGNIFICANCE OF THIS CHAPTER**

While certain additional risks are involved in international business, the potential rewards are also great. As the volume of international commerce increases, it will become more and more important for American business managers to have an appreciation for the rules of international law. Significant differences exist as to the sources, enforcement, and application of international law, as between it and our national U.S. law. Some of those basic differences were outlined in this chapter.

DISCUSSION CASE

PFIZER, INC. v. GOVERNMENT OF INDIA
434 U.S. 308 (1978)

FACTS: The plaintiffs are the Government of India, the Imperial Government of Iran, and the Republic of the Philippines. They brought separate actions in U.S. District Courts against the petitioners, six pharmaceutical manufacturing companies. The actions were later consolidated for pretrial purposes in the United States District Court of Minnesota. The complaints alleged that the petitioners had conspired to restrain and monopolize interstate and foreign trade in the manufacture, distribution, and sale of broad spectrum antibiotics, in violation of SS.1 and 2 of the Sherman Act. Among the practices the petitioners allegedly engaged in were price fixing, market division, and fraud upon the United States Patent Office. India and Iran each alleged that it was a "sovereign foreign state with whom the United States of America maintains diplomatic relations"; the Philippines alleged that it was a "sovereign and independent government." Each respondent claimed that as a purchaser of antibiotics it had been damaged in its business or property by the alleged violations and sought treble damages under S.4 of the Clayton Act on its own behalf and on behalf of several classes of foreign purchasers of antibiotics. The defendants, the pharmaceutical companies, asserted as an affirmative defense to the complaints that the respondents as foreign nations were not "persons" entitled to sue for treble damages under S.4. In response to pretrial motions the District Court held that the respondents were "persons" and refused to dismiss the actions. The Court of Appeals for the Eighth Circuit affirmed . . . and adhered to its decision upon rehearing en banc. The U.S. Supreme Court granted certiorari to resolve an important and novel question in the administration of the antitrust laws.

■

Justice Stewart stated:

In this case we are asked to decide whether a foreign nation is entitled to sue in our courts for treble damages under the antitrust laws. . . .

As the Court of Appeals observed, this case "turns on the interpretation of the statute.". . . [W]hether a foreign nation is entitled to sue for treble damages depends upon whether it is a "person" as that word is used in S.4. There is no statutory provision or legislative history that provides a clear answer; it seems apparent that the question was never considered at the time the Sherman and Clayton Acts were enacted.

The Court has previously noted the broad scope of the remedies provided by the antitrust laws. "The Act is comprehensive in its terms and coverage, protecting all who are made victims of the forbidden practices by whomever they may be perpetrated.". . . And the legislative history of the Sherman Act demonstrates that Congress used the phrase "any person" intending it to have its naturally broad and inclusive meaning. There was no mention in the floor debates of any more restrictive definition. Indeed, during the course of those debates the word "person" was used interchangeably with other terms even broader in connotation. For example, Senator Sherman said that the treble-damages remedy was being given to "any party," and Senator Edmunds, one of the principal draftsmen of the final bill, said that it established "the right of anybody to sue who chooses to sue.". . .

In light of the law's expansive remedial purpose, the Court has not taken a technical or semantic approach in determining who is a "person" entitled to sue for treble damages. . . .

The respondents in this case possess two attributes that could arguably exclude them from the scope of the sweeping phrase "any person." They are foreign, and they are sovereign nations. . . .

Yet it is clear that a foreign *corporation* is entitled to sue for treble damages, since the definition of "person" contained in the Sherman and Clayton Acts explicitly includes "corporations and associations existing under or authorized by . . . the laws of any foreign country.". . . Moreover, the antitrust laws extend to trade "with foreign nations" as well as among the several States of the Union. . . . Clearly, therefore, Congress did not intend to make the treble-damages remedy available only to consumers in our own country. . . .

Moreover, an exclusion of all foreign plaintiffs would lessen the deterrent effect of treble damages. The conspiracy alleged by the respondents in this case operated domestically as well as internationally. If foreign plaintiffs were not permitted to seek a remedy for their antitrust injuries, persons doing business both in this country and abroad might be tempted to enter into anticompetitive conspiracies affecting American consumers in the expectation that the illegal profits they could safely extort abroad would offset any liability to plaintiffs at home. If, on the other hand, potential antitrust violators must take into account the full costs of their conduct. American consumers are benefited by the maximum deterrent effect of treble damages upon all potential violators. . . .

The second distinguishing characteristic of these respondents is that they are sovereign nations. The petitioners contend that the word *person* was clearly understood by Congress when it passed the Sherman Act to exclude sovereign governments. The word *person,* however, is not a term of art with a fixed meaning wherever it is used, nor was it in 1890 when the Sherman Act was passed. . . . Indeed, the Court has expressly noted that use of the word *person* in the Sherman and Clayton Acts did not create a "hard and fast rule of exclusion" of governmental bodies. . . .

On the two previous occasions that the Court has considered whether a sovereign government is a "person"

under the antitrust laws, the mechanical rule urged by the petitioners has been rejected. . . .

It is clear that in *Georgia* v. *Evans* the Court rejected the proposition that the word *person* as used in the antitrust laws excludes all sovereign states. And the reasoning of that case leads to the conclusion that a foreign nation, like a domestic State, is entitled to pursue the remedy of treble damages when it has been injured in its business or property by antitrust violations. When a foreign nation enters our commercial markets as a purchaser of goods or services, it can be victimized by anticompetitive practices just as surely as a private person or a domestic State. The antitrust laws provide no alternative remedies for foreign nations as they do for the United States. . . .

Accordingly, the judgment of the Court of Appeals is affirmed.

■ IMPORTANT TERMS AND CONCEPTS

U.S. Constitution
supreme law of the land
multinational
ius gentium
ius civile
natural law
custom
treaty
International Court of
    Justice
jurisconsults
diversity of citizenship

ratification
arbitration
act of state doctrine
sovereign immunity
    doctrine
Sherman Antitrust Act
Foreign Corrupt Practices
    Act
CISG
letter of credit
UCC, Article Five

■ QUESTIONS AND PROBLEMS FOR DISCUSSION

1. A major United States corporation had a contract with a foreign government to supply certain goods and services. The foreign government accepts the goods and services and then refuses to pay. Can the U.S. corporation sue the foreign government in the International Court of Justice? Why or why not? If not, where can they bring suit?

2. What is the difference between the Act of State doctrine and the Sovereign Immunity doctrine?

3. Why are "Letters of Credit" used in foreign commerce? Why doesn't the buyer just send its check in payment for the goods?

4. Are decisions of national courts which apply to international legal situations as significant to the manage-

ment of international business as the decisions of the International Court of Justice? Why?

5. Armando Brile sold 5,000 tons of sheet steel to a customer in Ghana. The contract provided for payment by letter of credit, drawn against a Paris bank. The customer's bank in Ghana sent a cable to its correspondent bank in Paris, instructing the Paris bank to open a comforming letter of credit in the customer's name. For some unknown reason, the French government refused to permit the proposed transfer of funds from the Paris bank. Armando now sues the Ghana bank on the basis that its telegram was itself a letter of credit and that he is entitled to payment. What result, and why?

6. Fishing is very important to the economy of the small nation of Portos. Traditionally it had claimed exclusive fishing rights, or at least the right to regulate fishing by citizens of other nations, only out to a distance of 12 miles from its coastline. As Russia and Japan modernized their fishing fleets, however, it became apparent that they were having a substantial impact on Portos' fishing industry. The government of Portos then declared that henceforth it would claim exclusive fishing rights, or the right to regulate catches by foreigners, out to a distance of 200 miles. Japan and Russia challenge this claim before the International Court of Justice. Does the International Court of Justice have jurisdiction over this type of case? What do you feel the decision should be and why?

7. In response to certain U.S. foreign policy actions with which it violently disagreed, the government of Bwana nationalized all assets owned by American nationals within its jurisdiction. At that point, a large

freighter loaded with bauxite ore belonging to Metallics, Inc., was preparing to leave Bwana's main port. The ship and its cargo were subjected to the seizure order and were later sold by the Bwana government to Ivan Rushoff. Ivan then brought the ship and cargo to New York, to try to resell them at a profit. Metallics has learned what's happening and has filed an appropriate action in New York, asking for immediate possession of the ship and cargo which were illegally seized by Bwana. How should the court rule in this case? Explain.

8. The S.S. Cariba entered into a towing contract with Little Tug, a German vessel, in Germany. The contract required the tug to tow the Cariba from New York to Taiwan for scrapping and provided that any dispute be referred to the Supreme Court of Justice in London. The S.S. Cariba broke loose from Little Tug, became stranded in Apra Harbor on Guam, and finally broke up and sank. The United States commenced an action against Little Tug in District Court of Guam for damages caused by obstruction to navigation. The S.S. Cariba's owner also filed an action in Guam, naming Little Tug and its owners for damages for loss of the vessel and for indemnity from the action filed by the U.S. government. What will happen in this case and why?

5

Antitrust Law and Trade Practices Regulation

CHAPTER OBJECTIVES

THIS CHAPTER WILL:

- Introduce antitrust laws, including the Sherman Act, the Clayton Act, the Robinson-Patman Act, and the Federal Trade Commission Act.
- Review major decisions applying and interpreting the antitrust statutes.
- Summarize major changes in government policy toward mergers.
- Indicate the FTC's major areas of jurisdiction.

The word *antitrust* is used to describe laws that were passed by Congress to protect the public from monopolies. Actually we should refer to these laws as antimonopoly laws. They were called antitrust laws because during the late 1800s, companies in many industries transferred control of their companies to a voting trust. The trustee could be a separate corporation, an individual, or group of individuals, who now had control of manufacture, sale, distribution, and pricing of a large share of the products of the particular industry. The result was the elimination of competition among the sellers in the industry. Thus a *monopoly* was created and the public suffered, because without competition, the public must pay the price dictated by the monopoly, not the price that would be set by a competitive market. Antitrust or antimonopoly law consists not only of the famous Sherman Act but also other legislation, Supreme Court cases, and Justice Department guidelines.

■ THE SHERMAN ACT

It's hard to say whether Senator John Sherman of Ohio would be pleased with the growth of his century-old offspring. The Sherman Antitrust Act was passed in 1890 as the first attempt by the national government to deal with the perceived abuses of market power by the giant industrial corporations that had grown up after the Civil War.

In the broadest possible language, the Sherman Act stated: "Every contract, combination in the form of trust or otherwise, or conspiracy, in *restraint of trade* or commerce among the several States, or with foreign nations, is hereby declared to be illegal." Section 2 of the act defined another broad category of offenses: "Every person who shall monopolize, or attempt to monopolize, or combine or conspire with any other person or persons, to monopolize any part of the trade or commerce among the several States, or with foreign nations, shall be deemed guilty of a misdemeanor." The act was clearly aimed at the giant concentrations of economic power that existed in many industries—the "trusts." Firms that should have been competing against each other were working together and were in many cases tied together organizationally through voting trusts. Quite clearly, the act was intended to reach such anticompetitive schemes as price-fixing, bid-rigging, and market-splitting.

Is "bigness" unlawful?

The continuing dilemma of antitrust interpretation is whether or not the act was intended to go beyond those obvious, specific practices to prohibit "bigness" as such. If one company competes aggressively, builds a better product at lower cost, and succeeds in getting nearly all the potential customers to deal with it, has it violated the antitrust laws? Stated most simply, is market success illegal? This is where opinions diverge.

Two Conflicting Interpretations

There are two opposing schools of thought on the basic meaning and purpose of the Sherman Act and the other antitrust laws; for want of better terminology, the *legal school* and the *economic school.* The dispute is not quite as simple as the terms suggest, since some economists support the "legal" view and many lawyers and judges take the "economic" view.

The legal school

The legal approach starts with the premise that size alone is not made illegal by the Sherman Act; there is specific support for this approach in the 1890 debates in Congress. To be guilty of an antitrust violation, a company must be shown to have actually abused its position of market power. What counts are the methods used and the intent of those using them. Free and fair competition will result in winners *and losers* in the marketplace; the winners should not be penalized if they've won "fair and square." This view of antitrust emphasizes protecting the *process* of competition rather than trying to ensure the survival of specific *competitors*. If customers want to deal with GM and IBM, should the government step in to "preserve" other car makers and computer manufacturers? Supporters of the legal approach would answer no.

The economic school

The economic approach starts from the premise that large concentrations of economic power are bad per se, that our democratic society is endangered by such power blocs, and that Congress intended the antitrust laws as a vehicle for preserving an economic structure which embraces a number of smaller, independent economic units. In this view, economic efficiencies may at times have to be sacrificed to preserve this sort of market structure. The Robinson-Patman Act of 1936 (sometimes referred to as the "anti-chainstore act" and discussed later in this chapter) clearly points in this direction. What counts in this approach is the market structure; large size and market dominance are inherently bad. There is an antitrust violation if a company has the *potential* power to abuse, whether or not it has actually been guilty of any specific abuse. This view of antitrust is clearly most concerned with protecting *competitors,* even to the point of insulating them from the rigors of effective competition.

Unfortunately for students, teachers, lawyers, and most of all for businesses, the antitrust laws have been interpreted *both* ways by various courts with various combinations of judges. Depending in large part on the basic policy view taken by a majority of the justices on the U.S. Supreme Court, a given course of business conduct may or may not be deemed to violate the antitrust laws. If some of the case opinions in this chapter seem to conflict, that's because they probably do conflict.

Penalties for Violation

Criminal prosecutions

These basic questions of interpretation are of more than academic interest to the business community because of the broad reach of the antitrust statutes and the serious penalties that may be imposed for violations. The three basic enforcement mechanisms are *criminal prosecution, civil suit by the U.S. government* (the Justice Department or the Federal Trade Commission), and *civil suit by private parties.*

Criminal cases are usually pursued by the Justice Department only for conduct which is deemed to be illegal per se, without any test of "reasonableness." *Price-fixing* is one such example. If convicted, a corporation now faces a fine of up to $1 million. For individuals, criminal penalties include a fine of up to $100,000 and/or a maximum of three years in jail. Historically, jail sentences were rarely imposed, but the courts' attitude has been changing. Executives served more time in jail for price-fixing in 1978 than in the entire preceding 87 years of the Sherman Act's existence. The Justice Department was also able to establish in the electrical industry price-fixing cases in the 1960s that it does not have to accept a *nolo contendere* plea to the criminal charges. **Nolo contendere** means no contest. The ruling against automatic acceptance of *nolo*

The nolo contendere plea

pleas is important because a plea of guilty can be used by a civil plaintiff to help prove a case for damages; a *nolo* plea is not an admission of guilt and cannot be used by a civil plaintiff to prove his or her case.

Because of the much higher standard of proof required in a criminal case (beyond any reasonable doubt) and the general reluctance of juries to subject someone to the chance of prison for nonviolent, business-related conduct, the Justice Department and the FTC prefer to file civil actions in many cases. Anticompetitive conduct may be enjoined; divestiture (separation) may be ordered where an illegal merger between businesses has taken place; and other civil remedies may be involved. In 1974, for instance, the FTC agreed to a settlement of its complaint against Xerox, by the terms of which Xerox was required to make its entire portfolio of about 2,000 patents available to any other firm that wanted to enter the copier market. Much of the fear of antitrust lawsuits stems from the fact that private parties can recover *treble damages* (three times the actual injury shown) plus reasonable attorney fees. This measure of damages is a very real incentive to litigate, and thus a significant deterrent to antitrust violations.

Treble damages

Monopoly Power in One Company

Standard Oil case

Alcoa case

The first big case under the Sherman Act was against the Sugar Trust, which controlled about 98 percent of U.S. sugar production. The Sugar Trust escaped liability when the Supreme Court held that manufacturing was not "commerce" and was therefore not covered by the act. This interpretation was soon overruled, and in the famous *Standard Oil* case of 1911 a majority of five justices voted to apply a *rule of reason* in antitrust cases. The *Standard Oil* majority correctly concluded that a literal reading of the act ("every contract") would produce absurd results since every business contract "restrains" trade in the sense of denying a particular business opportunity to others. In other words, if you contract to buy Smith's used car, Smith has "foreclosed" others from selling you a used car, unless you need more than one. Likewise, you have "foreclosed" Smith's opportunities to sell his used car to other buyers.

Clearly, the act must have been aimed at something other than those normal business contracts with their normal business consequences. While the majority adopted a reasonableness test, they did not really apply it to the facts of the *Standard Oil* case, and ordered the combination split up without much investigation of actual economic performance.

In the landmark *Alcoa* case in 1945, Circuit Judge Hand stated that monopoly power was illegal per se, regardless of how it had been attained and regardless of whether or not it had been abused. The case had been started in 1937 in U.S. District Court, where Judge Caffey heard 155 witnesses, viewed 1,803 exhibits, and produced a trial record of 58,000 pages. After four years the court decided that Alcoa was not guilty on any of the 140 criminal counts. Hand and the Second Circuit Court of Appeals reversed Judge Caffey on *one* count and took that as the opportunity to radically reinterpret the Sherman Act. The appeals court found a monopoly by a very restrictive definition of the *relevant market,* which excluded aluminum made from reprocessed scrap and aluminum produced abroad. While the *Alcoa* decision was not reviewed by the Supreme Court, the principle stated there was generally accepted in the Supreme Court's 1946 decision in the *American Tobacco* case. A court's determination of the dimensions of the "relevant market" may thus be decisive in deciding whether or not there is a "monopoly."

In the famous "cellophane" case (*U.S.* v. *Du Pont,* 351 U.S. 377), the U.S. Supreme Court decided that the relevant market was all flexible packaging materials, not just cellophane. While Du Pont produced almost 75 percent of the cellophane made in the United States, its share of the much larger packaging market was less than 20 percent. With that larger market definition, Du Pont was held not guilty of the monopolization charge.

In the 1960s and 1970s, the government filed monopolization charges against such industrial giants as IBM and AT&T, and threatened several times to try to break up GM. In the early 1970s, the late Senator Philip Hart of Michigan sponsored an "Industrial Reorganization Act" that would have created a new government agency with the power to restructure industries where an oligopoly existed. An *oligopoly* was defined as four or fewer firms controlling over 50 percent of a market. In the late 1970s, as the energy crisis worsened, several states passed laws prohibiting oil companies (the large refiners) from also owning retail gas stations. Also, the FTC's long-pending case against the four large cereal makers, charging a "shared monopoly" in violation of the Sherman Act, was finally dismissed. Such a theory would have opened many firms to prosecution. Under the Reagan administration's more liberal view of "bigness," the *IBM* case was finally dropped and the *AT&T* case was settled. AT&T agreed to give up its local telephone businesses in return for the right to compete in computers and other high-tech fields.

Attempts to Monopolize. Section 2 of the Sherman Act also prohibits attempts to monopolize. Courts have disagreed as to what must be proved to show a violation of this section. Generally, it is necessary to show a specific intent to monopolize, but it is not necessary to show that the defendant already has monopoly power. The charge is that the defendant is *attempting* to achieve monopoly power. Disagreement exists over whether a "dangerous probability" of success in acquiring monopoly power must also be shown. Some courts have required this element; others have not. This other group of courts have found violations where the intent was coupled with an attempt to acquire a monopoly. Sometimes, in the second group of cases, the courts did not even seem too worried about establishing the relevant market.

Concerted Activities among Competitors

When competing companies get together to fix prices, limit output, or divide markets, the antitrust violation is clear. These practices are so inherently anticompetitive that they are classified as *per se violations;* that is, no "rule of reason" defense is available. In the 1927 *Trenton Potteries* case, the U.S. Supreme Court held that the defendants' good motives and the reasonableness of the prices they set were both irrelevant; the power to fix reasonable prices was also the power to fix unreasonable prices at some future time. In 1940, in the *Socony-Vacuum Oil* case, the Court said that the government did not have to prove that the defendants had been successful in raising prices, only that they had conspired with the intent to do so. In a 1933 decision that stands virtually alone, the Supreme Court did rule in favor of coal producers who had entered

Oligopolies under the Sherman Act

Trenton Potteries and Socony-Vacuum cases

into a "reasonable" price and output agreement; in the midst of a terrible depression, reasonable cooperation in the industry was permitted.

Trade Association Activities under the Sherman Act

One of the most troublesome *conspiracy* areas involves the cooperative activities of trade associations, especially the collection and reporting of price information. The government's problem in these cases is to prevent the trade association from being used as a price-fixing mechanism while permitting legitimate cooperative activities. In cases dealing with manufacturers of sugar, lumber, and linseed oil, the Supreme Court has indicated that "reporting" of specific prices charged to specific customers is probably evidence of an agreement to charge everyone the same prices. In a case involving cement manufacturers, the Court permitted such reporting, where there was a history of some firms delivering extra, "free" cement, billing the customer, and splitting the extra profits with the contractor.

American Tobacco and Theatre Enterprises cases

Another difficult problem relates to the proof necessary to substantiate the conspiracy charge. Price uniformity, in and of itself, does not necessarily indicate the existence of a conspiracy, especially where similar increases can be shown to have stemmed from uniformly increased costs of production and delivery. On the other hand, specific instances of joint price increases and *reductions,* when new firms entered the market, were held to show a conspiracy based on *conscious parallelism* in the 1946 *American Tobacco* case. This doctrine was limited by the 1954 *Theatre Enterprises* decision, which stated that parallel business behavior was not itself illegal nor was it conclusive proof of an illegal conspiracy. In most such cases the existence of a conspiracy is for the jury to decide.

Just as "it takes two to tango," it takes two to make up a conspiracy. There is no such legal animal as a "solo" conspiracy; two or more persons must be involved. Can a parent corporation and its wholly owned subsidiary be the *two* "persons" in an antitrust conspiracy? In an important 1984 decision (*Copperweld Corp.* v. *Independence Tube Corp.,* 467 U.S. 752), the Supreme Court said "no" to that question.

Resale Price Maintenance and Refusals to Deal

For many years the manufacturers of some products have attempted to control the prices at which retailers sell the products, usually by establishing a minimum retail price. Most states passed so-called *fair trade laws* by 1940. Fair trade laws are laws that allow the manufacturer to set a retail price for which the product must be sold. The retailer can sell the product for more, but not for less than the set price. Congress passed the Miller Tydings Amendment to the Sherman Act in 1937 to exempt such state laws from antitrust, and then passed the McGuire Amendment to the FTC Act in 1952, so that *nonsigner plans* were also exempt from antitrust. In a nonsigner plan, if one retailer in a state agreed to the minimum prices, all retailers in that state were bound to adhere to them. Even with this legislative support, manufacturers found it very difficult to "police" their minimum prices and they could not prevent an interstate shipment of goods at a lower price from a non-fair-trade state. In 1975, Congress brought the fair-trade movement to an end by repealing the 1937 and 1952 amendments; nearly any fair-trade arrangement would now be an antitrust violation.

Miller-Tydings and McGuire Amendments

Parke, Davis case

What about refusals to deal, as possible antitrust violations? Except for certain-businesses which are bound to deal with all members of the public on an

■ EXHIBIT 5–1
Product Distribution
Patterns

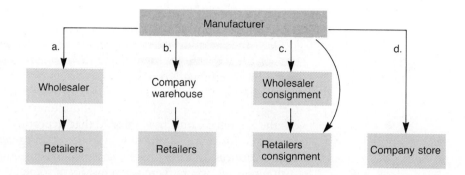

equal basis, such as innkeepers and common carriers, it is generally assumed that a business is free to decide with whom it will deal and on what terms. In the 1960 *Parke, Davis* case, however, the Court said that where the manufacturer entwined its wholesalers and retailers in a policing arrangement it had created an illegal conspiracy under the Sherman Act. Courts today continue to examine both of these restrictions very closely.

Territorial and Other Distribution Restrictions

Manufacturers may wish to restrict resales by their wholesalers or retailers. The manufacturer may get its distributor to agree not to resell the product outside a particular geographical area or not to resell to a particular class of customers. For example, the manufacturer may want to handle all sales of the product to the government or to institutional buyers, such as schools and hospitals. Where the manufacturer has granted exclusive sales territories to its several distributors, it doesn't want them stepping on each other's toes. Rather than having its distributors compete with each other for the same set of customers, it wants each of them to compete with other suppliers' products—within their assigned area. These restrictions are designed to increase *interbrand* competition, at the expense of *intrabrand* competition. The legal validity of such restrictions under the antitrust laws is at issue in the following case.

CONTINENTAL TV, INC. v. GTE SYLVANIA, INC.

433 U.S. 36 (1977)

FACTS GTE Sylvania Inc. manufactures and sells television sets through its Home Entertainment Products Division. Prior to 1962, like most other television manufacturers, Sylvania sold its televisions to independent or company-owned distributors who in turn resold to a large and diverse group of retailers. Prompted by a decline in its market share to a relatively insignificant 1 percent to 2 percent of national television sales, Sylvania conducted an intensive reassessment of its marketing strategy, and in 1962 it adopted the franchise plan challenged here. Sylvania phased out its wholesale distributors and began to sell its televisions directly to a smaller and more select group of franchised retailers. An acknowledged purpose of the change was to decrease the number of competing Sylvania retailers in the hope of attracting the more aggressive and competent retailers thought necessary to the improvement of the company's market position. To this end, Sylvania limited the number of franchises granted for any given area and required each franchisee to sell his Sylvania products only from the location or locations at which he was franchised. A franchise did not constitute an exclusive territory, and Sylvania retained sole discretion to increase the number of retailers in an area in light of the success or failure of existing retailers in developing their market. The revised marketing strategy appears to have been successful during the period at issue here, for by 1965 Sylvania's share of national television sales had increased to approximately 5 percent, and the company ranked as the nation's eighth largest manufacturer of color television sets.

Dissatisfied with its sales in the city of San Francisco, Sylvania decided in the spring of 1965 to franchise Young Brothers, an established San Francisco retailer of televisions, as an additional San Francisco retailer. The proposed location of the new franchise was approximately a mile from a retail outlet operated by petitioner Continental TV, Inc., one of the most successful Sylvania franchisees. Continental protested that the location of the new franchise violated Sylvania's marketing policy, but Sylvania persisted in its plans. Continental then canceled a large Sylvania order and placed a large order with Phillips, one of Sylvania's competitors.

The jury found that Sylvania had engaged "in a contract, combination or conspiracy in restraint of trade in violation of the antitrust laws with respect to location restrictions alone," and assessed Continental's damages at $591,505, which was trebled, to produce an award of $1,774,515. On appeal, the Court of Appeals for the Ninth Circuit, sitting en banc, reversed by a divided vote.

ISSUE   Are these location restrictions an antitrust violation?

DECISION   No. Judgment for defendant is affirmed.

REASONS   **Justice Powell thought that there were valid reasons for the restraint:**
"The traditional framework of analysis under Section 1 of the Sherman Act is familiar and does not require extended discussion. Section 1 prohibits '[e]very contract, combination. . . , or conspiracy, in restraint of trade or commerce.' Since the early years of this century a judicial gloss on this statutory language has established the 'rule of reason' as the prevailing standard of analysis. . . . Under this rule, the factfinder weighs all of the circumstances of a case in deciding whether a restrictive practice should be prohibited as imposing an unreasonable restraint on competition. Per se rules of illegality are appropriate only when they relate to conduct that is manifestly anticompetitive. As the Court explained in *Northern Pac R. Co.* v. *United States,* 356 U.S. 1 . . . 'there are certain agreements or practices which because of their pernicious effect on competition and lack of any redeeming virtue are conclusively presumed to be unreasonable and therefore illegal without elaborate inquiry as to the precise harm they have caused or the business excuse for their use.' . . .

"The market impact of vertical restrictions is complex because of their potential for a simultaneous reduction of intrabrand competition and stimulation of interbrand competition. Significantly, the Court in *Schwinn* did not distinguish among the challenged restrictions on the basis of their individual potential for intrabrand harm or interbrand benefit. Restrictions that completely eliminated intrabrand competition among Schwinn distributors were analyzed no differently from those that merely moderated intrabrand competition among retailers. The pivotal factor was the passage of title: All restrictions were held to be per se illegal where title had passed, and all were evaluated and sustained under the rule of reason where it had not. The location restriction at issue here would be subject to the same pattern of analysis under Schwinn.

"It appears that this distinction between sale and nonsale transactions resulted from the Court's effort to accommodate the perceived intrabrand harm and interbrand benefit of vertical restrictions. . . . The Court's opinion provides no analytical support for these contrasting positions. Nor is there even an assertion in the opinion that the competitive impact of vertical restrictions is significantly affected by the form of the transaction. Nonsale transactions appear to be excluded from the per se rule, not because of a greater danger of intrabrand benefit, but rather because of the Court's unexplained belief that a complete per se prohibition would be too 'inflexible.' . . .

"Vertical restrictions reduce intrabrand competition by limiting the number of sellers of a particular product competing for the business of a given group of buyers. Location restrictions have this effect because of practical constraints on the effective marketing area of retail outlets. Although intrabrand competition may be reduced, the ability of retailers to exploit the resulting market may be limited both by the ability of consumers to travel to other franchised locations and, perhaps more importantly, to purchase the competing products of other manufacturers. None of these key variables, however, is affected by the form of the transaction by which a manufacturer conveys his products to the retailers.

"Vertical restrictions promote interbrand competition by allowing the manufacturer to achieve certain efficiencies in the distribution of his products. These 'redeeming values' are implicit in every decision sustaining vertical restrictions under the rule of reason. Economists have identified a number of ways in which manufacturers can use such restrictions to compete more effectively against other manufacturers. . . . For example, new manufacturers and manufacturers entering new markets can use the restrictions in order to induce competent and aggressive retailers to make the kind of investment of capital and labor that is often required in the distribution of products unknown to the consumer. Established manufacturers can use them to induce retailers to engage in promotional activities or to provide service and repair facilities necessary to the efficient marketing of their products. Service and repair are vital for many products, such as automobiles and major household appliances. The availability and quality of such services affect a manufacturer's goodwill and the competitiveness of his product. Because of market imperfections such as the so-called free rider effect, these services might not be provided by retailers in a purely competitive situation, despite the fact that each retailer's benefit would be greater if all provided the services than if none did. . . .

"Economists also have argued that manufacturers have an economic interest in maintaining as much intrabrand competition as is consistent with the efficient distribution of their products. . . . Although the view that the manufacturer's interest necessarily corresponds with that of the public is not universally shared, even the leading critic of vertical restrictions concedes that *Schwinn's* distinction between sale and nonsale transactions is essentially unrelated to any relevant economic impact. . . . Indeed, to the extent that the form of the transaction is related to interbrand benefits, the Court's distinction is inconsistent with its articulated concern for the ability of smaller firms to compete effectively with larger ones. Capital requirements and administrative expenses may prevent smaller firms from using the exception for nonsale transactions. . . .

"In sum, we conclude that the appropriate decision is to return to the rule of reason that governed vertical restrictions prior to *Schwinn*. When anticompetitive effects are shown to result from particular vertical restrictions they can be adequately policed under the rule of reason, the standard traditionally applied for the majority of anticompetitive practices challenged under § 1 of the act. Accordingly, the decision of the Court of Appeals is affirmed.

■ THE CLAYTON ACT

Section 1 of the Sherman Act of 1890 had stated: "Every contract, combination in the form of a trust or otherwise, or conspiracy, in restraint of trade or commerce among the several states, or with foreign nations, is hereby declared to be illegal." The *Standard Oil* case added the rule of reason when judging these contracts and combinations. Still, courts lacked a real definition or classification of what was illegal and what was legal. This need for specific classifications of contracts or combinations which may be illegal brought about the passage of the Clayton Act in 1914. The important sections of the Clayton Act which affect antitrust are Sections 2, 3, 7, and 8.

Section 2 prohibits price discrimination, subject to certain exclusions and exceptions. *Price discrimination* is simply selling products of the same kind and quality to different customers for different prices. This topic will be discussed later in this chapter.

Tying Contracts and Exclusive Dealing Agreements

Northern Pacific case

Rule of reason for exclusive dealing contracts

Section 3 prohibits tying contracts and exclusive dealing agreements. A *tying contract* is an arrangement whereby the customer is required to buy a product or service it may not want in order to buy the product it does want; in the retail trade, this is sometimes referred to as *full-line forcing*. Tying contracts, said the Supreme Court in the 1958 *Northern Pacific Railway* case, are presumed to be illegal "because of their pernicious effect on competition and lack of any redeeming virtue." Unless some very special facts are present, tying contracts are hard to justify.

Exclusive dealing agreements should be analyzed quite differently from tying contracts, since in many situations both the seller and the buyer benefit from such commitments. The buyer has an assured supply and protection against price fluctuations; the seller has an assured market and can plan production more realistically. Such agreements therefore must be tested on a case-by-case basis, under the rule of reason. The motives of the parties are important, and so is the impact of the particular agreement on the relevant market.

Mergers

Types of mergers

Celler-Kefauver Amendment

Section 7 of the Clayton Act prohibits certain mergers where the effect of the merger may be to substantially lessen competition.

Mergers may be divided into three basic classifications: (1) horizontal mergers, (2) vertical mergers, and (3) conglomerate mergers. A *horizontal merger* occurs when two competing firms merge. For example, one retail grocery chain merges with another retail grocery chain, both of which compete in the same geographic area. A *vertical merger* is one in which a manufacturer merges with a wholesale distributor or a retail chain, which does business in the same product market as the manufacturer. For example, a manufacturer of shoes owns no retail outlets so it merges with a company that runs a chain of retail stores selling shoes. A *conglomerate merger* is a merger where the acquiring firm is not in the same line of commerce as the firm being acquired, and thus the acquired firm was neither a competitor nor a supplier nor a former customer. An example of a conglomerate merger would be a firm which manufactures bicycles buying a company that makes water beds. The key question in all three of these types of mergers is whether or not the merger may substantially lessen competition.

Section 7 of the Clayton Act of 1914 was largely ineffective during its first 40 years on the statute books, due to restrictive Supreme Court interpretations and a lack of enforcement vigor. Section 7, in its original version, established a kind of per se rule which prohibited any acquisition by a company of a controlling stock interest in a competitor. In several cases in the 1920s and 1930s, the Supreme Court held that an acquisition of a competitor's *assets* was not prohibited. The Du Pont/GM case, filed in 1949, resulted in a drastic reinterpretation of the original Section 7, but it really set no precedent because

Congress had in the meantime passed the 1950 Celler-Kefauver Amendment, which substantially reworked Section 7.

The amended Section 7 covered one corporation's acquisition of the stock or the assets of another "where in any line of commerce in any section of the country, the effect of such acquisition may be substantially to lessen competition, or to tend to create a monopoly." This new version clearly established an *incipiency test;* the acquisition was illegal if there was a reasonable probability that it would have future anticompetitive effects.

Brown Shoe case

Using the revised Section 7, the government was able to stop the proposed merger of Bethlehem Steel and Youngstown Sheet & Tube in 1958 (but Youngstown was subsequently merged into Lykes and Lykes into LTV). The first case to come to the Supreme Court under the new Section 7 was the Brown Shoe acquisition of Kinney Shoes, a merger which had both vertical and horizontal aspects, since both companies were manufacturers and retailers. Using a very restrictive definition of the market which excluded shoe retailers such as Sears, Montgomery Ward, and J. C. Penney, and ignoring the fact that Kinney stores bought *more* shoes from independent manufacturers after the merger than it had before, the Supreme Court found the merger illegal.

Merger Guidelines. To resolve some of the uncertainty as to which mergers would be challenged, the Justice Department in 1968 issued its *merger guidelines*. These guidelines did little more than summarize the existing case law: horizontal mergers between competitors in a highly concentrated market would be challenged where each firm had as little as 4 percent of the market; vertical mergers would be challenged where the supplier had 10 percent of the sales and the purchaser firm bought at least 6 percent of the goods involved; conglomerate mergers would be brought to court where the acquiring firm was a "potential entrant" into the market through internal expansion, or where the merger created a danger of reciprocal buying, or where the acquiring firm's resources were so extensive as to give the acquired firm an unfair advantage over its smaller competitors.

1968 Justice Department merger guidelines

1982 merger guidelines

The new merger guidelines issued by the Justice Department in 1982 focus primarily on horizontal mergers. A mathematical formula—the *Herfindahl-Hirschman Index (HHI)*—is used to describe the approximate level of concentration already existing in an industry. If the level is too high, the proposed merger will be challenged by the Justice Department, as occurred with two proposed steel mergers in early 1984. The market share of each existing competitor is squared, and these figures are totaled. If the total is 1,000 or less, indicating a relatively unconcentrated market, the proposed merger will probably not be challenged. If the total is over 1,800, the Justice Department will probably object. Between these figures, the department will evaluate the amount of concentration which the proposed merger would add to the industry. The market shares of the proposed merger partners will be added together and squared, and totaled with the other firms' squared market shares. The original total will be subtracted from this new total, to see how many points have been added. If more than 100 points would be added to the HHI, the merger will probably be challenged; under 50, probably not. Between these extremes, the department will have to weigh other industry factors and then decide whether to permit the merger or to challenge it. Vertical and conglomerate mergers are generally not viewed as posing serious marketplace threats by the current

Justice Department. The FTC has indicated that it too will generally follow the guidelines using the HHI.

Interlocking Directors

Section 8 of the Clayton Act prohibits certain interlocking directorates. An *interlocking directorate* exists when a person is a director in any two or more competing corporations. Section 8 would prohibit an interlocking directorate if any one of the corporations has capital, surplus, and undivided profits aggregating more than $1 million, and if the companies are engaged in commerce, and if they are not banks, banking associations, trust companies, or common carriers.

W. T. Grant and Sears, Roebuck cases

Similar to the history of Section 7, there were very few proceedings against "interlocking" directors for the first 40 years after the Clayton Act was passed. Cases against W. T. Grant and Sears, Roebuck & Co. were decided in 1953, and Section 8 of the Clayton Act was revived. A District Court forced the common director of Sears and B. F. Goodrich to resign from the Sears board, and five years later the same District Court held that its decree would be violated if the same person served on the Goodrich board and as a director of Sears' Savings and Profit Sharing Pension Fund. There was renewed emphasis on enforcement of this section in the 1970s, and a common director of Chrysler and General Electric was forced to resign from the GE board because both companies made air conditioners. Potentially, there is a considerable area of antitrust violation under this section.

It is important to note that the Sherman Act is an *"after the fact"* law, which means you cannot be prosecuted until you have committed a violation. The Clayton Act is a *"before the fact"* law, meaning that its purpose is not to punish someone for having done a wrongful act, but to prevent damage to competition in the marketplace. For example, under Section 7 of the Clayton Act a proposed merger may be stopped before it is consummated if the merger might tend to substantially lessen competition. If the merger has already been consummated, as in the case of *U.S. v. E.I. du Pont Nemours & Co.,* and if a substantial lessening of competition appears possible, even though there is no evidence of wrongdoing, the court will order divestiture.

This "before the fact" purpose of the Clayton Act is also evident in Section 2 and Section 3 cases, as it is not necessary to show actual damage has occurred, only that such competitive damage may occur if the specific actions are not discontinued. Section 8 also does not require showing that a director who happens to be on the board of directors of two competing companies is actually a bad person who is doing something wrong. The director may be removed before the opportunity to do anything wrong arises.

■ ROBINSON-PATMAN ACT

One of the most difficult antitrust problems occurs when a seller charges different prices to two or more buyers for the same type of goods. As mentioned earlier, this is price discrimination. The original Section 2 of the Clayton Act of 1914 did contain a provision aimed at the seller who cuts prices in competitive locations and maintained higher prices everywhere else. The early cases, however, interpreted this section to prohibit only discrimination between *competing* buyers, and thus there were few prosecutions under it. By the mid-1930s, grocery

Morton Salt case

store chains had become very powerful buyers and were demanding and getting quantity discounts. As the Supreme Court noted in the *Morton Salt* case, volume discounts of the large chains enabled them to sell Morton Salt at retail for less than the price at which independent wholesalers could sell it to their retail-store customers. In 1936, under intense pressure from small independent retailers and wholesalers, Congress passed the Robinson-Patman Act to amend Section 2 of the Clayton Act.

The Offense

The Robinson-Patman Act basically states that it is unlawful for any seller to discriminate in price between different purchasers, if the sale involves goods and not services, if the sales constitute interstate rather than intrastate commerce, if the goods are of *like kind and quality,* and provided the effect of such discrimination may be to substantially lessen competition or tend to create a monopoly in any line of commerce. The responsibility for prosecuting Robinson-Patman violations rests with the Federal Trade Commission. As is true for other antitrust violations, any private parties who are injured by the illegal price discrimination may also bring their own case for damages.

Borden case

A common practice among large manufacturers and food processors is to package products under their own brand name and also produce and package the product for certain volume customers under the customer's private label. The question arises, Must the manufacturers charge the same price for the private label goods as they do for their own brand name goods? In the 1966 case of *F.T.C.* v. *Borden Company,* the Supreme Court found the two products to be of like kind and quality regardless of the difference in the label.

Nonprofit Institutions Exemption

Only two years after passage of Robinson-Patman, Congress adopted the *Nonprofit Institutions Act,* as an amendment. The NIA exempts from the application of Robinson-Patman "purchases of their supplies for their own use by schools, . . . hospitals, and charitable institutions not operated for profit." Manufacturers and other suppliers can thus provide special prices to these kinds of nonprofit agencies without violating Robinson-Patman.

Even here there have been definitional problems. The agencies themselves are usually easy enough to categorize. (There may be some question about some of the self-defined "nonprofit" agencies which solicit funds on television and elsewhere.) But there are some tough issues involved in deciding what is an agency's "own use." Can professors get the special discount, as well as the school itself? How about students? How about participants in a one-day seminar at the school? How about librarians at the school? Noninstructional staff? Spouses? "Significant others"? Alumni? Some difficult line-drawing may have to be done when these various groups also demand the special pricing.

The "Meeting Competition" Defense

Recognizing that in many cases a seller firm must cut its price to meet a lower price quoted by a competitor, Congress specifically provided for such a defense. A seller relying on this defense must be acting in good faith; knowledge that the competitor's lower price is itself illegal would probably prevent a finding of good faith. The following case is one example of this defense in action.

GREAT ATLANTIC & PACIFIC TEA CO., INC. v. FEDERAL TRADE COMMISSION

440 U.S. 69 (1979)

FACTS

The alleged violation was reflected in a 1965 agreement between A&P and Borden under which Borden undertook to supply "private label" milk to more than 200 A&P stores in a Chicago area that included portions of Illinois and Indiana. This agreement resulted from an effort by A&P to achieve cost savings by switching from the sale of "brand label" milk (milk sold under the brand name of the supplying dairy) to the sale of "private label" milk (milk sold under the A&P label).

To implement this plan, A&P asked Borden, its longtime supplier, to submit an offer to supply under private label certain of A&P's milk and other dairy product requirements. After prolonged negotiations, Borden offered to grant A&P a discount for switching to private label milk provided A&P would accept limited delivery service. Borden claimed that this offer would save A&P $410,000 a year compared to what it had been paying for its dairy products. A&P, however, was not satisfied with this offer and solicited offers from other dairies. A competitor of Borden, Bowman Dairy, then submitted an offer which was lower than Borden's.

At this point, A&P's Chicago buyer contacted Borden's chain store sales manager and stated, "I have a bid in my pocket. You [Borden] people are so far out of line it is not even funny. You are not even in the ball park." When the Borden representative asked for more details, he was told nothing except that a $50,000 improvement in Borden's bid "would not be a drop in the bucket."

Borden was thus faced with the problem of deciding whether to rebid. A&P at the time was one of Borden's largest customers in the Chicago area. Moreover, Borden had just invested more than $5 million in a new dairy facility in Illinois. The loss of the A&P account would result in underutilization of this new plant. Under these circumstances, Borden decided to submit a new bid which doubled the estimated annual savings to A&P, from $410,000 to $820,000. In presenting its offer, Borden emphasized to A&P that it needed to keep A&P's business and was making the new offer in order to meet Bowman's bid. A&P then accepted Borden's bid after concluding that it was substantially better than Bowman's.

An Administrative Law Judge found, after extended discovery and a hearing that lasted over 110 days, that A&P had acted unfairly and deceptively in accepting the second offer from Borden and had therefore violated Section 5 of the Federal Trade Commission Act as charged in Count I. The Administrative Law Judge similarly found that this same conduct had violated Section 2(f) of the Robinson-Patman Act. Finally, he dismissed Count III on the ground that the Commission had not satisfied its burden of proof.

On review, the Commission reversed the Administrative Law Judge's finding as to Count I. Pointing out that the question at issue was what amount of disclosure is required of the buyer during contract negotiations, the Commission held that the imposition of a duty of affirmative disclosure would be "contrary to normal business practice and, we think, contrary to the public interest." Despite this ruling, however, the Commission held as to Count II that the identical conduct on the part of A&P had violated Section 2(f) of the Robinson-Patman Act, finding that Borden had discriminated in price between A&P and its competitors, that the discrimination had been injurious to competition, and that A&P had known or should have known that it was the beneficiary of unlawful price discrimination. The Court of Appeals for the Second Circuit held that substantial evidence supported the findings of the Commission, and that as a matter of law A&P could not successfully assert a meeting competition defense because it, unlike Borden, had known that Borden's offer was better than Bowman's. Finally, the court held that the Commission had correctly determined that A&P had no cost justification defense. The U.S. Supreme Court granted certiorari.

ISSUE Did A&P violate Section 2f of the Robinson-Patman Act by knowingly inducing an illegal price discrimination from Borden?

DECISION No. Judgment reversed.

REASONS **Justice Stewart did not think any offense had been committed:**

"The Robinson-Patman Act was passed in response to the problem perceived in the increased market power and coercive practices of chain stores and other big buyers that threatened the existence of small independent retailers. Notwithstanding this concern with buyers, however, the emphasis of the Act is in Section 2(a), which prohibits price discrimination by sellers. While the phrase 'this section' refers to the entire Section 2 of the Act, only subsections (a) and (b) dealing with seller liability involve discriminations in price. Under the plain meaning of Section 2(f), therefore, a buyer cannot be liable if a prima facie case could not be established against a seller or if the seller has an affirmative defense. In either situation, there is no price discrimination 'prohibited by this section.' The legislative history of Section 2(f) fully confirms the conclusion that buyer liability under Section 2(f) is dependent on seller liability under Section 2(a). . . .

"Congress did not provide in Section 2(f) that a buyer can be liable even if the seller has a valid defense. The clear language of Section 2(f) states that a buyer can be liable only if he receives a price discrimination 'prohibited by this section.' If a seller has a valid meeting competition defense, there is simply no prohibited price discrimination. . . .

"In a competitive market, uncertainty among sellers will cause them to compete for business by offering buyers lower prices. Because of the evils of collusive action, the Court has held that the exchange of price information by competitors violates the Sherman Act. . . . Under the view advanced by the respondent, however, a buyer, to avoid liability, must either refuse a seller's bid or at least inform him that his bid has beaten competition. Such a duty of affirmative disclosure would almost inevitably frustrate competitive bidding and, by reducing uncertainty, lead to price matching and anticompetitive cooperation among sellers. . . .

"The test for determining when a seller has a valid meeting competition defense is whether a seller can 'show the existence of facts which would lead a reasonable and prudent person to believe that the granting of a lower price would in fact meet the equally low price of a competitor.' . . . Since good faith, rather than absolute certainty, is the touchstone of the meeting competition defense, a seller can assert the defense even if it has unknowingly made a bid that in fact not only met but beat his competition. . . .

"Borden was unable to ascertain the details of the Bowman bid. It requested more information about the bid from the petitioner, but this request was refused. It could not then attempt to verify the existence and terms of the competing offer from Bowman without risking Sherman Act liability. . . . Faced with a substantial loss of business and unable to find out the precise details of the competing bid, Borden made another offer, stating that it was doing so in order to meet competition. Under these circumstances, the conclusion is virtually inescapable that in making that offer Borden acted in a reasonable and good faith effort to meet its competition, and therefore was entitled to a meeting competition defense.

"Since Borden had a meeting competition defense and thus could not be liable under Section 2(b), the petitioner who did no more than accept that offer cannot be liable under Section 2(f)."

The "Cost Justification" Defense

In an important proviso to Section 2(a), Congress indicated that it did not wish to outlaw price differentials that could be justified by cost savings. If genuine cost savings could be realized on larger orders, a seller ought to be able to pass them on to the buyer. The theory of this defense is that if a price differential can be justified to the customer, it is lawful to pass that savings along to the customer.

For example, Company X wants to purchase 100,000 items which you produce and ship without separate wrapping and packaging. Company Y orders 5,000 of the identical item and wants each item individually packaged. Obviously, your cost per item for Company Y's order is going to be far greater than your cost per item to fill Company X's order. If you can prove a cost savings you can charge Company X less per item than you charge Company Y. However, be sure you have good records as to costs, because if a case of price discrimination is brought against you, you have the burden of proving the cost justification and its exact amount.

The "Obsolete or Perishable Goods" Defense

This defense is a rather obvious one. A seller who has obsolete or perishable goods needs to get rid of them for the best price. Also, since the quantity of these goods is limited, they present little likelihood of any substantial lessening of competition in the market.

■ PREDATORY PRICING

Another potentially significant limitation on a business's pricing decisions exists under Section 2 of the Sherman Act, which outlaws *attempts* to monopolize, as well as an accomplished monopolization. The courts have generally recognized that a violation of this section has occurred where a business has a specific intent to control prices or destroy competition, and has engaged in predatory or anticompetitive conduct designed to accomplish that unlawful purpose, and has a "dangerous probability" of success. These elements are often difficult to define in a particular situation. Intent may be inferred from conduct, and market power is certainly one factor in deciding whether there is a likelihood of successful monopolization, but the courts have also been careful not to make these inferences too quickly or too easily.

Areeda-Turner test for predatory pricing

One indication the courts have used in such cases is the practice of pricing a product below its cost, usually described as ***predatory pricing***. The idea is that a large firm can stand such losses on one of its products longer than a small firm, which may be selling only the targeted product line. Traditionally, the courts used a concept of *total costs*—both variable costs for labor and materials and fixed costs for such things as buildings and research. In 1975, Harvard law professors Phillip Areeda and Donald Turner suggested that the legal test for predatory pricing should be based only on *variable costs*. The fixed costs would be incurred anyway, and a business could very well decide to sell additional units at a price that covered variable costs for perfectly legitimate reasons. The company would probably wish to keep its workers employed, and to maintain or increase its market share, by making additional sales at a price that covered the variable costs. A number of U.S. Courts of Appeals have adopted the Areeda-Turner analysis. In those circuits it has become more difficult to prove a charge of predatory pricing. *Potential* predatory pricing was alleged in the following case.

CARGILL, INC. v. MONFORT OF COLORADO, INC.

107 S.Ct. 484 (1986)

FACTS Monfort of Colorado, Inc., the plaintiff below, owns and operates three integrated beef-packing plants, that is, plants for both the slaughter of cattle and the fabrication of beef. Monfort operates in both the market for fed cattle (the input market) and the market for fabricated beef (the output market). These markets are highly competitive, and the profit margins of the major beef packers are low. The current markets are a product of two decades of intense competition, during which time packers with modern integrated plants have gradually displaced packers with separate slaughter and fabrication plants.

Monfort is the country's fifth-largest beef packer. Petitioner Excel Corporation (Excel), one of the two defendants below, is the second-largest packer. Excel operates five integrated plants and one fabrication plant. It is a wholly owned subsidiary of Cargill, Inc., the other defendant below, a large privately owned corporation with more than 150 subsidiaries in at least 35 countries.

On June 17, 1983, Excel signed an agreement to acquire the third-largest packer in the market, Spencer Beef, a division of the Land O'Lakes agricultural cooperative. Spencer Beef owned two integrated plants and one slaughtering plant. After the acquisition, Excel would still be the second-largest packer, but would command a market share almost equal to that of the largest packer, IBP, Inc.

Monfort brought an action under Section 16 of the Clayton Act to enjoin the prospective merger. Its complaint alleged that the acquisition would "violat[e] Section 7 of the Clayton Act because the effect of the proposed acquisition may be substantially to lessen competition or tend to create a monopoly in several different ways. . . ." After the trial, the court entered a Memorandum Opinion and Order enjoining the proposed merger. The Court of Appeals affirmed.

ISSUE Has Monfort alleged it would be injured as the result of an *antitrust violation*, not just because of increased competition?

DECISION No. Judgment reversed (injunction denied).

REASONS Justice Brennan did not think that the antitrust acts protected businesses against "injuries" which resulted from increased competition. He felt that that was all Monfort was complaining about—tougher competition after the merger.

"Monfort's first claim is that after the merger, Excel would lower its prices to some level at or slightly above its costs in order to compete with other packers for market share. Excel would be in a position to do this because of the multiplant efficiencies its acquisition of Spencer would provide. . . . To remain competitive, Monfort would have to lower its prices; as a result, Monfort would suffer a loss in profitability but would not be driven out of business. The question is whether Monfort's loss of profits in such circumstances constitutes antitrust injury.

"To resolve the question, we look again to *Brunswick* v. *Pueblo Bowl-O-Mat*. . . . In *Brunswick*, we evaluated the antitrust significance of several competitors' loss of profits resulting from the entry of a large firm into its market. We concluded:

> [T]he antitrust laws are not merely indifferent to the injury claimed here. At base, respondents complain that by acquiring the failing centers petitioner preserved competition, thereby depriving respondents of the benefits of increased concentration. The damages respondents obtained are designed to provide them with the profits they would have realized had competition been reduced. The antitrust laws, however, were enacted for 'the protection of *competition*, not *competitors*.' . . . It is inimical to the purposes of these laws to award damages for the type of injury claimed here.

"The loss of profits to the competitors in *Brunswick* was not of concern under the antitrust laws, since it resulted only from continued competition. Respondent argues that the losses in *Brunswick* can be distinguished from the losses alleged here, since the latter will result from an increase, rather than from a mere continuation, of competition. The range of actions unlawful under Section 7 of the Clayton Act is broad enough, respondent claims, to support a finding of antitrust injury whenever a competitor is faced with a threat of losses from increased competition. We find respondent's proposed construction of Section 7 too broad, for reasons that *Brunswick* illustrates. *Brunswick* holds that the antitrust laws do not require the courts to protect small businesses from the loss of profits due to continued competition, but only against the loss of profits from practices forbidden by the antitrust laws. The kind of competition that Monfort alleges here, competition for increased market share, is not activity forbidden by the antitrust laws. It is simply, as petitioners claim, vigorous competition. To hold that the antitrust laws protect competitors from the loss of profits due to such price competition would, in effect, render illegal any decision by a firm to cut prices in order to increase market share. The antitrust laws require no such perverse result, for '[i]t is in the interest of competition to permit dominant firms to engage in vigorous competition, including price competition.' . . . The logic of *Brunswick* compels the conclusion that the threat of loss of profits due to possible price competition following a merger does not constitute a threat of antitrust injury.

"The second theory of injury argued here is that after the merger Excel would attempt to drive Monfort out of business by engaging in sustained predatory pricing. Predatory pricing may be defined as pricing below an appropriate measure of cost for the purpose of eliminating competitors in the short run and reducing competition in the long run. It is a practice that harms both competitors *and* competition. In contrast to price cutting aimed simply at increasing market share, predatory pricing has as its aim the elimination of competition. Predatory pricing is thus a practice 'inimical to the purposes of [the antitrust] laws,' . . . and one capable of inflicting antitrust injury. . . .

"Although the Court of Appeals did not explicitly define what it meant by predatory pricing, two interpretations are plausible. First, the court can be understood to mean that Monfort's allegation of losses from the above-cost 'cost-price squeeze' was equivalent to an allegation of injury from predatory conduct. If this is the proper interpretation, then the court's judgment is clearly erroneous because (a) Monfort made no allegation that Excel would act with predatory intent after the merger, and (b) price competition is not predatory activity, for the reasons discussed . . . supra.

"Second, the Court of Appeals can be understood to mean that Monfort had shown a credible threat of injury from below-cost pricing. To the extent the judgment rests on this ground, however, it must also be reversed, because Monfort did not allege injury from below-cost pricing before the District Court. The District Court twice noted that Monfort had made no assertion that Excel would engage in predatory pricing. . . . We conclude that Monfort neither raised nor proved any claim of predatory pricing before the District Court. . . .

"We hold that a plaintiff seeking injunctive relief under Section 16 of the Clayton Act must show a threat of antitrust injury, and that a showing of loss or damage due merely to increased competition does not constitute such injury. The record below does not support a finding of antitrust injury, but only of threatened loss from increased competition. Because respondent has therefore failed to make the showing Section 16 requires, we need not reach the question of whether the proposed merger violates Section 7. The judgment of the Court of Appeals is reversed and the case is remanded for further proceedings consistent with this opinion."

■ FEDERAL TRADE COMMISSION ACT

In 1914 Congress not only passed the Clayton Act but also the Federal Trade Commission Act. This act created a new administrative agency with very broad powers in the area of trade regulation. The FTC has the responsibility of investigating alleged violations of Sections 2, 3, 7, and 8 of the Clayton Act and has the authority to issue cease and desist orders to stop certain illegal practices and activities. Failure to comply with a cease and desist order from the Federal Trade Commission can result in fines of up to $10,000 for each day the violation continues.

The FTC and False Advertising

Section 5 of the Federal Trade Commission Act of 1914 prohibited unfair methods of competition and unfair or deceptive acts or practices. The FTC's original enforcement emphasis was against deceptive advertising. Many of the states had statutes that outlawed deceptive advertising, but enforcement varied from state to state. This sort of violation obviously injured both competitors and consumers, so it was probably a good place to start. While the FTC's approach to unfair methods of competition has become much broader over the years, especially since the 1970s, it continues to be alert for false and deceptive advertising. The "Man in the Sandpaper Mask" commercial is being tested in the following case.

FTC v. COLGATE-PALMOLIVE CO.

380 U.S. 374 (1965)

FACTS Ted Bates & Company, Inc., an advertising agency, prepared for Colgate three one-minute commercials designed to show that Rapid Shave could soften even the toughness of sandpaper. Each of the commercials contained the same "sandpaper test." The announcer informed the audience that, "To prove RAPID SHAVE's super-moisturizing power, we put it right from the can on this tough, dry sandpaper. It was apply [pause] soak [pause] and off in a stroke." While the announcer was speaking, Rapid Shave was applied to a substance that appeared to be sandpaper, and immediately thereafter a razor was shown shaving the substance clean.

The Federal Trade Commission issued a complaint against respondents Colgate and

Bates charging that the commercials were false and deceptive. The evidence before the hearing examiner disclosed that sandpaper of the type depicted in the commercials could not be shaved immediately following the application of Rapid Shave, but required a substantial soaking period of approximately 80 minutes. The evidence also showed that the substance resembling sandpaper was in fact a simulated prop, or "mock-up," made of plexiglass to which sand had been applied. However, the examiner found that Rapid Shave could shave sandpaper, even though not in the short time represented by the commercials, and that if real sandpaper had been used in the commercials the inadequacies of television transmission would have made it appear to viewers to be nothing more than plain, colored paper. The examiner dismissed the complaint because neither misrepresentation—concerning the actual moistening time or the identity of the shaved substance—was in his opinion a material one that would mislead the public.

The FTC overruled the trial examiner, and issued a cease and desist order against the ad. The Court of Appeals disagreed with the FTC and refused to enforce its order.

ISSUE   Is the use of the plexiglass mock-up "false and misleading"?

DECISION   Yes. FTC decision affirmed; Court of Appeals reversed.

REASONS   **Chief Justice Warren thought that a violation had been proved, with substantial evidence in the record.**

"We are not concerned in this case with the clear misrepresentation in the commercials concerning the speed with which Rapid Shave could shave sandpaper, since the Court of Appeals upheld the Commission's finding on that matter and the respondents have not challenged the finding here. We granted certiorari to consider the Commission's conclusion that even if an advertiser has himself conducted a test, experiment, or demonstration which he honestly believes will prove a certain product claim, he may not convey to television viewers the false impression that they are seeing the test, experiment, or demonstration for themselves, when they are not because of the undisclosed use of mock-ups.

"We accept the Commission's determination that the commercials involved in this case contained three representations to the public: (1) that sandpaper could be shaved by Rapid Shave; (2) that an experiment had been conducted which verified this claim; and (3) that the viewer was seeing this experiment for himself. Respondents admit that the first two representations were made, but deny that the third was. The Commission, however, found to the contrary, and, since this is a matter of fact resting on an inference that could reasonably be drawn from the commercials themselves, the Commission's finding should be sustained. For the purposes of our review, we can assume that the first two representations were true; the focus of our consideration is on the third which was clearly false. The parties agree that Section 5 prohibits the intentional misrepresentation of any fact which would constitute a material factor in a purchaser's decision whether to buy. They differ, however, in their conception of what *'facts'* constitute a 'material factor' in a purchaser's decision to buy. Respondents submit, in effect, that the only material facts are those which deal with the substantive qualities of a product. The Commission, on the other hand, submits that the misrepresentation of *any* fact so long as it materially induces a purchaser's decision to buy is a deception prohibited by Section 5. . . .

"We agree with the Commission, therefore, that the undisclosed use of plexiglass in the present commercials was a material deceptive practice, independent and separate from the other misrepresentation found. We find unpersuasive respondents' other objections to this conclusion. Respondents claim that it will be impractical to inform the viewing public that it is not seeing an actual test, experiment, or demonstration, but we think it inconceivable that the ingenious advertising world will be unable, if it so desires, to conform to the Commission's insistence that the public be not misinformed. If, however, it becomes impossible or impractical to show simulated demonstrations on television in a truthful manner, this indicates that television is not a medium that lends itself to this type of commercial, not that the commercial must survive at all costs. Similarly unpersuasive is respondents' objection that the Commission's decision discriminates against sellers whose product claims cannot be 'verified' on television without the use of simulations. All methods of advertising do not equally favor every seller. If the inherent limitations of a method do not permit its use in the way a seller desires, the seller cannot by material misrepresentation compensate for those limitations. . . .

"The Court of Appeals has criticized the reference in the Commission's order regarding the 'test, experiment, or demonstration' as not capable of practical interpretation. It could find no difference between the Rapid Shave commercial and a commercial which extolled the goodness of ice cream while giving viewers a picture of a scoop of mashed potatoes appearing to be ice cream. We do not understand this difficulty. In the ice cream case the mashed potato prop is not being used for additional proof of the product claim, while the purpose of the Rapid Shave commercial is to give the viewer objective proof of the claims made. If in the ice cream hypothetical the focus of the commercial becomes the undisclosed potato prop and the viewer is invited, explicitly or by implication, to see for himself the truth of the claims about the ice cream's rich texture and full color, and perhaps compare it to a 'rival product,' then the commercial has become similar to the one now before us. Clearly, however, a commercial which depicts happy actors delightedly eating ice cream that is in fact mashed potatoes or drinking a product appearing to be coffee but which is in fact some other substance is not covered by the present order. . . .

"The judgment of the Court of Appeals is reversed and the case remanded for the entry of a judgment enforcing the Commission's order."

The FTC and Unfair Trade Practices

As it moved beyond false advertising cases, the FTC's basic difficulty became one of definition. Just what did its statute mean? What exactly are **unfair methods of competition?** To some persons, "all's fair in Love and War"—and Business. The drafters of the statute had clearly left the phrase vague and flexible, so that the FTC would be able to deal with new unfair devices as they were developed. If only specific practices had been prohibited, business firms and their lawyers could quickly circumvent the act by restructuring their operations. Although the uncertainty was intentional, it has nevertheless caused problems.

Unfair methods clearly include violations of the Sherman Act and the Clayton Act (including Robinson-Patman) and incipient Sherman Act violations. The Supreme Court has also held that methods that violate the "basic policy" of the Sherman and Clayton Acts, even though not specifically listed in the acts, can be reached under Section 5. Practices that injure customers can be prosecuted without necessarily showing that any competitor has been injured. All types of behavior that might be classified as "bad business morals" can also be reached under Section 5, including such things as tampering with a competitor's goods, deceptive packaging, and delivering unordered goods. In 1972 the Supreme Court decided that the FTC had general rule-making power; that is, the FTC did not have to proceed on a case-by-case basis but could promulgate rules of behavior, just like the NLRB, the SEC, and other agencies. Since then, the

FTC has been quite aggressive in adopting rules for competitive conduct. Most recently, there have been attempts in Congress to curb the FTC's growing power over commercial practices.

Other FTC Jurisdiction

The FTC was also given the responsibility for enforcing a series of labeling acts passed in the 1940s and 1950s: the Wool Products Act (1941), the Fur Products Act (1952), the Textile Fibre Act (1958), and the Flammable Fabrics Act (1954). The enforcement mechanisms include both cease-and-desist orders and criminal penalties. The FTC also enforces the 1975 Magnuson-Moss Warranty Act, discussed in Chapter 20.

Other consumer protection statutes

As part of the consumerism movement of the 1960s and 1970s, the FTC was given increased enforcement jurisdiction under several new statutes. The Truth in Lending Act, which requires disclosure of the true annual percentage rate of interest and other information to the consumer or farmer borrower, places primary enforcement in the Federal Reserve Board. The Fair Credit Reporting Act creates new debtor rights against credit bureaus, as does the Fair Credit Billing Act in disputes with creditors. Congress also limited debt collection practices with the Fair Debt Collection Practices Act. Many of these new statutes provide the possibility of private damage suits as well as administrative agency action. The FTC was given joint jurisdiction with the Department of Health and Welfare (now Department of Health and Human Resources) to enforce the new Fair Packaging Act, which requires label disclosures and limits sellers' claims.

Probably because Congress felt that more specific engineering and technical expertise was needed to deal with the problem, the FTC was not given enforcement responsibility under the 1972 Consumer Product Safety Act. A new Consumer Product Safety Commission (CPSC) and a new Advisory Council were created by the act. The CPSC collects and distributes data on product safety and product-related injuries. Injured consumers can bring suits in the U.S. courts if the alleged damages are $10,000 or more, and the further distribution of the "unsafe" product may be enjoined. The manufacturer may also be fined $2,000 for each violation, but the total fine for a single product cannot exceed $500,000.

■ SIGNIFICANCE OF THIS CHAPTER

The antitrust laws are significant because to maintain a competitive marketplace we must prevent anticompetitive schemes, such as price fixing, market splitting, resale price maintenance, and tying contracts. The antitrust laws try to prevent actions which may restrain competition.

Pricing decisions are at the heart of the competitive process and are the essence of the free enterprise system. Our national laws nonetheless impose significant restrictions on a business's freedom to make such decisions. Even though the Robinson-Patman Act seems outdated and incompatible with a free marketplace, it lurks in the statute books, waiting to trap the unwary marketer. Persons responsible for pricing and other marketing decisions need to be aware of these basic rules of the game.

Likewise, while the FTC Act does not provide a complete list of "unfair methods of competition," a marketing executive can get a good idea of the outer boundaries by reading some of the landmark cases. This chapter is designed to provide a sensitivity for these legal boundaries on competition.

DISCUSSION CASE

NATIONAL COLLEGIATE ATHLETIC ASSOCIATION V. BOARD OF REGENTS OF THE UNIVERSITY OF OKLAHOMA AND UNIVERSITY OF GEORGIA ATHLETIC ASSOCIATION
468 U.S. 85 (1984)

FACTS: The NCAA has approximately 850 voting members. The regular members are classified into separate divisions to reflect differences in size and scope of their athletic programs. Division I includes 276 colleges with major athletic programs; in this group only 187 play intercollegiate football. Divisions II and III include approximately 500 colleges with less extensive athletic programs. Division I has been subdivided into Divisions I-A and I-AA for football.

Some years ago, five major conferences together with major football-playing independent institutions organized the College Football Association (CFA). The original purpose of the CFA was to promote the interests of major football-playing schools within the NCAA structure. The Universities of Oklahoma and Georgia, respondents in this Court, are members of the CFA.

Beginning in 1979 CFA members began to advocate that colleges with major football programs should have a greater voice in the formulation of football television policy than they had in the NCAA. CFA therefore investigated the possibility of negotiating a television agreement of its own, developed an independent plan, and obtained a contract offer from the National Broadcasting Co. (NBC). This contract, which it signed in August 1981, would have allowed a more liberal number of apppearances for each institution, and would have increased the overall revenues realized by CFA members.

In response the NCAA publicly announced that it would take disciplinary action against any CFA member that complied with the CFA-NBC contract. On September 8, 1981, respondents commenced this action in the United States District Court and obtained a preliminary injunction preventing the NCAA from initiating disciplinary proceedings or otherwise interfering with CFA's efforts

to perform its agreement its agreement with NBC. The Court of Appeals affirmed.

■

Justice Stevens was convinced that the NCAA rules did violate the Sherman Act.

There can be no doubt that the challenged practices of the NCAA constitute a "restraint of trade" in the sense that they limit members' freedom to negotiate and enter into their own television contracts. In that sense, however, every contract is a restraint of trade, and as we have repeatedly recognized, the Sherman Act was intended to prohibit only unreasonable restraints of trade.

Horizontal price-fixing and output limitation are ordinarily condemned as a matter of law under an "illegal per se" approach because the probability that these practices are anticompetitive is so high; a per se rule is applied when "the practice facially appears to be one that would always or almost always tend to restrict competition and decrease output." In such circumstances a restraint is presumed unreasonable without inquiry into the particular market context in which it is found. Nevertheless, we have decided that it would be inappropriate to apply a per se rule to this case. This decision is not based on a lack of judicial experience with this type of arrangement, on the fact that the NCAA is organized as a nonprofit entity, or on our respect for the NCAA's historic role in the preservation and encouragement of intercollegiate amateur athletics. Rather, what is critical is that this case involves an industry in which horizontal restraints on competition are essential if the product is to be available at all.

As Judge Bork has noted: "[S]ome activities can only be carried out jointly. Perhaps the leading example is league sports. When a league of professional lacrosse teams is formed, it would be pointless to declare their cooperation illegal on the ground that there are no other professional lacrosse teams." What the NCAA and its member institutions market in this case is competition itself—contests between competing institutions. Of course, this would be completely ineffective if there were no rules on which the competitors agreed to create and define the competition to be marketed. A myriad of rules affecting such matters as the size of the field, the number of players on a team, and the extent to which physical violence is to be encouraged or proscribed, all must be agreed upon, and all restrain the manner in which institutions compete.

. . . Thus, the NCAA plays a vital role in enabling college football to preserve its character, and as a result enables a product to be marketed which might otherwise be unavailable. In performing this role, its actions widen consumer choice—not only the choices available to sports fans but also those available to athletes—and hence can be viewed as procompetitive. . . .

Throughout the history of its regulation of intercollegiate football telecasts, the NCAA has indicated its concern with protecting live attendance.

There is, however, a . . . fundamental reason for rejecting this defense. The NCAA's argument that its television plan is necessary to protect live attendance is not based on a desire to maintain the integrity of college football as a distinct and attractive product, but rather on a fear that the product will not prove sufficiently attractive to draw live attendance when faced with competition from televised games. At bottom the NCAA's position is that

ticket sales for most college games are unable to compete in a free market. The television plan protects ticket sales by limiting output—just as any monopolist increases revenues by reducing output.

Petitioner argues that the interest in maintaining a competitive balance among amateur athletic teams is legitimate and important and that it justifies the regulations challenged in this case. We agree with the first part of the argument but not the second.

The NCAA does not claim that its television plan has equalized or is intended to equalize competition within any one league. The plan is nationwide in scope and there is no single league or tournament in which all college football teams compete. . . .

The television plan is not even arguably tailored to serve such an interest. It does not regulate the amount of money that any college may spend on its football program, nor the way in which the colleges may use the revenues that are generated by their football programs, whether derived from the sale of television rights, the sale of tickets, or the sale of concessions or program advertising. The plan simply imposes a restriction on one source of revenue that is more important to some colleges than to others. There is no evidence that this restriction produces any greater measure of equality throughout the NCAA than would a restriction on alumni donations, tuition rates, or any other revenue-producing activity. At the same time, as the District Court found, the NCAA imposes a variety of other restrictions designed to preserve amateurism which are much better tailored to the goal of competitive balance than is the television plan, and which are "clearly sufficient" to preserve competitive balance to the extent it is within the NCAA's power to do so. Affirmed.

■ IMPORTANT TERMS AND CONCEPTS

Sherman Act
monopoly
attempt to monopolize
restraint of trade
legal school
economic school
Clayton Act
Robinson-Patman Act
Federal Trade
   Commission Act
nolo contendere
price-fixing
treble damages
rule of reason

relevant market
oligopoly
conspiracy
conscious parallelism
fair trade laws
resale price maintenance
refusal to deal
interbrand competition
intrabrand competition
price discrimination
tying contract
exclusive dealing
   agreement
merger

horizontal merger
vertical merger
conglomerate merger
merger guidelines
Herfindahl-Hirschman
   Index
interlocking directors
like kind and quality

Nonprofit Institutions Act
meeting competition defense
cost justification defense
predatory pricing
false advertising
unfair trade practices
unfair methods of
   competition

■ QUESTIONS AND PROBLEMS FOR DISCUSSION

1. Why is resale price maintenance a violation of the antitrust law? What is the difference between resale price maintenance and refusal to deal?

2. Why should the government regulate corporate mergers? Is any merger good, or are they all bad? Where should we draw the line? What are the merger guidelines?

3. What is the role of the Federal Trade Commission with regard to antitrust laws? What specific laws does the FTC have authority to enforce?

4. It is often said that the Sherman Act is an "after the fact" law, whereas the Clayton Act is a "before the fact" law. Explain what this means.

5. Sticky Stamp Company, Inc. provided grocery stores and other retailers trading stamps to give to customers as "bonuses." Customers might collect books of these stamps and then redeem them for merchandise at Sticky's "gift centers." Each of Sticky's collection books contained a printed notice that the stamps were not for resale. Sticky enforced this provision by bringing injunction suits against "trading centers" where customers tried to exchange one brand of trading stamp for stamps from another company and where customers could buy additional stamps to fill uncompleted books. Sticky had been very successful in closing down these stamp trading centers. The FTC, after an investigation, charges Sticky with unfair methods of competition under Section 5 of the FTC Act. Should the Commission and the courts sustain this charge? Discuss.

6. Fritter's Appliance Company had a retail store in Anytown, Ohio. Two blocks away was an Ace Department Store, which also sold appliances. Ace was a large statewide chain of 50 stores. Fritter had only one location. Ace and the other large chain stores in the area contacted most of the national appliance manufacturers and asked them not to supply merchandise to Fritter, whose discount prices were hurting sales from the chain stores. As a result, Fritter was unable to buy many brand name appliances. Fritter sues Ace and several manufacturers, alleging violations of Section 1 and 2 of the Sherman Act and asking for treble damages and an injunction. What is the result, and why?

7. Marner-Silas Co. has been selling Blisteine, a mouthwash, for nearly 40 years. The formula for the product has not changed during this period, but at various times, Marner-Silas has advertised that Blisteine relieves colds and sore throats. The FTC has solid medical evidence that these claims are not true. How should the FTC proceed, and what remedy should it require of Marner-Silas? Explain.

8. Leon Rippof advertised eyeglasses for sale at his store, "from $7.50 complete, including lenses, frames, and case." Some of his ads mentioned a "modest examination fee"; others did not. Of the 1,400 pairs of eyeglasses he sold during the prior year, only 9 were sold at $7.50; most cost considerably more than that. Has Rippof committed false advertising? Discuss.

6

Criminal Law

CHAPTER OBJECTIVES

THIS CHAPTER WILL:

- Define *crime*.
- Compare and contrast civil and criminal proceedings.
- Explain why a corporate executive could be found guilty of a crime for acts committed in the name of the corporation.
- Review the rights a person accused of a crime has under criminal law.

Traditionally the businessperson has been less concerned about criminal law than about contract law, tort law, corporation law, and other mainstream business law subjects. This is changing. Criminal law, particularly as it applies to *white-collar crimes,* is becoming an area of considerable concern. The businessperson needs to be aware of a number of business crimes, including one of the newest types of crime: computer theft. Computer theft encompasses embezzlement of funds, theft of programs, and theft of confidential business information and records—all through the use and manipulation of computers and other electronic devices.

In addition to having to concern themselves with white-collar or business crimes, corporate officers and directors need to know what kinds of circumstances can make them subject to both civil lawsuits and criminal charges.

■ DEFINITION OF CRIME

A *crime* can be defined as a public wrong. To maintain an orderly society, the government must set standards of conduct which the members of society must observe. Failure to observe these standards must be enforced by some form of societal pressure, such as fines or imprisonment. A crime may involve either the commission of a specific act or the omission or failure to act under certain circumstances. For the commission or omission of an act to be classified as a crime, the legislature, either national or state, must have passed a statute declaring the commission or omission of that act to be a crime. Usually, it is also necessary to prove that the act was done with wrongful intent.

Crimes and torts

Many of the acts or omissions which have been defined as crimes may also be torts. A tort, as defined in Chapter 7, is a private wrong for which the wronged person may recover monetary damages. If someone is mugged on the street, the mugger may be punished in a criminal court by a fine or imprisonment. The person who has been mugged, as the victim of a private wrong, has a legal right to bring a civil action at his or her own expense to recover monetary damages from the mugger.

■ CLASSIFICA-TIONS OF CRIME

Crimes are usually classified as felonies or misdemeanors. Traditionally *felonies* have been serious crimes, such as murder, rape, robbery, burglary, arson, theft, and larceny. A crime is not a felony, however, unless a statute designates it as such. Felonies are normally punishable by jail sentences of at least one year, plus possible fines.

Different state definitions

Misdemeanors are criminal offenses other than felonies. Typically, misdemeanors are punished by small fines or jail sentences not exceeding one year, or both a fine and imprisonment. Normally the person who has been convicted of a misdemeanor is confined in a county jail rather than the state penitentiary. The fines imposed for misdemeanors are normally smaller than the fines imposed for felonies. No standard is common to all states; different states have different crime classifications and different levels of punishment. Each state is responsibile for creating its own criminal law, but state criminal law cannot conflict with any applicable national law.

■ BUSINESS CRIMES

Since this textbook focuses on business-related legal matters, we will only discuss crimes that are relevant to the operation of a business. The following are some typical business crimes.

Larceny. Larceny, or theft as it is commonly called, is simply the unlawful taking of another person's personal property with the intent of depriving the owner of the property. Shoplifting is an example of larceny with which the businessperson has to be concerned. Larceny is also committed by employees who carry off goods and merchandise.

Robbery. Robbery, like larceny, involves the unlawful taking of personal property. However, the unlawful taking in a robbery involves the use of force, putting other persons in fear of injury. Thus, robbery is a more serious crime than larceny since it has the potential of physical harm to individuals.

Embezzlement. With embezzlement, a person who had lawful possession of someone else's money or property used the property or money for his or her own purposes. A typical case here would be a bank employee who was in charge of certain funds and used some of the funds for personal purposes. Many embezzlers borrow money with the intent of paying it back later. In most jurisdictions the person who takes money with the intent of returning it is still guilty of embezzlement.

Arson. Arson is willfully setting fire to and burning someone else's building. In old English common law, arson referred primarily to the burning of someone else's dwelling house. Under most state statutes, arson now covers the burning of business buildings as well as dwellings.

Defrauding Consumers by Use of the Mails. Using the mails to solicit money for fraudulent purposes is a crime. This could include schemes to sell phony corporate stocks and bonds, false statements about products which when received are not as advertised, and numerous other situations in which people use the mails to convey false information for the purpose of committing fraud. National laws also make it a crime to send pornographic materials through the mails.

Intent to defraud a necessary element

Defrauding Consumers by Using False Labels, Measures, and Weights. In recent years a number of national and state laws have been passed concerning false weights, measures, and labels. Again, intention is a key factor in this crime. A simple mistake in weight or measurement is not a crime. There must be an intent to defraud or cheat the consumer.

Falsification of legal documents

Forgery. Forgery is the false or fraudulent making, or the material alteration with the intent to defraud, of any writing which, if genuine, would be of legal effect and create legal liability.

Credit Card Fraud. Illegal and fraudulent use of stolen credit cards has become a major concern to credit card companies. In 1971 Congress passed a law that limited an individual's liability to $50 per stolen credit card. While an individual cannot be liable for more than $50 per stolen card, the loss of credit card companies is not limited.

Liability for unauthorized use of credit cards

Computer Crime. This is the newest and perhaps the most important area of criminal law of concern to business managers. Computer-related crimes range from the theft of a computer program worth thousands of dollars to the use of computers to embezzle millions of dollars.

The following case discusses one of the procedural problems in prosecuting computer crime—*where* is the crime committed?

COMMONWEALTH v. KATSAFANAS

464 A.2d 1270 (Pennsylvania, 1983)

FACTS

Nicholas Katsafanas (also known as Nick Perry) and Edward Plevel worked out a scheme to enrich themselves by the means of the computer-run state lottery. They first decided that the winning number combination (always one with three numerals) for the draw of April 24, 1980 would consist of only the numerals four (4) and six (6). There are eight possible three digit number combinations using only 4 or 6.

They purchased lottery tickets for all the possible number combinations from retail ticket vendors at various locations. The rigging, or "fix," took place in the studio of WTAE in Pittsburgh, Allegheny County, by means of placing counterfeit balls in the machines used in the drawing. When the winning number combination, 666, was drawn, Plevel telephoned Michael Keyser, an administrative officer in the Lottery Bureau in Harrisburg, Dauphin County. Keyser programmed 666 into the computer, and the conspirators or their agents subsequently cashed in their winning tickets.

Katsafanas and Plevel were convicted of conspiracy, theft by deception, criminal mischief, rigging a publicly exhibited contest, and perjury. They moved for a new trial. Defendants claim that they were erroneously brought to trial in Dauphin County (the locus of the computer) because none of the manipulation of the lottery equipment used to select the winning numbers took place in Dauphin County. The trial judge denied their motion and they appealed.

ISSUE

Was the trial properly held in the county where the computer used to commit the fraud was physically located?

DECISION

Yes. Judgment affirmed.

REASONS

Judge Beck explained the reasoning behind the venue rules.
"This appeal, challenging the venue of a trial for crimes which made use of a computer-based operation, requires an examination of ancient rules of law in light of today's technology. The common law adopted a territorial theory as the basis of jurisdiction over crimes. Jurisdiction is concerned with the authority or power of a court to entertain a case. A state has the power to make certain conduct criminal if that conduct, or its

results, occurs within the state's territorial limits. The rules of venue determine the place of trial within a jurisdiction. Issues relating to venue address the criteria for holding a trial in a particular court among several which may be jurisdictionally correct. The law relating to venue limits the general territorial rule by the concept that each crime has its own situs or locus which determines the correct place within the jurisdiction for the trial to take place. . . .

"[T]he rules of venue [are] designed to protect the accused from being forced to stand trial far from home or far from the place where the crime was committed. Venue guarantees also safeguard criminal defendants from unfairness resulting from 'forum shopping' by government prosecutors. . . .

"Clearly, the functions of the Harrisburg computer were the essential operations in obtaining tickets and cashing them. Every purchase of a ticket and every validation of a win occurred in and by the operation of the Harrisburg computer. The informations filed against Perry and Plevel charge them with purchasing lottery tickets and causing others to make purchases for them. Much more than the telephone call from Pittsburgh to Harrisburg was at stake, and the locus of the computer in Harrisburg makes Perry and Plevel's statement that Harrisburg was 'incidental' to the crimes erroneous. . . .

"[T]he computer in Harrisburg was central and essential to the operation of the lottery. . . .

"[I]t was the mechanism without which the lottery operation could not function. . . .

"Thus, venue may lie at the location of the central computer, whether the crime involved direct manipulation of the computer itself, or whether the crime involved use of the central computer as an essential part of the plan or scheme giving rise to the criminal activities as in the instant case.

"We find ample reason for concluding that acts of crime occurred in Dauphin County, where the number 666 was programmed into the state computer and where all the computer-based data relating to purchases, odds, and authorization of payments originated. In the lottery fraud, criminal activity occurred in numerous places throughout the state. Essential to the entire operation was the functioning of the computer in Dauphin County. Since we regard appellants' argument that only the conspiracy charge and only the telephone call to Keyser in Harrisburg have any relationship to Dauphin County as specious, we find it unnecessary to respond to their contention that all of the offenses charged against Perry and Plevel have been 'piggy-backed' onto that single event. If the computer is essential to and part and parcel of the crime, then the locus of the computer is one of the places where venue lies. We therefore hold that venue in Dauphin County was correct for the charges of conspiracy, theft by deception, criminal mischief and rigging a publicly exhibited contest."

CPA criminal liability

Criminal Liability of Accountants. This is also a new area of criminal law. Traditionally, professionals such as accountants, lawyers, and doctors were found liable for civil damages for malpractice but were not prosecuted criminally for acts of mere negligence. In recent years a number of criminal cases have been brought against accountants, particularly in connection with their failure to discover and report fraud by corporate officers or employees.

The following case is one of the first cases where accountants were criminally prosecuted. In Chapter 8, we will discuss the liability of accountants and other professionals in more detail.

UNITED STATES v. NATELLI

527 F.2d 311 (U.S. Second Circuit, 1975)

FACTS   National Student Marketing Corporation ("Marketing") was formed in 1966. It charged fees to businesses for marketing their products and services directly to students in an "attractive package" of merchandise. Marketing stock went public in 1968 at $6 a share; five months later it was selling at $80 a share.

Peat, Marwick, Mitchell & Co. ("Peat") became Marketing's auditors in August 1968. Anthony Natelli was the engagement partner for the account and the manager of PMM's office in Washington, D.C. Joseph Scansaroli was the audit supervisor for the account.

Many of Marketing's fee arrangements were only oral commitments. Using their estimates of the completion of its services on the accounts, a 1968 year-end adjustment for "unbilled accounts receivable" of $1.7 million turned a loss into a profit twice that of the previous year. About $1 million of the oral commitments were written off by May 1969. Marketing's 1968 income thereby went down more than $200,000 but Scansaroli and Natelli covered this by "reversing" a deferred tax credit for about the same amount. The financial statements which were filed with a proxy statement proposing a merger with six other firms did not show any adjustment in Marketing's profit figure for 1968. A $12 million commitment from Pontiac (GM) was backdated so as to be included in the period through May 31, 1969. When Natelli questioned this practice, he was told that there was a commitment from Eastern Airlines for a similar amount that could be included, so he let it pass. The financial statements did not show that Marketing had written off $1 million of its 1968 sales and more than $2 million of the unbilled sales for 1968 and 1969. Marketing should have showed no profit for 1969, but instead the financial statement prepared by Natelli and Scansaroli and filed with a proxy statement that was relied upon by other companies in a proposed merger showed tremendous profits and was in fact false and misleading. Anthony Natelli and Joseph Scansaroli were criminally prosecuted under Section 32(a) of the 1934 Act for willfully and knowingly making false and misleading statements in a corporation's proxy statement. Both were convicted in U.S. District Court, which imposed a one-year sentence and a $10,000 fine upon Natelli, suspending all but 60 days of imprisonment, and a one-year sentence and a $2,500 fine upon Scansaroli, suspending all but 10 days of the imprisonment. Both appealed.

ISSUE   Did the defendants *knowingly* issue false statements of material facts?

DECISION   Yes. Judgment affirmed.

 REASONS   Circuit Judge Gurfein reviewed the standard of proof.

"It is hard to probe the intent of a defendant. Circumstantial evidence, particularly with proof of motive, where available, is often sufficient to convince a reasonable man of criminal intent beyond a reasonable doubt. When we deal with a defendant who is a professional accountant, it is even harder, at times, to distinguish between simple errors of judgment and errors made with sufficient criminal intent to support a conviction, especially when there is no financial gain to the accountant other than his legitimate fee.

"Natelli argues that there is insufficient evidence to establish that he knowingly assisted in filing a proxy statement which was materially false. After searching consideration, we are constrained to find that there was sufficient evidence for his conviction. . . .

"The claim of Scansaroli with respect to insufficiency of the evidence is somewhat more difficult. As Judge Tyler noted after both sides had rested, 'It is a close question, I think frankly as to Scansaroli, as I see it. Certainly if I were the factfinder, I would be more troubled with his case for a variety of reasons.'

"Scansaroli contends that there was insufficient evidence to prove beyond a reasonable doubt that (1) he participated in a criminal act with respect to the footnote or (2) that he made an accounting judgment permitting Marketing to include in sales certain contracts-in-progress with the requisite criminal intent. We hold that there was enough evidence to establish the former, but not the latter. . . .

"There is some merit to Scansaroli's point that he was simply carrying out the judgments of his superior Natelli. The defense of obedience to higher authority has always been troublesome. There is no sure yardstick to measure criminal responsibility except by measurement of the degree of awareness on the part of a defendant that he is participating in a criminal act, in the absence of physical coercion such as a soldier might face. Here the motivation to conceal undermines Scansaroli's argument that he was merely implementing Natelli's instructions, at least with respect to concealment of matters that were within his own ken.

"Judgment affirmed as to appellant Natelli; as to appellant Scansaroli judgment reversed and remanded for a new trial."

[The United States petitioned the court for a rehearing concerning the court's reversal of the conviction of Scansaroli, and after rehearing Judge Gurfein reversed his previous decision and affirmed the conviction of Scansaroli as well as the conviction of Natelli.]

Commercial Bribery.   Over the past two decades the press has exposed many cases of commercial bribery, payoffs to politicians, and illegal campaign contributions. A problem in many of these cases is that a corporation made the illegal contribution or paid the bribe. You can fine a corporation, but you can't put one in jail. Shouldn't the executive who made the decision to have the corporation disobey the law also be criminally liable? Such activities by U.S. corporations in other countries were the major reason behind passage of the Foreign Corrupt Practices Act, discussed earlier in Chapter Four.

FCPA and foreign bribery

Criminal Liability of Corporate Executives.   In stockholder actions against managers, corporate directors, and corporate officers, corporate executives have always been individually accountable in civil court for their acts of negligence in the operation of the business. If criminal charges were filed, however, typically the corporation was charged with the crime. Since a corporation cannot be jailed, the corporation simply paid the fine and the case was closed. For many years a protective shield seemed to exist between the manager, corporate directors, and corporate officers, and the criminal prosecutor. This corporate shield was first pierced in the electrical industry price-fixing conspiracy case in 1960. In that case several corporate executives were sent to jail. The corporate shield has been disintegrating ever since, as Mr. Park learns in the next case.

Corporate vs. individual criminal liability

U.S. v. PARK

421 U.S. 658 (1975)

FACTS   Mr. Park was the president of Acme Markets Inc., a large retail food chain, with 12 warehouses, 874 stores, and 36,000 employees. The Food and Drug Administration (FDA) advised the company and its president of unsanitary conditions in its warehouses and requested that the conditions be cleaned up. Some cleanup was done, but the warehouses still did not meet minimum standards. The U.S. government then filed a criminal action against both the company and Park for the continued violation. The company pleaded guilty, and Park pleaded not guilty. He did not feel personally responsible for the failure of other employees in the company. The trial court still found him guilty. The appeals court reversed, and the U.S. Supreme Court granted certiorari.

ISSUE   Can a corporate officer be found guilty of criminal violation of the Food, Drug, and Cosmetic Act?

DECISION   Yes, trial court decision affirmed. Court of Appeals is reversed.

REASONS   Chief Justice Burger, speaking for the Court, commented:

"The rule (that corporate employees who have a responsible share in the furtherance of the transaction which the statute outlaws are subject to the criminal provision of the Act) was not formulated in a vacuum. . . . [T]he principle had been recognized that a corporate agent, through whose act, default, or omission the corporation committed a crime, was himself guilty individually of that crime. The principle has been applied whether or not the crime required consciousness of wrongdoing, and it has been applied not only to those corporate agents who themselves committed the criminal act, but also to those who by virtue of their managerial positions or other similar relations to the Act could be deemed responsible for its commission. . . ."

In this case, by his own admission, Mr. Park stated that as Acme's chief executive officer he was responsible for 'any result which occurs in our company.'"

▪ YOUR RIGHTS UNDER CRIMINAL LAW

Civil penalties versus criminal penalties

Your rights under criminal law are considerably different from your rights under civil law. Under civil law, if you are sued for breach of contract or for the commission of a tort, the usual remedy is monetary damages. None of us wants to lose money. However, if we are unfortunate enough to have a very large judgment assessed against us and we do not have the funds to satisfy it, we have the opportunity to file for bankruptcy. (Bankruptcy will be covered in Chapter 23.) A person who is adjudicated a bankrupt is free from most prior debts and is, in effect, born again, as far as his or her financial life is concerned.

Severe possible penalties

On the other hand, a person who is convicted of a crime may be jailed and/or fined. If the crime is a felony, the person also may lose certain civil rights. In some states convicted felons lose the right to vote, the right to serve on juries, and the right to hold public office. Also, professional practitioners convicted of a crime may lose their right to practice their profession. For instance, a lawyer may face disbarment if convicted. Thus, the consequences of a criminal conviction are more serious than those of civil judgment for money. A person convicted of a crime will carry this record for life. In fact, if capital punishment is allowed, the person may lose his or her life. Thus the guarantees the law must give to a person charged with a crime are much greater than the guarantees that must be given in a civil trial for monetary damages.

Strict procedural requirements

Following are some of the guarantees that are essential in a criminal trial, but need not be provided in a civil trial.

Sixth Amendment guarantees of jury and speedy trial

Right to a Speedy, Public Trial by Jury. The *Sixth Amendment* to the U.S. Constitution guarantees a speedy public trial by jury in criminal cases. In civil cases in large metropolitan areas, the trial may be delayed several years after the time the lawsuit was filed. A person charged with a crime should have his or her day in court promptly, and it must be public. The trial must be before a jury, unless the defendant waives the right to a jury trial.

In addition to having the right to a speedy, public trial by jury, an accused in a criminal case also has the right to be judged by a fair and impartial jury, one not subjected to the pressures and prejudices of the newspaper and television media during the trial. The *Sheppard* case illustrates this point.

SHEPPARD v. MAXWELL, WARDEN

384 U.S. 333 (1966)

FACTS

Sheppard was arrested, tried, and convicted of murdering his wife. The trial was held in the common pleas court of Cuyahoga County, Ohio. Sheppard's conviction was affirmed by the Supreme Court of Ohio. Sheppard filed a petition for habeas corpus in U.S. District Court against the prison warden, seeking release from custody. His intention was that he was denied a fair trial because the trial judge failed to protect him from inherently prejudicial publicity which saturated the community and also because the judge allowed extensive newspaper, radio, and television coverage of his trial in the courtroom itself. The District Court ruled in favor of the petition for habeas corpus; the U.S. Court of Appeals reversed; and the Supreme Court of the United States granted certiorari.

ISSUE

Was Sheppard denied a fair trial?

DECISION

Yes. Judgment reversed.

REASONS

Justice Clark spoke for the Supreme Court:

"On July 7, the day of Marilyn Sheppard's funeral, a newspaper story appeared in which Assistant County Attorney Mahon—later the chief prosecutor of Sheppard—sharply criticized the refusal of the Sheppard family to permit his immediate questioning. From there on, headline stories repeatedly stressed Sheppard's lack of cooperation with the police and other officials. . . . The newspapers also played up Sheppard's refusal to take a lie detector test and 'the protective ring' thrown up by his family. Front page newspaper headlines announced on the same day, 'Doctor Balks At Lie Test; Retells Story.' . . .

"On the 20th, the 'editorial artillery' opened fire with a front-page charge that somebody is 'getting away with murder.' The editorial attributed the ineptness of the investigation to 'friendships, relationships, hired lawyers, a husband who ought to have been subjected instantly to the same third-degree to which any other person under similar circumstances is subjected. . . .' The following day, July 21, another page-one editorial was headed: 'Why No Inquest? Do It Now, Dr. Gerber.' The Coroner called an inquest the same day and subpoenaed Sheppard. It was staged the next day in a school gymnasium; the Coroner presided with the County Prosecutor as his advisor and two detectives as bailiffs. In the front of the room was a long table occupied by reporters, television and radio personnel, and broadcasting equipment. The hearing was broadcast with live microphones placed at the Coroner's seat and witness stand. A swarm of reporters and photographers attended. Sheppard was brought into the room by police who searched him in full view of several hundred spectators. Sheppard's counsel were present during the three-day inquest but were not permitted to participate. When Sheppard's chief counsel attempted to place some documents in the record, he was forcibly ejected from the room by the Coroner, who received cheers, hugs, and kisses from ladies in the audience. . . .

"With this background the case came up for trial two weeks before the November general election at which the . . . trial judge . . . was a candidate to succeed himself. Twenty-five days before the case was set, 75 veniremen were called as prospective jurors. All three Cleveland newspapers published the names and addresses of the veniremen. As a consequence, anonymous letters and telephone calls, as well as calls from friends, regarding the impending prosecution were received by all of the prospective jurors. The selection of the jury began on October 18, 1954.

"The courtroom in which the trial was held measured 26 by 48 feet. A long temporary table was set up inside the bar, in back of the single counsel table. It ran the width of the courtroom, parallel to the bar railing, with one end less than three feet from the jury box. Approximately 20 representatives of newspapers and wire services were assigned seats at this table by the court. Behind the bar railing there were four rows of benches. These seats were likewise assigned by the court for the entire trial. The first row was occupied by representatives of television and radio stations, and the second and third rows by reporters from out-of-town newspapers and magazines . . . Representatives of the news media also used all the rooms on the courtroom floor, including the room where cases were ordinarily called and assigned for trial. Private telephone lines and telegraph equipment were installed in these rooms so that reports from the trial could be speeded to the papers. . . .

"There can be no question about the nature of the publicity which surrounded Sheppard's trial. We agree, as did the Court of Appeals, with the findings of Judge Bell's opinion for the Ohio Supreme Court:

> Murder and mystery, society, sex, and suspense were combined in this case in such a manner as to intrigue and captivate the public fancy to a degree perhaps unparalleled in recent annals. Throughout the preindictment investigation, the subsequent legal skirmishes, and the nine-week trial, circulation-conscious editors catered to the insatiable interest to the American public in the bizarre. . . . In this atmosphere of a "Roman Holiday" for the news media, Sam Sheppard stood trail for his life.

Indeed, every court that has considered this case, save the court that tried it, has deplored the manner in which the news media inflamed and prejudiced the public.

"Since the state trial judge did not fulfill his duty to protect Sheppard from the inherently prejudicial publicity which saturated the community and to control disruptive influences in the courtroom, we must reverse the denial of the habeas petition. The case is remanded to the District Court with instructions to issue the writ and order that Sheppard be released from custody unless the State puts him to its charges again within a reasonable time."

Presumption of Innocence. The judge must instruct the jury in a criminal trial that the defendant is innocent until proven guilty. The jury is instructed that the case against the defendant must be proved beyond a reasonable doubt, unlike a civil case where the plaintiff must simply prove the case by a preponderance of the evidence. This means that the jury must simply believe the plantiff's story more than it believes the defendant's story. In a criminal case the jury in most jurisdictions has only one thing to decide, and that is guilt or innocence. The jury's verdict must be unamimous. Punishment is normally decided by the judge or at a second deliberation of the jury. In civil cases the jury not only decides whether the plaintiff gets a verdict or the defendant gets a verdict, it may also decide how much money the plaintiff will be awarded.

Criminal case standard of proof versus civil case standard of proof

Privilege against Self-Incrimination. In a criminal case the person charged with a crime cannot be forced to testify against himself or herself. This, of course, is the guarantee against self-incrimination which is provided by the Fifth Amendment of the U.S. Constitution. In an ordinary civil trial a defendant may be required to testify or be found in civil contempt of court.

Fifth Amendment guarantee versus self-incrimination

Right to Counsel. The Sixth Amendment to the U.S. Constitution provides that the accused in a criminal trial shall have the right to assistance of counsel. If the accused cannot afford an attorney, an attorney will be appointed for the accused by the court at the expense of the state. In most civil cases no attorney is appointed for a defendant. The defendant must personally hire an attorney or act as his or her own counsel. Many metropolitan areas and many university towns now have legal aid societies which furnish free legal counsel to people who cannot afford the services of an attorney.

Sixth Amendment guarantee of right to counsel

Right to a Miranda-Type Warning. The famous case of *Miranda* v. *Arizona,* 384 U.S. 436 (1966) initiated the so-called Miranda-type warning which now must be given to an accused at the time of arrest. Briefly, the accused must be told that he or she has the right to remain silent, that any statements made can be used in court by the prosecution, that he or she has the right to have an attorney present when being questioned, and that an attorney will be appointed by the court if the defendant cannot afford one.

Miranda case

Prohibition against Double Jeopardy. In criminal trials there is also the Fifth Amendment guarantee against double jeopardy. If a person charged with a crime has been found innocent, even though later evidence may prove that the person was in fact guilty of the crime, the person may not be tried again. The state may not appeal a verdict of not guilty. Once a person has been tried and found innocent, that is the end of the case. In a civil case either party may appeal a decision.

Fifth Amendment guarantee against double jeopardy

Requirement of Mens Rea. In a criminal case a person may not be found guilty of a crime unless the person had a mental intent to commit the crime. We often hear about the defense of temporary insanity in criminal cases. If a person charged with the commission of a crime did not know what he or she was doing, then the person is not guilty of the crime since there was no mental intent to commit it. Some states have a doctrine called *irresistible impulse.* In

Criminal intent required

those states, a person who can convince a jury he or she had an irresistible impulse to commit the criminal act is not guilty. The typical case here would be a husband or wife finding the spouse in bed with another person, and striking or shooting them in a fit of rage.

A person who is intoxicated or under the influence of drugs may not be guilty of acts committed while in that condition. However, in such cases the question arises as to whether the person became intoxicated or fell under the influence of drugs voluntarily or involuntarily, and whether the person was incapable of having a mental intent. If the person became intoxicated or fell under the influence of drugs voluntarily and was still capable of a mental intent, then the majority of courts would find the person guilty. For example, Sam Soak went to a party, voluntarily imbibed too much liquor, got into his car to drive home, and while swerving down the street, hit and killed a pedestrian. Sam may very well be found guilty of manslaughter.

If the person who committed a crime was a child under the age of reason, then the child would not legally have sufficient *mens rea,* or mental intent, to be guilty of the crime. In most states a child under seven years of age is presumed to be incapable of the mental intent to commit a crime. Over the age of seven years the individual child's capacity of mental intent becomes an open question. Here again, state laws differ.

■ CRIMINAL PROCEDURE

The procedure in a criminal trial differs considerably from the procedure in a civil trial, which we reviewed in Chapter 2.

In a civil case the injured party simply chooses a lawyer and proceeds to file a civil lawsuit at his or her own expense. That party can control the lawsuit; that is, the injured party, the plaintiff, can settle the case out of court, pursue the case through trial, or dismiss the case entirely at any point during the proceedings. In a criminal case the injured party simply reports the commission of a crime to the proper authority, and the state or national government takes over. The injured individual has no further control over the case.

The first step in the procedure of a criminal case is the report of the crime and the investigation. If the investigators are unable to find evidence sufficient to prosecute, then no arrest is made. Many cases will fall into the unsolved category. If the investigation does produce evidence which would support prosecution of the case, then an arrest is made. At the time of the arrest the arresting officer must inform the suspect of the rights in the *Miranda* warning. After having been arrested, the person will be booked. This process involves photographing and fingerprinting the subject and making up a record containing the subject's name, address, age, weight, height, and other pertinent information. The person now has a "police record."

The accused then is entitled to an appearance before a judge, and will be informed that he or she has the right to have counsel present. At this hearing the judge must determine whether the person shall be released on bail or without bail, or returned to jail. If the person is to be released on bail, then the judge must set the amount. Bail must be paid or pledged to the court before the defendant is released, although in many minor cases the judge will release the person without bail.

■ **EXHIBIT 6–1**
Procedure in a Criminal
Trial

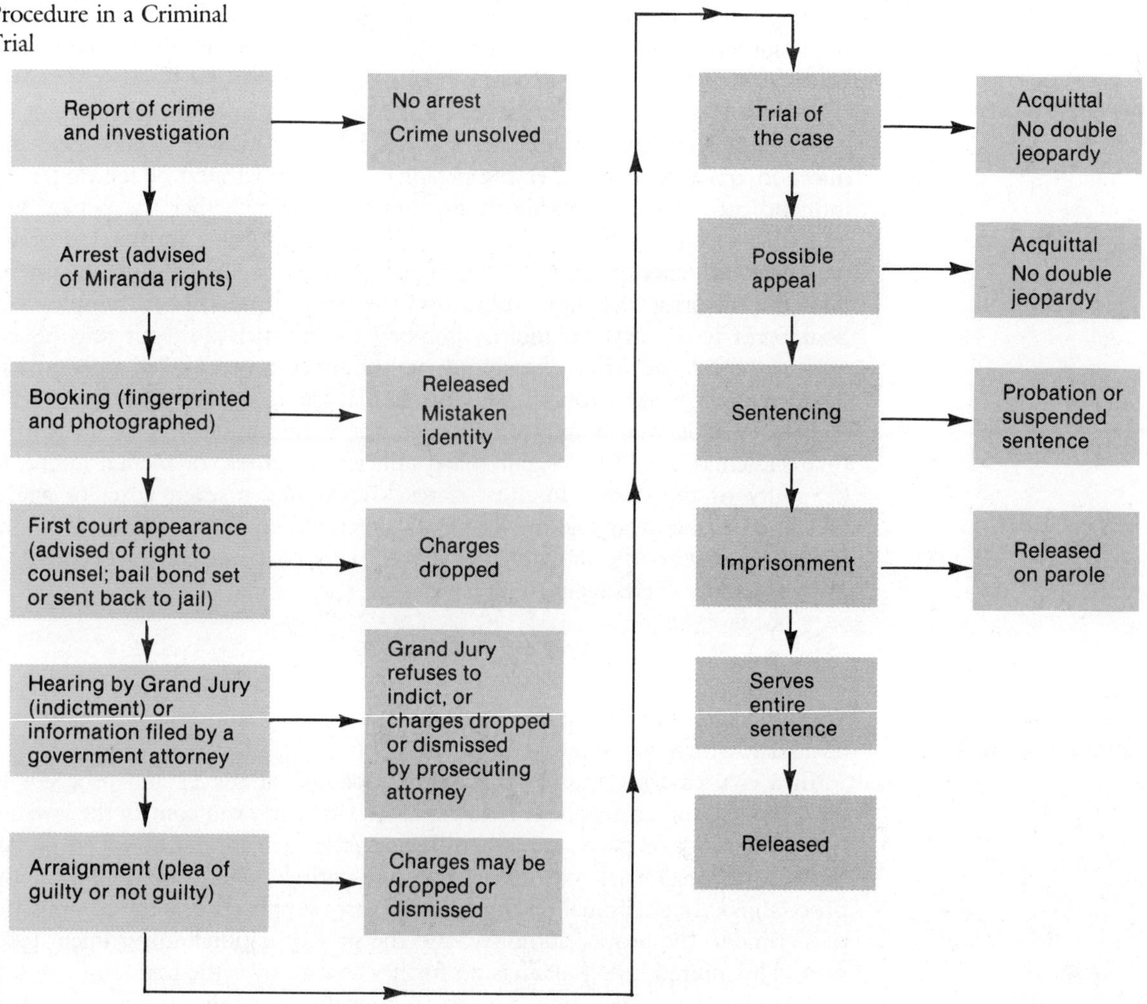

Report of crime and investigation	→	No arrest Crime unsolved
↓		
Arrest (advised of Miranda rights)		
↓		
Booking (fingerprinted and photographed)	→	Released Mistaken identity
↓		
First court appearance (advised of right to counsel; bail bond set or sent back to jail)	→	Charges dropped
↓		
Hearing by Grand Jury (indictment) or information filed by a government attorney	→	Grand Jury refuses to indict, or charges dropped or dismissed by prosecuting attorney
↓		
Arraignment (plea of guilty or not guilty)	→	Charges may be dropped or dismissed

Trial of the case	→	Acquittal No double jeopardy
↓		
Possible appeal	→	Acquittal No double jeopardy
↓		
Sentencing	→	Probation or suspended sentence
↓		
Imprisonment	→	Released on parole
↓		
Serves entire sentence		
↓		
Released		

Indictment versus information

The next step in the criminal process is to determine whether or not there is sufficient evidence to try the person for the crime charged. In serious crimes a *grand jury* may be impaneled to hear evidence to determine whether or not there is sufficient cause to proceed to a regular trial. If the grand jury finds sufficient evidence, it will issue an *indictment.* In other cases the prosecuting attorney will file an *information,* or formal statement of the charges, which will allow the case to proceed to a regular trial.

Plea bargaining

At this stage of the proceeding the prosecutor must decide what crime the accused should be prosecuted for. Probably the prosecution and the defense will engage in the process called *plea bargaining.* A very typical example of plea bargaining would take place where a person was arrested for drunken driving—normally punishable by a fine, possible imprisonment, and suspension of driving privileges. If the blood alcohol test or the breath-analyzer test was borderline or just slightly over the legal limit, the prosecuting attorney will often agree to reduce the charge to speeding or reckless driving, which are lesser offenses, if the accused will plead guilty. The prosecutor realizes that the case is not too strong and a conviction for a lesser offense is better than a possible "not guilty" verdict on the drunken driving charge.

Plea, trial, and sentencing

The next step is the ***arraignment hearing.*** Here the accused party must plead to the charges—either not guilty or guilty. If the party pleads guilty, then, of course, the next step is ***sentencing.*** If, on the other hand, the party pleads not guilty, a trial must be scheduled. The accused person has a right to a jury trial and a right to a speedy trial. After the trial the party is either acquitted and released, or, if the jury found the party guilty, there is the possibility of appeal. The appellate court may affirm the conviction, or it may reverse and order a retrial. If the appellate procedure has been exhausted and the party has not been acquitted or released, then the party is sentenced to a jail term and/or fine. At this point the judge may decide to put the person on ***probation,*** or to suspend the sentence, or to send the person to jail. If the person goes to jail, he or she can be paroled within a stated period of time or serve out the entire sentence, before being released to go back into society.

Although increases in the crime rate are often blamed on weak judges and a weak criminal law system, a system can only be as good as the persons who operate it. We must remember that under our system of law, a person charged with a crime is presumed innocent until proven guilty beyond a reasonable doubt. In most of the cases that go to trial, the crucial decision of guilty or not guilty is made, not by the judge, but by a jury of people selected at random from the community.

■ SIGNIFICANCE OF THIS CHAPTER

The study of criminal law was not traditionally a subject of concern for the businessperson. However, with the increase in the volume and types of white-collar crimes, businesspeople need to be aware of situations which invite prosecution under criminal law. This chapter reviews the various types of business-related crime and the steps and requirements of criminal procedure.

DISCUSSION CASE

CARPENTER v. U.S.
108 S.Ct. 316 (1987)

FACTS: Petitioner Winans was coauthor of a Wall Street Journal investment advice column which, because of its perceived quality and integrity, had an impact on the market prices of the stocks it discussed. Although he was familiar with the Journal's rule that the column's contents were the Journal's confidential information prior to publication, Winans entered into a scheme with petitioner Felis and another stockbroker who, in exchange for advance information from Winans as to the timing and contents of the column, bought and sold stocks based on the column's probable impact on the market and shared their profits with Winans. On the basis of this scheme, Winans and Felis were convicted of violations of the federal securities laws and of the federal mail and wire fraud statutes, 18 U.S.C. §§ 1341, 1343, which prohibit the use of the mails or of electronic transmissions to execute "any scheme or artifice to defraud, or for obtaining money or property by means of false or fraudulent pretenses, representations, or promises." David Carpenter, Winans' roommate, was convicted for aiding and abetting the scheme. The Court of Appeals affirmed.

∎

Justice White delivered the opinion of the Court:

Petitioners assert that their activities were not a scheme to defraud the Journal within the meaning of the mail and wire fraud statutes; and that in any event, they did not obtain any "money or property" from the Journal, which is a necessary element of the crime under our decision last Term in *McNally v. United States*. We are unpersuaded by either submission and address the latter first.

We held in *McNally* that the mail fraud statute does not reach "schemes to defraud citizens of their intangible rights to honest and impartial government," and that the statute is "limited in scope to the protection of property rights." Petitioners argue that the Journal's interest in prepublication confidentiality for the "Heard" columns is no more than an intangible consideration outside the reach of § 1341; nor does that law, it is urged, protect against mere injury to reputation. This is not a case like *McNally*, however. The Journal, as Winans' employer, was defrauded of much more than its contractual right to his honest and faithful service, an interest too ethereal in itself to fall within the protection of the mail fraud statute, which "had its origin in the desire to protect individual property rights." . . . Here, the object of the scheme was to take the Journal's confidential business information—the publication schedule and contents of the "Heard" column—and its intangible nature does not make it any less "property" protected by the mail and wire fraud statutes. *McNally* did not limit the scope of § 1341 to tangible as distinguished from intangible property rights. . . .

Petitioners' arguments that they did not interfere with the Journal's use of the information or did not publicize it and deprive the Journal of the first public use of it . . . miss the point. The confidential information was generated from the business and the business had a right to decide how to use it prior to disclosing it to the public. Petitioners cannot successfully contend based on *Associated Press* that a scheme to defraud requires a monetary loss, such as giving the information to a competitor; it is suffi-

cient that the Journal has been deprived of its right to exclusive use of the information, for exclusivity is an important aspect of confidential business information and most private property for that matter.

We cannot accept petitioners' further argument that Winans' conduct in revealing prepublication information was no more than a violation of workplace rules and did not amount to fraudulent activity that is proscribed by the mail fraud statute. Sections 1341 and 1343 reach any scheme to deprive another of money or property by means of false or fraudulent pretenses, representations, or promises. As we observed last Term in *McNally*, the words "to defraud" in the mail fraud statute have the "common understanding" of " 'wronging one in his property rights by dishonest methods or schemes,' and 'usually signify the deprivation of something of value by trick, deceit, chicane or overreaching.' " The concept of "fraud" includes the act of embezzlement, which is "the fraudulent appropriation to one's own use of the money or goods entrusted to one's care by another.' ". . .

We have little trouble in holding that the conspiracy here to trade on the Journal's confidential information is not outside the reach of the mail and wire fraud statutes, provided the other elements of the offenses are satisfied. The Journal's business information that it intended to be kept confidential was its property; the declaration to that effect in the employee manual merely removed any doubts on that score and made the finding of specific intent to defraud that much easier. Winans continued in the employ of the Journal, appropriating its confidential business information for his own use, all the while pretending to perform his duty of safeguarding it. In fact, he told his editors twice about leaks of confidential information not related to the stock-trading scheme, . . . demonstrating both his knowledge that the Journal viewed information concerning the "Heard" column as confidential and his deceit as he played the role of a loyal employee. Furthermore, the District Court's conclusion that each of the petitioners acted with the required specific intent to defraud is strongly supported by the evidence. . . .

Lastly, we reject the submission that using the wires and the mail to print and send the Journal to its customers did not satisfy the requirement that those mediums be used to execute the scheme at issue. The courts below were quite right in observing that circulation of the "Heard" column was not only anticipated but an essential part of the scheme. Had the column not been made available to Journal customers, there would have been no effect on stock prices and no likelihood of profiting from the information leaked by Winans.

The judgment below is *Affirmed*.

■ IMPORTANT TERMS AND CONCEPTS

crime
white-collar crime
felony
misdemeanor
embezzlement
computer crime
accountants' criminal
   liability
commercial bribery
executives' criminal
   liability
Sixth Amendment
trial by jury
presumption of
   innocence

privilege against self-
   incrimination
right to counsel
Miranda-type warning
double jeopardy
mens rea
grand jury
indictment
information
plea bargain
arraignment
sentencing
probation

■ QUESTIONS AND PROBLEMS FOR DISCUSSION

1. How can a business manager prevent being held criminally liable for company actions? Discuss.

2. What is the "Miranda-type" warning? To whom is this warning given and when?

3. Should we continue to allow plea bargaining in the criminal justice system? What are the pros and cons of this process?

4. What is the purpose of the grand jury hearing?

5. Acting on a tip from an informant, two police officers went to Tommy's home while he was at school. They identified themselves and explained that they had a tip that Tommy had been taking dangerous weapons to school. They asked Tommy's mother if they could search his room. She let them do so, and they found a zip gun and a switchblade. Possession of either of these items is a crime under state law. If Tommy is prosecuted, can he ask that the evidence be thrown out because the search was unlawful? Would it make any difference how old Tommy was? Discuss.

6. Scott was a student at State University (SU). He received two tickets on his car windshield on October 1, one for parking in a restricted area and one placed under the windshield wipers for failing to register the car with the university, as required by university regulations. The tickets stated that the fines would be doubled if not paid within one week. Scott also testified that a "wheel lock" was put on his car so that he could not move the vehicle without contacting the university police. The SU Traffic Appeals Committee upheld the validity of the tickets. Scott now sues the university alleging that the university's procedures for issuing and enforcing traffic tickets violated his rights to due process of law. Will Scott win? Why or why not?

7. Andy was a student at West Side High School. The school officials were concerned about what they perceived as the widespread use of marijuana by the students, so they asked the city police for assistance. The city police came to the high school with a dog which had been trained to sniff out the scent of marijuana. The dog indicated that there was marijuana in Andy's locker. When the locker was opened by the school officials, marijuana was found there. If Andy is prosecuted, can he claim that the use of the dog constituted an illegal search and seizure of the evidence? Discuss.

8. Hogg was charged with having robbed three men who were together in a tavern at the time of the robbery. He was acquitted by a jury. The state then charged Hogg with having robbed a fourth man who was also in the group at the tavern. This time, Hogg was found guilty by the jury. On appeal, Hogg says that the second prosecution violated his due process rights. How should the court rule? Discuss.

7

Tort Law

CHAPTER OBJECTIVES

THIS CHAPTER WILL:

- Define a tort.
- Explain the three general categories of torts.
- Discuss what types of acts or omissions constitute negligence.
- Review possible defenses open to a defendant in a tort lawsuit.
- Introduce the theory of strict liability.
- Explain workers' compensation laws.
- Discuss the pros and cons of the no-fault system of automobile tort compensation.

While businesspersons may face legal problems resulting from crimes, they are also fair game for civil lawsuits. Customers may sue for injuries received if they slip or fall on the premises, or they may sue for injuries resulting from defective products. Competitors may sue for alleged slander or libel. This list could go on and on. We live in a litigious society, and to survive we must know our rights and duties regarding potential lawsuits. This chapter discusses the various types of torts, and the defenses that may be raised against tort claims.

■ DEFINITION OF A TORT

Breach of a general legal duty

Tort versus crime

Tort versus contract

A *tort* is a civil wrong committed when one individual breaches a legal duty not to invade the legal rights of another, causing damage to the person, property, or reputation of that other individual. The person whose rights have been invaded and who has suffered damage may then bring action in a civil court to recover monetary damages suffered because of the invasion of rights. These rights and duties may be derived from statutory or common law. When we speak of an individual we mean a legal individual, such as a corporation, as well as a natural individual, a human being.

As discussed in Chapter 6, conduct which is a tort may also be a crime. For example, a drunken driver runs a red light and hits your car in the intersection. You have a cause of action in tort against that person for your property damage and personal injury. The drunken driver may also be prosecuted criminally for driving a motor vehicle under the influence of intoxicating beverages. Most nonintentional torts, however, are not crimes.

Also, a tortious civil wrong must be distinguished from a contractual civil wrong, where the rights and duties between the parties arise out of their own specific contractual agreement. In a tort the rights and duties are imposed by general laws which apply to all persons under similar circumstances, such as traffic laws and general laws of negligence.

■ CLASSIFICA-TION OF TORTS

Torts can be classified into three general categories. First, there are *intentional torts*. These are wrongs which the wrongdoers intended to commit. Second, there are *negligent torts*. These are wrongs which the wrongdoers did not mean to commit. They simply failed to act as ordinary, prudent, reasonable persons would have acted under similar circumstances. For example, in the typical automobile accident, the driver of the automobile does not mean to strike another automobile and damage either vehicle. He or she was simply not careful and was not acting as a reasonable and prudent person. Third, there are *strict liability torts*. This classification encompasses situations in which, by law, persons are held liable for injuries that result from their actions, without regard to intent or fault. The plaintiff need not prove negligence on the part of the defendant. The defendant is simply liable, as a matter of law, for the harmful results caused.

■ INTENTIONAL TORTS

An intentional tort is an intentional breach of one's legal duty to another person, which causes physical or mental damage to that person or damage to that person's reputation or property. To discourage such intentional wrongful conduct, courts frequently award large amounts as *punitive damages*. The winning plaintiff receives these extra dollars in addition to all actual damages proved.

Intentional torts can be subdivided into three categories: torts against the physical person, torts against the reputation of the person, and torts against the property of the person.

Torts against the Physical Person

Mere words≠Assault

Assault.   An assault is an intentional act by one person which causes another person to be in immediate apprehension for his or her safety. Apprehension does not necessarily mean fear, since fear is a very subjective term. Some persons may be in apprehension for their safety without actually being frightened, whereas other persons may be frightened without justifiable cause. Courts have held that mere words are not sufficient to prove a case of assault, even if the words are provoking or insulting. Also, threats of future injury are not the basis for assault. To prove a case of assault, it must be shown that the defendant committed a specific act or acts which put the plaintiff in apprehension for his or her immediate safety, not simply future safety. Although the tort of assault is classified as an intentional tort, it is not necessary to prove that the defendant actually intended to harm the plaintiff. It is sufficient to show that a reasonable person under the circumstances would have been in apprehension for his or her safety.

Intent to harm need not be proved

Battery.   Battery is the intentional contact or touching of another person without that person's permission and without legal justification. The contact or touching must cause injury. It is not necessary that there be a specific intent to cause harm. Nor is it necessary that the contact be directly with the person. For example, the tort of battery is committed if one person puts in motion an object which strikes another person, say, by shooting a gun or throwing a knife, or if one person strikes another person with an object in hand.

Not all touching or contact is considered battery. For example, people are often bumped, pushed, and jostled when they walk through the crowded aisles of department stores or walk out of crowded sports stadiums. Here there is physical contact and touching by other persons which may cause discomfort and which may be offensive. From a legal standpoint, however, these are not considered batteries because there is an implied consent to such "touching."

A technical battery occurs when the person gives consent to physical contact of one sort and then a different kind of contact occurs, or the terms of the consent are exceeded. Damages may be claimed under this theory against a surgeon who performs "extra" surgical procedures while the patient is under anesthesia. In the absence of some sort of emergency, the surgeon's act is tortious and the patient could recover damages. This is a very different kind of liability than that in a malpractice action, in which the claim is that the physician did not perform the agreed treatment or procedure in accordance with reasonable professional standards.

Intentional Infliction of Mental Distress.

Some state courts now recognize the intentional infliction of emotional or mental distress as a tort. Plaintiffs need not show either physical injury or a threat of physical contact, such as one would find in the torts of assault and battery. This tort may be defined as an act or the use of words by a person with the intent of causing another person to experience anxiety, fright, terror, or some other form of emotional and mental distress.

No physical contact necessary

The courts are still concerned about potential misuse of this tort. Generally, courts have held that to recover damages a plaintiff must prove that the mental distress or disturbance goes beyond an annoyance or hurt feelings. Actual mental injury must be shown. The courts also require that the plaintiff show that the defendant's conduct has been of an outrageous, intolerable character.

False Imprisonment.

False imprisonment can be defined as the intentional detention of a person without that person's permission. Actual physical detention is not necessary. However, the courts have required that the detained person be detained by at least a threat of force, either expressed or implied. Also, the detention must be for more than a reasonable time.

The majority of false imprisonment cases arise from the detention of persons accused of shoplifting, as illustrated by the next case.

SOUTHWEST DRUG STORES OF MISSISSIPPI, INC. v. GARNER

195 So.2d 837 (Mississippi, 1967)

FACTS

Mrs. Garner entered the drugstore, found the bar of soap she wanted, took it to the cashier, paid for it, and received a sales ticket. The cashier put the soap in a small bag. Mrs. Garner walked out of the store, but before she got to her car, the manager of the store yelled out at her, telling her to stop, and accused her of stealing the bar of soap. She denied it, but he told her she would have to go back into the store with him to prove that she hadn't stolen the soap. There were a number of people in the parking lot who heard the manager's loud and rude accusations. When the manager and Mrs. Garner got back to the store, the cashier verified that Mrs. Garner had paid for the soap. Mrs. Garner was then released. She became ill and distressed as result of the incident. She required medical treatment for her distress.

A Mississippi statute allows a merchant to stop and question a person if the merchant has reasonable grounds to believe that the person is attempting to commit the crime of shoplifting. Mrs. Garner sued Southwest Drug Stores for false imprisonment and slander, and a verdict for $8,000 was rendered in her favor in the lower court. Southwest Drug Stores appealed.

ISSUE   Is Southwest Drug Stores liable to the plaintiff for slander and false imprisonment, despite the statute?

DECISION   Yes. Judgment affirmed.

REASONS   **Justice Inzer thought that the privilege granted by the statute had been exceeded.** "Appellants . . . argue that the proof shows a qualified privilege existed and it was not exceeded; that Ratcliff investigated what he believed to be a case of shoplifting upon probable cause in a reasonable manner, and therefore under the laws of Mississippi such an investigation was privileged and no action was maintainable thereon. . . .

"Appellants argue that Ratcliff had observed Mrs. Garner and believed by her actions that she was committing an act of shoplifting; that her actions gave him probable cause to investigate, and that he acted in good faith and upon an occasion of privilege in carrying out his duties to protect his employer's property.

"Although the occasion was one of qualified privilege, the privilege was lost by the manner in which it was exercised. Mrs. Garner testified and the jury found that she was wrongfully accused of stealing in a rude and loud voice in the presence of other people outside the place of business. Granting that Ratcliff had reason to believe that Mrs. Garner had put a bar of soap in her purse and left the store without paying for it, and that he had probable cause to make inquiry, still he was careless and negligent in his method of ascertaining whether Mrs. Garner had paid for the soap."

False Arrest.   False arrest is similar to false imprisonment in that it is the intentional detention of an individual without that person's permission. In the case of false arrest the detention is imposed under an asserted legal authority. If, in fact, the person making the arrest does not have proper legal authority to do so, then we would have the tort of false arrest. In the case of false arrest, as in the case of false imprisonment, it is not necessary that the person detaining the suspect use force.

Torts against the Reputation of the Person

Next we come to intentional torts which injure the person's reputation. These are often called *defamation of character.*

Publication to a third person required

Libel and Slander.   Libel and slander are both torts involving intentional defamation of character by the tort-feasor. *Libel* is defamation of character which can be read or seen, and *slander* is defamation of character which can be heard. In both libel and slander cases it must be proven that a defamatory statement or defamatory material was published. In the case of libel, this means that the defamatory material was published in a book, magazine, newspaper, movie, picture, or some other physical form whereby the material was seen by one or more third persons. If you write defamatory statements about an individual in a personal letter to that individual, this does not constitute publication, since no one other than the individual to whom you are writing is intended to see the letter.

In the case of slander, publication means that the statement was heard by someone other than the person about whom the defamatory statement was made. If no third person heard, read, or saw the statement or material, then there is no slander or libel.

The next issue is the truth of the defamatory statement or material. Generally, truth is a defense to slander or libel. The exception is a situation where the party publishing the defamatory statement or material is doing so with a malicious intent to injure the other party. This is called a *technical tort*. An example of this would be the publication of the fact that a person now well established in society committed a crime while a teenager. Here, even though the statement is true, if it was made for malicious purposes, there would be a right of action for this defamation of character.

There are also cases where defamatory statements may be either absolutely ***privileged*** or ***conditionally privileged.*** Lawyers and judges cannot be sued for slander for the statements made by them during the trial of a lawsuit. Also, if a member of Congress makes a defamatory statement on the floor of Congress, the congressman can not be held liable for the statement. There is also a different standard with regard to slander and libel when the statement is made about a public official or other public figure, rather than a private individual. The public person must show, not only that the defamatory statement was false, but that it was made with malice, or with reckless disregard for whether it was true or false.

Invasion of Privacy. Individual privacy has been a highly publicized topic in recent years. Several state and national statutes have been passed to protect the individual's right to privacy, especially when regard to credit and bank records stored in computers.

Other, more traditional concerns about invasions of the individual's privacy have also surfaced. One of the most controversial intrusions on privacy is eavesdropping by wiretapping or other electronic devices. Such eavesdropping is a national crime as well as a tort, and it is prohibited except in the rare cases authorized by national statute.

Another invasion of privacy is the use of a person's photograph under objectionable circumstances. Simply turning the television cameras and taking pictures of the persons in the bleachers at a baseball game is not an invasion of privacy. However, if someone takes an embarrassing picture of you and uses it without your permission, you may have an action for invasion of privacy.

As with libel and slander, the right to privacy may conflict with the constitutional protection of freedom of speech and freedom of the press. A person's involvement in matters of public interest affects his or her privacy rights. For example, if you are involved in an automobile accident, newspaper photographers may snap pictures of you at the scene of the accident; if you are arrested, the TV cameras may be directed toward you. Here you are news; thus your right of privacy must be secondary to the freedom of the press to publish the news. For similar reasons a public figure, one who is known because of his or her actions or position, a movie star, a famous sports person, or a president's wife, for example, does not have the same right of privacy as an ordinary citizen. An illustration of the right of privacy of a public figure is the case of *Galella* v. *Onassis.*

GALELLA v. ONASSIS

487 F.2d 986 (U.S. Second Circuit, 1973)

FACTS Ronald Galella is a free-lance photographer specializing in the making and sale of photographs of well-known persons. Jackie Onassis is the widow of the late President John F. Kennedy, mother of the two Kennedy children, John and Caroline, and the widow of the late Aristotle Onassis, widely known shipping figure and reputed multimillionaire. Galella has been harassing Mrs. Onassis and her children, jumping out from behind bushes to take their pictures and invading the children's private schools to get pictures of the children at play. The children are protected by U.S. Secret Service agents, who under law must protect the children of a deceased president until they are 16. One day Galella jumped out from bushes into the path of young John Kennedy as he was riding his bicycle in Central Park. The Secret Service men protecting John were fearful for his safety and arrested Galella. He was tried and acquitted of any crime.

Mr. Galella then filed a lawsuit against the Secret Service agents and Mrs. Onassis. He alleged that, under orders from Mrs. Onassis, he had been falsely arrested and maliciously prosecuted. The suit was dismissed against the Secret Service agents as they are immune from prosecution while acting within the scope of their authority. Mrs. Onassis answered, denying any role in the arrest or in the claimed interference with his attempts to photograph her. She also counterclaimed for damages and injunctive relief, charging that Galella had invaded her privacy, assaulted and battered her, intentionally inflicted emotional distress, and engaged in a campaign of harassment.

The action was removed to the United States District Court. At the same time, the U.S. government intervened, requesting injunctive relief from the activities of Galella which obstructed the Secret Service's ability to protect Mrs. Onassis's children.

After a six-week trial the court dismissed Galella's claim and granted injunctive relief to both Mrs. Onassis and the government. Galella appeals.

ISSUE Does Galella's wrongful conduct justify injunctive relief, to prevent future wrongs?

DECISION Yes. Judgment affirmed.

 REASONS **Circuit Judge Smith thought an injunction was needed.**

"We conclude that grant of summary judgment and dismissal of Galella's claim against the Secret Service agents was proper. Federal agents when charged with duties which require the exercise of discretion are immune from liability for actions within the scope of their authority. . . . The protective duties assigned the agents under this statute . . . require the instant exercise of judgment which should be protected. The agents saw Galella jump into the path of John Kennedy who was forced to swerve his bike dangerously as he left Central Park and was about to enter Fifth Avenue, whereupon the agents gave chase to the photographer. Galella indicated that he was a press photographer listed with the New York City Police; he and the agents went to the police station to check on the story, where one of the agents made the complaint on which the state court charges were based. Certainly it was reasonable that the agents 'check out' an individual who has endangered their charge and seek prosecution for apparent violation of state law which interferes with them in the discharge of their duties. . . .

"Discrediting all of Galella's testimony, the court found the photographer guilty of harassment, intentional infliction of emotional distress, assault and battery, commercial exploitation of defendant's personality, and invasion of privacy. Fully crediting defendant's testimony, the court found no liability on Galella's claim. Evidence offered by the defense showed that Galella had on occasion intentionally physically touched Mrs. Onassis and her daughter, caused fear of physical contact in his frenzied attempts to get their pictures, followed defendant and her children too closely in an automobile, and endangered the safety of the children while they were swimming, water skiing, and horseback riding. Galella cannot successfully challenge the court's findings of tortious conduct. . . .

"Galella's action went far beyond the reasonable bounds of news gathering. When weighed against the de minimis public importance of the daily activities of the defendant, Galella's constant surveillance, his obtrusive and intruding presence, was unwarranted and unreasonable. If there were any doubt in our minds, Galella's inexcusable conduct toward defendant's minor children would resolve it.

"Galella does not seriously dispute the court's findings of tortious conduct. Rather, he sets up the First Amendment as a wall of immunity protecting newsmen from any liability for their conduct while gathering news. There is no such scope to the First Amendment right. Crimes and torts committed in news gathering are not protected. . . .

"The injunction, however, is broader than is required to protect the defendant. Relief must be tailored to protect Mrs. Onassis from the 'paparazzo' attack which distinguishes Galella's behavior from that of other photographers; it should not unnecessarily infringe on reasonable efforts to 'cover' defendant. Therefore, we modify the court's order to prohibit only (1) any approach within twenty-five (25) feet of defendant or any touching of the person of the defendant Jacqueline Onassis; (2) any blocking of her movement in public places and thoroughfares; (3) any act foreseeably or reasonably calculated to place the life and safety of defendant in jeopardy; and (4) any conduct which would reasonably be foreseen to harass, alarm, or frighten the defendant. . . .

"Likewise, we affirm the grant of injunctive relief to the government, modified to prohibit any action interfering with Secret Service agents' protective duties. Galella thus may be enjoined from *(a)* entering the children's schools or play areas; *(b)* engaging in action calculated or reasonably foreseen to place the children's safety or well-being in jeopardy, or which would threaten or create physical injury; *(c)* taking any action which could reasonably be foreseen to harass, alarm, or frighten the children; and *(d)* from approaching within thirty (30) feet of the children. . . .

"As modified, the relief granted fully allows Galella the opportunity to photograph and report on Mrs. Onassis' public activities. Any prior restraint on news gathering is miniscule and fully supported by the findings."

Torts against the Person's Property

Trespass to Real Property. The general rule of law with regard to trespass to real property is that the owner of real property has the right not only to exclusive possession of a specific piece of ground and the buildings and other things on that ground, but also to exclusive possession of the airspace above the ground and the area below the ground. The old common-law rule was that the owner of the land owned all of the airspace above the land and the area below the land all the way to the middle of the earth. This rule had to be modified when we started to use airspace for airplane travel. Now the landowner still owns the airspace above the land, subject, however, to the right of airplanes to fly through that airspace. With regard to the space below the land, the possessor of the land surface also possesses the soil and space below the surface to the extent that he or she can effectively use that soil or space, either now or in the future. When we talk about space below the land we are talking about the ownership of the oil, gas, water, and other valuable minerals and resources which may be present under the surface. Mineral rights are frequently sold apart from the land itself. If that has happened, the owner of the land would not own them.

In order to have the tort of trespass to your land, it is not necessary that there be actual damage to your land. In all of the other torts previously mentioned, damage had to be proven before a recovery could be made. In the tort of trespass to land, you can sue the trespasser even though there was no actual damage and the court will award nominal damages, perhaps $1, and court costs.

The following case dealt with the question of how much force a landowner can use to repel trespassers.

KATKO v. BRINEY

183 N.W.2d 657 (Iowa, 1971)

FACTS

In 1957 defendant Bertha L. Briney inherited her parents' farmland in Mahaska and Monroe Counties. Included was an 80-acre tract in southwest Mahaska County where her grandparents and parents had lived. No one occupied the house thereafter. Her husband, Edward, attempted to care for the land. He kept no farm machinery thereon. The outbuildings became dilapidated.

For about 10 years, 1957 to 1967, there occurred a series of trespassing and house-breaking events with loss of some household items, the breaking of windows, and "messing up of the property in general." The latest occurred June 8, 1967, prior to the event on July 16, 1967, herein involved.

Defendants through the years boarded up the windows and doors in an attempt to stop the intrusions. They had posted "no trespass" signs on the land several years before 1967. The nearest one was 35 feet from the house. On June 11, 1967 defendants set "a shotgun trap" in the north bedroom. After Mr. Briney cleaned and oiled his 20-gauge shotgun, defendants took it to the old house where they secured it to an iron bed with the barrel pointed at the bedroom door. It was rigged with wire from the doorknob to the gun's trigger so it would fire when the door was opened. Briney first pointed the gun so an intruder would be hit in the stomach but at Mrs. Briney's suggestion it was lowered to hit the legs. He admitted he did so "because I was mad and tired of being tormented" but "he did not intend to injure anyone." He gave no explanation of why he used a loaded shell and set it to hit a person already in the house. Tin was nailed over the bedroom window. The spring gun could not be seen from the outside. No warning of its presence was posted.

Plaintiff lived with his wife and worked regularly as a gasoline station attendant in Eddyville, seven miles from the old house. He had observed it for several years while hunting in the area and considered it as being abandoned. Prior to July 16, 1967 plaintiff and McDonough had been to the premises and found several old bottles and fruit jars which they took and added to their collection of antiques. On that date about 9:30 P.M. they made a second trip to the Briney property. They entered the old house by removing a board from a porch window which was without glass. As plaintiff started to open the north bedroom door, the shotgun went off, striking him in the right leg above the ankle bone. Much of his leg, including part of the tibia, was blown away. Only by McDonough's assistance was plaintiff able to get out of the house and after crawling some distance was put in his vehicle and rushed to a doctor and then to a hospital. He remained in the hospital 40 days.

Plaintiff's doctor testified he seriously considered amputation but eventually the healing process was successful. Some weeks after his release from the hospital plaintiff returned to work on crutches. He was required to keep the injured leg in a cast for approximately a year and wear a special brace for another year. He continued to suffer pain during this period.

There was undenied medical testimony plaintiff had a permanent deformity, a loss of tissue, and a shortening of the leg.

Plaintiff sued defendants and at defendants' request plaintiff's action was tried to a jury consisting of residents of the community where defendants' property was located. The jury returned a verdict for plaintiff and against defendants for $20,000 actual and $10,000 punitive damages. Defendants appeal.

ISSUE   Was defendants' use of the shotgun trap privileged?

DECISION   No. Judgment affirmed.

REASONS   **Chief Justice Moore had no doubt that the use of the shotgun was excessive.**

"The primary issue presented here is whether an owner may protect personal property in an unoccupied boarded-up farmhouse against trespassers and thieves by a spring gun capable of inflicting death or serious injury.

"We are not here concerned with a man's right to protect his home and members of his family. Defendants' home was several miles from the scene of the incident. . . .

"Plaintiff testified he knew he had no right to break and enter the house with intent to steal bottles and fruit jars therefrom. He further testified he had entered a plea of guilty to larceny in the nighttime of property of less than $20 value from a private building. He stated he had been fined $50 and costs and paroled during good behavior from a 60-day jail sentence. Other than minor traffic charges this was plaintiff's first brush with the law. On this civil case appeal it is not our prerogative to review the disposition made of the criminal charge against him.

"The main thrust of defendants' defense in the trial court and on this appeal is that 'the law permits use of a spring gun in a dwelling or warehouse for the purpose of preventing the unlawful entry of a burglar or thief.' They repeated this contention in their exceptions to the trial court's instructions 2, 5, and 6. They took no exception to the trial court's statement of the issues or to other instructions.

"In the statement of issues the trial court stated plaintiff and his companion committed a felony when they broke and entered defendants' house. In instruction 2 the court referred to the early case history of the use of spring guns and stated under the law their use was prohibited except to prevent the commission of felonies of violence and where human life is in danger. The instruction included a statement breaking and entering is not a felony of violence. . . .

"The overwhelming weight of authority, both textbook and case law, supports the trial court's statement of the applicable principles of law.

"Prosser on Torts, Third Edition, pages 116–118, states:

> The law has always placed a higher value upon human safety than upon mere rights in property, it is the accepted rule that there is no privilege to use any force calculated to cause death or serious bodily injury to repel the threat to land or chattels, unless there is also such a threat to the defendant's personal safety as to justify a self-defense. . . . spring guns and other man-killing devices are not justifiable against a mere trespasser, or even a petty thief. They are privileged only against those upon whom the landowner, if he were present in person would be free to inflict injury of the same kind. . . .

"The legal principles stated by the trial court in instructions 2, 5 and 6 are well established and supported by the authorities cited and quoted supra. There is no merit in defendants' objections. . . . Defendants' various motions based on the same reasons stated in exceptions to instructions were properly overruled."

Trespass to Personal Property. This tort allows the owner of personal property to bring an action against a person or persons who interfere with his or her exclusive possession of an item of personal property. Unlike the plaintiff in a case involving trespass to real property, the plaintiff in a case involving trespass to personal property must show and prove monetary damage in order to get a verdict against the trespasser.

Conversion. The tort of conversion is the unlawful taking and use of personal property owned by another person. In other words, it is the conversion of another person's property to your own use. This sounds like theft. However, you will recall that in order to have theft, one has to have a mens rea, or mental intent, to steal. In the tort of conversion, the person converting the property to his or her own use does not necessarily have the intent to steal. The person may feel that he or she has the right to use the property. A good example of conversion would be a case where the branches of your neighbor's apple tree hang over the lot line so that the apples are over your property. You honestly feel that you have a right to these apples; after all, they are over your property in your airspace. After you pick the apples, your neighbor tells you that the apples belong to him and that you should give them to him. If you fail to give your neighbor the apples, you are guilty of the tort of conversion. The apples and the branches that hung over the lot line are in effect trespassing on your airspace; however, you do not have the right of ownership to them. You may, however, cut off the branches at the lot line and put them on your neighbor's land. You cannot keep them.

Deceit (Fraud). The tort of deceit, also called fraud, involves a situation where one or more parties, fraudulently and with the intent to deceive, misrepresent certain facts, either through oral or written statement or through an artifice or device of some type, and another party relies upon the misrepresentation and is damaged. Fraud in connection with the making of a contract is discussed more fully in Chapter 14.

Interference with Economic Relations. This tort concerns your right to conduct your business free from malicious and intentional interference which might destroy the business. The free enterprise system is based on the competitive marketplace. However, competition must be kept within reasonable bounds. It is certainly permissible for one business to lower its price in an effort to competitively secure a market advantage. However, when a person or a business intentionally uses economic resources to injure another person or business for reasons other than the legal reasons for competition, the tort of interference with economic relations has been committed.

The tort of interference with economic relations also encompasses interference with contractual relations. If Johnny Rich, a nightclub owner, knowingly induces a famous entertainer to breach a contract with another nightclub to come to work for him, the employer who had a contract with the entertainer can sue Johnny Rich for interference with his contractual relations.

The *Pennzoil* case in Chapter 9 is based on this theory. It resulted in the largest damages award ever—over $10 *billion!*

Nuisance Torts to Person and Property.   Nuisance torts are wrongs that arise from the unreasonable or unlawful use by a person of his or her own property in a manner as that interferes with the rights of others, with resulting damages. Nuisance torts may be classified as private or public. An example of a private nuisance would be a situation in which your neighbor has a dog that howls all night.

Private nuisance

Public nuisance

A public nuisance can be defined as the doing of something or the failure to do something as a result of which the safety, health, or morals of the public are injuriously affected. Public nuisances may be criminal as well as civil. Examples of public nuisances are the storing of explosives on a person's premises or allowing persons to smoke marijuana on the premises. If the public nuisance also injures private parties, those private parties may have their own actions separate from the government, since private parties are concerned with damages for their own injuries. Restrictions on land use will be discussed further in Chapter 36.

The legal test in a nuisance case is whether the interference with your enjoyment of your property is substantial and unreasonable and whether that interference would be offensive or inconvenient to a reasonable or prudent person. The victim may sue for money damages, an injunction, or both remedies.

■ NEGLIGENT TORTS

Each person in society is bound to take reasonable care not to injure the person, reputation, or property of those persons likely to be affected by his or her behavior. Any act or omission in breach of that duty which causes damage to others may cause a person to be liable for damages to the person or persons affected by that act or omission.

Definition of Negligence.   The standard for determining the absence or presence of negligence is very simple: Did the person act as a *reasonable and prudent person* would have acted under the same or similar circumstances? Would the reasonable and prudent person have foreseen the dangers of this action, and was the damage or injury proximately caused by the action or the failure to act of the individual being charged with the tort? The question then arises: Who is this reasonable and prudent person? The reasonable and prudent person is an imaginary person. When deciding a case involving a negligent tort, jurors are instructed not to use themselves as examples of the reasonable and prudent person. The jurors must determine not what they individually would have done in the same or a similar situation but what that imaginary reasonable and prudent person would have done. Obviously, this standard is not very precise and it is certainly subject to great variations. The standard, however, has operated very successfully over the years since it does take into consideration changes in technology and changes in societal mores which the jury will impute to the reasonable and prudent person. Also, it would be impossible to have a specific statutory code that would cover every possible act or omission which could be considered negligent. Thus negligence continues to be decided on a case-by-case basis.

Reasonable person test

Proximate Cause.

Defendant's action must be the cause of plaintiff's injury

A person may commit a negligent act or may negligently fail to act under certain circumstances. However, that person will not be liable to any person who is damaged or injured as a result of such act or omission unless it can be shown that the damage or injury was proximately caused by the negligent act or omission. For a negligent act or omission to be a proximate cause of damage or injury, it must be a cause which in a natural and continuous sequence, unbroken by any intervening cause, produced the injury, and it must be a cause without which the injury would not have occurred.

There are situations where the actions or omissions of more than one person are a proximate cause of damage or injury to a person or property. If two cars collide in an intersection and one of the cars strikes a legally parked car, it may be found that the negligence of both of the drivers in the collision proximately caused the damage to the parked car. Thus, it is not necessary that any one act or omission be the sole proximate cause of damage or injury.

Foreseeability.

Injury must be foreseeable

For a defendant to be liable to a plaintiff for a tortious act or omission to act, not only must the act or omission be a proximate cause of the damage or injury, but the ultimate damage or injury must also be foreseeable by the reasonable and prudent person. It is not enough that an injury was caused by an unbroken chain of events. It must also have been foreseeable to the reasonable and prudent person that the actions which triggered the chain of events could ultimately cause injury to the plaintiff.

■ DEFENSES TO NEGLIGENT TORTS

There are three basic defenses to negligent torts. They are (1) contributory or comparative negligence, depending upon state law, (2) assumption of risk, and (3) act of God.

Contributory or Comparative Negligence.

Both parties at fault

Contributory negligence on the part of the plaintiff bars the plaintiff from recovering damages in a state which has adopted the contributory negligence doctrine.

Historically, most states followed the contributory negligence doctrine. A plaintiff who was guilty of negligence, no matter how slight, could recover nothing from the defendant. This admittedly was a very harsh rule, but states accepted it nonetheless. A recent rend, however, has been toward the doctrine of *comparative negligence,* also referred to as *comparative fault.* This doctrine is not as harsh as the contributory negligence doctrine; plaintiffs are not denied any recovery whatsoever simply because they were in the estimation of the juries, slightly negligent. Today most states have some form of comparative fault law.

Party less at fault may recover damages

Under one type of comparative fault law, a plaintiff will be entitled to recover against a defendant if the plaintiff's comparative fault is not greater than the comparative fault of the defendant or the combination of defendants. Thus, if the plaintiff's fault exceeds 50 percent, then the plaintiff will not recover at all. However, if the plaintiff's comparative fault is less than 50 percent, the plaintiff's recovery will be reduced by the percentage of the plaintiff's fault. Let's consider a situation where the plaintiff's damages are $100,000, the defendant's comparative fault is 50 percent, and the plaintiff's comparative fault is

50 percent. Under the old contributory negligence doctrine the plaintiff would recover nothing. Under the comparative fault doctrine, the plaintiff would still recover $50,000, which would be 50 percent of the plaintiff's damages. If, however, the jury found the plaintiff's comparative fault to be in excess of 50 percent (i.e., 51 percent or 52 percent), the plaintiff would recover nothing. The problem, of course, is how do you determine the percentage of fault of each party? This is a question that has to be resolved on a case-by-case basis by the jury, or when the case is being tried without a jury, by the judge.

The existence of negligence and comparative negligence, plus issues of foreseeability and damages, were involved in the *Walt Disney World* case.

WALT DISNEY WORLD CO. v. GOODE

501 So.2d 622 (Florida, 1986)

FACTS

On August 11, 1977, four year old Joel Goode drowned in a man-made waterway or moat at Walt Disney World. He was with his mother, Marietta Goode, who noticed that he was missing shortly after 11 P.M. Approximately three hours later, Joel's body was found in five feet of water a short distance from where he had become separated from his mother. An autopsy found no evidence of foul play and established the cause of death as drowning. No one saw Joel enter the waterway.

Joel's parents sued Walt Disney World for the wrongful death of their son. The jury returned a verdict of $1,000,000 for Joel's father, Harry Goode, and $1,000,000 for Joel's mother, Marietta. The jury also determined that Disney and Joel's mother were each 50 percent negligent. Accordingly, a judgment was entered for $500,000 dollars for the mother and $1,000,000 for the father. On appeal, Disney argues that the artificial waterway was not unreasonably dangerous nor did it constitute a trap, and thus as a matter of law, Disney was not negligent. Even assuming some negligence on its part, Disney contends that the damages awarded were excessive.

ISSUES

Was defendant negligent? Was the injury foreseeable? Are the damages awarded excessive?

DECISION

Yes. Yes. No. Judgment affirmed.

REASONS

Judge Orfinger was reluctant to disturb the lower court's decision, since there was evidence in the record to support the jury's verdict on each issue.

"The legal principles which should be applied in this case are exactly the same as those which would be applied had Joel Goode fallen at night into an open hole dug by Disney employees on one of its walkways and left without barricades, lights or other warning, or in cases where a plaintiff drives his motor vehicle off an unbarricaded dead end street into a bay or canal. . . . Under these circumstances Joel would not have become a trespasser and Disney's liability would not depend on the attractive nuisance doctrine or upon a finding that Joel's injury was caused by a trap or some unusual element of danger. Instead, the issue of liability would turn upon the issue of whether Disney had used ordinary or reasonable care for the protection of the safety of its patron.

"There is no evidence in this case that Joel Goode entered the waterway to swim or bathe. Instead, the evidence leads itself to the conclusion that he fell in. Joel Goode did not become a trespasser by falling into the moat. Disney employees testified that they were aware of the fact that young children frequently climbed the short fences to play in the grassy area adjacent to the moat. . . .

"Both the manager of safety and occupation and the manager of loss prevention for Disney testified that the fences around the grassy area adjacent to the moat were not designed to keep children out of the moat but rather were designed for crowd control and to keep people off the grass. The fences separating the walkway from the grassy slopes to the moat were approved at a height of 31 inches, with a 24 inch 'stepping distance' between the bottom and top horizontal rails. Disney's own standards required a fence with a minimum 36-inch-stepping distance anywhere there was an interface with a water hazard. There was no fence or other barrier directly adjacent to the moat itself. There was evidence presented from which the jury could conclude that a fence with a 36-inch-stepping distance would have effectively prevented children of Joel Goode's age from climbing over it, whereas the lower fence could be easily scaled by such children. The Disney employee who designed the fences in question testified that the short fence was not intended as a safety barrier for the moat nor was it adequate for that purpose. . . .

"Disney employees testified that they frequently observed children going over the fences into the grassy area surrounding the moat. Additionally, the moat was built to a depth of 5 feet and it was undisputed that the depth of a similar moat at Disneyland (in California) was only between 1½ to 3 feet deep. Regarding the foreseeability of the accident, Disney's supervisor for guest relations testified that in the 12 months preceeding the accident 11,420 children were reported lost at Disney, although in her four years of experience none had been found harmed or injured. Disney had instituted elaborate procedures for reuniting separated children and parents. From the testimony presented there was evidence from which a jury could determine that Disney had failed in its duty to keep and maintain the premises in a reasonably safe condition commensurate with the business conducted. . . .

"Whether Disney breached its duty of reasonable care to the decedent by leaving the moat unprotected under the circumstances presented here was a factual question to be determined by the jury. It is peculiarly a jury function to determine what precautions are reasonably required in the exercise of a particular duty of due care. . . . Similarly, proximate causation was also a jury question. . . . Based on the evidence presented, the jury found that Disney had not complied with its duty of due care and that this failure proximately caused the child's death, and we will not disturb those findings because the evidence supports them. . . .

"We are unable to say, as a matter of law, that the award was so inordinately large as to exceed the maximum limit of the reasonable range within which the jury could properly operate. There was unrebutted evidence before the trial court that the Goodes suffered almost complete, full personality changes since the loss of Joel and that their grief was overwhelming, genuine, and crushing. The jury saw the parents and heard their testimony, and were in a better position to evaluate the reality of their anguish and suffering than are we from a reading of a cold record. We should not substitute our judgment for theirs."

Voluntarily taking a chance

Assumption of Risk. The defense of assumption of risk may be a complete defense to a plaintiff's negligent tort action. When a person is aware of the danger in a situation, yet continues to expose himself or herself to that danger and is then injured, that person cannot complain of the defendant's negligence.

Natural causes of damage

Act of God. If lightning strikes a large tree in your yard, causing the tree to fall on and crush your neighbor's car, you would not be liable. The proximate cause of the damage is legally considered an act of God. Similarly, if a tornado swept your tree into your neighbor's house, you would not be liable. If, however, you had a dead tree in your back yard which you intended to cut down because the tree was rotten and dangerous, and one day a strong wind toppled the tree onto your neighbor's car, then you would not be able to use the defense of act of God. You were aware of the tree's condition and also should have realized the possibility that a windstorm would cause it to fall and do damage to others.

▪ STRICT LIABILITY

Reason behind strict liability

Strict liability is liability without fault. In a strict liability case the defendant will be liable for injuries caused by his or her actions, even though the defendant was not negligent in any way and the defendant did not intentionally injure the plaintiff. This concept of liability without fault is comparatively new in our legal system. The traditional theories of tort involve either intentional wrongful acts, negligent acts, or omissions where someone was injured through unintentional carelessness or negligence. In developing the theory of *no-fault* or *liability without fault,* the courts and the legislatures are not really looking at right or wrong, but at who can best bear the cost of the loss. In other words, someone engaging in dangerous activities must realize that persons might be injured by those activities, even though the person does nothing legally wrong and does not intend to hurt anyone. The person exposing the public to this extra risk of harm must simply be prepared to pay for the consequences of those actions, regardless of any legal fault.

Owners of wild animals

Strict liability has been imposed on owners or possessors of wild animals. If you keep a wild animal, you are going to be strictly liable for any damages that animal does to other persons or to their property. The owner or possessor of hard-hooved animals, such as cattle, horses, and donkeys, may also be held strictly liable for injuries caused by those animals. The owner or possessor of a dog or a cat would not normally be liable unless he or she knows the animal to be dangerous. The common-law rule was that a dog is entitled to its first bite. This means that a dog is generally not known to be dangerous until it has bitten someone. However, the owner of a large Doberman that was constantly growling and baring its teeth at anyone who came near it would be strictly liable for any injury it caused since the dog appeared to be dangerous. In some states, by statute, the pet owner may be held liable even for the first bite.

Attractive nuisance

Strict liability has also been imposed on persons who are responsible for activities or conditions on their property that are unreasonably dangerous and that might cause injury to other persons. The theory of **attractive nuisance** comes under this area of strict liability. For example, if an old refrigerator and an old junk car are sitting on your premises, these are called attractive nuisances, because they simply invite young children to come over and climb around on them. If these children are injured, you are strictly liable for injuries to them, even though you did not intentionally do anything wrong and, in fact, the children were trespassing on your property. Another example would

Hazardous activities

Product liability

be a contractor blasting out stumps or blasting hard rock in excavating for a building. If the blasting caused structural damage to nearby buildings or homes or if personal property within the buildings or homes were damaged by the concussion of the explosions, then the contractor would be strictly liable.

A third area of strict liability involves product liability. Traditionally, we had the theory of *caveat emptor,* which meant "let the buyer beware." The theory was that the buyer had a duty to inspect the goods when delivered, and unless there was fraud, the buyer was simply stuck with them if defects later appeared. This area of the law has changed radically over the past 30 years. Product liability is discussed in depth in Chapter 20.

▪ NO-FAULT SYSTEM OF WORKERS' COMPENSATION

Common-law rules

Historically, if an employee were injured on the job, the employee could sue the employer for medical bills incurred and for lost wages. However, the employer had three defenses: assumption of risk, contributory negligence, and the fellow servant rule. Thus, if the employee knew the machine being operated was faulty, and continued to operate it, and was injured, the employer would not be liable. If the employee removed a safety guard to clean out scrap, and forgot to replace it, and the employee was injured, the employer could defend under the doctrine of contributory negligence. If a fellow employee negligently bumped another employee, causing the first employee to fall against a machine and be injured, the employer again could successfully defend the action. The net result of the use of the traditional tort system for claims for work-related injuries to employees was that most employees simply could not collect from the employer due to these defenses, and the cost of litigation often exceeded the claimed damages. Thus, the system of no-fault compensation for employees' work-related injuries and diseases was developed.

Statutory changes

Every state now has a *workers' compensation* statute. Essentially these statutes provide that if an employee is injured on the job or becomes ill or disabled due to an occupational disease, the employer or its insurance carrier will have to pay all reasonable medical bills and a percentage of the lost wages during the period of disability. A settlement, or periodic payments, will be made if the employer suffered some permanent disability, such as the loss of an eye, or the partial loss of function of an arm or leg.

The key concept in workers' compensation is that it is no-fault. The employee may have negligently left the safety guard off the machine or continued to operate a machine the employee knew to be faulty, but the employee will still collect all the statutory benefits if the employee is accidentally injured.

If the employee intentionally and knowingly injures himself or herself then, normally, no benefits will be awarded.

▪ NO-FAULT SYSTEM OF AUTOMOBILE TORT COMPENSATION

Traditionally, the party whose negligence proximately caused injury to another person or to another person's property would be found liable in tort, provided there was no defense, such as contributory negligence or assumption of risk. As indicated earlier in this chapter, the defense of contributory negligence as a complete defense was found to be harsh and unjust in many cases. The doctrine of comparative negligence has now replaced the traditional contributory negligence doctrine in most states.

Common-law rules

Statutory changes

This fault system works satisfactorily in the majority of tort cases. However, there is one specific class of tort claims—automobile accident cases—where certain states have replaced the fault system with a no-fault system of compensation. The proponents of the automobile no-fault system argue that it will cut insurance rates because it will save litigation expenses, such as attorney fees and court costs. No-fault systems can reduce court congestion and can be an effective method for promptly resolving minor automobile property damage and less serious injury claims. The theory of a *no-fault auto insurance* system is simple. Each automobile owner-driver carries insurance. If that person has an accident, his or her own insurance company pays the doctor bills, lost wages, and car repair bills.

Fair results without a lawsuit?

Critics of the no-fault system argue that no-fault statutes take away the injured person's right to a trial by jury, and provide no recovery for pain and suffering. To overcome these criticisms, some no-fault laws allow claimants to sue in court if their injuries are serious or their damages exceed a certain dollar amount.

■ OTHER THEORIES OF LIABILITY FOR TORT

Res Ipsa Loquitur. The term *res ipsa loquitur* means "the thing speaks for itself." The plaintiff normally has the burden of proving that the defendant failed to act in a reasonable and prudent manner, that the accident was foreseeable, and that the damage or injury was a proximate cause of the defendant's action. Normally the plaintiff has available various types of evidence, such as skid marks and eyewitnesses.

Presumption of negligence

In some cases it is obvious that the accident would not have happened had it not been for negligence on the part of the defendant, but the plaintiff does not have access to information which would verify or prove such negligence. An example would be a situation where a person was a passenger in an airplane and the airplane struck a mountain. The plane was demolished, and all its occupants died. In this case the next of kin of the passengers will bring suit for the wrongful deaths. However, a plaintiff here lacks access to the physical evidence needed to prove this case. We know that airplanes normally do not run into mountains, and that someone's negligence probably caused the accident. The cause may have been a malfunction or a breakdown in the aircraft itself; it may have been a manufacturing defect; or it may have been a failure on the part of the airline to properly service and inspect. It may also have been pilot error or error on the part of air traffic control. In such cases plaintiffs plead the theory of *res ipsa loquitur,* and the burden is shifted to the defendants, to prove that they were not negligent.

Burden of proof shifts to defendant

Respondeat Superior. This doctrine provides that "the boss will pay." You might also call this the "deep pocket" doctrine. Under the doctrine of *respondeat superior,* a principal may be liable for the tortious acts of an agent, provided the agent was acting in the scope of employment for the principal. A similar rule applies to the employer-employee relationship. It is important to note here that the agent or employee is still liable for his or her own actions. In

Agency law rule

■ EXHIBIT 7-1
The Tort Case

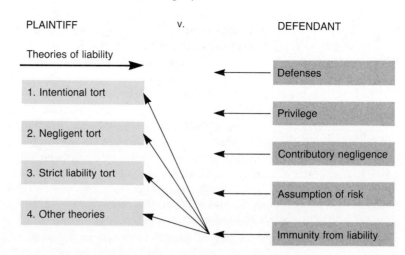

other words, both employee and employer or both agent and principal could be liable in tort. This rule is discussed further in the chapters on agency.

Last Clear Chance Doctrine. Simply stated, this doctrine provides that the liable party is the one who had the last clear chance to avoid damage or injury to the other party. This doctrine imposes a duty upon one party to exercise care in avoiding injury to another party who has negligently placed himself or herself in a situation of danger. For example, suppose that a motorist on a very cold day started up his or her automobile, drove up to an intersection while the motor was still cold, and proceeded to enter the intersection. The motor died, causing the car to stall crosswise in the intersection. Cars approaching the stalled vehicle would then have a duty to exercise reasonable care to avoid injury to the driver who had negligently placed himself or herself in a position of peril. Thus, if an oncoming motorist could swerve to the right or the left, go around this stalled car, or could stop before hitting it, then the driver would have a duty to do so.

Who could have avoided the accident?

■ IMMUNITY FROM TORT ACTION

Certain persons, organizations, and governmental bodies have traditionally been immune from tort liability under certain circumstances.

At common law a husband could not sue his wife and a wife could not sue her husband for personal torts. Also, traditionally, a child could not sue either parent. The courts' theory was that such litigation would destroy family unity. These common-law intrafamily immunities are gradually being eroded. Today, we generally believe that injured parties should be able to sue wrongdoers, whoever they may be. In most cases the spouse or the child is not actually suing the other spouse or the parent, but is, in effect, going after insurance proceeds. The spouse or the parent is a defendant in name only.

Charitable organizations traditionally were immune from tort liability. The theory was that to impose tort liability on the funds of the charitable organization would cripple its good work and would discourage donations to the organization. This immunity is also being eroded, if not eliminated, in many states. Here again, the original reasons for the immunity are no longer valid. A charitable

Intrafamily immunity from tort liability

Charitable immunity eroding

Statutory changes in sovereign immunity

organization today can buy liability insurance and have as much protection against liability claims as any business. An example would be the charitable hospital. A person negligently injured in a charitable hospital should have the same rights of recovery in tort as he or she would have against a profit-making hospital. In either case, the injury to the patient is the same, and the fault is the same.

The third traditional immunity is called *sovereign immunity;* simply stated, this means that the government may not be sued for its torts. Here "government" can mean national, state, municipal, or county governments. The U.S. Tort Claims Act, enacted in 1946, established certain conditions for lawsuits and claims against the national government. Many states have also passed tort claims acts or other laws limiting the sovereign immunity of the state, cities, and other governmental units. Some states, however, have established dollar limits on claims that can be recovered from them. The trend in this area is toward eliminating sovereign immunity. Here again, the state, city, or other governmental subdivision can purchase liability insurance, and thus budget the cost on an annual basis.

■ SIGNIFICANCE OF THIS CHAPTER

We live in a legalistic society, and the law of torts is a very important concern for individuals and businesspeople. Anything we do or say in our personal or business lives could subject us to liability. This chapter reviews the various types of torts that may occur, the main defenses that are available against such claims, and some of the recent developments in this area of the law.

DISCUSSION CASE

MIDLER v. FORD MOTOR CO.

849 F.2d 460 (U.S. 9th Circuit, 1988).

FACTS: Ford Motor Company and its advertising agency, Young & Rubicam, Inc., in 1985 advertised the Ford Lincoln Mercury with a series of nineteen 30- or 60-second television commercials in what the agency called "The Yuppie Campaign." The aim was to make an emotional connection with Yuppies, bringing back memories of when they were in college. Different popular songs of the 70s were sung on each commercial. The agency tried to get "the original people," that is, the singers who had popularized the songs, to sing them. Failing in that endeavor in 10 cases the agency had the songs sung by "sound alikes." Bette Midler, the plaintiff and appellant here, was done by a sound alike.

Neither the name nor the picture of Midler was used in the commercial; Young & Rubicam had a license from the copyright holder to use the song. At issue in this case is only the protection of Midler's voice. The district court described the defendants' conduct as that "of the average thief." They decided, "If we can't buy it, we'll take it." The court nonetheless believed there was no legal principle preventing imitation of Midler's voice and so gave summary judgment for the defendants. Midler appeals.

■

Circuit Judge Noonan:

The First Amendment protects much of what the media do in the reproduction of likenesses or sounds. A primary value is freedom of speech and press. . . . The purpose of the media's use of a person's identity is central. If the purpose is "informative or cultural" the use is immune; "if it serves no such function but merely exploits the individual portrayed, immunity will not be granted." . . . Moreover, federal copyright law preempts much of the area. "Mere imitation of a recorded performance would not constitute a copyright infringement even where one performer deliberately sets out to simulate another's performance as exactly as possible." . . . It is in the context of these First Amendment and federal copyright distinctions that we address the present appeal. . . . Midler does not seek damages for Ford's use of "Do You Want To Dance," and thus her claim is not preempted by federal copyright law. Copyright protects "original works of authorship fixed in any tangible medium of expression." . . . A voice is not copyrightable. The sounds are not "fixed." What is put forward as protectible here is more personal than any work of authorship. . . .

[W]e do not find unfair competition here. One-minute commercials of the sort the defendants put on would not have saturated Midler's audience and curtailed her market. Midler did not do television commercials. The defendants were not in competition with her. . . .

California Civil Code section 3344 is also of no aid to Midler. The statute affords damages to a person injured by another who uses the person's "name, voice, signature, photograph, or likeness, in any manner." The defendants did not use Midler's name or anything else whose use is prohibited by the statute. The voice they used was Hedwig's, not hers. The term "likeness" refers to a visual image not a vocal imitation. The statute, however, does not preclude Midler from pursuing any cause of action she may have at common law; the statute itself implies that such common law causes of action do exist because it says its remedies are merely "cumulative." . . .

The companion statute protecting the use of a deceased person's name, voice, signature, photograph, or likeness states that the rights it recognizes are "property rights." By analogy the common law rights are also property rights. . . .

Why did the defendant ask Midler to sing if her voice was not of value to them? Why did they studiously acquire the services of a sound-alike and instruct her to imitate Midler if Midler's voice was not of value to them? What they sought was an attribute of Midler's identity. Its value was what the market would have paid for Midler to have sung the commercial in person.

A voice is more distinctive and more personal than . . . automobile accouterments. . . . A voice is as distinctive and personal as a face. The human voice is one of the most palpable ways identity is manifested. We are all aware that a friend is at once known by a few words on the phone. At a philosophical level it has been observed that with the sound of a voice, "the other stands before me." . . . A fortiori, these observations hold true of singing, especially singing by a singer of renown. The singer manifests herself in the song. To impersonate her voice is to pirate her identity. . . .

We need not and do not go so far as to hold that every imitation of a voice to advertise merchandise is actionable. We hold only that when a distinctive voice of a professional singer is widely known and is deliberately imitated in order to sell a product, the sellers have appropriated what is not theirs and have committed a tort in California. Midler has made a showing, sufficient to defeat summary judgment, that the defendants here for their own profit in selling their product did appropriate part of her identity.

Reversed and remanded for trial.

▪ IMPORTANT TERMS AND CONCEPTS

tort	nuisance
intentional tort	reasonable person test
negligent tort	proximate cause
strict liability in tort	foreseeability
false imprisonment	contributory negligence
defamation	comparative negligence
libel	attractive nuisance
slander	workers' compensation
privilege	no-fault auto insurance
invasion of privacy	*res ipsa loquitur*
trespass	*respondeat superior*
conversion	last clear chance doctrine
deceit	immunity
interference with economic relations	

▪ QUESTIONS AND PROBLEMS FOR DISCUSSION

1. How does a tort differ from a crime? Explain how a person's action or failure to act can be both criminal and tortious.

2. If you were the manager of a retail store, what instructions would you give to your salespersons about apprehending shoplifting suspects?

3. Explain the rationale for prohibiting a public official from winning a libel or slander judgment unless the official proves that the defamation was made with malice.

4. What does *res ipsa loquitur* mean? Give an example where this theory of liability would be used.

5. Russo and Olive Dribble owned a large male goat, which they kept in a pen. One morning the Dribbles'

two sons, aged 10 and 7, missed the school bus. Their parents had already left for work, so the boys were home alone. They let the goat out of his pen to play with him. At this point the goat was still within the Dribbles' fenced-in front yard. When the boys went across the street to visit their friend Mr. Pappe, the goat jumped the fence and followed them. Pappe poked the goat in the side with his cane to try to get it off his property. The goat attacked Pappe and seriously injured him. Pappe was taken to the hospital, treated for a month, and then released. He was readmitted about three months later and died about a month after that. Pappe's estate sues the Dribbles. Is there any basis for tort liability here? Discuss.

6. Mrs. Wilma Winsomme, married and the mother of two sons, aged 8 and 10 years, has lived in Culpepper County, Tennessee, all her life (35 years). While they were attending the county fair, her sons wanted to go into the "Fun House" but wanted her to come with them. Wilma had never been in a "fun house" before and didn't quite know what to expect, but she went anyway. As she was coming out the exit door, a blast of air from holes in the floor blew her skirt up, exposing the lower part of her body. At that moment, without her knowledge, a newspaper photographer snapped her picture. Three days later the picture appeared on the front page of the local paper. Wilma sues the newspaper. What is the result, and why?

7. Farley Fan went to Fenway Park in Boston to watch a baseball game between the Baltimore Orioles and the Boston Red Sox. Freddie Fastball, a pitcher for Baltimore, was warming up by throwing a baseball in the bull pen located near the right field bleachers. The Boston fans heckled Freddie. After the heckling had gone on for some time, Freddie faced the right field bleachers, moved as if he were pitching in the direction of the plate in the bull pen, and threw the baseball. The ball, traveling at a speed of over 80-miles-per-hour, went directly toward the hecklers in the right field bleachers and struck Farley Fan, who filed a civil action against Freddie. How would you rule on this claim? Explain your decision.

8. Ralph Nader, an attorney, author, and lecturer on automobile safety, had been a severe critic of General Motors' products for many years. Shortly before Nader's publication of his book, "Unsafe at Any Speed," GM decided to conduct a campaign of intimidation against Nader. Nader filed suit against GM and alleged that GM and their agents conducted interviews with acquaintances of Nader to learn intimate details about him, kept him under surveillance, made threatening and obnoxious phone calls to him, tapped his telephone by means of mechanical and electrical equipment, and conducted an harassing investigation of him. If these allegations are proved to be true, is GM guilty of invasion of privacy? Discuss.

8

Liability of Accountants and Other Professionals

CHAPTER OBJECTIVES

THIS CHAPTER WILL:

- Summarize accountants' contract liability.
- Define professional negligence.
- Discuss the states' disagreements on the scope of an accountant's duty.
- Discuss CPA liability under the Securities Acts.
- Define potential liability under RICO.

In the previous chapter we discussed the various types of torts that the business-person should be aware of, defined the types of negligence that could bring about liability claims, and discussed the defenses that could be raised against such claims. We reserved discussion of a very important area of liability for this chapter. This area of liability is often referred to as *malpractice liability* or *professional liability.*

In the previous chapter we also noted that we live in a litigious society. That comment is certainly appropriate when we discuss malpractice or professional liability, as the number of claims made and the amounts of the various verdicts in this area of liability have increased tremendously in recent years. These increases have resulted in an enormous increase in the cost of malpractice liability insurance for professionals.

The costs associated with malpractice claims are not only payment of the claims themselves, but also the costs of legal defense that professionals are faced with. Thus, even if the professional is innocent of any wrongdoing, he or she still might have to pay several thousand dollars for defense costs. Remember, even if the verdict is in your favor, the cost of your attorney for your defense is still your responsibility.

There is a tort known as *abuse of process*. This tort has been used successfully as a counterclaim in many malpractice cases where the plaintiff obviously did not have a valid cause of action, but simply field a lawsuit hoping for an out-of-court settlement because the professional might wish to limit adverse publicity and the costs of legal defense. In that type of case the abuse of civil process tort may well be used. However, in cases where there is reasonable evidence that malpractice did occur, the tort of abuse of civil process would not be effective, as filing of the law suit would probably not be viewed as an intentional misuse or abuse of the civil process.

In this chapter our primary concern will be the liability of accountants. The common law applicable to accountants' liability is similar to the liability of other professionals such as physicians, attorneys, engineers, architects, and other persons classified as professionals. Accountants, however, in addition to being liable under common law principles, are also subject to statutory liability under the national securities laws and the U.S. internal revenue laws.

■ LIABILITY OF ACCOUNTANTS OR OTHER PROFESSIONALS TO CLIENTS UNDER CONTRACT LAW

The professional, whether an accountant, attorney, physician, or other professional, may be liable to the client for failure to perform in accordance with the terms of the contract with the client. An accountant or other professional sells services to clients. If the accountant or other professional fails to perform the services in accordance with the terms of the agreement, then the professional will be liable to the client under the theory of breach of contract. The client will be entitled to money damages sufficient to compensate the client for the out-of-pocket damages the client suffered as a result of the breach. An example would be a situation where the client had contracted with an accountant to furnish a financial statement to the client's bank by a certain date, as the client had a loan commitment and guaranteed interest rate up to that date, of which the accountant was aware. If the accountant failed to deliver the financial report to the bank within the required time period, and as a result of the accountant's failure, the client's loan was turned down or the interest rate went up, then the client could sue the accountant for breach of contract and recover any out-of-pocket loss. The professional may not avoid this liability by delegating the duties to other persons. If an accountant delegates the duty of preparing your tax returns to a subordinate, the accountant will still be liable if a breach of contract occurs. Contract law will be reviewed and discussed in more detail in Part Two, which follows this chapter. The liability of accountants or other professionals to their clients under contract law is essentially the same as the liability of any party to a contract who fails to perform in accordance with the terms of the contract.

■ LIABILITY OF ACCOUNTANTS OR OTHER PROFESSIONALS TO THE CLIENT FOR NEGLIGENCE

An accountant or other professional owes a duty to the client to exercise *reasonable care* in the performance of his or her duties under the terms of the contract. Failure to exercise this reasonable care may be considered negligence on the part of the professional. The obvious question here is what constitutes reasonable care and what does not. Generally speaking, reasonable care has been defined as the exercise of the same degree or amount of skill and care that other similar professionals practicing in the same locality would exercise under the same or similar circumstances. The professional being judged may also be judged by established standards of the specific profession, as well as the standard of skill and care of other similar professionals in the locality. For example, individual states have enacted codes of ethics and/or rules of professional conduct for the practice of law, the medical profession has its ethical standards, certified professional engineers have ethical codes to comply with, and Certified Public Accountants (CPAs) also have standards of care required by their profession. These standards are the generally accepted accounting principles known as *GAAP,* and the generally accepted auditing standards known as *GAAS.*

Examples of situations where a professional would be liable to the client for negligence would be the case of an attorney who failed to file a lawsuit for the client within the statutory period, causing the client to lose the right to receive damages from the adverse party; a physician who prescribed the wrong medication which injured the patient, or the CPA who miscalculated or made omissions or other errors in the tax report for the client, causing the client to have to pay tax penalties.

■ LIABILITY OF AN ACCOUNTANT OR OTHER PROFESSIONAL TO THIRD PARTIES

It is in this category of liability that the CPA is often in a more precarious liability position than other professionals. CPAs are often found liable to third parties (nonclients) who foreseeably and justifiably relied on the CPA's report to the client. In the other professions we do not find the same degree of liability to third parties. For example, if a surgeon performs an operation and sews up the incision leaving a sponge in the wound, the only person who can claim against the surgeon is the patient, or perhaps the patient's estate or his dependents if the patient died as a result of negligence in the surgical process. Similarly in the case of an attorney, the major threat of a malpractice claim is

■ EXHIBIT 8–1
Scope of Accountants
Liability—To Whom Is a
Duty of Care Owed?

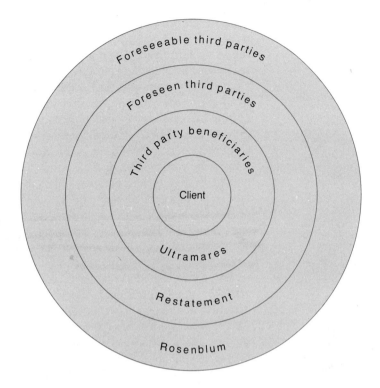

from clients, not third parties. Thus CPAs find themselves in a unique situation with regard to third party liability.

The *Ultramares* Doctrine

Accountants do more than simply make up tax returns for clients. One of the most common tasks the accountant performs for the client is the auditing and certification of the business organization's financial reports. Obviously the accountant would be liable to the client for a mistake in the auditing and preparation and certification of a financial report if the client suffered damages as a result of the mistake, because the accountant and the client are "in privity of contract." This means they have a contractual arrangement, and therefore have responsibilities to each other.

The question arises, what happens if the client takes this audited and certified financial report to a bank to convince the bank that the client is solvent and has assets to repay the loan being requested. If the accountant negligently made a mistake in the audit and certification of the financial report and in fact the client's financial status is not as portrayed in the report, can the bank sue the accountant if they suffered damages as a result of their reliance on the report? In 1931 Chief Judge Benjamin Cardozo of the New York Court of Appeals, the highest court of the state of New York, addressed the problem of liability of accountants to third persons (nonclients) in *Ultramares Corp.* v. *Touche,* 174 N.E. 441 (1931). Judges in courts all over the United States followed the precedent set by that decison for many years. It was referred to as the *Ultramares* doctrine.

In the *Ultramares* case, Touche, the accounting firm, had audited the financial records of Fred Stern & Co. and prepared a financial statement as a result of the audit. Ultramares Corporation, relying on the financial statement prepared by Touche, loaned money to Fred Stern & Co. Later Fred Stern & Co. couldn't pay back the loans and declared bankruptcy. Actually Fred Stern & Co. was insolvent at the time the financial statement was made. Judge Cardozo in the *Ultramares* case stated that an accountant has a duty and responsibility not only to the client, but to all third parties who relied on their reports, if the accountant was guilty of fraud. However, if the mistake or misstatement was simply the result of negligence, then the accountant would not be liable to nonclients, that is third persons, unless the nonclient was known by the accountant to be an intended user who would be relying on the accountant's reports. This case established the "primary beneficiary" test. That is, unless the third party (nonclient) was known by the accountant to be a primary beneficiary of the accountant's work product, then the accountant would not be liable to such third party for negligence.

The *Ultramares* doctrine gave accountants a special protection that is not available to all professionals. For example, take the case of the architect who designed a building in Minneapolis, Minnesota and miscalculated the roof weight load factors. After the building was erected the roof fell in following the first heavy snowfall, and hundreds of persons were injured. Those injured people can sue and collect damages from the architect even though the error was not the result of fraud but simply negligence. In that case the court would find it was foreseeable that people occupying the building would be injured if the roof collapsed. The architect was aware of this potential liability when the design was made and had a duty, not only to its clients but to all foreseeable users, to design the building to withstand natural and expected roof loads. Accountants under the *Ultramares* doctrine are not liable to any and all persons who might be damaged by relying on their work product.

Restatement Rule

In recent years courts in many states have refused to follow the *Ultramares* doctrine and have extended the liability of accountants not only to the client who is in privity of contract and the primary beneficiary nonclient, but also to nonclients who were not known to the accountant but who were in a foreseen class of users of the accountant's work product, and some courts have extended liability to foreseeable users generally. The foreseen class of users doctrine has been adopted in the *Restatement (Second) of Torts*. The relevant section reads as follows:

§ 552. Information Negligently Supplied for the Guidance of Others

(1) One who, in the course of his business, profession, or employment, or in any other transaction in which he has a pecuniary interest, supplies false information for the guidance of others in their business transactions, is subject to liability for pecuniary loss caused to them by their justifiable reliance upon the information, if he fails to exercise reasonable care or competence in obtaining or communicating the information.

(2) Except as stated in Subsection (3), the liability stated in Subsection (1) is limited to loss suffered

(a) by the person or one of a limited group of persons for whose benefit and guidance he intends to supply the information or knows that the recipient intends to supply it; and

(b) through reliance upon it in a transaction that he intends the information to influence or knows that the recipient so intends or in a substantially similar transaction.

(3) The liability of one who is under a public duty to give the information extends to loss suffered by any of the class of persons for whose benefit the duty is created, in any of the transactions in which it is intended to protect them.[1]

The *Restatement* rule expands the class of third party nonclients who can sue and recover from the accountant beyond the limits of the *Ultramares* doctrine. The *Restatement* extends liability to certain *foreseen* beneficiaries but not to any and all *foreseeable* users of the accountant's work product.

Foreseeable Users Doctrine

This doctrine, which is most recent in origin and most liberal in extending liability of the accountant, holds that accountants may be held liable not only to nonclients who are primary beneficiaries (the *Ultramares* doctrine) or to reasonably foreseen beneficiaries (the *Restatement* concept) but also to **foreseeable third parties**. In 1983, the New Jersey Supreme Court in the following case found it was not in the public interest to give accountants the special protection against lawsuits by nonclients who were neither primary beneficiaries nor reasonably foreseen beneficiaries which the Ultramares doctrine and the *Restatement (Second) of Torts* grant the accountant. Instead, the court felt accountants should be liable for their negligence to the foreseeable users of their work product, just as other professionals, such as the Minnesota architect in the previous example, would be.

ROSENBLUM v. ADLER

461 A.2d 138 (New Jersey 1983)

FACTS   Giant, a Massachusetts corporation, operated discount department stores, retail catalog showrooms, and art and gift shops. Its common stock was publicly traded. Giant was required to file audited financial statements with the SEC as part of its annual report to stockholders, and Touche conducted those audit examinations during the fiscal years 1969 through 1972.

In November 1971 Giant commenced negotiations with the plaintiffs for the acquisition of their businesses in New Jersey. The merger negotiations culminated in an agreement executed on March 9, 1972. During the discussions two significant events occurred. First, on December 14, 1971, Giant made a public offering of 360,000 shares of its common stock. The financial statements included in the prospectus of that offering contained statements of annual earnings for four years ending January 30, 1971, as well as balance sheets as of January 30 for each of those years, which had been audited by Touche. Touche's opinion affixed to those financials stated that it had examined the statements of earnings and balance sheets "in accordance with generally accepted

---

[1] Copyright 1977 by The American Law Institute. Reprinted with the permission of The American Law Institute.

auditing standards" and that the financial statements "present[ed] fairly" Giant's financial position. Similar data had been incorporated in Giant's annual report for the year ending January 30, 1971. Second, Touche began its audit of Giant's financials for the year ending January 29, 1972. This audit was completed on April 18, 1972. The attached Touche opinion bore the same language affixed to the 1971 statements.

The merger agreement provided that the Rosenblums would receive an amount of Giant stock shares, depending upon the net income of their enterprises for their fiscal year ending December 31, 1971. The closing was to be scheduled between May 15 and May 31, 1972. Giant agreed that as of the closing it would represent and warrant that there had "been no material adverse change in the business, properties, or assets of Giant and its Subsidiaries since July 31, 1971." The plaintiffs claim they relied upon the 1972 audited statements before closing the transaction on June 12, 1972. The Rosenblums received Giant common stock, which had been listed on the American Stock Exchange in February 1972 and was being traded on that Exchange when the merger was effected. After the Rosenblum closing, Giant made another public offering of common stock in August 1972. Touche furnished for this Giant registration statement the audited financial statements for each of the five fiscal years ending January 29, 1972, to which was affixed Touche's unqualified opinion.

Giant had manipulated its books by falsely recording assets that it did not own and omitting substantial amounts of accounts payable so that the financial information that Touche had certified in the 1971 and 1972 statements was incorrect. The fraud was uncovered in the early months of 1973. Trading in Giant stock on the American Stock Exchange was suspended in April 1973 and never resumed. On May 22, 1973, Touche withdrew its audit for the year ending January 29, 1972. Giant filed a bankruptcy petition in September 1973. The Giant stock received by the plaintiffs in the merger had become worthless.

The plaintiff's complaint, based on the audited financials for the years ending January 30, 1971 and January 29, 1972, charged fraudulent misrepresentation, gross negligence, negligence, and breach of warranty. Touche moved for partial summary judgment. It sought to have the courts dismiss the claims based on alleged negligence in making the audit for the year ending January 30, 1971 and on alleged negligence, gross negligence, and fraud in making the audit for the year ending January 29, 1972. The trial court granted the motion with respect to the 1971 financials and denied it as to the 1972 financials. Plaintiffs appealed.

The Appellate Division affirmed the trial court's dismissal of the negligence claim based on the 1971 audit. The defendants also appealed from the denial of their motion for partial summary judgment addressed to claims predicated on the 1972 financials. The Appellate Division denied that motion. The defendants subsequently appealed the Appellate Division's denial to the New Jersey Supreme Court.

ISSUE   Should CPAs be liable to foreseeable third parties?

DECISION   Yes. Judgment affirmed.

REASONS   **Justice Schreiber thought a duty was owed to plaintiffs.**

"This case focuses upon the issue of whether accountants should be responsible for their negligence in auditing financial statements. If so, we must decide whether a duty is owed to those whom the auditor is in privity, to third persons known and intended by the auditor to be the recipients of the audit, and to those who foreseeably might rely on the audit. Subsumed within these questions is a more fundamental one: to what extent does public policy justify imposition of a duty to any of these classes? . . .

"An independent auditor is engaged to review and examine a company's financial statements and then to issue an opinion with respect to the fairness of that presentation. That report is customarily attached to the financial statements and then distributed by the company for various purposes. Recipients may be stockholders, potential investors, creditors, and potential creditors. When these parties rely upon a negligently prepared auditor's report and suffer damages as a result, the question arises whether they may look to the auditor for compensation. In other words, to whom does the auditor owe a duty? The traditional rule is that the auditor's duty is owed only to those with whom he is in privity or to those who are known beneficiaries at the time of the auditor's undertaking. This rule is commonly attributed to an opinion of Chief Judge Cardozo in *Ultramares* v. *Touche*. . . . A second rule has been expressed in Section 552 of the *Restatement (Second) of Torts*. Under the *Restatement*, liability is extended to a known and intended class of beneficiaries. . . .

"A third rule is that the auditor's duty is owed to those whom the auditor should reasonably foresee as recipients from the company of the financial statements for authorized business purposes. . . .

"The fundamental issue is whether there should be any duty to respond in damages for economic loss owed to a foreseeable user neither in privity with the declarant nor intended by the declarant to be the user of the statement or opinion. . . .

"The imposition of a duty to foreseeable users may cause accounting firms to engage in more thorough reviews. This might entail setting up stricter standards and applying closer supervision, which should tend to reduce the number of instances in which liability would ensue. Much of the additional costs incurred either because of more thorough auditing review or increased insurance premiums would be borne by the business entity and its stockholders or its customers.

"Recently Justice Wiener, in his article 'Common Law Liability of the Certified Public Accountant for Negligent Misrepresentation,' concluded:

> The time has come to absolve the negligent accountant of this anachronistic protection. Accountant liability based on foreseeable injury would serve the dual functions of compensation for injury and deterrence of negligent conduct. Moreover, it is just and rational judicial policy that the same criteria govern the imposition of negligence liability, regardless of the context in which it arises. The accountant, the investor, and the general public will in the long run benefit when the liability of the certified public accountant for negligent misrepresentaton is measured by the foreseeability standard. . . .

"When the defendants prepared the Giant audit, they knew or should have known that Giant would probably use the audited figures for many proper business purposes. They knew that it was to be incorporated in Giant's annual report, a report that would be transmitted to each Giant stockholder, and would be filed with the SEC in conjunction with Giant's proxy solicitation material for its annual stockholder meeting. The defendants also knew or should have known that the audited financial statements would be available and useful for other proper business purposes, such as public offerings of securities, credit, and corporate acquisitions. These were clearly foreseeable potential uses of the audited financials at the time of their preparation. Giant and the defendant auditors knew that these financial statements would be used at least until the next financial statements had been audited and released.

"Defendants became aware of plaintiffs' existence and their intended use of these statements before the plaintiffs relied on the accuracy of these financials. The defendants knew that the merger agreement included a representation that the prospectus used for the public offering in December 1971 contained no untrue statement of a material fact and did not omit to state any material fact. The defendants knew that this prospectus included their opinion that the financials had been prepared in accordance with generally accepted accounting principles and fairly presented Giant's financial condition. The defendants' representations were of a continuing nature and their obligation was a continuing one. . . .

"Irrespective of whether the defendants had actual knowledge of Giant's proposed use of the 1972 audit in connection with the merger, it was reasonably foreseeable that Giant would use the audited statement in connection with the merger and its consummation. This is particularly so since the defendants were familiar with the merger agreement and had been engaged by Giant to audit the books and records of the plaintiffs' enterprises for the purpose of the merger. The trial court properly denied defendants' motion."

The New York Court of Appeals in 1985 again addressed the question of liability of accountants to third persons (nonclients) in *Credit Alliance Corporation* v. *Arthur Andersen & Co.,* 483 N.E.2d 110. The court in that case essentially reaffirmed the original *Ultramares* doctrine and went on to list three requirements that must be met before a nonclient can hold an accountant liable for negligence. These requirements are: (1) the accountants must have been aware that their work product was to be used for a particular purpose; (2) in the furtherance of which a known party was intended to rely; and (3) some conduct on the part of the accountants linking them to that party must show the accountant's understanding of that party's reliance. Thus we have a considerable difference in opinion among the various states as to the liability of accountants to third party nonclients. The accountant should be aware of which of the three legal concepts his or her state has adopted: the *Ultramares* doctrine, the *Restatement* concept, or the foreseeable users doctrine.

■ LIABILITY OF AN ACCOUNTANT FOR FRAUD

An accountant may be found liable to the client or third persons for "actual" fraud. *Actual fraud* occurs when the accountant intentionally misstates or omits material facts intending to mislead the client or third persons who will rely on the accountant's work product. Material facts are facts that would be considered to be important to decision making based on the accountant's work product. If the client or the third party justifiably relied on the misstatement or the omission and suffered damage then the accountant will be liable for that person's out-of-pocket damages. Also in some cases the courts may allow punitive damages to be awarded against the accountant. *Punitive damages* are a method of punishing the fraudulent wrongdoer in addition to making the wrongdoer pay for the actual damage caused by the wrong.

There are other cases where the accountant is not guilty of an intentional misstatement or omission of material facts and the accountant did not intend to mislead anyone, but the actions of the accountant were not simply negligent actions; they were grossly negligent. By this we mean the accountant was guilty of an uncaring and reckless disregard for the accuracy and possible consequences of the use of his or her work product. If there were misstatements or omissions of material fact in the work product the accountant could be found guilty of *constructive fraud.* Typically the plaintiff, who has justifiably relied on an erroneous financial report which was audited and certified by an independent accountant, where there is no evidence of actual fraud, will allege negligence, constructive fraud, and also breach of contract, thus covering all the bases.

■ ACCOUNTANT'S LIABILITY UNDER THE NATIONAL SECURITIES LAWS

Securities Act of 1933

The Securities Act of 1933 requires issuers of securities to file a *registration statement.* This registration statement must contain financial statements and other information relating to the security. The purpose of this registration statement is to give the prospective buyers an opportunity to learn about the security before making a purchase. The 1933 Securities Act is often referred to as "The Truth in Securities Law." Chapter 48 discusses the 1933 Securities Act in more detail.

Section 11 of the 1933 Securities Act makes an accountant who provides inaccurate financial information used in a securities registration statement liable to a purchaser of the securities. Section 11(a), which specifically refers to accountants' liability, reads in part as follows:

> In case any part of the registration statement, when such part became effective, contained an untrue statement of a material fact or omitted to state a material fact required to be stated therein or necessary to make the statements therein not misleading, any person acquiring such security . . . may sue . . . every accountant . . . who has with his consent been named as having prepared or certified any part of the registration statement.

The first question to be answered is what constitutes a material fact. Briefly, a *material fact* is a factual statement which would have been important to the purchaser in making the decison to purchase or not to purchase.

Once it has been determined that there has been a mistatement of a material factor or an omission of a material fact, the next question is whether the accountant exercised *due diligence* in the preparation of the material and whether the accountant made reasonable efforts to determine the accuracy of the factual statements prior to the time the registration statement was made available to purchasers.

Section 11 does not require the purchaser of securities issued based on a registration statement that contained misstatements of material fact or omissions of material fact to prove that the purchaser actually relied on the misstatements or omissions when purchasing the securities. Also the purchaser doesn't have to prove the accountant/auditor was negligent. The burden is on the accountant to prove that he or she used due diligence in preparation and presentation of the material in the registration statement. Section 11 lawsuits against the accountant are also subject to a statute of limitations. The purchaser has only one year from the date the misstatement or omission is discovered, or in some cases, from the date the misstatement or omission should have been discovered. In no instance can a purchaser file suit against the accountant once a period of three years has elapsed after the securities were first offered to the public.

Escott v. *BarChris* explains the "due diligence" defense available to the accountant/auditor.

ESCOTT v. BARCHRIS CONSTRUCTION CORP.

283 F.Supp. 643 (New York, 1968)

FACTS

This is an action by purchasers of convertible subordinated 15-year debentures of BarChris Construction Corporation (BarChris). BarChris got into financial trouble in early 1962 and defaulted on the interest payments on the debentures. In October 1962 BarChris filed bankruptcy. The action is brought under Section 11 of the Securities Act of 1933 (15 U.S.C. § 77k). Plaintiffs allege that the registration statement with respect to these debentures filed with the Securities and Exchange Commission, which became effective on May 16, 1961, contained material false statements and material omissions.

Defendants fall into three categories: (1) the persons who signed the registration statement; (2) the underwriters, consisting of eight investment banking firms, led by Drexel & Co. (Drexel); and (3) BarChris's auditors, Peat, Marwick, Mitchell & Co. The signers, in addition to BarChris itself, were the nine directors of BarChris, plus its controller, defendant Trilling. Defendants claim the defense of due diligence.

ISSUE

Did defendants use "due diligence" in preparing the registration statement?

DECISION

No. Judgment for plaintiffs.

REASONS

District Judge McLean was not convinced.

"On the main issue of liability, the questions to be decided are (1) did the registration statement contain false statements of fact, or did it omit to state facts which should have been stated in order to prevent it from being misleading; (2) if so, were the facts which were falsely stated or omitted 'material' within the meaning of the Act; (3) if so, have defendants established their affirmative defenses? . . .

"It is a prerequisite to liability under Section 11 of the Act that the fact which is falsely stated in a registration statement or the fact that is omitted when it should have been stated to avoid being misleading, be 'material.' . . .

"The average prudent investor is not concerned with minor inaccuracies or with errors as to matters which are of no interest to him. The facts which tend to deter him from purchasing a security are facts which have an important bearing upon the nature or condition of the issuing corporation or its business.

"Judged by this test, there is no doubt that many of the misstatements and omissions in this prospectus were material. This is true of all of them which relate to the state of affairs in 1961, i.e., the overstatement of sales and gross profit for the first quarter, the understatement of contingent liabilities as of April 30, the overstatement of orders on hand, and the failure to disclose the true facts with respect to officers' loans, customers' delinquencies, application of proceeds, and the prospective operation of several alleys. . . .

"Before considering the evidence, a preliminary matter should be disposed of. The defendants do not agree among themselves as to who the 'experts' were or as to the parts of the registration statement which were expertised. . . .

"To say that the entire registration statement is expertised because some lawyer prepared it would be an unreasonable construction of the statute. Neither the lawyer for the company nor the lawyer for the underwriters is an expert within the meaning of Section 11. The only expert, in the statutory sense, was Peat, Marwick, and the only parts of the registration statement which purported to be made upon the authority of an expert were the portions which purported to be made on Peat, Marwick's authority. . . .

"The underwriters other than Drexel made no investigation of the accuracy of the prospectus. One of them, Peter Morgan, had underwritten the 1959 stock issue and had been a director of BarChris. He thus had some general familiarity with its affairs, but he knew no more than the other underwriters about the debenture prospectus. They all relied upon Drexel as the 'lead' underwriter.

"Drexel did make an investigation. The work was in charge of Coleman, a partner of the firm, assisted by Casperson, an associate. Drexel's attorneys acted as attorneys for the entire group of underwriters. Ballard did the work, assisted by Stanton. . . .

"After Coleman was elected a director on April 17, 1961, he made no further independent investigation of the accuracy of the prospectus. He assumed that Ballard was taking care of this on his behalf as well as on behalf of the underwriters.

In April 1961 Ballard instructed Stanton to examine BarChris's minutes for the past five years and also to look at 'the major contracts of the company.' Stanton went to BarChris's office for that purpose on Arpil 24. He asked Birnbaum for the minute books. He read the minutes of the board of directors and discovered interleaved in them a few minutes of executive committee meetings in 1960. He asked Kircher if there were any others. Kircher said that there had been other executive committeè meetings but that the minutes had not been written up. . . .

"As to the 'major contracts,' all that Stanton could remember seeing was an insurance policy. Birnbaum told him that there was no file of major contracts. Stanton did not examine the agreements with Talcott. He did not examine the contracts with customers. He did not look to see what contracts comprised the backlog figure. Stanton examined no accounting records of BarChris. His visit, which lasted one day, was devoted primarily to reading the director's minutes. . . .

"The other underwriters, who did nothing and relied solely on Drexel and on the lawyers, are also bound by [their failure.] It follows that although Drexel and the other underwriters believed that those portions of the prospectus were true, they had no reasonable ground for that belief, within the meaning of the statute. Hence, they have not established their due diligence defense, except as to the 1960 audited figures.

"The same conclusions must apply to Coleman. Although he participated quite actively in the earlier stages of the preparation of the prospectus and contributed questions and warnings of his own, in addition to the questions of counsel, the fact is that he stopped his participation toward the end of March 1961. He made no investigation after he became a director. When it came to verification, he relied upon his counsel to do it for him. Since counsel failed to do it, Coleman is bound by that failure. Consequently, in his case also, he has not established his due diligence defense except as to the audited 1960 figures . . . .

"Peat, Marwick's work was in general charge of a member of the firm, Cummings, and more immediately in charge of Peat, Marwick's manager, Logan. Most of the actual work was performed by a senior accountant, Berardi, who had junior assistants, one of whom was Kennedy.

"Berardi was then about 30 years old. He was not yet a CPA. He had had no previous experience with the bowling industry. This was his first job as a senior accountant. He could hardly have been given a more difficult assignment.

"After obtaining a little background information on BarChris by talking to Logan and reviewing Peat, Marwick's work papers on its 1959 audit, Berardi examined the results of test checks of BarChris's accounting procedures which one of the junior accountants had made, and he prepared an 'internal control questionnaire' and an 'audit program.' Thereafter, for a few days subsequent to December 30, 1960, he inspected BarChris's inventories and examined certain alley construction. Finally, on January 13, 1961, he began his auditing work, which he carried on substantially continuously until it was completed on February 24, 1961. Toward the close of the work, Logan reviewed it and made various comments and suggestions to Berardi. . . .

"The purpose of reviewing events subsequent to the date of a certified balance sheet (referred to as an S-1 review when made with reference to a registration statement) is to ascertain whether any material change has occurred in the company's financial position which should be disclosed in order to prevent the balance sheet figures from being misleading. The scope of such a review, under generally accepted auditing standards, is limited. It does not amount to a complete audit.

"Peat, Marwick prepared a written program for such a review. I find that this program conformed to generally accepted auditing standards. . . .

"Berardi made the S-1 review in May 1961. He devoted a little over two days to it, a total of 20½ hours. He did not discover any of the errors or omissions pertaining to the state of affairs in 1961 which I have previously discussed at length, all of which were material. The question is whether, despite his failure to find out anything, his investigation was reasonable within the meaning of the statute.

"What Berardi did was to look at a consolidated trial balance as of March 31, 1961 which had been prepared by BarChris, compare it with the audited December 31, 1960 figures, discuss with Trilling certain unfavorable developments which the comparison disclosed, and read certain minutes. He did not examine any 'important financial records' other than the trial balance. As to the minutes, he read only what minutes Birnbaum gave him, which consisted only of the board of directors' minutes of BarChris. He did not read such minutes as there were of the executive committee. He did not know that there was an executive committee, hence he did not discover that Kircher had notes of executive committee minutes which had not been written up. He did not read the minutes of any subsidiary.

"In substance, what Berardi did is similar to what Grant and Ballard did. He asked questions, he got answers which he considered satisfactory, and he did nothing to verify them. . . .

"There had been a material change for the worse in BarChris's financial position. That change was sufficiently serious so that the failure to disclose it made the 1960 figures misleading. Berardi did not discover it. As far as results were concerned, his S-1 review was useless.

"Accountants should not be held to a standard higher than that recognized in their profession. I do not do so here. Berardi's review did not come up to that standard. He did not take some of the steps which Peat, Marwick's written program prescribed. He did not spend an adequate amount of time on a task of this magnitude. Most important of all, he was too easily satisfied with glib answers to his inquiries.

"This is not to say that he should have made a complete audit. But there were enough danger signals in the materials which he did examine to require some further investigation on his part. Generally accepted accounting standards required such further investigation under these circumstances. It is not always sufficient merely to ask questions.

"Here again, the burden of proof is on Peat, Marwick. I find that that burden has not been satisfied. I conclude that Peat, Marwick has not established its due diligence defense."

Securities Act of 1934

The Securities Act of 1934 was passed to regulate the day-to-day trading of securities sold through the national stock exchanges. The 1934 Securities Act also set up the Securities and Exchange Commission. The companies regulated are typically those with more than $3 million in assets and having over 500 stockholders. The 1934 Act is also covered in more detail in Chapter 48.

Under the 1934 Act businesses whose securities are regulated are required to register their securities and to file quarterly and annual reports with the

SEC. The quarterly report is called a *10-Q report* and the annual report is called a *10-K report.* These reports contain financial information which must be certified by an independent public accountant. These reports are available to the public.

Most suits brought against accountants under the 1934 Act are based on Section 10(b), SEC rule 10b-5 or Section 18 of the 1934 Act. Section 10b reads as follows:

> It shall be unlawful for any person, directly or indirectly, by the use of any means or instrumentality of interstate commerce or of the mails, or of any facility of any national securities exchange
>
> (b) To use or employ, in connecton with the purchase or sale of any security registered on a national securities exchange or any security not so registered, any manipulative or deceptive device or contrivance in contravention of such rules and regulations as the commission may prescribe as necessary or appropriate in the public interest or for the protection of investors.

Section 10b allows the SEC to make further rules and regulations as necessary. *Rule 10b-5* reads as follows:

> It shall be unlawful for any person, directly or indirectly, by the use of any means or instrumentality of interstate commerce, or of the mails, or of any facility of any national securities exchange
>
> (a) to employ any device, scheme, or artifice to defraud,
>
> (b) to make any untrue statement of a material fact or to omit to state a material fact necessary in order to make the statements made, in the light of the circumstances under which they were made, not misleading, or
>
> (c) to engage in any act, practice, or course of business which operates or would operate as a fraud or deceit upon any person, in connection with the purchase or sale of any security.

Section 10b and SEC Rule 10b-5 are very broad. They apply to any false statements or omissions made by the accountant, even though the statement was not made in an application document or report filed with the SEC. These provisions are primarily concerned with fraud.

Section 18 of the 1934 Act is really a disclosure provision. It only applies to statements made in applications, reports, and documents filed with the SEC. Section 18 reads as follows:

> Any person who shall make or cause to be made any statement in any application, report, or document filed . . . which . . . was . . . false or misleading with respect to any material fact, shall be liable to any person . . . who, in reliance upon such statement, shall have purchased or sold a security at a price which was affected by such statement, for damages caused by such reliance, unless the person sued shall prove that he acted in good faith and had no knowledge that such statement was false or misleading.

An accountant's liability under the 1934 Act, Section 10b, or SEC Rule 10b-5 must be based on fraudulent conduct, not mere negligence. As you will recall, under the 1933 Act, the accountant was liable if there was a false statement or omission in the registration statement even though the purchaser had not relied on such statement or omission. The accountant's only defense was "due diligence." In other words the accountant was guilty until he or she proved a defense of due diligence. The burden of proof is on the accountant under the 1933 Act.

Under Section 10b and SEC Rule 10b-5, the accountant is not liable unless fraud is proved by the purchaser. The purchaser has the burden of proving reasonable reliance on the alleged false and material statement and a financial loss as a result of such reliance. Thus the burden is entirely on the purchaser under Section 10b and SEC Rule 10b-5. Here the accountant is innocent until proven guilty.

In the following 1976 case the Supreme Court, in a lawsuit based on Section 10b and SEC Rule 10b-5, found negligence on the part of the Ernst & Ernst accounting firm, but not fraud, and therefore dismissed the case against the accountants.

Why didn't they sue under 1933 the

ERNST & ERNST v. HOCHFELDER

425 U.S. 185 (1976)

FACTS Leston B. Nay, president and owner of 92 percent of the stock of First Securities Company of Chicago, was involved in a fraudulent securities scheme in which Hochfelder and the other plaintiffs had invested. From 1942 to 1966 Hochfelder invested in so-called escrow accounts which supposedly carried a very high interest rate. In fact, no such accounts were listed on the books of First Securities or in the disclosure filings which First Securities sent to the SEC and the Midwest Stock Exchange. Nay was using the money for his own purposes as soon as he got it. To try to hide what he was doing, Nay had a strict rule that any incoming mail addressed to him was not to be opened by anyone else, whether or not he was there at the time. The plaintiffs argued that Ernst & Ernst had failed to use proper auditing procedures on First Securities' accounts and that if they had, they would have discovered Nay's strange rule and thus the fraud. (The fraud was not discovered until 1968, when Nay committed suicide.) The U.S. District Court said that there was no case against Ernst & Ernst for *fraud* under Rule 10b-5. The Seventh Circuit Court of Appeals reversed.

ISSUE Can a CPA be held liable under Section 10-b for mere negligence?

DECISION No. Judgment reversed.

 REASONS Justice Powell agreed with the District Court.

"We granted certiorari to resolve the question whether a private cause of action for damages will lie under § 10(b) and Rule 10b-5 in the absence of any allegation of 'scienter'—intent to deceive, manipulate, or defraud. We conclude that it will not and therefore we reverse. . . .

"Section 10(b) makes unlawful the use or employment of 'any manipulative or deceptive device or contrivance' in contravention of Commission rules. The words *manipulative or deceptive* used in conjunction with *device or contrivance* suggest strongly that § 10(b) was intended to proscribe knowing or intentional misconduct. . . .

"Although the extensive legislative history of the 1934 Act is bereft of any explicit explanation of Congress' intent, we think the relevant portions of that history support our conclusion that § 10(b) was addressed to practices that involve some element of scienter and cannot be read to impose liability for negligent conduct alone.

"The most relevant exposition of the provision that was to become § 10(b) was by Thomas G. Corcoran, a spokesman for the drafters. Corcoran indicated:

Subsection (c) § 9(c) of H.R. 7852—later § 10(b) says, "Thou shalt not devise any other cunning devices." . . . Of course subsection (c) is a catch-all clause to prevent manipulative devices. I do not think there is any objection to that kind of clause. The Commission should have the authority to deal with new manipulative devices.

"This brief explanation of § 10(b) by a spokesman for its drafters is significant. The section was described rightly as a 'catch-all' clause to enable the Commission 'to deal with new manipulative (or cunning) devices.' It is difficult to believe that any lawyer, legislative draftsman, or legislator would use these words if the intent was to create liability for merely negligent acts or omissions. Neither the legislative history nor the briefs supporting Hochfelder identify any usage or authority for construing 'manipulative (or cunning) devices' to include negligence. . . .

"In its *amicus curiae* brief, however, the Commission contends that nothing in the language 'manipulative or deceptive device or contrivance' limits its operation to knowing or intentional practices. In support of its view, the Commission cites the overall congressional purpose in the 1933 or 1934 Acts to protect investors against false and deceptive practices that might injure them. . . . The argument simply ignores the use of the words *manipulative, device,* and *contrivance,* terms that make unmistakable a congressional intent to proscribe a type of conduct quite different from negligence. Use of the word *manipulative* is especially significant. . . . It connotes intentional or willful conduct designed to deceive or defraud investors by controlling or artificially affecting the price of securities. . . .

"Thus, despite the broad view of Rule 10b-5 advanced by the Commission in this case, its scope cannot exceed the power granted the Commission by Congress under § 10(b). . . . When a statute speaks so specifically in terms of manipulation and deception, and of implementing devices and contrivances—the commonly understood terminology of intentional wrongdoing—and when its history reflects no more expansive intent, we are quite unwilling to extend the scope of the statute to negligent conduct."

Section 18 does not require the proof of fraudulent conduct on the part of the accountant before the accountant may be found liable. It simply provides that if there is a false or misleading statement made by the accountant in an application, document, or report filed with the SEC, the accountant could be found liable to a purchaser of the security involved, provided the purchaser reasonably relied on the false or misleading statement and suffered a loss due to the reliance. The accountant can escape such liability by proving a lack of knowledge that the statements were either false or misleading, and that he or she acted in good faith. What constitutes good faith? This means the accountant made a reasonable effort to be truthful and did not intentionally put in false or misleading information. On the other hand, if the accountant did not actually know that the statements were false or misleading, but had been grossly negligent—he or she clearly did not follow standard procedures and was guilty of obvious misconduct in conducting the investigation—then the court would no doubt find the accountant guilty. The accountant will not be held civilly liable for simple, honest mistakes, only for mistakes that result from gross inattention and misconduct.

There is also a statute of limitations which applies to actions filed under the provisions of the 1934 Act. The same one-year and three-year limitations that apply to actions filed under the 1933 Act apply to actions filed under the 1934 Act.

ACCOUNTANT'S CIVIL LIABILITY UNDER RICO

In 1970, the U.S. Congress passed the Racketeer Influenced and Corrupt Organizations Act, known as RICO. The intent of this law was to control the influence of organized crime on legitimate businesses. The act has criminal penalties and civil provisions which allow the imposition of treble damages. Under this law stockholders can bring civil suits for treble damages and even get their attorney fees paid.

Originally the act was aimed at so-called organized crime, but when Congress defined the types of crimes it applied to, they included such crimes as mail fraud and fraud in the sale of securities, which were not previously considered to be the types of crimes in which organized crime was involved. At any rate this poorly and broadly worded law has been used to bring civil law suits against certified public accountants who may have been involved with a business which has been accused, but not necessarily convicted, of a pattern of racketeering activity. Almost any fraud committed by a business may be interpreted as being a violation of this act. The *Sedima* (discussion) case decided by the U.S. Supreme Court in 1985 explains the operation of this law.

PROCEDURAL ISSUES IN CIVIL LIABILITY CASES

In Chapter 2 we discussed procedural issues, specifically the right of the court to compel testimony or production of documents. It was pointed out that there is a recognized privilege of confidentiality for certain professions. For example, attorneys cannot be forced to reveal matters communicated to them in confidence by their clients.

The question arose as to whether a similar privilege of confidentiality exists between the client and his or her accountant. Chief Justice Burger, speaking for the Supreme Court of the United States in the case of *U.S.* v. *Arthur Young & Company* in 1984, found there was no privilege of confidentiality concerning an accountant's work product.

As a consequence of this case many clients who are concerned about the confidentiality of their records will engage an attorney to handle their specific problems. The attorney then hires an accountant to assist. Thus the accountant's work is the attorney's work product and protected by the attorney-client privilege of confidentiality.

ACCOUNTANT'S CRIMINAL LIABILITY

We briefly introduced you to the problem of criminal liability of accountants in Chapter 6, and we will now cover this area in more detail.

The Securities Act of 1933 and the Securities Act of 1934

Section 24 of the 1933 Act makes an accountant criminally liable if the accountant willfully makes a false statement regarding a material fact or willfully omits a material fact in a registration statement. The penalty can be a fine of up to $10,000, or five years in prison, or both.

Section 32(a) of the 1934 Act makes an accountant criminally liable if the accountant willfully makes a false or misleading statement regarding a material fact in a report required to be filed under the 1934 Act such as the 10-K reports. The penalty can be a fine of up to $10,000, or five years in prison, or both.

The Mail Fraud Statute

This statute imposes criminal liability upon persons who either send false financial statements in the U.S. mails or conspire to send false financial statements in the U.S. mail.

In the case of the *United States* v. *Simon,* often referred to as the *Continental Vending* case, decided by the U.S. Second Circuit in 1969, accountants were found criminally liable. That case involved violations of Section 32(a) of the 1934 Act as well as the Mail Fraud Statute. This statute was also applied in the *Carpenter* case in Chapter 6.

The Foreign Corrupt Practices Act

This act was passed by the U.S. Congress in 1977 to discourage payment of bribes by U.S. corporations to foreign officials for favors in business dealings.

This act prohibits both businesses registered under the provisions of the 1934 Securities Exchange Act and U.S. businesses not so registered from offering or giving anything of value to a foreign official to obtain a new business relationship or to retain a business relationship previously established. A willful violation of the provisions of this act can result in a criminal conviction with penalties of up to $10,000 and/or five years in prison for the individual or individuals involved and fines to the corporation of up to one million dollars.

Accountants are concerned with this law because it amended section 13(b) of the Securities Exchange Act of 1934. The law now requires businesses that are registered with and report to the SEC to keep accurate and complete records of all transactions and dispositon of assets. Also the company must maintain a system of internal accounting to check on all cash payments and see that they are specifically authorized by management. The accountant is now charged with new responsibilities, violation of which could result in severe criminal charges. The SEC is the watchdog; they will investigate and then refer the case to the Justice Department for criminal prosecution if they suspect a violation.

The Internal Revenue Code

The Internal Revenue Code provides for criminal penalties including fines and imprisonment for accountants (tax preparers) who willfully prepare false tax returns or willfully assist a client to evade taxes.

■ SIGNIFICANCE OF THIS CHAPTER

Accountants' legal liability as well as the legal liability of other professionals has become a real concern in recent years due to the increased amount of litigation and the increased amounts of the various awards. Future accountants must be aware of the potential liability problems they face in their profession. They must be prepared to adhere to a high standard of care in order to avoid civil and criminal liability.

DISCUSSION CASE

SEDIMA, S.P.R.L. v. IMREX CO. INC.
473 U.S. 479 (1985)

FACTS: In 1979, petitioner Sedima, a Belgian corporation, entered into a joint venture with respondent Imrex Co. to provide electronic components to a Belgian firm. The buyer was to order parts through Sedima; Imrex was to obtain the parts in this country and ship them to Europe. The agreement called for Sedima and Imrex to split the net proceeds. Imrex filled roughly $8 million in orders placed with it through Sedima. Sedima became convinced, however, that Imrex was presenting inflated bills, cheating Sedima out of a portion of its proceeds by collecting for nonexistent expenses.

In 1982, Sedima filed this action in the U.S. District Court for the Eastern District of New York. The complaint set out common-law claims of unjust enrichment, conversion, breach of contract, fiduciary duty, and constructive trust. In addition, it asserted RICO claims under § 1964(c) against Imrex and two of its officers. Two counts alleged violations of § 1962(c), based on acts of mail and wire fraud. Claiming injury of at least $175,000, the amount of the alleged overbilling, Sedima sought treble damages and attorney's fees.

The District Court held that for an injury to be "by reason of a violation of section 1962," as required by § 1964(c), it must be somehow different in kind from the direct injury resulting from the acts of racketeering activity.

While not choosing a precise formulation, the District Court held that a complaint must allege a "RICO-type injury," which was either some sort of distinct "racketeering injury," or a "competitive injury." It found "no allegation here of any injury apart from that which would result directly from the alleged . . . acts of mail fraud and wire fraud," and accordingly dismissed the RICO counts for failure to state a claim. The Court of Appeals affirmed.

■

Justice White adopted a broad interpretation of the Act.

The Racketeer Influenced and Corrupt Organizations Act (RICO) . . . provides a private civil action to recover treble damages for injury "by reason of a violation of" its substantive provisions. . . . The initial dormancy of this provision and its recent greatly increased utilization are now familiar history. In response to what it perceived to be misuse of civil RICO by private plaintiffs, the court below construed § 1964(c) to permit private actions only against defendants who had been convicted on criminal charges, and only where there had occurred a "racketeering injury." While we understand the court's concern over the consequences of an unbridled reading of the statute, we reject both of its holdings.

RICO takes aim at "racketeering activity," which it defines as any act "chargeable" under several generically described state criminal laws, any act "indictable" under numerous specific federal criminal provisions, including mail and wire fraud, and any "offense" involving bankruptcy or securities fraud or drug-related activities that is "punishable" under federal law. . . . Section 1962, entitled "Prohibited Activites," outlaws the use of income derived from a "pattern of racketeering activity" to acquire an interest in or establish an enterprise engaged in or affecting interstate commerce; the acquisition or maintenance of any interest in an enterprise "through" a pattern of racketeering activity. . . .

Underlying the Court of Appeals' holding was its distress at the "extraordinary, if not outrageous," uses to which civil RICO has been put. . . . Instead of being used against mobsters and organized criminals, it has become a tool for everyday fraud cases brought against "respected and legitimate enterprises.". . . Yet Congress wanted to reach both "legitimate" and "illegitimate" enterprises. . . . The former enjoy neither an inherent incapacity for criminal activity nor immunity from its consequences. The fact that § 1964(c) is used against respected businesses allegedly engaged in a pattern of specifically identified criminal conduct is hardly a sufficient reason for assuming that the provision is being misconstrued. Nor does it reveal the "ambiguity" discovered by the court below. "[T]he fact that RICO has been applied in situations not expressly anticipated by Congress does not demonstrate ambiguity. It demonstrates breadth." . . . It is true that private civil actions under the statute are being brought almost solely against such defendants, rather than against the archetypal, intimidating mobster. Yet this defect—if defect it is—is inherent in the statute as written, and its correction must lie with Congress. It is not for the judiciary to eliminate the private action in situations where Congress has provided it simply because plaintiffs are not taking advantage of it in its more difficult applications.

We nonetheless recognize that, in its private civil version, RICO is evolving into something quite different from the original conception of its enactors. . . . Though sharing the doubts of the Court of Appeals about this increasing divergence, we cannot agree with either its diagnosis or its remedy. The "extraordinary" uses to which civil RICO has been put appear to be primarily the result of the breadth of the predicate offenses, in particular the inclusion of wire, mail, and securities fraud, and the failure of Congress and the courts to develop a meaningful concept of "pattern." We do not believe that the amorphous standing requirement imposed by the Second Circuit effectively responds to these problems, or that it is a form of statutory amendment appropriately undertaken by the courts.

Sedima may maintain this action if the defendants conducted the enterprise through a pattern of racketeering activity. The questions whether the defendants committed the requisite predicate acts, and whether the commission of those acts fell into a pattern, are not before us. The complaint is not deficient for failure to allege either an injury separate from the financial loss stemming from the alleged acts of mail and wire fraud, or prior convictions of the defendants. The decision below is accordingly reversed, and the case is remanded for further proceedings consistent with this opinion.

▪ IMPORTANT TERMS AND CONCEPTS

malpractice liability	constructive fraud
professional liability	punitive damages
abuse of process	Securities Act of 1933
negligence	registration statement
reasonable care	material fact
foreseeable third parties	due diligence
foreseen third parties	Securities Act of 1934
primary (third party)	10-K report
beneficiaries	10-Q report
Restatement of Torts	SEC Rule 10b-5
GAAP	scienter
GAAS	RICO
Ultramares doctrine	Mail Fraud Statute

▪ QUESTIONS AND PROBLEMS FOR DISCUSSION

1. What is the significance of the *Ultramares* doctrine? Explain.
2. What is the difference in the scope of the accountant's duty under the *Restatement* rule, as opposed to the *Ultramares* doctrine?
3. What is the nature of the accountant's potential liability under the 1933 Securities Act?
4. What is the nature of the accountant's protential liability under the 1934 Securities and Exchange Act?
5. International Factors, Inc. is a U.S. corporation that does business in many foreign countries. Sam Sleazy is the general manager of the company's office in Rome, Italy. He believes "when in Rome, do as the Romans do." He noticed that a few extra bucks on the side often bring good results in a business transaction, so he established what he called an advertising and entertainment account which was basically a cash disbursement account with no receipts to show to whom or how much was paid. The disbursements from the account amount to roughly $100,000 to $150,000 per year. You are the accountant. What law should you be concerned with and what type of records and verification would you require from Sam?
6. Race Cars International is a manufacturer of specialty equipment for racing cars all over the world. They want to expand their production facilities so they have decided to go public and offer $3 million in shares to the public. They engage Lazy Louie, a local CPA, to prepare the financial statement to be included in the registration statement which they file with the SEC. Louie did not really check the company's records very carefully. He knows all the officers and he figured they were honest, so he just accepted the figures they gave him and put them in the financial statement unaudited. Later, it was found that the material given to Louie was false and misleading and that there were misstatements of material fact and omissions of material information. Paul Purchaser had purchased $100,000 worth of the stock and it is now worthless. Paul sues Louie. Will Paul win? Discuss.
7. Archie Starch, a famous prizefighter, was interested in investing in an oil and gas tax shelter being arranged by Minerals Corporation. Minerals went to their accounting firm and asked them to prepare an opinion letter to reassure their client, and other investors, as to the benefits of this tax shelter. The opinion letter was prepared and delivered to Minerals. When the accountants found out that the letter was being used as a sales tool, they wrote a revised, more complex letter which was sent out under the partnership name.

There were both misrepresentations of material fact and omissions of material information in this letter. After a number of persons had invested, the Internal Revenue Service denied deductions taken for the investment in this tax shelter. The investors now sue the accountants alleging a violation of rule 10b(5) of the SEC. Who should win this case? Why?

8. An accounting firm was employed by Ace Car Rental Company to do an audit of their records and to prepare an audit statement showing the company's net worth. The client specifically requested that the accountants not audit accounts receivable. The accountant complied with that request and made an appropriate notation on the balance sheet and also qualified their audit opinion with an appropriate notation that accounts receivable had not been audited. Ajax Industries, relying on the audit report, purchased two thirds of the stock of Ace Car Rental Co. Shortly thereafter, Ace Car Rental Co. became insolvent and had to file bankruptcy. Ajax Industries then sued the accountant alleging they misrepresented the status of the accounts receivable and they should be liable for the losses Ajax suffered. If you were the judge, how would you rule on this case? Why?

PART TWO

Contract Law

Contract law affects every transaction in which an individual or a business may be involved. Every sale of goods or services to a customer is a contract. Investments made by stockholders are contracts. Purchases or rentals of land and equipment are contracts. Hiring agreements are contracts. Agreements with professional firms for advertising, accounting, and legal services are contracts. Contract law is important to you as a consumer and as a future business manager.

Contract law principles also form the basis for many other specialized bodies of law, such as sales of goods, secured transactions, insurance, suretyship, and commercial paper. Although each of these other topics is covered later in this text, it is important to understand contract law principles before studying those more specific topics. Contract law is the foundation; the particular rules and exceptions for each of these specialized topics are the rooms of the house.

For these reasons, contract law is given extensive coverage in Part Two. We first gave you some basic definitions and terminology, then we examine the formation of the agreement and its enforceability. We then proceed to discuss the major defenses a party may assert against liability on a contract. We also explain and discuss the situations where persons other than the two parties who made the agreement may have rights under it. We then review the various ways in which contract liability may be excused or discharged. Finally, we review the remedies available when one party breaches a contract. These 10 chapters obviously cannot cover the subject in the same depth as a full year's work in law school. After studying them, however, you will have a very good overview of the major rules involved in the formation, performance, and enforcement of contracts.

9

Introduction to Contract Law

CHAPTER OBJECTIVES

THIS CHAPTER WILL:

- Introduce contract law.
- Define the term *contract*.
- Outline the elements of a valid contract.
- Explain the main classifications of contracts.
- Provide an overview for following chapters.

Contract law is perhaps the most basic area of civil law. Every transaction, be it oral or written, for the purchase or sale of goods, land, or intangible personal property, involves principles of contract law. Contract law is the foundation upon which other areas of law are built.

For example, suppose that two persons want to establish a business. Whether they propose a partnership, a corporation, or any other type of organization, their venture involves principles of contract law. If employees are to be hired, any agreement between employer and employees involves contract law. The business must operate from physical premises and use machinery and equipment, and each of these necessities may be purchased or perhaps leased. Either way, principles of contract law apply.

When the organization begins transacting business, it must purchase raw materials, and those purchases involve contract law. After the raw materials are processed into products, the manufacturer's sales to wholesalers, wholesalers' subsequent sales to retailers, and retailers' sales to consumers are all controlled by principles of contract law.

Thus we must understand the principles of contract law before we study the laws governing sales, commercial paper, secured transactions, agency, business organizations, employer-employee relations, ownership of property, and the various other areas that affect the businessperson and the daily operation of the business entity.

■ SOURCES OF CONTRACT LAW

Common law and the UCC

Contract law stems from case law, the *Uniform Commercial Code,* and other state statutes. As noted in Chapter 1, all states have adopted the UCC except Louisiana, which has enacted only those parts of the UCC that do not conflict with its variation of the Napoleonic Code.

As you study contract law, remember that the common law governs some contract transactions, or parts of them, while the Uniform Commercial Code governs others. If the contract involves the sale of land or the sale of services, traditional common-law rules will normally apply unless some specific state statutory law pertains to that transaction. If the transaction involves the sale of personal property, then any applicable provisions of the Uniform Commercial Code will supersede the common-law rules.

The sale of land or services in transactions not covered by any specific state statutory law normally will be covered by the general contract rules summarized by the *Restatement of Contracts.* As we noted in Chapter 1, the *Restatement* is a treatise prepared by the American Law Institute. These *Restatements* are presented in an encyclopedia-like form, and give the generally accepted rules of law on specific topics. The *Restatements* are not the actual law, only a reference to the generally applied rules.

When confronted with new or difficult questions, or when prior cases have reached differing results, courts frequently use textbooks and law review articles. Such sources are not themselves the law, but they can assist a court in seeing the issues involved. Two of the most widely cited contracts texts are those by Professor Williston and Professor Corbin.

Just what is a "contract"? In simplest terms, it is a private agreement which imposes legal duties on the parties which agree to it. Of course, there are

■ **EXHIBIT 9–1**
Sources of Contract Law

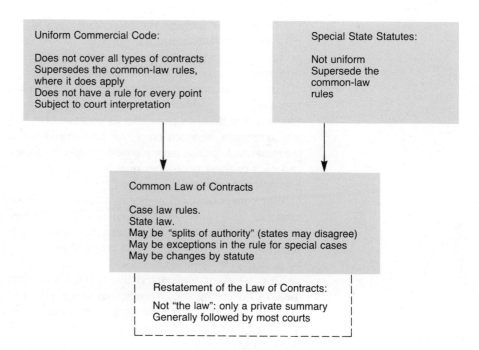

Uniform Commercial Code:

Does not cover all types of contracts
Supersedes the common-law rules,
where it does apply
Does not have a rule for every point
Subject to court interpretation

Special State Statutes:

Not uniform
Supersede the
common-law
rules

Common Law of Contracts

Case law rules.
State law.
May be "splits of authority" (states may disagree)
May be exceptions in the rule for special cases
May be changes by statute

Restatement of the Law of Contracts:

Not "the law": only a private summary
Generally followed by most courts

many refinements and exceptions to this overall definition. That's why there are 10 chapters on Contracts.

■ **DEFINITION OF A CONTRACT**

UCC definition of contract

UCC definition of agreement

For the commercial contracts which it covers, the Uniform Commercial Code, in Section 1–201(11) defines a contract as the "total legal obligation which results from the parties' agreement as affected by this Act and any other applicable rules of law." Upon reviewing this definition, we find the term *agreement* is not defined. Is an agreement always legally binding on the parties? Do all agreements create a legal obligation? Must an agreement be in writing and signed by the parties to create legal obligations? Section 1–201(3) of the UCC defines *agreement* as *"the bargain of the parties in fact as found in their language or by implication from other circumstances including course of dealing or usage of trade or course of performance as provided in the Act. Whether an agreement has legal consequences is determined by the provisions of this Act if applicable, otherwise by the law of contracts."*

The agreement is simply the bargain agreed upon by the parties. It may or may not create legal obligations against the parties, depending on the terms of the bargain and the applicable law. For example, a promise between two friends to meet and go to the movies constitutes an agreement, since both parties agreed to meet at a certain time and place. However, the obligations created are only social and not legally enforceable as a contract.

Section 1–201(3) of the UCC makes it clear that an agreement need not be in writing and signed by the parties. It can be oral; it can even be implied from nonverbal actions of the parties. Oral contracts are fully enforceable, unless terms of the oral agreement conflict with the provisions of the Statute of Frauds. The Statute of Frauds, which requires that certain types of contracts be proved by a signed writing, will be discussed in Chapter 12.

The next case shows how the courts use the UCC, in combination with the general rules, to decide contract disputes involving *sales of goods.*

FIBER INDUSTRIES v. SALEM CARPET MILLS

315 S.E.2d 735 (North Carolina, 1984)

FACTS

Prior to 1980, Fiber Industries (Celanese) sold fiber to carpet manufacturers for their use in the making of carpets. Beginning in 1975, Salem Carpet bought trademarked "Fortrel" and "Fortron" fiber from Celanese on an order-by-order basis. Celanese and Salem Carpet had no written agreement other than the individual purchase orders.

On August 14, 1980, Celanese announced that it was withdrawing from the carpet industry and would cease production of nylon and polyester staple by December 31, 1980. In its announcement, Celanese stated that "all carpet fiber customers will be supplied fiber in an orderly fashion until phase-outs are complete."

Salem Carpet continued to purchase the nylon fiber from Celanese after the decision to withdraw was announced and placed one final order in December of 1980, which was delivered and accepted. Salem Carpet refused to pay the purchase price of $407,128.40 and claimed an offset and counterclaim for approximately $400,000 for losses allegedly suffered as a result of Celanese's withdrawal from the carpet industry.

On March 25, 1981, Celanese filed suit against Salem Carpet for the purchase price plus interest. In its answer and counterclaim, Salem Carpet denied liability and asserted breach of contract on the part of Celanese. On February 21, 1983, the trial court granted Celanese's motions for summary judgment on all claims. From that order Salem Carpet appeals.

ISSUE

Can Salem prove a trade custom as part of the contract?

DECISION

No. Judgment affirmed.

 REASONS

Judge Arnold was not convinced that any extra terms should be added to what seemed like a very clear agreement.

"Salem Carpet contends that the trial court erred in granting Celanese's motion for summary judgment in that Celanese breached an implied warranty established by 'usage of trade' within the carpet industry. It is claimed that, in accordance with customary practice, Celanese was obligated to fill all orders made by Salem Carpet during the projected market life of any carpet style which utilized fiber manufactured by Celanese. We do not agree with this contention and affirm the order of the trial court.

"The Uniform Commercial Code, as embodied in Chapter 25 of the North Carolina General Statutes, defines 'usage of trade' as:

any practice or method of dealing having such regularity of observance in a place, vocation or trade as to justify an expectation that it will be observed with respect to the transaction in question . . . G.S. 25–1–205(2).

In short, Salem Carpet claims that it was justified in expecting that all orders made on Celanese would be filled because, as was stated in the affidavit of J. Terris Hagan, vice president of marketing for Salem Carpet:

> in the carpet industry where a manufacturer of fiber makes available a branded fiber for use by a carpet manufacturer in the introduction of a new line or style, it is standard practice, custom, and usage of trade in the carpet industry that the fiber manufacturer will fill all orders submitted by the carpet manufacturer for use in producing that style carpet and further that the fiber manufacturer will continue to make its branded fiber available for the useful life of the carpet style or for sufficient time to allow the carpet manufacturer to produce and sell sufficient carpet to recoup the large start-up expenses incurred in introducing and marketing a new line of branded carpet.

Before considering what constituted the standard practice in the carpet industry during the time Salem Carpet and Celanese contracted to buy and sell carpet fiber, it is necessary to examine the actual agreement which existed between them. . . . Salem Carpet periodically placed orders for a stated amount of fiber and Celanese filled these orders as they were received. The standard Celanese order acknowledgment form provided:

> These terms and conditions [set out in the acknowledgment form] constitute the entire contract. No modification, limitation, waiver, or discharge of this contract or of any of its terms shall bind Seller unless in writing and signed by Seller's authorized employee at its headquarters.

Salem Carpet's purchase order form contained similar language:

> This purchase order contains all the terms and conditions of the purchase agreement and shall constitute the complete and exclusive agreement between Seller and Purchaser. No modification, rescission or waiver of this purchase order or of any of its terms shall be effective unless in writing signed by the parties.

Since it is clear that both Salem Carpet and Celanese intended their respective purchase order forms to comprise any and all obligations they might have owed the other party, the question arises as to whether Salem Carpet can now introduce evidence to show that the usage of trade inherent in the carpet industry required Celanese to continue to fill its orders. . . .

"The code . . . allows Salem Carpet only to supplement or explain the terms of the written purchase orders. Since neither the forms of Salem Carpet nor those of Celanese contain any mention of a continuing obligation to sell carpet fiber or, in any way, to compensate Salem for its loss, it would appear that evidence as to usage of trade in the carpet industry is irrelevant as a matter of law. G.S. 25–2–202(a) clearly limits the use of trade usage evidence to that which *explains* or *supplements* the terms of the written agreement. We find the usage of trade evidence urged by Salem Carpet goes beyond merely explaining or supplementing existing terms, but, in fact, imposes additional obligations on Celanese. . . . '[E]xplanatory or supplemental information is not to be admitted when the ". . . court finds the writing to have been intended also as a complete and exclusive statement of the terms of the agreement."' . . .

"It is important to note that even if trade usage evidence were admissible in this case, Salem Carpet failed to establish a question of fact sufficient to survive Celanese's motion for summary judgment. The evidence proposed to show a 'regularity of observance' in the carpet industry actually amounted to no more than self-serving affidavits of Salem Carpet employees. There was no independent evidence that the customary practice of the carpet industry places on a manufacturer of carpet fiber a continuing obligation to fill all orders of the maker of a carpet which utilized that fiber. We find that Salem Carpet failed to meet its burden of showing a genuine issue of material fact as to the existence of such trade usage in the carpet industry. . . . The granting of the motion for summary judgment is, therefore, affirmed."

BASIC REQUIREMENTS OF A VALID CONTRACT

Not all discussions, or even all agreements, are enforced as contracts. A contract requires two basic elements, but several other factors may affect its enforceability. These requirements are:

1. That an agreement be made between the parties. To have such an agreement, there must be an *offer* and an *acceptance,* each intended as such. The process of making the agreement is discussed in the next chapter.

2. That the agreement indicates an exchange of values. The technical legal term here is *consideration,* which usually means that benefits and burdens are involved on both sides. A totally one-sided agreement, such as a promise of a gift, generally can not be enforced as a contract. These technical rules are discussed in Chapter 11.

The combination of elements 1 and 2 indicate a contractual agreement. In determining whether the contract is fully valid and enforceable, however, the courts may also consider several other matters. These are usually raised as defense arguments, when there is a lawsuit to enforce the alleged contract.

3. That the agreement be in the form required by the applicable law. Some types of contracts, such as those for land, are subject to the *Statute of Frauds,* which requires a signed writing for the contract to be enforceable. If this special statute applies, and there is no writing which meets its requirements, the contract is unenforceable in court. This writing requirement is discussed in Chapter 12.

4. That there is legal capacity to make a contract. *Capacity* here refers (normally) to mental competence. The law recognizes that minor children and mental incompetents should not be held liable, as a rule, for their contracts. Such persons' contracts are usually voidable, at their option. These rules, and those for other persons with special legal status, are discussed in Chapter 13.

5. That the agreement be based on the real consent of the parties, without fraud, coercion, or mistake. Where someone has been forced or tricked into making a contract, it is voidable at his or her option, and sometimes, totally void. These rules are discussed in Chapter 14.

6. That the purpose and performance of the contract be legal. Where the agreement involves the commission of some criminal act, the courts will generally refuse to recognize it at all. It will be deemed totally null and void, as far as any civil case is concerned. If the parties agreed to a criminal conspiracy, however, they may be prosecuted under the criminal law. Various types of illegality which may occur in contracts are discussed in Chapter 15.

CLASSIFICATIONS OF CONTRACTS

Contracts are classified with regard to their formation, the nature of the required acceptance, their enforceability, and the extent to which the terms of the contract have been performed. The same contract may thus be placed in four different categories, depending on which feature is being examined. (See Exhibit 9–2.)

Method of Formation

Express Contract. An express contract is a contract, either oral or written, in which the terms of the contract are clearly and openly stated, in words.

■ EXHIBIT 9–2
Classifications of Contracts

Method of formation	Nature of acceptance	Extent of performance	Enforceability
Express contract	Bilateral	Executed	Valid
Implied contract	Unilateral	Executory	Void
Quasi-contract (implied in law)			Voidable
			Unenforceable

Agreement expressed by conduct

Implied Contract.   An implied contract is a contract in which the agreement between the parties was not stated orally or in writing; however, the fact that a contract was intended can be implied from the circumstances or the conduct of the parties. This type of contract is very common. For example, suppose that you call the plumber to come repair a leaky faucet. You are at work, and you tell the plumber that the key is under the doormat. When you come home the key is back under the doormat, the door is locked, and the faucet is repaired. You owe the plumber a reasonable fee for the repair even though you gave no oral or written promise to pay. The fact that you called the plumber, who is in business for profit, is evidence of an implied promise to pay for services rendered.

ROTH v. LIESKE

201 N.W.2d 846 (Nebraska, 1972)

FACTS   Plaintiff was formerly a patrolman with the Nebraska State Patrol. He filed an action for overtime pay. The claim was denied. He then appealed to the district court for Lancaster County, Nebraska, and the court also denied his claim. He states he was hired on the basis of a 50-hour week and paid a stated monthly salary. Plaintiff states he worked many hours overtime and if he determined his hourly rate by dividing his monthly salary on the basis of 50 hours per week then he is entitled to $2,142.53 in overtime pay. He states that he is entitled to overtime under the theory of implied contract. He appeals.

ISSUE   When there is an express contract as to wages and no provision is made for overtime, can an employee collect overtime under the theory of implied contract?

DECISION   No. Judgment affirmed.

REASONS   **The court denied plaintiff's claim for overtime, stating as follows:**
"The plaintiff relies upon a theory of implied contract to the effect that since the basic work was 50 hours, he is entitled to pay for time over 50 hours per week at an hourly rate determined as previously mentioned. . . . Here the evidence shows an express contract, namely, a hiring at a monthly salary for a basic workweek of 50 hours but with the understanding that additional hours would be worked when de-

manded. The evidence negates any expectation by the plaintiff of additional pay for overtime or any intention on the part of the employer to pay overtime. It is the universal rule that there can be no implied contract where there is an express agreement between the parties relative to the same subject matter."

Quasi Contract, or Implied in Law Contract. A quasi contract is not really a contract at all, since there has been no agreement between the parties. Quasi contract is simply a remedy which the courts have developed to prevent *unjust enrichment.* It is an obligation implied by law rather than by the parties' conduct. In a quasi-contract situation one party receives a benefit that had been neither ordered nor requested. Still, the law will not allow one party to be unjustly enriched at the expense of the other party. Persons cannot use a quasi-contract lawsuit to recover for benefits which they voluntarily conferred on another party without that person's knowledge or consent, or for benefits conferred under conditions which justify the receiving party to believe that they were a gift. Any recovery made is based solely on the extent of the unjust enrichment to the receiving party and not necessarily the loss which the plaintiff suffered.

> *A remedy to recover for benefits conferred*

To recover on the basis of quasi contract, the plaintiff not only must show that the defendant has been "enriched," but also that the retention of the benefit by the defendant without compensation to the plaintiff would be "unjust." This means that there must be proof that the defendant is guilty of some misconduct, or fault, or undue advantage. Money paid by mistake must nearly always be returned, since the defendant can easily do so without harm or damage. On the other hand, if someone mows your lawn by mistake while you were not at home to tell them not to do so you have probably received a free mowing job. You don't have to pay for this "benefit," since you were in no way to blame for the other party's mistake, had no chance to prevent the mowing, and since the mowing service can't really be returned. (Try "un-mowing" a lawn sometime.)

Nature of Acceptance

> *A promise for a promise*

Bilateral Contract. In a bilateral contract, one person promises to do something in exchange for a promise from another person. Simply stated, a bilateral contract is a promise for a promise. An example of a bilateral contract would be a situation where Phil offers to sell his car to George for $1 million. George accepts the offer. Phil has promised to sell his car to George and George has promised to buy the car for the agreed price. Thus a promise to sell was exchanged for a promise to buy, and a bilateral contract was made.

> *A promise for an act or a forebearance*

Unilateral Contract. A unilateral contract is a contract in which a promise is made in exchange for an act or for refraining from an action. The promisor promises certain benefits if another person or persons will act in a certain way, or perhaps not do a certain act. At any rate, there is no contract until the requested act is performed or the forbearance occurs.

A good example of a unilateral contract would be the posting of a reward for a lost dog: "I will pay $50 to anyone who will return my lost dog." No contract exists until someone shows up with the dog in response to the offer. At that point, the offeror will have to give that person the promised amount in exchange for that person's handing over the dog.

An example of a unilateral contract where the promise is made in exchange for refraining from action would be a situation where Mr. Jones had expressed an interest in bidding on a certain item at an auction. Ms. Smith was aware of this and told Mr. Jones, "I will give you $100 if you refrain from bidding on that certain item." No promise was made by Mr. Jones. When the item came up for sale, Mr. Jones refrained from bidding. He accepted the offer of Ms. Smith by *not* bidding. This example also shows the important difference between unilateral and bilateral contracts. Since Mr. Jones made no *promise* not to bid, he was thus free to do so if he wished. Had he entered into a bilateral contract, he would have promised not to bid, and would have been legally bound not to do so.

Extent of Performance

Executed Contract. An executed contract is one wherein the obligations created by the contract have been fulfilled by the parties and nothing is left to be done. In other words, the case is closed.

Executory Contract.   In an executory contract something remains to be done. A contract can be wholly executory when there has been no performance at all yet, but each party has merely made a promise to the other. Or the contract can be partially executory when one party has performed partially or when one party has completely performed and the other has performed partially but still owes some additional performance.

Enforceability

Valid Contract.   A contract that contains all the necessary requirements for formation and enforcement is a valid contract.

Void Contract.   A void contract is not a legal contract. As the term *void* implies, the agreement which was bargained for is null and void without legal effect. A "contract" between a person and a hit man to murder someone for insurance benefits would be an example of a void contract because the contract lacks an essential element; namely, a lawful purpose. This point was raised in the famous *Marvin* case.

MARVIN v. MARVIN

557 P.2d 106 (California, 1976)

FACTS

Plaintiff (Michelle Triola "Marvin") alleges she and defendant (Lee Marvin) "entered into an oral agreement" that while "the parties lived together they would combine their efforts and earnings and would share equally any and all property accumulated as a result of their efforts whether individual or combined." Furthermore, they agreed to "hold themselves out to the general public as husband and wife" and that "plaintiff would further render her services as a companion, homemaker, housekeeper, and cook to . . . defendant."

Shortly thereafter plaintiff agreed to "give up her lucrative career as an entertainer and singer" in order to "devote her full time to defendant . . . as a companion, home-maker, housekeeper, and cook"; in return defendant agreed to "provide for all of plaintiff's financial support and needs for the rest of her life."

Plaintiff alleges that she lived with defendant from October of 1964 through May of 1970 and fulfilled her obligations under the agreement. During this period the parties, as a result of their efforts and earnings, acquired in defendant's name substantial real and personal property, including motion picture rights worth over $1 million. In May of 1970, however, defendant compelled plaintiff to leave his household. He continued to support plaintiff until November of 1971, but thereafter refused to provide further support.

Following extensive discovery and pretrial proceedings, the case came to trial. Defendant renewed his attack on the complaint by a motion to dismiss.

After hearing argument the court granted defendant's motion and entered judgment for defendant. Plaintiff appealed.

ISSUE   Is plaintiff prevented from trying to prove this alleged contract?

DECISION   No. Judgment reversed; case remanded for trial.

REASONS   Justice Tobriner knew he was dealing with a precedent-setting case, in an important area of social custom.

"Although the past decisions hover over the issue in the somewhat wispy form of a Chagall painting we can abstract from those decisions a clear and simple rule. The fact that a man and woman live together without marriage, and engage in a sexual relationship, does not in itself invalidate agreements between them relating to their earnings, property, or expenses. Neither is such an agreement invalid merely because the parties may have contemplated the creation or continuation of a nonmarital relationship when they entered into it. Agreements between nonmarital partners fail only to the extent that they rest upon a consideration of meretricious sexual services. Thus the rule asserted by defendant, that a contract fails if it is 'involved in' or made 'in contemplation' of a nonmarital relationship, cannot be reconciled with the decisions. . . .

"In summary, we base our opinion on the principle that adults who voluntarily live together and engage in sexual relations are nonetheless as competent as any other persons to contract respecting their earnings and property rights. Of course, they cannot lawfully contract to pay for the performance of sexual services, for such a contract is, in essence, an agreement for prostitution and unlawful for that reason. But they may agree to pool their earnings and to hold all property acquired during the relationship in accord with the law governing community property; conversely they may agree that each partner's earnings and the property acquired from those earnings remains the separate property of the earning partner. So long as the agreement does not rest upon illicit meretricious consideration, the parties may order their economic affairs as they choose, and no policy precludes the courts from enforcing such agreements. . . .

"We are aware that many young couples live together without the solemnization of marriage, in order to make sure that they can successfully later undertake marriage. This trial period, preliminary to marriage, serves as some assurance that the marriage will not subsequently end in dissolution to the harm of both parties. We are aware, as we have stated, of the pervasiveness of nonmarital relationships in other situations.

"The mores of the society have indeed changed so radically in regard to cohabitation that we cannot impose a standard based on alleged moral considerations that have apparently been so widely abandoned by so many. Lest we be misunderstood, however, we take this occasion to point out that the structure of society itself largely depends upon the institution of marriage, and nothing we have said in this opinion should be taken to derogate from that institution. The joining of the man and women in marriage is at once the most socially productive and individually fulfilling relationship that one can enjoy in the course of a lifetime. . . .

"Since we have determined that plaintiff's complaint states a cause of action for breach of an express contract, and, as we have explained, can be amended to state a cause of action independent of allegations of express contract, we must conclude that the trial court erred in granting defendant a judgment on the pleadings."

Voidable Contract. A contract can be classified as voidable when one or both of the parties has the legal right to terminate the obligation. If the promisor is a minor and decides to assert that minority to avoid the contract, then the minor's contract obligation will be avoided. If the party with the power to avoid liability chooses not to do so, however, the contract will be enforceable.

Unenforceable Contract. A contract can be unenforceable even though its formation was valid because it does not meet some specific statutory requirement.

Unenforceable oral contracts

For example, consider an oral contract for the sale of goods over $500. Under the Statute of Frauds, such a contract must be in writing or it will not be enforced. This is not to say that oral contracts for the sale of goods over $500 are illegal or void. It simply says that in case a party to that oral contract challenges its existence, the courts will not grant a remedy unless the party against whom enforcement is sought has signed a writing.

Another example of an unenforceable contract could occur when one of the parties did not perform. The statute of limitations may preclude the other party's claim for breach of contract. The statute of limitations requires that a lawsuit be filed within a prescribed time after the breach of contract occurs. If the party alleging a breach by the other party does not file a lawsuit in the prescribed time, the court will not enforce the contract. Other regulatory statutes, such as the bankruptcy act, also could affect enforceability.

The *Eriksen* case involves a new statute requiring a written contract. The statute was passed as a response to the *Marvin* case.

IN RE ESTATE OF ERIKSEN

337 N.W.2d 671 (Minnesota, 1983)

FACTS

Jorgen Eriksen and Pamela Potvin began living together in June 1977. They lived together in rented premises for about two years, and then decided to buy a home. Potvin had been paying her half of their living expenses by giving Eriksen a check, and they agreed that the new home would be owned and paid for by both of them. Since Potvin was still married, they decided to have the title to the home, and the mortgage, listed in Eriksen's name. That way, Potvin's husband would have no interest in the property and would not have to agree to the mortgage on it. Also, Potvin would not be a registered property owner and thereby lose her AFDC benefits. The home was purchased in early 1979. Potvin and her husband were divorced on January 8, 1981. Eriksen died on May 13, 1981. Potvin claimed a one-half interest in the home; Karen Wicklund, representing Eriksen's estate, says that the claim is barred by a Minnesota statute which requires "co-habitation agreements" on finances and property to be in writing. The probate court granted Potvin's claim. Estate of Eriksen appealed.

ISSUE   Was this contract for joint ownership of the house required to be in writing?

DECISION   No. Judgment affirmed.

REASONS   **Justice Wahl did not think that the statute applied.**

"The Minnesota legislature addressed this developing area of law when it enacted sections 513.075 and 513.076. Section 513.075 provides that a contract which deals with the property and financial relationship of an unwed, cohabiting man and woman will be enforced if it is written and if the parties seek to enforce it after the relationship ends. Conversely, section 513.076 provides that a trial court cannot hear claims by parties where there is no written contract if the consideration for the oral contract was, as in *Marvin,* the intimate relationship of the couple. Reading these statutes *in pari materia,* as did the probate court, and for the reasons stated below, we conclude that sections 513.075 and 513.076 were not intended to apply to the facts of this case where the claimant does not seek to assert any rights in the property of a cohabitant but to preserve and protect her own property, which she acquired for cash consideration wholly independent of any service contract related to cohabitation.

"As the probate court noted, Potvin's claim to one half of the home in this case is based on the agreement between Potvin and Eriksen to join in the purchase of a home. Although they lived together 'out of wedlock' and 'in contemplation of sexual relations,' their sexual relationship did not provide the sole consideration for the agreement. Each party contributed money equally toward the expenses of purchasing and maintaining the home, and each contributed equally to the premiums for the credit life insurance policy which ultimately paid $48,334.63 on the mortgage when Eriksen died. Potvin's claim is similar to the claim made by a joint venturer or partner, as the probate court noted in its memorandum. Sections 513.075 and 513.076 and the cases dealing with division of property between an unmarried cohabiting man and woman are not apropos. Those statutes will apply only where the *sole* consideration for a contract between cohabiting parties is their 'contemplation of sexual relations . . . out of wedlock.' They do not apply in this case. The probate court properly exercised jurisdiction. . . .

"Here, where Pamela Potvin contributed equally to the acquisition and maintenance of the home, and where she contributed equally to the premiums on the insurance which ultimately paid the mortgage after Eriksen's death, failure to award her one-half interest in the home would result in unjust enrichment of the estate."

■ **SIGNIFICANCE OF THIS CHAPTER**

This chapter set the foundation for further study of contracts in Chapters 10 through 18. A contract is defined as the total legal obligation which results from the parties' agreement as affected by the Uniform Commercial Code and by any other applicable rules of law. An agreement is defined as the bargain agreed upon by the parties. This chapter also outlined the basic requirements of a contract and defined the various classifications of contracts.

DISCUSSION CASE

TEXACO, INC. v. PENNZOIL CO.

729 S.W.2d 768 (Texas, 1987)

FACTS: This is an appeal from a Texas trial court's judgment in favor of Pennzoil for $7.53 billion in actual damages, plus $3 billion in punitive damages—by far the largest verdict ever. Texaco filed the lawsuit which appears in Chapter 2 to try to challenge the constitutionality of Texas' court procedures. While that case was working its way up through the U.S. courts, this case was being appealed in the Texas court system.

Pennzoil's claim, as indicated in the case in Chapter 2, was that Texaco had intentionally induced Getty stockholders, including the Getty Trust and the Getty Museum, to breach a contract which they had made with Pennzoil to sell their Getty Oil shares to Pennzoil. In order to prove its claim, Pennzoil had to prove that there was in fact a valid contract between it and the Getty Oil shareholders for the sale of their shares of stock. Along with several other defenses, Texaco asserted that there never was a valid contract, because the parties never reached a final agreement, and/or because they did not intend to be bound until a written contract had been signed, and/or because the contract was required to be in writing to be enforceable, and/or because the contract was based on mutual mistake, and/or because the contract would have been illegal and thus void under SEC Rule 10b-13 and under state laws regulating corporate directors, controlling stockholders, and trustees. The Texas trial court had rejected Texaco's defense arguments. What follows is the section of the Texas Court of Appeals' opinion which discusses the validity of the contract between the Getty Oil shareholders and Pennzoil.

■

Judge Warren gave the opinion:

The main questions for our determination are: (1) whether the evidence supports the jury's finding that there was a binding contract between the Getty entities and Pennzoil, and that Texaco knowingly induced a breach of such contract; (2) whether the trial court properly instructed the jury on the law pertinent to the case; (3) whether the evidence supported the jury's damage awards; (4) whether the trial court committed reversible error in its admission and exclusion of certain evidence; (5) whether the conduct and posture of the trial judge denied Texaco a fair trial;

and (6) whether the judgment violates certain articles of the United States Constitition. . . .

Validity of the Contract

Texaco's last contention regarding the sufficiency of the evidence is that Pennzoil failed to prove that the alleged contract was valid and enforceable, so there could be no interference. Texaco argues that the alleged contract would have violated SEC Rule 10b-13; that it would have violated state law governing fiduciary duties of directors, controlling stockholders, and trustees; that it would have been unenforceable because of mutual mistake; and that it would have violated the statute of frauds. . . .

We find that Texaco has waived its claim of mutual mistake . . . and insufficiency under the statute of frauds . . . because these affirmative defenses were not properly alleged in Texaco's amended trial pleadings. In its appellate brief, Texaco alleges generally that a mutual mistake about the possible tax treatment of the Museum's shares would have made the agreement unenforceable. Texaco's amended pleading alleges only a mistake by Pennzoil and Gordon Getty, and not one mutually shared by all the parties. There was also no request for a jury issue on the question of mistake, nor was the statute of frauds asserted in Texaco's operative pleadings. These contentions are waived, and Points of Error 55 and 56 are overruled.

Illegality as an affirmative defense is not limited to contracts prohibited by law, but also includes contracts rendered unenforceable because of some failure to comply with the law. . . .

Texaco contends that the alleged contract would have been void as violating SEC Rule 10b-13, which provides that once a party has publicly announced a tender offer, the offeror may not buy stock of the target company, except through the tender offer, for as long as the tender offer remains open. . . . Texaco alleges that any contract made in violation of the rule is void.

Texaco points out that even under Pennzoil's version of the facts, Pennzoil allegedly contracted to buy the Museum's shares immediately and the public shares later at $110 plus a $5 stub per share—a higher price than the $100 tender offer price—at a time when the tender offer was still open. Texaco claims that this constituted a per se violation of the rule, whether or not any shareholder received a special benefit from the purchase occurring outside the tender offer. But Texaco also argues that the Museum did receive a substantial benefit that the public shareholders did not, in that it was to have received payment for its shares "immediately," which could possibly have been months before the public shareholders would be paid. Texaco contends that this timing difference could have amounted to millions of dollars in interest, and it was exactly this kind of treatment favoring large shareholders that the SEC rule was designed to prevent. . . .

Although Texaco is not a party whom the rule is intended to protect in any way, it complains that Pennzoil's transaction violated the rule, was automatically void for that reason, and therefore could not give rise to an action for tortious interference. The express exemption provision of the rule negates the suggestion that any infraction of the rule automatically makes the transaction void. If the transaction is only voidable, Texaco has no standing to assert the rule, and we may not speculate on whether a proper party would have successfully asserted it. . . .

In any event, Pennzoil amended its SEC tender offer statement on January 4 to incorporate the information about its agreement with the Getty entities contained in the press release and to state that the tender offer at $100 would be withdrawn upon the execution of the definitive merger contract. Texaco's contention in Point of Error 51 that the alleged contract would have been void under rule 10b-13 is overruled.

Next, Texaco claims that the alleged contract would have violated Delaware state law governing the fiduciary duties of various parties. Texaco contends that agreeing to a contract that provided for the sale of Getty at a "bargain basement" price would have been a breach by Gordon Getty of his fiduciary duty as a controlling shareholder, and also a breach by the Getty Oil directors of their fiduciary duty to Getty stockholders.

Gordon Getty, as trustee, owned approximately 40.2 percent of the shares of Getty Oil. In addition to the fact that this does not constitute legal "control" of the corporation, the record does not support Texaco's implication that Gordon Getty had de facto control of Getty Oil, in spite of the Trust's large ownership percentage. On the contrary, the record evinces Gordon Getty's continual conflicts with the Getty Oil board of directors and management, which acted independently of and sometimes without the knowledge of Gordon Getty.

The jury found, in response to a special issue, that the agreed price was a fair price for the Getty shares. There was evidence that at the January 2 Getty Oil board meeting, the Trust and Museum had both been willing to sell at $110 or above. The Trust and the Museum had received opinions from their investment bankers that $110 plus the minimum $5 stub was a fair price. Prior to that board meeting, there had been discussions of having the company itself propose a self-tender to its shareholders at $110 per share to respond to Pennzoil's $100 tender offer.

Though the Getty entities eventually sold to Texaco at a higher price per share than they had agreed to accept from Pennzoil, that fact alone does not prove that selling to Pennzoil would have been a breach of fiduciary duty to the minority shareholders. There was evidence that public minority stockholders, with no direct claim to a company's assets, are primarily interested in the return on their investment in realizing a profit from the increase in market value of their shares. Pennzoil's price represented a significant premium over the previous trading price of Getty's shares.

The test of fairness in a merger situation is that a minority shareholder receives the substantial equivalent in value of what he had before. . . . Thus, the fairness of the price that the public minority shareholders received is not to be judged by the pro rata value of Getty's assets, as Texaco implies, but rather by the value of the shares in the hands of those minority shareholders, who had no direct right to the company's assets. In the two years before the Pennzoil agreement, Getty stock had traded at $83 per share or less, and the jury found that $110 plus the $5 stub was a fair price. Agreeing to sell to Pennzoil at this price did not constitute a breach of fiduciary duty to the minority shareholders.

Finally, Texaco argues that the Getty directors had an obligation to exercise informed business judgment and to maximize Getty Oil's sale value, based on the information available to them. It claims that agreeing to any implied no-shop provision or good faith obligation to complete negotiations with Pennzoil would have breached its duty to get the highest price possible for the Getty Oil shares. . . .

The evidence shows that the board made an informed decision to enter the agreement with Pennzoil. It had notice of other companies' interest, but there is some evidence that the board might have thought it more prudent to commit to a sure thing, rather than to speculate on whether other offers would eventually materialize. Getty's CEO was quoted in Fortune magazine some months later, "it was a bird-in-the-handish situation. We approved the deal but we didn't favor it." Once the agreement was made, Getty could not evade it, citing fiduciary duty, just because a higher offer came along. . . . Points of Error 52, 53, and 54 are overruled.

[Judgment for Pennzoil affirmed.]

■ IMPORTANT TERMS AND CONCEPTS

contract law
Uniform Commercial Code
Restatement of Contracts
agreement
sales of goods
Statute of Frauds
offer
acceptance
consideration
capacity
express contract
implied in fact contract

quasi contract
implied in law contract
bilateral contract
unilateral contract
executed contract
executory contract
valid contract
void agreement
voidable contract
unenforceable contract
unjust enrichment

■ QUESTIONS AND PROBLEMS FOR DISCUSSION

1. What is the difference between a void agreement and an unenforceable contract?
2. What is the difference between a voidable contract and an unenforceable contract?
3. What is the difference between an implied-in-fact contract and an implied-in-law contract?
4. What is the difference between a bilateral contract and a unilateral contract?
5. Helen has a doll collection, and she wants a Cabbage Patch doll to add to her collection. She tried to get one at the local stores, but they were sold out. Little Suzy, age nine, who lives next door, had a Cabbage Patch doll she got for Christmas. Helen offered Suzy $100 for her doll, and Suzy accepted. Suzy brought the doll to Helen and took the $100 bill. Suzy proudly told her parents about the sale, and they told her to get the doll back. Can Suzy get the doll back? Explain.
6. Plaintiffs operated a partnership which cleaned buildings by sandblasting. Defendant saw Communale, plaintiff's foreman, and three laborers at work on a job, and hired them to sandblast his swimming pool floor. For four or five hours' work, defendant paid Communale $80, which he split with the workmen. Plaintiffs got nothing, even though Communale used their equipment and sand. Communale testified that defendant told him not to tell his boss about this contract; but defendant testified that he thought Communale was the owner of the business and dealt with him in good faith on that basis. Plaintiffs claim that defendant owes them the full value of the job—$250. How much can plaintiffs collect from defendant? Explain.
7. Telly and Nellie Smith, husband and wife, sued Dumpy Department Stores for breach of contract. The Smiths had applied for, received, and used a credit card from Dumpy. Payments on their account were overdue, but the Smiths say that was because they had moved and their mail wasn't being forwarded properly. When Mrs. Smith tried to use her card to charge some merchandise, Dumpy's clerk took the card and refused to return it.

   Assuming that the Smiths' excuse about the late payments is valid, has Dumpy breached a contract for the use of the card? Discuss.
8. Anthony and Diane Hofstede contracted with Northland Homes for the construction of a home on a residential lot in Minneapolis. Northland Homes subcontracted plumbing work to Krunholz Plumbing, which in turn accepted a bid of $900 from Skjod to connect the water and sewer lines to the Hofstedes' residence. The Hofstedes had no contracts or communications with Skjod and no knowledge of any work performed by Skjod. Skjod's court claim against the Hofstedes alleges that Skjod installed water and sewer lines and "never received payment after complete performance of the contract," and that the Hofstedes were enjoying the benefits of Skjod's work. How should this case be decided?

10

Formation of the Agreement

CHAPTER OBJECTIVES

THIS CHAPTER WILL:

- Emphasize the consensual nature of contracts.
- Define an offer.
- Indicate the essential elements of an offer.
- Explain when and how an offer terminates.
- Explain when an acceptance takes effect so as to form a contract.
- Indicate the essential elements of an acceptance.
- Alert the reader to special cancellation rules.

Our basic contract formula may be stated as follows: **Contract = Agreement + Consideration.** That is, for promises to have legal consequences as contracts, there must be an agreement between the parties that they will have such consequences, and that agreement must involve an exchange of legally sufficient considerations, or values.

This chapter examines the "Agreement" part of the formula, which may be stated as a subformula: Agreement = Offer + Acceptance. To learn whether there was a contractual agreement, we will need to know the answers to three main questions: What is an "offer"? How long is an offer open for acceptance? What is an effective acceptance?

■ DEFINITION OF AN OFFER

Preliminary Negotiations Distinguished from Offers. Parties may engage in extended preliminary discussions before one of them finally makes a direct business proposition to the other. Buyers typically want to compare prices and payment terms, and therefore may request such information from several prospective sellers. Sellers may have only one or a limited number of items available, but they will contact a number of prospective buyers to see whether any of them is interested. Thus, a buyer who asks, "What will you take for your car?" is only seeking price information and is not making an offer to buy. Likewise, a would-be seller who responds, "$400," is only supplying the requested information and is not making an offer to sell at that price, to this buyer, or to anyone else.

The element that distinguishes an offer from such preliminary negotiations, the thing that makes it an offer, is a **promise** to do business. The promise may be stated expressly, in so many words ("I'll give you $400 for your car"), or it may be implied from the language used and the surrounding facts and circumstances. This promise gives the **offeree,** the person to whom the offer is made, the power to change the legal relationships between the parties by accepting the offer and forming a contract. Because, typically, price quotations and advertisements do not contain such promises, they are not considered to be offers. However, stores which advertise products for sale to the public are required by state **false advertising** statutes and by Federal Trade Commission regulations to have "reasonable quantities" of the advertised items available for sale. They can't, in other words, rely on the general contract law rule that "advertisements are not offers" without being liable for fines under the "false advertising" laws.

No promise = No offer

Identity of Offeree. Since, as a general rule, you have no legal duty to do business with anyone unless and until a contract is made, you can as an **offeror** specify the person or persons to whom your offer is made. You can make the offer to as many or as few persons as you wish, on whatever basis you wish. Today, however, an offeror's power to pick and choose the persons with whom to do business is subject to some important limitations by both state and national civil rights acts.

Offeror controls who offerees are

Not all types of contracts, or all potential offerors, or all possible bases of "discrimination" between offerees, are prohibited by these acts. Each such statute must be read carefully to see exactly what forms of discrimination are covered.

Usually it is illegal to discriminate on the basis of race, color, religion, sex, or national origin, for contracts involving employment, real estate purchase or rental, or places of "public accommodation." Employment discrimination is discussed further in Chapter 41.

Law professors and students everywhere should be grateful to Mr. Lefkowitz for having had the tenacity to litigate the following case to his state's supreme court. It is a classic illustration of the application of these first two points about "offers."

LEFKOWITZ v. GREAT MINNEAPOLIS SURPLUS STORE

86 N.W.2d 689 (Minnesota, 1957)

FACTS   On April 6, 1956, the defendant published the following advertisement in a Minneapolis newspaper:

> SATURDAY 9 A.M. SHARP
> 3 BRAND NEW
> FUR COATS
> Worth to $100.00
> First Come
> First Served
> $1
> EACH

On April 13, the defendant published a similar advertisement:

> SATURDAY 9 A.M.
> 2 BRAND NEW PASTEL
> MINK 3-SKIN SCARFS
> Selling for $89.50
> Out they go
> Saturday. Each . . . $1.00
> 1 BLACK LAPIN STOLE
> Beautiful,
> Worth $139.50 . . . $1.00
> FIRST COME
> FIRST SERVED

On each Saturday the plaintiff was the first to present himself at the appropriate counter in the defendant's store. On the first Saturday he demanded the advertised coat, and on the second Saturday he demanded the advertised stole. On both occasions he indicated his readiness to pay the sales price of $1, and on both occasions the defendant refused to sell the merchandise to the plaintiff, stating at the time of the plaintiff's first visit that by a "house rule" the offer was intended for women only and sales would not be made to men, and at the time of the second visit that the plaintiff knew the defendant's house rules. The defendant appealed the trial court's award of $138.50 damages.

ISSUE   Were the newspaper advertisements offers? If so, was Lefkowitz an intended offeree?

DECISION   Yes. Yes. Judgment affirmed.

REASONS

Justice Murphy first cited Professor Williston:

"The test of whether a binding obligation may originate in advertisements addressed to the general public is whether the facts show that some performance was promised in positive terms in return for something requested."

Justice Murphy then stated that "where the offer is clear, definite, and explicit, and leaves nothing open for negotiation, it constitutes an offer, acceptance of which will complete the contract. Whether in any individual instance a newspaper advertisement is an offer rather than an invitation to make an offer depends on the legal intention of the parties and the surrounding circumstances. We are of the view on the facts before us that the offer by the defendant of the sale of the Lapin fur was clear, definite, and explicit, and left nothing open for negotiation. The plaintiff having successfully managed to be the first one to appear at the seller's place of business to be served, as requested by the advertisement, and having offered the stated purchase price of the article, he was entitled to performance on the part of the defendant. We think the trial court was correct."

This case thus tells advertisers who only wish to consider offers from others to be very careful in their choice of words. Don't say "First come, first served" or "First $400 takes it away," or anything else from which a court can imply your promise to do business.

Communication to Offeree.   It's really no more than common sense to say that an offer has no legal effect as an offer until it has been communicated to the intended offeree or offerees. If I mail you a letter containing an offer, but then change my mind and get the letter back from the post office before it's delivered to you, no offer has been made. Even if you somehow learn what happened, there would be nothing for you to "accept." If the letter were on my desk waiting for my signature, and you or one of your agents happened to be in my office and read the letter without my having authorized you to do so, no offer would have been made to you. In other words, it's *my* offer, and it's not effective until I intend that it be effective.

Manner of Acceptance.   Also, since it's my offer, I determine the manner of acceptance; I tell you what you have to do to accept it. The required acceptance can be as ridiculous, as stupid, or as difficult as I choose to make it; if you want to accept, you must do so on whatever terms I specify. Of course, you are not obligated to accept my terms; you can propose your own terms or ignore the offer completely. Your counterproposal, however, does not create a contract; it is a counteroffer which has the effect of rejecting (and thus terminating) my original offer.

Return promise as acceptance

Where the offeror requests a return promise, that person has offered a ***bilateral contract***—a promise in return for a promise. If the offeree accepts by making the requested return promise, each party is then both a ***promisor*** making a promise and a ***promisee*** receiving a promise from the other party. In order for a bilateral contract to exist, then, both parties must be bound to perform, or neither is bound. Most contracts are bilateral in form. My offer to sell you a used book is really my promise to transfer ownership of the book to you if you promise to pay me the requested contract price.

Act as acceptance   If instead the offeror requests the performance of some act, the offer is for a ***unilateral contract.*** A newspaper ad that states: "I offer $100 reward for the return of my lost poodle, Fifi" is offering a unilateral contract. To accept, one would have to perform the requested act—bring the lost dog back to the owner. Promising to look for the dog would not be an acceptance in this case, because that is not what the offeror requested as the price of the promise. On the other hand, since no return promise has been made, no one is obliged to look for the dog, and there is no case for breach of contract if the dog is never returned.

(Reasonably) Definite Terms Necessary.   Courts do not require that exact agreement be reached on all points for a contract to be enforceable. Obviously, the more specific and complete the terms are, the less chance there is for misunderstanding and possible lawsuit. However, the courts are aware that parties very often intend agreements but do not bother to spell out the terms completely.

At some point, however, the "terms" become so vague and indefinite that a court can only hold that there was no contract made because the parties never really agreed on anything. Confronted with an employee's claim that he had been promised "some share of the profits" of the business, a Wisconsin court had to say that there was no way for it to enforce such a "promise," since it could not know what share the parties might have had in mind.

Definiteness under UCC   **UCC Special Rules for Goods.**   The UCC (Sections 2–204, 2–305, 2–306) has liberalized this requirement to some extent for sales of goods contracts, by permitting the parties to use "requirements" or "output" as quantity terms and to leave the price term open, that is, unspecified. Even here, however, there are limits. There must be a real promise, not just an illusory one, such as, "I promise to buy as much as I want to buy." To be enforceable, the promise must be definite enough to restrict the promisor's freedom of action if the offer is accepted.

Importance of intent   **Intent to Contract.**   In most cases where the parties have exchanged promises, there probably has been a real "meeting of the minds"; that is, each party intended a promise in the same way that it was understood by the other. Such a mutual understanding obviously forms the contractual agreement.

There are cases, however, where one of the parties claims that no contract was ever formed because he or she did not "intend" that the promise be taken seriously—that it have contractual effect. In such cases a court will not require the other party to prove an actual meeting of the minds; it is enough if the trier of fact is convinced that a reasonable person would have believed that the promise was seriously intended. What counts, in other words, is not what the promisor really intended but the impression that those words and actions created in the mind of the other party. If the "joke" was convincing enough to fool a reasonable person and if the other party was not aware of the joke when accepting the offer, there is a contract. (See the *LUCY* case at the end of this chapter.)

Signing unread documents   Another aspect of the intent to contract problem arises when one party claims that certain parts of a signed, written contract are not binding because he or she did not read the contract or did not understand it. Absent special facts, such as fraud or illiteracy, courts generally will not accept this argument. In general, the rule is that you are bound by what you sign—read or unread, understood or not understood.

■ DURATION AND TERMINATION OF OFFERS

Lapse of Time. Even though no specific termination date or length of time during which the offer will remain open is stated, the offer will not be open for acceptance forever. In such cases the offer will terminate at the expiration of a *"reasonable time."* What constitutes a reasonable time depends on the facts of the particular case, and litigations will result because one party claims to have accepted in time and the other party claims that the acceptance was too late because a reasonable time had already elapsed. Where an offer is made during a person-to-person conversation, either face-to-face or over the telephone, and nothing is stated about its being open for some period of time, the presumption is that the offer terminates when the conversation ends.

Reasonable time for acceptance

Where an offer states that it will terminate on a specific date, as in "This offer will end August 14, 1990," the day named is the last day on which an acceptance can occur. Unless facts and circumstances indicate otherwise, an acceptance which took legal effect any time on that date would form a contract. Where an offer was made by a retail store with regular business hours, it would normally have to be accepted during business hours, by the date specified in the offer. Actual communication of the acceptance to the retail store, within the specified time period, would also usually be necessary.

Where an offer sent by letter indicates that it will be open for a period of time, as in "This offer is good for 30 days," the time period normally begins to run as of the date of the writing, even though the letter is not received through the mails for several days. But if the offer says that the offeree has a certain period of time within which "to consider" or "to accept" it, the time period does not commence until the letter is delivered.

General rule: No consideration = Offer revocable

Revocability of Offers. In most cases, even though the offeror has stated that the offer will remain open for a period of time, the offeror has both the power and the right to revoke it if such a revocation takes legal effect prior to an acceptance. Since these so-called *continuing offers* are not supported by any value given by the offeree to the offeror, the offeror is not bound by his or her promise to keep the offer open. Usually, therefore, to be sure to have the promised 30 days to investigate and consider the offer, an offeree must "buy" the 30 days by forming a preliminary *option contract* with the offeror. An offeror who has received the agreed money or other value in exchange for his or her "30-day" promise is no longer free to revoke the offer without being liable for breach of the option contract. (Note that there is still no contract on the main offer; the offeree may decide, after thinking about the main offer for the 30 days, that he or she does not wish to do business after all.)

UCC exception: Firm offers by merchants for goods

For offers to buy or sell goods, the UCC (2–205) contains a special rule on revocability. If such an offer is made by a *merchant,* is in a signed writing, and by its terms gives assurance that it will remain open for some period of time, it is not revocable, even though nothing has been paid to the merchant to keep it open. The merchant is bound to keep the *firm offer* open for the time period stated, or for a reasonable time if the offer gives such assurance, but does not state a specific cutoff date. In no case is the merchant bound for more than three months under this rule. As defined in the UCC, a merchant is a dealer or other expert with respect to the type of goods involved in the contract.

Implied Revocation. If an offer is revocable, it may be revoked expressly or impliedly. ***Implied revocation*** occurs when the court feels that underlying facts and circumstances have changed to such an extent that the agreement contemplated by the parties can no longer be made. The death or insanity of either the offeror or the offeree, for instance, impliedly revokes any outstanding offers, because one of the intended parties no longer has the capacity to contract. Likewise, the destruction of the intended subject matter of the contract operates to terminate any unaccepted offers for its purchase or sale. A sale of the only item available does not, however, impliedly revoke an outstanding offer. In a situation where a seller-offeror sells an item to a third party, the offeror's first offer to Buyer 1 is not terminated unless and until Buyer 1 learns of the sale. If, in the meantime, Buyer 1 has effectively accepted the offer, the seller is bound to two contracts for the same item and will be guilty of breaching one of the contracts unless one of the buyers will accept a substitute.

Express Revocation. With an ***express revocation,*** the offeror's intent is usually clear enough: "I revoke"; "The deal's off"; "My offer is hereby canceled." The main problem in these cases is not whether the offeror meant to revoke but whether the offeror's revocation took legal effect before the offeree's acceptance. If a revocation takes legal effect before the intended acceptance, there is no contract, and the would-be acceptance is only a counteroffer. If an acceptance takes legal effect first, there is a contract, and the revocation is inoperative.

Communication of Revocation. Where the parties are dealing face-to-face or over the telephone, the jury or judge must determine, as a matter of fact, which party spoke the "magic words" first. Where the parties are communicating by letter or telegram, there is an additional complexity in the case because communications may cross each other in transit—a revocation and an acceptance may be in the mail at the same time. Many such problems are solved by applying two presumptions that courts have worked out as to when communications take legal effect: generally, a revocation is not effective until it is *received,* while an acceptance letter takes legal effect as soon as it is *mailed.* In general, a letter is received when the post office finishes handling it; that is, when the letter is delivered at the place a party has designated for receipt of such communications. If you have a mailbox on your front porch and you have left a letter of acceptance of my offer in the mailbox for the mail carrier to pick up, the jury will then have to decide whether the mail carrier dropped my letter of revocation in the mailbox first and then took out your letter of acceptance, or vice versa. In the first case, there is no contract; in the second case, there is a contract.

The UCC establishes a special ***rule for communications*** to an organization, for all types of contracts that it covers, such as sales of goods, secured transactions,

Revocation due to events

Timing of revocation

UCC rule for communciation

commercial paper, and investment securities. "Organization" includes businesses, such as partnerships and corporations, and also trusts, decedents' estates, and governmental agencies. Such organizations do not "receive" a notice or notification until it comes to the attention of the person who is conducting the transaction, or within the time when it would have come to that person's attention if the organization had a proper procedure for handling incoming communications. If you were negotiating a UCC contract with a large automobile company, for example, your notice would not be received when the post office delivered a sack of mail to the company. Your notice would be received when it actually reached the desk of the individual you were dealing with or when it should have reached that person if the company had a proper mail-handling system. This may not sound like a big difference, but it could be important. If that company executive mailed a letter accepting your offer to sell steel before your revocation letter got to the sender's desk, a contract would exist. Under prior law, and even now for non-UCC contracts, your letter of revocation would be presumed effective when received by the *company,* and your offer would terminate at that point.

Revocation of Offer of Unilateral Contract. There is one other conceptually difficult problem regarding revocations. This problem arises where the offeror has offered a unilateral contract. Suppose an offeree, intending to accept, has started to perform the requested act and is then notified by the offeror that the offer is revoked. There is no acceptance unless and until the offeree completes the performance requested, but shouldn't the offeree, in all fairness, be given the chance to finish? Courts disagree here; there are at least three rules. Some states, following the old common law, permit the offer to be withdrawn any time prior to complete performance of the requested act, on the basis that every offeree should know that this can happen in a unilateral contract situation. Most courts use a rule which says that an offeree's commencement of performance makes the offer irrevocable for a reasonable period of time, which gives the offeree a chance to finish the performance. If the offeree does render complete performance as requested, then the offeror must perform as promised. A few states go one step further and say that where an offeree has made substantial preparations to perform, the offeree must be given a chance to do so.

The following case illustrates the older common-law rule for unilateral contracts as well as the rules for revoking a "public" offer.

Attempted revocation after offeree starts to perform

SHUEY v. UNITED STATES

92 U.S. 73 (1875)

FACTS

Henry B. Ste. Marie sued in the U.S. Court of Claims to recover the sum of $15,000, the balance alleged to be due him of the reward of $25,000 offered in a proclamation by the secretary of war on April 20, 1865, for the apprehension of John H. Surratt, one of Booth's alleged accomplices in the murder of President Lincoln. The proclamation also promised that "liberal rewards will be paid for any information that shall conduce to the arrest of either of the above-named criminals or their accomplices." The proclamation was not limited in terms to any specific period, and it was signed "Edwin M.

Stanton, Secretary of War." On November 24, 1865, President Andrew Johnson published an order revoking the reward offered for the arrest of Surratt.

In April 1866, both Surratt and the claimant were Zouaves in the military service of the papal government. During that month the claimant communicated to Mr. King, the American minister at Rome, the fact that he had discovered and identified Surratt, who had confessed to him his participation in the assassination plot against President Lincoln. The claimant subsequently communicated further information to the same effect and kept watch over Surratt at the American minister's request. Thereupon, certain diplomatic correspondence passed between the government of the United States and the papal government regarding the arrest and extradition of Surratt; and on November 6, 1866, the papal government, at the request of the United States, ordered that Surratt, who was then at Veroli, be arrested and brought to Rome.

Surratt was arrested under this order of the papal government, but as he left the prison at Veroli he escaped from the guard who had him in custody and, crossing the frontier of the papal territory, embarked at Naples and escaped to Alexandria in Egypt. Immediately after Surratt's escape, and both before and after his embarkation at Naples, the American minister at Rome, having been informed of the escape by the papal government, took measures to rearrest him. This was done in Alexandria, from which he was conveyed by the American government to the United States. Before this departure the American minister, having procured the discharge of the claimant from the papal military service, sent the claimant to Alexandria to identify Surratt.

From the time of the claimant's first interview with the American minister until the final capture of Surratt, both the claimant and the American minister were ignorant of the fact that the reward offered by the secretary of war for Surratt's arrest had been revoked by President Johnson. The discovery and arrest of Surratt were due entirely to the claimant's disclosures to the American minister at Rome; but the arrests at Veroli and Alexandria were not made by the claimant.

Shuey, representing Ste. Marie's estate, appealed from a judgment for the U.S. government.

ISSUE   Had the government's offer been revoked before Ste. Marie accepted by performance?

DECISION   Yes. Judgment of the Court of Claims affirmed.

 REASONS   Justice Strong thought that, at most, Ste. Marie had earned the $10,000. Technically, not even that amount would be owed.

"We agree with the Court of Claims, that the service rendered by the plaintiff's testator was, not the apprehension of John H. Surratt, for which the War Department had offered a reward of $25,000, but giving information that conduced to the arrest. These are quite distinct things, though one may have been a consequence of the other. The proclamation of the Secretary of War treated them as different; and, while a reward of $25,000 was offered for the apprehension, the offer for information was only a 'liberal reward.' The findings of the Court of Claims also exhibit a clear distinction between making the arrest and giving the information that led to it. . . .

"But, if this were not so, the judgment given by the Court of Claims is correct. The offer of a reward for the apprehension of Surratt was revoked on the twenty-fourth day of November, 1865; and notice of the revocation was published. It is not to be doubted that the offer was revocable at any time before it was accepted, and before any thing had been done in reliance upon it. There was no contract until its terms were complied with. Like any other offer of a contract, it might, therefore, be withdrawn before rights had accrued under it; and it was withdrawn through the same channel in which it was made. The same notoriety was given to the revocation that was given to the offer; and the findings of fact do not show that any information was given by the claimant, or that he did any thing to entitle him to the reward offered, until five months after the offer had been withdrawn. True, it is found that then, and at all times until the arrest was actually made, he was ignorant of the withdrawal; but that is the immaterial fact. The offer of the reward not having been made to him directly, but by means of a published proclamation, he should have known that it could be revoked in the manner in which it was made."

Rejection or Counteroffer. A rejection by the offeree indicates that the offeree does not wish to do business at all. A counteroffer indicates that the offeree is willing to contract, but on terms different from those stated in the original offer. Either of these responses by an offeree operates to terminate the original offer; each of them takes legal effect when it is received by the offeror. A counteroffer gives the original offeror the power to form a contract on the basis of the new terms, by accepting the counteroffer. If the offeree inquires about the possibility of alternative terms but does not indicate an unwillingness to accept the terms offered, such an inquiry is not considered a rejection.

■ REQUIREMENTS FOR AN EFFECTIVE ACCEPTANCE

Mailbox rule for acceptance

When Effective. Like all other person-to-person communications, words of acceptance spoken during a conversation and heard at almost the same instant take legal effect immediately. As we have seen, most litigations arise where the parties have been negotiating by correspondence and their communications have crossed in transit.

As a convenient method of solving some of these problems, the courts have created the *mailbox rule,* which states that a letter of acceptance is effective when it is *mailed*. This has the effect of placing the risk of lost, delayed, or misdelivered communications on the offeror. The rule holds that there is a contract at the instant the letter is placed in the mailbox, even though the letter is delivered late or not delivered at all. The *Morrison* case shows one situation where the mailbox rule is important.

MORRISON v. THOELKE

155 So.2d 889 (Florida, 1963)

FACTS

The Thoelkes, owners of certain realty, sued to quiet title, specifically requesting that the Morrisons be enjoined from making any claim under a recorded contract for the sale of the subject realty. The Morrisons counterclaimed, seeking specific performance of the same contract and conveyance of the subject property to them. The lower court, after a hearing, entered a summary decree for the Thoelkes, and the Morrisons appeal.

On November 26, 1957, the Morrisons, as purchasers, executed a contract for the sale and purchase of the subject property and mailed the contract to the Thoelkes, who were in Texas. On November 27, 1957, the Thoelkes executed the contract and mailed it to the Morrisons' attorney in Florida. It was also undisputed that after mailing the contract, but prior to its receipt in Florida, the Thoelkes called the Morrisons' attorney and canceled and repudiated the execution and contract. Nonetheless, the Morrisons, upon receiving the contract, caused it to be recorded.

ISSUE   Was the sellers' revocation by telephone effective?

DECISION   No. Judgment for buyers; decree for sellers reversed.

REASONS   Judge Allen stated:

The question is whether a contract is complete and binding when a letter of acceptance is mailed, thus barring repudiation prior to delivery to the offeror, or when the letter of acceptance is received, thus permitting repudiation prior to receipt.

"The rule that a contract is complete upon deposit of the acceptance in the mails . . . had its origin, insofar as the common law is concerned, in *Adams* v. *Lindsell.*

"Examination of the decision in *Adams* v. *Lindsell* reveals three distinct factors deserving consideration. The first and most significant is the court's obvious concern with the necessity of drawing a line, with establishing some point at which a contract is deemed complete, and their equally obvious concern with the thought that if communication of each party's assent were necessary, the negotiations would be interminable. A second factor, again a practical one, was the court's apparent desire to limit but not overrule the decision in *Cooke* v. *Oxley,* 3 T.R. 653 (1790), that an offer was revocable at any time prior to acceptance. In application to contracts negotiated by mail, this latter rule would permit revocation even after unqualified assent unless the assent was deemed effective upon posting. Finally, having chosen a point at which negotiations would terminate and having effectively circumvented the inequities of *Cooke* v. *Oxley,* the court, apparently constrained to offer some theoretical justification for its decision, designated a mailed offer as 'continuing' and found a meeting of the minds upon the instant of posting assent. Significantly, the factor of the offeree's loss of control of his acceptance is not mentioned.

"A better explanation of the existing rule seems to be that in such cases the mailing of a letter has long been a customary and expected way of accepting the offer. It is ordinary business usage."

Insufficient postage or address

Exceptions to the Mailbox Rule.   There are several situations where a response intended as an acceptance is not effective when it is sent, but only if and when it is received. Perhaps the most obvious of these is the situation where the letter does not give the offeror's correct address or does not have sufficient postage to be delivered through regular postal procedures. Here the risk of misdelivery should be borne by the offeree and the letter is an effective acceptance only when it is delivered (if it is delivered at all).

Earlier rejection

Section 40 of the *Restatement of Contracts, Second,* also indicates that there is no mailbox presumption in effect where the offeree first sends a rejection communication and then tries to accept. The second communication is only a counteroffer unless it overtakes the earlier rejection and is received by the offeror before the rejection is received.

Offer requires receipt of acceptance

A third exception occurs when an offer specifies that the offeror must *receive* the offeree's acceptance communication before the acceptance is effective. The mailbox rule is only a presumption; it applies unless the offeror says otherwise.

For example, "We must have your acceptance in our main office by the close of business next Friday."

Fourth, there may be no mailbox rule where the offeree responds by using a communication means different from the means of communication that the offeror used for the offer. Generally, if the offeror did not specify the use of a particular means of communication, the offeree may use a different, but still reasonable means of communicating an acceptance, and have the acceptance effective when sent (e.g., offer by letter, acceptance-response by telegram). However, if the offeree uses another means of communication which the court feels is "unreasonable" and therefore not "intended" by the offeror, the acceptance is effective only if and when it is delivered (e.g., offer by letter, acceptance-response by carrier pigeon). Finally, if the offeror has specified *the one means* by which the acceptance must be communicated, a response by any other means is not an acceptance, but only a counteroffer. When you make an offer, you can specify exactly when and how acceptance is to occur.

Different and unreasonable means of communication

Nature of an Effective Acceptance

Three main problems arise regarding the nature of an effective acceptance. First, what happens when an offeree responds by saying that the offeree wants to do business but adds, deletes, or modifies one or more of the terms of the offer? Second, what happens when a seller-offeree responds to an order for goods by shipping "nonconforming" (different) goods? And third, when, if ever, does silence by an offeree constitute an effective acceptance?

Offeree Changes Terms. At common law, to be an effective acceptance, a response-communication must agree exactly with the terms of the offer; courts often say it must be a *mirror image* of the offer. This mirror image rule does not mean that the acceptance must literally restate all the terms of the offer, just that it must *agree* with all of them. Given the right set of facts, a response as simple as "OK" could be interpreted as an acceptance. What the rule does mean is that a response that changes one or more terms is most likely a counteroffer rather than an acceptance, so that no contract is formed when the response is sent. If, for example, an employer writes you a letter offering you a job starting June 1 and you reply, "I accept, but I can't start until June 20," at that point you do *not* have a job. You have simply made a counteroffer.

As applied by the courts, this rule meant that there was no contract on the buyer's terms in the very frequently occurring situation where the buyer-offeror sends the seller an order for goods and the seller responds with an acknowledgment/invoice form which contains additional or different terms. If the seller ships the goods and the buyer receives and uses them, there is a contract on the seller's terms. The buyer's use is an acceptance of the seller's counteroffer. If the buyer refused to accept the goods on those terms (e.g., "There are no warranties, express or implied"), there is no contract, and the seller will have to absorb the shipping charges. Dissatisfaction with these results led to a specific UCC provision, 2–207, to deal with this problem in the sale of goods situation.

UCC 2–207 first says that a response from the seller which indicates that the seller wants to do business is an acceptance, not a counteroffer, even though it contains terms "additional to or different from" those in the offer. The only way for the offeree (seller) to avoid this result is to make the acceptance *expressly*

Mirror image rule for acceptances

Different UCC rule for goods contracts

"conditional on assent to the additional or different terms"—in other words, to clearly make it a counteroffer.

Having thus created a contract for the sale of goods, the Code then proceeds to answer the question: On whose terms? The *UCC rule for goods* states: "The additional terms are to be construed as proposals for addition to the contract." In other words, they are *not* part of the contract unless they are specifically agreed to by the offeror; otherwise, there is a contract on the terms of the original offer. Where *both* parties are "merchants," the additional terms become part of the contract unless *(a)* the original offer said otherwise, or *(b)* they materially alter the original offer, or *(c)* the offeror objects to their inclusion within a reasonable time after the offeror has notice of them. Where the offeree-merchant has included such terms and the offeror-merchant has said nothing specific about their inclusion, the litigation will focus on whether or not the new terms "materially alter" the original offer. The *Leonard Pevar* case applies these rules.

LEONARD PEVAR CO. v. EVANS PRODUCTS CO.

524 F.Supp. 546 (Delaware, 1981).

FACTS   Marc Pevar asked several manufacturers for price quotes on the medium density overlay plywood which his company needed. Evans made the lowest quote, in a telephone conversation on October 12, 1977. Pevar claims that it called Evans back on October 14 and ordered the plywood. Evans admits getting the call, but denies that it accepted that order. Pevar later sent Evans a written purchase order for the plywood. This written order specified the price, quantity, and shipping instructions, but did not mention warranties or remedies for breach. On October 19, Evans sent Pevar a written acknowledgment of the order. Evans's form said that the contract was expressly conditional on Pevar's agreement to all its terms, including a disclaimer of most warranties and a limitation of remedies. Evans shipped the plywood, which was accepted and paid for by Pevar. Pevar later brought suit for breach of warranty; Evans claimed its acknowledgment form controlled the terms of the contract. Both parties moved for summary judgment.

ISSUE   Is the contract governed by the seller's acknowledgment form?

DECISION   No. No summary judgment. (There must be a trial on the facts.)

 REASONS   Chief Judge Latchum first disposed of the argument that the contract was unenforceable because it was for more than $500 worth of goods and was oral. Section 2–201 of the UCC makes such oral contracts enforceable between merchants if either one sends the other a written confirmation of the oral agreement. Pevar's purchase order complied with this section. Besides, neither party really disputes the existence of a contract; the argument is over what its terms are.

UCC Section 2–207 provides the rules for this case. "Section 2–207 was intended to eliminate the 'ribbon matching' or 'mirror' rule of common law, under which the terms of an acceptance or confirmation were required to be identical to the terms of the offer or oral agreement, respectively. . . . The drafters of the Code intended to preserve an agreement, as it was originally conceived by the parties, in the face of additional material terms included in standard forms exchanged by merchants in the normal course of dealings. . . . Section 2–207 recognizes that a buyer and seller can enter into a contract by one of three methods. First, the parties may agree orally and thereafter send confirmatory memoranda. . . . Second, the parties, without oral agreement, may exchange writings which do not contain identical terms, but nevertheless constitute a reasonable acceptance. . . . Third, the conduct of the parties may recognize the existence of a contract, despite the previous failure to agree orally or in writing. . . .

"Evans argues that by inserting the 'unless' proviso in the terms and conditions of acceptance of the acknowledgment, it effectively rejected and terminated Pevar's offer, and initiated a counteroffer; and when Pevar received and paid for the goods, it accepted the terms of the counteroffer. . . .

"The consequence of a clause conditioning acceptance on assent to the additional or different terms is that *as of the exchanged writings there is no contract*. Either party may at this point in their dealing walk away from the transaction or reach an express assent. . . . Without the express assent by the parties no contract is created pursuant to § 2–207(1). Nevertheless, the parties' conduct may create a contract pursuant to § 2–207(3). . . .

"In this case, the parties' conduct indicates that they recognized the existence of a contract. If this Court finds after trial that Pevar and Evans did not enter into an oral agreement, Section 2–207(3) will apply. The terms of the contract will include those terms in which Pevar's purchase order and Evans' acknowledgment agree. For those terms where the writings do not agree, the standardized 'gap filler' provisions of Article Two will provide the terms of the contract."

■ EXHIBIT 10–1
Formation of the Agreement

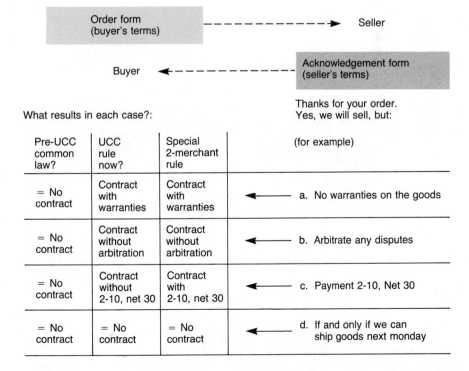

What is an effective acceptance?

What happens when an offeree changes the terms of the offer?

| Order form (buyer's terms) | | - - - - - - - - → | Seller |

| Buyer | ← - - - - - - - - | Acknowledgement form (seller's terms) |

Thanks for your order. Yes, we will sell, but:

What results in each case?:

Pre-UCC common law?	UCC rule now?	Special 2-merchant rule	(for example)
= No contract	Contract with warranties	Contract with warranties	← a. No warranties on the goods
= No contract	Contract without arbitration	Contract without arbitration	← b. Arbitrate any disputes
= No contract	Contract without 2-10, net 30	Contract with 2-10, net 30	← c. Payment 2-10, Net 30
= No contract	= No contract	= No contract	← d. If and only if we can ship goods next monday

Seller Ships Nonconforming Goods. Exactly the same sort of problem, with exactly the same results under the common-law rules, is presented by the seller who responds to an order by shipping goods which do not conform to the terms of the order. Buyers were frequently placed in a situation where they either had to accept the nonconforming goods and make whatever use they could of them, paying for any modifications out of their own pocket, or send the nonconforming goods back and sustain "shut-down-the-plant" losses. (Buyer orders blue widgets; seller ships green. If buyer uses green, buyer has accepted seller's counteroffer and there is a contract for *green*.)

UCC says nonconforming shipment = Acceptance

■ **EXHIBIT 10–2**
Formation of the Agreement

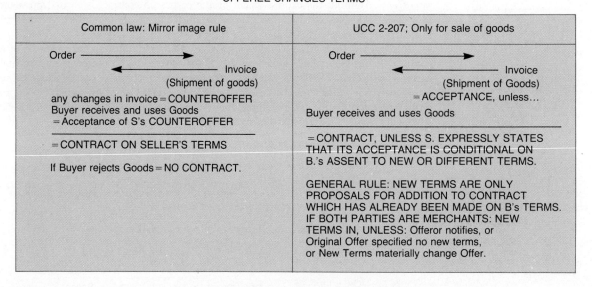

OFFEREE CHANGES TERMS

Common law: Mirror image rule	UCC 2-207; Only for sale of goods
Order ⟶ ⟵ Invoice (Shipment of goods) any changes in invoice = COUNTEROFFER Buyer receives and uses Goods = Acceptance of S's COUNTEROFFER = CONTRACT ON SELLER'S TERMS If Buyer rejects Goods = NO CONTRACT.	Order ⟶ ⟵ Invoice (Shipment of Goods) = ACCEPTANCE, unless… Buyer receives and uses Goods = CONTRACT, UNLESS S. EXPRESSLY STATES THAT ITS ACCEPTANCE IS CONDITIONAL ON B.'s ASSENT TO NEW OR DIFFERENT TERMS. GENERAL RULE: NEW TERMS ARE ONLY PROPOSALS FOR ADDITION TO CONTRACT WHICH HAS ALREADY BEEN MADE ON B's TERMS. IF BOTH PARTIES ARE MERCHANTS: NEW TERMS IN, UNLESS: Offeror notifies, or Original Offer specified no new terms, or New Terms materially change Offer.

SELLER SHIPS NONCONFORMING GOODS

Common law	UCC 2-206-1(b)
Order (BLUE widgets) ⟶ ⟵ Ships GREEN = COUNTEROFFER: "GREEN" Buyer receives and uses Goods = ACCEPTANCE OF S' COUNTEROFFER = CONTRACT FOR GREEN; SELLER HAS NOT BREACHED, BUYER GETS NO DAMAGES. or- Buyer rejects Goods; no contract ever existed; no breach by Seller, Buyer gets no damages	Order (BLUE widgets) ⟶ ⟵ Ships GREEN = ACCEPTANCE: "BLUE", UNLESS = CONTRACT FOR BLUE, WHICH SELLER HAS BREACHED, UNLESS S. NOTIFIES BUYER THAT GOODS OFFERED FOR ACCOMODATION.

The UCC also has a specific provision, 2–206(1)(b), to deal with this sale of goods problem. The new Code rule states that even a shipment of nonconforming goods by the seller, in response to an order, is to be interpreted as an acceptance rather than a counteroffer. (Under the Code, in the example above, there is a contract for *blue* widgets and the seller has breached this contract and is liable for damages unless the seller sends blue widgets to the buyer within the time permitted by the contract.) The buyer is protected; whether the buyer uses the nonconforming goods or rejects them and buys elsewhere, the buyer can still collect whatever damages are sustained.

Silence as Acceptance.   Since, normally, an offeree has no duty to respond to an offer, the offeree's failure to respond cannot be given any particular legal significance. The offeree's silence is therefore not effective as an acceptance in most cases. The common law did, however, recognize four exceptions to this general rule.

Exceptions, where silence is acceptance

First, where an offeree has the opportunity to reject offered services but instead takes the benefit of them, the offeree's silence does imply an acceptance. By permitting the offeror to perform services which a reasonable person should have known were not being offered for nothing, the offeree has impliedly agreed to pay a fair market price for them.

Second, where the offeror has told the offeree that he or she can accept the offer by not saying or doing anything, just by remaining silent, and the offeree *actually* does intend his or her silence to have that effect, it does.

Third, where because of previous dealings, such as a standing order with a book or record club, the offeree has indicated to the offeror that nonnotification by the offeree means that the standing order should be continued, the offeree's silence has the effect of continuing the standing order.

Finally, where nonordered merchandise is sent to the offeree and the offeree exercises "dominion" over it, this dominion has the effect of an acceptance and an implied promise to pay the offered contract price. An example would be reading an unordered book or magazine, or giving it to someone else.

Statutory changes

The second and fourth rules have not been substantially changed because nearly all states have **unordered goods statutes.** These laws vary; the strongest ones make such unsolicited goods an absolute, out-and-out gift to the recipient, who has no obligation to return them, to pay for them, or to account for them in any way.

■ SPECIAL "CANCELLA-TION" RULES

At the point where the agreement had been formed by offer and acceptance (and assuming an exchange of legally sufficient considerations), the common-law analysis would have said there was a binding contract. This result still occurs in the vast majority of contract situations. However there is a growing trend under new statutes and regulations to give the consumer/buyer a "cancellation" privilege for at least a limited period of time, even after the contract has been entered into.

FTC Home solicitation rule

For example, FTC regulations and statutes in several states give the consumer a three-day cancellation option where the contract is entered into in the consumers' home and is for more than a specified minimum amount. Each of these

National statutes

new laws is likely to contain some exceptions; life insurance sales and emergency home repairs may not be covered, for instance.

The *U.S. Truth-in-Lending Act* gives a similar three-day rescission option where the borrower's residence has been used as security for a loan, except for the first mortgage to finance the original purchase of the house. The National Interstate Land Sales Act gives a buyer 48 hours to revoke a purchase of land where the buyer has not been given the required "property report" on the land. Many of the states have separate laws covering these same general areas.

UCCC

If the proposed Uniform Consumer Credit Code *(UCCC)* is widely adopted by the states, it will cover more transactions than any of the above examples; its three-day cancellation privilege applies to any consumer transaction for goods *or* services, with no dollar minimum, where the sale is made in the buyer's home, or where the home is used as collateral (other than in the original purchase of the home). The UCCC has not yet been widely adopted.

For consumer transactions, at least, it appears that we will have to ask this fourth question about many agreements in the very near future.

■ SIGNIFICANCE OF THIS CHAPTER

Whenever a claim for breach of contract is asserted, the other party may argue that no agreement was ever reached and thus there was no duty to perform. As we have seen, this "no agreement" argument may be made as to the entire alleged contract or only as to paritcular terms. When this argument is presented, the claimant must prove that an offer had been made and that it was accepted while still open for acceptance. Failure to prove any of these points means that there was no contract and, therefore, no breach and no liability.

Typically, actual cases will involve other defense arguments along with "no agreement." For discussion purposes in the remaining contracts chapters, we will assume that an agreement did exist.

The next chapter will discuss the second part of our contract formula: the requirement that the parties' agreement provides for an exchange of values or that it involves one of the recognized alternate bases for enforcement.

DISCUSSION CASE

LUCY v. ZEHMER
84 S.E.2d 516 (Virginia, 1954)

FACTS: W. O. Lucy and J. C. Lucy sued A. H. Zehmer and Ida S. Zehmer, his wife, to have specific performance of a contract by which the Zehmers were alleged to have sold to W. O. Lucy, a tract of land known as the Ferguson Farm for $50,000. J. C. Lucy, the other complainant, was a brother of W. O. Lucy, to whom W. O. Lucy had transferred a half interest in his alleged purchase.

■

Justice Buchanan gave the opinion for the court:

The instrument sought to be enforced was written by A. H. Zehmer on December 20, 1952, in these words: "We hereby agree to sell to W. O. Lucy the Ferguson Farm complete for $50,000.00, title satisfactory to buyer," and signed by the defendants, A. H. Zehmer and Ida S. Zehmer.

The answer of A. H. Zehmer admitted that at the time mentioned W. O. Lucy offered him $50,000 cash for the farm, but that Zehmer considered that the offer was made in jest; that so thinking, and both he and Lucy having had several drinks, he wrote out "the memorandum" quoted above and induced his wife to sign it; that he did not deliver the memorandum to Lucy, but that Lucy picked it up, read it, put it in his pocket, attempted to offer Zehmer $5 to bind the bargain, which Zehmer refused to accept, and realizing for the first time that Lucy was serious, Zehmer assured him that he had no intention of selling the farm and that the whole matter was a joke. Lucy left the premises insisting that he had purchased the farm. . . .

In his testimony Zehmer claimed that he "was high as a Georgia pine," and that the transaction "was just a bunch of two doggoned drunks bluffing to see who could talk the biggest and say the most." That claim is inconsistent with his attempt to testify in great detail as to what was said and what was done. It is contradicted by other evidence as to the condition of both parties, and rendered of no weight by the testimony of his wife that when Lucy left the restaurant she suggested that Zehmer drive him home. The record is convincing that Zehmer was not intoxicated to the extent of being unable to comprehend the nature and consequences of the instrument he executed, and hence that instrument is not to be invalidated on that ground. It was in fact conceded by defendants' counsel in oral argument that under the evidence Zehmer was not too drunk to make a valid contract.

The appearance of the contract; the fact that it was under discussion for 40 minutes or more before it was signed; Lucy's objection to the first draft because it was written in the singular, and he wanted Mrs. Zehmer to sign it also; the rewriting to meet that objection and the signing by Mrs. Zehmer, the discussion of what was to be included in the sale, the provision for the examination of the title, the completeness of the instrument that was executed, the taking possession of it by Lucy with no request or suggestion by either of the defendants that he give it back, are facts which furnish persuasive evidence that the execution of the contract was a serious business transaction rather than a casual, jesting matter as defendants now contend.

Not only did Lucy actually believe, but the evidence shows he was warranted in believing, that the contract represented a serious business transaction and a good faith sale and purchase of the farm.

In the field of contracts, as generally elsewhere, "We must look to the outward expression of a person as manifesting his intention rather than to his secret and unexpressed intention. The law imputes to a person an intention corresponding to the reasonable meaning of his words and acts." At no time prior to the execution of the contract had Zehmer indicated to Lucy by word or act that he was not in earnest about selling the farm. They had argued about it and discussed its terms, as Zehmer admitted, for a long time. Lucy testified that if there was any jesting, it was about paying $50,000 that night.

The mental assent of the parties is not requisite for the formation of a contract. If the words or other acts of one of the parties have but one reasonable meaning, his undisclosed intention is immaterial except when an unreasonable meaning which he attaches to his manifestations is known to the other party.

An agreement or mutual assent is of course essential to a valid contract, but the law imputes to a person an intention corresponding to the reasonable meaning of his words and acts. If his words and acts, judged by a reasonable standard, manifest an intention to agree, it is immaterial what may be the real but unexpressed state of his mind.

So a person cannot set up that he was merely jesting when his conduct and words would warrant a reasonable person in believing that he intended a real agreement.

Whether the writing signed by the defendants and now sought to be enforced by the complainants was the result of a serious offer by Lucy and a serious acceptance by the defendants, or was a serious offer by Lucy and an acceptance in secret jest by the defendants, in either event it constituted a binding contract of sale between the parties.

■ IMPORTANT TERMS AND CONCEPTS

contract	acceptance	false advertising	unilateral contract
agreement	preliminary negotiations	promise	definite terms
consideration	offeror	identity of offeree	UCC special rules for
offer	offeree	communication to offeree	goods
		manner of acceptance	intent to contract
		bilateral contract	duration of offer

reasonable time for offer
revocation of offer
continuing offer
option contract
firm offer for goods
merchant of goods
implied revocation
express revocation
communication of
    revocation
UCC rule for
    communication
revocation of unilateral
    contract offer
rejection

counteroffer
mailbox rule
exceptions to mailbox rule
mirror image rule
offeree changes terms
UCC rule for goods
seller ships nonconforming
    goods
silence as acceptance
unordered goods statutes
special cancellation rules
FTC home solicitation rule
U.S. Truth-in-Lending Act
UCCC

■ QUESTIONS AND PROBLEMS FOR DISCUSSION

1. What is the meaning and significance of the "mailbox rule"?
2. What is the difference between a firm offer and continuing offer?
3. When can the offer of a unilateral contract be revoked?
4. When is an offeree's silence in response to an offer an effective acceptance of that offer?
5. Reinhold Miller leased a building from George Bloomberg. The lease contained the following provision: "At any time during the original term of the lease or any extension thereof, lessee shall have the option to purchase the premises for the then prevailing market price." After three years of occupancy Reinhold notified his landlord of his intention to exercise the option. Both parties ordered an appraisal of the property. After receiving the appraisal report of the landlord, Reinhold offered $80,000 for the property. The offer was rejected, and Reinhold sued George Bloomberg for specific performance. What arguments can George use, and who will win?
6. Henna and Gertrude rented a house while they attended business school at Barely Normal College.

There was room to park six cars on the property, so they decided to rent out the five extra spaces. They rented four spaces for $20 a month each. Lola and Bertram both wanted the last available space. Henna and Gertrude told Lola she could have the space for $30 a month. The next day, Lola sent them a check for $25, saying that's all she'd pay per month. Henna and Gertrude returned Lola's check and rented the space to Bertram for $30 a month. Lola has been unable to find another suitable parking space and now sues for specific performance. What is the result, and why?

7. Compo, Inc., mailed out an advertising circular to a large number of businesses. The circular was mailed in August and was headlined "Christmas comes early at Compo." It described a list of premiums that could be selected, based on the size of an order. Deal 25E gave the customer a new LeCount convertible and 50 Dazzo cameras for only $1,000 extra with an order of $500,000 or more. The Piggie Bank ordered over $500,000 worth of computers and software and indicated that it wanted Deal 25E. Compo telephoned Piggie and told them that their order was refused. Piggie bought their computers elsewhere and now sues Compo for damages. What is the result, and why?

8. As a special attraction at the 1988 annual Labor Day Golf Tournament, sponsored by the Ritzy Country Club of Smalltown, Frederick Fender, the local Buick dealer, offered a brand-new Buick to "the first entry who shoots a hole in one on the eighth hole." The golf course of the Ritzy Country Club had only 9 holes, but it could be played as an 18-hole course by going around it twice. Each hole thus carried two numbers, and hole 8 was also marked as hole 17. Archibald Green scored his hole in one on hole 8 on the first day of the tournament while playing from the 17th tee in an 18-hole match. When he claimed his prize, Frederick Fender refused to give it to him. Who wins in a suit by Archibald against Frederick? Explain.

11

Consideration

CHAPTER OBJECTIVES

THIS CHAPTER WILL:

- Define the term *consideration*.
- Discuss the four methods of complying with the consideration requirement.
- Explain the various types of exchanges which do not provide a legally sufficient consideration.

This chapter is concerned with the second part of our contract "formula"—the requirement of "consideration." Once again, we need to know the answers to three main questions: What does the law mean by consideration? What are the basic methods of complying with this requirement? What do the courts accept as legally sufficient consideration?

We will use Uncle Ned and his nephew Johnny to provide some factually simple hypothetical examples of how the consideration rules work.

■ DEFINITION OF THE CONSIDERATION REQUIREMENT

General rule: No exchange = No contract

Basic Definitions.   In our legal system a promise is generally not enforceable as a contract, even if it is agreed to by the promisee, unless the promise is supported by legally sufficient *consideration.* In other words, a completely one-sided promise of benefits (a promise of "something for nothing") does not generally bind the *promisor* to performance or make the promisor liable in the event of nonperformance. If Uncle Ned promises to give Johnny $5,000 as a Christmas present and then changes his mind, Johnny cannot sue and collect the $5,000, even if the promise was written and signed or was made in front of witnesses. The consideration requirement, most simply stated, means that unless *something* is given in return for the promise, the promise is not legally enforceable.

From whom, to whom consideration passes

Source and Recipient of Consideration.   The required consideration may be supplied by the *promisee* or by a third person. Uncle Ned would be contractually obligated if he had promised Johnny the $5,000 in return for a house-painting job and Johnny saw to it that the job was done, whether or not Johnny did the work. When Uncle Ned gets his house painted according to the terms of the agreement, he owes Johnny the $5,000. (See Exhibit 11–1).

Likewise, the benefits given in return for the promise may be given to the promisor or to a third person. If Uncle Ned promised the $5,000 to Johnny if Johnny would paint H. O. Moaner's house, he is bound to pay the money if Johnny does the job. Even if no one receives anything that most people would think of as a "benefit," there is legally sufficient consideration if the promisee has assumed a *burden,* by doing something which he or she was not already legally bound to do. If Uncle Ned promises the $5,000 to Johnny if Johnny stops smoking until age 21, and Johnny does so, Uncle Ned is legally obligated to pay the money. In each of these last two examples, Uncle Ned has received a *legal* benefit, in the sense that he got the performance he bargained for as the price for his promise, and he has therefore received consideration.

■ COMPLIANCE WITH THE CONSIDERATION REQUIREMENT

There are four ways in which the consideration requirement may be satisfied, so that the promisor is legally bound to perform his or her promise: (1) a bargained-for exchange of values; (2) a change of legal position by the promisee in reliance on the promise; (3) the seal; or (4) a statutory exception to the requirement. In each of the last three cases, the promise is enforced even though there was no exchange or bargain in the usual sense.

■ EXHIBIT 11–1
Consideration

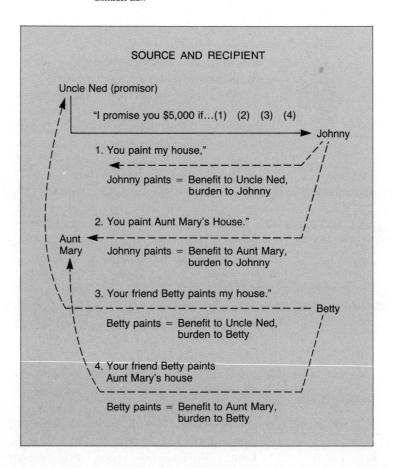

SOURCE AND RECIPIENT

Uncle Ned (promisor)

"I promise you $5,000 if…(1) (2) (3) (4)

→ Johnny

1. You paint my house,"

Johnny paints = Benefit to Uncle Ned,
burden to Johnny

2. You paint Aunt Mary's House."

Aunt
Mary

Johnny paints = Benefit to Aunt Mary,
burden to Johnny

3. Your friend Betty paints my house."

Betty

Betty paints = Benefit to Uncle Ned,
burden to Betty

4. Your friend Betty paints
Aunt Mary's house

Betty paints = Benefit to Aunt Mary,
burden to Betty

Bargained-For Exchange of Values

The basic meaning of the consideration requirement is that there must be a "bargain" for there to be a contract; promises to make gifts, with nothing given in return, are not legally enforceable. The usual method of complying with the consideration requirement, therefore, is to prove the existence of a bargain, to prove that something *was* given or promised in return. Since the law generally does not concern itself with whether the bargain was a good one or a bad one, but only with the question of whether there was in fact a bargain, the promisee should be able to enforce the promise by showing that there was an agreement for any sort of exchange of benefits.

In most cases the existence or nonexistence of a bargain can be seen pretty clearly, but the facts are somewhat ambiguous in a few situations. One of the most difficult distinctions to draw is that between a condition attached to the promise of a gift (no contract) and a burden undertaken as part of a bargain (contract).

Suppose that Uncle Ned says to Johnny, "Come over to the house Saturday night, and I'll fix you a steak dinner." Is Uncle Ned contractually obligated to provide a steak dinner when Johnny arrives as requested? No, he's not—for two reasons. First, Uncle Ned's promise is not intended by him, or reasonably understood by Johnny, as a contractual arrangement. Second, "coming over to the house" is neither intended nor understood as the price of the steak dinner.

Exchange versus gift on condition

Something done in return for promised benefit

What about the case where Uncle Ned tells Johnny, "When you get married, I'll give you $5,000," and Johnny does in fact get married? Whether Johnny's marriage supplies consideration for Uncle Ned's promise depends on the parties' intent, as derived by the court from the surrounding facts and circumstances. If Johnny already had his wedding planned and the date set and Uncle Ned was just making a promise of a cash wedding gift, there is probably no consideration for the promise and thus no contract. But if Uncle Ned is trying to induce Johnny away from life as a "swinging single," the initiative for the marriage comes from *Uncle Ned* rather than Johnny, and Johnny in response to the promise does as his uncle requests and gets married, Uncle Ned is contractually bound to pay the money. (Such a promise would probably have to be made in a signed writing to be enforceable.)

In the next case example, it appears that Mr. Pitts may have provided some benefits to the company, but was unable to show any *agreement* for an *exchange* of benefits.

PITTS v. McGRAW-EDISON COMPANY

329 F.2d 412 (U.S. Sixth Circuit, 1964)

FACTS

Plaintiff was a manufacturer's representative in Memphis, Tennessee, for a period of many years prior to July 1, 1955. For approximately 25 years preceding that date, he sold the products of the defendant, McGraw-Edison Company, on a commission basis in an assigned territory comprising several southern states. In his capacity as a manfuacturer's representative he was an independent businessman, hiring and firing his own employees, paying his own expenses and overhead, and managing his business as he saw fit. He had no written contract with the defendant, and the defendant had no obligation to him except to compensate him on a commission basis for sales made in the assigned territory. It was terminable at will, without notice, by either party at any time. The plaintiff was free to handle any other products he desired, including those of competitors of the defendant, and he did so until early in 1954, when on his own volition and without any requirement by the defendant, he discontinued his representation of other manufacturers.

In April 1955, when the plaintiff was approximately 67 years of age, he accompanied O. Dee Harrison, the sales manager for the defendant, to Little Rock, Arkansas, for a meeting with one Paul Thurman, who had formerly worked for the plaintiff but at the time was working in the State of Arkansas as a factory representative for the defendant and others. At that meeting Mr. Harrison told the plaintiff that the defendant was making arrangements for the plaintiff to retire at a time shortly thereafter and for Thurman to take over the plaintiff's territory, with the plaintiff receiving an overwrite commission of 1 percent from the defendant on all sales made in the territory. Thereafter the plaintiff received a letter dated July 1, 1955, from O. Dee Harrison, reading in part as follows:

Dear Lou:

Whether you know it or not, you are on retirement effective July 1st. But to make the matter of retirement a little less distasteful, we are going ahead as you and I talked last time we were together by paying each month 1 percent of the . . . sales from the Mississippi and Tennessee states. You will get your check each month just as you have been in the habit of getting our check on commissions. Let us hope that there is enough to help keep a few pork chops on the table and a few biscuits in the oven.

We are going to keep you on the list for bulletins, Lou, so that you will know what is going on. I know that you will help Paul in every way that you can, and I know that your help will be greatly appreciated by Paul.

A letter dated July 20 also said:

We will keep you on the mailing list and any time you can throw a little weight our way we will appreciate any effort you make, Lou. And any time you have any questions, don't be afraid to ask us about them.

The plaintiff received a check from the defendant each month regularly from July 1955 through June 1960 covering the 1 percent commission on sales in the specified territory.

On July 23, 1960, the defendant sent a letter reading in part as follows:

Dear Mr. Pitts:

I am enclosing our check #50064752 for $238.51 which, according to our records, completes the five-year series of payments to be paid after your retirement from the Company.

Pitts sued for $15,000 damages. Following a trial to the court without a jury, the District Judge held that the plaintiff was not entitled to recover any amount whatever and dismissed his complaint.

ISSUE

Had Pitts promised or provided any benefits to the company *in exchange for* the 1% commission?

DECISION

No. Judgment affirmed.

REASONS

Circuit Judge Miller did not think the parties had ever bargained out an agreed exchange.

"Plaintiff contends that the negotiations between the Company and him leading to his retirement were in substance an offer on the part of the Company that if he would retire as a manufacturer's representative on July 1, 1955 and turn over to his successor representative all of his customer account records containing valuable information on active and inactive accounts, which had been built up over a period of 20 years or more, the Company would pay him monthly thereafter a 1 percent overwrite commission on sales by the defendant in the territory which was at that time allotted to him; that after considering the offer, he accepted it and thereafter carried it out by retiring as a manufacturer's representative and turning over to his successor the stipulated records; and that the defendant breached the contract by refusing to make the payments after July 1, 1960. . . .

"Assuming, without so holding, that there was a promise by the defendant to pay the plaintiff the retirement benefits claimed, we are faced with the question of what consideration passed from the plaintiff to the defendant to make this promise enforceable.

"Plaintiff vigorously argues that although he did not *promise* to do anything or to refrain from doing anything, as plainly appears from the two letters, and so conceded by him, consideration nevertheless exists because of the action taken by him at the request of the defendant, namely, his retirement as a manufacturer's representative, including other manufacturers as well as the defendant, and his turning over to the defendant his personal records, pertaining to customers and sales over a period of years in the past. There would be merit in this contention if it was supported by the facts. . . .

"However, these factual contentions of the plaintiff were disputed by the evidence of the defendant. The District Judge made findings of fact that the plaintiff was not required by the terms of the letters, or by any other statements on the part of the defendant, or its agents, to do anything whatsoever; that upon his retirement of July 1, 1955, the plaintiff was free to handle the products of any other manufacturer or competitor if he so desired, to seek other employment, or to do as he pleased; that nothing in the arrangement circumscribed the plaintiff's actions or rights in any manner;

and that the plaintiff was not obligated to perform any duties on behalf of the defendant. These findings are fully supported by the evidence. In fact, they were substantially conceded by the plaintiff in the cross-examination of him as a witness, in which he apparently contended that he did certain things for the defendant after his retirement although he was not required to do so.

"On the basis of these facts, the District Judge ruled that the payments to the plaintiff over the period of July 1, 1955, to July 1, 1960, were without consideration, were the result of voluntary action on the part of the defendant, and were mere gratuities terminable by the defendant at will."

Change of Position in Reliance

Promise which induces action in reliance

Most courts today accept the rule stated in Section 90 of the *Restatement of the Law of Contracts, Second:* "A promise which the promisor should reasonably expect to induce action or forbearance of a definite and substantial character on the part of the promisee or a third person, and which does induce such action or forbearance is binding if injustice can be avoided only by enforcement of the promise." In other words, where the promisee, reasonably relying on the promise of benefits, makes a substantial change in his or her legal position, a court will estop (prevent) the promisor from using the "no consideration" argument when he or she is sued on the promise. The courts usually refer to this concept as ***promissory estoppel.***

■ **EXHIBIT 11–2**
The Consideration Element in a Litigation

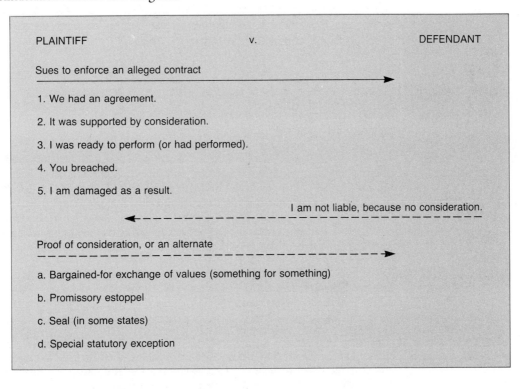

PLAINTIFF   v.   DEFENDANT

Sues to enforce an alleged contract ⟶

1. We had an agreement.

2. It was supported by consideration.

3. I was ready to perform (or had performed).

4. You breached.

5. I am damaged as a result.

                          I am not liable, because no consideration.
⟵ –

Proof of consideration, or an alternate
– ⟶

a. Bargained-for exchange of values (something for something)

b. Promissory estoppel

c. Seal (in some states)

d. Special statutory exception

If, when Uncle Ned makes his promise of a $5,000 gift, Johnny goes out and buys a new car, which he would not have bought except for his reliance on the promise, Uncle Ned is probably estopped from asserting a no consideration defense when Johnny sues him for the money. Johnny would have to prove that his reliance was reasonable.

The Seal

As an alternative method of holding persons to promises made and accepted, the common law said that if the promise was made in writing and "sealed," there was a *conclusive presumption* that consideration had been given in return. Promisors, in other words, were not able to make the no consideration argument against their signed and sealed written promises. The use of the word *seal* or the initials "L. S." before or after the promisor's signature was sufficient.

Seal (L.S.) on contract

Only a few states follow this rule today. In about half of the states, a seal on the signed writing supplies a *rebuttable presumption* of consideration, meaning that the promisor still has a chance to prove that no consideration was given for the promise. Similarly, in many states the presence of a corporate seal on a document creates a rebuttable presumption that the document was executed by someone who had authority to act for the corporation.

UCC Rule on the Seal. In about half of the states, the presence of a seal on a signed, written document creates no presumption at all as to consideration: the promisee must prove consideration by one of the other methods. This last, "no-effect-at-all" rule is adopted by the UCC (2–203) for the sale of goods, so that many states now have two rules on the seal—one for goods and one for other contracts. The problem of the seal is further complicated by the fact that many states allow a longer "statute of limitations" period in which to bring suit where the contract is "sealed."

McGOWAN v. BEACH

86 S.E.2d 763 (North Carolina, 1955)

FACTS
Lois McGowan claimed that her husband Wade (now deceased) had borrowed $15,000 from her and, as evidence of the debt, had given her the following memorandum: "January 2, 1945. I owe my wife Lois McGowan $15,000. Wade H. McGowan (Seal)." In answer to specific questions in their instructions, the jury found that Wade had in fact written, signed, sealed, and delivered the memorandum. Beach, the administrator of Wade's estate, objected to the trial judge's refusal to ask the jury for a finding as to whether Wade had in fact borrowed the money. Beach appeals from a judgment in favor of Lois.

ISSUE
Must a claimant under a sealed instrument prove that the deceased received consideration for the promise in the instrument?

DECISION
No. Judgment for Lois affirmed.

REASONS
Justice Denny stated that Lois's "right to recover must turn solely upon the legal effect of the instrument as written, including the seal, since the jury found that W. H. McGowan executed it as alleged in the complaint."

"It is said in 12 Am.Jur., Contracts under Seal, section 74 page 567: 'At common law a promise under seal, but without any consideration, is binding because no consideration is required in such a case or, as is sometimes said, because the seal imports, or gives rise to a presumption of, consideration. It has been said that the solemnity of a sealed instrument imports consideration or, to speak more accurately, estops a covenantor from denying a consideration except for fraud.' . . .

"Hoke, Jr. (late Chief Justice), in speaking for the Court in [one] case, said: 'It is the accepted principle of the common law that instruments under seal require no consideration to support them. Whether this should rest on the position that a seal conclusively imports a consideration, or that the solemnity of the act imports such reflection and care that a consideration is regarded as unnecessary, such instruments are held to be binding agreements enforceable in all actions before the common-law courts.'

"Whether we construe the instrument under consideration to be a . . . note, a due bill, or merely an acknowledgment by W. H. McGowan of a debt to his wife in the sum of $15,000, the fact that it was executed under seal, which in the absence of proof to the contrary, imports a consideration, the instrument is sufficient as an acknowledgment of such debt."

Statutory Exceptions to the Consideration Requirement

A respectable body of legal opinion holds that the consideration requirement has caused more problems than it has prevented, and that people should be bound to perform whatever they promised to perform, at least where the promise was made in a signed writing, whether or not the person gets anything in return. These same ideas may have been the rationale for the common-law rule on the seal; they find their modern expression in various statutes which provide that certain promises are enforceable even though no consideration was given in return. One such provision is the *firm offer rule* discussed in Chapter 10. If a merchant's signed, written offer to buy or sell goods says that the offer will remain open for acceptance, it is not revocable by the merchant (within certain time limits) even though the merchant has received no consideration for the promise to keep the offer open. Similarly, the Model Business Corporation Act, Section 17, provides that an offer to subscribe to shares of stock is not revocable for a period of six months unless otherwise agreed.

UCC firm offer rule

Subscription for stock

UCC Waiver Rule. The UCC contains two other "no-consideration-required" sections that have very broad potential application (and are thus very important). UCC 1–107 permits a party to a contract to waive any claim the party may have for an alleged breach of the contract by means of a signed writing. No special form is required, and no consideration need be received by the person giving up the contract claim. Since this section is in Article 1 of the Code, it applies to all of the types of contracts covered in any other section of the Code.

UCC written waiver

UCC Modification of Sale of Goods. UCC 2–209(1) applies only to contracts for the sale of goods, but it is also a very significant exception to the consideration requirement. It provides that any agreement modifying a preexisting contract for the sale of goods needs no consideration to be binding. (Normally, any change in an existing contract must be a "two-way" change—each party must receive consideration.) Suppose that you contract to buy a new

UCC rule for modification of goods contracts

car, but decide after you've driven it for two days that you'd like rear-seat stereo speakers for the radio. You call up the dealer and talk to your salesman, and the salesman promises to install the speakers for no additional charge if you bring the car in next Monday. If the jury believes your testimony that such a modification of the original car contract was agreed to, the dealer is now contractually bound to install the speakers. Without 2–209(1), the dealer would *not* be bound, since the dealer received no new consideration for the speakers. (*Remember* that this Code rule applies *only* to goods contracts. If you want to modify other types of contracts, such as those for land or services, there must be consideration moving both ways.)

Special (No Consideration) Statutes. In addition to these Code provisions, special statutory provisions applying the no-consideration-required rule to other types of contracts have been adopted by some states. The following statute, adopted by Michigan in 1941, is an example: "Agreements to Modify or Discharge Contracts, Sec. 1. An agreement hereafter made to change or modify, or to discharge in whole or in part, any contract, obligation, or lease, or any mortgage or other security interest in personal or real property, shall not be invalid because of the absence of consideration: Provided, that the agreement changing, modifying, or discharging such contract, obligation, lease, mortgage or security interest shall not be valid or binding unless it shall be in writing and signed by the party against whom it is sought to enforce the change, modification, or discharge."

Special state statutes

▪ COURTS' DEFINITIONS OF LEGALLY SUFFICIENT CONSIDERATION

Legal Sufficiency versus Adequacy. As noted previously, the courts do not generally concern themselves with whether the parties have made a "good deal" or a "bad deal"; they will enforce stupid and unreasonable contracts as well as wise and reasonable ones. To be legally sufficient, a consideration need not be "adequate," in the sense of being a reasonable estimate of a jury's idea of fair market value. Unless there are unusual circumstances, such as fraud, duress, or undue influence, it is enough that something of value was received in return as the price of the promise, even though that "something" does not seem very desirable to the judge or jury. Freedom of contract means that you have the power to make your own bargains and that you are generally bound by the bargains you make once you have agreed to them.

Adequate consideration

Courts continue to state these general rules, and yet they seem more and more willing to "remake" contracts so as to arrive at "fair" results. For one thing, the *gross* inadequacy of the consideration received by one party is *some* evidence to support that party's claim to have been defrauded or subjected to duress or undue influence. Also, where a court finds such gross inadequacy it will generally refuse to exercise its equity powers to order specific performance of the unfair contract, since "He who seeks equity must do equity." A court may even refuse to award money damages in such a case, by using the newly popular concept of ***unconscionability,*** which means that the contract is so terribly unfair that it should not be enforced as written.

For the purpose of calculating amounts due under the U.S. estate and gift taxes, the Internal Revenue Code requires examination of alleged "contracts" to make sure that each party has received "an adequate [and full] consideration in money and money's worth." For example, if Uncle Ned promises Johnny $50,000 for painting a picket fence, there may technically be a contract, but the IRS will view the transaction as a gift by Uncle Ned of the difference between $50,000 and the fair market value of the painting job.

As noted in Chapter 10, moreover, the courts do require that the promise given in return be definite enough to impose some restrictions on that party's freedom of action. An ***illusory promise,*** such as one to buy as many parts as one *wanted* to order, imposes no real obligation to do any business at all. It seems as if a promise is being made, but there is no real commitment. An illusory promise thus does not supply consideration for a promise made in return. There is no contract in this situation, and *neither* party is bound to any performance. Because the buyer provided no consideration to the seller, the seller would not be bound to sell any parts at the stated price, even if the buyer later had ordered some. The order would be an offer to buy, which the seller is absolutely free to reject since there was no contract originally.

The following pages discuss some of the other "returns" which the courts do *not* generally accept as supplying a legally sufficient consideration.

Nominal Consideration. *Nominal* means "in name only" or "very small." ***"Nominal consideration"*** usually refers to the recital of $1 as consideration. Nothing is inherently wrong with $1 or any other very small amount as consideration for a return promise, if that amount is *in fact* intended and agreed to as the price of the bargain. Most courts, however, do not accept the mere recital of a fictitious dollar bill as legally sufficient consideration. The *O'Neill* case at the end of the chapter discusses this point further.

Good Consideration. As it appears in most legal forms ("and other good and valuable consideration"), *good* seems to be used as a synonym for *valuable* (and thus legally sufficient) consideration. However, that is not the meaning given to the term by most authoritative legal texts; they generally define *good consideration* in terms of a promise to be a "good relative," and thus *not* legally sufficient. "Nice family feelings" do not provide a legally sufficient consideration. When Johnny promises to be a "good nephew" (kind, loyal, and loving) in return for Uncle Ned's promise of $5,000, there is no consideration for Uncle Ned's promise, and Uncle Ned is not contractually bound to pay the money.

Past Consideration. A promise of benefits is not changed from a gift into a contract by the fact that the promisee has given something to the promisor in a previous, separate transaction. Such so-called past consideration is no consideration for the new promise of benefits. It is this rule which requires that a modification of a preexisting contract must be supported by a new exchange of considerations in order to be enforceable, except for UCC 2–209(1). Likewise, this rule generally prevents a "good Samaritan" from enforcing a promise to repay the good Samaritan for benefits previously conferred on the promisor as a gift. Since no contract was entered into or intended at the time the benefits were originally provided, those benefits—a completed gift—constitute past consideration.

Moral Consideration. Generally, the courts treat the existence of a moral obligation in the same way that they treat past consideration. The fact that a person is morally obligated to provide certain benefits does not supply consider-

Illusory promise ≠ Consideration

Recited promise of fake $1 ≠ Consideration

Family member's promise of love and affection ≠ Consideration

Past benefits given ≠ Consideration

General rule: Moral obligation ≠ Consideration

ation for that person's promise to provide them. By most standards the person who received aid and comfort from the good Samaritan would be morally obligated to repay the good Samaritan when able to do so, but the courts do not regard this moral obligation as a legally sufficient consideration.

Exception: New promises to pay old debts barred by bankruptcy or statute of limitations

In three situations the courts *will* generally enforce a promise on the basis of some idea of moral obligation. Two of them are closely related—new promises to pay a debt barred by a discharge in bankruptcy or by the running of the *statute of limitations*. In each of these cases the debtor has received the values the debtor contracted for but has not paid for them; in each case the debtor has a technical defense which would prevent a successful lawsuit to collect the debt. Nevertheless, when the debtor makes a *new promise to pay the bankruptcy debt* in either of these cases, most courts will hold the debtor to the new promise, even though the debtor has received no *new* consideration, on the theory that "a person ought to pay his or her debts." In most states one or both of these new promises must be made in a signed writing to be enforceable.

Exception: Promises to charities

The third situation relates to promises made to charitable organizations. *Charitable promises* are almost uniformly enforceable, though the courts do not always agree on why they are. Some courts imply mutual promises between and among the donors not to revoke their pledges to the charity. Where the charity has "moved in reliance" on the promises, the doctrine of promissory estoppel can be applied. An example would be hiring an architect to design a new building, or taking an option on land. Even without applying either of these ideas, some courts apparently enforce promises to charitable organizations on the basis of some underlying "moral obligation" to support good works.

Preexisting Duty Rule. A promise to do or the actual doing of something which one is already bound to do anyway does not supply consideration for a return promise. Thus, when a landowner promises an extra bonus to a builder if the builder will get a job done on time, in accordance with the terms of the original contract, the builder cannot collect this promised bonus even if the builder does get the job done on time. The builder was already legally obligated to do so and has promised nothing new in return for the bonus. Similarly, police officers usually cannot collect rewards offered for the capture of criminals when they make the arrest in their own jurisdiction, in the line of their official duties. The following case presents the application of this rule in a slightly different factual context.

Performing a duty already owed ≠ Consideration

LEONE v. PRECISION PLUMBING AND HEATING OF SOUTHERN ARIZONA, INC.

591 P.2d 1002 (Arizona, 1979)

FACTS

Sam Leone worked as a foreman for Precision, which was a subcontractor on a construction project. Sam was covered under a collective bargaining contract between Precision and the construction workers' union. Sam sues to enforce an alleged oral promise of a bonus of one half of the difference between the estimated cost of the project and its actual cost. The jury found for Sam, and the trial judge refused Precision's request for a judgment notwithstanding the verdict. Precision appeals.

ISSUE   Was Precision's promise to Sam supported by a legally sufficient consideration?

DECISION   Yes. Judgment affirmed.

REASONS   Judge Hathaway had no difficulty in agreeing with the trial court that consideration was supplied by Sam to Precision. Although Sam was already an employee, he supplied consideration for the bonus promise in two ways.

"A promise lacks consideration if the promisee is under a preexisting duty to counter-perform. The rule is inapplicable, however, if the promisee undertakes any obligation not required by the preexisting duty, even if the new obligation involves almost the same performance as the preexisting duty. If bargained for, an employee's extra effort is a new duty sufficient to support a bonus offer. In this case, appellant bargained for appellees' extra efforts. The estimated cost for the project included projections of labor costs based on wages paid to union members working at union standards. Appellee, working at union standards, was obliged to direct and induce his crew to work at union standards. He could earn the bonus only if he induced his crew to perform at better than union standards. To encourage appellee to use extra effort as foreman to maximize his crew's efficiency, appellant offered the bonus. The bonus, therefore, was supported by consideration.

"The trial judge instructed the jury that if an employee at will continues his employment after a modification of contract, '[c]ontinued employment by an employee constitutes sufficient consideration to support a modification.' Applied to this case, the instruction was correct. It is undisputed that if continued employment is bargained for in making a bonus offer, continued employment is sufficient consideration. The same rule should apply if continued employment, although not expressly bargained for, is a condition of receipt of a bonus. To receive the bonus, appellee had to continue his employment. His staying on the job attempting to gain the bonus constituted consideration supporting the bonus agreement."

Sam Leone was entitled to $17,789.28 as a bonus.

Part Payment. One of the most common applications of the preexisting duty rule is in cases where a debtor offers to pay part of the debt if the creditor will accept the part payment as full satisfaction of the debt. Obviously, in most cases the creditor is willing to agree to anything to get some cash, especially if the debt is past due and the debtor is in questionable financial condition. Does such an agreement prevent the creditor from later suing to collect the unpaid balance of the original debt? At common law the general rule was clear: no, the creditor is not prevented from collecting the balance, because the debtor's part payment was nothing more (in fact less) than the debtor was already legally obligated to pay.

Only under special circumstances would the part payment legally discharge the debt in full. If the part payment was made and accepted by the creditor as payment in full before the debt was in fact due, the creditor would be bound by the acceptance of this "early payment." The creditor in this case

General rule: Paying a debt already owed ≠ Consideration

Exceptions:
1. *Early payment*
2. *Some new item*
3. *Honest dispute*

did receive new consideration for the agreement to surrender the balance of the debt because the creditor had no right to receive any payment on the date that the payment was actually made. There is likewise consideration for the discharge of the entire debt if the part payment is accompanied by "some new item," received and accepted by the creditor, which the creditor was not previously legally entitled to receive. There is consideration (at least technically), and the debt is (probably) discharged, when a creditor agrees to accept a ballpoint pen and $600 in cash in full satisfaction of a $1,000 debt. Finally, where there is an honest, good faith dispute over the amount that is actually owed and the creditor agrees to take a lesser sum in full payment, the creditor is bound and the debt is discharged.

The following case shows that the courts are likely to be quite liberal in their definition of such a "new item."

JAFFRAY v. DAVIS

26 N.E. 351 (New York, 1891).

FACTS   On December 8, 1886, the defendants owed the plaintiffs for goods sold between that date and the previous May at an agreed price, the sum of $7,714.37. On December 27, 1886, the defendants delivered to the plaintiffs three promissory notes amounting in the aggregate to $3,462.24 secured by a mortgage on the stock, fixtures, and other property of the defendants, located in East Saginaw, Michigan. These notes and the mortgage were received by plaintiffs under an agreement to accept them in full satisfaction and discharge of the indebtednesss.

ISSUE   Did the creditor receive new consideration for his promise to discharge the debt in full?

DECISION   Yes. Judgment for the debtor (Jaffray). Trial court reversed.

REASONS   The court first stated the general rule:

"One of the elements embraced in the question presented upon this appeal is whether the payment of a sum less than the amount of a liquidated debt under an agreement to accept the same in satisfaction of such debt forms a bar to the recovery of the balance of the debt. This single question was presented to the English court in 1602, when it was resolved (if not decided) in *Pinnel's* case, 'that payment of a lesser sum on the day in satisfaction of a greater, cannot be any satisfaction for the whole,' and that this is so, although it was agreed that such payment should satisfy the whole. This simple question has since arisen in the English courts and in the courts of this country in almost numberless instances, and has received the same solution, notwithstanding the courts, while so ruling, have rarely failed, upon any recurrence of the question, to criticize and condemn its reasonableness, justice, fairness, or honesty. No respectable authority that I have been able to find has, after such unanimous disapproval by all the courts, held otherwise."

The court then described the exceptions to the rule. "Lord Blackburn said in his opinion in *Foakes* v. *Beer.* . . , while maintaining the doctrine 'that a lesser sum cannot be satisfaction of a greater sum, but the gift of a horse, hark or robe, etc., in satisfaction is good,' quite regardless of the amount of the debt. And it was further said by him in the same opinion 'that payment and acceptance of a parcel before the day of payment of a larger sum would be good satisfaction in regard to the circumstance of time, and so if I am bound in 20 pounds to pay you 10 pounds at Westminister, and you request me to pay you 5 pounds at the day at York, and you will accept it in full satisfaction for the whole 10 pounds, it is a good satisfaction. . . . [A] negotiable security may operate, if so given and taken in satisfaction of a debt of a greater amount; the circumstance of negotiability making it in fact a different thing and more advantageous than the original debt which was not negotiable.' "

The court then decided that this was an "exception" case. "Under the cases above cited, and upon principle, this new agreement was supported by a sufficient consideration to make it a valid agreement, and this agreement was by the parties substituted in place of the former. The consideration of the new agreement was that the plaintiffs, in place of an open book account for goods sold, got the defendants' promissory notes, probably negotiable in form, signed by the defendants, thus saving the plaintiffs perhaps trouble or expense of proving their account, and for security upon all the defendants' personal property for the payment of the sum specified in the notes, where before they had no security."

UCC Rules on Part Payment. Some legal writers have suggested that under UCC 1–107, 2–209(1), and 3–408, the cashing of a part-payment check discharges the debt in full if the check so indicates, even if there is no dispute. Most of the cases decided since the adoption of the Code, however, continue to apply the common-law rules discussed above, without reference to any of these Code sections. It is thus not clear how a court would apply these sections if they were properly briefed and argued. It certainly appears that creditors would be much safer in sending such checks back and suing for the entire balance due. At the very least, a creditor should be aware that cashing such a check *may* cancel the right to sue for the balance of the debt.

UCC sections may provide exception

■ SIGNIFICANCE OF THIS CHAPTER

Not all promises are contractually enforceable, even if proved to have been made and accepted. The basic idea of the consideration requirement is that a person ought not to be required to perform a promise made to another unless the promisor received something of value in return for the promise. While it is inevitable that some promisors will be disappointed in what they have received in return, that in itself is no basis for not performing their promises. But it is also true that courts are more and more willing to examine the agreement to make sure that a genuine exchange of values was promised, particularly where one of the parties lacks education and experience.

Fairness also underlies the concept of promissory estoppel as an alternate basis for enforcement. It's just not fair to let someone make the "no consideration" argument after a promise has been relied on by another party. Courts may also use the estoppel concept to prevent someone from using the Statute of Frauds to deny liability on an oral promise. The next chapter will discuss this point in more detail.

DISCUSSION CASE

O'NEILL v. DELANEY
92 Ill.App.3d 292 (Illinois, 1980)

FACTS: In this action plaintiff seeks a declaratory judgment that he is the owner of a valuable painting. Essentially, plaintiff maintains that the painting was sold to him by James Paul DeLaney on August 18, 1970. Following a bench trial, the trial court found the purported sale of the painting from James Paul DeLaney to plaintiff was void because of inadequate consideration and lack of delivery. On appeal from that judgment, Jeannette DeLaney is the sole appellee.

Defendants were married on January 17, 1953. Approximately three to five years later, they acquired a painting allegedly the work of Peter Paul Rubens and entitled "Hunting of the Caledonian Boar." . . . This painting was a part of the art collection acquired by the defendants during their marriage. In 1966, defendants moved into an apartment building in which the plaintiff and his wife resided. The two couples soon became friends. Jeannette DeLaney characterized the friendship between plaintiff and her husband as "casual" for the next four years. After 1970, however, she noticed that plaintiff and her husband had become close friends, and in fact, the two couples went on a vacation together.

On August 18, 1970, James Paul DeLaney purportedly sold the painting to plaintiff for $10 and "other good and valuable consideration." A written contract, embodying the terms of the agreement, was prepared and signed by plaintiff and James Paul DeLaney. Jeannette DeLaney was not a party to that contract. The painting was then brought to plaintiff's apartment where it was hung on the wall.

When asked what the contract term "other good and valuable consideration" meant to him, plaintiff stated:

That to me and Mr. DeLaney means our friendship and favors that we have done; and as you put it earlier, the love and affection that one had for another. Mr. DeLaney didn't have any children, and I assume he looked upon me as a son.

Under cross-examination, plaintiff was asked whether he gave James Paul DeLaney anything else other than $10 and love and affection in exchange for the painting. Plaintiff responded: "No, not really."

At the time of the sale of the painting, plaintiff believed it was worth $100,000 if not authenticated as a Rubens original, and if authenticated, several hundred thousand dollars. James Paul DeLaney told plaintiff the painting was a genuine Rubens. Plaintiff, however, had no formal education in art and had no experience in art research.

During the next four years, plaintiff stated that the painting was either in his apartment or in DeLaney's. The painting apparently never remained in plaintiff's apartment for a sustained period of time. Since James Paul DeLaney was plaintiff's agent for the purpose of selling the painting, it was kept in DeLaney's apartment to be viewed by prospective buyers. Both plaintiff and DeLaney felt the painting's value would be enhanced if viewed by prospective buyers with the rest of the DeLaney art collection. Also, plaintiff considered the painting to be safer in DeLaney's apartment. Despite plaintiff's concern for the safety of the painting, he never insured the painting during this period.

According to Jeannette DeLaney, the painting hung on the south wall of the sunroom of their apartment during the years 1970 to 1974. It was only removed from the apartment for art exhibitions and restoration work. At no other time was she aware that the painting was outside her apartment.

Mrs. DeLaney denied that she was ever informed by her husband that the painting had been sold to plaintiff. Nor did plaintiff mention this transaction to Mrs. DeLaney. She stated that she first became aware of plaintiff's claim of ownership in 1974 during the course of her divorce proceedings.

Irving Friedin, a friend of the plaintiff, visited plaintiff's apartment approximately 40 to 50 times during the period from August 1970 to December 1974. On one of these visits, he recalled seeing the painting inside the plaintiff's apartment.

In Jeannette DeLaney's complaint for divorce, filed in 1974, she claimed "special equities" in the painting and prayed for an equitable share thereof. Although plaintiff was, in his own words, a good friend of the DeLaneys, he was unaware of the marital problems confronting the couple or that Mrs. DeLaney had filed for divorce. On December 19, 1974, Mrs. DeLaney obtained an injunction enjoining her husband from transferring or encumbering the title to the painting. In an affidavit, filed January 8, 1975, on behalf of James Paul DeLaney, plaintiff stated that the painting had been placed in storage on December 12, 1974. More specifically, plaintiff stated: "On or about December 12, 1974, I personally examined certain works of art *owned and possessed by Mr. James Paul DeLaney* and assisted in their placement in certain vaults on the premises of Reebie Storage and Moving Company, Inc." (Emphasis added.) Identified as one of these works of art was the painting allegedly sold to plaintiff on August 18, 1970.

After a full hearing on May 11, 1976, the trial court, which was hearing the divorce action, found the purported sale of the painting by James Paul DeLaney to plaintiff void.

Five weeks after that hearing, on June 21, 1976, plaintiff initiated this action for declaratory judgment against James and Jeannette DeLaney.

■

Justice Loren gave this opinion:

An offer, an acceptance, and consideration are the basic elements of a contract. Consideration to support a contract is any act or promise which is of benefit to one party or disadvantage to the other. Whether there is consideration for a contract is a question of law for the court. Generally, courts will not inquire into the sufficiency of the consideration which supports a contract. However, where the amount of consideration is so grossly inadequate as to shock the conscience of the court, the contract will fail. Professor Corbin in his treatise on contracts explained the underlying analysis employed by courts to strike down contracts for grossly inadequate consideration as follows:

> The gross inadequacy of the consideration, as measured by the opinions of other men, may tend to support the conclusion that the parties did not actually agree upon an exchange, that the 'peppercorn' [a term signifying a useless and valueless item used as consideration] was not in fact bargained for by the promisor. If it was not bargained for, it was not a consideration, according to the definition that makes agreed bargain the test. Persons sometimes say that they have bargained, when their other conduct shows that they have not; and they sometimes actually bargain for something when their written or oral statement is that they have bargained for something else. . . . The rule that market equivalence of consideration is not required, and that the value of the consideration is to be left solely to the free bargaining process of the parties, leads in extreme cases to absurdities. When the consideration is only a 'peppercorn' or a 'tomtit' or a worthless piece of paper, the requirement of consideration appeared to Holmes . . . to be as much of a mere formality as is a deal.

In such extreme cases, Professor Corbin concluded that "the stated consideration is a mere pretense" and no contract exists. This analysis of contract law can also be seen in those cases which have examined the attempts of one spouse to transfer marital property prior to either divorce or death, and thereby defeat the marital interests of the other spouse.

Generally, a spouse has an absolute right to dispose of his or her property during marriage without the concurrence of the other spouse. Moreover, the spouse may do so even if the transfer is made for the express purpose of minimizing or defeating the marital interests of the surviving spouse. There is only one exception to this rule: when the transaction is merely "colorable" or "illusory" and is tantamount to fraud. This fraud, as explained by our supreme court, relates to the absence of a present intent to transfer title and ownership of the property, not the presence of an intent to defeat the marital interest or right of the other spouse.

In the present case, the painting was purportedly sold to the plaintiff on August 18, 1970, for $10 and other good and valuable consideration. Plaintiff expressly testified that "other good and valuable consideration" meant the love and affection plaintiff and James Paul DeLaney had for one another. In Illinois, love and affection does not constitute legal consideration. Thus, the only remaining valid consideration for the transaction was the tender of $10. As we noted above, the adequacy of the consideration must be determined as of the time of entering the contract. Plaintiff stated that at the time he purchased the painting, it was worth $100,000 if not authenticated and several hundred thousand dollars if authenticated as an original Rubens. James Paul DeLaney told him at the time of transfer that the painting was an original Rubens. A purchase price of $10 for such a valuable work of art is so grossly inadequate consideration as to shock the conscience of this court, as it did the trial court's. To find $10 valid consideration for this painting would be to reduce the requirement of consideration to a mere formality. This we will not do. By finding this to be inadequate consideration, we are not trying to protect one party against a bad deal entered into voluntarily, but rather are questioning the existence of the alleged contract.

We hold that no valid sales contract existed between plaintiff and defendant James Paul DeLaney. Both the grossly inadequate consideration and the conduct of plaintiff and James Paul DeLaney demonstrate that this sales contract was colorable and a mere pretense. No present intent to transfer title to the painting to plaintiff existed here. Accordingly, the order of the circuit court is affirmed.

■ IMPORTANT TERMS AND CONCEPTS

consideration	bargained-for exchange	change of position in	conclusive presumption
promisor	of values	reliance	rebuttable presumption
promisee	promissory estoppel	seal	UCC rule on the seal

firm offer rule
UCC waiver rule
UCC modification of sale
  of goods
special (no consideration)
  statutes
legal sufficiency
adequate consideration
unconscionability
illusory promise
nominal consideration

good consideration
past consideration
moral consideration
charitable promises
new promise to pay
  bankruptcy debt
Statute of Limitations
preexisting duty rule
part payment of a debt
(possible) UCC changes
  on part payment rules

■ QUESTIONS AND PROBLEMS FOR DISCUSSION

1. When will a promisor be estopped from arguing that he or she is not bound to perform the promise because he or she received no consideration for it?

2. What is the effect of a promisor's placing a "seal" on a written promise?

3. What is the meaning and significance of "past" consideration?

4. When will part payment of a debt, if offered and accepted "in full payment," actually discharge the whole debt?

5. Crachit had lived in his uncle Ebenezer's house for several years and had worked as a clerk in Ebenezer's office. In 1988 Ebenezer suggested that Crachit would benefit from a trip to Europe and said that he would repay all Crachit's expenses for the trip. Crachit did go to Europe, but his uncle died a short time later without having repaid Crachit's expenses. The executor of Ebenezer's estate denies liability for this claim, since the trip had nothing to do with Ebenezer's business and did not benefit him in any way. Can Crachit collect his expenses from the estate?

6. On October 19, 1985, Ellis Valente and Jarle Ottesen engaged in a barroom brawl in which Ottesen was seriously injured and consequently sued Valente for assault and battery. About six weeks after the fight Valente (70 years old) transferred all of his assets except for a small amount of cash to his wife and children for estate-planning purposes and in consideration of love and affection. In April 1986 Ottesen instituted an action to set aside the transfer of assets, claiming that the transfer had had the effect of defrauding him. Who wins the case? Why?

7. In June Richard Axminster listed his house with Speedy Real Estate Company in an exclusive selling agreement. The contract specified a 6 percent commission if the house were sold during the three-month listing period or within three months thereafter either by Speedy or by the owner. No buyer was procured by Speedy, and in October Richard sold the house to a buyer with whom he had negotiated directly. Speedy still wants to collect the commission, which Richard refuses to pay since Speedy never showed the property to anyone, never made an offer, and did not even know the final buyer. Can Speedy collect? Why or why not?

8. Natalie was driving along the road one day when she saw her dream house up for sale. She didn't have the money at the moment, but she decided that if she could get a loan she would purchase the house. After explaining her situation to Stuart, the owner of the home, she signed an option agreement. Natalie's consideration for the option was stated as $1 and her "efforts to obtain a loan." The moment her loan went through, Natalie attempted to exercise her option to buy the house. Stuart had just found out that selling his home would increase his income tax liabilities, so he decided not to sell it. Stuart told Natalie that due to the fact she had only given him $1 the offer was revocable. Natalie refused to see her dreams crushed and sued Stuart for specific performance. How should the court rule, and why?

12

Statute of Frauds and Parol Evidence Rule

CHAPTER OBJECTIVES

THIS CHAPTER WILL:

- Explain the need for written proof of a contract.
- Indicate the major types of contracts which are subject to this requirement.
- Discuss the methods of complying with this requirement.
- Indicate the results if the Statute of Frauds applies to a contract and has not been satisfied.
- Explain the major exceptions to the unenforceability result if the Statute has not been satisfied.
- Explain the operation of the parol evidence rule.
- Indicate the situations where the rule does not apply.
- Indicate the major exceptions to the rule.

Although the parties have entered into an agreement and their agreement is supported by an exchange of legally sufficient considerations, courts, in many situations, will refuse to enforce some or all of the promises exchanged unless the alleged promises can be proved by something more than oral testimony. The *Statute of Frauds* requires that certain types of contractual promises be contained in a signed writing to be enforceable in court. The *parol evidence rule* prevents a party from contradicting the terms of a complete written contract, once signed, by the use of outside, or parol, evidence.

■ STATUTE OF FRAUDS: ORIGINS, DEVELOPMENT, AND BASIC PURPOSE

Reasons for requiring written evidence of contract

One year after the United States celebrated its bicentennial, the Statute of Frauds celebrated its tricentennial. The English Parliament passed the original statute in 1677 to deal with what was perceived to be a serious legal problem: the possibility that a court would force a party to perform a contract which had never really been made, solely on the basis of perjured oral testimony. The solution to this problem seemed simple enough: require that a contract be proved by something more than oral testimony before you enforce it. Thus, the Statute of Frauds ("An Act for Prevention of Frauds and Perjuries") was adopted.

Parliament did not go as far as requiring that *all* contracts be evidenced by a signed writing to be enforceable in court. Rather, it confined this new requirement to what seemed to be "important" contracts and to other situations where intentional perjury or mistaken testimony seemed likely. As a result, the following types of contracts had to be in writing to be enforceable in court: the sale of any interest in real estate; the sale of goods worth £10 or more; any contract which by its terms could not possibly be completed within one year from the date it was made; any promise to pay the debt of another party; any promise by the executor or administrator of a decedent's estate to pay the estate's debts out of his or her own funds; any promise made "in consideration of marriage." This list formed the basis for similar statutes in nearly all of our states.

To see how the Statute of Frauds works today, we need to know the answers to three questions: What contracts are now subject to the Statute of Frauds? How does one comply with the Statute of Frauds requirement? What results follow if the Statute of Frauds applies and has not been satisfied? We will now consider each of these questions in turn.

■ CONTRACTS SUBJECT TO THE STATUTE OF FRAUDS

Transfer of any interest in real estate

Pre-UCC Holdovers. Three provisions of the 1677 statute that have general commercial significance have, on the whole, survived in their original form: the transfer of any interest in real estate, any promise to pay the debt of another, any contract which by its terms cannot be performed within one year. Prior to the UCC, many states had also adopted a Statute of Frauds provision which required all *assignments, or transfers, of contract rights* to be made in writing. (Assignments are discussed more fully in Chapter 16.)

Real Estate Transfers. "Any interest" in land means just that: every case where one or more parties are voluntarily creating such an interest in another or divesting themselves of such an interest. Most courts agree that leases, mortgages, easements, and options on real estate are all subject to this requirement, although options might be excluded in some states. Also, most states do have a statutory exception for short-term leases; if the term of an oral lease is not more than one year, the lease is enforceable. Although real estate brokers do not have an "interest" in the real estate under this section of the Statute of Frauds, in most states real estate brokers are required by a separate statutory provision to have their commission arrangements in writing to make them enforceable.

Coverage of things in or on the land

Some definitional problems arise where the contract relates to things which are growing on, attached to, or contained in the land. Generally, these questions will be answered by reference to UCC 2–107. If the contract requires the seller to "sever" minerals or the like, or a structure or its materials, the contract is a sale of goods within Article 2. If the buyer is to do the severing, until the buyer does so, the contract would be assumed to deal with an "interest" in the land. Where the subject matter of the contract is timber, growing crops,

■ Exhibit 12–1
Statute of Frauds: Debt of Another?

What is a promise to pay the debt "of another"?			
Promisor:	to	Promisee:	= Debt of Another
a. Uncle Ned		Johnny	
You need the European experience. If you go, I will pay your first $3000 in expenses.			= No. (oral OK) Not made to third party creditor
b. Uncle Ned		Eaters Club	
My nephew is going to Europe. Send him a set of the luggage you advertised, and bill me.			= No. (oral OK) Promisor is making the purchase, even though goods are going to Johnny
c. Uncle Ned		Amex Credit	
My nephew is going to Europe. He is authorized to use my Amex Credit card for the next two weeks			= No. (oral OK) Oral authorization of Johnny as agent; Johnny is making debts for Uncle Ned
d. Uncle Ned		Harolds Store	
My nephew will probably need some new suits for his European trip. Go ahead and sell them to him. I will pay if he doesn't pay.			= Yes. (writing required) Uncle Ned is promising to pay Johnny's debt if Johnny does not
e. Uncle Ned		Bigger Bank	
My nephew will be in to borrow some cash for his European trip expenses. Please let him have the loan. I will pay it if he can't.			= Yes. (writing required) Uncle Ned is promising to pay Johnny's debt if Johnny can not pay

"or other things attached to realty and capable of severance without material harm thereto," but not covered under the first rule, the contract is a sale of goods, regardless of who does the severing. The significance of the distinction can be seen later, in the discussion of what is a sufficient compliance with the Statute of Frauds provision which applies to the contract.

Promises to Pay the Debt of Another. Parliament probably included this provision because both the principal debtor and the creditor have an incentive to commit perjury in this case. Here, too, there are definitional questions to be resolved. This section does not apply to direct, "original" promises to confer benefits on a third party—only to "secondary" or supplemental promises. This section of the Statute of Frauds does not apply where the promisor's main motive in making the promise is to benefit *himself* or *herself* rather than just to "backstop" the principal debtor's credit. Finally, the section does not apply where the secondary promise is made to the principal debtor rather than to the creditor. As seen in the *Peterson* case, the Court must examine the facts carefully, to see exactly what kind of promise was made.

Promises to pay debts of other persons

PETERSON v. ROWE

314 P.2d 892 (New Mexico, 1957)

FACTS   Between the approximate dates of July 26, 1955, and September 11, 1955, the plaintiff provided hospital care, laboratory facilities, and medication to the patient William H. Rowe. Rowe's sons, M. H. Rowe and William W. Rowe, had asked Dr. Peterson to do so, and had promised to pay him. When Dr. Peterson sued the sons, the trial court gave him $2,739.25, the account balance. The sons appealed.

ISSUE   Are the sons' promises subject to the Statute of Frauds, and therefore unenforceable, because they were made orally?

DECISION   No. Judgment for Dr. Peterson affirmed.

REASONS   **Justice Compton reviewed the nature of the promises which the sons had made:** "A review of the evidence convinces us that appellants are original promisors and not guarantors. . . .

"The evidence discloses at least four conversations between the parties concerning payment for services to be furnished the patient. Appellants were at the hospital the day after William H. Rowe was admitted, and while there, discussed with appellee the matter of making financial arrangements. Appellee explained to appellants that the patient was very ill and would require extensive treatment. Appellants informed appellee that their father had no financial means; nevertheless, appellant M. H. Rowe stated that appellants themselves would pay for such service. His exact statement was: 'You go right ahead and give him whatever is necessary to save his life and I will pay for it.' Subsequently, on July 29, appellants, accompanied by their wives, came to the hospital, and again appellant M. H. Rowe stated to appellee: 'Well, we want you to do everything you can to save his life, and we don't want you to spare any expense, because whatever he needs, doctor, you go ahead and get it and I will pay you.' On July 31, the date of the operation, appellants were at the hospital, and again the question of payment of expenses was renewed. At that time, M. H. Rowe voluntarily authorized the services of special nurses, stating: '[B]ecause whatever he needs, I want him to have it and I will pay you for it.' To which appellant William W. Rowe assented as follows: 'That is correct, anything that—any expense. Do not spare any expense on my father, and I will pay you for it.' The testimony of both Dr. Kinne and Dr. Andrews lends strong support to appellee. This evidence is substantial. Further, some three weeks later, the business manager of the hospital phoned appellants and advised them that the expenses were continuing to mount, and asked them to come in and discuss the matter. They did, but stated that they were just then short of cash. Appellant M. H. Rowe said: 'We will pay you $200 now, and then we will pay you $200 every month.' He stated further: 'My father has some property back in Missouri, and we will put it on the market for sale, and when we sell the property, why, we will pay the entire balance off in full.' Appellant William W. Rowe spoke up, saying, '[T]hat is correct.' They then paid $200, and $45 later when threatened with litigation.

"Of course, in the absence of an expressed contract, appellants would have been under no legal obligation to pay for the services rendered to their father. But it was at appellants' request, and for their benefit, that the services were furnished; hence, the promise to pay was an original undertaking and is without the statute."

Contracts Impossible to Perform within One Year. The probable reason for inclusion of the *year clause* was the likelihood that the parties and witnesses would tend to forget the provisions of the contract, or would remember them differently, where the performances extended over a relatively long period of time. Thus, if on the day a contract is made, the parties can see that there is absolutely no way to perform it within one year from that date, the contract must be evidenced by a signed writing. As applied by the courts, the test is not how long the performances were likely to take or, with hindsight, how long they actually took. The test is whether there was any conceivable way that the contract *could* have been fully performed, according to its terms, within a year from the date it was made. If it *could* have been performed within a year, the oral contract is perfectly valid and perfectly enforceable in court (assuming that the jury believes the oral testimony).

Contracts which will definitely take over one year to fully perform

Thus, an oral *contract for lifetime employment,* where performance is to start within one year of the date the contract is made, is enforceable, since the employee could conceivably die within the first year. But where the employee is hired for more than one year, or is not to start performing until some future date and then is to work for at least a year, the oral contract is not enforceable.

KIYOSE v. TRUSTEES OF INDIANA UNIVERSITY

333 N.E.2d 886 (Indiana, 1975)

FACTS

Gisaburo Kiyose taught in the Department of East Asian Languages on the Bloomington campus of Indiana University. From 1964 to 1966, he was a teaching associate; from 1966 to April 1973, a lecturer. He received his Ph.D. in 1973 and was appointed an assistant professor. He claims that he was promised lifetime employment, beginning with a three-year appointment as assistant professor. He was notified in 1973 that he would not be reappointed for 1974–75. He further claims that he turned down five offers from other schools because of Indiana's promise. The trial court granted defendants' motion to dismiss.

ISSUE   Is this oral promise subject to the year clause of the Statute of Frauds?

DECISION   No. Judgment reversed, and case remanded.

REASONS   Judge Lybrook analyzed this promise as one of "lifetime" employment, despite the initial three-year period.

"The courts of this State have consistently held that the one-year clause of the Statute of Frauds has no application to contracts which are *capable* of being performed within one year from the making thereof. . . . Thus, an oral agreement the performance of which is dependent upon the happening of a certain contingency is not encompassed by the Statute, provided the contingency is one which could possibly occur within one year. . . . In a contract of lifetime employment, death is the contingency which renders the agreement fully performed. Since the contingency is one which may occur at any time, such a contract by *its terms* is capable of being performed within one year and is therefore not within the Statute. . . ."

As Judge Lybrook interpreted the promised contract, it was indeed for lifetime employment, commencing in 1973, although it called for periodic reappointments.

"Defendants in one instant case argue that the claimed 'lifetime' contract of employment was not to *commence* until the expiration of plaintiff's initial three-year appointment to the rank of Assistant Professor. Thus, defendants envision their required performance under the contract to be a single appointment for the period of plaintiff's life which, due to an intervening three-year appointment as Assistant Professor, could not have been made within one year of the formation of the contract. However, as we interpret plaintiff's allegations, the performance to which defendants were bound was that of making successive appointments for the period of plaintiff's life, *commencing* with a three-year appointment as Assistant Professor."

UCC Statute of Frauds Provisions

The Code contains several specific Statute of Frauds provisions. Contracts for the sale of goods with a price of $500 or more, investment securities, or intangible personal property over $5,000 in amount, and contracts creating a security interest or establishing a letter of credit must be evidenced by some sort of writing. In addition, "negotiable instruments" under Article 3 and "documents" under Article 7, by definition, involve signed writings with particular characteristics.

Sales of Goods for $500 or More.   As defined in Section 2–105(1), *goods* means tangible, movable personal property, but it can also refer to things which are currently attached to land, as noted earlier in this chapter. There can be a contract for the sale of goods which do not exist yet, with the seller promising to produce them or get them from a third party prior to the delivery date specified in the contract.

Sales of goods with contract price of $500 or more

In some cases, it is hard to decide whether the contract is a contract for the sale of goods or a contract for services. The distinction is very important here since there is no Statute of Frauds which is generally applicable to services contracts. If a services contract, such as a promise to construct a building on land already owned by the customer, can be performed within one year, it can be oral and still be enforceable, no matter how much money it involves. If a contract is for goods worth $500 or more, Section 2–201 applies.

A contract to buy a $600 color TV is clearly a contract for the sale of goods even if the seller also promises to deliver and "set up" the TV as part of the contract. Likewise, if you buy all the parts for a TV set in a "kit," and then hire a TV technician to put the set together for you, your contract with the technician is clearly a services contract. Many contracts are more ambiguous, however, such as your contract for the purchase of a custom-made suit from a tailor, or your contract with an artist to have your portrait painted, or your contract to have your car fixed or your house aluminum-sided, all of which involve both labor and materials. (Most probably, a court would decide that the suit and portrait contracts are primarily for goods and that the car repair and aluminum siding contracts are primarily for services.)

Sales of Investment Securities.   Simply put, ***investment securities*** are stocks and bonds. Stock warrants and other such special devices, which are commonly traded in securities markets, would also be covered here. No dollar minimum is specified, so that every contract for the sale of securities must be in writing to be enforceable. However, nearly all the cases in point have held that this Statute of Frauds section (8–319) does not apply to your "agency" contract with your broker, so you can sue your broker for failing to follow your oral instructions. (Agency is covered in Chapters 39 and 40.)

Sales of stocks and bonds

Sales of Intangible Personal Property for $5,000 or More.   After eliminating goods, investment securities, and security agreements, Section 1–206 covers "personal property." Included here are the sales of ***miscellaneous intangible property,*** such as copyrights, patents, royalties, trademarks, and trade names, and tort claims for damages. If the contract amount of such items is $5,000 or more, there must be a signed writing.

Security Agreements.   Where a creditor ("secured party") wishes to use a piece of personal property as collateral for the payment of some obligation, the creditor must have a written security agreement which creates or provides for such a "security interest" and the writing must be signed by the debtor. Without such a writing the creditor has no rights against the specific collateral when the debtor goes into default unless the creditor actually has possession of the collateral. (***Secured transactions*** are explained in Chapters 24 and 25.)

Letters of Credit.   Letters of credit are widely used in international trade, where the credit standing of a buyer may not be known to the seller. Before leaving his or her country, the buyer arranges to have a bank honor drafts (orders for money) up to a certain amount. With such a written agreement from a recognized bank in the buyer's own country, the buyer can have ready access to funds from banks in a foreign country. Obviously, any such letter of credit, and any modification thereof, must be contained in a signed writing.

Contract modifications under common law

Modifications. Because of the common-law requirement that a document must contain all the material terms to comply with the Statute of Frauds, subsequently agreed-to modifications of such contract must also be evidenced by a signed writing to be enforceable. Such changes can be written on the original document and initialed, or a new document covering the modifications can be prepared and signed by the parties. In a real estate transaction, for example, any later agreement to modify the signed writing by changing the total contract price, the monthly payments, the acreage involved, the interest rate, or even such things as the date of possession, almost certainly has to be written to be enforced in court.

UCC rules on modifications

UCC Rule for Modification of Goods Contract. For sales of goods, however, the rules are quite different because of the wording of the applicable Code provisions. Because the signed writing here does *not* have to contain all the terms agreed on, or even all the material terms, oral modifications of a previous written contract for goods should be enforceable in nearly every case.

The one thing which Section 2–201(1) does not permit is an oral modification which increases the quantity term stated in the signed writing. (For example, the parties enter into a written contract for 1,000 bushels of wheat at $3 per bushel. They can later orally agree to raise or lower the price, to change the delivery date, or to lower the quantity to 700 bushels. What they cannot do without a new writing is to increase the quantity to 1,200 bushels. The quantity term in the original writing can't be increased orally, and 200 more bushels means $600 worth of goods, so this "modification" has to be evidenced by a new writing.) Where there was originally an enforceable oral contract for under $500 and the agreed modification brings the price to over $500, the contract as modified must be evidenced by a writing, or else the modification cannot be enforced and the original terms stand. (For example, the parties orally agree to a contract for 150 bushels of wheat at $3 per bushel. Later they agree to raise the price per bushel to $3.50, for a total price of $525. This modification must be in writing to be enforced.)

Remember from the last chapter that such modifications need no new exchange of considerations in a sale of goods case; they can be completely one-sided and still be binding under Section 2–209(1). For other types of contracts, however, there has to be new consideration moving both ways for such modifications to be enforceable, even if the modifications are in writing.

Writing as substitute for consideration

Consideration Substitutes. Chapter 11 contained several examples of statutory provisions which made certain kinds of promises enforceable even without consideration. Typically, such promises will have to be contained in a signed writing to be enforceable. UCC 2–209(1) does not require modifications of a preexisting sale of goods contract to be in writing, nor, in some states, do the statutes which cover new promises to pay debts barred by the statute of limitations or by a bankruptcy discharge. (As always, of course, it's a good idea to have the promise in writing even though no statute requires it, simply because a signed, written promise is easier to prove in court.)

■ COMPLIANCE WITH THE STATUTE OF FRAUDS

General rule for common law S/F: All material terms in signed writing

General Common-Law Rule. The method of compliance intended by the original 1677 statute was a signed writing. As interpreted by the courts, this requirement came to mean that the writing had to contain "all the material terms" and that a writing which did not clearly spell out all the important provisions of the contract was not sufficient to comply with the statute. In general, this *all-material-terms rule* continues to be used for those Statute of Frauds provisions described above as common-law "holdovers."

The all-material-terms rule can be seen operating most clearly in real estate transactions, where most courts have used the *4-P's* interpretation. To comply with the statute for real estate, the signed writing has to at least contain the Parties, the Property, the Price, and the Payment terms. If the terms are simple, a very short memorandum conceivably could contain all these elements. In the *Lucy* case in Chapter 10, Zehmer signed a writing which identified Lucy as the buyer and the property as the Ferguson Farm, which named the price ($50,000), and which specified the payment terms ("cash"). All of the necessary terms were included. More typically, however, payment for real estate is to be made over an extended period of time, interest must be calculated on the unpaid balance and paid periodically, and other special provisions are agreed to. In such cases the parties run a very real risk that a court may later find their document to be insufficient to comply with the statute.

Sales of Goods Compliance: Five Alternatives. The UCC, Section 2–201, provides five alternative methods of compliance: a signed writing, a writing in confirmation, special manufacture, admission in court, and part performance.

UCC rules for goods:
1. Quantity term, contract for sale, signature

Unlike the common-law rule, the *signed writing* for the sale of goods need not contain all the material terms: "a writing is not insufficient because it omits or incorrectly states a term agreed upon." The writing must indicate that a contract for sale has been made; it must be signed by the party against whom enforcement is sought or by that party's authorized agent; and it must contain the quantity term ("the contract is not enforceable under this paragraph beyond the quantity of goods stated"). Price, packaging, and delivery terms can all be omitted and then filled in by supplementary evidence. A very simple notation on the check given for the down payment would be sufficient, for example, "Down payment on one 1979 Buick." The buyer's signature on the check binds the buyer to the contract; the seller is also bound when the seller indorses the check so that the check can be cashed.

2. Writing in confirmation, where both parties are merchants

Where both parties are merchants and there is no writing which evidences a contract because agreement has been reached over the telephone or in personal conversation, the Code provides a method of compliance called a *writing in confirmation.* This is a brand-new Code concept, unknown in prior law. It is a "bootstrap" method: our contract becomes enforceable by me against you on the basis of a writing signed by *me,* not by you. If within a reasonable time after the oral contract has been made, one *merchant* sends the other a written confirmation of the contract and the confirmation is a sufficient writing against the sender-merchant, it also becomes a sufficient writing against the receiver-merchant unless the receiver-merchant sends back notice of objection to its contents within 10 days after receiving it. This Code rule is saying two things to merchants: first, to be on the safe side, always send written confirmation of the contract (preferably by registered mail) before you expend time and money in reliance on an oral agreement; and second, *read your mail!*

SIERENS v. CLAUSEN

328 N.E.2d 559 (Illinois, 1975)

FACTS

Kenneth Sierens and James Thompson sued Edwin Clausen for breach of two alleged oral agreements to sell them a total of 3,500 bushels of soybeans. They said they sent Clausen a written confirmation, in accordance with UCC 2–201(2). Clausen had been a farmer for 34 years, was then cultivating 180 acres of corn and 150 acres of soybeans, and had for the past five years sold his crops to grain elevators in both cash sales and futures contracts. The trial court held that Clausen was a farmer, and not a "merchant" for the purposes of UCC 2–201(2). It dismissed the complaint, and the appellate court affirmed.

ISSUE

Is an experienced farmer selling his own crops a "merchant" under UCC 2–201(2)?

DECISION

Yes. Judgment reversed, and case remanded for trial.

REASONS

Justice Goldenhersh recognized that prior decisions in his own state and in other states were split on this point of law, so he adopted what he thought was the fairer rule.

"The briefs of the parties, and our own research, indicate that the question whether a farmer may under the circumstances here shown be a 'merchant' under the Uniform Commercial Code, has been decided on three prior occasions. In *Campbell* v. *Yokel,* 20 Ill. App. 3d 702. . . , the appellate court held that farmers who marketed their crops on a regular basis are merchants within the contemplation of section 2–201 of the Uniform Commercial Code. In *Cook Grains, Inc.* v. *Fallis* (1965), 239 Ark. 962 . . . , the court held that a merchant under Section 2–104(1) of the Uniform Commercial Code is one who trades in goods or commodities on a professional basis and a farmer who 'sells the commodities he has raised' is not a merchant. In *Ohio Grain Co.* v. *Swisshelm* (1973), 40 Ohio App. 2d 203, . . . the court held that the defendant, an experienced farmer who had previously sold soybeans and kept abreast of the market, was a 'merchant' when selling his current crop of soybeans.

"The practice of grain and soybean growers in selling their products in the manner described in plaintiffs' amended complaint is well known and widely followed. We know of no reason why under the circumstances shown here the defendant, admittedly a farmer, cannot at the time of the sale be a 'merchant.' On this record we hold that he was a merchant and that Section 2–201 of the Uniform Commercial Code applied to those transactions.

"In his motion to strike the complaint defendant has attacked the sufficiency of the written confirmations of the agreements sent by plaintiffs. We have examined the documents and hold them to be sufficient under the provisions of Section 2–201 of the Uniform Commercial Code.

"Although for purposes of the motion all facts well pleaded are taken as true, defendant's letter 'repudiating' the agreements, which appears in the record as an exhibit attached to plaintiffs' amended complaint, purports to raise the question whether the parties entered into the oral contracts. Although we have determined as a matter of law defendant's status and the sufficiency of the confirmations, the remaining question is one for the trier of fact."

3. Special manufacture

To protect the seller of goods against a potentially unfair result, UCC Section 2–201 provides a separate alternative for *specially manufactured goods.* Where the buyer has a change of mind and tries to cancel an oral order for custom-made goods, the seller can enforce the oral contract by convincing the jury that the goods the seller is making are "for the buyer," that the seller has substantially started to produce the goods or has made commitments to get them from someone else, and that the goods cannot be readily resold in the ordinary course of the seller's business. This case thus raises several fact questions; basically, the jury has to be convinced that the seller will be stuck with the proverbial "white elephant" if the oral contract, actually made, is not enforced.

4. Admission in court

The oral contract is also enforceable against a party who *admits its existence in pleadings, testimony, or otherwise in court.* As with the "writing" alternatives, the contract is not enforceable under this provision beyond the quantity of goods admitted.

5. Part of goods received by buyer, or part of contract price received by seller

Finally, the *part performance* alternative has been substantially changed by the Code. Previously, either party could use the other's receipt and acceptance of a partial performance as evidence of a much larger contract. For example, a seller who could prove having delivered 50 bushels of wheat to a buyer who had accepted the goods might then allege that this was merely the first installment on an oral contract for 1,000 bushels of wheat; if the jury believed the seller, the seller could get the contract enforced on that basis. The drafters of the Code felt that this result circumvented the policy of the Statute of Frauds, so they provided that partial performance by one party makes the contract enforceable against the other party only to the same, *pro rata* extent. Thus, in the above example the seller can only collect the contract price for the 50 bushels of wheat delivered and accepted; the rest of the oral contract remains unenforceable. However, if the goods are an indivisible unit, such as a car or a Boeing 707, the buyer's payment of part of the contract price, received and accepted by the seller, does have the effect of making the entire contract enforceable.

UCC rules for stocks and bonds

Compliance Alternatives under Other Code Sections. The Code permits the use of these same basic *alternatives for investment securities* with the exception of "special manufacture." To be sufficient, a writing under this section (8–319) must also contain the price term. The writing in confirmation procedure can be used between any buyer and seller; it is not limited to situations where both parties are, or are represented by, brokers or other securities "experts." Since these securities would normally exist in divisible units, partial performance here should nearly always result in only partial enforceability.

For security agreements, there must be a writing by which the debtor grants the secured party a security interest in the described collateral, and only if the *debtor* signs the writing will the secured party have the right to repossess and resell the collateral if the debtor goes into default. The only instances where such a writing is not required are in cases where the secured party has possession of the collateral, such as "pledge" or "pawn" transactions.

For sales of miscellaneous intangibles at a contract price of $5,000 or more, no alternative to the writing is provided. The signed writing must indicate that a contract has been made, must describe the subject matter of the contract, and must contain a price term.

■ Exhibit 12–2

Statute of Frauds: Compliance?

	Signed Writing	Writing in Conformation	Admission in Court	Part Performance	Special Manufacture
ALTERNATIVE METHODS OF COMPLIANCE WITH THE STATUTE OF FRAUDS					
Real estate	All material terms, signed PTBC	No	Split	Yes = Buyer possession + payment of improvements	N.A.
Year clause	All material terms, signed PTBC	No	Split	Quasi-K for benefits conferred	N.A.
Debt of another	All material terms. signed PTBC	No	Split	N.A.	N.A.
Goods $500 or more	Contract QUANTITY signed PAWEIS	To: PAWEIS(M) contract QUANTITY signed SENDER M	Yes—up to QUANTITY admitted	Yes—for a pro rata part if divided,	Yes—if all elements proved.
Investment securities	Contract QUANTITY PRICE signed PAWEIS	To: PAWEIS contract QUANTITY PRICE signed SENDER	Yes—up to QUANTITY admitted	Yes—for a pro rata part.	N.A.
Secured trans.	SECURITY INT. DESCRIPTION signed DEBTOR	No	No	Yes—possession of collateral by Creditor.	N.A.
Miscellaneous intangibles $5000 or more	Contract PRICE SUBJECT MATTER signed PAWEIS	No	No	No	N.A.

└── Notice that only the signature of the "party to be charged" / "party against whom enforcement is sought" is required on the writing.

With a sale of real estate, for example:
(a) If only BUYER has signed a 4Ps writing, the SELLER could sue for enforcement, but the BUYER could not.
(b) If only SELLER has signed a 4Ps writing, the BUYER could sue for enforcement, but the SELLER could not.
(c) If NEITHER has signed a 4Ps writing, NEITHER could sue for enforcement.
(d) If BOTH have signed a 4Ps writing, EITHER could sue for enforcement.

■ RESULTS IF THE STATUTE OF FRAUDS APPLIES AND IT HAS NOT BEEN SATISFIED

General rule: No compliance = Contract is unenforceable in court

Unenforceable in Court. In the vast majority of cases where the Statute of Frauds applies and has not been complied with, the contract is unenforceable in court. This does not mean that the contract is illegal in any way or that the parties have violated any criminal law. Nor does it mean that if the parties perform the contract in full, one of the parties can later move to rescind the performances on the basis that the contract should have been evidenced by a writing and never was. *Unenforceable contract* as applied here simply means that there will be no court remedy for the enforcement of such a contract, that the court will not assist either party with its sanctions for nonperformance of the contract unless the contract can be proved by the required writing.

This result is not changed by the fact that one party has relied in good faith (but stupidly) on the existence of the unenforceable oral contract. Courts do not generally feel that they are permitted to work out a result forbidden by the Statute of Frauds just because a particular plaintiff presents an appealing set of facts. The following case illustrates this point, with the court refusing to override the legislative policy expressed in the statue even though it doesn't particularly like the results produced.

DAVIS v. CROWN CENTRAL PETROLEUM CORP.

483 F.2d 1014 (U.S. Fourth Circuit, 1973)

FACTS The plaintiffs were small independent oil dealers with their main operations in North Carolina. The defendant was a refiner, dependent almost entirely on producers for its supply of crude oil. It had for some years been selling its product to the plaintiffs. In anticipation of the oil shortage, which all parties in the industry apparently foresaw, discussions as to future supplies were held among the parties. It was contended by the plaintiffs that the defendant agreed to supply them with certain fixed quantities of gasoline. As the energy crisis deepened, the defendant's suppliers drastically reduced its supply of crude oil. The defendant accordingly proceeded to allocate on a lower percentage its deliveries to its contract customers and to notify customers such as the plaintiffs, whom it denominated noncontract customers, that it would make no further sales to them. Preliminary injunctive relief was granted in both instances. In each case the defendant appealed.

ISSUE Can these contracts be enforced despite the Statute of Frauds?

DECISION No. Judgment for defendant in both cases.

REASONS Justice Russell stated:

"It is true, as the plaintiffs have argued, that in exceptional cases, courts of equity will find an estoppel against the enforcement of the statute, but such an estoppel can arise in North Carolina only 'upon grounds of fraud' on the part of him who relies on the statute. The District Court in neither case made a finding of 'fraud' on the part of the defendant, and, absent such finding, there can be no estoppel. Nor, on the facts in the record before us, would it appear that any such findings would have been in order. . . .

"A mere failure or refusal to perform an oral contract, within the statute, is not such fraud, within the meaning of this rule, as will take the case out of the operation of the statute, and this is ordinarily true even though the other party has changed his position to his injury.

"After all, as the district court in one of the cases observed, the plight of the defendant was not substantially different from that of the plaintiffs. It was experiencing hardships which forced it to take action it obviously did not relish.

"The claim of the plaintiffs is appealing, and our sympathies are with them. As the district courts indicated, it is equitable in periods of scarcity of basic materials for the government to inaugurate a program of mandatory allocations of the materials. This, however, is a power to be exercised by the legislative branch of government. The power of the Court extends only to the enforcement of valid contracts and does not comprehend the power to make mandatory allocations of scarce products on the basis of any consideration of the public interest."

"Part Performance" Exceptions. The UCC's exceptions where part performance of an oral contract for goods or securities has taken place, have already been discussed as "alternatives." In addition, courts have worked out limited exceptions to the unenforceability result for contracts involving real estate or the one-year clause.

Where one party has in good faith conferred benefits on the other under an oral contract which is unenforceable because of the one-year clause, a court will generally permit recovery in *quasi contract* of the fair market value of the benefits so as to prevent *unjust enrichment.* An employee who worked for three months under a two-year oral contract would thus be able to recover the fair market value of any services for which he or she had not been paid already. This exception would not, however, permit the recovery of moving expenses, bonuses, or other special compensation promised as part of the unenforceable oral agreement. The entire contract is enforceable, according to the *Restatement of Contracts, Second,* only where one party has *fully* performed his or her obligations; that party can then enforce the other party's full return performance.

For real estate contracts, the courts have developed a doctrine called *equitable estoppel,* which prevents a party from relying on the Statute of Frauds under certain limited circumstances and thus has the effect of making an oral contract enforceable. The courts have permitted either party to enforce an oral contract where the buyer has taken possession of real estate with the seller's permission and has made substantial permanent physical improvements or (perhaps) where the buyer has taken possession and has made a part payment on the contract price. This doctrine is generally not applicable in cases where there has been only a part payment of the price or only a taking of possession by the buyer, or only "reliance" expenditures such as preparation of documents by the seller or moving expenses by the buyer.

It is never advisable to rely on the slim chance that a court will salvage your situation by applying one of the exceptions to the Statute of Frauds. The only safe course is to *Get it in writing!* (And make sure the other party signs the writing!)

Exceptions for contracts over one year, if part performance

Exception for real estate, if payment—plus

■ PAROL EVIDENCE RULE

Reasons for parol evidence rule

Results under parol evidence rule

P.E.R. not applicable:

1. No final writing = No P.E. rule

Nature and Operation of the Rule.   Just as the operation of the Statute of Frauds can be summarized in the sentence "Get it in writing," so can the significance of the parol evidence rule be summarized by slightly modifying the sentence to read: *"Get it **all** in writing!"* The rule says that prior "outside" evidence cannot be used to change the terms of a complete, final written contract. It is a rule that limits the evidence a court can consider in interpreting the parties' agreement.

Although the application of the parol evidence rule may seem to produce harsh or unfair results in particular situations, the equities are not all on one side. There are sound, practical reasons for the rule's existence. It is, ultimately, another example of the courts' efforts to find and enforce the intent of the parties. The contracting parties may have engaged in extended negotiations before reaching their agreement. They may have exchanged numerous oral and written proposals and counterproposals, some accepted by the other side, some rejected. Then, at the end of this lengthy process, they signed a document which either expressly or impliedly stated that it was intended by them as the full, final, and complete written expression of their agreement.

At this point, the parol evidence rule comes into operation. Once a party has signed such a document, the rule prevents that party from unilaterally changing or modifying its terms by using parol, or outside, evidence. The document means what it says: "blue" means blue, not green; "10 tons" means 10 tons, not 100 tons or 10 pounds. If a term or a provision on a particular subject is not contained in the document, the presumption is that it was left out on purpose, because the parties did not intend that it be included. In short, the rule operates against the "add-on-a-term" person, who is trying to say, "Yes, that's the contract I signed. Yes, that's the deal I made. But—there's something else that we agreed on that's not in the document." In general, the "add-on" person will (and should) lose this argument; parol evidence will not be admitted to change the terms of the written document.

In other words, the parol evidence rule operates to protect *both* parties, by guaranteeing the integrity of the document they both signed and intended as "the contract." The rule is really not saying anything more "unfair" than that a person is, generally, bound by what he or she has signed. If the document isn't "right," if it doesn't contain all the terms you have agreed on, *Don't sign it!*

Situations Not Covered by the Rule.   Since the purpose of the parol evidence rule is to make final a document which the parties intended to be final, the rule has no application in contract situations where no such full, final, and complete document has ever been signed. In these cases, there is no "rule" that prohibits the court from looking at all relevant evidence. If the seller has simply given the buyer a sales receipt, or if the parties have merely exchanged letters, no such complete document exists, so all evidence is admissible to show what the parties intended to include as part of the contract. For sales of goods, a *final writing* may be "explained or supplemented," but not "contradicted," by "consistent additional terms," "unless the court finds the writing to have been intended also as a complete and exclusive statement of the terms of the agreement" (UCC, 2–202[b]). What this means in plain English is that a court *may* be a little more reluctant to apply the parol evidence rule in a sale of goods case where the contract does not contain a specific, "This is it" statement.

2. Extra promise made after final writing signed

Again remembering the basic purpose of the parol evidence rule, it obviously has no application in situations where the alleged modification of the terms in the document occurred *after* the document was signed. The document is presumed final as of the time it was signed. The parties may decide to modify it later, and the parol evidence rule does not prevent either of them from trying to convince a jury that such modifications were in fact agreed to. (There may, however, be both consideration and Statute of Frauds problems as to such subsequent modifications, as noted previously.)

3. Second separate oral contract

Third, and even more obviously, the rule has no application where there are *two* contracts, one evidenced by a complete writing, the other oral. The fact that one contract is written does not prevent a party from trying to prove that there was a second, oral contract. If you buy a used car from your next-door neighbors for $900, and they also agree to let you park the car in their garage for the next six months for $10 a month, the fact that you have signed a complete written contract for the sale of the car will not prevent you from trying to prove the existence of the separate oral contract to rent the garage space.

Exceptions to the Operation of the Parol Evidence Rule

Like many of the other rules of evidence, the parol evidence rule is subject to some important exceptions. That is, the trier of fact can consider parol evidence in some situations, at least for some purposes, even though a complete written document exists and even though the evidentiary facts occurred before the document was signed.

Stated most simply, parol evidence is admissible where it is being offered to help the court interpret the terms of the written contract or to show the existence of a defense against the written contract, not to *change* the terms of the written contract. The line is not always easy to draw, although in some cases the correct result seems fairly obvious.

1. Evidence to explain ambiguities in final written contract

Ambiguities.   The easiest cases to decide are those where the writing makes no sense by itself, due to ambiguities, contradictory provisions, or coded "nonsense" terms. In these cases a court must use extrinsic evidence to discover what the parties "really meant." Where both parties are engaged in a particular trade or business and certain words have acquired a customary meaning in that business, courts generally permit either party to prove that special meaning even though the words have a "plain English" meaning, too. Thus, an Oregon court permitted a seller to prove that "50 percent protein" really meant *49.50 percent* protein in the dog food business, and the seller could therefore collect the full contract price per ton for all shipments of dog food scraps with a protein content of at least 49.50 percent. For sales of goods, the UCC now permits the parties to explain or supplement a "final" writing by course of dealing, usage of trade, or course of performance.

2. Evidence that final written contract is conditional

Oral Conditions.   Most courts will also allow a party to show that the written contract was intended to be subject to an orally agreed-upon condition precedent, that they intended no deal at all unless and until some special condition was satisfied. Similarly, if the writing states as a fact something that is just not so, a party can usually prove the truth. For instance, if your contract to buy a new TV set not only describes the set and states the price and the payment terms, but also goes on to say that the set "has been delivered," when in fact it has not been delivered, you can prove that you didn't get the TV set as promised. (But the parol evidence rule will generally prevent you from changing "one TV" into *two* TVs, or "$600" into $450, or "TV" into stereo.)

Defenses. Courts are quite liberal in allowing proof of the existence of a defense against liability on the written contract. In most cases this is not really a "contradiction" of the writing because the writing does not usually contain such provisions as "This contract is legal" or "There was no duress." The contract may, however, contain a representation that the party signing it is of full legal age, and there are some courts which prevent a minor from asserting lack of capacity if the minor has stated otherwise in writing. (The next chapter has a more complete discussion of this point, and other defenses are covered in Chapters 14 and 15.)

3. Evidence of a defense against final written contract

■ SIGNIFICANCE OF THIS CHAPTER

Knowledge of the two major rules discussed in this chapter—the Statute of Frauds and the parol evidence rule—could save you and any organization you represent from many unnecessary lawsuits. This chapter contains the most significant legal "first-aid" rules in the entire book: *Get it in writing—and get it **all** in writing!* In some cases, you don't have any enforceable contract at all if you don't follow the rules. In other cases, you may wind up with a contract other than the one you intended, if you don't follow the rules.

People tend to forget promises and guarantees once they have your contract price, or your goods, land, or services. Promises are harder to "forget" if you have them in a signed writing. Take a little extra time and write up the agreement, or rewrite it, if it doesn't state the terms correctly. If the written agreement isn't clear and understandable, you should probably have your lawyer check it over for you. Once you sign it, you'll be bound by it, so make sure you know what it says—and make sure the *other* party signs it too, and that you get a signed copy. An ounce of written "prevention" is worth several pounds of lawyers.

DISCUSSION CASE

SHEPHERD REALTY CO., INC. v. WINN-DIXIE MONGOMERY, INC.

418 So.2d 871 (Alabama, 1982)

FACTS: On May 11, 1971, the Eugene Wylie Corpration and Winn-Dixie Montgomery entered into a 20-year lease for occupancy by Winn-Dixie of 30,000 square feet of premises for the operation of a supermarket in a development known as Brookwood Village Convenience Center immediately adjacent to the then proposed Brookwood Mall. Shepherd Realty is the current owner of the premises and the assignee of the rights of the landlord-lessor party to the 1971 lease to Winn-Dixie.

The 1971 lease was the result of arm's-length negotiations. Part of these negotiations centered around a letter of intent addressed to Winn-Dixie by Shepherd Realty dated October 22, 1970. That letter dealt with many of the preliminary negotiations needed for creation of the lease, including the following: location, amount of space to be occupied by lessee, amount of rentals, and the term of occupancy. Section 6 of the letter contained the following provision:

> (c) Tenant agrees to join the Brookwood Merchants Association when formed and pay for the first _____ years of the term $_____ and for the _____ years immediately following $_____ monthly as dues. Tenant agrees to contribute $_____ toward the opening promotion of the center.

The letter of intent was never signed by Winn-Dixie.

Winn-Dixie prepared a draft of the lease and it was reviewed, discussed, and modified by both parties until agreement was reached regarding terms of the lease, which were then reduced to writing. There was no specific reference requiring membership in the Brookwood Village Merchants Association contained in the lease. There was, however, paragraph 42, entitled "Rules and Regulations," that stated:

> 42. Tenant agrees to abide by all reasonable rules and regulations promulgated by Landlord from time to time, the purpose of which rules and regulations is to promote the best interests of the shopping center and its customers. Tenant intends to operate its business in keeping with the dignity and reputation of the shopping center, and will make every reasonable effort to work harmoniously with Landlord, other merchants in the Center and residents of the surrounding area.

Shepherd Realty contends that paragraph 42 was intended to require Winn-Dixie to join the merchants association and to remain a member. A major conflict in the evidence arose when James Wylie Shepherd, president of Shepherd Realty, testified that Bamber Cox, an employee of Winn-Dixie with whom Shepherd Realty was negotiating, acknowledged that paragraph 42 required Winn-Dixie to become a member of the merchants association and to thereafter continue to be a member. Cox testified that he did not recall such an acknowledgment. Cox did recall, however, that Winn-Dixie agreed to contribute monies to the merchants association.

The Brookwood Village Merchants Association was formed in 1974 upon completion of the Brookwood Village Mall area. The yearly dues for membership were set at 20 cents per square foot of space occupied by a lessee.

Winn-Dixie paid monthly dues from the time the merchants association was organied in 1974 until the dues were increased to 28 cents per square foot in August 1979. It initially refused to pay the increased dues; later it sought to discontinue paying any dues. Shepherd Realty threatened to declare Winn-Dixie's lease in default for nonpayment of dues, whereupon Winn-Dixie agreed to pay the increased dues under protest.

Shepherd Realty filed a complaint against Winn-Dixie on May 9, 1979 for breach of contract based upon Winn-Dixie's refusal and protest of payment of the increased dues.

Shepherd Realty Company, Inc. appeals from a final judgment, which denied recovery against Winn-Dixie Montgomery, Inc. for breach of contract.

■

Justice Embry stated that:

There was no error in the trial court's ruling that Winn-Dixie was not required to be a member of the Brookwood Village Merchants Association. There is no specific language in the lease requiring Winn-Dixie to join the merchants association. Furthermore, the record reflects that specific language requiring such membership was found in the leases of other tenants of Brookwood Village but not in the Winn-Dixie lease.

Shepherd Realty vigorously argues that paragraph 42 of the lease should be construed as requiring Winn-Dixie to become and remain a member of the merchants association. Upon a careful reading of that paragraph, together with the other terms of the lease, we conclude that paragraph 42 cannot be construed as requiring Winn-Dixie's membership in the merchants association. Rather, we conclude that this paragraph, on its face, only provides a means by which Shepherd Realty may compel Winn-Dixie to comply with rules affecting the normal operation of Brookwood Village Convenience Center of a nature regarding parking, maintenance, etc., insofar as its premises and appurtenant facilities are concerned. Once a contract between two parties is reduced to writing, absent mistake or fraud, the courts must construe the contract as written. "Furthermore in the absence of ambiguity the court cannot interpret the contract but must take it as it is written." . . .

Paragraph 33 of the lease also militates against a liberal construction of paragraph 42. Paragraph 33 provides:

> 33. The written lease contains the complete agreement of the parties with reference to the leasing of the demised premises except plans and specifications for tenant's store and related improvements to be formally approved by the parties prior to the effective date of this lease.

We agree with Winn-Dixie that "Paragraph 33 clearly indicates the lease constitutes the complete agreement between the parties."

The trial court was correct in refusing to admit parol evidence to show the "true intent" of the parties. It is fundamental that the parol evidence rule prohibits the contradiction of a written agreement by evidence of a prior oral agreement. The rule provides, generally, that when the parties reduce a contract to writing, intended to be a complete contract regarding the subject covered by that contract, no extrinsic evidence of prior or contemporaneous agreements will be admissible to change, alter, or contradict such writing. . . .

Under the facts of this case we conclude the trial court did not err in its findings or entry of judgment. The judgment below is due to be and is hereby affirmed.

■ IMPORTANT TERMS AND CONCEPTS

Statute of Frauds
parol evidence rule
assignment of contract rights
real estate transfer
promise to pay debt of another
year clause
lifetime contract
sale of goods
investment securities
secured transaction
miscellaneous intangible property
letter of credit
modification of prior contract
UCC rule for modification of goods contract
consideration substitutes
all material terms rule

4Ps
signed writing
writing in confirmation
merchant
specially manufactured goods
admission in court
part performance of goods contract
alternatives for investment securities
unenforceable contract
quasi contract
unjust enrichment
Restatement of Contracts, Second
equitable estoppel
final writing
ambiguity in contract
oral condition to contract
defenses against contract

■ QUESTIONS AND PROBLEMS FOR DISCUSSION

1. When is an oral contract enforceable in court?
2. What happens when the Statute of Frauds applies to a contract and only one party signs a writing which is sufficient to comply with its requirements?
3. When does the Statute of Frauds apply to an employment contract?
4. What must a writing include, under the Uniform Commercial Code, to comply with the Statute of Frauds?
5. On May 30, 1988 Roger entered into an oral contract with Merc Motors whereby he was to be employed as sales manager for a one-year period starting June 6, 1988. He was to receive a salary of $2,200 per month plus a bonus to be later agreed upon but with a guaranteed yearly minimum of $40,000. In addition, the employer was to pay plaintiff's moving expenses, provide him with a company automobile, and reduce the agreement to writing on June 6, 1988. Roger quit his job in St. Louis, moved his family to Champaign, Illinois, and assumed his duties pursuant to the agreement. However, Merc Motors did not abide by the agreement, so Roger quit on March 18, 1989. He claimed damages of $22,527. Can he collect? Explain.

6. On June 29, Irma Embea, eager to get started in a business of her own, entered into a written agreement for the purchase of Sweet Corner Candy Shop from retiring John Olds. She paid earnest money of $1,000, with the remaining $15,000 due on July 26, the agreed closing date. When Irma could not obtain financing by July 26, she telephoned John Olds, who extended the deadline until August 31. Irma was not able to meet this deadline either and asked for a new extension over the phone. She claims that it was granted to her. John Olds, however, denies having granted a second extension. He subsequently sold the candy store to a third party. Now Irma Embea sues John Olds for specific performance of the contract. What is the decision? Discuss.

7. Eugene Feudal brings this action against Mr. and Mrs. Trustee. The two parties had entered into an oral rental agreement which continued for several years. In September the Trustees suddenly stopped payment. When they had not paid any rent by December, Eugene brought an action against them. The Trustees countered by claiming that they were the owners of the disputed premises, which Eugene Feudal had sold to them in an oral contract two years ago. They said that they had stopped payment when their obligation under the oral contract had been fulfilled. Mrs. Trustee testified that she had heard her husband and Feudal discussing the possibility of a sale. Mr. Trustee told his attorney that Feudal would contact him to draw up a contract. Was there an enforceable contract? Why or why not?

8. Solar Service, Inc., contracted with Sheet Metal Co. to do about $500 of sheet metal fabrication work. Later, Solar Service again wanted to contract with Sheet Metal Co. to do much more extensive work. Solar Service had never paid the original bill, so Sheet Metal refused to do the work until credit arrangements were made. Roger Sun, the president, a director, and a shareholder of Solar Service, orally guaranteed payment of the work. Sun had a falling out with the other corporate officers and directors and as a result resigned from his positions in the company. Solar Service, Inc., never completed payments for the work so Sheet Metal Co. sues Sun for the remainder due. What result, and why?

13

Defenses—Lack of Capacity

CHAPTER OBJECTIVES
THIS CHAPTER WILL:

- Discuss the effect of lack of capacity on a contract.
- Explain the three main theories of liability that may be asserted against a minor who makes a contract.
- Indicate possible results when a minor misrepresents his or her age.
- Discuss other groups of persons with special legal status or limited contractual capacity.

Even though parties have entered into a contract that appears complete, and the agreement is enforceable under the Statute of Frauds, they still may have defenses against liability on the contract. Depending on the defense proved, the contract may be voidable at the option of one or both parties, the whole contract may be unenforceable, or the entire agreement may be void.

We consider, first, defenses based on a party's lack of capacity to contract. Capacity questions may be raised with regard to minors, insane persons, persons under the influence of alcohol or other drugs, aliens, American Indians, convicts, married women, and private and governmental corporations. Rulings on these questions are usually made according to the law of the place where the contract is entered into, except where real estate is involved; for realty, the law of the state where the realty is located determines capacity questions.

■ MINORS, OR "LEGAL INFANTS"

It is sometimes said that "minors can't make contracts." That is patently not so; minors can and do make millions of dollars' worth of contracts every day. What is distinctive about the minor's contract is that it is voidable at his or her option; the minor can later elect not to be bound by it. But make no mistake; the other party, unless that party too lacks full contractual capacity, *is* bound to the agreement with the minor. The common-law judges were concerned with the possibility that the "infant" might be taken advantage of, and so gave the minor the virtually absolute right of disaffirmance. Although minors today may be more sophisticated at an earlier age, this rule continues to be applied by the courts.

Minors' special legal status

We need, then, to examine the scope of minors' power to disaffirm their contracts and to see when minors may be liable under five different legal bases for liability (Exhibit 13–1).

Scope of the Minor's Power to Disaffirm. The common law set the age of legal majority at 21; until quite recently that was also the age used for full contractual capacity in nearly all states. The adoption of the Voting Rights Amendment, setting the voting age at 18, has led most states to similarly lower their age of majority to 18 (except perhaps for the age at which one can lawfully buy alcoholic beverages). Different ages, however, may still exist in some states for such matters as criminal responsibility, marriage without parental consent, and making a valid will. However, we are concerned here only with the legal capacity to make fully binding contracts.

Whatever age is established in a state, it refers strictly to chronological age. How old the minors "look," or how "experienced" they are, is completely irrelevant to minors' power to disaffirm their contracts. Equally irrelevant is the fact that the minors might be living away from their parents and are totally free of their control (i.e., emancipated). These facts would, however, be relevant in deciding whether an item was a "necessary," as discussed below.

In general, minors have the power to disaffirm any contract they make while still a minor. In some states, certain contracts are made binding against the minor by special statutes (bank accounts and life insurance contracts are typical examples), but these are special, and very limited, exceptions.

■ EXHIBIT 13-1
Litigation Against the
Minor: Five Theories of
Liability

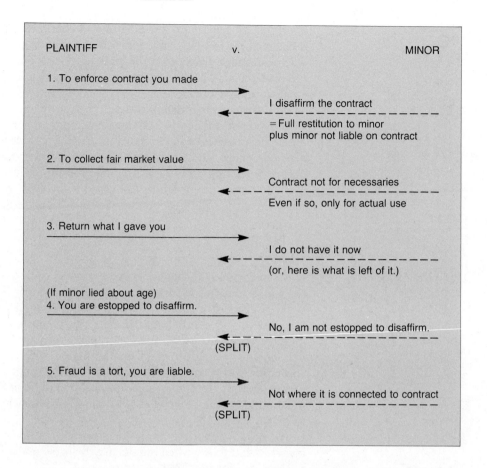

PLAINTIFF   v.   MINOR

1. To enforce contract you made

              I disaffirm the contract

              = Full restitution to minor
              plus minor not liable on contract

2. To collect fair market value

              Contract not for necessaries

              Even if so, only for actual use

3. Return what I gave you

              I do not have it now

              (or, here is what is left of it.)

(If minor lied about age)
4. You are estopped to disaffirm.

              No, I am not estopped to disaffirm.

       (SPLIT)

5. Fraud is a tort, you are liable.

              Not where it is connected to contract

       (SPLIT)

In most states, minors can disaffirm a contract any time while they are still minors and for a reasonable time after arriving at the age of majority. For contracts involving real estate, most states say that minors cannot disaffirm until reaching the age of majority, and then they have a reasonable time to elect to affirm or disaffirm. What is a reasonable time within which to disaffirm is a question to be determined by the facts of each case, with the courts paying particular attention to whether the minor was aware of the right to disaffirm.

Method of disaffirmance

Any words or actions which indicate the minor's intent not to be bound by the contract are sufficient notice of disaffirmance. Asking for the money back or offering to return items bought while a minor would be clear indications of an intent to disaffirm. Where the contract is completely "executory" (i.e., not performed by either side), even the minor's silence may amount to a disaffirmance. The minor's failure to confirm the unperformed contract after age 18 indicates an unwillingness to be bound by it, but the receipt and retention of benefits or the making of a payment on the contract by the former minor would probably be a ratification of the contract. Silence has the opposite implication where the minor has received the performance of the other party and has, in return, performed under the contract while still a minor, and then turns 18 but says nothing about wanting to disaffirm. In this case, silence beyond the reasonable time for disaffirmance equals ratification.

Ratification by minor

All states agree that *ratification* by the minor can occur only after the minor has arrived at the age of majority; otherwise, any "ratification" can be disaffirmed since it too occurred while the person was a minor. In addition to the "silence" case described above, ratification can be made by express statements, such as "I'll keep the car," or it may be implied from the retention of benefits, or from payments made after the minor has reached age 18.

The question in the following case is whether the defendant waited too long to disaffirm.

BOBBY FLOARS TOYOTA, INC. v. SMITH

269 S.E.2d 320 (North Carolina, 1980)

FACTS

Defendant Charles Edward Smith, Jr., purchased an automobile from plaintiff on 15 August 1973. On that date defendant was 17 years old and would have his 18th birthday on 25 September 1973. Defendant executed a purchase money security agreement to finance $2,362, the balance due on the purchase price of the automobile, payable in 30 installments of $99.05 each. Plaintiff subsequently assigned the purchase money security agreement to First Union National Bank. After having made 11 monthly payments pursuant to the installment loan contract, 10 of which were made after his 18th birthday, defendant voluntarily returned the automobile to plaintiff and defaulted on his payment obligations. Upon default, First Union reassigned the purchase money security agreement to plaintiff, which proceeded to sell the automobile at public auction. At the time of sale a balance was owing on the purchase money security agreement of $1,521.52. The car was sold for $700, leaving a deficiency of $821.52. From the judgment dismissing plaintiff's complaint, plaintiff appeals.

ISSUE

Did the minor buyer wait too long to disaffirm?

DECISION

Yes. Judgment reversed.

REASONS

Judge Morris cited several precedents.

"The rule in North Carolina regarding a minor's contract liability is as follows:

> It is well settled that the conventional contracts of an infant, except those for necessities and those authorized by statute, are voidable at the election of the infant and may be disaffirmed by the infant during minority or within a reasonable time after reaching majority. . . .
>
> '[W]hat is a reasonable time depends upon the circumstances of each case, no hard-and-fast rule regarding precise time limits being capable of definition.' . . .
>
> The most reasonable rule seems to be that the right of disaffirmance should be exercised within a reasonable time after the infant attains his majority, or else his neglect to avail himself of this privilege should be deemed an acquiescence and affirmation on his part of his conveyance. The law considers his contract a voidable one, on account of its tender solicitude for his rights and the fear that he may be imposed upon in his bargain. But he is certainly afforded ample protection by allowing him a reasonable time after he reaches his majority to determine whether he will abide by his conveyance, executed while he was a minor, or will disaffirm it. And it is no more than just and reasonable that if he silently acquiesces in his deed and makes no effort to express his dissatisfaction with his act, he should, after the lapse of a reasonable time, dependent upon circumstances, be considered as fully ratifying it.

"In the instant case, we believe that 10 months is an unreasonable time within which to elect between disaffirmance and ratification, in that this case involves an automobile, an item of personal property which is constantly depreciating in value. Modern commercial transactions require that both buyers and sellers be responsible and prompt.

"We are of the further opinion that defendant waived his right to avoid the contract. The privilege of disaffirmance may be lost where the infant affirms or otherwise ratifies the contract after reaching majority. Our Supreme Court has held that, under the particular circumstances, certain affirmations or conduct evidencing ratification were sufficient to bind the infant, regardless of whether a reasonable time for disaffirmance had passed. . . . Application of this rule often leads to an equitable result, particularly where the infant can be fairly said to have recognized and adopted as binding a contract under which the infant accepts the benefits of the contract to the prejudice of the other party.

"In the present case, it is clear that defendant Smith recognized as binding the installment note evidencing the debt owed from his purchase of an automobile. It is undisputed that he continued to possess and operate the automobile after his 18th birthday, and he continued to make monthly payments as required by the note for 10 months after becoming 18. In fact, defendant's conduct in returning the automobile and acquiescing in default being entered against him is strong evidence that defendant recognized the security agreement, which provided for repossession after default, as controlling. There is no evidence to indicate that defendant ever made a demand for rescission of the contract because of his infancy or that he ever had any intention of doing so. We hold, therefore that defendant's acceptance of the benefits and continuance of payments under the contract constituted a ratification of the contract, precluding subsequent disaffirmance."

Effect of Minor's Disaffirmance on the Contract. Once a minor has effectively exercised the power to disaffirm a contract, the minor can no longer be held liable for any promises made therein; the minor's contract was voidable, and the minor has elected to avoid it. Thus, where a minor purchased an automobile and promised to make installment payments for the balance of the contract price, if the minor disaffirms, then the minor is no longer liable for the balance still due. Likewise, a minor who disaffirms such a voidable contract generally has the legal right to receive all benefits already transferred to the other party under the contract. For example, in the car purchase case, the minor is entitled to the return of all monies already paid to the seller of the car. A minor who gave the seller a trade-in car as part of the down payment is entitled to the return of that too, or of its fair market value if the seller no longer has it.

Minor's right to restitution

Where the benefits given by the minor have been retransferred to third parties, the minor can generally sue such third parties and demand the return of such property. Thus a minor who sells real estate while a minor would be able to reclaim it even as against a good faith third party who bought the real estate from the minor's buyer. As exceptions to the general third-party rule, the UCC protects good faith purchaser third parties against such claims by minors in two situations: where the minor's goods have been resold by the initial buyer to a good faith purchaser or where a promissory note or other negotiable instrument executed by a minor has gotten into the hands of a *holder in due course* (basically, just another name for a good faith purchaser). This HDC rule is discussed in detail in Part Five, Commercial Paper. In each of these two exception situations, the minor could not recover the instrument or the goods from the third party. The minor could, however, still use minority to avoid liability as the seller/transferor of the property.

Liability in Quasi Contract for Necessaries. To prevent **unjust enrichment** and to provide a remedy for persons who have transferred benefits but have no enforceable contract claim for their price, the common-law courts developed the concept of **quasi contract.** While acknowledging that there is no enforceable contract claim, this theory permits a plaintiff to collect the reasonable market value of benefits that the plaintiff has conferred, "as if" a contract existed.

Minor's liability in quasi contract for necessaries

A minor is liable in quasi contract for the reasonable market value of **necessaries** actually furnished to the minor pursuant to the minor's now-disaffirmed contract. The other party has the burden of proving that whatever was furnished was actually a necessary to the *particular* minor whom the party dealt with; proof that general categories of necessaries, such as food, clothing, shelter, or medical services, were furnished to the minor is not sufficient to establish the seller's right to recovery. It must also be shown that the minor in question had no source of supply of these items and that the items were furnished to the minor in reasonable amounts. An apartment would not be a necessary, for example, for minors who could live with their parents; and even if *an* apartment were a necessary for the particular minor, a 10-room penthouse would probably not be. Although the courts today are somewhat more liberal in defining necessaries, sellers of such obvious "luxury" items as stereos, TVs, and vacations probably have no case under this theory. Even where an item is found to be a necessary, the proper measure of recovery is only its fair market value (a fact question), not its contract price, and that *only* for the benefits already conferred on and used by the minor. In the case of the apartment found to be a necessary, the landlord can collect only what a jury determines to be the fair market value and only for the period of time that the minor stayed in the apartment.

Fair market value = recovery

Minor's Duty to Make Restitution. Under the general rule, as applied in most states, a minor who wishes to disaffirm a contract has the duty to return to the other party whatever contract benefits are still in the minor's possession at the time of disaffirmance. In most states the minor has no duty to reimburse the other party for that portion of the consideration which the minor has lost, wasted, or disposed of during infancy. In the classic example, a 16-year-old boy buys a new Cadillac, drives it until he is almost 18, then "totals" it in an accident. In most states the minor's only duty of restitution is to return the wreck; the minor is not liable for the use value of the car while the minor had it or for the extensive "depreciation" in the value of the car. Similarly, if the minor had resold the car and spent the proceeds, the minor would have nothing at all to restore but could still disaffirm the original purchase contract and get back whatever payment the minor had made to the original seller. (In short, car dealers are repeatedly warned: *"Don't sell to minors!"*) The same result—no restitution at all by the minor—occurs when the minor has received intangible benefits such as a vacation or services.

Minor's liability for restitution

The *Webster Street* case is a recent example of how these rules operate to protect minors.

WEBSTER STREET PARTNERSHIP, LTD.
v. SHERIDAN

368 N.W.2d 439 (Nebraska, 1985)

FACTS   Webster Street Partnership, Ltd. appeals from an order of district court which modified an earlier judgment entered by the municipal court of the city of Omaha. The municipal court entered judgment in favor of Webster Street and against Matthew Sheridan and Pat Wilwerding, in the amount of $630.94. On appeal the district court found that Webster Street was entitled to judgment in the amount of $146.75 and that Sheridan and Wilwerding were entitled to a credit in the amount of $150. The district court therefore entered judgment in favor of Sheridan and Wilwerding and against Webster Street in the amount of $3.25. It is from this $3.25 judgment that appeal is taken.

On September 18, 1982, Webster Street, through one of its agents, Norman Sargent, entered into a written lease with Sheridan and Wilwerding for a second-floor apartment at 3007 Webster Street. The lease provided that Sheridan and Wilwerding would pay to Webster Street by way of monthly rental the sum of $250 due on the first day of each month until August 15, 1983. The lease also required the payment of a security deposit in the amount of $150 and a payment of $20 per month for utilities during the months of December, January, February, and March.

At the time the lease was executed both tenants were minors and Webster Street knew that fact. At the time the lease was entered into, Sheridan was 18 and did not become 19 until November 5, 1982. Wilwerding was 17 at the time the lease was executed and never gained his majority during any time relevant to this case.

The tenants paid the $150 security deposit, $100 rent for the remaining portion of September 1982, and $250 rent for October 1982. They did not pay the rent for the month of November 1982, and on November 5 Sargent advised Wilwerding that unless the rent was paid immediately, both boys would be required to vacate the premises. The tenants both testified that, being unable to pay the rent, they moved from the premises on November 12.

Webster Street thereafter commenced suit against the tenants and sought judgment in the amount of $630.94, which was calculated as follows:

Rent due November	$250.00
Rent due December	250.00
December utility allowance	20.00
Garage rental	40.00
Clean up and repair broken window, degrease kitchen stove, shampoo carpet, etc.	46.79
Advertising	24.15
Rerental fee	150.00
	780.94
Less security deposit	150.00
	$630.94

Following trial, the municipal court of Omaha found in favor of Webster Street and against both tenants in the amount of $630.94.

The tenants appealed to the district court for Douglas County. The district court found that the tenants had vacated the premises on November 12, 1982, and therefore were only liable for the 12 days in which they actually occupied the apartment and did not pay rent. The district court also permitted Webster Street to recover $46.79 for cleanup and repairs. The tenants, however, were given credit for their $150 security deposit, resulting in an order that Webster Street was indebted to the tenants in the amount of $3.25.

ISSUE   Was the apartment a "necessary"?

DECISION No. Judgment for Webster Street reversed; judgment for minors for $500.

REASON   Chief Justice Krivosha first stated the rules, and then reviewed the facts.

"As a general rule, an infant does not have the capacity to bind himself absolutely by contract. . . . The right of the infant to avoid his contract is one conferred by law for his protection against his own improvidence and the designs of others. . . . The policy of the law is to discourage adults from contracting with an infant; they cannot complain if, as a consequence of violating that rule, they are unable to enforce their contracts. . . . 'The result seems hardly just to the [adult], but persons dealing with infants do so at their peril. The law is plain as to their disability to contract, and safety lies in refusing to transact business with them.'

"However, the privilege of infancy will not enable an infant to escape liability in all cases and under all circumstances. For example, it is well established that infant is liable for the value of necessaries furnished him. . . . An infant's liability for necessaries is based not upon his actual contract to pay for them but upon a contract implied by law, or, in other words, a quasi contract. . . .

"The undisputed testimony in this case is that both tenants were living away from home, apparently with the understanding that they could return home at any time. Sheridan testified:

Q. During the time that you were living at 3007 Webster, did you at any time, feel free to go home or anything like that?
A. Well, I had a feeling I could, but I just wanted to see if I could make it on my own.
Q. Had you been driven from your home?
A. No.
Q. You didn't have to go?
A. No.
Q. You went freely?
A. Yes.
Q. Then, after you moved out and went to 3417 for a week or so, you were again to return home, is that correct?
A. Yes.

It would therefore appear that in the present case neither Sheridan nor Wilwerding was in need of shelter but, rather, had chosen to voluntarily leave home, with the understanding that they could return whenever they desired. One may at first blush believe that such a rule is unfair. Yet, on further consideration the wisdom of the rule is apparent. If, indeed, landlords may not contract the minors, except at their peril, they may refuse to do so. In that event, minors who voluntarily leave home but who are free to return will be compelled to return to their parents' home—a result which is desirable. We therefore find that both the municipal court and the district court erred in finding that the apartment, under the facts in this case, was a necessary.

"Having therefore concluded that the apartment was not a necessary, the question of whether Sheridan and Wilwerding were emancipated is of no significance. The effect of emancipation is only relevant with regard to necessaries. If the minors were not emancipated, then their parents would be liable for necessaries provided to the minors. . . .

"If, on the other hand, it was determined that the minors were emancipated and the apartment was a necessary, then the minors would be liable. But where, as here, we determine that the apartment was not a necessary, then neither the parents nor the infants are liable and the question of emancipation is of no moment.

"Because the rental of the apartment was not a necessary, the minors had the right to avoid the contract, either during their minority or within a reasonable time after reaching their majority. . . . Disaffirmance by an infant completely puts an end to the contract's existence, both as to him and as to the adult with whom he contracted. . . . Because the parties then stand as if no contract had ever existed, the infant can recover payments made to the adult, and the adult is entitled to the return of whatever was received by the infant. . . .

"The record shows that Pat Wilwerding clearly disaffirmed the contract during his minority. Moreover, the record supports the view that when the agent for Webster Street ordered the minors out for failure to pay rent and they vacated the premises, Sheridan likewise disaffirmed the contract. The record indicates that Sheridan reached majority on November 5. To suggest that a lapse of seven days was not disaffirmance within a reasonable time would be foolish. Once disaffirmed, the contract became void; therefore, no contract existed between the parties, and the minors were entitled to recover all of the moneys which they paid and to be relieved of any further obligation under the contract. The judgment of the district court for Douglas County, Nebraska, is therefore reversed and the cause remanded with directions to vacate the judgment in favor of Webster Street and to enter a judgment in favor of Matthew Sheridan and Pat Wilwerding in the amount of $500, representing September rent in the amount of $100, October rent in the amount of $250, and the security deposit in the amount of $150."

Estoppel to Assert Minority. As applied in most states, the above rules are hard enough on the adult seller, but even harsher results occur when minors have misrepresented their age and thus have induced the other party to contract on the assumption that they were adults.

General rule: no estoppel of minor

Estoppel, remember, is the legal rule that prevents a party from denying the legal effectiveness of a previous statement, after another party has changed his or her position in reliance on the earlier statement. Shouldn't that rule be applied where the other party has made a contract in reliance on the minor's statement that the minor was of legal age to contract? Shouldn't the minor, in other words, be estopped from asserting minority in such a case? Some courts do apply estoppel against the minor here, but the majority do not. A special California statute provides a procedure for court approval of employment contracts for minor athletes and artists; the minor-employee is bound to the contract once the court approves it.

Tort Liability for Misrepresentation of Age. Minors are, as a general rule, liable for their own torts, and intentional misrepresentation is a tort—fraud. Should not the other party, having been damaged by reasonable reliance on the minor's misrepresentation of age, be able to sue the minor on a tort theory of liability even though the contract has been disaffirmed? Once again, the courts are split on this point. A slight majority still follows the older view that the minor cannot be sued in tort, where to do so would amount to

Courts split on tort liability for misrepresenting age

holding the minor liable on his or her contract. The policy protecting the minor against unnecessary contracts is more important to most courts than the policy of holding the minor liable for torts.

It probably should also be noted at this point that a minor's parents are not generally liable for the minor's torts or the minor's contracts, although they are legally obligated to support the minor with the necessities of life. Some states do have statutes which make parents liable for their minor children's intentional torts, up to a specific dollar amount of damages.

■ PERSONS WHO ARE INSANE, INTOXICATED, OR DRUGGED

Contracts made by persons who lack contractual capacity because their ability to make decisions has been impaired by mental disease or defect, or by alcohol or drugs, are treated in much the same way as contracts made by minors. As a general rule, where a person's mental faculties are so impaired that the person does not understand the nature and consequences of the transaction, the resulting contract is voidable at the person's option when the person recovers, or at the option of a subsequently appointed guardian. If any such person has previously been taken before a (probate) court, adjudged incompetent to manage his or her own affairs, and had a guardian appointed, then later contracts made by that person are not just voidable but totally void. The person need take no action to disaffirm the contracts; they simply will not be recognized by the courts.

Such persons are generally liable in quasi contract for the fair market value of necessaries furnished to them during their period of disability (assuming that these needs are not already being met by a guardian), under basically the same rules as those that apply to minors. Much more strictly than with the minor, the courts require the mentally disabled person to make full restitution in money or the equivalent in order to disaffirm contracts entered into in good faith by the other party. Note the "good faith" of the plaintiff doctor in the following case.

KRASNER v. BERK

319 N.E.2d 897 (Massachusetts, 1974)

FACTS

The plaintiff and the defendant, both doctors, occupied a suite of medical offices from 1964 to 1969, and shared the rent equally. In April 1969, they renewed the lease for three years beginning June 1, 1969, and on May 22, 1969, they agreed in writing that each would pay half the rent and taxes due under the lease, even if one of them moved out or was "unable to occupy his suite as a result of disability or for any other reason." The written agreement was drawn up by the plaintiff's attorney. The defendant, aged fifty-three, was diagnosed in November 1969, as suffering from presenile dementia, and in July 1970, he closed his office and moved out. It was stipulated that his share of the rent and taxes for the period from August 1, 1970, to the expiration of the lease, May 31, 1972, was $7,754.18.

The defendant's wife and brother testified to his behavior. In September 1967, he began to be absentminded and confused, he missed appointments with patients, and records piled up in his office. He was unable to answer direct questions with direct answers, and was forgetful and oversolicitious of everyone. While skiing in New Hampshire, he would get lost and be unable to find the lifts. On a trip in August 1968, he kept getting lost and sometimes could not find his hotel room or his tickets. He failed to keep an appointment with his brother in 1968. In the fall of 1968 he began to consult doctors about his health. As of 1968 his brother could no longer permit him to write prescriptions for patient-employees at the brother's company in Maine, although he continued to examine them. In the winter or spring of 1969 he went to the movies and climbed over the seats while his brother walked down the aisle. Early in 1969 he could not use his dictaphone; he ran over his medical bag in the parking lot several times; if his watch stopped, he would not know how to fix it. He would forget there were patients waiting for him. Sometimes he would leave his car at his ski lodge in New Hampshire and hitchhike home to Newton; at least once every two weeks he would forget his car at the office and hitchhike home. The defendant's wife talked to the plaintiff about these matters and the plaintiff said that he knew her husband and he seemed to be the same as he always was.

A neurologist called as a witness by the defendant testified that the defendant was referred to him on June 5, 1969, and was found to be a friendly, cooperative man with a disorder of immediate recall; beyond this the neurological examination was entirely unrevealing. At this time there was discussion about the defendant's giving up his practice. In November 1969, the witness saw the defendant again. This time the hospital record showed a diagnosis of disturbance of brain function manifested by memory impairment and episodic confusion. The patient's history included the fact that his mother had a presenile dementia (loss of high intellectual function, memory, judgment) beginning at the age of 50, accounting for the patient's terrible fear of the problem. The patient refused a definitive study because of the fear that it might demonstrate a pathology of which he was fearful. A neuropsychological test showed a verbal IQ of 116 (above average) and a performance IQ of 76 (very dangerously low, at the moronic level), indicating that the defendant was unable to reason, unable to form proper judgment, and unable to learn new material.

Based on the findings, the diagnosis was of presenile dementia. The patient had a disease in which there was premature senility of the brain; at the age of 53, he had a loss of higher mental abilities resembling that of very-old-age dementia. The condition had been developing slowly for a matter of years and was permanent. The witness advised the defendant to give up his practice.

The trial court found for the defendant, but the Appellate Division reversed.

ISSUE   Did the defendant lack mental capacity to make a contract?

DECISION   Yes. Judgment reversed.

REASONS   Justice Braucher got right to the main question:

"The sole question presented to us in this action of contract is whether the evidence was sufficient to warrant a finding that at the time the contract was entered into by the defendant he was of unsound mind and mentally incapable of making the agreement. The trial judge denied the plaintiff's requested ruling that the evidence was insufficient, and found for the defendant, but the Appellate Division ordered the finding vacated and judgment entered for the plaintiff. We hold that the evidence warranted a finding that the defendant did not understand in a reasonable manner the nature and consequences of the transaction. . . .

"We have said that in an inquiry into capacity to contract, 'the true test is, was the party whose contract it is sought to avoid in such a state of insanity at the time as to render him incapable of transacting the business.' If he 'could not understand the nature and quality of the transaction or grasp its significance, then it was not the act of a person of sound mind. There may be intellectual weakness not amounting to lack of power to comprehend. But an inability to realize the true purport of the matter in hand is equivalent to mental incapacity.' We have required proof that the person in question 'was too weak in mind to execute the deed with understanding of its meaning, effect, and consequences.' These expressions do not differ in substance from the statement of the rule in *Restatement (Second) of Contracts.* . . . 'A person incurs only voidable contractual duties by entering into a transaction if by reason of mental illness or defect. . . . he is unable to understand in a reasonable manner the nature and consequences of the transaction.'

"Even where there is sufficient understanding, a contract may in some circumstances be voidable by reason of failure of will or judgment, where the person contracting, by reason of mental illness or defect, is unable to act in a reasonable manner in relation to the transaction and the other party has reason to know of his condition. There was evidence in the present case to support a finding that the defendant had a terrible fear of presenile dementia and could not bring himself to face that prospect. There was evidence also that the defendant's wife discussed the defendant's condition with the plaintiff, and that the plaintiff's attorney drew up a written agreement referring explicitly to inability to occupy the suite 'as a result of disability.' Perhaps it might be inferred that the plaintiff, contrary to his testimony, had reason to know of the defendant's condition.

"On the sufficiency of understanding, the case is a close one. We have little doubt that on a record like this one a finding that the defendant had testamentary capacity, as distinguished from capacity to contract, would be upheld.

"We think, however, that we would invade the province of the trial judge if we drew inferences as to capacity to understand from actions of the defendant which in the setting may have been equivocal. 'Where a person has some understanding of a particular transaction which is affected by mental illness or defect, the controlling consideration is whether the transaction in its result is one which a reasonably competent person might have made.' When the defendant made the lease and the agreement, his medical practice had already been curtailed, and the judge could infer that this was the result of his mental condition. Within two weeks after signing the agreement he consulted a doctor specializing in brain disease and discussed giving up his practice, and within six months that doctor advised him to give up the practice of medicine. The agreement made was an improvident one for a doctor who was about to consider whether he should give up his practice. We think the judge could find that he was not competent to make it."

ALIENS

Aliens in the United States are not generally subject to any contractual disability unless they are in the country illegally or their country is at war with ours. In either case, they will usually not be able to use our courts to enforce contracts. Aside from these two exceptional cases, some states—and even the national government—have made efforts to reserve to citizens certain rights and privileges, such as real estate ownership, practice of such professions as law and medicine, and government employment.

Constitutional protections for aliens

Aliens do not have to be given the "privileges and immunities of citizenship" under the Fourteenth Amendment, since they are obviously not citizens. But they are "persons," and thus they are protected by the due process of law clauses of the Fifth and Fourteenth Amendments and by the equal protection clause of the Fourteenth Amendment. The courts' problem, when such "citizens only" laws are challenged, is to try to decide which rights and privileges fall into which category. Voting in political elections and holding political office are obviously rights which do not have to be extended to aliens. The present tendency of the courts is to invalidate all other restrictions on aliens. A new U.S. statute does, however, require employers to verify the legal residency of all aliens who apply for employment.

Currently, because of the large number of illegal aliens residing in this country, a significant question persists: To what extent do such persons qualify for government benefits, such as education, housing, and workers' compensation? Here again, the tendency is to require that such benefits be made available to illegal aliens, too. Even the traditional rule which denies illegal aliens access to our courts is being changed, as seen in several recent cases.

■ AMERICAN INDIANS

Special legal status of Native Americans

It sounds very strange to say it, some 200 years after the birth of the United States, but it is nonetheless true: The original inhabitants of this country, the American Indians, may still be subject to different legal rules because of their "national origin." This special legal status is not necessarily all bad; it may involve special privileges and immunities as well as disabilities. As noted in Chapter 1, Albert B. LeBlanc, a full-blooded Chippewa Indian, did not have to get a commercial fishing license from the Michigan Department of Natural Resources since an 1836 treaty with the U.S. government reserved such fishing rights to the Chippewa nation. Likewise, a Navajo woman, Rosalind McClanahan, could not be required to pay Arizona state income tax on income she earned on the Navajo reservation. Inheritance of property, particularly for Indians living on reservations, may still be governed by tribal law rather than the general inheritance law of the particular state. Reservation businesses and the Bureau of Indian Affairs may engage in preferential hiring of Indians without violating the 1964 Civil Rights Act.

While the foregoing examples would probably be thought of as advantages enjoyed by Indians because of their special status, members of particular Indian tribes may still be subject to some residual contractual disabilities under old U.S. treaties and statutes.

■ CONVICTS

Upon conviction for certain crimes, a person may be sentenced to confinement in a U.S. or state prison. Such a sentence does not, however, mean that the person loses the general capacity to contract and to own property. Likewise, even in prison the person is still protected by the U.S. and state constitutions. Even prisoners have the capacity to appoint agents and attorneys and through them to make contracts and manage their property and affairs; such contracts made on a prisoner's behalf are, generally, fully enforceable by and against the prisoner.

Conviction of crimes involving force or fraud may, however, carry certain other disabilities. A person who has been released after having served the required sentence may be prevented from holding political (or labor union) office for some period of time. The person may also be prevented from practicing a licensed profession, such as law or medicine. Spiro Agnew, for example, was disbarred as a lawyer after pleading "no contest" to tax evasion charges.

■ MARRIED WOMEN

Common law coverture rule

At common law, husband and wife are regarded legally as one person. As applied in contract and tort situations, this doctrine of *coverture* meant that the wife lacked the capacity to manage even her separately owned property or separate income and that no tort liability could exist between the spouses. The contracts which a married woman attempted to make were totally void. The wife could, however, obligate her *husband* in quasi contract for necessaries furnished to her for herself, their children, or their home.

Modern statutes

In nearly all states these rules have been changed by statute or constitution, so that a married woman enjoys the same legal rights and powers as her husband. She can own, manage, and dispose of her own property and has joint control of the jointly owned property. She, not he, is legally entitled to receive her earnings from her job. State courts have also been permitting the spouses to sue each other in tort, at least in some cases. Also, under modern interpretations, a wife would be similarly obligated in quasi contract for necessaries furnished to her husband where she had income or property and he did not.

Remaining exceptions

Residues of the common-law rules remain in a few states, where a married woman may not be able to convey real estate, to mortgage jointly owned property, or act as a guarantor of someone else's debt without the husband's consent. Until 1963, Texas continued to apply the basic rules of coverture, so that a married woman lacked the capacity to contract unless she went through a special court procedure which removed her disability. Michigan continued to apply the coverture rules into the 1970s, and it did so despite Article 10, Section 1 of its 1963 constitution, which says: "The disabilities of coverture as to property are abolished." A 1982 Michigan statute appears to make the married woman liable in most cases where she has cosigned a contract with her husband.

The Equal Rights Amendment to the U.S. Constitution, if ever ratified, will almost certainly overturn any state laws that provide for different legal results based solely on sex. The restriction in the *Peddy* case is being challenged under the Alabama Constitution, as well as under the equal protection clause of the U.S. Constitution.

PEDDY v. MONTGOMERY

345 So.2d 631 (Alabama, 1977)

FACTS

A. N. Peddy contracted to buy certain real estate from Bessie Montgomery, a married woman. Title 34, § 73 of the Alabama Code denies a wife the power to convey or mortgage her lands without her husband's consent. If he does not join in signing the deed or mortgage it is void. Bessie changed her mind about selling, and, since her husband had not cosigned the land contract, she relied on the statute as a defense. When Peddy sued for specific performance of the contract, the trial court gave Bessie a summary judgment.

ISSUE   Does this statute deny married women equal protection?

DECISION   Yes. Judgment reversed.

REASONS   **Justice Shores thought the statute was clearly discriminatory under modern tests.** "This section contains the only statutory provision left in the law of Alabama limiting the right of a married woman to contract. . . .

"We, therefore, turn to the constitutional question presented. There is no dispute that Title 34, § 73 treats married women differently than married men and unmarried females. The question is whether that difference in treatment is permissible under the Constitution of Alabama and the Constitution of the United States.

> By the common law, husband and wife were regarded as but one person, for many purposes. The legal existence of the wife was lost, or, as most often expressed, merged in that of the husband. She was without capacity to contract, and had not the administration of her property. By the marriage, if she was seized of an estate of inheritance, the husband became seized thereof, taking the rents and profits during their joint lives, and, by possibility, during his life. . . . Her chattels real passed to the husband, who had power to sell, assign, or make other disposition of them, at pleasure. . . .

"The foregoing was true, not only in Alabama, but in most, if not all, of the other states. In 1839 Mississippi passed the first of the Married Women's Property Acts, and other states rapidly followed. This legislation was designed to remove many of the severe disabilities placed on married women by the common law. The first of a series of such laws was enacted in Alabama in the 1840s. These acts had for their purpose securing to married women their separate estates, and generally provided, insofar as material to this discussion, that under certain circumstances a married woman could go into chancery to have herself declared a 'freedealer' which, in turn, allowed her to purchase and hold property in her own name as if she were a femme sole.

"Although the purpose of this legislation was to protect the wife, and 'not to limit her power of alienation,' the issue is reduced to whether it is constitutionally permissible when its effect is to treat married women, in dealing with their separate property, different from all other adult persons. Single women, divorced women, widowed women, and all men are free to transact business, contract, and alienate property, free of all legislative restraints. Only married women are perceived to require restrictions on one of such rights (i.e., alienation of their property), theoretically to protect them against their own actions. In the exercise of all other rights, they are as unrestricted as all other adults. . . .

"Article X, Section 209, Constitution 1901, assures that all real and personal property of any female in this state, whether acquired before or after marriage, '. . . shall be and remain the separate estate and property of such female. . . .' As noted earlier, that provision was first placed in the Constitution of 1868 to ensure that there would be no restoration of the common-law rule. Obviously, the invalidation of a provision requiring the husband to join in a wife's conveyance could not have the effect of restoring the wife to her common-law status. That, too, is precluded by the Constitution.

"Nor are we persuaded that the legislature has the unbridled authority to govern all aspects of our social and economic life. That legislative discretion is limited by the Constitution to the enactment of laws which do not deny to persons of this state the equal protection of the laws. To hold that all conveyances of a wife's land, or any interest therein, must, to be valid, carry the signature of her husband, is to deny to a married woman rights which are freely exercised by every other adult person, male or female, in Alabama.

"To justify such a holding on the legal presumption that all married women are incapable of dealing with their own land, without the guidance of their husbands, is to ignore the realities of life as we know it.

"We hold that Title 34, § 73, Code, limiting the freedom of a married woman to alienate or mortgage her lands, or any interest therein, without the assent and concurrence of her husband, violates the provisions of Article 1, Constitution of 1901, in that it denies to that category of adult landowners rights guaranteed to all other adult landowners by the Constitution and laws of this state. . . .

"There is no provision of the Constitution which would permit the legislature to deny to married women rights possessed by all other adults. Its authority to do so must be found in that document, and cannot rest upon an ancient myth that married women are presumed to be more needful of protection of their own interests than other adults, male or female."

■ CORPORATIONS

Private Corporations. Since corporations are "artificial" persons, existing only in the eyes of the law, they can have and exercise only those powers which the law gives them. In this sense, they have limited legal capacity; they can make contracts only in those areas of activity in which they have been authorized to be engaged. Modern corporation statutes are generally very liberal in granting corporate powers, and even if a corporation makes a contract which is outside its charter powers, most courts today do not permit either of the parties to the contract to raise that fact as a defense when sued on the contract. These matters are discussed more fully in Chapter 43.

Public (Municipal) Corporations. Like both profit and nonprofit private corporations, public corporations are creatures of limited legal authority, possessing only those powers given to them by constitutional or statutory provisions. The courts will normally not permit any enforcement of contracts made by a public corporation in excess of its powers, on the theory that to do so would injure the public through the illegal expenditures of public funds. Contracting procedures for public bodies are usually subject to very specific regulations, which must be complied with if one hopes to have an enforceable contract with them.

■ SIGNIFICANCE OF THIS CHAPTER

While it is certainly true that most minors do pay their debts and meet their other contractual obligations, it is important for the other contracting party to be aware of what *can* happen when a contract is made with a minor. Even though the age of majority has been lowered to 18 by most states, and even though more courts are willing to permit some recourse against a minor who makes an intentional misrepresentation of age, minors still enjoy a special legal status. Courts still will give them special protection where they act innocently. If you are contracting with minors, you need to know the possible results.

Similarly, while many courts and legislatures are moving to eliminate special restrictions on legal rights and privileges, some do still remain. You also need to be aware of these possibilities, because again there can be serious legal consequences when your contract is declared void or voidable due to the other party's lack of capacity.

DISCUSSION CASE

BABBITT FORD, INC. v. NAVAJO INDIAN TRIBE

710 F.2d 587 (U.S. Ninth Circuit, 1983)

FACTS: Babbitt is an Arizona car dealership doing business in Page and Flagstaff, Arizona. Both automobile dealerships are located within close proximity to the Navajo Indian Reservation. Each derives a substantial part of its income from sales to members of the Tribe. All automobile sales contracts with the Indians are negotiated at the dealership. Delivery of the automobiles also occurs off the reservation. The majority of these sales involve loan contracts that give the dealer the right to repossession by self-help upon default. Babbitt states it exercises this right approximately 10 times per month upon vehicles owned by members of the Tribe and kept within reservation boundaries.

In 1968, the Navajo Tribal Council enacted regulations governing self-help vehicle repossessions on the reservations. Sections 607 through 609 of the Navajo Tribal Code provide that written consent is required for repossession from either the owner of the vehicle or the tribal court.

In 1980, Babbitt entered the Navajo reservation and repossessed the vehicles belonging to the Sellers and the Joes. In neither case did Babbitt attempt to comply with the consent requirement of Section 607. Both the Sellers and the Joes brought suit in the tribal court for violation of Section 607. The tribal court found Babbitt to be in violation of 7 N.T.C. Section 607, and granted the Sellers and the Joes damages in accordance with 7 N.T.C. Section 609. The Sellers were awarded $476.75 and the Joes were awarded $4,455.75. Babbitt appealed this decision to the Navajo Appeals Court before bringing this action in U.S. District Court.

■

Judge Alarcon:

Indian tribes have long been recognized as sovereign entities, "possessing attributes of sovereignty over both their members and their territory. . . ." This sovereignty is not absolute. Tribal sovereignty is subject to limitation by specific treaty provisions, by statute at the will of Congress, by portions of the Constitution found explicitly binding on the tribes, or by implication due to the tribes' dependent status. . . .

Indian tribes also retain the inherent sovereign power to exercise "some forms of civil jurisdiction over non-Indians on their reservations. . . ." The Supreme Court has repeatedly recognized tribal courts "as appropriate forums for the exclusive adjudication of disputes affecting important personal and property interests of both Indians and non-Indians." . . . Tribal law-making institutions also have been recognized as competent legislatures. . . .

The Navajo consent regulation at issue in this matter is a necessary exercise of tribal self-government and territorial management: The regulation is designed to keep reservation peace and protect the health and safety of tribal members. The Navajo reservation covers a vast expansion of land. Repossession of an automobile has the potential to leave a tribal member stranded miles from his or her nearest neighbor. A repossession without the consent of the tribe member also may escalate into violence, particularly if others join the affray.

Such conduct, in our view, clearly "threatens or has some direct effect on the . . . health and welfare of the tribe." . . . The enactment of regulations aimed at preventing such occurrences reflects the Tribe's concern for the safety and welfare of persons on the reservation. For this reason, the regulations at issue here are a valid exercise of tribal jurisdiction. . . .

In their cross-appeal, the Sellers and the Joes contend the District Court erred in holding that the regulatory damage provision of Section 609 conflicts with overriding interests of the federal government. We agree.

Section 609 provides that any person who repossesses goods in violation of Section 607 is deemed to have breached the peace and "shall be civilly liable . . . for any loss caused [thereby]. . . ." If "consumer goods" are repossessed in violation of Section 607, the purchaser of such goods may recover either (1) actual damages or (2) in any event an amount not less than the credit service charge plus 10 percent of the principal amount of the debt or the time price differential plus 10 percent of the cash price." . . .

The language of Section 609 closely parallels other attempts at consumer protection legislation, and is in fact identical to the damage measure set out in Section 9–507(1) of the Uniform Commercial Code (UCC). This UCC section has been adopted without material modification by . . . Arizona. . . .

Numerous cases have held that under UCC Section 9–507(1) an improper auto repossession results in liability

for the statutory minimum. In each of these cases, proof of creditor's failure to give notice of resale, just as under Section 609 proof of the creditor's failure to obtain consent, is considered sufficient to support the minimum damage award. None of these cases require a showing of actual damage and all of the cases consider an automobile to be a consumer good. Those states that have adopted Section 9–507(1) of the UCC have acted to protect the safety and property of all persons within their boundaries. The adoption of Section 609 realistically increases the likelihood of achieving these same goals.

The District Court's judgment is affirmed in part and reversed as to Section 609.

■ IMPORTANT TERMS AND CONCEPTS

capacity to contract	rescission
minor (legal infant)	restitution
insane person	quasi-contract
alien	reasonable/fair market
American Indian (Native	value
American)	disaffirmance
convict	affirmance/ratification
married woman	estoppel
coverture	misrepresentation of age
private corporation	unjust enrichment
public corporation	voidable contract
necessaries	void agreement

■ QUESTIONS AND PROBLEMS FOR DISCUSSION

1. What happens when a minor disaffirms a contract for necessaries?
2. What is the special legal status of an alien living in the United States?
3. Why are persons who were intoxicated when they made contracts permitted to disaffirm them?
4. When will a minor be estopped from disaffirming a contract made while a minor?
5. Goodie, the minor son of a rich architect, was an undergraduate at State University. Trash sold him about $2,000 worth of expensive clothing items. Goodie later refused to pay, and Trash sued for the contract price, alleging that these items were necessaries. Goodie's father, Lord Toshues, testified that

Goodie was already being supplied with sufficient clothes for school. What is the result, and why?
6. Rodrigo, an alien who had entered the United States illegally, was injured while he was working on a farm in Florida. Florida has a statute that provides for the payment of certain benefits to employees injured on the job. Is Rodrigo entitled to these benefits? Explain. Would it make any difference in the result if the Florida statute specifically included aliens as "employees"?
7. Bluff Credit Company unsuccessfully attempted to collect payment from Freddy Freeloader for medical services he requested. Freddie's wife Fanny has been trying to divorce Freddy for several years, but due to a court decree, Freddy is still allowed to live in Fanny's home. Fanny and Freddy have separate rooms, eat separate meals, and do their laundry separately, just strangers sharing a home. Bluff Credit Company now sues Fanny for payment of her husband's medical expenses. Is Fanny liable? Explain.
8. Yolanda, using money that she had saved from her newspaper route, bought an expensive stereo set when she was 15 years old. She paid cash for the set. After using it for about two and one-half years, Yolanda decided that she would rather have a sports car instead, so she asked the seller (Big Bennie) if she could have her money back. She offered to give the set back to Bennie. Bennie refused to take the set and give her her money back unless she agreed to compensate him for the depreciation on the set. Yolanda sues to recover the contract price of the stereo set. What result, and why?

14

Defenses—Lack of Real Consent

CHAPTER OBJECTIVES

THIS CHAPTER WILL:

- Explain the results that may occur when one or both parties fail to truly agree.
- Indicate the different types of fraud.
- Discuss the five elements needed to prove a fraud case.
- Differentiate innocent misrepresentation, undue influence, and duress.
- Indicate the different types of mistakes that may occur in a contracting situation.
- Discuss the most common mistake arguments.

A second group of defenses centers on the idea that one of the parties did not really consent to the terms of the contract which the other wishes to enforce. While courts generally continue to require both parties to live up to the bargain they made, the problem in many cases is to discover exactly what they really did agree to. Included here are cases involving *fraud, innocent misrepresentation, duress, undue influence,* and *mistake. Unconscionability,* as discussed in the next chapter, is a related idea.

■ FRAUD

Many types of fraud may be crimes, so that criminal charges can be filed against the wrongdoer. False advertising and other deceptive practices may also result in administrative proceedings before the Federal Trade Commission and/or similar state bodies. We are concerned here, however, with the civil aspects of fraud, with its impact on the contract.

Types of fraud

Civil fraud is of two kinds: fraud in the execution and fraud in the inducement. *Fraud in the execution* describes a situation where one party is deceived as to the very nature of the transaction. The party is not aware that a contract is being made, or at least that he or she is making the one which the plaintiff now seeks to enforce. Elvis Presley, for example, fighting his way toward the exit from a concert hall, in the midst of a screaming mass of fans, was signing autograph books as fast as he could. One clever person shoved a folded piece of paper at him, and Elvis signed, not knowing that the unseen part of the paper contained a contract to buy a new set of encyclopedias. On these facts, there is fraud in the execution, and the purported "contract" is totally void. Elvis was deceived as to the very nature of the "transaction" he was entering into, without having had a reasonable opportunity to discover the truth.

The far more common kind of civil fraud is *fraud in the inducement,* where the defrauded party is aware of entering into a contract and intends to do so, but has been deceived about some aspect of the contract. Usually fraud in the inducement involves misrepresentation of what the defrauded party is to receive. A used car falsely represented as being in A-1 mechanical condition illustrates this concept.

Elements of fraud in the inducement

Although different courts may use slightly different formulations, the typical fraud case requires proof of five elements: (1) misrepresentation of a material fact, (2) knowledge of falsity, (3) intent to deceive, (4) reasonable reliance by the other party, and (5) damage to the defrauded party. Because fraud is so easily alleged by anyone having second thoughts about a contract, courts typically require proof of fraud by independent evidence which is clear and convincing. The plaintiff's testimony, by itself, is not sufficient proof of the fraud case, unless admitted by the defendant. (See Exhibit 14–1.)

Misrepresentation of Material Fact. A statement must contain a factual assertion to provide the basis for a fraud case. *Statements of opinion* are therefore not generally treated as statements of fact, so long as the statements do in fact represent the speaker's honestly held opinion. Sellers are also given some latitude in "puffing" their wares, so that such statements as, "It's the best car for the money," or, "It looks great on you," are not normally intended or understood as factual descriptions. Thus, a statement by an individual selling

General rule: Opinion ≠ Facts

■ EXHIBIT 14–1
Defenses—Lack of Real
Consent

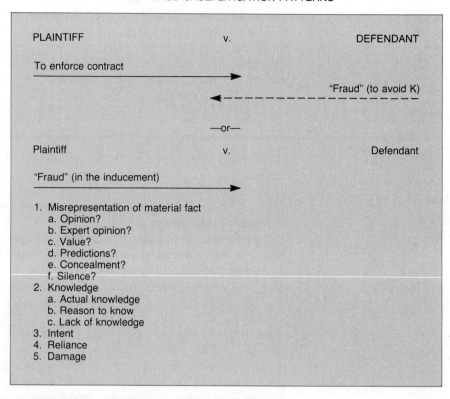

THE FRAUD CASE: LITIGATION PATTERNS

PLAINTIFF   v.   DEFENDANT

To enforce contract ————————————▶

◀ – – – – – – – – – – – – – – – – "Fraud" (to avoid K)

—or—

Plaintiff   v.   Defendant

"Fraud" (in the inducement) ————————————▶

1. Misrepresentation of material fact
   a. Opinion?
   b. Expert opinion?
   c. Value?
   d. Predictions?
   e. Concealment?
   f. Silence?
2. Knowledge
   a. Actual knowledge
   b. Reason to know
   c. Lack of knowledge
3. Intent
4. Reliance
5. Damage

a used car that it is "in good shape mechanically" would not be fraudulent unless the buyer could show that the seller knew that there were mechanical defects in the car at the time of the statements. A car dealer making the same kind of statement, however, would be making a misrepresentation of fact, since "expert opinions" are generally treated as statements of fact.

General rule: Predictions ≠ Facts

Predictions of future events over which the speaker has no control are generally not regarded as statements of fact. Where the speaker's promises concern the speaker's own future behavior, however, a misrepresentation of fact can be proved by showing that the speaker had no such intention at the time of the statements. If a buyer promises to use a piece of land for residential purposes only, there is fraud where the seller can show that the buyer had already signed construction and lease contracts for a gasoline station at the time the "residential use" statement was made.

General rule: Nondisclosure ≠ Misrepresentation

Although a party to an "arm's-length" transaction between equals generally has no affirmative duty to disclose every known fact, in several situations nondisclosure or *silence* can be interpreted as a fraudulent misrepresentation. The most obvious case requiring affirmative disclosure occurs when the party knowing the facts has created a mistaken belief in the mind of the other person through actions ***(concealment)*** or prior communications (which were true when spoken but have become false).

A second case requiring full disclosure occurs where the transaction is not arm's length but rather involves a ***fiduciary relationship,*** such as lawyer-client or guardian-ward. A lawyer who buys a piece of real estate from a client and has a resale deal with Wonder World already lined up, would have a duty to tell the client about the resale deal, whereas a buyer in an ordinary transaction would not.

Exception: Hidden safety defects

A third group of cases is more difficult to define. Most courts today are increasingly willing to impose fraud remedies for nondisclosure where one party (usually the buyer) has had no reasonable opportunity to discover the truth and where the undisclosed fact is so significant that the contract might not have been made at all if the fact had been known. Examples are the house with a serious termite infestation and the used car with dangerously defective brakes. The following case is another example of this last rule in operation.

JANINDA v. LANNING

390 P.2d 826 (Idaho, 1964)

FACTS

In December 1961 Harold M. Janinda was transferred by his employer from Denver, Colorado, to Mountain Home, Idaho. In looking for housing for his family and for income-producing property, he consulted a local real estate agency. A Mr. Swearingen of that agency showed him several parcels of real estate, including Mrs. Lanning's rental and residence property consisting of duplex apartments, six trailer spaces, and a three-bedroom house. This property was located a short distance outside the city limits of Mountain Home, within the county, and obtained its water supply from two shallow wells on the property.

On January 24, 1962, Mrs. Lanning received information indicating that one of the wells was contaminated, but she did not disclose this fact to Mr. Swearingen when he asked about the water supply. About two weeks later, Janinda bought the property. Janinda now sues to rescind the contract.

ISSUE

Was Mrs. Lanning's nondisclosure a fraudulent misrepresentation?

DECISION

Yes. Judgment for plaintiff affirmed.

REASONS

Justice Smith felt that there were several aspects of the case that required Mrs. Lanning to make disclosure of the poisoned water, despite the fact that the parties were dealing at arm's length.

"Particularly, the duty of disclosure is required to be observed 'in cases involving latent dangerous physical conditions of land' *Prosser on Torts,* § 87 at 535 (2d ed. 1955). Appellant regarded her property as income-producing property and was fully aware, as was her agent, that respondents intended buying it for the same purpose; and admitted on cross-examination that if 'I had gone on owning the place and I had had contamination, . . . I probably would have put in a chlorine system.' Respondents relied upon appellant's representations and were under no duty to make an independent investigation of their own.

"The rule decisive of the issue is stated in *Restatement of Contracts,* sec. 472, Comment b (1932):

. . . if a fact known by one party and not the other is so vital that if the mistake were mutual the contract would be voidable, and the party knowing the fact also knows that the other does not know it, nondisclosure is not privileged and is fraudulent."

Three ways to prove knowledge
of misrepresenter

Knowledge of Falsity. There is no fraud unless it can be shown that the speaker made a misrepresentation with knowledge that it was false. However, there are three ways to prove this *knowledge,* or *scienter,* element. One way is to show that the speaker knew the statement was a lie at the time of the statement. The speaker knew the car was not in "A-1 mechanical shape" because the day before the garage mechanic said to get rid of the car or be prepared to spend a lot of money, because it needed a lot of work.

Even if the speaker didn't actually know from personal inspection or from the mechanic that the car was in bad shape, there was "knowledge" if the speaker had *reason to know* that he or she was not telling the truth about the car's condition. Presumably, every reasonable car driver knows that a car in A-1 mechanical shape does not burn a quart of oil every 100 miles or require repeated pumping of the brake pedal to get the car to stop. A speaker who knew of these operating characteristics would certainly have reason to know that the car was not in A-1 shape.

Finally, "knowledge" can be proved by proving *lack* of knowledge. Assume that a car dealership has just taken a used car as a trade-in; no complete mechanical inspection of the car has been made. Nevertheless, when a buyer comes to the used-car lot and inquires about the car, the buyer is told that it is in "A-1 shape" and buys it on that basis. If the car has serious defects, fraud has been committed in this case. The salesperson who made the "A-1" statement *knew* that he or she didn't know anything at all about the car's real mechanical condition; thus the salesperson was lying and was *aware* of lying about the extent of information he or she had on the car.

Proof of intent to injure not
required

Intent to Deceive. In most cases, knowledge of the lie and intent to deceive go so closely hand in hand that some courts do not even consider them separately. But what about the person who says, "Yes, I knew I was lying. But I didn't intend that the other party should be hurt by it. I thought things would come out all right in the end." For want of a better label, we might refer to this as the Nixon defense: "Yes, I lied, and I knew I was lying, but I did it for your own good." The few cases that have considered this argument have rejected it; the requirement is not proof of intent to *injure* or do harm, only of intent to *deceive.* Deception for any motive, good or bad, is fraud, assuming that the other four elements are also proved.

Reliance on misrepresentation
must be reasonable

Reasonable Reliance. Even though the liar is the nastiest person imaginable, the liar has not committed fraud unless the other party can show that he or she reasonably relied on the misrepresentation. It is not enough to show that the person was in fact deceived; the person complaining must also convince the trier of fact that it was reasonable to rely on the misstatement. There is clearly no fraud if the other party knows the truth but goes ahead and makes the contract anyway. On the other hand, reliance is reasonable where an independent verification of the representation would require considerable time, money, and effort. Where the truth is readily ascertainable, it is probably not reasonable to rely on the misstatement. If the used-car salesman tells you the car has only 25,000 miles and the odometer in the car shows the mileage is 48,000, most juries would probably decide that a reasonable person would have checked the odometer before relying on the salesperson's statement. Each case ultimately rests on its own facts, as indicated in the Haleys' case.

CAPITOL DODGE, INC. v. HALEY

288 N.E.2d 766 (Indiana, 1972)

FACTS

Thomas Haley, with his parents, Loren M. Haley and Edna Haley, executed a retail installment contract on April 10, 1970, for the purchase by the son of an automobile from Capitol Dodge.

Thomas Haley testified that he had told Allen, the salesman, before the contract was signed that he had to make sure that he could have "full coverage" and "that [he] wouldn't have anything to do with the car unless it had full coverage insurance." According to Loren Haley, Allen assured him that he had nothing to worry about and that Thomas would be fully covered. Mr. Haley then signed the contract. He indicated, however, that he had not read the contract prior to signing it.

No liability coverage was afforded by the contract. The face of the contract, otherwise printed in blue ink, contained a provision in red letters near the point at which the Haleys signed as follows:

> The Insurance Contracted for in Connection with This Retail Installment Sale Does Not Provide for Liability Insurance for Bodily Injury and Property Damage.

Nothing of record, however, indicates that Haley's attention was specifically called to the exclusionary language.

The line immediately above the space provided in the contract for the purchaser's signature read as follows:

> NOTICE TO THE BUYER: Do not sign this contract before you read it or if it contains any blank spaces. You are entitled to an exact copy of the contract you sign.

Thomas Haley demanded that the contract be rescinded, and that his down payment of $395 and the sum of $495.70, representing a trade-in by Haley, be returned to him. Upon refusal of his demand and having discontinued payments, he returned the car to Capitol Dodge. Chrysler Credit, in turn, repossessed the car and sued Haley for the deficiency.

A jury returned a verdict in favor of Haley for $874.90 as compensatory damages and $2,000 punitive damages. Chrysler in its suit received a verdict against Haley and his parents for $1,226.44, representing the deficiency balance upon the auto.

ISSUES

Did the evidence support Haley's fraud case? Is this a proper case for punitive damages?

DECISION

Yes. Yes. Judgment affirmed.

REASONS

Judge Sullivan first stated that punitive damages were particularly appropriate in cases of "consumer fraud."

"There can be no dispute that the installment contract in question did not provide for liability insurance coverage. The 'full coverage' representation by Capitol's salesman, Mr. Allen, was therefore patently false.

"The statements heretofore alluded to as made by Capitol's salesman could have reasonably been found by the jury to have been made recklessly and without regard to their truth or falsity. Such unconcern for the truth may serve as an imputation of scienter.

"Capitol's most plausible argument concerns the matter of reliance by Haley upon the representations made by Allen, and we are inclined to agree that it perhaps harbors a measure of naïveté to conclude, without reservation or hesitance, that a literate adult who insists upon the inclusion of a particular subject in a purchase contract would bind himself to that contract without availing himself of the opportunity to read the document in order to satisfy himself that the desired subject was within the contract terms. Nevertheless, the question whether Thomas Haley reasonably relied upon Allen's assurances, which were in conflict with the limited insurance coverage specifically recited in the contract, was for the jury's determination. We are not at liberty to substitute our assessment of the evidence. It is but to repeat a truism that the question of reliance is one of fact to be determined by the jury, and that upon appeal from a jury verdict this court will not weigh the evidence."

Damage to the Defrauded Party. As a final essential part of a fraud case, the defrauded party must prove having sustained damage as a result of the misrepresentation. Suppose that a seller of land fraudulently represents that there is gold on it, and there is no gold, but there is oil. The land with oil is worth more than it would have been with gold, so the buyer probably does not have a case of fraud. (The buyer probably will not want to rescind anyway.) Even in the gold/oil case, however, the buyer has wound up with a contract different from the one the buyer intended to have, so in that sense the buyer may have suffered an "injury" which would permit the buyer to rescind if the buyer wanted to.

Generally, to justify rescission of the entire contract, the misrepresented fact must relate to an essential part of the bargain. If the defrauded party wishes to keep the contract in force and collect *"make-it-right"* or *difference-in-value damages,* the party must prove the amount of the dollar loss which the party has sustained because of the fraud. Since fraud is an intentional tort, punitive damages (over and above the actual loss) may also be collected in many of these cases.

■ **INNOCENT MISREPRESEN-TATION**

In some cases, speakers may have honestly and reasonably believed they were telling the truth and may have had no intent to mislead anyone. Still, if the speaker in fact misrepresented the truth, damages to the other party may be as bad as if there had been fraud. The net effect is the same, whether the misrepresentation was made fraudulently or "innocently." For this reason, where the fact innocently misstated has been proved to be a very important part of the contract, most courts will permit rescission by the other party. In most states, if the misrepresented fact is not material enough to justify rescission, the contract stands as is; no damages remedy is given. In a few states damages can be recovered even for an innocent misrepresentation, as an alternative remedy to rescission. Since there has been no intentional tort, punitive damages are not recoverable for innocent misrepresentation.

■ UNDUE INFLUENCE

As noted in our discussion of fraud, where any sort of fiduciary relationship exists, as in lawyer-client, guardian-ward, or doctor-patient, one of the parties to the transaction may have misused the trust and confidence which the other has given to benefit at the other's expense. One party may rely on the advice of the trusted lawyer, doctor, or guardian as the basis for entering into a contract with that person. Where such an underlying relationship exists between the contracting parties, the courts will examine their bargain very carefully to make sure that it represents the true intent of the "subordinate" party and that all the facts had been disclosed to that party.

Even without an underlying fiduciary relationship, it is possible to prove that a contract exists because of undue influence rather than by free choice, although this case is not nearly as easy to prove. Such cases might arise in the context of an emotional or romantic relationship between the parties to the contract. Where proved, undue influence makes the contract voidable by the party of whom advantage was taken.

■ DURESS

Closely related to the idea of undue influence is that of *duress*. Duress means something more than just pressure or "hard selling." The most obvious cases involve violence or threats of violence against the contracting party. Threats to commence a criminal prosecution unless money is paid or promised also constitute duress, but simply threatening to bring a civil suit for money allegedly owed is not duress. While sales pressure or hard selling is not considered duress, threats of economic harm against the buyer by the seller, if the buyer does not accept seller's terms, is *economic duress,* and courts will recognize such threats as duress. A person can be injured by being struck by a baseball bat, but can also be injured by the misuse of economic power by an adversary. The violence-type duress makes the resulting contract totally void. Other duress makes the contract voidable by the party who was pressured into making it.

The discussion case for this chapter illustrates the newer idea of "economic duress."

■ MISTAKE

The contracting parties can be "mistaken" about so many things that it is impossible to catalog all of the conceivable factual combinations. Mistakes may occur in the formation of the agreement, in writing up the deal, or in performance. Rather than a comprehensive list, what follows is a discussion of some of the most frequent kinds of mistakes: mutual mistake in basic assumptions, material unilateral mistake, mistake in integration, and mistake in performance.

Mutual Mistake in Basic Assumptions.   Where both parties enter into a contract assuming the existence of some particular fact or condition which later turns out not to have been so, there is no contract at all if the fact is "basic" (material) to the contract. Efrem Zimbalist, Sr., the famous concert violinist, bought two violins which both he and the seller assumed were a genuine Stradivarius and a genuine Guarnerius. In fact, both violins were merely good copies. When he discovered the truth, Zimbalist was entitled to get his money back; neither party intended a contract for *fake* violins. *Beachcomber Coins* involves a similar misunderstanding.

BEACHCOMBER COINS, INC. v. BOSKETT

400 A.2d 78 (New Jersey, 1979)

FACTS   Beachcomber, a retail coin dealer, sued to rescind its purchase of a 1916 dime from Boskett for $500. The "D" stamped on the coin indicated it had originated at the Denver mint, making it a rare issue. Beachcomber's owner spent some 15 to 45 minutes closely examining the coin before buying it. He later had an offer to resell it for $700, but that buyer determined that the coin was counterfeit. The trial judge, on the basis of testimony of customary "coin dealing procedures," held that the plaintiff-buyer had assumed the risk of nongenuineness. Beachcomber appeals.

ISSUE   Was there a mutual mistake in basic assumptions, so that the contract should be rescinded?

DECISION   Yes. Judgment reversed.

REASONS   For Judge Conford, this was a textbook case of mutual mistake, just like *Zimbalist*. He cited Professor Williston:

> Where parties on entering into a transaction that affects their contractual relations are both under a mistake regarding a fact assumed by them as the basis on which they entered into the transaction, it is voidable by either party if enforcement of it would be materially more onerous to him than it would have been had the fact been as the parties believed it to be.

Judge Conford continued, "Moreover, negligent failure of a party to know or to discover the facts as to which both parties are under a mistake does not preclude rescission or reformation on account thereof. It is undisputed that both parties believed that the coin was a genuine Denver-minted one. The mistake was mutual in that both parties were laboring under the same misapprehension as to this particular, essential fact. The price asked and paid was directly based on that assumption. That plaintiff may have been negligent in his inspection of the coin (a point not expressly found but implied by the trial judge) does not, as noted above, bar its claim for rescission.

"Defendant's contention that plaintiff assumed the risk that the coin might be of greater or lesser value than that paid is not supported by the evidence. It is well established that a party to a contract can assume the risk of being mistaken as to the value of the thing sold. The *Restatement* states the rule this way:

> Where the parties know that there is doubt in regard to a certain matter and contract on that assumption, the contract is not rendered voidable because one is disappointed in the hope that the facts accord with his wishes. The risk of the existence of the doubtful fact is then assumed as one of the elements of the bargain.

However, for the stated rule to apply, the parties must be conscious that the pertinent fact may not be true and make their agreement at the risk of that possibility. In this case both parties were certain that the coin was genuine. They so testified. Plaintiff's principal thought so after his inspection, and defendant would not have paid nearly

$450 for it otherwise. A different case would be presented if the seller were uncertain either of the genuineness of the coin or of its value if genuine, and had accepted the expert buyer's judgment on these matters."

Ambiguities causing mistakes

Many "mutual mistake" cases arise from a latent ambiguity in the terms of the contract; that is, a word or phrase really describes more than one thing, and each party understands it to mean something different. In the classic example, a buyer and a seller contracted in England for "certain goods, to wit, 125 bales Surat cotton to arrive ex ship Peerless from Bombay." Unknown to either the buyer or the seller, there were *two* ships called *Peerless,* and both were in Bombay and both had some Surat cotton on board. To make the story complete, incredible though it may seem, they were both bound for London, one to arrive in October, and one in December. The buyer knew only about the "October" *Peerless;* the seller knew only about the "December" *Peerless.* When the buyer's cotton was not delivered in October and the buyer sued for breach of contract, the English court correctly held that no damages were recoverable since no contract had ever really been made. The parties were talking about two different things and had never really agreed.

No mistake where parties are aware of uncertainty

There is no mistake, and thus there is a binding contract, where both parties are aware that they lack knowledge about a particular fact of condition, and take their mutual ignorance into account in setting the terms of the contract. In a Wisconsin case, the finder of a pretty stone in a field took the stone to a friend and asked the friend what he thought it was worth. The friend said he didn't know either, but that he'd pay the finder $1 for it. After the sale the stone was identified as an uncut diamond, worth $700. There was no mistake in this case, in the legal sense, since both parties were aware when they contracted that they did not know the true identity or worth of the stone.

Because much of modern commerce is based on differing estimates of the value of land, goods, and securities, most courts also adhere to a rule which says that mistake relief will not be given where the only error concerns the *value* of an item rather than its *identity.* The mistake in the *Zimbalist* case, for example, was not as to the value of fake violins but as to whether the violins were genuine or fake. This difference is probably easy enough to see in most instances, but some cases are a little harder to decide.

Material Unilateral Mistake.   Generally, the fact that one party to the contract has made a mistake of some sort affords no basis for relief, so long as the other party was unaware of the mistake and was acting in good faith. Most courts do, however, say that there is no contract where the mistake was so "gross" that the other party should have been aware of it. This situation arises most frequently where bids are being solicited for a certain job. Several bid offers are submitted, and one is way out of line. Courts usually will not permit the offeree to "snap up" what the offeree has good reason to know must be a mistaken bid, thus binding the honestly mistaken bidder to an unfair contract. Just how gross the mistake has to be to trigger this rule is a question of fact. The *Kemper* case illustrates this rule.

KEMPER CONSTRUCTION CO. v.
CITY OF LOS ANGELES

235 P.2d 7 (California, 1951)

FACTS   Kemper sued to rescind a bid it had submitted to do the piping work for a sewer project. The City requires that 10 percent of the bid price be posted as a bond, in favor of the City, guaranteeing that the bidder would do the job for the bid price if awarded the contract. Three of Kemper's employees worked until 2 A.M. of the day the bids were due in preparing Kemper's bid. Over 1,000 different items were involved in preparing these estimates. When the work of these three men was combined and the estimates were totaled, a $301,769 item was omitted. Kemper's bid came in at $780,305. The three competing bids were $1,049,592, $1,183,000, and $1,278,895. The mistake was discovered a few hours after the bids were opened. Kemper explained what had happened and withdrew its bid, but the City accepted the bid anyway. When Kemper refused to enter into a contract at the mistaken price, the City awarded the contract to the next lowest bidder and claimed that Kemper's 10 percent bond was forfeited to the City. The trial court held that Kemper was entitled to rescind its bid *and* its bond.

ISSUE   Should rescission be granted for this unilateral mistake?

DECISION   Yes. Judgment affirmed.

REASONS   Chief Justice Gibson was convinced that all the equities were on Kemper's side—the mistake was obvious, the City was actually notified of it before it formally accepted Kemper's bid, it would be grossly unfair to hold Kemper to the mistaken price, and the City really would sustain no damage by getting the job for a correct and fair price.

"Omission of the $301,769 item from the company's bid was, of course, a material mistake. The City claims that the company is barred from relief because it was negligent in preparing the estimates, but even if we assume that the error was due to some carelessness, it does not follow that the company is without remedy. . . . The type of error here involved is one which will sometimes occur in the conduct of reasonable and cautious businessmen, and, under all the circumstances, we cannot say as a matter of law that it constituted a neglect of legal duty such as would bar the right to equitable relief.

"The evidence clearly supports the conclusion that it would be unconscionable to hold the bid at the mistaken figure. The City had knowledge before the bid was accepted that the company had made a clerical error which resulted in the omission of an item amounting to nearly one third of the amount intended to be bid and, under all the circumstances, it appears that it would be unjust and unfair to permit the City to take advantage of the company's mistake. There is no reason for denying relief on the ground that the City cannot be restored to status quo. It had ample time in which to award the contract without readvertising, the contract was actually awarded to the next lowest bidder, and the City will not be heard to complain that it cannot be placed in status quo because it will not have the benefit of an inequitable bargain."

Mistake in Integration.   Both the courts and the *Restatement* continue to state as the general rule that one is bound by what he or she signs. Yet, almost in the same breath, courts everywhere also continue to grant relief ("reformation") for what is commonly termed *mistake in integration*—an alleged mistake in writing up the terms agreed on. Much of the seeming conflict between the two rules can be explained by the difference between the specifically bargained-out terms and the printed terms in a form contract. Many printed contracts use fairly standardized terms—what lawyers refer to as "boilerplate." When you sign a form contract, you are bound by all this standardized language. On the other hand, where a specifically agreed-on term has been written up incorrectly, courts are willing to correct the error. In such a case one party alleges that a written document is incorrect, that it does not accurately state the terms actually agreed on. If there is evidence to support this claim, a court with equity powers can "reform" the document to make it agree with the actual intent of the parties, and then enforce the document as corrected. The document is rewritten, and then enforced.

Mistake in Performance.   Perhaps the most difficult cases of all in which to work out a mutually fair result are those involving a "mistake in performance." Someone performs for the wrong person, or at the wrong time, or in the wrong place, or when the party was not really contractually obligated to perform at all. Where the performance involves money or a tangible object which can be easily returned, the solution is simple; the person who has received the money or other item by mistake must return it.

Where construction or demolition takes place at the wrong site, however, the problem is not so easily resolved. What does one do for the owner of the apartment house which the wrecking crew tore down "by mistake"? Even if the owners are given the full fair market value of the old building, plus lost rentals, until a new one is built, they have still been the unwilling participants in a forced sale of the old building, with all sorts of possible adverse tax consequences. How about the landowners who get a new house put up on their lot "by mistake"? Should these people have to pay for the new house, and if so, how much? Or should they be able to force the removal of the house and the restoration of the pristine ecology? For these, as for many other "mistake" questions, there are no easy or universal answers.

■ SIGNIFICANCE OF THIS CHAPTER

The basic idea of a contract is that it is a relationship which we have entered into voluntarily, because we wished to do so. It's not something that's imposed on us by someone else; it's a relationship which we have imposed on ourselves. Where our consent to the contract has occurred because of factual misrepresentation by the other party, legal relief from the terms of the contract is available—either rescission or damages. If the misrepresentation was intentional, punitive damages should be available against the person who has committed an intentional wrong. Where no agreement ever really occurred, either because the parties were talking about two different things and didn't know that, or because they both assumed the existence of a material fact which was not so, no contract exists, and legal relief should be given. Even where only one party has made a serious mistake, there is no contract if the other is aware of the mistake. In all of these situations, what appears at first to be a contract may not be enforceable because one or both parties were unaware of the true facts.

DISCUSSION CASE

INTERNATIONAL UNDERWATER CONTRACTORS v. NEW ENGLAND T. & T. CO.

393 N.E.2d 968 (Massachusetts, 1979)

FACTS: The plaintiff, International Underwater Contractors, Inc. (IUC), appeals from the entry of summary judgment for the defendant, New England Telephone and Telegraph Company (NET).

The plaintiff, which had entered into a written contract with the defendant to assemble and install certain conduits under the Mystic River for a lump sum price of $149,680, to be paid semimonthly in installments in proportion to the progress of the work, seeks additional compensation in a total amount of $811,816.73 for a major change in the system from that specified in the contract. The plaintiff asserts that the change, which was necessitated by delays caused by the defendant, forced the work to be performed in the winter months instead of during the summer, as originally bid, making the equipment originally specified unusable. This major change was made, the plaintiff alleges, at the direction of the defendant, and upon the defendant's assurances that it would pay the resulting additional costs.

The defendant moved for summary judgment with a supporting affidavit, wherein it argued in defense a release signed by the plaintiff settling the additional claim for a total sum of $575,000. The plaintiff, which submitted countervailing affidavits in opposition to the motion, argues that the release is not binding because it was signed under economic duress.

A special master appointed to hear summary judgment motions found that "as a matter of law, the economic duress required to vitiate the subject release was not present." Summary judgment was entered for the defendant, and the plaintiff's motions for reconsideration and to vacate judgment were denied. The instant appeal ensued. Justice Brown gave the opinion:

■

We must, therefore, examine the standard for economic duress and the pleadings and affidavits in this case to determine whether issues of material fact have been raised, and whether the facts set forth by the plaintiff, if true, would show economic duress invalidating the release.

A release signed under duress is not binding. . . . "Coercion sufficient to avoid a contract need not, of course, consist of physical force or threats of it. Social or economic pressure illegally or immorally applied may be sufficient.". . .

To show economic duress (1) a party "must show that he has been the victim of a wrongful or unlawful act or threat, and (2) such act or threat must be one which deprives the victim of his unfettered will.". . . "As a direct result of these elements, the party threatened must be compelled to make a disproportionate exchange of values.". . .

The elements of economic duress have also been described as follows: "(1) that one side involuntarily accepted the terms of another; (2) that circumstances permitted no other alternative; and (3) that said circumstances were the result of coercive acts of the opposite party.". . . "Merely taking advantage of another's financial difficulty is not duress. Rather, the person alleging financial difficulty must allege that it was contributed to or caused by the one accused of coercion." . . . Thus "[i]n order to substantiate the allegation of economic duress or business compulsion . . . [t]here must be a showing of acts on the part of the defendant which produced [the financial embarrassment]. The assertion of duress must be proved by evidence that the duress resulted from defendant's wrongful and oppressive conduct and not by plaintiff's necessities.". . .

Here the affidavit submitted in behalf of the defendant stated that amendments to the agreement were executed in January and February 1974, which provided for "additional compensation for certain additional work.". . .

[T]he affidavits show a dispute as to whether NET gave assurances to IUC that if IUC made the change in installation of equipment and continued to perform that work to completion, NET would pay the additional costs and would not permit IUC to lose money. The affidavits also raise a question whether IUC's financial difficulties were attributable to such acts of the defendant and whether the plaintiff was forced because of such difficulties to accept a disproportionately small settlement which it would not otherwise have accepted.

Such allegations are material, and, if true, would make out a case for duress. Here, if the plaintiff's allegations are true, the defendant's acts in (1) insisting on a deviation from the contract and repeatedly assuring the plaintiff that it would pay the additional cost, which was substantially greater than the original, if the plaintiff would complete the work and (2) then refusing to make payments for almost a year caused the plaintiff's financial difficulties. Such acts could be considered "wrongful" acts and indications of bad faith. . . .

In the present case, the fact that the assurances may have been given by NET's representatives and never agreed to by the company's board of directors does not lessen the company's responsibility. "[T]he test of good faith should be the same for an entity which must act through agents as for an individual acting for himself. If the aggregate of the actions of all of the agents would, if all done by one individual, fall below the standard of good faith, the entity for whom the various agents acted should be held to have violated that standard.". . .

The unequal bargaining power of the two parties (both in terms of their comparative size and resources as well as the financial difficulties into which the plaintiff had fallen, allegedly, because of the defendant's acts) is a factor to be considered in determining whether the transaction involved duress. . . . In addition, the disparity between not only the plaintiff's alleged costs ($811,816) but also the amount NET's engineers had recommended in November 1974 to the board for settlement ($775,000) and the amount offered on a "take-or-leave-it basis" in December and accepted in settlement ($575,000) raises the possibility there may have been a disproportionate exchange of values and should be considered in determining whether the release was signed under duress. . . .

The defendant argues that it did not have to settle the case but could have "exercised its lawful right to litigate the rights of the parties under the agreement" and that "[d]oing or threatening to do what a party has a legal right to do cannot form the basis of a claim of economic duress.". . . However, if the assertions of the plaintiff are true, the defendant did more than assert a legal right, as its acts created the financial difficulties of the plaintiff, of which it then took advantage. The defendant also argued that the plaintiff cannot be found to have acted under duress because it had an adequate remedy at law. . . . However, "if recourse to courts of law is not quick enough to save the victim's business or property interests, there is no adequate legal remedy.". . . Here, if the allegations of the plaintiff are true, the plaintiff, as a result of the defendant's wrongful acts, was not "free either to rely on [its] legal rights or . . . voluntarily to accept the terms proposed.". . .

In summary, we find that the affidavits raise issues of material fact, and we are therefore unable to say as matter of law that the signing of the release was voluntary. Accordingly, it was error to enter summary judgment.

Judgment reversed.

■ IMPORTANT TERMS AND CONCEPTS

fraud
fraud in the execution
fraud in the inducement
innocent misrepresentation
duress
economic duress
undue influence
mistake
mutual mistake in basic
    assumptions
material unilateral mistake
mistake in integration

mistake in performance
misrepresentation of
    material fact
opinion statements
predictions
concealment
silence
knowledge
reason to know
reasonable reliance
fiduciary relationship

■ QUESTIONS AND PROBLEMS FOR DISCUSSION

1. Why is a defrauded party permitted to rescind a contract?
2. Why is there generally no relief given where both parties were mistaken as to the value of the subject matter of the contract?
3. When can a contract be rescinded because of duress?
4. What is the meaning and significance of the "knowledge" element in a fraud case?

5. Billy Joe Smith contracted to purchase a certain piece of land from Jeremiah Bluegrass. The land consisted of the Bluegrass homesite, 1.65 acres, and an 80-acre tract of land containing the famous tourist attraction Wildcat Cave. After Billy Joe had paid for the 81.65 acres, he discovered that the homesite was on U.S. Forest Service land, that the cave had been flooded during the previous year, that the gross income was $6,000 rather than $9,000, and that the number of billboards advertising the cave was considerably less than represented. What can Billy Joe do?
6. Hi-Way Motor Company entered into an agreement with International Harvester to become an IH franchised dealer. Orally, International Harvester assured Hi-Way Motor Company that it would not franchise any other dealers, but the written contract which was drawn up later did not mention any such promise. Three years later another franchise was granted to an area dealer. Hi-Way Motor Company unilaterally terminated its franchised agreement and sought damages, claiming fraud. What is the decision? Explain.
7. Cora owned a farm which she had never seen. Ringer came to her home and said that he wanted to buy the pasture portion of the farm. Ringer told Cora that the pasture was poor land and worth only $400

and that the only reason he wanted to buy it was because it adjoined a piece of land that he owned and that was being used for access to the pasture. Ringer said that he just wanted to end the annoyance of having the access over his land. Cora told Ringer to see her lawyer, Fumble. Ringer told Fumble the same story. As a result, Cora sold the entire farm to Ringer for $4,000. She later learned that there was a valuable, undeveloped granite quarry on the farm. She now sues for rescission of the contract and deed. What decision? Why?

8. Joe Cleen purchased a Laundromat operation from Shirley Bubbles. The agreement mentioned that all equipment was in good condition. It also stated that in 1982 the business had grossed $26,000, with $16,000 in taxable income, and that the business had been growing steadily. The buyer was given the right to examine the books for the years 1980, 1981, and 1982. It is uncertain whether Joe actually looked at the books before the purchase. Soon after he took over the business, the equipment started to break down, business was less than expected, and upon examination he found that the 1982 gross receipts had been $25,761, with taxable income of $8,774. He claims that he has been defrauded by Shirley Bubbles and wants to rescind the contract. Will the court allow rescission in this case? Why or why not?

15

Defenses—Illegality and "Public Policy"

CHAPTER OBJECTIVES

THIS CHAPTER WILL:

- Explain the results that may occur when a contractual performance is illegal.

- Indicate the most frequently occurring types of illegality.

- Discuss those illegalities having special importance for business operations, including noncompliance with licensing laws, Sunday laws, and usury laws.

- Explain the possible results if a court decides that a contract is unconscionable or against public policy.

In the vast majority of cases, both the formation of the contract and the performances it requires are lawful. Where a bargain transaction is illegal, either in its formation or in the performances required, the court attempts to do exactly the opposite of what it normally does; instead of enforcing the intent of the parties, the court tries to frustrate it. Since the bargain is illegal in some respect, the court will try to prevent the illegality from occurring and to discourage similar illegal bargains in the future. Specific results vary from case to case, yet this policy underlies all "illegality" cases.

This chapter discusses the results which the courts work out in some of the most frequent illegality cases as well as several examples of courts refusing to enforce contract provisions that are not specifically illegal, but just against public policy (see Exhibit 15–1).

■ ILLEGAL BARGAINS

Contracts requiring illegal acts

Commission of Crime or Tort. The clearest case for the application of these illegality rules occurs where the would-be contract calls for a performance specifically defined as criminal under applicable state statutory law or involves the commission of an intentional tort against some third party. In popular jargon, the arrangement between the local Big Boss and Murder, Inc., which calls for the removal of the crosstown competition is called a "contract." Clearly, the courts should not (and will not) have any part in the enforcement of such a contract, regardless of the stage of performance or nonperformance in which it is brought to the attention of the court. Whether the hit man has taken the money and has refused to perform or has done the job in an unworkmanlike way, or the Big Boss has refused to pay for the services rendered, the court should refuse to recognize any rights or duties flowing from such a contract and simply leave these equally guilty parties where it finds them, with no relief to either. Conspiracy to commit murder is itself a crime, so very few such contracts are brought to the attention of a court.

Gamblers can repent and rescind before bet paid to winner

Gambling, Lotteries, and Games of Chance. Nearly all forms of gambling are illegal in most states, and the parties to an illegal bet are clearly *in pari delicto;* that is, they are equally guilty of violating the law, so that there should be no reason to prefer one over the other. Still, different legal rules are applied to the bet case. Since the illegal purpose of a bet is to pay money to the winner based on the outcome of a game, race, fight, or whatever, the courts attempt to frustrate that purpose by permitting the losers of the bets to "repent" and repudiate their bets *(and* get their money back) at any time before the money is actually paid to the winner. If you "see the light" only after your team has lost, you can still (legally) repudiate your bet and keep your money (or get it back from the stakeholder), as long as you indicate your intent to do so before the money is actually paid over to the winner. The same rule applies when you try unsuccessfully to fill an inside straight in poker: you can take your money back from the pot (though you may lose a lot of friends, and hands, in doing so).

Most state gambling statutes are broad enough to cover lotteries, license plate bingo, and similar games of chance; some states also have separate statutes to cover these other forms of gambling. States are also attempting to prohibit

■ EXHIBIT 15–1

Defenses—Illegality and Public Policy

Type of illegality	I.P.D.?	Results?
(A) Commission of crime or tort	Yes	Leave as is (No court remedies)
(B) Gambling: Lottery	Yes	Repent and rescind
(C) Licensing (1) Revenue	No	Get license, then sue (or) sue without license
(2) Regulatory	No	Collect no contract price Collect no quasi contract Refund $ paid already Liable for any damages
(D) Usury: Split on definition	No	Collect no excess interest (or) collect no interest (or) forfeit some principal (or) forfeit all principal
(E) Sunday laws	Yes	Leave as is (or) permit weekday affirmance
(F) Restraint of trade (1) Common law	Yes/no	O.K. if reasonable Split if not reasonable
(2) Statutes (a) National	Yes/no	Leave as is if I.P.D. If not, give remedies to innocent party
(b) State	Yes/no	Leave as is if I.P.D. If not, give remedies to innocent party
(G) Interference with governmental processes (1) Lobbying = not illegal, so long as no improper methods		
(2) Bribery, etc.	Yes	Leave as is (same as A)
(H) Against public policy -or- unconscionable (not illegal)	No	U.C.C., 2-302 choices 1. Void whole contract 2. Void unconscionable clause, then enforce K 3. Interpret unconscionable clause to avoid unconscionable results.

newer forms of risk taking, such as so-called chain letter and pyramid forms of selling. All of these statutes are subject to judicial interpretation as to just what they prohibit and just what the courts should refuse to enforce.

Licensing Statutes. In a 1969 study the U.S. Labor Department estimated that over 500 different occupations required a license of some sort from at least one governmental body, including such jobs as beekeeper, rainmaker, tattoo artist, and fund raiser. The "illegality" problem here occurs when an

Regulatory versus revenue licensing statutes

unlicensed person performs services for which a license is required. Should the client-customer be required to pay for the services received from the unlicensed practitioner?

Courts usually try to answer this question by first categorizing the licensing statute in question as either **regulatory** or **revenue raising.** Of course, many statutes will include both legislative purposes, but what the court is trying to decide is whether the basic reason for the license is to protect persons from unqualified or unscrupulous practitioners or just to raise some money for the government. If the licensing statute contains educational and experiential requirements and specifies that a standardized test must be passed to get a license, it is pretty clearly regulatory in character. The fewer such standards it contains, the more it looks like just a revenue raiser.

Statutes licensing professionals, such as lawyers, accountants, dentists, and physicians are clearly regulatory in nature. On the other hand, a statute which required one to have a license to keep bees, but which permitted anyone to be licensed by paying $200, is only designed to raise revenue.

Results of noncompliance with regulatory licensing statute

If a statute is regulatory in nature, the results of not being properly licensed under it are serious. In addition to being liable for whatever punishments are provided for practicing without the required license and for any malpractice against the client, unlicensed practitioners will usually be denied any recovery for the service performed even if they later get licensed. On the other hand, if the statute is only designed to bring in money, the worst that will happen to unlicensed practitioners is being required to get licensed before being able to sue to recover for services already performed.

The question in the next case is whether Tom Welch was properly licensed to do the work he was doing.

TOM WELCH ACCOUNTING SERVICE v. WALBY

138 N.W.2d 139 (Wisconsin, 1965)

FACTS   Tom Welch, d/b/a Tom Welch Accounting Service, sued to recover $1,429.75 for bookkeeping services performed and bookkeeping materials furnished for the defendant, Roger Walby, at his request between July 5, 1960, and September 26, 1961. Welch was not licensed under a statute which required that public accountants and CPAs be licensed; he was licensed as an accountant.

Judgment was entered April 7, 1965, in behalf of the plaintiff against the defendant for $1,029.75 together with costs. The defendant appealed.

ISSUE   Did the plaintiff violate the licensing statute for public accountants?

DECISION   No. Judgment for plaintiff affirmed.

REASONS   Chief Justice Currie stated:

> The principal contention advanced by defendant on this appeal is that plaintiff, although not licensed as a public accountant or CPA, held himself out to defendant as being such, and, therefore, is precluded from recovering for the services rendered for which recovery is sought in the instant action. . . .

"When this court stated . . . that the work of a nonregistered accountant 'cannot be put before the public as work of a public accountant or certified public accountant' it put its finger upon the public aspect of the practice of accountancy which the statute prohibits. The statute does not concern itself with the methods used by a nonregistered accountant to gain employment from members of the public so long as these means do not deceive the public into believing he is a public accountant or CPA. Ch. 135, Stats., has now been in effect for 30 years, and we believe that the distinction between a nonregistered accountant and a public accountant is generally recognized. One has only to turn to the yellow pages of a telephone directory to see the distinction maintained.

"We conclude that plaintiff did not violate sec. 135.11(5) and (6), Stats., when he did business under the name of 'Tom Welch Accounting Service' or listed himself under that name in the Shawano telephone directory under the occupational heading of 'Accountants.' No claim is here made that the services he actually performed for defendant violated any of the prohibitions of ch. 135. Therefore, because plaintiff did not violate the statute, there is no illegality in his contract of employment by defendant which would bar him from recovering the reasonable value of the services rendered."

Sunday Laws. About half of the states have some sort of statute prohibiting the doing of business, or at least some types of business, on Sunday. Some of the more recently enacted statutes give the target merchants the option of closing either Sunday or Saturday. These statutes are an obvious outgrowth of the old colonial **Blue Laws** which prohibited doing almost anything on Sunday except going to church. Although these laws clearly interfere with the "free exercise of religion," and clearly "establish" the Christian Sunday (in most cases) as *the* official day of rest, the U.S. Supreme Court upheld their constitutionality in 1961.

Merchants who wish to remain open on Sunday have fared better by challenging these laws in state courts, under the state's own constitution, either on the "religion" ground or on the ground that the legislation arbitrarily discriminates between products and businesses.

Results where illegal Sunday contract

Where there is a valid Sunday law in force, some rather surprising results may occur, as illustrated by an old New Hampshire case where two cows were sold on a Sunday with the price to be paid later. When the buyer didn't pay and the seller repossessed the cows, the seller was held liable for trespass since an absolute ownership of the cows had passed to the buyer. But when the seller sued for the contract price, the court permitted the buyer to use the illegality defense since the contract had been made on a Sunday! The court's main reason for this result was that the parties were equally guilty and should therefore have been left where they were when performance of the illegal bargain ceased—the buyer with the cows, the seller without the money. In many states today, a court would construct an "implied promise" to pay the contract price if the buyer retained the property and would say that this promise was legal because it was "made" on a weekday.

The *Cameron* case shows that the Sunday statute must be read carefully, to see exactly what it prohibits.

CAMERON v. GUNSTOCK ACRES, INC.

348 N.E.2d 791 (Massachusetts, 1976)

FACTS

Gunstock Acres is a vacation and retirement home development in New Hampshire. Solicitations are made by mail and through the media for a free weekend to review the development. In response to such an invitation, Cameron went to the development with friends on Friday, January 24, 1969. On Sunday morning, January 26, 1969, after discussions with a salesman, he signed the contract, dated January 25, 1969, and delivered a check for $100.

Subsequently, Cameron made a down payment and paid 28 monthly installments, paying more than $3,800 toward the purchase price of $6,495. He made several visits to the property, the last in October 1972, and observed roads in rough condition. He had correspondence with the seller relating to delinquent payments and possible sale of the lot. In August 1971, he went to the seller's office in Fitchburg, Massachusetts, and was told that finding a buyer would be his responsibility. He was unsuccessful in finding a buyer.

Cameron filed this action in equity, asking the court to declare the contract void because it was executed on Sunday. He lives in Massachusetts; both states have Sunday laws. The trial court dismissed the case.

ISSUE

Is this contract void because it violates a Sunday law?

DECISION

No. Judgment affirmed.

REASONS

Justice Braucher first noted that the findings in the trial court indicated that the development had not been abandoned by the seller, although work was proceeding slowly, and that there was no fraud involved. The only question related to the possible Sunday law violation.

He first determined that the New Hampshire law was the one which applied, since the land was located there, the contract had been made there, and the contract specified that it would be governed by New Hampshire law. The New Hampshire law had been repealed in 1973, but as it was in force in 1969, it prohibited only secular work "to the disturbance of others." Braucher agreed with the interpretation of an earlier case, which had involved the signing of a real estate listing agreement with a broker:

"It appeared that the parties were willingly assembled in the defendants' private home, without solicitation by the plaintiff, for the purpose of executing an agreement authorizing the sale of the defendants' home by the plaintiff. Under any realistic meaning of the phrase in the twentieth century this cannot be considered an activity 'to the disturbance of others' as used in RSA 578:3. In the present case there was solicitation by the seller, but there is no indication that it took place on Sunday."

Usury.   Usury is very easy to define: it is the charging of an illegally high rate of interest. This simple definition is not always so easy to apply to particular cases. Each state must decide two subsidiary questions: What is interest, and what is an illegally high rate? States do not agree on the answers to these questions.

Credit charges as interest

Interest is generally defined as the charge for a loan of money or for the forbearance of a debt. Since the impact on the buyer-debtor is the same in either case, and since the seller-lender ought not to be able to evade the maximum rate by merely calling interest something else, most courts today would probably hold that a **time-price differential** charged in a credit sale is in fact interest, but there are cases reaching the opposite result. Monthly **service charges** on revolving charge accounts have been held to be interest by nearly every court to consider the problem since 1970. Some states have specific statutes regulating these special kinds of credit arrangements and permitting the creditor to charge a higher rate of interest than that permitted by the state's general usury law. Nearly all courts agree that *bona fide* charges for separate services, such as credit reports on the debtor, appraisals of collateral, and filing fees, are valid and are not to be calculated as part of the interest charge.

Many different limits for different credit transactions

How high is too high? The general usury law in most states specifies a maximum annual interest rate of from 7 to 10 percent. In most states corporations are not protected by usury laws, and this same idea has been extended in several states to any loan to a business, incorporated or not. Small loan companies are typically governed by their own statute, which permits them to charge a much higher interest rate (usually 24 to 36 percent). Credit unions and other special lenders may also have their own special statutory rate. One of the main objectives of the proposed Uniform Consumer Credit Code is to simplify this hodgepodge of existing laws.

Courts split on results if usury shown

The states disagree not only on the definition of interest and the rate permitted but also on what the remedy should be when a lender tries to charge a usurious rate. At least four types of results have been worked out: (1) forfeiture of only the excessive amount of interest; (2) forfeiture of all interest; (3) forfeiture of double or triple the amount of interest charged; and (4) forfeiture of the entire debt, both principal and interest.

Common-Law Restraint of Trade. Contracts which produce unreasonable restraints of trade were illegal under the common law and they continue to be prohibited by many modern state and national statutes. However, the courts have long recognized that certain types of restraints serve a legitimate business function. In two situations in particular, the courts have recognized and enforced reasonable restraints of trade. When someone buys a business, that person is also buying *goodwill*. The courts permit the buyer to protect this goodwill by requiring the seller not to engage in a competing business within a reasonable geographic area for a reasonable period of time. If this restraint or **covenant not to compete** were not permitted, the seller could immediately regain most or all former customers by going back into business right across the street. Similarly, former employees, partners, or other business associates can be restrained from going to work for a competing firm, within reasonable area and time limits, if this is necessary to protect a former employer's goodwill, customer lists, or trade secrets.

Reasons for agreements not to compete

Courts split on results if restraint unreasonable

Where the area or time limitations are unreasonable, and therefore illegal, the courts do not agree on what should happen. Some courts throw out the restraint entirely, thus giving the restrained party a better bargain than was made originally. Other courts use a "blue pencil" and rewrite the limitations to make them reasonable. The problem with this approach is that it encourages the buyer or employer to write in unreasonable limitations since, if these are challenged in court, the worst outcome is that they will only be made reasonable.

The accompanying case illustrates the common use made of such restraints in professional partnerships.

MIDDLESEX NEUROLOGICAL ASSOCIATES, INC. v. COHEN

324 N.E.2d 911 (Massachusetts, 1975)

FACTS

A neurosurgeon named Fusillo engaged in discussions with the defendant in the summer and fall of 1971 which led to an oral understanding that the defendant would associate with Fusillo in the practice of neurology in Malden and vicinity, where Fusillo had been in practice since 1963. The association began on November 6, 1971. About a week later Fusillo asked the defendant to sign an "employment agreement," which stated that it represented the entire agreement of the parties and contained the restrictive covenant. The defendant expressed reluctance to sign it, but did so after consulting with an attorney. The plaintiff corporation, of which Fusillo was president and sole stockholder, was chartered on December 3, 1971, and Fusillo assigned the employment agreement to it on December 7. Cohen left the corporation and began his own practice. Middlesex got an injunction from the trial court.

ISSUE

Is the covenant enforceable as a reasonable restraint?

DECISION

Yes. Judgment for plaintiff affirmed.

REASONS

Justice Armstrong first rejected the defendant's arguments that he received no consideration for his promise not to compete and that the plaintiff had not lived up to its part of the contract.

"The defendant further contends that the restrictive covenant is unreasonably broad in its territorial coverage. The defendant's argument is addressed to the inclusion in the restriction of the entire 'Malden, Melrose, Wakefield, Everett, Winchester, Stoneham community,' which, according to the defendant's brief, exceeds 250,000 in population. In view of the master's finding that Fusillo actively practices throughout the area, the covenant's territorial scope is not broader than the plaintiff's legitimate interests require. Several neurologists and neurosurgeons other than Fusillo and the defendant practice (although not exclusively) in the area, and . . . no patients have suffered due to the unavailability of a neurologist.

"The duration of the restriction (two years) was reasonable. The goodwill sought to be protected by the restrictive covenant was of long-term significance, relating not only to Fusillo's patients during the period of employment but also to the medical community from which a neurologist must derive patients by referral.

"The defendant [also] argues that enforcement of the restrictive covenant is not necessary for the economic protection of the plaintiff. . . .

"But even if the subsidiary findings did establish that the plaintiff has suffered no loss in volume of business, that without more would not establish that the plaintiff has not suffered a loss of the goodwill which it is the lawful purpose of the covenant to protect. On the contrary, the master's findings that the defendant has been treating former patients of the plaintiff and has accepted referrals from doctors who formerly made referrals to the plaintiff suggest loss of goodwill in fact."

Improper Interference with Governmental Processes.   In the wake of Watergate, with the absolutely unprecedented loss through resignation of both a President and a Vice President of the United States and with the disclosures of illegal political contributions by some of our largest national corporations, many people have been made much more aware of the possibilities for the corruption of governmental processes. Coercion or bribery of public officials is clearly illegal, and any "contract" involving such "services" would be void. *Lobbying,* on the other hand, is perfectly lawful and an essential part of the democratic process, and lobbying contracts which do not involve any improper means are valid and enforceable in court.

In most states mere failure to report a crime, called *misprision,* is no longer criminal; however, a person who actively aids in concealing a crime or agrees not to file criminal charges in return for a consideration is committing a criminal act. Perjury and jury tampering are both crimes. While at one time *maintenance* (stirring up litigation) was a crime, this rule has been modified as a result of the activities of such organizations as the NAACP Legal Defense Fund and Nader's Raiders. The old common-law judges were so jealous of their prerogatives that they even held arbitration agreements to be illegal "obstructions of justice," but this view has been almost completely repudiated.

The Watergate scandal has left this entire area of the law somewhat unsettled, as new legislation has been adopted to limit private political contributions and new attempts are under way to permit political activities by employees of the U.S. government.

■ BARGAINS AGAINST PUBLIC POLICY AND UNCONSCIONABLE CONTRACTS

Courts more willing to oversee contract provisions

Courts have become increasingly willing to refuse enforcement of contract provisions which are not specifically illegal but which they just plain don't like. Traditionally the emphasis of the common law has been on freedom of contract, or letting the parties make any sort of contractual arrangement they want so long as it is not illegal. More and more, however, recognizing that contracts in modern society do not always represent real bargaining between equals, courts have been rewriting contracts by refusing to enforce provisions which they regard as unduly harsh, oppressive, or unjust. As the following case shows, courts have been discovering that they have always had a common-law power to refuse enforcement of such ***unconscionable*** provisions, even without Section 2–302 of the UCC.

WILLIAMS v. WALKER–THOMAS FURNITURE COMPANY

350 F.2d 445 (District of Columbia Circuit, 1965)

FACTS

During the period from 1957 to 1962 Ora Lee Williams purchased a number of household items from Walker–Thomas, for which payment was to be made in installments. The terms of each purchase were contained in a printed form contract which set forth the value of the purchased item and purported to lease the item to her for a stipulated monthly rent payment. The contract then provided, in substance, that title would remain in Walker–Thomas until the total of all the monthly payments equaled the stated value of the item, at which time Williams could take title. In the event of a default in the payment of any monthly installment, Walker–Thomas could repossess the item.

The contract further provided that "the amount of each periodical installment payment to be made by [purchaser] to the Company under this present lease shall be inclusive of and not in addition to the amount of each installment payment to be made by [purchaser] under such prior leases, bills or accounts; *and all payments now and hereafter made by [purchaser] shall be credited pro rata on all outstanding leases, bills and accounts* due the Company by [purchaser] at the time each such payment is made." (Emphasis added.)

ISSUE

Is the *pro rata* payment clause valid?

DECISION

No. Judgment reversed and case remanded.

REASONS

Chief Judge Wright did not think that "unconscionability" applied only under UCC 2–302.

"Appellants' principal contention, rejected by both the trial and the appellate courts below, is that these contracts, or at least some of them, are unconscionable and, hence, not enforceable. . . .

"We do not agree that the court lacked the power to refuse enforcement to contracts found to be unconscionable. In other jurisdictions, it has been held as a matter of common law that unconscionable contracts are not enforceable. While no decision of this court so holding has been found, the notion that an unconscionable bargain should not be given full enforcement is by no means novel. . . .

"In determining reasonableness or fairness, the primary concern must be with the terms of the contract considered in light of the circumstances existing when the contract was made. The test is not simple, nor can it be mechanically applied. The terms are to be considered 'in the light of the general commercial background and the commercial needs of the particular trade or case.' Corbin suggests the test as being whether the terms are 'so extreme as to appear unconscionable according to the mores and business practices of the time and place.' We think this formulation correctly states the test to be applied in those cases where no meaningful choice was exercised upon entering the contract.

"Because the trial court and the appellate court did not feel that enforcement could be refused, no findings were made on the possible unconscionability of the contracts in these cases. Since the record is not sufficient for our deciding the issue as a matter of law, the cases must be remanded to the trial court for further proceedings."

Among other kinds of provisions challengeable as *against public policy* are those attempting to insulate landlords, employers, and bailees from liability for their own negligence and those which purport to waive or give up specific statutory protections. Anyone who has ever rented a house or an apartment knows that landlords' lawyers are particularly adept at coming up with objectionable lease provisions: no pets, no motorcycles, no waterbeds, no alcohol; tenant waives right to trial by jury; landlord may inspect the premises at any hour of the day or night, with or without notice to the tenant. While the landlord surely has a legitimate concern with what happens on the premises, some of the preceding seem to constitute an unwarranted intrusion into the tenant's affairs; this balance has not yet been fully and finally defined.

These are not closed categories. As society's values change, provisions which are readily accepted and enforced today may become "against public policy" and thus unenforceable. In any case where the results called for by the terms of the contract seem unduly harsh, this additional defense argument should be presented to the court. What can you lose?

■ SIGNIFICANCE OF THIS CHAPTER

As statutes and administrative regulations multiply, it becomes increasingly possible that contracting parties may on occasion agree to do some illegal act. Generally, for successful criminal prosecution, criminal intent must be proved. Intent is usually irrelevant, however, as far as the enforcement of an illegal bargain is concerned. Both parties are presumed to know the applicable criminal law; whether or not they do in fact is usually irrelevant—their purported contract is void or voidable. Where a statute or regulation is designed to protect one of the parties to the transaction, the courts will try to work out results which achieve that objective. Otherwise, where both parties are equally guilty, the court's general approach will be to leave all parties as is. Since either of these rules can result in the forfeiture of substantial economic values, you need to be alerted to the major types of illegality which may occur in contracting situations.

DISCUSSION CASE

ROUSE v. PEOPLES LEASING CO.
638 P.2d 1245 (Washington, 1982)

FACTS: Plaintiffs brought a class action. Each of them had gone to a car dealership seeking to lease a new car and, as is the normal practice, the plaintiffs and other customers selected cars and negotiated purchase prices with the dealer. The dealer supplied credit application forms and contacted PLC for credit approval. Upon approval of credit, PLC paid the dealer the purchase price and the customers took possession of the cars, and PLC retained title although the customers were the registered owners. The agreement is termed a "lease." The lessees can gain full title by tendering the outstanding balance, the guaranteed residual value (established at the time of the original transaction), and a termination fee.

The nine lease forms used by PLC have the following similar characteristics:

(1) a term of 24 to 48 months with monthly payments;

(2) the lessee assumes all risks, insures, licenses and maintains the vehicle at the lessee's own expense;

(3) the lessor is guaranteed repayment of its entire capital outlay plus a predetermined profit within the term of the lease or termination; and

(4) the agreements are "open-ended" in that if the vehicle is sold for less than the guaranteed residual value then the lessee is liable for the difference and, if it is sold for more, then PLC is liable to the lessee for the difference.

The plaintiffs claim these arrangements are in substance loans disguised as leases and are usurious because the "interest" exceeded the maximum allowed by statute (12 percent per annum).

In granting defendants' summary judgment motion dismissing plaintiffs' claims, the trial court found the contract was not usurious because it could be explained by another hypothesis: that is, that the parties entered into a lessor-lessee rather than a loan relationship.

■

Justice Dolliver gave this opinion:

Washington courts have held that in any case involving an alleged usurious transaction the person attempting to use usury either affirmatively or defensively must establish five elements in order to carry the burden of proof. . . . These five elements are:

(1) a loan or forbearance, express or implied; (2) money or its equivalent constituting the subject matter of the loan or forbearance; (3) an understanding between the parties that the principal shall be repayable absolutely; (4) the exaction of something in excess of what is allowed by law for the use of the money loaned or for the benefit of the forbearance; and, in some jurisdictions; (5) an intent to exact more than the legal maximum for the loan or forbearance.

The finding of all five elements indicates the transaction is usurious irrespective of the form in which the parties put the transaction. . . .

The court thus seems to be faced with a conflict in the application of its rules: (1) substance should prevail over form to determine whether usury is present and (2) when there is a question of usury if a contract is susceptible of two constructions, one lawful and the other unlawful, the former will be adopted. . . .

On a question of usury, the court must first look at the transaction, regardless of what the parties might choose to call it, to see whether it is in fact a loan or forbearance—the first element to be proved where either party claims usury. . . . In making this initial determination the two-hypotheses rule is not used. It is only after determining the transaction was in fact a loan or forbearance that the court will employ the two-hypotheses test and uphold the lawful construction. To hold as the trial court did that the two-hypotheses test applies to the question of whether the transaction is a loan or forbearance would allow a skillful party to negate the application of the usury laws simply by characterizing a transaction so that it would not be a loan or forbearance in form but would accomplish the same end and not be susceptible to usury laws. This is not nor should it be the law in Washington.

The present case revolves on the question of whether a loan or forbearance exists. The trial court, basing its opinion on the two-hypotheses theory, held that, because the parties clearly intended the transaction to be a lease, it must magically be turned into one. As noted previously, this triumph of form over substance, if followed, could have an emasculating effect on the usury laws. While finding intent is important in determining the computation of charges pursuant to a contract, it is irrelevant as it pertains to the determination of the transaction being a loan or forbearance as posed to a lease. . . .

The transactions cannot be both loans and lease agreements. . . . We agree with Judge Morell E. Sharp who, in holding open-ended leases to be loans stated:

The defendant banks . . . conceive of vehicle leases as a species of legal chameleon: they resemble bona fide leases whenever resting upon a tax return or an interest disclosure form; yet they cannot be distinguished from ordinary loans when examined against the background of the National Bank Act.

In categorizing the transaction as a loan, the court continued at page 1295:

[T]he open-end motor vehicle lease, which is the usual form, is merely a variation in the traditional manner of extending credit and is the functional equivalent of a loan on personal security.

We hold as a matter of law that the open-end motor vehicle lease is the functional equivalent of a loan and that it is a "loan or forbearance, express or implied" for the purpose of the usury statutes. The case is remanded to the trial court to determine whether these transactions which are loans for the purpose of the usury statutes are usurious.

On the matter of the class action, the reason given by the trial court for decertification no longer applies given our holding. The question is remanded to the trial court for action not inconsistent with this opinion.

■ IMPORTANT TERMS AND CONCEPTS

gambling/lottery
licensing statute
revenue-raising statute
regulatory statute
usury
time-price differential
service charge
Sunday law
restraint of trade

covenant not to compete
lobbying
bribery
interference with
   government process
against public policy
unconscionable
in pari delicto

■ QUESTIONS AND PROBLEMS FOR DISCUSSION

1. What results occur when a credit contract specifies an illegally high rate of interest on the debt?
2. When and how can the seller of a business be prevented from competing with it after selling it?
3. To what extent are Sunday contracts illegal?
4. What happens when a person contracts to perform services without having the required license to do so?

5. R. E. Fuse operates a garbage collection service in the towns of Cleen and Teidy. In June 1984 he made an oral agreement with Wesley Trashy to hire him as a garbage truck driver. In November R. E. Fuse handed Wesley a written document which stated that, upon severance of employment, Trashy would not engage in garbage collection within 15 miles of Cleen and Teidy for a period of five years. Trashy, who knew that his signature on the document was a precondition for continued employment, signed the agreement. In September 1985 Wesley Trashy quit his job and immediately went into the garbage collection business for himself. R. E. Fuse now brings an action against Trashy for breach of contract. What decision? Why?

6. Sinkin Beverage Company was licensed by Blitz Beer as a wholesale distributor in 1975. The written contract which the parties signed at that time provided that either one could cancel at any time, for any reason or for no reason at all. Sinkin was the exclusive distributor for Blitz products in Suffould County 1975 to 1986, and its Blitz sales constitute a large part of its wholesale business. In 1986 Blitz notified Sinkin that the contract would be terminated in 10 days. Sinkin sues for an injunction against the termination, claiming that the contract clause is unconscionable. Should this injunction be granted? Explain.

7. After some lengthy negotiations, Hammermill Paper Company agreed to appoint Nashua River Supply Company as its exclusive sales agent for the State of Massachusetts. A comprehensive written contract was drafted and executed. One provision of the contract read as follows: "no action at law or in equity shall be instituted or maintained by Nashua in any court of any State of the United States, or in any United States District Court, or elsewhere, against Hammermill, other than in the state courts of Pennsylvania." Disputes arose over the terms of the agency agreement, and Nashua sued in Massachusetts. Hammermill asks the Massachusetts court to dismiss the case, based on the above-quoted contract clause. What is the result, and why?

8. Plaintiffs, desirous of purchasing a home, and defendant entered into a promissory note secured by a mortgage on the home. The promissory note was for the principal amount of $30,000 with interest at 9.5 percent per annum, for a period of five years, with monthly payments of $279.64. The mortgage agreement contained the following clause: "Balance due in five years with option to renew at current rate of interest." A statute provides that "a note, mortgage, contract, or other evidence of indebtedness shall not provide that the rate of interest initially effective may be increased for any reason whatsoever."

Plaintiffs sue to have the note and mortgage declared illegal. How should the court rule, and why?

16

Assignment and Third-Party Beneficiary Contracts

CHAPTER OBJECTIVES

THIS CHAPTER WILL:

- Indicate how persons other than the contracting parties may acquire rights under a contract.
- Explain third-party beneficiary contracts.
- Differentiate donee beneficiaries, creditor beneficiaries, and incidental beneficiaries.
- Explain the difference between assignment of rights and delegation of duties.
- Discuss the rules for assigning rights.
- Explain how a debtor's rights may be affected when a creditor assigns the right to receive the contract price.

The problems discussed in this chapter are quite different from any we have considered so far. Here our basic question is whether persons other than the parties who actually negotiated and agreed to the contract should be given the right to demand performance under it. The answer given by the early common law was simple: No! Today, however, courts do recognize the rights of these "strangers"—both assignees and third-party beneficiaries—at least in some situations and subject to many complicated and technical limitations.

■ THIRD-PARTY BENEFICIARY CONTRACTS

Basic Concepts and Definitions. A *third-party beneficiary contract* is one in which at least one of the performances called for is intended for the direct benefit of a person or persons other than the parties who actually made the contract. *Donee beneficiaries* are persons who receive this benefit as a gift, without any prior duty on anyone's part to provide them with the benefit. In most cases, persons named as the beneficiaries in life insurance policies are

■ EXHIBIT 16–1

Assignment and Third-Party Beneficiary Contracts

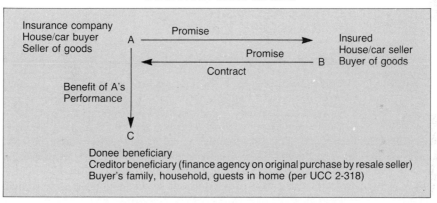

THIRD PARTY BENEFICIARIES

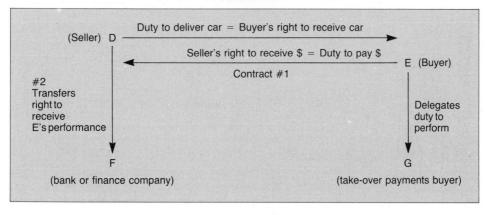

ASSIGNMENT

Intended beneficiaries of others' contracts

donees. A **_creditor beneficiary_** is one to whom the benefit was already owed, as a result of a prior legal relationship. If creditors have sold or financed purchases of such items as cars, appliances, or real estate to buyers who resell the as-yet-unpaid-for items to purchasers who agree to take over the payments, the creditors are third-party creditor beneficiaries of the take-over-the-payments contracts. In these cases, the creditor beneficiary has two parties to look to for payment: the original debtor and the takeover buyer.

UCC warranties to third parties

UCC Rule on Third-Party Beneficiaries of Warranties. The Uniform Commercial Code does not deal with third-party beneficiaries in any comprehensive way. It does, however, contain one very important third-party provision: 2–318, which provides that whatever warranties are made by a seller of goods are also by law extended at least to members of the buyer's family and household and to guests in the buyer's home. (Alternative wordings of this section extend the warranties to cover any reasonably anticipated "human" person, or even to any person, who may be affected by the goods.) The section further provides that its effect cannot be limited by any contrary agreement between the seller and the buyer.

The *Brown* case illustrates another kind of third-party beneficiary situation.

BROWN v. NATIONAL SUPERMARKETS, INC.

679 S.W.2d 307 (Missouri, 1984)

FACTS

Plaintiff-appellants Pauline and George Brown appeal from a summary judgment in favor of the three defendants, National Super Markets, Sentry Security Agency, and T. G. Watkins, a security guard employed by Sentry.

Pauline and George Brown brought a negligence action against the defendants after Pauline was shot and seriously injured by an unknown assailant in National's parking lot. The Browns allege that the defendants have a duty to protect National's patrons both in the store and in the parking lot and that they breached that duty. Defendants denied that they have such a duty and filed a motion for summary judgment. The trial court granted the motion.

Appellants maintain that summary judgment should not have been granted because as a matter of law their petition properly stated a claim of actionable negligence. The petition claims that in the two years prior to Mrs. Brown's assault there were 16 incidents of reported robbery involving a firearm and 7 incidents of reported strong-arm robberies as well as 136 other reported crimes on National's premises. Appellants maintain that this known criminal activity and conduct creates special facts and circumstances giving rise to a duty on behalf of the defendants to protect store patrons against assaults.

ISSUE

Did the defendants have a duty to protect store patrons from criminal attacks?

DECISION

Perhaps, depending on the specific facts. Summary judgment reversed and case remanded.

REASONS

Judge Karohl.

"As to National the question here is whether as a matter of law a store owner, the security company it had hired under a contract to provide security services, and an on-duty security guard have a duty to protect store patrons from criminal assaults by third parties when the store owner knows that repeated violent crimes have occurred recently on the premises. . . .

"[W]hile there is no general duty for the owner of a business to protect a plaintiff against the intentional criminal conduct of unknown persons, the duty can arise where special relationships or special circumstances exist. . . . Included among the special circumstances and facts [is] the frequent and recent occurrence of violent crimes on the business premises. . . . [I]f a business owner has notice, actual or constructive, of prior acts committed by third parties on the premises which might cause injuries to the patron, he or she may be liable if reasonable care to provide appropriate precautions is not taken. . . . [I]n order to prevail under this rule a plaintiff must allege that specific crimes occurred on the premises. . . . In the case at bar the plaintiffs have attached and incorporated a detailed list of prior violent crimes that have occurred on National's premises.

"Based on the legal theory . . . that a business owner may have a duty to patrons, summary judgment as to National was error.

"The question as to Sentry and its employee is whether they assumed a duty to plaintiff if, as alleged, they contracted with National to provide protection National may owe to its patrons. The cases do not clearly establish whether a security company or security guard working for a business owner under contract has a duty to protect patrons from crime. It is the general rule that a private person has no duty to protect another from a deliberate criminal attack by a third person. . . . We find that Sentry may or may not have assumed such a duty when it entered into the security contract. . . . The existence of a duty will turn on the terms of the contract and the circumstances.

"Plaintiffs allege in their amended petition that Sentry contracted with National to provide security against criminal activities for National *and its patrons*. (our emphasis). In effect plaintiffs claim that the contract between National and Sentry is an attempt to perform National's previously established duty. The provisions of the contract are not in evidence. However, the National store manager testified by deposition that although he had never seen the contract he understood it to cover the area both inside and outside the store. T. G. Watkins, the security guard, stated in his deposition that he was never told to patrol the parking lot. As it is unclear whether the security company assumed any duty through the contract, an issue of fact remains and summary judgment was in error.

"Plaintiffs may be third party beneficiaries to this contract. As such they may sue in tort or contract for any contract breach by Sentry or its employees.

> Third party beneficiary is the nomenclature given to one who is not privy to a contract nor its consideration but to whom the law gives the right to maintain a cause of action for breach of contract. . . . Only those third parties for whose primary benefit the contracting parties intended to make the contract may maintain an action. . . . The intention of the parties is to be gleaned from the four corners of the contract, and if uncertain or ambiguous, from the circumstances surrounding its execution. . . .

"Privity of contract is no longer always necessary to maintain a suit for breach of contract. . . .

> [T]here are situations in which the making of the contract creates a relation between the defendant and the promise, which is sufficient to impose a tort duty of reasonable care. . . . Where an agent or servant has accepted the control of property under a contract with his principal, and under circumstances where there is an obvious risk of harm to outsiders if he does not use reasonable care, the obligation of affirmative conduct has been imposed upon him. . . .

"As a matter of law both National and Sentry may have a duty to protect National patrons from criminal assaults. Summary judgment was inappropriate because questions of fact remain.

"We reverse the trial court decision for summary judgment and remand the cause for an action consistent with this opinion."

Incidental Beneficiaries. Many courts are still quite reluctant to permit "non-participant" third parties to enforce contracts which they had no part in making. Such courts, therefore, demand clear proof of an intent to benefit a third party. *Incidental beneficiaries,* persons who derive some indirect benefit from a contract but cannot show such an intent on the part of the contracting parties, have no right to sue to enforce the contract.

It is not necessary that the third party be specifically named or identified at the time the contract is made. A shopkeeper-tenant was held to have enforceable rights against a contractor who had promised the owner-landlord that the remodeling job would be done "in such a way as to cause a minimum of disturbance to the daytime operations in the building." Courts will, however, look very carefully for the contracting parties' intent.

Mutual Rescission of the Contract. Generally, the parties to a contract can agree to call off the deal any time they want to. The problem is complicated by the presence of a third-party beneficiary: Must the original contracting parties also have consent to the rescission from the third party?

Rescission where third party beneficiary

In answering this question, the *Restatement* distinguishes between the donee beneficiary and the creditor beneficiary. In the case of the donee beneficiary, the gift is considered to be complete, and therefore nonrescindable, when the contract is made. Thus, the parties to a life insurance contract, for example, cannot rescind the gift by agreeing to a change of beneficiaries unless the right to change beneficiaries has been reserved. On the other hand, where a creditor beneficiary is involved, there is a preexisting contract with the original debtor. The creditor can still demand performance from that party. The contract made for the benefit of a third-party creditor can thus be rescinded until the creditor relies on it in some way. The creditor might let the original debtor remove collateral from the state, for instance, relying on the fact that the substitute debtor was still there. Once that had happened, the original debtor and the substitute debtor would not be able to rescind their agreement.

■ **ASSIGNMENT OF CONTRACT RIGHTS**

Basic Concepts and Definitions. *Assignment* simply means transfer; the "owner" of the right to receive benefits under a contract is simply transferring this right to someone else. The transfer may itself be part of a second contract (as it usually is), or it may be made as a gift. No special language is required for an effective assignment; any manifestation of an intent to make such a transfer is sufficient. Some states require all assignments to be in writing to be enforceable; others do not. For the kinds of assignments it covers (9–102[1][b], 9–104[f], 9–106), Article 9 of the UCC requires assignments to be in writing.

Early Common-Law Rule.   The common law emphasized freedom of a contract; no one should be required to deal with another person without first agreeing to do so. Contract prohibitions against assignment were given full force and effect. An *obligor,* the person who had a duty to perform, could in effect veto an assignment by refusing to perform for the new *obligee.* Although the validity of transfers of contract rights is now generally recognized and such assignments provide the mechanism for financing a large part of modern business, there are still many technical legal rules on this subject.

Delegation of Duties.   One of the first distinctions which must be drawn is the difference between assigning a right and delegating a duty. Duties can never be assigned, only delegated, the difference being that someone who delegates his or her own duty of performance to another remains personally responsible for its proper and timely performance. In our example above, if the repurchaser of the car in the take-over-the-payments deal does not make the payments as promised, the original buyer remains personally liable and can be sued by the original seller. Where a right has been validly assigned, however, the assignee completely displaces the original owner of the right, to whom performance was due. However, the original debtor is free of liability for a delegated duty only if the original obligee (creditor) agrees to the substitution of the new obligor (debtor) in place of the original one and agrees to discharge the original one. This change of parties, called a *novation,* is discussed further in the next chapter. Without the obligee's consent, the performance of a duty cannot even be delegated to another person if the duty involves an individualized service or if there is a particular reason for dealing with one certain person.

Distinction between assignment and delegation

These rules are illustrated by the *Loftus* case.

LOFTUS v. AMERICAN REALTY COMPANY

334 N.W.2d 366 (Iowa, 1983)

FACTS   Raymond and Connie Loftus sue for damages to their home, which they were trying to sell. Plaintiffs entered into an exclusive contract with American Realty, under which American Realty was given the exclusive right to offer plaintiff's home for sale. Plaintiffs moved out of the house, and shut off all of the appliances with the exception of the furnace.

Under the contract the realty company was to assume the responsibility for performing any tasks necessary for the closing of the transaction, including turning on utilities. An offer was made for plaintiffs' house, which offer was accepted by plaintiffs. Prior to the closing, American Realty hired Fitzpatrick to light the gas water heater. In opening the gas valve to the water heater, Fitzpatrick also opened an uncapped gas line. As a result, the house exploded and burned, resulting in damages totaling $22,500.

Defendant Fitzpatrick was discharged in bankruptcy prior to trial in this matter.

ISSUE   Is American Realty liable for the negligence of Fitzpatrick?

DECISION   Yes. Judgment reversed.

REASONS   Chief Judge Oxenberger agreed with the trial court that Fitzpatrick was not American's agent, but rather an independent business operator. American thus could not be held liable under principles of agency law. There was, however, another basis under which American could be held—delegation of a duty.

"The general rule regarding obligations under a personal service contract is that they are not delegable. This rule is relaxed in the case where the duties which are delegated are purely ministerial. However, even then, the performance of such delegated duties is regarded as performance by the obligor and liability remains with him. 'One who contracts to perform an undertaking is liable to his promise for the negligence of an independent contractor to whom he delegates performance.'

"In the present case, defendant American Realty assumed a number of obligations when it entered into a contract with plaintiffs to act as their agent in the sale of their home. It assumed the obligation to light the water heater as part of this contract. Although this obligation was clearly ministerial, the fact that American Realty could delegate the duty to a third party, and did so delegate it, did not excuse it from liability for the faulty performance of the subcontractor.

"The judgment of the trial court is reversed with instructions to enter judgment for plaintiffs in the amount of $22,500."

Assignability of Contract Rights.   To determine whether or not rights are assignable, we must consider contracts in three categories. First, there are contracts whose rights are not assignable unless the obligor specifically agrees to the assignment. This category includes contracts involving some personal element, such as the personal service of the obligor or the personal credit or requirements of the obligee, and contracts where the performance of the duty would be materially changed if the assignment were recognized. The UCC adopts this same basic approach for sales of goods in Section 2–210(2).

> Contracts with personal element not assignable

Probably the vast majority of contracts fall into the second category, in which the rights are assignable unless there is a specific contract prohibition against assignment. In most cases, contract rights for such things as land, securities, or goods would be presumed to be transferable to others unless the parties had specifically agreed otherwise. Section 2–210(3) of the UCC says that in order to prohibit assignment of the right to receive goods, a contract clause must very clearly specify that result; a general prohibition of transfer of "the contract" is only effective to prohibit a delegation of duties.

> Most contracts assignable unless agreed otherwise

The third group of contracts results from the Code's effort to make sure that businesses will be able to use their accounts as financing collateral without having to get each account debtor's consent. Section 9–318(4) says that even if the contract specifically prohibits assignment of the right to receive payment for goods sold or leased or services performed, the creditor can go ahead and assign the account anyway, without the debtor's consent; the contract provision will not be enforced. For example, when you buy your new TV on time, even getting a specific clause written into your contract will not enable you to avoid dealing with a finance company if the dealer wants to assign your contract.

> Accounts receivable assignable despite contrary agreement

As a rule, present assignments of future rights are fully effective; that is, one can effectively transfer ownership now of the right, under an existing

> Assignment of future rights

contract, to receive a performance at some future date. However, any purported assignment of rights under a contract which does not exist yet, but is merely anticipated, is totally void. An unemployed person has not made an effective assignment by signing a contract with an employment agency which purports to assign one third of the first month's wages to the agency when it gets that person a new job. In addition, most states have specific regulatory statutes covering wage assignments and limiting the percentage share that can be assigned.

Due on Sale Clauses in Real Estate Mortgages. A due on sale clause does not, technically, prohibit the resale of real estate before an existing mortgage is paid off. What it does say is that when such a resale occurs, the entire remaining mortgage balance becomes immediately due and payable. As a practical result, this means that no assignment of the existing mortgage to the resale purchaser can occur; the resale purchaser will have to qualify for new financing. As interest rates soared in the late 1970s and early 1980s, mortgage lenders did not want to be bound on the 20- and 30-year mortgages which they had written at 6 to 9 percent interest rates. The lenders began to enforce their due on sale clauses vigorously.

U.S. statute validates due on sale clauses

Although outright prohibitions on assignments by real estate buyers would generally be enforceable, some state courts refused to enforce due on sale clauses. For a time, there was a distinction based on whether the lender was state chartered or U.S. chartered. U.S. regulations specifically recognized the validity of the due on sale, but a state lending institution, competing for the same business, might not be able to enforce the clause. As a result of the 1982 Garn-St. Germain statute passed by Congress, due on sale clauses are now generally enforceable.

Warranties of Assignor to Assignee. Where a contract right has been transferred for value, the **Restatement** says that the assignor makes three implied warranties to the assignee:

1. That the assignor will do nothing to defeat or impair the value of the assignment and that he or she has no knowledge of any fact which would do so.

2. That the right, as assigned, actually exists and is subject to no limitations or defenses good against the assignor, except those stated or apparent.

3. That any writing given or shown to the assignee as evidence of the right is genuine and what it purports to be.

Assignor's express warranties

In addition, the seller/assignor of the right can be sued for breach of warranty and/or fraud for any express statements made which are not true, such as a statement that a credit check had been made on the buyer/debtor, or that the buyer/debtor had a steady job. Note, however, that there is no implied guarantee that the buyer/debtor is solvent or will in fact perform as promised. In most cases where accounts receivable are being assigned on a regular basis, as with a car dealer to a manufacturer's financing subsidiary, the assignment agreement itself will include a specific recourse provision. The assignor may have to buy back all uncollectible accounts, or none of them, or only some of them. The parties are free to work this out as they choose.

Delegation of Duty to Assignee. Courts are not agreed as to whether, in taking the assignment, an assignee is also impliedly agreeing to perform any remaining duties owed by his or her assignor to the other original party. Most of the older cases say that no such promise is implied; many of the newer ones have adopted a contrary rule. In any event, all of the surrounding facts and circumstances, and especially the language of the assignment itself, will be examined to see whether such a promise should be implied. The simplest solution to this problem is to specify the result desired in the assignment itself.

Assignee may impliedly agree to perform duties

For the sale of goods, the Code adopts the view of the newer cases, so that an acceptance by the assignee of a general assignment also constitutes the assignee's promise to perform all of the assignor's remaining duties, unless the language of the assignment or the circumstances indicate otherwise.

UCC rule for goods

The significance of such a promise by the assignee is that nonperformance of the reciprocal duty gives (or may give) the other party an excuse for withholding the required return performance or even a basis for bringing a lawsuit against the assignee for breach of contract.

Notice to Obligor. All courts agree that, as between the assignor and the assignee, the assignment is effective when it is made, even though notice of the assignment has not been communicated to the obligor. However, notice (or its absence) does have some important legal consequences. Payment or other performance that the obligor gives to the assignor, before receiving notice that the obligation has been assigned and that the performance should now be made to the assignee, completely discharges that part of the original contract obligation. The assignee cannot sue the obligor and force a repeat performance but instead would have to sue the assignor. Similarly, the obligor can assert defenses or counterclaims against the assignee even on totally unrelated transactions between the obligor and the assignor if such claims arose before the obligor received notice of the assignment. For example: Dull buys a used car and a new car from Sharpie. Dull pays cash for the used car and finances the new car. Sharpie assigns the financing contract on the new car to the Bigger Bank. Until Dull gets notice of this assignment he can use as a defense against paying the balance due, not only any defects in the new car but also any defects in the used car. Once Dull gets notice of the assignment of his new car contract to Bigger Bank he can use only defects in the new car as his reason for nonpayment. After notice has been received, any additional problems with the used car will have to be taken up separately with Sharpie.

Importance of notice to obligor

FIRST NATIONAL BANK OF RIO ARRIBA v. MOUNTAIN STATES TELEPHONE AND TELEGRAPH CO.

571 P.2d 118 (New Mexico, 1977)

FACTS   Vernon Siler contracted to work on a project for Mountain States. To help finance the project, he got a loan from First National, and assigned to them the payment he was to receive when he finished the job for Mountain States. The written assignment was delivered to Mountain States. First National made no specific demand for payment.

Mountain States paid Siler. The trial court granted summary judgment in favor of First National.

ISSUE Did the account debtor (Mountain States) wrongfully pay the assignor (Siler) after receiving notice of the assignment?

DECISION Yes. Judgment affirmed.

REASONS Justice Payne noted that the written assignment was very clear as to its meaning and intent: Siler had transferred all his rights to the money to First National. Justice Payne also thoroughly reviewed the UCC provisions and Official Comments pertaining to assignments. The UCC does not specify the form for an assignment or for a notice of assignment, only that the account debtor be reasonably notified of what has been assigned. If he has any doubt, he can not simply proceed to pay the assignor, but must instead notify the assignee that there is a problem. Here, Mountain States blithely proceeded to pay the assignor after receiving the assignment. That was clearly improper.

"Mountain Bell could readily determine from the assignment form that First National had purchased Siler's *right, title* and *interest* in the contract proceeds and was therefore entitled to payment. There was no reason for the bank to instruct Mountain Bell not to pay Siler because Siler retained no right to payment. The unconditional language of the assignment was notice that 'payment [was] to be made to the assignee.' . . .

"Mountain Bell takes the position that it was not an account debtor at the time it received notice, as the contract had not been performed and nothing was owed to Siler. Thus it argues that notice of the assignment was untimely since Siler had nothing to assign. Section 50A–9–105(1)(a) . . . defines an account debtor as follows:

> 'Account debtor' means the person who is obligated on an account, chattel paper, *contract right* or general intangible (emphasis added).

"Siler had contracted to perform work for Mountain Bell prior to the date of the assignment and the date of acceptance of the assignment by Mountain Bell. At the time of the assignment there was a contract, and Siler had a right to payment upon performance of the contract work."

Multiple assignments of same contract

Notice is also significant in working out the problems encountered when the assignor has made more than one assignment of the same right. Although this should not occur, and the assignor is clearly liable for breach of implied warranties to both assignees, the situation does arise and rules have been developed to deal with it. To a retailer or a construction firm caught in a temporary cash flow squeeze, a "temporary" double assignment of the accounts receivable looks like a painless solution, with no one ever being the wiser. Too often, however, the optimism is not justified, and the double financing is discovered in a bankruptcy proceeding. The problem, then, is that there is only one sum of money to be paid, and there are two assignee-claimants. Which one should be paid first?

Courts split as to which assignee gets paid

The states do not agree on the answer to this question. In the states which follow the *English rule* (probably still the minority), the assignee who first gives notice to the obligor is entitled to priority of payment. In the states which follow the *American rule,* the first assignment in point of time is given priority, but subject to several exceptions where notice has not been given. Under these exceptions, the first assignee loses if:

1. The first assignment was revocable or voidable by the assignor.

2. Payment has been made to the second assignee.

3. A judgment has been entered in favor of the second assignee.

4. A substitute contract has been negotiated by the second assignee and the debtor.

5. A specific writing representing the account, such as a savings account passbook, has been given to the second assignee.

Even in an American-rule state, therefore, it is important to give notice to the obligor immediately.

BOULEVARD NATIONAL BANK OF MIAMI v. AIR METALS INDUSTRIES, INC.

176 So.2d 94 (Florida, 1965)

FACTS   Air Metals was a subcontractor on a construction job for Tompkins-Beckwith Co., and was required to furnish a surety bond guaranteeing its proper performance of the job. American Fire & Casualty issued the bond for Air Metals, but required that Air Metals give them a conditional assignment of all moneys due under the construction contract "in the event of default" by Air Metals. Air Metals did so, but Tompkins-Beckwith was not notified. Air Metals borrowed money from Boulevard National Bank, and gave them an absolute assignment of all moneys due or to become due, from Tompkins-Beckwith, who again were not notified. Then Air Metals defaulted on the construction contract. American Fire notified Tompkins-Beckwith of their assignment, and Tompkins-Beckwith agreed to pay them what was owed to Air Metals. Boulevard then notified Tompkins-Beckwith of their assignment, which was actually the "first" in time, since the one to American Fire was to take effect only if and when Air Metals went into default. Boulevard lost in the trial court. Boulevard appealed from the judgment for American Fire.

ISSUE   Which assignee has priority?

DECISION   American Fire, under the English rule. Judgment affirmed.

 REASONS   Justice Willis discussed the choice he had between the two rules.

"The question which was passed upon by the certifying court is whether the law of Florida requires recognition of the so-called English rule or American rule of priority between assignees of successive assignments of an account receivable or other similar chose in action. Stated in its simplest form, the American rule would give priority to the assignee first in point of time of assignment, while the English rule would give preference to the assignment of which the debtor was first given notice. Both rules presuppose the absence of any estoppel or other special equities in favor of or against either assignee. The English rule giving priority to the assignee first giving notice to the debtor is specifically qualified as applying 'unless he takes a later assignment with notice of a previous one or without a valuable consideration.' The American rule giving the first assignee in point of time the preference is applicable only when the equities are equal between the contending assignees, and if a subsequent assignee has a stronger equity than an earlier one, he would prevail.

"In the case here there are no special equities and no rights, such as subrogation, which would arise outside of the assignments. Also we regard that any conditions precedent to the assignments, which the parties have expressly or impliedly stipulated, have occurred. In this posture, we are thus free to adjudicate which of these two rules, described as being 'clearly defined and irreconcilable,' is in harmony with our jurisprudence.

"The American rule for which petitioner contends is based upon the reasoning that an account or other chose in action may be assigned at will by the owner; that the notice to the debtor is not essential to complete the assignment; and that when such assignment is made, the property rights become vested in the assignee so that the assignor no longer has any interest in the account or chose which he may subsequently assign to another. . . .

"It is undoubted that the creditor of an account receivable or other similar chose in action arising out of contract may assign it to another so that the assignee may sue on it in his own name and make recovery. Formal requisites of such an assignment are not prescribed by statute, and it may be accomplished by parol, by instrument in writing, or other mode, such as delivery of evidences of the debt, as may demonstrate an intent to transfer and an acceptance of it. . . .

"It seems to be generally agreed that notice to a debtor of an assignment is necessary to impose on the debtor the duty of payment to the assignee, and that if before receiving such notice he pays the debt to the assignor, or to a subsequent assignee, he will be discharged from the debt. . . . It would seem to follow that the mere private dealing between the creditor and his assignee unaccompanied by any manifestations discernable to others having or considering the acquiring of an interest in the account would not meet the requirement of delivery and acceptance of possession which is essential to the consummation of the assignment. Proper notice to the debtor of the assignment is a manifestation of such delivery. It fixes the accountability of the debtor to the assignee instead of the assignor and enables all involved to deal more safely. . . .

"We thus find the so-called English rule which the trial and appellate court approved and applied is harmonious with our jurisprudence, whereas the so-called American rule is not."

[Judgment for American Fire affirmed as they were first to give notice to the debtor Tompkins-Beckwith.]

UCC rules require public filing of assignments

The Code will be of some help in dealing with this problem, since Article 9 covers most assignments for value as *secured transactions,* and generally requires the filing of a *public notice* that such financing arrangements are in force in order for them to be effective against third parties. Where such a filing is required by *Article 9* and has not yet occurred, a subsequent assignee of the accounts who gave value for them, had no knowledge of the first assignment, and filed its own public notice would be entitled to priority. It is, therefore, important for the first assignee to file the required public notice as well as to notify the obligor.

Availability of Defenses against Assignee. As it began to recognize the validity of assignments, the common law developed a rule which said that the assignee took the assigned contract right subject to all claims and defenses which the obligor could assert against the assignor. The assignee stepped into the assignor's legal shoes, and the shoes didn't get any bigger just because someone else was wearing them. While the assignee could at least cut off the

General rule: Assignee subject to debtor's defenses

obligor's claims on unrelated transactions by getting notice to that person, there was no way that the assignee could stand in any better enforcement position than assignor with respect to the assigned contract itself.

Obviously, a promise to pay money or render some other performance becomes much more uncertain and, therefore much less valuable, if it is subject to all sorts of unknown contingencies. To deal with this problem, the merchant community developed the **_negotiable instrument,_** which is basically just a written promise to pay money stated in a particular way. The law merchant said that if a promise to pay money was in negotiable form and was properly transferred to a good faith purchaser, then the debtor would not be able to assert most voidable-type defenses against the transferee. This was a "negotiation," not just an assignment. Where the buyer-debtor had signed a negotiable promissory note for 100 bushels of wheat which the seller had never delivered, the buyer would have to pay the amount of the note to the bank or finance company to which the note had been sold and then bring a lawsuit for breach of contract against the seller. Article 9 of the Code permitted the parties to work out this same basic result without using a negotiable instrument, by simply placing a provision to that effect, called a **_waiver-of-defenses clause,_** in the contract itself. (See Exhibit 16–2.)

These two "exceptions"—the negotiable instrument and the waiver-of-defenses clause—came into such widespread and common use that they all but

Exceptions:
1. Debtor signs negotiable instrument

2. Debtor signs waiver of defenses

■ **EXHIBIT 16–2**
Assignment and Third-Party Beneficiary Contracts

AVAILABILITY OF DEBTOR'S DEFENSES AGAINST ASSIGNEE

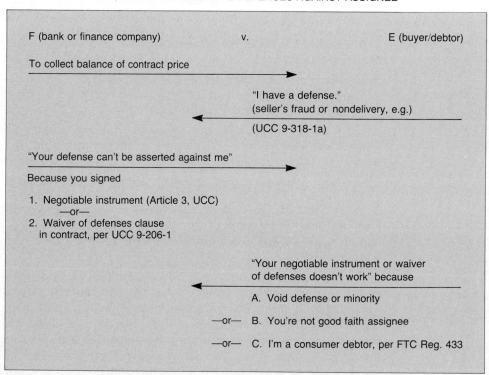

swallowed up the general rule. The result was that many, many buyers had to pay for a "dead horse"—the undelivered wheat, the fraudulently represented car, the unperformed services. As a result of the consumer movement of the 1960s and 1970s, first some of the states and then the *Federal Trade Commission* (FTC) adopted rules which invalidated both of these devices in consumer contracts. As the law stands today, these devices are available only where the debtor is a business or other "nonconsumer." One important loophole does remain, however: where the consumer personally negotiates a direct loan from the financing agency, and *then* gives the cash to the seller, the dead horse result still occurs. The consumer who is referred to the financing agency by the seller is protected, however.

■ SIGNIFICANCE OF THIS CHAPTER

Modern business operations require the free assignability of contract rights. Much business at all levels of production and distribution is done on credit, and sellers often do not have sufficient capital to do their own accounts receivable financing. The solution, of course, is to assign the accounts receivable to a bank or finance company, for cash, so that ongoing business operations can continue. Even individuals—such as inventors and authors—need to be able to assign patents and copyrights, for tax, estate, and other purposes. It is also true that there are situations where performance by a substitute party is necessary or desirable. In all of these situations, the law is concerned with meeting the practical necessities of trade and commerce, while at the same time maintaining the basic terms of the original contract. For this reason, and also because many of these transactions are themselves quite involved, the legal rules for assignments are quite complex.

Modern law also needs to recognize that there are many situations where promises are made for the benefit of third parties, and rules need to be provided for these cases, too.

Both of these concepts will almost certainly apply to transactions throughout your personal and professional activities.

DISCUSSION CASE

FIRST NEW ENGLAND FINANCIAL CORP. v. WOFFARD
421 So.2d 590 (Florida, 1982).

FACTS: When Woffard decided to buy a 36-foot sailing yacht from a yacht broker, the broker suggested that he contact FNEFC to finance the deal. FNEFC represented out-of-state banks which were interested in making marine loans. FNEFC approved Woffard's credit, and he signed a printed retail installment contract to buy the yacht. By its terms the contract was simultaneously assigned to

FNEFC, which reassigned it the next day to City Trust, a Connecticut bank. City Trust's name, address, and telephone number were on the contract, under that of FNEFC. Woffard got a coupon payment book from City Trust several weeks later.

On Woffard's first sea voyage, he discovered several manufacturing defects in the yacht. He notified the broker, the manufacturer, FNEFC, and City Trust. He kept making his payments for eight months, but finally stopped when no one agreed to fix the defects. City Trust and FNEFC sued for the balance due, $42,054.25. Woffard counterclaimed for the return of his $12,349.56 down payment, his monthly payments, and costs for docking and maintenance.

■

Judge Dauksch gave the opinion for the court:

The Contract in the present case, entitled "Marine Security Agreement–Retail Installment Contract" contains the provision set forth in 16 CFR § 433.2:

> NOTICE
> Any holder of this consumer credit contract is subject to all claims and defenses which the debtor could assert against the seller of goods or services obtained pursuant hereto or with the proceeds hereof. Recovery hereunder by the debtor shall not exceed amounts paid by the debtor hereunder.

This provision allows a consumer to set up, against one who finances a purchase, those claims and defenses which could be asserted against the seller of goods. Immediately following that provision is:

NOTICE ABOVE DOES NOT APPLY IF:

> a. The amount financed . . . exceeds $25,000.00. In such case, holder, nevertheless, shall be subject to all defenses which Buyer may have against Seller under this contract pursuant to the applicable State Law since the Notice above is a Federal rule rather than a State rule and does not eliminate defenses under State law.

or

> b. This Consumer Contract form is used for a boat purchased primarily for commercial or business use. In such case, Buyer agrees not to assert any claim or defense arising out of this sale against Seller as a defense, counterclaim, or setoff to any action by any assignee for the unpaid balance of the total of payments or for possession of the boat.

As the amount financed in this consumer transaction exceeds $25,000.00, we look to applicable state law to determine whether appellant is subject to appellee's claims/defenses. Under section 679.206(1), an agreement by a buyer waiving any claims/defenses against the seller is enforceable by an assignee who takes his assignment for value, in good faith and without notice of any claim/defense. Such an agreement waiving claims/defenses often appears in the form of a waiver of defenses clause in a contract. There is no such clause in this contract. Section 679.206(1) also provides that a buyer who, as part of one transaction, signs both a negotiable instrument and

a security agreement makes such an agreement waiving claims/defenses. The contract does not meet the requisites of negotiability and does not appear to be a negotiable instrument. Thus, section 679.206(1) is inapplicable.

The contract created a purchase money security interest to be retained by the seller or seller's assignee. Section 679.206(2) provides that "when a seller retains a purchase money security interest in goods, the chapter on sales (Chapter 672) governs the sale and any disclaimer, limitation or modification of the seller's warranties." Before reaching the merits of appellee's counterclaim for breach of warranty, governed by Chapter 672, we must first see if any other state law prevents appellee's assertion of the claim against the assignee. . . .

An assignee has traditionally been subject to defenses or set-offs existing before an account debtor is notified of the assignment. When the account debtor's defenses on an assigned claim arise from the contract between him and the assignor, it makes no difference whether the breach giving rise to the defense occurs before or after the account debtor is notified of the assignment. The account debtor may also have claims against the assignor which arise independently of that contract: an assignee is subject to all such claims which accrue before, and free of all those which accrue after, the account debtor is notified. The account debtor may waive his right to assert claims or defenses against the assignee to the extent provided in section 679.206. . . . This is in accord with the general rule in sales transactions that the assignee takes his assignment subject to the purchaser's defenses, set-offs and counterclaims against the seller. . . .

Just as an assignee is subject to defenses and claims accruing before the obligor receives notification, so a sub-assignee is subject to defenses and claims accruing between the assignee and obligor before the obligor receives notice of the sub-assignment. Defenses and claims arising from the terms of the contract creating the right are available to the obligor regardless of when they accrue. . . .

Appellee's claim of breach of warranty arose out of the terms of the contract and also accrued before receipt of notification of assignment. Testimony during trial proved that appellee told the seller that he specifically wanted to buy a sailing yacht that he could live aboard full time and also use for pleasure sailing. Appellee told the seller the yacht must be suitable for "blue water" sailing (i.e., ocean sailing). Thus, if there was a breach of warranty, it arose out of the terms of the contract (as incorporating the sale agreement) and accrued before appellee received notification of assignment, in this case by receipt of the coupon payment books. . . .

To be effective, a seller's disclaimer of warranties in the sale of consumer goods must be part of the basis of the bargain between the parties. . . . The evidence indicates that appellee and seller entered into the sales agreement on the premise that the yacht was suitable for appellee's purposes. Circumstances indicate that seller's disclaimer of warranty of fitness for a particular purpose was not made a part of the bargain; to the contrary, seller's warranty of fitness for the particular purpose was an essential factor in the initial agreement between the parties.

Appellant has not convinced this court that the lower court erred in ruling in appellee's favor on the damages claim. The contract provides for payment by the installment buyer of court costs plus attorney's fees upon default. The lower court correctly awarded costs and attorney's fees to appellant in the replevin action. As appellee has not presented any contractual or statutory authority supporting an award of attorney's fees on the counterclaim, such request is denied.

Affirmed.

■ IMPORTANT TERMS AND CONCEPTS

assignment of contract
  rights
third-party beneficiary
  contracts
creditor beneficiary
donee beneficiary
incidental beneficiary
delegation of duty
UCC rule on third-party
  beneficiaries of warranties
rescission of third party
  contract
obligor
obligee
UCC rule on assignability
  of contract rights

due on sale clause
warranties of assignor
Restatement of Contracts
notice to obligor
American Rule
English Rule
secured transaction
public notice
Article 9, UCC
express waiver of defenses
  as against assignee
implied waiver of defenses
  in negotiable instrument
Federal Trade Commission
special rule for consumer
  defenses

■ QUESTIONS AND PROBLEMS FOR DISCUSSION

1. What is an incidental beneficiary?
2. When can contract duties be delegated?
3. When can a debtor not assert defenses to the assigned contract obligation against the assignee of the contract?
4. When does an assignee have recourse against the assignor?
5. American Bridge, assignee from Coburn of "all the moneys due or which may hereafter become due" to Coburn under two building contracts which Coburn had with the city of Boston, sues to collect the alleged contract balances. After notification of the assignment had been received by Boston, Coburn defaulted on his performance obligations. Boston wishes to deduct the damages caused by Coburn's default from the amounts due under the contracts. What is the result, and why?
6. Ethel Wido sued Pipeline Oil Corporation and its franchised service station operator on the New York State Thruway, Carl Pump, for failure to provide road services to her husband. Their car developed a flat tire, and a passing state trooper ordered Carl Pump to come to the aid of the stranded motorists. Carl neglected to do so, and after waiting for over two hours, Ethel's husband, a stout accountant, tried to change the tire himself. The work exhausted him, so that he collapsed. He died shortly thereafter of a heart attack. What is the result, and why?
7. Fred and Ethyl signed a $55,000 mortgage in favor of the Redondo Bank when they bought their house. About five years later, they sold their house to Luci and Ricki, who agreed to pay off the then existing mortgage balance. Shortly thereafter, Luci and Ricki sued to rescind their purchase contract, claiming that the house had been fraudulently misrepresented to them. The court ordered rescission of the purchase contract. Since no one was making mortgage payments, Redondo Bank sued to foreclose the mortgage, naming Luci and Ricki defendants along with Fred and Ethyl. Who, if anyone, is liable on the mortgage? Explain.
8. Pitzoo Snak Shops agreed to have Kookie Cola vending machines installed in each of its 23 Pitzoo locations. Kookie Cola was later bought by Burpsi Cola, and this contract with Pitzoo was assigned to Burpsi. Pitzoo objected to doing business with Burpsi and attempted to terminate the contract. Burpsi sued Pitzoo for breach. What result, and why?

17

Excuses for Nonperformance

CHAPTER OBJECTIVES

THIS CHAPTER WILL:

- Explain how contract duties may be excused or discharged.
- Differentiate conditions concurrent, conditions precedent, and conditions subsequent.
- Indicate how a breach by one party may impact on the other party's performance obligations.
- Define the various types of new agreements which the parties may use to modify their prior contract.
- Explain how the court's judgment in a contract dispute supersedes all claims under the original contract.
- Discuss the kinds of changes in circumstances which may excuse the parties' contract duties by operation of law.

While the vast majority of contracts are performed according to their terms, many are not. Not all nonperformances will produce liability for breach of contract, however; in some of these cases nonperforming parties will have legal excuses for their failure. These legal excuses, or discharges of liability, can be placed in five general groupings: (1) conditions, (2) breach by other party, (3) discharge by new agreement, (4) discharge by merger, and (5) discharge by operation of law. We now proceed to consider each of these groups.

■ CONDITIONS

Basic Concepts and Definitions. A ***condition*** is an act, event, or set of facts to which the parties have attached some special legal significance. The parties have included it in their contract with the intent that its occurrence or nonoccurrence will operate to modify, suspend, or completely discharge a performance duty under the contract. Conditions may be expressly stated or implied from the facts and circumstances.

Different types of conditions

In terms of how they operate, conditions are classified as precedent, concurrent, and subsequent. A ***condition precedent*** prevents a contract duty from arising until it occurs. If a tailor promises that you will be personally satisfied with your new custom-made suit, and you're not satisfied, you don't have to take the suit and pay for it—no "personal satisfaction" (the condition precedent), no duty to take the suit. ***Concurrent conditions,*** which are usually ***implied by law,*** operate so that each party's duty to perform is conditioned on the other party's being ready, willing, and able to render the required return performance. The most typical example of concurrent conditions in action is the cash sale transaction, but they also may arise in other contexts, as in the *Shaw* case.

SHAW v. MOBIL OIL CORP.

535 P.2d 756 (Oregon, 1975)

FACTS

In 1972 the parties entered into a service station lease and retail gasoline dealer agreement. John Shaw agreed to buy not less than 200,000 gallons of gasoline per year, and Mobil agreed to supply his requirements, up to a maximum of 500,000 gallons per year. Shaw agreed to pay rent on the station on the basis of 1.4 cents per gallon delivered, with a minimum of $470 per month. To meet the minimum rental, Mobil would have to deliver 33,572 gallons each month. In July 1973, Shaw ordered 34,000 gallons, but Mobil delivered only 25,678 gallons, due to the gasoline shortage caused by the Arab oil embargo. The U.S. Energy Office had required Mobil to allocate available supplies among its dealers, and Shaw's allocation was 25,678 gallons. Shaw sued for a judgment that he was not liable for the minimum rental for July. The trial court held for Mobil.

ISSUE

Does Mobil's failure to deliver the full order excuse Shaw's duty to pay the minimum rental for that month?

DECISION

Yes. Judgment reversed.

REASONS

Justice Denecke examined several prior cases, and quoted extensively from an Oregon precedent:

"Whether convenants are dependent or independent is a question of the intention of the parties as deduced from the terms of the contract. If the parties intend that performance by each of them is in no way conditioned upon performance by the other, the covenants are independent, but if they intend performance by one to be conditioned upon performance by the other, the covenants are mutually dependent. . . .

While there is no fixed definite rule of law by which the intention in all cases can be determined, yet we must remember, as stated by Professor Williston, that, since concurrent conditions protect both parties, courts endeavor so far as is not inconsistent with the expressed intention to construe performances as concurrent conditions. . . .

"In the present case we believe it equally apparent that the dealer undertook his obligation to pay a minimum rental in reliance on Mobil's fulfillment of its obligation to deliver the quantity of gasoline ordered by the dealer.

"We conclude that the dealer's promise to pay the minimum rental was conditioned or dependent upon Mobil's delivery of the amount of gasoline ordered by the dealer. . . .

"A party has no obligation to perform a promise that is conditioned upon the other party's performance when the other party failed to perform even though the other party's failure to perform is excused and is not a breach of contract."

Conditions subsequent discharge or excuse an existing duty of performance. An automobile liability insurance policy, for example, may provide that the insurance company's duty to defend liability claims under the policy is excused where the insured admits liability for the accident. Or, a property insurance policy may specify that coverage lapses where a structure is unoccupied for more than a certain period of time. Whether a condition exists or has occurred is generally a question of fact, to be proved like any other.

Conditions of Approval or Satisfaction. Especially in large construction contracts, the parties may specify that a third party's approval is required before the final payment has to be made. In construction, this third party is typically the architect who drew the plans and specifications for the job. Until the builder can convince the architect that the job conforms to the plans, the landowner/customer does not have to make the final payment on the contract price. Where the architect is withholding approval in bad faith, or as part of a fraudulent scheme against the builder, most courts would probably hold this condition to have been satisfied and require the landowner/customer to pay the balance due.

In some contracts, *personal satisfaction* of the buyer/customer is guaranteed: the parties' intent is that if they are not satisfied, they are not bound to pay the contract price. In trying to determine whether or not such a condition has been met, so that the seller can collect the contract price, the courts use two different tests: an individualized, or *subjective,* test and a reasonable person, or *objective,* test. The individualized test requires that the particular buyer be satisfied before payment is due, whereas the objective test says that if a reasonable person would be satisfied with the performance offered by the seller, the buyer must pay.

Where the contract is for an item involving personal taste, such as a custom-tailored suit, a portrait, or a statue, "personal satisfaction" probably means

Third party's approval

Two tests for personal satisfaction

just that: no deal unless the individual buyer indicates that he or she is satisfied. Where the contract involves an item of everyday mechanical utility, such as a furnace, "personal satisfaction" is probably a jury question under the reasonable person test: either the furnace is working properly, or it is not; if it is, the buyer ought to be satisfied with it.

Besides the nature of the item, the other main factor considered by the courts in determining which test to use is what happens to the item if the satisfaction condition is not met. The suit, portrait, or sculpture stays with the seller; there is no unjust enrichment of the buyer, though the seller may be stuck with an unmarketable item. With something like an aluminum siding job, however, the situation is quite different. Since it is somewhat uneconomical to remove aluminum siding from a house, the courts would almost certainly apply the reasonable person test to the job.

Timely Performance as a Condition Precedent. What happens when one party is late in performing or offering to perform contract obligations? Any provable damages resulting from the delay in performance should be collectible without question. The real question, however, is whether or not the other party can refuse to accept the offered late performance and use the failure to perform on time as a basis for rescinding the whole contract. Courts generally consider this problem in terms of whether or not *time is of the essence,* meaning that the parties have either expressly or impliedly made timely performance a condition precedent.

In a few early cases, time was presumed to be of the essence in a sale of goods, but this does not seem to be the general rule, and it is clearly not the rule for real estate or construction contracts. Where the parties have not clearly specified in the contract that time is of the essence, the court must determine, as a question of fact, whether or not such a condition precedent should be implied.

Failure to perform on time as a breach of contract

Doctrine of Substantial Performance. Courts are reluctant to excuse a party's contractual obligations completely just because the other party has committed a relatively minor breach. Just as many cases involve the simple, one-shot performances completed exactly in accordance with the contract terms, many other cases, such as construction contracts, deal with more complex performances which extend over a considerable period of time. In construction contracts, jobs are rarely completed *exactly* in accordance with the agreed plans and specifications. Should minor deviations by the builder permit the buyer to rescind the whole contract?

The courts have answered this question in the negative, by applying the doctrine of *substantial performance.* What this doctrine says is that if the builder has acted in good faith and has done the job in *substantial* compliance with the contract, the builder can enforce the contract and collect the contract price. Any damages which result from any noncompliance, no matter how trivial, can be collected by the buyer or deducted from the amount of the contractor's recovery. Perfection is not required. The buyer of a new house would not be able to rescind the contract just because the kitchen was painted green instead of blue, but that buyer could force the builder to repaint, or deduct the price of the paint job from the contract price if the builder refused.

Failure to perform exactly as promised as breach of contract

■ EXHIBIT 17–1
Excuses for
Nonperformance

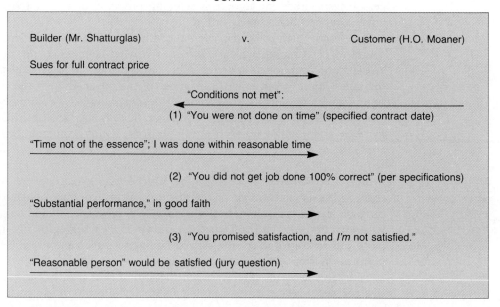

CONDITIONS

The doctrine of substantial performance will not be applied where the builder has intentionally substituted inferior materials or used other production shortcuts in a fraudulent attempt to make extra money. Nor will it be applied where the builder has only partially, rather than substantially, performed. In such cases buyers can rescind the whole contract. If the partially built structure has been placed on land already owned by the buyers, they are probably liable in quasi contract for the fair market value of the labor and materials, but even in this case they can probably deduct any provable damages they have sustained. (See Exhibit 17–1.)

■ **BREACH BY
OTHER PARTY**

In General. When the plaintiff brings an action for breach of contract, a possible response by the defendant is the argument "You breached first." That is, the defendant argues that his or her own nonperformance was not a breach, because the plaintiff's prior nonperformance justified the defendant's refusal to perform. Although in some cases the courts have treated the reciprocal performances as "independent," they generally accept this argument as a sufficient excuse where the prior breach by the plaintiff was a material one. It would, generally, be unfair to require the defendant to perform or hold the defendant liable for not performing if he or she has not received what the plaintiff promised in return. However, it would be equally unfair for the defendant to repudiate the whole contract and completely refuse to perform if the plaintiff has committed only a minor, relatively insignificant breach.

Breach of Installment Contract. It is even more difficult to work out a fair result where the contract calls for a series of performances by one or both parties, rather than a single exchange. What should be the measure of recovery when a party partially performs and then fails to deliver one or more of the installments still due?

When breach of installment contract is a material breach

The courts usually try to solve this problem by first determining whether the contract is divisible or indivisible. If the contract is held to be divisible into a series of pro rata exchanges, the court will usually permit the breaching party to recover the agreed reciprocal performance, less any damages the breach has caused to the other party. An employee who quits after having worked for three months under a one-year contract would usually be able to collect the agreed contract salary for the three months worked, less any damages which the employer sustains as a result of the breach. If the contract is held to be indivisible, or "entire," a party guilty of a material breach should collect only the fair market value of any benefits retained by the other party, less damages caused by the breach.

Anticipatory Repudiation. An *anticipatory repudiation* occurs when one party, by words or conduct, indicates unwillingness or inability to perform contract duties when the time for performance arrives. In other words, the party announces in advance that he or she is not going to perform as scheduled. In nearly all cases the courts treat such an unequivocal repudiation of the contract as a present breach, giving the injured party the right to make other arrangements immediately and sue for any damages caused, if in fact performance does not occur. The courts do not apply this rule to promises to pay money at a future date; a present statement of intention not to pay a future debt normally does not accelerate the due date of the debt unless there is a special provision to that effect. The courts also normally permit a party to retract a repudiation, provided the retraction is made before the other party has substantially changed legal position because of the repudiation.

Advance repudiation as breach

Adequate Assurance. For the sale of goods, the UCC's rules for dealing with breach and repudiation problems are substantially the same as the common-law principles discussed above. The Code does, however, give the injured party one very important new protection: the right to demand *adequate assurance* (2–609).

A breach by one of the parties to a goods contract may not be material enough in itself to justify rescission of the whole contract; for example, a two- or three-day delay in delivery of one month's shipment of goods on an installment contract. Still, such a breach may create a doubt in the mind of the other party as to whether or not the breaching party will be able and willing to continue to perform. The same is true where one party has repudiated and then retracted: Does this person mean it or not? When will this person do the same thing again?

UCC rule for goods contracts

A party who has reasonable grounds for feeling "insecure," may make a written demand that the other party furnish "adequate assurance of due performance." So long as the insecure party is being commercially reasonable, any performance for which the agreed return has not already been received may be withheld until receipt of such adequate assurance. Where a proper demand for assurance has been made, the other party's failure to respond within a reasonable time (not over 30 days) is treated as a repudiation of the contract. At that point, the party who made the demand can go ahead and make other arrangements, without being guilty of a breach, and can sue for any damages sustained because of the other party's repudiation.

■ DISCHARGE BY NEW AGREEMENT

The parties themselves created their reciprocal rights and duties by making the agreement. It's their contract, and unless the rights of third parties are involved in some way, the parties can call off their agreement anytime they both wish to do so, or they can substitute a new arrangement for the old one. There are many technical terms to describe the different types of new agreements, but they all come down to the same basic argument: "My nonperformance under the original contract was excused because we made a new deal." We now consider the main types of "new deals."

Parties can agree to cancel contract

Mutual Rescission. As a rule, the parties can call off their existing contract any time they wish, as long as they both agree to do so. This case is called a *mutual rescission,* to distinguish it from the case where the *remedy* of rescission is given to one party because of a material breach by the other. If the parties have mutually agreed to a rescission, neither can later claim that the other's nonperformance of the contract was a breach.

Where partial performance has already occurred, the mutual rescission agreement should provide for part payment or restitution. If there is no such provision in the rescission agreement, any retained benefits would almost certainly have to be paid for at fair market value.

Parties can agree to a substitute debtor

Novation. Although the derivation and common sense meaning of the term *novation* would seem to apply to any new agreement which the parties intend to substitute for their existing contract, the courts generally apply the term only to those new arrangements which involve a substitution of parties. That is, a new debtor is substituted for the original debtor, with the consent of the creditor, or the obligation is assigned to a new creditor for whom the debtor agrees to perform.

If, in the take-over-the-payments example used in the last chapter, the mortgagee/creditor agrees to accept the resale buyer as the sole obligor and to discharge the original mortgage/debtor, there has been a novation. Whether the new agreement is called a novation or simply a new contract, it must itself be a valid contract to have the effect of discharging the original one. (See Exhibit 17–2.)

Parties can agree to a substitute performance

Accord and Satisfaction. This term is usually applied to a situation where the obligee/creditor has agreed to accept a substituted performance, in place of the original one. For example, Dan Debtor owes Carl Creditor $1,000. Dan does not have the cash, but he does own a used car, which he offers to convey to Carl in lieu of the $1,000. Carl, of course, does not have to take the car; he can sue Dan for the $1,000 if it is not paid when due. If Carl does agree to take the car, there is an accord. At that point, the $1,000 debt

■ EXHIBIT 17–2
Excuses for
Nonperformance

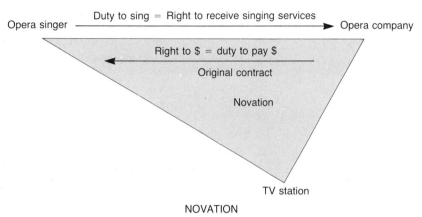

NOVATION

Singer agrees to perform for TV station, and/or to look
only to TV station for payment of contract price

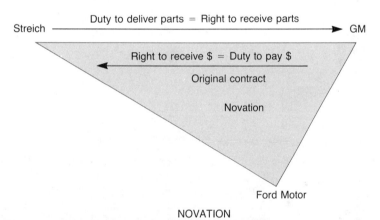

NOVATION

Streich agrees to deliver parts to Ford Motor and/or to look
only to Ford Motor for payment of contract price

is not yet discharged; if Carl does not get the car, he can sue Dan either for $1,000 or for breach of the accord. When Dan delivers the car as agreed, however, the $1,000 debt has been discharged by an *accord and satisfaction.*

Unfortunately, from the standpoint of clarity, courts also use the term *accord and satisfaction* to refer to situations involving part payment of a debt, especially where the debt is in dispute. (See our earlier discussion of this problem in Chapter 11.) The creditor's cashing of the "in full" check is that person's agreement to the accord and satisfaction and acceptance of the substituted performance thereunder.

Waiver or Estoppel. A *waiver* is the intentional surrender of a known right or benefit; a person simply chooses not to demand that something which is due be given. Your apartment lease, for example, specifies that the rent must be paid in advance on the 1st of each month, but the landlord tells you that

A party can waive contract rights

payment can be made by the 10th; this is a waiver of the right to insist on payment by the 1st. Ordinarily, this kind of waiver "before breach" can be retracted by proper notice to the other party, unless consideration was given for the waiver or unless the other party has made a substantial change of position in reliance on the waiver. Contrariwise, courts usually hold that a waiver of the right to sue for a breach which has already occurred does not require any new consideration to be binding. (See UCC 1–107, previously referred to in Chapter 11.) A waiver may also be inferred from a party's conduct.

Release. A *release* also involves the giving up of some right, but it is based on a written contract. Releases are commonly used in situations where there is a contingent or disputed liability, as in auto accident cases or in employment termination agreements. The law generally favors compromises and settlements of disputes, particularly in light of the tremendous backlog of civil litigation that is clogging the courts. Traditionally, therefore, courts have been reluctant to permit parties to avoid the effect of a release they have previously given unless there is very strong evidence of fraud, undue influence, mistake, or other defense. While courts today are more and more willing to stretch a point in favor of the "little guy," the *Stetzel* case shows that they will still look for some evidence to support the claimed defense against the effect of a release.

A party can release contract rights

STETZEL v. DICKENSON

174 N.W. 2d 438 (Iowa, 1970)

FACTS   Ms. Stetzel sustained personal injuries as the result of an intersection collision in Iowa City on September 27, 1965. She was thrown sideways, and her head struck the window. She went to the University Student Health Center for treatment of her headache, was kept overnight, and was sent home the next day. Her headaches continued for several weeks, interfering with her studying; she was taking a prescribed medication for these headaches. After being pestered by an insurance adjuster, she finally signed a release on December 2, in return for $400. She admits she knew what the paper was when she signed it. Shortly thereafter, her symptoms became more serious; the headaches became more severe, she had difficulty picking things up; her eyes tired more easily; she seemed to be forgetful. Alleging that the release was invalid due to mutual mistake and/or undue influence, she sued for her injuries. The jury agreed and gave her $3,000. Defendant appeals.

ISSUE   Was the release invalid due to mutual mistake? Was it invalid due to undue influence?

DECISION   No. No. Judgment reversed; judgment entered for defendant.

REASONS   **Justice LeGrand first reviewed the rules for releases; they are contracts, and are subject to the same invalidity arguments as other contracts. As to mutual mistake, he quoted from an Iowa precedent:**

> "Here there was a settlement for a lump sum having no relation to any computation based on estimated loss of time and expense. The parties clearly intended to cover future developments, whatever they might be." The parties were aware of the possible medical uncertainties, and clearly intended a final settlement.

As to the claim of undue influence, he was equally unsympathetic.

"We find no evidence here to support a finding that plaintiff executed the release as the result of undue influence. The fact that the adjuster was boorish and intruded upon plaintiff's privacy is not significant unless it resulted in depriving her of her independence of action and substituted his will for hers at the time the release was signed. There is a total absence of evidence that it did. In fact the record proves conclusively to the contrary.

"Plaintiff places great importance on her testimony that she did not want to sign. This is by no means the same as saying undue influence was exercised upon her. Plaintiff was a well-educated, highly intelligent young lady. Her scholastic record was outstanding. Before signing the release, she sought independent advice from her landlady, in whom she apparently had considerable confidence, and from an Iowa City lawyer—not counsel now representing her—whose help she now denounces. Whether his advice was good or bad is not the question we here consider. The fact that she sought and received independent advice is a proper matter to consider on the question of undue influence.

"In addition to all this is the testimony heretofore set out in which plaintiff concedes she knew the purpose of the instrument, read it, understood it, and realized its consequences before signing. We hold all these circumstances refute undue influence as a matter of law."

Account Stated. The *account stated* is based on the same fundamental principle as accord and satisfaction: the law favors settlements. Where, after a series of transactions between them, the parties have agreed on a final statement of the net amount due, there is an account stated. No further reliance can be placed on the earlier transactions; the amount which is now due and owing is that agreed to in the account stated. An account stated can arise when the creditor sends a summary statement of the account and the debtor retains the statement without objection beyond a reasonable time. In other words, the agreement to the account stated can be implied as well as expressed.

■ DISCHARGE BY MERGER

In General. As used here, the doctrine of *merger* means that the prior obligation has been superseded by a "better" one, better in the sense of being easier to prove, to transfer, or to collect. Merger may be effected by a new agreement between the parties or by *judgment*. The three most common examples of such better legal obligations (other than a judgment) are the sealed contract, the negotiable instrument, and the secured debt. Since many states have abolished by statute the common-law effect of the seal on the presumption of consideration, there would be no merger effect in those states, if a sealed contract were given in satisfaction of an unsealed one. In a state where the seal makes the contract easier to prove in court, or (perhaps) even if the seal only has the effect of keeping the debt alive for a longer time, the acceptance of a sealed contract by the creditor in place of the unsealed one should have the merger effect.

Contract can be merged into a better legal obligation

A negotiable instrument is clearly a much better form of legal obligation than an ordinary "open-book account." For example, you owe your dentist, Dr. Paul Pullit, $300 for services rendered. If he sues to collect, he will have to produce office records, witnesses, and so forth, to prove that he in fact gave you this consideration and that you agreed to pay for it at his prices. Such a collection suit would involve substantial disruption of his regular office routine and a loss of time and money, even though he would ultimately win. If he accepts your offer of a 90-day negotiable promissory note for $250 as satisfaction of the account, he could in fact be net dollars ahead even if he is forced to sue on the note, since the note carries a presumption of consideration which *you* would have to overcome with evidence. Because of this fact, the note is much more readily transferable than the account. If your dentist doesn't want to wait the 90 days and collect the interest, he will have a much easier time selling your note to a bank than he would have in assigning your account.

Finally, if the debt is made more certain of collection because the debtor gives the creditor a mortgage or other security interest against a specific piece of the debtor's property, that is clearly a better deal for the creditor. If your dentist agrees to take your new contract promise to pay $250, secured by your used car as collateral, in satisfaction of the $300 open-book amount, there has been a merger and the old account debt is discharged.

A judgment supersedes the underlying contract

Judgment. The doctrine of *res judicata* says that once "the thing has been adjudicated," it cannot be relitigated. Whatever rights and duties may have been alleged as the result of the prior legal relationship have been superseded by the court's final judgment; the prior obligations have been merged into the judgment.

The following case illustrates the doctrine of *res judicata* and also shows the important distinction between a ***joint obligation,*** in which all debtors must be sued at the same time if they are to be held liable, and a ***joint and several obligation,*** in which the creditor may get a judgment against one or more of the debtors and still retain the right to sue the others. The same result would follow if the creditor released one joint debtor; such action releases the entire debt against all the joint debtors.

B-OK, INC. v. STOREY

473 P.2d 426 (Washington, 1970)

FACTS

For several years prior to April 30, 1962, the Storeys were partners in the petroleum products business at Cle Elum, doing business as Storey Distributing Company. On April 30, 1962, the defendants dissolved their partnership. At the time of dissolution of the partnership, defendants' account with plaintiff had a balance of $3,515.80.

On December 27, 1963, plaintiff obtained a judgment against defendant Earl Storey for $3,735.47. Defendant William E. Storey was not a named defendant in that case. Having failed to collect that judgment, B-OK brought this suit on the same account. The trial court held for William Storey.

ISSUE

Is William Storey still liable on this partnership obligation?

DECISION

No. Judgment affirmed.

REASONS

(Opinion by Chief Justice Evans.)

"The conclusion by the trial court that defendant William E. Storey should be dismissed is based on the Uniform Partnership Act and *Warren* v. *Rickles,* 129 Wash. 443 . . . holding that:

> It is a very generally accepted rule of law that, where an obligation is joint and not joint and several, a judgment rendered on such obligation against one or more, but less than the whole number of obligors, is a bar to any action on the same claim against the obligors not parties to the judgment, because the claim is merged in the judgment and is extinguished thereby.

"We hold the trial court correctly concluded that after dissolution the liability of the retiring partner William Storey to plaintiff remained a joint liability, and that plaintiff's claim against him was merged in the prior judgment taken against the continuing partner, Earl Storey. The trial court, therefore, did not err in dismissing William Storey."

■ DISCHARGE BY OPERATION OF LAW

Expiration of time makes contract unenforceable

Bankruptcy discharges most ordinary contract debts

Statute of Limitations. At least in most states, debts do not last forever. At some point, it becomes rather unfair for an alleged creditor to revive ancient history and begin a litigation over a matter which should have been long forgotten (and probably has been by nearly everyone else). Again, the law encourages the parties to settle their disputes and requires them to commence any necessary litigation before memories fade completely. At some point, if no action has been taken to enforce an alleged obligation, it is good public policy to declare that the debtor has a defense if that person does not wish to pay the ancient debt. This *statute of limitations* defense is a technical one, and it is not particularly favored by the courts, but where it does apply it is a complete defense against a lawsuit based on the old debt or breach of contract claim. In most states the limitations period for tort actions is considerably shorter than the one for contracts.

Bankruptcy; Composition with Creditors. A discharge in a bankruptcy proceeding also operates as a technical defense in favor of the debtor, as to all debts and claims provable under bankruptcy rules. This same result occurs whether the debtor has filed a "voluntary" petition with the bankruptcy court or has been forced into an "involuntary" bankruptcy by one or more creditors. Like the statute of limitations, a *bankruptcy discharge* is a technical defense which can be waived by the debtor when that person makes a new promise after bankruptcy to pay the old debt. Where the debtor is a consumer, there are strict rules for such "new promises," as discussed in the bankruptcy chapter.

To avoid the administrative costs and (some of) the legal expenses incident to a bankruptcy proceeding, a person's creditors may, as a group, voluntarily agree to accept less than full payment in full satisfaction of their debts. A creditor cannot be forced to make such an agreement, but may wish to do so to receive payment for a higher percentage of the claim paid than if the debtor were forced through bankruptcy. Such a *composition with creditors* operates like an accord and satisfaction.

Subsequent Illegality. Where the performances called for by the contract were legal when made but were subsequently made illegal by statute or administrative regulation, the now-illegal contract duties are discharged by operation of law. This is clearly the only fair result: neither party normally assumes this kind of risk, and neither ought to be forced to perform if by doing so, he or she is breaking the law. The adoption of the Eighteenth Amendment and the Volstead Act, which made it illegal to manufacture, transport, or sell alcoholic beverages, provided one illustration of this rule in effect. More current examples might involve changes in the legal rules pertaining to foreign investments, currency exchange, ownership of gold by U.S. citizens, and sales of "strategic" materials to Communist-bloc countries.

Contract duty excused if impossible to perform

Impossibility. Where a contract specifies performance by one certain party or where the performance requires the existence of a particular thing, the death or disability of the party or the destruction of the thing will normally discharge the performance obligation through *objective impossibility.* That is, because the contract is so specific, no one at all can render the required performance. A promise to deliver "all of my tomato crop" is discharged if the tomato crop is destroyed without any fault on the part of the grower. A promise to deliver "1,000 tons of tomatoes" is probably not discharged when the grower's own crop fails, because the grower could buy other tomatoes on the market and deliver them; where no specific thing is identified, there is only *subjective impossibility,* which does not operate to discharge contract obligations.

CHRISTY v. PILKINTON

273 S.W.2d 533 (Arkansas, 1954)

FACTS   The parties executed a valid written contract by which the Christys agreed to buy an apartment house from Mrs. Pilkinton for $30,000. The vendor's title is admittedly good. When the time came for performance, the purchasers, although not insolvent, were unable to raise enough money to carry out their contract. Mrs. Pilkinton, after having tendered a deed to the property, brought this suit. At the trial the defendants' evidence tended to show that, as a result of a decline in Christy's used car business, they do not possess, and cannot borrow the unpaid balance of $29,900.

ISSUE   Does defendants' financial inability to perform constitute "impossibility"?

DECISION   No. Judgment affirmed.

 REASONS   (Opinion by Justice Smith.)
"Proof of this kind does not establish the type of impossibility that constitutes a defense. There is a familiar distinction between objective impossibility, which amounts to saying, 'The thing cannot be done,' and subjective impossiblity—'I cannot do it.' The latter, which is well illustrated by a promisor's financial inability to pay, does not discharge a contractual duty and is therefore not a bar to a decree for specific performance.

"Much of the appellants' brief is devoted to a discussion of the difficulty that the chancellor may have in enforcing his decree; but that problem is not now before us. By the decree the defendants were allowed a period of 20 days in which to perform their obligation. If their default continues, it will, of course, be for the chancellor to say whether further relief should be granted, as by a foreclosure of the vendor's lien or by other process available to a court of equity. At present it is enough to observe that foreseeable obstacles to the enforcement of a judgment are not a sufficient reason for denying the relief to which the plaintiff is entitled."

UCC rule on impracticability

Commercial Impracticability and Frustration. Closely related to the idea of impossibility are the ideas of ***impracticability*** and ***frustration.*** A performance may not actually be impossible to render, but it may be financially impracticable to do it, in the sense that it is stupid or nonsensical to require the performance. If a trucking company has a contract to transport a racehorse to Churchill Downs for the Kentucky Derby, and the horse dies, it would clearly be commercially impracticable to require the owner to pay the trucking company for transporting a dead horse to Churchill Downs, although that performance is not impossible. The UCC contains specific provisions, in Section 2–615, for dealing with this impracticability problem in sale of goods cases.

Frustration is closely related to impossibility. Again, the performance specified in the contract is not technically impossible, but the entire *purpose* or reason for making the contract no longer exists because of the happening of some unforeseeable event. The classic case of frustration involved the renting of rooms in London for exorbitant prices to enable the guests to see the coronation parade of King Edward VII. On the day designated in the "leases," there was no parade because the king had caught a cold and postponed it. Although there was nothing impossible about performance by either the landlord or the tenant, at least one English court agreed that the contract duty should be discharged.

■ SIGNIFICANCE OF THIS CHAPTER

As noted by the great Scots poet, Robert Burns, "the best laid plans of mice and men, gang aft a-glee." This chapter has indicated some of the reasons why the plans laid in a contract may "go astray." Our discussion has covered at least the main bases for excuse or discharge of a party's contractual obligations. The parties themselves may provide for such excuses, either in the original contract, or in a subsequent modifying agreement, or through their subsequent conduct. Even without express contract excuse clauses, courts will sometimes grant relief from a contract duty where the anticipated circumstances have changed very substantially. Since not every nonperformance is a breach of contract, the parties in many of these situations would be better served by a negotiated settlement than an extended litigation.

DISCUSSION CASE

TRANSATLANTIC FINANCING CORP. v. UNITED STATES
363 F.2d 312 (District of Columbia, 1966).

Facts: On July 26, 1956, Egypt nationalized the Suez Canal. On October 2, the U.S. government hired Transatlantic to transport a cargo of wheat from a U.S. Gulf port to Bandar Shapur, Iran. On October 27, the *SS Christos* sailed from Galveston, Texas on a course which would have taken her through the Suez Canal. On October 29 Israel invaded Egypt; France and Great Britain invaded two days later. Egypt retaliated by closing the canal with sunken ships. On November 7, Beckmann (representing Transatlantic) called the U.S. Department of Agriculture to ask for further instructions on how to proceed with the shipment. Potosky, who had no authority to bind the government, told Beckmann that Transatlantic was expected to deliver the wheat as agreed and that he did not think extra compensation would be paid for going around the Cape of Good Hope, but that Transatlantic was free to file a claim if they wanted to do so. The wheat was delivered on December 30, and Transatlantic was paid the full original contract price, $305,842.92. The U.S. District Court dismissed Transatlantic's claim for additional payment.

■

Circuit Judge Wright gave the opinion for the court:

The doctrine of impossibility of performance has gradually been freed from the earlier fictional and unrealistic strictures of such tests as the "implied term" and the parties' "contemplation."

It is now recognized that " 'A thing is impossible in legal contemplation when it is not practicable; and a thing is impracticable when it can only be done at an excessive and unreasonable cost.' " The doctrine ultimately represents the ever-shifting line, drawn by courts hopefully responsive to commercial practices and mores, at which the community's interest in having contracts enforced according to their terms is outweighed by the commercial senselessness of requiring performance. When the issue is raised, the court is asked to construct a condition of performance based on the changed circumstances, a process which involves at least three reasonably definable steps. First, a contingency—something unexpected—must have occurred. Second, the risk of the unexpected occurrence must not have been allocated either by agreement

or by custom. Finally, occurrence of the contingency must have rendered performance commercially impracticable. Unless the court finds these three requirements satisfied, the plea of impossibility must fail.

The first requirement was met here. It seems reasonable, where no route is mentioned in a contract, to assume the parties expected performance by the usual and customary route at the time of contract. Since the usual and customary route from Texas to Iran at the time of contract was through Suez, closure of the Canal made impossible the expected method of performance, but this unexpected development raises rather than resolves the impossibility issue, which turns additionally on whether the risk of the contingency's occurrence had been allocated and, if not, whether performance by alternative routes was rendered impracticable.

Proof that the risk of a contingency's occurrence has been allocated may be expressed in or implied from the agreement. Such proof may also be found in the surrounding circumstances, including custom and usage of the trade. The contract in this case does not expressly condition performance upon availability of the Suez route. Nor does it specify "via Suez" or, on the other hand, "via Suez or Cape of Good Hope." Nor are there provisions in the contract from which we may properly imply that the continued availability of Suez was a condition of performance. Nor is there anything in custom or trade usage, or in the surrounding circumstances generally, which would support our constructing a condition of performance. The numerous cases requiring performance around the Cape when Suez was closed indicate that the Cape route is generally regarded as an alternative means of performance. So the implied expectation that the route would be via Suez is hardly adequate proof of an allocation of the promises of the risk of closure. In some cases, even an express expectation may not amount to a condition of performance. The doctrine of deviation supports our assumption that parties normally expect performance by the usual and customary route, but it adds nothing beyond this that is probative of an allocation of the risk.

If anything, the circumstances surrounding this contract indicate that the risk of the Canal's closure may be deemed to have been allocated to Transatlantic. We know or may safely assume that the parties were aware, as were most commercial men with interests affected by the Suez situation, that the Canal might become a dangerous area. No doubt the tension affected freight rates, and it is arguable that the risk of closure became part of the dickered terms.

We do not deem the risk of closure so allocated, however. Foreseeability or even recognition of a risk does not necessarily prove its allocation. Parties to a contract are not always able to provide for all the possibilities of which they are aware, sometimes because they cannot agree, often simply because they are too busy. Moreover, that some abnormal risk was contemplated is probative but does not necessarily establish an allocation of the risk of the contingency which actually occurs. In this case, for example, nationalization by Egypt of the Canal Corporation and formation of the Suez Users Group did not necessarily indicate that the Canal would be blocked even if a confrontation resulted. The surrounding circumstances do indicate, however, a willingness by Transatlantic to assume abnormal risks, and this fact should legitimately cause us to judge the impracticability of performance by an alternative route in stricter terms than we would were the contingency unforeseen.

We turn then to the question whether occurrence of the contingency rendered performance commercially impracticable under the circumstances of this case. The goods shipped were not subject to harm from the longer, less temperate Southern route. The vessel and crew were fit to proceed around the Cape. Transatlantic was no less able than the United States to purchase insurance to cover the contingency's occurrence. If anything, it is more reasonable to expect owner-operator of vessels to insure against the hazards of war. They are in the best position to calculate the cost of performance by alternative routes (and therefore to estimate the amount of insurance required), and are undoubtedly sensitive to international troubles which uniquely affect the demand for and cost of their services. The only factor operating here in appellant's favor is the added expense, allegedly $43,972.00 above and beyond the contract price of $305,842.92, of

extending a 10,000 mile voyage by approximately 3,000 miles. While it may be an overstatement to say that increased cost and difficulty of performance never constitute impracticability, to justify relief there must be more of a variation between exected costs and the cost of performing by an available alternative than is present in this case, where the promisor can legitimately be presumed to have accepted some degree of abnormal risk, and where impracticability is urged on the basis of added expense alone.

We conclude, therefore, as have most other courts considering related issues arising out of the Suez closure, that performance of this contract was not rendered legally impossible. Even if we agreed with appellant, its theory of relief seems untenable. When performance of a contract is deemed impossible, it is a nullity. In the case of the charter party involving carriage of goods, the carrier may return to an appropriate port and unload its cargo, subject of course to required steps to minimize damages. If the performance rendered has value, recovery in quantum meruit* for the entire performance is proper. But here Transatlantic has collected its contract price, and now seeks quantum meruit relief for the additional expense of the trip around the Cape. If the contract is a nullity, Transatlantic's theory of relief should have been quantum meruit for the entire trip, rather than only for the extra expense. Transatlantic attempts to take its profit on the contract, and then force the Government to absorb the cost of the additional voyage. When impracticability without fault occurs, the law seeks an equitable solution, and quantum meruit is one of its potent devices to achieve this end. There is no interest in casting the entire burden of commercial disaster on one party in order to preserve the other's profit. Apparently the contract price in this case was advantageous enough to deter appellant from taking a stance on damages consistent with its theory of liability. In any event, there is no basis for relief.

Affirmed.

---

*Quasi contract for fair market value.

■ IMPORTANT TERMS AND CONCEPTS

condition	personal satisfaction	waiver	statute of limitations
condition precedent	breach by other party	estoppel	bankruptcy discharge
condition subsequent	breach of installment	release	composition with creditors
concurrent condition	contract	account stated	subsequent illegality
substantial performance	anticipatory repudiation	merger	impossibility
time is of the essence	UCC adequate assurance	judgment	commercial frustration
express condition	mutual rescission	joint obligation	impracticability
implied in fact condition	novation	joint and several	objective impossibility
implied in law condition	accord and satisfaction	obligation	subjective impossibility

■ QUESTIONS AND PROBLEMS FOR DISCUSSION

1. When is the original contract obligation discharged by an accord and satisfaction?
2. What is the difference between "impossibility" and "impracticability"?
3. What is the difference between a condition precedent and a condition subsequent?
4. What is the difference between a joint obligation and a joint and several obligation?
5. In 1985 Edwin Shaw, a tenured professor in the School of Pharmacy of Carlisle University was fired because a cutback in funds to the pharmacy school greatly increased the pharmacy school's already existing deficit. Shaw's contract stated that he could be fired in the event of financial exigency on the part of the institution. Financial exigency was defined to include bona fide discontinuance of a program or department of instruction or reduction in size thereof. The university as a whole was not in financial trouble, and Shaw claimed that he could not be fired unless that were true. Can he get his job back? Explain.
6. Dr. Slycce filed a claim against the estate of Leroy, who had been one of the doctor's patients, for $19,000 in unpaid medical bills. Dr. Slycce said that she had been treating Leroy for nearly 25 years, and that he had made only a few payments during that time. She had let the bill go for so long because Leroy was a good friend, but she did expect payment for the medi-cal services. The state's statute of limitations period for contract claims is six years. Leroy died in 1983, and Dr. Slycce filed her claim at that time. She began treating him sometime in 1958 or 1959, and had continued to do so up until his death. How should the doctor's claim be resolved by the court? Explain.
7. Gordie and Flora Myres bought an acre of land in a proposed retirement village in New Texaco. The purchase agreement they signed said that the developer, Cackle Bros., agreed to pay all taxes on the property until the purchase price is paid in full. This agreement was signed on January 18, 1982, and the Myres paid $220 of the $4,220 purchase price at that time. The Myres paid the $4,000 balance on October 8, 1982. They then received a deed to the land which recited that it was subject to taxes for 1981 and 1982. The Myres did pay taxes on the land for 1983 and 1984. The land was sold by the county for nonpayment of the 1981 taxes. The Myres sued for breach of contract. How should the court handle this case? Explain.
8. By written contract, Vidal agreed to buy four used airplanes from Transcontinental Airlines. Payment was to be made by certified check on delivery of the planes, which was to occur at the Kansas City Municipal Airport on June 1. Transcontinental was ready to deliver only one plane on June 1; the other three could have been delivered sometime before July 10. No offer of performance was ever made by either party. On October 8, Vidal sued for breach of contract. What is the result, and why?

18

Remedies for Breach

CHAPTER OBJECTIVES

THIS CHAPTER WILL:

- Indicate the general purpose of court remedies for breach of contract.
- Explain the necessity of choosing between inconsistent remedies.
- Discuss the four factors that must be proved to collect compensatory damages for breach on contract.
- Differentiate nominal damages, punitive damages, and liquidated damages.
- Discuss alternate remedies for breach of contract.

■ GENERAL PRINCIPLES

A rational decision to litigate a claim must be based on economic, psychological, and legal factors. In many cases, a party can be a legal winner (that is, get a favorable judgment) and still be an economic loser, by not being compensated for all economic losses, to say nothing of the psychological strains endured during the litigation process. The potential litigant faces the distinct possibility of not recovering all out-of-pocket expenses for court costs and attorney fees. In addition, the person's "downtime" during litigation is not compensable; that is, the plaintiff may collect "lost revenue" resulting from a breach of contract, but will not collect "lost revenue" resulting from having to be in court. Also, any mental stress resulting from the pressures of the litigation process is not compensable.

Court Costs and Attorney Fees. *Court costs,* which include filing fees, jury fees, witness fees, and transcripts, are usually assessed against the losing party. Where a public question is involved, however, the court may decide to let the taxpayers, rather than one of the parties, bear the costs of the litigation. The trial judge generally has great discretion in determining which items of costs were really necessary to the litigation and should, therefore, be paid by the loser.

Almost alone among the legal systems of the civilized world, the common-law system did not permit victorious litigants to recover their lawyers' charges as part of court costs. In large part, this rule resulted because each lawyer-client contract was created through a private agreement, with no official fee schedule limiting the amount that could be charged. Since there was no general court control over legal fees, it was felt that the court could not properly charge them against the losing party. *Attorney fees* are still not generally included as court costs. To assess them against the losing party, there must be a specific provision to that effect in the contract of the parties or in a statute covering the kind of claim being litigated.

General rule: Attorney fees not part of court costs

All of these factors should be very carefully considered by anyone contemplating litigation. Even if you win legally, you may still lose financially.

Election of Remedies. The strict application of logical principles does not always produce justice in particular cases, and the early common law always tried to be logical. Common-law rules of pleading, for example, required a plaintiff who had two alternative remedies for an alleged breach of contract to choose between them if they were "inconsistent." The two most clearly inconsistent remedies are specific performance and rescission and restitution. In the first, the plaintiff insists that the contract be performed as agreed, in the second, the plaintiff wants to call off the whole deal and put everything back where it was.

Plaintiff must choose if remedies are inconsistent

The plaintiff's main difficulty under these early rules was that the choice had to be made when the complaint was filed; that is, at a time when the plaintiff did not yet know whether or not a case for restitution could be proved. A court might find that the plaintiff had waited too long to rescind, for example, and deny the restitution remedy. But if the plaintiff then tried to sue for damages in a second case, the early civil procedure rules would prohibit the suit because a binding "election of remedies" had been made when the first lawsuit was filed. As a result, some plaintiffs received no remedy at all, just because they (or their lawyers) had guessed wrong initially.

Some of the injustice inherent in these rules has been removed by the adoption of civil procedure rules which permit the plaintiff to file a complaint asking for such inconsistent remedies in the alternative ("I want *either* rescission and restitution *or* damages"). Such alternative pleading is possible in a majority of states and in the U.S. District Courts. Even with this liberalization, however, the plaintiff must still make an election of remedies at some point in the litigation. Such an election might mean deciding whether or not to keep the house with the leaky basement and get damages for the wet furniture and for fixing the leak, or to ask for the money back and a rescission of the house deal. If rescission is granted, no dollar damages for the wet furniture will be awarded. Because of the potential harshness of these election rules, it becomes important to know which remedies are inconsistent and thus require an election.

UCC rule for goods

The best possible rule for the plaintiff is found in the **UCC *rules for the sale of goods*,** which do not require the plaintiff to make any election at all. Buyers of goods who prove their case for rescission can get their money back and also can collect all provable damages which they have sustained while the goods were in their possession. The *Riley* case illustrates a buyer's recovery under both of these "inconsistent" theories.

RILEY v. FORD MOTOR COMPANY

442 F.2d 670 (U.S. Third Circuit, 1971)

FACTS

Riley purchased his new 1969 Lincoln Mark III from a Florida dealer at a cost of $8,476.00, and Ford issued a self-styled "New Vehicle Warranty." Shortly thereafter he took the car to Robinson Brothers, an Alabama Ford dealer, for repair of a window and removal of a noise in the rear end. According to Riley these defects were not corrected. At trial he testified that in the weeks following the requested repairs, and before the car was returned to Robinson Brothers for further repairs, these additional malfunctions developed: air conditioning did not work, speed control did not function, power seats became inoperative, the radio aerial functioned spasmodically, the rear seat did not fit, headlight panels were not synchronized, the cigarette lighter was missing, windshield wipers were defective, engine knocked upon acceleration, the transmission did not function properly, gear shift lever would not function, and the left door would not close properly.

Riley wrote to Ford setting forth in detail his complaints, and requesting Ford "to direct me to a dealer employing trained service personnel, or furnish me with someone capable of overseeing service personnel available in order to insure that the defects in my automobile are properly corrected in an expert and dependable manner." Ford dispatched a Technical Service Representative who road-tested the automobile, agreed that it was not functioning properly, and offered to take it to Robinson Brothers where he would personally supervise its repair. Riley believed he had a better idea. He sued Ford and was awarded $30,000 by a U.S. District Court jury.

ISSUES

Was the dealer acting as Ford's agent? Was the jury's award of damages supported by the evidence?

DECISION

The jury must be free to decide this issue on the facts. No, the damage award was clearly incorrect. Judgment reversed and case remanded for a new trial.

🏛 REASONS   Judge Aldisert's opinion first noted that the trial court had committed reversible error by telling the jury that the dealer was "acting for Ford Motor Company" rather than letting the jury decide this as a question of fact. He then discussed the award of damages.

"[W]e cannot validate the jury's award of $30,000. The District Court correctly instructed as to the measure of damages:

> Now, I charge you that if you find that the defendant Ford Motor Company, has breached its warranty and that they were given a reasonable opportunity to repair it, and they didn't, then the proper measure of damages for breach of warranty is this: the difference in the value of the automobile as it was represented and warranted to be and the value it really was at the time of its delivery.
>
> The measure of damages may also include any incidental damage, as you may think is proper, such as any expenses, reasonably incurred, in acquiring any substitute means of transportation during such reasonable time as it would take to repair the defects in the automobile. . . .

"The purchase price of the automobile was $8,476. In response to questions propounded by the trial court, plaintiff declared that the car 'hasn't been worth anything to me.' Even accepting this testimony as sufficient to establish that the automobile was worthless at the time of delivery, 'the difference in the value of the automobile as it was represented and warranted to be and the value it was at the time of delivery' could not have exceeded the price of $8,476. Adding to this the reasonably incurred cost of a substitute means of transportation, which, at the most, amounted to $430.43, plaintiff's total recovery would have been limited to $8,906.43."

▪ DAMAGES

Underlying Factors. In determining the amount of damages that a plaintiff can collect for a breach of contract, the court will subject the claimed damages to four tests: *causation, certainty, foreseeability,* and *mitigation.* To be collectible, compensatory damages must meet each of these tests.

Requirements for collecting compensatory damages: Causation

First, the plaintiff must prove that the alleged damages were caused by the breach and not by something else. Lost profits which result when a supplier fails to deliver may be recoverable, but if the plaintiff's lower sales are due to a general economic downturn, the breaching seller should not be liable because his or her breach did not cause the "injury."

Certainty

Second, the plaintiff must be able to prove the amount of damages with *reasonable* certainty. Damages for lost profits and for *mental stress* are difficult to collect, in part, for this reason. Courts are reluctant to permit jury speculation and sympathy to substitute for solid evidence of amount of injury.

Foreseeability

A third significant limitation on the amount of damages awarded is that the damages sustained must have been reasonably foreseeable at the time the contract was made. That is, a party is not held legally responsible for damages which result from a breach of contract unless the party ought to have known that damages of that sort would result from the nonperformance. Damages for lost profits which result from a "shut down the plant" situation are especially difficult to collect because of the application of this foreseeability principle. Obviously, your safeguard here is to make sure that your suppliers and contractors are fully informed as to your requirements and of the consequences of their failure to perform.

Mitigation

Finally, it is only common sense to require the injured party to take reasonable steps to mitigate, or hold down, losses. Even though one party has breached, it wouldn't be fair to that party to allow the other party to simply sit back and watch the damages mount up, without making any effort to get an alternative performance from someone else. The law, therefore, generally requires injured parties to make reasonable efforts to mitigate their damages. If a car manufacturer did not get an expected shipment of needed parts from a supplier, the car maker would have to try to buy them from another source. The car maker couldn't just close the plant when they used up their existing inventory of the part, without making reasonable efforts to get more somewhere else.

Because a lease of real estate is a conveyance of an interest in the land as well as a contract, courts at one time did not apply the mitigation rule to landlords. Landlords could simply sue for the agreed rental price whether the tenant was using the premises or not. There is now a growing trend toward removing this exception, thereby forcing the landlord to mitigate by rerenting the premises before collecting damages against a tenant who has moved out prior to the expiration of the lease.

Compensatory Damages. The basic purpose of the damages remedy is to compensate the injured party for the loss sustained by the other party's breach; that is, to put the injured party, so far as possible, in the place he or she would have been if the contract had been properly and fully performed. The measure of *compensatory damages* is the difference between the performance promised and the performance given; thus general compensatory damages are sometimes called *difference-money damages*. For example, if a used car is represented to be in "A-1 shape," and it is not, compensatory damages would give the buyer the amount of money necessary to put the car into "A-1 shape."

Damages to compensate for injury caused by breach

Special compensatory damages, or *consequential damages,* are awarded for losses which are further down in the chain of causation, losses over and above the difference-money losses which are caused by the breach. For example, if the buyer of the above used car had to take a cab to work twice because the car wouldn't start, special compensatory damages should be given to cover the cab fare. Again, there may be questions here of causation and of foreseeability.

Nominal Damages and Punitive Damages. Where there has been a breach of contract, but the injured party is unable to show any actual losses as a result, the plaintiff will be awarded *nominal damages* (almost always $1) and court costs, provided the case is proved. Obviously, most such cases will not be litigated. But nominal damages play an important part in a case which contains the right combination of facts for *punitive damages* to be awarded. Once the injured party proves a case for breach of contract, an award of punitive damages can be added on, to punish the defendant who has been guilty of repeated, willful violations of the rights of others (again, even though no actual damages can be proved). Cases involving fraudulent or other intentionally tortious conduct are particularly appropriate for punitive damage awards, as seen in the *Nader* case.

Damages to punish party who breached (rarely given)

NADER v. ALLEGHENY AIRLINES, INC.

426 U.S. 290 (1976)

FACTS

Ralph Nader was scheduled to make several appearances for the Connecticut Citizens Action Group on April 28, including a noon rally in Hartford and a speech on the Storrs campus of the University of Connecticut. On April 25, he bought a ticket for Allegheny's 10:15 A.M. flight from Washington, D.C., to Hartford, which was scheduled to arrive at 11:15 A.M. His reservation was confirmed. When he arrived at the airport about five minutes before his flight, he was told there were no more seats. Only 100 seats were available for the 107 reservations which had been confirmed one hour before the flight. No one would give up a seat when Allegheny asked. Nader refused Allegheny's offer to fly him to Philadelphia, where he would have 10 minutes to catch a flight due to arrive in Hartford at 12:15. He flew to Boston, where a CCAG staff member picked him up and drove him to Storrs. Nader refused the $32.41 compensation offered to him under the Civil Aeronautics Board's rules, and brought a common-law suit for damages, alleging fraudulent misrepresentation. Nader was awarded $10 compensatory damages and $25,000 punitive damages; CCAG was awarded $51 compensatory damages and $25,000 punitive damages. The Court of Appeals reversed.

ISSUE

Must a decision in this case be delayed until the CAB rules on whether overbooking is an "unfair practice"?

DECISION

No. Judgment reversed, and case remanded for further proceedings.

 REASONS

Justice Powell first reviewed the facts, noting that domestic airlines had "bumped" about 82,000 passengers in 1972 and 76,000 in 1973. The CAB had adopted compensation rules to deal with this problem, and revisions were being considered. The only issue before the Supreme Court was whether Nader could proceed with his common-law suit prior to a CAB decision on "bumping."

"Section 1106 of the Act . . . provides that 'nothing contained in this chapter shall in any way abridge or alter the remedies now existing at common law or by statute, but the provisions of this chapter are in addition to such remedies.' The Court of Appeals found that 'although the saving clause of section 1106 purports to speak in absolute terms it cannot be read so literally.' . . .

"The present regulations dealing with the problems of overbooking and oversales were promulgated by the Board in 1967. They provide for denied boarding compensation to bumped passengers and require each carrier to establish priority rules for seating passengers and to file reports of passengers who could not be accommodated. The order instituting these regulations contemplates that the bumped passenger will have a choice between accepting denied boarding compensation as 'liquidated damages for all damages incurred . . . as a result of the carrier's failure to provide the passenger with confirmed reserved space,' or pursuing his or her common-law remedies. The Board specifically provided for a 30-day period before the specified compensation need be accepted so that the passenger will not be forced to make a decision before 'the consequences of denied boarding have occurred and are known.' After evaluating the consequences, passengers may choose as an alternative 'to pursue their remedy under the common law.'"

Damages can be agreed on in
advance, in contract itself

Liquidated Damages. The general policy of the law to favor settlements of claims after they arise also operates to validate remedy provisions agreed to in advance, as part of the original contract. The parties are generally free to specify in advance what steps can be taken if their contract is breached by one of them. However, since many contracts are entered into between parties with unequal bargaining power, and since in many cases form contracts drafted by one party are used, the courts examine such *liquidated damages* provisions very carefully. These clauses must be basically fair, and a substantial forfeiture of rights must not result from a relatively minor breach. Where a valid liquidated damages provision exists, the amount specified can be collected for a breach without any proof of actual damages. If the court decides that an unreasonably large amount has been specified as a *penalty* for a breach of the contract, the clause will not be enforced. That rule protects Miller in the next case.

AMERICAN FINANCIAL LEASING & SERVICE CO. v. MILLER

322 N.E.2d 149 (Ohio, 1974).

FACTS   Miller started a car wash/gasoline station in Columbus, Ohio. He leased his equipment from American in 1967, under a five-year lease which was renewable for three one-year periods. At the end of eight years, American would "abandon" the equipment to Miller (he would have paid for it in full). In May 1971, Miller defaulted. American repossessed and resold the equipment. In addition to its costs and expenses, and the difference between the resale price and the balance of the lease payments, American claimed $2,119.79 under a lease provision which said they could collect 10 percent of the equipment's total cost in the event of any default. Miller appeals from the trial court's award of the $2,119.79; he is not contesting the actual damages.

ISSUE: Is the contract clause a valid liquidated damages provision?

DECISION: No. Judgment reversed.

 REASONS: **Judge Holmes reviewed the requirements for such clauses.**
"It is quite generally accepted that a clause in a contract providing for liquidated damages in the event of a default is valid and enforceable. . . .

"Most Ohio cases hold that there must be three elements appearing in order that the provision may be construed as one for liquidated damages, rather than a penalty. . . . 'It must, according to most cases, appear that the sum stipulated bears a reasonable proportion to the loss actually sustained; . . . the actual damages occasioned by the breach are uncertain or difficult to ascertain; and most important of all, . . . that a construction of the contract as a whole evinces a conscious intention of the parties deliberately to consider and adjust the damages that might flow from the breach. . . .'

"It is our belief that the main element to be considered in arriving at the determination of the validity of such a provision is whether it expressed the intention of the parties that any such stipulated amount represents the reasonable damages for the breach of the general provisions of the contract, which damage, because of the nature of the transaction, would be difficult to ascertain.

"If the provision is not on its face unconscionable, the element of fraud is not present, and the amount can reasonably be related to the loss that may have been experienced by a party due to the breach, the reviewing court should uphold the provisions of the contract.

"However, where, upon a review of the terms of the specific agreement, all of the elements in the rule do not fall into place, a contrary conclusion must be reached. Such is the case before this court.

"In the first instance, the actual damages that would be sustained by the lessor, in the event of a breach by the lessees, would not be difficult to ascertain or prove. There would be little or no uncertainty in determining actual damages. Such damages would be the unpaid portion of the lease and, if the property had been repossessed, the costs of repossession and sale, and any deficiency remaining after such sale.

"Secondly, we must look to the reasonableness of the 10 percent to be exacted from the lessees pursuant to the 'Default' paragraph of the contract. It should be noted that in the 'Default' paragraph, upon the occurrence of one of the events constituting a default, the lessor had a wide range of options available to him. . . . It being inconceivable that the print used in the production of the instrument could have been any smaller, it appears that the only way in which additional default provisions favorable to the drafter could be included would be by way of adding further pages to the contract.

"In any event, going specifically to the reasonableness of the stipulation extracting 10 percent of the contract price in the event of default, we hold that such amount, in light of the other provisions covering the recoupment of the lessor's actual damages in the event of a breach, neither bears a reasonable relationship to such damage, nor is in a reasonable proportion thereto. Such amount is patently in excess of the actual damage which could be suffered by the lessor, and therefore must be considered as a 'penalty' rather than a stipulated 'liquidated damage.'

"Further, a reading of the contract in its totality, and most particularly the paragraph entitled 'Default,' shows that there are ample provisions which reasonably consider and adjust any damages which might flow from a breach. On the other hand, we are not convinced that it was the intent and understanding of the parties hereto that the enforcement of the clause questioned would reasonably adjust the actual damages that might flow from any breach.

"As previously stated, the courts are generally reluctant to step in and reform contracts of individuals, in that our business world demands, and should be afforded, a free right of contract. Yet the underlying philosophy pertains that our courts abhor penalties, and such legal philosophy must be applied to the instant contract.

"Therefore, the single assignment of error is sustained, and the judgment of the Court of Common Pleas of Franklin County is hereby reversed and a final judgment is entered accordingly."

OTHER REMEDIES

In addition to the damages remedy, several other remedies may be available to the injured plaintiff, depending on the facts of the case. Most of these alternative remedies were first developed by the courts of equity to deal with situations where the "remedy at law," that is, damages, was felt to be inadequate to solve the plaintiff's problem. The main alternative remedies for breach of contract are discussed below; certain special remedies for breach of sale of goods contracts and secured financing contracts are discussed in later chapters.

In special cases, court may order contract performance

Specific Performance. Where the parties have contracted for the purchase and sale of a unique item, the buyer, particularly, may want the court to specifically enforce the contract, because it will usually be very hard to prove damages in the absence of an established market, and because even with damages, the buyer would still not be able to get the thing bargained for. In the eyes of the law every piece of land is unique, so the specific performance remedy is available to either party to a real estate contract. Goods and securities are legally unique if no alternative source of supply is reasonably available. Fifty shares of stock in a small, closely held corporation might very well be unique; 50 shares of U.S. Steel would not be. A 1983 Ford is probably not unique; a 1904 Stanley Steamer almost certainly is.

As a general rule, specific performance is not available as a remedy for breach of personal services contracts, for two main reasons. First, courts traditionally have been reluctant to get involved in extensive supervision of contract performances on a day-to-day basis. And second, an order forcing one person to work for another smacks of "involuntary servitude," which is prohibited by the U.S. Constitution. Because performance under construction contracts can normally be judged against an agreed set of plans and specifications, specific performance is available in such cases.

In special cases, court may order a party not to perform for others

Injunction. *Injunction* is another remedy that was developed by equity courts; a court orders someone to do something or to stop doing something. In breach of contract situations, a *negative* injunction may be granted to prevent a breaching party from performing for others while still under a contractual duty to perform for the plaintiff. For the reasons stated above, the plaintiff does not get a positive decree ordering the defendant to perform; the plaintiff only gets a negative order directing the defendant not to perform for others. In the following case, Professor Felch (or his lawyer) failed to appreciate this difference.

FELCH v. FINDLAY COLLEGE

200 N.E.2d 353 (Ohio, 1963)

FACTS

William E. Felch alleges, among other things, that he was employed by the defendant as a member of its faculty on a continuing basis and that contrary to and without compliance with the provisions for dismissal contained in administrative memoranda purporting to require certain hearings, the board of trustees of defendant on August 22, 1961, approved the action of its president on July 20, 1961, dismissing the plaintiff effective August 11, 1961. Plaintiff asks that "defendant be enjoined from carrying into effect the dismissal of this plaintiff as a member of the faculty . . . and that the defendant may be ordered to continue plaintiff as such member of the faculty of Findlay College, Findlay, Ohio, and that defendant be ordered to pay to this plaintiff the salary therefore agreed upon."

ISSUE

Is an injunction a proper remedy in this case?

DECISION

No. Judgment affirmed.

🏛 REASONS   Judge Guernsey first stated that Felch "in essence and in legal effect" was really asking for specific performance. He then cited three authorities to support the court's denial of that remedy.

"In *Masetta* v. *National Bronze & Aluminum Foundry Co.,* 159 Ohio St. 306, . . . the Supreme Court held that '[a] court of equity will not, by means of mandatory injunction, decree specific performance of a labor contract existing between an employer and its employees so as to require the employer to continue any such employee in its service or to rehire such employee if discharged.' . . .

"In 81 C.J.S. Specific Performance § 82, p. 591, the rule is stated as follows:

> In general, specific performance does not lie to enforce a provision in a contract for the performance of personal services requiring special knowledge, ability, experience, or the exercise of judgment, skill, taste, discretion, labor, tact, energy, or integrity, particularly where the performance of such services would be continuous over a long period of time. This rule is based on the fact that mischief likely to result from an enforced continuance of the relationship incident to the service after it has become personally obnoxious to one of the parties is so great that the interests of society require that the remedy be denied, and on the fact that the enforcement of a decree requiring the performance of such a contract would impose too great a burden on the courts. . . .

"Assuming plaintiff's claim of continuing contract status, the services to be performed would 'be continuous over a long period of time' and although his services might once have had a unique and peculiar value, they no longer have any value as far as the defendant is concerned. . . .

"The same rule is reiterated in 2 *Restatement of the Law of Contracts.*"

Rescission and Restitution.   Two remedies are really involved here—calling off the deal, and returning any benefits already transferred. A court will not lightly undo the parties' whole agreement and order the restoration of benefits already given. The rescission and restitution remedy is provided only if there has been fraud, material breach, or similar failure; only if the injured party asks for this remedy with reasonable promptness; and only if the rights of third parties or other equitable factors have not intervened. The objective of "R & R" is to terminate the contract *and* to put the parties back where they were before it was made. The more difficult and complex it is to achieve this objective, the less likely it is that R & R will be used as a remedy.

For serious breach, injured party may cancel contract

Quasi Contract.   Because the old common-law courts only heard cases which fell into certain categories, lawyers became somewhat creative in constructing fact combinations to fit those categories. *Quasi contract* means in essence "almost like a real contract, but not quite"; it describes a situation where a party has received and retained benefits but has made no actual promise to pay for them. It is in fact a remedy which the courts developed to prevent such a party from being "unjustly enriched." The circumstances are such that it wouldn't be fair for the person to keep the benefits without paying anything for them. The *unjust enrichment* principle is the justification for requiring a minor to pay the fair market value for necessaries received, even though the minor has exercised the option of disaffirming the contract made to pay for them. Quasi contract also applies to all sorts of other situations, such as benefits conferred on the wrong person by mistake or partial performance given to one party prior to a breach of contract.

Even though no enforceable contract, a person may be ordered to pay for benefits received

■ SIGNIFICANCE OF THIS CHAPTER

Since you are not reading this text to become lawyers, we have deemphasized most procedural aspects of the law, and concentrated instead on the nature of your rights and liabilities. The purpose of this chapter on remedies is to acquaint you with the options you may have in the event the other party is guilty of a breach of contract. Since not every remedy is available for every situation, you need an appreciation of the limits of what the courts, and your lawyer, can do for you if you are successful in proving your case. You need to know what the possible outcomes might be to make a rational decision whether or not to bring the litigation—or to continue it.

Since a court will not (and should not) give unrequested remedies, one of the lawyer's main jobs is to figure out the remedy or the combination of remedies which will best solve the client's problem. If you do go to litigation, make sure you fully understand what your options are and what your chances are of receiving each possible remedy.

DISCUSSION CASE

JONES v. HONCHELL
470 N.E.2d 219 (Ohio, 1984)

Facts: On April 8, 1979, plaintiffs-appellees, Charles and Bobbie Jones, entered into an agreement with defendant-appellant, William Honchell, wherein appellant agreed to construct a single-family residence for appellees for the sum of $57,881. Construction of the home began shortly afterward and proceeded normally until early July 1979, when appellees expressed dissatisfaction with the brickwork. Appellees were particularly concerned about the construction of the chimneys and fireplaces. They considered the workmanship in these areas to be so poor that the only way to correct the problem was to remove the existing chimneys and fireplaces and rebuild them.

The parties made several attempts to settle their differences regarding the construction of the house, including the alleged defective brickwork. These discussions culminated in a meeting between the parties and their respective attorneys in late July or early August 1979. At the meeting, appellant agreed to remedy a number of relatively minor problems with the partially constructed residence but refused to completely rebuild the fireplaces and chimneys. Shortly thereafter, appellees refused to permit appellant to complete construction of the residence and proceeded to complete construction themselves by purchasing various necessary materials and hiring their own subcontractors.

After the residence was substantially completed, appellees filed suit in the Butler County Court of Common

Pleas charging appellant with a breach of the construction contract due to his failure to construct the home in a workmanlike manner. The matter was, pursuant to local court rules, scheduled for nonbinding arbitration. The decision of the panel of arbitrators was then appealed to the trial court, and a trial *de novo* was begun on June 1, 1983. The trial court, in an opinion filed June 13, 1983, found in favor of appellees in the amount of $8,450.

■

Per Curiam:

Appellant's first assignment of error asserts that the trial court erred in its finding that appellant waived the arbitration provisions of the written contractual agreement.

The language . . . without question requires both parties to submit any disputes arising under the contract to binding arbitration. However, we believe that the actions of both parties indicate a waiver of the agreement to arbitrate.

Appellees' waiver of the arbitration provision may be inferred from the filing of the instant suit in the Butler County Court of Common Pleas in lieu of pursuing arbitration. . . . Appellant did not raise the arbitration provision of the contract in his answer, which may also be construed to be a waiver of the clause. . . .

In his second assignment of error, appellant asserts that the trial court erred by finding that he improperly constructed the residence and failed to remedy the improper construction.

The record reveals conflicting testimony at trial as to the quality of the brickwork. Appellant testified that while he did not consider the brickwork to be a "first class job," he did not feel it was so defective that it could not be remedied without completely tearing down the existing structure and rebuilding it. Appellees did not share appellant's optimism and, in support of their position presented the expert testimony of Roger P. Davis, a builder and general contractor. Davis testified that the brickwork on appellees' home was, in his opinion, not of acceptable quality based on prevailing practice in the area. Davis added that he believed that the chimneys and fireplace could not be fixed without tearing them down and completely rebuilding them. Appellees further presented a large number of photographs depicting the alleged defective workmanship. . . .

As the record reflects some competent, credible evidence which supports the trial court's finding, we must affirm the trial court's determination that appellees' residence was improperly constructed and that appellant failed to remedy the improper construction. . . .

Appellant's third assignment of error states that the court below erred in finding that appellees' expenditures to complete the residence were reasonable and necessary.

When a construction contract has been breached, the proper measure of damages is the reasonable cost of placing the building in the condition contemplated by the parties at the time they entered in the contract. . . . The burden of proof is on the party seeking damages, appellee in the case *sub judice,* who must prove by a preponderance of the evidence the necessary and reasonable cost to complete the building in accord with the original tenor of the agreement. . . .

In the instant case, appellees attempted to carry their burden by presenting at trial the testimony of Roger P. Davis as an expert witness in the area of home construction. Davis testified that, based on his training and experience as a contractor, the cost to complete the . . . home . . . would be $58,746. . . . Jones . . . presented a series of canceled checks indicating that the various amounts described had been paid. The actual subcontractors hired by the appellees to finish the house did not testify.

Appellant in his brief contends that because appellees failed to present the testimony of the actual contractors hired to complete the residence, he was denied the opportunity to cross-examine them to determine if the work performed was reasonable and necessary. We feel that this concern goes merely to the weight of the evidence presented by appellees. . . .

As the record contains some competent, credible evidence to support the trial court's finding that the amounts expended by the appellees were reasonable and necessary for the completion of their residence under the terms of the building contract, we are unwilling to disturb such finding on appeal. . . .

Appellant, in his fourth assignment of error, contends that the trial court erred by finding as a matter of law that he failed to prove his counterclaim below. The counterclaim at issue asserted that appellant was entitled to a draw of $18,300 for work already completed on appellees' residence before appellees became so dissatisfied with the brickwork that they decided to complete the construction of the residence themselves and sue appellant for damages. The record indicates that appellant received draws for the amounts of $5,000 and $18,000, but was refused a third draw because appellees were dissatisfied with the brickwork and did not wish to continue with the construction until the brickwork problem had been solved to their satisfaction.

It is undisputed that appellant was not entitled to his third draw until the brickwork on appellees' residence was completed. The trial court, in its findings of fact, found that appellees' house was improperly constructed. While the finding did not specifically refer to the brickwork, it is clear from the record that the brickwork was the principal source of dispute between the parties. Therefore, as appellee did not consider this work to be done properly and proved this contention to the satisfaction of the trial court, appellant is not entitled to his draw.

Appellant further asserts, possibly as an alternative to his $18,300 counterclaim, that there was approximately $10,000 owed to subcontractors for work performed on appellees' house prior to the third draw and that he is therefore entitled to be paid the above amount by appellees. This position is an untenable one because once the contract was breached, appellees were entitled to the difference between the contract price and the cost of completing the residence. . . . Were appellees to pay appellant $10,000, it would only increase the cost of completing the residence by the same amount and cause appellant to owe that amount to appellees as consequential damages.

Therefore, the trial court properly found appellant's counterclaim to be without merit, and appellant's fourth assignment of error is, accordingly, overruled. . . .

Judgment affirmed.

■ IMPORTANT TERMS AND CONCEPTS

court costs   compensatory damages
attorney fees   difference-money damages
election of remedies   special compensatory
UCC election rule for   damages
    goods   consequential damages
causation of damages   nominal damages
certainty of damages   punitive damages
foreseeability of damages   liquidated damages
mitigation of damages   penalty clause
mental stress damages   specific performance
injunction   rescission and restitution
quasi contract   unjust enrichment

■ QUESTIONS AND PROBLEMS FOR DISCUSSION

1. What is the difference between nominal damages and punitive damages?
2. When will a liquidated damages clause be enforced?
3. When is specific performance available as a remedy for breach of contract?
4. What is the "causation" element which the injured party must prove to collect compensatory damages for breach of contract?
5. Larry lost the use of his airplane for 75 days because of damage caused by the negligence of an employee of Airserv, Inc. He sued Airserv, proved his case, and was awarded $900 damages by the trial court. The trial court measured damages based on Larry's actual out-of-pocket costs, including the cost of several plane rentals. On appeal, Larry contends that he should receive damages based on his loss of the use of his plane for the entire 75 days, or $3,500, even though he didn't actually rent the plane each day. What is the proper measure of Larry's damages?
6. Tom sold his junk auto and salvage business, Trusty's Auto Parts, to Lem. As part of the contract, Tom agreed not to compete in the auto salvage business for a period of five years, within a radius of 100 miles. When Lem took over, he changed the business name to Loosewheel's Auto Salvage. Lem's business volume is only about half of what Tom was doing. After some investigation, Lem has learned that Tom has been buying scrap copper and aluminum wire from two of his former business contacts and has generally been buying and selling auto scrap and salvage. Lem wants to sue for breach of contract. What difficulties will he face in winning a lawsuit on these facts? Explain.
7. Fasttime Construction Company contracted with Richie School District to construct an athletic track and certain other improvements at the high school. The contract specified that the work was to be completed within 60 days of the School District's "notice to proceed," and that $150 per day would be assessed for each day the contractor was late in completing the project. The total price of the project was $120,996.97. The contractor was 50 days late in finishing the project, and the School District wishes to deduct $7,500 from the balance due. Can it do so? Explain.
8. On August 20, 1980, Armand signed a 10-year lease for a "book and bottle" shop in Peachtree Plaza, a shopping center which was under construction. Cash shortages and construction delays occurred, and Octopus Bank, which had provided the financing, foreclosed against Peachtree Plaza's owners and took over the project. When the center was finally completed, Armand's space was rented to someone else. Octopus claimed that it had never seen a copy of his lease and thought the space was available for rental. Octopus offered Armand another space in Peachtree, but he said it wasn't suitable for his type of business. Armand sues for specific performance and/or damages. How should the court handle this case? Explain.

PART THREE

Sales of Goods

A sale of goods is one particular type of contract, so the general rules of contract law apply, unless replaced by a specific rule from the Uniform Commercial Code. We have already seen many examples of such changes in the various chapters in Part Two. There were special goods rules for offer and acceptance, consideration, Statute of Frauds, assignment, and other topics. We will not repeat all those special rules in this part.

Our focus here is the other major areas of difference between general contract law and the UCC's rules for sales of goods. Chapter 19 discusses the rules for transferring the various ownership interests in the goods from the seller to the buyer. Chapter 20 covers the very important area of products liability, one of the two or three most important legal developments in the past 50 years. Chapter 21 summarizes the UCC's special rules for performance of sales contracts and the remedies given to each party by the UCC in the event of breach. Finally, Chapter 22 looks at two situations involving problems with the transfer of ownership—defects in the seller's title to the goods, and claims of the bulk seller's unsecured creditors against the goods.

19

Sales: Title, Risk of Loss, and Other Interests

CHAPTER OBJECTIVES

THIS CHAPTER WILL:

- Define "goods" as the subject of a sale contract.
- Review the special goods rules from the contract law chapters.
- Identify and explain the six different ownership interests that can exist in goods.
- Explain the rules for transferring these ownership interests.
- Summarize the rules in four special sale arrangements.
- Indicate how documents of title are used in sale transactions.

■ BASIC CONCEPTS AND DEFINITIONS

The sale of goods is certainly one of the most basic types of commercial transaction. Each of us probably enters into several such "sales" every day, buying school supplies, books, hamburgers, groceries, toothpaste, shoes, and similar items. Less frequently, we buy "big ticket" items such as TVs, furniture, cars, and boats. The transactions we're talking about in this chapter are familiar ones. But the problems we're discussing, and the technical language we're using, are probably less familiar. Most of us don't think about the problems discussed in this chapter as we do our daily business, and usually we don't have to do so. Most of the time, our "sale" transactions do go through as planned. Most of the time, the goods don't get lost or stolen between the time we buy them and the seller delivers them to us. Most of the time, no third parties try to assert rights against "our" new goods.

This chapter is concerned with the statistically unusual "what if" cases. *What if* something happens to the goods in transit, while they're on the way to the buyer? *What if* some third party has a claim against the goods? *What if* a third party alleges injury caused by someone with the goods? These problems do arise in the real world. Not every sale goes as planned, every time. Businesses and consumers need to know what the rules are for handling these problems when they arise. One "record-of-the-month" might not be worth a lawsuit, but a half-million-dollar shipment of computers might very well be worth arguing about. Businesses are also buyers, as well as sellers, and some sales transactions involve millions of dollars of "goods." Car manufacturers, for example, buy large amounts of steel, plastic, glass, machinery, and auto parts. They certainly need to know what's what in these dealings with their suppliers.

UCC Coverage

Since a "sale of goods" is one specific type of contract, the general principles of contract law apply to such sales, but most of the rules relating specifically to sales of goods have been codified, supplemented, and sometimes changed by the Uniform Commercial Code. Article 2, the longest article in the Uniform Commercial Code, specifically covers sales of goods, but other portions of the UCC may also apply. If the goods are to be stored or transported as part of the transaction, Article 7 may apply. The general principles and definitions stated in Article 1 apply to all Code transactions.

Many of the special sales rules have already been discussed in the contracts chapters covering offer and acceptance, consideration, the Statute of Frauds, and assignments. This chapter and the next three chapters will focus on other major differences between the law of sales and general contract law.

Definitions

The basic purpose of a contract for the sale of goods is to pass the various ownership interests recognized by the Code from the seller to the buyer, for a consideration called the price. The transaction is not a gift of the goods, because the seller is receiving a price for them; it is not a bailment of the goods, because the buyer will become the owner of them. Whether a particular contract is a sale of goods or a services contract depends on which element— goods or services—predominates.

As defined in 2–105(1), *goods* means tangible, movable personal property.

Goods = Tangible, movable
personal property

Investment securities, such as stocks and bonds, and other "things in action" (intangibles) are excluded from the definition of goods; specifically included are such things as growing crops, the unborn young of animals, and specially manufactured goods. Goods which are not both existing and identified when the contract is made are called *future goods,* and a contract involving such goods is a *contract to sell. Fungible goods* are goods whose units are indistinguishable from one another, such as grain in a grain elevator, fuel oil in a tank car, or coal in a pile.

The *price* is whatever value is received by the seller for the goods; it may be money, other goods, services, or land—or a promise by the buyer to deliver any of these things.

A *merchant* (2–104[1]) is defined as a person who *(a)* deals in goods of the kind being sold; or *(b)* by his or her occupation holds himself or herself out as having special knowledge about the goods or practices involved in the sale; or *(c)* is represented by someone who is held out as having such special knowledge. The question of whether or not a farmer is a merchant for Code purposes has not been answered uniformly by the courts. (See the *Siĕrens* case in Chapter 12.)

Implied quality guarantees on
goods

Another important difference between sales of goods, services, and land has to do with quality guarantees: What sort of performance standards does the law require of the seller? There are some very important distinctions between goods, on the one hand, and services or land, on the other. For land, although many states now follow a different rule (at least for the seller of a new home), the original rule is that the buyer takes the land as is; unless the buyer can prove that the seller committed fraud or made a specific guarantee as part of the contract, the buyer has no case for alleged defects in the real estate. For services, unless a specific guarantee of results has been made, the buyer-customer has to prove malpractice to recover; that is, the buyer-customer has to show that the seller's performance fell below the standard of a reasonably competent practitioner. For sales of goods, however, a merchant-seller is held to an automatic quality *warranty* that the goods are merchantable, even though the merchant-seller has said nothing specific about their quality and even though the merchant-seller is not guilty of any negligence in handling or delivering the goods. These warranty rules will be discussed in the next chapter.

▪ PASSING OF OWNERSHIP INTERESTS IN THE GOODS

Six sticks of ownership

One special (and somewhat complicated) problem in the law of sales is that of determining when the various ownership interests recognized by the Code pass from the seller to the buyer. The UCC recognizes six different ownership interests in the goods—*special property, insurable interest, title, risk of loss, right to possession,* and *security interest.* These six interests represent packages of rights and duties with respect to the goods. They can all exist at the same time, as to the same goods, and they may be parceled out among the seller, the buyer, and different third parties in any number of combinations. Part of the complexity in Article 2 is caused by the need to provide rules for all these situations.

The simplest case occurs when you buy a used book from a friend for cash, or items from a drugstore, or grocery store. If you pay by check, things get a bit more complicated since the check will only be paid by your bank if there is enough money in the account. If you use a credit card or some other credit arrangement, the seller is taking a still greater risk of nonpayment. Where you order goods by mail, as many businesses do, all sorts of things can happen while the goods are in transit. When the goods are delivered to the buyer they may not conform to the contract, and either party may decide not to go through with the deal. The Code must provide appropriate rules to deal with all these "what if" situations.

Under the Code, most of the disputes between the buyer and the seller will be "risk of loss" cases, as shown by the examples in this chapter. Where third parties are involved in the litigation, the solution will nearly always depend on the location of one of the other five interests. For example, "title" is frequently important in deciding liability claims by or against third parties.

Presumptions

Article 2 contains a rather extensive set of statutory presumptions as to when each of the various interests in the goods passes to the buyer; the most important sections are 2–401, 2–501, and 2–509. In general, these presumptions may be overcome by the parties' specific agreement. That is, the parties are free to make any specific agreement they wish as to when a particular ownership interest will pass to the buyer, but if they say nothing, the Code presumptions apply. In most cases the contract probably will not say anything specific about when these ownership interests pass.

Goods must be existing and identified

One inflexible rule is stated in the Code (2–105[2]): "Goods must be both existing and identified before any interest in them can pass." In other words, even if they both agree to do so, the buyer and the seller cannot pass any interest to anyone unless the goods are both existing and identified. This is just common sense. Until we know whose goods are whose, no ownership in any goods can pass to anyone. Once the goods come into existence and are identified as the goods for the given contract, the buyer and the seller are free to parcel out the six ownership interests in any way they choose. The *Lamborn* case illustrates what happens when goods are not identified.

LAMBORN v. SEGGERMAN BROTHERS, INC.

240 N.Y. 118 (1925)

FACTS

Lamborn as the buyer and the Seggermans as the sellers entered into a written contract for the sale of "1200/50 lb. boxes Calif. Evap. apples—Extra Choice Quality—1919 crop." (The Seggermans had, in turn, made arrangements to buy 1,200 boxes of dried apples from a supplier, Rosenberg Brothers.) Lamborn was to pay 22½ cents per pound "FOB Pacific Coast Rail Shipping Point. . . . Payment to be made against draft with documents attached." The Rosenbergs loaded a Southern Pacific railroad car with 1,770 boxes of dried apples and received an "order" bill of lading which provided for shipment to New York. Once they knew the apples were on the way, the Seggermans billed Lamborn for 1,200 boxes and gave Lamborn an order addressed to their delivery clerk at their place of business. Seeing these documents, Lamborn paid the contract price as agreed—$13,377. The apples never arrived in New York; they were seized en route by agents of the U.S. government, for reasons not disclosed by the court. Lamborn sued for a refund but lost in the lower court.

ISSUE Has the risk of loss on the 1,200 boxes of apples passed to Lamborn?

DECISION No. Judgment reversed (Lamborn gets the contract price back).

REASONS Since this was a pre-Code case, the New York Court of Appeals talked about the passing of title as implying the passing of risk of loss, and used the word *appropriation* rather than the word *identification* in referring to specific goods. The underlying principles are the same under the UCC.

Judge Lehman pointed out that neither the Rosenbergs nor the Seggermans had ever set aside 1,200 specific boxes for Lamborn. "[I]n the present case there has been no . . . appropriation by the defendant of any ascertained goods to the plaintiffs' contract. . . . A delivery by a seller to a carrier, even for the purpose of transmission to the buyer, of a quantity greater than the amount called for by the contract does not constitute an appropriation of goods to the buyer's contract . . . sufficient to pass property in any of the goods." Further, said Judge Lehman, the sellers had exceeced the "shipment" authority given to them by Lamborn and had not really complied with the contract. "The plaintiffs never agreed to purchase an undivided share in a mass; they never authorized shipment of 1,200 boxes of apples as part of a mass or even as part of a pool car, for their contract refers to a specific carload and to 1,200 boxes of apples to be ascertained and appropriated before shipment and no title to any apples has ever passed to the plaintiffs."

Identification

Which goods are for this buyer?

Identification is the act of specifying exactly which goods are to be delivered by the seller to the buyer to satisfy the terms of a particular **shipment contract.** Identification may be made by either the seller or the buyer, in any manner they agree to have it made. As an important change from prior law, the goods do not necessarily have to be in "deliverable condition" per the terms of the contract, for identification to occur. If the parties so agree, individual shares of a mass of fungible goods can be "identified," and thus sold, even though these shares have not yet been parceled out. For example, the parties could agree to buy and sell one half of the fuel oil in Penn-Central railroad car no. 35790; that would be a sufficient identification.

In the absence of any specific agreement, Section 2–501 says that identification is presumed to occur: *(a)* when the contract is made, if it is for goods already existing and identified in the parties' negotiations (a particular used car, for example); *(b)* for future goods generally, when the goods are "shipped, marked, or otherwise designated" by the seller (when the seller tags one new car in an inventory with the buyer's order number, for example); or *(c)* for agricultural products such as crops and the young of animals when the crops are planted and the as-yet-unborn young are conceived.

Once identification has occurred, ownership interests can then be passed to the buyer as the parties wish. "Special property" and "insurable interest" are presumed to pass to the buyer as soon as identification occurs.

Special Property

The first ownership stick

The special property interest, which the UCC gives to the buyer once particular goods have been identified to the contract, is a very different concept. Nothing like it existed under pre-Code law. The purpose of this new Code interest is to provide some protection for the buyer, both as to the seller and as to third parties, as soon as the buyer's goods have been identified, even though the buyer is not yet technically "the owner" of the goods, that is, legal title has not yet passed to the buyer.

In addition to an "insurable interest," the buyer's special property interest gives the buyer a package of three rights against the goods:

a. The buyer has the right to inspect the goods at a reasonable time and place.

b. The buyer has the right to recover damages that the buyer sustains if a third party wrongfully interferes with the buyer's possession of the identified goods.

c. The buyer has a right to sue for possession of the identified goods where the seller refuses to deliver them and the buyer can't get substitute goods or where the seller goes insolvent within 10 days after receiving the first installment on the contract price.

Insurable Interest

The second ownership stick

As soon as the goods are identified, the Code gives the buyer an *insurable interest,* meaning that the buyer can then get a valid insurance policy protecting the buyer against financial losses relating to these goods. The extent to which a preexisting "blanket" insurance policy on all property "owned" by the buyer would apply to such identified goods has not yet been determined in most states. Even so, this question can be resolved by a carefully drafted policy provision.

More than one person may have an insurable interest in the same goods at the same time. This does not mean that several persons will recover for the same damages, but that several persons may suffer different financial losses when the goods are lost or damaged. Each such person has an insurable interest to the extent of his or her potential loss. The seller, for example, retains an insurable interest so long as it holds title to the goods or a security interest against the goods. Where the goods are shipped or stored, the carrier or the warehouse has an insurable interest in the goods while they are in its possession. Any party with an insurable interest in the goods can sue a third party who has caused a financial loss by injuring the goods.

Title

The third ownership stick

The concept of *title* generally refers to legal ownership, with all its attendant rights and liabilities. For the purpose of Article 2, however, title is given a much more restricted meaning, since most of the litigations between the buyer and the seller, and even some litigations involving third parties, are solved by using other ownership interests and the location of the legal title is irrelevant. Title is still an important concept because even under the Code many cases involving third parties will depend on whether the buyer or the seller had title to the goods at some particular point in time. Such cases might involve liability for required taxes, registration, or insurance on the goods, or liability

■ **EXHIBIT 19–1**

Passing of Title (presumptions)

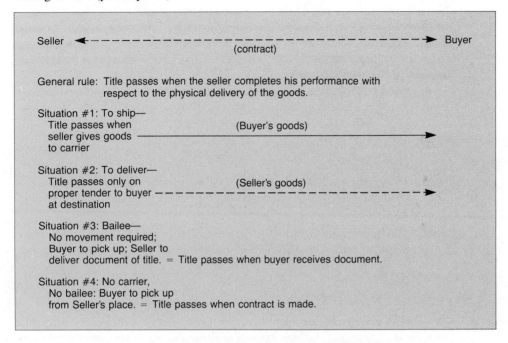

Seller ◄ – ► Buyer
(contract)

General rule: Title passes when the seller completes his performance with
respect to the physical delivery of the goods.

Situation #1: To ship—
Title passes when
seller gives goods ——————— (Buyer's goods) ————————————►
to carrier

Situation #2: To deliver—
Title passes only on
proper tender to buyer – – – – – – – – (Seller's goods) – – – – – – – – – – ►
at destination

Situation #3: Bailee—
No movement required;
Buyer to pick up; Seller to
deliver document of title. = Title passes when buyer receives document.

Situation #4: No carrier,
No bailee: Buyer to pick up
from Seller's place. = Title passes when contract is made.

resulting from use of the goods, or adverse claims against the goods by the creditors of the buyer or the seller.

The main presumptions as to when title passes are contained in Section 2–401; this section states a general rule and four specific applications. These presumptions are all based on common sense; if the parties want a special result, they will have to so expressly agree. On one point, however, the Code controls the parties' agreement: a seller cannot retain title to goods which have been shipped to, or delivered to, the buyer. The general rule is that title passes to the buyer "at the time and place at which the seller completes his [or her] performance with respect to the physical delivery of the goods." This rule applies even though, for financing reasons, using the goods as collateral for the unpaid balance of the purchase price, the seller has reserved a "security interest" in the goods, or even though a "document of title" (bill of lading or warehouse receipt) is to be delivered to the buyer at a different time or place. These documents are discussed more fully later in this chapter.

—Limits on parties' agreement
—General presumption

Four Specific Applications. The four specific rules cover the two common arrangements where the goods are to be moved as part of the contract for sale and the two common situations not involving any further movement of the goods by the seller. If the contract merely authorizes the seller to make the arrangement for shipping the goods to the buyer, but it does not require the seller to deliver the goods at their destination, title is presumed to pass at the time and place of shipment. In the other "movement" case, where the seller is required to make delivery of the goods at their destination, a proper

—Two movement situations

tender means that the seller must get the goods to the place where they are to be delivered to the buyer and give the buyer any notice reasonably necessary to enable the buyer to receive delivery.

In the two "nonmovement" cases, the goods are already at the location where the buyer is to take delivery. In one case, they are in the possession of a third party (usually a warehouse); in the other, they are in the seller's possession. If the seller is not required to move the goods but is required to deliver to the buyer a "document of title" (warehouse receipt or bill of lading) covering them, title is presumed to pass when the required document is delivered. (In this case the seller is only required to give the buyer the document. The buyer can then go over to the warehouse whenever he or she wants to and get the goods.)

Where the seller is not required to move the goods or to deliver any documents, and the specific goods to which the contract applies have already been identified, title is presumed to pass "at the time and place of contracting"; that is, at the instant the contract is made. And the Code assumes that the place of delivery is the seller's place of business. In the typical used-car purchase, for example, "title" to the used car passes to the buyer at the instant he or she says, "I'll take it," since the seller has possession and is not required to move the car to any other location to make delivery. In most states this presumption would hold even though the state's motor vehicle registration requirements had not yet been complied with, as seen in the *Waggoner* v. *Wilson* case.

The language in Wilson's State Farm auto insurance policy is fairly typical, and is there for a reason. Car insurers don't want to be held liable for all accidents with all the cars owned by a family if they have insured only *one* car. For instance, Mom, Dad, and Junior each has a car to drive. Mom buys a State Farm policy on *her* car. She is, of course, covered under *her* policy while she's driving *her* car. But if she is listed as a co-owner of the car Dad drives, she is *not* covered under *her* policy when she drives *Dad's* car. And if she has registered Junior's car in her name, she is *not* covered under *her* policy when she drives that car. Even if she was not listed as owner or co-owner on either of the other two cars, she would not be covered under her policy while driving either of them if any family member could use any of the three cars at any time. Mom *would* be covered under her policy if she had an accident while driving a rented car.

In the *Waggoner* case, Arlene Wilson has a State Farm policy on her new car, but has cancelled her insurance on the T-Bird she is selling to Beucker. She then had an accident while driving the T-Bird.

WAGGONER v. WILSON

507 P.2d 482 (Colorado, 1973)

FACTS   Plaintiff was struck by a 1961 Ford Thunderbird driven by the defendant. Plaintiff received a judgment against the defendant in the sum of $39,727.80. Defendant did not appeal, and the judgment became final. Subsequently, plaintiff served a writ of garnishment upon State Farm Mutual Automobile Insurance Company. State Farm filed an answer. The court determined that State Farm was not indebted to the defendant,

—Two nonmovement situations

and, hence, was not subject to garnishment by plaintiff. Judgment was entered against plaintiff, who appeals.

State Farm admitted that it had issued an automobile liability policy insuring Arlene Louise Wilson, defendant, regarding a certain automobile she owned other than the 1961 Ford Thunderbird involved in the accident. Such coverage would satisfy plaintiff's judgment only if defendant were driving a "non-owned automobile," defined by the policy as follows:

> Non-owned Automobile—means an automobile, trailer, or detachable living quarters unit, not
>
> (1) owned by,
> (2) registered in the name of, or
> (3) furnished or available for the frequent or regular use of the named insured, his spouse, or any relative of either residing in the same household, other than a temporary substitute automobile.

Charles Beucker was purchasing the T-Bird from defendant and her husband pursuant to an oral sales agreement entered into on June 10, 1969. Beucker had made payments to defendant and her husband, but neither the license plates nor the certificate of title had been transferred to him. Defendant and her husband delivered possession of the automobile to Beucker and retained the title as security for the balance of the purchase price.

ISSUE   Had title to the T-Bird passed to Beucker, so that it was "non-owned" by Wilson?

DECISION   Yes. Judgment against State Farm.

REASONS   **Judge Smith reviewed the UCC title rules.**

"The oral sales agreement was a sales contract covered by the Uniform Commercial Code. . . . Although the certificate of title was not transferred to Beucker, delivery of possession of the car to Beucker constituted a transfer of its ownership to him. . . . Notwithstanding the provision of C.R.S. 1963, 13–6–8, that no purchaser 'shall acquire any right, title or interest in and to a motor vehicle purchased by him unless and until he shall obtain . . . the certificate of title thereto,' nondelivery of the certificate of title does not prevent change of ownership as between the parties to the transaction. . . . Thus, as a matter of law, the automobile in question was not owned by defendant.

"The parties stipulated that defendant's name appeared on the records of the Department of Revenue as owners of the car at the time of the accident. Consequently, a question arises concerning the word 'registered' in the insurance contract. The concept of registration is commonly understood to be a function of the law of each state. 'Registered in the name of' should be construed to have the meaning accorded it by the applicable state law, especially where the phrase is used on an insurance company form given multistate distribution. Colorado law . . . provides in pertinent part:

> Whenever the owner of a vehicle registered under the provisions of this article transfers or assigns his title or interest thereto the registration of such vehicle shall expire . . .

As indicated above, defendant had transferred her interest in the automobile prior to the accident, and, consequently, the registration of the vehicle had expired at that time. Thus, under the terms of the policy, the automobile in question was not registered in the defendant's name at the time of the accident.

"The court found as a matter of fact that the automobile in question 'was not used by the Wilsons more than two or three times' in the four-month interval between the sale and the accident in which plaintiff was injured. The court also expressly found that defendant had obtained permission from Beucker to use the automobile on the date of the accident. These findings were supported by the evidence. . . .

"We conclude, as a matter of law, that the use shown by the evidence is not sufficient to establish that the car was 'furnished or available for the frequent or regular use of the insured.'

"Having determined the automobile in question was not owned by, registered in the name of, or available for the frequent or regular use of defendant it follows that, in the terms of the policy, the automobile in question was a 'non-owned automobile.' Therefore, defendant was entitled to coverage under her insurance policy with State Farm. Judgment is reversed and the cause remanded with directions to sustain plaintiff's writ of garnishment against State Farm Mutual Automobile Insurance Company and for the entry of appropriate orders thereon."

Return of Title to Seller.   Where title has already passed to the buyer under the above presumptions, it is passed back to the seller either by the buyer's rejection of the goods, whether the rejection is justified or not, or by the buyer's revocation of his or her previous acceptance, but only if such revocation is justified. In other words, if the buyer refuses delivery and sends the goods back, the goods again "belong to" the seller on the way back. But if the buyer has accepted the goods and *then* tries to revoke that acceptance by sending the goods back, title is not revested in the seller unless the buyer can show a justification for his or her action.

Risk of Loss

The fourth ownership stick

Article 2 treats "risk of loss" as a separate and distinct ownership interest. Stated most simply, *risk of loss* means responsibility for the goods. As between the buyer and the seller, who gets stuck for the value of the goods when they are destroyed or damaged by an "act of God" or by a third party. Who has to try to recover from the third party or from an insurance company?

Once the goods are identified, the parties can allocate the risk of loss on the goods in any way they wish. Merely giving the buyer a right to inspect the goods at a particular time and place does not postpone the passing of risk of loss, unless that result is also specified. If the parties have not made any specific agreement as to when risk of loss passes, Article 2 again provides a set of commonsense presumptions in section 2–509.

—Two movement situations

In the two "movement" cases, the presumptions for risk of loss are basically the same as those for the passing of title. If the seller is authorized to ship but is not required to deliver, risk passes when the goods are delivered to the carrier, even though the seller has reserved the right to possession (COD shipment) or a security interest against the goods. A seller who is required to deliver keeps the risk of loss until the goods arrive at their destination and are duly tendered to the buyer.

—Nonmovement situation with bailee

Where the goods are in the possession of a bailee, such as a warehouse or a carrier, and are to be delivered to the buyer without further movement to another place, risk of loss passes when any one of three things happens:

    a.   When the buyer receives a negotiable document of title on the goods.

    b.   When the buyer receives a nonnegotiable document of title or other written

■ **EXHIBIT 19–2**

Passing of Risk of Loss (presumptions)

No general rule.   As with title, a specific contract clause controls.

Situation #1: To ship—
 Risk passes when seller ————————————— (Goods at buyer's risk en route) ——————————————▶
 gives goods to carrier

Situation #2: To deliver—
 Risk passes only on   (Goods at seller's risk en route)
 proper tender to buyer – ▶
 at destination.

Situation #3: Bailee—
 No movement required:
 A. If negotiable document = When buyer gets document, buyer gets risk.
 B. If nonnegotiable document = Buyer gets risk when s/he gets document,
      and has had a reasonable time to present it to the bailee.
 C. If bailee acknowledges buyer's right to possession, buyer gets risk.

Situation #4: No carrier,
 No bailee, buyer to pick up:
 A. Buyer gets risk when non-merchant seller tenders goods.
 B. Buyer gets risk only on receipt of goods from merchant seller.

delivery order on the goods *and* has had a reasonable amount of time to present the bailee with it and to pick up the goods.

   c. When the bailee acknowledges the buyer's right to possession of the goods.

The reason for the difference between negotiable and nonnegotiable documents is that the negotiable document requires the carrier or the warehouse to give the goods to the bearer of the document, or to the order of someone named in the document. Whether issued to the bearer or to someone's order, the document itself thus indicates that someone other than the party who originally turned over the goods may present the document and demand redelivery. Since the carrier or warehouse is alerted to this possibility from the beginning of the transaction, no extra time is allowed for the buyer to present the document. Nonnegotiable documents require that buyers be given a reasonable chance to identify themselves and explain why they, rather than the sellers, are picking up the goods.

—Nonmovement situation with seller

Where the goods are in the seller's possession and the buyer is to come over and pick them up, there are two different rules as to when risk passes, depending on whether or not the seller is a merchant. Sellers who are not merchants pass risk when they tender delivery to the buyer; but sellers who are merchants do not pass risk to the buyer until actual receipt of goods by the buyer. This special "risk" rule where the seller is a merchant represents an important change from prior law.

—Effect of breach on risk of loss

Where the seller's tender of delivery or the seller's delivery "fails to conform to the contract" so as to give the buyer the right to reject the goods, the risk of loss stays with the seller until the seller "cures" the problem or until the buyer agrees to accept the goods anyway. Where the buyer rightfully revokes a prior acceptance, the seller must bear any loss not covered by the buyer's insurance. Where the buyer breaches after conforming goods have been identified to the contract but before risk has passed to the buyer, the buyer must bear any loss not covered by the seller's insurance. In these breach cases, the basic risk of loss rule is: "The bad guy loses." Carole Chevrolet is the "bad guy" in the next case.

JAKOWSKI v. CAROLE CHEVROLET, INC.

433 A.2d 841 (New Jersey, 1981)

FACTS   Stanley Jakowski bought a new 1980 automobile from Carole Chevrolet. As part of the contract, Carole promised to undercoat the car and to apply a polymer sealant to the exterior finish. When Jakowski picked up the car on May 19, 1980, these two operations had not been done. Carole realized what had happened the next day, called Jakowski and asked him to return the car for these treatments. Stanley brought the car back on May 22, and it was stolen from the lot that night, before the coatings had been applied.

ISSUE   Had risk of loss passed to the buyer?

DECISION   No. Judgment for buyer.

REASONS   Justice Newman said that this was a case under Section 2–510, rather than Section 2–509, since the goods as originally delivered did not conform to the contract.

"Seller argues that the risk of loss passed to the buyer upon his receipt of the auto. This is consistent with UCC § 2–509(3) pursuant to which the risk of loss passes to the buyer upon his receipt of the goods. Section 2–509(4), however, expressly provides that the general rules of § 2–509 are subject to the more specific provisions of § 2–510 which deals with the effect of breach upon risk of loss. . . .

"Application of this section to the instant facts requires that three questions be answered. First, did the car 'so fail to conform' as to give this buyer a right to reject it? If so, did the buyer 'accept' the car despite the nonconformity? Finally, did the seller cure the defect prior to the theft of the auto? . . .

"The contract provided that the car would be delivered with undercoating and a polymer finish, and it is disputed that it was delivered without these coatings. The goods were thus clearly nonconforming. . . .

"Secondly, did buyer 'accept' the auto by taking possession of it? . . . The mere taking of possession by the purchaser is not equivalent to acceptance. Before he can be held to have accepted, a buyer must be afforded a 'reasonable opportunity to inspect' the goods. . . .

"Seller's actions in this matter preclude analysis in conventional 'acceptance' terms. Buyer had no opportunity, indeed no reason to reject, given seller's own communication to buyer shortly after delivery, to the effect that the goods did not conform and that the seller was exercising its right to cure said nonconformity. . . .

"As to the final question of whether the seller effected a cure, there is no evidence—in fact defendant does not even contend—that cure was ever effected.

"Given the undisputed facts, the operation of § 2–510(1) is inescapable. The goods failed to conform, the buyer never accepted them, and the defect was never cured. Accordingly, the risk of loss remained on the seller and judgment is granted for plaintiff."

Right to Possession of the Goods

The fifth ownership stick

The Code also recognized that a party may have title and risk of loss and yet not have an immediate "right to the goods." One obvious case where this result occurs is the COD (collect on delivery) contract: When the seller ships the goods as agreed, the buyer has title, risk of loss, and a special property interest and an insurable interest in the goods, but does not yet have the right to possession because the COD term requires payment to get delivery. Another common separation of the right to possession from title and risk occurs when goods are shipped or stored by a carrier or a warehouse. Article 7 of the Code gives such persons a possessory "lien" for their services, meaning that they can hold (and if necessary sell) the goods until their charges are paid. Either the buyer or the seller may have title and risk of loss, but neither of them has the right to possession of the goods until the carrier or warehouse gets paid.

Security Interest

The sixth ownership stick

Finally, where the goods are being used as collateral to secure payment of the balance due on the contract price, the financing agency, which could be the seller, a bank, or other lender, has a "security interest" in them. Stated most simply, this *security interest* means that if the debtor defaults, the creditor, the "secured party," has the right to get possession of the goods, to resell them, and to apply the proceeds to pay off the balance due on the debt. Section 2–401(1) says that any attempt by the seller to withhold "title" on goods which are shipped or delivered to the buyer "is limited in effect to a reservation of a security interest." What the seller has to do is to make sure that there is a valid security interest. The legal requirements of such secured transactions are covered in Article 9 of the UCC; Chapters 24 and 25 will discuss secured transactions at greater length.

Special Sale Arrangements

The Code also provides specific rules to cover several frequently used special sale arrangements: sale on approval, sale or return, consignment, and sale by auction. Where the buyer has the option of returning goods even though they conform to the contract, the transaction is presumed to be a sale on approval if the buyer bought primarily for personal use, and a sale or return if the goods were purchased primarily for resale to others.

In a *sale on approval*, the buyer has possession of someone else's goods as a bailee, to use them according to the terms of the trial contract; the seller still "owns" the goods that is, the seller has both title and risk of loss. Title and risk do not pass to the buyer until the buyer accepts the goods, either expressly or by doing something which indicates an intent to exercise ownership, or until the agreed trial period expires with the buyer still in possession and not having notified the seller that they will be returned.

In a *sale or return,* title and risk pass to the buyer under the normal presumptions, but with the option of returning the goods in accordance with the terms of the contract. Any such "return" is at the buyer's risk and expense, unless otherwise agreed.

In a *consignment* arrangement, the "buyer" (a retail store, for example) is not really a buyer at all, but rather a bailee-agent who has possession of someone else's goods and the power to sell the goods to third parties. As between this *consignee,* the retail store, and the *consignor,* a manufacturer, for example, the consignor retains title and risk on the goods until they are sold to third parties. Out of fairness to the creditors of the consignee, however, the Code says that they can treat the transaction as if it were a sale or return, unless the consignee's creditors know generally that the consignee engages in such transactions or unless the consignor publicly files a financing statement under Article 9's provisions or posts a sign on the consignee's premises in accordance with an applicable state statute.

Auction rules

Section 2–328 contains some special "offer and acceptance" rules for sales by *auction.* When the auctioneer, Colonel Fasthammer, receives offers in the form of bids, his acceptance occurs when he raps his hammer (and hollers "Sold!") or in any other customary manner. Until the hammer falls, any bid can be withdrawn, but such a withdrawal does not revive any previous bid. Whether the goods have to be sold to the highest bidder depends on whether the sale is *with reserve* or *without reserve.* Unless specific notice is given otherwise, it is assumed that the auction is with reserve, meaning that the auctioneer "may withdraw the goods at any time until he announces completion of the sale." Since the goods are already identified and (usually) no further delivery by the seller is required, title and risk would be presumed to pass to the buyer when the auctioneer's acceptance occurs. In a sale without reserve, each bid is an acceptance of the auctioneer's offer to sell. Each such contract is conditional on there being no higher bid. The last, highest bid has thus formed a final contract, and title and risk would pass to that buyer when the auctioneer announces the end to bidding on that item.

■ SHIPMENT AND STORAGE OF GOODS

Bill of Lading—A Document of Title.   Most goods shipped have no specific title registration certificates. The shipper simply delivers the goods to the common carrier with instructions to transport and deliver them, or the common carrier comes to the residence or business of the shipper and picks up the goods with instructions as to their transportation and delivery.

Receipt, contract, and evidence of ownership

At the point where the shipper turns over possession to the common carrier a document showing ownership of the particular goods is necessary. This document is called a *bill of lading* if the transportation is by land or sea, and it is called an *air bill* if the transportation is by air. The bill of lading or air bill serves as both a receipt for the goods and as a contract which states the terms of the agreement to transport and deliver the goods. Title to the goods may be transferred from the shipper to another person or organization by transferring the bill of lading or air bill.

Negotiable versus nonnegotiable

A bill of lading or an air bill can be negotiable or nonnegotiable. If the bill is negotiable, it will state that the goods are to be delivered to the *bearer* of the bill or to the *order* of a specific person or organization. If the bill simply consigns the goods to a specific person or organization at the point of delivery, then it is nonnegotiable and it is called a **straight bill of lading** or a **straight air bill.**

The bill of lading or air bill must describe the goods. Typically, it will state the weight of the goods and describe the number of items and the content of the shipment in such a manner that the person receiving the goods will be able to identify them as those which were entrusted to the carrier for shipment.

Article 7 of the UCC contains specific provisions governing the issuance and use of bills of lading. Normally, the bill of lading is issued to the shipper. The shipper can then mail the bill of lading to the person or organization that is to receive the goods at their final destination. However, UCC Section 7–305(1) allows the shipper to request that the common carrier issue the bill of lading directly to the person or organization receiving the goods at the final destination or at any other place which the shipper may request. Obviously, situations arise where mailing the bill of lading to the receiver of the goods would be unwise. It would be better to have the bill of lading issued by the carrier directly to the person or organization receiving the goods prior to, or at the time of, delivery.

If the bill of lading is negotiable, then the carrier may not deliver the goods without getting the bill of lading properly indorsed by the person or organization receiving them. If the goods are shipped under a nonnegotiable bill of lading, the carrier can simply deliver them to the person or organization named as consignee in the bill, and the bill of lading need not be indorsed by the receiving party. With a nonnegtiable bill, the carrier must verify that the receiving party is in fact the party to whom the shipment was supposed to be delivered. If the carrier delivers the goods to the wrong person, the carrier will be responsible to the shipper.

Definition of a Warehouse. A **public warehouse** presents itself to the public as a business engaged in storing goods for members of the public for a fee. A **private warehouse** is a storage business which is not open to the public, but only leases storage space to one person or company or to a select number of persons or companies.

Contents of warehouse receipt

Warehouse Receipts—Another Document of Title. Every warehouse that stores goods for the public must issue a **warehouse receipt** to the bailor when the bailor leaves goods for storage. There is no specific statutory form that must be used. However, the receipt must contain certain essential terms, such as the *location* of the warehouse, the *date* the receipt was issued, and the *consecutive number* of the receipt. It also must contain a statement about *delivery*. Will the goods be delivered to the *bearer* of the receipt, or to the *order* of a specified person? If so, the receipt is negotiable. Or, will the goods be delivered only to a specified person, thus making the receipt nonnegotiable? The rates to be charged must also be stated, and the goods described. The receipt must be signed by an agent of the warehouse, and if any advances have been made or any liabilities incurred, an explanation must be made on the receipt. The special duties of both carriers and warehouse are discussed further in Chapter 33.

Common Shipping Terms. Since in the "movement" cases the location of title and risk will probably depend on whether the seller has met contractual duties, it is important to know what certain commonly used shipping terms require the seller to do. In addition to the *COD* (collect on delivery) term discussed earlier, the abbreviations *FOB* (free on board), *FAS* (free alongside), and *CIF* (cost, insurance, and freight) are commonly used.

The FOB term is used in combination with a named city, for example, FOB Chicago. The seller's obligation is to get the goods into the possession of a *carrier* and to get them to the specified place. Whether this is a shipment contract or a delivery contract depends on whether "Chicago" is the seller's city or the buyer's city. If the FOB contract also specifies a vessel, car, or other vehicle, the seller must also "at his own expense and risk load the goods on board"; in other words, the seller is responsible for getting the goods into the buyer's designated carrier.

The FAS term is used in connection with a particular vessel, for example, FAS *S.S. Mariner*. The seller must deliver the goods alongside that vessel in accordance with the port's custom, or on a dock specified by the buyer. The seller must also get a receipt for the goods and tender it to the buyer so that the buyer can get a bill of lading from the vessel's operator.

The CIF contract provides the buyer with the convenience of making one lump-sum payment to the seller, after the seller has made all the arrangements for shipping the goods. The seller is obligated to pay the carrier's freight charges (or to get credit from the carrier) and to obtain the customary insurance policy on the goods while they are in transit. (A *C&F* contract omits the insurance requirement.) The seller then forwards to the buyer all the required paperwork: the freight receipt, the bill of lading, the insurance policy, the seller's own invoice for the package price, and a negotiable draft for the total invoice price. Normally these papers will be sent to a bank in the buyer's city where the buyer has made credit arrangements; the bank has instructions to give the buyer the negotiable bill of lading (without which the buyer can't get the goods) only after the buyer signs the negotiable draft, thus indicating that the buyer will pay the draft when it becomes due. The bank then buys the draft from the seller and sends the seller the cash. Everyone's happy: the buyer has the goods and whatever credit period is specified in the draft in which to pay for them; the seller has the cash, with no risk of nonpayment; and the buyer's bank earns the interest rate provided for in the draft. This very common transaction shows how Articles 2, 3, 4, and 7 come together to cover the various aspects of a single commercial transaction.

The importance of the seller's complying exactly with the agreed shipping terms can be seen in the following case.

RHEINBERG-KELLEREI GMBH v. VINEYARD WINE CO.

281 S.E.2d 425 (North Carolina, 1981)

FACTS   Plaintiff, a West German wine producer and exporter, sued for $8,621.25, the purchase price of a shipment of wine sold to defendant and lost at sea en route between Germany and the United States. Defendant, a North Carolina corporation, is a distributor of wine, buying and selling foreign and domestic wines at wholesale. Frank Sutton is a licensed importer and seller of wines. During 1978–79 Sutton served as an agent for plaintiff and was authorized to sell and solicit orders for plaintiff's wine in the United States. During 1978 and early 1979, Randall F. Switzer, then of Raleigh, North Carolina, was a broker soliciting orders of wine on behalf of several producers and brokers, including Sutton, on a commission basis. Defendant gave Switzer an order for 620 cases.

On or about November 27, 1978, plaintiff issued notice to Sutton giving the date of the shipment, port of origin, vessel, estimated date of arrival, and port of arrival. Sutton did not give any of such information to defendant or to Switzer and did not notify defendant of anything. There was never any communication of any kind between plaintiff and defendant, and defendant was not aware of the details of the shipment.

Plaintiff delivered the wine ordered by defendant, consolidated in a container with the other wine, to a shipping line on November 29, 1978, for shipment from Rotterdam to Wilmington, North Carolina, on board the *MS Munchen*. Defendant did not request the plaintiff to deliver the wine ordered to any particular destination, and plaintiff and its agent, Sutton, selected the port of Wilmington for the port of entry into the United States. The entire container of wine was consigned by plaintiff to defendant, with freight payable at destination by defendant.

After delivering the wine to the ocean vessel for shipment, plaintiff forwarded the invoice for the entire container, certificate of origin, and bill of lading, to its bank in West Germany, which forwarded the documents to Wachovia Bank and Trust Company, in Charlotte, North Carolina. The documents were received by Wachovia on December 27, 1978. The method of payment for the sale was for plaintiff's bank in West Germany to send the invoice, certificate of origin, and bill of lading to Wachovia whereupon defendant was to pay the purchase price to Wachovia and obtain the shipping documents. Wachovia then would forward payment to plaintiff's bank, and defendant could present the shipping documents to the carrier to obtain possession.

Wachovia mailed to defendant on December 29, 1978 a notice requesting payment for the entire consolidated shipment, by sight draft in exchange for documents. The notice was not returned by the post office to the sender.

On or about January 24, 1979, defendant first learned that the container of wine left Germany in early December 1978 aboard the *MS Munchen,* which was lost in the North Atlantic with all hands and cargo aboard between December 12 and December 22, 1978.

Defendant did not receive any wine from plaintiff and did not pay Wachovia for the lost shipment. Plaintiff released the sight draft documents to Frank Sutton. Defendant was not furnished with any copy of said documents until receiving some in March and April 1979 and the others through discovery after this action was filed.

The order and "Special Instructions," mailed by Sutton to plaintiff, but not to defendant, provided: (1) "Insurance to be covered by purchaser;" (2) "Send a 'Notice of Arrival' to both the customer and to Frank Sutton & Company;" and (3) "Payment may be deferred until the merchandise has arrived at the port of entry."

From judgment in favor of the defendant, dismissing plaintiff's action, plaintiff appealed.

ISSUE   Had risk of loss passed to the buyer?

DECISION   No. Judgment affirmed.

REASONS   Judge Wells spoke for the court:

"The first question presented by plaintiff's appeal is whether the trial court was correct in its conclusion that the risk of loss for the wine never passed from plaintiff to defendant due to the failure of plaintiff to give prompt notice of the shipment to defendant.

. . . Our review on appeal is limited to determination of whether the facts found support the court's conclusions and the judgment entered. . . .

"All parties agree that the contract in question was a 'shipment' contract, i.e., one not requiring delivery of the wine at any particular destination. . . . The Uniform Commercial Code, as adopted in North Carolina, dictates when the transfer of risk of loss occurs in this situation. . . .

"Before a seller will be deemed to have 'duly delivered' the goods to the carrier, however, he must fulfill certain duties owed to the buyer. In the absence of any agreement of the contrary, these responsibilities [are] set out in G.S. 25–2–504. . . .

"The trial court concluded that the plaintiff's notification of the defendant of the shipment after the sailing of the ship and the ensuing loss was not 'prompt notice' within the meaning of G.S. 25–2–504, and therefore, the risk of loss did not pass to defendant upon the delivery of wine to the carrier pursuant to the provisions of G.S. 25–2–509(1)(a). We hold that the conclusions of the trial court were correct. The seller is burdened with special responsibilities under a shipment contract because of the nature of the risk of loss being transferred. . . . Where the buyer, upon shipment by seller, assumes the perils involved in carriage, he must have a reasonable opportunity to guard against these risks by independent arrangements with the carrier. The requirement of prompt notification by the seller, as used in G.S. 25–2–504(c), must be construed as taking into consideration the need of a buyer to be informed of the shipment in sufficient time for him to take action to protect himself from the risk of damage to or loss of the goods while in transit. . . . It would not be practical or desirable, however, for the courts to attempt to engraft onto G.S. 25–2–504 of the UCC a rigid definition of prompt notice. Given the myriad factual situations which arise in business dealings, and keeping in mind the commercial realities, whether notification has been 'prompt' within the meaning of UCC will have to be determined on a case-by-case basis, under all the circumstances. . . .

"In the case at hand, the shipment of wine was lost at sea sometime between December 12 and December 22, 1978. Although plaintiff did notify its agent, Frank Sutton, regarding pertinent details of the shipment on or about November 27, 1978, this information was not passed along to defendant. The shipping documents were not received by defendant's bank for forwarding to defendant until December 27, 1978, days after the loss had already been incurred. Since the defendant was never notified directly or by the forwarding of shipping documents within the time in which its interest could have been protected by insurance or otherwise, defendant was entitled to reject the shipment pursuant to the terms of G.S. 25–2–504(c)."

| **SIGNIFICANCE OF THIS CHAPTER** | Although millions of sales contracts are made and performed each day without any problem ever arising, things go wrong in some cases. One of the parties fails to perform properly, or the goods are lost without the fault of either, or a third party asserts claims against the goods or otherwise tries to interfere with the transaction. The law needs to provide a set of rules to deal with these problem situations. The Code's approach is to provide a set of presumptions as to when the various ownership interests in the goods pass from the seller to the buyer, or exist in favor of third parties. |

As between the buyer and the seller, the most important presumptions are those dealing with risk of loss, since most such cases will involve that issue.

Where one or more third parties are involved in the dispute, the case will usually require application of the presumptions for the other ownership interests: special property, insurable interest, title, right to possession, and security interest. A case pitting the seller or the buyer against a third party will usually have to be decided by applying the rules for one of these other five ownership interests. Both the parties to the sales transaction and third parties such as financing agencies thus need to know the rules governing the transfer of the various ownership interests from seller to buyer.

DISCUSSION CASE

LUMBER SALES, INC. v. JULIOUS BROWN, d/b/a JULIOUS BROWN LUMBER COMPANY
469 S.W.2d 888 (Tennessee, 1971)

FACTS: On November 6, 1968, the defendant purchased from plaintiff five carloads of lumber, which the plaintiff agreed to deliver to defendant at a certain railroad siding near Radnor Yards in Nashville, Tennessee, which siding was designated by the railroad carrier as No. 609–A.

Plaintiff contends that all five carloads of lumber were delivered to defendant at said railroad siding in Nashville, Tennessee, and the defendant admits that four carloads thereof were received by him, but he denies that the fifth carload of lumber, which was to consist of two-by-four pine studs, was ever delivered to him or received by him.

The Circuit Judge gave a judgment for plaintiff for $5,163.20 and costs. Defendant appeal(s).

The railroad siding at which the lumber was to be delivered is located about one-half mile from the defendant's place of business and is known as a "team track," which means that it is available for use by several parties, including the defendant. Track location 609–A on this siding is a point where a loading platform is located.

During the early morning hours of November 27, 1968, the Louisville and Nashville Railroad Company placed a boxcar loaded with lumber for the defendant on this siding at track location 609–A.

This boxcar was designated as NW 54938, and it was inspected by an employee of the carrier between 8:00 A.M. and 8:30 A.M. on November 27, 1968, at which time it was found loaded with cargo and so designated upon the carrier's records.

At 11:07 A.M. on November 27, 1968, the carrier notified one of defendant's employees that the carload of lumber had been delivered at track location 609–A.

At approximately 4:00 P.M. on that same day an employee of the carrier again inspected this boxcar at track location 609–A, found one of the seals on it to be broken, and resealed it at that time. The evidence does not show whether the car was still loaded with cargo at that time or not.

The following day, November 28, was Thanksgiving Day, and the record does not disclose that the carrier inspected the boxcar on that date. But on November 29, 1968, between 8:00 A.M. and 8:30 A.M. an employee of the carrier inspected the car and found it empty.

∎

Judge Puryear:
From evidence in the record before us it is impossible to reach any logical conclusion as to what happened to this carload of lumber without indulging in speculation and conjecture, but the defendant earnestly insists that he did not unload it and there is no evidence to the contrary. . . .

The trial Court held that the risk of loss in this case did, in fact, pass to the defendant buyer. . . .

There is competent evidence in the record which shows that on November 27, 1968, at 11:07 A.M. the carrier notified the defendant's employee, Mr. Caldwell, at defendant's business office, that the carload of lumber had been delivered at track location 609–A. Mr. Caldwell did not testify, so this evidence is uncontroverted.

There is no evidence in the record to the effect that the defendant declined to accept delivery at that time or asked for a postponement of such delivery until a later time.

The defendant testified that it would normally require about four or five hours for him and his employees to unload a carload of lumber and that on November 27, 1968, he and his employees were so busily engaged in other necessary work that he could not unload the lumber on that day and since the following day was Thanksgiving, he could not unload it until November 29, at which time, of course, the carrier found the car to be empty.

The defendant also testified, on cross-examination, as follows:

Q. Mr. Brown, did you, in fact see NW 54938?
A. I did see that car somewhere on some track.
Q. And that was at Radnor Yards?
A. I said I seen the car on some track because I have a crossmark where I have seen the car. When I see a car I put a crossmark. When I unload a car I mark him out.
Q. All right, Mr. Brown, let me ask you this: Is this your records right here?
A. Yes.

[*Tendering documents.*]

Q. All right, sir, so you have—now, these are your business records?
A. Yes, sir, I keep that in my car, I go by the railroad and check for my cars. I knew several cars were coming in at that time.
Q. Yes, sir, and you keep this memo in your car?
A. In my car, so when I go to breakfast I go by and check; when I go to lunch I go by and check. At night I check. I carry the bookkeeper home. I have a night-time bookkeeper, and when I carry the bookkeeper home I go by and check.
Q. All right, sir, you put down in your book NW 54938 and you put a check by it, is that correct, sir?
A. That is correct.
Q. All right.
A. That shows I have seen the car.
Q. You have physically seen the car?
A. Yes.
Q. Now, does that mean, also, that you have opened the door on the car to check its contents?

A. No, sir, it does not.
Q. Then when you have unloaded it you scratch it off, is that correct, sir?
A. That is right, sir. . . .

One Kenneth E. Crye, freight agent of the carrier, Louisville and Nashville Railroad Company, testified that on Thanksgiving Day, November 28, he saw what he believed to be a railroad car being unloaded at track location 609–A, but he could not identify the car or the persons whom he believed to be unloading it. He qualified this testimony by saying that he was not positive that the car was being unloaded, but there was some lumber and some kind of activity on the platform, none of which appeared to be unusual. . . .

Counsel for defendant argues that the lumber in question was not duly "so tendered as to enable the buyer to take delivery." . . .

However, this argument seems to be based upon the premise that it was not convenient for the defendant to unload the lumber on November 27, the day on which it was delivered at track location 609–A and defendant was duly notified of such delivery.

This was an ordinary business day, and the time of 11:07 A.M. was a reasonable business hour. If it was not convenient with the defendant to unload the lumber within a few hours after being duly notified of delivery, then he should have protected himself against risk of loss by directing someone to guard the cargo against loss by theft and other hazards.

To hold that the seller or the carrier should, under the circumstances existing in a case of this kind, continue to protect the goods until such time as the buyer may find it convenient to unload them would impose an undue burden upon the seller or the carrier and unnecessarily obstruct the channels of commerce. . . . 2–509 does not impose such a burden upon the seller, in the absence of some material breach of the contract for delivery, and we think a reasonable construction of such language only requires the seller to place the goods at the buyer's disposal so that he has access to them and may remove them from the carrier's conveyance without lawful obstruction, with the proviso, however, that due notice of such delivery be given to the buyer. . . .

[T]he judgment of the trial court is affirmed.

■ IMPORTANT TERMS AND CONCEPTS

goods	merchant	bill of lading	FOB
future goods	warranty	air bill	CIF
contract to sell	special property	COD	insurable interest
fungible goods	shipment contract	carrier	title
price	document of title	sale or return	risk of loss
		auction with reserve	right to possession

security interest   warehouse
existing goods   sale on approval
identification   consignment sale
delivery contract   auction without reserve
warehouse receipt   FAS
tender of delivery   C & F

■ QUESTIONS AND PROBLEMS FOR DISCUSSION

1. What is "identification" in a sale of goods contract, and when does it occur?
2. What is the buyer's "special property" in the goods, and when does it pass to the buyer?
3. When does the seller have an insurable interest in the goods which are the subject-matter of a sale of goods contract?
4. When do title and risk of loss pass to the buyer in a delivery contract?
5. Shabby Trading Company sold used, scrap, and waste fabrics, which were baled up, sent to cloth manufacturing companies, and used by them in the production of new cloth materials. Shabby sent 40 bales to Margo Corporation, one of its regular buyers. Margo told Shabby that it could only use five bales at that time, because its production of cloth had slowed down. Shabby told Margo to store the remaining 35 bales at Margo's factory, and to send payment as it used any of those 35 bales. Margo agreed to this arrangement. Margo went bankrupt about six months later, not having used any of the remaining 35 bales. Shabby says those 35 bales belong to it and are not part of the debtor's (Margo) assets. Margo's trustee in bankruptcy is refusing to return the 35 bales, claiming them as an asset of Margo's. Who is right, and why?
6. About 5 P.M. on December 26, 1983, Irwin Busse telephoned Decker's place of business in Piqua, Ohio, and bought a truckload of dressed hogs for Armour, at a price of $8,885.51. The hogs were to be shipped C & F to Western Pork Packers, Inc. in Worchester, Massachusetts. The truck left Piqua at 12:25 P.M. on December 27. Sometime before 3 P.M. on December 28, the truck driver called Armour's manager in Worchester and reported mechanical trouble with the truck. The manager said that delivery by 6 A.M. on December 29 would be acceptable, but the truck did not arrive until December 31, at which time Armour refused the shipment. Decker resold the shipment for $7,203.99 and sued for damages. Armour's written confirmation indicated its "desire to unload these hogs not later than 3:00 P.M. Friday 12/28 and as much sooner as possible." Should Decker collect damages? Explain.
7. EXIM Corporation bought 4,000 pounds of yarn from Knitwear Corporation at $1.35 per pound, to be loaded into a container at the seller's premises for reshipment to South America. EXIM had a trucking company deliver an empty semitruck container to the seller's premises. Knitwear loaded the container with the yarn and notified EXIM that the container was ready to be picked up. Before EXIM's driver appeared, a thief drove up with another semicab, signed for the goods, hooked up the container, and drove off. Seller sues for the contract price. Discuss and decide.
8. Freda Construction Company, working on a large electrical project, ordered three reels of burial cable from Cableus, Inc. By mistake, Cableus shipped one reel of burial cable and two reels of aerial cable, although all three cartons were labeled "burial cable." Freda's foreman rejected the two reels of aerial cable but left them at the construction site because of their size and weight. Cableus was notified of the rejection but did not come out to pick up the two reels. Freda was unable to reship the two reels because of a trucker's strike. About four months later, the two reels of aerial cable were stolen from the construction site. Cableus sues for the contract price for the two cables. Discuss and decide.

20

Warranties and Products Liability

CHAPTER OBJECTIVES

THIS CHAPTER WILL:

- Indicate the need for product liability rules.
- Summarize the traditional theories of product liability—fraud, innocent misrepresentation, mistake, and negligence.
- Explain the UCC changes on express warranties.
- Define the implied warranty of merchantability and its application.
- Define the implied warranty of fitness.
- Explain the UCC's limitations on disclaimers of warranties.
- Indicate how strict liability in tort applies to defective products.
- Discuss the defenses that may be available in a product liability case.
- Explain recent state and national changes in this area of the law.

Stop and think for a minute. How many times each day do you entrust your health and safety, and even your life, to a manufactured product? Your new electric blanket that you left on all night, the can of frozen orange juice that you opened for breakfast this morning (and the electric can opener that you used to open the orange juice), the car or bus that you used to get to school (and all the other motor vehicles that were on the highway at the same time)— a malfunction in any one of these or in thousands of other products that we encounter every day could produce sickness, injury, or even death. No product can be made absolutely safe, under any and all circumstances. Malfunctions do occur, with resulting personal injury, property damage, and financial loss. The law's function in this area is to provide the rules by which the burden of such losses will be allocated.

Early rule: Leave loss with party who suffered it

Earlier legal doctrine tended to "leave the loss where it was incurred"; that is, to force the injured parties to pay for their own injuries, or to buy their own insurance to cover such losses. The modern legal trend,which has accelerated sharply during the past two decades, is to pass these losses back up the chain of distribution, to sellers and manufacturers, as one of the costs of doing business. The net result of the modern product liability rules is that all of us as consumers will pay higher prices for products and that some of the smaller manufacturers in high-risk industries, such as chemicals and machinery, may be forced out of business because they cannot absorb these additional overhead costs. The courts' willingness to apply these modern theories of liability and to disallow traditional defenses has produced a crisis of major proportions and worldwide impact.

▪ PLAINTIFFS, DEFENDANTS, AND THEORIES OF LIABILITY

Manufacturers as defendants

In addition to the buyer of defective goods, other possible plaintiffs include members of the buyer's family and household, guests in the buyer's home, the buyer's employees and customers, and bystanders who have had no previous relationship with the buyer. In addition to the seller, possible defendants include the manufacturer or assembler of the product, the designer, the supplier of the defective component part, and any intermediate distributors. The availability of the manufacturer as a defendant becomes crucial in those cases where the seller is unable to pay the judgment, or where the injured buyer cannot remember where the brand name product that caused the injury was purchased, or where the injury resulted from long-continued use of the brand name product, such as lung cancer from smoking.

Modern courts have a wide selection of theories of liability which can be used to impose damages back up the chain of distribution: fraud, innocent misrepresentation, negligence, breach of express or implied warranty, and strict liability. Although these different theories of liability require different forms of proof and are subject to different defenses and different statutes of limitations, the courts are not always careful to distinguish which theory is being applied to produce liability in a particular case. (See Exhibit 20–1).

■ **EXHIBIT 20–1**
Theories of Liability, and Defenses

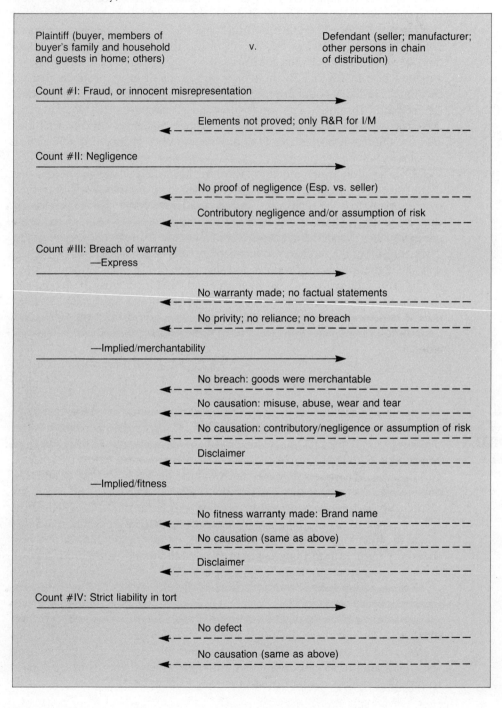

Plaintiff (buyer, members of buyer's family and household and guests in home; others)

v.

Defendant (seller; manufacturer; other persons in chain of distribution)

Count #I: Fraud, or innocent misrepresentation

Elements not proved; only R&R for I/M

Count #II: Negligence

No proof of negligence (Esp. vs. seller)

Contributory negligence and/or assumption of risk

Count #III: Breach of warranty
—Express

No warranty made; no factual statements

No privity; no reliance; no breach

—Implied/merchantability

No breach: goods were merchantable

No causation: misuse, abuse, wear and tear

No causation: contributory/negligence or assumption of risk

Disclaimer

—Implied/fitness

No fitness warranty made: Brand name

No causation (same as above)

Disclaimer

Count #IV: Strict liability in tort

No defect

No causation (same as above)

▪ FRAUD AND INNOCENT MISREPRESENTATION

The most obvious case for ***product liability*** is against the seller (or manufacturer) who has fraudulently misrepresented the product. The defrauder should clearly be held liable for all the losses which are caused by the misrepresentation, and probably for punitive damages as well. However, as noted in Part Two, Contract Law, fraud is easy to allege, but difficult to prove, and it probably applies to only a tiny fraction of product liability cases.

Restatement of Torts rule

As noted in Chapter 14, most courts permit rescission (but not recovery of damages) where a buyer has been damaged because of reasonable reliance on the seller's honest, but mistaken, statement of fact. The most recent version of the ***Restatement of the Law of Torts, Second,*** includes a revised Section 402B, which would substantially modify this general rule for sales of goods. Under Section 402B, a seller of goods is liable for "physical harm to a consumer" which results from reliance on the seller's material misrepresentation, even though "not made fraudulently or negligently" and even though "the consumer has not bought the chattel from or entered into any contractual relation with the seller." Essentially, what this section does is to restate the law of express warranty, without the requirement of ***privity*** (relationship) of contract.

▪ NEGLIGENCE

Like fraud, negligence is easy to allege but sometimes very difficult to prove. The fact that one part fails and causes injury is not much evidence of negligent manufacture, if tens of thousands of identical parts have been and are functioning properly. Indeed, in most cases such statistics would present a pretty convincing case that the manufacturer was doing an excellent job of product design, manufacture, and inspection. Where negligence can be proved against either the manufacturer or the seller or both, the injured party should be able to collect all the damages which result. Courts today generally recognize that the manufacturer's liability for negligence extends not only to the buyer of the product but also to other persons "whom he should expect to be endangered by its probable use" (if the product is not properly made). In a few situations, such as the case of the dead mouse in the bottle of cola, the courts may apply the doctrine of ***res ipsa loquitur*** ("the thing speaks for itself"), meaning that such things do not occur without negligent or purposeful conduct.

Proof of fault required

The following case is a classic application of negligence as a theory of product liability.

MACPHERSON v. BUICK MOTOR CO.

111 N.E. 1050 (New York, 1916)

FACTS

MacPherson bought a Buick from a retail dealer. He was injured while driving the car when the wooden spokes on one of the wheels crumbled into fragments. The defective wheel had been supplied to Buick Motor Company by a parts manufacturer. There was evidence tending to show that a reasonable inspection by Buick would have disclosed the defective wheel but that Buick failed to make such an inspection. The trial court held for the plaintiff.

ISSUE   Does a manufacturer owe a duty of care to the ultimate purchaser (consumer) who has bought the item from an independent distributor?

DECISION   Yes. Judgment affirmed.

REASONS   Justice Cardozo first discussed many of the precedents in the field of products liability. The basic New York case imposing such liability on the manufacturer-producer involved a mislabeled poison, where there was a clearly foreseeable risk of injury to persons other than the initial buyer-distributor. Other cases imposed liability for a collapsing scaffold and an exploding coffee urn. Justice Cardozo then concluded that the rule should be applied to any product which was dangerous if negligently made, not just to products which were inherently dangerous (such as poisons and explosives).

"From this survey of the decisions, there thus emerges a definition of the duty of a manufacturer which enables us to measure this defendant's liability. Beyond all question, the nature of an automobile gives warning of probable danger if its construction is defective. This automobile was designed to go 50 miles an hour. Unless its wheels were sound and strong, injury was almost certain. It was as much a thing of danger as a defective engine for a railroad. The defendant knew the danger. It also knew that the car would be used by persons other than the buyer. . . . The dealer was indeed the one person of whom it might be said with some approach to certainty that by him the car would not be used. Yet the defendant would have us say that he was the one person whom it was under a legal duty to protect. The law does not lead us to so inconsequent a conclusion. Precedents drawn from the days of travel by stagecoach do not fit the conditions of travel today. The principle that the danger must be imminent does not change, but the things subject to the principle change. They are whatever the needs of life in a developing civilization require them to be."

▪ BREACH OF WARRANTY

Old rule: Caveat emperor

Warranty is simply another word for guarantee. Depending on the facts and circumstances, the seller may make several different types of warranties on the goods being sold—warranties relating to the title to the goods or to the characteristics, qualities, or capabilities of the goods. In a simpler economy, where most sellers produced what they sold, where such manufactured goods as there were could be readily inspected and understood by the buyers, and where there was a rough equality in the bargaining power of the parties, *caveat emptor* ("let the buyer beware") may have been a workable rule for the law of sales. As products became more intricate and the distribution system became more impersonal, courts and legislatures saw the necessity of changing this early rule to provide more protection to buyers and users. It is one thing to say that Walter Woodcutter ought to be able to tell a bad ax from a good one when he deals with the village blacksmith; it is quite another to apply the same standard to a weekend hobbyist who buys a gasoline-driven chain saw from the local hardware store. The law of warranty has changed, and is still changing, to meet changes in the economy.

The UCC does not make any revolutionary changes in the law of warranties, but it does contain several provisions which extend warranty liability, or which

Warranty of good title

make such liability more difficult to disclaim. The Code sections cover three types of warranties: *express, implied,* and *title* warranties.

Although the title warranties are not specifically labeled "implied," they are such, in the sense that they are automatically written into the transaction by the law unless the parties agree otherwise or the circumstances clearly indicate otherwise. The seller guarantees that he or she has a good title to the goods, and that he or she has the right to sell them, and that there are no liens or encumbrances against them. In addition, where the seller is a merchant regularly dealing in such goods, there is also a warranty that the sale will not subject the buyer to suit by any third party claiming *infringement* on a patent, copyright, trademark, and the like.

■ EXPRESS WARRANTIES

Under the Code, express warranties are created in one of three ways:

1. An *affirmation of fact* or a promise, which relates to the goods and becomes part of the basis of the bargain.

2. A *description of the goods.*

3. A *sample or model* of the goods.

In each of these three cases, the assumption is that the seller and the buyer have specifically included the guarantee as an integral part of their sales contract.

An express warranty is thus virtually impossible to disclaim by form language in a written sales contract. It is not necessary to prove that the seller used the word *warranty* or *guarantee,* or had the specific intent to make a warranty. If the statement is a factual one and it is made in the context of negotiations on the sales contract, it is assumed to be a warranty unless the facts clearly indicate otherwise. In the case of a description, sample, or model, there is an express warranty that the goods will conform to the description, sample, or model. Even statements made in advertisements, if factual, may be held to be express warranties.

Factual statements = Warranties

■ IMPLIED WARRANTY OF MERCHANT-ABILITY

Where the seller is a merchant with respect to the type of goods involved in the contract, there is an implied warranty that the goods are "merchantable." This is a minimum quality guarantee, defined in UCC 2–314, which is imposed on the seller unless the buyer and the seller clearly agree otherwise. Among other requirements, to be merchantable goods must at least be "fit for the ordinary purposes for which goods are used"; be "adequately contained, packaged, and labeled as the agreement may require"; and "conform to the promises or affirmations of fact made on the container or label if any."

Merchantability = Guarantee of fair, average quality

Merchantability of Food. Prior to the adoption of the Code some courts drew a distinction between food purchased in carryout restaurants, to be consumed off the premises, and food purchased in service restaurants, where the diners ate on the premises. The latter case was held to be a services contract, not a sale of goods, and thus there was no implied warranty that food or drink purchased for consumption on the premises was "merchantable." The

Code specifically repudiates this distinction, so that your hamburger must be merchantable whether you eat it on or off the restaurant premises.

Whether a particular product is merchantable is a question of fact, to be decided in each case. There is still a split of authority where an injury is caused by the presence in a food product of something which is a natural part of the food at some stage of production. For example, is a chicken sandwich which contains a chicken bone unmerchantable? Some courts would say no, since the chicken bone is a "natural" part of a chicken. The same reasoning would apply to a cherry pit in cherry pie or cherry ice cream. Other courts apply a different test: What should the consumer reasonably expect to find in the food product? Clearly, no one expects to find a piece of glass in a hot dog. But neither does one expect to find a sharp piece of bone there—even though bones are a "natural" part of the beef and pork from which the hot dog was made. The "naturalness" of the object is therefore merely one fact to be considered in determining whether the food product is merchantable. Under this second test, a chicken sandwich with a bone is not merchantable, but a serving of roast chicken containing a chicken bone would be.

Similar fact questions may arise when other products are alleged to be unmerchantable. The fact that someone was injured while a product was being used does not always mean that the product was not merchantable. The Code does not require that the goods must be perfect, or that they will do anything and everything which the buyer wishes. They need only be fit for the *ordinary* purposes for which such goods are used. Experts in design and production may be called to testify on the safety and suitability of the goods. It may be appropriate to have the use of the goods demonstrated for the judge and jury. Even if the goods are found to be defective, it is also necessary to show that the injury complained of was caused by the defect, and not by the actions of the user or someone else.

Merchantability is at issue in the *Webster* case.

WEBSTER v. BLUE SHIP TEA ROOM, INC.

198 N.E.2d 309 (Massachusetts, 1964)

FACTS

On Saturday, April 25, 1959, about 1 P.M., the plaintiff, accompanied by her sister and her aunt, entered the Blue Ship Tea Room operated by the defendant. The group was seated at a table and supplied with menus.

This restaurant, which the plaintiff characterized as "quaint," was located in Boston "on the third floor of an old building on T Wharf, which overlooks the ocean."

The plaintiff, who had been born and brought up in New England, ordered clam chowder and crabmeat salad. Within a few minutes she received tidings to the effect that "there was no more clam chowder." Presently, there was set before her "a small bowl of fish chowder." "The fish chowder contained haddock, potatoes, milk, water, and seasoning. The chowder was milky in color and not clear. The haddock and potatoes were in chunks." "She agitated it a little with the spoon and observed that it was a fairly full bowl. . . . After three or four spoonfuls she was aware that something had lodged in her throat because she couldn't swallow and couldn't clear her throat by gulping and she could feel it." This misadventure led to two esophagoscopies at the

margin note: Guarantees on food products

Massachusetts General Hospital, in the second of which, on April 27, 1959, a fish bone was found and removed.

ISSUE   Was the fish chowder merchantable?

DECISION   Yes. Judgment for defendant.

REASONS   **Justice Reardon gave the opinion for the court:**
"We must decide whether a fish bone lurking in a fish chowder, about the ingredients of which there is no other complaint, constitutes a breach of implied warranty under applicable provisions of the Uniform Commercial Code. . . . As the judge put it in his charge, 'Was the fish chowder fit to be eaten and wholesome? . . . [N]obody is claiming that the fish itself wasn't wholesome. . . . But the bone of contention here—I don't mean that for a pun—but was this fish bone a foreign substance that made the fish chowder unwholesome or not fit to be eaten?' . . .

"We are asked to rule in such fashion that no chef is forced to 'reduce the pieces of fish in the chowder to minuscule size in an effort to ascertain if they contained any pieces of bone. In so ruling,' we are told (in the defendant's brief), 'the court will not only uphold its reputation for legal knowledge and acumen, but will, as loyal sons of Massachusetts, save our world-renowned fish chowder from degenerating into an insipid broth containing the mere essence of its former stature as a culinary masterpiece.' Notwithstanding these passionate entreaties we are bound to examine with detachment the nature of fish chowder and what might happen to it under varying interpretations of the Uniform Commercial Code.

"Chowder is an ancient dish preexisting even 'the appetites of our seamen and fishermen.' It was perhaps the common ancestor of the 'more refined cream soups, purees, and bisques.' The word *chowder* comes from the French *chaudière,* meaning a 'cauldron' or 'pot.' In the fishing villages of Brittany . . . 'faire la chaudière' means to supply a cauldron in which is cooked a mess of fish and biscuit with some savoury condiments, a hodgepodge contributed by the fishermen themselves, each of whom in return receives his share of the prepared dish. The Breton fisherman probably carried the custom to Newfoundland, long famous for its chowder, whence it was spread to Nova Scotia, New Brunswick, and New England. [*A New English Dictionary* (MacMillan, 1893). p. 386.] Our literature over the years abounds in references not only to the delights of chowder but also to its manufacture. A namesake of the plaintiff, Daniel Webster, had a recipe of fish chowder which has survived into a number of modern cookbooks and in which the removal of fish bones is not mentioned at all. One old-time recipe recited in the *New English Dictionary* study defines chowder as 'A dish made of fresh fish (esp. cod) or clams, stewed with slices of pork or bacon, onions, and biscuit. Cider and champagne are sometimes added. A chowder variant, cod 'Muddle,' was made in Plymouth in the 1890s by taking 'a three or four pound codfish, head added. Season with salt and pepper and boil in just enough water to keep from burning. When cooked, add milk and piece of butter.' . . . The recitation of these ancient formulae suffices to indicate that in construction of chowders in these parts in other years, worries about fish bones played no role whatsoever. This broad outlook on chowders has persisted in more modern cookbooks. The all-embracing Fannie Farmer states, in a portion of her recipe, fish chowder is made with a 'fish skinned, but head and tail left on. Cut off head and tail and remove fish from backbone. Cut fish in 2-inch pieces and set aside. Put head, tail and backbone broken in pieces, in stewpan; add 2 cups cold water and bring slowly to boiling point. . . .' The liquor thus produced from the bones is added to the balance of the chowder. . . .

"Thus, we consider a dish which for many long years, if well made, has been made generally as outlined above. It is not too much to say that a person sitting down in

New England to consume a good New England fish chowder embarks on a gustatory adventure which may entail the removal of some fish bones from his bowl as he proceeds. We are not inclined to tamper with age-old recipes by an amendment reflecting the plaintiff's view of the effect of the Uniform Commercial Code upon them. We are aware of the heavy body of case law involving foreign substances in food, but we sense a strong distinction between them and those relative to unwholesomeness of the food itself, e.g., tainted mackerel, and a fish bone in a fish chowder. Certain Massachusetts cooks might cavil at the ingredients contained in the chowder in this case in that it lacked the heartening lift of salt pork. In any event, we consider that the joys of life in New England include the ready availability of fresh fish chowder."

■ MERCHANT-ABILITY OF LEASED GOODS AND OF REAL ESTATE

New rules for leases and for real estate

As noted in the last chapter, courts have been extending the merchantability concept to cover other sorts of commercial transactions. Nearly all courts which have had to decide the question have imposed an implied warranty of merchantability on a business which rents goods to others. (See the *Cintrone* case in Chapter 33.) Many states now hold sellers of new houses to a similar standard. (See the discussion in Chapter 34.) Statutes in some states now require that real estate leased for residential purposes be reasonably "habitable." (See the discussion in Chapter 35.) In each of these situations, the courts and legislatures have determined that social policy requires that at least a minimum level of quality be guaranteed to the buyer or lessee. It now seems to be only a question of time until all states adopt similar rules.

■ IMPLIED WARRANTY OF FITNESS

Suitable for buyer's particular needs

The Code has also made an important extension in the seller's liability under the implied warranty of fitness. Where this warranty applies, the seller is not only guaranteeing that the goods are of fair, average quality and that they will do what most buyers expect them to do but also that they are suitable for the *particular* needs of the given buyer. The fitness warranty does not arise unless the buyer makes known to the seller some special needs and the fact that the buyer is relying on the seller to select or furnish suitable goods to meet those special needs. Prior to the Code, this fitness warranty could not apply where the goods were sold under a **brand name** or a **trade name.** Under UCC 2–315, a brand name on the goods is only one fact to be considered in determining whether the buyer relied on the seller to furnish suitable goods.

■ EXCLUSION OR MODIFICATION OF WARRANTIES

The Code generally makes it more difficult for the seller to disclaim warranties once they are made. For all practical purposes, it is impossible for the seller to disclaim an express warranty unless the entire transaction is renegotiated or unless the parties agree on a final written contract which does not include the express warranty and which indicates that it is intended as a complete statement of all the terms of the contract. With such a clause in the final contract, any prior express warranty would be excluded by the operation of the parol evidence section of Article 2 (2–202). Otherwise, where an express warranty has been made it overrides any attempted disclaimer of warranty to the extent that the two provisions are inconsistent.

Parol evidence rule

Code's requirements for disclaimers

Theoretically, at least, a seller can disclaim the implied warranties of merchantability and fitness by complying with the appropriate Code sections. As a practical matter, however, courts have been reluctant to enforce such disclaimers unless there is evidence that the buyer understood and intended that result. An example would occur where a used item is bought *as is* or where the buyer is also a business, such as TWA buying jumbo jets from Boeing. To stand *any* chance of being enforceable, the disclaimer of warranties must comply with the Code's requirements. Merchantability may be disclaimed either orally or in writing, but the word *merchantability* must be used, unless the goods are being bought "as is." Moreover, if the disclaimer is part of a written contract, it must be stated "conspicuously" in the writing. The fitness warranty cannot be excluded except by a writing, and the disclaimer must be a conspicuous part of the writing. UCC 1–201(10) defines *conspicuous* as being "so written that a reasonable person against whom it is to operate ought to have noticed it." A contrasting type style or color might be used to meet this requirement.

Even where all the Code's requirements for language and form of the disclaimer have been met, a court may still refuse to enforce the disclaimer, on the grounds that it is an attempt to avoid the seller's basic obligations of "good faith, diligence, reasonableness and care" (1–102[3]), or that it is *unconscionable* (2–302), or that it is against "public policy." The *Henningsen* case is perhaps the most significant single case on product liability. It started the modern trend by repudiating the "privity" requirement and by refusing to enforce the auto manufacturer's form disclaimer.

Code's limits on disclaimers

There are two other important limitations on warranty disclaimers. A seller who has made warranties to the buyer cannot "exclude or limit" the operation of Section 2–318, which extends the warranties automatically to "any natural person who is in the buyer's family or household or who is a guest in the buyer's home." Also, although Section 2–316 permits the parties to agree to *limit the remedies* for breach of warranty, Section 2–719 states that any limitation "of consequential damages for injury to the person in the case of consumer goods is prima facie unconscionable" (and therefore not enforceable).

The Code also provides that warranties, whether express or implied, are to be construed as consistent with each other and *cumulative,* (meaning that *all* the warranties which apply on the facts are made) unless such a construction is unreasonable.

HENNINGSEN v. BLOOMFIELD MOTORS, INC.

161 A.2d 69 (New Jersey, 1960)

FACTS
Clause Henningsen bought his wife a new Plymouth as a Mother's Day present. Ten days later, while driving the car, she heard a loud noise from under the hood; she said it "felt as if something had cracked." The steering wheel spun in her hands, and the car veered sharply to the right and crashed into a brick wall. The Henningsens sued Bloomfield (the dealer) and Chrysler (the manufacturer.) The sales contract stated that

the manufacturer's only warranty on the car was a promise to replace defective parts at the factory and that the warranty was given in lieu of all other warranties, express or implied. The trial court held for the plaintiffs, and the defendants appealed.

ISSUE   Should the disclaimer of warranties be given full effect?

DECISION   No. Judgment affirmed.

REASONS   Justice Francis held that the "large scale advertising programs" of Chrysler and others, to the extent that they contained factual representations, "constitute an express warranty running directly to a buyer who purchases in reliance thereon." He then noted that the form disclaimer was "a sad commentary upon the automobile manufacturers' marketing practices." Even though he recognized the fundamental principle of freedom of contract, he felt that this provision should not be enforced. "[W]arranties originated in the law to safeguard the buyer and not to limit the liability of the seller or manufacturer. It seems obvious in this instance that the motive was to avoid the warranty obligations which are normally incident to such sales. The language gave little and withdrew much. In return for the delusive remedy of replacement of defective parts at the factory, the buyer is said to have accepted the exclusion of the maker's liability for personal injuries arising from the breach of the warranty. An instinctively felt sense of justice cries out against such a sharp bargain. . . .

"The warranty before us is a standardized form designed for mass use. It is imposed upon the automobile consumer. He takes it or leaves it, and he must take it to buy an automobile. No bargaining is engaged in with respect to it. In fact, the dealer through whom it comes to the buyer is without authority to alter it; his function is ministerial— simply to deliver it. . . .

"The gross inequality for bargaining position occupied by the consumer in the automobile industry is thus apparent. There is no competition among the car makers in the area of express warranty. . . .

"In the area of sale of goods, the legislative will has imposed an implied warranty of merchantability as a general incident of sale of an automobile by description. The warranty does not depend upon the affirmative intention of the parties. It is a child of the law; it annexes itself to the contract because of the very nature of the transaction. . . . The disclaimer of the implied warranty and exclusion of all obligations except those specifically assumed by the express warranty signify a studied effort to frustrate that protection."

STRICT LIABILITY IN TORT

Historically, strict tort liability was imposed only on the keepers of dangerous wild animals and on persons who engaged in "extra-hazardous activities." What the courts have done, in effect, is to extend this theory of liability to manufacturers, sellers, and renters of products, so that the supplier of a defective product will be liable for the damage it causes, irrespective of any contract.

Plaintiff's case easier to prove

Of course, the plaintiff must still prove the case, but this is a much easier case to prove, and a much more difficult case to defend, than either negligence or breach of warranty. The fact that only this one product failed out of 5 million produced and used may prevent recovery for negligent manufacture, but it will not prevent recovery based on strict liability. The plaintiff need only prove that the product was made by the defendant, that it was "defective," that the defect caused the injury, and that damages have been sustained in a certain amount. The defendant can then try to show that the product was not defective, but instead failed as the result of normal wear and tear, or improper maintenance, or misuse by the plaintiff.

Definition of "defect"

Although strict liability for defective products has been recognized for at least 20 years, the concept is not uniformly applied by all states. The types of transactions covered differ, as do the third parties protected, and ways possible defenses may apply. Results may vary because different triers of fact analyze similar situations in different ways. Opinions as to what constitutes a *defect*, legally and factually, may differ. Is a car "defective" if its gasoline tank explodes when the car is struck from behind by another vehicle? How about a car with an unpadded dashboard? Almost by definition, if the vehicle is not made in accordance with U.S. government safety standards, it would be "defective" in the legal sense. But is the reverse also true? Does compliance with these government standards mean that the product is *not* defective? The courts have generally said no; compliance with government or industry standards does not necessarily prevent liability.

■ DEFENSES AGAINST PRODUCT LIABILITY CLAIMS

As indicated previously, it may be possible to avoid liability by disproving the main element of the plaintiff's case. For negligence, a defense would be proof that reasonable care was in fact exercised throughout the production and distribution process. For warranty, liability might be avoided by proving either that no warranty was made, or that all warranties were disclaimed, or that all warranties were in fact met. For strict liability, the defense would be proving that the product was not in fact defective.

Foreseeable misuse

Where evidence suggests that the product failed, and personal injuries were sustained, the courts have generally been reluctant to permit the seller and the manufacturer to escape liability on a "technicality." Even misuse of the product may not be a defense, if the misuse was foreseeable by the seller and the manufacturer. They may be held liable if they have not taken reasonable precautions to avoid *foreseeable misuses*, such as providing safety devices, warnings, and detailed instructions for use of the product.

Contributory or comparative negligence

Historically in a negligence case, *contributory negligence* on the part of the plaintiff was a complete defense. So was the plaintiff's voluntary *assumption of a known risk*. In product liability cases, these two defenses may not completely absolve the seller and the manufacturer. As noted in Chapter 7, many states have now adopted *comparative negligence* in place of contributory negligence. If the jury is permitted to offset the fault of the seller and the manufacturer of the defective car against the fault of the injured buyer, who happened to be speeding when the front tire fell off, clearly most of the buyer's damages will be awarded. Where the product failure occurs due to abuse or misuse, however, the defendants may be able to convince the trier of the fact that there was really no defect, no breach of warranty, and no negligence in manufacture. The machine failed not because it was defective, but because it was used constantly without proper servicing. Likewise, even where a defect exists, if the buyer continues to use the product after discovering it, without service or

Product failure caused by abuse

repair, the defendants can argue that the defect did not really *cause* the buyer's injuries.

The *Baker* case shows how these defenses may be used against the injured plaintiff.

BAKER v. ROSEMURGY

144 N.W.2d 660 (Michigan, 1966)

FACTS   Baker bought a rifle from Rosemurgy. He paid for the gun even though he knew "there was something wrong with the safety" on it. He used the gun during the hunting seasons of 1959, 1960, and 1961. While he was deer hunting in 1961, he dropped the rifle, and it fired, even though the safety was in the "on" position. Baker sustained severe and permanent leg injuries. He sued Rosemurgy; Gamble-Skogmo, which had distributed the rifle to Rosemurgy; and Olin, the manufacturer. The trial court granted summary judgment for all three defendants.

ISSUE   Does the buyer's contributory negligence and/or assumption of risk prevent that person from recovering for the injuries which were caused by the defective safety mechanism?

DECISION   Yes. Judgment affirmed.

 REASONS   Judge Fitzgerald agreed with the trial court that there wasn't even a case for the jury here, since Baker's own testimony showed that he knew the gun was dangerously defective, and kept using it without getting it repaired.

"A sampling of the general tone of the transcript will reveal that there was little doubt in plaintiff's mind but that something was wrong with the safety mechanism on the rifle, indeed his doubts appear to have been substantial.

Q. And knowing that there was something wrong with the safety you still went ahead and paid for the rifle, isn't that right?
A. That's right. Knowing in my mind that there was something wrong. . . .
Q. Your wife was not anywhere near you when you fell; true or false?
A. Well, due to the condition of the gun, I refused to hunt and have her in the immediate vicinity. . . .
Q. Even, Mr. Baker, when you were walking here on the by-path out to the woods you were very much afraid of the gun?
A. Yes sir. . . .
Q. Why didn't you write to Winchester or go to Mr. Rosemurgy and say, "there's something wrong with the rifle?"
A. There was a little question in my mind whether it was me or the rifle. . . .
Q. Were you satisfied with this rifle after the hunting season of 1959?
A. In all respects except that. It was a beautiful gun, and I loved it.
Q. Did you think you should do something about the safety device?
A. Yes, I did.
Q. Did you do anything about it?
A. But I didn't know, and I waited until I'd try it the next year and see if it was me.

"In general, his statements admitting knowledge of a defect in the rifle for 3 years prior to the accident, his failure to communicate this to anyone, all in the light of his admitted expertise in the use of a rifle over a period of 40 years, adds up to contributory negligence as a matter of law."

▪ MAGNUSON–MOSS WARRANTY ACT

One might have imagined that if any field of law under the sun required additional "protective" legislation, it was not the law of product liability. Indeed, if a problem in this field required legislative attention, it was exactly the opposite problem: how to *limit* skyrocketing product liability costs before all but the very largest manufacturers were driven out of business. Congress, however, did not see it that way. Either unaware of or unimpressed by the product liability "revolution" which had occurred during the preceding 15 years, Congress in 1975 passed the Magnuson-Moss Warranty Act, thereby adding one more large straw to the already weakened camel's back.

Requirement for clear warranty information

The act does not provide that product warranties must be made; its basic purpose is to make warranties which are made more understandable. Warranty information must be made available prior to purchase of a product and must be displayed prominently with it. Moreover, the terms of the warranty must be stated in "plain English." The purpose of these requirements is to better enable buyers to shop for the best warranty, just as they shop for the best price and credit terms. Enforcement of the act is entrusted to the Federal Trade Commission, which has the power to adopt appropriate regulations to achieve the act's purposes.

Full warranties vs. limited warranties

For products over $15, any express warranty must be stated to be a ***full warranty*** or a ***limited warranty***. The act provides standards for each type. A full warranty:

  a. Must provide that the seller will remedy any defect, without charge, within a reasonable time.
  b. Must provide that the buyer will have the choice of replacement or refund if the seller is unable to correct a defect after a reasonable number of attempts.
  c. May not limit the duration of any implied warranty.
  d. Must conspicuously state any clause which attempts to limit or exclude liability for consequential damages.

Such a full warranty, once made, extends for the entire time period specified, even if the product is resold. Injured third parties are protected by the warranty under its provisions, and under applicable state law on warranties (UCC 2–318, for example).

Any other written warranty on a consumer product must be labeled as a limited warranty, no matter how broad its coverage or how liberal its remedies. Such a limited warranty must specify its coverage and duration, the procedures to be followed, and any mechanism provided for resolving disputes. These warranties cannot be made contingent on the consumer's return of a warranty card, or on a requirement that the goods be serviced only by authorized dealers.

Like most "remedial" legislation, the act has high-minded objectives which are impossible to oppose: to provide consumers with clearer and truer warranties and to give dissatisfied consumers a remedy for defective products. The net result in the marketplace so far has been that very few manufacturers have tried to claim that they are giving full warranties on their products, and some have stopped giving written warranties altogether. Faced with the act's uncertainties, only the very hardiest (or foolhardiest) manufacturers will run the risk of extended jousting with the FTC staff. Whether this act represents a net gain for consumers remains to be seen.

▪ NEW STATE LEGISLATION

State statutory reform

Confronted with manufacturers' and sellers' claims that they were being driven out of business by excessive judgments and by soaring premiums for liability insurance, state legislatures have been considering the need for statutory changes in product liability laws. Most of the product liability "crisis" is perceived to result from overexpensive judicial interpretations, and overgenerous jury verdicts. Several types of changes are being considered, and, in some states, have already been adopted.

One proposal is to create a strong statutory presumption that a product is not "defective" where a claim is made a certain number of years after the initial sale of the product—10 years, for example. Under existing law, an injured party could claim that a product which had been in use for 20 or 30 years was defective, and thus have the benefit of the strict liability rules. Manufacturers and sellers would also like to see a specific statutory statement of contributory negligence and *assumption of risk* as defenses to product liability claims, even though most courts already do apply them in appropriate cases. Manufacturers would also like to be immune from liability where they have complied with all applicable government regulations and industry standards, as of the date of manufacture. This is the *state-of-the-art* argument. They do not feel that they should be held liable if they fail to recall and modify a product which has already been sold. These and similar changes are being pushed hard by producer and seller organizations. Further legislative action seems likely.

▪ A NATIONAL PRODUCTS LIABILITY STATUTE?

National statutory reform

In recent years, the Senate Commerce Committee has discussed proposals that would drastically change the products liability rules in the United States. They would require the injured party to prove that the manufacturer's *negligence* caused the injury. If adopted as reported, these proposals would thus preempt all state law on implied quality warranties and all state applications of strict liability to defective products. They would repeal nearly all of the judicial revolution that has taken place in this area over the last 25 years. Obviously, this legislation is of vital concern to all U.S. manufacturers and sellers of products, and to international firms interested in the U.S. market.

▪ EUROPEAN COMMON MARKET RULES

Strict liability in EEC

Meanwhile, the European Common Market countries have moved in exactly the opposite direction. A new EEC regulation requires all member-nations to provide legal recourse to injured consumers, on the basis of strict liability in tort. Prior to this regulation, some countries (such as France and West Germany) did have legal rules covering defective products which approximated strict liability. Many of the members, however, did not. The United Kingdom, for example, still required privity of contract, or proof of negligence, to recover for product-related injuries.

This change is obviously very important to anyone dealing in the European market, as buyer or seller.

■ **SIGNIFICANCE OF THIS CHAPTER**

The product liability revolution is one of the two or three most important developments in commercial law in the last 50 years. A whole new range of potential liability exposure, of vast and unknown dimensions, has been created. Entire industries are threatened and have been forced to rethink completely their production and distribution processes. Some businesses have decided to terminate their operations. The consumer is king, with many new rights and protections. Some observers have suggested that the price (which we all are paying) may be too high. It is to deal with this question, and to strike a fair balance between rights and costs, that the state legislatures and Congress are now considering changes.

DISCUSSION CASE

NATIONAL CRANE CORP. v. OHIO STEEL TUBE CO.
332 N.W.2d 39 (Nebraska, 1983)

FACTS: Ohio sold National sections of welded steel tubing for use in the tilt cylinder mechanism of cranes which National manufactured. Over a period of about five years, National sold 1,232 cranes in which Ohio's tubing had been used. When cylinder failures began to occur as the buyers were using the cranes, National notified Ohio. Ohio agreed that two failures might be due to imperfect welding, but otherwise denied liability. National was told by its engineering consultants that the tubing in the cranes was defective and dangerous. (One death had already been caused by a failure.) National then tested for, and replaced, all defective cylinders at a cost of $1,078,960. Ohio's last sale to National occurred in 1975; National brought suit in 1980. Ohio says it is liable only for the damages caused by the actual failures, not for the expenses of refitting all the other cranes. The trial court sustained Ohio's demurrer to the complaint.

■

Justice McCown: The great majority of courts which have considered the issue have held that the purchaser of a product pursuant to contract cannot recover economic losses from the manufacturer on claims based on principles of tort law, in the absence of property damage or personal injury from the use of the product. . . .

The line of demarcation between physical harm and economic loss has been said to reflect the line of demarcation between tort theory and contract theory. . . .

Chief Justice Traynor analyzed the distinction which the law has drawn between tort recovery for physical injuries and warranty recovery for economic loss. "He [the manufacturer] can appropriately be held liable for physical injuries caused by defects by requiring his goods to match a standard of safety defined in terms of conditions that create unreasonable risks of harm. He cannot be held for the level of performance of his products in the consumer's business unless he agrees that the product was designed to meet the consumer's demands. A consumer should not be charged at the will of the manufacturer with bearing the risk of physical injury when he buys a product on the market. He can, however, be fairly charged with the risk that the product will not match his economic expectations unless the manufacturer agrees that it will. Even in actions for negligence, a manufacturer's liability is limited to damages for physical injuries, and there is no recovery for economic loss alone. . . .

Dean Prosser, after pointing out that a seller's liability for negligence covers any kind of physical harm, including not only personal injuries but also property damage, said: "But where there is no accident, and no physical damage, and the only loss is a pecuniary one, through loss of the value or use of the thing sold, or the cost of repairing it, the courts have adhered to the rule . . . that purely economic interests are not entitled to protection against mere negligence, and so have denied the recovery." . . .

The rule that the purchaser of a product pursuant to contract cannot recover economic losses from the manufacturer under a claim of strict liability in tort has been adopted by this court. . . . "From a review of the authorities and giving maximum import to the basic doctrine of strict tort liability, we feel that the doctrine of strict tort liability was not conceived as a substitute for warranty liability in cases where the purchaser has only lost the benefit of his bargain. . . . If the loss is merely economic, the Uniform Commercial Code has given the purchaser an ample recourse under the particular provisions and requirements of the Code." . . .

Sections 323, 395, and 402 A and B of the *Restatement (Second) of Torts* (1965) all apply to tort liability for "physical harm." The title of § 402 A is "Special Liability of Seller of Product for Physical Harm to User or Consumer." The section then provides: "(1) One who sells any product in a defective condition unreasonably dangerous to the user or consumer or to his property is subject to liability for physical harm thereby caused to the ultimate user or consumer, or to his property, if. . . ."

The *Restatement* sections referred to are applicable only where the product causes physical harm. Nowhere in the comments or illustrations does the *Restatement* indicate that the doctrine of strict liability covers economic loss in the absence of physical harm caused by the product. In addition, Neb.Rev.Stat § 25–21,180 (Reissue 1979) defines a product liability action as an action brought "for or on account of personal injury, death, or property damage caused by" the product. The statute refers only to physical harm, not to economic loss.

Section 402 A specifically applies to liability for physical harm caused to the ultimate user or consumer or to his property. It is the unanimous view of the courts that plaintiffs may utilize a strict liability cause of action to recover for damage to property other than the defective product. That consensus is not present, however, as to damage to the defective product itself.

Damage to the product itself is sometimes characterized as economic loss or indirect loss resulting from the inability to make use of the defective product or loss of the benefit of the bargain. The difficulty in determining whether to apply strict liability for any type of economic loss results from the distinction between tort doctrine of strict liability and contract theory embodied in the Uniform Commercial Code.

A majority of courts that have considered the applicability of strict liability to recover damages to the defective product itself have permitted use of the doctrine, at least where the damage occurred as a result of a sudden, violent event and not as a result of an inherent defect that reduced the property's value without inflicting physical harm to the product. . . .

In the case at bar the facts pleaded establish that the damages sought to be recovered are the costs and expenses of removing the defective tubing manufactured by the defendant and replacing it. Such damages are not damages resulting from physical harm caused by the defective product. Instead, they are damages resulting from the purchase of defective or unsatisfactory products. . . .

At this point it should be noted that the parties tacitly concede that, upon the facts pleaded in the instant case, the plaintiff stated a cause of action against the defendant under a warranty or contract theory of liability. That cause of action, however, was barred by the statute of limitations under the Uniform Commercial Code, and the plaintiff does not seriously contend that the sustaining of the demurrer to the first cause of action on that ground was erroneous. Instead, plaintiff's position is that the facts pleaded gave rise to two separate causes of action, one in tort and one in contract under a theory of express or implied warranty.

The proper relationship between tort law and the Uniform Commercial Code dictates that a cause of action for "economic loss" under the facts of the present case be pursued under a warranty or contract theory. The fact that the incurring of replacement costs here also removed a potential future tort liability to ultimate users or consumers does not convert economic loss into physical harm, nor transform a contract warranty cause of action into a product liability tort action. It should again be noted that the 15 cases in which actual failures of defendant's product occurred are not involved in this litigation.

We hold that the purchaser of a product pursuant to contract cannot recover economic losses from the seller manufacturer on claims in tort based on negligent manufacture or strict liability in the absence of physical harm to persons or property caused by the defective product. . . .

The action of the District Court in sustaining demurrers to the petition and amended petition was correct and is affirmed.

▪ IMPORTANT TERMS AND CONCEPTS

product liability	negligence	affirmation of fact	merchantability of
fraud	warranty	lien or encumbrance	leased goods
innocent	express warranty	implied warranty of	brand name or trade
misrepresentation	title warranty	merchantability	name

exclusion or modification
of warranties
as is
third party beneficiaries
of warranties
cumulative warranties
defect (in product)
foreseeable misuse
comparative negligence
Magnuson-Moss
Warranty Act
limited warranty
legislative reform of
product liability
Restatement of Torts
privity
res ipsa loquitur
caveat emptor
implied warranty

description of goods
sample or model
infringement
merchantability of food
merchantability of real
estate
implied warranty of
fitness
conspicuous
unconscionable
limitation of remedies
strict liability in tort
contributory negligence
assumption of risk
full warranty
state-of-the-art defense
European Common
Market/European
Economic Community

■ QUESTIONS AND PROBLEMS FOR DISCUSSION

1. To what extent is contributory negligence or assumption of risk a defense against a product liability action based on strict liability in tort?
2. What is the difference between the implied warranty of merchantability and the implied warranty of fitness?
3. How can the implied warranties of merchantability and fitness be disclaimed?
4. What happens when an express warranty and an express disclaimer are both part of a sales contract, and they conflict with each other?
5. Millicent Innocent purchased a "ski weekend" vacation package at Nobby Nob Lodge. She was injured while using a rope-tow at the skiing facility operated by the Lodge. She sues the Lodge, on the theories of negligence, breach of warranty, and strict liability. The Lodge moves to dismiss all three counts of the complaint. How should the trial judge rule, and why?

6. Gladys Flippo went into a ladies clothing store in Batesville, operated by Rosie Goforth, and known as Mode O'Day Frock Shops of Hollywood. Mrs. Flippo tried on two pairs of pants, or slacks, which were shown to her by Mrs. Goforth. The first pair proved to be too small. When Mrs. Flippo put on the second pair, she suddenly felt a burning sensation on her thigh; she immediately removed the pants, shook them, and a spider fell to the floor. An examination of her thigh revealed a reddened area, which progressively grew worse. Mrs. Flippo was hospitalized for 30 days. According to her physician, the injury was caused by the bite of a brown recluse spider. She sued Mode O'Day Frock Shops. Explain how the three major theories of products liability would apply to Flippo's case.
7. Two-year-old Herman Murt was playing with two-year-old Freddie Sper in the basement of the Sper home. The boys were playing with a gasoline can which had been purchased by Wayne Sper, Freddie's father, at Belles Department Store. The children were playing near a gas furnace and a hot water heater when gasoline, which they had poured from the can, ignited. Herman was severely burned. Mrs. Sper, who was home at the time, had not checked on the boys for some time. The gasoline can, manufactured by Hufto Company, did not have a child-proof cap. Which parties may be liable for Herman's injuries . . . and on what theories?
8. Lem Hardluk worked as a busboy at Beefy's Bar & Grill. Lem moved several cases of Boffo Beer from a locked and dry storage area to a place near the coolers behind the bar. After a 15-minute break, he started to take the bottles out of the cases and put them into the coolers. One bottle exploded in his hand and some flying glass severely injured his right eye. Lem testified that he handled the bottles carefully at all times. There is no proof of who delivered the cases to Beefy's, but it may have been an independent distributor. Lem sues Boffo for his injury. Boffo moves for dismissal. How should the court rule, and why?

21

Special Performance and Breach Rules

CHAPTER OBJECTIVES
THIS CHAPTER WILL:

- Explain the UCC's basic performance rules for sales contracts.
- Discuss the buyer's basic alternatives of acceptance or rejection of the goods.
- Define the seller's remedies for a breach by the buyer.
- Define the buyer's remedies for a breach by the seller.

Article 2 of the Uniform Commercial Code covers in some detail the respective performance requirements of the buyer and seller, and the remedies available to each in the event of breach by the other. Many of these points, however, have already been discussed in Part Two, Contracts Law. This chapter thus emphasizes those major "performance and breach" rules which have not yet been mentioned.

■ PERFORMANCE REQUIREMENTS OF SELLER AND BUYER

Code's limits on freedom of contract

Basic Requirements.   Article 2 generally permits the parties to structure their contract for the sale of goods as they wish and to specify what will or will not be required of each. This general *freedom of contract* is, however, subject to a few qualifying provisions. Any clause of the contract, or the entire contract, is subject to modification if the court finds it to be *unconscionable* under Section 2–302. One of the generally applicable provisions of Article 1 (1–102[3]) also states that a party cannot disclaim the *basic obligations* of "good faith, diligence, reasonableness and care" or effectively agree to "manifestly unreasonable" standards by which the performance of such obligations is to be judged. A court may also rely on its general notions of "public policy" to refuse enforcement of a particularly unfair contract term. Within these very broad limits, the buyer and the seller can pretty much "do their own thing."

The most succinct statement of the parties' obligations is Section 2–301: "The obligation of the seller is to transfer and deliver and that of the buyer is to accept and pay in accordance with the contract." Each party thus has the right to expect the other to perform these minimum obligations in accordance with the specific agreement. These expectations may become uncertain because one party has delegated a performance to another person, or because a party has repudiated the contract and then tried to reinstate it, or for some other reason. When that happens, the party having reasonable grounds for "insecurity"

Demand for adequate assurance

may demand in writing that the other party provide *adequate assurance* of due performance; that is, some sort of guarantee that performance will occur as promised. Until some reasonable assurance is received, the insecure party can withhold any performance of his or her own for which the agreed return has not yet been received. A seller who received notice of the buyer's bankruptcy, for instance, could demand a guarantee that all future shipments would be paid for, and would not have to deliver any more goods until the buyer provided a sufficient guarantee of payment. If the insecure party receives no such assurance of due performance within a reasonable time not over 30 days, he or she can treat the other party's silence as a repudiation of the whole contract. The basic performance duties of the parties to a contract may also be discharged or suspended by a party's "anticipatory repudiation" (2–610) or by *impracticability* (2–615), as discussed in Chapter 17. The *Mishara* case is an example of one sort of impracticability.

MISHARA CONSTRUCTION CO., INC. v. TRANSIT-MIXED CONCRETE CORP.

310 N.E.2d 363 (Massachusetts, 1974)

FACTS   Mishara was the general contractor on a housing project. Mishara contracted with Transit to supply all the ready-mixed concrete for the project at $13.25 per cubic yard, with deliveries as ordered by Mishara. The contract was signed on September 21, 1966, and it was performed satisfactorily until April 1967. In April there was a labor dispute at the jobsite. Work resumed on June 15, but a picket line was maintained until the job was completed in 1969. Transit made only a "very few" deliveries during this period, despite repeated requests by Mishara. After notifying Transit, Mishara met the balance of its concrete requirements elsewhere. It then sued Transit for difference-money damages and for the costs involved in finding the second source. The trial court jury held for Transit.

ISSUE   Was the seller's duty discharged by impracticability due to the strike and picket line at the buyer's jobsite?

DECISION   Yes, as properly submitted to the jury and determined by it. Judgment affirmed.

REASONS   Justice Reardon gave the court's opinion:
"It is, of course, the very essence of contract that it is directed at the elimination of some risks for each party in exchange for others. Each receives the certainty of price, quantity, and time, and assumes the risk of changing market prices, superior opportunity, or added costs. It is implicit in the doctrine of impossibility (and in the companion rule of 'frustration of purpose') that certain risks are so unusual and have such severe consequences that they must have been beyond the scope of the assignment of risks inherent in the contract. . . . To require performance in that case would be to grant the promisee an advantage for which he could not be said to have bargained in making the contract. . . . The question is, given the commercial circumstances in which the parties dealt: Was the contingency which developed one which the parties could reasonably be thought to have foreseen as a real possibility which could affect performance? . . . If it were, performance will be required. If it could not be so considered, performance is excused."

Justice Reardon then rejected Mishara's claim that a labor dispute could *never* provide such an excuse; it might or it might not. "Much must depend on the facts known to the parties at the time of contracting with respect to the history of and prospects for labor difficulties during the period of performance of the contract, as well as the likely severity of the effect of such disputes on the ability to perform." The determination was thus properly made by the jury in this case.

Delivery and Payment.   Unless otherwise agreed, the Code assumes that the seller's duty to deliver the goods and the buyer's duty to pay the price are each conditioned on the other party's tender of the reciprocal performance; this is the doctrine of concurrent conditions, as also discussed in Chapter 17. The requirements for the seller's **tender of delivery** of the goods are spelled out in 2–503 (and the parties' contract). Generally, tender "requires that the

Concurrent conditions of
performance

seller put and hold *conforming goods* at the buyer's disposition and give the buyer any notification reasonably necessary to enable him to take delivery." It is generally assumed that the place for delivery is the seller's place of business, unless there is a specific agreement or trade practice that it should be otherwise. Where the goods must be sent to the buyer in another location, the contract is assumed to be one for shipment rather than delivery unless otherwise agreed.

The buyer's *tender of payment* can be made "by any means or in any manner current in the ordinary course of business," including check or credit card. If the seller wants cash, he or she must demand cash and he or she must give the buyer "any extension of time reasonable necessary to procure it." If the buyer does pay by check, the payment is conditional, the condition being that the check will be honored by the buyer's bank when it is duly presented.

Inspection. Unless otherwise agreed, where goods are tendered or delivered or have been identified, the buyer has the right to inspect them before accepting or paying for them. This *inspection* of goods must be at a reasonable time and place and in a reasonable manner, and the assumption is that the buyer bears the expenses of such inspection, though the buyer can recover such expenses against the seller if the goods do not conform to the contract. Where there is a specific agreement on the place or manner of inspection, that place or manner is presumed to be exclusive, unless compliance becomes impossible. The impossibility of performing the inspection as agreed may or may not discharge the whole contract, depending on how the court views the parties' intent. As a rule, where the contract requires a COD delivery or payment as soon as shipping documents are presented to the buyer, payment for the goods must be made prior to inspection.

Buyer's right to inspect

When a claim or dispute arises as to whether the goods conform to the contract, either party has the right to inspect, test, and sample goods in the possession of the other party by giving that party reasonable notification, so that the facts can be ascertained and evidence preserved. Further, the parties may by agreement provide for such an inspection by a third party (who acts as a sort of arbitrator) and may agree that those findings shall be binding upon them in any subsequent litigation.

Buyer's Acceptance of Goods. Under the Code, *acceptance of the goods* occurs when, having had a reasonable opportunity to inspect them, the buyer indicates that they do conform to the contract or that they are acceptable in spite of some nonconformity, or when the buyer simply fails to effectively reject them. Any act by the buyer which is inconsistent with the seller's ownership of the goods is likewise an acceptance, but if the act is wrongful as against the seller, it is an acceptance only if it is ratified by the seller. "Acceptance of a part of any commercial unit is acceptance of that entire unit."

Once the buyer has accepted the goods, they must be paid for at the contract rate. Further, the burden is now on the buyer to prove any alleged breach with respect to the accepted goods. The buyer must also prove that the seller was notified of the breach within a reasonable time after the buyer discovered it or should have discovered it. If the buyer has accepted the goods, it follows logically that they can no longer be rejected. Nor can an acceptance be revoked where the buyer knew of the nonconformity at the time of acceptance, unless the buyer accepted with the reasonable assumption that the nonconformity would be cured. Except for the foregoing provisions, acceptance does not prevent the buyer from pursuing any other remedy provided for nonconformity of the goods.

Buyer's Revocation of Acceptance.   The buyer may revoke or withdraw an acceptance of any lot or commercial unit which is subsequently discovered to have a substantial nonconformity if the defect could not reasonably have been discovered before acceptance, or if the buyer was induced to accept the goods by the seller's assurance that a known defect would be cured, and the seller has not seasonably cured the defect. The buyer must revoke the acceptance within a reasonable time after he or she discovers, or should have discovered, the defect "and before any substantial change in condition of the goods which is not caused by their own defects" (2–608[2]). The buyer, after having notified the seller of such a proper revocation, has the same rights against the goods as if they had been rejected initially. The *McCullough* case illustrates these rules.

McCULLOUGH v. BILL SWAD CHRYSLER-PLYMOUTH, INC.

449 N.E.2d 1289 (Ohio, 1983)

FACTS   Ms. McCullough bought a car from Bill Swad Chrysler-Plymouth. When defects appeared in the car's steering, transmission, and brakes, she notified the seller and brought the car back in for repairs. Not only did the dealer not correct the defects, after several tries, but new defects also continued to appear. McCullough kept driving the car, and bringing it back in for repairs, over the course of several months. Finally, she had had enough, and demanded that the dealer take back the car and give her her money back. The lower courts held in her favor.

ISSUE   Did the buyer waive her right to revoke her acceptance?

DECISION   No. Judgment affirmed.

REASONS   Justice Locher gave the opinion for the court:
"The case at bar essentially poses but a single question: Whether appellee, by continuing to operate the vehicle she had purchased from appellant after notifying the latter of her intent to rescind the purchase agreement, waived her right to revoke her initial acceptance. After having thoroughly reviewed both the relevant facts in the present cause and the applicable law, we find that appellee, despite her extensive use of the car following her revocation, in no way forfeited such right. . . .

"Although the legal question presented in appellant's first objection is a novel one for this bench, other state courts which have addressed the issue have held that whether continued use of goods after notification of revocation of their acceptance vitiates such revocation is solely dependent upon whether such use was reasonable. . . . Moreover, whether such use was reasonable is a question to be determined by the trier of fact. . . .

"The genesis of the 'reasonable use' test lies in the recognition that frequently a buyer, after revoking his earlier acceptance of a good, is constrained by exogenous circumstances—many of which the seller controls—to continue using the good until a suitable replacement may realistically be secured. Clearly, to penalize the buyer for a predicament not of his own creation would be patently unjust. . . .

" 'It does not lie in the seller's mouth to demand the utmost in nicety between permissible and impermissible use, for the perilous situation in which the purchaser finds himself arises from the imperfections of that furnished, for a consideration, by the seller himself.'

"In ascertaining whether a buyer's continued use of an item after revocation of its acceptance was reasonable, the trier of fact should pose and divine the answers to the following queries: (1) Upon being apprised of the buyer's revocation of his acceptance, what instructions, if any, did the seller tender the buyer concerning return of the now rejected goods? (2) Did the buyer's business needs or personal circumstances compel the continued use? (3) During the period of such use, did the seller persist in assuring the buyer that all nonconformities would be cured or that provisions would otherwise be made to recompense the latter for the dissatisfaction and inconvenience which the defects caused him? (4) Did the seller act in good faith? (5) Was the seller unduly prejudiced by the buyer's continued use? . . .

"It is manifest that, upon consideration of the aforementioned criteria, appellee acted reasonably in continuing to operate her motor vehicle even after revocation of acceptance. First, the failure of the seller to advise the buyer, after the latter has revoked his acceptance of the goods, how the goods were to be returned entitles the buyer to retain possession of them. . . .

"Appellant, in the case at bar, did not respond to appellee's request for instructions regarding the disposition of the vehicle. Failing to have done so, appellant can hardly be heard now to complain of appellee's continued use of the automobile.

"Secondly, appellee, a young clerical secretary of limited financial resources, was scarcely in position to return the defective automobile and obtain a second in order to meet her business and personal needs. A most unreasonable obligation would be imposed upon appellee were she to be required, in effect, to secure a loan to purchase a second car while remaining liable for repayment of the first car loan. . . .

"Additionally, appellant's successor (East), by attempting to repair the appellee's vehicle even after she tendered her notice of revocation, provided both express and tacit assurances that the automobile's defects were remediable, thereby, inducing her to retain possession. Moreover, whether appellant acted in good faith throughout this episode is highly problematic, especially given the fact that whenever repair of the car was undertaken, new defects often miraculously arose while previous ones frequently went uncorrected. Both appellant's and East's refusal to honor the warranties before their expiration also evidences less than fair dealing. . . .

" '[A]t some point after the purchase of a new automobile, the same should be put in good running condition, that is, the seller does not have an unlimited time for the performance of the obligation to replace and repair parts.' Clearly, the hour glass has run on appellant's efforts to place the car in good running order."

Buyer's Rejection of Goods. A buyer wishing to reject goods because of their nonconformity must do so within a reasonable time after delivery or tender and must "seasonably" notify the seller of the rejection. Once the buyer has rejected the goods, any exercise of ownership over them by the buyer is wrongful as against the seller. The buyer, unless entitled to retain possession under 2–711(3), is required to take reasonable care of the seller's rejected goods until the seller has had a reasonable chance to remove them. Where

Buyer's duties as to rejected goods

the buyer is a merchant and the seller does not have an agent or a place of business nearby, the buyer must follow the seller's reasonable instructions with respect to the disposition of the rejected goods. If the goods are perishable or otherwise subject to a rapid decline in value, the buyer must make reasonable efforts to resell them even if the seller has not sent instructions. Under those circumstances, it would not be fair or reasonable to permit the buyer to watch the goods spoil without making some effort to salvage them.

Seller's Right to "Cure" Defects. UCC 2–508 gives the seller a "second chance" in two situations where the buyer rejects a delivery or tender of goods because of their nonconformity to the terms of the contract. If the contract time for performance has not yet expired, the seller can seasonably notify the buyer of its intent to cure the nonconformity, and then make a conforming delivery within the contract time. For example, if the buyer rejected a tender of 500 units, because the contract called for 700 units, the seller could notify the buyer that it would deliver the full 700, and then do so within the contract period. The buyer would be required to take the second shipment of 700 units.

Where the buyer rejects goods the seller had reasonable grounds to believe would be acceptable, the seller is allowed a reasonable time *after* the contract date to substitute a conforming delivery. The purpose of this rule is to avoid unfair, "surprise" rejections, for technical reasons, where the goods are substantially conforming and would usually be accepted in the trade or business involved. As several cases have pointed out, however, the seller's right to cure is not unlimited. The seller must be acting honestly and reasonably, not trying to knowingly pass off inferior goods or to force the buyer into an acceptance. The *Gappelberg* case illustrates the limitations on the seller's right to cure defects.

GAPPELBERG v. LANDRUM

666 S.W.2d 88 (Texas, 1984)

FACTS On September 5, 1980, Nathan Gappelberg purchased a large screen Advent television set from Neely Landrum, doing business as The Video Station. Gappelberg paid $2,231.25 cash and was allowed a $1,500 credit for his old set. Gappelberg immediately experienced numerous problems with the new set. Landrum and Alpha Omega, the authorized repair agency, made several house calls in an effort to repair the set. On September 26, 1980, the set totally ceased operating. Gappelberg allowed the television set to be removed from his home but refused offers to make further repairs on the set, saying he simply wanted his money and old set returned to him. Landrum felt he was in no position to return the old set, as he had promised it as a prize for a promotional sweepstakes, and offered Gappelberg another Advent as replacement. Gappelberg refused to accept the substitute and brought suit against Landrum. The trial court rendered judgment for Landrum, and the court of appeals affirmed that judgment.

ISSUE Can the seller still "cure" by delivering a new set?

DECISION No. Judgment reversed.

🏛 REASONS

Justice Kilgarlin spoke for the court:

"This case presents an issue previously undecided in Texas, or for that matter, any other American jurisdiction. Under the Uniform Commercial Code, does the seller have the right to cure a substantial defect by making a replacement of the product after the buyer has revoked acceptance?

"The concept of revocation of acceptance is relatively new. During early years of the Code, 'the courts did not take to it.' . . . Early court decisions interpreting the Code confused the terms *revocation* with *rescission* and *rejection*. Gradually, however, the concept of revocation of acceptance has taken hold. Its principle is simple. The right of a buyer to revoke exists only when the buyer has initially accepted the goods in question. Rejection, however, is an initial act of the buyer, meaning there was never an acceptance.

"The right of the seller to cure by repair or replacement clearly exists in instances of rejection. . . . This, of course, is not a rejection case. It is a case in which, under the fact findings, the buyer was clearly entitled to revoke his acceptance. Revocation of acceptance is controlled by UCC § 2.608. . . .

"It will be noted that paragraph (a)(2) is applicable to this case. The only reference to cure in § 2.608 is in situations when the buyer knew of the defects at the time of acceptance of the goods. There is no reference to cure for our situation where Gappelberg accepted the television set without knowing of the defects. The court of appeals, in its opinion, has listed the numerous cases from other jurisdictions which hold that once a buyer properly revokes acceptance, the seller no longer has the right to cure by repair. This is likewise the conclusion of White and Summers . . . , who state the revocation of acceptance is not limited by the right to cure. We do not consider paragraph (c) in UCC § 2.608 as having any reference to UCC § 2.508. It is more logically related to UCC § § 2.603 and 2.604 as UCC § 2.608(c) makes absolutely no mention of seller's rights. . . .

"The court of appeals in this case notes that in none of the cases in which a seller's right to cure has been denied once revocation of acceptance occurs was the buyer presented with such a generous offer as Landrum's offer to replace. The court of appeals concluded that 'in the spirit of the Code,' cure by replacement even in revocation situations should be authorized.

"Although a rejection case, in *Zabriskie Chevrolet, Inc.* v. *Smith*, 99 N.J.Super 441, 240 A.2d 195 (1968), the court observed that 'for a majority of people, the purchase of a new car is a major investment, rationalized by the peace of mind that flows from its dependability and safety. Once their faith is shaken, the vehicle loses not only its real value in their eyes, but becomes an instrument whose integrity is substantially impaired and whose operation was fraught with apprehension.' In *Zabriskie*, a new 1966 Chevrolet ceased to operate within one mile of being removed from the showroom because of a faulty transmission. The buyer was not forced to take the Chevrolet with a different transmission in it, his faith in the whole automobile having been shaken. By the same token, Gappelberg had seen one Advent television perform, or fail to perform as the case may be, and there certainly is justification for his not wanting to go through [similar] experiences with another Advent.

"Professor Wallach states, 'the seller is ordinarily in a better position to maximize the return on the resale of the goods, and his disposition of the goods eliminates the storage and other incidental expenses that may be involved in the unsatisfactory transaction.' . . . This is probably the best policy reason of all for denying replacement after revocation—the relative position of the parties. It is true that a new machine provided by Landrum could have proved perfectly free of defects. It is equally possible that such a new machine would have defects, perhaps similar to those of the old Advent or entirely different ones. No one contends that the seller's right to cure is limitless. Even Landrum, in argument, admits that a day of reckoning must come, although he earnestly contends that the three weeks in the situation at bar was not adequate time to allow cure.

"We are cited no good policy reason why different rules should attain as to cure by replacement instead of cure by repair. Indeed, we cannot envision any basis for a distinction. Thus, we state that once a buyer has properly revoked acceptance of a product, the seller has neither the right to cure by repair nor by replacement."

■ **EXHIBIT 21–1**
Performance of Sales Contract

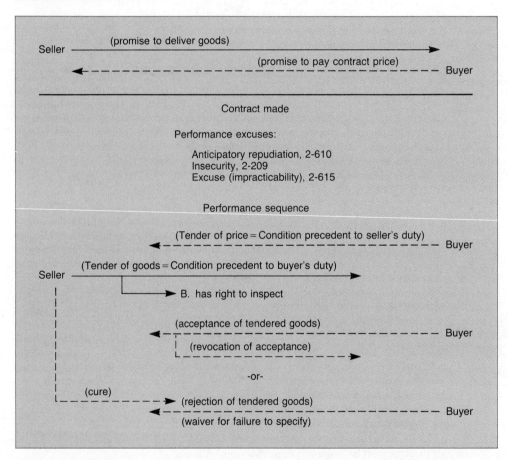

■ REMEDIES OF THE SELLER

In General. The basic policy of Article 2 is that the injured party should have available whatever combination of remedies best solves the problems created by the breach. The technical doctrine of election of remedies is officially rejected; the remedies listed for the seller in 2–703 are "essentially *cumulative* in nature." "Whether the pursuit of one remedy bars another depends entirely on the facts of the individual case" (Comment 1). Further, the drafters of the Code

Cumulative remedies

intended that its remedies of breach "be liberally administered" (Comment 4). The intent of the Code is to put the injured party where he or she would have been had the breach not occurred.

Against the Goods. Whether the seller discovers that the buyer is insolvent, the seller may withhold delivery of the goods, unless the buyer is prepared to pay cash, including payment for all goods already delivered under the same contract. Where the goods are already in transit, the seller can order the bailee to stop delivery if the bailee has not acknowledged the buyer's right to possession and if the buyer has not received a negotiable document of title covering the goods.

Limited right to repossess

Where the goods have already been delivered on credit to an insolvent buyer, the seller has a very limited right to reclaim them. The seller must demand their return within 10 days after the buyer received them, unless the buyer made a written statement of solvency within three months prior to the delivery; then the 10-day limitation does not apply. In any case, however, the seller's **right of repossession** is subject to the rights of **buyers in the ordinary course** of business or other **good faith purchasers,** and to the rights of **lien creditors.** Where the seller decides on repossession, this remedy excludes all others.

The court in the next case is trying to decide how these rules should be applied.

IN RE BEL AIR CARPETS, INC.

452 F.2d 1210 (U.S. Ninth Circuit, 1971)

FACTS

Bel Air applied for a line of credit at Mand Carpet Mills in late June or early July 1969. Bel Air submitted a financial statement dated June 30, 1968. Bel Air's president told Mand's credit manager not to worry about the statement's being a year old, that a new one was being prepared, and that it would show Bel Air to be in substantially the same financial condition. The new statement was never given to Mand, but Mand extended credit to Bel Air anyway, on July 9, 1969, and within five weeks Bel Air had bought $10,365.52 worth of goods on credit. Mand delivered the last shipment, worth $539.08, on August 13. The next day Bel Air declared that it was insolvent, and on September 10 it filed an involuntary bankruptcy petition. Meanwhile, another carpet mill had sued Bel Air in California and had attached almost all of its carpet inventories. Mand filed a third-party claim in that case, and it recovered goods worth $3,871.92, taking delivery on September 19.

ISSUE

Is the unpaid seller permitted to recover these goods under UCC 2–702, even against the buyer's trustee in bankruptcy?

DECISION

Yes. The referee's decision is affirmed.

REASONS

Judge Choy first decided that the key date for establishing Mand's rights was August 19, when it filed its third-party claim in the California lawsuit. That was the date of the "transfer" to Mand, and it was prior to the date of bankruptcy. Normally a seller must make its demand for the return of goods within 10 days after delivery to the buyer. Mand was relying on the exception to that rule which existed where the buyer had made a written misrepresentation of solvency within three months prior to the delivery. The Code section itself said only that the misrepresentation must have been *made* within the prior three months, but the official comment to that section said that the written misrepresentation must have been *dated* within the prior three months. Judge Choy disregarded the official comment.

"The protection afforded the seller would be severely limited by allowing the loophole the Trustee would have us create. Reliance upon a financial statement such as that delivered to Mand takes place on the date the statement is delivered, not on the date in the past on which it was purportedly prepared. . . .

"There would be little doubt that, had the Bankrupt sent Mand the 1968 financial statement with a current cover letter incorporating the enclosed statements, S.2–702(2) would be fully operative. There is no reason for a different result in this case. . . . Whatever the reason behind the arbitrary time requirement, it was not designed to achieve such an anomalous result as the Trustee espouses, which is patently contrary to common sense and to the intent of the Code. Mand was entitled to rescind its contract with the Bankrupt and to retain the entire sum it recovered."

If the buyer breaches before the seller has finished manufacturing the goods, the seller, if exercising "reasonable commercial judgment," has the options of completing the goods and identifying them to the contract, or of selling the unfinished goods for scrap or salvage, or of pursuing any other reasonable alternative.

For Damages.   The general measure of the seller's damages is difference money; that is, the difference between the contract price and the (lower) market price at the time and place of tender. Obviously, if another buyer pays more for the goods and the seller had only one item for sale, the seller should not collect any ***difference-money damages.*** The seller can also recover any "incidental" damages which were sustained because of the buyer's breach, such as additional storage charges on the goods or the cost of an advertisement needed to resell the goods. Where the buyer's breach means that the seller "loses" that sale, in the sense that the seller, a car dealer for instance, has many of the same items for sale and could have sold another one to Buyer 2, the seller should collect the profit which would have been made on that other sale as damages from Buyer 1.

Difference money versus lost profits

Right to Full Contract Price.   The seller can sue and collect the full contract price from the buyer only in certain limited situations. The seller can, of course, sue for the full price on any goods which the buyer has accepted. The seller can also get the contract price for conforming goods which have been lost or damaged within a commercially reasonable time after the risk of loss passed to the buyer. Finally, the buyer owes the contract price for goods which have been identified to the contract and which cannot be resold at a reasonable price.

Limited right to collect for contract price

REMEDIES OF THE BUYER

Specific performance

Against the Goods. The buyer's right to *specific performance* of the contract by the seller has been expanded by the Code. In addition to cases involving "unique" goods, such as works of art, this remedy is also available "in other proper circumstances," such as "output and requirements contracts involving a particular or peculiarly available source or market" (2–716[1]). As to any goods which have been identified to the contract, the buyer can sue for possession when similar goods are not available elsewhere or if the goods were shipped under reservation of a security interest and the buyer has made or tendered the required performance. A computer manufacturer, for example, could sue to force a supplier to deliver silicon chips which were not available elsewhere, due to a market shortage.

In the "extreme hardship" case, where the seller has become insolvent within 10 days after receiving the first installment on the contract price, the buyer has the right to obtain possession of identified goods by tendering any unpaid part of the contract price. This is part of the buyer's *special property* in the goods once they have been identified to the contract. If the buyer has made the identification, this right to possession exists only if the goods conform to the contract.

A buyer in possession or control of goods which were rightfully rejected because of their nonconformity has a security interest in them for any payments already made on the price and for all reasonable expenses incurred in inspecting and handling them. The buyer can sell such goods and apply the proceeds to satisfy this claim.

To Cancel. Where the seller has been guilty of a material breach, the buyer has the right to *cancel the contract* and to recover any payments already made on the price and any damages sustained. On an installment contract the breach is material and justifies cancellation of the whole contract if it "substantially impairs the value of the whole contract."

Difference money, plus incidental damages

For Damages. If the seller has failed to deliver or the buyer has rightfully rejected or justifiably revoked an acceptance, the buyer may obtain substitute goods from another source and sue the seller for difference-money damages. The buyer may also recover any *incidental and consequential damages*, which are defined as any expenses incurred in inspecting or handling the goods or obtaining substitute goods and any other reasonable expenses incident to the delay ("incidental"), any loss resulting from the buyer's requirements for the goods of which the seller had reason to know and which could not be avoided, and any injury to person or property resulting from breach of warranty.

As to goods which the buyer has accepted but which are nonconforming, damages may be recovered for any "loss resulting in the ordinary course of events" from the seller's breach. For a breach of warranty the buyer may recover damages for the difference between the value of the goods accepted and what the value of the goods would have been if the warranty had been met, "unless special circumstances show proximate damages of a different amount."

Limitation of Remedies.   In accordance with its general "freedom of contract" approach, the Code permits parties to the sale of goods contract to specify what remedies will or will not be available in the event of breach. Such contract provisions are not enforceable, however, if they are unreasonable or unconscionable. One important limitation is Section 2–719(2): "Where circumstances cause an exclusive or limited remedy to fail of its essential purpose, remedy may be had as provided in this Act." If, in other words, enforcement of the contract clause would mean that the injured party wound up with no real remedy at all, the Code's remedy sections apply. Further, subsection (3) of Section 2–719 provides that a limitation of consequential *damages for personal injuries* caused by defective consumer goods is prima facie unconscionable. The seller or manufacturer of the consumer goods would have a heavy presumption to overcome to make such a limitation enforceable. Where a commercial loss is caused by defective goods, there is no presumption that a contract clause limiting consequential damages is invalid. If an airline and a plane manufacturer included such a limitation in their contract, for example, the limitation would not be presumed unconscionable.

Where the contract contains a *liquidated damages* provision, the amount specified must be "reasonable," under essentially the same test used prior to the Code. If the amount set is unreasonably large, it is void as a penalty.

Unreasonable contract limitations not enforceable

■ SIGNIFICANCE OF THIS CHAPTER

The UCC outlines the performance obligations of the parties and their available remedies in the event of breach in some detail. Generally, the parties are free to write the contract as they wish, but several Code sections try to ensure fair results in all cases. Parties who are aware of the Code's rules are in a better position to negotiate their own contract so that it recognizes their situations and provides for the variations they wish. If they are also aware of the outer limits set by the Code, they are in a better position to provide for a different, but still reasonable, package of remedies in the event of a breach.

■ IMPORTANT TERMS AND CONCEPTS

freedom of contract
basic obligations
impracticability
conforming goods
inspection of goods
revocation of acceptance
    of goods
right to cure defects
right to repossess goods
good faith purchaser
difference-money damages
specific performance
cancel the contract
consequential damages
personal injury damages

unconscionable
adequate assurance
tender of delivery
tender of payment
acceptance of goods
rejection of goods
cumulative remedies
buyer in ordinary course
lien creditor
right to full contract
    price
special property interest
incidental damages
limitation of remedies
liquidated damages

■ QUESTIONS AND PROBLEMS FOR DISCUSSION

1. When does the buyer have the right to inspect the goods?
2. When is the buyer deemed to have accepted the goods in satisfaction of the seller's performance obligations under the contract for sale?
3. Under what circumstances can the buyer revoke an earlier acceptance of the goods?
4. When can the seller collect the full contract price as a remedy for the buyer's breach of the sale contract?
5. Sweet Tooth Sugar Company supplied 800 bags of sugar to Red Cheek Apple Orchards, which used the sugar in processing frozen diced applies under contract for J. Fussy Company. An inspector for Red Cheek noticed the presence of a contaminant, and Red Cheek

returned 68 bags of sugar to Sweet Tooth. They were promptly replaced. Red Cheek used the other 732 bags, even though its inspectors had noticed the presence of some contaminants in them as well.

When delivering the frozen apples to its customer some months later, Red Cheek was told that they did not measure up to J. Fussy Company's exacting quality standards. Red Cheek had to take them back and later sold them at a great loss. Red Cheek then refused to pay for the defective 732 bags of sugar, and Sweet Tooth sued Red Cheek. Red Cheek brought a countersuit for breach of warranty. What is the decision? Why?

6. On April 30, 1987, Fleet purchased from Lang an ice-cream freezer and a refrigeration compressor unit, paying only $200 down, though agreeing to pay $860 down and the balance, plus interest, in 18 payments of $78.72. (Total cash price was $2,160.) Fleet made no further payments. On July 30, 1989, Lang brought suit for replevin, because of Fleet's failure to pay.

Before this, Fleet had disconnected the compressor from the freezer and connected it to an air conditioner. Yet he now alleged that the equipment was defective and was wholly unusable for the purpose intended, and he demanded the return of the contract price down payment. What is the result and why?

7. Joseph Versatile conducted a profitable hide, fur, and junk business. To branch out, he bought batteries from Louie Loaded, a distributor for the Waterless Battery Company, in order to sell them to retail customers. Each battery carried a warranty promising free replacement of any faulty battery unless it showed signs of abuse.

Joseph received 150 batteries, all of which were allegedly defective and had to be replaced. When he applied for refund, Louie wanted to see the defective batteries in order to make sure that the defect was not due to abuse. Joseph, however, could produce only 30 batteries. He claimed that the other 120 had been junked for $1 each. Joseph sues for a refund. What is the result? Why?

8. Ralph Red verbally agreed to sell Arthur Adobe a pile of bricks located at Ralph's property for a unit price. Later he made Arthur another offer for building materials located at a second site which Ralph could purchase for $1,000. Arthur removed some materials from both sites and sent Ralph a check for $150, the unit price for the materials he had taken. Ralph refused to take the check, claiming that Arthur must pay for the whole lot, even though he had only removed parts of it so far. Arthur, on the other hand, claimed that he had never agreed to anything but a sale per unit. Who is right? Why?

22

Special "Entrusting" and Bulk Sales Rules

CHAPTER OBJECTIVES

THIS CHAPTER WILL:

- Explain the difference between a void and voidable title to goods.
- Discuss the UCC change in the law where an owner entrusts goods to a merchant who deals in goods of that kind.
- Define a bulk sale.
- Explain the requirements under the UCC for a valid bulk transfer of goods.
- Discuss the rights of BFPs (bona fide purchasers).

Two special situations involving claims by third parties against the goods have arisen frequently enough to require special legal rules. The "title" sections of Article 2 provide the rules for settling disputes which occur because of "defects" in the seller's title to the goods. "Bulk sales" problems are dealt with in Article 6.

■ SALE BY SELLER WITH VOID OR VOIDABLE TITLE

Original owner versus BFP

Void title versus voidable title

Bailee who appears to be agent of owner

Defects in Seller's Title. In any number of situations, a person might possess goods which he or she doesn't own, or have a voidable title to such goods because someone else has the power to rescind a previous sale transaction. What happens when the person in possession of such goods sells them to a good faith purchaser? Which of the two innocent parties should the law protect— the original owner or the good faith purchaser? Since only one of these parties can win the litigation for ownership of the goods, the other party will sustain a loss unless he or she can find and collect against the "middleman." If you lend one of your books to a friend, and that person sells it along with some of his or her own books, either intentionally or by mistake, you can clearly sue your friend for the value of the book. The more basic question, however, is whether or not you can locate the buyer and get the book back.

The Code's basic approach to this sort of problem is to distinguish between a seller who has a *void title*; that is, no title at all, and a seller whose title to the goods is *voidable* because of some irregularity in that person's acquisition of the goods. Except for the very special case you are about to read, the general rule is that a person with no title passes no title to his or her buyer. Where your watch is lost, stolen, or lent and then sold by the finder, thief, or bailee, you get the watch back from the buyer if you can prove what happened, even if the buyer was acting in good faith. On the other hand, where there was in fact a sales transaction between the original owner and the reseller and the original owner intended at that time to make the reseller the owner of the goods, a *good faith purchaser* from the reseller keeps the goods, even though the original sale is voidable because of minority, fraud, duress, nonpayment, or similar irregularity.

Appearance of Authority to Sell. However, where the original owner created a situation in which it appeared to reasonable third parties that the *bailee* was really the owner of the goods or that the bailee had the power to sell the goods for the owner, a good faith purchaser from the bailee would keep the goods. The main problem in such a case, both before and after the adoption of the Code, has been to determine what actions by the original owner are sufficient to create this *"appearance of authority" to sell*. Generally, the courts held that mere possession of goods by a bailee was not enough to create this appearance. The following pre-Code case illustrates this problem.

ZENDMAN v. HARRY WINSTON, INC.

111 N.E.2d 871 (New York, 1953)

FACTS

On November 28, 1947, Jane Zendman bought a diamond ring for $12,500 at an auction held at the gallery of Brand, Inc., on the boardwalk of Atlantic City, New Jersey.

The ring had been entrusted to Brand by the defendant, Harry Winston, a diamond merchant located in New York City, under memorandums stating that the goods were for the jeweler's examination only and that title was not to pass until he had made his selection and had notified the defendant of his agreement to pay the stated price. Records disclosed that in the past other goods had been sent and later sold with payment accepted. A judgment in Zendman's favor in the trial court was reversed by the appellate division, and she appealed to the Court of Appeals.

ISSUE

Did Brand, Inc., have "apparent authority" to sell the diamond ring?

DECISION

Yes. Judgment reversed (for plaintiff).

REASONS

Justice Fuld discussed the policies underlying the "estoppel" rule.

"Generally, we seek a proper balance between the competing interests of an owner who has entrusted his property to another for purposes other than sale, and of an innocent purchaser who has in good faith bought that property from the latter without notice of the seller's lack of title or authority to sell. . . . 'As between two innocent victims of the fraud, the one who made possible the fraud on the other should suffer.' . . .

" 'The rightful owner may be estopped by his own acts from asserting his title. If he has invested another with the usual evidence of title, or an apparent authority to dispose of it, he will not be allowed to make claim against an innocent purchaser dealing on the faith of such apparent ownership.' . . .

"The trial court was fully justified in holding that defendant was precluded from denying Brand's authority to sell. For more than a month, defendant acquiesced in Brand's public display of the ring unsegregated from other wares properly up for sale. Defendant's officer, Raticoff, knew of the ring's display, and yet no effort was made to inform the public that it was exhibited only to solicit offers and not for immediate sale. Moreover, as noted above, the evidence revealed a regular course of dealing between Brand and Winston regarding jewelry received 'on memorandum,' under which Winston appears to have accepted either Brand's check or money or customers' checks for sales made by Brand, without insisting on compliance with the limitations of the memoranda. Winston was thus responsible for the appearance of a general, unrestricted authority in Brand to sell items received on such memoranda. And, relying on Brand's apparent authority to sell the diamond, plaintiff bid at the auction sale and bought the ring."

Code rule where bailee is merchant

Entrusting to a Merchant. The Code creates a conclusive presumption of such an "appearance of authority" in only one situation—an "entrusting" of possession of goods to a merchant who deals in goods of that kind. *Entrusting* is defined in Section 2–403(3) as including any delivery of possession or any acquiescence in retention of possession. Where such an entrusting occurs, the

■ **EXHIBIT 22–1**
Defects in Seller's Title

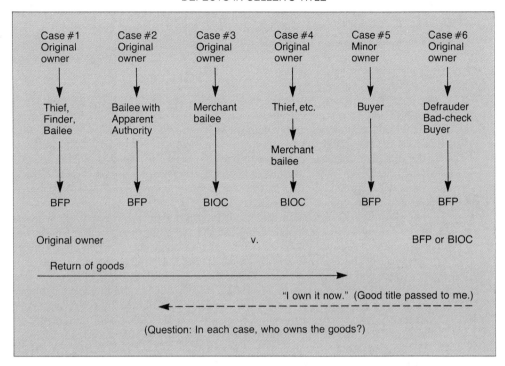

DEFECTS IN SELLER'S TITLE

Case #1 Original owner	Case #2 Original owner	Case #3 Original owner	Case #4 Original owner	Case #5 Minor owner	Case #6 Original owner
↓	↓	↓	↓	↓	↓
Thief, Finder, Bailee	Bailee with Apparent Authority	Merchant bailee	Thief, etc.	Buyer	Defrauder Bad-check Buyer
			↓		
			Merchant bailee		
↓	↓	↓	↓	↓	↓
BFP	BFP	BIOC	BIOC	BFP	BFP

Original owner   v.   BFP or BIOC

Return of goods ———————————————————————→

←- "I own it now." (Good title passed to me.)

(Question: In each case, who owns the goods?)

merchant has the *power* (not the right) to transfer all rights of the *entruster* to a ***buyer in the ordinary course*** of business **(BIOC).** If you left your watch for repair at a jewelry store that sold watches, or if you bought a new watch at the store but left it there on a layaway plan until you could pay for it, you have given the watch merchant the power to transfer all your rights in the watch to a good faith purchaser (BIOC). The buyer keeps "your" watch; you have to sue the merchant for wrongfully selling your property. Notice, however, that if a thief stole your watch and left it for repair, you could still recover it from a BIOC, since the merchant only had the power to pass whatever title the thief had (none). This section thus goes further than the law ever has in protecting good faith purchasers. The *Couch* case illustrates this point.

COUCH v. COCKROFT

490 S.W.2d 713 (Tennessee, 1972)

FACTS   Couch, a dealer in new and used cars, sold a new 1967 Cadillac to Sartain, also a dealer in used cars. The related papers of sale were held by Couch and were to be sent to Sartain after Sartain's check cleared. After Couch had delivered the car, but before the check had cleared, Sartain sold the car to Cockroft, a BFP (bona fide purchaser).

The check bounced. Couch filed for replevin, regained the Cadillac, and then resold it.

The chancery court held that the seller had no right to replevy the car and that Cockroft was entitled to the value of the automobile from the seller for wrongful replevy. Couch appealed.

ISSUE

Was Cockroft a BIOC (buyer in the ordinary course of business) even though he had not yet received a motor vehicle registration certificate?

DECISION

Yes. Judgment affirmed.

REASONS

Judge Matherne quickly got to the main issue:

"We do not find a reported Tennessee case on the issue. This Court has, however, repeatedly held a failure to comply with the title and registration laws does not render the sale of the automobile void. . . .

"We therefore conclude the failure of the purchaser to obtain from the seller a certificate of title, or other instrument showing compliance with the Motor Vehicle Title and Registration laws, does not in and of itself deny the purchaser the status of a buyer in ordinary course of business. . . .

"The plaintiff further insists the defendant Cockroft did not act in 'good faith' wherein he had experience as an automobile dealer, but he accepted a new Cadillac automobile from a nonfranchised dealer without receiving the manufacturer's certificate of origin to that vehicle. The evidence reveals Cockroft had about 10 years' experience as a dealer in used and new automobiles. This experience ended, however, about 15 years prior to the trial date of this lawsuit. . . . The good faith of Cockroft is further challenged on the ground he knew the Cadillac was purchased by Sartain by telephone to fill Cockroft's specific order and therefore Cockroft in good faith would be required to demand complete title papers with the delivery to him of the automobile. . . .

"The legislative intent by the enactment of T.C.A. § 47–2–403(2) and (3) was to protect the purchaser of goods entrusted to another who is engaged in the business of selling goods of that kind. We hold the fact Sartain obtained the Cadillac from some source unknown to the defendant Cockroft in order to meet the demand of the defendant for a certain type vehicle did not put the defendant on notice to demand proof the vehicle was clear of liens. Under the facts of this case, all elements of the 'entrustment statutes' were met. The Cadillac in the possessin of Sartain was subject to sale the same as any other vehicle on Sartain's lot."

■ BULK SALES

Seller's unsecured creditors versus bfp

The Problem Defined. *Bulk sales* also involve third parties who may have claims against the seller's goods and who wish to assert those claims even though the goods are now in the hands of a good faith purchaser. This problem, however, arises in a different context. It occurs because some sellers want to play "take the money and run": they sell all their inventory to an innocent buyer, pocket the cash, and leave town without paying off their business creditors.

The seller here is a *merchant* "whose principal business is the sale of merchandise from stock, including those who manufacture what they sell." This definition excludes farmers, contractors, and service enterprises. The seller *does* own the goods involved—the inventory—but instead of selling it in the normal course of business, a *bulk transfer* is made; that is, a single transfer involving a "major part" of the inventory. The purpose of prior bulk sales laws and of Article 6 of the Code is to try to protect both the seller's creditors and the buyer by specifying a required procedure for bulk transfers, with the main burden of compliance placed on the bulk seller.

The court in the following case was trying to decide what is the "ordinary course of business."

STERNBERG v. RUBENSTEIN

305 N.Y. 235 (1953)

FACTS Three weeks before Christmas 1948, Fink opened a family shoe store in Buffalo, New York. In May he still had $19,000 worth of winter-style shoes. He sold 1,300 pairs for $3,549 to Rubenstein to clear his shelves of off-season shoes as well as to obtain cash to pay his debts and thus obtain credit for the purchase of new summer stock. Fink continued in business for six months after the sale, until the filing of a petition in bankruptcy in November 1949. The plaintiff, the trustee in bankruptcy, acting on behalf of the creditors, sued to hold the defendant, Jack Rubenstein, accountable under the Bulk Sales Act. The trial court held for Rubenstein, but the appellate division reversed. Rubenstein appealed.

ISSUE Is a retailer's bulk disposition of off-season merchandise "in the ordinary course of business"?

DECISION Yes. Judgment reversed (for Rubenstein).

REASONS The majority opinion emphasized the policy and spirit of the Bulk Sales Act:

"The record here shows that in the business of shoe retailing the sale of 'off-season' wares is no rare and irregular occurrence, but rather an established operating pattern, no attempt to defraud creditors, but rather an inevitable incident to the conduct of business. Shoe styles may vary sharply from season to season and year to year, with the result that last year's 'rage' may clog this season's shelves. As seasons change, a merchant seeks to clear his store, and as rapidly as possible, of shoes still unsold. Larger stores may resort to much publicized 'clearance sales' or operate their own 'special outlet' stores. But the smaller, independent retailer, lacking the means for extensive advertising or a separate store, must, of necessity, rely on dealers specializing in unseasonable obsolete shoes. Thus, as the record reveals, Rubenstein alone regularly dealt with as many as 'several hundred' retailers in 'smaller towns . . . throughout northern and western New York.'

"Such recurring sales, vital as these may be to the operation of the smaller independent retailer, must be regarded, in the words of the statute, as sales made 'in the ordinary course of trade and in the regular prosecution of said business.' Indeed, to subject such transactions to the requirements prescribed by section 44 would tell creditors little more than they already know. They are forewarned, by industry and trade custom, that 'off-season' sales are regular occurrences and, entirely apart from the Bulk Sales Act, they may anticipate usual sales of obsolete leftovers and scrutinize such transactions beforehand. And, if fraud or covert advantage is later unearthed, a creditor may set it aside as a fraudulent conveyance under state law or as a preference or fraudulent conveyance under federal statute."

Basic Requirements. In most cases the required procedure should be easy enough to follow. The buyer and seller prepare a schedule of the goods to be transferred. The seller furnishes the buyer with a *list of the seller's creditors* and their addresses; this list must be sworn to by the seller, and the buyer is not liable for any inaccuracies unless that person actually knows that a creditor's name has been omitted. The buyer is then responsible for notifying each listed creditor, either in person or by registered or certified mail, that the bulk transfer is to occur. This notice must be given at least 10 days before the buyer takes possession of the goods or makes a payment on the price. The notice must also contain the names and business addresses of the seller and the buyer and, if provision has been made for paying off the creditors, the address to which they should send their bills for payment. If no arrangement has been made for paying off the creditors, a *"long form" notice* must be used, which includes the estimated total of the seller's debts, the description and location of the goods to be transferred, the address where the creditor list and property schedule may be inspected, and the consideration received by the seller for the goods. The buyer must either preserve the schedule and list for six months, for inspection, or simply file this information with the specified public official.

If these steps have been followed, the buyer owns the goods free and clear of any claims of the seller's unsecured creditors, except in those few states which have adopted optional Section 6–106. This part of the Code makes the buyer personally responsible for seeing to it that the purchase price is applied to pay off the seller's creditors. If the required steps have not been followed, the seller's creditors can have the bulk goods seized and sold to satisfy their claims if they bring suit within six months after the transfer occurred or, if the transfer was *concealed*, within six months after they discover what happened. In any case, a good faith purchaser from the bulk transferee owns the goods free and clear of claims of the original seller's creditors.

In those states which have adopted optional Section 6–106, the bulk buyer needs to be much more careful, since noncompliance can make the buyer personally liable to the unpaid creditors.

Exceptions. Certain extraordinary transfers are not subject to the requirements of Article 6. Transfers pursuant to judicial processes or to satisfy certain preexisting obligations and transfers of property which is exempt from creditors' claims can be made without complying with Article 6. Article 6 also contains two exemptions that were not found in most of the old bulk sales statutes.

These two new exemptions will permit the sale of a business, including its *inventories,* without the necessity of compliance, where the buyer has an established, solvent business and agrees to *assume the seller's debts,* or where the buyer is a *new enterprise* organized to take over and continue the seller's business and the seller receives nothing from the bulk transfer except an interest in the new enterprise which is subordinate to the claims of its creditors. In both cases an unspecified "public notice" must be given, but otherwise these exceptions should provide considerable flexibility in reorganizing an existing business.

Tax and Other Special Statutes. In addition to the bulk sale problems discussed above, the buyer of a business will also need to be aware of possible claims against the business for unpaid taxes. Accrued social security and withhold-

Procedure followed = Buyer owns free and clear

New exceptions: takeover and incorporation

■ EXHIBIT 22–2

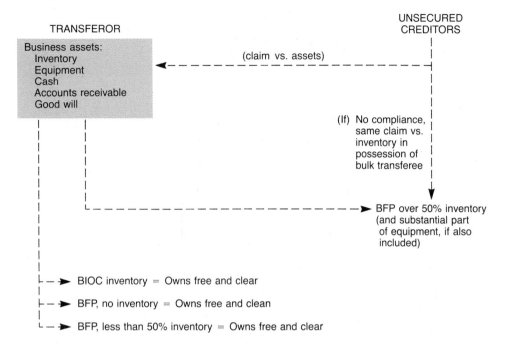

TRANSFEROR

Business assets:
Inventory
Equipment
Cash
Accounts receivable
Good will

(claim vs. assets)

UNSECURED CREDITORS

(If) No compliance, same claim vs. inventory in possession of bulk transferee

BFP over 50% inventory (and substantial part of equipment, if also included)

BIOC inventory = Owns free and clear

BFP, no inventory = Owns free and clean

BFP, less than 50% inventory = Owns free and clear

ing taxes may be owed to the national government. Payments may be due to the state government for sales taxes, unemployment taxes, and workers' compensation coverage. Local real estate taxes and special assessments may not have been paid. In some cases, the tax statutes will provide that these accrued liabilities become liens against the business' assets. The buyer of the business may not be protected against such liens simply by complying with the Code's bulk sales requirements.

Also, if a transfer of real estate is involved in the sale of the business, the buyer needs to be aware of the possibility of adverse claims against the land. These matters are discussed more fully in Chapter 34. Article 6 has no application to transfers of land, only to bulk sales of inventory.

■ **SIGNIFICANCE OF THIS CHAPTER**

A modern economy cannot function effectively unless most buyers are assured that they will, in fact, own the goods which they buy in good faith. The basic policy of the Code is to protect such good faith buyers against most adverse claims which might be made against the goods. Where one buys goods from a merchant-dealer in an ordinary business transaction, the Code states a conclusive presumption that the merchant was authorized to sell them if the owner voluntarily left them in the merchant's possession. Where one is buying a merchant's inventory "in bulk" and not in the ordinary course of business, Article 6 provides a relatively simple procedure to validate the transaction. In both cases, buyers are protected if they act in good faith and follow the law.

DISCUSSION CASE

KUNSTSAMMLUNGEN ZU WEIMAR v. ELICOFON
678 F.2d 1150 (U.S. Second Circuit, 1982)

FACTS: In this diversity suit involving two foreign countries (East Germany and West Germany), a foreign national, and an American citizen, the courts must determine the ownership of two priceless Albrecht Duerer portraits executed around 1499. They were stolen in 1945 from a castle located in what is now East Germany and fortuitously discovered in 1966 in the Brooklyn home of Edward I. Elicofon, an American citizen, where they had been openly displayed by him to friends since his good faith purchase of them over 20 years earlier without knowledge that they were Duerers. The search for an answer to the deceptively simple question, "Who owns the paintings?" involves a labyrinthian journey through 19th-century German dynastic law, contemporary German property law, Allied Military Law during the post-War occupation of Germany, New York State law, and intricate conceptions of succession and sovereignty in international law.

The Grand Duchess of Saxony-Weimar ("Grand Duchess"), who intervened as plaintiff in the lawsuit, which was initiated in 1969 by the Federal Republic of Germany ("FRG"), the government of West Germany, claims that the paintings were and remain the private property of the successive Grand Dukes of Saxony-Weimar and that title to the paintings was assigned to her by her husband Grand Duke Carl August. Kunstsammlungen zu Weimar ("KZW"), or the Weimar Art Collection, also intervened as plaintiff representing the interests of the German Democratic Republic ("GDR"), the government of East Germany, claiming that title to the paintings passed to the GDR as a successor in interest to the public property of predecessor sovereignties. Elicofon claims title based on his good faith purchase and uninterrupted possession of the paintings for 20 years.

In separate opinions, Judge Jacob Mishler of the Eastern District of New York granted summary judgment in favor of KZW and dismissed the claims of both intervenor-plaintiff Grand Duchess and defendant Elicofon.

This consolidated appeal raises two distinct issues: (1) as between the Grand Duchess and KZW, who owned the Duerer paintings when they were stolen in 1945; and (2) whether Elicofon subsequently acquired valid title at the expense of the true owner, either upon his purchase or at some later time as a result of his uninterrupted

good faith possession of them for 20 years from 1946 to 1966.

Elicofon's claim of ownership arises out of his uninterrupted possession of the Duerer paintings from the time of his good faith purchase of them in 1946 from an American serviceman in Brooklyn to his discovery in 1966 of the identity of the paintings. Until 1943 the Duerer paintings had remained on exhibit in a museum in Weimar, Thuringia, known as the Staatliche Kunstsammlungen zu Weimar, the predecessor to the intervenor-plaintiff KZW. To protect the exhibited artworks from anticipated bombardment, they were in 1943 stored in a nearby castle, the Schloss-Schwarzburg, located in the District of Rudolstadt in the Land of Thuringia. They remained there until stolen some time between June 12 and July 19, 1945. Their disappearance coincided with the withdrawal of the temporary American occupation forces which were replaced by the Russian Army on July 2, 1945. Dr. Scheidig, the Director of the Weimar Museum from 1940 to 1967, who discovered the theft on an inspection of the castle, immediately reported the theft and thereafter engaged in diligent efforts to locate the paintings. These efforts included contacting various German museums and administrative organs, the Allied Control Council, the Soviet Military Administration, the United States State Department, and the Fogg and Germanic museums at Harvard (which were active in locating stolen art), all to no avail.

In the meantime, unbeknownst to Dr. Scheidig or the art world generally, Elicofon purchased the unsigned Duerer paintings in the spring of 1946 for $450 from a young American ex-serviceman who appeared at his Brooklyn home and claimed to have purchased the paintings in Germany. Elicofon framed and displayed them on the wall in his home along with his many other collected art objects. In the years that followed his house was used for numerous charity functions and other large gatherings and his collection was viewed by many people, including some who were knowledgeable about art.

In May of 1966 Elicofon discovered the identity of the Duerer paintings through a friend who had recently seen them listed in a German book describing stolen art treasures of World War II. His discovery was publicized in a front-page article in *The New York Times* of May

30, 1966, and was described by one official of the Metropolitan Museum as the "discovery of the century." Thereafter the FRG, the Grand Duchess and KZW all demanded the return of the paintings; KZW's demand was made in September 1966. These demands were refused.

■

Judgment: Circuit Judge Mansfield:

Judge Mishler's holding that the State's ownership of the paintings was established by the 1927 Agreement is fully supported and indeed strengthened by the earlier occurrences, including the 1918 abdication and the 1921 Agreement, which unequivocally rebut the erroneous assumption underlying the Grand Duchess' interpretation of the 1927 Agreement, namely, that the Grand Ducal Art Collection was originally private property and not Krongut or Kammervermoegen, and is therefore governed by §§ 8 and 9 rather than by § 1 of the 1921 Agreement. Moreover, it is undisputed that the 1913 Museum Catalogue, which clearly designates those objects owned privately by the Grand Duke, failed to designate the Duerer paintings as privately owned. Thus the Collection as a whole constituted Krongut or Kammervermoegen and not private property. We hold, therefore, that the paintings, as acknowledged by § 1 of the 1921 Agreement and § 1 of the 1927 Agreement, were the "exclusive property" of the Territory of Weimar.

We also reject the Grand Duchess' "reversion" theory, under which she claims that even if the paintings became public property in 1921 she regained title to them when the annuity payments ceased in 1945. By its terms the 1921 Agreement does *not* condition the State's title to the Collection under § 1 on the continued payment of annuities. . . .

Elicofon's third argument is that KZW is barred by New York's statute of limitations from suing to recover the paintings. The essential facts are that in October 1966 Elicofon refused to comply with KZW's demand for return of the paintings and in April 1969 KZW moved to intervene in this action, which was begun by FRG, thereby commencing KZW's action. . . . The applicable New York statute provides a three-year limitation period. . . . The question is when the limitation period began to run, or, in other words, when KZW's claim against Elicofon accrued. If it accrued only upon Elicofon's refusal in 1966, then the suit was timely commenced. If, on the other hand, it accrued in 1946, when Elicofon bought the paintings, the action would be barred by the then-applicable limitation period of six years unless it was tolled by a subsequent disability before it expired. Judge Mishler held that under New York law KZW's claim accrued in 1966 and that, even if it accrued earlier in 1946, the then-applicable limitation period was tolled under New York's judicially created "nonrecognition" toll because the United States did not recognize GDR until 1974, which precluded the KZW from intervening until then. We agree with both conclusions.

Under New York law an innocent purchaser of stolen goods becomes a wrongdoer only after refusing the owner's demand for their return. Until the refusal the purchaser is considered to be in lawful possession. . . .

Even were we to assume that under New York law KZW's cause of action accrued in 1946, we would affirm Judge Mishler's holding that the statute of limitations was tolled under New York's judicially created "nonrecognition" toll until 1974, when the United States first recognized the GDR. . . .

Accordingly, we affirm the district court's holding that KZW is entitled to possession of the paintings and order that the judgment entered below be enforced.

■ IMPORTANT TERMS AND CONCEPTS

defect in seller's title
voidable title
buyer in ordinary course
appearance of authority
  to sell
bulk sale/bulk transfer
list of seller's creditors
concealed transfer
transfer to new business
void title

good faith purchaser
bailee
entrusting to a
  merchant
merchant
long form notice to
  creditors
assumption of debts
  of seller
inventory

■ QUESTIONS AND PROBLEMS FOR DISCUSSION

1. When does a person in possession of goods, other than the owner, have an "appearance" of authority to sell them?
2. Why does the UCC protect the buyer in ordinary course of business who has bought goods from a merchant to whom they have been entrusted by the owner?
3. What businesses are covered by the bulk sales article of the UCC?

4. What must a bulk buyer do to comply with the requirements of Article 6?

5. Savvy Drug Store owned First Bank $100,000 on a loan which had been personally guaranteed by Savvy's president, Don Rennis. Rennis also owned First Bank for personal loans. Savvy sold all its inventory to Hermit Drugs for $92,000 and immediately endorsed and transferred Hermit's check to First Bank. Savvy did not give Hermit a list of its creditors, nor was a notice of the sale sent to them. At the time of the sale, Savvy owed Drug Dealers, Inc. over $14,000 for drugs that had been sent on credit. What rights does Drug Dealers have here? Explain.

6. Jaybird Corporation, a mass marketing organization, transferred almost all of its assets, including its merchandise inventories, to Marketers, Inc. Prior to the transfer, Deliverance, Inc., had performed delivery services for Jaybird, totaling more than $57,000, and had not been paid. Jaybird was insolvent, and Deliverance wants to assert its claim against Marketers. Marketers argues that it should not be held liable, since its contract with Jaybird indicates that a fair consideration was to be paid for the merchandise. No notice of the transfer was given to Deliverance or any of Jaybird's other creditors. What is the result, and why?

7. Friedrich was interested in trading in his used car for a newer model. He went to Karl, a used-car dealer, to discuss the possibility of a trade-in. Karl said he could allow only $1,500 on the trade-in. Friedrich said he thought the car was worth at least $2,000. Karl told Friedrich to leave the car and said that he would show it to customers and see if anyone would pay $2,000 for it. Karl sold the car for $1,800 but never turned the money over to Friedrich or got Friedrich's specific approval for the sale at that price. Karl is now bankrupt. Friedrich sues to recover his car from the buyer, Nikolai. What is the result, and why?

8. Road Machinery Company was a dealer in heavy equipment. It leased a set of truck scales to Ore Company for a period of 24 months, at $600 per month. At the end of the lease, Ore had an option to buy the scales if it wished to do so. Ore never made any lease payments, but instead resold the truck scales to Clyde for $9,000. Prior to buying the scales, Clyde checked the public records and found no financing statements or any other indication that anyone had a claim against them. Road sues Clyde for the return of the scales. What is the result, and why?

PART FOUR

Creditors and Debtors

Since many sales of goods are made on credit, and since goods and documents of title covering goods are frequently used as collateral in business financing arrangements, the material in Part Four logically follows Part Three. Here we review various aspects of short-term commercial financing and risks of nonpayment.

The core of the legal rules for short-term commercial financing is found in Article Nine of the UCC, "Secured Transactions." Article Nine covers all types of financing that use personal property or real estate fixtures as collateral. This very complex legal topic is covered in Chapters 24 and 25. Chapter 24 also covers the use of cosigners ("sureties") in credit transactions. To help you better appreciate the need for being a secured creditor rather than an unsecured one, the first chapter in this part summarizes the U.S. bankruptcy law. With hundreds of thousands of bankruptcies occurring each year, an unsecured creditor is taking a substantial risk of not receiving full payment. Bankruptcy is the problem; secured transactions are the solution.

In addition to establishing the legal rules in these two areas, both national and state governments have moved aggressively in the last two decades to protect consumers and debtors. Chapter 26 outlines the major consumer protection statutes now in force in the area of credit transactions.

23

Bankruptcy

CHAPTER OBJECTIVES

THIS CHAPTER WILL:

- Explain the purpose and history of bankruptcy laws.
- Review the different types of proceedings in bankruptcy which are authorized by the law.
- Discuss the procedure for filing bankruptcy by debtor or by debtor's creditors.
- Explain the exemptions allowed to the debtor under national and state law.
- Review the terms of the bankruptcy law regarding discharge of debts.

DEFINITION, GOALS, AUTHORITY, HISTORY

Bankruptcy is the process of settling the debts of persons or firms that are no longer able to meet their obligations. Under court supervision, the debtor's assets (or most of them) are collected and sold, and the proceeds are distributed to creditors. Creditors with equal *priority* status should receive the same proportion of their claims against the debtor. If the correct procedures have been followed, at the end of the process the debtor's obligations (or most of them) are discharged even though they have not been paid in full. The debtor gets a "fresh start."

Congress is empowered to establish uniform bankruptcy laws by the U.S. Constitution, Article I, Section 8. The first national bankruptcy law was passed in 1800. The Bankruptcy Act of 1898 was in force for 80 years, though it was substantially revised by the Chandler Act of 1938. To deal with the administrative problems which had arisen under the Bankruptcy Act and to better implement changes in consumer credit laws and in the UCC, Congress enacted the Bankruptcy Code of 1978, which became generally effective October 1, 1979.

ADMINISTRATION

The 1978 Code provided for a new system of bankruptcy courts as of April 1, 1984. The plan was that each U.S. judicial district would then have a bankruptcy court as an adjunct to the U.S. District Court, with one or more bankruptcy judges, each appointed for a 14-year term. These courts would have jurisdiction to decide all controversies affecting the debtor or the debtor's estate. In 1982, the Supreme Court in the *Northern Pipeline* case, found that the portion of the 1978 Bankruptcy Code which created the new system of bankruptcy courts violated Article III of the U.S. Constitution. The Court did state that its decision in this case would apply prospectively rather than retroactively, to avoid upsetting previously decided cases. In July 1984, the Bankruptcy Amendments and Federal Judgeship Act was adopted to replace those sections of the 1978 code which had been held unconstitutional. The 1984 Amendments also made many other changes in the details of bankruptcy law.

TYPES OF PROCEEDINGS

Liquidation versus debt adjustment

Chapter 7 of the 1978 code provides for *straight bankruptcy,* or *liquidation.* The trustee gathers and sells the debtor's property and pays the creditors; the debtor receives a discharge from all listed debts. Generally, straight bankruptcy proceedings may be voluntary or involuntary; that is, either the debtor or the creditors may institute such proceedings. Involuntary straight bankruptcy proceedings may not be commenced against a farmer or a nonprofit corporation.

Chapter 9 provides for adjustment of the debts of municipal corporations, where this is authorized by applicable state law.

Chapter 11 gives corporations in financial difficulty a chance to *reorganize* their financial affairs by staying in business and making periodic payments to their creditors. Chapter 11 proceedings may be voluntary or involuntary. Railroads are limited to Chapter 11 procedures.

Chapter 13 permits similar debt readjustments and payoffs for individuals with regular income. Chapter 13 proceedings can only be voluntary on the part of the debtor.

Insurance companies, banks, savings and loans, and similar financial institutions are governed by their own regulatory agencies and are not subject to the Bankruptcy Code.

In 1986, Congress added Chapter 12 to the Bankruptcy Code to provide for debt adjustment plans for "family farmers." As defined, a family farmer is an individual, or individual and spouse, engaged in a farming operation, whose total debts do not exceed $1,500,000 and at least 80 percent of which arise out of farming operations. In addition, such person(s) must have received more than 50 percent of the prior year's taxable income from farming operations. A corporation or partnership is included if more than 50 percent of the equity is owned by one family, or by one family and relatives, *and* the family or relatives conduct the farming operation. Additionally, more than 80 percent of the firm's business assets must be related to farming operations; its debts must not exceed $1,500,000 and must be 80 percent farming related; and if a corporation, its stock must not be publicly traded. *Farming operation* is defined as including ranching, raising of crops or livestock, and production of such unprocessed farm products as milk, eggs, and wool.

Chapter 12 provides for the filing and approval of a debt readjustment plan by the family farmer. The procedure is similar in most respects to the individual plans under Chapter 13, but it is specifically tailored to the needs of farmers. The family farmer is a business operation, and thus not quite the same as the typical consumer debtor who uses Chapter 13. Likewise, family farmers probably do need a slightly different procedure than the typical business reorganization under Chapter 11. In any event, Congress decided that a special procedure for *farm reorganizations* was justified.

■ PROCEDURE

The debtor commences voluntary proceedings under Chapters 7, 9, 11, 12, or 13 by filing a petition, under the appropriate chapter, with the bankruptcy court. Spouses may file a joint petition to reduce administrative costs; the bankruptcy court has the power to allocate joint and separate property and debts.

Involuntary petitions

Where the debtor has 12 or more creditors, an involuntary petition under Chapters 7 or 11 must be joined in by three of them, who must have unsecured claims totaling at least $5,000. In determining this number, employees and insiders of the debtor are not counted. Where there are fewer than 12 creditors, any one of them with an unsecured claim of $5,000 can file an involuntary petition. In addition, in an involuntary case the petitioning creditor or creditors must show either that the debtor is not paying his or her debts as they fall due or that the debtor has made a general assignment of assets for the benefit of creditors within 120 days prior to the filing of the petition.

Court's order for relief

In a voluntary case the court's "order for relief" is automatic; this operates to stay collection proceedings against the debtor in state courts. In an involuntary petition the court must determine whether or not relief should be ordered. Where the creditors' allegations are not proved, the debtor may be awarded court costs and damages for the lost use of property turned over to a trustee as well as actual and punitive damages if the filing was made in bad faith. Once an order for relief has been entered, the debtor is required to prepare schedules of creditors, assets, and liabilities. Where the debtor is claiming personal exemptions, a schedule of those exemptions must also be filed with the court. Based on the list of creditors, the court sends out a notification of the first creditors' meeting.

The court may appoint an interim trustee to hold and manage the debtor's property until a trustee is elected by the creditors. If the creditors fail to elect a trustee, the interim trustee continues to administer the debtor's estate. The trustee's job is to collect all the debtor's property, to separate out exempt property, to determine whether creditors' claims are secured or unsecured, and finally to pay off claims according to their legal priority status.

■ DEBTOR'S AVAILABLE PROPERTY

State exemptions

The 1898 act permitted each state to specify what items of property the debtor could exempt from the bankruptcy proceeding; these exemptions vary considerably from state to state. The Michigan exemptions, for example, include all family pictures, wearing apparel, "provisions and fuel" for comfortable subsistence for the family for six months, up to $1,000 of household goods and appliances, burial plots, up to $1,000 in the tools of the debtor's trade, disability insurance benefits for sickness or injury, the cash surrender value of life insurance, benefits to be paid under workers' compensation, up to $3,500 for a "homestead" exemption (the debtor's equity in the family home), and to each householder "10 sheep, 2 cows, 5 swine, 100 hens, 5 roosters and sufficient hay and grain growing or otherwise to keep such animals and poultry for six months." The foregoing list seems fairly generous if one remembers that the debtor is getting a discharge from most debts and a fresh start.

The 1978 code gives the debtor the option of choosing the state exemptions or those provided in the 1978 code, unless the particular state specified its exemptions must be used. Some 30 states have done so. For most debtors with the option, the national exemptions will be a better choice.

U.S. exemptions

Exempt Property. The exemptions of the 1978 code include a residence exemption of up to $7,500; up to $1,200 for one motor vehicle; and up to $200 per item, with a $4,000 limit on total value, for household goods, wearing apparel, appliances, animals, crops, or musical instruments. Additional exemptions include up to $500 in jewelry owned by the debtor or a dependent; up to $400 for any property plus up to $3,750 from any unused amount from the $7,500 residence exemption; up to $750 for the tools or books of the debtor's or a dependent's trade; any unmatured life insurance policy owned by the debtor other than a credit life policy; up to $4,000 in cash surrendered or loan value for a life insurance policy owned by the debtor and on the debtor's life; professionally prescribed health aids for the debtor and dependents; alimony and child support payments; "future earnings" such as social security and veterans' benefits, unemployment compensation, disability payments, and pension plan payments; and up to $7,500 in payments from a personal injury lawsuit. The debtor is also given the power to avoid *judicial liens* and nonpossessory, ***nonpurchase-money security interests*** that impair his or her exemptions

Recovery of property

for most listed items of tangible personal property (but not liens against the motor vehicle).

The trustee may recover any items of property which the debtor *fraudulently transferred* to others within one year prior to the filing of the bankruptcy petition. A transfer is fraudulent if the debtor actually intended to hide the asset from his or her creditors' claims or if the debtor received less than fair consideration for the asset and was insolvent at the time (or became so as a result of the transfer). The trustee may also recover *preferential payments* made by the debtor 90 or fewer days to the petition. A payment is preferential if it is made for a prior unsecured debt, if it gives a creditor more than that creditor would have received in a bankruptcy proceeding, and if the debtor was insolvent at the time the payment was made. The debtor is presumed to have been insolvent during the 90-day period, and the creditor's good faith is irrelevant. A payment is not preferential if it was made in the ordinary course of business.

The question in the *Lynn* case is whether a professional degree and license are "property."

MATTER OF LYNN

18 B.R. 501 (U.S. Bankruptcy Court, D. Connecticut, 1982)

FACTS   Robert Isaac Lynn and Bonnie Marie Ryan had been married in 1971, while he was still in medical school. When they were divorced in 1979, the New Jersey court held that his medical degree and license to practice medicine were "property" and thus subject to "equitable distribution" between the spouses in the divorce proceeding. The New Jersey court then awarded Bonnie 20 percent of this "property," valued at $306,886. Robert was ordered to pay that amount ($61,377.20) in semiannual installments over the next six years. When Robert filed for bankruptcy, he indicated that he practiced medicine as a physician, but did not list his medical degree and license in his schedule of property owned. Bonnie and her attorney (Stephen Roth) objected to Robert's receiving a discharge in bankruptcy because he failed to schedule all his "property."

ISSUE   Is an academic degree, or a professional license to practice, "property" under the U.S. Bankruptcy Reform Act of 1978?

DECISION   No. (Neither one is.) Judgment for defendant Lynn.

REASONS   **Bankruptcy Judge Krechevsky did not consider himself bound by the state divorce law of New Jersey; what mattered were the definitions of property in the Bankruptcy Act.**

"Without questioning the reasoning of the New Jersey court in determining what constitutes 'property' subject to equitable distribution under New Jersey law, I find that the debtor's medical degree and license are not property for purposes of bankruptcy law. Section 541 of the Bankruptcy Reform Act of 1978 contains a fulsome description of what constitutes property of the estate. In subsection (a)(6), Congress has specifically excluded 'earnings from services performed by an individual debtor after the commencement of the case' from the definition of property included in the estate. A medical degree and license to practice medicine are related to a debtor's future earning ability and are not susceptible to conversion into money for distribution to creditors. The cases cited by the plaintiffs, which generally hold that the Bankruptcy Reform Act has expanded the concept of property of the estate, do not approach the concept of property urged in this proceeding. The holding of the New Jersey court that the medical degree and license are property under New Jersey law is not binding on a bankruptcy court.

"[W]here the Bankrupt Law deals with property rights which are regulated by the state law, the federal courts in bankruptcy will follow the state courts; but when the language of Congress indicates a policy requiring a broader construction of the statute than the state decisions would give it, federal courts cannot be concluded by them."

■ CREDITORS' CLAIMS AND PRIORITIES

A claim under the 1978 code includes nearly any sort of right to payment, whether or not it is reduced to judgment, liquidated or unliquidated, fixed or contingent, matured or unmatured, disputed or undisputed, legal or equitable, secured or unsecured. It includes the right to equitable remedies where the breach also gives a right to payment. A creditor who has such a claim files a document called a *proof of claim.* A secured creditor need not do so unless the claim exceeds the value of the security and the creditor wishes to try to collect the balance in the bankruptcy proceeding. The creditor's "proof" is accepted as prima facie evidence of the existence and the amount of the debt, and such claims will be allowed and paid (to the extent that funds are available) unless objection is made to them by another creditor, the trustee, or the debtor. Under current practice, proofs of claim must be filed within six months after the first date set for the first meeting of creditors.

Secured versus unsecured claims

Not all claims arc paid at the same time or to the same extent. *Secured creditors,* that is, creditors who have taken the proper steps to establish their rights against specific pieces of collateral, will be paid first from the proceeds of that collateral. If the value of their collateral is sufficient, secured creditors may be paid in full; if not, they are *unsecured creditors* for the remainder of their claims. In addition to the claims of secured creditors, there are other claims which are given priority under the Bankruptcy Code. Administrative expenses, including the payment of accountants, appraisers, attorneys, and trustees, are paid first; so are creditors' expenses in discovering and recovering property which the debtor has transferred or concealed.

Payment priorities

The 1978 code changes priorities by giving second-payment status to unsecured claims for goods, services, or credit which arose in the normal course of the debtor's business between the filing of an involuntary petition and the court's order for relief or appointment of a trustee. Similarly, third priority is given to *wage claims* of up to $2,000 each which were earned by the debtor's employees in the 90 days preceding the filing of the petition or the cessation of business, and fourth priority is given to claims for contributions to employee benefit plans, which were earned within the prior 180 days, for up to $2,000 per employee, less any payments on wage claims. The 1984 amendments inserted a new fifth-priority claim, for up to $2,000 each, in favor of grain growers and U.S. fishermen against persons who store their products.

Consumers now have a sixth-priority claim of up to $900 per claimant for the return of money deposited with the debtor for purchased or leased goods which were not delivered or for services which were not performed. *Claims for unpaid taxes* owed to various governmental units have been lowered to seventh-priority status. Only after all of the above priority claims have been paid in turn will the general, unsecured creditors receive any money. In most bankruptcy cases this means that the general creditors will receive little or nothing. (And remember that the debtor is allowed to keep all "exempt" property.)

The 1978 Bankruptcy Code makes one other significant priority change. The creditors of a *bankrupt partnership* are now entitled to share equally with the unsecured creditors of individual partners against the partners' personal assets. Under the old rule in the Uniform Partnership Act, the firm's unpaid creditors had no claim against personal assets until all the personal creditors had been paid in full. The Bankruptcy Code also contains special rules for community property, and it gives the court general power to change priorities on equitable grounds after a hearing.

■ DISCHARGE, OBJECTIONS, AND GROUNDS FOR REFUSAL

Most of the individual debtors who file under Chapter 7 will receive a *discharge* from most of their previous debts at the conclusion of the bankruptcy proceedings. This is the whole idea of the "fresh start." Generally, an individual can be so discharged only once within any six-year period. However, where an individual has worked out a voluntary repayment plan under Chapter 13, has paid off at least 70 percent of the claims filed under it, and has made his or her best efforts in good faith, a discharge may be granted more frequently than once in six years.

Objections to discharge

Any single creditor or the trustee acting for all of them may file an *objection to a discharge.* The court must then determine whether or not there is some reason for denying the discharge. The Bankruptcy Act lists several grounds

■ **EXHIBIT 23–1**

The Bankruptcy Process— Chapter 7 Liquidation

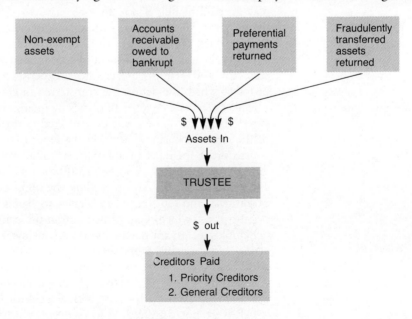

for denial, including the debtor's destruction or concealment of property with the intent of delaying or defrauding creditors; destroying, concealing, falsifying, or failing to keep books and records; committing a "bankruptcy crime," such as giving a false oath or participating in bribery to obtain some special advantage; failing to explain losses or deficiencies in existing assets; and failing to obey court orders or to answer questions (but *not* including refusals properly based on the constitutional privilege against self-incrimination). Also, even a debtor who is entitled to a discharge may in writing waive the right to one.

Where a discharge has been properly granted, the 1978 code extends the protection given the debtor from the unpaid creditors' further collection efforts for discharged debts. The discharge, of course, voids all existing and future judgments based on such debts. The 1898 act also prohibited creditors from employing "any process" to collect discharged debts; the 1978 code forbids any *act* by creditors to recover such debts.

The *Boydston* case considers whether certain acts by the debtor spouses should prevent their being discharged in bankruptcy.

MATTER OF BOYDSTON

520 F.2d 1098 (U.S. Fifth Circuit, 1975)

FACTS

In November of 1969 Arland Boydston, a 40-year-old Army Lt. Colonel, married Carolyn Conner. Their financial downfall began in March 1970 when they borrowed $3,000 to start a wig business, the Chateau De Monique Wig Salon in Mineral Wells, Texas. By September, the shop's business had sharply deteriorated because of the projected closing of nearby Fort Wolters. At this time Boydston retired from the service, cutting his income by more than half, to $708 per month. Aside from his retirement income and the small amount of money the couple was taking in from the salon, the Boydstons had no other income. The bankrupt was also involved in a prospective low-income housing project from which he hoped to make a windfall by sharing in the net profits. In January 1971, the project fell through when FHA approval was denied, again because of the closing of Fort Wolters.

Despite their strained financial condition, however, the Boydstons went on a spending spree which lasted from the latter part of August 1970 until they filed their petition in bankruptcy on February 15, 1971. During this six-month period they incurred almost $32,000 in new indebtedness, the overwhelming portion of which was for luxury items and nonessential personal expenses rather than for salvaging the wig business. Merchandise purchased included a new Cadillac, a mink coat, a very expensive shotgun, a houseful of new furniture, and $1,300 in personal travel expenses. A $6,000 bank loan ostensibly intended to acquire new inventory for the wig salon was diverted to the purchase of a new home in Dallas, and on several occasions personal financial statements submitted to creditors flagrantly failed to disclose a majority of their indebtedness. Most of the debt was incurred after the Boydstons were no longer able to meet existing obligations when due, and had written at least two creditors requesting extension of payment deadlines.

During this period, $2,923.73 worth of personal merchandise was charged at Sears and $2,540.03 at Neiman Marcus. No payments were ever made on either account. Appellants claim that the factors detailed above clearly indicate a purpose to acquire merchandise on credit with no intention of paying for it. Sears also complains that, in completing a credit application with the store in November, Mrs. Boydston grossly overstated the wig salon's monthly earnings and omitted the family's major financial obligations in order to secure an extension of credit which otherwise would not have been granted. The application, however, contained only three blanks for listing present creditors.

Neiman Marcus thwarted Mrs. Boydston's discharge from any of her debts under S. 14(c)(1) of the Bankruptcy Act by showing that she had altered documents pertaining to her bankruptcy for the purpose of deceiving the court and had given perjured testimony concerning the exhibits. The referee found that there was no evidence to show that Mr. Boydston participated in or knew of these changes, and granted him a discharge. The U.S. District Court affirmed.

ISSUE   Is there sufficient evidence of fraud to deny a discharge?

DECISION   No. Judgment affirmed.

REASONS   **Judge Coleman reluctantly agreed with the prior decisions:**

"Appellants contend that the discharge should have been denied under S. 17(a)(2) of the Bankruptcy Act . . . because the bankrupts were engaged in a scheme to obtain property on credit with the secret intention of not paying for it. Although Boydston's actions appear so highly questionable that if we were hearing this case in the first instance, we would be inclined to deny discharge, we are unable to say as an appellate tribunal that the referee's findings are clearly erroneous. Therefore, we affirm the judgment of the District Court. . . .

"In mitigation of the husband's apparent disregard of his financial responsibilities, factors cited by the referee or which appear in the record include Boydston's contemplated business venture, the approach of the Christmas gift season, his lack of business experience, the fact that his wife made many of the purchases, particularly furniture and household goods, to replace items that had been used by his deceased wife, and his testimony that he was unaware of the precarious nature of his financial situation or the possibility of bankruptcy until he spoke with an attorney in February. The bankruptcy judge had the opportunity to see and hear the Boydstons firsthand, to weigh the credibility of all the witnesses, and to thoroughly examine the record. In his words, 'The evidence offered impresses me more as reckless, irresponsible naivete on the part of a recently married military man, who had just remarried, than cold, calculating, sophisticated planning by one bent on financial deception.' Based on Sears and Neiman Marcus' failure to demonstrate Boydston's insolvency at the time the debts were incurred or to provide sufficient evidence of his subjective intent not to repay the debts, the discharge was granted. . . .

"There is sufficient evidence in the record before us to sustain the original findings of fact. Boydston could feasibly have felt his financial slump was only temporary. Although he was unable to meet certain obligations as they came due, he did not try to permanently avoid payments, but merely postpone them. His reluctance to attempt to curb his wife's spending may be explained by his desire to stabilize his marriage rather than a secret desire to bilk creditors. The Sears credit application was not materially false since the store asked for the names of only three creditors, not for all outstanding obligations. The wig salon had just begun its decline when Mrs. Boydston stated its earnings in the application, a statement which may have been more optimistic than intentionally deceptive. The bankrupts' expectancy of a windfall from the housing project, the fact that bankruptcy was not contemplated when they made the purchases, and their lack of business expertise all militate against denying a discharge."

■ DEBTS NOT DISCHARGED

Some debts survive the bankruptcy discharge; that is, the debtor's liability still exists, and the creditor may use appropriate enforcement procedures. Such nondischargeable debts include taxes incurred for three years prior to the bankruptcy; **_alimony and child support_** payments; sums owed by a fiduciary because of fraud, misappropriation, or embezzlement; liability based on fraudulent representations or false pretenses; and liability for **_intentional torts_** ("willful and malicious injury"). As to debts in the last three groups, the creditor involved must specifically request a determination by the court that the debt is not dischargeable; if there is no such request, such debts would be discharged.

Because of the increasing frequency with which bankruptcies were being filed by recent college graduates, the 1978 code added another category of nondischargeable debts: **_educational loans,_** unless the first due date was more than five years before the filing of the bankruptcy petition or unless the continuing liability would impose an "undue hardship" on the debtor or the debtor's dependents. The 1984 amendments add liability for drunk driving to the list. Also, under the 1984 act, a debt of over $500 for luxury items bought within 40 days prior to the filing, and certain cash advances of over $1,000 made within 20 days prior to filing are presumed to be nondischargeable. These last two were clearly added in response to cases like *Boydston.* The question of "undue hardship" on a student debtor is discussed in the *Hemmen* case.

MATTER OF HEMMEN

7 B.R. 63 (1980)

FACTS

Michael Hemmen has no accumulated wealth. He recently obtained a divorce and his wife got everything. He has no savings account and only $40 in his checking account. He lives with his parents and pays them $60 per month room and board. He is unemployed and has made several unsuccessful attempts to obtain a job. He does not have a car. He only has three years of college with Business Administration as his Major. He receives $90 per week unemployment. He owes $4,039 plus interest on several educational loans. The total unsecured debt less the educational loans is over $13,000.

ISSUE

Is there sufficient "hardship" to discharge the student loans?

DECISION

No. Judgment for U.S. Government.

REASONS

Judge Coleman thought Michael still had prospects:

"While this loan is not the main debt, it is a substantial part of it. It seems that a discretion exists in the Bankruptcy Court to determine the remedy of undue hardship resulting from temporary lack of income, which by its nature can ameliorate or change. Unemployment or inability to earn is the most common casualty together with divorce, separation, and illness, both mental and physical. Unemployment is a status that requires some consideration and critical examination, even where it is not the result of the debtor's own disinclination or lack of effort.

"But circumstances may change. Permanent disability and disaster may occur rendering a blow to his plans and dreams. Unemployment or inability to earn can be cured by a change in the economy and the creation of jobs which we hope will soon occur. Unemployment is a status that requires some consideration and critical examination, even where it is not the result of the debtor's own disinclination or lack of effort. Unemployment is always possible, but can be followed by employment.

"Unemployment coupled with the other factors in this case causes the debtor to live in an almost poverty-level style of living, but the chances of his obtaining a job are very real. Employment is always possible.

"One of the main purposes of the Bankruptcy Code is to provide a 'fresh start' for the debtor. If unemployment continues for an indefinite time period, to require the debtor to repay this debt might frustrate the fresh start policy of the Code; however, the purpose of education is to enable the student to fit himself for a better life and a better ability to earn and produce. Here three years of college might help the debtor *obtain* a job. . . .

"This is a temporary lack of income rather than permanent. The Court therefore [recommends] supervision of the judgment for a short term of years, with an adjustment of payments according to some formula related to income to be earned in the future.

"Applying this formula and the principles announced to the facts in this case, the Court finds that undue hardships exists because of the very low earnings of the debtor and his lack of employment and inability to find a job paying a living wage. He is capable of earning considerably more, in which event he should pay.

"The Court will by separate order render judgment in favor of The UNITED STATES OF AMERICA for the principal amount of $4,039.46 plus interest in the amount of $203.95 as of August 1, 1980, making a total of $4,243.41, and interest thereafter on the principal at 7 percent per annum until paid but provide that the judgment may be discharged and satisfied if the debtor uses his best efforts to find suitable employment in a reasonable length of time and pays and applies on the judgment all funds received by him over $3,600 per annum, after taxes, to the payment of the judgment for the period of five years from the maturity of the last loan made by him with this creditor."

■ REAFFIRMA-
TION OF DEBTS

Protection for individual debtors

The 1978 code changes the rules on debtor's new promises to pay scheduled bankruptcy debts by adding several extra requirements for such promises to be enforceable. First, the new promises must be enforceable under the applicable state (nonbankruptcy) law; you'll recall from Chapter 12 that many states require such new promises to be made in writing. The 1978 code requires such new promises to have been made before the bankruptcy discharge becomes effective, and the code further states that such a promise may be rescinded by the debtor for 60 days after it becomes enforceable. In addition, where the debtor is an individual, the court must hold a hearing and advise the debtor of the legal effects of such a promise. The court also must tell the debtor that the promise is not required as a condition of the discharge. Where the new promise relates to a consumer debt that is not secured by real property, the court in addition must approve the promise as being in the debtor's "best interest" and not imposing an "undue hardship" or as being part of a good faith agreement for the redemption of some of the debtor's property or for the settlement of a dispute as to whether the debt was or was not dischargeable.

■ INDIVIDUAL REPAYMENT PLANS

Adjustment of debts

Objections to plan

Broader discharge under Chapter 13

An individual in financial difficulty may file a voluntary petition for "adjustment" of debts under Chapter 13 of the 1978 code and thus prevent nearly all further actions by creditors to collect their claims. This Chapter 13 procedure is available to persons who have less than $100,000 in unsecured debts, less than $350,000 in secured debts, and a "regular income." Proprietors of businesses, social security recipients, and wage earners can file under Chapter 13. Within 10 days of filing the petition, the debtor must file with the court a plan which provides for payments of future income to a trustee, for full payment to creditors with priority, for equal treatment of all claims in the same class, and for retention of liens by secured creditors. Such plans usually ask for an extension of time within which to pay the debts; the plan maximum is three years unless the court grants an extension of up to five years for good cause. The debtor may also ask for a *composition* of debts in which the creditors may receive less than 100 percent of their claims.

A bankruptcy judge presides at the hearing for confirmation of the proposed plan. Unsecured creditors do not get to vote on confirming the plan, but the plan must give them at least what they would have received if the debtor had gone through a Chapter 7 bankruptcy/liquidation. Priority claimants must be paid in full, to the extent that money is available, unless these creditors agree to lesser payments. Secured creditors do get to vote on whether or not to accept the plan, but if a secured creditor disapproves, the court may confirm it anyway if the debtor gives the dissenting creditor the property which secures the claim or if the dissenting creditor retains a lien and the subject property is worth at least as much as the allowed amount of the secured claim. A secured claim against the debtor's principal residence cannot be modified by the plan; other secured claims may be. The payment arrangements of the plan itself may be modified after confirmation, subject to the above limitations, after proper notice and a hearing.

After completing the payments required by the plan, the debtor is discharged from all debts except long-term unsecured debts not covered by the plan and debts for child support, maintenance, and alimony. In cases of "hardship," where modification of the plan is not practicable and where the amounts already paid are equal to Chapter 7 liquidation values, the debtor may receive a hardship discharge if the failure to complete the plan is not his or her fault. Such a hardship discharge does not affect any nondischargeable debts under Chapter 7, or long-term debts not dealt with by the plan, whether secured or unsecured; or debts incurred without the trustee's permission after confirmation of the plan. If the plan was a composition, the debtor cannot receive a second discharge for six years unless the amounts paid were his or her best effort, made in good faith, and at least 70 percent of the required payments were made.

■ REORGANIZA-TION OF BUSINESS DEBTOR

In many cases businesses get into financial difficulty because of dislocations in the production/distribution/collection process over which they have little, if any, control. Embargoes, wars, strikes, materials shortages, defaults by major customers, and other economic occurrences may have serious impact on a business that does not have substantial financial reserves. If a basically sound firm has a temporary cash flow problem, it probably makes sense to try to save the firm rather than push it into a Chapter 7 liquidation. Most reorganizations under Chapter 11 are designed to salvage the debtor businesses, although the creditors sometimes require management changes and the business may be run temporarily by a trustee.

Voluntary or involuntary

Chapter 11 cases, like Chapter 7 liquidations, may be voluntary or involuntary; most of the same rules apply to both types of proceedings. Under Chapter 11, however, the court must appoint a creditors' committee, usually composed of the seven largest unsecured creditors. This committee examines the affairs of the business to decide whether to continue the business, or to ask the court for a liquidation, or to ask that a trustee be appointed to operate the business in place of the existing management. For the first 120 days after filing, only the debtor can propose a plan for reorganization, but the debtor would normally develop such a plan in consultation with the creditors. A debtor who files a plan within that time has a further 60 days to get the creditors to approve it. The court can reduce or extend these time periods for good cause. After the first 120 days, any party in interest (a creditor or the trustee) can propose a plan.

Requirements of plan

The proposed plan must classify claims and ownership interests and must spell out which will and which will not be impaired; it must provide equal treatment for all claims or interests in the same class unless the persons with that class or interests agree otherwise; and it must provide adequate means for implementing the plan's payment arrangements. Further, where the debtor business is a corporation, the plan must require that stockholders' voting rights be protected, that no nonvoting stock be issued, and that directors and officers be selected so as to protect the interests of creditors and stockholders. Generally, the plan may modify the rights of creditors and owners, but these persons have the right to vote on whether or not to accept the plan. Normally the bankruptcy court will not confirm a reorganization plan unless it has received the required majority vote of each class of creditors or owners whose rights were modified ("impaired"). Two thirds in dollar amount of each class of such owners must vote in favor of the plan. Each class of such creditors must approve by a majority in number and by two thirds in the dollar amount of allowed claims. The plan may be confirmed without the consent of owners or creditors whose rights were not impaired.

It is possible for the court to confirm a plan which has not received the consent of an impaired class if the persons in that class are treated in a "fair and equitable" manner—for instance, if all members of the class will receive the full current value of their claims or if all members of the class will receive an equal proportion of their claims and classes whose claims and interests have lower priorities will receive nothing. In any case, dissenters are protected by the rule that they must receive from the plan at least what they would have received through a Chapter 7 liquidation. These points are illustrated in the *White* case.

■ **SIGNIFICANCE OF THIS CHAPTER**

Even honest and hard-working persons can suffer financial difficulties. Economic trends and technological changes can have adverse impacts on both businesses and individuals. When financial pressures become too severe, bankruptcy offers the debtor a "fresh start."

All businesspersons must therefore be aware of the existence of the bankruptcy laws. They should know how the bankruptcy laws operate and who is covered by them. This chapter gives the reader a basic understanding of this area of the law.

DISCUSSION CASE

IN RE WHITE
41 B.R. 227 (S.D. Tennessee, 1984)

FACTS: One of the debtors, Thomas C. White, has owned and operated a small land surveying business, Thomas C. White & Associates, in Waverly, Tennessee, over the past 11 and a half years. In his business, Mr. White employs his wife, the codebtor, and his two sons as well as three other employees. In order to secure financing for his business, Mr. White borrowed funds from a number of creditors including his largest creditor, Midland. In 1981, Mr. White's business began experiencing financial difficulties due in large part to the depressed economic conditions in Waverly, Tennessee. As a result of these difficulties, the debtors were unable to make a number of mortgage payments and, on October 28, 1983, filed a voluntary petition under Chapter 11 of the Bankruptcy Code.

The objecting creditor, Midland, was listed by the debtors as holding a claim totaling approximately $146,000. Midland's claim was secured by mortgages on four parcels of real property owned by the debtors. By an agreed order entered into between the debtors and Midland on January 12, 1984, Midland was allowed to foreclose upon three of these parcels of real property. Midland is presently seeking relief from the stay imposed by 11 U.S.C. § 362 (West 1979) in order to proceed with foreclosure on the fourth parcel of property, an 87-acre farm in Waverly, Tennessee.

On February 22, 1984, the debtors filed a plan of reorganization with this court. The plan provided for payment of claims identified in 10 separate classes. The debtors proposed funding their plan by tendering payments of $2,800 per month received from the debtors' surveying business and by subdividing a portion of the 87-acre farm property. Midland, the sole member of class IX, rejected the plan; members of class IV and VI abstained from voting; and, all other classes of creditors accepted the plan.

The debtors' plan provides for the payment of two claims asserted by Midland. The first claim will be secured by the accounts receivable of Mr. White's business to the extent of $12,000 and shall be paid at a rate of $270 per month with interest accruing at the rate of 12 percent per annum until the claim is paid in full. Midland's second claim is in the amount of $88,200 and will be secured by a security interest in the 87-acre farm owned by the debtors. This latter claim, accruing interest at a rate equal to the FMHA mortgage rate modified in accordance with the current FMHA mortgage rates on May 15 and November 15 of each year, will be paid over a 10-year period. Midland will also receive any funds from the sale of the debtors' subdivided farm land, which will accordingly reduce the debt to Midland.

■

Judge Paine:

The debtors testified that they intended to subdivide 28.78 acres of wooded farmland located on Cane Creek Road, two tenths of a mile from the city limits of Hohenwald, Tennessee. The debtors' remaining farmland is separated by Cane Creek Road from that which the debtors intend to subdivide. The farmland has been owned by Mr. White's family since 1961 and Mr. White's mother presently resides on the farm. The debtors claimed that the only improvements necessary to allow subdivision of the farm property would be the improvement of a dirt road and the installation of water mains. They estimated that the road could be improved for $1,500 and that the water mains could be installed for a small amount. Although no contracts for sale were tendered, Mr. White stated that an adjoining landowner as well as a local company had expressed interest in purchasing a combined total of approximately 10 to 12 acres.

Several exhibits were tendered and evidence was presented concerning the history and probable future of Mr. White's surveying business. Although Mr. White's business had grossed only $52,000 a year over the past two years, Mr. White projected that gross income for 1984 would total $102,787.23. Mr. White's projections were based on the value of new projects acquired in the first three and two-thirds months of 1984, current work in progress, current accounts receivable, the general economic conditions in Humphreys and surrounding counties and his significant work experience. On cross-examination, Mr. White admitted that he could not have funded the proposed plan in either of the prior two years; however, the volume of new work acquired by his business in the first few months of 1984 reflects that his business is indeed expanding.

Midland presented the testimony of Mr. Hines, a vice president of Midland Bank with experience in the foreclosure and resale of real property, who had visited the farm property in question. He testified that in order to subdivide this property, the debtors would need to improve the existing road at a probable cost of $30,000 to $32,000. He further testified that the market for real property in Humphreys County is presently very weak. Finally, Mr. Hines testified that the bank felt the interest rate provided to the bank under the plan for repayment of the $12,000 secured by accounts receivable and the $88,000 secured by real property was too low. He stated that both loans had been commercial loans which the bank expected the debtors would repay in a short period of time.

In order for a plan of reorganization to be approved by this court, the plan must comply with all the requirements of Chapter 11 as stated in 11 U.S.C. § 1129(a)(1). The court has a duty to examine the plan and determine whether or not the plan conforms to the requirements of 11 U.S.C. § 1129, regardless of whether objections are filed. . . . In fulfilling this duty, the court concludes that the specific objections raised by Midland are without merit.

First, Midland asserts that the plan was not proposed in good faith as required by 11 U.S.C. § 1129(a)(3). Essentially, a reorganization plan is proposed in good faith when there is "a reasonable likelihood that the plan will achieve a result consistent with the objectives and purposes of the Bankruptcy Code." . . . Herein, the debtors have proposed a plan which provides for payments to both secured and unsecured creditors. The secured creditors will receive the value of their collateral plus interest while the unsecured creditors will receive payment contingent upon both the surveying business and the subdivision of the debtor's property. The court finds that the financial assumptions underlying the debtors' plan are reasonable and there is a likelihood of success. Thus, the requisite good faith has been established by the debtors.

Midland also claims that the proposed plan does not comply with § 1129(a)(11) in that it is not feasible and will most likely be followed by liquidation. Courts have held that in order to determine whether a plan is feasible, the court must examine ". . . the adequacy of the capital structures; the business's earning power; economic conditions; management's ability; the probability of the present management's continuation; and any other factors related to the successful performance of the plan." . . . The court need not find that the plan is guaranteed of success, but only that a reasonable expectation of success exists. . . . At trial, the court heard testimony concerning the present earning power of the surveying business and the projected earning power of the business based on work in progress. The court also heard testimony concerning prospective purchasers of the subdivided farmland. Based on this evidence, as well as the debtors' demonstrated expertise in the surveying business, the court has determined that the plan is feasible within the meaning of § 1129(a)(11).

Finally, Midland alleges that the debtors' plan does not meet the fair and equitable requirements of § 1129(b)(2) and thus, may not be confirmed over its objection. The court finds that the debtors' plan allows Midland to retain its lien on the property securing its claims, provides Midland with deferred cash payments totaling the allowed amount of its claims plus appropriate interest, and provides that Midland receive any proceeds obtained from the sale of its collateral. With respect to Midland, the court finds that the debtors' plan meets both the fair and equitable requirement of 1129(b)(2) and the requirement that the plan not discriminate unfairly pursuant to 1129(b)(1). . . . The plan proposed by the debtor not only conforms to all of the applicable requirements of § 1129(a), but also conforms to the requirements of § 1129(b) with respect to each class of dissenting creditors. Therefore, the court hereby orders that the plan proposed by the debtor is confirmed.

■ IMPORTANT TERMS AND CONCEPTS

bankruptcy
straight bankruptcy
income earner plans
exempt property
preferential payment
nonpurchase-money
    security interest
secured creditor
wage claims
partnership bankruptcy
objection to discharge
intentional tort debts
educational debts
approval of corporate
    reorganization plan

priority
corporate reorganization
farm reorganization
fraudulent transfer of
    property
judicial lien
proof of claim
unsecured creditor
tax claims
discharge of debtor
debts not discharged
alimony and child support
reaffirmation of debts
composition

■ QUESTIONS AND PROBLEMS FOR DISCUSSION

1. What is the difference between a Chapter 7 proceeding and a Chapter 11 proceeding?
2. When can a person be forced into bankruptcy?
3. How much of a debtor's property is exempt from a bankruptcy proceeding?
4. What debts are not discharged by bankruptcy?
5. Tessie Boble stored several valuable antiques with Louie Looper in the warehouse he operated. When Tessie failed to pay the storage charges as required, Louie sold the items to enforce his warehouse lien. Unfortunately, Louie did not comply with all of the required procedural steps in the lien statute. Tessie sued Louie and received a judgment for $50,000, $10,000 of which was a jury award of punitive damages. Louie filed for bankruptcy, listing Tessie as one of his creditors. She says her claim is not dischargeable in bankruptcy. Is she right? Why or why not?
6. Rex Ruthor, doing business as Poisson Chemicals, was enjoined by the State of New York from continuing to do business, was ordered to clean up the hazardous wastes at his business site, and was fined $175,000. Some of Rex's chemical wastes had leaked into a nearby lake, polluting the water and killing fish and wildlife. Rex filed a petition in bankruptcy, listing the cleanup order and the fine as a "debt" or "claim" for which he was liable. The State argues that these obligations are not dischargeable "debts" under the Bankruptcy Act. How should the court rule?
7. Delbert Dedalus sued in the state courts of Vermont, asking for enforcement of an $18,000 Idaho state court judgment against Ike Icarus for the conversion of Delbert's airplane. The Idaho judgment had been taken by default. Delbert introduced a certified copy of his Idaho judgment. Ike then introduced a certified copy of his discharge in bankruptcy, entered after the Idaho judgment, and asked the Vermont court to dismiss Delbert's case. Delbert says that his claim was not discharged by Ike's bankruptcy. How should the court rule, and why?
8. Prior to filing his petition in bankruptcy, Bobby Boggle borrowed $1,500 from Detrimental Finance Company. Bobby gave Detrimental a security interest in certain household goods, appliances, cameras, and his Browning shotgun. Detrimental filed a proper financing statement to perfect its security interest in these items. Bobby now claims that all these items are exempt "household goods" under Section 522 of the Bankruptcy Code. Detrimental admits that its lien is invalid as to all the items except the shotgun, since "household goods" are exempt from "nonpossessory, nonpurchase money" liens. How should the bankruptcy court decide the exemption claim on the shotgun?

24

Suretyship and Secured Transactions

CHAPTER OBJECTIVES

THIS CHAPTER WILL:

- Explain the legal rights of cosigners.
- Define the term *secured transactions*.
- Review the Uniform Commercial Code (UCC) provisions relating to secured transactions.
- Discuss the creation of security interests, their validity and enforceability.
- Explain the use and contents of a financing statement.

Perhaps no single area is so crucial to the functioning of a modern economy, or so little understood by the "average" participant in the economic game, as secured financing. It is hard to imagine a modern business enterprise functioning effectively on a "cash on the barrelhead" basis; credit is the oil that keeps the economic wheels turning. Of course, some holdout consumers still insist that they always "pay cash for everything," but for most individuals this is just as much a credit economy as it is for business firms. The great majority of us will have an occasion, not just once but many times, to buy things on credit and to borrow money. Credit buying, borrowing, and financing is the name of the modern economic game, and that's what "secured transactions" are all about.

Cash versus credit

This chapter and the next are intended to convey to you the basic concepts and problems involved in *secured financing* and to give you some idea of what you need to do to protect your rights, either as an individual or as a businessperson. This chapter first explains the legal consequences of *cosigning* another person's obligations. It then focuses on the basic concepts involved in creating a *security interest* in personal property: What types of *collateral* may be involved? What has to be done to create a valid security interest in favor of the creditor, in the debtor's property? Chapter 25 examines the requirements for "perfecting" a security interest against third-party claimants—usually the debtor's other creditors, or a buyer of the collateral from the debtor. It also covers the rules for determining which creditor has the best claim to the collateral ("priority"), where there is more than one claim, and the rules for handling the collateral when the debtor defaults.

■ SECURITY AND PRE-CODE LAW

Creditor's Need for Security. Creditors as a group are notoriously unwanted, unloved, misunderstood, and *insecure*. A *creditor* is someone who has permitted another party to receive his or her goods, services, or other value without their having been fully paid for by return value. This other party, the *debtor*, has been permitted to enjoy the benefits of the transaction but has not yet returned the full value which was promised to the creditor. The unsecured creditor thus has only the debtor's word that he or she will fulfill that promise, subject to all the human and economic infirmities which may come "twixt the cup and the lip."

In many personal business situations the debtor's word may be good enough. The debtor's financial standing may be such that there is little risk of nonpayment. In many other situations the creditor has good reason to feel insecure, particularly since in the event of bankruptcy general creditors are paid only after a long line of preferred claims.

Types of Security, or Collateral. The creditor seeking the warm feeling of "security" may use any one of the three basic types of "collateral" to try to ensure the payment of the debt. A second person may be required to back up the debtor by also agreeing to pay the debt (a *surety*) or by agreeing to pay the debt if the debtor does not (a *guarantor*). The parties may agree that the creditor will have certain rights against some of the debtor's real estate if the debtor defaults. Finally, the parties may agree that the creditor will have certain rights against an item or items of personal property as collateral if the debtor defaults. It is this third situation which is defined by the UCC as a *secured transaction.*

■ NATURE OF SURETYSHIP

Cosigning versus bonding

Where a lender or seller does not feel that the debtor's personal financial situation warrants the extension of credit, the lender or seller may require a *cosigner;* that is, another person who also agrees to become liable for payment of the debt. This sort of arrangement may be the only additional security the creditor requires, or it may be combined with personal property or real estate as specific collateral security for the debt. The person who actually receives the money or credit is spoken of as the *principal debtor;* the cosigner is the *surety.*

The other frequently occurring suretyship transaction involves *bonding.* Here a company issuing a surety bond promises to pay a certain sum of money if the "debtor" defaults on performance obligations. For example, with the performance bonds required of building contractors, the bonding company promises to pay the landowner/customer in the event of nonperformance or of improper performance by the builder. Because courts do not agree that such a bond also covers the claims of unpaid laborers or material suppliers, the builder may also be required to furnish a bond which specifically provides for the payment of these claims.

Many public officials, particularly those who have custody of public funds, must file bonds guaranteeing that the bonding company will replace any missing monies. Bonds are also required in many types of judicial proceedings to protect the other party and to guarantee performance of court-imposed obligations. An example is a bail bond to ensure a party's appearance for trial. Although perhaps not technically surety bonds, fidelity bonds are frequently required by employers for employees in "sensitive" jobs; specified defaults by such an employee give the employer the right to recover the amount of the bond from the bonding company.

Suretyship versus guaranty

Most courts continue to draw a distinction between *suretyship,* strictly defined, and *guaranty.* A surety makes the same promise to the creditor as does the principal debtor; the surety says, "I will pay." When the debt falls due, the creditor can sue the surety without first demanding payment from the principal debtor. A guarantor makes a different sort of promise; this person says, "If the principal debtor doesn't pay, then I'll pay." The creditor is required to demand the money from the principal debtor and to notify the guarantor of the principal debtor's default before the guarantor becomes liable to "pick up the check." The guarantor's promise is similar to the conditional contract liability of the indorser of a negotiable instrument. A *guarantor of collectibility* makes an even more limited promise; the creditor normally must get a judgment against the principal debtor and have the judgment returned unsatisfied before the guarantor of collectibility becomes liable. Many of the following legal rules, however, are applied by the courts to both suretyship and guaranty.

■ CONTRACT ASPECTS OF SURETYSHIP

Offer and acceptance

Since suretyship is a contract, an offer and acceptance (supported by consideration) must be present. Whether or not the creditor-offeree must give notice of acceptance to the surety-offeror depends on the facts and circumstances of the particular situation. In many cases the creditor's acceptance of the surety's offer will be obvious. Where a continuing guaranty of payment covers a number of possible transactions, many courts will require notice of a creditor's acceptance, so that the guarantor knows the extent of the obligations which the creditor has undertaken.

Consideration

In the simplest transaction, both the principal debtor and the surety sign the loan agreement at the same time. The bank's payment of the loan funds to the principal debtor is consideration for both promises of payment. Since a contract of guaranty is typically a "reassurance" of payment sometime after the primary debt was made, new consideration is required to bind the guarantor to the promise. This new consideration may be an extension of the time for payment, smaller monthly installments, forbearance from suit, or any other agreed modification by the creditor, but *some* new consideration has to be present to hold the guarantor liable.

Statute of frauds

The precise form in which the "backstop" promise is made may also determine whether or not the **Statute of Frauds** applies. Clearly the guarantor's "if-then" promise is covered, and it must be evidenced by a signed writing. Courts may not always draw the technical distinction between suretyship and guaranty, however, and they may require a writing for suretyship contracts as well. Special state statutes may also produce the same result. As always, it's a good idea to "get it in writing."

■ SPECIAL RIGHTS OF THE SURETY

The promise to pay someone else's debt places the surety in a rather special position. Therefore, the law gives the surety a set of special rights to produce fair ultimate results wherever possible.

Exoneration is the right of the surety to demand that the principal debtor pay the debt when it falls due and before the creditor collects it from the surety. The surety can also get a similar equity order against cosureties, forcing each to pay a proportionate share of the debt where the debtor is insolvent or otherwise in default.

The surety, after paying some or all of the debt, is entitled to *reimbursement* or *indemnification* from the debtor. This was really the debtor's obligation, and it's only fair that the debtor repay the surety. If there were two or more cosureties, any of them who paid more than a fair share is entitled to *contribution* from the cosureties, so that each surety bears the agreed proportionate part of the loss. To assist the surety in obtaining reimbursement from the principal debtor, the surety who has paid off the creditor acquires, through a process called *subrogation,* the same legal status that the creditor had. The surety automatically acquires whatever rights the creditor had in property which served as collateral for the debt, and can take whatever enforcement steps the creditor could have taken against the collateral.

■ DEFENSES OF THE SURETY

The law provides the surety with some special defenses because of the surety's unique situation. The surety can use some, but not all, of the defenses that can be used by the principal debtor as well as any defenses which may be personal to the surety.

Because of the surety's special legal situation, and to prevent unfair results, the courts generally hold that any of the following acts by the creditor will discharge the surety's liability.

Release of the Principal Debtor.

A release of the principal debtor also releases the surety, *unless* the surety consents to such a release, or the creditor specifically reserves rights against the surety, or an arrangement is made to indemnify the surety, such as turning over to the surety sufficient collateral to cover the debt.

Where the creditor releases the principal debtor but reserves the right to sue the surety, the surety's rights against the principal debtor must be preserved too, so that the principal debtor ultimately pays.

Release of Collateral.

The courts have generally said that a release of rights against property held as collateral security for the debt also will release the surety *if* it can be shown that the surety's rights are prejudiced in some material way by such release. Some courts have reached similar results where the value of the items held as collateral has been substantially diminished by negligence of the creditor.

Material Alteration of Terms.

The surety agrees to assume the debt of another person under certain terms and conditions. Therefore, any material change in those terms, if not agreed to by the surety, should discharge his or her liability. Materiality here is a fact question, but changes in the amount of the debt, the maturity date, or the place of payment would almost certainly be held to be material. Most modern cases require that a surety who has been paid for acting as such must show that the change in terms prejudices the surety's rights. The *Wexler* case involves a parent as cosigner.

WEXLER v. McLUCAS

121 Cal. Rptr. 453 (California, 1975)

FACTS   Floyd McLucas and his wife wanted to buy some furniture but were told by the store that the sale could not be made to them on credit. (Floyd was 22 years old; his wife 18). Floyd was told that he needed a cosigner. He brought his friend James McWilliams to the store, and McWilliams also signed the contract. The store was still not satisfied, so Floyd brought his mother, Catherine McLucas, and she cosigned too. At that point, the sale was made. The store assigned the contract to the plaintiff, Wexler, who sued Catherine when Floyd and his wife defaulted on their payments. The trial court held for Wexler, and Catherine McLucas appealed. After the complaint was served on Catherine, Floyd had gone to Wexler's office and Wexler had agreed to let him pay off the account at $10 per week, thereby lengthening the term of the contract.

ISSUES   Was Catherine a principal or a surety? If a surety, did the change in the payment terms exonerate her from further liability?

DECISION   A surety. Yes. Judgment reversed.

REASONS   After reviewing the facts and the testimony of the parties, Judge Marshall examined the word cosign. He said that its meaning had not been previously adjudicated and that it had not acquired a clear common meaning. In other words, Catherine could have "cosigned" *either* as a principal or as a surety. The terms of the contract were not conclusive as to how she had signed. Further, a state statute provided that a person who appeared to be a principal might show that he or she was in fact a surety except as against persons who had relied on the appearances. There was no evidence to put the store or Wexler within the exception; in fact, the contract named only Floyd and his wife, Roseanna, as purchasers in its first paragraph. Oral testimony was therefore admissible.

"The uncontradicted testimony indicates that the defendant intended to be a surety and not a principal or purchaser (even though she may have been asked to sign as a co-signer). Her testimony, corroborated by her son, was that she neither bought nor possessed the furniture and that she only agreed to pay for it if her son failed to do so. Such agreement is that of a surety: one who promises to answer for the default of another. . . . The defendant is a classic example of a nonprofessional surety: a mother who seeks to help her 22-year-old son and her 18-year-old daughter-in-law to acquire furniture. Suretyship law throws up many defenses around such a person.

"Among such defense is exoneration of liability where the principal obligation is altered in any respect or where the remedies of the creditor are impaired or suspended in any way."

Judge Marshall held that Wexler's agreement to change the payment terms automatically discharged Catherine, as did Wexler's failure to ask in his complaint for repossession of the furniture.

Creditor refuses payment = Surety discharged

Rejection of Tender of Payment.   Where the creditor refuses a valid tender of payment by either the principal debtor or the surety, the surety is discharged. If the debtor is willing to pay the amount as agreed and the tender is refused by the creditor, it certainly wouldn't be fair for the creditor to then be able to sue the surety. If the surety's tender of payment is refused, it wouldn't be fair to extend the liability any further since the surety could have sued the principal debtor immediately if the creditor had taken the money.

Other defenses

Like any other party liable on a contract, the surety has available any defense which applies to the individual situation. Some examples are lack of agreement, lack of consideration, lack of contractual capacity, and fraud. However, most courts will not allow a surety sued by a creditor to use fraud by the principal debtor against the surety as a defense unless the creditor is somehow responsible for the fraud.

The special suretyship arrangement entitles the surety to assert many of the defenses of the principal debtor, especially those relating to the formation or performance of the agreement. Where a defense such as fraud or duress against the principal debtor makes the contract voidable, the surety can use the same defense if the principal debtor elects to avoid the contract. If the

■ EXHIBIT 24–1
Secured Transactions: Preview/Review

(loan or credit sale)

SECURED PARTY ◄─────────────────────────► DEBTOR

1. Debtor signs SECURITY AGREEMENT, or Secured Party POSSESSES Collateral.
   +
2. Secured Party gives VALUE ($; merchandise).
   +
3. Debtor has ownership RIGHTS in Collateral
   =

   Security Interest, + "Attached" to Collateral

If Debtor DEFAULTS,
   Secured Party can REPO Collateral (lawfully)
   +
   RESELL Collateral (reasonably)
   +
   APPLY Proceeds to pay balance due on debt.

   NOT ENOUGH $ = Debtor still owes balance.
   TOO MANY $ = Debtor gets surplus.

If Secured Party ASSIGNS to Bank or Finance Company,
—Debtor can still use all Defenses s/he had vs. Secured Party.
—Unless Debtor signed a waiver of defense clause or a negotiable
   instrument, in which case s/he can't use "Personal" Defenses,
—If Bank or Finance Company is a BFP Assignee
   AND IF Debtor is not a Consumer.

If Debtor TRANSFERS Collateral, goes BANKRUPT, gives S/I #2 to SP #2,

SECURED PARTY # 1 must Perfect to Protect:

Methods:	Consumer Goods	Inventory	Equity	Farm Products	Documents	Instruments	Chattel Paper	Accounts	General Intangibles
FILING	X	X	X	X	X		X	X	X
F/S	*		*	**					
POSS'N.	X	X	X	X	X	X	X		
AUTOM.	X								
PMSI									
-not Fix.									
-not Veh.									

*F/S must describe real estate, for Fixtures.

**F/S must describe real estate, for growing Crops.

Special priority rules: Cons, Goods PMSI, PMSI vs. Blanket, Fixtures,
   Proceeds, BIOC Inventory.

principal debtor elects to affirm the contract, the surety remains bound. Where the whole contract is void because of illegality, that defense would, of course, be available to the surety. Where the principal debtor's defense is a personal lack of capacity, the surety would still be bound. Such lack of capacity would in many cases be the very reason for having a cosigner. However, where a minor has disaffirmed the contract and returned the consideration received to the creditor, the surety is discharged, at least to the extent of the value of the consideration when returned. Bankruptcy of the principal debtor does not discharge the surety.

■ SECURED TRANSACTIONS, ARTICLE 9, UNIFORM COMMERCIAL CODE

Purpose, Policy, and General Characteristics. The basic objectives of Article 9 in the field of personal property secured financing are uniformity, unity, and simplicity. Lawyers and nonlawyers struggling with the Code concepts and terminology may wonder whether the third objective has really been advanced very far, but it is clear that the first two have. The Code is now in force, with only relatively minor variations, in all U.S. jurisdictions except Louisiana, thus ending the pre-Code jungle of drastically conflicting state laws and the attendant conflict-of-laws problems. And even though it was necessary to make distinctions in Article 9 and to deal with different security situations and problems in different ways, such differences were placed within the context of an overall scheme of security law and their nature and effects were carefully calculated.

The following hypothetical examples show the range of Article 9's coverage:

Types of Article 9 transactions

1. Carole Consumer wants to buy a new car on credit. Whether she arranges her own financing at her bank or credit union, or signs a time payment contract which her car dealer sells to a bank or finance company, this is a "secured transaction" if the new car is used as collateral to secure payment of the balance of the purchase price.

2. Dan Debtor needs to borrow $1,500. His bank (or credit union, or finance company) will not make the loan on Dan's signature alone, but requires collateral. Dan owns an expensive stereo set and a refrigerator-freezer, which are both paid for and which his bank accepts as sufficient collateral. This is a "secured transaction."

3. Big Bennie's Appliance Store orders a shipment of new TVs on credit. This is a "secured transaction" if the credit seller (manufacturer or wholesaler) wants to use the TVs as collateral for the unpaid contract price. Alternatively, Bennie could borrow the contract price from a bank or finance company and use the TVs as collateral for the loan. Either way, since the creditor (the "secured party") wants to use the TVs as collateral, this is a "secured transaction."

4. Mr. Shatturglas (the home improvement king) needs to borrow $50,000 for added working capital. His bank (or finance company) will not lend him the money without collateral. His only available asset is his accounts receivable—the amounts due him for work performed. Whether Shattur-

glas merely pledges his accounts to the bank or sells the accounts outright for cash, this is a "secured transaction."

5. Freddy Farmer leases a new tractor from an equipment rental company for two years for $300 per month. At the end of the two-year lease term, Freddy has the option of buying the tractor for an additional $1. This is a "secured transaction."

In sum, all credit transactions in which **personal property** or a **fixture** is used as collateral are defined by the UCC as secured transactions.

Article 9, while "comprehensive" in intent and organization, does not embrace all the law dealing with interests in personal property. It is, after all, part of the Code; all the "General Provisions" of Article 1 apply to a particular transaction, and other parts of the Code may also be involved. For example, if the secured transaction involves a credit sale of **goods,** the warranty sections and other parts of Article 2 may be relevant.

Applicable non-UCC laws

The most important single piece of non-Code law applicable to financing transactions is the U.S. Bankruptcy Act; one of the main contenders that a secured creditor is trying to defeat is the trustee in bankruptcy, who is seeking the debtor's assets for pro rata distribution to all of the debtor's creditors. Problems as to priority of claims between the secured creditor and persons such as a garage operator who is given a statutory lien also require reference to sources outside the Code. A secured transaction involving a motor vehicle will probably require reference to the state's motor vehicle code. And so on. Moreover, in some areas the coverage of the Code will depend on prior state law, such as the definition of a "fixture," and in other areas the Code's applicability is unclear—mobile homes, for example.

General Characteristics. Like the Code generally, Article 9 is characterized by a considerable degree of **freedom of contract.** Some sections contain rules which are explicitly made subject to a different agreement by the parties, usually with the words *unless otherwise agreed* (see, e.g., 9–207[2]). A few sections specifically state that they cannot be varied by the parties (see, e.g., 9–501[3]). But most of Article 9 sections contain no specific statement as to whether the parties may, by agreement, change or modify the rules the sections contain. In light of the Code's general commonsense approach and its downgrading of legal technicalities, it would seem that the parties would be given considerable latitude to "do their thing" in their own agreement, unless otherwise specified, subject only to the requirements of good faith, reasonableness, diligence, and care (the "Four Horsemen" of 1–102[3]) and to the idea of unconscionability expressed in 2–302.

General rule: Freedom of contract

The organizational pattern of Article 9 is based on a practical, step-by-step, problem-solving approach in dealing with a secured transaction. The first question we must answer is whether Article 9 applies to the transaction; the answer will be based on the 9–100 sections in Part 1 and on the general definitions contained in 1–201. Our next problem is to create a security interest in the collateral which will be effective as between the immediate parties to the transaction; here we use the 9–200 sections. Our next job is to perfect the security interest to maximize our rights against third parties; here we need to consult the 9–300s and 9–400s. Where there are conflicting claims against the collateral, we need to determine the relative priorities of these claims; for this we will use the 9–300s. And finally, in the event of a default by the debtor, we need to know what we can or must do to enforce our security interest against the collateral; these procedures are outlined in the 9–500 sections. We now proceed to consider each of these matters in greater detail.

■ APPLICABILITY AND DEFINITIONS

Transactions Covered. The coverage intended by the drafters of Article 9 is very broad indeed. Coverage is extended by 9–102(1):

a. to any transaction (regardless of its form) which is intended to create a security interest in personal property or fixtures including goods, documents, instruments, general intangibles, chattel paper, or accounts; and also
b. to any sale of accounts, or chattel paper.

In 9–102(2) the drafters reiterate their intent to cover all security interests created by contract, "including pledge, assignment, chattel mortgage, chattel trust, factor's lien, equipment trust, conditional sale, trust receipt, other lien or title retention contract and lease or consignment intended as security." The comment states that this listing of the old pre-Code security devices is illustrative only; any contractual arrangement, new or old, which is intended to create a security interest in personal property is included.

Parties' intent in leases and consignments

Since in many cases Article 9's applicability is made dependent on the intent of the parties to the transaction, litigation frequently arises as to what the parties did intend. A third-party claimant will usually raise the question that the parties' arrangement is not effective as against third parties because it was really "intended" as a secured transaction and it was not properly filed as such. The "lease" and "consignment" cases are particularly troublesome. The problem arose so often that a special new section on consignment was added by the 1972 amendments. In general, this section requires the cosigner to give the same kind of notice to other inventory financers as if it were selling on credit rather than consigning.

In 1–201(37) the Code also provides that "leases" are intended as security devices when the debtor can become the owner of the collateral by paying an additional nominal consideration.

Exclusions. Having made such brave claims for the comprehensiveness of Article 9's coverage, we must now consider the lengthy list of specific exclusions (*a* through *k*) which the Code enumerates in 9–104. Generally, these exclusions refer to liens and transactions which are outside the scope of normal financing arrangements. For example, landlords' liens, wage assignments, and transfers of insurance claims, tort claims, and bank deposits are among the exclusions. Also excluded are security interests that are subject to a supervening national statute, such as the Ship Mortgage Act of 1920. The general theme underlying these exclusions is to omit Code coverage for transactions which are not normally used in commercial situations, particularly transactions which are already adequately covered under existing law.

Which state's law applies

Conflict-of-Law Rules.   Section 9–103 lays down some basic rules for dealing with multistate transactions in three situations which caused problems under prior law. The validity and perfection of security interests against accounts, general intangibles, and mobile equipment is to be determined according to the law of the state where the debtor has its chief executive office.

Where personal property of other kinds already subject to a security interest is brought into a Code state, its validity is to be determined by the law of the state where the property was located when the security interest attached. If such an interest was already perfected when the property was brought into the state, it generally remains perfected in the new state for four months, within which time it may also be perfected in that state. Where a certificate of title is issued on property under a state statute which requires notation on such a certificate in order to perfect a security interest, then perfection is governed by the law of the state which issued the certificate.

Although the adoption of the Code in all jurisdictions except Louisiana has had the effect of substantially minimizing the areas of interstate conflict, these 9–103 rules retain considerable significance. One still needs to know where to file to perfect a security interest, whether or not to have a notation made on a vehicle's certificate of title, and what to do to protect the interest where the debtor will be using the collateral in more than one state. The *L.M.S.* case at the end of the chapter illustrates some of these conflicts.

Definitions.   To avoid as many ambiguities and differences in interpretation as possible, the drafters of the Code provided a set of definitions, some found in 1–201 and generally applicable throughout the Code and some contained in each article. For secured transactions the drafters felt it desirable to use new terminology which would not be encumbered and encrusted with residues from pre-Code law. The *secured party* (lender, credit seller) and the *debtor* enter into a contract (the *security agreement*) which provides that the secured party shall have a *security interest* in the described *collateral*. This is a *secured transaction* (see 9–105).

Collateral is classified generally into nine categories. The definitions used are essentially functional definitions, based on the nature of the item and/or the use to which it is being put by the debtor at the time the security interest attaches to it. The significance of these categories stems from the different treatment given the different types of collateral. Such differences are observable: in the available methods of perfecting the security interest; in the place of filing and the necessity therefor; in the priority of claims against the collateral; in determining the rights of buyers from the debtor; and in the respective rights and remedies of the parties on default.

Section 9–109 recognizes four classes of "goods":

Four types of goods

(1) "consumer goods" if they are used or bought for use primarily for personal, family or household purposes;
(2) "equipment" if they are used or bought for use primarily in business (including farming or a profession) or by a debtor who is a non-profit organization or a governmental subdivision or agency or if the goods are not included in the definitions of inventory, farm products or consumer goods;

(3) "farm products" if they are crops or livestock or supplies used or produced in farming operations or if they are products of crops or livestock in their unmanufactured states . . . , and if they are in the possession of a debtor engaged in . . . farming operations . . . ;

(4) "inventory" if they are held by a person who holds them for sale or lease or to be furnished under contracts of service or if he has so furnished them, or if they are raw materials, work in process or materials used or consumed in a business. . . .

The comment to this section makes clear that these categories are mutually exclusive. While the same goods can fall into different categories at different times, "the same property cannot at the same time and as to the same person be both equipment and inventory, for example." "Equipment" is the residuary category; if the goods do not fit one of the other definitions, they are equipment.

The *Nicolosi* case is an illustration of the differences in legal results that may flow from these differences in categorization of the collateral. One of the special rules for "consumer goods" is that a security interest for the purchase price is automatically "perfected" (effective) against *almost* all third parties. The credit seller loses, however, if the collateral is sold to another consumer. The court is trying to apply these rules to the ring Nicolosi bought.

■ **EXHIBIT 24–2**
Classification of Goods

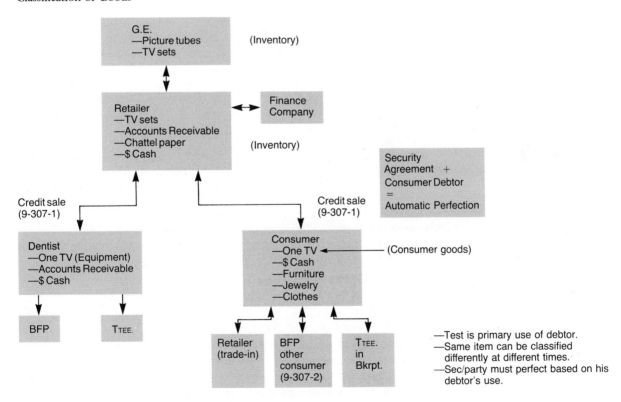

IN RE NICOLOSI

4 UCC Rptr. 111 (U.S. District Court, Southern District Ohio, 1966)

FACTS   Nicolosi bought a diamond engagement ring for his fiancée for $1,237.35 from Rike-Kumler Company. He executed a purchase-money security agreement for the unpaid contract price, with the ring as collateral. Rike-Kumler did not file a financing statement. Nicolosi gave the ring to his fiancée prior to his bankruptcy. After he was declared bankrupt, she called off the engagement and gave the ring to the trustee in bankruptcy. The trustee wanted to sell the ring for the benefit of all of Nicolosi's creditors; Rike-Kumler claimed priority as a secured party.

ISSUE   Was Rike-Kumler's security interest automatically perfected against the ring so as to give priority against the trustee in bankruptcy?

DECISION   Yes. Rike-Kumler takes priority.

REASONS   The court first considered whether the ring was indeed "consumer goods." Apparently the question was raised because Nicolosi did not buy the ring to wear himself. It was purchased, however, for his own "purposes," that is, a gift to his fiancée. The court also noted that "by a process of exclusion," a diamond engagement ring (as to the debtor Nicolosi) could not be defined as "equipment," "farm products," or "inventory." The court then felt it necessary to consider whether the trustee had succeeded to the fiancée's special status as another consumer who had "bought" the goods in good faith.

"Is a promise, as valid contractual consideration, included under the term 'value'? In other words, was the ring given to his betrothed in consideration of marriage (promise for promise)? If so, and 'value' has been given, the transferee is a 'buyer' under traditional concepts. . . .

"The Uniform Commercial Code definition of 'value' . . . very definitely covers a promise for a promise. The definition reads that 'a person gives value for rights if he acquires them . . . (4) generally, in return for any consideration sufficient to support a simple contract.'

"It would seem unrealistic, nevertheless, to apply contract law concepts historically developed into the law of marriage relations in the context of new concepts developed for uniform commercial practices. They are not, in reality, the same juristic manifold. The purpose of uniformity of the code should not be defeated by the obsessions of the Code drafters to be all inclusive for secured creditors.

"Even if the trustee, in behalf of the unsecured creditors, would feel inclined to insert love, romance, and morals into commercial law, he is appearing in the wrong era, and possibly in the wrong court."

Two types of intangibles

Section 9–106 defines two kinds of intangible property which may serve as collateral: *account* and *general intangible*.

"Account" means any right to payment for goods sold or leased or for services rendered which is not evidenced by an instrument or chattel paper, whether or not it has been earned by performance. "General intangibles" means any personal property (including things in action) other than goods, accounts,

Three types of paper intangibles

chattel paper, documents, instruments, and money. The distinction between an account and a contract right has been eliminated by the 1972 amendments.

The last three general types of collateral under Article 9 are also "intangible," but they relate to rights which are embodied in pieces of paper which are physically transferred from party to party as the rights they represent are sold, pledged, or mortgaged. In other words, these pieces of paper are used as a convenient way of handling any transfer of these intangible rights. These three categories are "documents," "instruments," and "chattel paper." ***Document*** means a document of title, defined in 1–201(15) as including bills of lading, warehouse receipts, and the like, covering goods in the possession of a bailee and giving the possessor of the document the right to dispose of it and of the goods it represents. ***Instrument*** means a negotiable instrument as defined in 3–104 (notes, drafts, checks, and certificates of deposit), or an investment security as defined in 8–102 (stocks and bonds), or any other similar writing. Under the UCC, "Chattel paper means a writing or writings which evidence both a monetary obligation and a security interest in or lease of specific goods." ***Chattel paper*** is thus the retail installment contract you sign when you buy your new car; you promise to pay the balance of the contract price in easy monthly installments, and the seller (or its financing agency) reserves a security interest in the goods in the event that you default. This piece of paper has value to the car dealer; it can be sold to a financing agency, or used as collateral for the dealer's own loan.

Article 9 also singles out certain specific types of collateral for special treatment under some of the provisions to be discussed below. Motor vehicles, fixtures, and the proceeds derived from the sale of collateral are examples of collateral to which such special treatment is applied.

Sufficiency of Description of Collateral.   Both the immediate parties to the secured transaction and third parties need to know the identity of the collateral which it covers. Thus, both the security agreement itself and any financing statement which is to be publicly filed require a description of the collateral. Once again, the drafters of Article 9 clearly express their intent that this requirement should not become encumbered with extreme technicalities and legalisms. Section 9–110 says:

> For the purpose of this Article any description of personal property or real estate is sufficient whether or not it is specific if it reasonably identifies what is described.

The *Waychus* case, involving "farm products," provides an illustration of the "reasonableness" approach of the courts to this Article 9 requirement. The *National Cash Register* case in Chapter 25 also discusses this reasonableness rule.

FIRST STATE BANK OF NORA SPRINGS v. WAYCHUS

183 N.W.2d 728 (Iowa, 1971)

FACTS

From time to time during 1968 Waychus had borrowed money from the bank and had executed promissory notes and security agreements. A financing statement had been filed on October 17, 1968, with the recorder of Cerro Gordo County. The financing statement identified the collateral as "All Farm Machinery, All Brood Sows & the increase, All Crops, feed and roughage." The financing statement also contained a real estate description of land located in Floyd County, whereas Waychus in fact resided in Cerro Gordo County.

Johnson, who had no actual knowledge of the bank's interest, bought hogs from Waychus. The trial court held that Johnson was subject to the bank's perfected security interest. Johnson appealed.

ISSUE

Was the financing statement with the erroneous real estate description "seriously misleading" so as to make the filing invalid?

DECISION

No. Judgment for the bank affirmed.

REASONS

Justice Rees rejected Johnson's attempt to use a pre-Code case as a precedent. He held that the old chattel mortgage acts were quite different since they required a filing of the chattel mortgage itself rather than a simple notice. He did not think the mistaken real estate description was very serious.

"It is apparent there is no present requirement under the law that the location of livestock be set out in the financing statement. Certainly the erroneous description would be insufficient to impart constructive notice as to a claimed security interest in crops, but the erroneous description or for that matter the lack of a description entirely would not impair the efficacy of the financing statement insofar as it imparts constructive notice as to a security interest in hogs or other livestock. . . .

"[T]he test of the sufficiency of a description of property is that the description does the job assigned to it—that it makes possible the identification of the thing described. Certainly the financing statement was sufficient to direct inquiry and therefore to impart constructive notice."

As for Johnson's claim that the financing statement was "fatally misleading," Justice Rees noted that Johnson never checked the records and never saw the financing statement, so he could hardly claim that it had misled *him* in any way. In any case, it clearly stated "*All* Brood Sows & the increase," which should have put any hog buyer on notice of the bank's possible claim.

(Note: Even though Johnson was probably a buyer in the ordinary course of Waychus' business, he was not protected by the special BIOC rule of UCC 9–307[1] because "farm products" are specifically excluded from that section. This is another example of the different rules for different categories of collateral.)

VALIDITY OF SECURITY AGREEMENT AND RIGHTS OF PARTIES THERETO

General Validity. As noted previously, both the Code generally and Article 9 specifically provide for a great deal of freedom of contract between the immediate parties to a transaction.

Section 9–201 says, in part:

> Except as otherwise provided by this Act a security agreement is effective according to its terms between the parties, against purchasers of the collateral and against creditors.

EXHIBIT 24–3
Security Agreement

MICHIGAN MOTOR VEHICLE SECURITY AGREEMENT
(DIRECT LOAN FORM, NOT A DEALER LOAN)

MAKER *Annie Maize*   DUE *Sept. 1, 1989*

The undersigned, hereinafter called the Debtor, for value received promises to pay to

ANN ARBOR BANK, Ann Arbor, Michigan

hereinafter called the Secured Party, the sum of *Eight Thousand* ———— Dollars ($*8000.00*) in successive monthly installments each of $ *300.00*, except the final installment which shall be the balance due on this note, commencing on the *1st* day of *September*, 19 *89*, and on the same date of each month thereafter until paid with interest at the rate of *12* per cent per annum, after maturity. All persons signing this instrument agree that they shall all be jointly and severally liable.

The Debtor for the purpose of securing punctual payment of said debt and the performance of all covenants and conditions hereof hereby grants a Security Interest to the Secured Party in the following described property, to-wit:

NEW OR USED	YEAR MODEL	NO. CYL.	TRADE NAME MAKE	TYPE OF BODY IF TRUCK, GIVE TONNAGE	MODEL. LETTER OR NUMBER	MOTOR OR SERIAL NO.
New	*1989*	*6*	*Chevy. Citation*	*4 Door*	*Sprint*	*ZW2X3115A*

CHECK OPTIONAL EQUIPMENT USED ON THIS CAR

☒ RADIO ☒ HEATER ☒ AUTO. TRANS. ☒ POWER STEER. ☒ POWER BRAKES ☒ POWER SEATS ☒ POWER WINDOWS ☒ TINTED GLASS
☐ HIGH H/P ENGINE ☐ H-SPEED TRANS. ☒ AIR COND. ☐ DESCRIBE OTHER

together with all parts, tires, equipment and accessories, now or hereafter attached thereto, which said will be kept at the below mentioned address.

TO HAVE AND TO HOLD the same forever, provided that if said Debtor shall fully pay said Secured Party the amounts due herein and shall keep and truly perform all agreements and covenants herein contained, then this agreement shall be void, otherwise to remain in full force and effect. The Debtor, covenants and agrees with the Secured Party and its successors and assigns as follows, to-wit:

(1) Debtor is the lawful owner of said property which is free and clear from all liens. The CERTIFICATE OF TITLE is in the name of the Debtor.

(2) Debtor shall keep said property free of all taxes and liens, shall maintain it in good condition and repair, and shall keep it properly insured, against substantial risk of damage, destruction and theft in an amount at least equal to the unpaid balance of the debt secured hereby. All policies of insurance shall contain endorsements making losses payable to said Secured Party as its interest may appear, and such policies or certificates evidencing such endorsements shall be deposited with said Secured Party. If the Debtor fails to effect and keep in force such insurance or fails to pay the premiums thereon, said Secured Party may do so for the Debtor's account, and any amounts so paid shall become immediately due and owing.

(3) In case of any default by the Debtor in the performance of any of the conditions of this agreement, or in the payment when due, of any installment upon the note, or if the said Secured Party shall at any time deem itself insecure or its security inadequate, then in any such event, said Secured Party may declare the entire amount then remaining unpaid hereunder; to be due and payable forthwith, without notice, and it shall be lawful for the said Secured Party or its duly authorized agent, to enter upon the premises where the said automobile may be, and without making any demand for possession, to take possession thereof with or without process of law, using whatever force may be necessary, and to sell and dispose of the same in accordance with the statutes of the State of Michigan and the taking of possession and the sale of said automobile by the Secured Party shall not in any manner release the Debtor from liability for any deficiency.

(4) The Debtor may at any time prepay all or any part of the amount then remaining paid hereunder, and upon complete prepayment the Debtor will receive a rebate of any unearned finance charges, but not more than the total finance charges less $15.00 if such unearned finance charges equal $1.00 or more.

(5) If any installment is not paid when due, said Secured Party may collect default charges of 5% per month (or fraction of a month in excess of ten days) on the amount of any payment or payments in arrears. Said Secured Party may collect such default charges when earned or may accumulate and collect them at the time of final maturity. No default charge shall be collected on any payment in default because of any acceleration provision. This provision shall not be construed to extend the due date of payment.

(6) No warranties, express or implied, representations, promises or statements, have been made by the Secured Party unless endorsed hereon in writing.

(7) The waiver or indulgence of any default shall not operate or be construed as a waiver of any subsequent default.

The debtor represents that the above described collateral is:

☐ Used for personal, family or household use,   ☒ Used as equipment in a business (including farming or a profession).

Debtor represents that the County of *WASHTENAW* is my/our County of ☐ Residence ☒ Principal place of business.

Executed and delivered by the said Debtor this *15th* day of *APRIL* 19 *89*.

Approved by

X _____ *Annie Maize*
  Debtor
X _____
  Debtor
Address *918 N. 7th*   *Ann Arbor*   *48103*
  No. Street   City   Zip Code

IN DUPLICATE

FORM NO. 79

The section then goes on to point out that Article 9 is not intended to modify in any way any existing *regulatory* legislation in the state pertaining to financial transactions.

Location of "title" irrelevant

Section 9–202 makes it clear that for the purposes of Article 9 distinctions based on whether the secured party has "title" to the collateral or "only" a lien on the collateral are no longer applicable. The parties are still free to structure their approach either way, but for the purposes of rights and remedies under Article 9 it makes no difference which form they choose to use. The location of "title" to the collateral may still be important for other reasons, however; tax, regulatory, and other non-Code liability problems may be solved by reference to the location of title.

Enforceability; Formal Requisites. Article 9 does include a *statute of frauds*

Signed writing or possession required

requirement, 9–203(1), which states a general rule requiring a security interest to be in writing to be enforceable either against the *debtor* or against third

■ **EXHIBIT 24–4**
UCC Financing Statement

STATE OF MICHIGAN
UNIFORM COMMERCIAL CODE — FINANCING STATEMENT — FORM UCC-1
(Approved by the Secretary of State)

INSTRUCTIONS
1. **PLEASE TYPE** all of the information on this form. Fold only along perforation for mailing.
2. Send the top 2 copies with interleaved carbon paper intact to the Secretary of State, Lansing, Michigan.
3. Enclose filing fee of $1.00.
4. If **ADDITIONAL SPACE IS NEEDED FOR ANY ITEMS ON THIS FORM,** continue the items on separate sheets of paper (5'' X 8''). One copy of these additional sheets should accompany the forms. **USE PAPER CLIPS** to attach these sheets to the forms. **DO NOT USE STAPLES, GLUE, TAPE, ETC.,** and indicate in item 2 the number of additional sheets attached.
5. If collateral is crops or goods which are or are to become fixtures, describe generally the real estate and give name of record owner.
6. At the time of original filing, Filing Officer will return second copy as an acknowledgment. At a later time secured party may date and sign termination legend and use second copy as a Termination Statement.

This **FINANCING STATEMENT** is presented to a Filing Officer for filing pursuant to the Uniform Commercial Code.	1. Maturity date (if any)	2. No. of additional sheets presented (if any) (See Instruction 4)	
3. Debtor(s) (Last Name First) and address(es):	4. Secured Party(ies) and address(es):	For Filing Officer (Date, Time, Number, and Filing Office)	
5. Name and address(es) of assignee(s) (if any)	Check [X] if covered: 6. ☐ Proceeds of collateral are also covered. 7. ☐ Products of collateral are also covered. 8. ☐ Collateral was brought into this state subject to a security interest in another jurisdiction.		

9. This financing statement covers the following types (or items) of property:

by: _____
Signature(s) of Debtor(s)

By: _____
(Signature of Secured Party or Assignee of Record. Not Valid until Signed).

(4) File Copy — Debtor(s)

FORM UCC-1

parties. As an alternative to the writing (the "security agreement"), the secured party may keep possession of the collateral, under an oral security agreement. There are also three limited exceptions to this writing requirement: the security interest of a collecting bank in items it is handling for collection (4–208), and security interests arising under Article 2 on Sales of Goods (9–113) or under Article 8 on Investment Securities (8–321).

Writing must grant a security interest

What is a sufficient writing to make the security interest enforceable under Article 9? On its face, Section 9–203(1) is deceptively simple. It provides that the security interest is not enforceable, generally, unless "the debtor has signed a security agreement which contains a description of the collateral and in addition, when the security interest covers crops growing or to be grown or timber to be cut, a description of the land concerned." The deception arises because the term *security agreement* is itself defined in Section 9–105(1) as "an agreement which creates or provides for a security interest." In other words, to be effective as a security agreement, the writing signed by the debtor must not only *describe* the collateral; it must also *create* or *provide for* a security interest in that collateral in favor of the creditor. (See Exhibit 24–3.)

■ FINANCING STATEMENTS

The document which is publicly filed to give notice to all the world of the existence of the security interest is called a *financing statement*. This is not the lengthy and detailed *financial* statement often required from the debtor, showing all prior credit transactions, assets, and liabilities. The Code's *financing* statement is a simple, half-page form which merely announces the existence of a security interest in certain collateral. (See Exhibit 24–4.)

Minimal contents

Contents of Financing Statement. What must a financing statement contain to be effective? Since the only purpose of the financing statement is to serve as a "red flag" to third parties who may wish to deal with the collateral, the requirments are held to a minimum. A valid financing statement must contain the signature of the debtor, the names and addresses of both the debtor and the secured party, and "a statement indicating the types, or describing the items, of collateral." In addition, where crops or fixtures are involved, there must also be a description of the real estate involved. (Remember that any description is sufficient which "reasonably identifies" the collateral.) No legal mumbo jumbo is required—no witnesses, no affidavits, no notarization. Moreover, substantial compliance is sufficient.

As previously noted, *security agreement* and *financing statement* are not used synonymously in Article 9; they are distinct terms, with distinct functions. It would be possible for a security agreement which contained the names and addresses of both parties to be filed as a valid financing statement. The disadvantage of this procedure is that it puts all the "gory details" of the transaction on the public record. But the greater potential danger to the secured party arises by attempting to have the financing statement do double duty as the security agreement. Since the typical financing statement form will not embody any agreement, or provide for the creation of a security interest in the collateral, the secured party may very well wind up with an interest which is not even enforceable against the debtor. The *Mosley* case shows what happens if the proper documents are not signed.

MOSLEY v. DALLAS ENTERTAINMENT CO., INC.

496 S.W.2d 237 (Texas, 1973)

FACTS Dallas Entertainment operated a private club known as the Music Box. In June 1970, Dallas sold the entire club to Follies Buffet; included was a certain cash register. The parties prepared and filed a financing statement which described the collateral as including all equipment, but which did not specifically mention the cash register. Mosley bought the cash register from Follies, and then resold it. Dallas sued Mosley for conversion and received a judgment for $950.

During the trial, Peggy Foley, the president of Dallas, testified that Dallas had received a promissory note and a security agreement from Follies at the time of the purchase. There was an objection to the introduction of the alleged security agreement because it had not been signed, and it does not appear in the trial court record. There was no other writing.

ISSUE Can a security agreement be established by oral testimony? Was the financing statement itself a valid security agreement?

DECISION No. No. Judgment reversed (in favor of Mosley).

REASONS Justice Moore had little difficulty in finding that the trial court had made an error. The Code sections were perfectly clear; so were the precedent cases.

"Since the foregoing statute requires the secured party to show that the debtor has signed a security agreement containing a description of the collateral, we hold that the oral testimony of the secured party is without probative force to establish a security interest for the simple reason that it fails to satisfy the statutory requirement that the security agreement be in writing and signed by the debtor.

"This brings us to the question of whether the judgment may be sustained on the theory that the financing statement amounts to a security agreement. The financing statement in this case appears to have been written on the Secretary of State's standard form. As noted above, it recites a general description of the collateral in which a security interest is claimed. It is signed by the creditor, appellee, and by a party alleged to be the agent of Follies, though the character of that signature was never established in the trial of this case. Nowhere in the instrument does it grant the creditor a security interest in the collateral nor does it identify the obligation owed to the creditor.

"The code makes no provision for a naked financing statement to be enforced as a security agreement. It merely gives notice of the existence of a security interest but in itself does not create a security interest. . . . A financing statement cannot serve as a security agreement where it does not grant the creditor an interest in the collateral and does not identify the obligation owed to the creditor. . . . Since the financing statement offered by appellee fails to contain any language showing the alleged debtor granted the creditor (appellee) an interest in the collateral and since appellee was unable to produce a written security agreement signed by appellant, appellee failed to establish a cause of action."

Continuation Statement; Termination Statement. When properly filed, the original financing statement is effective for the period it specifies, up to five years. It lapses at the end of the five-year period or 60 days after the expiration date where a shorter period is specified. "Upon such lapse the security interest becomes unperfected" (9–403[1]).

If an extension of time is desired, a ***continuation statement*** may be filed by the secured party anytime within the six-month period prior to the specified expiration date or within the 60-day grace period referred to in the preceding paragraph. The requirements for this continuation statement are absolutely minimal: "Any such continuation statement must be signed by the secured party, identify the original statement by file number and state that the original statement is still effective." As long as it complies with the provisions each time, secured party may renew the filing any number of times and thus preserve perfection against the collateral.

When the secured debt has been paid and the secured party has no obligation to make further advances of money or credit to the debtor, the secured party must on written demand by the debtor send the debtor a ***termination statement,*** saying that "he no longer claims a security interest under the financing statement, which shall be identified by file number." A termination statement signed by someone other than the secured party of record must be accompanied by a statement of assignment from the secured party of record. Where the secured party fails to send the statement within 10 days after a proper demand by the debtor, the debtor can recover a penalty of $100 in addition to any loss sustained because of the secured party's refusal.

When the termination statement is presented to the filing officer, it must be noted in the index. The filing officer must then remove the financing statement, any continuation statement, and any statement of assignment or release. These are marked "terminated" and sent to the secured party. Sections 9–405 and 9–406 contain provisions for handling an "Assignment of Security Interest" and a "Release of Collateral," respectively.

▪ RIGHTS IN THE COLLATERAL

Attachment of the Security Interest. The words ***attach*** and *attachment* as used in Article 9 merely refer to the coming into existence of the security interest with respect to the collateral involved. The point in time at which the security interest "attaches" to the collateral is significant for several reasons. It is at this point in time that the collateral is classified under the definitions discussed above. Some priority rules among conflicting claims to the collateral will hinge on "attachment." And so on.

Attachment = Existence of security interest

Section 9–203(1) also contains the rules determining when a security interest attaches. There must be an agreement, evidenced either by a writing signed by the debtor or by the creditor's possession of the collateral. Value must have been given by the secured creditor. And the debtor must have ***"rights" in the collateral.*** The security interest attaches to the collateral as soon as all three of these events have occurred unless the parties expressly agree to postpone the time of attaching. To rephrase the rules: the parties may provide that the security interest attaches to the collateral at any time *after* these three conditions exist. But even by agreement, they cannot provide for attachment *prior* to the occurrence of the three conditions.

When does debtor have "rights" in collateral?

The general rules of contract law and sales law would normally determine when the debtor had "rights" in the collateral. As pointed out in Chapter 19, for instance, UCC 2–105(2) provides: "Goods must be both existing and identified before any interest in them can pass." If you were borrowing money from your credit union to buy a new car, the credit union could not have an effective security against the new car until it had been "identified" (i.e., until you and the dealer had agreed on exactly which one you were buying). If the new car had to be ordered from the manufacturer, your credit union's security interest could not "attach" until your car was assembled, and identified as yours—with your name or order number. In other words, even though a security agreement has been signed and cash or credit has been extended by the secured party, there can be no effective security interest until we know what things are being used as the collateral.

Subject to an exception for consumer goods, the Code expressly permits the parties to provide in their agreement "that collateral, whenever acquired, shall secure all obligations covered by the security agreement." For all subsequent creditors, the word is: "Look out for the person with this *security blanket.*"

This section also permits the security agreement to cover "future advances" of value by the secured party, whether that party is obligated to make them or has the discretion to make them.

Use of Collateral by Debtor; Statement of Account. Article 9 expressly validates financing arrangements using a debtor's inventory or accounts, and lets the parties determine to what extent the debtor should "police" the inventory or accounts. In general, third-party creditors in such situations should be adequately protected by the requirement that a financing statement on the shifting stock of collateral be publicly filed. Where there has been no such filing and the validity of the security interest depends on possession of the collateral by the secured party, the common-law rules on "pledge" still apply.

> Shifting collateral OK

For the protection of both the debtor and any third parties involved, Section 9–208 provides that the debtor can require the secured party to verify periodic "progress reports" on the total amount the debtor believes to be due and on the collateral which is believed to be subject to the security agreement. The secured party must comply with such a request within two weeks after it is received, by sending a written correction or approval, and may become liable to the debtor and to third parties if it fails to comply without "reasonable excuse." The debtor can request one such statement without charge every six months; the secured party may charge a fee of up to $10 for each additional statement.

Collateral in Possession of Secured Party. In general, Section 9–207 continues the case law rules which had been developed under the common law of pledge. Where the collateral is being held by the secured party, he or she has the obligation of using reasonable care in its custody and preservation—and of keeping collateral other than fungible goods identifiable. However, the risk of loss or damage to the collateral remains on the debtor to the extent of any deficiency in effective insurance coverage.

The secured party has the right to recover all reasonable expenses from the debtor, to hold any increase or profits (except money) received from the collateral as additional security for the debt, and to repledge the collateral so long as the debtor's right to redeem is not impaired. The secured party also has the right to use or operate the collateral to preserve it or its value, or pursuant to a court order, or in accordance with the provisions of the security agreement itself.

The secured party is liable for any loss caused by a failure to meet these obligations, but does not thereby lose the security interest in the collateral.

■ SIGNIFICANCE OF THIS CHAPTER

Creditors require a second party's obligation on many personal and business loans or credit sales to ensure an additional source of payment if the principal debtor defaults. Any of us may be called on to cosign for another person, or may be required to get a cosigner for our own obligation. Likewise, if we're representing the creditor company, we may want to require a cosigner. Whichever of the three parties we may be, it's nice to know the rules of the game.

Once again, the basis for suretyship law is general contract law, but some special rules apply. This chapter reviewed the special status of the surety/guarantor, the application of general contract rules, and the special rights and remedies of the surety/guarantor.

Since secured credit arrangements are so necessary and so frequently used in modern commercial society, it is important to know when and how they occur. All types of personal property may be used as collateral, and the debtor may be a single consumer or the very largest industrial corporation. The credit transaction may be structured as a sale, a loan, or a transfer of accounts receivable. For the purposes of Article 9, the form is generally irrelevant; what counts is the function—the extension of credit, with personal property used as collateral. This chapter discussed the rules for creating an effective security interest between the immediate parties. The next chapter will cover the secured party's rights against other persons who have claims against the same collateral, and the rights of both the secured party and the debtor when the debtor defaults on the credit contract.

DISCUSSION CASE

IN RE L. M. S. ASSOCIATES, INC.

18 B.R. 425 (S.D. Florida, 1982)

FACTS: The trustee in this case filed a complaint to determine amount, validity, and priority of lien against Capital Bank, a lender of the debtor, and the bank counterclaimed for modification of the automatic stay. The trustee consents to a lifting of the automatic stay if the court finds that he does not have priority over the bank.

The debtor is a Florida corporation, with its headquarters in Florida. It operates gift shops aboard cruise ships which sail in the Caribbean and Mediterranean and stop at ports in several countries, primarily not in Florida. The ships are all of non-American registry.

Capital Bank made loans to debtor of $140,000 on August 2, 1979 and $40,000 on November 23, 1979. The notes were renewed, and the outstanding principal is now $125,734.10. On August 2, 1979, the debtor entered into a security agreement with Capital Bank covering, among other things, the inventory of the ship gift shops, including after-acquired property. The bank filed financing statements as to this collateral with the Secretary of State of Florida on August 7, 1979 and with the Dade County Clerk of Court.

As the debtor continued the operation of its business, it would obtain goods and air ship them to the various cruise ships. Most, but not all, of the goods originated

in or came through Florida. They were never sent to or
kept in any foreign cities, but would be held by customs
agents in a given port only for delivery onto a vessel
when it arrived in port. Goods continued to be shipped
in this manner until four or five weeks before bankruptcy.
Approximately a week before the petition in bankruptcy
was filed, and in anticipation of it, goods were taken off
the S.S. Victoria, S.S. Britannus, and S.S. Vera Cruz
and placed in a sealed, bonded warehouse in San Juan,
Puerto Rico. It is these goods, of a present liquidation
value of approximately $75,000–$80,000, which the
trustee seeks.

∎

Judge Gassen:

In the present case, the financing statement had been
filed prior to acquisition by the debtor of the collateral
in question. Therefore, under UCC substantive law, the
"last event . . . on which is based the assertion that the
security interest is perfected" would be acquisition by
L.M.S., UCC 9–303. . . . In some cases the goods were
located in Florida when they were acquired by L.M.S.
but not in all cases. The trustee has also asserted that
the security interests became unperfected by being removed from Florida for more than four months. However,
he relies on Section 679.103(1)(d), Fla. Stats., which
leads to the disperfection of security interests brought
to Florida, but not the reverse. Since there is no other
event which leads to an assertion of perfection or unperfec-
tion, under Florida law (and UCC) choice of law provisions, this court should look to the substantive law of
the respective jurisdictions where each part of the collateral
was located when L.M.S. acquired it. . . .

It is not . . . easy to reach the conclusion that Florida
and federal conflicts law would be the same in the case
before this court. First of all, most of the jurisdictions
where the collateral was located at various times were
non-UCC jurisdictions and this court cannot assume that
their law would be the same as that of Florida.

[T]here was a printed choice of law provision in the
security agreement executed August 2, 1979. . . . "Paragraph 16: This agreement has been delivered in the State
of Florida and shall be construed in accordance with the
laws of Florida." However, the UCC conflicts provision
here is not 1–105(1), which authorizes the parties to
designate the applicable law, but 9–103(1)(b) which does
not.

The difference between 1–105 and 9–103 is appropriate, because the issue at 9–103 is not one of general commercial law, but specifically of perfection of security inter-

ests. *Perfection* does not affect the rights and obligations
between a debtor and his secured creditor, but relates
to rights among competing creditors or others with interests in the collateral. It defines what notice is necessary
to "the world," and without which the secured creditor
may not assert his priority interest in the collateral. The
concept is inherently connected with the location of the
collateral because third parties who are interested in the
collateral will most naturally look to the jurisdiction where
the collateral is located for notice of prior interest. There
will always be problems, of course, when collateral is
moved from one jurisdiction to another. In 9–103 the
Uniform Commercial Code has created an intricate framework of choice of law rules to cover situations where
various types of collateral are moved for various purposes,
to provide the best combination of efficiency in protecting
security interests and fair notice to third parties. Since
the framework depends on the reciprocal uniform provisions of other UCC jurisdictions, however, it collapses
when the collateral is removed to a non-UCC jurisdiction,
and may lead to an unfair result. . . .

The importance of the physical location of property
is also demonstrated by the comment:

> In any event, the tendency of the courts is to treat the law
> of the situs of property at the commencement of the case as
> governing to the extent that Section 544(a) refers to non-
> bankruptcy laws. . . .

None of these rules seems effective to carry out the
intent of the perfection provisions of secured transactions
law on the facts of this case, however. At the time of
perfection, the various items of collateral were either in
Florida or in another jurisdiction where they were acquired
by the debtor. In either case, they were immediately transported to ships of some other registry, and operated by
corporations of yet another jurisdiction. On the high seas
the collateral would be deemed to be constructively within
the territory and therefore within the jurisdiction of a
given ship's registry. It would probably continue to be
subject to that jurisdiction although a ship would be in
port in several additional jurisdictions. . . . Finally,
at the commencement of the case the collateral was located in Puerto Rico, placed there only for the purpose
of liquidation. Throughout it all the secured creditor and the debtor operated their businesses in Florida,
and their contracts were executed and performed in
Florida.

On these facts and because there is no binding authority
on this court against the exercises of its independent judgment as to choice of law, this court concludes that the
internal (substantive) law of Florida as to the method
of perfection of security interests will be applied. The

only other possibly appropriate internal law would be the law of the nation to which each vessel was registered. The physical location of the property is not of major significance here, however, because of the unique nature of its location on a (comparatively speaking) small and moving ship, and the fact that the physical location is not connected with the physical location of the jurisdiction. Normal commercial relations would not relate to the physical location of the goods. The primary "local" persons who would be interested in property would be retail customers, and their rights are protected under Florida law. In this instance, the most logical place to search for prior liens would be Florida, not the location of the property. Similarly, it would not be logical, and it would be difficult to ascertain and search the jurisdictions where the goods were located when acquired, if other than Florida (as would be required by application of UCC 9–103(1)(b).)

In concluding that the substantive law of Florida should

be applied, the court discounts the bank's argument of convenience to the secured party. It would not be unduly burdensome for the secured party to additionally perfect its security interest in the jurisdiction of a ship's registry, and convenience to secured parties is not the overriding factor in a policy determination. The same is true of the bank's argument that it cannot have been required to perfect in Puerto Rico because it did not know the collateral was there. Difficult as it often is, secured party by taking collateral assumes the burden of keeping track of it.

Applying the internal law of Florida, the secured party filed its financing statements as required under Section 679.302 and Section 679.401, Fla. Stats. to perfect this security interest in the goods. It has priority over the trustee, Section 679.312(5), Fla. Stats. Therefore, the automatic stay will be modified to permit the bank to foreclose on its collateral.

■ IMPORTANT TERMS AND CONCEPTS

secured financing
credit transaction
collateral
guarantor
secured transaction
exoneration
contribution
release of principal debtor
material alteration of
  terms
defenses of surety
fixture
personal property
documents
general intangibles
accounts
assignment
conditional sale
conflict of laws rules
debtor
equipment
inventory
security agreement
continuation statement
attachment of security
  interest
after-acquired property
  clause
cosigning

security interest
surety
principal debtor
bonding
Statute of Frauds
reimbursement/
  indemnification
subrogation
release of collateral
rejection of tender
  of payment
Bankruptcy Act
freedom of contract
goods
instruments
chattel paper
pledge
chattel mortgage
lease or consignment
  intended as security
secured party
consumer goods
farm products
description of collateral
financing statement
termination statement
rights in the collateral
security blanket

■ QUESTIONS AND PROBLEMS FOR DISCUSSION

1. What is the difference between a "secured transaction" and a suretyship contract?
2. What types of property may be used as the collateral in a secured transaction?
3. What is the significance of defining certain collateral as being in one category of "goods" rather than another category?
4. What is the difference between a security agreement and a financing statement?
5. Delilah filed for bankruptcy, listing among her secured creditors one Erlene Lertz. Erlene held a security agreement and had filed a financing statement, both of which described the collateral as "Lot 8, Lake Minotaur, & cabin at same location." Delilah leased Lot 8 and owned the cabin, so both were items of personal property rather than real estate. The trustee says that Erlene does not have a secured claim because the description of the collateral is insufficient. What is the result and why?
6. Denver and Gary were both officers of Sunny Mobile Homes, Inc. Both of them had indorsed several of the company's notes for loans to it. They had also signed a guaranty agreement for the loans, which stated: "Liability hereunder is not affected or impaired by any surrender, compromise, settlement, release, renewal, extension, authorization, substitution, exchange, modification, or other disposition of any said indebtedness and obligations." At one point, all of

the company's outstanding loans were consolidated into one renewable note. Gary signed the renewal note, but Denver did not. Denver now claims that his liability as guarantor was discharged by a novation between the bank (lender), the company (Sunny), and Gary, since the renewal note did not include his signature. What result, and why?

7. Piggy Bank sued Hot Dog Shops, Inc. on a promissory note for $35,000. Piggy also sued Clem, Hot Dog's president, on a guaranty contract which he had signed personally at the same time he had executed the note for the corporation. No dollar amount appeared on the guaranty contract. In one blank space on the guaranty form, someone filled in "Hot Dog Shops, Inc." before the word *Dollars*. The other space provided on the form for writing in an amount was simply left blank. The trial court gave summary judgment for Piggy against both defendants. Clem appeals. How should the appeals court rule, and why?

8. Tom Billing bought a truck in Mythigan on credit. Whirly Credit Union, which had loaned Tom the money, perfected its security agreement by filing a financing statement in Mythigan. Tom drove the truck to Floridated where it was seized under a court order to satisfy his creditors there. The truck was sold by the Floridated court to Biff Bumble, even though Whirly's lawyer wrote a letter to the court, stating that Whirly had a prior secured claim against the truck. Biff drove the truck back to Mythigan with a load of produce. After he made his delivery Biff stopped for lunch. While he was inside, one of Whirly's agents drove the truck away. Biff now sues to get the truck back. As between Biff and Whirly, who is entitled to the truck? Explain.

25

Secured Transactions: Priorities and Remedies on Default

CHAPTER OBJECTIVES

THIS CHAPTER WILL:

- Explain the methods of making a security interest effective against third parties as well as the parties to the transaction.
- Review the UCC rules which assign priorities with regard to creditors' claims against the secured collateral.
- Discuss the UCC requirements for filing notice of a security interest in collateral.
- Explain the debtor's rights after default.
- Review the remedies available to the secured party after default.

■ RIGHTS OF THIRD PARTIES; PERFECTED AND UNPERFECTED SECURITY INTERESTS; PRIORITIES

Perfect to get prior rights versus collateral

Reasons for Perfection. For the purpose of Article 9, the term *perfection* is used to describe a process—the steps which a secured party must take to make the security interest effective against third parties, particularly the debtor's general creditors or their representative in an insolvency proceeding. The very idea of "security" is to have an available source of funds from which the secured debt can be paid in the event of default by the debtor; that objective is defeated if the asset in question or its proceeds are distributed *pro rata* to all creditors.

To be more specific and more technically correct, perfection of the security interest in the collateral is necessary to beat "a person who becomes a lien creditor without knowledge of the security interest and before it is perfected" (9–301[1][b]). *Lien creditor* is defined to include a creditor with a levy or attachment against the property involved, or an assignee for the benefit of creditors, or a receiver in equity, or a *trustee in bankruptcy*. (As of the date of bankruptcy, the trustee becomes a "perfect" lien creditor against all the debtor's nonexempt property.) The secured party needs to perfect to prevent these people from making priority claims against that item of collateral. A secured party who has provided the purchase-money credit or loan (which enabled the debtor to purchase the collateral) does have a 10-day grace period within which to perfect a security interest and still beat out these lien creditors, but as a rule the secured party must perfect *before* the lien creditor becomes such, or lose priority. Subsections 9–301(1)(c)&(d) extend similar protection to certain unknowing transferees of goods, instruments, documents, chattel paper, accounts, and general intangibles; they too will beat the *unperfected security interest* of the would-be secured party to the extent that they give value without knowledge of the security interest.

Perfection will also assist the secured party in beating out some other kinds of third-party claimants, at least in some situations. But since it is possible to have more than one perfected security interest in the same collateral, and since even a perfected security interest is subordinate to certain types of third-party claims in certain situations, it must be remembered that a secured party with a perfected security interest is not always "the first to be paid." Priorities of payment under Article 9 are discussed below.

Filing, possession, or automatic

Methods of Perfection. There are three general methods of perfection—*filing* a financing statement, *possession* of the collateral, and *automatic perfection*—plus some variations (such as different places to file for different types of collateral). Filing is effective for every type of collateral except "instruments." Filing is the only method of perfecting against accounts and general intangibles since there is nothing in these situations that can really be effectively "possessed." Possession of the item of collateral by the secured party is an effective method of perfection for all types of goods and for the "paper intangibles"—documents, instruments, and chattel paper. Since these pieces of paper are commonly dealt with in the commercial world as embodying the rights they represent, and since they are capable of being physically possessed, the drafters of Article 9 provided that a security interest in such pieces of paper could be perfected by the retention of them. Indeed, for instruments, except for a limited 21-day perfection against the debtor's other creditors, possession is the only acceptable method of perfection.

Place of Filing. The "uniformity" desired by the drafters of the Code has broken down in the requirements for a valid "filing" to give notice to third parties of the existence of a security interest against the collateral. Solid policy arguments can be made both for central filing (there's only one place to check, particularly for a mobile debtor) and for local filing (it's much more convenient). The Code originally contained a simple filing scheme: for fixtures, file with the registrar of deeds in the county where the real estate is located; for motor vehicles required to be licensed, file by making a notation on the vehicle registration certificate; for all else, file with the secretary of state. Alternatives provided in the Code, combined with the effects of having each state legislature "do its own thing," have produced some major variations in these filing requirements. Each state's filing requirements must be checked to ensure the validity of a filing there.

Where the secured party makes a good faith attempt to file but files in an improper place or in only one of two required places, the filing is nonetheless effective as to anyone who has knowledge of the contents of the financing statement and also for any types of collateral as to which the filing is correct. An effective filing is not invalidated by a change in the debtor's residence or place of business or in the location of the collateral, but some states have adopted alternative language which requires a new filing in the new county, even within the same state. *Filing* is defined as meaning *either* "[p]resentation for filing of a financing statement and tender of the filing fee" *or* "acceptance of the statement by the filing officer." (The alternative language is included just in case the local filing officer gets funny and refuses to accept your financing statement for some reason, such as "it's not in proper form.")

Automatic Perfection. For *purchase-money security interests* in most consumer goods, Article 9 provides a third alternative. The "purchase-money person" (the seller or the financing agency that provided the cash or credit which the debtor used to buy the collateral) is given the benefit of an "automatic" perfection as soon as that person's security interest attaches to the collateral. (This automatic perfection alternative is *not* available where the consumer good is defined as a fixture or is a motor vehicle required to be licensed.) Even without filing and with the debtor in possession of the consumer good, the purchase-money person will still be protected against nearly all other possible claimants—lien creditors, other general creditors, the trustee in bankruptcy, another dealer to whom the collateral was given, or a buyer who had knowledge of the security interest.

Aside from the common priority problems, only one sort of claimant—a *bona fide purchaser (BFP)*—takes the collateral free and clear of the *unfiled* purchase-money security interest. The BFP must buy without knowledge of the unfiled security interest for value, and for his or her own personal, family, or household purposes (consumer goods). Given this extensive protection of the unfiled security interest, the retailer or financer of these types of collateral can then decide whether or not protection against BFPs is worth the filing fee and the clerical expense involved in filing a financing statement. If the dealer does file, it will prevail even against a BFP, so buyers of consumer goods from other individuals do have to check these filing records to make sure that the item they are buying is indeed "free and clear." Note again that

Local vs. central filing

Improper filing

PMSI in most consumer goods

Resale consumer BFP

this third perfection alternative applies only to the purchase-money person; all other secured parties must file or possess to perfect.

Perfection against Proceeds.   Section 9–306 provides an extensive and careful coverage for security interests in *proceeds,* meaning "whatever is received when collateral or proceeds is sold, exchanged, collected or otherwise disposed of. Money, checks, and the like are 'cash proceeds.' All other proceeds are 'noncash proceeds.'" The general intent of this section is to give the secured party with a security interest in collateral a similar security in anything which the debtor received from third parties in exchange for that collateral.

Things received for collateral

As a rule, unless the debtor was authorized to make the sale or exchange of the collateral, a secured party can elect to pursue the collateral in the hands of a third party as well as the proceeds in the hands of the debtor. A dealer who filed against a TV set which was bought on credit could, for example, repossess the TV from a third party to whom the set was sold if the debtor was in default under the original security agreement. The secured party will not get the debt paid twice, but will have two sources to look to for payment. This general rule is subject to several exceptions, including the *buyer in the ordinary course of business (BIOC)* who buys goods (usually from a dealer's inventory). This BIOC takes the goods free and clear of a security interest created by the seller, even though that interest is perfected and even though the BIOC knows about it. For other exceptions, see Sections 9–301, 9–308, and 9–309.

Ten-day grace period to perfect

What does the secured party need to do to perfect a security interest against "proceeds"? If a financing statement which indicates the security interest applies to proceeds as well as the original collateral has been filed, nothing more need be done; there is a continuously perfected security interest against the proceeds. Where the original financing statement does not so indicate, or where perfection against the original collateral occurred by another method, that perfection still applies to proceeds, continuously and automatically, for a 10-day grace period. Within that period, the secured party needs to file or to take possession of the proceeds to perfect.

In the event of insolvency proceedings then, the secured party with a perfected security interest against proceeds will be able to assert rights in any of the debtor's assets which can be identified as being derived from the original collateral and in "all cash and bank accounts of the debtor," even if the cash proceeds cannot be identified because they have been commingled with other funds.

Subsection (5) of 9–306 contains a detailed set of priority rules to cover situations where "a sale of goods results in an account or chattel paper which is transferred by the seller to a secured party, and . . . the goods are returned to or are repossessed by the seller or the secured party."

Perfection against Fixtures.   Many complex problems may arise where goods are attached to real estate and both the goods and the real estate are subject to the claims of financing agencies or good faith purchasers. The Code was not intended to regulate real property law, but in this area Article 9 does have an impact on real property doctrines. In general, fixtures are defined by the general law of the state where the realty is located. The Code does exclude structural materials from the "fixtures" definition.

Construction mortgage—No. 1

The 1972 revision of Section 9–313 changed the rules, in favor of the realty claimants. First, a construction mortgagee (who makes advances of funds to finance the building of structures on the land) is given a special priority over all fixture financers even as to such items as dishwashers and refrigerators. As to other existing interests in the real estate (such as a land contract seller or the holder of the purchase mortgage), the fixture financer must make a *fixture filing* either before or within 10 days after the goods become attached to the real estate. This is a special rule for purchase-money security interests in the fixtures. Otherwise, there is a first-to-file rule for fixtures. For example, the seller of a new furnace on credit could obtain priority over the holder of an existing mortgage by making the proper fixture filing. But if the existing mortgage had already been properly recorded, a nonpurchase-money creditor who wished to use existing fixtures as collateral could not take priority over the mortgagee unless the latter agreed.

Fixture financer can beat other claimants

Readily removable machines and appliances

Financers of "*readily-removable* factory or office *machines* or *readily-removable replacements of domestic appliances which are consumer goods*" are given priority over conflicting real estate interests if their security interest is perfected before the goods become fixtures. Most stoves, refrigerators, washers, and dryers would seem to be "readily removable"; most furnaces would not. A catchall provision indicates that a conflicting real estate interest takes priority against any security interest that is not properly perfected.

To avoid the problem that arose in states where the fixture financer did not have to file on the real estate records but merely in the *office* where real estate claims were filed, the 1972 amendments specify that a fixture filing must be made in the real estate records. It must include a legal description of the real estate to which the fixture is being attached and also the name of the real estate owner if that person is not the debtor who is using the fixture as collateral. Thus, the fixture claim should appear in any title search of the real estate records.

The "fixture" definition is at issue in the following case.

METROPOLITAN LIFE INSURANCE COMPANY v. REEVES

389 N.W.2d 295 (Nebraska, 1986).

FACTS

In this foreclosure action the district court found that a grain storage facility erected by defendant-appellant, Production Sales Co., on land then owned by the buyers, defendants-appellees Lawrence C. and Donna J. Reeves and Philip R. and June L. Gustafson, became a fixture subject to the first and second liens of the real estate mortgagees, plaintiff-appellee Metropolitan Life Insurance Company and defendant-appellee Comag Credit Corporation. Production Sales appeals.

The facility was contracted for and erected after the subject mortgages came into being and were filed. Thus, none of the proceeds of the mortgages were used in connection with the facility, which cost $171,185.30.

The facility consists of a number of steel structures bolted onto concrete slabs which are partially embedded into the ground, and includes 50 to 60 feet of underground tubing through which air is electronically pumped in order to move grain from the dryer to either of two storage bins. Most of the structures were transported to the site in a disassembled state, assembled with numerous bolts (over 1,000 of them in each of the two storage bins), lifted into the air, and then placed and bolted onto the slabs. Disassembly and removal of the steel structures would require a period of over two weeks.

Although the site was taxed as realty and the buyers stated they intended that the facility remain in place more than a season, the purchase agreement between Production Sales and the buyers provides that the facility not become a part of the realty until paid for in full. The buyers had paid but $16,137.77 of the purchase price. Production Sales failed to make the "fixture filing" permitted by § 9–313(1)(b), and it has no perfected security interest in the facility.

ISSUE   Is the grain storage structure a fixture?

DECISION   No. Judgment reversed.

REASONS   Justice Caporale got right to the point:

"The threshold question, then, is whether the facility is, as the trial court found, or is not a fixture. Once that question is resolved, § 9–313 dictates the result. If the facility is a fixture, the interest of Production Sales is subordinate to the liens of the mortgagees; if it is not a fixture, the interest of Production Sales never became subject to the mortgages and, thus, is free of the liens they create.

"Three main factors determine whether an article, or combination of articles, is a fixture. They are (1) whether the article or articles are actually annexed to the realty, or something appurtenant thereto; (2) whether the article or articles have been appropriated to the use or purpose of that part of the realty with which it is or they are connected; and (3) whether the party making the annexation intended to make the article or articles a permanent accession to the freehold. . . .

"[T]he third factor, the intention of the annexing party to make the article or articles a permanent accession to the realty, is the factor which is typically given the most weight.

"It is true, as Metropolitan Life points out, that *Tillotson v. Stephens,* . . . in holding that a mortgage took priority over an improperly filed security interest in a steel grain-drying bin, states that as a general proposition special agreements fixing the status of property as realty or personalty are binding only on the contracting parties and their privies, and are not binding on third parties who do not have notice of the agreement. However, in *Tillotson* the mortgage came into being after the bin had been erected. That is a significant distinction, for when the mortgagees in the present case made their loans, they could not have taken into account the value the facility added to the realty.

"[W]hen the rights of third parties are not adversely affected, and unless otherwise controlled by statute or unless the articles were so completely merged with the realty as to prevent their removal without material injury to the latter, courts generally will uphold the characterization put upon the property by parties to a purchase contract. Thus, while assuming that as to innocent third parties, a boiler, burner, and tank would be classified as fixtures, the court nonetheless held that the rights of the seller of the equipment under a conditional sales contract were superior to those of the prior vendor of the real estate under an executory contract of sale; however, the real estate vendor's rights in refrigeration equipment upon which she relied in making monetary advancements to the vendee of the real estate were superior to those of the equipment seller.

"We conclude, therefore, that under the circumstances the provision of the purchase agreement, that the facility not become part of the realty until after full payment, is to be enforced. Since full payment has not been made, the facility did not become a fixture."

Debtor defaults: Who gets paid first?

Priorities. For the creditor, priority of payment is what the "security" game is all about. Obviously, if the debtor had enough funds to go around, there would be no problem of who got paid first and no need for this sort of litigation. Litigation to establish priority occurs because someone who has extended credit to an insolvent debtor is going to get "stuck" for some or all of that claim against the debtor. Other types of claimants, such as good faith purchasers of collateral from the debtor, will also be interested in determining whether they hold the property in question free and clear, or subject to the claims of a creditor or creditors. Different potential claimants and different types of financing transactions combine to produce a great range of specific fact situations. Part of what appears to be a terrible complexity in Article 9's priority rules stems directly from the need to provide a number of different rules to deal with a number of quite different fact variations. We thus need to consider both the "general rules" and about 15 special situations covered by a special priority rule.

For the first general rule on priority, we return to 9–201:

> Except as otherwise provided by this Act a security agreement is effective according to its terms between the parties, against purchasers of the collateral and against creditors.

In other words, the security agreement itself controls priority unless a Code provision covers the situation and provides otherwise. Nearly all typical priority situations are in fact covered by a Code rule, so that the security agreement itself operates only within a limited range with regard to priority rules.

One of the special priority rules (9–316) does provide that secured parties may agree among themselves as to their relative priority positions. Such an arrangement, of course, would be effective only as between the parties who agreed to it.

A second look at 9–301 indicates that even a secured party with an unfiled, unperfected security interest receives some protection in terms of priority. If the interest has attached to the collateral, the secured party does have rights in the collateral as against the debtor, and *generally* that interest will take priority as against buyers of the collateral or lien creditors who have *knowledge* of the security interest when they become such.

Section 9–312 is the basic priorities section. It provides the general rules for determining priorities between conflicting security interests in the same collateral; it spells out special purchase-money rules for inventory and noninventory collateral; it provides a special priority rule where "crops" are used as collateral; and it cross-references other sections containing special priority rules.

General priority rules

The general priority rules from 9–312(5) are simple and logical. As between competing perfected interests, priority is determined according to the time of filing or perfection. For example, Mabel is shopping for a new car. She agrees to buy a particular car from Big Bennie's dealership. Mabel goes to her credit union and borrows $8,000 to buy the car, giving her credit union a security interest against the car. The credit union files a financing statement which identifies the new car as collateral. Mabel then goes back to Bennie's and signs a purchase-money security agreement for the car—buying it on credit. Bennie's gives her the car, and then files a financing statement (without checking the records under Mabel's name). Mabel then drives back to her credit union and picks up her $8,000 check. Even though Bennie's security interest was *perfected* first, Mabel's credit union takes priority if she defaults on these two obligations. The credit union *filed* first, even though their interest was perfected after Bennie's. Bennie should have checked the records before giving Mabel the car.

So long as neither security interest has been perfected, priority is given in the order in which they attached to the collateral.

For the purposes of applying these priority rules, the date of filing or perfection as to the collateral is also the effective date as to any proceeds of that collateral.

Special PMSI rules

Special purchase-money rules for inventory and noninventory collateral are set out in 9–312(3) and (4). A purchase-money security interest in inventory collateral has priority over a conflicting security interest in the same collateral if the purchase-money security interest is perfected when the debtor gets possession of the collateral; *and* written notification of the purchase-money security interest is received by any other "known" or "filed" secured party before the debtor gets possession of the collateral; *and* the notification states that the purchase-money person has or intends to acquire a purchase-money security interest in the debtor's inventory, "describing such inventory by item or type." Because there is much less of a commingling problem with noninventory collateral, the purchase-money person's requirements for priority in such collateral are much simpler. The interest just has to have been perfected when the debtor takes possession of the noninventory collateral, or within 10 days thereafter. Under this rule, Bennie could take priority over Mabel's credit union (in our last example) if he filed within the 10-day period.

As the *NCR* case shows, a creditor can lose collateral to a security interest already on file, if these rules are not followed.

NATIONAL CASH REGISTER CO. v. FIRESTONE CO.

191 N.E.2d 471 (Massachusetts, 1963)

FACTS

On June 15, 1960, NCR sold a new cash register to Edmond Carroll, who was doing business as the "Kozy Kitchen" in Canton, Massachusetts. This sale was designated as a conditional sale. The cash register was delivered sometime between November 19 and November 25. NCR filed financing statements on December 20 and 21.

Meanwhile, Carroll had borrowed $1,911 from Firestone on November 18 and had executed a security agreement covering "the following goods, chattels, and automobiles, namely: The business located at and numbered 574 Washington Street, Canton Mass. together with all its goodwill, fixtures, equipment, and merchandise. The fixtures specifically consist of the following: *All contents of luncheonette including equipment such as: booths and tables; stand and counter; tables; chairs; booths; steam tables; salad unit; potato peeler; U.S. slicer; range; case; fryer; compressor; bobtail; milk dispenser; Silex; 100 class air conditioner; signs; pastry case; mixer; dishes; silverware; tables; hot fudge; Haven Ex.; 2-door station wagon 1957 Ford a57R107215,* together with property and articles now, and which may hereafter be, used or mixed with, added or attached to, and/or substituted for, any of the foregoing described property." Firestone filed financing statements on November 18 and 25 which identified the collateral with the italicized words.

When Carroll went into default on both contracts, Firestone repossessed and sold the contents of the luncheonette, including the cash register. NCR sued for the tort of conversion of "its" cash register. The lower courts held for NCR.

ISSUE   Was the cash register covered by Firestone's financing statement, without a specific mention of after-acquired property or of a cash register?

DECISION   Yes. Judgment reversed; Firestone takes priority.

 REASONS   Chief Justice Wilkins first dismissed NCR's argument that Carroll did not intend to give Firestone security interest in the cash register:

"The debtor's intent must be judged by the language of the security agreement. Even if Firestone had enough security without the cash register (which is not apparent from the facts), Firestone is entitled to whatever priority it received by compliance with the Code. . . .

"The description in the security agreement is clearly broad enough to reach the cash register. It said 'All contents'; 'equipment such as': and 'used . . . with.' The cash register is covered by all of these phrases. Likewise, the financing statements cover the cash register by their use of the first two phrases—'All contents': 'equipment such as.'"

NCR also tried to argue that the financing statement was defective because it spelled "Kozy" with a C ("Cozy") rather than with a K. The court felt that this error was not seriously misleading because the filing was done under Carrol's name and because the address of the business was correctly stated.

The court held that the words *All contents . . . including equipment* "were enough to put the plaintiff on notice to ascertain what those contents were. This is not a harsh result as to the plaintiff, to which, as we have indicated, 5.9–312(4) made available a simple and sure procedure for completely protecting its purchase money security interest."

Some other sections as containing special priority rules have already been referred to above; 9–301, dealing with unperfected security interest and lien creditors; 9–306, covering proceeds and repossessions; 9–307, on good faith purchasers of goods (more on this in the next section of this chapter); 9–313, on fixtures; 9–316, on contractual subordination. For the sake of brevity, the remaining special priority rules are summarized:

Other special priority rules   Section 4–208 gives a bank which has given credit against an item being handled for collection a high-priority security interest against the item itself and any accompanying documents, even without a separate security agreement and without filing.

Section 9–304 provides a set of special rules for dealing with instruments, documents, and goods covered by documents, including a provision for limited and temporary (21 days) perfection without filing and without possession.

Section 9–308 provides a special rule protecting BFPs of chattel paper or nonnegotiable instruments where the conflicting security interest is perfected under 9–304's rules on permissive filing or temporary perfection.

Section 9–309 preserves the superior rights of good faith buyers of negotiable pieces of paper—instruments, documents, and investment securities; filing under Article 9 is not notice of the security interest to these parties.

Section 9–310 grants priority to any lien created by statute or case law in favor of a person who furnishes services or materials with respect to goods subject to a security interest.

Section 9–314 adopts a set of detailed rules for dealing with the common problem of *accessions* where goods become installed in or affixed to other goods, for example, the new motor in the old car; these rules are similar to the 1962 fixture rules.

Section 9–315 attempts to cover the situation where goods are commingled or processed so that they lose their distinct identity; the general idea is that the security interest continues against the mass or product; where there is more than one such security interest, they have equal priority and share pro rata in the product.

BIOC protected

Protection for Certain Good Faith Purchasers. Section 9–307 contains two special rules designed for the protection of good faith purchasers of goods. These rules were referred to in the preceding section of this chapter; and the *Nicolosi* case in Chapter 24 illustrates their application in one fact situation.

■ **EXHIBIT 25–1**

Perfection and Priorities

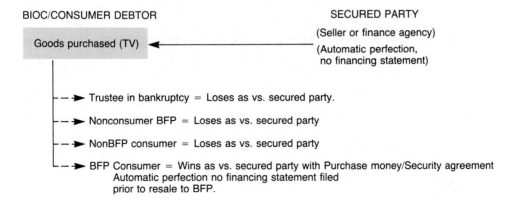

BUSINESS DEBTOR   SECURED PARTY

Business assets:
  Inventory
  Equipment
  Fixtures
  Accounts receivable
  Cash
  Good will

Security agreement and financing statement

BFP: Anything covered by Security agreement & Financing statement = Loses as vs. secured party.

Trustee in bankruptcy: Anything covered by Security agreement & Financing statement = Loses as vs. secured party.

BIOC: Inventory = Wins as vs. secured party

(If) BIOC is consumer debtor, who financed his/her purchase, with goods purchased as collateral

BIOC/CONSUMER DEBTOR   SECURED PARTY

Goods purchased (TV)

(Seller or finance agency)
(Automatic perfection, no financing statement)

Trustee in bankruptcy = Loses as vs. secured party.

Nonconsumer BFP = Loses as vs. secured party

NonBFP consumer = Loses as vs. secured party

BFP Consumer = Wins as vs. secured party with Purchase money/Security agreement Automatic perfection no financing statement filed prior to resale to BFP.

Subsection (1) of 9–307 protects the "buyer in the ordinary course of business," who is defined by 1–201(9) as follows:

"Buyer in ordinary course of business" means a person who in good faith and without knowledge that the sale to him is in violation of the ownership rights or security interest of a third party in the goods buys in ordinary course from a person in the business of selling goods of that kind.

Stated more simply, the BIOC is a buyer from a dealer's inventory. The BIOC "takes free of a security interest created by this seller even though the security interest is perfected and even though the buyer knows of its existence."

The limitations inherent in 9–307(1) have been brought out by several car dealer cases. In one such case, the Supreme Court of New Hampshire held that BIOC Jones was not protected under either 9–307(1) or (2) because a security interest had not been created by *his* seller and because the bank's security interest had been filed. Jones had bought the car in good faith from the dealer to whom it had been resold by the original buyer. When the original buyer went into default on his installment payments, the bank sued to foreclose on its security interest and won.

Moreover, where the BIOC not only knows of the existence of a security interest but also knows that the sale to him is in violation of it, he takes subject to the security interest.

Section 9–307(1) also specifically excludes from its protection "a person buying farm products from a person engaged in farming operations." Thus Buyer Johnson did not get BIOC protection in the *Waychus* case in Chapter 24.

Consumer BFP protected

Equally significant is the limitation which 9–307(2) places on the operation of the automatic perfection alternative for consumer goods. Where the secured party is relying on automatic perfection, a BFP takes free of the security interest if buying without knowledge and for personal, family, or household purposes.

Debtor's Defenses against Assignee. The great bulk of time-sale contracts are not held by the seller until maturity, but are transferred or "assigned" to a bank or other financing agency. The early common law absolutely prohibited such assignments since it was felt that they forced the debtor to do business with a stranger. Only within the last hundred years has their validity been accepted, and "traces of the absolute common law prohibition have survived almost to our own day."

One of the most significant common-law rules developed to protect account debtors in the assignment situation is the one which makes the assignee subject to all defenses which the debtor has against the assignor (seller). The assignee steps into the assignor's shoes; they don't get any larger just because someone else is wearing them; if they pinch a little bit, too bad. For its own protection, the financial community has been able to get statutes passed in some states which modify this general rule. The seller could also insulate the financing agency from most of the debtor's usual defenses (nondelivery, defective merchandise, fraud in the inducement) by having the debtor sign a negotiable instrument and then negotiating it to the financing agency as a "holder in due course."

General rule on debtor's defenses

The drafters of Article 9 continued the general rule on debtors' defenses against the assignee in substantially unchanged form, in 9–318(1). As under the common law, therefore, the account debtor can assert any defense under the assigned contract against the assignee, and can use any defense or claim against the assignor on totally unrelated matters, until receiving notice that the account has been assigned. For example, Biff Baker buys two cars, one new and one used, from Able's Auto Sales. Biff pays cash for the used car and finances the new car over 36 months. Able's Auto assigns the financing contract to the E-Z Money Company. If anything goes wrong with *either* car, Biff can use that defect (breach of warranty) as a defense when he is sued by E-Z Money, up to the point when Biff is notified of the assignment. After that, Biff can only assert claims he has under the new-car contract against E-Z and he has to go back to Able's Auto for any claims on the used car which arise after Biff gets notice.

Debtor can waive defenses

The references in 9–318(1) to Section 9–206 are important because 9–206 specifically validates a contractual agreement by the debtor-buyer "that he will not assert against an assignee any claim or defense which he may have against the seller." For an assignee to claim the protection afforded by this section, it must take the assignment "for value, in good faith, and without notice of a claim or defense." Moreover, this section does not prevent the debtor from asserting defenses which could be asserted against the holder in due course of a negotiable instrument, such as minority, illegality, and fraud in the execution. And finally, and perhaps most significantly, 9–206 states that it is subject to "any statute or decision which establishes a different rule for buyers of consumer goods."

FTC protection for consumers

If a state wishes to modify the seeming harshness of this third section to protect consumers, this is easily done, either legislatively or judicially. Massachusetts took the lead by passing the bill which abolished the "holder in due course" concept for consumer sales; most states have now adopted such legislation. Under its rule-making powers, the FTC held extensive hearings and then adopted an "unfair method of competition" rule at the national level. As a result, the **holder in due course doctrine** has been largely removed from the consumer-sales field. Such waiver clauses are valid for nonconsumer buyers (who, presumably, are better able to take care of themselves from a legal and contractual standpoint).

Section 9–206 makes it clear that any "disclaimer, limitation or modification of the seller's warranties" must be made in accordance with Article 2 and not under this section.

■ DEFAULT AND REMEDIES

Most of our discussion of secured transactions in this chapter has concerned the problems confronted by the secured party when third-party claimants contest the right to "priority" against the collateral. Most of Article 9 is directed toward those problems, but Part 5, Default, does step into the transaction between the immediate parties, to regulate the rights and remedies as between them in the event that the debtor defaults.

Cumulative Remedies; Minimum Requirements after Default. Section 9–501(1) makes clear the intent of the UCC drafters that the secured party should be entitled to pursue all available remedies until the debt to him or her is satisfied. The secured party has the rights and remedies provided by Part 5 and 9–207, those provided in the security agreement itself (subject to the limitations in 9–501[3], and "any available judicial procedure" for debt enforcement under applicable state law. "The rights and remedies referred to in this subsection are cumulative" (9–501[1]).

Limits on freedom of contract

Similarly, the debtor has the rights and remedies provided in Part 5, in Section 9–207, and the security agreement. The policy of the Code and of Article 9 is to provide substantial *freedom of contract* between the immediate parties to the particular transaction. That policy is continued, to a degree, as regards default procedures, but 9–501(3) imposes a set of "minimum procedural requirements" on default, for the protection of the debtor. In addition to these prescribed minima, the parties' freedom to agree to "whatever they want" may also be limited by 1–102[3] and 2–302, as noted above.

The objective in these default sections, then, is to balance the rights and remedies of both parties and ensure that the debtor is protected by requiring that certain steps be taken when default occurs. *Default,* however, is not specifically defined; its definition is left to the agreement itself and to generally applicable legal principles.

Collection.

On default, or whenever so agreed, the secured party has the right to notify an account debtor or the obligor on an instrument to start making payments directly and the right to take control of any proceeds under Section 9–306. This rule applies even though the assignor, called the "debtor" in the security agreement, was previously making the collections and then remitting them to the secured party.

When the agreement provides that the secured party is entitled to charge back against the debtor any "uncollected" collateral and the secured party elects to collect personally, that must be done "in a commercially reasonable manner." The reasonable expenses incurred in the collection process can be recovered from the assignor-debtor. Provision is also made for both "deficiency" and "surplus" situations (9–502[2]):

> If the security agreement secures an indebtedness, the secured party must account to the debtor for any surplus, and unless otherwise agreed, the debtor is liable for any deficiency. But, if the underlying transaction was a sale of accounts or chattel paper, the debtor is entitled to any surplus or is liable for any deficiency only if the security agreement so provides.

Repossession.

The creditor's classic remedy on default has been to "repo" the collateral. This remedy is continued for the secured party, pretty much as it existed under prior law, by 9–503:

> Unless otherwise agreed, a secured party has on default the right to take possession of the collateral. In taking possession a secured party may proceed without judicial process if this can be done without breach of the peace or may proceed by action.

No breach of peace permitted in taking collateral

Traditionally, the main question in these cases has been the definition of what constitutes a *breach of the peace* by the creditor repossessing without court order. Parked on the street or in a public parking lot, the debtor's car seems to be fair game for the repo person. Even if it's in the debtor's driveway or parked on private property, the repo person can probably still seize it and drive or tow it away. The line of demarcation seems to be the point at which the repo person opens a door or gate, either by force or fraud, or threatens the debtor in any way. These lines of decision under prior law will presumably continue under 9–503.

Section 9–503 also provides two new repo alternatives:

> If the security agreement so provides the secured party may require the debtor to assemble the collateral and make it available to the secured party at a place to be designated by the secured party which is reasonably convenient to both parties.

And:

> Without removal a secured party may render equipment unusable, and may dispose of collateral on the debtor's premises under Section 9–504.

These two provisions give the secured party additional options under the general right to repossession.

The *Raffa* case applies these self-help repossession rules.

RAFFA v. DANIA BANK

321 So.2d 83 (Florida, 1975)

FACTS   On September 27, 1972, while Nancy Raffa and her husband were entertaining friends in their home at Lighthouse Point, her 1970 Cadillac Eldorado was taken by a "collection agent" (the repo man). She was over a month behind in making the 16th of 36 monthly payments on the car. The car was gone when Mrs. Raffa and her guests came out of the house, and she said she was embarrassed by the incident. She has paid off the loan and retrieved the car, and now sues for compensatory and punitive damages for wrongful repossession. She claims that the repo man committed an unlawful trespass, and that the Dania Bank failed to give her specific notice of their intent to repo the car. The trial court granted summary judgment for the defendants.

ISSUE   Was Mrs. Raffa entitled to notice prior to repossession?

DECISION   Yes (probably). Judgement reversed in part, and case remanded.

REASONS   Judge Schwartz first disposed of the allegation of "unlawful trespass." On this point, he agreed with the trial court that summary judgment was proper. All that had happened was that the secured party's agent had come onto the land to retake the collateral, as it was authorized to do by the security agreement. The agent hadn't even had to open a door, much less break one in, to get the car. (The Eldorado was so long that it stuck out of the Raffas' carport.) There was absolutely no conduct which could be construed as a breach of the peace.

As to the second argument, however, Judge Schwartz disagreed with the trial court. A trial was necessary to determine whether Dania Bank had waived its right to repo without notice, by its acceptance of prior late payments.

"Mrs. Raffa also claims, however, that, under the circumstances of this case, and despite the provisions of the agreement to the contrary, she was entitled to notice from the Bank before the repossession took place. . . . [P]ast acceptances of late payments without repossession might give rise to a right by the purchaser to rely upon that course of conduct and a concomitant duty by the creditor to notify the buyer prior to his changing the pattern by retaking the property. In this record there are indications that Mrs. Raffa had in fact been allowed in the past to make up late payments and that the Bank had accordingly not repossessed her automobile. At the very least, the defendants did not discharge their affirmative duty, on motion for summary judgment, of conclusively establishing the absence of a genuine issue of material fact as to this contention. . . . Accordingly, the cause is remanded for appropriate determination below of the claim that, under these circumstances, notice or demand was required prior to the retaking of Mrs. Raffa's car."

Disposition. After default by the debtor, the secured party has the right to dispose of the collateral and to apply the proceeds—first, to pay all reasonable selling expenses; second, to satisfy the security interest; and third, to pay any subordinate security interest as to which a written demand for payment is received prior to distribution of the proceeds. Where there is an underlying debt, "the secured party must account to the debtor for any surplus, and, unless otherwise agreed, the debtor is liable for any deficiency." But if the transaction was a sale of accounts or chattel paper, "the debtor is entitled to any surplus or is liable for any deficiency only if the security agreement so provides."

Commercially reasonable disposition required

As regards the disposition itself, Section 9–504 allows maximum flexibility as to details. The disposition may be made by public or private sale, in one or more contracts, as a unit or in parcels, at any time and place, and on any terms. The secured party may buy the collateral at any public sale, or at a private sale if the collateral is of a type sold in a recognized market or subject to widely distributed standard price quotations. This considerable flexibility is, however, subject to a basic good faith limitation: "every aspect of the disposition including the method, manner, time, place and terms must be commercially reasonable." Except where the collateral is perishable, or threatens to decline speedily in value, or is customarily sold on a recognized market, the secured party must give the debtor reasonable notification of the intended sale. Except for consumer goods, notification must also be sent to any other secured party who had filed against the collateral or whose interest is known to the secured party. The debtor can thus challenge the legal effects of the sale either under the ***commercially reasonable*** requirement or on the basis that he or she did not get ***reasonable notification.*** The issue is most often raised when the debtor is sued for a deficiency judgment, where the secured party says that the sale did not bring enough to pay off the debt.

Section 9–504(4) deals with the rights acquired by the purchaser of the collateral at the disposition sale. The disposition gives the purchaser all rights of the debtor, and it discharges the security interest under which the sale was made and any subordinate interest or lien. Even though the secured party does not follow proper sale procedures, the purchaser is protected at a public sale if there is no knowledge of the defects in the sale or collusion, and in any other case if acting in good faith. These code requirements are discussed in the following case.

FIRST MISSOURI BANK & TRUST CO. v. NEWMAN

680 S.W.2d 767 (Missouri, 1984)

FACTS

In 1975 and 1976, defendant entered into four financing agreements with plaintiff bank. Each of the four promissory notes was secured by a motor vehicle. Defendant defaulted on all four notes. On May 20, 1976, the bank sent four notices informing defendant that the bank had repossessed all four vehicles. Each notice also stated:

> You have ten (10) days to redeem the collateral by presenting [the total amount owed on the note] in certified funds, to First Missouri Bank & Trust Co. . . . In the event you do not choose to redeem the above described collateral, it will be sold pursuant to the Uniform Commercial Code, through the competitive bidding process to the highest bidder. You will be liable for any resulting deficiency if the proceeds of the sale are not sufficient to cover the payoff figure. . . .

After making repairs to the vehicles, the bank sold all four of them for prices below the amounts still owed by defendants. The bank then filed this action to recover the deficiencies. Defendant filed a general denial. The trial court awarded a deficiency judgment. Defendant appeals.

ISSUE

Who has the burden of proof as to compliance or noncompliance with the Article 9 requirements?

DECISION

Plaintiff does. Judgment reversed; case remanded.

REASONS

Justice Reinhard:

"We first address defendant's argument that the bank did not meet the statutory notice requirements. Section 400.9–504(3) requires that when a secured party intends to sell collateral of the type presented here, reasonable notice of sale must be sent to the debtor. The statutory requirements for reasonable notice of a public sale are different than those for a private sale. . . . Here, the bank's notice meets the requirements for a private sale but not for a public sale because no time or place was given.

"Because no competent evidence was introduced on the type or manner of sale, it is impossible to discern from the record whether the notice was sufficient. Thus, the issue is whether the bank or the defendants had the burden of proving compliance or noncompliance with the notice requirements. Defendant argues that, as a prerequisite to obtaining a deficiency judgment, the bank must prove that notice was sufficient. The bank argues that by failing to affirmatively plead and prove lack of notice, defendants waived that defense.

"Neither the applicable Missouri statute, Section 400.9–504, nor the Uniform Commercial Code Section 9–504 expressly allocates the burden of proof. We are unable to find any Missouri cases on point, and neither party has cited any. However, we note that the Uniform Commercial Code Comment following Section 9–504 states, '[T]his Section follows the provisions of the Section on resale by a seller following a buyer's rejection of goods (Section 2–706). . . . Construing the notice requirements of Section 400.2–706, . . . this court has stated:

> We hold that when a seller avails himself of the remedy afforded by 400.2–706 he must comply with all of the terms of that section and the burden of showing compliance is upon the seller. In this case there was no finding upon this issue. . . . Defendant [seller] offered no

proof. As this case now stands defendant has not pleaded or proved that he complied with 400.2–706 and it may not recover the difference between the sale price and the contract price. . . .

"[B]ecause a deficiency judgment after the sale of repossessed collateral is strictly a creature of statute, the right to the deficiency accrues only when there is strict compliance with the statutory requirements. . . . [T]his court has expressly rejected the notion that lack of notice under Section 400.2–706 was an affirmative defense which must be pleaded by the defendant. . . . Here, because the bank offered no competent evidence of the public or private nature of the sale, we cannot determine whether the notice was sufficient to comply with the statute. The bank did not meet its burden of proof. We rule this point for defendant.

"Defendants' contention that the bank failed to prove the sale was commercially reasonable under the statute is also well taken. . . . However, the statute does not indicate which party bears the burden of proving that the sale complied or failed to comply with the statutory requirements.

"Plaintiff bank maintains that because defendant failed to affirmatively plead the defense of commercial unreasonableness, the issue has been waived. Again, neither part cites nor can we find a Missouri case on point. Some jurisdictions hold that the secured party bears the burden of proving commercial reasonableness; others place the burden of proving commercial unreasonableness on the debtor. . . . We believe the better view is that the party seeking the deficiency judgment bears the burden of proving compliance with the statutory requirement of commercial reasonableness, regardless of whether the debtor affirmatively pleaded a defense of commercial unreasonableness. We so hold because the secured party is the moving party in a deficiency action. . . . Our holding on this issue is in keeping with the Missouri policy requiring strict statutory compliance for the protection of the debtor. . . . This point is also ruled in favor of defendant."

Compulsory Disposition. A secured party who has repossessed the collateral *must* dispose of it in accordance with Section 9–504 where the consumer-debtor has paid 60 percent of the cash price or of the loan and has not signed *after default* a statement renouncing or modifying his or her rights under Part 5. If the secured party fails to comply with this section within 90 days after taking possession, the debtor may either sue for conversion of the collateral or recover damages and a penalty as specified under 9–507(1).

Except for the above consumer goods situation, a secured party who is in possession of the collateral may propose *after default* that he or she will retain it in satisfaction of the debt. The secured party must send written notice of this "proposal" to the debtor and, except for consumer goods, to any other secured party who has filed or who is known to the secured party with possession. The debtor or any secured party entitled to notification has 21 days from receipt of the notification to object in writing to the proposal; any other secured party claiming an interest in the collateral has 21 days from the time that secured party 1 obtained possession of the collateral. If anyone does object, secured party 1 cannot retain the collateral as proposed but must dispose of it under 9–504; if there is no objection, the secured party can keep the collateral in satisfaction of the obligation.

Redemption by Debtor. At any time before the secured party has disposed or contracted to dispose of the collateral under 9–504 or has discharged the obligation by retention of the collateral under 9–505(2), the debtor or any other secured party has the right to redeem the collateral. To redeem, there must be a tender to the secured party of *(a)* all obligations secured by the collateral; *(b)* "the expenses reasonably incurred by the secured party in retaking, holding, and preparing the collateral for disposition, in arranging for the sale;" and *(c)* "to the extent provided in the agreement and not prohibited by law, his reasonable attorneys' fees and legal expenses."

The debtor or any other secured party may agree *in writing, after default,* to waive this right to redeem.

Secured Party Liability for Failure to Comply. Section 9–507 does two things. It defines more precisely the requirement that the secured party proceed after default in a "commercially reasonable" manner and it provides remedies for the debtor where the secured party does not proceed in accordance with the provisions of Part 5.

Section 9–507(2) establishes several principles regarding "commercial reasonableness," and the debtor's right to recover for a secured party's violation of the default provisions of Part 5. Where such violation has occurred:

a. [D]isposition may be ordered or restrained on appropriate terms and conditions.

b. If the disposition has occurred the debtor or any person entitled to notification or whose security interest has been made known to the secured party prior to disposition has a right to recover from the secured party any loss caused by a failure to comply with the provisions of this Part.

c. If the collateral is consumer goods, the debtor has a right to recover in any event an amount not less than the credit service charge plus 10 percent of the principal amount of the debt or the time price differential plus 10 percent of the cash price.

These Code sections thus provide significant protections for both consumer and nonconsumer debtors even after they have gone into default on their obligations under a security agreement.

■ **SIGNIFICANCE OF THIS CHAPTER**

Since debtors do default with some frequency, creditors need to be assured that they will have priority claims against "their" pieces of collateral. This priority is really the whole purpose of structuring the credit arrangement as a secured transaction. The entire motive for being a *secured* creditor is to have a specific source of funds in the event the debtor defaults, rather than having to rely on the debtor's general financial condition. Creditors thus need to know what to do to establish priority, and what payment sequences the Code provides.

Similarly, both debtors and creditors need to be aware of their rights when a default does occur. In general, a secured creditor who is proceeding in a reasonable manner is well protected by Article 9. On the other hand, the Code also tries to assure that the debtor is treated fairly, even though guilty of a default. Because abuses occurred in the past, Article 9 gives consumer debtors the right to recover a penalty in the event their secured parties do not follow proper procedures. The Code has attempted to strike a fair balance between the parties in this very common and very important commercial transaction.

DISCUSSION CASE

JAMES TALCOTT, INC. v. FRANKLIN NATIONAL BANK OF MINNEAPOLIS
194 N.W.2d 775 (Minnesota, 1972)

FACTS: This is an appeal taken from a summary judgment in favor of defendant, Franklin National Bank of Minneapolis. The action was commenced for the recovery of possession of several motor vehicles, or their value, in which plaintiff, James Talcott, Inc., claimed a superior security interest.

On February 20, 1968, Noyes Paving Company, hereinafter referred to as "debtor," entered into a conditional sales contract with Northern Contracting Company, as seller, covering the purchase, on an installment basis, of two dump trucks and other construction equipment. On that same day, the seller assigned, without recourse, the conditional sales contract to plaintiff, together with all sums payable thereunder and all right, title, and interest in and to the equipment covered by the contract. On February 21, 1968, a financing statement was filed with the secretary of state naming Noyes Paving Company as debtor, Northern Contracting Company as secured party, and James Talcott, Inc., as assignee of the secured party. The financing statement covered the following items of property: "Construction Equipment, Motor Vehicles."

On May 1, debtor entered into an equipment lease with defendant bank covering one dump truck; and on May 31, a similar lease agreement was entered into between the same parties covering two additional dump trucks and other equipment. Each lease provided that debtor, if not in default, could purchase the leased goods at the end of the lease term for the sum of $1. Defendant did not at that time file a financing statement regarding the equipment described in the two lease agreements.

During the latter part of the year 1968, debtor experienced difficulty in making payments on the conditional sales contract. On January 20, 1969, debtor and plaintiff entered into an agreement extending the time for payment. In consideration of the extension granted, debtor gave plaintiff a security interest *"in all goods (as defined in Article 9 of the Uniform Commercial Code) whether now owned or hereafter acquired."* No additional financing statement was filed in connection with the extension agreement of January 30. At that time, plaintiff did not know of the existence of the motor vehicles and other equipment listed in defendant's two equipment leases and did not rely upon their existence in entering into the extension agreement.

Following the date of the exension agreement, debtor ran into more financial difficulty and defaulted in payments with respect to both the conditional sales contract and the equipment leases. On May 21, 1970, copies of the leases were filed by defendant bank as financing statements with the secretary of state. Sometime during May 1970, defendant repossessed the equipment in question and this action ensued. The precise date on which defendant made the repossession is not clear from the record. The parties agreed that it took place during the month of May 1970. All of the equipment was located with the exception of one item. By agreement between plaintiff and defendant, the equipment was sold, and the proceeds were placed in a special account pending the outcome of this case.

■

Justice Hackey gave the opinion for the court:

The issues on appeal are: (1) Whether an equipment lease which gives the lessee the right to acquire title to the equipment for $1 upon compliance with the lease terms is a "security agreement" within the meaning of Article 9; (2) whether debtor had sufficient ownership of the leased equipment so that it became secured property under the extension agreement with plaintiff; (3) whether the description of the secured property, as it appeared in the extension agreement, was sufficient to meet the requirements of Art. 9. . . ; (4) whether the financing statement filed at the time the first security agreement was assigned to plaintiff was sufficient to perfect a security interest in the property covered by the extension agreement; and (5) which security interest was entitled to priority. . . .

1. Were the leases security agreements?

This question is extremely significant because plaintiff's right to recovery is dependent upon a finding that the lease agreements between defendant and debtor were, in effect, security agreements. . . .

The language of the code specifically determines whether or not a lease creates a security interest in the collateral. . . . The words of that section are unequivocal. An option given to the lessee to purchase the leased property for a nominal consideration does make the lease one intended for security. Hence, the options to buy the equipment in the instant case for the combined sum of $2, a nominal amount when compared to the total rental of $73,303.32, created security interests. The leases in question were precisely the type that Art. 9 was intended to cover, i.e., transactions in goods which were in substance, although not in form, security agreements. . . .

2. Did the debtor "own" the leased property so that it was included as secured property under plaintiff's security agreement?

This question is a part of the critical issue in the case inasmuch as the second security agreement between plaintiff and debtor (the extension agreement of January 30, 1969) gave plaintiff a security interest in "all goods . . . whether now owned or hereafter acquired" by debtor. The issue turns on whether or not debtor can be deemed to have owned the leased property at the time it entered into the extension agreement. . . .

[T]he draftsmen of the code intended that its provisions should not be circumvented by manipulation of the locus of title. For this reason, consignment sales, conditional sales, and other arrangements or devices whereby title is retained in the seller for a period following possession by the debtor are all treated under Art. 9 as though the title had been transferred to the debtor and the creditor-seller had retained only a security interest in the goods. For the purpose of analyzing rights of ownership under Art. 9, we hold, based upon the stipulated facts of this case, that defendant had only a security interest in the equipment despite a purported reservation of title and that debtor "owned" the equipment at the time that the extension agreement was executed.

3. Was the description of the secured property, as it appeared in the extension agreement, sufficient to meet the requirements of Art. 9; that is, did the description reasonably identify what was being described?

The description of the collateral in the extension agreement did what it was meant to do—namely, it included all of the goods then owned, or to be owned in the future, by the debtor. The term "goods" was defined to be those goods as comprehended within the meaning of Art. 9 of the code. The definition selected is embodied in the statute, a definition that is used and applied frequently. The parties sought to create a security interest in substantially all of the debtor's property. That is what was stated, and that is what was meant. The parties did not particularize any further, and the statute does not require it. . . .

A security agreement should not be held unenforceable unless it is so ambiguous that its meaning cannot reasonably be construed from the language of the agreement itself. Such a test appears to have been intended by the draftsmen of the code and should be applied in this case. We fail to find an impelling reason why we should not approve the description used in this case, and we hold that it suffices within the terms of the statute. We further hold specifically that the description used in the extension agreement between debtor and plaintiff includes the equipment financed by defendant bank.

4. Was the financing statement, filed at the time the first security agreement was assigned to plaintiff, sufficient to reflect a security interest in the property covered by the extension agreement?

Section 336.402(1) provides that "[a] financing statement may be filed before a security agreement is made or a security interest otherwise attaches." This is what happened in the instant case. The financing statement filed February 21, 1968, met all requirements of the code since it described by type ("Construction Equipment, Motor Vehicles") not only the property covered by the original sales agreement which was assigned to plaintiff but also the property, which likewise consisted of motor vehicles and construction equipment, financed by defendant. The code does not require a reference in the financing statement to after-acquired property. . . .

The whole purpose of notice filing would be nullified if a financing statement had to be filed whenever a new transaction took place between a secured party and a debtor. Once a financing statement is on file describing property by type, the entire world is warned, not only that the secured party may already have a security interest in the property of that type (as did plaintiff in the property originally financed), but that it may later acquire a perfected security interest in property of the same type acquired by the debtor in the future. When the debtor does acquire more property of the type referred to in the financing statement already on file, and when a security interest attaches to that property, the perfection is instantaneous and automatic. . . .

5. Priority. . . .

Defendant's security interest did attach first, but (assuming it was filed after repossession) it was not perfected.

Plaintiff's security interest attached later—actually after its filing had occurred. But neither of these factors is material in the application of the first-to-perfect rule. Accordingly, when the conflict arose (still assuming it was before defendant had filed), plaintiff was entitled to priority. Once plaintiff's priority had been acquired, no subsequent filing by defendant (more than 10 days after debtor received possession) could alter the situation. Moreover, even if . . . 312(5)(a) should apply, plaintiff would still have priority under the first-to-file rule as its filing preceded defendant's by many months. . . .

The summary judgment for defendant is reversed, and the matter is remanded with directions to enter judgment for plaintiff. . . .

▪ IMPORTANT TERMS AND CONCEPTS

perfection
perfected security interest
lien creditor
trustee in bankruptcy
filing a financing
    statement
automatic perfection
consumer goods
perfection against
    proceeds
perfection against fixtures
construction mortgages
readily-removable replace-
    ments of consumer-
    good domestic
    appliances
priority
first to file
noninventory collateral
    rule
waiver of defense
holder in due course
    doctrine
default
collection of accounts
breach of the peace
commercial reasonableness
compulsory disposition

secured party liability
insolvency proceeding
unperfected security
    interest
bankruptcy
purchase-money security
    interest
taking possession of the
    goods
attachment alone
bona fide purchaser
    consumer
buyer in ordinary course
fixture filing
readily-removable
    machines
first to perfect
inventory collateral rule
debtor's defenses against
    assignee
FTC consumer protection
    rule
cumulative remedies
freedom of contract
repossession of collateral
disposition of collateral
reasonable notification
redemption by debtor

▪ QUESTIONS AND PROBLEMS FOR DISCUSSION

1. What is the difference between "attachment" and "perfection"?
2. What are the three different methods of perfecting a security interest?
3. What happens when a security interest is not perfected?
4. When does a buyer from a merchant take free and clear of a security interest which has been perfected against the goods being sold?
5. Kelly Goodheart, registered owner of a highway tractor, leased his tractor to Morse Crash. However, the rental agreement was in actuality a conditional sales or title-retaining contract, under which Morse agreed to pay $300 for 15 weeks and then was to receive title. Morse also was to pay all repair bills and to provide insurance coverage. The vehicle was damaged in an accident and later repaired by Frank Hammer's Collision Service for $600. Morse decided to move for destinations unknown, leaving Kelly and Frank to fight over the tractor. How would you decide these conflicting claims?
6. Ned Ninepins, owner of Lucky Lane bowling alley, bought six automatic pinsetters from Leisure Equipment, Inc. He entered into a retail installment contract with the seller which specified that upon default the total contract price would become due. After several payments Ned defaulted, and six months later Leisure Equipment, Inc. brought a foreclosure action against him. Under a warrant of seizure the local sheriff entered the building and rendered the pinsetters inoperative but left them in their place. Ned counterclaimed for damages, arguing that personal property had been converted and that the sheriff's failure to remove the seized equipment made it impossible for Ned to use the building in any other way. Was the seizure legal? Explain.
7. Becky Miller, M.B.A., decided to open a Texaco station. She purchased equipment from Leek Oil Equipment Company, for which she delivered to the seller a promissory note for $3,000. Under the conditional sales agreement she was to pay monthly installments, and title to the equipment would remain with the seller until the entire purchase price was paid. After making three payments, she defaulted. Leek repossessed the equipment, estimated to be worth $2,000, credited the promissory note for this amount, and sued Becky for another $1,000. Becky protests, claiming that the repossession wipes out the entire debt. What is the decision. Discuss.

8. In 1986 Pedro Agricola, a farmer, bought a pickup for which he executed a promissory note to Flatland Bank. The note was secured by a properly executed and perfected security agreement. Pedro also had other loans outstanding with Flatland Bank which were secured by mortgages on other equipment and on his 16 pigs. Two years later Pedro borrowed money from his neighbor Lilly White and gave her a promissory note, but soon afterward he defaulted on both notes. Lilly took possession of the truck, claiming that the bank should satisfy its claim by taking possession of Pedro's other assets, namely the 10-year-old equipment and the 16 two-year-old pigs. Who has prior claim on the truck? Why?

26

Consumer Protection in Credit Transactions

CHAPTER OBJECTIVES
THIS CHAPTER WILL:

- Review consumer protection laws already discussed.
- Explain the Consumer Credit Protection Act (the Truth in Lending Act).
- Indicate how the Equal Credit Opportunity Act protects credit applicants.
- Review the various prohibitions against misuse of credit information.
- Explain the new limitations on creditors' billing and collection practices.

■ NEW GOVERNMENT ACTIVISM ON CONSUMER ISSUES

Consumerism was surely one of the major social movements in the United States during the 1970s. The national government, and to a lesser extent the states, moved to correct what were seen as abuses by sellers and lenders. Inexperienced and unwary consumers were being pressured into paying for shoddy or undelivered merchandise, or misperformed or unperformed services. High-pressure sales tactics produced contracts with harsh and unfair provisions. Confronted with these marketplace manipulations, judges and legislataors rebelled.

Product liability changes

The *Henningsen* case (see Chapter 20) is probably the single most important piece of consumer law ever written. It was the opening salvo in the product liability revolution, which has continued through the 1960s and 1970s, into the 1980s. That part of consumer protection law is discussed throughout Chapter 20.

Other aspects of the consumer protection movement have also been discussed in prior chapters. The FTC's authority over unfair trade practices and deceptive advertising is discussed in Chapter 5. The new legal rules on unordered goods and in-home sales are discussed in Chapter 10. Usury laws, limiting the rate of interest that can be charged, are covered in Chapter 15. Also discussed in Chapter 15 is the concept of "unconscionability," which courts can use to invalidate contract provisions that are grossly unfair, although not specifically illegal.

■ CONSUMER CREDIT PROTECTION ACT (TRUTH IN LENDING ACT)

Full Disclosure in Credit Transactions. As several philosophers have said, "knowledge is power." A consumer who was aware of the terms of a proposed credit transaction would be better able to compare them with those of other possible lenders, and to object to those which were most unfair. Congress passed the Truth in Lending Act (TILA) in 1969, as the first major part of the Consumer Credit Protection Act (CCPA), which now also includes sections on other topics, such as consumer leasing and credit billing. A required disclosure form must be given to the consumer at or before the signing of the credit contract. It must disclose the interest rate as an annual percentage and show the total dollar figure for the "finance charge," which includes loan fees, credit report fees, and required insurance charges. TILA does not limit the amount of these charges; it only specifies that the amounts must be disclosed.

Required disclosures

Similarly, ads for credit which mention a down payment, a monthly payment, or an interest rate must go on to specify the other terms as well.

Recission rule

Where the purchaser's home is used as collateral, the purchaser is given three business days after the purchase, or after the creditor gives written notice of the right to cancel, within which to rescind the whole contract. This rescission rule does not apply to the first mortgage on the home, but only to later credit contracts, such as those for home improvements.

Under its rule-making authority, the Federal Reserve Board has stated that TILA applies to any consumer transaction which calls for payment in more than four installments. This rule is found in FRB Regulation Z.

Consumer leasing

Since the original TILA covered only consumer *purchases* on credit, Congress added the Consumer Leasing sections to CCPA in 1976. Leasing of cars, computers, and other equipment has become increasingly common, even for

TILA penalties

persons defined as consumers (personal users). Similar disclosures are required in these lease transactions.

Where a creditor has violated TILA or CLA, the consumer may recover twice the finance charge, but not less than $100 nor more than $1,000, plus attorneys' fees. Criminal penalties for a willfull and knowing failure to comply are a fine up to $1,000, or imprisonment up to one year, or both. Because of the detail and complexities involved in complying with TILA, amendments passed in 1980 exempt a creditor from liability if the error is corrected within 60 days after it is discovered. The *Young* case illustrates the TILA results prior to the 1980 amendments.

YOUNG v. OUACHITA NATIONAL BANK IN MONROE

428 F.Supp 1323 (Louisiana, 1977)

FACTS   Ruby Young financed her purchase of a 1976 Ford pickup truck with a loan from Ouachita Bank. Ouachita Bank took a chattel mortgage on the pickup as collateral for the loan. After Ruby took possession of the pickup, she discovered it was a 1975 model, rather than the 1976 it had been presented to be. She then alleged numerous violations of TILA in the bank's loan forms and sued for TILA's statutory damages. The bank had failed to itemize the $10 license plate fee, the $3.50 title fee, and the $1 recording fee for the mortgage, but had instead lumped them together as $14.50 for "official fees."

ISSUE   Does this violation of TILA's requirements entitle the debtor (Young) to TILA's statutory damages (twice the finance charge)?

DECISION Yes. Judgment accordingly. (Young gets $726.66, plus attorney's fees.)

REASONS   Judge Dawkins felt that the meaning of TILA, as interpreted in several precedent cases, was clear.

"[I]t is clear that lending institutions must choose, as plaintiff argues, either to include the various expenses in the finance charge, or itemize them in detail; merely summarizing or categorizing fees and expenses is not adequate disclosure.

"It makes no difference that this error was unintentional and made without willful purpose to mislead. Although these factors might have some weight were we faced with possible criminal penalties under the Act. . . , the reference to 'unintentional error' in section 1640(c) has been held to apply only to clerical error. . . .

"Here, there was a clerical error in the finance charge listed on the credit disclosure statement. The amount actually should have been $348.83 . . . rather than $345.83, the amount shown. To arrive at the finance charge, one of the measuring sticks in assessing statutory damages (plaintiff, here, is not seeking actual damages) . . . we must add the improperly disclosed expenses, $14.50, to the $348.83 set forth in the disclosure. Therefore, the total finance charge is $363.33. . . .

"Plaintiff argues that the life insurance charge, $66.89, likewise should be added to the above total in calculating the finance charge. As previously noted, plaintiff is entitled to but a single recovery for disclosure infractions, and improperly disclosed charges must be added to the finance charge in calculating the quantum of statutory damages.

"On the credit disclosure statement, the cost of life insurance was disclosed separately. Mrs. Young signed the statement twice, once at the bottom and once in the middle—

the portion of the form dealing with insurance. The date of her signature, which showed she desired credit life insurance, was typed next to her signature there. Thus, she clearly knew that purchase of life insurance was optional. The form itself sets forth that the borrower has the option, and is not required to purchase insurance. Moreover, in her deposition, at pages 8 through 9, plaintiff indicated that she knew she did not have to purchase this insurance."

Credit Card Liability. Other sections of the CCPA have drastically changed the law relating to the issuance and use of credit cards. Prior to the CCPA, gasoline companies and other issuers were free to send out cards by mass mailings, using computerized lists of potential customers. Under general contract law rules, retention and use of the credit card would constitute acceptance of the issuing company's offer. The issuer's terms could include a provision making the cardholder liable for its unauthorized use. These contract provisions were sometimes enforced by the courts, at least where the merchant taking the card as payment had made a reasonable effort to verify the identity of the person using the card.

Liability for use by others

It is now unlawful to issue cards that have not been requested by the customer. Further, the customer/cardholder's liability for unauthorized use is limited to $50. Even this $50 amount is conditioned on the card issuer's compliance with CCPA's requirements. The issuer must have notified the customer of this potential $50 liability, have provided a notification form to be sent to the issuer in the event of loss or theft of the card, and have provided either a signature or photo on the card so that the merchant can identify the user. If all these requirements have been met, the customer can be held liable for up to $50 of unauthorized charges that occur before the issuer is notified that the card has been lost or stolen. How this $50 limit applies is at issue in the *Cities Service* case.

$50 limit per card

CITIES SERVICE CO. v. PAILET

452 So.2d 319 (Louisiana, 1984)

FACTS

Cities Service Company appeals the dismissal of its suit on open account for $1,148.70, representing purchases made on defendant Ellis Jay Pailet's Citgo credit card.

The disputed invoices, except for one, were for charges made at a Pearl, Mississippi Citgo Service Station from January 21, 1982, through May 20, 1982. Copies of the invoices, signed "E. Pailet" and a monthly statement from February through June, 1982 were introduced into evidence.

John Bilbow, plaintiff's collection supervisor, testified that between April 21, 1982, and July 20, 1982 Cities Service made numerous phone calls to Pailet and left messages with his secretary in an attempt to collect on the delinquent account. According to Bilbow, Pailet returned only the call of May 4, to say that he was "checking on something." The card was cancelled, subsequently recovered by a service station, and returned to Cities Service. Plaintiff had no record, however, indicating that the card had been lost or stolen, or that the charges were unauthorized.

Defendant Pailet, on the other hand, testified that he had given his credit card to Connie Jordan, an employee of his wholesale beauty products company, for a limited business purpose in Gulfport, Mississippi. According to Pailet, before receiving calls from plaintiff about the balance due, he had "revoked" Jordan's authority to use the card. After Cities Service's call in "the beginning of 1982," Pailet called Jordan who informed him that she had stopped using the card and no longer had it. In response to a question whether Jordan told him what had happened to the card, Pailet stated, "I think she said she lost it. I just let it go at that." Jordan, the employee, did not testify.

Pailet further testified that the signatures on the invoices at issue are definitely not his, and that the charges in Pearl, Mississippi were 100 miles from the Gulfport area where Jordan was authorized to use the card. He felt that he had notified Cities Service "very specifically" that he no longer had the credit card and that the billings were not authorized.

ISSUE   Were the pre-April charges "unauthorized"?

DECISION   No. Judgment reversed.

REASONS   Judge Gulotta saw only a limited application here of TILA.

"Applying the statute to the facts of the instant case, we conclude that Pailet is not liable for any invoices dated after he had notified the company that the charges may not have been authorized. Although the evidence is conflicting, a reasonable inference from Pailet's testimony is that he specifically notified Cities Service as early as April 21, 1982. Considering this testimony, and recognizing the trial judge's express credibility determination in Pailet's favor, we conclude charges on the card made after April 21 were not authorized, and cannot be recovered by plaintiff.

"The more troubling question, however, is whether or not the unpaid invoices dated prior to April 21, 1982 are recoverable as 'authorized' charges.

"Although we have found no Louisiana authority directly on point, an Alabama decision, *Martin v. American Express, Inc.,* 361 So.2d 597 (Ala.Civ.App.1978), is persuasive. In *Martin,* a cardholder gave his credit card to his associate for use in their joint business venture but orally authorized the agent only to charge up to $500 on the card. When the associate ignored the cardholder's directions by charging in excess of this amount, the cardholder attempted to avoid payment by relying on the $50 maximum liability provision of the Truth in Lending Statute for 'unauthorized' use of the card.

"In rejecting the cardholder's argument, the *Martin* court concluded the statutory limit of liability for unauthorized use of a credit card may be warranted where the card is obtained from the cardholder 'as a result of loss, theft, or wrongdoing' but not 'where a cardholder voluntarily and knowingly allows another to use his card and that person subsequently misuses the card.'

"Like the cardholder in *Martin,* Pailet loaned his card to his employee for a limited business purpose. Although there is no evidence that Pailet's employee misused the card, neither is there a concrete explanation in the record to show what happened to the card after Pailet entrusted it to her. Pailet's vague testimony that he thought Jordan said she had lost it sheds little light, if any, in establishing the charges as 'unauthorized.' In the absence of sufficient evidence that the card was obtained from Pailet as a result of loss, theft, or wrongdoing, he is responsible for purchases made through the use of his card prior to April 21, 1982.

"The balance due on Pailet's account for charges through April 29, 1982 was $698.75. We deduct a $50.25 charge dated April 27 since it was made after Pailet's notification to plaintiff on April 21. Plaintiff is therefore entitled to recover $648.50."

■ EQUAL CREDIT OPPORTUNITY ACT

Sex discrimination

Marital status

Originally, the problems dealt with by the Equal Credit Opportunity Act (ECOA) were denials of credit on the basis of sex or marital status. Women who had been divorced or widowed were denied credit in many cases because they had had no separate credit history or because they had been codebtors with their husbands, who had defaulted on the debts. Either way, they were unable to obtain credit in their own names. ECOA now prohibits such discrimination, and also that based on race, color, religion, national origin, or age. These protections are similar to those given to employees under the national civil rights acts, as discussed in Chapter 41.

Creditors are prohibited from discouraging applications for credit, from refusing to grant a separate account to a married woman, and from asking the applicant's marital status where such a separate account is requested. Because marital property laws differ from state to state, however, a creditor may ask about marital status where collateral is required for the credit transaction. Similarly, minors cannot demand credit under ECOA, since they lack full capacity to contract and can disaffirm contracts which they make while minors. The marital status rules are illustrated by the *Markham* case.

MARKHAM v. COLONIAL MORTGAGE SERVICE CO. ASSOCIATES, INC.

605 F.2d 566 (District of Columbia, 1979)

FACTS   Jerry Markham and Marcia Harris, prior to their marriage, signed a contract to purchase a home, and submitted a loan application to Illinois Federal Savings and Loan, through Colonial Mortgage. One of Colonial's subsidiaries conducted a credit check on Markham and Harris. Their real estate agent told them that their loan application had been rejected because they were not married. The trial court granted defendants' motions for summary judgment, and plaintiffs appealed.

ISSUE   Can a lender treat joint applicants differently because they are not married?

DECISION   No. Judgment reversed, and case remanded for further proceedings.

REASONS   Judge Swygert did not think Illinois Federal's refusal could be justified under the act.

"We fail to see the relevance of any special legal ties created by marriage with respect to the legal obligations of joint debtors. This was not an instance where a single person is applying for credit individually and claiming income from a third party for purposes of determining creditworthiness. In such an instance, the absence of a legal obligation requiring continuance of the income claimed by the applicant from the third party would reflect on the credit applicant's creditworthiness. Inasmuch as the Markhams applied for their mortgage jointly, they would have been jointly and severally liable on the debt. Each joint debtor would be bound to pay the full amount of the debt; he would then have a right to contribution from his joint debtor. . . . Thus, inasmuch as the state laws attaching in the event of marriage would not affect the creditworthiness of these joint applications, section 1691d(b) may not be used to justify the refusal to aggregate the plaintiffs' incomes on the basis of marital status.

"We turn to a consideration of whether the Equal Credit Opportunity Act's prohibition of discrimination on the basis of sex or marital status makes illegal Illinois Federal's refusal to aggregate plaintiff's income when determining their creditworthiness. Illinois Federal contends that neither the purpose nor the language of the Act requires it to combine the incomes of unmarried joint applicants when making that determination. . . .

"This language is simple, and its meaning is not difficult to comprehend. Illinois Federal itself has correctly phrased the standard in its brief: The Act forbids discrimination 'on the basis of a person's marital status, that is, to treat persons differently, all other facts being the same, because of their marital status. . . .' Illinois Federal does not contend that they would not have aggregated plaintiffs' income had they been married at the time. Indeed, Illinois Federal concedes that the law would have required it to do so. Thus, it is plain that Illinois Federal treated plaintiffs differently—that is, refused to aggregate their incomes—solely because of their marital status, which is precisely the sort of discrimination prohibited by section 1691(a)(1) on its face. . . ."

■ USE OF CREDIT INFORMATION

It is true that businesses have always kept records about individuals, but record-keeping was limited, due to the obvious problems of storage, access, and retrievability. The computer has minimized those problems, and consequently more and more information is kept about the individual. There is more possibility of error and less access by the individual to the records to determine just what they say. A major concern has been the gathering, storage, and retrieval of information about individuals by various credit bureaus and local merchants' associations, which have computerized their files and have dossiers on nearly every American adult.

Fair Credit Reporting Act. To curb the abuses of credit bureaus, Congress passed the Fair Credit Reporting Act, which became effective on April 25, 1971. The following is a summary of its major provisions.

FCRA requirements

1. Credit reporting agencies are authorized to furnish credit information only in connection with credit, insurance, and employment applications, a goverment license for which a consumer has applied, or any other business transaction in which a consumer is involved; or by written consent of the consumer concerned; or in compliance with a court order.

2. The reporting of adverse information more than seven years old regarding suits, arrests, and other matters is generally prohibited. However, information on bankruptcies can be made available for 14 years, and if the inquiry concerns an application for a life insurance policy of $50,000 or more or an application for a job with an annual salary of $20,000 or more, then there is no age restriction on records and all information may be furnished. Thus the bureaus have an excuse not to clear out the computers periodically.

3. The reporting of adverse information from investigative reports more than three months old is generally prohibited unless the information is reverified.

4. All reporting agencies are required to "follow reasonable procedures to assure maximum accuracy of the information" contained in reports.

5. The type of information which can be furnished to government agencies without a court order is limited.

6. Upon the request of a consumer, a reporting agency must disclose to the consumer all information about him or her in the agency's files, except for medical information or the sources of the information.

7. A person or business ordering an investigative report must notify the consumer that an investigation is being made.

8. An agency must disclose to a consumer on request the names of persons and businesses that have been furnished credit information about the consumer in the preceding six months (two years for employment purposes).

9. An agency must reinvestigate information disputed by a consumer "within a reasonable period of time" unless "it has reasonable grounds to believe that the dispute by the consumer is frivolous or irrelevant." If the information is found to be inaccurate, then the agency must delete the information from the record. The consumer also has the right to have the agency put in the file a statement of not more than 100 words explaining that the information is disputed, and the agency, at the consumer's request, must send copies of the statement to the persons and businesses that had been sent the disputed information.

10. A person or business that rejects a consumer for credit, insurance, or employment on the basis of a credit report must advise the consumer of the reason for the rejection and identify the reporting agency.

11. A consumer is granted the right to file a civil action in U.S. District Court to recover damages resulting from willful and negligent noncompliance with the law.

12. Obtaining information under false pretenses for credit reporting and willfully giving out such information to unauthorized persons is punishable by a fine of up to $5,000 and imprisonment for up to one year.

FCRA penalties

As noted above, this law gives the aggrieved individual the right to file an action charging that a credit bureau, its informant, or a user of its report violated the Fair Credit Reporting Act. The violation doesn't have to be intentional, but it must have caused demonstrable financial damage. In a successful action a consumer can collect actual damages, legal costs, and attorney's fees. For willful violations, a credit bureau may also have to pay punitive damages and may be subject to criminal penalties. The *Millstone* case shows how these rules operate.

Privacy Act. In passing the Privacy Act of 1974, Congress recognized the problems of invasion of privacy caused by governmental computer record-keeping. The act placed many restrictions on computerized record-keeping and the handling of computerized records by the various governmental agencies. This act applies only to the records of national governmental agencies, not to those of state agencies or private businesses. In addition to placing restrictions on governmental record-keeping and the handling of governmental records, the act gave individuals access to such records about themselves and the right to copy, correct, and challenge personal information held by the national government. The act also prohibited the nonroutine dissemination of records without notification to the individuals involved, and it placed restrictions upon the expanded use of social security numbers.

Many states have passed privacy laws similar to the 1974 Privacy Act. These laws have placed restrictions on record-keeping and the handling of computerized information by the various state agencies. The subject of computers and privacy is certainly a key issue in our society today. To date, the major thrust of the various privacy bills has been to regulate only national and state computerized record-keeping, and there are still many unsolved legal problems concerning privacy and the record-keeping practices of private business.

Electronic Funds Transfer Act. On November 10, 1978, Congress recognized the problems associated with EFT and passed the Electronic Funds Transfer Act. Congress stated that the purpose of this law was to provide a basic framework establishing the rights, liabilities, and responsibilities of participants in electronic funds transfer systems. The primary objective of the law was to ensure a basic level of protection for the individual consumer's rights.

The Electronic Funds Transfer Act allows the various states to enact more comprehensive and more protective legislation if they desire to do so. A few states have enacted regulatory legislation in the EFT area, and many others are considering such legislation.

MILLSTONE v. O'HANLON REPORTS, INC.

528 F.2d 829 (U.S. Eighth Circuit, 1976)

FACTS   James Millstone applied to Firemen's Fund Insurance for insurance on his Volkswagen bus. Firemen's issued the policy, but also ordered a credit report from O'Hanlon. About a month later, O'Hanlon furnished a report, based on information from Washington, D.C., where Millstone had previously lived. The report stated that he "was a hippie-type person, with shoulder-length hair and with a beard on one occasion, who participated in many demonstrations in the Capitol, carried demonstrators back and forth to his home, where he housed them in his basement and wherever else there was room." It also said that "he was strongly suspected of being a drug user, that he was rumored by neighbors to have been evicted from three previous residences in Washington, D.C., and that he was very much disliked by his neighbors there." Based on this information, Firemen's ordered its agent to cancel the insurance policy on the VW. When the agent explained that Millstone was a highly respected assistant managing editor of the St. Louis Post-Dispatch, and that he had been a White House reporter in Washington, Firemen's withdrew its cancellation order. When O'Hanlon refused to give satisfactory answers to him about the credit report, Millstone sued. The trial court awarded $2,500 actual damages and $25,000 punitive damages, plus $12,500 attorney's fees.

ISSUE   Did O'Hanlon violate FCRA?

DECISION   Yes. Judgment affirmed.

REASONS Justice Clark found that O'Hanlon had "willfully violated both the spirit and the letter" of FCRA, "by trampling recklessly upon Millstone's rights thereunder." He rejected the defendant's claim to First Amendment protection, since commercial speech of the type involved here is subject to reasonable regulation.

"The next contention is that O'Hanlon did not violate the accuracy or disclosure provisions of the Act, §§ 1681c(b) and g, and that even if it did, Millstone was not damaged. Given the detailed account of the facts found in the record, we believe this contention merits a short answer.

"To us it seems amazing that O'Hanlon makes the claim that its agent followed reasonable procedures promulgated by it to attain the maximum possible accuracy. Everything in the record is to the contrary. It shows that O'Hanlon's agent devoted at most 30 minutes in preparing his report. His report was rife with innuendo, misstatement, and slander. Indeed, the recheck of his investigation shows that he depended solely on one biased informant; made no verification of the same despite O'Hanlon's requirement that there must be verification; and, finally, it took three days to recheck the original investigation, and every allegation therein was found untrue.

"O'Hanlon further asserts that its disclosures to Millstone completely revealed the nature and substance of the derogatory matters in its report. Again, the report proves otherwise. O'Hanlon sought at every step to block Millstone in his attempt to secure the rights given to him by the Act. Not only did O'Hanlon delay and mislead Millstone on the occasion of his first request, but it even did so on a second and third occasion. Not until Millstone brought pressure to bear, through the Federal Trade Commission, and, ultimately, through this lawsuit, did O'Hanlon make the disclosure required by § 1681g."

FAIR CREDIT BILLING ACT

Another area where abuses were thought to occur was disputes over charges to a credit account. Formerly, the creditor would bill charges it thought were valid, and then press the customer for payment. If the customer could not convince the creditor that disputed charges were incorrect, the creditor could report the delinquency to credit bureaus or take steps to collect the account through court process. Now, the FCBA has set up certain procedures that must be followed if there is a dispute.

FCBA procedures

The consumer-debtor has 60 days after receiving a billing to notify the creditor of any claimed errors. The creditor then has 30 days to notify the debtor of receipt of the claim. The creditor must correct the account, or investigate and explain its reasons for not correcting the account, within 90 days or two billing cycles. Claimed delinquencies cannot be reported to credit bureaus unless FCBA has been complied with. The debtor must be notified of the persons to whom the delinquency has been reported. A creditor who fails to comply with FCBA forfeits its right to collect the first $50 of the disputed amount, including finance charges.

HDC rule

FTC Regulation 433. Another very important consumer protection law has already been noted in Chapters 15 and 25, and will be further discussed in Chapter 28. The Federal Trade Commission adopted a rule in 1976 which abolished the "holder in due course" concept for most consumer transactions. Basically, this is the concept which says that an assignee of an account receivable which is in negotiable form, or which contains an express waiver of defenses clause, owns the account free and clear of most common defenses that the debtor might assert to try to avoid payment. The FTC has said, in effect, that a consumer-debtor can always assert any defense which can be proved.

■ FAIR DEBT COLLECTION PRACTICES ACT

Finally, Congress took action in 1977 to curb some of the worst abuses in the credit field—collection agencies' scare tactics and harassment. Most states had already acted to stop these abuses, and FDCPA allows these state regulations to continue if they contain adequate enforcement provisions. The national act covers only agencies that are collecting debts for others, not banks and businesses that are trying to collect their own accounts.

FDCPA restrictions

The FDCPA contains a number of restrictions on collection practices. The collector may not contact the consumer at work, if the employer objects, or at unusual or inconvenient times, or at all if the consumer has an attorney. The collector may not use harassing or intimidating tactics, or abusive language against any person, or false or misleading tactics. Unless so authorized by a court, the collector may not contact third parties other than a spouse, parent, or financial adviser about the account. The collector may not contact the consumer-debtor about the account after receiving a written refusal to pay, except to notify the consumer of possible actions which may be taken. A debt collector may not deposit a postdated check prior to its effective date. These are significant limitations on prior practices.

Garnishment Limitations. *Garnishment* is a court process for seizing money or property belonging to the debtor, but in the possession of third parties. Bank accounts and wages owed are typical subjects of garnishment.

Due process problems

Under its authority to interpret the constitutional phrase "due process of law," the U.S. Supreme Court has held that prejudgment garnishment of wages is unconstitutional (*Sniadach* v. *Family Finance Corp.,* 395 U.S. 337). It has also said, however, that some prejudgment remedies may be permissible (*Mitchell* v. *W.T. Grant,* 416 U.S. 600). Prejudgment garnishment of a bank account was specifically invalidated in *North Georgia Finishing, Inc.* v. *Di-Chem, Inc.,* 419 U.S. 601 (1975).

Amount limits

The CCPA also limits garnishments of wages. No more than 25 percent of an individual's aftertax earnings, or the amount by which the wages exceed 30 times the minimum wage, whichever is less, can be garnished. These limits do not apply if the claim is for taxes, wife or child support, or subject to an order in a bankruptcy Chapter 13, adjustment of debts.

■ SIGNIFICANCE OF THIS CHAPTER

Nearly everyone is a debtor, creditor, or both, at some time during their lives. Congress and the state legislatures have moved aggressively to regulate this aspect of commercial transactions. Important new protections have been developed for the consumer-debtor. This area of the law seems sure to expand further. Every businessperson needs to know the current debtor-creditor rules of the game.

DISCUSSION CASE

CARROLL v. EXXON CO., U.S.A.

434 F.Supp. 557 (Louisiana, 1977)

FACTS: In August of 1976, Kathleen Carroll, a single working woman, applied for an Exxon credit card. In response to her application, the plaintiff received correspondence from defendant, dated September 14, 1976, whereby she was informed that her application for credit was denied; but no specific reason for the denial was provided. Thereafter, by her letter of September 28, 1976, Ms. Carroll requested Exxon to furnish her with the specific reasons for the credit denial. An undated response to this request revealed that the credit bureau which was contacted in regard to plaintiff's application did not respond adversely, but was unable to furnish sufficient information regarding her established credit. However, this undated letter, like that of September 14, 1976, did not contain the name of the credit bureau used by Exxon to investigate certain aspects of plaintiff's credit application.

This lawsuit was filed on October 26, 1976. Subsequently, on November 2, 1976, Exxon sent another letter to the plaintiff. This correspondence did contain the name and address of the credit bureau which had been contacted with regard to plaintiff's application.

■

Judge Mitchell gave the opinion for the court:

As her first cause of action, the plaintiff alleges that Exxon violated the terms of the Fair Credit Reporting Act (FCRA) by failing to properly identify the consumer reporting agency which handled her credit application. . . .

Exxon's defense to this part of the complaint is threefold. The major thrust of Exxon's argument is based upon the premise that it did not deny credit to the plaintiff because of information contained in the report from the consumer reporting agency, Credit Bureau Services. Reliance upon such a defense is tenuous, at best. A mere cursory reading of Exxon's undated letter to the plaintiff reveals that the credit denial was, in fact, based on the report. . . .

Exxon next argues that it did actually furnish the plaintiff with the information required by the FCRA in its letter of November 2, 1976, which identified the credit bureau used in plaintiff's case. Like the first, this defense can be dismissed in short order. Assuming . . . (as defendant argues) that the FCRA does not impose a minimum time standard upon the user of a credit report for the

identification of the reporting agency to the consumer, it is obvious that full compliance with the Act is impossible after two violations have already been committed. Neither Exxon's letter of September 14, 1976, nor its subsequent undated letter to the plaintiff properly identified the consumer reporting agency used by Exxon in investigating Ms. Carroll's application. Exxon's *third* letter to the plaintiff, which supplied the name and address of the credit bureau, and which was written after notification of the instant lawsuit, does not constitute compliance with the FCRA, . . . when viewed in the context of the events and circumstances of this action.

Defendant's third defense to this part of the action is also unacceptable to this Court. Exxon seeks to avail itself of the "reasonable procedures" defense set out in the FCRA, 15 U.S.C. § 1681m(c):

> No person shall be held liable for any violation of this section if he shows by a preponderance of the evidence that at the time of the alleged violation he maintained reasonable procedures to assure compliance with the provisions of subsections (a) and (b) of this section.

Exxon has supplied various affidavits in the hope of showing that it has established and maintained reasonable procedures to assure compliance with the FCRA. However, as counsel for the plaintiff points out, at least one of defendant's supporting affidavits actually supports plaintiff's position. According to that affidavit:

> Exxon Company, U.S.A. has established and maintained since prior to August 19, 1976, a procedure whereby it furnishes specific reasons for denial of credit to a credit applicant *upon receipt of a request for such information.* (Emphasis added.). . .

Having found that Exxon has violated the FCRA, our next task is to determine whether or not its violation was "willful" within the meaning of 15 U.S.C. § 1681n. There is no doubt that Exxon's letter of September 14, 1976, which informed the plaintiff that her credit application had been denied, neither supplied the identity of the consumer reporting agency whose report formed part of the basis for the denial, nor even attempted to do so. In fact, as we have already mentioned, Exxon would not furnish its reasons for a denial of credit to an applicant unless it was first specifically requested to provide such information. We find that Exxon's failure to properly identify the consumer reporting agency in its letter of September 14, 1976, under the facts and circumstances of this case, constitutes willful noncompliance with the requirements of the FCRA, within the meaning of 15 U.S.C. § 1681n.

Therefore, IT IS ORDERED, ADJUDGED, AND DECREED that the motion of plaintiff, Kathleen Carroll, for summary judgment on the issue of liability under FCRA, be and the same is hereby GRANTED; . . .

IT IS FURTHER ORDERED, ADJUDGED, AND DECREED that this matter be referred to a Magistrate for a determination of the amount of damages, both actual and punitive, and attorney's fees, pursuant to 15 U.S.C. § 1681n.

The plaintiff also contends that Exxon violated the terms of the Equal Credit Opportunity Act (ECOA) by failing to provide her with the specific reasons for the credit denial, and by discriminating against her on the basis of marital status in evaluating her credit application. . . .

Even if we view Exxon's undated response to the plaintiff to have been properly amended and corrected by the letter of November 2, 1976, it is clear that Exxon has failed to meet the requirements of 15 U.S.C. § 1691(d)(3) and 12 CFR 202.5(m)(2). Exxon's responses to plaintiff's request for specific reasons for the credit denial fail to achieve the informative purposes legislated in the ECOA. We do not feel that this decision will place any heavier burden on creditors than that intended by Congress to aid the consumer in the search for reliable and informative credit information.

■ IMPORTANT TERMS AND CONCEPTS

consumerism
Federal Trade Commission
deceptive advertising
in-home sales
unconscionability
Truth in Lending Act
consumer leasing
finance charge
willful violation
unsolicited credit cards
Equal Credit Oppportunity Act
Privacy Act
Fair Credit Billing Act
holder in due course
Fair Debt Collection Practices Act
Henningsen case

unfair trade practices
unordered goods
usury laws
full disclosure in credit transactions
Consumer Credit Protection Act
credit billing
F.R.B. Regulation Z
correction of errors
credit card liability
Fair Credit Reporting Act
Electronic Funds Transfer Act
FTC Regulation 433
waiver of defense clause
garnishment limitations

■ QUESTIONS AND PROBLEMS FOR DISCUSSION

1. When can credit reporting agencies legally furnish credit information about persons in their files?
2. What are the consumer's rights where he or she disagrees with information in a credit reporting agency's file?
3. What penalties are provided for violation of the Fair Credit Reporting Act?
4. What are the legal restrictions against discrimination in the granting of credit?
5. Hermoine purchased a new stereo which had been advertised in the fall catalog sent out by Monty Warp's, Inc. to all its credit card customers. The ad stated; "No Monthly Payments Till February. No Increase in Monthly Payments Till Next Year." The ad did not disclose that a finance charge would be added to the account on any purchases made, for each month until the account balance was paid. When Hermoine discovered that she was being billed each month for an additional finance charge on her new stereo, she brought an action under TILA. Has Monty Warp's violated the Act? Explain.
6. Corner Company applied to Useless Express Company for several U.E. credit cards, which would be used by Corner's officers on business trips. After the cards had been used for some time, a dispute arose over certain billings for flight insurance that one of the officers, Brad Corner, had charged with his company card. Useless Express cancelled all cards issued to Corner Company, and when Brad tried to use "his" card, it was rejected. Brad sues Useless Express for cancelling the card without complying with the Fair Credit Billing Act. Should he recover damages under FCBA? Discuss.
7. Norbert Sawdown sold "lifetime memberships" in his health club for $360, payable in 24 equal monthly installments of $15 each. While he sold a few memberships for cash, at a discount of 10 to 15 percent of the installment price, over 90 percent of his customers paid over 24 months' time. Each time the customer signed a promissory note, which was then sold to a financing company. The finance company paid Norbert $275 for each note. The notes did not disclose any credit or finance charge. Margie James brought a class action suit against Norbert and the finance company, alleging violation of TILA. Does she have a case? Explain.

8. Olga and Miguel bought a new car from Bravura Motors on credit. The contract they signed did indicate that Bravura would retain a security interest in the new car until it was paid for. The contract also required the buyers to keep the car insured. On the back of the contract was a provision which stated that the buyers automatically assigned to the seller any unearned insurance premiums, which an insurance company might be required to refund. The seller would then be permitted to appy these refunded amounts to any balance remaining on the price of the car. This assignment provision was not mentioned on the front of the contract, where the buyers signed. Olga and Miguel sue Bravura, alleging violation of TILA. Has Bravura violated the Act? Discuss.

PART FIVE

Commercial Paper

Part Five deals with credit, but with a different aspect of the credit transaction than Part Four. Whereas the main focus of Part Four was on setting up the credit arrangement in a way that assures payment, this part deals with the problems involved in using nonmoney pieces of paper as a method of payment. Article Three of the UCC calls these pieces of paper *commercial paper;* the earlier term was *negotiable instruments*.

Nearly everyone is familiar with the use of personal checks as a payment instrument. The check is one form of commercial paper. This part covers the various types of liability on such instruments, the rules for enforcement of those liabilities, and the circumstances that will discharge such liabilities. Chapter 31 also covers the relationship between the customer and a bank where such instruments are deposited, or against which they have been issued.

Many students have signed promissory notes in loan transactions—for school expenses, car purchases, and the like. The promissory note is another form of commercial paper. Because it is a promise to pay, rather than an order to a bank to pay, some of the rules for a note are different than those for a check. These differences are also covered in this part.

The rules for dealing with these pieces of paper used as substitutes for money are complex, but very important to business operations. Millions of checks circulate through the banking system every day. Promissory notes are a key part of short-term financing arrangements, both for individuals and for businesses. A basic understanding of commercial paper rules is important to help you avoid or minimize liability, and to protect your rights in transactions where these pieces of paper are used.

27

Types of Instruments; Requirements of Negotiability

CHAPTER OBJECTIVES

THIS CHAPTER WILL:

- Indicate the need for negotiability in commercial credit transactions.
- Explain the concept of negotiability and the special results it produces.
- Outline the requirements an instrument must meet in order to be negotiable.
- Discuss each of these requirements.

Negotiable instruments were developed by Western European merchants several centuries ago to meet the needs of trade and commerce. Highwaymen and bandits made carrying large sums of money a risky operation. Goods and services conceivably could have been purchased on the buyer's credit, but that arrangement also entailed substantial risks of nonpayment in the days before Dun & Bradstreet and credit bureaus. What the merchant wanted was something, as acceptable as money in most commercial transactions, that could be carried from place to place more safely than currency.

Through custom and usage, merchants and their special commercial courts came to agree that instruments written in the proper form would have the characteristics they desired. These traits were:

Characteristics of negotiable instruments

1. Such instruments would be freely transferable from person to person (under the old English common law, at least, a transferee of contract rights could not sue the debtor directly).

2. They would be presumed to have been issued for value, and the debtor would have the burden of proving otherwise.

3. The debtor would not be able to assert certain defenses (generally, "void-able" defenses) when a good faith purchaser ("holder in due course") sued to enforce an instrument and collect the money.

Negotiable instruments law, as part of the law merchant, was assimilated into English common law during the 17th and 18th centuries. An English statute codifying these practices was passed in 1882, and in 1896 the Uniform Negotiable Instruments Law (NIL) was proposed and later adopted by nearly all states in the United States. The UCC's Article 3, Commercial Paper, now supersedes the NIL. Article 4, Bank Deposits and Collections, brings together the rules regarding bank processing of such instruments. More recently, several states and the FTC have adopted new rules eliminating the "no defenses" result where the instrument was executed by a consumer-debtor.

■ MAJOR LEGAL ISSUES

Negotiable instruments law is technical and complex and tends to confuse many beginners. Since it's so easy to get lost in the details of the cases and the UCC provisions, the student needs an overall picture of what's happening in these situations. One or more persons allegedly have signed a piece of paper that contains some sort of promise to pay money, and the plaintiff is trying to collect the money. The primary significance of that piece of paper's being *negotiable* is that a person to whom it was transferred as a good faith purchaser can force a party who is liable on it to pay the money even though that party has a defense against liability. If the instrument is negotiable, and it gets into the hands of the special sort of bona fide purchaser called a ***holder in due course (HDC),*** a business debtor who had signed it would have to pay it as promised. This is true even when the merchandise or services exchanged for the instrument were never delivered or were misrepresented. In other words, a negotiable instrument in the hands of an HDC can be enforced as written, despite the existence of certain defenses. The instrument's negotiability prevents the defendant from using some defenses, such as fraud or nonperformance, to avoid paying the HDC.

Basic purpose: Protection of HDC

In analyzing a negotiable instruments problem, then, we need to determine whether or not this special "negotiability" result should occur. Should the person who signed the instrument have to pay it, even if the goods or services for which it was issued were not delivered or were misrepresented? First, to get these special negotiability results, the instrument must be in negotiable form. It must comply with the requirements for negotiability, as discussed later in this chapter. If the instrument is not negotiable, any defense against liability on it can be asserted as a reason for not paying it.

Second, in order for the plaintiff to enforce the instrument and collect the money, the terms of the instrument must make the plaintiff the holder of the instrument. It must have been issued to the plaintiff or properly transferred ("negotiated") to the plaintiff. The requirements for becoming a "holder" of these instruments are discussed in Chapter 28. If the plaintiff is not a holder, the plaintiff should not collect on the instrument.

Third, if some of the persons who may be liable on the instrument have defenses against liability (reasons for not paying it), the plaintiff must also qualify as a "holder in due course" in order to overcome certain defenses and collect the money anyway. What it takes to become a holder in due course (HDC) is also discussed in Chapter 28. If the plaintiff is not an HDC of the negotiable instrument, any defense that can be proved can be used to defeat or reduce the plaintiff's recovery on the instrument. If there are no reasons for not paying the instrument, plaintiff collects merely by being a holder. The significance of HDC status relates to cases where there are reasons for not paying the instrument or disputes over its ownership.

Fourth, to collect against a particular person, plaintiff must prove that that person is liable on the instrument in some way. In most cases, liability is based either on a defendant's having signed the instrument, thereby making a contractual promise to pay it, or having transferred it for value, thereby assuming certain implied warranties as to its validity. In some cases, a tort theory based on negligence or conversion may also be used to collect the amount of the instrument from a particular defendant. It's not enough, in other words, for plaintiff to prove that he or she is the proper party to be paid. To collect against a particular person, the plaintiff must prove that that person is liable, under some theory, for payment of the instrument. These theories of liability are discussed in Chapter 29.

Finally, since some defenses against liability can be asserted against HDCs and some can not, we need to know which are which. These two types of defenses are discussed in Chapter 30, along with the events that discharge a party's liability on a negotiable instrument.

Text discussion in these chapters will follow the applicable sections of Article 3 of the UCC, which covers all these points in some detail. The cases in this area will focus on interpretation of the Code sections in particular fact situations.

▪ TYPES OF COMMERCIAL PAPER

Promise to pay or order to pay

When someone issues a negotiable instrument in exchange for cash, goods, or services, the instrument is written in either of two basic ways. It may be a *promise* by the issuer to pay the indicated amount, or it may be an *order* to someone else (a bank, or some other party who owes the issuer money) to pay the stated amount. The UCC says that a promise is "an undertaking to

■ EXHIBIT 27–1
Types of Commercial Paper

Note (Promissory note)

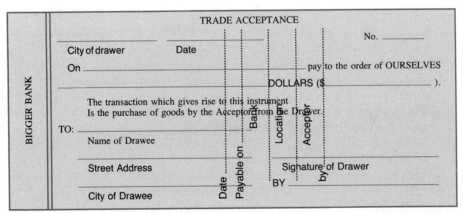

$ _____   _____ , 19 _____
                         City   State

On Demand, for value received, I/We promise to pay to the order

of _____

the sum of _____ Dollars.

at _____ ,
        Address

together with interest at the rate of _____ per year. If
lawsuit be commenced to enforce payment of this note, I promise to pay such added sum as the court
may determine as reasonable attorney's fees in connection with said lawsuit.

_____

_____

Draft (Bill of exchange)

TRADE ACCEPTANCE

No. _____

City of drawer   Date

On _____ pay to the order of OURSELVES

_____ DOLLARS ($ _____).

The transaction which gives rise to this instrument
Is the purchase of goods by the Acceptor from the Drawer.

TO: _____
    Name of Drawee

_____
    Street Address

_____
    City of Drawee

Signature of Drawer

BY _____

BIGGER BANK

Date Payable on

Location of Acceptance

Bank by Acceptor

pay and must be more than an acknowledgment of an obligation." An "IOU" is therefore not a negotiable instrument, even though it is in writing and signed, because it is merely an "acknowledgment" of the debt. An order is defined as a "direction to pay and must be more than an authorization or request." If you have a checking account, look at your checks—they don't say "Please pay," just "Pay." Some smart lawyer might otherwise try to argue that the use of courteous language made the "order" only a "request," and that the check was thus not negotiable.

The Code identifies four specific types of commercial paper—two promissory types and two order types. A **note** is a promise by a **maker** to pay money to a payee. A **certificate of deposit** is "an acknowledgment by a bank of receipt of money with an engagement to repay it." A **draft** (or bill of exchange) is an order from a *drawer* directed to a *drawee* and ordering the drawee to pay the stated amount of money to a named payee. A *check* is an order directed to a bank as drawee and indicating that the money is to be paid "on demand," that is, any time the payee requests it. The UCC says that these same four terms may be used to refer to nonnegotiable instruments as well, depending on the context of the particular UCC section involved.

In addition to these four basic types, several special kinds of negotiable instruments are widely used. *Installment notes* are frequently used for credit purchases of appliances, cars, and other large consumer items. Rather than being payable all at once, an installment note specifies monthly required payments. *Mortgage notes* are typically used in connection with the purchase of real estate. Again, monthly payments on the real estate mortgage are usually required. Businesses buying goods on credit also use the *trade acceptance,* which is a form of draft. Rather than ordering a bank to pay, the trade acceptance orders the buyer of the goods to pay the contract price of the goods, plus interest for the agreed credit period. The seller issues the trade acceptance as the drawer; the buyer is the drawee, who is ordered to pay the amount stated to the seller, as payee. When the buyer signs this order as well, meaning that the buyer promises to pay it according to its terms, the seller can then sell the trade acceptance to a bank (usually a bank where the buyer of the goods has established credit). The buyer of the goods gets the time to pay for the goods, the seller of the goods gets cash, and the buyer of the trade acceptance gets the interest on it, plus any discount. Trade acceptances are very useful where the seller of the goods cannot afford to carry the buyer as an account receivable for the length of time the buyer requires. A *certified check* operates in much the same way as a trade acceptance. The order to pay the money is directed to the drawee bank. When the drawee bank agrees that it will pay the check, it "certifies" the check by writing its name on the face of the check. At that point, the bank has directly promised to pay the check. A *cashier's check* is a check written by a bank ordering itself to pay the stated amount. Again, the bank is directly liable for payment of the cashier's check.

Article 3 of the Code specifically excludes "investment securities" (stocks and bonds) from its coverage, along with money and "documents of title." Article 8 covers investment securities, and documents of title are covered in Article 7. Both securities and documents may be issued in "negotiable" form, but they are not used as money substitutes in the same way as "negotiable instruments."

■ REQUIRE-MENTS OF NEGOTIABILITY

Negotiability is strictly a matter of form. If an instrument is written to comply with the requirements of UCC 3-104(1), it is negotiable; if not, it is not negotiable, though it may be enforceable as an ordinary written contract. *Negotiability,* in other words, does not depend on the parties' intent, or their agreement, or their understanding, but on their compliance with the Code's requirements. The drafters of the Code have expressed this policy very clearly in several of their official comments:

> The negotiability of an instrument is always to be determined by what appears on the face of the instrument alone (3–119, Comment 5). Either the language of the

section or a clear equivalent must be found, and . . . in doubtful cases the decision should be against negotiability (3–104, Comment 5).

The courts are thus directed not to produce the very special negotiability results unless the debtor has signed a writing which clearly conforms to Article 3's requirements.

What are these requirements? As listed in Section 3–104(1), the writing must:

Code's requirements for negotiability

a. Be signed by the maker or drawer.

b. Contain an unconditional promise or order to pay a certain sum in money and no other promise, order, obligation, or power given by the maker or drawer except as authorized by this Article.

c. Be payable on demand or at a definite time.

d. Be payable to order or to bearer.

■ **EXHIBIT 27–2**
Requirements of
Negotiability—Signatures
by Agents

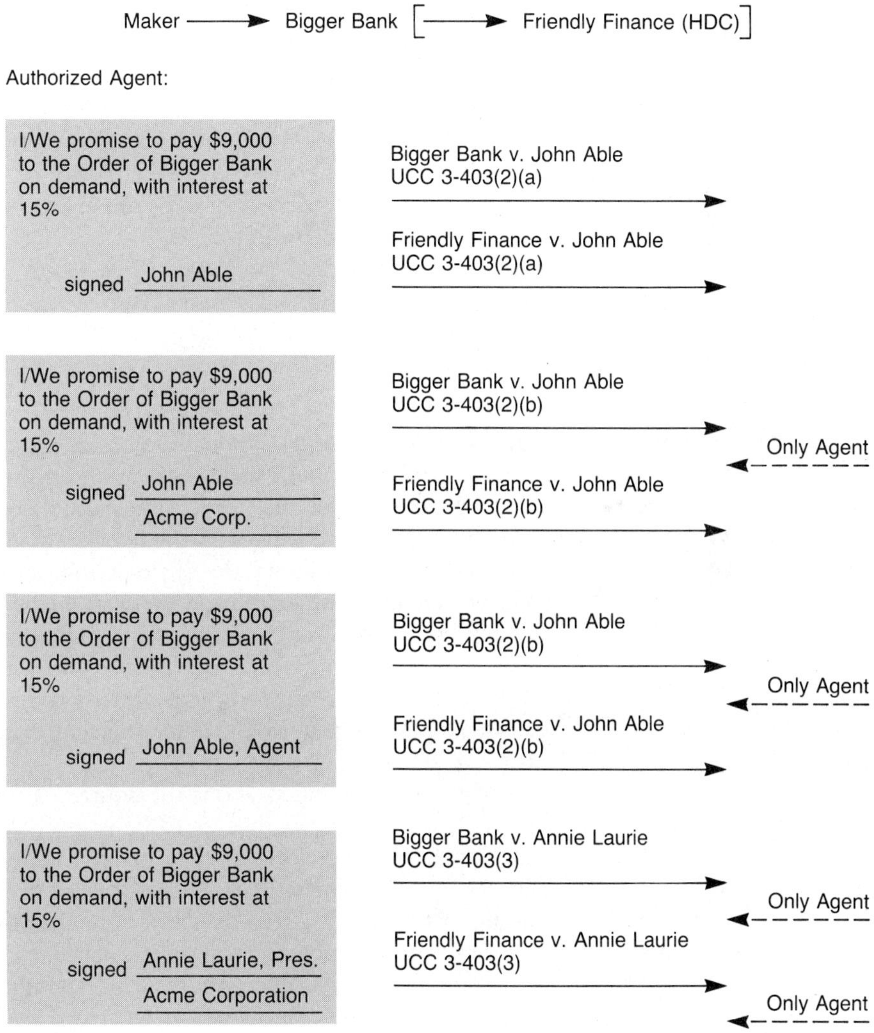

Each of these requirements is further defined and explained in other Code sections. Often, the defendant-debtor will argue against liability, claiming that the signed instrument is not negotiable. If true, the plaintiff-creditor would be subject to any provable defense.

■ SIGNED BY MAKER OR DRAWER

Signed, in the general definitions section of Article 1, includes "any symbol executed or adopted by a party with present intention to authenticate a writing." Thus, a signature need not be written out fully in script; it can be printed, typed, stamped, initialed, or reproduced mechanically by a checkwriter. Because of the special characteristics of negotiable instruments, Section 3–401(1) states a very important rule for them: "No person is liable on an instrument unless his signature appears thereon." A person may be liable on some other basis to the plaintiff, but cannot be liable *on an instrument* unless that person's signature is on the instrument, though it does not necessarily have to appear at the bottom. It may be made by trade name, assumed name, mark (X), or even thumbprint. It may be made by a properly authorized agent, though the agent may be held personally liable to subsequent holders of the instrument if the agent does not clearly indicate that the signing is being done only on behalf of the principal. Where someone who is not authorized to sign another's name does so, the signature operates as that of "the unauthorized signer in favor of any person who in good faith pays the instrument or takes it for value" (3–404). (See Exhibit 27–2.)

No signature = No liability on instrument

The application of these rules to Ms. Cook, a corporate treasurer, is the subject of this chapter's Discussion Case.

■ UNCONDITION-AL PROMISE OR ORDER

Section 3–105 lists a number of rules for determining when a promise or an order is or is not "unconditional"; most of these rules are designed to meet particular problems which have come up in prior cases. Instruments frequently refer to the transaction out of which they arose, or to the consideration received or to be received for them, or to the fact that payment is secured by mortgage or otherwise. Within limits, the Code permits such references; the promise or order is still "unconditional," and the instrument is still negotiable. But when a promise or order states "That it is subject to or governed by any other agreement," it is conditional and thus not negotiable. (The instrument may still be enforced like any ordinary written contract, however; *not negotiable* just means that the plaintiff's claim is subject to any defense that the defendant can prove.)

Conditional promise = Not negotiable

Similar rules are stated about the source of funds to pay the instrument. Generally, an instrument that "is to be paid only out of a particular fund" is conditional (and therefore not negotiable), because that one source may or may not be sufficient to pay the obligation. The instrument can, however, indicate that it is to be charged against or reimbursed from a particular account, for bookkeeping purposes, so long as it is issued in general terms. As an exception to the *particular fund* doctrine, the Code permits negotiable instruments to be issued against the "entire assets" of a partnership, unincorporated association, trust, or estate. As a further exception, governmental agencies can issue negotiable instruments with payment limited to a particular fund or source.

▪ SUM CERTAIN

The Code also provides some detailed rules for determining when the amount to be paid is a *sum certain.* Most typical provisions regarding interest, installment payments, and discounts or penalties for early payment require only a little mathematics to determine the "sum" due and are thus permissible. The interest rates and other percentages must be specified, however, so that the calculations can be made from the information appearing on the face of the instrument. Many instruments, particularly promissory notes, will include a provision requiring the payment of collection costs and attorney fees if the debtor defaults and litigation is necessary; the Code validates such provisions. Aside from the fact that "attorneys" drafted the Code, the rationale for this provision is that the basic sum due at maturity is "certain" and that these additional costs arise only because of the debtor's default.

▪ IN MONEY

Money is defined in the general definitions section of the Code as "a medium of exchange authorized or adopted by a domestic or foreign government as a part of its currency." The official comment to this section says that the "official governmental currency" test is broader than just saying "legal tender"; thus an instrument is payable in "money" even though it is payable in the United States in foreign currency. Unless it specifies otherwise, such an instrument may be paid in dollars equivalent to the stated amount of foreign currency on the due date.

The bank in the *Aztec* case tried to anticipate inflation's effect on a fixed sum of dollars by providing for payment of an "indexed" amount. Notice that no third party transferee is involved, so the negotiability of the note is not at issue. The only question is whether the indexing is legal.

**AZTEC PROPERTIES, INC. v.
UNION PLANTERS NATIONAL BANK
OF MEMPHIS**

530 S.W.2d 756 (Tennessee, 1975)

FACTS

On July 12, 1974, Aztec Properties, Inc. executed a promissory note payable to Union Planters National Bank of Memphis in exchange for a $50,000 loan. The promisor agreed to pay the promisee $50,000, "in constant United States Dollars adjusted for inflation (deflation)" with interest at 10 percent per annum. The adjusted principal was to be calculated according to a formula contained in the note, to wit:

> Amount of principal due shall equal the amount of original principal multiplied by the consumer price index adjustment factor. This adjustment factor shall be computed by dividing the consumer price index at maturity by the consumer price index on date of borrowing. Said consumer price index numbers shall be for the most recent month available preceding borrowing and maturity dates. This consumer price index shall be the index not seasonably adjusted for all items as reported by the United States Department of Labor.

On maturity of the note Aztec Properties repaid to the bank $50,000, with discounted interest at the rate 9.875 percent, in the amount of $419.35 (which is an effective yield of 9.96 percent per annum), but the borrower refused to pay the additional "indexed principal" of $500 based on the inflation adjustment formula.

Whereupon, the bank sued Aztec Properties in chancery court for the "indexed principal" together with interest from maturity at the rate of 10 percent per annum. Both parties filed motions for summary judgment, the chancellor holding in favor of the bank. Aztec Properties appeals.

ISSUE   Is the money added by the indexing formula really extra interest?

DECISION   Yes. Judgment reversed.

REASONS   Justice Brock reviewed both commercial custom and national policy:

"The first issue to be resolved is whether this note is usurious, whether it charges interest in excess of the legal rate of 10 percent per annum. . . . A defendant sued for money may avoid the excess over legal interest, by a plea setting forth the amount of the usury. . . . Interest includes *all* compensation for the use of money. 'Any payment to the lender in addition to the rate of interest legally permissible, whether called by the name of bonus or commission or *by any other name,* is usurious.' (Emphasis added.) *Restatement, Contracts,* Section 526. Compensation is determined not by what the borrower pays but by what the lender receives: thus, if the borrower is the beneficiary of a payment it will not be interest. . . . Nor are expenses incident to making a loan and furnishing the lender with satisfactory security for its repayment compensation or interest. . . .

"We have found no case holding that an intentional increase in the face value of the principal to account for inflation does not constitute interest. In practice the lender has long borne the risk of inflation in this state. The interest charged by a lender is not profit, strictly speaking, but compensation for the use of money and for bearing the risk that the borrower might not repay or the principal might depreciate in value. We accordingly hold that the 'indexed principal' constitutes usurious interest. . . .

"We are not concerned in this case with the exchange of currencies upon an international market, nor does the case involve the sale of any commodity. In this case a domestic customer borrowed funds from a national bank in a principal amount expressed in and repayable in United States dollars. It would be contrary to the national policy, as expressed by the Congress and as interpreted in several cases by the United States Supreme Court, to permit a lender to require of a borrower a different quantity or number of dollars from that loaned, insofar as the principal amount is concerned. . . .

"Accordingly, even if the reserved interest in the present case were only 5 percent or some other rate clearly free from any question of usury, we are of the opinion that a national or state banking institution would not be authorized to 'index' the principal amount of money loaned to a domestic customer on a primissory note, so as to vary the number of dollars which may be required to be paid in satisfaction of the debt.

"It is recognized, of course, that 'indexing' is a current and very legitimate concept in modern business transactions. Nothing in this opinion should be taken to suggest that there is an impropriety in measuring future rentals by a consumer price index, or some comparable standard, in leasing agreements. Nor is there anything improper in computing future wages or salaries by such an index in collective bargaining or employment contracts. As long as there is a national currency, however, which by law is legal tender for the payment of public and private debts, we hold that the indexing device cannot properly be applied to the principal of a debt evidenced by a promissory note payable in that currency."

■ NO OTHER PROMISE OR ORDER EXCEPT AS ARTICLE 3 AUTHORIZES

Most extra promises = Not negotiable

Negotiable instruments used to be described as "couriers without luggage." The obligations they imposed were to be stated clearly and simply; thus any language providing for performances in addition to the payment of money was to be regarded with suspicion. The UCC continues that same basic policy, but does state some rules more specifically. Comment 3 to Section 3–104 refers to Section 3–112 for a list of provisions permitted to be included in (or omitted from) an instrument without destroying its negotiability. Provisions relating to collateral given to secure payment of the instrument may be included. A draft may contain a statement that "the payee by indorsing or cashing it acknowledges full satisfaction of an obligation of the drawer."

Section 3–112 permits the inclusion of terms that waive the benefit of any law intended to protect debtors and by which the debtor authorizes the creditor to go into court on the debtor's behalf and "confess judgment" (admit that the debtor owes the money). Many states would probably not permit their consumer protection laws to be overridden in this way, and only a few states recognize the confession of judgment procedure; section 3–112 merely permits such provisions where they are otherwise lawful. An instrument need not state the consideration received for it, nor need it include any indication of where it was drawn or where it is to be paid.

These rules on "other promises" are discussed in the *Ingel* case.

UNIVERSAL C.I.T. CREDIT CORP. v. INGEL

196 N.E.2d 847 (Massachusetts, 1964)

FACTS   Albert and Dora Ingel had an aluminum siding job done on their home by Allied Aluminum Associates, Inc. In payment, they executed a promissory note for $1,890. The note, together with a certificate indicating that the job had been completed, was transferred for value to the plaintiff. After making several monthly payments, the Ingels alleged that the job had not been done properly and that Allied was guilty of breach of warranties, breach of contract, and/or fraud. C.I.T. sued for the balance due, claiming that it was a holder in due course, and recovered $1,630.12 in the trial court. The Ingels appealed, alleging that the note was nonnegotiable and that the holder (C.I.T.) was subject to any defense that the Ingels could prove.

ISSUE   Did the "other promises" in the completion certificate make the note nonnegotiable?

DECISION   No. Judgment affirmed.

REASONS   Justice Spiegel reviewed the negotiability rules:
"It appears that the note was a form note drafted by the plaintiff. The meaning of Fahey's general testimony that the note and the completion certificate were 'together' when given by the plaintiff to Allied is unclear. However, we see nothing in this testimony to justify the inference urged upon us by the defendants that in this case the note and completion certificate were 'part of the same instrument' and that an additional obligation in the completion certificate rendered the note nonnegotiable. . . . Similarly, we are not concerned with any variance between the written contract (entered into by Allied

and the defendants) and the note, since there is nothing in the note to indicate that it is subject to the terms of the contract. We are equally satisfied that the insurance clause in the note does not affect negotiability under § 3–104(1) (b) since it is clear that the 'no other promise' provision refers only to promises by the maker.

"The provision in the note for 'interest after maturity at the highest lawful' rate does not render the note nonnegotiable for failure to state a sum certain as required by § 3–104(1) (b). We are of opinion that after maturity the interest rate is that indicated in G.L. c. 107, § 3, since in this case there is no agreement in writing for any other rate after default. This being the case, we do not treat this note differently from one payable 'with interest.' The latter note would clearly be negotiable under G.L. c. 106, § 3–118(d).

"The note in question provides that payment shall be made 'commencing the 25 day of July, 1959.' It appears that there is an alteration on the face of the note in that 'July' was substituted for 'June,' the 'ly' in the former word being written over the 'ne' in the latter. The alteration has no effect in this case, where the defendants admitted that they had paid a particular sum on the note and where the sum still owing (assuming the note to be enforceable on its face) is not in dispute. . . .

"We thus conclude that the note in question is a negotiable instrument." (Spiegel also ruled that C.I.T. was a holder in due course, even though it had worked with Allied on various aspects of the financing arrangement and even though it knew of complaints from some of Allied's previous customers.)

▪ PAYABLE ON DEMAND OR AT A DEFINITE TIME

For an instrument to be negotiable, its amount must be certain and the holder must be able to determine when the money may be demanded. Where the instrument is payable "on demand," the money is due whenever the holder asks for it. *Demand instruments* include "those payable at sight or on presentation" (essentially the same thing as saying "on demand") and those "in which no time for payment is stated." Checks, for example, usually do not include any statement as to when they are to be paid, so they are assumed to be demand instruments.

The rules for determining whether an instrument is payable at a definite time are a little more complicated. The clearest cases are those where the instrument is payable "on or before a stated date or at a fixed period after a stated date." Also fairly easy to decide are those where the instruments are payable "at a fixed period after sight." The *acceleration clause* and the *extension clause,* two provisions frequently inserted in instruments, may cause some difficulties with respect to the "definite time" requirement. An acceleration clause advances the due date; an extension clause delays it.

The UCC permits the use of acceleration clauses, within reason. If the acceleration of the date for payment can be made by the maker, a note is essentially payable "on or before" the due date, and thus still negotiable. Payment must be made at least by the due date, but can be made earlier if the maker so wishes. If acceleration of the due date can be made by the holder of the instrument, such acceleration must be made in good faith. The holder must honestly believe that "the prospect of payment or performance is impaired." A default in paying several monthly installments, or perhaps only one installment, could produce such a good faith belief. The holder's good faith is presumed here; the party against whom the acceleration is occurring must prove that the holder acted in bad faith in advancing the due date. An instrument could also specify that acceleration would occur automatically when a specified event happens, such as filing of bankruptcy by the debtor, or sale of its business assets, or similar occurrences.

Some extension clauses OK

Since the holder of an instrument could always extend the time for payment anyway, giving the holder express permission to do so in the instrument does not affect its negotiability. If the maker is given an express option to extend the time for payment, it must be for a specified additional time. Similarly, if there is a provision for an automatic extension of the time for payment, it must be for a specified additional time. In these latter two cases, there is thus still a known date on which payment can definitely be demanded. If the holder is doing the extending, he or she can demand payment by simply refusing to give any further extensions. With both extensions and accelerations, the drafters of the Code wanted to give the parties some flexibility in making their payment arrangements, but subject always to reasonableness and good faith.

Uncertain event = not negotiable

Section 3–109(2) states one further rule, intended to cover the "death notes" sometimes issued by the beneficiaries of estates ("90 days after Uncle Ned's death"). The section states, "an instrument which by its terms is otherwise payable only upon an act or event uncertain as to time of occurrence is not payable at a definite time even though the act or event has occurred." The drafters of the Code made a conscious policy choice that such instruments should *not* be negotiable and that all the maker's defenses should be preserved as against subsequent holders of such notes.

A different kind of "contingency" is at issue in the *Barton* case.

BARTON v. SCOTT HUDGENS REALTY & MORTGAGE, INC.

222 S.E.2d 126 (Georgia, 1975)

FACTS   Barton signed a promissory note for $3,000 which would become due and payable "upon evidence of an acceptable permanent loan of $290,000 for Barton-Ludwig Cains Hill Place Office Building, Atlanta, Georgia, from one of SHRAM's investors and upon acceptance of the commitment by the undersigned." Barton admitted that SHRAM did get such a loan commitment and that Barton did execute the commitment. Barton claimed, however, that since the loan had not in fact been made, he didn't owe the $3,000 loan fee. The trial court entered judgment for SHRAM on the pleadings. Barton appealed.

ISSUE   Was the note negotiable?

DECISION   No, but summary judgment for SHRAM affirmed anyway, since Barton had no reason not to pay.

REASONS   Judge Deen said this note was just an ordinary contract.
"This 'promissory note' by its terms was made payable 'upon evidence of an acceptable permanent loan . . . and upon acceptance of the [loan] commitment;' however under

Code Ann. § 109A–3–104(1)(c) a negotiable instrument must 'be payable on demand or at a definite time.' The 'note' here was not payable on demand . . . and '[a]n instrument which by its terms is otherwise payable only upon an act or event uncertain as to time of occurrence is not payable at a definite time even though the act or event has occurred.' The language of the 'promissory note' therefore reveals that it was not payable on demand or at a definite time, was therefore not negotiable. . . .

"The 'promissory note' is rather a contract to pay money when certain contingencies are satisfied—'upon evidence of an acceptable permanent loan . . . and upon acceptance of the [loan] commitment.' There is no dispute that the loan commitment was accepted by the appellants. Appellee contends that this commitment itself, without more, wherein one of its investors agreed to make the loan in the desired amount, satisfied the requirement of evidence of an acceptable permanent loan. Appellant, apparently relying on the fact that the loan was never finally consummated, denies that 'an acceptable permanent loan was obtained.' Thus the controversy between the parties turns upon the construction of the contract language making the amount due and payable 'upon evidence of an acceptable permanent loan.'. . .

"[T]he whole contract should be looked to in arriving at the construction of any part. The contract provides specifically that it is for a loan origination fee; there is nothing which requires as a prerequisite to recovery evidence that the loan in fact be accepted. All that is required is that there be '*evidence* of an acceptable permanent loan.' . . . The record reveals that by their signatures, the appellants signified their '*acceptance* of the terms and conditions' of the loan commitment. . . . We agree with the appellee's construction of the document, that the loan commitment is evidence of a permanent loan in the desired amount and that the admission by the appellants of its execution acknowledges its acceptability and further supplies the necessary requirement for recovery under the contract. In short, the appellants contracted for the procurement of a loan and the signed loan commitment is 'evidence of an acceptable permanent loan.' The broker having successfully originated a loan, its fee was earned and the appellants were bound by their contract."

PAYABLE TO ORDER OR TO BEARER

Pay "anyone" = bearer

These are "the magic words of negotiability"; they indicate clearly that an instrument is intended to pass freely from hand to hand, to circulate in commerce as a money substitute. Sections 3–110 (order) and 3–111 (bearer) specify the words and phrases used to achieve these results. *Bearer instruments* include those made payable to bearer, to the order of bearer, to a specified person or bearer, to cash, to the order or cash, or to "any other indication which does not purport to designate a specific payee." As examples of the last phrase, Comment 2 lists "Pay bills payable" and "Pay to the order of one keg of nails."

Order instruments are those payable to "the order or assigns of any person therein specified with reasonable certainty, or to him or his order, or when it is conspicuously designated on its face as 'exchange' or the like and names a payee." The section then goes on to list the various possible types of order-payees: (1) the maker or drawer; (2) the drawee; (3) a payee who is not a maker, drawer, or drawee; (4) two or more payees together or in the alternative; (5) an estate, trust, or fund; (6) an office or an officer by his title as such; and (7) a partnership or an unincorporated association. (See Exhibit 27–3.)

■ **EXHIBIT 27–3**
Requirements of Negotiability—Order Instruments

ORDER INSTRUMENTS

Pay to the order of _____(Maker)_____

Pay to the order of _____(Drawer)_____

Pay to the order of _____Drawee_____

Pay to the order of _____John Smith_____

Pay to the order of bearer or _____John Smith_____

Pay to the order of _____John and Jane Smith_____

Pay to the order of _____John or Jane Smith_____

Pay to the order of _____Estate of John Smith_____

Pay to the order of _____Ham Harbour City Treasurer_____

Pay to the order of _____Redfront Grocery_____

BEARER INSTRUMENTS

Pay to _____Bearer_____

Pay to the order of _____Bearer_____

Pay to the order of _____John Smith or Bearer_____

Pay to _____Cash_____

Pay to the order of _____Cash_____

Pay to the order of _____Anybody_____

Pay to the order of _____Superman_____

Examples of order instruments   If you fill in your own (drawer's) name on your check to get some cash at the bank, that check would fall in to the first category of order paper. An example of the second type would be a check made out to your own drawee bank as an installment loan payment. Checks to the landlord or a grocery store would be in the third group. An income tax refund check payable to a husband and wife would fall into the fourth category. A check for a donation to a scholarship fund would be an example of the fifth category. When you make out your check for a parking ticket in favor of "City Treasurer, Ham Harbor, Mythigan," that's the sixth category; the check is payable to the city, but the incumbent officeholder may indorse and deposit it as a holder. A check made out to a partnership or an unincorporated association (such as a fraternity or a sorority), the seventh category, "may be indorsed or transferred by any person thereto authorized" (3–110[1][g]).

Finally, a requirement in an instrument not otherwise payable to order that is payable when "properly indorsed" does not make the instrument negotiable (3–110[2]). In other words, a nonnegotiable instrument cannot be made negotiable simply by requiring that it be indorsed when it is transferred to another person. The "indorsement required" clause in the nonnegotiable instrument does not make it payable "to order."

The drastically different results which occur if this one little word—"order"—is missing can be seen in the following case.

FIRST INVESTMENT CO. v. ANDERSEN

621 P.2d 683 (Utah, 1980).

FACTS
On September 6, 1965, defendants entered into a franchise agreement with Great Lakes Nursery Corporation, hereinafter identified as the "Nursery," a Wisconsin corporation. Defendants, as the franchisees, were to grow and sell nursery stock and Christmas trees. The Nursery was to provide and to deliver 65,000 trees as planting stock for the purchase price of $9,500. The franchisor, the Nursery, under the agreement was to provide the number, size, and variety therein specified, as well as to furnish replanting stock, chemicals, fertilizers, and other articles to be used in the production and sale of the trees; to root prune the trees; and to provide technical training and supervision necessary for the planting, shearing, pruning, marketing, and sale, and other technical information affecting the growth, production, harvest, and sale of the trees.

Contemporaneously with the franchise agreement, the defendants, as makers, executed two promissory notes, each in the amount of $6,412. The notes were payable "to Great Lakes Nursery Corp." Nursery indorsed the notes to "First Investment Company or order."

During 1967, defendants made no further payments on their notes for the reason that the Nursery had failed to perform in accordance with the franchise agreement. In their answer, defendants pleaded a failure of consideration as an affirmative defense. The trial court found there was a failure of consideration on the part of the Nursery for the following reasons: It did not furnish the number, size, and variety of trees specified in the agreement; it did not furnish the replanting stock; it did not furnish any chemicals, fertilizers, and other articles; it did not root prune the trees; and it did not provide technical training, supervision, and information. There is substantial evidence in the record to sustain the findings. Judgment was entered for the Andersens.

ISSUE
Were the notes negotiable?

DECISION
No. Judgment affirmed.

REASONS
Justice Maughan thought the decision was an easy one.

"Under both the NIL and the UCC (70A–3–104(1)(d)), one of the requirements to qualify a writing as a negotiable instrument is that it contain the time-honored 'words of negotiability,' such as 'pay to the order' or 'pay to the bearer.' The mere promise to pay, absent the magic words 'payable to order or to bearer' renders the note nonnegotiable, and the liability is determined as a matter of simple contract law.

"In the instant case, the notes were payable simply to the payee, and were not payable to the order of the payee or to the payee or its order and were thus not negotiable instruments. Since the notes were not negotiable, the transfer by the Nursery to plaintiff must be deemed an assignment, and the assignee (plaintiff) stood in the shoes of the assignor and took subject to existing equities and defenses.

"Significantly, the trial court found that the notes and franchise agreement constituted one integrated contract. This finding is substantiated by the recital concerning consideration in the note, and the absence of words of negotiability. Where there is a failure of consideration under a bilateral contract consisting of a breach by the assignor, such failure is a good defense to an action by the assignee whether it occurred before or after the assignment. Such a defense, although acquired after notice of the assignment, is based on a right of defendant inherent in the contract by its terms. Therefore, where payments under an executory contract are assigned, the debtor may set up failure of the assignor to fulfill his part of the contract though such failure occurs after the assignment, for the assignor cannot give another a larger right than he has himself. The trial court did not err in its ruling that failure of consideration constituted a valid defense to plaintiff's action."

■ **SIGNIFICANCE OF THIS CHAPTER**

The special negotiability results can occur only where the written promise to pay money is in negotiable form: a written, unconditional promise or order to pay a sum certain in money, signed by the maker or drawer, payable on demand or at a definite time, payable to order or to bearer, and containing no other promise or order not authorized by the provisions of Article 3. The special holder in due course status, which is explained in Chapter 28, can only exist with respect to negotiable instruments. As a general rule, even an assignee who takes an account receivable in good faith and for value holds it subject to any defense which the debtor had against liability on the underlying contract. To prevent the debtor from asserting most voidable-type defenses, the instrument must be in negotiable form. Unless it is, the holder's good faith and lack of notice of the defenses is irrelevant.

On the other hand, just because an instrument is nonnegotiable does not mean that it is totally invalid. If the debtor has no defenses to assert anyway, or is estopped to assert them, the holder of the nonnegotiable instrument will get the money represented by the instrument.

The requirements for negotiability are simply the first hurdle that the plaintiff must clear in establishing the special elimination-of-defenses result.

DISCUSSION CASE

VALLEY NATIONAL BANK, SUNNYMEAD
v. COOK
665 P.2d 576 (Arizona, 1983)

FACTS: On October 21, 1977, appellee J. M. Cook (Cook), the treasurer of Arizona Auto Auction and R. V. Center, Inc. (Arizona Auto Auction, Inc.), issued three corporate checks to Central Motors Company. Central Motors deposited these checks in its corporate account which was held by appellant Valley National Bank, Sunnymead, a California corporation (Bank). The Bank then sent each of these checks for payment to Arizona Auto Auction, Inc.'s drawee bank, First National Bank of Arizona. However, a stop payment order had been put on these checks and the First National Bank dishonored each of the checks. The checks were returned to the Bank, and the account of Central Motors was charged back for the amount of the checks which totaled $9,795. The Bank was unable to recover this amount from Central Motors. The Bank demanded payment from Arizona Auto Auction, Inc., but the demand was not honored. On March 27, 1978, the Bank commenced suit against Arizona Auto Auction, Inc. and J. M. Cook and her spouse.

After trial, the court found that the Bank was a holder in due course and that the Arizona Auto Auction, Inc. was obligated as drawer for the face amount of the checks, $9,795. However, the judgment provided that Cook was not personally liable on the checks and awarded her attorney fees as a prevailing party against the Bank. Arizona Auto Auction, Inc. does not appeal from the judgment against it. However, the Bank appeals from that portion of the judgment which is in favor of Cook and her husband as to liability and the award of attorneys' fees.

■

Judge Corcoran:

The question of whether Cook signed in her individual or representative capacity is governed by section 3–403 of the Uniform Commercial Code (UCC) as adopted in this state. . . . The Bank argues that this section conclusively establishes Cook's personal liability on the checks. We do not agree. Admittedly, the checks fail to specifically show the office held by Cook. However, we do not find that this fact conclusively establishes liability since A.R.S. § 44–2540(B)(2) imposes personal liability on an agent who signs his or her own name to an instrument only "if the instrument . . . does not show that the representative signed in a representative capacity." Thus, we must look to the entire instrument for evidence of the capacity of the signer. . . .

The checks are in evidence and are boldly imprinted at the top "Arizona Auto Auction, Inc." and also "Arizona Auto Auction, Inc." is imprinted above a signature line appearing at the lower righthand corner. Under the imprinted name of the corporate defendant appears the signature of appellee Cook without any designation of office or capacity on each of the checks before us on appeal. Appellee Cook did not endorse the checks on the back. The record does not reflect appellee Cook made any personal guaranty of these checks or any other corporate obligation. . . .

[I]t is important to draw a distinction between a check and a note:

The payee of a corporate check with the corporate name imprinted on its face probably expects less from the individual drawer than the payee of a corporate note may, where both the corporate name and the maker's name may be either handwritten or typewritten. Further, it is common for creditors to demand the individual promise of officers on corporate promissory notes, specially in the case of small corporations. Thus, we think a court should be more reluctant to find an agent personally liable who has signed a corporate check than in the case of a similar indorsement of a corporate note. This does not mean that the drawer of a corporate check will never be personally liable; indeed, more than a few have been stuck. Rather, we hope that courts will be more conscious of differences in business practices with respect to different types of instruments when they evaluate the extrinsic evidence presented by the parties. . . .

Thus, while it may be common for creditors of small corporations to demand that corporate officers personally obligate themselves on corporate notes, it would be most unusual to demand the individual obligation of an officer on corporate checks.

The fact that common business expectations may not be consistent with a strict reading of UCC § 3–403(2), as that section relates to corporate checks, as opposed to notes, is exemplified by the record before us. Regarding the checks, a branch manager employed by the Bank, testified during the trial as follows:

Q. Would it be fair to say that when a bank receives an instrument that designates at the top a name of a corporation designated by Inc., that it would deal with that item at all times as a corporate instrument?
A. That is correct.
Q. And in the custom and usage of banking practices that would be considered a corporate instrument, would it not?
A. Yes.
Q. And you receiving those instruments assumed, did you not, that Mrs. Cook was writing that instrument as a representative of the corporation, did you not?
A. I would assume that she would have the authority to sign on that account.
Q. And having that authority, you presume that she was writing that for and on behalf of the corporation; is that not correct?
A. I would assume so, to pay these funds.
Q. You didn't expect Mrs. Cook to individually pay these funds out of her pocket, did you? You expected the corporation to do it, did you not?
A. I expected these funds to come from the account number coded at the bottom of this particular check.
Q. And as far as you know, that account number was the account of the Arizona Auto Auction, Incorporated, is that not correct?
A. That is correct.
Q. You were not mislead by the fact that she wrote on the instrument "J. M. Cook" were you?
A. No.

This testimony is consistent with the common business and banking expectation that where a corporate name is printed on a check any accompanying signatures relating to the corporate drawer will be the signatures of officers authorized by the bylaws or corporate resolutions to sign the instrument in a representative capacity without regard to whether there is a specific reference to the representative capacity. This is especially clear where, as here, the check is drawn against a corporate checking account.

In this case the checks clearly show the name of the corporation in two places, and the money was payable from the account of Arizona Auto Auction, Inc., over which Cook as an individual had no control. Considering the instruments as a whole, we conclude under these circumstances that they sufficiently disclose that Cook signed them in a representative and not an individual capacity.

Our conclusion is further supported by the actions of the Bank which accepted the checks as that of the corporate defendant, Arizona Auto Auction, Inc. In its complaint it so avers. . . . As the [precedent case] stated:

On that basis it proceeded against the corporate defendant and secured a judgment. That judgment was predicated on a proper execution of the instrument by that defendant, which required the signature of its representative. Therefore it accepted appellant's signature as that representative. In fact, in his complaint against appellant he avers the checks were those of the corporation.

Having secured a judgment on that basis against the corporate defendant, we are at a loss to see how he may now contend that appellant's signature was on his own individual behalf and not in a representative capacity. It must be one or the other. It cannot be both. . . .

The only objection made by the Bank on appeal regarding the award of attorneys' fees is predicated upon the assumption that this court reverses the judgment in favor of appellees Cook. Since we affirm the judgment, we also affirm the award of attorneys' fees.

■ IMPORTANT TERMS AND CONCEPTS

negotiable instrument
holder in due course
draft (bill of exchange)
note
direction to pay
investment securities
signed writing
sum certain
in money
payable on demand
event uncertain as to time
payable to bearer
conditional promise to
    pay
acceleration clause
holder who feels insecure
trade acceptance
mortgage note

installment note
bona fide purchaser
voidable-type defense
check
certificate of deposit
undertaking to pay
documents of title
unconditional promise or
    order
no other promise or order
payable at definite time
payable to order
signature by agent
particular fund doctrine
extension clause
good faith acceleration
certified check
cashier's check

■ QUESTIONS AND PROBLEMS FOR DISCUSSION

1. From transferee's point of view, what are the advantages of an instrument's being "negotiable," rather than nonnegotiable?
2. What is the difference between a note and a draft?
3. Why is a promise which is conditional not negotiable?
4. What is the difference between an instrument payable to order and one payable to bearer?
5. Myrna signed a promissory note for $9,000, which was dated May 5, 1985, and which stated that it was payable "within ten (10) years after date." The business equipment which she received in return for the note from Systems, Inc., never functioned properly. Systems negotiated the note to Creditors Corp., a good faith purchaser, for value and without notice of the equipment problems. Systems would be an HDC and could enforce the note if it is negotiable. Myrna said that the note is not negotiable because of the indefinite due date. Is she correct? Explain.
6. Conan Briggs signed a promissory note for $3,498.45. The note permitted the holder to accelerate the due date if it felt insecure and authorized a "confession of judgment" if the note were not paid when due. After the phrase "promise to pay to the order of," the note read: "Three Thousand Four Hundred Ninety Eight and 45/100 -------- Dollars." No payee's name had been filled in, just the amount. The trial court entered a "judgment by confession" and issued a garnishment order against a third party who was holding stock certificates owned by Briggs. Briggs appealed. Should the trial court be reversed? Why or why not?
7. Charter sued to foreclose on a note and mortgage given by Holly Hill. The note contained the following provision: "The terms of said mortgage are by this

reference made a part thereof." Rogers and Blythe had sold to Holly Hill, received the note and mortgage, and then assigned both to Charter. Holly Hill alleged that Rogers and Blythe had committed fraud in the sale. The trial court entered summary judgment against Holly Hill, since it ruled that Charter was a holder in due course of a negotiable instrument. How should the Appeals Court rule? Why?

8. Ellinger had furnished labor and materials to Greenway Building Company, of which Griffin was president. Griffin signed three drafts, totaling $3,950, in payment for the work done. The drafts were drawn against Greenway's account at the Northeast Bank of Houston, which refused payment because of insufficient funds. Griffin's signatures did not show that he was signing in a representative capacity only. Ellinger was not told who owned the building project, or who would pay him, or who would be responsible for the payments. Ellinger had received other payments from Greenway officers and had never looked to them personally for payment. Can Ellinger collect from Griffin? Explain.

28

Negotiation and Holders in Due Course

CHAPTER OBJECTIVES

THIS CHAPTER WILL:

- Explain the difference between negotiation of commercial paper and assignment of an ordinary contract.
- Indicate why proper indorsements are needed to negotiate an instrument.
- Discuss the different types of indorsements.
- Define holder in due course.
- Discuss the requirements a transferee must meet to become a holder in due course.
- Explain the shelter rule for holders through a holder in due course.

We now have an instrument which is negotiable and on which one or more parties are liable as signers. To get the special "negotiability" results, however, a plaintiff seeking to enforce the instrument must meet an additional set of requirements. Unless the plaintiff has taken the instrument through a special form of transfer called *negotiation* and under circumstances which qualify the plaintiff as a "holder in due course," our plaintiff holds the instrument subject to all the defenses and claims which would be available against the assignee of a simple written contract. Only a person with the rights of an HDC holds the negotiable instrument free of adverse claims and defenses.

■ NEGOTIATION

Negotiation = A transfer to holder

Missing required indorsement = No holder

Today, as indicated in Chapter 16, most contracts can be assigned. Only a negotiable instrument, however, can be "negotiated." *Negotiation* is a trai sfer "in such form that the transferee becomes a holder." There must be physical delivery of the instrument and, if the instrument is payable to order, it must be indorsed. A *holder* is a person who is in possession of an instrument "drawn, issued, or indorsed to him or to his order or to bearer or in blank." Where you make your check payable to "cash," or where you indorse your paycheck on the back by simply signing your name, any person who subsequently gains possession of the instrument is a holder, even without any further indorsements. Not every holder is a *holder in due course (HDC),* however. That status depends on the circumstances under which the holder acquired the instrument.

Where an instrument is drawn to someone's order (your rent check to your landlord, for example) or is indorsed to someone's order (you indorsed a dividend check to your bank as payment on a loan), negotiation cannot occur unless the person to whose order the instrument is now payable has properly indorsed the instrument. In other words, the finder of an unindorsed order instrument would not be a holder nor would any subsequent transferee from the finder. The missing required indorsement breaks the "chain of title" to the instrument, so that no later person, even though in possession of the instrument itself, is a "holder."

To qualify as a holder in due course so as to own an instrument free of most claims and defenses, a person must first be a holder. The proper indorsement of an order instrument is therefore crucial to the HDC status of later possessors. If you simply sign your name on the back of your paycheck and then lose it on the way to the bank, the finder would not be an HDC (since that person gave no value for it), but the finder would be a *holder* and the store where he or she used it to buy merchandise could qualify as an HDC. The net result is that you lose the value represented by your paycheck just as if you had cashed it and then lost the cash.

To change this example: If you lost your paycheck before you indorsed it, the finder would not be a holder and neither would the store, even if the finder forged your indorsement on the back of the check. The net result is that you get your money back and the store gets stuck. For this reason, many stores and banks are reluctant to cash checks where the person asking for the money is not the original payee.

The UCC rules for indorsing checks made out in the wrong name are used to settle the "family feud" between father and son Agaliotis.

AGALIOTIS v. AGALIOTIS

247 S.E.2d 28 (North Carolina, 1978)

FACTS   Louis Agaliotis, the defendant, purchased a life insurance policy from Occidental, on the life of his son, Robert Agaliotis. A provision in the policy states that all transactions relating thereto which occur prior to Robert's reaching age 21 shall be entered into with Louis, as the policy owner. Pursuant to another provision in the policy, Louis requested that $1,852 be paid to him. Through a clerical error, the Occidental check was made payable to Robert, but it was (correctly) delivered to Louis. Louis indorsed Robert's name on the check and cashed it. Louis appeals from the trial court's granting of a summary judgment in favor of Robert.

ISSUE   Is Louis guilty of conversion by wrongfully indorsing the check?

DECISION   No. Judgment reversed, and case remanded for summary judgment for Louis.

REASONS   **For Judge Erwin, this simple case of an administrative mistake in making out the check was precisely the sort intended to be covered by UCC 3–203.**

"The findings of fact show, and it was not contradicted, that defendant was entitled to receive the proceeds of the insurance policy in question, that the insurance company intended to deliver the check to defendant and did so, and that only by administrative error was the check made payable to Robert L. Agaliotis.

"Thus, it appears to us that plaintiff's position is that defendant should be liable to him merely because of the administrative error and defendant's having indorsed the check Robert L. Agaliotis. G.S. 25–3–203, 'Wrong or misspelled name,' provides in pertinent part:

> Where an instrument is made payable to a person under a misspelled name or one other than his own he may indorse in that name or his own or both . . .

Plaintiff must show some basis, other than a mere misnomer, to recover of defendant; he has not done so. In fact, the trial court concluded that plaintiff was not entitled to the proceeds of the policy and yet granted summary judgment for plaintiff. In reality, defendant, not plaintiff, was the payee, and defendant did no more than indorse the check in a manner permitted under the Uniform Commercial Code."

▪ INDORSEMENT

Ambiguous signature = indorsement

General Rules.   An indorsement is made by signing your name on the instrument, normally on the back. An indorser could sign on the front of the instrument, but this would entail the risk of being held liable as a comaker of the note or as a codrawer of the draft if that's what the signature seemed to be. Section 3–402 is some help: "Unless the instrument clearly indicates that a signature is made in some other capacity it is an **indorsement.**" The Code also presumes the sequence in which indorsers are liable: "in the order in which they indorse, which is presumed to be the order in which their signatures appear on the instrument." Where an instrument has been transferred so many times that there is no room on it for further indorsements, these may be made on a "permanently" attached piece of paper called an *allonge*.

Partial transfer ≠ Indorsement

An indorsement is effective for negotiation only when it conveys the entire amount due on the instrument. Any attempt to indorse over only part of what's due is not a negotiation, rather a partial assignment. (Therefore, no transferee under such a partial indorsement could be an HDC.) Additional words of assignment, condition, waiver, or limitation of liability "do not affect its character as an indorsement." Where the name of the person to whose order the instrument is payable is misspelled or otherwise incorrect, he or she may indorse with the incorrect name or the correct name or both. Anyone giving value for the instrument can require the double indorsement of both the incorrect and the correct names. Unless the instrument is already payable to the bearer, any transferee for value can demand that the transferor indorse.

"A and B" = Need two indorsements

Where an instrument is payable to two or more persons jointly ("pay to the order of Jones and Green"), all of them must indorse to be able to negotiate the instrument. Where an instrument is payable to two or more persons in the alternative ("pay to the order of Jones or Green"), the single indorsement of either of them is sufficient to negotiate it.

Impostors and Defrauders. Article 3 contains some very special rules to cover situations where instruments are issued to impostors, crooked employees and agents, and other defrauders. In the impostor case, someone who is not Henry Forge comes into your office, says "I am Henry Forge," convinces you that he is, and persuades you to enter into a transaction which results in your making out a check payable to the order of "Henry Forge." He tricked you.

Impostor = Anyone can indorse in fake name

The Code says that *anyone* can effectively indorse this instrument by signing "Henry Forge." The fake Henry Forge can do so. If he loses it or it's stolen from him, the thief or finder can indorse "Henry Forge" and effectively negotiate the instrument. This doesn't mean that some or all of the persons can't be prosecuted criminally; it just means that subsequent transferees can be holders and can therefore qualify as HDCs if they meet all of the other requirements.

Padded payroll = Anyone can indorse in fake names

The same rule applies where a corporation's bookkeeper or payroll clerk "pads the payroll" with extra fake names and then indorses and cashes these extra checks. The crook's indorsements in the names of the named payees are effective; the drawee bank honoring these checks when presented has paid the right party; and the corporation is stuck unless it can get the money back from the crook. Most simply, the Code's rule for these cases is: "The sucker always pays!"

These "fictitious payee" rules are applied by the court in the *Kraftsman* case at the end of this chapter. Notice that the scheme of Kraftsman's crooked treasurer/bookkeeper was not detected by the company's accountants for *four years*.

The Code also provides for similar results where the negotiation of an instrument is subject to rescission because of minority or other incapacity, illegality, breach of duty, or fraud, duress, or mistake. Such a negotiation is at least temporarily effective, and these "defects" in the transaction cannot be used to recover the instrument from a later HDC. A minor's negotiation of an instrument, for example, would make all later transferees "holders," so that one of them could qualify as an HDC. If there were a subsequent HDC in the chain of title, the minor could not get the instrument back; if there were no subsequent HDC the minor could recover the instrument from the current holder. In either case, the minor could use minority as a defense against having to actually pay the instrument.

■ TYPES OF INDORSEMENT

Every indorsement has at least three features: the method it requires for making further negotiations, or at least the next one; the nature of the liability it imposes on the indorser; and the kind of restrictions, if any, which it attempts to place on further transfers. These three features may be combined in various ways.

Blank Indorsements and Special Indorsements.   The last indorsement controls the status of the instrument as order paper or bearer paper, regardless of the form in which it was originally issued. A *blank indorsement* consists merely of the indorser's signature: "John Smith." If the last or the only indorsement is a blank indorsement, the instrument is now *bearer paper* and may be negotiated henceforth by delivery, without further indorsement. A *special indorsement* names the next transferee: "Pay to Judy Jones. John Smith." Regardless of how it was originally made payable, this instrument is now *order paper* and Judy must now indorse to negotiate the instrument further. (Note that the words of negotiability—*order* or *bearer*—do not have to be used in an indorsement. The preceding example is payable to the order of Judy Jones.)

Fred Klomann obviously didn't understand how these indorsement rules are supposed to work.

Last indorsement controls whether now bearer or order

KLOMANN v. SOL K. GRAFF & SONS

317 N.E.2d 608 (Illinois, 1974)

FACTS
Graff & Sons, a real estate brokerage partnership, represented Fred Klomann in his trading of certain real estate for the Countryside Shopping Plaza. The firm owed Klomann $13,000 as a result, and Robert Graff (a partner) gave him three notes, one for $5,000 and two for $4,000 each. Klomann hired Graff & Sons to manage the shopping center and orally promised that the commissions which the firm earned for that work could be offset against the amount that Graff owed him. Robert Graff estimated that his salary of $300 a month (total $14,700) more than offset the firm's debt to Klomann. Klomann specially indorsed the notes to his daughter, Candace Klomann. She examined them and then handed them back to her father so that he could collect them for her. Klomann later scratched out Candace's name, inserted his wife Georgia's name, and delivered the notes to Georgia. Georgia sued to collect. The trial court ruled that the money earned by Robert as manager of the shopping center could not be offset against the money that Graff & Sons owed Klomann, and it entered a summary judgment for Georgia.

ISSUE
Is Georgia Klomann a holder, and therefore entitled to collect the notes?

DECISION
No. Judgment reversed and case remanded.

▥ REASONS After reviewing the facts, Justice Dieringer thought that the case was controlled by UCC 3–204 and 3–201, regarding the propriety of the indorsement as vesting ownership in the transferee.

"Fred Klomann specially indorsed the promissory notes to his daughter, Candace, in August, 1967. The notes, therefore, could only be further negotiated by Candace. Examination of the record further reveals Candace, the special indorsee, has never negotiated the notes. . . . When Fred Klomann assigned the notes in question to his daughter he no longer had any interest in them. His attempted assignment to Georgia approximately three years later conveyed only that interest which he had in the notes, which was nothing. Plaintiff, therefore, has no interest in the notes sued on in the instant case. We do not believe, as the plaintiff contends, that the Uniform Commercial Code intends . . . to not allow the maker of the note to look into the situation and see where title really lies."

Qualified and Unqualified Indorsements. An indorser may disclaim secondary contract liability by using the words *without recourse* or similar language. This is called a *qualified indorsement.* If such language is not used, the indorsement is unqualified, meaning that the indorser is assuming the normal secondary contract liability—to pay the instrument on dishonor. These rules are discussed in detail in the next chapter.

Restrictive Indorsements. Indorsers sometimes attempt, in various ways, to restrict or limit the further negotiation of an instrument. Under the Code's rules, some such restrictions are fully effective, some are partially effective, and some are without legal effect. Section 3–206(1) states that no indorser can effectively prohibit the further negotiation of a negotiable instrument. If John Smith indorsed "Pay only Judy Jones" or "Pay Judy Jones and no one else," the "only" language is completely ineffective. Judy can indorse and renegotiate the instrument just as if John had indorsed "Pay to the order of Judy Jones." Furthermore, Comment 2 to Section 3–206 says that such an "only" indorsement "does not of itself give notice to subsequent parties of any defense or claim, of the indorser." It is not necessarily an indication that something is wrong back up the line, which would prevent later holders from qualifying as HDCs.

> "Pay only Jones" = Pay Jones or order

The promise or order contained in the body of the instrument itself cannot be conditional without destroying its negotiability. This is not true, however, of indorsements. Conditions can be included in indorsements without affecting an instrument's negotiability. What's more, the Code makes such conditions fully effective against all subsequent holders of the instrument other than banks handling it for collection purposes.

> Conditional indorsement binds all later holders

For example, Biff Bosox buys a new TV from Big Bennie's Appliance Store. As payment, Biff indorses his payroll check: "Pay to Big Bennie if he delivers one new Zenith TV to my home. Biff Bosox." Bennie is not supposed to get the money unless he delivers the TV as promised, and the Code says that all later holders of the instrument are responsible for verifying that he has done so before they take the instrument. If Bennie has not delivered the TV but

■ EXHIBIT 28–1
Types of Indorsements

TYPES OF INDORSEMENTS

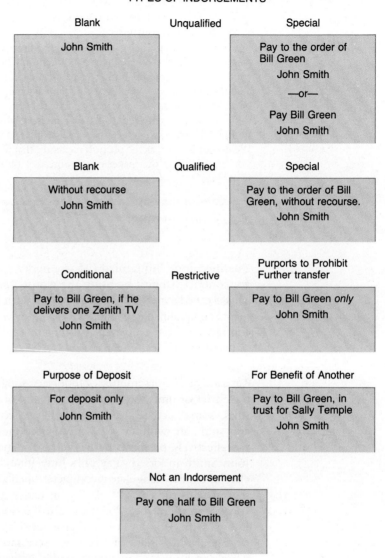

gets the money from someone anyway, that later holder of the instrument is not an HDC. Similarly, all subsequent holders other than intermediary banks are fully bound by such language in the indorsement as "For deposit only" or "For collection." It is very hard to imagine a situation where a nonbank person taking an instrument after such an indorsement could ever qualify as an HDC. Such language clearly indicates that the instrument is intended to circulate only through the bank collection process.

Indorsement in trust binds only immediate transferee

Where the restrictive indorsement indicates that the proceeds are to be paid to one person for the benefit of another ("Pay to Ollie Orkin for the benefit of Shirley Trample"), only the first taker after the indorsement is bound by it. To be the holder for value so as to (perhaps) qualify as an HDC, the immediate transferee must pay any value given "consistently with the indorsement." Unless later holders of the instrument actually know that the trustee or other fiduciary has misapplied these funds, they are not affected in any way by the "benefit" type of restrictive indorsement.

■ HOLDER IN DUE COURSE

HDC = H + BFP

Generally. The essence of the whole concept of negotiability is the elimination or nonassertability of most common defenses when the instrument gets into the hands of a good faith purchaser. The technical term for such a BFP in the negotiable instruments context is ***holder in due course.*** The requirements for becoming an HDC are set out in section 3–302, and then they are more specifically defined in other sections. Whether or not a particular person has met this set of requirements presents a complex combination of legal and factual issues which have been subject to considerable litigation. Since, as previously noted, consumer debtors are now permitted to assert any defense they may have against anyone, HDC status has become virtually meaningless in consumer transactions. For businesses, however, these issues are still vital where merchandise has been fraudulently misrepresented or has not been delivered at all. Whether a business debtor will be able to assert such defenses or will be forced to pay for the proverbial ***dead horse,*** will depend on a later holder's status as an HDC.

A holder in due course first has to be a holder (as discussed above) and then must have taken the instrument "for value, and in good faith, and without notice that it is overdue or has been dishonored or of any defense against or claim to it on the part of any person." Section 3–302 also contains several specific rules: a payee can qualify as an HDC; a purchaser of a limited interest in an instrument can be an HDC only to that extent; and a person cannot become an HDC by buying an instrument at a judicial sale or as part of a bulk transaction not in the ordinary course of business or by acquiring it through legal process or in taking over an estate.

"Value" = Delivered consideration

Value. As used here, *value,* is a much more limited concept than "consideration." A holder ***for value*** must have performed the agreed consideration for the note. If Axle Greez promises to buy a certain promissory note from Henna Rinz for $600, there is a contract, but Axle is not a holder for value until he actually pays Henna the $600. If he is notified of an existing defense before he pays, he can't become an HDC. A person who acquires security interests or other liens against instruments, other than by judicial process, is a holder for value. So is a person who "takes the instrument in payment of, or as security for, an antecedent claim against any person whether or not the claim is due." Similarly, someone who makes an "irrevocable commitment to a third person" (a binding agreement for an extension of credit, for example) is thereby a holder for value. Finally, value is given by giving another negotiable instrument. In the above example, if Axle had given Henna his check for $600 in payment for the promissory note he bought from her, Axle would be a holder "for value" of the note.

The *Korzenik* case shows that even lawyers may be confused by these UCC rules.

KORZENIK v. SUPREME RADIO, INC.

197 N.E.2d 702 (Massachusetts, 1964)

FACTS

On October 31, 1961, Armand Korzenik's law firm had received $15,000 in trade acceptances from its client, Southern New England Distributing Corporation, "as a retainer for services to be performed." Korzenik had been retained by Southern on October 25 in connection with certain antitrust litigation. He did some work for Southern from October 25 to October 31, but there was no evidence as to its value. He also paid cocounsel in the antitrust case some money, but there was no indication of the specific amount. Korzenik sued to collect on two of the trade acceptances, due November 1 and December 1, 1961, in a total amount of $1,900. Southern had defrauded Supreme, although Korzenik didn't know that when he took the trade acceptances. The lower courts found for Supreme Radio.

ISSUE

Had Korzenik given "value" for the trade acceptances, so that he qualified as an HDC?

DECISION

No. Judgment for Supreme Radio affirmed.

REASONS

According to Justice Whittemore, the key was UCC 3–303(a): "A holder takes the instrument for value (a) to the extent that the agreed consideration has been performed." The agreement with Korzenik clearly related to future legal services, and the burden was on him to prove the extent to which those services had already been performed when he learned of the fraud defense.

"The Uniform Laws Comment to S.3–303 points out that in this article 'value is divorced from consideration' and that except as provided in paragraph (c) '[a]n executory promise to give value is not . . . value. . . . The underlying reason of policy is that when the purchaser learns of a defense . . . he is not required to enforce the instrument, but is free to rescind the transaction for breach of the transferor's warranty.'. . .

"The only other possible issue under S.3–303 is whether, because of or in connection with taking the assignments, Korzenik made 'an irrevocable commitment to a third person.' There is no evidence of such a commitment. The finding as to a payment to cocounsel shows only that some of the proceeds of other assigned items have been expended by Korzenik."

Good Faith. Article 3 contains no special definition of *good faith* other than that in the general definitions section (1–201[19]). It is a subjective test, to be applied by the trier of fact: "honesty in fact in the conduct or transaction concerned." Such facts as the relationship between the parties, the size of any discount from the face amount of the instrument, the proximity of the transfer to the instrument's due date, the appearance of the instrument, and the time and place of the transfer would be relevant in deciding whether a particular holder had bought in "good faith."

No Notice of Claim or Defense. Article 3 (3–304) does contain several specific rules for determining when a purchaser has *notice* that an instrument is overdue, has been dishonored, or is subject to a claim or defense. The basic

Irregular instrument = Notice of defense; no HDC

rule is nothing more than common sense: A purchaser has notice of a claim or defense where "the instrument is so incomplete, bears such visible evidence of forgery or alteration, or is otherwise so irregular as to call into question its validity, terms or ownership or to create an ambiguity as to the party to pay." A purchaser who is made aware "that the obligation of any party is voidable in whole or in part, or that all parties have been discharged" also has notice. Where a fiduciary has negotiated an instrument for his or her own benefit, the purchaser must have had knowledge of that fact when taking the instrument.

"Knowledge" vs. "Notice"

Remember the difference between "knowledge" and "notice"; *knowledge* means actual, "inside-the-head" information, whereas *notice* includes both acts from which a reasonable person should infer other information and the receipt of notices containing information, whether those notices are actually read or not. Knowledge is therefore only one form of "notice." This section does say that the filing or recording of a document does not of itself constitute notice so as to prevent a person from being an HDC. It also says that for notice to be effective, it must be received "at such time and in such manner as to give a reasonable opportunity to act on it."

Section 3–304 also specifies conditions that do *not* necessarily give the purchaser notice of a claim or defense and thus prevent him or her from qualifying as an HDC. These include the fact that the instrument is antedated or postdated; that the instrument was originally incomplete and has been completed (unless there is also notice that the completion was improper); that one or more persons have signed the instrument as accommodation parties; that any person negotiating the instrument is or was a fiduciary; that the instrument was issued or negotiated in return for an executory promise or was accompanied by a separate agreement; that there has been a default in interest payments on the instrument or in payment on any other instrument, except where the defaulted instrument was part of a series with this one (a series of corporate notes, for example).

The application of these HDC rules can be seen in the *Money Mart* case.

MONEY MART CHECK CASHING CENTER v. EPICYCLE

667 P.2d 1372 (Colorado, 1983)

FACTS

Money Mart cashes payroll and government checks for a fee. Epicycle Corporation is a Colorado employer that pays its employees by check. On February 16, 1980, Epicycle issued a payroll check, payable to John Cronin, in the amount of $278.59. During the term of his employment, Cronin had borrowed money from Epicycle to be offset by subsequent wages.

The sequence of events is not clear, but Cronin's employment was terminated, and an Epicycle employee who was unaware of Cronin's indebtedness gave Cronin his final payroll check. Epicycle ordered payment on the check stopped. Cronin cashed the check at one of Money Mart's locations on February 22, 1980. Money Mart deposited the check, sending it through normal banking channels. The check was returned to Money Mart marked "Payment Stopped."

Money Mart brought suit in the Small Claims Division of the Denver County Court for the amount of the check, claiming that as a holder in due course of the dishonored check it was entitled to recover from Epicycle. Judgment was entered in favor of Money Mart for $278.59.

The Denver Superior Court reversed, holding that Money Mart was negligent in not verifying that the check was good prior to cashing it and was therefore not entitled to holder-in-due-course status. The court based its decision, at least in part, on the fact that Money Mart is in the business of cashing checks.

ISSUE   Is Money Mart an HDC?

DECISION   Yes. Superior Court's judgment reversed.

REASONS   Justice Rovira saw no need to impose extra requirements on a check-cashing business.

"The question before us is whether Money Mart is a holder in due course. If it is, it takes the check free of any of Epicycle's claims to the check or defenses against Cronin. . . . That Money Mart took the check for value is undisputed, leaving the questions of 'good faith' and 'notice.'

" 'Good faith' is defined as 'honesty in fact in the conduct or transaction concerned.' . . . The drafters of the Uniform Commercial Code intended that this standard be a subjective one. . . . Thus, the question is: '[W]as this alleged holder in due course acting in good faith, however stupid and negligent his behavior might have been?'

"The only testimony on the question of good faith is that Money Mart cashed the check without knowing that a stop payment order had been issued on it. The Superior Court concluded that Money Mart was not a holder in due course because it 'did not inquire as to the check itself and had no knowledge as to whether the check was stolen, incomplete, or secured by fraud.' Under a subjective standard, an absence of knowledge is not equivalent to a lack of good faith. . . . Consequently, if the Superior Court's reversal was based upon a lack of good faith on the part of Money Mart, it was in error.

"We now consider whether Money Mart had 'notice' of the fact that payment had been stopped on the check or that Cronin had obtained the check improperly. A person has 'notice' of a fact when:

(a) He has actual knowledge of it; or
(b) He has received a notice or notification of it; or
(c) From all the facts and circumstances known to him at the time in question he has reason to know that it exists. . . .

As can be seen, tests other than 'actual knowledge' may be used in determining whether a person is a holder in due course. . . . There is no allegation that Money Mart had received notification of the defenses so we must now determine whether Money Mart had 'reason to know' of them.

"The County Court referee found that Money Mart had no reason to know of the defenses because there was nothing inherently suspicious in the transaction, and Money Mart had no duty to inquire about any possible defenses or ensure that the check was good. The Superior Court held that Money Mart's failure to inquire about the validity of the check constituted negligence. However, there is nothing in the Uniform Commercial Code and nothing in the record to support such a conclusion.

"A determination of whether a holder has 'reason to know' is based upon 'all the facts and circumstances known to him.' A person 'knows' of a fact when he has 'actual knowledge' of it. . . . The question therefore is whether Money Mart had actual knowledge of facts giving it reason to know that a defense existed. There is nothing to distinguish the facts of this case from any other of the thousands of checks that Money Mart and others cash each year: A man came to Money Mart to cash his paycheck;

Money Mart is in the business of cashing paychecks; the face of the check disclosed nothing to raise even a suspicion that there was something wrong with it.

"It has often been held that where an instrument is regular on its face there is no duty to inquire as to possible defenses unless the circumstances of which the holder has knowledge are of such a nature that failure to inquire reveals a deliberate desire to evade knowledge because of a fear that investigation would disclose the existence of a defense. . . . There is nothing in using a check-cashing service instead of a bank that would lead to a rule imposing different standards on the two kinds of institutions. . . .

"Accordingly, we hold that Money Mart is a holder in due course and, as such, is not subject to the defenses Epicycle may have against Cronin. Epicycle raises other arguments concerning the question of Money Mart's entitlement to holder-in-due-course status that we find to be without merit."

No Notice that Instrument Is Overdue.   Section 3–304(3) provides a few rules for determining when a purchaser has notice that an instrument is "overdue." With a demand instrument, rather than one with a specific due date, the purchaser has notice that it's overdue if he or she is taking it after a demand for payment has already been made by a prior holder or after more than a reasonable time from the date issued. The section contains a presumption that 30 days is such a reasonable time for an uncertified check payable in the United States, but it does not contain similar guidelines for drafts or notes. (Presumably, the reasonable time for these other instruments would be longer than that for an uncertified check.)

The purchaser who is aware that a prior acceleration of the due date has been made also has such notice. Finally, there is notice that an instrument is overdue when the purchaser has reason to know that part of the principal is overdue (a missed installment payment, for example) or that "there is an uncured default in payment of another instrument of the same series." There is no stated rule for the most obvious case: the stated due date is July 1, and you buy the instrument on July 2. You can clearly see that the instrument is overdue when you buy it, and you are not an HDC.

Demand = "Overdue" after a reasonable time

■ SHELTER RULE

H/HDC had HDC rights

Under the Code, a transferee of a negotiable instrument (including one who is not even a holder) in most instances receives whatever rights its transferor had. A holder who is not an HDC (a donee, for example) would nevertheless have whatever enforcement rights the transferor had. Because of this general rule, any holder of an instrument after an HDC succeeds to all the rights of the HDC, even though the later holder or holders don't personally meet all the requirements for being an HDC. The donee of the instrument can't personally qualify as an HDC, because he or she gave no value for it. But if the donor or some prior party was an HDC, the donee would have all the rights to the instrument that the HDC did. In simplest terms, once there is an HDC in an instrument's chain of title, all later holders of the instrument receive the "shelter" of that person's HDC status even though they can't meet the HDC tests personally.

There are two exceptions to this shelter rule. A person who is a party to some fraud or illegality affecting an instrument cannot improve his or her legal position by transferring the instrument to an HDC and then reacquiring it. Nor can a person who has notice of a claim or defense to an instrument, then transfers the instrument to an HDC, and then later reacquires the instrument.

■ SIGNIFICANCE OF THIS CHAPTER

Since the major purpose of the merchant community in developing negotiable instruments was to protect holders in due course to whom they had been transferred, and to permit HDCs to enforce them free of most common defenses, an understanding of how one becomes an HDC is crucial to understanding the uses and the significance of commercial paper.

The requirements for HDC status are relatively easy to list but sometimes more difficult in specific fact situations. Always, to be an HDC, one must first be a holder, which means that there can be no required indorsements missing. The holder's good faith is usually assumed, but circumstances may indicate otherwise. It is usually easy enough to determine whether the holder has given value for the instrument. Most litigations seem to center on whether or not the holder had notice of a claim or defense when the instrument was acquired. Generally, one who acquires an instrument from an HDC acquires all the HDC's rights to enforce it, even if the acquirer cannot personally qualify as an HDC. This shelter rule thus further protects the HDC, by providing greater marketability for the instrument. Although FTC Regulation 433 has made HDC status less significant in most consumer transactions, it is still very important in all other commercial transactions involving negotiable instruments.

DISCUSSION CASE

KRAFTSMAN CONTAINER v. UNITED COUNTIES TRUST

404 A.23 1288 (New Jersey, 1979)

FACTS: Kraftsman maintained a checking account with defendant bank. Kraftsman's treasurer, who also acted as bookkeeper, was authorized to draw and sign checks on its behalf. Over a four-year period ending in December 1975 the treasurer drew and signed over 100 checks payable both to fictitious parties and to actual creditors. He retained the checks and then cashed them at the bank, converting the funds to his own use. The checks ranged in amounts from $200 to $3,000 with the sum of the embezzled funds totaling $46,714.28. In most instances the treasurer indorsed the checks, usually illegibly, although the bank's tellers cashed some of the checks without any indorsement. It was the normal procedure of the bank to require that any party cashing a check indorse it, but the tellers did not obtain the treasurer's personal indorsement, nor did they make any inquiry regarding any of the illegible or missing payee indorsements. Kraftsman had employed accountants throughout the four-year period to review its cancelled checks and its monthly bank statements, but the scheme remained undetected for four years. Kraftsman sued the bank to recover the amounts paid by the bank on the checks cashed without indorsement. The trial court granted the bank's motion for summary judgment. Kraftsman appealed.

Judge Dreier:

The bank claims by way of the present motion that it is shielded from liability by the terms of the UCC, specifically N.J. S.A. 12A:3–405(1)(b). Plaintiff responds that the bank's failure to exercise reasonable care in guarding against improper payment of the checks renders the bank liable for the amount embezzled. The application of a "reasonable care" negligence standard to a bank in a fictitious-payee endorsement case is the novel proposition urged upon this court.

Articles 3 and 4 of the UCC . . . set forth the duties, rights, and liabilities of banks and their customers concerning commercial paper. Under § 4–401(1) a bank may charge a customer's account only for checks that were properly payable by the bank. Wrongful payment by the bank renders it liable to the customer, who must be reimbursed. This broadly defined duty of the bank is modified by other provisions which define the obligations of the customer. Section 3–406 precludes a customer from claiming wrongful payment when its own negligence has substantially contributed to the making of a material alteration or an unauthorized signature. The customer is required by § 4–406(1) to (3) to be reasonably careful and prompt in examining the periodic bank statements and cancelled checks to discover and report alterations or the unauthorized use of its signature. Failure of the customer to discharge these duties may relieve the bank from liability under § 4–406(2) and (3).

The customer acknowledges that its treasurer was authorized to draw and sign its checks. Therefore none of the drawer's signatures were unauthorized, and plaintiff cannot have been negligent in failing to discover an unauthorized signature. Section 3–406 is thus inapplicable, as are the provisions of § 4–406(1) and (3) which impose upon the customer the duty of discovering its own unauthorized signatures or alterations. The dispute here is over the relative duties of the parties regarding indorsements. The only reference to indorsements in § 4–406 is found in subsection (4), where the time limitation for "asserting against the bank such unauthorized signature or indorsement" is set at three years from the availability to the customer of the relevant bank statement and checks, "Without regard to care or lack of care of either the customer or the bank."

Liability for payment on a forged instrument is treated by the UCC as a separate concept. The basic rule is that a bank which pays a check on a forged indorsement is liable, since a forged indorsement is wholly inoperative as the signature of the actual payee (§ 3–404), and is thus not properly payable under § 4–401. A check validly issued but wrongfully paid by the bank on a forged indorsement entitles the customer to a credit. . . .

The risk of loss may shift. Section 3–405 deems effective an indorsement by anyone in the name of a fictitious payee. The treasurer in the instant case, drawing and signing checks on behalf of the customer, plainly had the requisite intent under the statute. . . .

There is no qualifying language in § 3–405 setting forth a standard of care to be applied to either the bank or its customer. This is in contrast to § 3–406, which would specifically penalize the customer for negligence substantially contributing to a material alteration or an unauthorized signature. In that situation a bank is required to pay the item "in good faith and in accordance with the reasonable commercial standards of the drawee's or payor's business" under § 3–406, but the preclusion of a customer from asserting the unauthorized signature or material alteration under § 4–406(2) is inapplicable if the customer establishes the bank's "lack of ordinary care" under § 4–406(3). The conspicuous absence in § 3–405 of either an "ordinary care" or "good faith" standard signals that a test for a bank's liability for payment on improper indorsements must be found elsewhere. . . . Plaintiff urges that a standard of simple negligence applies. Defendant asserts that it is shielded from liability by § 3–405. There are no New Jersey cases construing the standard to be applied.

Read independently of other UCC provisions, § 3–405 apparently shifts the fictitious-payee indorsement loss to the customer without regard to any lack of care on the part of the bank. . . . Yet the bank may not pay over such an indorsement with impunity. Section 1–203 of the UCC imposes on every contract subject to its provisions an obligation of good faith which, under § 1–102(3), may not be disclaimed by agreement. Although § 4–103(1) specifies that a bank may not disclaim responsibility for its own lack of good faith or failure to exercise ordinary care, § 4–401(2) allows the bank to charge its customer's account only when payment has been in good faith. "Good faith" itself is defined in § 1–201(19) as "honesty in fact in the conduct or transaction concerned."

While the good faith requirement is invariable throughout the UCC by way of § 1–102(3), the more rigorous and objective negligence standard of ordinary care does not have such general applicability. Simple negligence on the part of a bank should not, and has been found not to affect the operation of § 3–405; only bad faith should bar the bank from invoking § 3–405 to defeat the customer's claim. . . .

[The] authorities are in accord with UCC Comment No. 6 to § 4–406:

Nothing in this section is intended to affect any decision holding that a customer who has notice of something wrong with an indorsement must exercise reasonable care to investigate and to notify the bank. *It should be noted that under the rules relating to impostors and signatures in the name of the payee (Section 3–405) certain forged indorsements on which the bank has paid the item in good faith may be treated as effective notwithstanding such discovery and notice.* If the alteration or forgery results for [sic] the drawer's negligence the drawee who pays in good faith is also protected. Section 3–406. [Emphasis supplied]

The bank must fulfill at least a threshold requirement to invoke the protection of § 3–405. The provision requires "[a]n indorsement by any person in the name of a payee."...

Defendant bank seeks here to invoke § 3–405(1)(b) to defeat plaintiff customer's claim. The bank must have at the very least required indorsements in the name of the named payee.... This court construes § 3–405 as requiring an indorsement substantially identical to the name of the named payee.

Those checks cashed by defendant bank without any indorsement must be excluded from § 3–405 protection. Summary judgment is therefore denied the bank regarding the unindorsed checks. Summary judgment is also denied as to those checks exhibiting illegible indorsements; the illegibility of the indorsements raises a question of fact as to whether payment by the bank constituted a lack of "good faith" on the part of the bank....

Finally, plaintiff has raised a material question of fact as to the propriety of the bank's conduct over the entire four-year period. The transactions are to be viewed as a whole, since bad faith may be evidenced by a consistent failure by the bank to monitor and investigate a series of irregular transactions.... Effective indorsements do not relieve the bank from liability if there is proof of a course of dealing so irregular in nature that the bank is shown to have violated its own policies and to have failed to act according to the standard of honesty-in-fact.... Although there is no evidence that any bank employees were acting as confederates, not once was the treasurer asked to indorse the checks himself; nor was he ever questioned regarding the illegible or missing payee indorsements.

Viewing all of the evidence in the light most favorable to the customer, this court cannot say that as a matter of law defendant bank acted in good faith.... This matter, therefore, is also reserved for trial.

[Reversed and remanded for trial.]

▪ IMPORTANT TERMS AND CONCEPTS

negotiation
assignment of contract
indorsement
ambiguous signature
joint payees
impostor rule
blank indorsement
bearer paper
qualified indorsement
restrictive indorsement
indorsement in trust
consumer transaction
  rule
for value
without notice overdue
without notice of defense
notice vs. knowledge
holder through a holder
  in due course
holder in due course
  (HDC)

physical delivery of
  instrument
holder
partial transfer of
  instrument
alternative payees
padded payroll rule
special indorsement
order paper
unqualified indorsement
conditional indorsement
bona fide purchaser
  (BFP)
dead horse result
in good faith
without notice of
  dishonor
without notice of claim
shelter rule

▪ QUESTIONS AND PROBLEMS FOR DISCUSSION

1. Why can't a person in possession of an unindorsed order instrument be a "holder" of it?
2. What is the significance of the UCC's "impostor rule"?
3. Why must a person have given value to qualify as a holder in due course of commercial paper?
4. What is the meaning and significance of the "shelter rule"?
5. Malson bought a promissory note which had originally been issued by Commcred Company to Rusty Motors. Rusty Motors indorsed the note in blank and gave it to the Universal Bank. Universal typed out a special two-page indorsement of the note to Malson. The note was then stapled to these two pages and given to Malson. When Malson sued Commcred, it said that he wasn't a holder because the indorsement to him was not contained on the note itself and that even if he was, he was not an HDC and was thus subject to its defense of fraud (which had been committed against Commcred by Rusty). Can Malson collect from Commcred? Explain.

6. Roxanne gave Hamlet her promissory note for $8,500, as an investment in an oil well he was developing. Hamlet told her that he had over $50,000 of his own money invested in the venture; in fact, he had invested no money of his own. The note was dated April 23, 1983, and was due and payable "one year after date." The note was still unpaid when Hamlet negotiated it to Exray Bank on June 1, 1984. Exray Bank sues Roxanne to collect on the note. How should the court rule in this case? Explain.

7. Midtown Market had a checking account at Status Bank. Midtown's general manager, Leslie Schultz, was authorized to withdraw funds from the account. Midtown kept sums of cash on hand to pay farmers for fresh produce, eggs, and cheese. One day Schultz took two checks, totaling about $1,500 and payable to Midtown, and cashed them at Status Bank. The checks were drawn on another bank and had been indorsed by Schultz with Midtown's rubber stamp: "Pay Status Bank." After Midtown had discharged Leslie about a year later, they discovered what she had done and sued to recover these funds from Status Bank. What is the result, and why?

8. Emile, a state employee who had retired and was receiving monthly pension checks, died. The state, unaware of his death, continued to send checks to the same address. His daughter, Lillian, indorsed and cashed these checks each month. Her scheme was not discovered until she died some eight years after her father. The state sues its drawee bank to recover the funds. How should the court decide this case? Explain. (Looking ahead, what other argument should the drawee bank make against being held liable?)

29

Liabilities of Parties

CHAPTER OBJECTIVES
THIS CHAPTER WILL:

- Explain the distinction between primary contract liability and secondary contract liability.
- Discuss the conditions—presentment, notice of dishonor, protest—that are necessary to hold secondary parties liable for payment of the instrument.
- Define and explain warranty liability on commercial paper.
- Indicate how tort liability may arise from dealing with commercial paper.

Having determined that an instrument is negotiable and in the hands of a holder, we next need to ascertain whether or not the defendant is liable on it and, if so, the nature of that liability. Negotiable instruments combine property and contract concepts, so liability may stem from the contract which a person has made concerning the instrument or from that person's transferral of a piece of property. In addition, persons who intentionally or negligently cause loss to others when dealing with such instruments may be held liable on a tort theory. We now proceed to examine each of these types of liability.

■ DISTINCTIONS BETWEEN PRIMARY AND SECONDARY LIABILITY

"I'll pay" = Primary contract liability

Acceptance = "I will pay."

Primary Contract Liability.   Someone who has made a direct, unqualified promise to pay an instrument when it is due has assumed *primary contract liability* on the instrument. Only two parties make such a primary promise—the maker of a promissory note and the acceptor of a draft or check. Where the draft has not been presented to the drawee (or drawee bank) and accepted (certified) by the drawee, *no one* has primary contract liability on the draft or check. The draft or check is an *order* to the drawee to pay, and the drawer's normal assumption is that the order will be honored by the drawee.

If the payee or some later holder of the draft has some doubts about whether or not it will be honored, or if the payee refuses to send merchandise or to perform services without receiving a certified check, then the instrument can be presented to the drawee to find out whether or not the drawee will agree to pay it when it is presented for payment. A drawee who agrees to the order and directly promises to pay the money when due, writes "accepted" or "certified" on the instrument, signs his or her name, and gives the instrument back to the holder. By doing this, the drawee becomes an acceptor with primary contract liability; until the drawee does this, no one has primary contract liability on the draft or check, and the drawee or drawee bank is not liable on the instrument at all—to anyone.

"If M or De doesn't pay, then I'll pay" = Secondary contract liability

Secondary Contract Liability.   A party with *secondary contract liability* does not expect to pay the instrument; if everything goes right, someone else will pay. The drawer's signature on the instrument implies a kind of backstop promise: I'll pay if necessary—*if* you make a proper, timely presentment of the instrument to the person who is supposed to pay, *and if* that person dishonors the instrument, *and if* you give me proper notice of the dishonor, *then* bring it to me and I'll give you your money. This kind of "if—then" promise is quite different from that of the party who simply says, "I'll pay." Drawers of drafts and checks and indorsers of all types of negotiable instruments make this secondary contract promise. Furthermore, the drawer or indorser may *disclaim* even this secondary promise by drawing or indorsing "without recourse." If the instrument is a draft which appears to be drawn or payable outside the United States, there is a further requirement: The holder must also send the drawer and indorsers a *protest,* which is an official notarized statement of the fact of dishonor.

Failure to Meet Conditions.   Implicit in the conditional promise of the drawer or indorser is the idea that if the above conditions are not met, the secondary liability is excused. For a drawer, this is true only to a limited extent. An unexcused failure to make a proper presentment or to send a notice of dishonor excuses the drawer only where the drawer "is deprived of funds maintained with the drawee or payor bank to cover the instrument" because the drawee or payor bank becomes insolvent during the delay.

Limited excuse for drawer

When such bank insolvency occurs, the drawer can become free of any further liability for such instruments by making a written assignment to the holder of any rights against the insolvent bank. As a practical matter, this means that few drawers will be excused by a holder's failure to present or to give notice of dishonor. Where a protest is required, failure of the holder to furnish it to the drawer will discharge the drawer. Any unexcused delay in complying with the requirements for presentment, notice, or protest is a complete discharge of indorsers. Adhering to these requirements thus becomes very important to the holder. The holder must make sure that the secondary contract liability of drawers and indorsers is preserved to keep them available if the instrument is dishonored. The details of these requirements are spelled out in various other provisions of Article 3.

■ PRESENTMENT, NOTICE OF DISHONOR, PROTEST

Presentment is the holder's demand for acceptance or payment of the instrument. It may be made by mail, through a clearinghouse, or in person at the place specified. The party to whom presentment is made may require the presenter to show the instrument, to provide personal identification, to note a receipt for partial or full payment on the instrument, and to surrender the instrument if it is paid in full.

Mechanics of presentment

When should presentment be made? If the instrument is payable on a specific date, presentment is also due then. If it is payable "after sight," it must "either be presented for acceptance or negotiated within a reasonable time after date or issue whichever is later." To enforce the instrument against a secondary party, presentment of any other instrument "is due within a reasonable time after such party becomes liable thereon." For an uncertified, domestic check, a "reasonable time" is *presumed* to be 30 days after date or issue, whichever is later, for the drawer to be held liable; for an indorser, 7 days after the indorsement. If presentment is due on a day which is not a full business day for either party, it is postponed to the next day which is a full business day for both. Presentment must be made at a reasonable hour; if it is made at a bank, during its banking day.

In some cases, the holder is required to present the instrument in order to hold secondary parties liable on it. In other situations, presentment is optional. Presentment for acceptance is necessary to charge the drawers and indorsers of a draft (1) where it so provides; or (2) where it is payable elsewhere than at the residence or place of business of the drawee; or (3) where its date of payment depends upon such presentment. Any other draft payable on a stated date may be presented for acceptance at the option of the holder.

Presentment for payment is necessary to charge any indorser, of any sort of instrument. To charge any drawer, or the acceptor of a draft payable at a bank, or the maker of a note payable at a bank, presentment for payment is required. As noted above, however, such drawers, acceptors, and makers are discharged only to a limited extent if the required presentment for payment is not made or is delayed. Only in the situation where they are deprived of funds due to the insolvency of the drawee or payor bank, during the delay period, will they be excused from further liability on the instrument.

Dishonor of the instrument occurs when it is properly presented and acceptance or payment is refused. The party to whom presentment is made has only a limited period to decide whether to pay or to accept. The time to decide whether or not to accept is limited to the close of the next business day, but the holder has the option of extending that deadline by one extra business day.

Payment, if requested, can be deferred "pending reasonable examination to determine whether it is properly payable," but only until the close of business on the day of presentment. There are only two exceptions to this "pay-same-day" rule: first, where the party to pay agrees to an earlier time for payment; second, where "documentary drafts" are being presented under a "letter of credit." In letter of credit cases, the bank to which such drafts are presented may defer honor until "the third banking day following receipt of the documents."

Where an instrument has not been properly indorsed, returning it to the holder to obtain the required indorsement is not a dishonor, but a bank may or may not certify the instrument before returning it for the proper indorsement.

Since a check is a demand instrument which is normally intended to have only limited circulation and then to be paid, the drawee bank "has no obligation to certify a check." The bank's refusal to pay the check would, of course, be a dishonor. The holder is entitled to have the instrument accepted as presented and can treat any variation or qualification in the acceptance as a dishonor. If the holder does agree to take the acceptance with the changed terms, that act discharges the drawer and indorser. The holder then has only the obligation of the drawee/acceptor according to the changed terms. In this situation, the holder must decide which course is more likely to produce the money.

Notice Requirements. Something has obviously gone wrong when a proper presentment has been made and the instrument has been dishonored; the original expectations of the parties have somehow been frustrated. Where such dishonor occurs, the drawer of a draft or check and indorsers of any sort of instrument are entitled to receive prompt notice, so that they can take steps to protect their rights. Notice is usually given by the holder, but 3–508(1) says that it may be given by "any other party who can be compelled to pay the instrument," such as a prior indorser.

"Any reasonable manner" of notification is sufficient; even oral notice is permitted, if it can be proved. The Code also specifically recognizes the validity of the common banking procedure of simply returning the item with a stamp or attached ticket indicating the dishonor, or just sending back a debit notice to the party who gave the instrument to the bank. Banks must give such required notice before their "midnight deadline," which means that a bank must send the word back up the line to others by midnight of the next banking day after the day of dishonor or the day of its own receipt from some other party of notice of dishonor. Nonbank parties are given until midnight of the *third* business day following dishonor or their receipt of notice.

Since a "written notice is given when sent although it is not received," it is important to be able to prove exactly when letters were posted or telegrams

Refusal to pay or accept = Dishonor

Mechanics of notice of dishonor

given to the telegraph company. Once properly given, "notice operates for the benefit of all parties who have rights on the instrument against the party notified." If a holder sent notice to prior indorsers Archie and Bernice, for example, Bernice's rights against Archie would be preserved even though *she* didn't send Archie any notice.

The effect of delaying notice of dishonor is seen in the *Hane* case.

HANE v. EXTEN

259 A.2d 290 (Maryland, 1969)

FACTS   John B. Hane was the assignee-holder of a note issued by Theta Electronics Laboratories, Inc., in the amount of $15,377.07, plus 6 percent interest. The note, dated August 10, 1964, provided that the first monthly payment of $320.47 would be due on January 10, 1965. The note contained an acceleration clause. Gerald M. Exten, Emil L. O'Neil, James W. Hane, and their wives all indorsed the note. The original payees, George B. and Marguerite F. Thompson, assigned the note without recourse to Hane on November 26, 1965. Some $2,222.13 had been paid on the note up to that point. Exten had originally been the corporate president of Theta but had been removed in April or May 1965. Although no more than six payments were made (through June 1965), Hane took no action until June 7, 1967, when he filed a confession of judgment against all of the indorsers except the Thompsons. The Extens demanded and received a trial on the merits, after which the judge found them not liable.

ISSUE   Have the conditions to the Extens' liability as indorsers been met?

DECISION   No. Judgment for the Extens affirmed.

REASONS   Judge Singley first reviewed the requirement of UCC provisions and noted: "S.3–502(1)(a) makes it clear that unless presentment or notice of dishonor is waived or excused, unreasonable delay will discharge an indorser." The record indicated that Hane waited about 18 months before making any sort of demand for payment. As to the giving of notice of Theta's dishonor, Hane's brother testified that demand for payment had been made on April 15, 1967, and that he was uncertain as to exactly when he notified Exten, but he said that it was "within a week." For nonbank parties, the UCC specifies that notice of dishonor must be given before midnight of the third business day following the dishonor. Exten denied receiving any notice at all prior to the default judgment on June 7.

Hane next tried to argue that the late presentment and notice were excused "because Exten himself had dishonored the note or had no reason to expect that it would be paid. . . . The court below rejected this contention on the ground that there was no evidence that Exten dishonored the note in his individual capacity.

"There is an even more persuasive reason which negates the contention that Exten had reason to expect that the note would not be paid. . . . While the manner in which $2,222.13 had been paid was unexplained, it would appear that at least six monthly payments of $320.47 had been met, with the result that payments were current for the period when Exten was president. . . . In the face of this Hane offered no proof that Exten, in his capacity as president of Theta, knew or should have known that the note would not be paid. An indorser's knowledge of the maker's insolvency, standing alone, will not excuse the giving of notice of dishonor."

Excuse for Failure to Meet Conditions. Parties with secondary contract liability may still be held on an instrument where there is an excuse for a delay in meeting these requirements or for a failure to meet them at all. If a holder does not know that an instrument has been accelerated by a prior holder, for example, a delay in making presentment would be excused. Similarly, where a delay is due to "circumstances beyond his control," a party has an excuse for late presentment, notice, or protest, so long as that person "exercises reasonable diligence after the cause of the delay ceases to operate."

Holder has an excuse for delay in presenting instrument

Any of these requirements is "entirely excused" where *(a)* the party to be charged has waived it, or *(b)* there is no reason to expect the instrument to be paid or accepted, such as when the drawer of a check issues a stop pay order to his or her drawee bank, or *(c)* the requirement cannot be met "by reasonable diligence." Presentment is also excused by the death or subsequent insolvency of the maker, acceptor, or drawee "of any instrument except a documentary draft," or where "acceptance or payment is refused but not for want of proper presentment." In line with general commercial understanding, a waiver of protest is also a waiver of presentment and notice, even though protest is not required. If the waiver language is part of the body of the instrument, it is binding on all secondary parties; if it is written above the signature of an indorser, it binds only that person.

The "circumstances" in this chapter's Discussion Case *(Port City)* involve the all-purpose excuse: "Computer Error."

■ OTHER TYPES OF LIABILITY

Liability of Accommodation Parties and Guarantors. In many cases the person desiring a loan or credit may not have sufficient income or assets to make the creditor feel reasonably secure about receiving repayment when it is due. One form of additional security which can be used is to have another person, someone who does have a good credit rating, also promise to pay the debt. These "backstop" promises on negotiable instruments can take several forms.

Cosigners' liability

An **accommodation party** is someone who has signed an instrument in some capacity (maker, indorser, acceptor) to lend his or her credit standing to another party to the instrument. Common sense and the Code dictate that the accommodation party be liable in whatever capacity he or she signs to third parties who take the instrument for value. If Jones can't get a bank loan in his own name and his friend Smith agrees to cosign the note with him as a joint maker, Smith (the accommodation party) is liable to third parties as a maker. Had Smith indorsed the note after Jones signed as a sole maker, Smith would be liable to third parties as an indorser (and entitled to presentment, notice, and protest). Generally, these results occur even if the third party knows that Smith signed only to accommodate Jones. As between Smith and Jones, however, Smith has the right to demand reimbursement from Jones if Smith has to pay a third party, regardless of the order or the capacity in which they signed the instrument. The debt is really owed by Jones, and Jones should repay Smith.

Betty Kail's status as a comaker with her company is at issue in the *Durbin* case.

IN RE I.A. DURBIN, INC.

49 B.R. 528 (Bankruptcy Court, S.D. Florida, 1985)

FACTS   I.A. Durbin, Inc. is a voluntary Chapter 11 debtor in possession, engaged in the construction and sale of single family homes in Broward County, Florida. Betty D. Kail is its president and sole stockholder. She operates the company.

In early 1984, Durbin was in need of additional financing to continue its business activities. Durbin had been financing its operations by real estate loans on the property being developed and by borrowing from American Bank of Hollywood. That bank held a security interest in a "collateral package" of property owned by Durbin.

In early 1984 Kail approached Jefferson Bank to borrow $500,000 to be secured by the "collateral package," including second mortgages on model homes owned by Durbin, a lien upon the model home furnishings, an assignment of purchase money mortgages held by Durbin, and an assignment of one half the closing proceeds from house sale contracts held by Durbin. Jefferson agreed to make the loan, provided Kail personally obligated herself and collateralized her promise by a second mortgage upon her personal residence. She agreed to this and the loan closed on March 30, 1984. Durbin defaulted on the note in May 1984.

ISSUE   Is Kail an accommodation maker, and thus discharged by "impairment of collateral"?

DECISION   No. Judgment for Jefferson Bank.

REASONS   Judge Weaver saw Mrs. Kail as a comaker. She could not claim to have been discharged.

"[E]ven if it is assumed the bank's failure to perfect a security interest in the contract receivables of Durbin was an unjustifiable impairment of collateral . . . there was no competent evidence at trial to prove the amount of impairment claimed. Damages for unjustifiable impairment is a question of fact to be proven as any other fact. . . . Failure to do so will bar any relief. . . . Kail claims the bank's failure to perfect resulted in a substantial portion of the collateral being lost. The evidence did not prove any loss resulted from the bank's actions. It reflects that the contract receivables in question were nothing more than contracts between home buyers and Durbin for the construction of homes. Any net profit from these contracts due Durbin would not be known or realized until the closing had occurred. This means that in fact there is no sum of money due Durbin until and unless it finished the home, built it at a profit, and closed with the buyer. Durbin prevented these events from occurring when it ceased operations in May 1984, some two months prior to the petition initiating these proceedings. There was no evidence presented to show how much it would cost to complete these homes, the net amount due Durbin after payment of increased construction costs and liens, or indeed, whether any of these contracts still exist after the passage of so much time. The court should not and will not speculate on what might have been the amount of net profit if the closings had occurred as originally scheduled where the failure to close was the fault of Durbin.

"A final and equally conclusive reason why the unjustifiable impairment of collateral defense of Mrs. Kail fails is that, because she is a comaker on the note in question, the defense is not available to her. Both a maker, who engages that he will pay the note according to its tenor . . . and an accommodation maker, who signs the note in order to lend his name to the maker . . . are normally liable to the payee. . . . However, as a surety, an accommodation maker has the right to release from his obligation to the extent he can show an impairment of collateral. This defense is not available to a maker. . . . Because comakers of notes retain only the right to contribution between themselves, and are not entitled to subrogation to the rights of the payee or to release upon release of a comaker, it follows that a comaker cannot complain of the release of collateral as a comaker as he continues to owe an independent duty to the payee which is not discharged until payment in full or express release is granted."

Words of guarantee may also be added to a signature. ***Payment guaranteed*** means that the holder of the instrument can present it directly to the person so signing if it is not paid when due. In other words, the person making the guarantee is directly and immediately liable when the primary debtor defaults. ***Collection guaranteed*** means that before the signer-guarantor is obligated to pay, the holder must first get a judgment against the maker or acceptor and show that the judgment is uncollectible. Where an indorser so guarantees payment or collection, presentment, notice, and protest are waived as to that indorser.

Warranty Liability. In addition to assuming contract liability by signing an instrument, a person may assume warranty liability by dealing with it as a piece of property. Warranty liability is imposed by the Code in two types of transactions—transfers of ownership of instruments and presentments of instruments for payment or acceptance. Where a person transfers an instrument and receives consideration in return, that person makes five warranties about the instrument. This person is not collecting final payment, but is simply transferring ownership of the instrument to someone else. If the transferee is a donee, receiving the instrument as a gift, the transferor makes no warranties. However, if the transferee is buying the instrument from the transferor, the five transfer

■ **EXHIBIT 29–1**
Commercial Paper—
Warranties

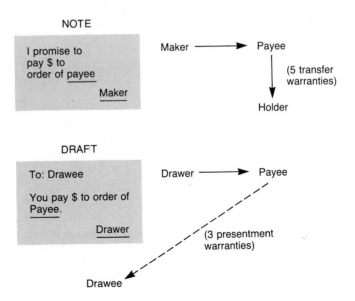

warranties are made by the transferor. The details of these five transfer warranties are explained in the next section.

A person who presents the instrument for payment or acceptance (discussed earlier in this chapter) also makes warranties to the party who in good faith pays or accepts. Someone who takes the instrument to the party who is supposed to pay it and gets the money from the party should at least make a guarantee that he or she is the proper party to be paid. The Code implies such a guarantee, as well as certain guarantees about the genuineness of the instrument. If the instrument is being presented for acceptance, the presenter is asking for a direct promise to pay it when it is finally presented for payment. In this case too, the presenter should be required to guarantee ownership and validity, and the Code so requires. The details of the three presentment warranties are also spelled out below.

Transfer warranties.   Because the parties are dealing with the instrument as a piece of property, the Code provides that certain implied warranties are made when the instrument is transferred for value. Just as implied warranties are imposed against the seller of goods under Article 2, so, too, five implied warranties are imposed on the person who transfers an instrument and receives consideration. If the transfer is by indorsement, these five warranties run to all subsequent good faith holders of the instrument; if the transfer is by delivery alone, they run only to the immediate transferee. If the instrument is payable to someone's order, that person must indorse it to negotiate it to someone else. No indorsement is required to transfer a bearer instrument, but the transferor will often indorse anyway.

The transferor for value warrants:

a. That he or she has good title, or is authorized to act for a person who has, and that the transfer is otherwise rightful.

b. That all signatures are genuine or authorized.

c. That the instrument has not been materially altered.

d. That no prior party who is liable on the instrument has a defense which is good as against the transferor.

e. That he or she has no knowledge of any insolvency proceeding instituted with respect to the maker, acceptor, or drawer of an unaccepted instrument.

Comment 1 to this section states that these warranties may be disclaimed by agreement between the immediate parties but that an indorser cannot escape such warranty liability to subsequent holders unless the disclaimer is part of the indorsement. Such a disclaimer might be stated as, "without recourse and without warranty of any kind."

Where the indorsement contains only the words *without recourse,* the indorser-transferor still makes five warranties. Warranty *(d),* however, changes to a warranty that *he or she has no knowledge* that any defense of a prior party is good as against him or her. A selling agent or broker who does not disclose that status makes all the warranties provided in this section. If such a seller does disclose that he or she is acting only as a representative, the seller warrants only his or her good faith and authority.

Without recourse indorser = one warranty changed

The *Oak Park* case shows the problems which can arise from indorsing a check for a friend.

OAK PARK CURRENCY EXCHANGE, INC. v. MAROPOULOS

363 N.E.2d 54 (Illinois, 1977)

FACTS   Oak Park sued James Maropoulos (defendant). Plaintiff's theory was that a check for $3,564 had been indorsed by defendant and cashed by plaintiff and that the prior indorsement of the payee was a forgery. After all of the evidence was presented, the trial court directed a jury verdict for defendant. Plaintiff appeals.

On July 24, 1971, Bugay requested assistance in cashing a check. Defendant suggested that they go to plaintiff currency exchange where defendant often transacted business and was known to plaintiff's employees. The check in question was a certified check drawn on American National Bank payable to the order of "Henry Sherman, Inc." and indorsed "Henry Sherman" on the reverse side.

Defendant testified that at the currency exchange he identified himself and asked the clerk if she would cash his friend's check. Though she was not the woman with whom he usually dealt, she recognized him. She answered that she would cash the check if defendant would indorse it. He indorsed the check and handed it to the clerk. He observed that she examined both sides of the check. She then handed him the money. He did not count this but gave it immediately to Bugay. Defendant testified unequivocally that he received no money from Bugay in return for his help.

Some time later a claim was made against plaintiff by Belmont National Bank where plaintiff had deposited the check because the indorsement "Henry Sherman" had been forged. Plaintiff determined that it was liable to the bank and paid the claim.

ISSUE   Is defendant liable for breach of warranty?

DECISION   No. Judgment affirmed.

 REASONS   Justice Goldberg very carefully reviewed the UCC rules:

"[D]efendant is an accommodation indorser and would be liable to plaintiff under his indorser's contract, provided that he had received timely notice that the check had been presented to the drawee bank and dishonored. . . . Because these conditions precedent to the contractual liability of an indorser have not been met, defendant is not liable on his contract as an accommodation indorser.

"Furthermore, the drawee bank, American National, did not dishonor the check but paid it. This operated to discharge the liability of defendant as an accommodation indorser. . . .

"The portion of the Code upon which plaintiff seeks to hold defendant liable is section 3–417 entitled 'Warranties on Presentment and Transfer.' . . . Section 3–417(1) sets out warranties which run only to a party who 'pays or accepts' an instrument upon presentment. . . . We note that presentment is defined as 'a demand for acceptance or payment made upon the maker, acceptor, drawee, or other payor. . . .' As applied to the instant case, the warranties contained in section 3–417(1) are limited to run only to the payor bank and not to any other transferee who acquired the check. In the case before us, plaintiff is not a payor or acceptor of the draft. This interpretation is strongly supported by the official comment which details the reasons for distinguishing warranties made to a payor or acceptor of an instrument from those made to a transferee.

. . . The case before us involves a transferee, not a party who paid or accepted the instrument. Thus it appears that reliance by plaintiff upon subsection 3–417(1) was misplaced. . . .

"An additional theory requires affirmance of the judgment appealed from. Subsection 3–417(2) of the Code provides that one 'who transfers an instrument and receives consideration warrants to his transferee . . .' that he has good title. . . . The Illinois comments to this portion of the Code confirm that this warranty is made only by any party who transfers an instrument for consideration. . . .

"The evidence presented in the case at bar establishes that defendant received no consideration for his indorsement. Though Mrs. Panveno testified that she saw Bugay hand defendant some money as the two left the currency exchange, she also testified that defendant stated that he was doing a favor for his friend; that she was not paying close attention to the two men and that she did not watch them as they walked away from her. Thus her testimony was considerably weakened by her own qualifying statements and it was strongly and directly contradicted by the positive and unshaken testimony of defendant that he received nothing in return for his assistance. The simple fact standing alone that this witness saw Bugay hand some money to defendant, even if proved, would have no legal significance without additional proof of some type showing that the payment was consideration for defendant's indorsement."

Presentment Warranties.   Primarily to assure that the proper party gets the money, Article 3 also imposes three warranties when the instrument is presented for payment or acceptance. These three warranties are imposed on both the person who obtains the payment or acceptance and on any prior transferor.

The warranties are:

Person who asks for $ or acceptance makes three warranties

a. That the person who presents the instrument has a good title to it or is authorized to act for someone who does.

b. That he or she has no knowledge of any unauthorized signature of a maker or drawer, except that a holder in due course does not warrant the maker's *own* signature to the maker, or the drawer's *own* signature to the drawer, or the drawer's signature to the acceptor if the holder took the instrument after acceptance or if the holder obtained the acceptance without knowledge of the unauthorized drawer's signature.

c. That the instrument has not been materially altered, except that a holder in due course does not make this warranty, either, to those persons who should know the original terms of the instrument—the maker, the drawer, and the acceptor.

The exceptions made under *(b)* and *(c)* are made to ensure fairness and are based on the old English case of *Price* v. *Neal,* 3 Burr. 1354 (1762). The idea is that at some point payment should be "final." The Code draws this line at the point where payment is made to a holder in due course, acting in good faith. If the maker, drawer, or acceptor isn't sharp enough to catch the fact that the instrument has been altered or that his or her signature has been forged (or in the case of the acceptor-drawee, that the drawer's signature has been forged), it's simply not fair to permit recovery of the money paid to a holder in due course who was acting in good faith. Probably the most typical situation where the money has to be paid back and the instrument has to be kicked back up the chain of title is the case where a required indorsement is missing, so that the person making the presentment did not really have a "good title." That is the claim made in the *Yagow* case.

IN RE YAGOW

61 B.R. 109 (Bankruptcy Court D. North Dakota, 1986)

FACTS   Sargent County Bank filed a complaint, alleging a right to indemnification from the debtor and a determination of nondischargeability to the extent of such indemnification. The Debtor, Merlyn Yagow, denies responsibility for the damages allegedly sustained and additionally argues that no damages have actually been sustained.

Commencing in 1980 the Debtor began to have disagreements with Production Credit Association. These disputes became so severe that by 1984, P.C.A., who claimed a security interest in all the Debtor's crops, required that all checks stemming from the sale of any crops name P.C.A. as copayee. At all times material the Debtor was aware of this requirement and knew that he would not be able to cash checks without P.C.A.'s indorsement. Yagow nevertheless cashed three checks without a P.C.A. indorsement.

P.C.A. commenced an action against the Bank in North Dakota State District Court for recovery of all sums paid over to the Debtor, alleging in its complaint that the Bank breached its duty as collecting bank in making payment of altered checks without obtaining the required indorsement.

ISSUE   Does Yagow's alteration prevent his discharge in bankruptcy?

DECISION   Yes. Judgment for the Bank.

REASONS   **Judge Hill had no trouble finding fraud by Yagow.**

"The Bank alleges in the present adversary case that the check alterations were made by Merlyn Yagow with the fraudulent intent to obtain payment without the necessary indorsement of P.C.A. and consequently, to the extent it may be liable to P.C.A., it is entitled to nondischargeable indemnity from the Debtor.

"For a creditor's right to indemnity from a debtor in bankruptcy to be rendered nondischargeable the indemnity obligation must meet one of the enumerated exceptions to debt dischargeability set out in section 523 of the Bankruptcy Code. In the instant case contingent nondischargeability is premised upon section 523(a)(2)(A) which provides in part:

(a) a discharge under section 727, 1141 or 1328(b) of this title does not discharge an individual debtor from any debt . . .

(2) for money, property, services, or an extension renewal, or refinancing of credit, to the extent obtained by—

(A) false pretenses, a false representation, or actual fraud.

"The fraud alleged to have occurred in this case is the material alteration to the checks by the Debtor, a joint payee, which caused the Bank to mistake the checks as being payable in the alternative to several payees including the Debtor. Fraud, whether alleged under state law or in a section 523 bankruptcy action, is never presumed but must be proved by clear and convincing evidence. . .

"As payee on a check, a person obtaining payment warrants to the collecting bank which cashes it that he has good title to the check or is authorized to obtain payment on behalf of one who has good title. He further warrants that the check has not been materially altered. . . . (UCC 3–116) specifies further that a check payable to the order of two or more persons and in the alternative payable to any one of them may be negotiated by any of them who has possession. If, however, the jointly issued check is not in the alternative payable to one, it is payable to all payees and can only be negotiated by all of them. Any alteration in a check is material which changes the contract of any party thereto in any respect including the number or relations of the parties and the addition or removal of any part of the check as originally signed. . . .

"Each of the three checks was originally drawn naming P.C.A. as joint payee and thereby requiring P.C.A.'s indorsement for negotiation. At the time of receiving payment on the three checks, Merlyn Yagow under applicable commercial law made two warranties. He first warranted he had good title to the checks and/or was authorized to receive payment on behalf of P.C.A. In addition, he warranted that the checks had not been materially altered. . . .

"The breach in the instance of each check was a misrepresentation and concealment of a material fact which if known to the Bank, as collecting bank, would have caused them not to cash the checks. The breach of UCC warranties has been recognized as sufficient to constitute a false representation under section 523(a)(2)(A). . . .

"A similar result must be reached in the case at bar. One who presents a check for payment cannot do so free of the UCC presentment warranties explicit in N.D.C.C. § 41–02–54 and breach of these warranties, by the making of a false statement or concealment of a material fact, constitutes fraud under section 523(a)(2)(A).

"This Court is satisfied that if Sargent County Bank is ultimately liable to P.C.A. and suffers damages thereby, those damages were proximately caused by the Debtor's fraud in the guise of breach of presentment warranties. If, of course, P.C.A. does not prevail in its action against the Bank, then no damages will have been sustained as a consequence of the Debtor's breach and no recovery under section 523(a)(2)(A) may be had. . . .

"For the reasons stated, IT IS ORDERED that Judgment be entered in favor of Sargent County Bank against the Debtor for indemnification in such amounts as the Bank may be found liable to P.C.A., but not to exceed $18,553.41, stemming from presentment of the three (3) checks referred to herein. Any sum for which the Bank is entitled to indemnity is declared to be nondischargeable under section 523(a)(2)(A)."

Tort Liability. Article 3 also has special sections imposing liability for the torts of negligence and conversion. Section 3–406 says:

Liability for negligence

> Any person who by his negligence substantially contributes to a material alteration of the instrument or to the making of an unauthorized signature is precluded from asserting the alteration or lack of authority against a holder in due course or against a drawee or other payor who pays the instrument in good faith and in accordance with the reasonable commercial standards of the drawee's or payor's business.

If you fill out a check with a blank space after "Six" and before "dollars," and you also leave a blank where you write "$6 .00" and if someone alters that check to read "Six Hundred" and the check is paid by your bank, you could not claim the alteration as a basis for having the bank put $594 back in your account. However, if the words *six* and *hundred* were written in ink of a different color, or if the handwritings were obviously dissimilar, your counter-argument would be that the bank had not paid the check in good faith or had not exercised reasonable care in doing so.

Another fairly typical case of this sort would involve the negligence of a business which printed its checks on a checkwriter. If the business had not taken reasonable precautions to prevent unauthorized persons from using the checkwriter, it could not assert their lack of authority where the drawee bank had paid the checks in good faith. The net result of this section is that the negligent party is stuck with the loss, unless that party can find and recover from the person who inserted the alteration or the unauthorized signature.

Liability for conversion

As with other types of personal property, a person who deals with an instrument in a manner inconsistent with the rights of the true owner commits the tort of conversion. Section 3–419 says that an instrument is converted where:

a. A drawee to whom it was presented for acceptance refuses to return it.

b. A person to whom it was delivered for payment refuses to either pay or return it.

c. It is paid on a forged (required) indorsement.

If any of these things occurs, the amount of tort damages which the owner can collect against the wrongdoer will usually be the face amount of the instrument. Banks which are merely acting as agents for their customers in trying to collect for deposited items are not liable as converters under this section, so long as they have exercised reasonable commercial standards in dealing with such an item and so long as they turn over any of the proceeds remaining in their possesion to the true owner. The customer is the converter, not the bank.

■ SIGNIFICANCE OF THIS CHAPTER

Both plaintiffs and defendants, creditors and debtors, need to know the circumstances under which they could become liable on a negotiable instrument. These rules are complicated, since they encompass different types of liability. Perhaps no other single topic so clearly combines all the basic legal concepts: contract, property, tort, and crime.

Although negotiable instruments are involved in many fraudulent schemes where criminal prosecution could occur, this chapter examined civil, rather than criminal, liability. We covered the contract liabilities of makers of notes, drawers and acceptors of drafts and checks, and indorsers of all types of instruments. Our discussion included warranties made by persons who transfer instruments for value or who present them for payment or acceptance, and tort liability for negligence or conversion. While these liabilities are primarily based on the provisions of Article 3 of the UCC, liabilities may also arise under general legal principles.

Because liability is easy to incur and hard to disclaim, extreme care should be exercised in signing, handling, transferring, and verifying all negotiable instruments.

DISCUSSION CASE

PORT CITY STATE BANK v. AMERICAN NATIONAL BANK, LAWTON, OKLAHOMA

486 F.2d 196 (U.S. Tenth Circuit, 1973)

FACTS: This appeal is from a judgment entered against appellant Port City State Bank in its suit to collect upon two checks forwarded to appellee and not returned as insufficient before the appropriate midnight deadline. Following a trial without jury, the U.S. District Court ruled that the failure to notify of dishonor prior to the deadline was excused by Regulation J of the Federal Reserve Regulations.

Appellant was the holder of two checks drawn upon the J. H. McClung Coin Shop account with American National. Both items were forwarded through collecting channels for payment. The first check arrived at American National on Friday, November 28, 1969. That check contained two conflicting amounts: in figures $72,000.00 and in words seventy-two dollars and no/100 dollars. It was processed manually and stamped insufficient funds on Saturday, November 29; however, it was not returned immediately but was placed in Monday's business to determine if any deposits were forthcoming on Monday which would balance the account. Notice of dishonor was given to the last indorser of the check, the Federal Reserve Bank of Oklahoma City, on Wednesday, December 3, and the check was returned to the Federal Reserve Bank at Oklahoma City, on Wednesday, December 3, and the check was returned to the Federal Reserve on December 4.

The second check, in the amount of $120,377.20, arrived at American National on Tuesday, December 2, 1969. The first notice of its dishonor was by telephone to the Federal Reserve on Friday, December 5; it was returned to the Federal Reserve the same day.

It was stipulated by the parties that the "midnight deadline" for these items as established by Regulation J was midnight December 1 for the first check and midnight December 3 for the second check. Additionally, it was stipulated that neither check was dishonored before the applicable deadline.

■

Judge Hill:

These facts establish a prima facie case for the application of 12 C.F.R. 210.12 and 12A O.S.A. 4–302(a),

both concerning the necessity of fulfilling the midnight deadline, and thus it became the obligation of appellee at the trial to prove an excuse from these provisions under 12 C.F.R. 210.14 and 12A O.S.A. 4–108(2). The latter regulations in essence prevent the operation of the midnight deadline in cases when the delay by the payor bank is caused by the interruption of communication facilities, suspension of payments by another bank, war, emergency condition, or other circumstances beyond the control of the bank, provided it exercises such diligence as the circumstances require.

In furtherance of its contention, American National presented evidence that prior to December 1, 1969, it had performed its bookkeeping functions by machine posting, a so-called manual system. During 1969, however, a decision was made to implement a computer bookkeeping operation, and a rental agreement was entered into with a large computer company. That lease provided that all repairs and maintenance were the obligation of the computer firm, and American National was not authorized to undertake any such tasks. After the installation of the computer, American National paralleled its manual system with computer operations for approximately two weeks. Finally the decision was made to change over to computer processing beginning on December 1. A last manual posting was made on Saturday, November 29, and the manual bookkeeping equipment was removed from the bank during that weekend.

At approximately 10 A.M. on December 1, the first day for use of computer operations, the American National computer developed a "memory error" which rendered it unusable. Though the computer manufacturer indicated repairs would not take "too long," they lasted until late Monday night and the testing procedure extended into the early hours of Tuesday, December 2.

In reliance upon the belief that the computer would be repaired without prolonged delay, American National took no extraordinary steps to process Monday's business during the business day. However, when it became apparent that evening that the computer was not going to be ready immediately, American National decided to utilize an identical computer in a bank which was a trip of some two and one half hours away, in accord with a backup agreement they had made with the other banking institution. Thus at about 11:30 P.M. personnel from American National and the computer company began processing Monday's business on the backup computer and continued processing through the night. This work had proceeded to the point of capturing the items on discs when, because the backup computer was required by its owner and because they were informed their own computer was operational, the American National personnel returned to their bank to complete the work on their own machine. After returning to American National, the work was processed to the point of completing the printing of the trial balances when another memory error developed which again rendered the computer unusable. No further use could be made of the appellee's computer until a new memory module was installed on Thursday, December 4.

Because of the second failure, American National was forced to utilize the backup computer both Wednesday and Thursday during times it was not required by its owner. Monday's business was completed and work was begun on Tuesday's items the evening of Tuesday, December 2. Tuesday's items were not completed until either Wednesday, the third, or Thursday, the fourth. When the second check arrived in Tuesday's business, it was held to determine if a later deposit had balanced the account. Through the use of the backup computer and then its own computer during the next weekend, American National was fully "caught up" by Monday, December 8. . . .

As to the first check, it is true that it was processed and stamped insufficient on Saturday; however, it was held for Monday's business to allow any deposits made on Monday to balance the account before notice was required. This procedure is reasonable, and only the subsequent computer breakdown prevented timely notice upon the check. In the case of the second check, appellant contends that problems involved in balancing the "proof batches" caused the delay, not the unavailability of the computer. Such a contention ignores the problems encountered by the bank on Tuesday as a result of the delay in processing Monday's business. Tuesday's work was delayed first by the necessity of driving two and one half hours each day before work could commence, and second by the necessity that Monday's business be completed first. Without doubt, both of these delays resulted from the computer problems at American National.

Further, appellant contends that a computer failure, as a matter of law, is not an event which can impose the application of 12A O.S.A. 4–108(2). In our opinion, such a determination is a mixed question of fact and law; however, neither treatment justifies the reversal of the trial court's determination in this case. Factually, it was in no way erroneous to conclude that the malfunction

created an emergency condition in the bank and was also a condition beyond the control of the bank. . . .

Port City next alleges that the trial court erred in its determination that American National exercised "such diligence" as the circumstances required. Basically, appellant asserts three alternative procedures that American National could have employed and asserts that if any of these alternatives would have resulted in meeting the deadline, then appellee did not exercise diligence under the circumstances. As the trial court correctly concluded, the statute does not require perfection on the part of the appellee, and American National's performance should not be judged on the basis of 20–20 hindsight.

It must first be noted that appellee quickly notified the computer firm of the breakdown, and that the company began an immediate repair effort. Further, there was evidence to indicate that such computer breakdowns are generally repaired very quickly. Thus it would appear that appellee was justified in its initial delay in adopting emergency procedures based on its belief such measures would prove unnecessary. Additionally, we must agree with the trial court that appellee's duty under these circumstances was much broader than one requiring merely that it meet its midnight deadline. It was further obligated to keep the bank open and to serve its customers. To abandon the orderly day-by-day process of bookkeeping to adopt radical emergency measures would have likely prolonged the delay in returning the bank to normal operations.

As to appellant's assertion that appellee should be returned to manual posting, it was shown that the equipment for this procedure was no longer in the bank. Further, no clear evidence was presented to indicate such a procedure would have allowed appellee to fulfill its deadlines if the procedure had been implemented. Any decision to return to manual posting would have to have been made very soon after the discovery of the initial failure. At that time, because of their own experience with computers and the industry history, and also because the manufacturer did not foresee the serious nature of the repairs, American National was justified in believing its computer would be back in service soon. Their delay in commencing emergency operations was reasonable, and these facts prevented a return to manual posting in time to fulfill the deadlines.

As to the possibility of utilizing another backup computer at the regional headquarters of the computer leasing firm, we must agree with the trial court that there was no evidence that this alternative would have proved any more successful than the method actually employed by appellee.

In regard to the last alternative, "sight posting," the evidence is conflicting but sufficient to indicate it is not clear this alternative was so obviously superior as to be mandated under these circumstances. There were differing estimates as to the time required, and it was indicated such a procedure would upset and delay the eventual computer bookkeeping required to return the bank to current status. And as in the consideration of the previous alternatives, it was not clearly demonstrated that this procedure would have allowed American National to meet its deadlines even if it had been adopted. . . .

[Judgment affirmed.]

■ IMPORTANT TERMS AND CONCEPTS

primary contract liability
acceptor of draft
presentment of draft/check
holder of draft/check
drawer of draft/check
indorsers of instruments
time for presentment
notice of dishonor
excuse for failure to meet
  conditions
payment guaranteed
collection guaranteed
warranty of good title
warranty of no material
  alteration
warranty of no knowledge
  of insolvency
warranty of no knowledge
  of prior party defenses
warranty of no knowledge
  of unauthorized maker
  or drawer signature
warranty of no material
  alteration

tort liability
conversion
maker of note (or CD)
certifier of check
drawee or drawee bank
secondary contract liability
failure to meet conditions
bank insolvency as excuse
  for drawer
dishonor
reasonable manner of
  notification
accommodation party
transfer by indorsement
warranty liability
warranty of genuine
  signatures
warranty of no prior
  party defenses
without recourse
presentment warranties
no warranties to maker,
  drawer, acceptor
negligence

■ QUESTIONS AND PROBLEMS FOR DISCUSSION

1. What is the difference between primary contract liability and secondary contract liability?
2. When are the conditions to secondary contract liability excused?
3. What is warranty liability as it relates to commercial paper?
4. What is the significance of indorsing an instrument with the words "without recourse"?
5. Keppos owned and operated Lighting, Inc. He issued three notes, totaling $36,000, to one of his suppliers, Rostuba Brassware. Each note was signed on the signature line "Howard Keppos." Typed above the signature were the words: "Lighting, Inc." The body of the note said: "We promise to pay." Lighting, Inc. defaulted on the notes, and Rostuba sued Howard Keppos individually. Is Howard personally liable for these notes? Why or why not?
6. Anne Berlin was employed by the State Department of Labor. Her job was to verify reports filed by employers for various taxes due and to indorse and deposit their checks to the state. Anne found several checks where the employer had left a space under the state's name as payee and wrote in the words "or Anne Berlin." She then deposited these checks in her personal account, later withdrew the money, and left town. The state sued her bank for conversion. What is the result, and why?
7. On June 5, 1980, Lucille indorsed a $3,000 check which was drawn by Wilber on his account at the Clayborn Bank and which was payable to his order. Lucille indorsed the check so that Wilber could cash it at the Volley Bank. On August 23, 1980, Volley Bank was notified by a collecting bank that the check had been dishonored by Clayborn Bank. On August 24, Volley Bank debited Lucille's account for $3,000 and notified her by mail that Wilber's check had been dishonored. Lucille sues Volley Bank to force them to put the money back into her account. What is the result and why?
8. Sparky drew a check payable to Wheaton, on Sparky's account at the Alfalfa Bank. The proceeds of this check were supposed to be paid over to Danno, by Wheaton. Wheaton received the check, but before he could cash it, Sparky filed a garnishment action to try to collect a separate debt owed to him by Danno. Sparky named Wheaton as the garnishee-defendant since he was holding the check that was to be paid over to Danno. The applicable state statute says that no garnishment action can occur against any person by reason of having ". . . accepted . . . any negotiable instrument." Wheaton said he has accepted this check and thus can't be named in the garnishment action. Is he correct? Explain.

30

Defenses and Discharge

CHAPTER OBJECTIVES

THIS CHAPTER WILL:

- Explain the difference between personal and real defenses.
- Define the major real defenses.
- Define the major personal defenses.
- Indicate the application of FTC Regulation 433.
- Show how a party may be estopped to assert a defense.
- Explain the major forms of discharge of liability.

HDC of NI = Free and clear of personal defenses

The merchant community's main purpose in developing negotiable instruments (NI) and the main significance of negotiability today is the nonassertability of most common defenses against liability when an instrument gets into the hands of an HDC. HDC status does not, however, eliminate *all* defenses. Some defenses can still be asserted against an HDC and, if proved, will defeat or reduce recovery on an instrument. Those defenses that cannot be asserted against an HDC or an HHDC (a *holder through a holder in due course)* are called *personal* or *limited defenses.* Personal defenses can still be asserted against anyone who is not an HDC or a holder through an HDC.

"Void" = no contract = real defense

Those defenses that can be used against anyone, including an HDC or an HHDC, are called *real* or *universal defenses.* The most obvious example of these defenses is forgery; certainly a person whose name has been forged on an instrument should not be required to pay it, even to an HDC. The basic distinction is between *void-type* defenses (= real) and *voidable-type* defenses (= personal), except for minority, which is recognized as a real defense. If a defense is one which "makes the obligation a nullity," it is a real defense. If there is no contract, there is no contract—even if the instrument is in the hands of an HDC. On the other hand, if a defense merely relates to some problem between two of the parties on an instrument, it is a personal defense, and it cannot be asserted against an HDC. The court is trying to decide which type exists in the *Berenyi* case.

NEW JERSEY MORTGAGE & INVESTMENT CORP. v. BERENYI

356 A.2d 421 (New Jersey, 1976)

FACTS

Apparently as a result of irregularities in its earlier dealings with customers, Kroyden Industries was under an injunctive order from a New Jersey court not to engage in certain sales practices in connection with the sale of carpeting. In violation of this injunction, an employee of Kroyden told Andrew and Anna Berenyi that they could have $1,100 worth of new carpeting in their home if they referred other customers to Kroyden. The Berenyis bought the carpeting and signed a negotiable promissory note for $1,521, with the understanding that they would receive credit for each referral they made. The note was negotiated to plaintiff, a holder in due course. In 1964 when the note was signed, neither the state nor the FTC had a consumer protection regulation in force. Anna Berenyi appeals from a trial court judgment for the plaintiff; Andrew is now deceased.

ISSUE

Does Kroyden's violation of the injunction make the whole transaction void?

DECISION

No. Judgment affirmed.

REASONS

The court discussed the difference between the two types of defenses.

"The controlling issue presented is whether the defense here asserted is a 'real' defense or a 'personal' defense. Real defenses are available against even a holder in due course of a negotiable instrument; personal defenses are not available against such a holder. We affirm since we are satisfied that the defense presented is not a 'real' defense.

"Defendant argues that since the transaction which resulted in the execution and delivery of defendant's note was engaged in by Kroyden in violation of the injunctive order, the transaction was 'illegal and thus a nullity. . . .'

"However, the fact that it was illegal for Kroyden to enter into the transaction did not by reason of that fact render defendant's obligation under the note she executed a nullity.

"On the contrary, as noted in the New Jersey Study Comment on N.J.S.A. 12A:3–305(2)(b):

> In New Jersey, a holder in due course takes free and clear of the defense of illegality, unless the statute which declares the act illegal also indicates that payment thereunder is void. . . . Where no such statute is involved, it has been held that a negotiable instrument which is rooted in an illegal transaction or stems from a transaction prohibited by statute or public policy is no reason for refusing to enforce the instrument in the hands of a holder in due course. . . .

"There being no statute ordaining that a note obtained in violation of an injunction is void or unenforceable, the illegality involved is not a 'real' defense; the note is enforceable in the hands of a holder in due course who had no knowledge or notice of the injunction."

■ REAL DEFENSES

Article 3's main list of real defenses is found in Section 3–305. In addition, 3–404 (unauthorized signatures) and 3–407 (alteration) describe real defenses.

Unauthorized Signature or Forgery. When someone signs your name to an instrument without your permission, you're not liable, even to an HDC. The result is the same whether your name is simply forged or whether it is signed with an indication of agency authority which doesn't exist. The section says that this unauthorized signature is "wholly inoperative" against you unless you ratify it or are estopped by your conduct from denying its validity. It is, however, effective to impose full liability on the instrument against the forger, in favor of someone who pays or takes the instrument in good faith.

Forged signature = No liability

Material Alteration. Where the contract of any party to an instrument has been changed "in any respect" by an alteration, Section 3–407 says that the alteration is material. If this material alteration is also fraudulent, the party whose contract is changed is discharged from further liability on the instrument unless that person assents to the change or is estopped from asserting it. As the one exception to this rule, an HDC can still enforce the instrument "according to its original tenor"; that is, the terms prior to the alteration. A nonmaterial or nonfraudulent alteration does not discharge any party.

HDC gets only original amount

As an example of these rules, if you signed a blank check and lost it, and the finder filled in $600 as the amount, an HDC could force you to pay the $600. If you signed a check and filled it in for $6.00 and someone found or stole the check and altered it to read $600, an HDC could force you to pay only the original $6.00. However, if you filled in the amount spaces with blanks after the number 6 and the word *Six*, so that the thief or finder could very easily add "oo" and "Hundred," you would be estopped from asserting the alteration and would have to pay the full $600.

In the *Thomas* case, the court is trying to decide whether the language added to the note is a "material alteration" of it.

THOMAS v. OSBORN

536 P.2d 8 (Washington, 1975)

FACTS
William Thomas sued to collect on a note executed by James and Bernice Osborn for $2,000, given in settlement of a dispute over the value of a redwood table and over claims for certain other work. The note was dated October 30, 1969, and was due one year later, subject to an acceleration clause which provided that if a certain described piece of real estate was sold before the due date, the note would become immediately payable. To make sure that any third-party buyer of the land knew about his claim against the Osborns, Thomas had the note recorded in the real estate records. To do so, he had a notary public write on an acknowledgment of James Osborn's signature and notarize it. Since the note was recorded, it was also so stamped by a clerk in the recorder's office. The trial court held for the plaintiff, and the Osborns appealed.

ISSUE
Did the acknowledgment, notarization, and recording stamp operate as material alterations, so as to discharge the Osborns from liability?

DECISION
No. Judgment affirmed.

REASONS
Judge Callow quickly disposed of the Osborns' claim that the table wasn't worth $2,000 and that there was no consideration for the note. It had been given in settlement of this dispute, he said. He then examined their argument that the recording of the note had added the relationship of mortgagor-mortgagee to that of maker-payee and thus constituted a material alteration.

"Ostensibly, the terms of the note include the legal description of the real property for the purpose of inserting an acceleration provision into the note. This is the apparent reason for the presence of the property description since the terms provide for payment in full on sale of the property rather than granting a security interest which might be looked to for recourse in the event of a default in payment. . . . The note was not ambiguous when it was signed by the makers, and it does not purport either a purpose to convey or to encumber the property. . . . The note does not contain the expression of an intent to impose a lien upon the property. . . .

"We conclude that neither the recording of the instrument nor the addition of the addendum to the instrument changed the relationship of the parties, materially affected the form of the document, the time of payment, or the sum payable. The alteration did not attempt to acquire for the payee any funds to which he was not entitled. . . .

"The actions of the parties here are best characterized by the term 'misguided.' The trial court did not find a dishonest, fraudulent intent in the payee, and the chaotic dealings of the parties reveal that their understanding of the legal ramifications of their actions was limited. While the plaintiff attempted to overreach his position as payee by his effort to achieve security for payment of the debt, his ineffective attempt was not such a fraudulent intent to achieve something to which he was not entitled as would justify excusing the liability of the makers and granting them a windfall."

Minority.   Although minority or infancy generally results in a voidable obligation rather than a void one, Section 3–305 makes it a real defense to liability on a negotiable instrument. Infancy is a defense to the same extent that it would be against liability on a simple contract. In other words, infancy can be asserted against an HDC. On the other hand, since this section distinguishes between "defenses" and "claims" and states that an HDC owns the instrument free of *all* adverse ownership claims, the minor cannot get back the instrument that he or she signed. Remember that the indorsement sections make the minor's indorsement fully effective to transfer ownership of the instrument, so that there can be later HDCs in the chain of title.

Minor not liable

Other Incapacity.   As to other types of contractual incapacity, 3–305 makes these a real defense only if they void the contract (render "the obligation of the party a nullity"). This rule thus refers us to the applicable state law on insanity, aliens, married women, and so on, as discussed in Chapter 13. Unauthorized acts by corporations or governmental agencies which resulted in the issuance of negotiable instruments would probably also fall into this category.

Void-Type Duress.   Duress may be either a real or a personal defense, depending on whether it results in a void or a voidable obligation. "Gun-to-the-head" duress "renders the obligation of the party a nullity" and can thus be asserted against an HDC. The "threat-of-criminal-prosecution" type of duress would make a contract only voidable, not void, and thus it cannot be asserted against an HDC.

Forced signature = No liability

Void-Type Illegality.   Where some part of a transaction violates a criminal statute, the state's statutory and case law may make the contract involved either void or voidable. Section 3–305 again refers us to these state law distinctions to see whether the particular illegality is a real or only a personal defense. The following case illustrates how the courts will try to make this determination.

COMMERCIAL BANK & TRUST CO. v. MIDDLE GEORGIA LIVESTOCK SALES

182 S.E.2d 533 (Georgia, 1971)

FACTS   Middle Georgia bought some stolen cattle at an auction sale and paid for them with a check. When it learned that the cattle were stolen, it ordered its bank to stop payment on the check. Meanwhile, the plaintiff bank had cashed the check for the seller. When payment was refused by the drawee bank, the plaintiff bank sued the drawer, Middle Georgia. Middle Georgia appealed from the trial court's decision against it.

ISSUE   Did the fact that the consideration given for the check was stolen make the drawer's obligation a nullity?

DECISION   Yes. Judgment reversed.

REASONS   The court first indicated that the case must be decided by local state law, and it cited UCC 3–305(2)(b).

"The case then turns on the question of whether the sale of the stolen [cattle] . . ., presuming the seller possessed guilty knowledge of the fact but the buyer did not, represents an 'illegal consideration' so as to render it absolutely void. 'A contract to do an immoral or illegal thing is void.' . . . A sale of stolen goods, although to a bona fide purchaser for value, cannot transfer any lawful interest in the property and does not divest the title of the true owner.

"Knowingly disposing of stolen property is . . . a type of theft and a statutory offense. Being prohibited by statute, it is an illegal transaction within the meaning of Code Ann. 190A–3–305(2)(b). . . . This accords with the decisions of our courts. In *Smith* v. *Wood,* 36S.E.649, it was held: 'A note given for something . . . which the law absolutely prohibits and makes penal is based upon an illegal consideration, and is consequently void in the hands of any holder thereof. The thing for which the note is given is outlawed, and the note standing upon such a foundation is outlawed also.' . . .

"It follows that the note is unenforceable even in the hands of a holder in due course, and the trial court erred in granting summary judgment for the plaintiff."

Fraud in the Execution.   The most obvious example of fraud in the execution occurs when the nature of the instrument itself is misrepresented. You are told you're merely signing a receipt for delivery of merchandise, or an authorization form for repairs on your car, but the document is folded, or covered, or switched, so that you can't see it's really a negotiable instrument. The section also extends this defense to the case where you *do* know you're signing a negotiable instrument but you don't have a reasonable opportunity to obtain knowledge of its "essential terms." In either of these cases, you must show that your ignorance of the character and terms of the instrument was "excusable ignorance"—in other words, that you acted reasonably under the circumstances. This is a fact question, depending on such things as the signer's age, education, business experience, and literacy; the nature of the representations made to the signer and the signer's reasons for relying on them; the availability of independent information; and the need to act quickly. If your ignorance was "excusable," you have a real defense, good even as against an HDC; otherwise, you don't.

Discharge in Bankruptcy.   Section 3–305 also spells out a result that should be obvious anyway: the debtor's discharge in bankruptcy or other insolvency proceedings can be asserted against anyone, even the HDC of a negotiable instrument signed by the debtor.

Notice of Other Discharge.   A holder can't qualify as an HDC after taking the instrument with notice that *all* parties have been discharged. But it's possible to become an HDC with notice that one or more parties have been discharged, as long as there's no notice that *all* have been. The holder then qualifies as an HDC as to the remaining parties, but can't collect against the ones known to have been discharged when the instrument was transferred. Discharge of an indorser by canceling his or her signature would be a typical example of this rule. The HDC couldn't collect against that indorser, but would still be an HDC as to all the remaining parties.

No intent to sign NI = No liability

▪ PERSONAL DEFENSES

Since Section 3–305 says that an HDC can enforce an instrument free of "all defenses except" those listed, any other defense against liability on the instrument is only a personal defense. Section 3–306 lists some of these personal defenses.

Ordinary Contract Defenses.   Any defense a party could assert in a simple contract suit can be asserted against anyone who does not have the rights of an HDC. This general rule would include such things as undue influence, breach of contract by the plaintiff (including any counterclaim by the defendant), and setoffs which the defendant might have from unrelated transactions.

Consideration Defenses.   Section 3–306 mentions "want or failure of consideration" specifically because there is an initial presumption that the negotiable instrument was issued for legally sufficient consideration. If it was not, or if the promised consideration was not properly delivered, the burden of proving the defense is on the defendant. These consideration defenses are only personal ones, and thus they can't be used against an HDC.

Voidable Defenses.   Tying back into Section 3–305, any defense based on lack of capacity, duress, or illegality which does not "render the obligation of the party a nullity" (void) is only a personal defense. Remember that minority is a real defense even though the minor's contracts are voidable rather than void.

Fraud in the Inducement.   In contrast to fraud in the execution, fraud in the inducement, which is the typical fraud case, provides only a personal defense. Here the party does know that he or she is entering into a contract but is deceived as to the consideration to be received or the other terms and conditions of the contract. The following case shows that fraud in the inducement also exists where a party could *reasonably* have discovered the nature of the contract that was signed, but simply didn't bother to read it. The contract was misrepresented, but on the facts there's only a personal defense, and so the HDC collects. Since the Burchetts and the Beevers are consumers, the result in this case would have been reversed under the new FTC regulations.

BURCHETT v. ALLIED CONCORD FINANCIAL CORPORATION

396 P.2d 186 (New Mexico, 1964)

FACTS

John and Connie Burchett and Harold and Marie Beevers bought an aluminum siding job on their homes from a man named Kelly, who represented Consolidated Products of Roswell. In each case, Kelly promised that the buyers would receive a $100 credit off the price of their job for each other customer who signed up after seeing these "demonstration homes." Kelly said that the Burchetts and the Beevers would in effect be getting their own jobs for nothing. While these buyers were reading the contract forms given to them by Kelly, he was busy filling out other forms. In each case, these buyers signed the filled-in forms without reading them, although they had never seen

Kelly before. The signed, filled-in forms were notes and mortgages against the homes as security for the notes. Although the work was done, these buyers were not completely satisfied with the jobs, and there was nothing in the signed contracts about $100 credits. Consolidated negotiated the notes and assigned the mortgages to Allied Concord, an HDC. The trial court held the notes void, and Allied Concord appealed.

ISSUE Does the fraud involved here make the notes totally void?

DECISION No. Judgment reversed.

 REASONS **Judge Carmody's opinion started with UCC 3–305(2)(c) and its key phrase, "reasonable opportunity to obtain knowledge." He then cited Official Comment 7 to this section, which discusses "excusable ignorance" and the facts which may be considered in deciding whether there was reasonable care exercised by the party signing the instrument. He decided that in this case the reliance on Kelly's representations was not reasonable.**

"We recognize that the reasonable opportunity to obtain knowledge may be excused if the maker places reasonable reliance on the representations. The difficulty in the instant case is that the reliance upon the representations of a complete stranger (Kelly) was not reasonable, and all of the parties were of sufficient age, intelligence, education, and business experience to know better. In this connection, it is noted that the contracts clearly stated, on the same page which bore the signatures of the various appellees, the following: No one is authorized on behalf of this company to represent this job to be 'A SAMPLE HOME OR A FREE JOB.'

"Although we have sympathy with the appellees, we cannot allow it to influence our decision. They were certainly victimized, but because of their failure to exercise ordinary care for their own protection, an innocent party cannot be made to suffer."

Delivery Defenses. Numerous cases involve irregularities in the delivery or completion of an instrument. Where an instrument has been signed or indorsed in bearer form, the fact that it has been negotiated by a thief or finder will not prevent a later party from being an HDC and collecting on the instrument.

Irregularity in delivery or completion = Personal defense

The fact that you just signed your check as drawer, intending to fill in the payee's name and the amount later, and that the check was completed by the thief or finder, won't change this result; the HDC still collects. An HDC would also collect where you signed a check and delivered it to your intended payee with instructions to fill in the amount you owed, but your payee filled it in for a larger, unauthorized amount. Finally, an HDC is also protected where a check has been properly filled in and delivered, but delivered subject to some oral condition which is not expressed in the instrument. If the condition is not fulfilled, a defense exists which could be asserted only against someone not having the rights of an HDC.

Agency Defenses. Where someone signing on behalf of a corporation, a partnership, or an individual has general authority to sign negotiable instruments, the fact that a particular instrument was improperly signed is only a personal defense.

■ **EXHIBIT 30–1**
Defenses—All Defenses Good

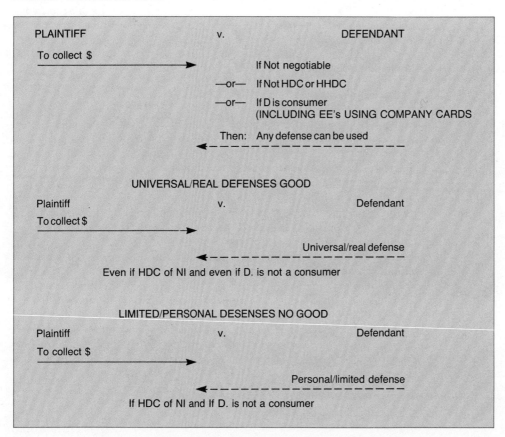

PLAINTIFF   v.   DEFENDANT

To collect $

           If Not negotiable

—or— If Not HDC or HHDC

—or— If D is consumer
(INCLUDING EE's USING COMPANY CARDS

Then: Any defense can be used

UNIVERSAL/REAL DEFENSES GOOD

Plaintiff   v.   Defendant

To collect $

Universal/real defense

Even if HDC of NI and even if D. is not a consumer

LIMITED/PERSONAL DESENSES NO GOOD

Plaintiff   v.   Defendant

To collect $

Personal/limited defense

If HDC of NI and If D. is not a consumer

■ **FTC REGULATION**

Consumer debtor = All defenses can be used

After the early 1970s court decisions that the FTC could issue rules with industrywide application, the FTC has been much more vigorous in the consumer protection field. One of the most important and widely discussed FTC rules relates to the HDC status of holders of consumer installment sales contracts. This rule, Regulation 433, was previously discussed in Chapters 16 and 25. It applies to a consumer's purchase or lease of goods with a price of $25,000 or less. Consumer purchases over that amount are subject to normal HDC rules. Regulation 433 does not apply to payments made by check, nor to purchases of land or securities.

While the rule does not say so in so many words, the net effect is that in most cases all of a consumer's defenses are real defenses. Likewise, no waiver-of-defenses clause in an installment contract for the purchase of goods or services is effective against the consumer-buyer. Holders and assignees are thus remitted to their position under the old common law: The assignee "steps into the shoes of the assignor" and is subject to all available defenses that the debtor can prove. While the exact dimensions of this FTC rule are still subject to litigation, revolving charge accounts (such as a Sears charge account) signed before August 1, 1977, and credit card accounts have been exempted from its operation.

▪ ESTOPPEL

Negligence may = Liability

It has been, and still is, true that a person with a claim or defense may be estopped by his or her conduct from asserting it. This is as true of real defenses as of personal defenses. If you typically signed your checks with a rubber stamp, and you lost the stamp and didn't bother to alert your bank, you probably ought to get stuck when your bank continues to honor the checks that someone else has prepared in your name with your lost signature stamp. Estoppel clearly applies where you have made out your check or note in such a way as to permit alteration very easily (large, inviting gaps after words and numbers, for example). A more interesting question for litigation is whether persons as gullible as the Burchetts and the Beevers ought to be permitted to assert the new FTC rule to avoid liability on the notes they signed, under circumstances similar to the fact pattern in that case.

▪ DISCHARGE

Discharge by payment not effective vs. later HDC

In addition to the defenses discussed above and the conditions precedent to indorsers' liability discussed in Chapter 29, parties may be discharged from liability on an instrument in several other ways.

Payment. The most obvious and most frequent method of discharge is payment of the instrument to the holder. Perhaps the most important rule for most of us is found in Section 3–802(1)(b): "unless otherwise agreed, where an instrument is taken for an underlying obligation . . . discharge of the underlying obligor on the instrument also discharges him on the obligation." In other words, when your check is paid by your bank, you are both discharged of liability on the check and liability on the underlying debt for which it was given as payment. The one danger point here is that this discharge is not effective against a later HDC of the instrument if the HDC does not have notice of it. If you pay your promissory note, but you don't get it back from the holder, and there's no indication on it that it has been paid or that it's overdue, a later HDC could make you pay it again.

Tender of Payment. Where payment is offered to a holder on or after the due date of the instrument and the holder refuses payment for some reason, the party offering full payment is discharged only to the extent of any additional interest, court costs, or attorney fees later incurred. This rule also applies where the maker or acceptor of a nondemand instrument is ready and able to make payment on the due date at the place or places specified in the instrument, and payment is not demanded by the holder. The holder's refusal of tender "wholly discharges" any party who has a right of recourse against the party making the tender.

Simple Contract Discharge. As between themselves, any two parties can agree that the liability of one to the other is discharged by any mechanism which is sufficient to discharge liability on a simple contract. All the forms of new agreements discussed in Chapter 17 also apply here: novation, rescission, release, waiver, and accord and satisfaction. Once again, no HDC unaware of these new arrangements is bound by them.

Cancellation or Renunciation. As a special negotiable instruments rule, Section 3–605 provides that any holder may discharge any party from further liability on an instrument by destruction or mutilation of the instrument, by canceling the party's signature, by surrendering the instrument to the party, or by a separate writing signed and delivered to the party. All of these but the last would seem to be sufficient to put third parties on notice of the discharge.

Reacquisition Rules. Because of the very special nature of indorsers' liability, Section 3–208 provides some specific rules for the discharge of intermediate parties where someone reacquires an instrument. As against the reacquirer, such parties are discharged. If Arnie, Bernice, and Carole have signed an instrument as indorsers and Arnie reacquires it, he can't sue Bernice or Carole. Arnie could, however, renegotiate the instrument to Donald, who could sue Bernice or Carole if he qualified as an HDC. On the other hand, if Arnie crossed out the signatures of Bernice and Carole, Donald would be on notice that they had been discharged and so he could not sue them either.

Suretyship Rules. As is true under the law of suretyship generally (see Chapter 24), a holder of an obligation who impairs someone's rights of recourse or repayment from another person discharges the party whose rights are impaired. In the above example, if Donald had crossed out Bernice's signature, he would have discharged her from liability on the instrument, thus impairing Carole's rights against Bernice, and so Carole would have also been discharged. A holder can avoid such an "automatic discharge" by expressly reserving rights against the other party (Carole), but when he (Donald) does so, that has the effect of preserving the right of secondary recourse (by Carole against Bernice). Donald can say: "I won't sue Bernice, but I reserve my right to sue Carole." This also preserves Carole's right to sue Bernice if Carole has to pay Donald.

Likewise, where some piece of property is being used as collateral for an obligation, and through the negligence or intentional conduct of the holder its value is lessened or lost, secondary parties are discharged to that extent.

Discharge of prior party = Discharge of parties who had recourse versus that party

---

■ **SIGNIFICANCE OF THIS CHAPTER**

Even HDCs will not necessarily collect every instrument from any party whose name appears on it. Some defenses, such as forgery and material alteration, involve such fundamental irregularities that they can be used against any plaintiff, including an HDC. Others, such as fraud in the inducement, are primarily just difficulties between two of the parties to the instrument, and should not be available when an HDC sues to enforce the instrument. Under FTC Regulation 433, consumers are generally able to assert any defense which they can prove, to defeat or reduce the claim of any plaintiff. For nonconsumers who have signed negotiable instruments, the distinction between real and personal defenses continues to be important.

In addition to defenses against liability which may be available, both claimants and obligors need to know the circumstances under which an existing liability may be discharged. Here, too, an HDC may be prevented from collecting the instrument from a particular party because that party's liability has been discharged.

DISCUSSION CASE

EXCHANGE INTERNATIONAL LEASING CORP. v. CONSOLIDATED BUSINESS FORMS CO.

462 F.Supp. 626 (Pennsylvania, 1978)

FACTS: Plaintiff, Exchange International Leasing Corporation, brought the instant suit to recover rental payments from defendant, Consolidated Business Forms, arising out of defendant's leasing of a Phillips business computer. Plaintiff is the named lessor of said computer by virtue of an assignment from the original lessor, third party defendant, Northern Leasing and Financial Corporation.

The aforesaid assignment conferred upon plaintiff the status of a holder in due course under Section 3–302 of the Uniform Commercial Code and the defendant's only plausible defense was misrepresentation under Section 3–305(2)(c). The matter now before the court is plaintiff's second motion for summary judgment in which it claims that no genuine issue of misrepresentation exists. After several weeks of discussion and correspondence with fourth party defendant, Benchmark Systems, Inc., a Pittsburgh area sales representative for third party defendant, Phillips Business Systems, Inc., Consolidated decided to acquire a Phillips computer. Because Consolidated was not in the position to purchase the $25,000 computer outright, a 66-month lease-purchase was arranged. Northern Leasing, not Phillips or Benchmark, was the lessor of the equipment under a lease signed on November 22, 1974. The lease contained a common waiver-of-defense clause, which stated essentially that rental obligations were not conditioned on the fulfilling of any express or implied warranties. Northern assigned the lease to Exchange in April 1975. Exchange subsequently instituted this suit alleging that shortly after the assignment Consolidated defaulted in its rental payments.

Consolidated filed an answer in which it claimed that its rental obligations had been excused by the breach of certain performance guarantees made to it by Benchmark during negotiations. In ruling on an earlier motion for summary judgment by Exchange, however, Judge Knox

of this court ruled that this defense was not available to Consolidated, since Exchange was a holder in due course within the meaning of Section 3–302 of the UCC and that therefore, Consolidated could only avail itself of the defenses enumerated in Section 3–305 of the UCC. Of those 3–305 defenses, the one contained in subsection (2)(c) dealing with misrepresentation was raised by Consolidated. Exchange had also sought summary disposition of the 3–305(2)(c) defense, but Judge Knox denied summary judgment in that regard for the reason that the record was insufficient to permit the conclusion that no genuine issue of material fact existed as to the 3–305(2)(c) claim.

Following the denial of summary judgment, Exchange incorporated into the record the deposition of one James E. Spohn, Chairman of the Board of Consolidated. Spohn was the Consolidated representative who negotiated for the acquisition of the Phillips computer and who also signed the lease with Exchange's predecessor-in-interest, Northern. Exchange then filed the instant motion for summary judgment, contending that Spohn's deposition sufficiently augmented the record to remove any genuine issue of fact concerning misrepresentation under 3–305(2)(c).

■

District Judge Diamond:

[T]o establish the defense, one must not only have had no knowledge of a document's character or essential terms, but also have had "reasonable opportunity" to acquire such knowledge. Comment 7 to 3–305 elaborates by stating that in determining what constitutes a "reasonable opportunity" factors such as the age, intelligence, and business experience of the signator, his ability to read

English, and the representations made to him and his reason to rely on them are to be considered.

The reported Pennsylvania decisions interpreting 3–305(2)(c) while few in number are nonetheless uniform in holding that only fraud in the factum, as opposed to fraud in the inducement, is a defense under 3–305. This view is in accord with Comment 7 and also the view expressed by certain scholars in the area.

As Comment 7 notes, the classic example of fraud in the factum is that of a person who is tricked into signing a note on the pretense that it is a mere receipt of some sort. Pennsylvania is apparently hesitant to expand the defense and afford relief to less obvious victims. . . .

With the foregoing in mind we consider the specific misrepresentations relied on by Consolidated. In its brief Consolidated contends that "Mr. Spohn was precluded from examining the contents of the agreement by the representations made to him" by employees of Phillips and Benchmark. Although defendant's brief does not disclose the specifics of those representations, Spohn's deposition indicates that they were in the nature of assurances that the computer would be removed with a complete refund if it failed to function properly. Spohn testified that the Benchmark representative with whom he was most actively involved, the person who suggested the lease arrangement and who was present for its signing, one Steve O'Connor, "assured me at all times that the guarantee was in force." . . . Spohn referred to two other statements "guaranteeing" the computer, both of which were made shortly after he initially approached Benchmark in regard to a possible purchase. One statement was made orally at a trade show by the president of Benchmark . . . , while the other was contained in a promotional brochure signed by another officer of Benchmark. . . .

Assuming without deciding that the statements referred to by Spohn could form the basis of a misrepresentation, nevertheless the court is of the opinion that no genuine issue exists as to the presence of a 3–305(2)(c) defense. For, even if it be true that Spohn did not have actual knowledge of the essential terms of the lease, it can hardly be said that he lacked a "reasonable opportunity" to acquire that knowledge—an essential element of a 3–305(2)(c)

defense. Spohn testified unequivocally that O'Connor in no way prevented him from reading the instrument before he signed it . . . , that he could have read the document in its entirety had he so desired . . . , and that he was not busy or otherwise distracted at the time of execution. . . . Spohn further testitifed that he read part of the lease but simply chose not to read the "fine print" because he had trust in O'Connor. . . .

The court notes that while the waiver-of-defense clause was not in boldface print, it was not inconspicuously buried in the document either. It appeared on the cover page of the lease immediately between the identification-of-the-transaction and the signatory portions of the instrument. The court further observes that there were three "fine print" clauses on the cover sheet and that, of the three, the waiver-of-defense clause was the most prominent. Considering all of these factors, the court concludes that there is no genuine issue of fact concerning the reason for Spohn's ignorance of the essential character and terms of the instrument which he executed on behalf of Consolidated. It was purely a matter of his choice not to read that which was readily and conveniently available for him to read.

Consolidated argues for a contrary result by emphasizing that portion of Comment 7 which states that in determining what constitutes a "reasonable opportunity" one is to consider the representations made to the signator and "his reason to rely on them or to have confidence in the person making them." The court does not find this argument persuasive because it simply ignores the other facts to be considered in determining whether one had reasonable opportunity to obtain knowledge of the instrument's character and essential terms. When these other factors, viz., age, intelligence, business experience, ability to read the document, necessity for acting speedily, are considered in the light of Spohn's deposition it is clear that there is no legal justification for the blind reliance which Spohn contends he had on the statements of O'Connor.

An appropriate order will be entered granting plaintiff's motion for summary judgment.

■ IMPORTANT TERMS AND CONCEPTS

defense against liability
voidable-type defense
personal/limited defense
holder through holder in
   due course (HHDC)
unauthorized signature

estoppel to assert defense
incapacity to make
   contract
illegality
fraud in the inducement
notice of discharge

consideration defenses
agency defenses
discharge
tender of payment
cancellation or renunciation
suretyship rules
void-type defense
real/universal defense

holder in due course
   (HDC)
forgery
material alteration
minority
duress
fraud in the execution
discharge in bankruptcy

ordinary contract defenses
delivery defenses
FTC regulation

payment of instrument
simple contract discharge
reacquisition rules

■ QUESTIONS AND PROBLEMS FOR DISCUSSION

1. What is the difference between a real defense and a personal defense?
2. Why is an unauthorized signature or a forgery a real defense for the party whose name was improperly signed?
3. Why is minority a real defense?
4. Why is it possible for illegality or duress to be either a real defense or a personal defense?
5. Sopel executed a promissory note in favor of Inenbe Bank for $8,000. He defaulted on the note, and Inenbe filed suit to collect the principal amount, interest, court costs, and attorney's fees (total due $10,000), as provided in the note. Sopel admitted that the note was in default but said that he had talked to one of the bank's officers about it and that the officer had told him that he could renew the note for the total amount due if he would give the bank a mortgage on certain real estate he owned. Sopel says that he has offered to deliver such a mortgage, but the bank now wants to enforce the original note. Should the bank be able to sue on the original note? Why or why not?
6. Carol Bolivia contracted to have certain improvements made on the building in which she operated a beauty shop. Myron Huxter, the builder, told Carol that he had already purchased most of the materials for the job and that he needed a $2,500 down payment so that he could rent the equipment that he needed to do the work. Myron cashed the check that afternoon at the Boring Bank. Meanwhile, Carol discovered that Myron had not in fact purchased any materials for her job and was planning to leave town. Carol told her drawee bank, the Worthy Bank, not to pay the check when it was presented. When Boring didn't get paid by Worthy, Boring sued Carol. What is the result, and why?
7. Larry Cobb executed and delivered to Security Bank a promissory note for $10,000, payment of which was secured by 80 acres of growing corn. The note was cosigned by I. M. Earnest as an accommodation party. Because Security Bank failed to identify the land on which the corn was growing in the financing statement which it filed, it lost its right against the corn to another creditor of Larry's. Security Bank now sues Earnest. What arguments can Earnest make against being held liable on this note? Will he be liable? Explain.
8. Herman wrote a note for $9,000 to pay certain gambling debts he had incurred. The payee on the note, Sharpie, transferred the note to his bank, Enbede, for value prior to its maturity date. When Enbede Bank sued Herman to collect the $9,000, he claimed that the note was void because it was issued in payment of gambling debts. Is this a valid argument? Why or why not? Would the result change if gambling were legal in this state?

31

Bank Deposits and Collections

CHAPTER OBJECTIVES
THIS CHAPTER WILL:

- Explain the process of collecting checks through the banking system.
- Define the various types of banks involved in this process, as covered in UCC, Article 4.
- Explain the relationship between the depositor and the depositary bank.
- Discuss the relationship between the depositor and the payor bank.
- Indicate when a drawee bank may charge its customer's account.
- Discuss a bank's liability to its customer for wrongful dishonor of an item properly payable.
- Alert the reader to the importance of electronic funds transfers.

UCC rules for banks and customers

Commercial banking in the United States is a huge industry. The nation's 10,000-plus commercial banks hold over $1 *trillion* in assets. Banks fund many business purchases of land, buildings, and equipment and provide many other services to business. The banking industry has been subjected to considerable governmental regulation, but the 1980s have seen a movement toward deregulation of many banking operations. This chapter will not attempt to cover all of the various banking regulations but will focus instead on Article 4 of the UCC, Bank Deposits and Collections. Article 4 sets out the basic legal rules for the relationship between a bank and its customers and for the processing of negotiable (and nonnegotiable) instruments.

■ CHECKS: THE COLLECTION PROCESS

Clearinghouses and Federal Reserve Banks. The next time you get back a canceled check that you've sent to an out-of-state creditor (a book club or a record club, for example), look at the back of it. All of those funny, multicolored stamps indicate that your humble little check has passed through several banks, and been processed by goodness knows how many computers on its way back to you.

If both the payee and the drawer do business at the same bank, the collection process is quite simple: out of one account and into the other. If both are in the same city, but are customers of different banks, a local clearinghouse association of banks probably handles the collection of the check. At the end of each business day, if a bank has presented more (total dollar) items for payment than have been presented against, it gets a check for the difference from the clearinghouse. If the reverse is true, it writes a check for the total dollar difference to the clearinghouse.

Collection of out-of-town items

Many *correspondent bank* arrangements also exist for collecting checks and other items, particularly between large metropolitan banks and smaller banks in the same region. The small local bank receiving a check for collection would forward it to its large correspondent bank, which would in turn present it directly to the payor bank or would forward it through one of the 13 federal reserve banks if the payor bank were located in a different federal reserve district.

Your check to your out-of-state creditor might pass through a local bank, a large nearby metropolitan bank, a federal reserve bank in that district, a federal reserve bank in your district, a large metropolitan bank close to your bank, and finally get presented at your bank for payment (by which time you had better have the money in your account). Over $50 million worth of checks is probably "floating" through this national collection process on any given day. It's therefore obvious that banks (and their customers) need a set of legal rules to ensure that this process goes smoothly.

Definitions of different banks in the collection process

Banks under Article 4. To better spell out the rights and duties of banks in the collection process, Article 4 defines different categories of banks according to their function in the various stages of that process. A *depositary bank* is "the first bank to which an item is transferred for collection even though it is also the payor bank." (The depositor, usually the payee/creditor of the drawer, or possibly a later holder of the instrument, takes the item to his or her bank and either cashes it or deposits it.)

The *payor bank* is the bank "by which an item is payable as drawn or accepted." (In the simplest case, where both the drawer and the "depositor" have accounts at the same bank, no other banks will be involved.) An *intermediary bank* is any bank "to which an item is transferred in course of collection except the depositary or payor bank." (In our earlier example, the correspondent banks and the federal reserve banks would be intermediary banks.)

Where the depositary bank is not also the payor bank, it and all intermediary banks are also called *collecting banks.* (They're collecting, or trying to collect, your paycheck for you.) The last bank in the collection process, the one that actually presents the item to the payor/drawee for payment, is called the *presenting bank.* (A payor bank presenting the item to itself is excluded from this definition.) Finally when the instrument is honored and the banks actually get the money (or a credit), all the banks passing the money back up the line to the depositary bank are called *remitting banks.* (This definition includes the payor bank, since it is the source of the funds and is remitting them to pay the instrument.)

■ DEPOSITOR AND DEPOSITARY BANK

Bank as agent of depositor

Agency Relationship. In the normal transaction, the depositor remains the owner of the check or other item which is being processed for collection by his or her bank. This rule protects the depositary and intermediary banks by leaving all the risks of ownership of the item with the depositor; all the banks in the collection process are protected so long as they exercise reasonable care in processing the item. This basic rule applies unless there is a clear agreement otherwise, regardless of the form of the indorsement or of the fact that the depositor is permitted to make withdrawals against these funds.

When deposits can be withdrawn

Withdrawals of Deposited Funds. A cash deposit can be withdrawn "as a matter of right" at the opening of the next banking day following its receipt by the bank unless the bank has the right to offset the deposited funds against amounts owed it by the depositor/customer. Where the deposit is in the form of a check or other instrument, however, the credit to the customer's account is only *provisional;* that is, the credit is subject to revocation if the instrument is not honored when it is presented to the drawee bank. The depositor/customer thus does not have the right to withdraw these funds until the depositary bank has received a "final settlement" for the item. Where the depositary bank is also the payor bank and the item is paid from the drawer's account, the depositor/customer has the right to withdraw the funds at the opening of the second banking day following receipt of the item.

Local check = $ in one day

Expedited Funds Availability Act. Congress passed the EFAA in 1987, to shorten the time period between the deposit of a check (or other item) and the availability of the dollars the check represents. The Federal Reserve Board has divided the country into check-processing regions. Any deposited check which is payable at another bank in the same region is a "local" check. As of September 1, 1990, the money from a local check must be available to the customer within *one* business day from the day of deposit. For checks drawn against banks outside the depositary bank's region, the funds must be available to the customer within four business days of the deposit.

Other one-day items

There is also a one day rule for cash deposits, wire transfers of money, certified checks, cashier's checks, government checks, checks drawn on branches of the same bank, and the first $100 of a day's check deposits. (The balance of a nonlocal, ordinary check would have to be available within the four business days specified by the general rule.)

Exceptions

Longer delay periods are permitted for more unusual transactions, or in special circumstances. Deposits made at automated teller machines which are not owned or operated by the depositary bank need not be made available for six days. Deposits in new accounts need not be available for eight days. The bank has an extra four days to verify deposits to accounts with repeated overdrafts, or where it suspects a check may not be collectible. It also has four extra days on deposits over $5,000, other than government or cashier's checks.

▪ CUSTOMER/ DEPOSITOR/ HOLDER (AND COLLECTING BANKS AS AGENTS) AND PAYOR BANKS

As between the holder of an instrument who is trying to collect on it and the payor/drawee bank that is supposedly going to pay it when it's presented, the most important rule is found in Article 3: "A check or other draft does not of itself operate as an assignment of any funds in the hands of the drawee available for its payment, and the drawee is not liable on the instrument until he accepts it" (3–409[1]). Even if the money is in the drawer's checking account, in other words, the drawee bank owes no direct duty to the holder to pay the instrument. The drawee bank may be liable to its customer, the drawer, for a wrongful dishonor of the instrument, as discussed below, but that does not mean that the holder/depositor has any direct claim against the payor bank.

Drawee bank owes no duty to holder

Obviously, a drawee bank which has certified a check or accepted a draft is primarily liable on it to the holder thereof and can be sued if it doesn't pay the check or draft when it is properly presented.

▪ CUSTOMER/ DEPOSITOR/ HOLDER AND DRAWEE

If a deposited item is not paid, for whatever reason, the holder who deposited the item for collection may proceed against the drawer on the basis of secondary contract liability, subject to the rules discussed in Chapter 29. In addition, the depositor/holder may have a case against one or more of the collecting banks, where their negligent mishandling of the instrument was the reason for its dishonor. However, a collecting bank is not liable solely on the basis of some *prior* bank's mishandling of the instrument; its own negligence must be established.

▪ DRAWER/ CUSTOMER AND DRAWEE/ PAYOR BANK

Article 4 also provides some detailed rules for handling the problems that may occur between a drawer and the drawee bank.

Charging Items against Customer's Account. The drawee bank has a general contractual duty to its drawer/customer to pay items when presented, assuming that there are sufficient funds in the account. As a general rule, when the

Drawee bank pays and charges customer's account

drawee bank does pay such items in good faith, it can charge the items against the customer's account. Even if an item causes an overdraft to a customer's account, the drawee/payor bank may honor the item anyway, and it has a claim against its customer for the amount of the *overdraft*.

The application of these overdraft rules to a joint account is discussed in the *McSweeney* case.

U.S. TRUST CO. OF NEW YORK v. McSWEENEY

457 N.Y.S.2d 276 (New York, 1982)

FACTS

Edward and Christine McSweeney, husband and wife, opened a joint checking account with the plaintiff bank in September 1976. Overdrafts commenced almost immediately, but the plaintiff regularly honored the checks. Edward gave the plaintiff two notes, totaling $181,000, to cover the overdrafts and some loans which the bank had made to him. The notes were given in April 1978. Between then and July 1978, when the account was closed, 195 checks were written, totalling $99,063.74. Christine wrote 95, totaling $16,811.43; Edward wrote 100, totaling $82,252.31. After deducting deposits to the account, the cumulative overdraft for this period was $75,983.06. The bank sued Edward on the two notes and sued both McSweeneys for the later overdrafts. The trial court gave summary judgment against Edward on both theories, but refused to enter summary judgment against Christine. Plaintiff bank appeals from this refusal.

ISSUE

Is one customer on a joint checking account liable for the overdrafts of the other?

DECISION

Perhaps, depending on the facts. Partial summary judgment entered against Christine for the $16,811.43 worth of checks which she herself wrote, and case remanded for trial.

REASONS

Justice Lynch turned first to UCC 4–401(1), which clearly permits a bank to honor a customer's overdrafts and to charge such payments against the account. Christine did not dispute her liability for the 95 checks she signed, but she said she should have been credited with a proportionate part of the deposits made during that period. The court dismissed this argument, since a creditor (the bank) may generally apply payments (the deposits) to either of two debts (Edward's or Christine's) where there is no specification as to which debt is to be credited.

On the main question of Christine's liability for Edward's overdrafts, the signature card was no help, since it did not contain any specific language.

"We find that, in the absence of a controlling provision in the account agreement, the liability of one cosignatory for the overdrafts of the other depends, as Special Term stated, upon the resolution of such issues as 'the knowledge of the cosignatory of the overdrafts, the degree of participation of the cosignatory in the day-to-day operations of the account, and the benefit allegedly derived by the cosignatory from the overdrafts'. . .

"Mrs. McSweeney would exculpate herself contending that her husband had complete control of the account and that she simply followed his directions. She also claims that many of the checks she wrote were of no benefit to her. These assertions, however, do nothing to change her status as a drawer, nor do they affect the liability to the bank that flows from that status. At best, they serve only to raise issues between the husband and wife that cannot be binding on the plaintiff."

Payment of overdrafts

The general rule for paying overdrafts is, however, subject to some important exceptions. The key phrase in Section 4-401 is "otherwise properly payable from that account." If the drawer's signature has been forged, the instrument is *not* "properly payable" from the drawer's account and the bank will have to put the money back even if it paid in good faith. The same result occurs where the required signature of an indorser is forged; the money must be returned to the drawer's account because the bank has not paid the right party. If the instrument has been materially altered, the bank which has paid it can charge the drawer's account only "according to the original tenor of his altered item." The drawer's own negligence may prevent the assertion of any of these irregularities against the drawee bank unless the bank was also negligent in paying the item; that is, the bank did not pay in good faith and according to reasonable commercial standards. Cairo Co-op raised these points in the next case.

CAIRO COOPERATIVE EXCHANGE v. FIRST NATIONAL BANK OF CUNNINGHAM

620 P.2d 805 (Kansas, 1980)

FACTS

K. C. Jones, the manager of Cairo's branch in Cunningham, was authorized to draw checks against Cairo's account. From September 30, 1969, to March 6, 1976, Jones drew 101 checks for various amounts to various customers of Cairo. Jones forged the customers' signatures on 10 of these checks and cashed them. As to these checks, Cairo made no claim for reimbursement from the bank. As to the other 91 checks, after forging the customers' indorsements, Jones used the co-op's own restrictive indorsement stamp, which read: "Pay to the order of First National Bank, Cunningham, Kansas. For Deposit Only, Cairo Co-op Equity Exchange, Farmer's Co-op." Jones got a total of $46,564.46 in cash at the bank for these checks. The trial court granted summary judgment for the bank, and Cairo appealed.

ISSUE

Is the bank guilty of conversion and/or failure to act in good faith and with reasonable care, in paying cash for checks which have been restrictively indorsed?

DECISION

Yes. Judgment reversed as to the 91 checks.

REASONS

Justice Herd reviewed the facts and the UCC provisions dealing with the effect of restrictive indorsements. He then stated that a "course of conduct" could not vary the duties imposed by a restrictive indorsement and to "monitor and investigate a series of irregular transactions." Further, he said that Jones could not modify the bank's obligations.

"We find no evidence to support modification. Jones and the bank entered in a contract commonly called a signature card. Nothing in that contract can be construed as an agreement to vary the application of K.S.A. 84–3–206(3). The only evidence of an agreement to vary is Jones' course of conduct. As we have previously indicated, good practice dictates that an agreement to vary a restrictive indorsement be in writing and noted on the instrument by a person with proper authority."

Wrongful Dishonor.   Whether mistakenly ("computer error") or intention-ally, the drawee bank may dishonor an instrument which it should have paid. When this happens, the drawer is at least temporarily embarrassed since his or her good credit is impugned when the check bounces. If this happens by an honest mistake, Article 4 protects the drawee bank by providing that the drawer can recover only damages which were "proximately caused" and "actually proved." There will be no punitive damages, in other words, for a simple mistake by the drawee bank. Further, the dishonor of a check is not per se defamation of a drawer's reputation, so that actual damages must be proved there, too. Finally, damages resulting from the arrest and prosecution of the drawer under an "insufficient funds" criminal statute may be recovered from the drawee bank *if* they are proved to have been proximately caused by the dishonor.

Actual damages for wrongful dishonor

Stop Payment Orders.   A check is an order by the customer/drawer to the drawee/payor bank to pay money to the order of the named payee. At least until the check is certified by the drawee bank, the drawer has the right to stop payment, in other words, to countermand the original order. An oral stop-pay order is valid for only 14 calendar days unless it is reconfirmed in writing within that period. A written stop-pay order is valid for six months unless it is similarly reconfirmed. In either case, the stop-pay order must be received by the drawee/payor bank "at such time and in such manner as to afford the bank a reasonable opportunity to act on it prior to any action by the bank with respect to the item."

Customer's right to stop payment

If the drawee/payor bank pays the item anyway, it can still charge its customer's account unless the customer can prove having suffered a loss as a result. (That would be the case, for example, where the customer had a defense which was valid against the holder, so that the holder really shouldn't have gotten the money. The bank would have to put that money back in its customer's account.) Obviously, once a check has been certified, the customer loses the right to stop payment.

The *FJS Electronics* case discusses the use of a bank's computer program to implement its customer's stop payment order.

FJS ELECTRONICS, INC. v. FIDELITY BANK

431 A.2d 326 (Pennsylvania, 1981)

FACTS

On February 27, 1976, FJS Electronics, Inc., trading as Multi-Teck, drew a check in the amount of $1,844.98 on Fidelity Bank. The number of the check was 896 and the payee was Multilayer Computer Circuits. On March 9, 1976, Mr. Frank Suttill, president of Multi-Teck, called Fidelity on the telephone and requested payment on check number 896 be stopped. Mrs. Roanna M. Sanders took the stop payment order. The amount given by Suttill was $1,844.48; otherwise the information he provided was essentially correct. A confirmation notice was subsequently sent to Multi-Teck, reciting the inaccurate amount, and Multi-Teck confirmed all the information it contained.

The confirmation notice also contained the request, "PLEASE ENSURE AMOUNT IS CORRECT."

The Bank used a computer to pull checks on which stop payment requests had been made. The computer keyed on the amount of the check which was typed in computer digits by the depository Bank on the bottom of each check. The Bank's computer program was designed so that all digits of the amount of the stop payment request had to agree with the computer digits of the amount on the bottom of the check before the check was pulled. The Bank's computer was not programmed to pull checks where there was a discrepancy in a digit of the amount of the stop payment request and the computer digits of the amount on the bottom of the check nor was it designed for stop payment purposes to read the number of the check. The Bank received approximately 100 to 150 stop payment requests a day during 1976.

On March 15, 1976, check No. 896 was paid by Fidelity, and Multi-Teck's account was charged. This charge resulted in a loss of $1,844.98 to Multi-Teck. The trial court held for Multi-Teck.

ISSUE

Did the customer's 50-cent error in the amount of the check on its stop-payment request excuse the Bank's failure to stop payment?

DECISION

No. Judgment affirmed.

REASONS

Chief Justice Haswell reviewed the U.C.C. rules:

"Section 4-403(1) of the Uniform Commercial Code addresses the problem of stop payment orders. . . . It is clear that the order here was timely received. The court below determined that even though it contained an error, the order was given in such manner as to give the bank a reasonable opportunity to act. Fidelity, in essence, asserts that the section should be read to require compliance with the procedures of a particular bank, regardless of what they are and regardless of whether the customer has been made aware of them. Fidelity argues that since its technique for ascertaining whether payment had been stopped required absolute accuracy as to the amount of a stopped check, this section would also require absolute precision in order for the notice to be reasonable. Such a narrow view is not consistent with the intent behind § 4-403, expressed in Comment 2 following the section:

> The position taken by this section is that stopping payment is a service which depositors expect and are entitled to receive from banks notwithstanding its difficulty, inconvenience, and expense. The inevitable occasional losses through failure to stop should be borne by the banks as a cost of the business of banking.

"Fidelity does not contend that it could not have used a technique which required less precision in the stop payment order. It does not contend that it could not have found the check had it used a more thorough system. It merely asserts that since it chose a system that searched only by amount, notice is not reasonable unless it conforms to the requirements of this system.

"Fidelity made a choice when it elected to employ a technique which searched for stopped checks by amounts alone. It evidently found benefits to this technique which outweighed the risk that an item might be inaccurately described in a stop order. This is precisely the type of inevitable loss which was contemplated by the code drafters and addressed by the comment quoted above. The focus of § 4-403 is the service which may be expected by the *customer,* and a customer may expect a check to be stopped after the bank is given reasonable notice. A bank's decision to reduce operating costs by using a system which increases the risk that checks as to which there is an outstanding stop payment order will be paid invites liability when such items are paid.

"An error of 50 cents in the amount of a stop payment order does not deprive the bank of a reasonable opportunity to act on the order. . . .

"Appellant further contends that appellee should bear the loss since it failed to ascertain whether check No. 896 had been paid before a replacement check had been issued. While . . . § 4403(c) places the burden of proof of loss on the customer, the purpose behind this requirement is to prevent unjust enrichment . . . and not to impose any additional burden on the customer beyond a showing of loss and payment over a binding stop order. The fact that payment occurred over a binding stop order was addressed above. Appellee's proof that a replacement check was issued and paid satisfied the trial court that a loss had been suffered due to Fidelity's payment of check No. 896. Appellant has made no argument that this loss did not occur."

Stale Checks.   Where an uncertified check has been circulating for more than six months, the drawee/payor bank is under no obligation to its checking account customer to pay the check. The bank may dishonor the check without any liability for damage even if there is enough money in the account to cover it. If the bank does pay the stale check, in good faith, it may charge the item against its customer's account. It's completely up to the bank, as long as the bank acts in good faith.

Check out over six months = Stale check

Customer's Death or Incompetence.   The Code's rules generally protect a bank from liability in the case where the customer dies or becomes legally incompetent. "Neither death nor incompetence of a customer revokes [a bank's] authority to accept, pay, collect or account until the bank knows of the fact of death or of an adjudication of incompetence and has reasonable opportunity to act on it" (4–405). Moreover, a bank, even after learning of its customer's death, may pay or certify previously issued checks for a period of 10 days, unless ordered not to by someone claiming an interest in the account. A customer's bankruptcy probably does not terminate the bank's authority to process items until the bank has knowledge or notice of it.

Bank can still pay after customer's death or incompetence

Customer's Duty to Inspect Statements.   When a bank makes available an itemized statement and the canceled items, its customer has a duty to exercise reasonable care and promptness in inspecting the charges and reporting any improper ones to the bank. Failure to do so may prevent a customer from forcing the bank to put money back in the account where an item has been altered or paid over a forged signature or indorsement. However, if the bank failed to exercise ordinary care in paying an item (for example, if it paid an item which was obviously altered), the customer could still force the bank to put the money back into the account. Finally, whether the customer, the bank, or both were guilty of negligence, this section protects the bank by imposing a one-year statute of limitations period for claims of alteration, or forgery of the drawer's signature, and a three-year period for claims of forged indorsements. In other words, if you don't notify the bank of the irregularities within those time periods, you can't make it put the money back in your account even if your signature on the check was forged. The lesson is clear: *Read your bank statement and verify your checks right away.* Antone Silvia learned this lesson the hard way.

Statute of limitations for customer's claims versus bank

SILVIA v. INDUSTRIAL NATIONAL BANK OF RHODE ISLAND

403 A.2d 1075 (Rhode Island, 1979)

FACTS   John Mahoney had prepared Antone Silvia's tax returns for over 25 years. Mahoney would make out the return and a check for any tax due to the IRS and would then take the documents to Silvia for his signature. In 1967, "apparently in need of some extra cash," Mahoney added $7,000 of nonexistent business profits to Silvia's return, thereby increasing Silvia's tax liability from about $2,000 to $4,625. Mahoney made out one of Silvia's checks to "Internal Revenue Services" and had Silvia sign the check and the return. Mahoney then added "by John J. Mahoney" in the space for the payee's name, indorsed the check "Internal Revenue Services by John J. Mahoney," and exchanged Silvia's check for several cashier's checks at Industrial National Bank. Mahoney used these cashier's checks to pay his personal creditors. Silvia did not notice the alterations made by his accountant when he received the canceled check with his bank statement in February 1968. Silvia first became aware of the problem in April 1969, when the IRS notified him that he had not paid his taxes for 1967. By that time, Mahoney had died. Silvia sued Industrial to force it to recredit his account. The trial court held for the bank; Silvia appealed.

ISSUE   Which UCC statute of limitations controls, the one-year period for alterations on the face of the item or the three-year period for unauthorized indorsements?

DECISION   The one-year statute controls. Judgment for the bank affirmed.

REASONS   **Justice Kelleher focused on UCC 4–406 and the policy underlying it. The reason for the two different time periods, he explained, was that the customer was not necessarily familiar with all the indorsers' signatures, so he or she needed a longer time in which to discover unauthorized indorsements.**

"Here, the alteration and unauthorized endorsement were identical, that is, 'Internal Revenue Services by John J. Mahoney.' Once the alteration was made, Mahoney could negotiate the check solely through the use of an unauthorized endorsement. Accordingly, discovery of the alteration would have been tantamount to discovery of the unauthorized endorsement. The presence of an altered payee on a canceled check should have automatically alerted Silvia to the existence of the unauthorized endorsement. Since the drafters of S.6A–4–406(4) considered one year more than sufficient time to discover a material alteration, we cannot allow Silvia to circumvent that policy when, as here, the unauthorized endorsement arises out of and is part of the scheme which caused the alteration. . . .

"Had he looked at the face of the check, he would have known that the instrument also contained an unauthorized endorsement. To allow Silvia to recover on this endorsement after the one-year period had elapsed would defeat the policies underlying prompt discovery and notice of material alterations. Such a suit is in actuality a suit upon the alteration itself."

Bank's Right to Subrogation. The drawee/payor bank is further protected by being subrogated to the rights of other parties where it has made a payment despite a stop order or under other circumstances where the drawer or maker has "a basis for objection." Where such an "improper" payment has occurred, the bank steps into the shoes of (1) an HDC, as against the drawer or maker;

Improper payment = Bank is subrogated

■ EXHIBIT 31–1

Bank Deposits and Collections

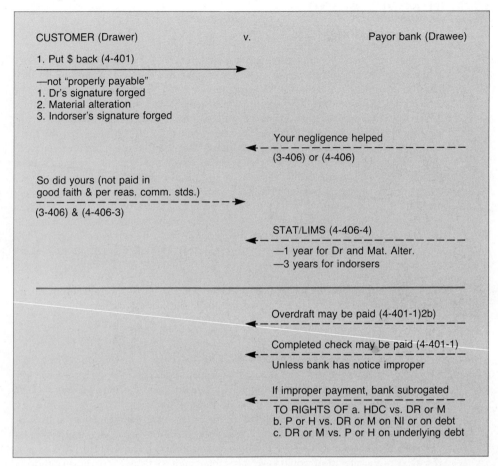

CUSTOMER (Drawer)   v.   Payor bank (Drawee)

1. Put $ back (4-401)

—not "properly payable"
1. Dr's signature forged
2. Material alteration
3. Indorser's signature forged

Your negligence helped

(3-406) or (4-406)

So did yours (not paid in
good faith & per reas. comm. stds.)

(3-406) & (4-406-3)

STAT/LIMS (4-406-4)

—1 year for Dr and Mat. Alter.
—3 years for indorsers

Overdraft may be paid (4-401-1)2b)

Completed check may be paid (4-401-1)

Unless bank has notice improper

If improper payment, bank subrogated

TO RIGHTS OF a. HDC vs. DR or M
b. P or H vs. DR or M on NI or on debt
c. DR or M vs. P or H on underlying debt

(2) the payee or any other holder, as against the drawer or maker, either on the paid item itself or on the underlying transaction; and (3) the drawer or maker, as against the payee or any other holder on the underlying transaction. In other words, if the bank has paid someone when it should not have done so, it shouldn't get stuck for the money but should have recourse against another party. The only problem may be finding that other party.

■ ELECTRONIC FUNDS TRANSFER

EFT = Instant $

Just as the use of checks and credit cards has made us, to a very large extent, a "cashless" society, use of computer-controlled electronic funds transfer (EFT) systems could make us a "checkless" society. With billions of checks being processed each year, the practical need for such a system is very clear. Properly implemented, it could speed payments, reduce errors, and lower costs. However, EFT presents its own set of problems, which the law is just beginning to confront.

Some phases of EFT are already in widespread use; probably the most common is the "24-hour money machine," located at bank branches and even many supermarkets. The machine enables a customer to use a magnetic card to receive cash, make deposits, pay bills, and transfer funds between accounts. Another frequently used EFT system makes direct deposits of paychecks to employees' bank accounts. More recently, banks have begun to offer their customers the option of paying bills with a telephone call to the bank's computer system; this method saves the customer's time and money. Not yet widely adopted is the most revolutionary EFT system: immediate payment from the customer's checking account through point-of-sale computer terminals located in stores.

It's not hard to imagine some of the problems involved in implementing each of these EFT systems. Inevitably, some customers who fear that they will lose control of their money will resist the change. Some workers like to see their actual paycheck, if only for a few minutes on the way to the bank. (Anyone who has ever been paid by an employer in cash can probably appreciate the different feeling you get from being able to actually see what you've earned in your own hands.)

Risks with EFT

The money machines are a great convenience, but they also involve security risks late at night and the possibility of lost cards and unauthorized withdrawals. The major difficulty involved with the point-of-sale payment, aside from the loss of the float period which would exist if the bills were totaled once a month and mailed out, is preserving consumer defenses where defective merchandise or services are delivered.

Customer-protection statutes

New legal rules to deal with these and other problems have been proposed, both as amendments to the UCC and as separate legislation. New laws have such provisions as: (1) the bank must send each customer a written agreement which includes rights of EFT card users; (2) the bank must provide a monthly statement of all EFT transactions to the customer; (3) the customer must be given a receipt for each EFT transaction; (4) the bank is liable for unauthorized use of the EFT card in the machine unless the customer has been negligent; (5) the bank may not send out unsolicited EFT cards unless the recipients are already its customers; and (6) the bank may not release a customer's financial records without the customer's permission or a court order. These statutes may provide civil and criminal penalties for violation by the bank.

Electronic Fund Transfer Act. Congress passed the EFTA in 1978 to protect consumers who were using these electronic banking services. Commercial accounts are not covered by the EFTA, only those used for personal, family, or household purposes. Nearly all types of consumer cash accounts, at nearly all kinds of financial institutions, are covered by EFTA. The major purpose of the EFTA is to provide information to the consumers who are using such services.

Required information to customer

Financial institutions must disclose the nature of the systems available; any limits on amounts or frequency of use; the charges for use; the right to see written receipts; how to correct errors; how to report a loss or theft; how to stop payment; the customer's liability for unauthorized use; the bank's liability to the customer; and the rules on disclosure of account information to third parties. The bank must provide monthly statements in any month where transac-

Limits on customer's liability

tions have occurred; otherwise, quarterly statements for the account must be provided.

EFTA limits the customer's liability for any unauthorized use to $50—*if* the customer notifies the institution within two business days after learning of the loss or theft of the access card. If the customer does not notify within that two-day limit, the liability goes up to $500. Where the customer receives a statement showing an unauthorized transfer of funds, and does not notify the institution of the problem within 60 days, the customer may be held liable for the full amount of the loss. Of course, the bank must prove that the loss would not have occurred if the customer had notified it.

UNPC

For commercial accounts, a Uniform New Payments Code (UNPC) is being developed by the American Law Institute and the Permanent Editorial Board for the UCC.

The entire area of electronic funds transfer will continue to challenge the ingenuity of judges, lawyers, and legislators.

■ SIGNIFICANCE OF THIS CHAPTER

Since most individuals and nearly all businesses issue and receive checks in significant numbers, we must have a clear set of rules for processing these instruments. Article 4 of the UCC supplements the general rules for commercial paper found in Article 3 by outlining the relationships between check issuers, check depositors, and the banks involved in the check collection process. Article 4 spells out the rules for charging a customer's checking account, and the circumstances under which the drawee bank has to put the money back in the account. In general, in dealing with their customers, banks will not incur liability if they act in good faith and with reasonable care. Even if they do, however, they may still be liable in cases involving forgery or alteration of instruments. For customer-depositors, it is important to have adequate internal financial controls and to verify bank statements and canceled items promptly.

DISCUSSION CASE

WOLVERTON FARMERS ELEVATOR v. FIRST AMERICAN BANK OF RUGBY
851 F.2d 223 (U.S. Eighth Circuit, 1988)

FACTS: Wolverton is a farmers' cooperative elevator located in Wolverton, Minnesota. In 1985 and early 1986 Wolverton was a supplier of corn to Dakota Crackin', Inc., a poultry operation located in Devils Lake, North Dakota. On January 13, 1986, Dakota Crackin', Inc. prepared two checks, numbers 7951 and 7952, in the amounts of $6,940.55 and $6,985, and sent them to Wolverton. When Wolverton received the checks on January 14, 1986, Allen Mashek, the manager of Wolverton at the time,

took them to Wolverton's bank, First National Bank of Breckenridge (First National) (the depositary bank) and had them forwarded directly to First American. Mashek testified that the checks were to be sent directly to First American to be presented for immediate payment. The teller at First National completed an "advice" form for the checks. Under the column entitled "Due" on the advice form is the word "now." The bottom of the advice form contains the following language:

Surrender documents only upon payment. Credit or remit only when paid. Do not hold after maturity or for the convenience of the payor. Return immediately if not paid, giving full reason. No protest, unless otherwise instructed.

The same collection procedure was followed for checks number 7956 and 7959, both in the amounts of $6,985, and received by Wolverton on January 15, 1986, and January 17, 1986, respectively.

Danny Stroh, an officer of First American, called Rick Steckler of First National to inquire as to how First American should treat the checks. Steckler informed Stroh that he did not know Wolverton's intentions concerning the checks. Stroh requested a letter from First National stating that the checks be held for 10 days to see if sufficient funds came into Dakota Crackin', Inc.'s account, but Steckler refused to draft such a letter.

First American ultimately treated the checks as "collection items," which are items forwarded outside normal banking channels and accompanied by an advice form; such items are held for a period of time while the account is checked each day for adequate funds. Stroh testified that his interpretation of the word "now" in the advice form under the column "Due" was that the underlying obligation for the check was due rather than that the check was to be either immediately paid or returned.

At the request of Wolverton's attorney, the checks were sent to First National on January 23, 1986. In early February 1986 Dakota Crackin', Inc. was adjudicated a bankrupt, and Wolverton never received payment for the amounts represented by the four checks at issue in this case.

Sitting without a jury, the U.S. District Court Magistrate held that First National was not liable for the checks.

■

Per Curiam:

On appeal, Wolverton reiterates its argument that the four checks "were presented for payment" within the meaning of the statute and that the midnight deadline rule therefore applied. Wolverton contends that because there was no agreement varying the terms of the midnight

deadline rule, First American is liable for the face value of the checks. . . .

[O]nly if the checks were presented for immediate payment does the midnight deadline rule apply. "Presentment is a demand for acceptance or payment made upon the maker, acceptor, drawee, or other payor by or on behalf of the holder," and requires a present demand. . . . Presentment can be waived, in which case the indorser or payee has no basis for complaint if the payor bank fails to give a timely notice of dishonor. . . . In addition, an exception to the midnight deadline rule exists where an agreement is reached between the payor bank and the payee that the bank should retain the check. . . .

In the present case, the magistrate determined from the trial testimony and advice forms attached to each check that the forms contained ambiguous language—some language apparently requesting payment now and other language apparently requesting payment whenever sufficient funds were available. Under North Dakota law, a document containing ambiguous language should be construed against the drafter, . . . and pursuant to . . . [U.C.C. § 4–201], a collecting bank acts as an agent for the owner of an item for the purposes of presentment, payment, and collection, unless a contrary intent is apparent. Thus, any ambiguous language in the advice form is also to be construed against Wolverton as First National's principal.

The magistrate made a factual finding that no presentment for payment was made, but, rather, that the checks sent directly to First American were sent for collection. Leaving a check with a bank to pay when the account on which it is drawn has sufficient funds does not constitute a presentment. . . . Upon careful review of the record, we conclude that it supports the magistrate's findings and conclusion that the midnight deadline rule was inapplicable.

Because the magistrate's finding that no presentment occurred is not clearly erroneous, Wolverton's argument that no agreement existed between the parties to waive the midnight deadline rule does not need to be reached.

Accordingly, the judgment of the district court is affirmed.

■ IMPORTANT TERMS AND QUESTIONS

bank collection process
Federal Reserve Banks
UCC, Article 4
payor bank
collecting bank
remitting bank

withdrawal rules
charging customer's account
wrongful dishonor
stale checks
duty to inspect statements

electronic funds transfer
clearinghouse
correspondent bank
depositary bank
intermediary bank
presenting bank
agency relationship with bank

check not assignment of funds
overdrafts
stop payment orders
customer's death or incompetence
right to subrogation
EFT customer protection

■ QUESTIONS AND PROBLEMS FOR DISCUSSION

1. What is the difference between a payor bank and a depositary bank?

2. What is the difference between a collecting bank and a remitting bank?

3. What happens when an item payable from a customer's account is presented to the payor bank, and paying it would create an overdraft?

4. What happens when a payor bank wrongfully dishonors an item?

5. Raskell sent two undated drafts to Lonnie, one for $21,000 and one for $27,000. Raskell's account balance at Rosie Bank, the drawee on both drafts, showed sufficient deposits to cover the drafts, but some of these deposits were checks and others were drafts for which Rosie had not yet collected the money. Without these uncollected items, Raskell's account did not have sufficient funds to cover his drafts to Lonnie. When Lonnie presented the drafts, Rosie Bank dishonored them. Lonnie sues Raskell and Rosie Bank on the drafts, and Raskell cross-claims against Rosie Bank for wrongful dishonor of his drafts. What is the result, and why?

6. Violet Mims deposited to her account at the Bigger Bank a $1,200 check, which was drawn on an out-of-town bank. Bigger's usual procedure was to delay crediting such deposits to the customer's account for three days to give the check time to clear. By mistake, Bigger's teller put a 10-day "hold" on the deposit. As a result, two checks written by Violet against this deposit "bounced." Because of all the delay in getting things straightened out, Violet suffered a case of "nerves," and her doctor advised her to take two weeks off from work, which she did. Violet now sues Bigger for the cost of telephone calls she had to make to discuss the account, for two weeks' lost wages, and for damages for embarrassment, humiliation, and inconvenience. What should Violet recover in this case? Explain.

7. Secured Bank was the authorized depositary for Blott Company's funds. Norm Muggi was Blott's manager and one of its three stockholders. By corporate resolution, Blott had authorized any of its officer-owners to indorse checks for it and to sign its checks to its creditors. Blott had a rubber stamp with a restrictive indorsement which was used to indorse checks made out to it, for deposit to its account at Secured. Norm Muggi took 23 checks made out to Blott, indorsed them in longhand in blank, and had Secured deposit them to his personal checking account. Muggi has withdrawn these funds from his account. Blott sues Secured for the face amount of the 23 checks. What is the result, and why?

8. Zepka drew a check for $4,800 on his account at Socie Bank, payable to SAB Company, and gave the check to Mishmash, one of SAB's sales agents. Mishmash forged SAB's indorsement, signed his own name, and exchanged the check for a cashier's check for the same amount at Socie Bank. The cashier's check was also made out to SAB, so Mishmash again forged SAB's signature and then deposited the check in an account titled "Doors, Inc.," which he had at Capie Bank. Capie Bank sent the check to Commie Bank for collection. Commie Bank collected on the check from Socie Bank. More than a year later, Zepka told Socie Bank that the indorsement on his original check had been forged and Socie put the money back in his account. Socie now sues Capie and Commie. What is the result, and why?

PART SIX

Property

The law governing the acquisition, ownership, and disposition of property, both real and personal, is basic to the management of business and of nearly all our personal affairs. Real property cannot be picked up and carried with us from place to place, and mere possession is not a presumption of ownership. Also, more than one person may have an ownership interest in real or personal property. Thus, ownership rights have to be defined and different forms of ownership are needed to fit the various situations that may arise in co-ownership.

In our society, we often rent or borrow personal property and lease real property. We need to know the rights and duties each party has in those transactions. Also since many areas in which we live and work have become densely populated, we can no longer do with our property as we wish if it offends or injures our neighbors. We must, therefore, have land use and environmental regulations. Lastly, what happens to your property when you die? You can't take it with you, so it must be distributed among those who survive you. If you have a will, you dictate to whom those rights are given; if not, the state law will make the decision for you. For all these reasons, it is important to understand property rights.

In Part Six we review the methods of acquisition and disposition of real and personal property and define the various forms of ownership. We examine the law regarding rental or use of personal property belonging to someone else (bailments), scrutinize the rights and duties of landlords and tenants, discuss zoning laws and environmental regulations and how they affect the use of land, and look at the laws regarding inheritance of personal and real property and methods of estate planning. Finally, we define the major types of property and personal insurance, and review some of the major legal rules used in interpreting insurance policies.

32

Forms of Co-Ownership; Personal Property

CHAPTER OBJECTIVES

THIS CHAPTER WILL:

- Define "property."
- Describe the different classifications of property.
- Describe different types of ownership a person or persons may have in property.
- Explain the process by which personal property can become real property, and real property can become personal property.
- Discuss the various ways title to personal property may be acquired.

■ HUMAN RIGHTS, PROPERTY RIGHTS, AND PERSONAL RIGHTS

Property has no rights; its owners do

You'll often hear people, particularly proponents of regulatory and wealth redistribution schemes, say that "human rights are more important than property rights." That statement is illogical and ridiculous. The *things* that are the subject matter of property rights—cars, books, TVs, parcels of real estate—have no "rights" at all, in and of themselves. Property rights belong to persons, including human beings, corporate persons, and various other kinds of legal entities. Among the most important rights of human beings are property rights—the right to acquire, possess, use, enjoy, and dispose of the things which are the subject of those rights. Your TV set has no "rights"; you do: the rights to acquire it, to watch it when you want to, to turn it off when you want to study, and to sell it or give it away (when it's paid for).

At least equally important is your property right in the results of your labor—the money and other rewards you earn through your physical and mental efforts. Those things are yours because you worked for them, and your "property rights" protect your freedom to save or spend, as you see fit, when you wish, where you wish. Property rights are very important to all of us. They enable us to enjoy music, art, poetry, literature, and all sorts of leisure and productive activity. In short, they are a large part of what separates us from the beasts of the jungle and makes life worth living.

■ DEFINITION OF PROPERTY

Property as a bundle of rights

Property may be defined as the **bundle of rights** concerning a specific parcel of land or any other thing of value, tangible or intangible, visible or invisible. Some of the rights included in this bundle are the right to possess, to use, to sell, to lease, to dispose of, or to destroy the land or thing in a legal way, and the right to exclude others from trespassing or interfering with the land or thing.

Since property may be described as the bundle of rights concerning land or a thing, we often find that we do not have absolute or unconditional property, since someone else may have certain rights in the land or thing. For example, the owner of a parcel of land may say, "That is my property," but the parcel of land may be leased to a tenant. Thus, the tenant has property rights in the land—the right to use it and the right to use the proceeds from it according to the terms of the lease contract. Also, a public utility company may have an easement across the parcel of land, allowing it to come in and repair or replace underground or overhead power lines. An *easement* is simply a right to enter someone else's land for a specific purpose. If there are mineral, oil, or gas deposits on the land, those deposits may be owned by a person or persons other than the landowner. Moreover, if the purchaser of the land took out a purchase-money mortgage (i.e., a loan to buy the land), the mortgagee has certain rights in the land as security for payment of the mortgage. Thus, it is not uncommon for several persons to have property rights in the same land.

We tend to think of property in terms of tangible and visible objects or things, such as cars, furniture, houses, and land. However, property can be intangible things, such as patents granted by the U.S. Patent Office or copyrights granted by the U.S. Copyright Office. Here the property is simply the right to prevent others from using an invention or copying a book, song, or other copyrighted material, and to secure damages from those persons who do so without permission.

Copyrightability of Computer Software. With the growth of the computer industry, more and more time and dollars are being invested in software development, and investors have become very concerned about the safety of their investments. The old copyright law did not mention software or computer programs, and even in 1976 when Congress revised the old copyright law, legislators failed to specifically include any mention of computer programs or the term *software*.

Finally, in December 1980, Congress passed the Computer Software Act (Public Law 96–517), which amended the copyright law to specifically include computer programs. The copyright office had been accepting computer programs for copyright purposes since the 1976 amended act was passed, under its own interpretation; however, the 1980 law clearly settled the issue of copyrightability of software. A major problem with the copyright is that it only prohibits copying. You are not granted an exclusive monopoly to that computer program; if someone else comes up with the same program or something similar, you still have no case unless you can prove there was copying. In the case of a patent, once you are granted it you have an exclusive monopoly on that process or machine. You can enforce your patent and prevent others who develop a similar product with no knowledge about you or your patent from using their own invention. Thus, patents remain the preferred protection.

The validity of Apple's copyrights is at issue in the following case.

APPLE COMPUTER, INC. v. FRANKLIN COMPUTER CORP.

714 F.2d 1240 (U.S. Third Circuit, 1983)

FACTS   Apple Computer, Inc. appeals from the District Court's denial of a motion to preliminarily enjoin Franklin Computer Corp. from infringing the copyrights Apple holds on 14 computer programs.

Apple, one of the computer industry leaders, manufactures and markets personal computers (microcomputers), related peripheral equipment (peripherals), and computer programs (software). It presently manufactures Apple II computers and distributes over 150 programs. One of the byproducts of Apple's success is the independent development by third parties of numerous computer programs which are designed to run on the Apple II computer.

Franklin, the defendant below, manufactures and sells the ACE 100 personal computer and at the time of the hearing has sold fewer than 1,000 computers. The ACE 100 was designed to be "Apple compatible," so that peripheral equipment and software developed for use with the Apple II computer could be used in conjunction with the ACE 100. Franklin's copying of Apple's operating system computer programs in an effort to achieve such compatibility precipitated this suit.

Franklin did not dispute that it copied the Apple programs. Its witness admitted copying each of the works in suit from the Apple programs. Its factual defense was directed to its contention that it was not feasible for Franklin to write its own operating system programs. Franklin's vice president of engineering testified he spent 30–40 hours in November 1981 making a study to determine if it was feasible for Franklin to write its own Autostart ROM program.

Franklin's principal defense is primarily a legal one, directed to its contention that the Apple operating system programs are not capable of copyright protection.

ISSUE   Are the Apple Computer, Inc. operating systems capable of copyright protection?

DECISION   Yes. Denial of preliminary injunction by the trial court is reversed.

REASONS   Justice Sloviter speaking for the court stated:

"In 1976, after considerable study, Congress enacted a new copyright law to replace that which had governed since 1909. . . . Under the law, two primary requirements must be satisfied in order for a work to constitute copyrightable subject matter—it must be an 'original wor[k] of authorship' and must be 'fixed in [a] tangible medium of expression.' . . .

"The 1980 amendments added a definition of a computer program:

A 'computer program' is a set of statements or instructions to be used directly or indirectly in a computer in order to bring about a certain result. . . .

"The amendments also substituted a new Section 117 which provides that 'it is not an infringement for the owner of a copy of a computer program to make or authorize the making of another copy or adaptation of that computer program' when necessary to 'the utilization of the computer program' or 'for archival purposes only.' . . . The parties agree that this section is not implicated in the instant lawsuit. The language of the provision, however, by carving out an exception to the normal prescriptions against copying, clearly indicates that programs are copyrightable and are otherwise afforded copyright protection. . . .

"We turn to the heart of Franklin's position on appeal which is that computer operating system programs, as distinguished from application programs, are not the proper subject of copyright 'regardless of the language or medium in which they are fixed.' . . .

"Franklin argues that an operating system program is either a 'process,' 'system,' or 'method of operation' and hence uncopyrightable. Franklin correctly notes that underlying Section 102(b) . . . is the distinction which must be made between property subject to the patent law, which protects discoveries, and that subject to copyright law, which protects the writings describing such discoveries. . . .

"Franklin's attack on operating system programs as 'methods' or 'processes' seems inconsistent with its concession that application programs are an appropriate subject of copyright. Both types of programs instruct the computer to do something. . . .

"Perhaps the most convincing item leading us to reject Franklin's argument is that the statutory definition of a computer program as a set of instructions to be used in a computer in order to bring about a certain result . . . makes no distinction between application programs and operating programs. Franklin can point to no decision which adopts the distinction it seeks to make. . . .

"We believe that the 1980 amendments reflect Congress' receptivity to new technology and its desire to encourage, through the copyright laws, continued imagination and creativity in computer programming."

Patentability of Computer Software.   The patent law itself does not specifically define a computer program as being patentable or unpatentable. The question of patentability is thus a question of interpretation by the courts.

The U.S. Supreme Court in earlier decisions pointed out that a computer program is no more than an algorithm, and as such simply a mathematical formula and is not patentable. The Supreme Court has, however, in recent cases allowed exceptions to that general rule. In 1981 the Supreme Court decided *Diamond* v. *Diehr* 450 U.S. 175 (1981). (Sidney Diamond, the petitioner, is the U.S. Commissioner of Patents and Trademarks.) In the *Diehr* case the respondent sought a patent on a software package (a process) for operating a rubber molding press with the aid of a digital computer. In this case the Supreme Court approved patentability. However, there was strong dissent.

It becomes obvious that there is a need for Congress to amend the patent law as it did the copyright law to settle the question of what types of software are patentable.

■ CLASSIFICATIONS OF PROPERTY

Real Property.   When we speak of *real property,* we are referring to land, buildings, or permanent fixtures which have been erected on or affixed to the land. Crops, trees, or any other objects that are growing on land are generally considered real property until they are severed from the land, or at least until they are sold separately.

Personal Property.   This term designates anything of value which is subject to ownership and is not classified as real property. *Personal property* can be divided into two classifications, tangible and intangible. *Tangible personal property* includes such items as animals, furniture, books, clothes, jewelry, and business inventories. *Intangible personal property* includes a person's rights in patents, copyrights, shares of corporate stock, insurance policies, and many similar legal documents.

Public Property.   *Public property* designates the land and things which are owned by the national government, a state government, a city, or some other political subdivision. Those things are, therefore, considered to be owned by the public. This classification includes parks, public buildings, and the national archives.

Private Property.   In contrast to public property, *private property* belongs to an individual, a corporation, or other private legal entity. The property of Notre Dame University is private property, whereas the property of Iowa State University is public property.

■ TYPES OF OWNERSHIP

Ownership in Severalty.   This is ownership in the name of one person. There is no co-owner of the property right.

Tenancy in Common.   Here, there are two or more co-owners of real or personal property. Under this type of co-ownership, the co-owners or co-tenants have equal rights to possess and use the property. A co-owner's interest in a tenancy in common may be transferred by a last will and testament. It may be sold without the consent of the other co-owners, and is subject to judicial sale by a creditor who has secured a judgment against the owner.

Tenants in common need not own equal shares

Tenants in common need not be equal owners. For example, Grandfather had a will which said that all of his property would be divided equally among his children and that any deceased child's share should go to that child's children. When Grandfather died only one of his children survived him. However, one of the deceased children had five children and the other had four. Thus, one third of Grandfather's real and personal property went to his surviving child, and the third which was willed to each of his other children was co-owned by their children. All of the heirs are tenants in common, yet the tenants in common do not have equal shares.

In this example, the heirs could continue as tenants in common and any rents or profits from the property would have to be divided in proportion to the share of each person, or the entire property or parts of the property could be sold and the money received from the sale would be divided according to each person's proportionate share.

Often, the parties prefer not to sell the property. Instead they ask the probate court to divide it in accordance with their various shares. With a divisible property, such as farmland, the court would divide the acreage according to the interests of the parties.

In addition to arising from inherited property, tenancy in common may arise when title to real or personal property is transferred to two or more persons and it is not declared to be joint tenancy or tenancy by the entirety.

Joint Tenancy. *Joint tenancy* is a second form of co-ownership in which land or personal property is owned by two or more persons. These persons enjoy equal rights to share in the use and profits of the property involved, but if any one of the joint tenants dies, the entire property passes to the surviving joint tenants. The interest of a joint tenant cannot be willed to the joint tenant's heirs because the deceased's interest terminates at death.

Joint tenancy has automatic survivorship

Joint tenants may sell and convey their separate shares in the joint tenancy. If this is done, the joint tenancy is severed, and the tenants or co-owners become tenants in common. Also, a joint tenant's interest is subject to the rights of creditors. The creditors of one joint tenant may secure judgment and have that co-owner's interest sold and the joint tenancy severed.

Historically, joint tenancy was only applicable to real estate. Today, however, one can have joint tenancy in almost any type of personal property—including bank accounts, stock shares, and automobiles.

Statutory modifications of joint tenancy

Many states have passed specific joint tenancy statutes which modify the common-law concept, and thus the applicable state law must be referred to in any case involving a joint tenancy relationship. The Illinois rules are at issue in the *Grassman* case.

MINONK STATE BANK v. GRASSMAN

432 N.E. 2d 386 (Illinois, 1982)

FACTS
Gustav Grassman executed a deed under which Agnes, Ida, and Frieda became owners in joint tenancy of a parcel of real estate. Frieda died in 1972 leaving Agnes and Ida as surviving joint tenants.

One week after the death of Frieda, defendant Ida Grassman executed a deed conveying this parcel of property from herself as a joint tenant to herself as a tenant in common. The deed recited that this action was for the sole purpose of dissolving any and all rights of survivorship as between the parties to the deed executed by Gustav Grassman. It is undisputed that Agnes was unaware of what Ida had done.

On February 16, 1977, Agnes died. Her will, dated March 13, 1963, was admitted to probate with Minonk State Bank as administrator. Minonk State Bank filed this action requesting a declaration by the court that Ida and Agnes held the property in tenancy in common. Defendant argued that the 1972 deed she executed was ineffective, so that she is the sole owner of the property by virtue of her having survived Agnes.

Plaintiff, the administrator of the estate of Agnes Grassman, appeals from an order declaring Ida Grassman, the sole surviving joint tenant.

ISSUE
Can one joint tenant terminate a joint tenancy by conveying her interest from herself as a joint tenant to herself as a tenant in common?

DECISION
Yes. The order of the Circuit Court is reversed.

REASONS
The court stated:

"If an individual can grant to himself and another individual property in joint tenancy, there is no reason why the same party should not be able to sever the joint tenancy by conveying an estate to himself. The individual has done with one piece of paper what otherwise would have required two . . . Allowing one party to destroy the joint tenancy by executing a deed from himself to himself merely dispenses with an outmoded charade which is of dubious legal and practical significance. We hold that a joint tenant may unilaterally sever a joint tenancy without the use of an intermediary."

Tenancy by the Entirety. *Tenancy by the entirety* is essentially a joint tenancy with the right of survivorship; however, the co-owners must be husband and wife to each other. The characteristic which distinguishes the two forms of property ownership is that tenancy by the entirety cannot be changed except by joint action of the husband and wife during their lifetimes, whereas a joint tenancy is terminated when any one of the tenants conveys his or her interest, or when a levy of execution is made by a creditor against a joint tenant's interest. If a husband and wife take title to a home as tenants by the entireties and the husband has a judgment rendered against him for damages that result from an automobile accident, the person who was awarded the damages cannot have the judgment executed against the home. If, however, both the husband and wife are jointly liable on a debt, then the creditor may secure a judgment and execute it against the home.

Creditors of one spouse can't reach entireties property

Like joint tenancy, tenancy by the entirety was historically confined to real estate ownership and did not extend to ownership of personal property. However, some states have extended the concept to personal property. About 20 states recognize tenancy by the entirety, but here again the state laws are not uniform and the individual state law must be referred to in each case. As seen in the *D'Ercole* case, for example, Massachusetts makes the husband the exclusive manager of such co-owned property.

D'ERCOLE v. D'ERCOLE

407 F. Supp. 1377 (Massachusetts, 1976)

FACTS Plaintiff and defendant bought a house in 1962 and separated in 1971. The husband was seeking a divorce. The wife was seeking a separation and opposed a divorce on religious grounds. The husband had refused to share their marital home with the plaintiff, either by selling the house and dividing the proceeds, by paying the plaintiff her share of the equity of the house, or by renting the premises and dividing the proceeds. In support of his position, the husband pointed out that the property in question was held under a tenancy by the entirety which gave both him and his wife an indefeasible right of survivorship, but gave him the exclusive right to possession and control during his lifetime. He stated that he would grant the plaintiff one half of the equity in the house if she would grant him an uncontested divorce.

ISSUE Does the separation of husband and wife end tenancy by the entirety? Does the common-law concept of tenancy by the entirety deprive the plaintiff of the due process and equal protection of the law guaranteed by the Constitution and the Bill of Rights?

DECISION No, the separation of married persons does not end tenancy by the entirety even if that separation is ratified by a formal court decree. No, the common-law concept of tenancy by the entirety does not deprive the plaintiff of her constitutional rights to due process and equal protection of the law.

REASONS The court stated:

"The tenancy by the entirety is designed particularly for married couples and may be employed only by them. This form of property ownership differs from the joint tenancy in two respects. First, each tenant has an indefeasible right of survivorship in the entire tenancy, which cannot be defeated by any act taken individually by either spouse during his or her lifetime. There can be no partition. Second, the spouses do not have an equal right to control and possession of the property. The husband during his lifetime has paramount rights in the property. In the event of divorce the tenancy by the entirety becomes a tenancy in common unless the divorce decree reflects that a joint tenancy is intended."

In answer to the charge that the law was illegal because it discriminated on grounds of sex, the court stated: "[I]t is true that the only Massachusetts tenancy tailored exclusively for married persons appears to be balanced in favor of males. There is no equivalent female-biased tenancy, nor is there a neutral married persons' tenancy providing for indefeasible survivorship but not vesting paramount lifetime rights in the male. Married couples may, it is true, elect a joint tenancy, a tenancy in common, or a sole tenancy. . . . A wife who wants the security of indefeasible survivorship can achieve it only by means of a male-dominated tenancy." The plaintiff, however, had made this choice knowingly, and is now bound by it.

Community Property.   The main feature of the community property system is that most property acquired after marriage by either the husband or the wife automatically becomes the common property of the husband and wife. Under the common law, if a husband earned $50,000 per year, he was legally obligated to provide the necessities for his wife's support with that amount; however, his wife had no rights in any money over and above the amount required to provide these necessities. Also, under the common law, if a wife were employed outside the home, her income was also her husband's. Under the community property theory, most income and property acquired by either spouse is owned by both, share and share alike. Probable exceptions to the co-ownership rule would be property acquired by gift or inheritance, or property received in exchange for property owned by one of the parties prior to the marriage. Income earned during the marriage by separately owned property may or may not be community property, depending on the state.

The community property system is a statutory type of ownership which, if adopted by a specific state, will cover all persons in the relationship of husband and wife who are subject to the laws of that state. Unlike the previous types of ownership discussed in this chapter, it is not voluntary. Also, the states that have adopted this form of ownership have not followed any uniform pattern. Answers to such questions as whether a spouse's share in community property will descend to his or her heirs or will automatically go to the surviving spouse, or whether or not the spouse's share is subject to levy of execution by creditors, or how the property is to be divided in case of divorce, must be determined by looking at the specific statute of the state involved. The nine states that have community property laws are Arizona, California, Idaho, Louisiana, New Mexico, Nevada, Texas, Washington, and Wisconsin.

Condominium Ownership.   Condominium ownership is a combination of ownership in severalty and tenancy in common. Condominiums are multiple-unit buildings or developments of several buildings where an owner owns an individual unit, and all of these owners share the land and common areas used by all tenants as tenants in common. The owners of the various individual apartments or buildings pay a management fee to a condominium corporation to manage the complex and to keep the common areas repaired and cleaned.

Nearly all of the states have enacted some type of condominium law to regulate condominium ownership and construction. These laws vary from state to state, and a person should be familiar with the particular state condominium law before making any decisions regarding condominium ownership or construction.

Condominium owners are joint owners of the common areas, and as such are liable on a pro rata basis for costs, expenses, and even liability for claims for damages arising out of the use of the common areas.

In the following Texas case the court was asked to decide whether the owners of a condominium unit were liable jointly and severally or liable simply on a pro rata basis, for damages arising out of the operation of the common area.

Common law rules versus community property

Nine community property states apply it differently

New laws on condo ownership

DUTCHER v. OWENS

647 S.W.2d 948 (Texas, 1983)

FACTS J. A. Dutcher, a resident of San Diego, California, owned a condominium apartment in the Eastridge Terrace Condominiums, located in Dallas County, which he leased to Ted and Christine Owens. Ownership of the apartment includes a 1.572 percent pro rata undivided ownership in the common elements of the project. The Owenses suffered substantial property loss in a fire which began in an external light fixture in a common area.

The Owenses filed suit in Tarrant County against Dutcher, the Eastridge Terrace Condominium Association, Joe Hill Electric Company, IHS-8 Ltd. (the developer) and a class of co-owners of condominiums in Eastridge Terrace represented by the officers of the homeowners' association. The case was tried before a jury, which found the following:

1. The fire was proximately caused by the lack of an insulating box behind the light fixture in the exterior wall air space;
2. The homeowners' association knew of this defect;
3. The homeowners' association alone was negligent in failing to install an insulating box with knowledge of the defect; and
4. The negligence of homeowners' association resulted in damage to the Owenses' property in the amount of $69,150.

The trial court rendered judgment against Dutcher on the jury's verdict in the amount of $1,087.04. The award represents the amount of damages multiplied by Dutcher's 1.572 percent pro rata undivided ownership in the common elements of the Eastridge Terrace Condominium project. The court of appeals reversed.

ISSUE Is a condominium co-owner jointly and severally liable or is he liable for a pro rata portion of the damages?

DECISION The liability of a condominium co-owner is limited to his pro rata interest in the condominium as a whole. Judgment of the Court of Appeals reversed and judgment of the trial court affirmed.

 REASONS Justice Ray, speaking for the court, stated:

"This is a case of first impression concerning the allocation of liability among condominium co-owners for tort claims arising out of the ownership, use and maintenance of 'common elements.' The defendant was found to be vicariously liable for the homeowners' associations' negligence. . . .

"In enacting the Texas Condominium Act, . . . the Texas Legislature intended to create 'a new method of property ownership.' . . . A condominium is an estate in real property consisting of an undivided interest in a portion of a parcel of real property together with a separate fee simple interest in another portion of the same parcel. In essence, condominium ownership is the merger of two estates in land into one: the fee simple ownership of an apartment or unit in a condominium project and a tenancy in common with other co-owners in the common elements. . . .

"Given the uniqueness of the type of ownership involved in condominiums, the onus of liability for injuries arising from the management of condominium projects should reflect the degree of control exercised by the defendants. We agree with the California court's conclusion that to rule that a condominium co-owner had any effective control over the operation of the common areas would be to sacrifice 'reality to theoretical formalism,' for in fact a co-owner has no more control over operations than he would have as a stockholder in a corporation which owned and operated the project. . . . This does not limit the plaintiff's right of action. The efficiency found in a suit directed at the homeowners' association and its board of directors representing the various individual homeowners, as well as any co-owner causally or directly responsible for the injuries sustained, benefits both sides of the docket as well as the judicial system as a whole.

"Such a result is not inconsistent with the legislative intent. While the Act creates a new form of real property ownership, it does not address the issue of the allocation of tort liability among co-owners. Nevertheless, we are guided in our decision by the other provisions in the Act which appear *in pari materia,* and which proportionately allocate various financial responsibilities. For example, the Act provides for pro rata contributions by co-owners toward expenses of administration and maintenance, insurance, taxes, and assessments. Pro rata provisions also exist for the application of insurance proceeds. . . .

"We hold, therefore, that because of the limited control afforded a unit owner by the statutory condominium regime, the creation of the regime effects a re-allocation of tort liability. The liability of a condominium co-owner is limited to his pro rata interest in the regime as a whole, where such liability arises from those areas held in tenancy-in-common."

Time-Sharing Ownership. This property concept has been developed particularly for resort properties. Time-sharing ownership is also called "interval ownership" in some areas.

Most recent development: Time-sharing

The theory of **time-sharing ownership** is very simple. In the past, you purchased a condominium in Florida, hoping to rent it out for most of the year and to reserve it for yourself for two months in the winter. The problem was that the capital investment was quite sizable. Now, you can simply buy the right to use a condominium unit in a resort area for a specific period of time, perhaps 2 weeks a year; the other 50 weeks are sold to other individuals. You have purchased two weeks' use per year for your life or forever, as the case may be. You can trade your two weeks to one of the other time-share owners if you want to use the property at a different time, or you can sell or lease your right to use it. The obvious benefit of time-sharing ownership is that you have to pay only a fraction of the total price of the unit, yet you own an exclusive right to use it for a specific time every year.

As with condominium ownership, state laws regulating this type of ownership vary. Before any decision is made regarding such purchases, the laws of the state where the real estate is located should be reviewed.

Cooperative Ownership. The cooperative is a type of housing ownership where the tenants must be owners of an interest in the cooperative, which is the landlord. However, they do not actually own the space in which they live like the person who owns a condominium or a time share ownership. Typically the cooperative is a corporation and the tenants are the owners of shares of stock of the corporation. The stockholders as tenants then lease apartments from the corporation and the rent which each tenant pays is based on the tenant's share of the expenses of the corporation, such as mortgage payment, maintenance, real estate taxes, insurance, etc. The corporation is the owner of the real estate and the tenants are simply owners of personal property, namely the shares of stock of the corporation. Also most cooperatives require that if a tenant moves out he or she must sell the shares of stock to a person who will then lease the apartment he or she is vacating, or some cooperatives might have a provision in their articles or by-laws requiring the tenant-stockholder to sell the shares back to the cooperative upon moving out. Cooperatives are typically not-for-profit organizations and are created and regulated under specific statutes in most states.

■ CHANGES IN FORM

Fixtures on real estate

When purchasing a home the buyer may ask, "Do these drapes go with the house?" "Does this chandelier stay with the house?" "Does the carpet in the family room go with the house?" The crucial legal question here is whether or not these items, which were once personal property, now have become fixtures to the real property, and thus an inseparable part of the real property.

Personal Property to Real Property

Here again, the specific law of the state in which the property is located will determine whether a particular item is still movable personal property, or whether it has become a fixture and part of the real property.

The best advice is "put it in writing." Specify in your agreement to purchase, what items go with the house.

Method of attachment

Affixation. Has the item become permanently affixed to the land or the building? If an item has been attached to the land or the building in such a manner that it cannot be removed without damaging the building or the land or the item itself, then the item is usually considered part of the real property. If carpet is glued to the concrete slab in the family room of a house, it is typically considered part of the real estate, since removing it would leave a bare, unusable floor and would no doubt destroy the carpet. Drapes or curtains can normally be removed from curtain rods or other types of hangers without damaging either the curtains or the fixtures upon which they are hanging. However, the curtain rods themselves are considered permanent fixtures because they are permanently attached to the wall and cannot be removed without leaving holes in it.

Intent of affixer

Trade fixtures

Intent. What was the intent of the owner of the personal property when the personal property was affixed to the real property? Here, we may go beyond the actual physical method of affixing the property and look to the owner's intention when the property was affixed. Did the owner intend to add the fixture to the real property or to maintain it as personal property? If a person rents a store building and installs counters, showcases, and other equipment necessary to run the store, will these items be considered personal property, or will they be part of the real estate? Counters, showcases and similar equipment installed for business purposes are called "trade fixtures." The general rule is that, if a person affixes personal property to the land or building of another, the owner of the land or building becomes the owner of the affixed items. But in a situation such as the above, which involves installation of trade fixtures, most courts would probably say that the business tenant remains the owner of the items even though it becomes necessary to unbolt them from the floor or to disconnect electric wires or water pipes before the items can be removed from the building. It is normally not the intent of the business tenant to make a gift of such items to the landlord, and the landlord has either expressly or impliedly agreed to such removals.

Business Records. How is the property being carried on the books of a business? Is it still considered as personal property, or is it considered as an improvement of the real estate? Business records can be used as evidence of the parties' intent.

Courts are generally more liberal in permitting removal of items attached for the tenant's specific business or agricultural use, or to add to the comfort and convenience of a residence. In all of these situations, however, it is advisable to have a clause in the lease specifying which items are removable by the tenant and are not to be considered part of the realty, even though permanently attached.

Real Property to Personal Property

Severance of things from land

When a fixture is severed from the real estate, it becomes personal property. A built-in stove in your kitchen is considered part of the real estate and goes with the house. However, if you decide to replace it with a new one, once the old stove has been physically severed from the real estate it returns to the status of personal property. Growing timber or crops are part of the real estate; however, once they are severed from the ground they become personal property. They can also be sold, as "goods" under the UCC, without already having been physically detached from the land. Coal in the ground is part of the real estate; however, when it is mined and severed from the ground it becomes personal property.

■ ACQUISITION OF TITLE TO PERSONAL PROPERTY

Title to personal property may be acquired in several different ways. Acquisition may be the result of voluntary action on the part of the former owner and the new owner, or it may occur simply by the operation of the law. Following are some of the common methods of acquiring title to personal property.

Purchase of Personal Property

When you go to the grocery store and buy groceries for the week, you have acquired personal property by purchase. No certificate of title is attached to each item in your grocery sack; mere possession is evidence of title to such items. If you purchase an automobile, a motorcycle, or a motor home, the seller will give you a bill of sale, which must be registered with the specific state authorities, so that title to the vehicle is registered in your name on state records. If you purchase the equipment and trade fixtures of a business, you will normally require that a bill of sale specifically describes each item or object which is part of the purchase. This bill of sale does not need to be recorded with the state or county; however, it will be your evidence of title.

Title to Personal Property by a Gift

Title to personal property may be transferred from one person to other persons by gift. A gift is a voluntary action on the part of the giver, with no value in return from the person receiving the gift. The transfer of personal property by gift can be divided into three basic classifications. An *inter vivos* gift is a gift made by a living person to another living person. A gift *causa mortis* is a gift which is given in contemplation of the giver's death. A *testamentary gift* is a gift which is given in a person's will.

Three types of gifts

The three types of gifts differ mainly with regard to revocability. Once an *inter vivos* gift has been delivered, it is generally irrevocable. Since a gift *causa mortis* is made in contemplation of death, if the giver recovers, then the giver can have the property back. The *causa mortis* gift may be revoked by the giver during the giver's lifetime, and it may be revoked if the recipient dies before the giver dies. A *testamentary gift* may be revoked by revoking or amending the will.

Intent of donor

The question often arises as to when an *inter vivos* gift becomes effective. Two tests must be met. First, it must be shown that the giver intended to divest certain rights in the property. It is not necessary that all rights be given for a gift to be valid. For example, an owner of corporate stock may give the dividends of the stock to another person, but retain ownership of the actual shares of stock. Intent may be evidenced by a written statement, by actions of the giver, or by other documents such as the signature card for a joint bank account.

Delivery to donee or another

The second test of a gift is delivery. *Delivery* is simply the transfer of possession or control from one person to another. Delivery does not have to be made to the recipient of the gift; it can be made to a third person as agent or trustee for the recipient. A bank will often be the trustee for the recipient if the recipient is a minor, or if the recipient is an elderly person who is incapable of handling the property. The key with regard to delivery is that the giver surrenders all rights to possession and control of the property which is the subject of the gift. In some instances, you cannot pick the gift up and hand it to the recipient. With an automobile, for example, delivery would consist of handing over the keys. This would be called symbolic delivery. If the gift involves intangible property, then delivery would consist of turning over some document which transfers title to the intangible property to the donee, such as an assignment of a patent or a copyright, or a properly indorsed stock certificate. The *Evans* case discusses the legal significance of delivering the key to a safe deposit box.

IN RE ESTATE OF EVANS

356 A.2d 778 (Pennsylvania, 1976)

FACTS

Arthur Evans had rented a safe-deposit box in which he had stored valuables. His niece, Mrs. Kellows, had worked for the family since she was 16, and she continued to care for Evans until he died. Before Evans went into the hospital, just prior to his death, he gave the keys to the box to Kellows. Reverend Cummings visited Evans shortly before he died, and Evans told Cummings that he was giving $10,000 to the church and that he had given the rest of his possessions and the keys to the safe-deposit box to Kellows. The executor considered the contents of the safe-deposit box, valued at approximately $80,000, to be assets of the estate and not the specific property of Kellows. Kellows filed objections, stating that there had been a gift and that she owned the contents of the box. She had the keys; however, her name was not on the rental agreement and the bank had no notice that she had any interest in the box.

The trial court held that the decedent's delivery of the keys did not constitute sufficient delivery where the box remained registered in the decedent's name and the claimant could not have gained access to it even with the keys. Kellows appealed from that decision.

ISSUE   Did the decedent's delivery of the keys to the safe-deposit box before his death constitute a gift of the contents of the safe-deposit box?

DECISION   No. Judgment affirmed.

REASONS   The court admitted there was evidence that decedent intended to give his estate to Mrs. Kellows. However, the court also noted that there had been ample opportunity for the decedent to remove the contents of the box and give them to Kellows or to take her to the bank and transfer the rental of the box to her. The decedent did in fact visit the bank and get out the safe-deposit box less than one month before he died. His delivery of the keys was intended to ensure the safekeeping of the keys and not to signify delivery of the contents of the safe-deposit box, as was indicated by the fact that Kellows could not get into the safe-deposit box without the decedent's specific authorization. Thus delivery of the keys to a safe-deposit box is not symbolic delivery of the contents of the safe-deposit box.

"In the instant case, appellant did not have dominion and control over the box even though she was given the keys to it. The box remained registered in Mr. Evans' name and she could not have gained access to it even with the keys. Mr. Evans never terminated his control over the box, consequently he never made a delivery, constructive or otherwise."

The Uniform Gifts to Minors Act.   In the past many parents who wanted to give money to their children would set up a savings account in a bank in the name of the minor child. The account would show one of the parents as parent and guardian, and normally the money could be taken out of the account only by the parent. The question arose as to whether or not there was an actual gift, since the parent still retained control over the property. Was there really delivery? The Uniform Gifts to Minors Act (UGMA) was drafted to set up a procedure for making legal gifts to minors. This act has been adopted in nearly all of the states. It provides a method for making gifts of money and of registered and unregistered securities to minors.

If the gift is money, the money may simply be deposited in a bank in the name of the giver or some other adult, or of some corporate trustee, such as a bank, with the statement that the party in whose name the account is registered is a custodian for the minor under the UGMA. If the gift is a registered security, then the giver registers the security as custodian for the minor under the UGMA. If the security is unregistered, it has to be delivered to another adult or to a bank or some other financial institution as trustee, together with a statement of the gift and an acknowledgment accepting the role of custodian of the security for and on behalf of the minor. The custodian has very broad powers as to the use and disposition of the property. The property can be exchanged or sold without the permission of the minor who is the beneficiary of the gift. Of course, the custodian is not permitted to use any of the property or any of the proceeds for personal benefit.

The Uniform Anatomical Gift Act. Traditionally, we do not think of the human body or parts of the human body as things of monetary value, so we were not concerned about property rights to our body or various parts of our body. Now that medical technology has developed processes for transplanting parts of one body to another body, the law must treat the human body and the parts thereof as property, and establish some procedure for making gifts of the human body or its parts. Under the Uniform Anatomical Gift Act (UAGA), people 18 years of age or older may make a gift of their entire body or any specified part of their body. However, the gift does not take effect until the death of the giver. Such gifts are revocable at any time. They are usually included in the giver's last will and testament. Also, many states have included an anatomical gift statement on the back of the driver's license. Persons wishing to donate their bodies or specific organs can so specify and sign and date the statement in the presence of two witnesses, who must also sign.

People also may sell or donate blood, a kidney, an eye, or some other organ the loss of which does not automatically cause death. Such gifts are not covered by the UAGA since they are not given at death.

Title by Inheritance

As indicated previously, you may become the owner of personal property as a result of a specific bequest in a deceased person's will. You may also become the owner of personal property through the process of *intestate succession*. This means that you are an heir under state statute and that you will receive a designated share of the decedent's personal property if there is no valid will which disposes of it.

Title by Accession

Accession simply means an addition to what you already have. An example of accession would be a situation where the lawn mower which your neighbor borrowed for the weekend broke down and he had to have it repaired. When your neighbor returned the lawn mower to you, you became the owner of the repairs by accession.

Values added to things

Problems of this type of acquisition of personal property arise when accession of considerable value is made without the property owner's consent and when the original item has been changed or altered so that identification is difficult. A trespasser cuts down small trees on my land, makes rustic lawn chairs from the trees, and sets up a stand along the highway to sell the lawn chairs. Who owns the lawn chairs which were previously my timber? There is no simple answer to this question because the courts have not agreed on one solution, especially if the original material was taken as the result of an innocent mistake.

If, on the other hand, the taking was intentional and wrongful, the original owner will no doubt be awarded the value of the chairs.

Title by Possession and Control

Title to personal property may be acquired in some instances by simply taking possession of an item and exercising rights of ownership and control over that item. Following are some common situations where title by possession could be legally exercised.

Title to Wildlife. Title to fish, birds, or wild animals may, in some instances, be acquired simply by taking possession and control of the fish, birds, or animals. Title by possession can only occur, however, where the fish, birds, or animals are not owned by another party or where such action would not violate national, state, or local laws for the conservation and protection of wildlife. If you trespass upon a farmer's land and catch fish in the farmer's private pond, the fish belong to the farmer, not you. If you go hunting when it is not legal to hunt a certain species of animal, then you will not be allowed to keep the slain animal, and you may have to pay a fine for your wrongful action.

Abandoned Personal Property. An item of personal property has been abandoned if the owner has intentionally and voluntarily relinquished control and possession of the item and has not transferred the title to the item in any manner to another person. The intent of the owner is simply to have nothing more to do with the item. The issue of whether or not the article has been abandoned will be a fact question in each case.

Lost or Mislaid Property. *Lost property* is property the owner accidentally dropped or property that was accidentally separated from the owner. The owner has no knowledge of the location of the lost property. *Mislaid property* is property which was voluntarily and intentionally placed somewhere by the owner and then forgotten. Lost or mislaid personal property, unlike abandoned personal property, is still the property of the owner who lost or mislaid it. However, it is generally held that the finder of lost property has a right to possession and control until the item is claimed by the true owner, if the item is found in a publicly accessible place, such as a street, a parking lot, or a store. On the other hand, if you find a billfold in an office or an apartment, the courts will generally say that the landowner or occupier has the right to possession of the billfold. Mislaid property generally stays with the owner or occupier of the place where it was discovered.

Lost versus mislaid property

The identity of the lost or mislaid item is also a factor in determining who has the better right to possession. A lost billfold will normally have the owner's identification in it, whereas a wristwatch that fell off the owner's wrist when the band broke would not be so identifiable. Courts may also consider the status of the finder. Trespassers usually have to turn over any property they find; so do employees whose jobs include such a duty.

Many states have finders' statutes which enable the finder to become the new owner of lost or mislaid property by advertising or posting notices. If the owner does not return and claim the property within the statutory period, usually one year, the finder can become the new owner. Some of these statutes require the finder to pay the state part of the value of the item.

Confusion

Things of different owners
mixed together

Title to personal property may be acquired when the property of different owners is so intermingled that the property of the individual owners cannot be identified or separated and returned to the specific owners. *Confusion* is most common when dealing with such fungible goods as corn, wheat, milk, and oil.

If three persons owning 1,000 bushels of wheat of the same grade and quality agree to intermingle their property for purposes of storage, there would be no problem since the intermingling was voluntary. Each party will simply have a one-third ownership in the total volume of wheat. The problem involving title to personal property arises where one owner intentionally and wrongfully intermingles goods with those of another person so that the goods of each owner can no longer be separated or distinguished. The majority of the courts, in a case where the commingling was deliberate and wrongful and without the permission of the other party, will simply grant the innocent party title to the entire volume of goods. The wrongdoer is punished by being deprived of any further right or title to the property. If the intermingling of the goods is not an intentional and wrongful act, and if the goods are of the same kind and quality, courts will usually hold that each owner now owns a proportionate share of the total mixed goods.

Title by Creation

Property is created when a new invention is made, when a new song or book is written, or when a new painting is created. These creations are the result of intellectual production. In title by creation, you are intellectually creating an expression of a new idea in which the law grants property rights. Earlier in this chapter we discussed the patent law which gives inventors certain property rights in the inventions they create, and the copyright law, which gives writers, composers, and producers of other copyrightable material certain property rights in their creations.

■ SIGNIFICANCE OF THIS CHAPTER

Ownership of property is one of the most basic concepts of the law. At one time it was said that "possession was nine tenths of the law," but in a civilized society we must have rules regarding the ownership of property, how it can be transferred, and who inherits what rights. Possession in itself may not mean very much. It is also important to understand the concept of the bundle of rights, as many things which we say we own are not wholly owned by us; that is, we do not own all the rights in that thing. Another very important question concerns things which may be attached to, or detached from, real estate. Landlords and tenants, and buyers and sellers of land, need to know which things are part of the land. As a tenant, before you attach any item of personal property, get permission from the landlord to do so, reserve the right to remove the item, and "get it in writing."

DISCUSSION CASE

FACTORS ETC., INC. v. CREATIVE CARD CO.

444 F.Supp. 279 (New York, 1977)

FACTS: On August 16, 1977, Elvis Presley died. During his life, his professional career and the commercial exploitation of his name were managed by "Colonel" Tom Parker. On March 26, 1956, Presley and Parker entered into a written management contract which, although it does not specifically cover souvenir merchandise, authorizes Parker to act exclusively for Presley "in any and all fields of public and private entertainment . . . embracing any and all branches thereof now known or hereafter coming into existence."

Plaintiff Boxcar Enterprises, Inc. entered into the Presley-Parker relationship as a corporation formed in January 1974. Col. Parker has testified that he owned 56 percent of the shares and that Presley and Tom Diskin, president of Boxcar, each owned 22 percent. On August 18, 1977, two days after the entertainer's death, Boxcar entered into an agreement with plaintiff Factors Etc., Inc., which purported to afford the latter an exclusive license to use the Presley likeness in connection with all souvenir merchandise. On August 24, 1977, Vernon Presley, father of the deceased and executor of his estate, agreed to a royalty arrangement with Boxcar as "Merchandising Representatives for the Elvis Presley Estate." Vernon Presley also wrote to Col. Parker on August 23, 1977, asking Col. Parker to "carry on according to the same terms and conditions as stated in the contractual agreement you had with Elvis."

Creative Card Co., after Presley's death, began to manufacture and sell souvenir merchandise with Presley's name or likeness on it. Boxcar and Factors filed suit for an injunction to stop Creative Card Co. from making or selling such merchandise.

■

District Judge Tenney gave the opinion for the court:

Plaintiffs have moved this Court for a preliminary injunction pursuant to Rule 65 of the Federal Rules of Civil Procedure ("Rules") to restrain defendant Creative Card Company from the manufacture, distribution and sale of any poster or other commercially exploitive souvenir merchandise bearing the likeness of the late entertainer Elvis Presley. Plaintiffs claim possession of an exclusive right to that activity, based on a "right of publicity" as-

signed by Elvis Presley in life. Defendant Creative Card Company, an Illinois corporation, disputes the existence and assignment of this right. . . .

The Presley/Parker/Boxcar/Factors Relationship

It is hornbook law that where there is ambiguity in a contract the intent of the parties may be ascertained by reference to their subsequent course of conduct. . . . For more than 20 years, Elvis Presley and Col. Parker had a working relationship where the division of labor was apparent: one performed, the other promoted. If some of the documents memorializing this activity are less artful than those which some professional counsel can draft, they are no less valid. Defendant points to inconsistencies in the statements of Col. Parker and others as to who held the right to "merchandise" the Presley image during his lifetime—Presley himself, Parker, or, eventually, Boxcar. In view of the Parker-Presley agreements, the uncontested allegation that Presley himself was a 22 percent shareholder of Boxcar and the fact that Boxcar paid royalties to Elvis Presley for souvenir merchandise sold, it seems clear enough, at least for purposes of a preliminary injunction, that Presley gave Parker leave to exploit his image through merchandise and that Boxcar was, in recent years, the vehicle through which such merchandising was carried on. Defendant's allusions to defective links in the chain of title in Boxcar, . . . lose sight of the true facts: these entities involved the same people. With the exception of Diskin they had been doing business together for 20 years. None of the parties to the Presley-Parker business relationship appears to have been dissatisfied. . . .

The Right of Publicity

By far the most interesting issue in this case is whether Boxcar had anything to transfer to Factors when it entered into the August 18, 1977 "exclusive licensing" contract. After consulting the case law and certain commentaries in this field, . . . I have concluded that it did. It appears that a recognized property right, the "right of publicity," inhered in and was exercised by Elvis Presley in his lifetime, that it was assignable by him and was so assigned, that it survived his death and was capable of further assignment.

The "right of publicity" is not a new concept, but, to the detriment of legal clarity, it has often been discussed only under the rubric "right of privacy." It is said that the right of privacy embraces "four distinct kinds of invasion of four different interests of the plaintiff, which are tied together by the common name, but otherwise have almost nothing in common *except that each represents an interference with the right of the plaintiff 'to be let alone.'* ". . .

Based on the foregoing analysis, . . . plaintiffs' request for preliminary relief pursuant to Rule 65 is granted. Defendant Creative Card Company will be enjoined from manufacturing, distributing, selling or by any other means profiting from souvenir merchandise bearing the name or likeness of the late Elvis Presley until the merits of the case are determined.

■ IMPORTANT TERMS AND CONCEPTS

bundle of rights
patentability of computer
   software
personal property
public property
ownership in severalty
joint tenancy
community property
cooperative ownership
fixtures
Uniform Anatomical
   Gift Act
accession
lost property
confusion

copyrightability of
   computer software
real property
private property
tenants in common
tenancy by the entirety
condominium ownership
time sharing
Uniform Gifts to Minors
   Act
inheritance
abandoned personal
   property
mislaid property
title by creation

■ QUESTIONS AND PROBLEMS FOR DISCUSSION

1. What are the different ways in which ownership of property can be acquired?
2. What are the two classifications of personal property, and what sort of things does each include?
3. What is the difference between joint tenancy and tenancy by the entirety?
4. How does the community property system work? How many states are now using this system?
5. Kalyvakis was employed as an assistant steward aboard the T.S.S. Olympia, a passenger ocean liner. While the ship was moored at a pier in New York City taking on passengers for a cruise, Kalyvakis found $3,010 in U.S. currency lying scattered on the floor of the men's restroom on the upper deck. He turned the money over to the chief steward to hold for the owner of the money, should he come and claim it. Now three years have elapsed, no one has even made a claim for the money, and Kalyvakis asks that the money be returned to him. The T.S.S. Olympia owner, a Greek corporation, refused to turn over the money, so Mr. Kalyvakis sued. What should the court decide? Explain.

6. Sergeant Morrison was in command of an infantry squad on a search and destroy mission in Vietnam. They were searching a cave in the hills and found $150,000 in U.S. currency and a large sum of South Vietnamese money. The Sergeant turned all the money over to his superiors, as representatives of the government of the United States. Now Sergeant Morrison files claim in the U.S. Claims Court alleging that he was the finder and he should be entitled to the money. Who is entitled to this money? Why?

7. Charley and Carla Loveless had been married for six years when they filed a joint petition for divorce. Carla had been employed full time throughout the marriage and has also done most of the couple's housework and cooking. Charley had worked only part time and had gone to school full time for four out of the six years. He had finished a B.S. in Engineering and had also received an M.B.A. The trial court found that the only marital "asset" of any value that the parties had accumulated during the marriage was Charley's M.B.A. degree. The court placed a value of $82,000 on his future extra earnings due to the degree, and it awarded Carla $33,000 of this amount, which Charley was to pay off at the rate of $100 per month. Charley appeals from this award, saying his M.B.A. isn't really "property." How should the appeals court rule? Explain.

8. Ralph Renter leased a commercial building from Owen Owner. Owen had been using the building for storage and so had never installed heating equipment. Ralph knew this when he leased the building. Ralph installed an oil burner and boiler in the basement so that he could heat the building, since he intended to use it as his workshop. Owen sold the building to Betty Bucks. When Ralph's lease expired, Ralph and Betty were unable to agree on terms for a renewal, so Ralph planned to move out—with the heating equipment. Upon learning that Ralph planned to remove the oil burner and boiler, Betty sued for an injunction. Should the injunction be granted? Why or why not?

33

Bailments

CHAPTER OBJECTIVES

THIS CHAPTER WILL:

- Define "bailment."
- Discuss the four essential elements needed to create a bailment.
- Describe the three types of bailments.
- Discuss the duty of care required of a nonprofessional bailee.
- Define the term *professional bailee*.
- Discuss the duty of care required of professional bailees.

Have you ever loaned your car to a friend? Have you ever taken your stereo back to the dealer for repairs, or checked your coat and hat at a restaurant? These are all *bailments*. A bailment exists when the possessor of personal property gives possession and control to another person with the agreement that there is no transfer of title to the object, and that the transfer of possession is temporary. The person who is giving up possession is a *bailor,* and the person who is receiving the personal property is a *bailee.*

■ ESSENTIAL ELEMENTS OF BAILMENT

Four essential elements must be present to create a bailment: (1) an agreement between the parties, (2) possession of the object to be bailed by the bailor, (3) delivery of the object to be bailed, and (4) a duty on the part of the bailee to return the object to either the bailor or to someone else as instructed by the bailor.

Agreement. The first essential element of a bailment, an agreement between the parties, can be expressed either orally or in writing, or it may be implied from the facts and circumstances of the situation. An express agreement of bailment would normally cover the consideration, if any, to the bailor for the use of bailed property or to the bailee for caring for it; what the property is going to be used for or how it is going to be used; when, where, and how the bailed item is to be returned to the bailor, delivered to someone else, or disposed of in some other manner; and other rights and duties of the parties.

Bailment may exist without a contract

Many bailments involve contracts. Many do not. If you rent a car, a contract between you and the rental company covers the bailment of the car. If you *borrow* your friend's car, there is an agreement between you, but no contract.

Possession by the Bailor. To have a bailment, the bailor must have possession of the object to be bailed. The bailor need not be the owner of the property. In fact, the bailor may be a bailee. For example, as the bailee of the car you rented, you may entrust it to a parking attendant and thus become its bailor, as to the parking lot.

No delivery = No bailment

Delivery of the Object to Be Bailed. There must be delivery of the object to be bailed from the bailor to the bailee, and the bailee must accept delivery of the object. As noted earlier, size, weight, and location prevent some items of personal property from being physically handed over to another person. Instead, we may have *constructive delivery,* such as handing a person the keys to a rental car in the parking lot and telling the person to go ahead and take the car. Where the bailed property contains other items, there is no bailment as to those items unless the bailee knows, or has reason to know, of their existence.

For example, suppose that a friend loans you a car to drive downtown. The friend asks you to bring it back to the parking garage, park it in an assigned space, and return the keys before 5 P.M. After making some purchases downtown, you open the trunk and find a pocket-size radio with earphones, the type used by joggers. You take it out and use it. Obviously the radio was not part of the car and it is not bailed property. You are using it without permission. The question in the *Theobald* case is whether Mae "delivered" her coat to the beauty shop.

THEOBALD v. SATTERTHWAITE

190 P.2d 714 (Washington, 1948)

FACTS   On December 24, 1946, Mae Theobald came to the beauty shop owned by Satterthwaite for a permanent wave. Mae hung her coat on a hook in the waiting room. On a prior visit, Mae had asked Helen whether it was safe to leave her coat there and Helen had told her that it was safe, that nothing had been stolen in 20 years. This time Mae's coat was stolen. The trial court gave Mae $300, the value of the coat, on the basis that there had been a bailment and that the waiting room was not a safe place since there was no bell or other warning device on the front door and since the waiting room was visible from the street. The Satterthwaites appealed.

ISSUE   Was there a bailment of the customer's coat?

DECISION   No. Judgment reversed.

REASONS   After reviewing the facts, Chief Justice Mallery first noted that on this occasion the proprietors of the shop had had no knowledge of the presence of Mae's coat and that therefore there could not be a bailment. But the main reason for the decision was that there had been no transfer of possession of the coat.

"[T]here is another and better ground upon which the appellants must prevail. That is that there was no change of possession or delivery in this case. . . .

"While we are not inclined to view the element of delivery in any technical sense, still we think there can be no delivery unless there is a change of possession of an article from one person to another.

"It follows that, in the absence of a bailment, the appellants owed the respondent no duty of care and were not negligent in failing to guard it effectively."

Bailee's Duty to Return Object to Bailor.   The bailee must have a duty to return the personal property to the bailor, to deliver the property to a third person, or to dispose the property in accordance with the bailor's wishes. Assume that you rent a truck to move your household goods from Los Angeles to New York. As the bailee, you will have a duty to return the specific property, the truck, to the bailor or to any person the bailor may designate. In this case, let's say that the bailor does not have an office in New York City, and therefore directs you to deliver the truck to a specific location in New York City where an employee of the bailor will pick it up and drive it back. The important factor here is that the object is still the bailor's property and that the bailee has the duty to give up possession of the object at the time and place that the bailor designates.

■ TYPES OF BAILMENTS

Who benefits from bailment

Basically, there are three types of bailment. First, there is a type where both parties benefit from the bailment. Before leaving school, you rent a rug shampooer from a rental agency to clean your apartment. You are paying to use the rug shampooer so the bailor benefits and, in exchange for your payment, you receive the right to possess, use, and control the rug shampooer for a specified time.

In a second type of bailment the bailor is the only person who benefits from the arrangement. For example, your neighbor is going to the store where you bought your stereo and you ask that person to take your stereo back for adjustment. Your neighbor agrees, and you deliver the set to that person for the purpose of taking it to the store for repairs. Obviously, your neighbor is doing you a favor for no personal gain.

A third type of bailment is one where only the bailee benefits. Your roommate borrows your car for the evening. No payment is to be made; the bailment is simply for the benefit of the bailee. In each of these last two situations, there is a bailment even though there is no contract.

Bailments also can be classified into two major categories: *gratuitous bailments,* where no fee is charged for the use or care; of the bailed object, and bailments where a fee is charged. Bailments made in exchange for payment can be further broken down into two areas: ***commercial bailors*** such as automobile or equipment rental companies, and ***professional bailees,*** such as common carriers, innkeepers (hotels and motels), and warehouses.

■ CUSTODY SITUATIONS WHERE A BAILMENT WILL NOT NORMALLY EXIST

Custody ≠ Bailment

Businesspeople need to understand the difference between bailments and custody situations where a bailment will not exist. By knowing what creates a bailment, business owners can reduce liability for damage or theft of customers' property by avoiding situations in which they would become bailees. For example, in the typical university parking lot you either pay by the month, or get a claim check upon entering and pay when leaving. Since you park your own car and keep the keys, no bailment exists. You have not entrusted your car to the parking lot owner; you simply rent space. If, however, a parking lot attendant gives you a claim check, takes your car, parks it, and retains the keys, then there is a delivery to and acceptance by the bailee. In the case involving the university parking lot there was no delivery or acceptance by the university. You simply drove your car in and parked it.

■ RIGHTS AND DUTIES OF THE BAILEE

Since a bailment is based on an express or implied agreement between two parties, each party has rights and duties with regard to the use, care, and eventual return of the object of the bailment.

Rights of the Bailee. The bailee has the right to possess, use, and control the object during the period of the bailment, subject to any legal restrictions and to the restrictions in any express or implied agreement. For example, a garage to which you had given your car for repairs would not have the right to make any other use of it.

Duty of Care for the Bailed Property.   The general rule is that the bailee must take reasonable care of the bailed object while it is in the bailee's possession and control. If something happens to the bailed object, does the bailee have to reimburse the bailor for the cost of repairs if damaged, or the value of the object if it was lost or stolen? If, in fact, the bailee exercised reasonable care and still the damage or loss occurred, the bailee owes nothing to the bailor. If, however, the bailee failed to use reasonable care, then the bailee would be liable to the bailor for the damages or the value of the object if lost or stolen.

Now the question is: How much care is reasonable? The courts look at various factors when determining what level of care is reasonable. First, the court will look to see what type of bailment is involved? Is it a mutual benefit bailment, a bailment solely for the benefit of bailee, or a bailment solely for the benefit of the bailor? Next, courts take into consideration the type of object, and when appropriate, the skill level of the bailee.

Even in the case where the bailment is for the sole benefit of the bailor, the bailee must still use reasonable care, however, some courts have required a lesser degree of care by a bailee where the sole benefit is for the bailor, than would be required in cases where there was a mutual benefit bailment or a bailment for the sole benefit of the bailee. The *Snyder* case which follows discusses the degree of care required by a bailee.

Bailee's duty to exercise reasonable care

SNYDER v. FOUR WINDS SAILBOAT CENTRE, LTD.

701 F.2d 251 (U.S. Second Circuit, 1983)

FACTS   On September 12, 1979, Snyder bought a 27-foot sailboat from Four Winds. Under the contract he was given "free" storage for the winter. Four Winds' president refused to pay storage and said that the storage price was to be paid out of the salesman's commission on the sale. Snyder took delivery of his boat at the Four Winds marina in mid-October and took it out with the salesman on two or three short shake-down cruises, at the conclusion of which the salesman told Snyder where to tie up. After each cruise, Four Winds kept the keys to the four locks on the boat. Four Winds did not maintain dock guards, alarms, or other security devices. It did have three mercury vapor lights in the docking and office area. It also had a locked boat storage building with an alarm.

On Sunday, November 4, 1979, Snyder told the salesman that he would not be using the boat any more and directed that it be put into the locked building. The salesman said the boat would be taken out of the water sometime that week.

The last time the boat was seen was on Tuesday, November 6, 1979, by the president of Four Winds, who was checking the boats at his marina because someone had been reported as burglarizing another marina 100 feet away. He discovered the Snyder boat missing the following morning. Four Winds reported the theft to the police and the Coast Guard, but the boat was never seen again.

Judge Mishler awarded Snyder the cost of the boat, $32,261, plus interest. Four Winds appealed.

ISSUE

Was there a bailment? If so, did the bailee exercise reasonable care for the safety of the bailed property?

DECISION

Yes. No. Judgment for Snyder affirmed.

REASONS

Per Curiam (an opinion by the whole court). The court found that:
"Four Winds makes four arguments on appeal: (1) there was no bailment; (2) if there were any bailment it was merely gratuitous; (3) if there were a bailment for the parties' mutual benefit, liability must be founded on negligence; and (4) plaintiff failed to meet its burden of proof.

"Four Winds' argument that there was no bailment rests on *Marino* v. *Gagliano,* . . . where a sailboat owner paid a fee for the opportunity to tie his boat at a slip assigned to him. But neither *Marino* nor *Blank* v. *Marine Basin Co., Inc.,* . . . a decision on which *Marino* is based, involves storage as in this case. Moreover, in neither case is there any indication that the marina owner had exclusive custody of the boat, as here, where Four Winds kept the keys.

"Judge Mishler correctly concluded that a bailment results for the mutual benefit of the vessel owner and the dock operator when a vessel is placed at a dock for storage. . . . Although Four Winds charged no storage fee, the bailment was not gratuitous, but rather was incidental to the contract of sale, a transaction involving compensation. Four Winds gave Snyder 'free' storage as an incentive to buy the yacht in the autumn; making the sale was a benefit to Four Winds resulting from the storage agreement.

"We accept it as a fact that Four Winds could not erect a fence in the navigable waterway. But although there was little testimony on the common practice in the marina industry, a member of the Marine Division of the Freeport Police Department testified that a few marinas on these waterways have fencing preventing access from the land, and a few employ watchmen. Four Winds, however, had no security whatsoever other than lights and it was surely chargeable with knowledge of the fact that Snyder's boat, which he had directed be placed in the locked storage building, bore no markings and consequently was, like an automobile with keys, more likely to be subject to theft. While a marina is not an insurer for the boat owner who stores his boat there, its duty of ordinary and reasonable care requires that it take some measures, such as private security service, to protect the boats it stores. . . .

"At the very least, Judge Mishler found, when Four Winds learned that there was a thief in the area, it should have taken some additional precautions, and this it failed to do."

■ CONTRACT LIABILITY OF THE BAILEE

In view of the uncertainty about what the common-law liability of the bailee may be, in certain circumstances it is advisable to specify the bailee's liability in the bailment contract. This is especially true for a commercial bailee, such as a garage or a repair shop. A parking garage will normally have a clause in the bailment contract stating that the garage will not be responsible for theft of, or damage to, the automobile while the automobile is in its custody. Typically,

Contract may change the duty of care

this clause is printed on a parking ticket which you receive as you enter the parking lot. Also, the terms are in very small print. This clause may be effective in relieving the bailee of liability for damage to your car if the clause is called to your attention when you leave the car, except in cases where the bailee or its agents or employees negligently or willfully damage the bailed property. If the parking attendant backed your car into a post, for example, the bailee would be liable for the damages even though a clause in the bailment contract disclaimed all liability. If, on the other hand, the brakes of another parked car failed and that car ran into your parked car, no negligence would be attributed to the bailee or its employees or agents; the clause would relieve the bailee of liability.

Disclaimers may be against public policy

Some courts have held such **disclaimers** to be against public policy, and thus not effective in limiting the professional bailee's liability.

The other extreme in contract clauses concerns the bailee's assumption of full liability for the bailed object. If you take your diamond ring to the jeweler for cleaning, the jeweler may issue a bailment contract which is, in effect, an insurance policy for the safety of your ring. If the jewelry store is broken into and your ring is stolen, the jeweler or its insurance company will reimburse you for the value of the ring. Rental contracts for cars, trailers, and equipment typically contain similar clauses, which purport to make the bailee liable for any loss to the property. They may or may not be fully effective.

■ BAILOR'S LIABILITY FOR DEFECTS

The traditional bailment litigation is that of a bailor suing a bailee for loss of, or damage to, the bailed property. Even though the amounts involved in many of these cases are relatively small, the results are important to the parties.

More and more, people are renting all kinds of items from professional rental companies. Hundreds of thousands of cars are rented each year. Many businesses have discovered that it is more economical to rent trucks when they need them than to own and maintain their own fleets. College students rent furniture, TV's, and refrigerators. Do-it-yourselfers rent all types of tools and equipment. Businesses rent computers, software, and other office equipment. As a result, legal rules have been formulated to deal with cases in which the rented property is defective in some way and causes injury to the bailee or to third persons. Most recently, an entire Article (2A) has been added to the Uniform Commercial Code to provide a more complete set of rules for such leases of personal property.

Where the bailor simply loans an item to a friend, the bailor's only duty is to inform the friend-bailee of any known hazards or defects in the item. The bailor has no obligation to inspect the item or to discover existing defects. If the bailee has been informed of all known defects, the bailor has no further liability.

Professional bailor is liable for any defects

In the mutual benefit bailment, the bailor's obligation is much more extensive. Most courts that have looked at this problem in recent years have applied to the professional bailor the same three theories of product liability that are applied to the seller of goods. In such cases, a bailor may be held liable for negligence because of a failure to exercise reasonable care in maintaining, servicing, and inspecting equipment which is being rented for immediate use. The bailor may also be held liable for breach of warranty—either express warranty or the implied warranties of merchantability and fitness. The most recent development has been the extension to professional bailors of strict liability in tort for defects in their rented items, as seen in the *Cintrone* case.

CINTRONE v. HERTZ TRUCK LEASING & RENTAL SERVICE

212 A.2d 769 (New Jersey, 1965)

FACTS Francisco Cintrone was injured when the brakes failed on a 1959 Ford truck which his employer had leased from Hertz. Cintrone had driven the truck for three days during the previous week. Cintrone said that he had complained to Hertz each day about the brakes. When the accident occurred, Cintrone was a passenger in the truck; the driver was Robert Sottilare. Sottilare said that prior to the accident he had had no difficulty with the brakes: "they wasn't perfect"; "they were a little low, but they held." Both men were injured when the top of the truck hit a low bridge; the brakes had failed completely. The trial judge refused to charge the jury on Cintrone's breach of warranty claim, and the jury found for Hertz on the negligence claim, apparently feeling that neither party had been guilty of any negligence. Cintrone appealed.

ISSUE Did the trial judge err in refusing to charge the jury on a breach of warranty theory?

DECISION Yes. Judgment reversed and case remanded for a new trial.

REASONS Justice Francis, speaking for the court, stated:

"[T]he offering to the public of trucks and pleasure vehicles for hire necessarily carries with it a representation that they are fit for operation. This representation is of major significance because both new and used cars and trucks are rented. In fact, . . . the nature of the business is such that the customer is expected to, and in fact must, rely ordinarily on the express or implied representation of fitness for immediate use. . . . [I]f a traveler comes into an airport and needs a car for a short period and rents one from a U-drive-it agency, when he is 'put in the driver's seat' his reliance on the fitness of the car assigned to him for the rental period whether new or used usually is absolute. In such circumstances the relationship between the parties fairly calls for an implied warranty of fitness for use, at least equal to that assumed by a new car manufacturer. The content of such warranty must be that the car will not fail mechanically during the rental period."

■ STATUTORY LIABILITY OF THE BAILEE

In certain types of bailments, the bailee has a statutory duty rather than a common-law duty of care. Common carriers and innkeepers are by law held to a higher degree of care with regard to bailed property. Some states also have special statutes for parking lots, repair shops, dry cleaners, and other specific categories of bailees. Such statutes typically give the bailee a lien for services performed and the power to sell the property, if necessary, to enforce the lien.

■ PROFESSIONAL BAILEES: SPECIAL RULES AND REGULATIONS

Common carriers, warehouses, and innkeepers are referred to as professional bailees, and as such they are subject to certain special rules and regulations.

Common Carriers

A *common carrier* is an organization, such as a railroad, a truckline, an airline, a bus company, a moving company, a pipeline, or any other type of business, that presents itself to the public as a transporter of goods or people. A common carrier must be licensed by the Interstate Commerce Commission (ICC) if it transports goods or persons over state lines, and also has to be licensed by the commerce commissions of the various states where it operates. The license designates the routes and territory over which the common carrier is allowed to travel and do business. The common carrier may also be restricted to the transportation of a certain type of cargo. For example, the large household-moving companies move only household goods and do not have to accept commercial goods for transportation. The rates of the common carrier may be subject to ICC regulation and the various state commerce commissions. Airlines, railroads, and bus lines are common carriers that carry passengers as well as goods. In the past, their rates were strictly regulated; however, the trend now is toward deregulation, which allows competition among the carriers.

Definition of common carrier

Common Carrier of Goods—Special Duty of Care. The basic difference between the duty of care required of the bailee in the ordinary bailment and that required in the common carrier bailment is that the bailee in an ordinary bailment must use reasonable care for the care and protection of the bailed goods, whereas the common carrier is by law virtually an *absolute insurer* of the goods being transported from the time that it receives the goods until it delivers them to their final destination. This is a very high duty of care, and there have been many instances where liability has been imposed for goods lost or damaged in transportation or delivery despite the fact that the common carrier used reasonable care.

Common carrier held strictly liable for damage to goods

The common carrier is strictly liable for damage to the bailor's goods while they are in its possession. At first glance, this rule may seem very harsh since loss or damage to goods could be caused by elements beyond the control or foreseeability of the common carrier. For this reason, five exceptions to the strict liability, or absolute insurer, rule have been adopted to reduce the common carrier's liability in certain circumstances. These exceptions are for damage to goods or the loss of goods which is caused:

Five exceptions to insurer rule

1. *By an act of God.* For example, a tornado destroys the shipment.
2. *By action of an alien enemy.* This would include damage in an invasion by enemy military forces.
3. *By an order of public authority.* For example, if goods in shipment were in close proximity to a radiation leak from a nuclear power plant, the public authorities might condemn the shipment and have it disposed of.

4. *By the inherent nature of the goods.* For example, if goods are perishable, the bailor who is contracting to have them transported must notify the bailee of the problem, and the bailee may not want to accept the goods unless it has proper facilities for refrigeration and some guarantee of speedy transportation and delivery.

5. *By the bailor's negligence in packaging or crating.* This one is the most used exception.

The courts tend to be very strict in their interpretation of the five exceptions. As a rule, for the carrier to avoid liability, the loss or damage must be due solely to one of the five excepted causes.

Liability among Connecting Carriers. One problem that seems to come up constantly is that of the liability of the initial bailee versus the liability of the various connecting carriers or subbailees. If you were shipping goods from New York City to Los Angeles, you would make a bailment contract with a shipper-bailee in New York City, and that shipper would accept the goods for transportation and final delivery. However, as we learned, common carriers are limited in the routes and territory over which they can operate. Therefore, the New York common carrier might transfer the goods to several connecting common carriers before the goods are finally delivered in Los Angeles. Assume that the goods were in good condition when the bailor delivered them to the bailee carrier but were severely damaged when they finally were delivered in Los Angeles. Who damaged them—the original bailee, one of the connecting carriers, or the delivering carrier?

Obviously, in many cases it is impossible to know which of the carriers caused the damage. Since there is strict liability for damage to the goods, the bailor may collect the full amount for the loss, and may make the claim against either the initial bailee or the delivering bailee. The bailee to whom the claim is made may, in turn, seek restitution from the other carriers involved. Thus, without proof as to which carrier actually caused the loss, the loss may be shared by all of the parties that handled the goods.

Common Carrier of Passengers—Special Duty of Care. What is the duty of the common carrier when the objects of transportation are persons rather than goods? Common carriers, such as railroads, airlines, and buses, that transport human beings, are not held to be absolute insurers of the safety of their passengers; however, their duty of care for their passengers' safety is still very high. The injured passenger must prove that the common carrier was guilty of at least some negligence.

Common Carrier—Right to Limit Liability to Bailor. In the absence of any specific state or national law or regulation, a common carrier has the right to limit its liability to its own negligence. Rather than accepting the strict liability or absolute safety standard, the carrier may include a limited liability provision in its contract with the shipper-bailor, provided, however, that the shipper-bailor is given a reduced rate in exchange for accepting the carrier's limited liability. In other words, if the shipper-bailor and the carrier-bailee agree to a limited liability contract, the courts generally will enforce the contract unless fraud, duress, or unconscionability was involved in the transaction. If

Limited liability in return for a lower rate

the shipper-bailor so requests, however, the carrier-bailee must accept the shipment from the shipper-bailor with full liability, charging the full rate.

Agreement as to goods value

The common carrier may also make an agreement with the shipper regarding the value of the goods being shipped. Generally, the courts will accept this figure for loss purposes unless the amount appears unreasonable. Specific regulations of the Interstate Commerce Commission have further limited the liability of certain common carriers which transport goods in interstate commerce. These regulations do not affect the legal liability of the carrier for loss or damage. The liability is still strict liability with the exceptions previously noted. These regulations simply place a limit on the amount that the carrier must pay for loss of, or damage to, the goods.

If the shipper-bailor desires protection up to the full value of the goods, then the shipper-bailor may buy value insurance from the carrier or the carrier's insurance company. Specific regulations also limit the liability of common carriers that handle commercial freight rather than household goods. The value per pound is usually less for commercial freight. It should also be noted that the Interstate Commerce Commission regulations will change from time to time.

International regulations

Shipper-bailors should make themselves aware of the pertinent regulations. Although Interstate Commerce Commission regulations govern the transportation of goods and persons in interstate commerce within the United States, many common carriers carry passengers and goods by air and sea outside the territorial limits of the United States. Thus, there is a need for treaties and regulations that limit the liability of common carriers involved in international commerce and travel. The Warsaw Convention is a treaty that limits the liability of airlines carrying passengers in international travel. The Carriage of Goods by Sea Act similarly limits the liability of carriers operating in international waters.

Liability limitations on baggage

Common carriers of passengers, such as airlines, railroads, and bus lines, are required to have certain facilities for carrying the passengers' baggage. Regulations stipulate the number of bags that each passenger can transport and the maximum weight of each bag or the maximum weight of each passengers' total baggage. If baggage exceeds the weight limit or if the number of bags checked exceeds the allowable number, an added fare is charged. Limits have also been set on the common carrier's liability for loss of, or damage to, the baggage. The common carrier is not an absolute insurer of the passenger's baggage, but is responsible only for its negligence in its handling. Such negligence is defined as a lack of reasonable care in handling the baggage.

Bill of Lading—A Document of Title. Except for automobiles, boats, airplanes, and other personal property which must be specifically licensed to be used, the owner of personal property normally does not have a specific ownership document for such property. This explains the expression, "Possession is nine tenths of the law." In other words, it is assumed that people own the objects in their possession unless such ownership is challenged by another person. Thus, for most of the goods that are shipped, such as household or commercial, there are no specific title registration certificates. The shipper-bailor simply delivers the goods to the common carrier with instructions to transport and deliver them, or the common carrier comes to the residence or business of the shipper and picks up the goods with instructions as to their transportation and delivery.

At the point where the shipper-bailor turns over possession to the common
carrier-bailee, a document showing ownership of the particular goods is necessary. This document is called a ***bill of lading*** if the transportation is by land
or sea, and it is called an ***air bill*** if the transportation is by air. The bill of
lading or air bill serves as both a receipt for the goods and as a contract
which states the terms of the agreement to transport and deliver the goods.

Title to the goods may be transferred from the shipper to another person or
organization by transferring the bill of lading or air bill.

A bill of lading or an air bill can be negotiable or nonnegotiable. If the
bill is to be negotiable, it will state that the goods are to be delivered to the
bearer of the bill or to the order of a specific person or organization. If the
bill simply consigns the goods to a specific person or organization at the point

of delivery, then it is nonnegotiable and it is called a *straight bill of lading* or
a *straight air bill*.

The bill of lading or air bill must describe the goods. Typically, it will
state the weight of the goods and describe the number of items and the content
of the shipment in such a manner that the person receiving the goods will
be able to identify them as those which were entrusted to the carrier for shipment.

Article 7 of the Uniform Commercial Code, Warehouse Receipts, Bills of
Lading, and Other Documents of Title, contains specific provisions governing
the issuance and use of bills of lading and warehouse receipts. Normally, the
bill of lading is issued to the shipper-bailor. The shipper-bailor can then mail
the bill of lading to the person or organization that is to receive the goods at
their final destination. However, Uniform Commercial Code Section 7–305(1)
allows the shipper to request that the common carrier issue the bill of lading
directly to the person or organization receiving the goods at the final destination
or at any other place the shipper-bailor may request. Obviously, situations
arise where mailing the bill of lading to the receiver of the goods would be
unwise. It would be better to have the bill of lading issued by the carrier
directly to the person or organization receiving the goods prior to or at the
time of delivery.

If the bill of lading is negotiable, then the carrier may not deliver the goods
without getting the bill of lading properly indorsed by the person or organization
receiving them. If the goods are shipped under a nonnegotiable bill of lading,
the carrier can simply deliver them to the person or organization named as
consignee in the bill, and the bill of lading need not be indorsed by the receiving
party. With a nonnegotiable bill, the carrier must verify that the receiving
party is in fact the party to whom the shipment was supposed to be delivered.
If the carrier delivers the goods to the wrong person, the carrier will be responsible to the shipper-bailor.

Warehouses

A public warehouse presents itself to the public as a business engaged in storing
goods for members of the public for a fee. A private warehouse is a storage
business that is not open to the public, but only leases storage space to one
person or company or to a select number of persons or companies.

Duties of a Warehouse as a Bailee.   A warehouse is liable for damage to,
or loss of, the goods being stored by the bailor only if the warehouse fails to

exercise reasonable care in their storage or handling. The warehouse is generally not held to the same standard of care as that required of the common carrier. What constitutes reasonable care has to be resolved in each case. The care required to store goods subject to damage or to deterioration by freezing would certainly be different from the care required to store lawn furniture for the winter. Fragile goods require more care than nonfragile goods. Stacking heavy cartons on top of fragile antique tables would not be reasonable care. Thus, the standard of care depends on the type and condition of the goods being stored, and the warehouse must provide facilities suitable for the goods being stored.

Rights of a Warehouse as a Bailee.   The public warehouse is entitled to a lien for the amount of the storage charges on the goods stored by the bailor. If the stored goods are not picked up by the bailor at the designated time, the warehouse, after giving proper legal notice to the owner or to any other person having an interest in the goods, may sell the goods to pay off the lien. Most states have specific laws relating to the operation of warehouses and setting out the rights and duties of warehouses with regard to the claiming of liens for storage fees and with regard to the sale of stored goods to satisfy their bills.

Rights of a Warehouse to Limit its Liability to Bailors.   Like common carriers, warehouses may arrive at an agreement with the bailor on the values of the items being stored, and the courts will generally accept these figures assessing losses unless the amounts appear unreasonable. Warehouses may also limit their liability as to the amount which they will pay if stored goods are lost or damaged. Such a limit on liability is a contractual agreement between the bailor and the warehouse. The warehouse gives the bailor a reduced rate, and the bailor agrees to a maximum amount for which the warehouse will be liable if the stored item is lost or damaged. The warehouse's liability limit must be stated for each item or each unit of weight and not simply as a standard dollar amount per customer.

Warehouse Receipts—Another Document of Title.   Every warehouse which stores goods for the public must issue a *warehouse receipt* to the bailor when the bailor leaves goods for storage. There is no specific statutory form that must be used. However, the receipt must contain certain essential terms, such as the *location* of the warehouse, the *date* the receipt was issued, and the *consecutive number* of the receipt. It also must contain a statement about *delivery*. Will the goods be delivered to the bearer of the receipt, or to the order of a specified person? If so, the receipt is negotiable. Or, will the goods be delivered only to a specified person, thus making the receipt nonnegotiable? The rates to be charged must also be stated, and the goods must be described so that they can later be identified. The receipt must be signed by an employee or agent of the warehouse, and if any advances have been made or any liabilities incurred, an explanation must be made on the receipt. Section 7–202 of the Uniform Commercial Code governs the contents of the warehouse receipt.

Reasonable care required

Warehouse has lien

Agreement as to value of goods

UCC Section 7–202 governs contents of receipt

Innkeepers

An *innkeeper,* more commonly known today as a hotelkeeper, is any person or organization that operates a hotel, motel, or other business that offers sleeping and living accommodations to transient persons. Owners of an apartment complex are not innkeepers, since they are not in the business of offering sleeping and living accommodations to transient persons.

Liability of the Innkeeper for Loss of or Damage to Goods of Its Guests. Traditionally, the innkeeper was an insurer of the safety of the goods of its guests. The innkeeper's liability was subject to exceptions similar to those applicable to the liability of the common carrier for the bailor's goods. Thus, the innkeeper was not liable for damage to the guest's goods caused by an act of God, a public enemy, the nature of the goods, some act of a public authority, or negligence or fault of the guest, who in this instance is the bailor. Today, most states have passed laws to limit the common-law liabilities of the innkeeper. Many statutes allow the innkeeper to limit its liability by posting a notice of the limitations. Frequently, a notice will be placed on the door of a hotel room or a card will be left in the room which states that the hotel will not be responsible for the theft of money, jewelry, or similar valuables. It advises guests to deposit these valuables with the innkeeper to be put in its safe until they are ready to leave.

Strict liability rule

The following case applies these rules.

FEDERAL INSURANCE CO. v. WALDORF-ASTORIA HOTEL

303 N.Y.S.2d 297 (New York, 1969)

FACTS   Cesar Caceras, a guest at the Waldorf, discovered that his gold cuff links had been stolen from his room. Each cuff link was decorated with a nine-millimeter pearl; the cuff links were worth $175. The hotel denied liability under the innkeeper statute, saying that the cuff links were "jewels," "ornaments," or "precious stones" which should have been placed in the hotel safe.

ISSUE   Were the cuff links "safe" property?

DECISION   No. Defendant's motion for summary judgment denied; plantiff's motion for summary judgment granted.

REASONS   Judge Schwartz indicated that the only question was one of statutory interpretation. As he saw it:

"Cuff-links are not used as jewels or ornaments but to close the cuffs, otherwise buttonless, of shirts. They are articles of utilitarian and ordinary wear in daily use, on all occasions, with business clothes as well as clothes designed for leisure, in the daytime as well as the evening. They are carried principally for use and convenience and not for ornament. Cuff-links, as with watches and other articles of ordinary wear, may be made of precious metals and even made more elaborate with precious stones, but these do not change their essential description as articles of ordinary wear."

Other states besides New York have enacted laws which limit the maximum amount for which an innkeeper can be held liable. Such a law might say that the innkeeper cannot be held liable for any amount in excess of $500 for loss or damage to the goods of a single guest. Some states have simply reduced the high standard of care that the common law required of innkeepers to a standard of ordinary care, basically the same care that any bailee must use with regard to bailed property. In no case, however, can an innkeeper be held liable for more than the actual value of the guest's goods. Moreover, the innkeeper is not liable for any consequential damages that may result from damage to, or loss of, the guest's property. For example, a manufacturer's representative rents a hotel room, and has two suitcases of samples used to demonstrate products to prospective customers. The innkeeper could be responsible for the value of the samples and the suitcases, but would not be liable for any lost sales caused by the representative's inability to show samples to prospective customers.

Innkeeper—Special Rights. The innkeeper is given a *lien* on all goods brought onto the premises by the guest for the charges for the accommodations. In most states, the innkeeper can hold those goods until the guest's debt is paid, and the innkeeper can ultimately sell those goods to enforce the lien.

■ SIGNIFICANCE OF THIS CHAPTER

Every person either has been or will be a bailor and a bailee. Most bailments in which we are involved from day to day are gratuitous, such as loaning a book to a friend, or letting neighbors use a lawn mower while theirs is getting repaired. Remember, even though no money changes hands, a bailment still exists in those situations, and there is a possibility of legal action if the bailed object is lost, stolen, damaged, or totally destroyed. If the bailment is a business agreement with a professional bailee, such as a common carrier, a warehouse, or an innkeeper, then there are special rules and regulations which will govern the parties' rights and duties.

Prospective bailors and bailees should understand these rules and regulations and also realize that the various states may have other special regulations affecting their rights and duties.

DISCUSSION CASE

KRAAZ v. LA QUINTA MOTOR INNS, INC.
410 So.2d 1048 (Louisiana, 1982)

FACTS: Plaintiffs, Larry and Joyce Kraaz, are in an itinerant business: buying, selling, racing, and betting on horses. Their only permanent home is the residence of his parents in Chicago.

On December 31, 1978, Mr. and Mrs. Kraaz were attending the race meeting at the Fair Grounds and were staying at the La Quinta Motor Inn in Metairie, Louisiana. At approximately 4 A.M. the 17-year-old desk clerk, David Ulmer, was approached by two men. One of them identified himself as Benson in 233, who had lost his key.

Since there was a Benson registered in 233 and no room key available, Ulmer gave the man a passkey to all the rooms in the motel. This was contrary to company policy. Subsequently, Ulmer became apprehensive, discovered that Benson knew nothing about the key request, and observed two men coming from the direction of the Kraaz's room, one of them with a gun in his waistband.

In the interim, the two men had unlocked the door of the room occupied by Mr. and Mrs. Kraaz and broken the chain. They hog-tied Larry Kraaz, physically abused Joyce Kraaz, and took a package containing about $23,000 from Mrs. Kraaz's purse. They also took a .25 caliber Smith & Wesson automatic but overlooked another $15,000 in cash which was lying near the gun. The thieves also failed to find an additional $3,000 in the purse. The money was intended for the purchase of race horses. The testimony was that these are generally cash transactions.

Larry Kraaz said he was knocked out of bed and pinned down on the floor by two men with a gun. His wife started screaming and got hit in the face. Kraaz feared he would be killed and his wife raped and killed. He heard the hammer clicking on a large caliber weapon being held against his head. After he was tied with wire and his mouth taped, they mauled his wife and put her in the bathtub. Then they came out of the bathroom, picked up her purse, emptied it out, grabbed the bundle of cash and ran. Kraaz broke the wire, threw his pants on and reached for his pistol, but it was gone. He got a .44 magnum from his car and tried unsuccessfully to intercept the thieves at the back door of the motel. While chasing through the motel with his gun, Kraaz observed the elderly security guard sound asleep on the steps behind the office. Since the crime, Joyce Kraaz has become paranoid about motels, and Larry has lost her companionship. She had previously travelled around the country with him 10 months of the year. Now Joyce Kraaz feels more secure in Chicago, where there are other people and a dog in the house. After the accident, he described her as "a complete basket case."

One of the two assailants wore a mask. Joyce Kraaz was convinced that she and her husband would be killed, because she could identify the man without the mask. Her mouth, leg and hip were bruised and swollen. She remained in the room until her husband took her to the hospital that afternoon about 5 P.M. She could not walk and thought her hip might be broken. The emergency room doctor told her that the swelling was just a very bad bruise and would go away in time. She has been too frightened and uncomfortable to resume her former life and now takes sleeping pills and tranquilizers regularly. She has lost weight and has no appetite. Because she needs help, she intends to undergo therapy with a Chicago psychiatrist.

Dr. Terry E. Passman, a board-certified psychiatrist, saw Joyce Kraaz shortly after the robbery on January 3, 1979. He described her as extremely frightened, apprehensive, and essentially unable to function. He gave her some medication to calm her down enough to converse. Dr. Passman diagnosed an acute traumatic neurosis. Despite her total incapacity, he decided hospitalization might aggravate the anxiety. Sodium Amytal, an extremely strong sleeping drug, was administered intravenously at a hospital emergency room to help her over the initial period of shock. According to Dr. Passman, Joyce Kraaz had experienced several traumatic incidents as an adolescent, which she has repressed. The experience at the La Quinta broke down this defense mechanism and caused an exaggerated reaction to the situation. In Dr. Passman's opinion, Mrs. Kraaz could have lived a normal life except for this incident.

A notice allegedly posted on the door of the Kraaz room quotes some "Louisiana Hotel Laws" in very small print. The entire notice measures approximately three inches by seven inches. When a safe is provided and a notice to that effect is "conspicuously posted," liability is limited to $100. Significantly, Civil Code Article 2969 exempts from this limitation losses that "occur through the fraud and negligence of the landlord, or some clerk or servant provided by him in such inn or hotel." *Laubie v. Sonesta Intern. Hotel Corp.*, (Louisiana, 1981) held that the limitation of liability in LSA–C.C. Art. 2971 only applies to the innkeepers' contractual liability as a depositary. The innkeeper remains liable for damages resulting from fault on the part of him or his employees.

Neither the investigating officers nor the Kraazs saw the notice allegedly posted in the room. Joyce and Larry Kraaz both said they didn't know the La Quinta had a safe.

The trial court concluded that La Quinta's employee was grossly negligent in providing a passkey to criminals and the motel was liable for the Kraazs' damages. Mrs. Kraaz was awarded $3,500 for physical injuries, $30,000 for traumatic neurosis, and future medical expenses of $13,000. Mr. Kraaz was awarded $2,500 for his physical and mental pain and suffering and $23,000 for the lost cash. The trial court was not satisfied that there was a notice posted on the motel door, but stated that, even if present, it was not sufficient to alert the Kraazs to the fact that a depositary was available for the protection of their valuables. The Court of Appeals affirmed. Defendant appealed.

■

Justice Watson:

Defendant relies heavily on LSA–C.C. Art. 2970 which provides:

He [the innkeeper] is not responsible for what is stolen by force or arms, or with exterior breaking open of doors, or by any other extraordinary violence.

The Court of Appeals held that Civil Code Art. 2970 was not applicable because, even though the chain on the door was broken, the initial entry to the room was made with a passkey. . . . If a forcible armed entry were unaccompanied by fault on the part of the innkeeper or his employees, there would be no liability. However, that is not the case. The elderly security guard was asleep. The 17-year-old boy on duty gave a passkey to the entire motel to two strangers. There was unquestionably negligence. Since the passkey was a key element in the robbery, Civil Code article 2970 does not exonerate the innkeeper from liability.

An innkeeper does not insure his guests against the risk of injury or property loss resulting from violent crime. . . . The innkeeper's position vis-a-vis his guests is similar to that of a common carrier toward its passengers. . . . Thus, a guest is entitled to a high degree of care and protection. The innkeeper has a duty to take reasonable precautions against criminals. Safeguarding the room keys is a minimum requirement. The duty to avoid handing a passkey to any stranger is even stronger. Breach of this duty was a direct cause of plaintiffs' physical, emotional, and financial damages. La Quinta's employee, Ulmer, was at fault in giving the two armed robbers a passkey. The employer is liable for the resulting damages. . . .

Contributory negligence of the Kraazs in having the money with them is urged as a defense. Mere possession of money does not constitute negligence. The trial court was unconvinced that a notice about safe keeping was posted in the room. . . . Even if posted and adequate, the notice was certainly not conspicuous. The Kraazs could not foresee that assailants would open their room door with a passkey in the middle of the night, leaving them no time to defend themselves or call for help. They were not negligent.

There is no abuse of discretion in the award of damages. . . . The facts more than support the amounts awarded.

For the foregoing reasons, the judgment of the Court of Appeals is affirmed.

Justice Blanche (dissenting):

Plaintiff, a horse-racing man who makes his living betting horses, called his wife in Chicago to bring him $25,000 out of the refrigerator where they kept their life savings. After a day at the Fairgrounds flashing their bankroll around, plaintiffs went out to dinner and then retired to their room in the LaQuinta Inn. In their possession at that time was $41,000 in cash. Although plaintiffs have a permanent home in the residence of their parents in Chicago, they are usually on the road, as the majority notes, travelling around the country about 10 months of the year. Thus, staying in motels should not be an unfamiliar surrounding, nor should hotel and motel rules concerning the deposit of valuables be unknown, especially to racing enthusiasts who carry such big bankrolls. . . .

With regard to the law, whose plain, unambiguous provisions were disregarded, the liability of an innkeeper for valuables is governed by C.C. Arts. 2968, 2969 and 2971. . . . An interpretation that these articles limit an innkeeper's liability only as a depositary renders C.C. Art. 2971 useless. The innkeeper would only have occasion to rely upon the limitation of liability found in C.C. Art. 2971 if the loss occurred through fraud or negligence, because without fraud or negligence, he is not liable at all. . . .

Considering the nature of the hotel business, the fact that the rooms are available to public access, and the number of people who are in and out of hotel rooms on a day-to-day basis (hotel guests, visitors, hotel employees, and others), there is always the potential for burglary. Realistically, in almost any instance of burglary, it is arguable that the hotel was negligent in some way. If the rule is established that innkeepers are liable for valuables, including large sums of money, where some degree of negligence can be established on the part of the hotel or one of its employees, the burden placed on the innkeepers of this state will be unduly inequitable and onerous. It is patently unfair to provide no limit on the amount a guest may claim, even if the innkeeper is negligent in some respect, when the innkeeper provides a safe deposit and notice that it is available and the guest instead chooses to undertake the safekeeping of his valuables himself.

For the reasons stated above, I am unable to agree with the majority opinion; therefore, I respectfully dissent.

■ IMPORTANT TERMS AND CONCEPTS

bailment	liability of innkeeper for guest's property
professional bailee	bailee
constructive delivery	bailor
commercial bailments	gratuitous bailments
contract liability of bailee	duty of care for bailed property
statutory liability of bailee	disclaimer
liability of common carrier	common carrier
air bill	bill of lading
warehouse receipt	warehouse
	innkeeper
	innkeeper's lien

■ QUESTIONS AND PROBLEMS FOR DISCUSSION

1. What is the bailor's duty to take care of the bailed property?

2. What is the professional bailor's liability regarding defects in the bailed property?

3. What is the liability of the common carrier of goods for damage to the bailor's goods while in its possession?

4. Is a warehouse held to the same standard of care as a common carrier with regard to bailor's goods? If not, what is the standard of care required of warehouses?

5. Ms. Laval was a patient of Dr. Leopold. One morning, when she came to his office for her weekly appointment, she was wearing her new fur coat, worth $1,800. She took off her coat and hung it in the small clothes closet located in the waiting room. Dr. Leopold and his partner each had a private consulting office attached to the waiting room, but there was no receptionist or other staff person regularly in the waiting room. When Ms. Laval came out after her appointment, her new coat was gone. Dr. Leopold denies liability. Can Ms. Laval recover for her coat? Why or why not?

6. Ms. Nickson, staying in town for a business conference, parked her car at the Saf-T Parking Garage on Thursday morning. Saf-T was a "valet" parking garage, where the customer drove up, turned over possession of the car to an attendant, and was given a claim check. When Ms. Nickson returned for her car late Friday afternoon and presented her claim check, the car could not be located. When Ms. Nickson described her car and its out-of-state license plates, one of the attendants said he remembered giving that car to someone else who had also presented a claim check for it. When the other claim check was examined closely, it proved to be a forgery. The number on the duplicate check matched the number on Ms. Nickson's car. Is Saf-T liable for the missing car? Discuss.

7. Gaspane Restaurant required its waitresses to wear uniforms while on the job. It provided a room, with a clothes rack and lockers, where the waitresses could change into their uniforms and leave their purses and other personal property. The room was unattended, although waitresses came in and out at various times, either on breaks or when their shift was over. The room was at the rear of the restaurant, which had a city alley running directly behind it. The rear window had been locked, but it had been jimmied open with a crowbar. Ms. Grana's new coat and purse were stolen. The coat was worth about $300, and the purse $45. Ms. Grana had just cashed her paycheck at the bank, and she had nearly $400 in the purse. Gaspane refused to reimburse her. Is Gaspane liable for the loss of any of this property? Discuss.

8. Harvey Smith parked his car on a parking lot owned by Sarbov Parking, Inc. He drove up, took his claim check from the automatic machine, parked his car, and took the keys. His car was about 100 feet from the attendant's office, which had windows on all sides. The lot was well lighted. Later that evening an unidentified customer told the attendant that something was happening to one of the cars on the lot. The attendant went over to Harvey's car and saw a man looking under the hood. The man told the attendant that something was wrong with the car, which was his brother's, and that he was trying to fix it. The attendant made no further inquiry or observation, nor did he call the police, as he had been told to do if he saw a car being tampered with by unknown persons. When Harvey got back, the transmission was missing from his car. When Harvey sued, Sarbov Parking denied liability on the basis that no bailment had been established. What is the result here, and why?

34

Real Property: Acquisition of Ownership

CHAPTER OBJECTIVES

THIS CHAPTER WILL:

- Define "real property."
- Explain the two basic methods of land description.
- Discuss the types of ownership in real property.
- Describe the ways in which ownership to real property may be acquired.
- Compare purchase of real property by land contract to purchase by deed and mortgage.
- Review the national laws which must be complied with when real property is purchased.

The law concerning the rights and duties of the owners of real property differs considerably from the law concerning the rights and duties of the owners of personal property. Some objects of personal property can be transported from state to state, or even from country to country.

When dealing with real property, we are concerned with land and with the permanent fixtures and buildings attached to it. The land cannot be picked up and taken across state lines; it is part of the earth's surface. The fixtures and buildings on the land may depreciate, burn down, or otherwise be destroyed; however, the land itself remains basically the same, century after century. Also, the land cannot be possessed physically in the same way that an item of personal property is possessed.

■ NATURE OF REAL PROPERTY

Real property is a term that describes the *bundle of rights* to a specific parcel of land. It includes not only buildings, and permanent fixtures attached to the surface of the land, but also rights to the ground below the surface of the land and rights to the air and sky above the land. Thus, the owner of a parcel of land has rights to the airspace above that parcel, to water on it, to things growing on or attached to its surface, and to the minerals, underground waters, and whatever else may be found below its surface.

Extent of landowner's interest

Technically, the owners of a tract of land, and therefore of the airspace above it, could prevent anyone from trespassing into their airspace. This presented a problem, since landowners could have restricted interstate or even international air travel. The American Law Institute formulated a rule to govern trespasses into the airspace above a landowner's parcel of land. Such an overflight is privileged if it is made at a reasonable height and if it is in accordance with all applicable government regulations. For example, the FAA regulations state that no aircraft may fly over a congested (populated) area at an altitude of less than 1,000 feet, and no aircraft may fly over a noncongested (farmland) area at an altitude of less than 500 feet. These rules do allow an exception for helicopters if they are operated without hazard and in accordance with specific regulations. An example would be the use of a helicopter for medical rescue operations in a congested populated area and the use of helicopters for crop spraying in a noncongested farm area.

The most obvious area of real property is the surface of the land. In Chapter 32, we discussed the question of when fixtures become real property and how certain things which are part of real property, such as growing crops, may be severed from the real property to become personal property. The rules are fairly clear concerning most of the land surface and the buildings, fixtures, trees, and other growing objects, which generally stay affixed until they are severed by people or by an act of God. The water that is present on the land surface is in constant motion, and it changes course and swells and shrinks in height and width with the seasons and the years.

Water rights—different state rules

Water rights, called **riparian rights,** are a concern of those who own land which abuts a lake, river, or other body of water. Generally, the owner of the land next to a stream, river, or lake may take or use the water as needed for natural and domestic purposes on the land adjoining the water. For example, water could be taken for use in irrigation, for washing, or for drinking. A riparian owner would not, however, have the right to divert the entire stream and thus deprive landowners downstream of its use. Riparian rights also concern the property boundary lines of land next to a river, stream, or lake. Does your ownership extend to the edge of the river, 10 feet out into the river, or just where? The river or stream will run at different levels depending on the time of year. The general rule is that the property line will be at the point of normal flow of the river or stream.

The law concerning riparian rights varies from state to state, because different areas of the country have different problems regarding water. In areas where water is scarce and irrigation is a necessity, rules governing the use of water from running streams will be strict. Also, different problems are involved if the property abuts a creek rather than a navigable river. In addition, many national and state statutes govern actions by a riparian landowner which might affect water quality.

Mineral rights

The law covering minerals, such as coal or metals, is quite clear. If you own the land, you own everything below the surface, unless the ***mineral rights*** were previously sold to someone else. Such sales of mineral rights are very common in Texas, Oklahoma, and other oil-producing states. If there is oil under your land and your neighbor's land, how much do you own? How much does your neighbor own? If you pump out the pool under your land, will you be taking your neighbor's oil? Since liquids seek their own level, you cannot just separate and take your part of the oil beneath your area of land if the pool extends beyond the boundaries of your property. Thus, the courts have often been called upon to resolve disputes as to the ownership of oil and gas taken from below the surface of the ground. Now, an entire area of the law, known as "oil and gas law," specifically addresses the problems of oil and gas ownership. While this is an area of interest, time and space do not permit a further discussion of this area of the law in this text. The *Acker* case does show how courts try to resolve these problems.

ACKER v. GUINN

464 S.W.2d 348 (Texas, 1971)

FACTS

J. P. Acker, Jr., brought this declaratory judgment action against M. M. Guinn to determine whether certain mineral rights passed under a deed executed in 1941. The deed conveyed "an undivided one-half interest in and to all of the oil, gas and other minerals in and under, and that may be produced from" a tract of 86½ acres in Cherokee County. Acker, who held through the grantee, claimed that the deed included an interest in the iron ore on the land; Guinn, who held under the grantor, said that the deed did not include the iron ore. Over the years the main use made of iron ore from Cherokee County had been as a foundation base for road construction; iron ore was also used in the manufacture of cement. Because of its high silica content, this iron ore had to be mixed with other ores to make pig iron. The ore deposits were solid beds, varying in thickness from a few inches to three or four feet. There were outcrops of the ore deposits at some places, and the deposits ranged in depth to as much as 50 feet below the surface. The ore had to be strip-mined, which would destroy or substantially impair the use of the surface for farming, ranching, or timber production. The trial court granted Acker's motion for summary judgment; the court of civil appeals reversed.

ISSUE   Did a deed conveying an undivided one-half interest in oil, gas and other minerals in and under the land include iron ore on the surface and slightly below the surface of the land?

DECISION   No. Judgment of Court of Appeals is affirmed.

REASONS   Justice Walker stated:

"A grant or reservation of minerals by the fee owner effects a horizontal severance and the creation of two separate and distinct estates: an estate in the surface and an estate in the minerals. . . . The parties to a mineral lease or deed usually think of the mineral estate as including valuable substances that are removed from the ground by means of wells or mine shafts. This estate is dominant, of course, and its owner is entitled to make reasonable use of the surface for the production of his minerals. It is not ordinarily contemplated, however, that the utility of the surface for agricultural or grazing purposes will be destroyed or substantially impaired. Unless the contrary intention is affirmatively and fairly expressed, therefore, a grant or reservation of 'minerals' or 'mineral rights' should not be construed to include a substance that must be removed by methods that will, in effect, consume or deplete the surface estate. . . .

"That is the rule to be applied in determining whether an interest in the iron ore was conveyed by the deed in this case. In terms of its location with respect to the surface, methods by which it must be mined, and the effect of production upon the surface, the ore is quite similar to gravel and limestone. Aside from the general reference to 'other minerals,' moreover, there is nothing in the deed even remotely suggesting an intention to vest in the grantee the right to destroy the surface. It is our opinion that in these circumstances the ore, like gravel and limestone, should be considered as belonging to the surface estate and not as part of the minerals. We accordingly hold that as a matter of law no interest in the ore passed by the deed."

■ LAND DESCRIPTION AND TITLE REGISTRATION

Personal property can be described fairly easily—for example, "a red 1980 Dodge Mirada two-door sedan." People can readily recognize the personal property in question by that description. On the other hand, if a man says that he owns 300 acres of land, we must have some method to designate the boundaries of the land. Moreover, the method of description must be similar to the method used to describe the adjoining parcels of land. For these reasons, some type of uniform system for describing and identifying land became necessary.

Two methods of describing land

Basically there are two methods of land description—the *metes and bounds description* and the *rectangular survey description*. The metes and bounds description is the traditional method. It involves picking a starting point and marking it with a permanent stake or post so that it can always be referred to and then simply measuring distances and angles until you return to the starting point. This system was used for land description in the original 13 states of the United States.

In 1875 the U.S. government adopted a rectangular survey system which is now used in most of the states. This system divides the land into rectangular squares called *sections*. These sections are divided into quarter sections and can be further subdivided as needed. A section is a square mile. Where the rectangular survey system has been adopted, there will be maps or *plats* of the entire surface area of the land in a county, divided into one-mile squares. Records of such plats are filed in the county courthouse. If the land involved lies within the limits of a city or town, it will be divided further into various subdivisions, which in turn are subdivided into lots.

Unlike personal property, for which physical possession is a strong indicator of ownership, ownership of land is proved by registration of title. If you purchase land, you will be given a deed transferring ownership from the previous owner to you. This deed has to be filed or registered with the proper authority in the county where the land is located. The title will then be public record, and anyone may check the county records to find out who owns that particular tract of land. Land registration is also needed for taxation purposes. Real estate is a prime source of tax revenue for municipal and county governments, and an *ad valorem* tax is imposed upon the registered title holder of a tract of land.

■ TYPES OF RIGHTS TO OWNERSHIP IN REAL PROPERTY

All of the rights of ownership to most objects of personal property are typically owned by one person. Seldom would a person have only a life interest in a book, a chair, or an automobile. This, of course, is because personal property typically does not have perpetual life; most items of personal property will be destroyed or deteriorate over time. Land, however, will always be there. This explains the need for a different set of ownership rights for real property than for personal property.

Fee Simple Estate. *Fee simple title* is the best title that an owner can have. This means that the owner has all of the rights associated with a parcel of real property, and that the owner has these rights forever. The owner of the fee simple estate can sell all of these rights in the real property, or any part thereof. When the owner dies, the heirs will inherit the fee simple estate, and the title can be passed on through generations.

Life Estate. A *life estate* is an interest in real property which is limited to the life of a designated person or persons. The owner of the life estate may not cause permanent injury to the real property, but simply has the right to use it during the specified lifetime. An owner of a life estate may be viewed as a tenant who has free rent until he or she dies. When the life estate owner dies, ownership of the real property will revert to the owner who gave the life estate. If that owner is now dead, it will go to that owner's heirs or to whomever that owner has designated in his or her will. The *Medlin* case discusses the extent of the life estate given to Minnie by her deceased husband's will.

MEDLIN v. MEDLIN

203 S.W.2d 635 (Texas, 1947)

FACTS Medlin died in 1939, survived by his wife Minnie and nine children. Five of the children sued Minnie and the other four children for a declaratory judgment interpreting T. W.'s will. The will gave Minnie all of T. W.'s property "to have the use and benefit of the same during her natural life, and at her death, all of such property in her hands shall completely vest in my children, share and share alike." In another paragraph the will gave Minnie "the full and complete management, use and enjoyment of all of my property during her said lifetime, including all rents and revenues to be derived therefrom." The plaintiffs argued that Minnie received only a limited life estate, for her use and benefit, rather than a general life estate and that, similarly, the rents and revenues earned during her lifetime were not hers absolutely but were only to be used for her reasonable support. The trial court rejected both of these arguments. The plaintiffs appealed.

ISSUE Did the will create a general life estate in Minnie?

DECISION Yes. Judgment affirmed.

REASONS Justice Stokes first reviewed the terms of the will and the parties' conflicting interpretations of it. He then tried to ascertain T. W.'s intent when the will was executed. "We find nothing in the will which indicates a purpose on the part of the testator to limit in respect to her welfare and support the life estate bequeathed to his surviving wife. The adjectives 'reasonable' and 'comfortable' are not used in the will and to ingraft their implications of limitation upon the bequest to her would be to change completely a material portion of the will and the benefits which obviously the testator intended to confer upon her. . . .

"From the entire will here involved, it is obvious that the main plan and purpose of the testator was to provide for the comfort, maintenance, and support of his wife. In order to make it certain that this purpose was carried out, the provision was inserted a number of times that her judgment should control, and he enjoined his children in most solemn and appealing terms to aid her and recognize the fact that he had utmost confidence in her judgment. He provided in terms that her judgment was to be exercised in any matter pertaining to the handling and management of his estate and our interpretation of the will is that the surviving wife, Minnie Medlin, took a life estate in the property, together with the power and authority to manage, control, mortgage, sell, and convey the property or any part of it for such purposes and under such conditions as she might see fit and proper in order to pay the debts, provide for her own comfort and support, and to keep and preserve the estate."

Leasehold Estate. The owner of a *leasehold estate* has the right to occupy and use the described real property. A leasehold estate may be for a specified period, such as a year or 10 years, or it may be a *tenancy at will,* which means that either the tenant or the owner-landlord may terminate the leasehold at any time without reason, simply by giving a required notice. If you rent an apartment during the school year and you sign a lease, you will have acquired a leasehold interest in real property. Leasehold estates are discussed more fully in the next chapter.

Right to use another's land

Easements. *Easements* may also be described as rights-of-way over real property. If you buy a lot in a subdivision on which you intend to build a home, no doubt there will be an easement across the back of the lot for the use of public utilities. The easement will allow the water company, the electric company, and the gas company to come upon that specific area of land and erect poles, dig trenches for water lines, bury cable lines, and do other tasks associated with their business. You still own the land covered by an easement, but the easement allows another person or persons to come upon that portion of the land for certain purposes. An easement is an interest in real property which is usually evidenced by a written document called a *deed of easement,* and this deed must be registered with the appropriate county official in the county where the real property is located. An exception to this general rule is called an *easement by prescription.* An easement by prescription is also known as an *easement by adverse possession,* in many jurisdictions. Here there is no written easement and, in fact, there is no agreement that there should be an easement. This is simply a situation where the owner of the land has allowed another person or persons to use a certain portion of the land continuously for a number of years, and the owner is now legally unable to deny the rights of that person or persons to continue to use the land. Most states have a specific statutory time before an easement by prescription will be effective. The *Downie* case illustrates these rules.

DOWNIE v. CITY OF RENTON

9 P.2d 372 (Washington, 1932)

FACTS   The city of Renton built a concrete reservoir. About once a year, from 1908 to 1929, the city had to drain and clean the reservoir to prevent the buildup of contamination. The wastewater pipe ran from the base of the reservoir and was discharged into a small gully. The wastewater then ran down into a small stream, which crossed Downie's land. Downie bought his two acres in 1921; it was then "unused, unimproved, unoccupied, unfenced, and covered with underbrush and second growth trees." In 1928 Downie dammed up the stream and created a one-third acre pond, which he stocked with 25,000 fish. The city's cleaning of the reservoir in September 1929 resulted in the discharge of wastewater, debris, and mud into Downie's pond. The trial court dismissed Downie's suit for an injunction, holding that the city had acquired an easement by prescription. Downie appealed.

ISSUE   Had the city acquired an easement by prescription?

DECISION   No. Judgment reversed and case remanded for a perpetual injunction.

REASONS   Justice Beeler stated:

"To acquire an easement by prescription the owner must know of and acquiesce in the adverse user, or the use must be so open, notorious, visible, and uninterrupted that knowledge and acquiescence will be presumed. . . .

"The inquiry then is whether the asserted adverse user by the city was of a sufficiently open, notorious, and hostile character so as to charge the appellant's predecessor in interest with presumptive knowledge or constructive notice of the isolated acts of user. The word 'notorious' is defined by Webster as 'generally known and talked about by the public; usually believed to be true; manifest to the world; evident.' . . .

"[T]he property from 1908 to 1921 was unfenced, unused, and unimproved, a wild stretch of acreage almost as nature left it. Neither the appellant's vendor nor the appellant himself when he became the purchaser could have discovered by passing over the land any indication of adverse user, and the acts of user relied upon by the respondent were of such a nature as to negative the very idea of presumptive notice. . . . Nor was there anything about the manner in which the reservoir was claimed [sic] or drained that would in any wise bring knowledge to his attention. This took but from 2 to 2½ hours and occurred, according to the most reliable testimony in the record, only once a year between 1908 and 1929. . . .

"In addition to having open, notorious, and hostile possession, it is also essential that such possession, in order to ripen into a prescriptive right, be shown to have been continuous and uninterrupted for the full statutory period. . . .

"The acts of user relied upon by respondent consist at most of desultory acts of trepass, of short duration, and occurring at widely separated intervals. . . . The separate acts of draining the reservoir were wholly lacking in continuity and were not sufficiently open and notorious so as to charge the appellant's grantor or the appellant himself with presumptive notice of such occasional sue."

Right to remove things from another's land

Profits. In the law of real property, a *profit* is the right to remove part of someone else's land; for example, timber, crops, or minerals. Most modern cases treat profits under the same general rules as are applied to easements. Like easements, a profit may be *appurtenant,* attached to the ownership of other land, or *in gross,* owned by someone other than the adjoining landowner, regardless of whether or not that someone owns other real estate. An example of an appurtenant profit would be a neighbor who has the right to cut as much wood as he needs for his fireplace. A profit in gross would exist where the landowner has simply sold or given someone the right to remove firewood from the land.

Licenses. A *license* in permission to enter upon the real property of another person. It is not an easement since it is not truly an interest in real property, but simply temporary permission to go upon another person's real property for a specific purpose. A friend has an apple orchard, for example, and agrees to sell you all of the apples in the orchard for a specific price. Part of the agreement is that you will have to go into the orchard, pick the apples, and take them to market. You do not have a permanent easement to traverse that area at a later time or for any other reason.

Dower Rights. Under the common law, a widow had *dower rights* in her husband's real property. This meant that she had a life estate in one third of all the real property which the husband had owned during his lifetime, provided she had not signed away her dower rights in a transfer of any of that real property to another person. The purpose of the dower interest was to ensure that the widow would have some means to support herself if her husband died. In those days, a woman typically was not a wage earner outside the home.

The widow's dower interest is still recognized in many states. However, some states have limited it to only that real property which the husband owned at the time of his death, thus preventing the widow from claiming an interest in real property which the husband had transferred to others during his lifetime.

Curtesy Rights. Under the common law, the husband, upon the death of his wife, was entitled to a life estate in all of the real property his wife owned which was subject to inheritance. One requirement had to be met before the husband was granted curtesy rights: a child who could have inherited the real property had to have been born alive. Most states have replaced the common-law right of curtesy with specific statutory provisions concerning a husband's right in his wife's estate.

Liens against Real Property. A *lien* is a claim which some person or persons may have against real property for the payment of some debt, obligation, or duty. A lien may be either voluntary or involuntary. An example of a ***voluntary lien*** would be the lien of a mortgage which is created when the owner of real estate borrows money and pledges the real estate as security for repayment of the loan. The lending institution, the mortgagee, then files the mortgage agreement with the county recorder in the county where the land is located, and thus has a lien against the property. The owner of the real property cannot sell the real property and give clear title until the mortgage lien is satisfied by full payment, or unless the mortgagee agrees to let the new buyer pay off the mortgage.

Examples of ***involuntary liens*** include a tax lien, a judgment lien, and a mechanic's lien. If the owner of real property fails to pay the property taxes, then the property taxes become a lien against the real property. As with a mortgage, the real property may not be sold with a clear title unless the lien is paid off. A ***judgment lien*** would involve a situation where the owner of real property has been sued, the court has rendered a judgment against the owner, and the owner has not paid off the judgment. A ***mechanic's lien*** is a lien of a person or persons who furnish building materials and/or labor for the improvement of real property. Here again, the real property cannot be sold with a clear title unless the mechanic's lien is paid off. In some states, if a mechanic's lien is not satisfied within a specified period of time, the person holding the mechanic's lien may sue the owner, get a judgment, and have the real property sold at a sheriff's auction to satisfy the lien. Since mechanic's lien statutes differ from state to state, it is advisable to find out what the law is in your state. Otherwise, you might find your home sold for a very minor debt.

■ ACQUISITION OF OWNERSHIP TO REAL PROPERTY

Real property may be acquired in various ways.

Legislative Grant. Real property may be acquired by legislative grant from the national government or by a patent. A *patent* is a document similar to a deed which the government issues to convey a portion of the public lands to one or more persons. In the early days of this nation, the national Homestead Act allowed settlers to establish their homestead on public land. After the passage of a specified period of time and compliance with the requirements of the act, the homesteader would be granted a patent to this land.

Purchase. Real property may be acquired by purchase. This, of course, is the most common method of acquisition.

Inheritance. Real property may be acquired by inheritance. You may inherit land from your parents, grandparents, or other persons who die and name you in their will, or if you are the legal heir, you would inherit by intestate succession.

Gift. Owners of land may decide to give a certain parcel of land to their children, to some other person or persons, or to some charity during their lifetime. A gift is not valid unless there is a proper deed which evidences a transfer of title from the donor, or giver, to the donee, that is, the person receiving the gift.

Accretion. *Accretion* simply means that the owner of land has acquired more land because of a change in the course of a river or stream which runs alongside the property. For example, over a period of years sand and soil have been deposited on your side of a stream, thus increasing the actual land that you can use. A stream may also recede, giving more land between the previous bank and the present level of the stream.

Adverse Possession. After you use or occupy real property continuously for a statutory period of time, the original owner loses the right to object to your possession of the land. By your possession, which was adverse to the owner's interests, and the failure of the owner to enforce his or her rights to evict you, you have acquired ownership by ***adverse possession.***

Eminent Domain. This method of acquiring land applies to governmental entities, such as school districts, cities, states, and the national government. This method of acquisition, ***eminent domain,*** also is often referred to as ***condemnation.*** It is the right of government to take private property for the use of the public. The owner of the private property must be paid a fair amount for the land taken.

Dedication. Acquisition through dedication is also a method of acquiring land which applies only to governmental entities. A real estate developer of a new subdivision dedicates the streets to the city. The streets then become public property. **Dedication** is a gift by the landowner to a governmental entity, and it is an effective acquisition only if the governmental entity accepts the gift. For example, a person may want to dedicate certain land to a city for use as a park that will be named after the donor. The city may or may not accept the gift with that condition. If the gift is accepted, then appropriate documents are executed and the land become public property that is owned and maintained by the city.

■ PROCESS OF TRANSFER OF OWNERSHIP

Two types of deeds

The transfer of land from the present owner to the acquiring owner must be evidenced by a written document which can be recorded in the records of the county where the land is located.

The transfer document used in an acquisition by purchase or by gift is a *deed*. This is a written document which is signed by the owner of the real property and which conveys or transfers the owner's rights, title, and interest in specifically described real estate to the person or persons who are acquiring the ownership. The present owner or owners are called the *grantors,* and the person or persons acquiring ownership are called the *grantees.* The grantors must sign the deed in the presence of a notary public who will verify that they signed it. The deed may be in the form of a **warranty deed** or a **quitclaim deed.**

In warranty deed, the grantor expressly guarantees that the ownership being transferred is free from the claims of others. That is, the grantor guarantees to the grantee that the grantor is transferring a clear and merchantable title. A quitclaim deed states that the grantor is transferring all of his or her rights, title, and interest in the real property to the grantee, but the grantor makes no guarantee that the grantee will have a clear title free from the claims of others.

Reservation of rights in deed

The grantor or grantors in a warranty deed may reserve some rights or may make the warranty subject to certain rights of others. For example, the grantors in a warranty deed may reserve subsurface mineral rights. Then, if oil is ever found under the land, it belongs to the grantor. If there is a mortgage on the land, the grantor-seller may deed the title subject to the rights of the mortgagee, normally a bank or other lending institution. Thus, the new purchaser gets title subject to the lien of the mortgage. If there are private restrictions on the real estate, the deed will transfer title subject to those restrictions. Since taxes are a lien, the deed will also specify that the transfer of title is subject to unpaid taxes if any remain unpaid at the time of the transfer of title.

These warranty rules are discussed in the *Brown* case.

BROWN v. LOBER

379 N.E.2d 1354 (Illinois, 1978)

FACTS

In 1957 James and Dolly Brown, husband and wife, purchased 80 acres of land from William and Faith Bost, joint tenants. The Bosts gave the Browns a statutory warranty deed. The deed was absolute on its face, and it purported to convey an estate in fee simple. In fact, a prior owner in the chain of title had conveyed a two-thirds interest in the mineral rights in 1947. This prior conveyance was not discovered in title searches which the Bosts had done in 1958 and 1968, when they used the land as collateral for loans. Faith Bost died in 1974; William had died earlier. Maureen Lober was appointed as executor of Faith's estate. On May 8, 1974, the Browns granted a coal option to the Consolidated Coal Company for $6,000. On May 4, 1976, the Browns learned that they owned only one third of the coal rights. They accepted $2,000 from the coal company and then sued Faith's estate for damages of $4,000. The trial court dismissed the lawsuit, holding that only the first two warranties in the Bosts' deed had been breached, that this had occurred in 1957, when the deed was delivered, and that the claim was thus barred by the 10-year statute of limitations. The Browns appealed.

ISSUE   Did the Bosts only breach the guarantees of ownership and right to convey?

DECISION   No. Judgment reversed and case remanded.

REASONS   Justice Wineland agreed with the trial court that some guarantees were either met or breached when the deed took effect and that a cause of action for their breach would accrue at that time. He felt, however, that the Bosts had also breached the guarantee of quiet enjoyment, and perhaps the guarantee against incumbrances. "In the instant case it is agreed by the parties that the plaintiffs had no knowledge of the previous grant of the sub-surface minerals until 1976. . . . It was at this time that the plaintiffs were advised by the coal company of the outstanding incumbrance in the underlying minerals. It was at this time that plaintiffs yielded as they had a right to do, to the paramount title to the two-thirds interest in the coal. The coal purchaser refused to pay them for the coal rights warranted to them by the Bosts. It would seem to be at this time that the covenant of quiet and peaceable possession was disturbed for the first time since 1957 and that this suit was brought. The Statute of Limitations could not be operative until plaintiffs' rights were disturbed in the possession of their title by the sale of the underlying coal. . . .

"It would appear here that the defect in title would constitute an incumbrance as it would seem to be a claim, lien, charge, or liability attached to and binding real property. . . .

"A covenant against incumbrances does not depend for its existence upon the extent or amount of diminution of value, but extends to cases where, by reason of the burden, claim, or right, the owner does not acquire complete dominion over the land conveyed by his conveyance or deed."

■ FINANCING OF REAL ESTATE TRANSACTIONS

The great majority of real estate transactions involve some type of financing arrangement, since few people have the cash required in exchange for the title to real property. Financing can be handled through either a land contract or a real estate mortgage.

A **land contract** is an agreement between a buyer and a seller regarding the purchase of a parcel of land. The contract is a conditional sale of the land, subject to payment of the purchase price by the buyer. Typically, the buyer will make a down payment and will agree to make periodic payments of interest and principal for a specified period of time, either until the entire

Installment purchase of land

balance of the principal is paid or until the principal balance is paid down to a level where the buyer can secure a real estate mortgage from a lending institution. The down payment required for a land contract transaction is often less than that required in a transaction involving a real estate mortgage.

Upon execution of a land contract, the buyer is entitled to possession and control of the land and the improvements thereon. The buyer is the equitable owner of the rights to possess and control the land, subject to the legal rights of the fee simple titleholder who is selling the real property. In other words, the buyer may not use the real property in any way he or she wants to; however, the buyer does have the duty to keep the premises insured against fire and other risks of loss. The buyer may not add to or tear down the improvements without the specific permission of the seller. The buyer has the right to use, control, and enjoy the land and improvements, but may not materially change the land or improvements.

Deed to buyer; mortgage to financing agency

A *real estate mortgage* is a document wherein the owner of real property pledges that real property as security for the payment of a debt or some other obligation. The owner of the property, who is called the mortgagor, does not transfer title to the land in this document. The *mortgagee,* normally a bank or other lending institution, obtains a nonpossessory interest in the real estate. If the debt or obligation is not satisfied in accordance with the conditions for repayment set out in the mortgage document, the mortgagee may commence legal proceedings to foreclose on the mortgage and to have the real property sold. The proceeds will then be applied to the balance owed on the mortgage. The owner-mortgagor will receive any proceeds from the sale of the real property which are left after the payment of the mortgage balance, plus reasonable attorney's fees and court costs.

■ FILING AND RECORDING REQUIREMENTS FOR MORTGAGE

A mortgage need not be recorded in any public office to be valid between the mortgagor and the mortgagee. However, if a mortgage is not filed in the office of the recorder of the county where the real property is located, the mortgagee's lien will not be superior to any subsequent liens which may be placed against the real property. For example, an individual borrows money, executes a promissory note, and signs a mortgage on the real property, but the mortgagee doesn't record the mortgage. Later, a judgment is rendered against the owner as the result of an automobile accident. If the mortgage was not recorded properly, it would not have priority over the judgment. Thus, immediately after a mortgage is executed, it is very important to file and record the mortgage with the recorder of the county where the real property is located.

■ DEFAULTS IN PAYMENT OF THE MORTGAGE

The mortgagor may default on the mortgage by failing to pay the mortgage payments, the real property taxes, or the payments for insurance as they become due, or by doing an act which would endanger the security interest of the mortgagee.

If the mortgagor defaults, then the mortgagee may file a suit of foreclosure

Procedure if buyer defaults on mortgage

against the mortgagor. At that time, the entire balance of the mortgage is due and payable, and if the court awards the mortgagee a *judgment of foreclosure,* the property will be sold at a sheriff's sale. The proceeds of the sale of the real estate will be applied first to the unpaid balance of the mortgage, interest, and the legal fees and court costs of the foreclosure suit. The balance will then be paid to the mortgagor. If the sale does not bring enough money to pay off the mortgage debt, the mortgagor will remain liable for the unpaid balance of the mortgage.

Many states have enacted statutes which allow the mortgagor to get a delay of foreclosure in certain hardship cases. Another statutory procedure that favors the mortgagor is called the *right of redemption.* This is the mortgagor's statutory right to repurchase the real estate within a specified time after the foreclosure. In other words, a mortgagor can have the property back by paying the amount for which it was sold plus the expenses incurred in the foreclosure and sale.

Where the real property is sold by the sheriff, the sheriff is authorized by law to execute to the purchaser a sheriff's deed which is free and clear of the mortgage lien.

■ WARRANTIES OF TITLE IN THE SALE OF REAL PROPERTY

Seller guarantees title

The person transferring title, the grantor, is presumed to have made certain warranties of title even though those warranties were not expressly stated in the deed. The grantor warrants that he or she owns the real property which is being conveyed, subject to restrictions, such as unpaid taxes, an unpaid mortgage, easements, or any other liens against the real property. The grantor also warrants that he or she has the right to convey the property. In the case of the transfer of title by a corporation, the officers signing the deed warrant that they have authority to act for the corporation. The grantor also guarantees that the land is not encumbered by any right or interest other than the liens or easements which are stated in the deed. Thus, the grantor is guaranteeing that the purchaser will have the right to enjoy the use of the property without interference by the grantors or others at a later date.

Even though the grantor guarantees that the buyer is being given a clear title, the buyer should request further assurances. After all, should there be problems later, the grantor who made those guarantees may have spent the money that the buyer paid for the real property, may have moved out of the area, may have died, may have filed bankruptcy, or may simply be judgment-proof. Before consummating the purchase of real property, the buyer should require from the seller either an *abstract of title* showing good and merchantable title certified to the date of the closing of the transaction or a *policy of title insurance* for the real estate.

Verification of public record of seller's title

An abstract of title is a history of the title to a piece of real estate. Usually beginning with the original transfer from the U.S. government to the homesteader, it then contains brief copies of every deed, mortgage, or other document which affects the title, from that date to the present. It also contains copies of any liens or encumbrances which have been filed against the real property. The abstract of title, however, only covers those documents which have been recorded in the county recorder's office in the county where the real property is situated. It does not cover any unrecorded documents which may have been agreed upon by parties involved in the chain of title.

The *abstractor,* the person preparing the abstract, does not certify that the title is clear from liens and encumbrances and is merchantable. The abstract must be taken to an attorney who will examine it and then give an opinion stating whether or not the title is merchantable.

A policy of *title insurance* is an insurance policy which requires the insurance company to pay any judgment, legal fees, and court costs, in any action brought by someone claiming title against you. Before the title insurance company issues a policy, it first verifies that the title is clear and merchantable. Only then will it issue a policy of title insurance.

General rule: Seller does not guarantee condition of structures

The warranties made by the seller-grantor, the issuance of a title insurance policy, and the preparation and examination of an abstract of title do not protect the buyer against any defects in the improvements on the real property, such as the house, the garage, or other buildings. The courts originally used the (doctrine of) *caveat emptor,* "Let the buyer beware," with regard to the condition of the improvements on the real property. Buyers have an opportunity to examine the real property, and if they do not request any express warranties or agreement as to the buildings, then they get what they see. Of course, an exception will be made where the seller is guilty of fraud or misrepresentation. If the seller lied to the buyer about some material fact and this concerned a condition that the buyer could not have checked with the use of ordinary inspection methods, then the courts will simply void the transaction. The buyer also may be able to secure additional monetary damages.

Another exception to the general rule of *caveat emptor* with regard to the buildings on the real property being transferred may occur when a new home has been constructed on the real property. Many states have specific laws which make the builder responsible for defects in the new home for a specific period of time, usually one year. Since this is a matter of state law, the buyer of real property should either secure an express warranty from the seller or check the statutory law in the given state.

■ NATIONAL LAWS AFFECTING THE TRANSFER OF TITLE TO REAL ESTATE

The *U.S. Real Estate Settlement Procedures Act (RESPA),* requires the disclosure of the costs of a real estate transaction to the buyer prior to the consummation of such a transaction. The costs which must be disclosed are the loan origination fees, loan discount points, appraisal fees, attorney's fees, inspection fees, charges for title search or title insurance, and land survey fee. This law was passed in 1974 primarily to let buyers know just what they are paying for.

Full disclosure of charges to buyer

RESPA also prohibits certain practices which are not in the best interests of the buyer. The lending institution is not allowed to give a kickback to any person for referring the borrower to them, to charge or accept fees except for services actually performed, or to require that the borrower purchase title insurance from any specific title insurance company that the lender prefers. The parties also cannot be forced to use an attorney which the lending institution selects. They are free to hire one of their own choosing.

■ **SIGNIFICANCE OF THIS CHAPTER**

Everyone needs to understand the various rights involved in ownership of real property, since both individuals and businesses may become parties to many legal relationships involving land. This chapter answers many of the questions that relate to the ownership of real property.

DISCUSSION CASE

HENDERSON v. WADE SAND & GRAVEL CO., INC.

388 So.2d 900 (Alabama, 1980)

FACTS: This action was brought by three Jefferson County homeowners to recover damages for injury caused to their property by the operation of a neighboring quarry. At the close of plaintiffs' case, the trial court directed a verdict in defendant's favor. The plaintiffs appealed.

■

Justice Shores:

There are occasions when it becomes necessary to reexamine an existing legal doctrine in the light of changed societal conditions. This case presents such an occasion.

The plaintiffs' houses were constructed roughly 50 years ago, and are located in a residential neighborhood. In 1977, the land on which their houses are situated began to sink, large sinkholes appeared, and their houses began to break up. Investigation disclosed that the sinking of their property was due to the activities of defendant, Wade Sand and Gravel Company, which operated a quarry one-half mile north of plaintiffs' homes. In the course of its operations, the quarry, which began operating in 1957, periodically pumps water from the bottom of its pits and empties it into a nearby creek. This resulted in ground water being leached from under plaintiffs' land, leaving large underground cavities. Heavy rains then caused water to flow through the empty cavities at an accelerated rate, destroying the structure of the land beneath plaintiffs' homes and carrying away much subsoil and surface soil.

In 1969, the U.S. Geological Survey began a study of the sinkhole problem in the Roberts Field area, which includes plaintiffs' homes and the quarry. The defendant cooperated in the study and was allegedly familiar with the contents of the report subsequently published. Plaintiffs contend that the study predicted that damage of the type complained of would occur if defendant continued to pump water from its pits. The trial court refused to admit the study into evidence.

The trial court held that a verdict for the defendant was dictated by the principles enunciated in *Sloss-Sheffield Steel and Iron Co.* v. *Wilkes,* . . . (1936), and *Sloss-Sheffield Steel and Iron Co.* v. *Wilkes,* . . . (1938) . . . [*Sloss I and Sloss II*]. Those cases adopted and applied the so-called "American rule" of reasonable use of percolating waters, holding that where a landowner who

> is conducting any sort of operations to which its land is adapted in an ordinary and careful manner, and as a consequence percolating water is drained, affecting the surface owner's water supply, either of that or adjoining land, no liability for his damages exists. But if the waters are drained without a reasonable need to do so, or are willfully or negligently wasted in such an operation in a way and manner as that it should have been anticipated to occur, and as a proximate result the damage accrued to the surface owners so affected, including adjoining landowners, there is an actionable claim. . . .

As to adjoining landowners, "there is no difference between the duty to avoid surface disturbances and that to avoid drainage of percolating water, since the duty of subjacent support is not existent." . . . The trial court directed a verdict for the defendant because it found that plaintiffs had presented no evidence which indicated that the water pumped by the quarry was other than percolating, or that it was pumped unnecessarily or negligently. While we agree with the trial court that *Sloss I & Sloss II* articulate the applicable law and require the result reached below, on reexamination of those cases, we are convinced that they must be overruled. . . .

In the eastern United States, the rules as to usage of underground waters have varied according to whether the waters were classified as "percolating water" or as an underground stream. The general rule is that "where a subterranean stream flows in a distinct, permanent, well-known and defined channel, it is governed by the same rules as apply to a natural watercourse on the surface." Where there is no definable channel, water is classified as percolating, and a different set of rules has evolved concerning its use. The English rule, which was followed by most of the eastern states in the 19th century, was based upon the doctrine "that a man owned from the top of the sky above his land to the center of the earth beneath him." . . . The *Restatement (Second) of Torts 857* . . . summarizes the doctrine in the following terms:

> The "English rule" . . . gave each landowner complete freedom to withdraw and use ground water and made no attempt to apportion the supply among possessors of overlying land on their grantees. It was based on the premise that ground water is the absolute property of the owner of the freehold, like the rocks, soil, and minerals that compose it, so that he is free to withdraw it at will and do with it as he pleases regardless of the effect upon his neighbors. . . . Although framed in property language, the rule was in reality a rule of capture, for a landowner's pump could induce water under the land of his neighbor to flow to his well, water that was in theory the neighbor's property while it remained in place. . . .
>
> The "American rule" was based on the same theory of property and power of capture as the English rule, with the addition of a definite prohibition against waste and of some protection for the wells and springs of adjacent owners. The rule was sometimes called the "rule of reasonable use," but "reasonable" was used in a very special and restricted sense. A waste of water or wasteful use of water was unreasonable only if it caused harm, and any nonwasteful use of water that caused harm was nevertheless reasonable if it was made on or in connection with the overlying land. . . .

It is important to note that the *Restatement* rules regarding interference with use of water were formulated to deal with situations in which an adjoining landowner's *water supply* is impaired by a defendant's use or waste of ground water, not, as in Alabama, where adjoining land is itself damaged. Although some jurisdictions have followed Alabama's approach, . . . [i]n a well-reasoned case from Florida, the Supreme Court of that state concluded that where a defendant diverts ground water from adjoining land, as an incident to his use of his own land, and does not utilize the water itself, traditional nuisance law is more appropriately applied than rules governing competing uses of percolating waters. The Court discussed the issue in language which could well be applied to the instant case:

> We are concerned with an interference with plaintiffs' use of the spring on their land, caused by conduct of the defendant not involving a competing use of water and in which the effect on the subterranean water is only incidental to the defendant's use of its land. Obviously, then, the rule of "reasonable use," as engrafted upon the old common-law rule of absolute and unqualified ownership of percolating waters, insofar as the proprietary beneficial use of the *water* is concerned, has no application here where we are concerned with the proprietary use of *land,* and in which the water is only incidentally affected. Under such circumstances, even at common law, a person was subject to liability for interference with another's use of water, either for (1) an intentional invasion when his conduct was unreasonable under the circumstances of the particular case, or (2) an unintentional invasion when his conduct was negligent, reckless or ultrahazardous. . . .

We agree with the reasoning of this case, and conclude that the reasonable use rule was inappropriately applied in *Sloss I & II*. While the *Sloss* rule may have been acceptable, even beneficial, in an earlier era of lower population density and more primitive technology, it could produce disastrous results today. Carried to its logical extension, it would allow a quarry owner to willfully sink the City of Birmingham with impunity, provided that it was done in furtherance of a legitimate enterprise and that due care was exercised in the pumping. A rule which provides no check on a landowner's ability to utilize his land to the detriment of society cannot be tolerated. The appellee admits that "at some point a balance must be struck between annoyance and inconvenience to plaintiff and the right of defendant to do business," although they omit to specify when the point is reached. Accordingly, we hold that where a plaintiff's use of ground water, whether it be for consumption or, as here, for support, is interfered with by defendant's diversion of that water, incidental to some use of his own land, the rules of liability developed by the law of nuisance will apply. These are codified in Alabama at Code 1975, Sections 6–5–120 through 6–5–127. We remand the case for further consideration by the trial court consistent with this opinion.

■ IMPORTANT TERMS AND CONCEPTS

riparian rights	leasehold estate	judgment lien	dedication
metes and bounds description	easement by prescription	legislative grant	quitclaim deed
fee simple title	licenses	accretion	mortgage
	curtesy rights	eminent domain	abstract of title

U.S. Real Estate
  Settlement Procedures Act
  (RESPA)
mineral rights
rectangular survey
  description
life estate
easements
profits
dower rights

involuntary lien
mechanic's lien
adverse possession
condemnation
warranty deed
land contract
right of redemption
judgment of foreclosure
policy of title insurance

■ QUESTIONS AND PROBLEMS FOR DISCUSSION

1. If you own an acre of land which fronts a lake, what are the boundaries of your real property ownership, above, below, and on the lakefront?

2. Under the rectangular survey method, land was divided into rectangular squares called sections. How large is a section?

3. What is eminent domain? Give an example when the legal process of condemnation would be used.

4. What is an abstract of title? Does the preparation of an abstract by an abstractor guarantee the title is merchantable? Discuss the use of an abstract of title in the purchase of real property.

5. Southwest Weather Research Inc. conducts weather modification programs. They seed clouds with certain chemicals. In this case, they were hired by a number of local farmers to seed the clouds in their area to suppress hail which had, in the past, been very damaging to these farmers' crops. There were other property owners in adjoining areas who alleged that the cloud seeding had retarded the normal rainfall over their lands. These property owners brought a lawsuit requesting an injunction to stop Southwest Weather Research Inc. from seeding the clouds, as they alleged it caused them damage by retarding normal rainfall. Discuss.

6. Fontainebleau Hotel is a large, luxury, beachfront hotel in Miami Beach, Florida. Fontainebleau Hotel Corporation decided to build a 14-story tower addition to the hotel. Eden Roc Hotel is also a large, luxury, beachfront hotel which adjoins the Fontaine-bleau on the north. If this addition is built it will block the sun to the Eden Roc. During the winter months, from around 2 P.M. for the remainder of the day, the shadow of the addition will extend over the cabana, swimming pool, and sunbathing areas of the Eden Roc, which are located in the southern portion of its property. Eden Roc files suit to secure an injunction to enjoin Fontainebleau from building this addition. The city had issued a building permit, and Fontainebleau had complied with all existing zoning and building requirements. How should the court rule and why?

7. Sam Squatter claims ownership of 36 acres of land by adverse possession, as against the record owner, Jamesville Hutterian Mutual Society. This parcel lies across the river from Jamesville's other land. Sam erected no fences around the parcel since it was bounded by the river and his other land. Sam regularly farmed 22 of the 36 acres, and Jamesville concedes that Sam owns that much by adverse possession. The other 14 acres were wooded and along the river. Sam had begun clearing trees in that area in 1965 and had cleared it off slowly over a number of years, with most the clearing occurring after 1968. In the meantime, Sam had grazed cattle on some of the uncleared land. Sam brought a quiet title action in 1986, claiming that the 20-year period for adverse possession had run and that he owned all 36 acres. Jamesville Huterian Mutual Society says that the 20 years could not start until he had completely cleared the land, and also since he hadn't fenced it off. Who's right, and why?

8. Jill Johnson brought a declaratory judgment action to clarify a deed which had been given by a prior owner of her land to the Burlington Northern Railroad. The deed had conveyed a strip of land to the railroad "for said railroad and for railroad purposes only, to have and to hold the same to said company, their successors and assigns, forever." Burlington Northern has now abandoned this railroad line, and Jill claims that the land has automatically been reverted to her, since the railroad had only an easement. Burlington Northern says it was granted a fee simple estate to the strip of land. How should the court rule here and why?

35

Real Property: Landlord and Tenant

CHAPTER OBJECTIVES
THIS CHAPTER WILL:

- Define "lease."
- Describe the types of tenancies.
- Explain the landlord's rights and obligations.
- Explain the tenant's rights and obligations.
- Discuss termination of leases.
- Explain the purpose and use of security deposits.

The problems, rights, and duties involved in the landlord-tenant relationship are very relevant to the students reading this textbook as nearly all of you are involved in such a relationship. A student who lives in a dormitory is part of a landlord-tenant relationship in which the university is the **landlord** and the student is the **tenant.** For a student who lives in an apartment, the landlord is the owner of the apartment complex. In this chapter, we will try to answer some of the questions that are often asked about the landlord-tenant relationship. We will start by looking at tenancy—the right of the tenant, or lessee—to occupy the premises.

■ TYPES OF TENANCIES

Termination at any time, with notice

No notice required

Tenancies at Will. The simplest form of tenancy, **tenancy at will,** occurs when the landlord allows the tenant to occupy the premises and there is no agreement as to a specific time period. Either the landlord or the tenant may terminate the tenancy at any time. Also, a tenancy at will is automatically terminated by the death of either party.

Most states require that the terminating party give the other party advance notice. The length of this notice varies from state to state, but 30 days is typical. This, of course, assumes that the rent has been paid. If the tenant fails to pay the rent, then the landlord can simply give the tenant notice that the lease has been terminated for that reason. In this situation a different notice requirement would be imposed.

No reason need be given to terminate the tenancy at will. Landlords may terminate the tenancy at will simply because they do not want a tenant living there any longer. Tenants, on the other hand, may terminate it simply because they want to move out.

Tenancies for a Specified Period. The great majority of residential tenancies are for a period of one year. In a college community, however, the period of tenancy may be governed by the school year. For example, the landlord may lease an apartment from August to May to one student and then lease the apartment for two months during the summer to a student going to summer school. For expediency, a commercial lease usually will be for a period longer than one year. A tenancy for a specified time is automatically terminated by the expiration of its term, and there is no requirement that either party give any notice. Both parties are aware of the term, and when the term ends, the tenancy ends.

Normally, tenancies for a specified period will be in writing because it is in the best interest of both parties to have written evidence of their agreement and the term of the tenancy. In this type of tenancy, neither party may terminate the tenancy until the term expires, or unless one of them breaches the agreement, in which case the other party may terminate the tenancy based on that breach. For example, if the landlord turns off the heat in subzero weather, the tenant certainly would have a right to terminate the lease and to move out of the premises since it would be unsafe to continue to live there.

Tenancies by Sufferance. This type of tenancy occurs after the tenancy for a specified period expires. For example, a student had a 10-month lease which expired on May 31. The student had a duty to move out on May 31, but for one reason or another needed to continue to occupy the premises. The student then became a tenant by sufferance. The landlord may treat the tenant by sufferance as a trespasser and have that person evicted, or the landlord may work out some type of rental agreement with such a tenant for the period of time that the tenant needs to stay. Until a landlord issues an eviction notice, or until the landlord and tenant agree to a new term of tenancy, the status of the tenant is that of a tenant by sufferance.

■ NATURE OF A LEASE

The *lease* is a contract, and thus must comply with the requirements for the formation and enforcement of a contract. There must be an *offer, acceptance, consideration, capacity to contract,* and *lawful purpose.* The lease contract may be oral or written. If it is oral and for a term exceeding one year, it will not be legally enforceable in most states. A few states, however, allow the enforcement of oral lease contracts for a period of up to three years.

Oral versus written leases

Many tenants have the misconception that an oral lease is better for them than a written one. Actually, a written lease provides better protection for both parties. A written lease states the rights and duties of both parties, and the landlord cannot raise the rent, evict the tenant, or impose any new rules during the term of the lease. In a college town where living space is limited, these protections can be very important. A written lease also prevents the tenant from moving out during the term of the lease except where the landlord has breached duties under terms of the lease. If the landlord fails to comply with the terms of the lease, then the tenant can move out legally, or force the landlord to comply with the terms, or sue for damages.

Right to Use Premises. The lease agreement must give the tenant-lessee the right to occupy, use, and enjoy the apartment or the parcel of land and the improvements thereon as defined in the agreement. Since the intent is not to permanently convey any rights to the lessee, the agreement must state when the landlord is allowed to retake possession. It must also state the rent the tenant is required to pay. The lease should specify what security deposit must be paid and when rental payments are due and to whom they are to be paid.

Provisions in written lease

There will also be lease terms which govern the tenant's use, enjoyment, and possession of the premises, and which preserve the landlord's right of inspection. Other terms may be inserted in a lease agreement. Many landlords do not want animals on the premises and, therefore, have a clause in the lease which prohibits the tenant from having a pet. Another common clause restricts the subletting of the premises. Normally, the tenant may sublet the premises to another person, provided the landlord agrees to the sublease. Landlords also frequently include clauses which purport to limit their liability for accidents on the premises. The following case illustrates the effect of such an *exculpatory clause.*

STATE FARM FIRE & CASUALTY CO. v. HOME INSURANCE CO.

276 N.W. 2d 349 (Wisconsin, 1979)

FACTS Kirsch and her son moved into a ground floor apartment in a building owned by Mendez. Mendez employed Middleton as caretaker for the building. Kirsch lived there for one month before she was required to sign a one-year lease. The lease contained a clause disclaiming the landlord's liability for any damage done by plumbing, gas, steam, water, or other pipes. Kirsch did not read this clause at the time, nor was it explained to her. Her apartment had a "sleeve" for an air conditioning unit, but there was no air conditioning unit. Intead, a piece of cardboard covered the opening where the unit would have been. Hickman and Cramer moved into the apartment above Kirsch's in November. Their air conditioner was also missing, and during the winter they filed about 50 complaints with Middleton about the cardboard blowing off the hole and letting in cold air. Middleton did nothing about the problem. Kirsch received a call at work telling her to come back to her apartment. A copper tube in the baseboard radiation system had broken, and her apartment was flooded with water. The cold air coming in upstairs had apparently frozen the pipe, and it broke. Kirsch was paid by her insurance company, State Farm, and it sued Mendez's insurance company, Home. State Farm won a jury verdict, but the trial court entered a judgment N.O.V. for Home. State Farm appealed.

ISSUE Does the disclaimer clause in the lease protect the landlord from liability?

DECISION No. Judgment reversed; case remanded for entry of judgment on jury's award:

REASONS **Judge Bode stated:**

"The general rule is that an exculpatory clause exempting a landlord from liability resulting from a condition of the premises does not apply where the damage sustained is caused by the active or affirmative negligence of the landlord. . . .

"Middleton's actions did not amount to mere inadvertent acts or omissions. . . . Hickman and Cramer had repeatedly brought the lack of insulation in the air conditioning sleeve to Middleton's attention. His intentional failure to take action to correct the defect under the circumstances was an affirmative act constituting active negligence. Having concluded that Middleton's negligence was active, the exculpatory clause may not be used to exempt Mendez from liability."

▪ LANDLORD'S RIGHTS AND OBLIGATIONS

Once a lease agreement has been made, the landlord has a duty to give the tenant possession of the premises specified in the lease agreement. The landlord also has the duty not to interfere with the right of the tenant to possess and enjoy the premises for the term of the agreement, provided that the tenant does not breach the lease. The landlord also has the right to inspect the premises at reasonable times, with the tenant's permission, to see that the premises are not being mistreated or damaged.

Common law rule: Caveat emptor

Under the common law, the landlord did not have to worry about the condition of the premises at the time they were rented to a tenant. The tenant

Statutory changes

was subject to the rule of *caveat emptor* and simply took the premises as they were or refused to rent them. If the premises were filthy or infested with rats and the tenant knowingly agreed to take them, then the tenant assumed the risk. The landlord would not be responsible for injuries and damages that the tenant might suffer as a result. The rule of caveat emptor has generally been replaced by the rule of *caveat vendor*—that is, "Let the seller (in this case, the landlord) beware." The landlord-tenant relationship has become the target of many consumer groups. As a result, many states, cities, and counties have enacted housing codes which set minimum standards with regard to the rental of premises for residential occupancy. Most cities and counties now have housing inspectors who will respond to the complaints of tenants. These inspectors check to see that rental units are in fact safe, habitable, and free from dangers such as bare electrical wires, or other unhealthy and unsanitary conditions.

Landlord's liability for security of premises

In many recent cases, landlords have been found civilly liable for injury to tenants because the landlords failed to provide sufficient security, or because the landlords' employees were responsible for theft from, or injury to, tenants. Whether or not the landlord is liable in such cases depends heavily on the circumstances. If the apartment complex advertises that it provides security for its tenants, then it has assumed that duty; if, however, no security has been promised or provided, then the tenant will be faced with caveat emptor. As to theft, the landlord will normally have a clause in the lease stating that the landlord is not responsible for theft. If an employee of the landlord commits a crime against a tenant, then the landlord will allege that the person who perpetrated the crime was not acting as an agent or employee, and that the employer is not responsible for criminal acts of employees. However, the pendulum of the law is swinging in favor of the consumer-tenant and against the seller-landlord. The wise landlord will insure adequately against such situations, as this is still a questionable area of landlord's rights and obligations. The *Rullman* case is a recent example of how these rules work.

RULLMAN v. FISHER

371 N.W.2d 588 (Minnesota, 1985)

FACTS

Helen Fisher owns a three-story building located at 117 North Washington Avenue in Minneapolis. The first floor is leased to a commercial sauna and massage parlor, and the second and third floors are each studio/loft apartments. Stacey Greene and two roommates leased the second floor.

The building entrance, facing Washington Avenue, is not locked and opens into a small vestibule. Inside the vestibule one door opens into the sauna and another onto a stairway leading up to the lofts. A door on the second floor opens off the stairway into Greene's loft, and the stairway continues up to the third floor.

On January 1, 1981, appellant Renae Rullman attended an impromptu New Year's party in Greene's loft apartment. Because the building had no intercom or buzzer system, guests entered by knocking on the door at the bottom of the stairway and waiting for someone to walk down the stairs to open the door. The deposition testimony varied on the type of door and lock but was consistent that the door did not lock automatically upon closing. The depositions were also conflicting as to whether the door at the top of the stairs could be effectively locked. In the early evening Greene followed departing guests down the stairs to make sure the door was locked because she worried about security, particularly the "sauna situation." She states that she became "frustrated," however, because guests "were always going in and out," and stopped checking the door. Rullman arrived with a group of friends shortly after midnight.

Greene stated in a deposition that she recognized everyone at the party except for one man. Rullman said she did not know the man either, but "he was there mingling, like everybody else," and she assumed he was a guest. Greene said that even though he was a stranger she thought at the time, "it's New Year's Eve, if he's okay, then we'll welcome him." She stated that the unknown man was not doing anything improper. None of the other guests knew the man or how he had come to the party.

Rullman danced with the man and introduced him to Greene as "Leon." When she went to use the bathroom, located at the back of the loft away from the area of the party, the man followed her, pushed her into the bathroom, beat her, broke her jaw, and sexually assaulted her. Another guest interrupted the attack, but the man fled and was never apprehended or identified.

Rullman brought this personal injury action, contending that Fisher was negligent in failing to maintain reasonable security and security devices in the building. The trial court granted a summary judgment in favor of the landlord. Plaintiff appealed.

ISSUE   Did the trial court err in granting summary judgment on the issue of Fisher's alleged failure to provide adequate security?

DECISION   No. Judgment of the trial court is affirmed.

REASONS   **Judge Lansing, speaking for the court, stated:**
"Rullman contends that summary judgment was improper because Fisher was negligent in failing to provide a dead-bolt lock on Greene's apartment and a doorbell or buzzer system for the building. . . .

"The Minnesota Supreme Court has recognized, in some cases, a landlord's liability for criminal actions of a third person. . . .

"The general rule that a third person's criminal act is an intervening . . . cause breaking the chain of causation . . . is not applicable when the criminal act is reasonably foreseeable. . . . Rullman argues that the assault was reasonably foreseeable because of the commercial and warehouse character of the neighborhood and because of past criminal activity at the first-floor sauna.

"Even assuming that Fisher should have reasonably foreseen a sexual assault on tenants or guests, Rullman's claim founders when analyzed in terms of actual causation. On the issue of causation, the plaintiff must produce evidence

> which affords a reasonable basis for the conclusion that it is more likely than not that the conduct of the defendant was a substantial factor in bringing about the result. A mere possibility of such causation is not enough; and when the matter remains one of pure speculation or conjecture, or the probabilities are at best evenly balanced, it becomes the duty of the court to direct a verdict for the defendant. . . .

In this case it is undisputed that Greene intentionally allowed the door to remain unlocked even though she was aware it was unlocked and expressed concern over security. Rullman argues that Greene's alleged negligence was not an intervening cause of the assault because the necessity of walking downstairs to admit guests and to relock the door after them increased the likelihood that the door would be left unlocked. Even granting an increased likelihood that the door would be left unlocked, we do not find the necessary nexus between the lack of a doorbell or buzzer system and the assault. Whether the assailant knocked and was allowed into the loft, walked in with a group, or merely wandered in through the unlocked door, it is undisputed that he was at the party for some time, mingled with guests and the host, and although recognized as a stranger, was not questioned or asked to leave. Under these circumstances, it is merely speculation to argue that the lack of a buzzer system was a substantial factor in causing the assault. . . . Even viewed in the light most favorable to Rullman, the record does not show the requisite causal connection between Fisher's breach of any duty and the criminal assault. . . .

"Rullman presented insufficient evidence of a causal connection between Fisher's alleged negligent failure to provide adequate security and the criminal assault to raise a genuine issue of material fact. Summary judgment was appropriate on the issue of Fisher's liability."

■ TENANT'S RIGHTS AND OBLIGATIONS

The most important right that a tenant has is what the law terms *quiet enjoyment of the premises*. This means that, with a few exceptions, tenants have the *right to use* the house or apartment which they are renting in generally the same manner as if they owned the premises. To be more specific, if you are a tenant, you may invite anyone you wish to visit you, and you may carry on any activities which are not forbidden by the lease or by law. The key here is reasonable use of the premises.

Right to use

For example, you rent a house with a large yard and the house is a considerable distance from other houses. In that case, you can play your stereo as loud as you want to and have loud parties, as long as you do not destroy or damage the rented property. On the other hand, if you live in an apartment building, your right to play the stereo loud and to have loud parties would be limited. As the tenant in an apartment, you not only have the right to quiet enjoyment of the premises, but you also have an obligation not to unreasonably disturb the other tenants, who also have the right to quiet enjoyment of the premises. The tenant should always read the fine print in the lease agreement, as the agreement may prohibit many activities which are not expressly forbidden by law. Such provisions are contractual and will generally be enforced by courts.

As stated earlier, the landlord has a right to inspect the rented premises. However, during the period of the lease the landlord does not have the right to enter the house or apartment at will and without the tenant's permission. The landlord who is going to inspect the premises must do so at reasonable times that will not interfere with the quiet enjoyment of the premises by the tenant. A landlord could be civilly liable in a trespass action for forcing entry into the rented premises or for entering the rented premises periodically when the tenant is not at home, simply to snoop.

Lease may specify who has to make repairs

Another common problem experienced by tenants is that of liability for repairs. What repairs are the landlord's duty, and what repairs are the duty of the tenant? The landlord's obligation to make repairs inside the rented house or apartment will vary from state to state and from locality to locality, and may also be dictated by the terms of the lease. As a general rule, however, the landlord is required to make major repairs except where the damage is caused by the tenant's negligence. If the tenant is having a wild party and something is thrown through the window, the tenant will be obligated to replace the window. If a windstorm blows off part of the roofing and water drips through the ceiling causing the plaster to fall, the landlord will be responsible for repairs.

A rule of thumb in these cases would be that the tenant has a duty to make minor repairs to keep the premises in as good a condition as when they were rented, excluding, of course, normal wear and tear. Most landlords require a security deposit for use in making such minor repairs when the tenant vacates the premises. If the tenant's furniture marked up the walls, then the tenant would be obligated to have the walls repainted in order to cover the damage. If the furnace broke down, that is a major repair which would be the landlord's obligation. The *Borders* case, which follows, applies these distinctions in another context.

BORDERS v. ROSEBERRY

532 P.2d 1366 (Kansas, 1975)

FACTS   Rienecker leased a single-family house from Agnes Roseberry in 1970. Agnes had just had some remodeling done on the house, including the installation of a new roof. The roofers had removed the gutters from the front of the house but had not reinstalled them. Without gutters, water ran off the front side of the roof onto the front steps. On January 9, 1971, ice had accumulated on the steps and Rienecker worked that afternoon to clean them off. Gary Borders arrived at about 4 P.M. in response to a dinner invitation. When Gary left that evening, about 9 P.M., he slipped and fell on the icy steps, and sustained personal injuries. Gary sued Agnes. He appealed from a trial court ruling that Agnes owed no duty to a social guest of the tenant in a single-family house where the injury was the result of a known hazard.

ISSUE   Is the landlord liable for a known defective condition which existed when the tenant took possession of the premises?

DECISION   No. Judgment affirmed.

REASONS   Justice Prager stated that:
"The sole point raised on this appeal by the plaintiff, Gary D. Borders, is that the trial court committed reversible error in concluding as a matter of law that a landlord of a single-family house is under no obligation or duty to a social guest of his tenant to repair or remedy a known condition whereby water dripped from the roof onto the front steps of a house fronting north, froze, and caused the social guest to slip and fall.

"At the outset it should be emphasized that we do not have involved here an action brought by a social guest to recover damages for personal injuries from his host, a possessor of real property. The issue raised involves the liability of a lessor who has leased his property to a tenant for a period of time. Furthermore, it should be pointed out that the plaintiff, a social guest of the tenant, has based his claim of liability against the landlord upon the existence of a defective condition which existed on the leased property *at the time the tenant took possession.*

"Traditionally the law in this country has placed upon the lessee as the person in possession of the land the burden of maintaining the premises in a reasonably safe condition to protect persons who come upon the land. It is the tenant as possessor who, at least initially, has the burden of maintaining the premises in good repair. . . .

The relationship of landlord and tenant is not in itself sufficient to make the landlord liable for the tortious acts of the tenant."

"A tenant's rights as to heat, water, and electricity will depend primarily upon the lease. If a landlord who is to provide heat turns the thermostats down to an unsafe or intolerable temperature, then the tenant may terminate the lease and leave, or pay to heat the premises and deduct the cost from the rent, or report the landlord to the local housing authority.

Another question that often arises is: Who bears the responsibility for the loss of the tenant's furniture, clothing, and personal effects if the rented apartment or house burns down? The lease will often expressly state that the tenants assume responsibility for carrying fire insurance on their personal belongings. If there is no such agreement in the lease, then the courts will usually hold the landlord responsible for damages to the tenants' contents if the fire or other damage was caused as a result of the landlord's negligence. The wise thing for the tenants to do is to carry renter's insurance on their contents, as the law and the obligation of the landlord will vary. Also, it is often difficult to determine who, if anyone, was negligent in a major fire or catastrophe.

Ownership of Fixtures. Another common question concerns the extent to which tenants can make changes or additions, such as putting pictures on the walls, installing shelves, or changing curtain rods. Again, the lease often specifies that tenants may not paint the premises, hang pictures, or make any alterations to the premises without the landlord's permission. If there is no such provision in the lease, then a reasonableness rule applies. If tenants install such things as bookshelves or room dividers, the landlord automatically becomes the owner of those fixtures when the tenants leave, unless the fixtures can be removed without causing any damage to the rented property.

Fixtures stay with premises

■ TERMINATION OF THE LEASE

Agreed termination

Termination due to breach

If the lease is for a fixed period of time, it is rather difficult for the tenant to break it. However, a landlord and a tenant can always end the lease by mutual agreement, regardless of its terms. Thus, if the tenant and the landlord agree that the tenant may move out before the lease expires, then the lease may be terminated. It is a good idea to put this agreement in writing to prevent the landlord from coming back later and trying to enforce the original lease.

The tenant may also terminate the lease without the landlord's agreement if the landlord has interfered with the tenant's quiet enjoyment or if the landlord has in some way failed to meet obligations specified in the lease and such failure has caused the premises to be uninhabitable or below minimum health standards.

The landlord can evict a tenant for nonpayment of rent. The landlord can evict a tenant if the tenant stays in possession of the premises after the term of the lease has expired, or if the tenant violates the rules and regulations of the lease. For example, if your lease states that no pets are allowed and you keep a cat, the landlord can evict you unless you get rid of it.

In the following case, a condominium owners' association is attempting to enjoin Mr. and Mrs. O'Connor from residing in their condominium because they now have a baby, and the condominium regulations prohibit residency by children under 18 years of age.

O'CONNOR v. VILLAGE GREEN OWNERS ASSN.

662 P.2d 427 (California, 1983)

FACTS The Village Green is a housing complex of 629 units in the Baldwin Hills area of Los Angeles. It was built in 1942 and was operated as an apartment complex until 1973, when it was converted to a condominium development. As part of the condominium conversion the developer drafted and recorded a declaration of CC and Rs [Covenants, Conditions and Restrictions] which run with the property and which contain a prohibition against residency by anyone under the age of 18. The CC and Rs also establish the Village Green Owners Association (Association) and authorize it to enforce the regulations set forth therein. The Association is a nonprofit organization whose membership consists of all owners of units at Village Green.

John and Denise O'Connor bought a two-bedroom unit in Village Green in 1975. On July 4, 1979, their son Gavin was born. Shortly thereafter, the Association gave them written notice that the presence of their son Gavin in the unit constituted a violation of the CC and Rs and directed them to discontinue having Gavin live there.

After making unsuccessful attempts to find other suitable housing, the O'Connors filed a complaint against the Association seeking to have the age restriction declared invalid and to enjoin its enforcement. The first amended complaint alleged, *inter alia*, that the age restriction violated the Unruh Civil Rights Act. The Association filed a general demurrer which the trial court sustained without leave to amend. The action was dismissed and the O'Connors appealed.

After the O'Connors' notice of appeal was filed, the Association filed an action to enjoin the O'Connors from residing in the condominium with their son. The trial court granted a preliminary injunction but stayed its enforcement for 90 days to allow the O'Connors to find other housing. The O'Connors filed a notice of appeal.

ISSUE Is the age restriction which discriminates against children under the age of 18 years enforceable?

DECISION No. The decisions of the trial court are reversed.

REASONS Justice Kaus, speaking for the court, stated:

"In *Marina Point, Ltd.* v. *Wolfson*, . . . 30 Cal.3d 721, we considered the question of whether the Unruh Civil Rights Act (the act) prohibited an apartment owner's discrimination against children. We reviewed the history of the act—Civil Code section 51—and noted that it had emanated from earlier 'public accommodation' legislation and had extended the reach of such statutes from common carriers and places of accommodation to cover 'all business establishments of every kind whatsoever.' . . . [W]e held that the act barred all types of arbitrary discrimination. The act's reference to particular bases of discrimination—'sex, color, race, religion, ancestry or national origin'—was illustrative rather than restrictive. . . .

"In sum, we held in *Marina Point* that the landlord's blanket exclusion of children from residency was prohibited by the act. . . .

"In *Marina Point* there was no question that the apartment complex was a 'business establishment' within the meaning of the act. The determinative question in that case was whether the act encompassed discrimination against children. Since that question was answered in *Marina Point,* the only question to be decided in the present case is whether the discriminatory policy against children is being invoked by a 'business establishment' within the meaning of the act. . . .

"The Village Green Owners Association has sufficient businesslike attributes to fall within the scope of the act's reference to 'business establishments of every kind whatsoever.' . . .

"Consistent with the legislature's intent to use the term 'business establishments' in the broadest sense reasonably possible . . . we conclude that the Village Green Owners Association is a business establishment within the meaning of the act."

■ SECURITY DEPOSITS

No interest due on security deposits

What are deductable repairs and cleaning

Most leases provide that a lessee must pay a security deposit, also referred to as a damage deposit, when the lease is signed. This security deposit is to be held by the landlord and to be applied to any repairs required as a result of damage caused by the tenant, other than normal wear and tear. Two problems exist. First, the landlord takes two or three hundred dollars of each tenant's money and holds it for the lease period, which may be a year or longer. During that time the landlord can invest this money and secure interest on it. Some states require landlords to pay interest to tenants on the security deposit when it is returned. Most states, however, still do not have such a requirement. Thus, a landlord with 100 apartments has a large amount of cash to invest and the landlord can earn a good income from the tenants' money.

The second problem is what type of repairs and what type of cleanup should come out of the security deposit. Some landlords use the money for improvements such as repainting the entire apartment, or purchasing new curtains on the contention that the walls were chipped or the drapes were stained. Obviously the walls could be patched and painted as necessary, but the landlord is not entitled to a complete paint job at the expense of the tenant. The same principle applies to the curtains and drapes. Cleaning may be allowable, but not the purchase of new drapes. The landlord is not supposed to gain by getting an improvement. The problem is that the landlord has the security deposit, and often refuses to return it, alleging it was used for repairs and clean up. For years tenants simply grumbled but did not go to court since the cost of paying a lawyer, court costs, and other expenses made collecting too expensive for the amount of money involved. Most jurisdictions now have small claims courts where the tenant can, for a minimal filing fee, file a lawsuit and have the case heard promptly. Landlord-tenant cases comprise a major portion of the court docket in most small claims courts.

■ LANDLORD'S RIGHTS TO DAMAGES

Where a tenant simply defaults in the payment of rent, the landlord may file suit to evict and to collect the back rent. Depending on the particular state, the landlord may be entitled to hold the tenant's possessions under a "landlord lien statute." The *Martin* case reviews the landlord's right to attach a tenant's possessions for nonpayment of back rent.

EX PARTE MARTIN

412 So. 2d 815 (Alabama, 1982)

FACTS

Petitioner is a former radio announcer known as William (Billy) Martin, residing in an apartment unit of East Bay Apartments, a complex located in Baldwin County. On January 13, 1982 respondent, East Bay Apartments, filed an action seeking damages for breach of a lease agreement against petitioner in the District Court of Baldwin County. It was alleged that Martin had defaulted in making rent payments under his lease for a period of three months, and had failed to pay late charges as required by the lease. The damages requested amounted to $2,280. Along with its complaint, respondent filed a petition for a writ of attachment and an accompanying affidavit of the resident manager of the apartment complex. The affidavit alleges that petitioner is in default for three months' rent and applicable late charges, and that the affiant believes that petitioner "intends to move to Florida, outside the jurisdiction of the courts of Baldwin County, Alabama in the event collection procedures are commenced against him." The affidavit failed to contain a statement to the effect that the writ was not sued out solely "for the purpose of vexing or harassing the defendant," as required by § 35–9–62, Code 1975, the provision dealing with a landlord's lien on the tenant's possessions for rent due and owing.

The district court granted respondent's petition for a writ of attachment. On January 19 respondent filed an attachment bond in double the amount of the damages requested, and on January 20 a writ of seizure and attachment was issued. Petitioner was duly notified, and the sheriff seized an automobile and two queen-size beds belonging to petitioner.

Petitioner appeals and requests a writ of mandamus directing the dismissal of the writ of attachment.

ISSUE

Does a landlord have the right to have the tenant's automobile seized to apply to payment of back rent?

DECISION

Yes. Judgment of the trial court is affirmed.

REASONS

Judge Bradley, speaking for the court, finds that:

"Petitioner asserts four grounds for the issuance of a writ of mandamus directing the dismissal of the writ of attachment. He first alleges that the original affidavit filed by respondent in conjunction with the request for a writ of attachment was invalid for failure to allege that the writ was not sued out solely 'to vex or harass the defendant,' as required by § 6–6–44, Code 1975. . . .

"Although the original affidavit did not contain the required statutory language, the trial court permitted an amendment to the affidavit to include the required language. Both §§ 6–6–143 and 35–9–62 permit 'the plaintiff, before or during the trial . . . to amend any defect of form or of substance in the affidavit.' Consequently the trial court properly permitted the amendment to the affidavit. . . .

"Petitioner lastly contends that the automobile seized by the sheriff under the writ of attachment is not within the class of property covered by a landlord's lien. Petitioner argues that a landlord's statutory lien extends only to those items of personal property contained within the four walls of the rented apartment. That contention is without merit. A landlord's lien on the goods, furniture, and effects of the tenant extends to such property of the tenant as is brought upon and enjoys the protection of the premises and is used by the tenant in connection therewith. . . . That class of property covered by the lien has been extended to include all property kept on the premises and used in connection with the tenancy, whether inside or outside of the leased premises. . . .

Respondent's lien would therefore extend to the property of petitioner used on the common ways and parking areas of the apartment complex. Petitioner's automobile would be squarely within the scope of coverage. . . .

"For the reasons above stated, petitioner's request for a writ of mandamus is denied."

Landlord's duty to mitigate

What happens if the tenant moves out of the leased premises before the end of the lease? The landlord now sues the tenant for any unpaid rent due at the time the tenant moved out, and for the balance of the rent due under the lease. What is the ***landlord's duty to mitigate;*** that is, to lessen, the amount due from the lessee by rerenting the premises to someone else? Traditionally, the landlord did not have a duty to rerent the premises and thus mitigate the loss. The trend in the recent landlord-tenant cases involving residential leases reflects a change in judicial thinking. Recent cases require the landlord in residential leases to make at least a reasonable effort to rerent the premises and thereby mitigate the damages.

With regard to commercial leases, the courts will not feel so sorry for the lessee. In a commercial lease situation the lease agreement is usually negotiated, with each party having legal counsel. Also in a commercial lease situation the parties will be on a more equal footing financially.

■ **SIGNIFICANCE OF THIS CHAPTER**

Most people will be involved in a lease at some time, either as a tenant, or as a landlord. This chapter reviews the contents of a lease and discusses the rights and duties of the tenant and the landlord.

DISCUSSION CASE

SOMMER v. KRIDEL

378 A.2d 767 (New Jersey, 1977)

FACTS: On March 10, 1972 the defendant, James Kridel, entered into a lease with the plaintiff, Abraham Sommer, owner of the "Pierre Apartments" in Hackensack, to rent apartment 6-L in that building. The term of the lease was from May 1, 1972 until April 30, 1974, with a rent concession for the first six weeks, so that the first month's rent was not due until June 15, 1972.

One week after signing the agreement, Kridel paid Sommer $690. Half of that sum was used to satisfy the first month's rent. The remainder was paid under the lease provision requiring a security deposit of $345. Although defendant had expected to begin occupancy around May 1, his plans were changed. He wrote to Sommer on May 19, 1972, explaining:

I was to be married on June 3, 1972. Unhappily the engagement was broken and the wedding plans cancelled. Both parents were to assume responsibility for the rent after our marriage. I was discharged from the U.S. Army in October 1971 and am now a student. I have no funds of my own, and am supported by my stepfather.

In view of the above, I cannot take possession of the apartment and am surrendering all rights to it. Never having received a key, I cannot return same to you.

I beg your understanding and compassion in releasing me from the lease, and will of course, in consideration thereof, forfeit the 2 months' rent already paid.

Please notify me at your earliest convenience.

Plaintiff did not answer the letter.

Subsequently, a third party went to the apartment

house and inquired about renting apartment 6-L. Although the parties agreed that she was ready, willing, and able to rent the apartment, the person in charge told her that the apartment was not being shown since it was already rented to Kridel. In fact, the landlord did not reenter the apartment or exhibit it to anyone until August 1, 1973. At that time it was rented to a new tenant for a term beginning on September 1, 1973. The new rental was for $345 per month with a six-week concession similar to that granted Kridel.

Prior to reletting the new premises, plaintiff sued Kridel in August 1972, demanding $7,590, the total amount due for the full two-year term of the lease. Following a mistrial, plaintiff filed an amended complaint asking for $5,865, the amount due between May 1, 1972 and September 1, 1973. The amended complaint included no reduction in the claim to reflect the six-week concession provided for in the lease or the $690 payment made to plaintiff after signing the agreement. Defendant filed an amended answer to the complaint, alleging that plaintiff breached the contract, failed to mitigate damages, and accepted defendant's surrender of the premises. He also counterclaimed to demand repayment of the $345 paid as a security deposit.

The trial judge ruled in favor of defendant. Despite his conclusion that the lease had been drawn to reflect "the 'settled law' of this state," he found that "justice and fair dealing" imposed upon the landlord the duty to attempt to relet the premises and thereby mitigate damages. He also held that plaintiff's failure to make any response to defendant's unequivocal offer of surrender was tantamount to an acceptance, thereby terminating the tenancy and any obligation to pay rent. As a result, he dismissed both the complaint and the counterclaim. The Appellate Division reversed.

■

Justice Pashman:

We granted certification in these two cases to consider whether a landlord seeking damages from a defaulting tenant is under a duty to mitigate damages by making reasonable efforts to relet an apartment wrongfully vacated by the tenant. Separate parts of the Appellate Division held that, in accordance with their respective leases, the landlords in both cases could recover rents due under the leases regardless of whether they had attempted to relet the vacated apartments. Although they were of different minds as to the fairness of this result, both parts agreed that it was dictated by *Joyce* v. *Bauman*, . . . a decision by the former Court of Errors and Appeals. We now reverse and hold that a landlord does have an obligation to make a reasonable effort to mitigate damages in

such a situation. We therefore overrule *Joyce* v. *Bauman* to the extent that it is inconsistent with our decision today. . . .

As the lower courts in both appeals found, the weight of authority in this State supports the rule that a landlord is under no duty to mitigate damages caused by a defaulting tenant. . . . This rule has been followed in a majority of states, . . . and has been tentatively adopted in the American Law Institute's Restatement of Property. . . .

Nevertheless, while there is still a split of authority over this question, the trend among recent cases appears to be in favor of a mitigation requirement. . . .

The majority rule is based on principles of property law which equate a lease with a transfer of a property interest in the owner's estate. Under this rationale the lease conveys to a tenant an interest in the property which forecloses any control by the landlord; thus, it would be anomalous to require the landlord to concern himself with the tenant's abandonment of his own property. . . .

Yet the distinction between a lease for ordinary residential purposes and an ordinary contract can no longer be considered viable. As Professor Powell observed, evolving "social factors have exerted increasing influence on the law of estates for years." . . . The result has been that

> [t]he complexities of city life, and the proliferated problems of modern society in general, have created new problems for lessors and lessees and these have been commonly handled by specific clauses in leases. This growth in the number and detail of specific lease convenants has reintroduced into the law of estates for years a predominantly contractual ingredient. . . .

Thus in 6 *Williston on Contracts* (3 ed. 1962), § 890A at 592, it is stated:

> There is a clearly discernible tendency on the part of courts to cast aside technicalities in the interpretation of leases and to concentrate their attention, as in the case of other contracts, on the intention of the parties. . . .

Application of the contract rule requiring mitigation of damages to a residential lease may be justified as a matter of basic fairness. Professor McCormick first commented upon the inequity under the majority rule when he predicted in 1925 that eventually

> the logic, inescapable according to the standards of a "jurisprudence of conceptions" which permits the landlord to stand idly by the vacant, abandoned premises and treat them as the property of the tenant and recover full rent, will yield to the more realistic notions of social advantage which in other fields of the law have forbidden a recovery for damages which the plaintiff by reasonable efforts could have avoided. . . .

Various courts have adopted this position. . . .

The preexisting rule cannot be predicated upon the possibility that a landlord may lose the opportunity to rent another empty apartment because he must first rent the apartment vacated by the defaulting tenant. Even where the breach occurs in a multi-dwelling building, each apartment may have unique qualities which make it attractive to certain individuals. Significantly, in *Sommer* v. *Kridel,* there was a specific request to rent this apartment vacated by the defendant; there is no reason to believe that absent this vacancy the landlord could have succeeded in renting a different apartment to this individual.

We therefore hold that antiquated real property concepts, which served as the basis for the preexisting rule, shall no longer be controlling where there is a claim for damages under a residential lease. Such claims must be governed by more modern notions of fairness and equity. A landlord has a duty to mitigate damages where he seeks to recover rents due from a defaulting tenant.

If the landlord has other vacant apartments besides the one the tenant has abandoned, the landlord's duty to mitigate consists of making reasonable efforts to relet the apartment. In such cases he must treat the apartment in question as if it was one of his vacant stock.

As part of his cause of action, the landlord shall be required to carry the burden of proving that he used reasonable diligence in attempting to relet the premises. We note that there has been a divergence of opinion concerning the allocation of the burden of proof on this issue. . . . While generally in contract actions the breaching party has the burden of proving that damages are capable of mitigation, . . . here the landlord will be in a better position to demonstrate whether he exercised reasonable diligence in attempting to relet the premises. . . .

The *Sommer* v. *Kridel* case presents a classic example of the unfairness which occurs when a landlord has no responsibility to minimize damages. Sommer waited 15 months and allowed $4,658.50 in damages to accrue before attempting to relet the apartment. Despite the availability of a tenant who was ready, willing, and able to rent the apartment, the landlord needlessly increased the damages by turning her away. While a tenant will not necessarily be excused from his obligations under a lease simply by finding another person who is willing to rent the vacated premises. . . . Here there has been no showing that the new tenant would not have been suitable. We therefore find that plaintiff could have avoided the damages which eventually accrued and that the defendant was relieved of his duty to continue paying rent. Ordinarily we would require the tenant to bear the cost of any reasonable expenses incurred by a landlord in attempting to relet the premises, . . . but no such expenses were incurred in this case.

The judgment in *Sommer* v. *Kridel* is reversed.

■ IMPORTANT TERMS AND CONCEPTS

lease
landlord
tenancy at will
tenancies by sufferance
caveat emptor
quiet enjoyment of premises
landlord's rights and duties
ownership of fixtures

landlord's duty to mitigate
tenant
security deposit
tenancies for a specified period
exculpatory clauses
caveat vendor
right to use premises
tenant's rights and duties
termination of lease

■ QUESTIONS AND PROBLEMS FOR DISCUSSION

1. Which is better, an oral lease or a written lease? Why?
2. What are the landlord's rights and duties?
3. Do tenants have any rights? What are they?
4. If a lease is for a fixed period of time it will cease when that period has elapsed. However, in many cases either the landlord or the tenant may desire to terminate the lease before it expires. Can either of these parties terminate the lease before the term of the lease has expired? If so, how?

5. Mr. Garcia rented an apartment in New York from Freeland Realty, Inc. He found that plaster and paint were flaking off the walls in two of the rooms in the apartment. His small children were eating the plaster, and he was afraid they would become ill. He asked the landlord to replaster and paint these rooms, and the landlord refused. Mr. Garcia then went out and purchased the necessary plaster and paint and replastered and repainted the walls that were bad. He now sues the landlord for $29.53 for materials and for 10 hours labor at the minimum wage. How should the court rule in this case? What if there was no problem of children eating flaking plaster—let's say the tenant just wanted newly painted walls? Would the decision be the same?

6. Alva Sprecher owned and operated a bar for several years. As part of the business, he had been granted a state liquor license. Alva sold the business to Cecil and Cindy Weston, but retained ownership of the building in which it was located. The Westons leased the building from Alva. One provision of the lease stated that on termination of the lease the lessee would

surrender all licenses to serve liquor to the lessor. The Westons were duly licensed by the state to serve liquor. About halfway through their one-year lease, they bought the building next door to Sprecher's. Then they applied to the local city council for permission to move the location of their licensed liquor establishment into the other building. The city council granted permission. Sprecher learned what was going on and sued for an injunction and damages. The Westons argue that the lease provision is invalid since state liquor laws control the issuance and transfer of liquor licenses. Who's right, and why?

7. Mr. and Mrs. Lillemoen rented an apartment from Mr. Gregorich on June 1, 1983. They never had a written lease on the apartment but simply paid the rent on a month-to-month basis. On January 28, 1985, at about 9:30 A.M., Mr. Lillemoen left the apartment to buy groceries. He went out the front door, which opened onto a staircase leading to the ground level. The staircase was for the sole use of the tenants of the apartment. A handrail extended the full length of the staircase on the right side; on the left side there was a railing from the ground level up to the side of the building. The edge of the building roof extended partially over the stairs, but there were no gutters. Water had dripped off the roof and frozen on the stairs. Mr. Lillemoen descended the stairs without slipping, got his groceries, and returned. Because he lacked two fingers on his right hand he carried the groceries in his right arm and held the left handrail as he ascended the stairs. When he reached the second or third step from the top he let go of the handrail to open the door. He then slipped and broke his hip. Mr. Lillemoen sues for damages. What is the result, and why?

8. Two tenants living in an apartment complex commenced legal actions against the landlord to recover damages for personal injuries they suffered in accidents which occurred in common passageways of the apartment complex. Tenant McCutcheon fell down an unlighted stairway, and tenant Fuller fell down an exterior wooden stairway. Both alleged negligence in maintenance by the landlord. In both cases the landlord defended on the basis of an exculpatory clause in the lease which said that the landlord would not be liable for any injury to the lessee or his family. The plaintiffs are asking the court to declare this exculpatory clause to be against public policy and thus invalid. How should the court rule? Why?

36

Real Property—Zoning, Environmental Regulation, and Eminent Domain

CHAPTER OBJECTIVES

THIS CHAPTER WILL:

- Discuss the need for environmental regulations for the use and occupancy of real property.
- Explain the purpose and effect of local zoning laws.
- Explain the use of private restrictive convenants that regulate the use of real property.
- Discuss national environmental policy and laws.

Need for land use controls

This chapter deals with the many problems involved in the use of real estate by its owner. The initial reaction from most people is: "It's my land, and I ought to be able to use it as I see fit." If we look back to the era of our grandfathers, or perhaps our great-grandfathers, we would find that owners of real estate could use their land in any way that they saw fit, provided their use did not cause a nuisance as defined by the law. Such a nuisance would do harm to the neighboring property owners or would interfere with their peaceable use and enjoyment of their real estate. There were no restrictions on house sizes, on the erection of fences or any outbuildings, on the number of families housed on a property, or on the use of a home to operate a beauty shop, a barbershop, a small appliance repair shop, or some similar type of business. In those days, we did not have the density problem or the traffic problem that we have today in most cities. Plenty of land was available, and far fewer people were making a demand for its use. Yet, cities grew and grew, in most cases without a master plan. Thus, we ended up with industrial plants, apartment complexes, and scattered commercial buildings in single-family residential areas.

The increased population density in our cities has brought environmental problems: namely, contaminated air and water, solid waste pollution, traffic congestion, and noise pollution. To solve such problems, we have had to resort to governmental regulation of the use of various land areas. Today most cities develop industrial parks and encourage industry to build and operate within these areas. Most cities have developed zoning ordinances which restrict the use of the land in various areas. For example, single-family dwellings will be allowed in some areas, two-family dwellings will be allowed in other areas, multifamily dwellings, such as large apartment houses will be allowed in still other areas, and commercial businesses will be excluded from certain areas.

At first glance, this may seem unfair to the owner of real estate since under these ordinances the owner is limited to the uses prescribed by the law. It is true that zoning ordinances do take away certain rights of the individual owner. However, when one looks at the overall picture, it is clear that some type of land use regulation is in the best interest of all the residents of the city. Such regulation guarantees a more peaceful enjoyment of the owners' premises for the purposes that are allowed in an area, and it also preserves the property values for the owners in that area. For example, if you live in an area of single-family dwellings, you certainly would object to having a developer put an apartment complex next to your home since this would increase the traffic in front of your residence, create a parking problem, and generally reduce the value of your real estate.

HISTORY OF ZONING LAWS

The first zoning law in the United States was an ordinance adopted in 1916 by New York City. It regulated both the location and the use of buildings in the city.

The basic constitutionality of *zoning laws* was upheld as a valid exercise of the local government's police power in the landmark case of *Euclid* v. *Ambler Realty Co.,* which was decided by the U.S. Supreme Court in 1926. Zoning and land use restrictions of other kinds may still be held unconstitutional, if they unreasonably interfere with a property owner's rights or if they violate some other constitutional restriction.

The need for zoning regulation was initially a problem of the cities, and through enabling legislation the various states granted their cities the power to pass zoning ordinances. As the population grew, new developments, both residential and commercial, sprang up outside the city limits and, therefore, outside the legal jurisdiction of the city. A need arose for county zoning regulation to prevent the misuse and haphazard development of land. The states again responded, with a majority of them passing legislation giving counties the power to enact zoning laws. Another approach to the problem was for a state to create planning regions which were not limited to the boundaries of any city or county, but could cover parts of some counties and all of others. Each planning region would then be delegated the authority to make zoning regulations for the entire region. A third approach was for a state to grant extraterritorial zoning powers to a city, giving it the power to regulate and control subdivisions contiguous to the city but not actually within its limits. This approach has been adopted by only a few states as it presents possible constitutional problems since the persons in the extraterritorial areas are subjected to regulations made by the city legislative body, yet they are not represented on that body.

Today, nearly every urban area is controlled by some form of zoning law. In addition, in most cities a master plan has been adopted for the purpose of guiding and coordinating the future development of the city. Zoning is only one phase of this master plan. Zoning laws do not regulate the installation of utilities or the location of schools and parks or other public recreational facilities. Nor do these laws regulate the outward appearance of buildings or the materials used in building construction. In the past, these matters have been covered by separate city ordinances. However, with the adoption of a master plan for city planning, many cities have combined all of the old separate ordinances into a comprehensive land development control ordinance.

▪ ZONING DEFINED

Location of structures

Zoning can be defined as the division of a city, a township, or a county or other governmental unit into specific districts for the purpose of regulating the type of building structure that may be built in each district, the placement of the buildings upon the land, and the permitted use or uses of the buildings and the land. For example, certain districts will be zoned R-1, which means that only single-family residential buildings would be allowed in them. Two-family buildings would be allowed in an R-2 district. Multifamily buildings such as apartment houses would be allowed in an R-3 district. A G-B district would allow general businesses, such as office buildings, stores, shopping centers, motels, and hotels. An L-I would allow light industry, such as assembly-type factories and warehouses. H-I zoning would allow heavy industry, such as manufacturing plants, with the potential for noise and air pollution. Typically, these industrial districts are located as far away from residential areas as possible. The use of the identifying terms R-1, R-2, R-3, G-B, L-I, and H-I is not universal. Some areas classify their zoning districts alphabetically, referring, for example, to A or B districts, or use other methods to identify their various zoning districts.

Within each zoning district there may be further regulations regarding the architecture, the location, and the occupancy of buildings. Examples of such regulations are restrictions on the height of buildings and regulations specifying a minimum distance from the front, side, and rear property lines within which no building may be constructed. This type of regulation helps control the density of buildings and protects property owners from encroachment upon their airspace and access to sunlight. For example, a neighbor would not be allowed to construct a 16-foot fence that blocks your view or blocks sunlight from your windows, or to build an addition that brings the neighbor's house right up to your property line and thus reduces the space between the houses.

Building materials

Most cities or counties now have specific building construction codes, primarily for safety and health purposes. These codes regulate construction methods and the use of construction materials, and typically set a minimum standard for the area. Building codes will differ throughout the country because different standards are dictated by regional characteristics, such as temperature, the density of buildings, the possibility of earthquakes, and freezing and thawing problems.

Prohibited businesses

In addition to physical regulations regarding the structure and placement of buildings, many zoning districts may have regulations concerning businesses that may be undesirable to property owners. For example, certain districts may not allow bars or the selling of intoxicating beverages, or may exclude funeral homes or cemeteries.

One of the problems that has plagued city planners is that zoning must be prospective rather than retroactive in effect. If a zoning ordinance zones a certain area exclusively for single-family residential dwellings, the little corner grocery store or the lady who has her beauty shop in her home cannot be forced to cease doing business. Thus, most zoning laws have a grandfather clause which allows a business that was in the area before the passage of the zoning ordinance to operate until it is sold or disposed of in some other manner.

Exceptions

Another exception to zoning regulations is the *variance.* Often there are situations where the strict adherence to a zoning regulation would cause undue hardship to a property owner. In such situations the regulatory agency can grant a variance to allow the land to be used in a manner not in strict conformance with the zoning regulation. Variances are, however, not automatic but are granted only in exceptional situations.

The following case involves the interpretation of a zoning law.

TALCOTT v. CITY OF MIDLAND

387 N.W.2d 845 (Michigan, 1985)

FACTS   Mr. Reer requested a building permit to establish a "Good Times Pizza" parlor in the City of Midland. After the city's building inspector told Reer that a carryout restaurant was not a permissible use in the Business A zoning district where Reer proposed to build, Reer's request for an interpretation of the zoning ordinance was heard by the zoning board of appeals on March 29, 1983. By a three-to-one vote, the board determined that a carryout pizzeria was a permissible use. On April 19, 1983, the city attorney requested the board to reconsider. The board took no action. On April 28, 1983, Reer obtained a building permit and began extensive renovation of the building he proposed to convert into a pizzeria. He also entered into a 10-year lease of the building.

On May 17, 1983, the zoning board of appeals again took no action to reconsider. On June 6, 1983, a group of citizens filed suit against the city asking for a review of the zoning board's interpretation, contending that the notice requirement of the zoning ordinance had not been followed before the board's prior determination. After stipulation for another hearing following proper notice was entered into by the parties, the zoning board reconsidered its prior interpretation on June 28, 1983. By a four-to-zero vote, the board found a carryout pizzeria was not a permissible use.

Subsequently, the trial court affirmed the zoning board's interpretation. On grounds of estoppel, the trial judge enjoined the city from enforcing the ordinance. However, the trial court granted a group of private citizens, plaintiffs Talcott, Burks, and Boots, an injunction enjoining Reer from operating the pizzeria. Mr. Reer appealed.

ISSUE   Is a carry-out pizza business a permissible use in the Business A zoning district in Midland?

DECISION   Yes. Reversed as to appellant Reer. The injunctive order granted to plaintiffs Talcott, et al., and the injunction against appellant City of Midland shall be vacated.

REASONS   The court stated that:

"When construing provisions of a zoning ordinance, the court seeks to discover and give effect to the lawmaker's intent. . . . The interpretation problem at issue arises when one attempts to reconcile the definitions in Article II of the ordinance with Article XIV, which regulates land uses within business districts. Section 14.1(a)(12) of Article XIV of the city zoning ordinance provides that "restaurants, excluding drive-ins" are permitted uses in Business A districts. Section 2.0 of Article II defines in subsecs (50), (51), and (52), respectively, 'restaurant,' 'restaurant, carry-out,' and 'restaurant, drive-in.' . . .

"The city and plaintiffs-appellees contend, and the zoning board of appeals and circuit court held, that the word *restaurants* in Section 14.1(a)(12) should be limited to the definition of Section 2.0(50), '[a]n establishment where food and drink is served to sit-down customers.' Reer contends that the language in Section 14.1(a)(12), 'restaurants, excluding drive-ins' requires an inference that Section 2.0(51) carryout restaurants are a permissible use since carryout restaurants were not expressly excluded.

"When interpreting the language of an ordinance to determine the extent of a restriction upon the use of property, the language must be interpreted, where doubt exists regarding legislative intent, in favor of the property owner. . . . Applying this principle of interpretation to Midland's zoning ordinance, we hold that a carryout pizzeria is a permissible use in a Business A district. . . .

"Finally, the interpretation advanced by Reer is consistent with the statement of intent found in Section 14.0. The primary intent of the Business A district is to serve the surrounding residential neighborhood with goods and services of day-to-day needs.

"Because we find that appellant Reer's proposed use is a permissible use, we need not consider the other issues raised by appellants Reer and City of Midland."

PRIVATE RESTRICTIVE COVENANTS

Zoning laws are usually general in character and often do not cover certain specific areas of land use. For example, zoning laws do not forbid the parking of large boats or campers in a driveway, yet such action may be unsightly and disturbing to the adjoining residents. Thus, a land developer may place certain

Private restrictions in deeds

restrictions in the land deeds to protect the value of the real estate in a new residential subdivision. When the land is being developed and sold, the contract of sale and deed will contain certain restrictions, such as the requirement to submit house plans not only to the public agency for a building permit but *also* to a committee in the subdivision for its approval. Other restrictions might ban outside clotheslines, the construction of outbuildings, the construction of fences without prior approval, and the parking of boats and campers on driveways. Homeowners who violate these restrictions may be taken to court. The court may enjoin further violations and cause the party to tear down the building or fence, move the camper or trailer, or perhaps pay damages to neighbors if damages to them were incurred. Failure to comply with the court order could result in fines and/or imprisonment for civil contempt of court.

Thus, we have public zoning and private restrictive zoning. Before purchasing any parcel of real estate, purchasers should be aware not only of public zoning restrictions but of any private restrictions which may affect their future use of this land. The relationship between these two types of restrictions is at issue in the *Lidke* case.

LIDKE v. MARTIN

500 P.2d 1184 (Colorado, 1972)

FACTS

Residents of Hillcrest Heights sued to enjoin defendants from erecting two apartment buildings on a platted lot owned by defendants and located in Hillcrest Heights Subdivision. Plaintiffs contended that defendants' proposed apartment buildings would violate the subdivision's protective covenants, based upon the following clause of the covenants: "A. All lots in this subdivision shall be Residential One (R-1) only. . . ."

Defendants admitted that this clause standing alone would prohibit the construction of the proposed apartment buildings. They contend, however, that since another clause in the restrictive covenants incorporates an existing zoning classification that allows apartment buildings, the apartment buildings would not violate the protective covenants. The clause relied on by defendants provides as follows:

"L. None of the foregoing shall be construed as conflicting with any terms or regulations of the present or future Jefferson County zoning ordinance which shall form a part of this instrument and shall govern their use of all land herein described." The trial court entered judgment for plaintiffs.

ISSUE

Are restrictive or protective covenants written into a subdivision plat and made a part of the land titles in such subdivision superior to zoning regulations if the zoning regulations are less restrictive?

DECISION

Yes. Judgment affirmed.

REASONS

The court did not agree with defendants that Clause L allowed a resident to make any use of his property permitted under applicable zoning regulations.

"Read as a whole, the protective covenants envision and provide for a single-family residential subdivision. Actually, Clause L provides a rule of construction for the covenants, the effect of which is to incorporate those portions of the applicable zoning ordinance which provide more restrictive standards than the covenants or which prescribe regulations not covered by the covenants. This result is consistent with section 31 of the applicable zoning ordinance which provides:

It is not intended by this Resolution to interfere with or abrogate or annul any easements, covenants or agreements between parties, provided, however, that wherever this Resolution imposes a greater restriction upon the use of buildings or land or upon the location or height of buildings or structures or required larger open spaces about buildings than are imposed or required by other laws, resolutions or by easements, covenants or agreements between parties, the provisions of this Resolution shall govern.

"In this case, the new zone permitted the construction of apartment buildings. However, the covenants are controlling because they require a more restrictive use of the land than is permitted under the applicable zoning requirements."

■ OTHER LAND USE REGULATIONS

As we learned earlier in this chapter, each state has inherent rights to exercise police power to regulate private property for the public interest, convenience, and necessity. The states have delegated this regulatory power to the local governments: namely, counties and cities.

In addition to zoning regulations, *housing codes,* and *building codes,* most cities and counties now have subdivision controls and regulations, since housing density is becoming more and more of a problem. When a group of new homes is to be built in an area, there must be a preliminary investigation to determine whether any health or other environmental hazard will be caused by this new group of dwellings. Today, many subdivisions are being created in areas where there are no public sewage systems or public water systems. In such areas it is important to make sure that the soil will allow proper drainage and filtering of wastes from the septic tanks of the new dwellings. It must also be determined that the water supply will not be contaminated by the septic systems. Another problem that must be considered is the drainage of storm water. For example, if a subdivision with 300 or 400 homes is built in a rural area which has had natural drainage across farmlands for years and no apparent drainage problems, each new home that is built changes the drainage situation by replacing land that ordinarily absorbs water with a concrete slab or basement and concrete or asphalt roadways. These changes reduce the absorptive capacity of the land. However, the storm water has to go somewhere, and since less of it is absorbed by the land, it will run across the land, where it may well cause damage to buildings, the erosion of topsoil, and other problems.

■ ENVIRONMENTAL CONCERNS

The freedom of landowners to use their property as they wished was a cherished right in our country for many years. One day, only a few decades ago, people saw that our streams, rivers, and lakes had become polluted to such an extent that we could not enjoy the waters. The air had become hazy, smelly, and acrid, often burning our eyes. The landscape was cluttered with old car bodies, beer cans, and solid waste of every description. Citizen groups began calling for governmental regulation of the environment.

National statutes

On the national level, Congress passed the *National Environmental Policy Act* and created the Environmental Protection Agency to act as the watchdog

State statutes

against continued pollution of our air, water, and land. To control specific areas of pollution, Congress also passed the *Clean Air Act,* the *Water Pollution Control Act,* the *Noise Control Act,* and the *Solid Waste Disposal Act.*

Many states, counties, and cities have enacted environmental laws. In some instances these laws have set even more stringent pollution standards than the national pollution laws. Many states have also created their own environmental protection agencies to control and regulate pollution within their boundaries. A recent development in the control of solid waste pollution has been the passage of so-called *bottle bills* by several states. These laws require stores to take deposits from the customer on beverage containers and to return the deposit when the cans or bottles are returned empty. These same laws have also banned the use of pull-top cans for beverages. The following case represents an unsuccessful challenge of a bottle bill by American Can Company and other industry members.

AMERICAN CAN CO. v. OREGON LIQUOR CONTROL COMMISSION

517 P.2d 691 (Oregon, 1974)

FACTS

In 1971 the Oregon legislature passed a bottle bill. The bill prohibited the sale of pull-top beverage cans in the state and required deposits on all cans and bottles of beer and carbonated soft drinks. The plaintiffs in this suit included can and bottle manufacturers, bottlers of beer and soft drinks, and the Oregon Soft Drink Association. The plaintiffs alleged that the statute was invalid under the Due Process and Equal Protection clauses of the Fourteenth Amendment and under the Commerce Clause. They said that it also violated similar provisions in the state constitution. The trial court held that the statute was valid.

ISSUE

Does the statute violate the U.S. Constitution, specifically the Commerce Clause, the Due Process Clause, or the Equal Protection Clause?

DECISION

No. Judgment affirmed.

REASONS

Judge Tanzer devoted most of his lengthy opinion to an analysis of the Commerce Clause, feeling that this clause was the plaintiffs' strongest argument.

"The cases consistently hold that the Commerce Clause bars state police action only where:

1. Federal action has preempted regulation of the activity.
2. The state action impedes the free physical flow of commerce from one state to another; or
3. Protectionist state action, even though under the guise of the police power, discriminates against interstate commerce.

"In this case there is no claim of federal preemption, so we are concerned only with the latter two concepts, interstate transportation and economic protectionism. No party cited and we were unable to find any case striking down state action under the Commerce Clause which did not come within one of these two categories. . . .

"The blight of the landscape, the appropriation of lands for solid waste disposal, and the injury to children's feet caused by pull tops discarded in the sands of our ocean shores are concerns not divisible by the same units of measurement as is economic loss to elements of the beverage industry, and we are unable to weigh them, one against the other. . . .

"The bottle bill is unquestionably a legitimate legislative exercise of the police power."

Further environmental problems have been caused by the expansion of our cities into what was previously the domain of the farmer. No cattle or hog feedlot is pleasing to the nostrils, and we must accept the fact that such farming operations are not desirable next door to a residential area. What happens when the city expands to the point where the rights of the parties conflict? The following case illustrates this problem, and the court was forced to make a difficult decision.

SPUR INDUSTRIES, INC. v. DEL E. WEBB DEVELOPMENT CO.

494 P.2d 700 (Arizona, 1972)

FACTS
The retirement community of Youngtown was founded in 1954, about 14 or 15 miles west of the urban area of Phoenix. Farming operations had been conducted in the area since 1911, and Spur's predecessors had started a feedlot about 2½ miles south of Youngtown in 1956. By 1959 there were 25 cattle feeding or dairy operations in the area. In 1959 Del Webb began planning the development of a large retirement community, Sun City. One year later, 450 to 500 homes were completed or under construction. The units sold well, but sales resistance increased as the location of the homes got closer and closer to the feedlots. By 1962 Spur had expanded its operation from 35 to 114 acres. By 1963 Del Webb's housing manager said that it was impossible to sell any home in the southwestern portion of Del Webb's land. By 1967 the properties were within 500 feet of each other at one point, and Spur was feeding between 20,000 and 30,000 head of cattle on its lots, producing over a million pounds of wet manure per day. Del Webb sued to enjoin Spur as a public nuisance, due to the flies and odor. The trial court entered an injunction, and Spur appealed.

ISSUE
Is the feedlot a public nuisance which should be enjoined?

DECISION
Yes. Judgment affirmed, but case remanded for a damages award to Spur.

 REASONS
Vice Chief Justice Cameron thought that the feedlot clearly met the definition of a public nuisance and that it should be enjoined from continuing to operate. But he also thought that there needed to be a balancing of the equities.

"The difference between a private nuisance and a public nuisance is generally one of degree. A private nuisance is one affecting a single individual or a definite small number of persons in the enjoyment of private rights not common to the public, while a public nuisance is one affecting the rights enjoyed by citizens as a part of the public. To constitute a public nuisance, the nuisance must affect a considerable number of people or an entire community or neighborhood. . . .

"It is clear that as to the citizens of Sun City, the operation of Spur's feedlot was both a public and a private nuisance. . . .

"In addition to protecting the public interest, however, courts of equity are concerned with protecting the operator of a lawful, albeit obnoxious, business from the result of a knowing and willful encroachment by others near his business. . . .

"It does not equitably or legally follow . . . that Webb, being entitled to the injunction, is then free of any liability to Spur if Webb has in fact been the cause of the damage Spur has sustained. It does not seem harsh to require a developer, who has taken advantage of the lesser land values in a rural area as well as the availability of large tracts of land on which to build and develop a new town or city in the area, to indemnify those who are forced to leave as a result."

The previous case illustrates the need for community planning and proper zoning to prevent such situations from occurring.

Thus, we no longer have the cherished right to use our land, water, and airspace in any way we choose; there are too many of us, and we live too close together for that. You can't burn trash in an outside incinerator any more in most large cities. The burning of leaves may also be banned. You can't install a septic system for your home unless it is approved by a local agency. You can't use your backyard to store your collection of junk cars.

Today, before you can construct a building on your land, or add to an existing one, or conduct any business, or manufacture any product, you must first check all applicable pollution regulations—national, state, and local. You must also secure a building permit before you can begin construction.

▪ EMINENT DOMAIN

The Fifth Amendment in the Bill of Rights of the U.S. Constitution provides that the national government shall not take private property without the payment of just compensation. The Fourteenth Amendment extended this provision to the various states. The states also have similar provisions in their constitutions, allowing them to exercise the power of eminent domain if just compensation is paid to the property owner.

Most simply stated, the power of *eminent domain* is the power of government to take real estate from a private owner for the use of the public. This very basic governmental power is necessary for the government to function properly and efficiently. For example, if the government is building a highway across the state, the highway must be laid out in as straight a line as possible, considering the topography of the land. It would not be in the best interest of the public if the highway had to jog around various pieces of property whose owners had decided not to sell to the government. The power of eminent domain is also used to acquire land for new school buildings, public parks, public housing projects, and other public buildings and projects.

The government simply must have the right to take over private property when doing so serves the best interest of the public. The owner of such property does, however, have a right to just compensation. The two key problems are: (1) that the land may be taken only for a public purpose, and (2) that the owner must receive just compensation. What constitutes a public purpose is often a question that must be resolved in the courts. What constitutes just compensation is also not an easy question to resolve in many cases, and thus a lawsuit may be filed and a jury called upon to decide the issue. The *Midkiff* [discussion] case is an important recent example of government's power of eminent domain.

■ **SIGNIFICANCE OF THIS CHAPTER**

In the early 1960s we saw a movement in the United States to save the environment, to clean the air and water, to control solid waste dumping, and to stop other forms of pollution. We finally realized the results of uncontrolled and unregulated land use, which had occurred over a period of many years, and which left many cities with unnecessary traffic congestion problems, fire and safety hazards, and lowered property values. Most cities, both large and small, now have a system of land use regulation as well as local regulation of environmental problems.

This chapter gives an overview of the law concerning these areas. All citizens must realize the importance of this type of regulation and the continued need for regulation in the areas of land use and environment.

DISCUSSION CASE

HAWAII HOUSING AUTHORITY v. MIDKIFF
467 U.S. 229 (1984)

FACTS: The Hawaiian Islands were originally settled by Polynesian immigrants from the eastern Pacific. These settlers developed an economy around a feudal land tenure system in which one island high chief, the *ali'i nui,* controlled the land and assigned it for development to certain subchiefs. The subchiefs would then reassign the land to other lower ranking chiefs, who would administer the land and govern the farmers and other tenants working it. All land was held at the will of the *ali'i nui* and eventually had to be returned to his trust. There was no private ownership of land.

Beginning in the early 1800s, Hawaiian leaders and American settlers repeatedly attempted to divide the lands of the kingdom among the crown, the chiefs, and the common people. These efforts proved largely unsuccessful, however, and the land remained in the hands of a few. In the mid-1960s, after extensive hearings, the Hawaii Legislature discovered that, while the state and national governments owned almost 49 percent of the state's land, another 47 percent was in the hands of only 72 private landowners. The legislature further found that 18 landowners, with tracts of 21,000 acres or more, owned more than 40 percent of this land and that, on Oahu,

the most urbanized of the islands, 22 landowners owned 72.5 percent of the fee simple titles. The legislature concluded that concentrated land ownership was responsible for skewing the state's residential fee simple market, inflating land prices, and injuring the public tranquility and welfare.

To redress these problems, the legislature decided to compel the large landowners to break up their estates. The legislature considered requiring large landowners to sell lands which they were leasing to homeowners. However, the landowners strongly resisted this scheme, pointing out the significant U.S. tax liabilities they would incur. Indeed, the landowners claimed that the U.S. tax laws were the primary reason they previously had chosen to lease, and not sell, their lands. Therefore, to accommodate the needs of both lessors and lessees, the Hawaii Legislature enacted the Land Reform Act of 1967 (act) which created a mechanism for condemning residential tracts and for transferring ownership of the condemned fees simple to existing lessees. By condemning the land in question, the Hawaii Legislature intended to make the land sale involuntary, thereby making the U.S. tax consequences less severe while still facilitating the redistribution of fees simple.

Under the act's condemnation scheme, tenants living on single-family residential lots within developmental tracts at least five acres in size are entitled to ask the Hawaii Housing Authority (HHA) to condemn the property on which they live. When 25 eligible tenants, or tenants on half the lots in the tract, whichever is less, file appropriate applications, the act authorizes HHA to hold a public hearing to determine whether acquisition by the state of all or part of the tract will "effectuate the public purposes" of the act. If HHA finds that these public purposes will be served, it is authorized to designate some or all of the lots in the tract for acquisition. It then acquires, at prices set either by condemnation trial or by negotiation between lessors and lessees, the former fee owners' full "right, title, and interest" in the land.

After compensation has been set, HHA may sell the land titles to tenants who have applied for fee simple ownership. HHA is authorized to lend these tenants up to 90 percent of the purchase price, and it may condition final transfer on a right of first refusal for the first 10 years following sale. If HHA does not sell the lot to the tenant residing there, it may lease the lot or sell it to someone else, provided the public notice has been given. However, HHA may not sell to any one purchaser, or lease to any one tenant, more than one lot, and it may not operate for profit. In practice, funds to satisfy the condemnation awards have been supplied entirely by lessees. While the act authorizes HHA to issue bonds and appropriate funds for acquisition, no bonds have issued and HHA has not supplied any funds for condemned lots.

In April 1977, HHA held a public hearing concerning the proposed acquisition of some of appellees' lands. HHA made the statutorily required finding that acquisition of appellees' lands would effectuate the public purposes of the act. Then, in October 1978, it directed appellees to negotiate with certain lessees concerning the sale of the designated properties. Those negotiations failed, and HHA subsequently ordered appellees to submit to compulsory arbitration.

Rather than comply with the compulsory arbitration order, appellees filed suit, in February 1979, in United States District Court, asking that the act be declared unconstitutional and that its enforcement be enjoined. The District Court temporarily restrained the state from proceeding against appellees' estates. Three months later, while declaring the compulsory arbitration and compensation formulae provisions of the act unconstitutional, the District Court refused preliminarily to enjoin appellants from conducting the statutory designation and condemnation proceedings. Finally, in December 1979, it granted partial summary judgment to appellants, holding the re-

maining portion of the act constitutional under the Public Use Clause. The District Court found that the act's goals were within the bounds of the state's police powers and that the means the legislature had chosen to serve the goals were not arbitrary, capricious, or selected in bad faith.

The Court of Appeals for the Ninth Circuit reversed. The court determined that the public purposes offered by the Hawaii Legislature were not deserving of judicial deference. The court concluded that the act was simply "a naked attempt on the part of the state of Hawaii to take the private property of A and transfer it to B solely for B's private use and benefit."

■

Justice O'Connor:

The Fifth Amendment of the United States Constitution provides, in pertinent part, that "private property [shall not] be taken for public use, without just compensation." These cases present the question whether the Public Use Clause of that Amendment, made applicable to the states through the Fourteenth Amendment, prohibits the State of Hawaii from taking, with just compensation, title in real property from lessors and transferring it to lessees in order to reduce the concentration of ownership of fees simple in the state. We conclude that it does not. . . .

The majority of the Court of Appeals . . . determined that the act violates the "public use" requirements of the Fifth and Fourteenth Amendments. On this argument, however, we find ourselves in agreement with the dissenting judge in the Court of Appeals.

The starting point for our analysis of the act's constitutionality is the court's decision in *Berman* v. *Parker,* 348 U.S. 26. . . . In *Berman,* the court held constitutional the District of Columbia Redevelopment Act of 1945. The act provided both for the comprehensive use of the eminent domain power to redevelop slum areas and for the possible sale or lease of the condemned lands to private interests. In discussing whether the takings authorized by that act were for "public use," . . . the court stated:

> We deal, in other words, with what traditionally has been known as the police power. An attempt to define its reach or trace its outer limits is fruitless, for each case must turn on its own facts. The definition is essentially the product of legislative determinations addressed to the purposes of government, purposes neither abstractly nor historically capable of complete definition. Subject to specific constitutional limitations, when the legislation has spoken, the public interest has been declared in terms well-nigh conclusive. In such cases the legislature, not the judiciary, is the main guardian of the public needs to be served by social legislation, whether

it be Congress legislating concerning the District of Columbia . . . or the States legislating concerning local affairs. . . . This principle admits of no exception merely because the power of eminent domain is involved. . . .

The "public use" requirement is thus coterminous with the scope of a sovereign's police powers.

There is, of course, a role for courts to play in reviewing a legislature's judgment of what constitutes a public use, even when the eminent domain power is equated with the police power. But the court in *Berman* made it clear that it is an "extremely narrow" one. . . . In short, the court has made clear that it will not substitute its judgment for a legislature's judgment as to what constitutes a public use "unless the use be palpably without reasonable foundation." . . .

To be sure, the court's cases have repeatedly stated that "one person's property may not be taken for the benefit of another private person without a justifying public purpose, even though compensation be paid." . . . But where the exercise of the eminent domain power is rationally related to a conceivable public purpose, the court has never held a compensated taking to be proscribed by the Public Use Clause. . . .

On this basis, we have no trouble concluding that the Hawaii Act is constitutional. The people of Hawaii have attempted, much as the settlers of the original 13 colonies did, to reduce the perceived social and economic evils of a land oligopoly traceable to their monarchs. The land oligopoly has, according to the Hawaii Legislature, created artificial deterrents to the normal functioning of the state's residential land market and forced thousands of individual homeowners to lease, rather than buy, the land underneath their homes. Regulating oligopoly and the evils associated with it is a classic exercise of a state's police powers. . . . We cannot disapprove of Hawaii's exercise of this power. . . .

The mere fact that property taken outright by eminent domain is transferred in the first instance to private beneficiaries does not condemn that taking as having only a private purpose. The court long ago rejected any literal requirement that condemned property be put into use for the general public. "It is not essential that the entire community, nor even any considerable portion, . . . directly enjoy or participate in any improvement in order [for it] to constitute a public use." . . . "[W]hat in its immediate aspect [is] only a private transaction may . . . be raised by its class or character to a public affair." . . . As the unique way titles were held in Hawaii skewed the land market, exercise of the power of eminent domain was justified. The act advances its purposes without the state taking actual possession of the land. In such cases, government does not itself have to use property to legitimate the taking; it is only the taking's purpose, and not its mechanics, that must pass scrutiny under the Public Use Clause.

Similarly, the fact that a state legislature, and not the Congress, made the public use determination does not mean that judicial deference is less appropriate. Judicial deference is required because, in our system of government, legislatures are better able to assess what public purposes should be advanced by an exercise of the taking power. State legislatures are as capable as Congress of making such determinations within their respective spheres of authority. . . . Thus, if a legislature, state or federal, determines there are substantial reasons for an exercise of the taking power, courts must defer to its determination that the taking will serve a public use.

The State of Hawaii has never denied that the Constitution forbids even a compensated taking of property when executed for no reason other than to confer a private benefit on a particular private party. A purely private taking could not withstand the scrutiny of the public use requirement; it would serve no legitimate purpose of government and would thus be void. But no purely private taking is involved in this case. The Hawaii Legislature enacted its Land Reform Act not to benefit a particular class of identifiable individuals but to attack certain perceived evils of concentrated property ownership in Hawaii—a legitimate public purpose. Use of the condemnation power to achieve this purpose is not irrational. Since we assume for purposes of this appeal that the weighty demand of just compensation has been met, the requirements of the Fifth and Fourteenth Amendments have been satisfied. Accordingly, we reverse the judgment of the Court of Appeals, and remand these cases for further proceedings in conformity with this opinion.

■ IMPORTANT TERMS AND CONCEPTS

zoning laws	National Environmental Policy Act	Solid Waste Disposal Act	housing codes
private restrictive convenants	Water Pollution Control Act	eminent domain	Clean Air Act
building codes		variances	Noise Control Act
			bottle bills

■ QUESTIONS AND PROBLEMS FOR DISCUSSION

1. What happens if a zoning law is passed stating only single-family dwellings and no businesses are allowed in your area, and in fact a family grocery store operates in one of the houses in the neighborhood? Must the business immediately close up? If not, why not? Explain.

2. Describe a situation where a zoning variance would be requested.

3. Who is affected by private restrictive covenants? Why are these restrictive convenants often used in real property transactions?

4. What are the so-called bottle bills? How does a typical bottle bill operate?

5. The Township of Mount Laurel, New Jersey, is a township covering approximately 22 square miles of land. The present township zoning ordinance provides for four residential zones designated R-1, R-1D, R-2, and R-3. However, attached townhouses, apartments (except on farms for agricultural workers), and mobile homes are not allowed in any of the zones. The NAACP brought suit against the township stating their system of land use regulation unlawfully excludes low- and moderate-income families from residing in the area. The trial court of Burlington County, New Jersey, ruled in favor of NAACP and declared the ordinance invalid. The case was then appealed to the New Jersey Appellate Court. What decision do you think the appellate court made? Why?

6. Bobby and Tessie Swinghammer owned a lot in the Scenic Vista Recreation Area. They bought the lot for camping on weekends and planned to leave their travel trailer on the lot during the week as well as on weekends. All property in the area was subject to a restrictive convenant which permitted the lot owner to use the lot for camping for a maximum of five years after purchase before building a permanent structure, so long as the owner did not leave camping equipment on the lot when it was not in use. After the Swinghammers had left their travel trailer on the lot for several weeks, even when they weren't there

to use it, and had indicated that they intended to continue to do so, the SVRA Property Owners' Association brought suit for an injunction to enforce the restrictive covenant. The Swinghammers argue that (1) their trailer is not "camping equipment" under the meaning of the covenant; (2) their trailer is "in use," even though only on weekends; and (3) the agent who sold them their lot said that they could use it in this way. Are any of these arguments valid? Explain.

7. Zane Fonder, president of the Nonukes Alliance, filed a lawsuit challenging certain actions of the U.S. Nuclear Regulatory Commission. The NRC had held general public hearings on the problem of nuclear waste disposal, after which it had adopted an administrative rule that approved the practice of storing such wastes on-site at nuclear power plants, with appropriate safeguards. It subsequently issued operating permits to two nuclear power plants which proposed to use on-site storage of wastes. Now, however, it was again considering the problem of how best to handle nuclear wastes. Zane says that the two operating permits were improperly issued because (1) a generic rule-making hearing on this subject was inappropriate and (2) no licenses should have been issued until the new rules were adopted. How should the court respond to this lawsuit? Discuss.

8. Sandy Snidely, doing business as the Misfit Cleaners, had his business property condemned by the State Highway Commission to make way for a new road. Sandy says he was told that he would be given a relocation payment but would not be compensated for any equipment left in the building. Relying on this advice, he removed his dry cleaning equipment. Because of the age and nature of the equipment and because of changes in the city's laws and building codes, Sandy says that he was prohibited from relocating his business in the city and that the equipment now has only scrap value. Sandy did accept a relocation payment, but now he says that he is also entitled to the difference in value of the equipment resulting from the condemnation of his business location. The state says that he can't have both. Who's right, and why?

37

Trusts, Estate Planning, and Administration of Decedents' Estates

CHAPTER OBJECTIVES

THIS CHAPTER WILL:

- Outline the objectives of estate planning.
- Summarize the requirements for a valid will.
- Discuss the establishment and uses of trusts.
- Review the process of administering decedents' estates.

In the preceding chapters we were concerned with personal and real property relationships during the lifetime of the property owners. In this chapter we are concerned with the law and the procedures governing the planning for and the eventual disposition of both real and personal property when the owner of that property dies. There is no national law that governs the descent and distribution of the property of a deceased person. Applicable statutes in this area are state laws, and they vary from state to state. The U.S. estate tax laws do have a considerable impact on estate planning. However, with the use of trusts, we can often reduce the impact of the U.S. estate tax.

■ DEFINITION OF ESTATE PLANNING

New goals when children are grown and educated

The word *estate* means the interest an individual has in an item of property. *Estate planning* is the process of planning for the future distribution of a person's property, both prior to and after that person's death. Estate planning is not just making a last will and testament, putting it in a safe-deposit box, and leaving it there until the testator dies. An estate plan should be made by an individual early in life and should be changed periodically as the goals of the plan change. For example, once the children are grown and educated, a new plan with new goals usually needs to be formulated. Also, as a person's accumulation of assets increases, changes need to be considered. Thus, estate planning should not be a one-shot proposition but a continuing plan thoughout the property owner's adult life.

■ GOALS OF ESTATE PLANNING

Provisions for care of spouse and children

Trust to conserve assets

The primary goal of any estate plan is to ensure that the deceased person's property will be distributed according to his or her wishes.

A second goal of an estate plan is to provide for the care and support of minor children and the surviving spouse. Especially where the deceased person's estate is quite large, there is the fear that if a child were to receive inheritance, the child might soon squander it. Thus, wills often set up a trust whereby a trustee manages the child's inheritance and pays out only specific amounts until the child reaches a certain age or accomplishes a specified act, such as completing college or getting married.

If the spouse inherits a large sum, there is always the danger that the spouse might remarry and that the new wife or husband would benefit from the inheritance to the detriment of the children who were to later inherit from the spouse. One method of handling this problem is to create a trust in the last will and testament whereby the property is deeded to a trustee and the trustee is instructed to pay the surviving spouse the income from the property being managed by the trust, with the understanding that in case of need the capital funds could be used for the care and support of the spouse and that upon the spouse's death the remainder of the assets in the trust would be distributed to the children. Thus, the spouse would be cared for and supported yet the assets of the estate would not be squandered. Another method is to give the surviving spouse a life estate in the real property, which means that the surviving spouse could live on or rent out the real property but could not sell a complete interest in it.

Minimize taxes

A third goal of an estate plan is to minimize the impact of taxes and estate settlement costs. The individual planning his or her estate should be aware of the national and state taxes which may be assessed upon the estate or the heirs at the time of his or her death. Taxes must be paid prior to the distribution of assets to the heirs. The tax liability can be reduced by distributing property as gifts before the owner dies, thus reducing the value of the assets owned at death. The current tax law allows individuals to make annual tax-free gifts to donees of up to $10,000 per year per donee (up to $20,000 per year if the spouse joins in making the gift). Thus, over a period of years, a considerable amount of cash or other assets may be distributed to children, grandchildren, charities, and other beneficiaries, without any taxes having to be paid.

Life insurance to cover expenses of estate

A fourth goal of an estate plan is to prevent the forced sale of assets from the estate to pay taxes and estate settlement costs. This goal is particularly important when the major asset in the estate is a family business or farm, or residential or commercial real estate. Too often in such cases, the liquid assets (cash, stocks, and the like) are insufficient to meet the necessary costs and taxes. When that happens, major assets or portions of them must be sold, quite often at less than their market value, since the sale must be made quickly and for cash. A good estate plan would provide for life insurance in a sum sufficient to meet all of the immediate cash needs of the estate and the survivors, and thus obviate the need for any forced sale of major assets.

■ NATURE OF A TRUST

Trust can be created for any legal purpose

A *trust* is any arrangement whereby the owner of property transfers its ownership to a natural or corporate person, called the *trustee,* who is instructed to hold the property for the benefit of a person or persons who are designated as **beneficiaries.** A trust can be created for any purpose that is legal and not against public policy. The owner of the property interest that is being transferred must instruct the trustee as to how that interest is to be administered for the beneficiaries. For example, an owner of an interest in property may transfer that interest to the trustee for a person's benefit and may instruct the trustee to distribute only the earnings on the property and not to distribute the principal, or corpus, of the trust until a later date. It is important that the trustee have

■ EXHIBIT 37–1
Flowchart of a Trust

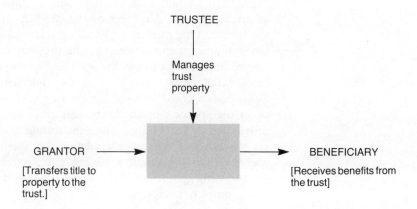

specific instructions as to how the property is to be administered for the beneficiaries.

▪ TYPES OF TRUSTS

Trusts are divided into two basic categories. A *living trust,* also called an *inter vivos trust,* is a trust that takes effect and is administered during the lifetime of the transferor of the property. A *testamentary trust* is created prior to the death of the person who sets it up but does not take effect until that person's death. These voluntary arrangements should be distinguished from a *constructive trust* which is a remedy for the fraudulent acquisition of property, imposed by a court of equity in favor of the real or intended owner. Equity says that the defrauder holds the property "in trust" for the rightful owner.

▪ CREATION OF TRUSTS

The giver is called the settlor

A trust is not necessarily a contract, since no consideration is required from the beneficiaries. It is in effect a gift from the giver, also called the *settlor,* to the beneficiary through a middle person; namely, the trustee. To create an express trust, there must be a written document, which is normally called a *trust agreement* or a *deed of trust.* While it is not necessary for any specific language to be used, certain requirements must be met. If the trust involves an interest in land, then the Statute of Frauds requires that the details of the transfer of that interest be set out in writing.

Rule against perpetuities must be complied with

There is also a limit to how long a trust may exist before the interest vests in beneficiaries. The rule to be complied with here is called the *rule against perpetuities.* This rule prohibits a person from creating a trust that remains in existence forever. A general statement of the rule is that an interest in property, if conveyed for the benefit of a beneficiary, must be turned over or vested in the beneficiary no more than 21 years plus the period of gestation of a new life after the expiration of the life or lives of some person or persons who were in being when the trust was created. There are exceptions to this rule if the purpose of the trust is charitable. Most states have a statutory maximum time during which a trust may remain operative. Here the specific state laws would govern.

▪ REVOCABILITY AND MODIFICATION OF TRUSTS

Inter vivos trust

Revocable trust

An *inter vivos* trust may be declared either revocable or irrevocable. If a person sets up an *irrevocable trust* for the benefit of beneficiaries, then that person, the settlor, may not revoke or change the trust at a later date. Such a trust may be modified, with the consent of all the beneficiaries, provided such modification would not frustrate its original intent. However, this would only be possible in exceptional circumstances, as the courts will not allow a change in a trust if this would change the trust's original intended purpose. If the settlor sets up a *revocable trust,* this means that this person transfers title to certain property to a trustee for the benefit of specific beneficiaries, but may at any time change his or her mind and take back the corpus of the trust from the trustee.

Many wealthy persons deed property over to a trustee so that the trustee can manage it for them. Thus, these persons are both settlor and beneficiary. Having a professional manage their property relieves them of the responsibilities of management, and gives them the income, less a managerial service charge. If such a trust is revocable, the settlor can terminate the trust at any time.

Testamentary trust effective at death

Testamentary trusts do not become effective until the death of the settlor, and they are not revocable after the settlor's death. But anytime before the settlor's death, such a trust may be revoked simply by changing the last will and testament that contains or refers to it.

■ TRUSTEE—RIGHTS AND OBLIGATIONS

Who can be a trustee

May not commingle funds

Fiduciary duties of trustee

A trustee can be an individual or an institution, such as a bank, a trust company, or a similar financial institution. The trustee is governed by a given state's laws concerning the handling of trust funds. A trustee generally has the right to make decisions concerning the investment of the trust corpus in accordance with the settlor's directions, provided those directions are not contrary to the law of the particular jurisdiction. For example, a trustee must generally invest trust funds more conservatively than he or she would invest personal funds.

A trustee may not commingle the property of a trust with property that the trustee owns individually or with property that the trustee is administering as the trustee of another trust. Generally speaking, the trustee owes a duty of loyalty to the beneficiaries; that is, the trustee's job is to conserve the corpus for the beneficiaries' benefit and yet to secure the best income and growth possible. The trustee will be required to use the skill, judgment, and care reasonably expected of a person in that capacity. Banks, trust companies, and other corporate trustees will of course be required to use a high degree of skill, care, and judgment in the management of trusts, since that is their profession. An individual who is acting as a trustee would not be required to use the same high degree of skill, care, and judgment but would be required to use reasonable care and judgment in the handling of the trust funds. Most trusts involving large sums of money or property will be administered by corporate trustees who have professional investment knowledge and expertise. The *Schug* case discusses these fiduciary duties of trustees.

SCHUG v. MICHAEL

245 N.W.2d 587 (Minnesota, 1976)

FACTS

James Michael, an attorney, was an original incorporator, the chairman of the board, and the owner of 50,000 shares (50 percent) of Mustang Investment Corporation. Kenneth Schug was a shareholder. Michael assigned the beneficial interest in 30,000 of his shares to various persons, including Schug. Schug purchased 7,000 of these shares for $0.50 per share through a "Trust Agreement" drafted by Michael. Schug as beneficiary was to receive the income for Michael's lifetime and then to receive the stock absolutely. Charles Quigley joined Mustang's board in 1969 and almost immediately had policy differences with Michael. Quigley made repeated offers to buy out Michael, but Michael never informed Schug of these offers. On November 2, 1970, Michael bought 6,000 shares back from Schug and then sold them and 24,000 more to Quigley for $3.50 per share. Morris, a lawyer representing Michael, then asked Schug to transfer the Trust Agreement to him, so that he could get the stock released by the commissioner of securities. Schug indorsed the agreement in blank and gave it to Morris. Morris later died, and the agreement could not be located. Michael said that he owned the other 1,000 shares as well. Schug also died. Schug's estate sued for damages of $15,000 on the repurchase of 6,000 shares and of $14,500 on the other 1,000 shares. The trial court gave damages. Michael appeals.

ISSUE   Was a trust created, and was defendant Michael guilty of a breach of his fiduciary duties?

DECISION   Yes. Yes. Judgment of the trial court is affirmed.

REASONS   Justice Kelly speaking for the court said:

"While use of the words 'trust agreement,' 'trustee,' and 'beneficiary' in the instrument executed by the parties is not dispositive of the question of a trust relationship . . . , it is persuasive evidence that defendant, an attorney who drafted the instrument himself, intended a trust relationship. . . .

"Defendant undertook to sell Schug a portion of his own insider stock and to retain control of that stock under the trust agreement. Defendant conceded that this was in direct violation of his escrow agreement that he not sell the stock and even argued before the trial court that this was criminal violation of Minnesota securities law which voided the trust agreement. Nevertheless, after having illegally sold a beneficial interest to Schug and other parties, defendant continued to seek for himself the best of all possible worlds. He apparently represented to others, including Quigley, that he owned a full 50,000 shares, and he even stated falsely in an affidavit in his own shareholder's action that he owned 50,000 shares. He then proceeded to engage in further trafficking of the escrowed shares by buying them back from Schug and other beneficiaries of similar trusts to aid in his control dispute with Quigley. The result was a substantial profit for him and a somewhat lesser return for his ill-used beneficiaries.

"Defendant's course of conduct reveals violations of several important duties to his beneficiary. First, he breached his duty of loyalty by purchasing (and trafficking in) trust property. . . . [H]e failed to disclose his offers from and disputes with Quigley, which were obviously material facts to Schug.

"Second, defendant also breached duties to take and keep control of trust property, to preserve trust property, and to keep trust property separate from his own."

■ USE OF TRUSTS IN ESTATE PLANNING

Conserve assets of estate

A primary use of trusts is to conserve estates. If the *testator*—the person making the will—has minor children, the testator may want to set up a testamentary trust in the will. This trust will become effective at the testator's death. At that time, certain specified property will be transferred to a person or organization named as the trustee. The trustee will then hold and manage the trust and will normally distribute its earnings to the beneficiaries. In some instances, if the amount involved is not sufficient to care for the beneficiaries' needs, the trustee is allowed to invade the trust principal and to pay out portions of that principal as necessary until the beneficiaries reach a specific age, at which time the trust will be dissolved and the remainder of the principal will be divided among the beneficiaries. A testator can also set up a testamentary trust fund for the benefit of a spouse. This is often done where the spouse is too ill or too old to be personally responsible. In effect, the testamentary trust allows the testator to control the distribution of his or her estate long after death since the testator's instructions to the trustee will dictate the handling and the distribution of the estate throughout the duration of the trust.

Save inheritance taxes

A second use of trusts is to save estate and inheritance taxes. Generation-skipping trusts serve this purpose. For example, if grandfather died and left his estate to grandmother, she would pay estate and inheritance taxes. Then, when grandmother died, her sons and daughters would inherit and would pay another round of estate and inheritance taxes. When they died, the grandchildren would inherit and would pay taxes again. Thus, a generation-skipping trust, whereby grandfather gives his property in trust for the grandchildren, would skip two levels of taxation. Grandfather pays a gift tax when he gives the property, and the grandchildren thus gain more net property than they would if the property went through the normal inheritance process and much of the principal were reduced by taxation. Generation-skipping trusts are, however, subject to Internal Revenue Service regulations, and recent regulations have limited the amount that can skip taxation.

Reduce estate settlement costs

A third use of trusts is to reduce estate settlement costs at death. Estate settlement costs are based on the value of the testator's estate at the time of death and on the legal procedures necessary to probate the estate. If a large portion of the estate has already been deeded to trusts, then the estate of the testator is relatively small and the probate process is much simpler and thus much cheaper.

■ ADMINISTRA-TION OF DECE-DENTS' ESTATES

Since our population is very mobile today and people often own property in several states, there is a need for uniformity in the descent and distribution laws of the various states. The National Conference of Commissioners on Uniform State Laws has drafted a Uniform Probate Code which it is hoped will be adopted by all the states. The first draft of the code was approved and submitted to the various state legislatures in 1969, and the code was amended in 1975. Thus far, only a few states have adopted the ***Uniform Probate Code.***

Uniform Probate Code

Testate distribution

Two procedures for the distribution of property are common to all the states. First, there is distribution by last will and testament. This procedure is called ***testate distribution.*** If a person makes a will, the property, after the payment of all valid debts, will be distributed according to the wishes of the deceased as set out in the will, unless the will is found legally invalid. If the deceased person did not make a will, then the real and personal property of the deceased person will be distributed to the legal heirs in accordance with specific statutory laws of descent and distribution. This procedure is called ***intestate distribution.*** Real property will be distributed in accordance with the statutes of the state where it is located; personal property will be distributed in accordance with the statutes of the state where the decedent resided. Thus, if a person with a legal residence in Minnesota and real estate in Wisconsin and Illinois dies in Florida, several different state laws would be involved in the distribution of the estate. If the person died without leaving a will or heirs, the property would be acquired by the state, through a process called *escheat.*

Intestate distribution

Last will and testament

The *last will and testament* is simply a written statement of a person's desires as to the distribution of any property owned at death. The person who makes a will is called a *testator* if a man and a *testatrix* if a woman.

In the following case, the testatrix in her last will and testament directed the executor to tear down the house on her real estate and then sell the land. The neighbors objected to the house being torn down as it would adversely affect their property interests and they filed suit asking for an injunction. Normally the court will honor the desires of a testator or testatrix as to the disposition of property; however to do so in this case would be against public policy, as it would clearly damage the property values of the neighbors.

EYERMAN v. MERCANTILE TRUST CO., N.A.

524 S.W.2d 210 (Missouri, 1975)

FACTS   Plaintiffs appeal from denial of their petition seeking injunction to prevent demolition of a house at #4 Kingsbury Place in the City of St. Louis. The action is brought by individual neighboring property owners and certain trustees for the Kingsbury Place Subdivision.

Louise Woodruff Johnston, owner of the property in question, died January 14, 1973, and by her will directed the executor "to cause our home at 4 Kingsbury Place . . . to be razed and to sell the land upon which it is located . . . and to transfer the proceeds of the sale . . . to the residue of my estate." Plaintiffs assert that razing the home will adversely affect their property rights, violate the terms of the subdivision trust indenture for Kingsbury Place, produce an actionable private nuisance, and be contrary to public policy.

The area involved is a "private place" established in 1902 by trust indenture which provides that Kingsbury Place and Kingsbury Terrace will be so maintained, improved, protected, and managed as to be desirable for private residences. The trustees are empowered to protect and preserve "Kingsbury Place" from encroachment, trespass, nuisance or injury, and it is "the intention of these presents, forming a general scheme of improving and maintaining said property as desirable residence property of the highest class." The covenants run with the land and the indenture empowers lot owners or the trustees to bring suit to enforce them.

Except for one vacant lot, the subdivision is occupied by handsome, spacious two- and three-story homes, and all must be used exclusively as private residences. The indenture generally regulates location, costs, and similar features for any structures in the subdivision and limits construction of subsidiary structures except those that may beautify the property, for example, private stables, flower houses, conservatories, play houses, or buildings of similar character.

On trial the temporary restraining order was dissolved and all issues found against the plaintiffs.

ISSUE   Should a provision in a decedent's last will and testament be enforced if it is against public policy and in violation of restrictive covenants of the subdivision?

DECISION   No. Judgment of trial court is reversed.

REASONS   **Judge Rendlen, speaking for the court, stated:**
"Plaintiffs clearly have standing to raise the issues of nuisance abatement and enforcement

of the restrictive covenants in the subdivision indenture. Persons threatened with wrongful interference of property rights may seek injunction against a threatened nuisance . . . and the trust indenture regulating Kingsbury Place empowers the trustee or any property owner to bring suit to enforce the covenants. . . . [T]rustees of an express trust may bring a civil action in their own names in such representative capacity. As to plaintiffs' standing to raise the public policy issue, we must determine whether plaintiffs alleged a legally protectible interest. . . . Though defendants cite no authority on the question of whether private individuals have a legally protectible interest sufficient to give them standing to raise public policy issues, the question has been examined by federal courts in recent years. . . . [T]he Supreme Court held that members of an environmental organization had standing to challenge a railroad surcharge on shipping rates of recyclable waste materials on allegation that the higher rates would discourage the use of recyclable waste materials and promote increased use of new raw materials, thus adversely affecting the environment. Plaintiffs pleaded, more specifically, that the environment surrounding their legal residences would be affected, causing them direct, personal injury. The Supreme Court recognized the test for standing as whether plaintiffs alleged that they had been or will in fact be perceptibly harmed by the challenged action, not merely that they can imagine circumstances in which they might be harmed or that the actions are generally undesirable. . . .

"These considerations are applicable even when plaintiffs raise aesthetic or environmental interests they wish to protect, or when these interests may be common to the entire community, so long as the named plaintiffs are threatened with specific, personal injury. 'Aesthetic and environmental well-being, like economic well-being, are important ingredients of the quality of life in our society, and the fact that particular environmental interests are shared by the many rather than the few does not make them less deserving of legal protection.'. . .

"Whether #4 Kingsbury Place should be razed is an issue of public policy involving individual property rights and the community at large. The plaintiffs have pleaded and proved facts sufficient to show a personal, legally protectible interest.

"Demolition of the dwelling will result in an unwarranted loss to this estate, the plaintiffs and the public. The uncontradicted testimony was that the current value of the house and land is $40,000; yet the estate could expect no more than $5,000 for the empty lot, less the cost of demolition at $4,350 making a grand loss of $39,350 if the unexplained and capricious direction to the executor is effected. Only $650 of the $40,000 asset would remain.

"Kingsbury Place is an area of high architectural significance, representing excellence in urban space utilization. Razing the home will depreciate adjoining property values by an estimated $10,000 and effect corresponding losses for other neighborhood homes. The cost of constructing a house of comparable size and architectural exquisiteness would approach $200,000.

"Although public policy may evade precise, objective definitions, it is evident from the authorities cited that this senseless destruction serving no apparent good purpose is to be held in disfavor. A well-ordered society cannot tolerate the waste and destruction of resources when such acts directly affect important interests of other members of that society. It is clear that property owners in the neighborhood of #4 Kingsbury, the St. Louis community as a whole, and the beneficiaries of the testatrix's estate will be severely injured should the provisions of the will be followed. No benefits are present to balance against this injury, and we hold that to allow the condition in the will would be in violation of the public policy of this state." . . .

■ TYPES OF WILLS

Formal Wills. The formal will is a written document specifically stating the desires of the testator or testatrix as to the disposition of property. The will is signed by the testator or testatrix in the presence of witnesses, who also sign the document. The testator or testatrix has indicated to the witnesses that he or she knows that the document is a last will and testament. Formal wills are recognized as legal in all jurisdictions. However, some states have particular requirements as to the formalities, such as the number of witnesses and whether or not they must also witness each other's signatures.

Dying (oral) wills

Nuncupative Wills. A *nuncupative will* is an oral will. It might also be called a *dying will* since it is an oral will made in a person's dying hours or minutes. Nuncupative wills are valid only for the distribution of personal property, and usually only the personal property the dying person has in his or her immediate possession. The problems in this type of will are to prove that the statements concerning the disposition of property were actually made and that the person who made them was of sound mind. In addition, there must be witnesses other than the persons benefiting from the will. Not all states recognize nuncupative wills. Some states extend the privilege of making nuncupative wills to wartime military personnel in a battle zone. Here again, the law would like to abide by the wishes of the dying person. However, problems of proof, fraud, undue influence, and perjury arise in these situations. Again, only personal property can be distributed by this type of will. Real property will be distributed to the heirs in accordance with the intestate succession laws of the state where the real estate is located if there is no valid formal will.

Holographic Wills. A *holographic will* is a will written out and signed by the testator or testatrix. There are no witnesses to the signature. Not all states recognize holographic wills as being legal wills. The problem with regard to a holographic will is that the person who made it is now deceased and cannot verify the handwriting and the signature. Thus, a court is faced with the possibility of forgery.

■ CAPACITY TO MAKE A WILL

Minor cannot make a will

Testator must be of "sound and disposing mind"

Heirs may contest will

As a rule, a minor cannot make a valid will. To execute a valid will, a person generally must have reached the age of majority, which is now 18 in most states. Some states do, however, permit persons under the age of majority to make valid wills, at least for their personal property.

The testator must be of "sound and disposing mind" at the time the will is executed. This requirement means that the person knows what property is owned and what disposition is being made of it. Many testators may have certain eccentricities, such as the wealthy elderly lady who leaves a small fortune to her cats. If, in fact, she knows what she is doing and wants to do it, the law will respect her wishes. The question as to whether or not the testator was indeed of sound and disposing mind may be the subject of a will contest. The heirs may well contest the will, alleging that the lady was not of sound and disposing mind when she made it. However, the presumption of validity will be in favor of the testatrix, and to invalidate the will the heirs will have the burden of showing incompetency on her part.

■ PROPERTY DISPOSED OF BY WILL

All real estate in which the testator or testatrix has a fee simple title and all personal property owned by the testator or testatrix may be disposed of by will. Real property in which the testator or testatrix has an interest as a tenant by the entirety or as a joint tenant with right of survivorship cannot be distributed by will because in such cases, when one tenant dies, the other tenant automatically inherits the property. Also, a life estate cannot be devised by will because such a legal interest dissolves upon the death of its possessor, and thus there is nothing to give away. In addition, depending upon the state law, dower statutes, widows' allowances, and exemption statutes may limit the right of the husband with regard to the disposition of property.

■ MODIFICATION OF WILL BY CODICIL

Codicil = change in original will

A will typically reflects the testator's or testatrix's desires, marital status, and family status at the time that the will is executed. As the years pass, children grow up, financial situations change, and perhaps the spouse dies, so the will may become obsolete and need modification. A will need not be completely rewritten every time a change in it is desired. It may be modified by adding a *codicil.* This is a separate written document which must be executed in accordance with the applicable state law. The codicil can add to or alter the will.

■ REVOCATION OF A WILL

Will is revocable up to death

Will may be revocable by operation of law

A will is revocable by the testator or testatrix at any time prior to death. The most common reason for revocation is that the testator or testatrix desires to make a new will and the changes are so extensive that it is desirable to revoke and remake the will rather than simply make the changes by codicil. The new will generally contains a clause stating that the testator or testatrix hereby revokes any and all prior wills. Also, a testator or testatrix may simply decide to tear up, burn, or otherwise destroy the will and not make another will. The party may simply want to let the property go through intestate succession rather than by specific bequest.

Some state statutes have provisions that would revoke a will by operation of law under certain circumstances. A common situation of this kind would be one like the following. A man made a will giving his property to his wife and his two sons, both of whom were named in the will. After the execution of the will, the man and his wife were divorced, he married again, his new wife gave birth to a daughter, and the man then died. In this situation these questions would arise: Does the daughter who was born after the making of the will have any rights in her father's estate? What are the rights of the surviving spouse in her husband's estate? Presuming that no alimony was owed to the divorced wife and that she had no legal right to inherit her ex-husband's property, what rights does she have? Does the will really reflect the testator's intent with regard to the distribution of his property? Obviously, the will does not reflect the testator's current family relationships. Thus, depending upon the state, part or all of the will may be revoked as a result of the changes in family relationships. The child born after the execution of the will should receive a share of the deceased parents' estate.

■ INTESTATE SUCCESSION

A person is considered *intestate* when he or she dies without leaving a will. *Succession* means the inheriting or succeeding to the ownership of the deceased person's property. Each state has specific statutes regulating the descent and distribution of the real and personal property of the deceased person where the deceased person did not leave a will or where the deceased person's will has been found to be invalid.

As a general rule, the intestate statutes order distribution of the entire estate to the wife or husband if living and to any children if living, or to children of the children who have predeceased the decedent. The shares are determined by the specific state statute. If the decedent had four children and his or her spouse had died previously, then the estate would be divided equally among the four children. If one child had died but was survived by two children, then those children would inherit their parent's share. This descent could go even further. If a grandchild had children and the grandchild was deceased, then the grandchild's share would go to his or her children.

Intestate statutes are based on blood relationships. In the same example, if one of the four children, a son, had died and was survived by a wife and two children, the wife would get nothing since she was not a blood relative. Only the son's children would inherit. The only exception to this restriction would be legally adopted children. Although not blood relatives, such children would be put in that category because of the legal adoption.

Where the decedent has no surviving spouse and no surviving children, grandchildren, or great-grandchildren, the law looks to the next preferred group of relations. The first in preference are the deceased's mother and father. If neither the mother nor the father of the decedent is living, then the estate is divided equally among his or her brothers and sisters, and if any of the decedent's brothers or sisters are deceased, then their share will go to their children or to the children of their children should the children be deceased.

In the case of an only child whose parents are both deceased and who had no children of his or her own, the intestate law will generally say that the estate will be divided among so-called ***collateral relatives.*** These are people who are not direct descendants of the decedent but are related in some way to the decedent through a common ancestor. This category would include grandparents, aunts, uncles, and cousins. Only in rare cases is this third level of descent and distribution used.

The fourth step in descent and distribution is taken if there are no direct descendants of the deceased person and no collateral relatives. Then the property is distributed to the state where it is located, if real estate, or to the state of the decedent's domicile if personalty. This is called ***escheat to the state.***

Escheat to state when no heirs

It can readily be seen that a person who wishes to have any effect on the distribution of his or her property should make a will. In the absence of a will, no part of a deceased person's estate can be given, for example, to a charity, to a friend, to the old alma mater, or to any other institution or person other than those persons designated by the particular state law which has jurisdiction over the property of the intestate deceased.

Uniform Simultaneous Death Act

With our high-speed motor vehicle and air travel, and with the other dangers which we face today, it is not uncommon for a husband and wife to die in the same accident. In such a situation, if the wife survived the husband for any period of time, however brief, then her estate would inherit from him. However, if she died first, then, of course, her estate would not inherit from the husband. The Commissioners on Uniform Laws, to whom we have referred previously, have formulated a *Uniform Simultaneous Death Act,* which has been adopted by many states. This act provides that where two people such as a husband and wife die in a situation such as an airplane or an automobile crash and it is impossible to determine which of them died first, then each of their estates would be handled and the property in that estate would be distributed as if each of the deceased persons had survived the other deceased person.

The obvious problem which this solved here is that if the husband owned a considerable amount of property and died first, the wife would inherit from him and her estate would have to pay tax on the inheritance, and then if she dies a few hours later, her estate would be distributed again and tax would be levied again. Thus, there would be the possibility of double taxation on both the state and the national level. With the Uniform Simultaneous Death Act, the property of each deceased spouse passes directly to other heirs of that spouse, disregarding the estate of the other deceased spouse. Thus, the property of each spouse is distributed only once and there is no immediate second taxation of the assets.

If a will is prepared, then the testator can provide for the possibility of simultaneous death in the will itself. For example, it is common to provide that property is willed to a spouse if the spouse survives the decedent by 30 days. In the event of simultaneous death or any other occurrence that prevents that from happening, the property does not pass to the spouse but directly to children or other beneficiaries.

■ PROBATING THE ESTATE

Pay all creditors of deceased

Whether the deceased left a will or not, there still has to be a legal procedure and administration to distribute the deceased's assets and to pay the deceased's estate and inheritance taxes and any income taxes that the deceased owed, to pay off the deceased's creditors and to pay any final doctor and hospital bills. Thus, one can see that a lot of details have to be handled when a person dies. Of course, if the deceased's property was of minimal value, the statutes in many states would waive the necessity of formally probating the estate.

Probate Court. Chapter 2 presented a diagram of the typical state court system and an explanation of the various courts. It was noted there that the probate court, also known as the surrogate court, generally handles the administration of decedent's estates and the guardianship of minor children and persons declared incompetent to handle their own affairs. In the smaller areas, the county court judge will act as both a probate judge and a trial court judge.

In the larger jurisdictions a special judge will handle only probate matters. The specific procedures with regard to the probating or administering of estates differ slightly from state to state.

Process of Probating the Deceased's Estate. When a person dies, the first step is for the immediate family to search through the deceased's papers and find out whether the deceased left a will and whether the deceased had insurance policies, savings accounts, a safe-deposit box, certificates of deposit, stocks and bonds, and so on. If the deceased had a safe-deposit box, the bank will not let an heir simply go to the bank and look into it. Before anyone is allowed to take anything out of the safe-deposit box, the county assessor's office or the local assessor, depending on the jurisdiction, will have to be informed of the person's death, and then a representative from the assessor's office will accompany one of the heirs to the bank and the bank will allow the parties to view the contents of the safe-deposit box. A listing and an appraisal of the contents will be made by the tax assessor, and the contents may not be distributed to any relatives or heirs until an estate has been opened if the estate falls within the dollar amount that requires a formal probate proceeding in the given jurisdiction.

If the deceased left a will, then the will should contain the name of the person or the financial institution that the deceased desired to act as the personal representative of the estate. (The Uniform Probate Code uses the term "personal representative" in place of executor, executrix, administrator or administratrix.) This person gathers all the assets, makes the required reports to the taxing authorities and to the court, and administers the estate in accordance with the desires of the deceased.

If the deceased left no will, then one of the heirs must petition the probate court to open an estate and appoint a personal representative to administer the assets and pay the debts of the deceased. Typically the court will appoint the surviving spouse, if that spouse is capable, or an adult child of the deceased, provided that person lives within the jurisdiction of the court. To be a personal representative, a person usually must live within the jurisdiction of the court.

The first step in the administration process is publication of legal notice advising creditors to present their claims against the estate of the deceased. The notice must be published in a newspaper of general circulation in the county where the estate is opened. The length of time that the notice must be published will depend upon the individual state laws. The notice will advise creditors that they have a limited time in which to present their claims. Generally, this will not exceed six months. Different states set different time limits for presentations against an estate.

The next step is to take care of the deceased's spouse during the period of administration, which could be up to six months or a year. Although the spouse may be entitled to inherit all of the decedent's money and property, he or she does not have the right to spend the money or to make any transfer of the property until settlement of the estate is approved by the court. Most states provide for the payment of an allowance during the period of administration. The allowance would have priority over other claims.

The third step is to make an inventory of all the assets the deceased owned prior to death. This, of course, would include all cash on hand, all bank accounts,

Gather assets of deceased

File reports with probate court

Publish notice to creditors

Care for spouse during administration

Inventory of assets

and all stocks and bonds. If real estate is involved, then a professional appraiser would be called in to appraise it, and if personal property is involved, an appraiser should be called in to appraise it. The executor or administrator is required to file a report to the court setting out a complete inventory of the real and personal property and its total value. This report is then used to determine whether national or state taxes will be due on the estate.

Pay debts of the deceased

The next step is to begin paying the debts of the deceased. First, the expenses of the deceased's last illness and his or her funeral and burial expenses must be paid. Next an income tax return must be completed for the period of the calendar year or fiscal year, depending on the tax year used by the deceased, up to the date of death. Then the personal representative must file tax return forms with the U.S. Internal Revenue Service and pay the appropriate *estate* tax. The state **inheritance taxes** are the liability of the individual or institution that was willed a gift by the deceased or the statutory share of an intestate estate where there was no will. The amount of state tax due depends not only on the amount of the gift or statutory share but on the relationship to the deceased of the person receiving it. No tax will be due unless the amount received exceeds the exemption amount, but the exemption amount will be larger for a spouse than for children. Generally, the exemption becomes smaller as the relationship to the deceased becomes more distant.

Pay inheritance taxes

If the deceased person left a will, it is possible to have all of the inheritance taxes paid out of the general funds of the estate which are not specifically given to persons or institutions. The will may simply state that its beneficiaries will not have to pay the inheritance taxes from their shares and that these taxes will be paid out of the general funds of the estate. This is especially helpful if the deceased gave his or her residential property to a son or daughter. If the son or daughter had to pay the inheritance taxes, he or she might have to sell the real estate to get the money to do so. The court in the next case enforces another type of arrangement for paying such taxes.

HAERRY v. HOFFSCHNEIDER

276 N.W.2d 196 (Nebraska, 1979)

FACTS

Elise Hoffschneider, a widow, had two children, Melba Marie Holm and Alfred Hoffschneider. In 1965 she gave Alfred a farm consisting of one-quarter section of land. On November 29, 1966, accompanied by Alfred, she consulted her lawyer and had him prepare three documents: (1) a deed conveying another quarter-section farm to Alfred but reserving a life estate for herself; (2) a will which left another quarter-section farm to Melba if she survived Elise; otherwise, this farm and the balance of Elise's estate would go to Alfred; and (3) an agreement which recited the execution of the deed and the will and said that in consideration thereof Alfred agreed to pay sufficient sums to cover the debts of Elise's estate, if necessary, so that the real estate left to Melba could pass to her. Elise signed all three documents, and Alfred signed the agreement. Elise died in 1975, leaving personal property assets of $2,270.28, debts and taxes due of $31,596.11, and the land devised to Melba. Haerry, as her executor, demanded payment from Alfred and then sued. Alfred appealed the trial court's award against him.

ISSUE | Is the agreement which was signed by Alfred at the same time Elise signed her last will and testament enforceable?

DECISION | Yes. Judgment of the trial court against Alfred is affirmed.

REASONS | **Judge Keens gave the opinion of the court:**

"It should be noted that the agreement simply recites the execution of the deed and the will and contains no independent provisions disposing of any property or rights belonging to Elise Hoffschneider. . . . The time of death is simply a time of performance. . . . A will is a unilateral disposition of property binding only from the death of the maker; a contract is an agreement drawing its binding force from the meeting of the minds of the parties. . . . Since the agreement is bilateral and not testamentary, execution in accordance with section 30–204, R.R.S. 1943, was not required. . . .

"Although the deed, the will, and the agreement were all executed upon the same date and may be read together for the purpose of ascertaining intention, it should be noted that the will refers to the previous conveyance by the deed and the agreement refers to the previous execution of the will. Appellant's argument . . . must fail because the agreement, although contemplated, was not in existence at the time of the execution of the will and for the further reason that such a revocation would be completely inconsistent with the general estate plan of Elise Hoffschneider that the devise to Melba should be subject only to the mortgage to the Federal Land Bank. . . . The testatrix was entitled to plan so that the land she had owned would stay in the family without being subject to possible sale by the executor to meet estate debts. The trial court construed the deed, the will, and the agreement correctly and properly imposed liability upon the appellant."

With regard to U.S. estate taxes, the Tax Reform Act of 1976 set up a unified tax credit system to replace separate schedules for estate tax and gift tax. The current unified tax credit for 1987 and beyond, as set by the *Economic Recovery Act of 1981* is roughly equivalent to a lifetime exemption of $192,800. This unified tax credit of $192,800 is equivalent to the U.S. estate tax that would be due on an estate valued at $600,000 after deductions for debts and expenses of administration of the estate, which includes attorneys' fees, executor's or administrator's fees, court costs and other required expenses of administration. The Economic Recovery Act of 1981 also provided that all property left by one spouse to a surviving spouse is free of U.S. estate taxes. Also, any and all material gifts from one spouse to another during the giver's lifetime, regardless of values, are free of gift tax.

No inheritance tax on property left to spouse

Thus, only estates where a person other than a spouse is the beneficiary, and where the value of the estate is over $600,000 will be subject to U.S. estate taxes. Thus U.S. estate tax is no longer a problem to be resolved in the great majority of decedents' estates.

U.S. estate tax only on estates of over $600,000

The next step in the administration of the estate is to sell real estate and personal property which is not specifically given to any particular person or institution. The cash is used to pay the creditors of the estate, provided they prove the validity of their claims to the satisfaction of the court. The personal representative must then submit a final report to the court, showing all the assets which have been accumulated, including interest earned on bank accounts, life insurance proceeds collected, cash received from the sale of assets, and

Sell property not specifically devised

other monies, as well as all debts which have been paid. A hearing is scheduled, to allow anyone with an interest in the estate to object to any part of the report. After the hearing the court will decide whether to approve or disapprove the final report of the personal representative.

File final return and close estate

Once the final report has been approved, the personal representative will distribute the assets in accordance with either the provisions of the will or the statutory law in the given jurisdiction. The personal representative's services will be paid for with a fee approved by the court or in accordance with a statutory fee schedule. After distribution of the assets and payment of the appropriate fee, the personal representative will again go back to the court for a final order to close the estate. At that time, the personal representative will also ask the court to release any bonds that the court required during the administration of the estate.

■ SIGNIFICANCE OF THIS CHAPTER

It has often been said that there are only two things that are certain in this world—death and taxes. This chapter addresses both of these important concerns. Proper planning for the distribution of property after death can save taxes. This chapter also explains the process by which property is distributed after the owner's death. All owners of property need to be aware of these legal rules and of the problems that may be involved.

DISCUSSION CASE

CHILDREN OF THE CHIPPEWA, OTTAWA, AND POTAWATOMY TRIBES v. THE UNIVERSITY OF MICHIGAN
305 N.W.2d 522 (Michigan, 1981)

FACTS: On September 29, 1817, the Treaty of Fort Meigs was executed. The Chippewa, Ottawa, and Potawatomy Tribes were signatories of the first part, and the government of the United States of America was the signatory of the second part. The treaty was drafted entirely by the representative of the United States. The defendant, the University of Michigan, was not party to the treaty.

Notwithstanding this latter fact, the plaintiffs, who are descendants of the members of the signatory Indian Tribes, brought an action in equity before the Circuit Court of Washtenaw County seeking to have a trust declared in their favor against defendant based on the provisions of this treaty. The trial court denied plaintiffs' request for a declaration of a trust in their favor. Plaintiffs appealed.

■

Per Curiam:

The original complaint was filed August 5, 1971. It was claimed that Article 16 of the treaty created a trust

whereby certain land, belonging to the Indians, was conveyed to defendant for purposes of ensuring that the Indians and their descendants would receive an education in the European fashion. In support of this contention, the complaint cited certain alleged historical events, including the vesting of title of the conveyed parcels of land in the defendant; the then-University president Lewis Cass's appointment of two trustees to locate and survey these lands; the patenting of these lands to defendant by the government of the United States in 1824; and the release by one Church of St. Anne of its interest of the lands in favor of defendant.

The inclusion of St. Anne's Church in the complaint was occasioned by the plaintiffs' assertion that the treaty compelled the church to provide for the primary and secondary education of the Indians. The complaint then contends that the treaty imposed a concomitant duty upon defendant to ensure the Indians' college education. It is then claimed that the aforementioned conveyance by the church to the defendant merged the foregoing duties wholly into defendant's realm of responsibility.

The complaint then charged that a breach of these duties had occurred and was continuing to occur. To remedy the alleged breach, plaintiffs proposed a broad spectrum of equitable remedies.

An accounting of the proceeds realized from sale of the subject parcels was sought. Plaintiffs proposed that upon completion of this accounting, a trust fund composed of proceeds from these sales should be established. Another trust fund, to be composed of monies accounted for from the sale of lands conveyed to defendant from St. Anne's Church, was also sought.

In addition to the foregoing, plaintiffs asked for an accounting of all the investments in both trusts, or, in the alternative, payment of a 15 percent interest fee thereon to be compounded annually from 1826 forward.

The complaint then went on to ask for an accounting of all lands received from the Indians which had not yet been sold together with an accounting of the accrued rent thereon to be computed annually with a compound rate of 15 percent interest to be added thereto.

It was finally requested that the circuit court should replace defendant as the trustee of these funds with a person of its own choosing and that the proceeds from the first trust fund should be directed toward providing plaintiffs with monies to continue their education at any collegiate institution of their choosing. The funds from the second trust were to be applied toward the primary and secondary education of the plaintiffs.

On March 28, 1977, plaintiffs filed an amended complaint and presented a two-pronged attack, again under the theory of equitable trust. After noting the 1974 decision of the trial court to treat the matter as a class action, plaintiffs proceeded to proffer a claim that the treaty had created an express trust, with the plaintiffs being the beneficiaries of that trust. The amended complaint went on to assert that defendant had sold the lands conveyed to it under the treaty without either dedicating the monies realized from the sales to the plaintiffs' educational needs or in any other way accounting to the plaintiffs for these proceeds. The amended complaint then sought a trial under the theories of express and/or constructive trust and otherwise repeated the earlier claims.

The treaty provision that is the primary focus of the present dispute, Article 16, reads:

> Some of the Ottawa, Chippewa, and Potowatomy Tribes, being attached to the Catholic religion, and believing they may wish some of their children hereafter educated, do grant to the rector of the Catholic church of St. Anne of Detroit, for the use of the said church, and to the corporation of the college at Detroit, for the use of the said college, to be retained or sold, as the said rector and corporation may judge expedient, each, one half of three sections of land, to contain 640 acres, on the river Raisin, at a place called Macon; and three sections of land not yet located, which tracts were re-

served, for the use of the said Indians, by the treaty of Detroit, in 1807; and the superintendent of Indian affairs, in the territory of Michigan, is authorized, on the part of the said Indians, to select the said tracts of land.

Trial commenced on August 21, 1978. During the trial numerous exhibits were received along with much expert testimony from all sides. On February 28, 1979, the trial judge issued a meticulously researched and well drafted written opinion, thoroughly discussing the historical and procedural facets of this novel action and carefully setting forth the law which he believed controlling of this case. The opinion denied relief on all counts.

We have painstakingly reviewed the findings of fact in that opinion and agree with the trial judge in respect to those findings. The task of leaping back over 160 years in time is most difficult, and the trial judge is to be commended for his efforts in that regard. . . .

[I]n setting forth the findings of fact, we choose to incorporate the entire opinion of the trial court as part of this opinion to accomplish that end. . . .

Following the issuance of the opinion of February 28, 1979, the present appeal was brought as of right. Five issues are raised by plaintiffs.

It is first asserted that the trial judge erred in finding that the Indians could not have owned fee simple title to any lands conveyed from the year 1790 forward. In so ruling, the trial court found *Oneida Indian Nation* v. *County of Oneida,* 414 U.S. 661 . . . (1974), to be dispositive. We agree. The thrust of *Oneida* is that the 1790 Nonintercourse Act created a right of occupancy rather than a title in fee simple in the Indians as to lands held by them. The trial court held that the federal government possesses power to convey the fee as to lands occupied by Indian Tribes and all questions with respect to rights of occupancy and conditions of extinguishment of Indian title are solely for the federal government. The trial court went on to say:

> This court will concede that in 1817 the Indians could have imposed an express trust on the lands possessed by them and granted to the Church and College by the 1817 Treaty, but this simply was not done at that time.

Given this recognition by the trial court, it is difficult to understand the plaintiffs' argument on the issue. The trial court's ultimate decision obviates further discussion in any event.

Plaintiffs assert that the trial court erred in relying upon the theories set forth in the first complaint as a point of reference for its opinion. While it is true that the opinion of February 28, 1979, assumes the claims of the earlier complaint in reference to grants of land, the error is not fatal. A fair reading of the opinion discloses that both theories of recovery in the second complaint were extensively discussed and refuted. The trial judge clearly comprehended the basis of the relief sought in the second complaint and carefully interwove those theories with the evidence adduced before ruling against them. . . .

A third issue raised by plaintiffs is whether the trial court was justified in holding that Article 16 of the Treaty of Fort Meigs constituted a gift of lands to Father Richard and to defendant. We believe that it did. . . .

The operative language in Article 16 provides that some of the plaintiffs' forefathers: "*do grant* to the . . . church . . . for the use of the said church, and to the . . . college . . . for the use of the said college, *to be retained or sold, as the said rector and corporation may judge expedient,* each. . . ." (Emphasis added.)

Clearly, the grant itself is a completed one and not conditional in nature. Nor do its terms encompass more than one transaction. The land is donated jointly to the church and to the corporation. The later division of the parcels was a consequence of Father Richard's discretion, a discretion Article 16 allowed him to exercise.

The evidence points to an almost reverential attitude toward Father Richard on the Indians' part. This attitude was commingled with an attitude of filial affection. The evidence also points to a clear donative intent on the Indians' part as regards Father Richard and encompasses a similar attitude toward the educational institution which the Indians very properly regarded as an extension of Father Richard's personality and influence.

We disagree with plaintiffs' continued assertions that the treaty, and particularly Article 16, were the sole product of Lewis Cass's efforts. The evidence does not support such a contention in any way. Rather, the treaty was the cumulative result of extended negotiations involving many leaders on both sides.

Both the expert testimony and the language of the treaty itself reflect the likelihood of a present donative intent on the part of the Indians at the time of the treaty's execution. . . .

The next claim of error challenges the trial court's decision that Article 16 created no express trust in the Indians' favor.

It is a general principle of trust law that a trust is created only if the settlor manifests an intention to create a trust, and it is essential that there be an explicit declaration of trust accompanied by a transfer of property to one for the benefit of another. . . . Further, an express trust in real property must be in writing, under the hand of the party to be charged. . . .

We find that the plaintiffs' substantive arguments in support of the theory of an express trust are based on speculation and irrelevancy. . . .

The last claim on appeal concerns the issue of a constructive trust. The trial court rejected this theory for several reasons: (1) the university was not a party to the negotiations and committed no misconduct in the treaty negotiations; (2) the Indians were represented by competent interpreters and a trusted Indian agent; (3) the United States evidenced no unjust conduct at the negotiations, its main intent being to secure a cession of a significant area in Ohio; (4) the Article 16 land was of minimal value when conveyed and when the university tried to sell it; and (5) the two cases cited by plaintiffs are distinguishable. We agree.

In a pristinely humane world, it might be honorable and fair to compel defendant to offer comprehensive scholarships in gratitude for the 1817 conveyance. Certainly, the cost of higher education is subject to the rigors of inflation as are all other things, and the plaintiffs, like everyone else, could benefit by the financial assistance they seek. However, constructive trusts are not used to requite obligations imposed solely where a balancing of equities discloses that it would be unfair to act otherwise. Where, as here, the language of the treaty and the historical evidence reflect a gift *inter vivos* and nothing more, the imposition of a constructive trust is neither equitably nor legally desirable.

Based on the foregoing, it is readily apparent that the judgment of the trial court should be and the same is hereby affirmed. No costs, questions of novel impression and public significance being involved.

■ IMPORTANT TERMS AND CONCEPTS

estate planning	formal will	trusts	last will and testament
settlor	holographic will	beneficiary	nuncupative will
living trust	testatrix	testamentary trust	testator
constructive trust	collateral relatives	deed of trust	codicil
rule against perpetuities	probating the estate	*inter vivos*	Uniform Simultaneous
irrevocable trust	of deceased	revocable trust	Death Act
testate distribution	Economic Recovery Act	Uniform Probate Code	inheritance taxes
escheat to the state	of 1981	intestate distribution	

■ QUESTIONS AND PROBLEMS FOR DISCUSSION

1. What are the four goals of an estate plan? Discuss.
2. What happens to a person's property if he or she dies and leaves no heirs?
3. What is intestate succession? Describe.
4. Briefly describe the process of probating a deceased person's estate.
5. Mr. Floyd Morris had made a will leaving everything to his youngest son. His wife was unhappy about the fact that she was left out of the will completely. One night after his wife complained about it in front of a friend he told her to go and get the will and then he would tear it up. The wife went and got a white envelope from the other room and tore it into shreds. Later Floyd died. His attorneys still had a signed copy. Was the tearing up of the envelope by the wife (not by Floyd) which may have contained the will a legal revocation of the will? Explain.
6. Hermoine Rance had six grandchildren—Irwin, Merwin, Jennie, Jasper, Torwald, and Rosco. Just before taking an airplane trip, she purchased $50,000 worth of life insurance from a machine at the airport. She filled out the policy, naming Irwin and Merwin as beneficiaries but telling her daughter, who was with her, "There's not enough room for all the kids' names, but if anything happens to me, make sure this gets divided among all of them." She then gave her daughter the insurance policy. Hermoine died when her flight crashed, and the insurance company wants to know who should be paid the $50,000. Irwin and Merwin claim it's theirs, since that's what the policy says. The other children claim Hermoine made Irwin and Merwin trustees for the benefit of all the children. Who's right, and why?
7. Leon Lucullus opened a bank account at the Zoomer National Bank, naming himself as "Trustee" for the benefit of his daughter Lucille. When Leon died several years later, the account contained over $20,000. Lucille claims that she now owns the money in the account. The administrator of Leon's estate says that the attempted trust was invalid, since Leon kept control of the account himself, and that it was really an attempt by Leon to make a will without complying with the necessary formalities. Who's right, and why?
8. Rembrandt Dauber's will created a testamentary trust, naming his nephews Ruben Dauber and Van Gogh Dauber as trustees for his controlling block of stock in Aroostok Airlines, Inc. In addition to Ruben and Van, beneficiaries of the trust included Rembrandt's wife, Zelda, and his son, Parsifal. Ruben and Van were the president and secretary of Aroostok. Aroostok's board voted to give them a large cash bonus, which they used to purchase shares of Aroostok. As a result of these purchases, the trust lost control of Aroostok. Zelda and Parsifal bring suit, alleging breach of fiduciary duties. What is the result, and why?

38

Insurance

CHAPTER OBJECTIVES

THIS CHAPTER WILL:

- Outline the various types of insurance.
- Review the formation of the insurance contract.
- Discuss the major parts of an insurance policy.
- Explain some of the special legal rules relating to insurance.

An insurance policy is a contract in which the risk of financial loss resulting from certain, specified occurrences is shifted from the insured to the insurance company. The company agrees to bear these risks and to reimburse the insured (or some other person) in return for the payment of the agreed premiums. In addition to being a method of *risk bearing,* insurance is also a method of *risk sharing,* since the insurance company collects a relatively small amount from each insured and reimburses only those insureds who suffer actual losses. Each insured pays a little so that none of the insureds loses a lot. Basically the same principle was used by the pioneer families who distributed their family possessions in several wagons in a wagon train so that if one wagon was destroyed, a family wouldn't lose everything.

■ HISTORY AND REGULATION

Arrangements similar to today's insurance have been known since the earliest historical times. Babylonian traders apparently used an insurance-like financing arrangement for assuming the risks of the caravan trade, a practice that was legally recognized in the Code of Hammurabi. The Phoenicians, the Greeks, and the Romans followed this precedent for seaborne trade. The Romans also appear to have worked out a sort of life insurance for the payment of burial expenses and survivor benefits. Marine insurance was widely used by the trading nations of medieval Europe; the oldest known marine insurance contract, from Genoa, is dated 1347. The first life insurance policy in the modern sense was issued in England in 1583. The oldest continuously existing insurance organization, the famous Lloyd's of London, was organized about 100 years later, in 1689, in Edward Lloyd's London coffeehouse. According to most sources, the term *underwriter* stems from the procedure used by the syndicates such as Lloyd's; members of the syndicate would sign their names and the amount of liability they wished to assume for particular ships.

Insurance law in the United States was originally subject to considerable English influence. Both life insurance and fire insurance existed in the colonies and continued to develop during the early years of nationhood. From a legal standpoint, the most important early precedent dealing with insurance was established in 1869, when the U.S. Supreme Court decided in *Paul* v. *Virginia* that insurance was not interstate commerce and therefore not subject to regulation by Congress. Based on this decision, the states constructed rather elaborate regulatory schemes of their own. While the details and the enforcement procedures vary considerably, the state insurance regulations typically include the qualifications foreign insurance corporations must meet to write insurance in the state, limitations on investments by insurance companies so as to provide protection against company insolvency, and the licensing and control of insurance agents and brokers.

State regulation of insurance companies

The states' comprehensive regulatory schemes were cast into question when, in *U.S.* v. *Southeastern Underwriters,* the U.S. Supreme Court reversed 75 years of precedents and held that insurance *was* interstate commerce. Congress responded by passing the McCarran-Ferguson Act, which delegated the regulatory power of Congress to the states. The insurance industry was given a broad exemption from the U.S. antitrust acts, stating that the antitrust acts apply to insurance only "to the extent that such business is not regulated by state law."

Since then, the Supreme Court has been experiencing continuing difficulties in defining the scope of this exemption. More recently, several proposals have been made in Congress to repeal or substantially amend the McCarran-Ferguson Act.

■ ORGANIZA-TIONAL FORMS OF INSURANCE COMPANIES

Stock companies

Mutual companies

The two major types of insurance companies are stock companies and mutual companies. *Stock companies* are organized as profit-making corporations, with the *policyholders* as the companies' customers. Some individuals may be both stockholders and customers, as is true with any publicly traded corporation, such as GM or Ford, but there is no necessary connection between the two groups. Except for life insurance, stock companies have historically dominated the insurance industry in this country. ***Mutual companies,*** at least theoretically, are a sort of "cooperative," in which each policyholder pays an initial "membership fee" to join the organization. If a mutual company is operated at a profit, this surplus is distributed to the owner-customers as rebates on the premiums charged. Little difference exists in most day-to-day operations of these two kinds of companies.

Relatively small amounts of life insurance and health insurance are written by fraternal organizations for their members. Governmental agencies may also issue life insurance and other insurancelike "guarantees." The U.S. government provides life insurance for members of the military. Social security provides certain kinds of insurance benefits. U.S. agencies also insure bank deposits and guarantee the payment of residential mortgages. State governmental agencies may be involved in a variety of other insurance programs.

■ TYPES OF INSURANCE

Six groups of insurance

Most types of insurance are well known. These can be grouped into six basic categories: life insurance, health and accident insurance, property insurance, marine insurance, liability insurance, and title insurance.

Life. There are many specific varieties of life insurance, containing different combinations of the "protection" element and the "savings" element and many different special clauses. Term life insurance commits the insurance for only a limited period (five years, for example); to renew coverage beyond that period, the insured must usually submit a new application, including evidence of good health. If a new term policy is issued, the premium is normally higher than that for the first five-year period since the insured is now five years older. Term insurance usually does not provide for "cash surrender value" or other savings features. Ordinary life insurance provides coverage, and level premium payments, throughout the insured's life. Ordinary life insurance accumulates a cash surrender value.

Greater emphasis on the savings feature of insurance is found in limited-payment life policies and endowment policies. In a limited-payment life policy, the premiums are paid only for a specified number of years, such as 10 or 20. At the end of that time, the policy is fully paid up and coverage continues for the life of the insured. This sort of policy is particularly appropriate for use

Endowment policies

during high earnings years, in contrast to term insurance, which is useful for persons who want maximum protection at minimum cost. An ***endowment policy*** also has a limited-pay feature, but the insured is to receive the face amount at a given age. If the insured dies before that date, the proceeds are payable to a named beneficiary. An annuity contract obligates the company to make regular periodic payments to the insured once that person reaches a certain age.

Health.   Health insurance provides for the direct payment or reimbursement of expenses incurred by the insured as a result of illness, such as hospital costs, doctors' fees, X-ray examinations, and medicines. It may also provide for periodic payments to make up for lost wages. Such "income maintenance" protection is especially important where the insured is the sole or principal wage earner in the family unit. Accident insurance provides similar coverage for costs arising from accidental injuries. It usually contains a provision for lump-sum payment in the event of accidental death, with a percentage of that amount payable for permanent disabilities such as the loss of an eye or an arm.

Property.   Property insurance of various kinds reimburses the insured for losses sustained from damage to, or destruction of, property. Fire insurance usually sets a maximum amount for which the company is liable, but the insured can collect only the actual cash value of the insured property at the time of the loss. Loss of a TV set that cost $500 new but had depreciated in value to $200 will permit the insured to recover only $200. A "valued" fire insurance policy, on the other hand, specifies the amount that will be paid in the event of loss by fire. An "extended coverage" indorsement to the policy would protect against loss due to other causes, such as windstorm, hail, aircraft, riot, vehicles, explosion, or smoke ("WHARVES" coverage). For an auto, collision coverage is appropriate if the vehicle has any value at all. Where property is used in a business so that its loss or nonfunctioning might prevent the business from continuing, "business interruption" coverage is also important.

Marine.   Both ocean marine and inland marine insurance are basically concerned with transportation losses, but there are some differences. The loss and liability rules for ocean marine rely heavily on concepts drawn from the law of the sea and international law generally. Because of the requirements for international uniformity, ocean marine is subject to much less regulation by the states. While inland marine basically covers losses due to transportation mishaps occurring within the United States, it may also provide protection against the loss of such things as tunnels, bridges, and pipelines. Inland marine companies also write "personal property floater" coverage for items which are used in different places at different times, such as a set of golf clubs or this book, or for property composed of different specific units at different times, such as the inventory of a shoe store.

Liability.   Liability insurance, sometimes classified as "casualty" insurance, is also very important for both business firms and individuals. Owners and occupiers of real estate need protection against the claims of persons who are injured while on the premises. Owners and operators of motor vehicles need similar protection. Professionals need insurance to cover malpractice liability claims.

Businesses need workers' compensation coverage for on-the-job injuries to employees. Manufacturers and sellers of products need product liability insurance (although today some firms may not be able to afford the premiums). The list could be extended considerably.

Title. Title insurance protection can be obtained in many locations. For a one-time premium, the title insurance company promises to litigate, if necessary, to maintain the validity of the title to particular real estate and to reimburse the purchaser and/or mortgage lender if another person proves to have a superior title to the real estate.

■ INSURANCE AS A CONTRACT

As noted earlier, an insurance policy is a contract, though subject to extensive regulation and to some special rules. All of the problems that can arise in the formation, execution, and enforcement of contracts generally can also arise with respect to the purchase of insurance. In general, contract law principles apply to insurance contracts unless these are superseded by special statutory rules or specific "insurance" precedents.

Offer and acceptance problems occur when it becomes necessary to determine the exact time at which insurance became effective because a loss occurred before the insured actually received the policy. In the absence of a specific agreement, the courts generally agree that a life insurance policy takes effect when it is mailed to the insured or even to the company's agent for delivery to the insured. Many insurance applications, however, also require that the insured be in good health as of the effective date of the policy and that the first premium be paid before the policy comes into force.

When insurance takes effect

For property and liability insurance, an authorized agent may be able to commit the company even without a written policy. In many cases the agent can at least issue a written *binder* which provides temporary insurance coverage until the company accepts or rejects the proposed policy. Once again, specific language as to what was intended should control, as seen in the *Turner* case.

Binder of coverage

TURNER v. WORTH INSURANCE COMPANY

464 P.2d 990 (Arizona, 1970)

FACTS

Mr. Wilson went to the Liken Insurance Agency on August 17, 1964, to buy the car insurance he needed in order to operate his car at the air base where he worked. He filled out an application, paid Liken $30.80, and received a receipt. Wilson said that he thought he was covered at this point, but Liken said that her intention was that coverage be subject to company approval. On August 25, Liken informed Wilson by letter that a higher premium would be required and asked him "to let us know if the policy should be issued." On September 18, not having heard from Wilson, Liken wrote him that his application had been rejected. Meanwhile, on August 23, Wilson had an accident with his car wherein the other driver-owner, Mr. Turner, suffered damages to his car and injury.

Worth brought a declaratory judgment action to have the court decide whether it was liable for a car accident under an alleged insurance contract entered into by Liken, its agent. The trial court decided that there was no valid contract, and Turner, the driver of the other car (who would have been able to file a claim against Worth if it were liable), appealed.

ISSUE   Was there a valid "binder" of insurance coverage made by the agent, Mrs. Liken?

DECISION   No. Judgment of trial court is affirmed.

REASONS   **Judge Hathaway, giving the opinion of the court, stated:**

"We shall first consider the contentions made by appellant Turner, who raises three questions: (1) Was there a written binder of insurance between Worth and Wilson? (2) Was there an oral binder of insurance between Worth and Wilson? and (3) Is Worth estopped to deny coverage by reason of its agent's acts and its retention of the premium paid by Wilson?

A.R.S. Section 20–1120 states in part:

> A. Binders or other contracts for temporary insurance may be made orally or in writing, and shall be deemed to include all the usual terms of the policy as to which the binder was given together with such applicable endorsements as are designated in the binder, except where superseded by the clear and express terms of the binder.

"We conclude that a written binder of insurance was not issued to Mr. Wilson. Although Mr. Wilson states that he did not read the application, a one-page uncomplicated form, that application is entitled in large print 'Special Risk Application for Automobile Insurance.' Right below Mr. Wilson's signature the following appears in bold type: 'No coverage is in effect until a binder in writing or a policy is issued by a policy writing office of International Service Group.'. . .

"While Mr. Wilson received a written receipt from Mrs. Liken, this appears to be for the $30.80 advance payment made by Wilson in applying for the insurance and not an insurance contract itself. And even though an application for insurance is accompanied by payment of premium a contract of insurance is not consummated until the acceptance by the company, . . . particularly where the express provisions of the application so state. . . .

"As in other contracts, an insurance contract must contain the requisite contractual elements. . . . One of these requisites is that there will be a meeting of the minds. . . .

"Mutual assent is based on objective evidence and does not depend upon the undisclosed intentions of the parties. . . . To protect one's reasonable expectancies in reliance on a contract it is imperative that a contracting party be able to rely upon the apparent intentions of the other party, without concern as to his secret thoughts or mental reservations. . . . However, 'there must be a distinct intention common to both and without doubt or difference and until all understanding alike there can be no assent.'. . . In this case each party had a different understanding of the contract, and thus there was no mutual assent.

"Due to Mr. Wilson's failure to list all of his moving traffic violations on his application, the amount of the premium to be paid was never agreed upon between the parties. This is, of course, one of the essential elements of the contract, without which mutual assent could not occur. While Worth was still apparently willing to insure Mr. Wilson, as indicated by Mrs. Liken's letter to Wilson on August 25, 1964, Mr. Wilson never responded to that letter letting Worth know 'if the policy should be issued.' In a situation where the testimony is conflicting as to the objective actions of Mr. Wilson and Mrs. Liken at the time the application was made, and where there is sufficient evidence to support the trial court's conclusion that there was no mutual assent between the parties as to the amount of the premium, the judgment below must be affirmed. . . .

Can a minor purchase life insurance?

By statute, many states permit minors to buy life insurance on their own lives and to designate certain persons as beneficiaries (usually spouse, parent[s], sibling[s]). In the absence of such a statute, a minor can usually disaffirm the purchase of insurance and recover all premiums paid since insurance is not viewed as a necessity.

Assignability of insurance contracts

Rules concerning the assignability of rights under insurance contracts vary, depending on the type of insurance. Since the identity of the user of property is a material element in determining the nature of the risk involved, property insurance normally is not assignable without the consent of the insurer before a loss occurs. Once claims under a property insurance policy arise, they are assignable, like any other contract claim. The right to receive the proceeds from a fire or extended coverage policy may be assigned to a creditor with a lien against the insured property; the nature of the risk does not change since the insured-owner is still using the property. Unless expressly prohibited by the terms of the policy, life insurance is normally assignable by the insured without the consent of the company. The policy may be assigned as a gift, or it may be assigned only temporarily as collateral for a loan. In either case, conflicting claims may arise between the assignee and the designated beneficiary. If the right to change beneficiaries has been expressly reserved in the policy, most courts hold that the assignee prevails. To avoid this problem, the named insured need only make himself or herself the beneficiary and then assign the policy.

▪ PARTS OF THE POLICY

The states regulate to a considerable degree the contents of insurance policies, including the basic coverages that may be written, the special provisions or *riders* that may be included, and to some extent even the actual wording. Recently, several states have tried to require by statute that insurance policies be written in "plain English." (If you don't think this is a real problem, try to read a policy sometime.) Most insurance contracts contain five major parts, though these are not always clearly separated or always in the same order: the definitions, the declarations, the insuring agreements, the exclusions, and the conditions.

Statutes require policies to be in "plain English"

Definitions. In any lengthy and detailed contract, it's a good idea to have a list of agreed definitions of terms. This is particularly true where technical terms are used, or where an everyday term has a technical meaning, or where one of the parties is a consumer or other nonexpert. The results of not carefully defining terms can be seen in the following case.

AMERICAN INDEMNITY CO. v. LANCER, VANDROFF & SUDAKOFF

452 So.2d.594 (Florida, 1984)

FACTS

The lower court rendered final summary judgment in favor of appellee finding that certain files of appellee were "in actual use" when a fire occurred and consequently were covered under a fire insurance policy.

Appellant issued the policy of fire insurance to appellee, a law firm. The policy contained a valuable papers endorsement which provided:

4. Protection of Valuable Paper and Records. Insurance under this policy shall apply only while valuable papers and records are contained in the premises described above, it being a condition precedent to any right of recovery hereunder that such valuable papers and records shall be kept in the following described receptacles at all times when the premises are not open for business, except while such valuable papers and records are in actual use . . .: Steel Cabinets

The endorsement had a $25,000 limit.

A fire occurred in appellee's office early one Monday morning before the office had opened for business. Files in attorneys' and secretaries' offices and not in steel cabinets were destroyed. Appellant denied coverage for the stated reason that appellee's office was not open for business when the fire occurred nor were the files "in actual use" as required by the policy endorsement.

Appellee brought suit seeking a determination of the issue of liability and of the amount of damages sustained. Appellee focused the damages issue on several destroyed bankruptcy files located in partner Lancer's office when the fire occurred. Lancer testified at deposition that no one was present or working in the office when the fire took place. As a general practice, active or open files, including the bankruptcy files in question, were not placed in steel cabinets at the end of each work day. Only passive or closed files were placed in steel cabinets. The bankruptcy files in question required daily work and were kept either in Lancer's office or at his secretary's desk. The cost of reproducing the bankruptcy files would exceed the $25,000 policy limits.

Ultimately, both parties moved for summary judgment, agreeing that the damages incurred exceeded the policy limit and that there were no genuine issues of material fact. Both motions alleged that the only question to be determined was a question of coverage, that being whether the destroyed files were "in actual use" when the fire started.

ISSUE   Were the files which were destroyed in "actual use" as required by the policy in order for them to be covered?

DECISION   No. Judgment of trial court is reversed.

REASONS   Chief Judge Ott, speaking for the court, stated:

"The phrase 'in actual use' is not defined in the policy. Terms in insurance contracts should be given their natural meaning. . . . If the terms are clear and unambiguous, they are to be taken and understood in their plain, ordinary, and popular sense. . . . We find no ambiguity in the phrase 'in actual use.' The American Heritage Dictionary defines 'actual' as '1. in existence; real; factual. 2. being, existing or acting *at the present moment*.' . . . Applying this definition to the case before us, files that Lancer planned or intended to use when he arrived at work were not 'in actual use' when the fire occurred.

"Apparently, this is the first time the term 'in actual use' has been interpreted in Florida. The parties have cited cases from other jurisdictions: *United States Automobile Association* v. *United States Fire Insurance Co.,* 36 Cal.App.3d 765 . . . and *Kaletta* v. *Merchants Mutual Insurance Co.* . . . 295 N.Y.S.2d 850 (1968). The court in *United Services* utilized a definition of 'actual use' similar to the one we adopt herein. However, *United Services* involved interpretation of an automobile liability policy vis-a-vis a homeowner's policy, and we do not purport to rely on it. *Kaletta* is also factually distinguishable.

"Appellee did not comply with the condition of the valuable papers endorsement requiring files not in actual use to be placed in a steel cabinet when the office was not open for business. Consequently, the trial court should have entered summary judgment in favor of appellant."

Declarations. Declarations are factual statements in the policy concerning such things as the name, age, residence, and occupation of the insured. Some such statements would obviously be material to the risk undertaken by the insurance company; others would not. The courts traditionally distinguished between "representations" and "warranties," holding that a false representation of fact not contained in the policy was a basis for rescinding the policy only if the misrepresented fact was material to the insured risk, whereas a false warranty (contained in the policy itself) was always a basis for rescission. Today, either by statute or newer decisions, most courts would probably require the insurance company to show that a false "warranty" by the insured was also material before permitting the company to deny liability under the policy. An error in stating the vehicle number or color of an insured car would probably not permit the insurance company to rescind the policy.

Insuring Agreements, Exclusions, and Conditions. The essence of the insurance policy is the insuring agreements. These are the company's statements of the risks it is agreeing to assume. The insuring agreements obviously need to be read very carefully, in conjunction with the exclusions, which are specific statements of the risks the insurance company is *not* assuming. These two parts of the policy must be read together to see exactly what occurrences are covered. Equally important are the policy's specifically stated conditions relating to such matters as what the insured must do to reinstate a lapsed policy, what notice and proof of loss are required, and what circumstances may cause termination of coverage. The next case shows how some of these provisions fit together.

STARK v. GRANGE MUTUAL INSURANCE COMPANY OF CUSTER COUNTY

277 N.W.2d 679 (Nebraska, 1979)

FACTS   Virgil Stark, doing business as Stark Electric, bought a fire insurance policy covering his building and its contents from Grange. The policy was written for five years, from December 5, 1973, to December 5, 1978, with annual premiums due on December 5. Stark did not pay the premium due on December 5, 1974, until December 18, 1974. Stark had not paid the premium due on December 5, 1975, when his building and its contents were destroyed by fire on December 13, 1975. Stark claimed that his late payment on December 18, 1974, gave him insurance for one year from that date, so that the fire loss was covered. The trial court denied recovery. Plaintiff appealed.

ISSUE   Did the late payment of the premium in 1974 extend coverage for one year from the date payment was due, December 5, or one year from the date the payment was actually made on December 18?

DECISION   Coverage expired on December 5. Judgment of the trial court is affirmed.

REASONS   Judge Caniglia, speaking for the court, stated:
"The key provision read in part as follows: 'This policy shall stand suspended if any default shall be made in the payment of any assessment on or before the date specified. . . . The company shall in no event be liable for any loss or damage occurring during

such period of suspension. This policy may be reinstated and placed in full force according to its terms to cover losses thereafter occurring and insured against under this policy, upon payment to and acceptance by the Company of such delinquent premium or assessment.'

"This provision is not ambiguous, nor is its meaning uncertain; its meaning is clear and since it is not illegal or opposed to public policy, it will be enforced as it is made. . . .

"This provision provides that the policy shall stand suspended if any default in the premium payment occurs on a certain date and the company shall not be liable for any loss occurring to the insured during the period of suspension. This provision is valid and enforceable. . . . Again referring to that part of the provision of the policy relating to delinquent payment of premiums and reinstatement of the policy, the provision provides, 'This policy may be reinstated and placed in *full force according to its terms* to cover losses thereafter occurring and insured against under this policy, upon payment to and acceptance by the Company of such delinquent premium. . . .' It is clear from these terms that the coverage of the policy extended from the fifth day of December of each year to the 5th day of December of the following year, and that the policy coverage would terminate and expire on December 5, 1978. Any other interpretation of this provision would stretch the policy period beyond December 5, 1978, and in effect make a new contract for the parties. The plaintiff was aware of this provision when he paid the premium on December 18, 1974. He was under no obligation to reinstate the policy. If he had desired coverage for a full year from December 18, 1974, he could have bought a new policy or made a new contract with the defendant. He chose instead to reinstate the policy according to its terms and thus when he paid the premium on December 18, 1974, he acquired coverage from December 5, 1974, to December 5, 1975, and when he did not pay the premium due on December 5, 1975, the policy stood suspended. Accordingly, he had no coverage on December 13, 1975, the date of the fire, and the decision of the trial court was correct and is affirmed."

■ **SPECIAL PROBLEMS AND POLICY PROVISIONS**

Insurable Interest. To prevent people from using insurance as another form of gambling and to discourage intentional destruction of the insured property or person, the law requires that the insured have an "insurable interest" in the subject matter of the policy. If such an insurable interest does not exist according to the applicable rules for the particular type of insurance, the policy is void and no recovery will be permitted.

Anyone who will suffer direct financial injury from the loss or destruction of an item of property has an insurable interest in it. The holder of the legal title to the property obviously has such an interest in its continued existence. But so has a tenant in a building, even though the lease gives the tenant only a temporary right to possession. So has a creditor with a mortgage or other security interest against the property. A partner has an insurable interest in the property of the partnership even though the partnership is the legal owner of its specific assets; by extension, a few cases have applied the same rule to the stockholders with respect to the property of a closely held corporation.

Insurable interest must exist at time loss occurs

The insurable interest must exist at the time the loss occurs; unless so provided by statute, it need not exist when the policy is issued. For example, a creditor who anticipates making a loan might buy insurance coverage on the building to be used as collateral. If the loan is made and a mortgage executed, the creditor would be able to recover under the policy. If the loan is not made, the would-be creditor has no insurable interest in the building and cannot recover if the building is destroyed. Likewise, if the loan is repaid by the debtor, the creditor no longer has an insurable interest in the building and cannot recover for any damage that occurs after the loan has been repaid.

UNIVERSAL C.I.T. CREDIT CORP. v. FOUNDATION RESERVE INSURANCE CO.

450 P.2d 194 (New Mexico, 1969)

FACTS

Norman Bowman bought a car for use by his 17-year-old cousin, Jimmy Don Bowman, during the school year 1965–66. Jimmy Don was living with Norman and needed transportation to school and to work. Norman bought, registered, and financed the vehicle in his own name. Knowing that Jimmy Don did not own the car, Foundation's agent nevertheless issued an insurance policy on the car to Jimmy Don. A specific policy provision stated that facts known to its agents would not estop the company from asserting lack of insurable interest.

When the school year ended, Jimmy Don returned to Washington to live with his father, leaving the car with Norman. In July Norman let a prospective buyer drive the car to try it out. The car was totaled in a one-car accident, and the (unpaid) finance company sued to collect under the policy which Jimmy Don had purchased. The trial court held for Foundation. Universal CIT Credit Corp. appealed.

ISSUE

Did Jimmy Don Bowman have an insurable interest in the automobile at the time of the loss?

DECISION

No. Judgment of the trial court is affirmed.

REASONS

Justice Compton gave the opinion of the court:

"Appellant attacks the court's conclusion. The court concluded that Jimmy Don Bowman had no insurable interest in the automobile. It is argued that Jimmy Don Bowman, the named insured, had an insurable interest in the automobile by virtue of the fact that he might incur liability because of his operation or use of it. . . . We think [the] cases . . . relied on by appellant are easily distinguishable on their facts. *Fulwiler* v. *Traders & General Insurance Company* . . . was a case where an assignee of a purchaser of an automobile on a conditional sales contract was substituted as insured for the original purchaser. Thereafter when the original purchaser repossessed the automobile without releasing the insured but was not substituted as insured, and the automobile was damaged, it was held that the named insured had an insurable interest because he had not been released of his liability on his purchase contract. We there adopted the following definition of 'insurable interest' . . .:

It is well settled that any person has an insurable interest in property, by the existence of which he will gain an advantage, or by the destruction of which he will suffer a loss, whether he has or has not any title in, or lien upon, or possession of the property itself.

"When the insured voluntarily abandoned the use of the vehicle, his insurable interest, if any, ceased to exist. An insurable interest must exist at the time of loss. . . . Where it may reasonably be done, it is our duty to liberally construe the findings of the court in such manner as to sustain the judgment entered thereon. . . . When all of the findings made by the court are considered together, the conclusion that the named insured had no insurable interest in the subject matter clearly rests on an ample foundation. . . . There was no contractual obligation between Jimmy Don Bowman with anyone. He could not have suffered loss by its destruction. He had no interest in the vehicle and he lost nothing.

"The judgment should be affirmed."

Every person has an insurable interest in his or her own life and can contract for insurance and designate anyone as beneficiary. In such a case the beneficiary need have no insurable interest in the life of the insured. Questions arise when one person buys life insurance on the life of another person. For such a policy to be valid, the buyer/beneficiary must have an insurable interest in the life of the person insured. In contrast to property insurance, this interest must exist when the policy is purchased but need not exist when the loss (death) occurs.

Just who has such interests in the lives of other persons is not absolutely clear since the courts generally test each case on its own facts. It is generally assumed that spouses and partners have an insurable interest in each other's lives, and by analogy, a corporation probably has an insurable interest in the lives of its key employees. A creditor usually has an insurable interest in the life of a debtor, at least to the extent of the debt. Based on specific sets of facts, parents and children and brothers and sisters may or may not have an insurable interest in each other's lives; the court will usually demand something more than just the blood relationship to validate the policy.

Incontestability Clause. By statute in many states and by common practice in others, life insurance policies typically contain a clause specifying that the insurance company cannot raise certain defenses to avoid liability after a policy has been in force for a stated period of time (usually two years). Not all of the company's defenses are removed by such a clause, however. Lack of an insurable interest, certain types of criminal fraud, no required proof of death, and the statute of limitations (and perhaps some other defenses) could still be asserted by the company.

Waiver and Estoppel. As is true with contracts generally, rights under an insurance contract may be waived or a party may be estopped by his or her conduct from asserting them. An insurance company, acting through its authorized agents, can waive its rights under the contract, such as its right to cancel a life insurance policy where the insured has been hospitalized prior to delivery of the policy. An insurance company may also be estopped by the conduct of its agents from asserting a defense on which it could otherwise have relied. It would be virtually impossible to prevent the company from asserting the lack of an insurable interest by either of these legal doctrines.

Waiver of premium clause

Nonforfeiture Provision. Since the insured's financial situation may change drastically and leave that person unable to pay premiums when due, many life insurance policies contain a nonforfeiture provision and/or a ***waiver-of-premiums clause.*** If the required premiums are not paid within the permitted grace period, the policy may provide that the insured can choose one of several options: a paid-up-for-life policy in a smaller amount, a term insurance policy for the original face amount for whatever term the accumulated values will cover, or return to the insured of the cash surrender value of the policy. Such a provision will also contain a presumption as to which choice is made if the insured does not specifically indicate a choice. Where sickness or other disability prevents the insured from paying the premiums, there may be a waiver-of-premiums clause which states that the policy remains in full force and effect for the duration of the disability. Obviously, such a clause is very important in a single-income family. It can usually be obtained for a slightly higher premium.

Double Indemnity Clause.   Life insurance policies frequently contain a provision requiring the company to pay twice the face amount of the policy in the event of *accidental death.* These clauses have produced much litigation as to what is an accidental death. An insured killed while playing Russian roulette? Probably not. An insured who dies of sunstroke after staying out in the sun too long? Possibly not. An insured who dies from serum hepatitis contracted as a result of a blood transfusion necessitated by a car wreck? Perhaps accidental, necessitating the double payment. The cases are not uniform.

What is accidental death?

Iron-Safe Clause.   To protect the insurance company against false claims of loss by fire or burglary, particularly where the property insured is a changing inventory of business goods, the policy may require the insured firm keep adequate inventory records and lock them in a fireproof safe when the firm is not open for business. These records will then have to be produced to substantiate any loss claimed under the policy.

Coinsurance Clause.   Unless prohibited by statute, property insurance policies typically require that coverage be purchased for some specified percentage of the total value if the insured wishes to collect the full amount of any loss. If a building had a value of $100,000 and the policy contained an 80 percent coinsurance clause, the insured would have to buy at least $80,000 worth of coverage to collect the full loss from the company. A person who bought only $60,000 worth of insurance on the building could collect only three fourths of any losses ($60,000/$80,000 × Amount of loss). With or without coinsurance clauses, the insured's recovery could not exceed the face amount of the policy.

No-Fault Auto Insurance.   No-fault automobile insurance was discussed in Chapter 7 in connection with tort liability. In those states that have statutes establishing a no-fault system for motor vehicle accidents, the parties involved in an accident generally can recover only from their own insurance companies. They can't sue each other to try to establish which party's fault—negligence—caused the accident. In some of these states it is possible to sue the negligent party who caused death or a serious injury. Some of these no-fault states also permit recovery for damage to a vehicle, up to a certain dollar amount. Even though no-fault auto rules are not yet in force in most states, there are already significant differences from state to state. The Fisher case, which follows, involved the no-fault statute in the state of Michigan.

FISHER v. LOWE

333 N.W.2d 67 (Michigan, 1983)

FACTS   Karen Lowe, driving a car owned by Larry Moffet and insured by State Farm, lost control of the car and ran into William Fisher's "beautiful oak tree." The no-fault statute in force at the time exempted owners and operators of motor vehicles from liability for damage caused with the vehicle. Fisher nonetheless sued all three. The trial court granted summary judgment for Lowe and Moffet because of the statute. The trial court also denied plaintiff's motion for a default judgment against State Farm since it had never properly been served with process. Fisher appealed.

ISSUE   Can the owner and operator of a motor vehicle be held liable for damage to plaintiff's tree which was struck by a vehicle driven by defendant Lowe?

DECISION   No. Judgment of the trial court is affirmed. The Michigan no-fault statute exempts owner and operator from this type of loss.

REASONS   Judge Gillis, evidently amused by Fisher's persistence in the face of a clear statutory result, wrote the court's entire opinion as a poem.
"We thought that we would never see
A suit to compensate a tree.
A suit whose claim in tort is prest
Upon a mangled tree's behest;
A tree whose battered trunk was prest
Against a Chevy's crumpled crest;
A tree that faces each new day
With bark and limb in disarray;
A tree that may forever bear
A lasting need for tender care.
Flora lovers though we three,
We must uphold the court's decree.
Affirmed."

    The Court of Appeals summarized the facts in a prose footnote to its rhythmical opinion. In preparing their annotated report of the case, the editors for West Publishing Company not only put their summary of the facts in rhyme, but their headnotes as well.

■ SIGNIFICANCE OF THIS CHAPTER

While living and functioning in modern society all of us are exposed to major personal and business risks. Unexpected events may result in property losses, large liabilities to others, or serious personal injuries. Insurance is the means by which we spread the risk of these occurrences. Each of us pays a relatively small amount as a premium to the insurance company to buy the protection, and the insurance company reimburses those of us who actually suffer the losses.

    While the insurance policy is a contract, it is a special type, with many technical terms and special provisions. An understanding of the basic rules of contract law provides a framework for understanding insurance policies. This chapter highlighted some of the special rules and terminology from insurance law.

DISCUSSION CASE

TITUS v. WEST AMERICAN INSURANCE COMPANY
362 A.2d 1236 (New Jersey, 1976)

FACTS: Gilford Titus is a young man who operates his own auto body repair shop and who has been an auto body mechanic all his working life. On March 16, 1972, he purchased a used 1966 Mustang convertible for a purchase price of $472.50 (including $22.50 in sales tax). About three weeks later he contacted his insurance broker, Robert Herdman, and requested that this vehicle be added to his current insurance policy underwritten by defendant. At this time he wanted only coverage for liability. . . .

In September 1972 he contacted his insurance broker again and requested that "comprehensive" (theft and property damage) coverage be added to his policy. The broker, Herdman, testified that when this coverage was added plaintiff never mentioned to him that the car was in the process of being extensively remodeled or customized. Herdman admitted that he knew from casual observation that plaintiff's car had been repainted and that new tires had been added, but he stated that this alone gave him no cause to suspect that the car was being customized or that these changes represented any increase in the insurable risk. The broker duly purchased this additional coverage at a cost of $9.18 a year.

Thereafter, plaintiff continued to improve and customize his vehicle. In March 1973 he rebuilt the engine at a cost of $156.10 (including labor). In May 1973 he purchased a second set of tires and a set of "mag wheels" at a total cost of $293.52 (including wheel locks). He also spent nearly $450 on other parts and equipment. During this time his automobile insurance policy was automatically renewed semiannually. At no time did plaintiff inform the company or his broker of the extensive modification he made on the automobile.

On February 23, 1974, plaintiff's automobile was stolen. To this date it has not been returned. Shortly therafter, plaintiff filed a claim with defendant insurance company giving a description of the car and indicating that the odometer read 89,000 miles at the time of the theft. Lengthy negotiations ensued but amicable settlement could not be made. Plaintiff filed suit seeking judg-ment in the amount of $2,000, together with interest and costs of suit, alleging that this amount represents the "actual cost value" (ACV) of plaintiff's automobile at the time it was stolen. Alternatively, plaintiff sought the appointment of a disinterested and competent umpire under Section 10, Part 3, of the insurance contract.

[T]he court ordered that Anthony Berezny of Sunset Tire Service, Inc., Route 12, Baptistown, New Jersey, be appointed the umpire for the purpose of making an award and determining the actual cash value of the automobile in question. . . .

Berezny and the appraisers met and agreed that the market value of plaintiff's particular car at the time of the theft was $2,000. However, they also agreed that the value of a vehicle of the same model and year in excellent condition, equipped with standard options, would be worth no more than $1,000. Neither of them knew which value was applicable under the law.

Thereafter, plaintiff's motion for summary judgment was denied and the matter proceeded to trial before the court on April 29, 1976. Defendant withdrew its jury demand and admitted liability. The case was then heard before the court without jury, limited to the issue of damages.

■

Judge Beetel:

At trial each side adduced expert testimony regarding the question of value and the method of evaluating auto insurance losses. Like the court-appointed umpire and defendant's appraiser, these experts were in substantial agreement regarding the market value of plaintiff's customized 1966 Mustang convertible. Among aficionados of such vehicles, plaintiff's car would have sold for $2,000 on the date of the theft. Plaintiff introduced pictures of his late beloved vehicle into evidence, and from viewing these photos this court finds that there is no question that the car was in excellent, indeed "cream puff" condition. Thus, this court finds as a fact that the market value of plaintiff's car, with the special equipment he added, was $2,000 on February 23, 1974.

The experts could not agree on the value of a 1966 Mustang convertible with full standard options in excellent condition. Defendant's expert, an appraiser with many years of experience, testified that the "book value" of such a car was $375. "Book value," he explained, refers to two publications used throughout the auto and insurance industries to evaluate used automobiles, the *Red Book* published by National Market Reports, Inc., and the *N.A.D.A. Official Used Car Guide* published by the National Automobile Dealer's Association. He testified, further, that the maximum value of such a vehicle would be double the "book" price, or $750. Plaintiff's experts testified that such a vehicle would have sold for about $1,000. They rejected the book value method of evaluation as the only guide toward the determination of actual cash value. Berezny, the umpire, agreed with plaintiff's experts and thus iterated his previous findings made during arbitration.

If this court were to make independent findings of fact on this issue, it might place the value of a fully equipped, "cream puff" 1966 Mustang convertible at something closer to the double book value standard espoused by defendant's expert. However, for the reasons which follow, this court finds that $1,000 was the actual cash value of such a vehicle on the date of the theft under the terms of the insurance contract in question. . . . The final question to be resolved is what automobile is to be evaluated. Plaintiff argues strenuously that it is his car, as he had equipped it, which should be the subject matter of the evaluation. Defendant argues with equal intensity that the subject matter of the evaluation is an automobile of the same model, year, and condition, equipped with standard options. Surprisingly, research had disclosed no case directly on point, nor do the commentators provide significant enlightenment.

Defendant insurer presented uncontradicted expert testimony by an experienced expert insurance underwriter regarding long-established industry custom and usage.

He stated that comprehensive coverage is geared to insure the ordinarily equipped automobile and that this was widely known and employed by all insurers. He further opined that the insurance buying public is aware of this custom, and that the extremely modest premiums payable for such coverage should, at a minimum, put the insured on notice that what was being insured was an ordinary risk. . . .

Based on this testimony defendant argues that the subject matter of this policy was a "1966 Mustang with standard options," not a "customized 1966 Mustang with a rebuilt high-powered engine, mag wheels, racing tires and front sloping chassis, and special paint." To point to the logical absurdity of plaintiff's position, counsel for defendant advanced a "horrible hypothetical"—a solid gold 1966 Mustang with mink seatcovers studded with precious gems. Surely, he urges, such a vehicle could not be insured at full value for the paltry sum of $9.18 a year. . . .

Here, plaintiff represented that his car was a "1966 Mustang convertible" when in fact is was (or became) a "customized 1966 Mustang convertible." Such a misstatement was certainly "material to the risk," since it both increased the potential liability of the insurer and the likelihood that the vehicle might be purloined. Had not defendant graciously admitted liability, it may well have been able to advance the argument that the policy should have been avoided on this ground.

There also exists another reason why plaintiff's claim for an additional $1,000 must be denied. . . .

In the instant case most of the modifications to the vehicle were made after plaintiff met with his broker and purchased the comprehensive coverage. These subsequent modifications (the rebuilt engine, the racing tires, and the mag wheels) were primarily responsible for the doubling of the car's market value.

For the reasons stated above, this court finds in favor of plaintiff in the amount of $1,000 plus taxed costs and interest. Because of the novel questions of law involved and defendant's lack of bad faith, taxed costs shall not include an award of counsel fees.

■ IMPORTANT TERMS AND CONCEPTS

risk bearing	title insurance	accidental death	binder
underwriter	rider	coinsurance clause	policy definitions
mutual companies	policy declarations	risk sharing	policy exclusions
life insurance	insurable interest	stock companies	incontestability clause
endowment policies	waiver and estoppel	policyholder	nonforfeiture provision
marine insurance	waiver of premiums clause	health insurance	double indemnity clause
		property insurance	iron-safe clause
		liability insurance	no-fault auto insurance

■ QUESTIONS AND PROBLEMS FOR DISCUSSION

1. Who has the authority to regulate insurance companies? Are they regulated by the states or exclusively by national regulation? Discuss.

2. There are six basic categories of insurance. List these six categories and briefly discuss each category.

3. What is a "binder"? Must a binder be in writing to be enforceable? Discuss.

4. What is an insurable interest? Discuss.

5. Employers had issued a standard form policy to Mr. and Mrs. Youse, covering their household goods and personal property "against all direct loss or damage by fire." Mrs. Youse was carrying one of her rings, wrapped in a handkerchief, in her purse. When she got home she put the handkerchief and some Kleenex tissues on the dresser in her bedroom. Her maid threw both the handkerchief and the Kleenex tissues into a wastebasket. Later, another member of the household staff emptied the wastebasket into the trash burner at the rear of the house and then burned the contents of the trash burner. About a week later, the missing ring was discovered in the ashes; it had been damaged to the tune of $900. Youse sued when Employers refused to pay for the damage. Will Mr. Youse win? Why or why not?

6. Humbert purchased automobile insurance from Civic Insurance. Coverage was included for income lost as a result of accidental injury. Humbert's daughter Lina was injured in a car accident and required constant nursing care for an extended period. Humbert's wife Olive cared for Lina in the family home during this period, and as a result, Olive lost her part-time job. Humbert sues Civic to collect for Olive's lost wages under the policy's lost-income clause. Will Humbert collect? Explain.

7. Romeo and Juliet have been living together as man and wife for over 10 years, although not legally married. The state does not recognize common-law marriages. Romeo's car insurance policy contains a family-exclusion clause, which says it does not provide coverage for bodily injury to Romeo or members of his family. Juliet was injured while riding in Romeo's car. Strange Insurance Company refused to pay her claim for personal injury damages. Can Juliet collect from Strange? Why or why not?

8. Merlin had allowed his life insurance policy with Trusty Insurance to lapse for nonpayment of premiums. Two days before he was killed in a car accident, he mailed a check to his insurance agent for the back premiums due, together with an application for reinstatement of the insurance. He did not have the reinstatement application completely filled out, nor did he submit proof of "insurability" (good health) as required by the reinstatement clause in the policy. Trusty Insurance had had no chance to consider his application and had not contacted him prior to his death in the car crash. Guinevere, Merlin's widow and named beneficiary, sues Trusty to collect under the policy. What is the result, and why?

PART SEVEN

Business Associations

Persons who intend to start a business may choose which of the various types of business associations to use in conducting their business. These choices range from the sole proprietorship, which is the least expensive to create, is not subject to extensive regulation, but has the disadvantage of unlimited liability against the owner; to the corporation, which is more expensive to create, may be subject to more extensive regulation, but offers limited liability. Part Seven reviews the various types of business associations and discusses the pros and cons of each. In Part Seven we also discuss the law of agency which allows us to have others, our agents, conduct business on our behalf. In this part we also review the law governing the issuance and sale of securities and, finally, we examine the issues of corporate social responsibility and business ethics.

39

Agency—Creation, Principal's Liabilities, and Termination

CHAPTER OBJECTIVES

THIS CHAPTER WILL:

- Define "agency."
- Distinguish independent contractors from agents or employees.
- Explain the methods of creating an agency relationship.
- Review the principal's liability for the agent's torts.
- Explain the methods of termination of an agency relationship.

Sources of agency law

Agency is a very ancient and very important legal concept. Agency law and contract law describe the two most basic legal relationships. On this foundation many of the other, more specialized legal relationships are erected. The modern law of agency can be traced to the Roman law concerning the owner and slave; the law merchant, a private system of rules and courts which traders and merchants established to govern themselves during the Middle Ages; and the English common law. Because individuals and businesses everywhere must on many occasions conduct their affairs through others, every legal system must somehow deal with the concept of *agency*. Every contract entered into by corporations and partnerships and many of the contracts made by individuals and unincorporated associations involve the principles of agency law.

Although the law of agency obviously has very great "commercial" significance, it is not covered in the Uniform Commercial Code. One reason for this omission may be that when the Uniform Commercial Code was formulated, the basic rules of agency law were already pretty well agreed on by the states and were already summarized in the *Restatement of the Law of Agency, Second*. The *Restatement* does not have the force of law, but it is considered to be an authoritative source and it is followed most of the time by most courts.

■ BASIC DEFINITIONS

An *agent* is one who has been authorized to act for another person, to conduct that other person's business dealings with one or more third parties. The person who authorizes another as agent is called the *principal*. The "third party" is the other person with whom the negotiations are to be conducted. The third party may also be represented in the transaction by an agent. Since all corporations must rely on human beings to conduct their actual business affairs, any contract between two corporations will be negotiated and finalized (and performed) by their agents.

An *employee* is a person who has been hired by someone to do a particular job for that person. Employees, as such, do not have the power to act as agents and make contracts with third persons on behalf of their employer. The same person, however, may be both an agent and an employee. The sales clerk in a retail store is clearly an employee of the store, but is also an agent, with the authority to make sales to customers and to receive payment for the goods sold. A friend taking your coat to the dry cleaners for you would be your agent, but not your employee. A factory worker with no authority to deal with third parties is an employee, but not also an agent.

Before we look at the various ways in which the agency relationship can be created (and terminated), it is necessary to distinguish another arrangement that involves the use of others to conduct one's affairs—the independent contractor.

■ INDEPENDENT CONTRACTORS

Independent Contractors Distinguished from Agents/Employees. As a rule, a person who employs an independent contractor to perform services is liable neither for torts committed by the independent contractor in performing the job nor for subcontracts made by the independent contractor to get the job done. Independent contractors are, of course, liable for their own torts (and for the torts of their agents and employees) and for their own contracts. Litigation frequently arises, however, when the independent contractor has gone out of business, or lacks the financial resources to cover a substantial claim, or is simply out of the jurisdiction and not available, or at least not conveniently available, for suit. The key issue in these cases is whether the relationship in question was really an independent contractor-employer relationship, which results in nonliability, or was a principal-agent or employer-employee relationship, which results in the principal/employer's being held liable in tort and/or contract.

Control test

The primary test used by the courts to distinguish these legal relationships is the degree of control the employer/principal exercises over the person in the middle; that is, the independent contractor or the agent/employee. The general idea is that with independent contractors the employer contracts only for results and leaves the details of the job to the independent contractors, although given the right set of facts, these too could be agents/employees.

I/C controls how job gets done

Put in the simplest terms, a person using an independent contractor controls *what* gets done, but the independent contractor decides *how* it gets done. With an agent/employee, the principal/employer not only determines *what* gets done but also has the power to determine *how* it gets done. If you hire an employee to help you put aluminum siding on your house, you can tell that person what size hammer to use, what size nails to use, where to place the nails, and so on. If you hire Mr. Shatturglas, "the aluminum siding king," to do the job for you, you contract only for a good, skillful job, and Shatturglas determines the nail placement and all the other details of how the job gets done.

Factors to be considered

The nature of the relationship the parties have created is essentially a fact question, for determination by the court. The label that the parties have attached to that relationship is not conclusive, nor is the "intent" of the parties, nor is what the parties "thought" they were creating. The facts speak for themselves in each case, since the parties may easily be mistaken as to what the law is or they may be attempting to avoid legal responsibilities by using the independent contractor label as a smoke screen. Among the factors which a court may consider significant are "whether the one employed is engaged in a distinct business, whether in the locality the work is usually done under supervision or by a specialist without supervision, skill required, furnishing of tools and equipment, time limit of employment, method of payment, whether [the] work is a part of [the] regular business of [the] employer, whether [the] parties believe they are creating one or the other relationship, and whether the principal is or is not in business." The *Newman* case illustrates the application of these tests.

NEWMAN v. SEARS, ROEBUCK & CO.

43 N.W. 2d 411 (North Dakota, 1950)

FACTS

Mr. Dale bought a folding bed from Sears to be installed in an apartment house he owned. It was the kind of bed that was designed to fold up into the wall when not in use. Mr. Dale had Mr. Nelson install it. When the tenant, Mr. Newman, went to bed, the bed folded up with him in it. In installing the bed, Nelson used ordinary wood screws rather than the lag screws which were designed to hold the bed in place as it was raised and lowered. The lag screws that came with the bed had a holding power four times that of the wood screws Nelson used. The trial court dismissed the action against Sears since there was no indication that the bed had been negligently designed or manufactured. It also held that Dale was not liable for Nelson's improper installation.

ISSUE   Was Nelson an independent contractor, so that Dale is not liable for his negligence?

DECISION   Yes. Judgment affirmed.

REASONS   Judge Grimson applied the "control" test as the basis for deciding this case. Here, it was clear that Nelson was indeed "independent."

"The evidence shows that Nelson was a carpenter of many years' experience . . . , that there was a general agreement between Dale and Nelson that Nelson should make repairs for Dale's apartments whenever called by Dale or his tenants; that the only instruction given by Dale to Nelson was to make the repairs called for according to his best judgment; that instructions were given by Dale to his tenants to call Nelson if carpenter repairs were needed. Nelson drew no salary. Instead such repairs were paid by Dale on a bill rendered at the completion of each job. Dale exercised no supervision over any particular job. Nelson had the right to hire help or to have others do the job for him in case he was otherwise employed. . . . From that evidence it is clear that Dale had no control and reserved no right of control over how Nelson performed the work of installation nor the methods he used. . . ."

Independent Contractors under Statutes Regulating Employer-Employee Relationships. The nonliability aspects of the independent contractor relationship as compared to the agent/employee relationship tend to make businesses and individuals prefer to conduct their affairs through independent contractors whenever possible. However, the tort and contract areas are not the only places where the law deals differently with independent contractors and their employers. In general, employers of independent contractors escape regulation under statutes designed to "protect" employees. Employers of independent contractors do not have to withhold state or national income tax, do not have to withhold or pay social security taxes, do not have to pay unemployment compensation taxes, do not have to provide workers' compensation coverage for the independent contractors, and are not subject to minimum wage or employment discrimination statutes. Moreover, independent contractors have no rights to organization and collective bargaining under the National Labor Relations Act.

I/C not protected by regulatory statutes

Statutes often contain their own definition, for their purposes, of who is an "employee" and who is an "independent contractor." Typically the board or agency charged with the enforcement of such a statute may make its own administrative determination as to who is subject to the statute's provisions, and often employers have to challenge the board or agency in court if they wish to claim an exemption for independent contractors employed by them.

Franchisees as Independent Contractors. A business that sells a widely advertised product or service through local franchised "dealers" (e.g., McDonald's, Kentucky Fried Chicken, and General Motors) must avoid overstepping the boundaries that separate the independent contractor relationship from the principal-agent relationship. The business wants to minimize its legal liability and regulatory exposures by using independent contractors to sell its products or services. At the same time, however, it wants to ensure that certain quality standards are met by each franchisee-dealer. The dilemma is that the greater the degree of "quality control" it exercises, the more likely it is that the franchisee will be held to be an agent-employee rather than an independent contractor for both liability and regulatory purposes. Ultimately, each case presents a fact question for the court.

Too much control = Liability

Exceptions to the Nonliability Rule for Contracts and Torts of Independent Contractors.

There are at least three well-recognized exceptions to the nonliability aspects of employing independent contractors.

Contracts by the Independent Contractor.   Nearly all states have mechanic's lien statutes, which provide that persons who supply labor or materials for improvements on real estate can file claims against the real estate if they are not paid. These laws generally do not make the owners of the real estate personally liable for the debts their independent contractors owe to laborers or materialmen, but the results have almost the same effect: Owners must pay off the claims to clear the title to the real estate. Of course, the landowner who is forced to pay off such third-party claims can recover from the independent contractor, if the contractor is still solvent and available for suit.

Mechanic's liens

Extra-Hazardous Activities.   Where the work for which the contractor is hired involves a clear risk of injury to others, the employer will be liable when such injuries occur. Examples of such activities include construction of dams and reservoirs, blasting, excavations near a highway, spraying of poisons, clearing land by fire, and razing buildings. These kinds of operations call for special precautions, and the employer should remain liable for any contractor negligence where such jobs are being done.

Nondelegable Duties.   Nondelegable duties may be created by statute, by contract, or by case law. In Chapter 16 we discussed contractual duties that could not be delegated due to their personal nature. Statutory and case-law rules create nondelegable duties on the part of a railroad to keep its crossings in good repair, a city to keep its streets in good repair, a business to provide a safe place for employees and customers, and others. In each of these cases, the employer can be held liable for the negligence of a contractor hired to perform the duty, at least where the negligence relates directly to the job itself. Of course, the employer could also be held liable for any personal negligence, such as providing the contractor with improper plans for the job or hiring a contractor who was not qualified to do the job. Most courts would also disallow the exemption where the employer reserved the right to supervise, or did in fact supervise, the performance of the job.

Personal Negligence by Employer of Independent Contractor

Quite apart from the issue of employer's liability for torts by the independent contractor, the employer can clearly be held liable for his or her own torts. The employer is liable for any personal negligence in connection with the work being done. The employer can be held liable for negligence in failing to select a qualified contractor, or for failing to require the contractor to take needed safety precautions, or for inadequate instructions or equipment furnished to the contractor. If the employer directs or controls part of the job, negligence in doing so would also make the employer liable. The employer would also be held negligent for failing to make a proper inspection after the job was done to make sure it had been done properly. In any of these cases, the negligence is the employer's own, not that of the independent contractor.

■ CREATION OF THE AGENCY RELATIONSHIP

In General. The agency relationship is created by the mutual consent of the parties thereto, the principal and the agent, but whether it exists or not depends on the legal significance of what the parties actually said and did rather than what they "really intended." In other words, a court may find that agency exists even though the parties did not really intend that result. As a general rule, agency may be created by oral or written words or by conduct. There is no generally applicable Statute of Frauds section for agency agreements, although many states require written authority when an agent is to execute real estate documents for the principal. Depending on the state, other particular types of agency agreements may also have to be in writing. A signed, written statement of agency authority is usually called a ***power of attorney,*** making the agent an "attorney in fact" for his or her principal as to the matters contained in the document.

Statute of frauds

Although agency is usually based on a contract, with the agent being compensated for his or her services, the relationship can also exist without any contract at all. For example, your roommate is going to the cleaner and agrees to take your coat there for you as well. Your roommate is acting as your agent when making the contract with the cleaner to have the coat cleaned, even though he or she is just doing it as a favor, with no compensation. If the cleaner ruins your coat, you could sue it for breach of contract. An agency was created. Your agent made an offer on your behalf, and the cleaner accepted the coat for cleaning. You would not, however, be able to sue your roommate for breach of contract if he or she decided not to take your coat to the cleaner after all, since there was no agency contract.

Contract with agent not required

Since the agent is to contract on behalf of the principal, the principal is the party who must have contractual capacity. Principals who are minors have the same rights of disaffirmance as they would have if they had made a contract in person, including the right to disaffirm whatever contract they may have made with their agents. The fact that agents are minors, or lack capacity for some other reason, would not generally have any impact on the contracts which they made on behalf of their principals. However, agents who are minors can disaffirm any employment contract which they made with their principals.

Capacity of parties

The burden of proving that an agency relationship exists is on the person alleging it, typically the third party who dealt with the alleged agent. The third party has no case against the alleged principal unless it can be shown that the principal gave the agent the authority to do the acts in question. To hold the principal liable for the agent's actions, the third party must show that the agent had **express authority, implied authority, apparent authority,** or **authority by ratification.**

Express Authority. Express authority is authority which has been given specifically, in so many words. Orally or in writing, the principal has told the agent to perform some specific act: "Sell my GM stock"; or "Go over to the lumberyard, and buy us 10 more two-by-fours." In these simple examples it's pretty clear what is intended, but there are many situations where the principal's meaning is not so easy to determine. Where the words used are more general, or where the agent is to conduct a series of complicated transactions, or where the agent is left "in charge" for a period of time, a court may be called on to see whether the principal's instructions did or did not include the acts in question.

Restatement definition of "manage"

The *Restatement of Agency, Second,* is of some help here, at least as to what is involved in "managing" a business. Section 73 lists these things: buying supplies and equipment, making repairs, hiring and firing employees, selling goods held for sale, paying and receiving payment of debts, and doing those things which are incidental, usual, necessary, or ordinary in such a business. In the following case the New York courts tried to define *manage* in another context.

KEYES v. METROPOLITAN TRUST CO.

115 N.E. 455 (New York, 1910)

FACTS

This was a lawsuit to collect a promissory note given in payment for the purchase of stocks. The note was signed in the name of Alexander McDonald by Edmund K. Stallo. Stallo was acting under powers of attorney executed by McDonald which gave him certain powers to act in McDonald's behalf. McDonald was now deceased, and it was his estate that was being sued. The defense of McDonald's estate was that the powers of attorney did not authorize Stallo to sign the promissory note in question. The power of attorney gave Mr. Stallo general powers to sell, but did not give him specific authority to buy property. It did have a management clause which reads as follows: "and generally in the sale and management of my personal property and in other matters above mentioned to do and to perform everything which I could do and perform if personally present." The trial court held that these powers of attorney conferred power upon Stallo to make the note in question. The Appellate Division reversed the trial court. Plaintiff appealed.

ISSUE

Did the powers of attorney executed by McDonald grant Stallo the authority to purchase property and execute a promissory note in payment of the purchase price?

DECISION

Yes. The decision of the Appellate Division was reversed, and the judgment of the trial court was reinstated.

REASONS

Justice McLaughlin stated:

"The purpose of a written power of attorney is not to define the authority of the agent, as between himself and his principal, but to evidence the authority of the agent to third parties with whom the agent deals. In order to enable Stallo to sell property belonging to McDonald, it was necessary that he should be able to prove to his vendees that he had authority to sell. But his authority to purchase property for McDonald was a matter which primarily concerned only McDonald and himself. If he purchased for cash, it did not matter to his vendors whether he was acting for himself or McDonald. It was not necessary in that case for him to show any power of attorney, and therefore the omission to specify therein authority to purchase property is of little significance.

If the property were not to be purchased for cash, it may well have been supposed that the authority to draw bills of exchange and promissory notes was enough, and that such authority was conferred for that very purpose. Third parties reading the powers of attorney would naturally be led to that conclusion. Certainly no reasonably prudent person would, after reading them, have any doubt on that subject. But, whether this be the correct view or not, it seems to me clear that a power of attorney to execute and deliver bills of exchange and promissory notes, as set forth in the instruments under consideration, would authorize an attorney to borrow money or purchase property for his principal, giving the latter's promissory note in payment thereof."

Most of the difficulty in the *Keyes* case centers on the fact that the courts are very reluctant to imply the power to issue negotiable instruments, since such a power, quite literally, gives the agent a blank check with the principal's name on it. As a general rule, third parties should not take such instruments signed by an alleged agent unless these parties have so dealt with the agent in the past or unless they have a clear, express statement of authority from the principal.

Implied Authority. Not every detail needs to be stated expressly for actual authority to exist. Once an agent has been given the express authority to do a particular job, the implication is that the principal also intended the agent to have the authority to do whatever was necessary and appropriate to get the main job done. By implication, the agent has the authority to take care of all

Incidental authority

incidental details. Also, when an emergency threatens the success of the enterprise, the agent on the spot, in charge of the principal's affairs, is assumed to have the authority to meet and deal with the emergency. And finally, implied authority may exist on the basis of a course of prior transactions between the principal and the agent or on the basis of custom in their trade or business.

Any implied authority which might otherwise exist would be negated by express instructions to the contrary, but third parties might still be able to rely on the "appearance" of authority unless they were aware of the specific instructions.

Customary authority

In addition to these fundamental ideas on implied authority, many rules as to whether particular powers have been given to the agent are generally agreed on, through long-established usage and custom and by expression in the *Restatement of Agency*. For instance, once an agency relationship has been established, notice to the agent is effectively notice to the principal, as to those facts related to the conduct of the agency. Likewise, admission by the agent, as to matters within the scope of that person's authority, bind the principal. And, although there are some earlier cases to the contrary, most courts today would probably hold the principal liable for representations made by the agent about the subject matter of the agency.

Third parties dealing with agents should be particularly careful about making payments to them, since the courts are reluctant to imply the power to receive payment unless there is a clear industry custom or a history of prior dealing between the parties. Store clerks who sell merchandise usually have the power to receive payments; traveling salespersons who merely solicit orders for goods or services usually do not. An agent who does have authority to receive payments can only accept money, checks (usually), or credit cards (in accordance with the principal's policies). The agent cannot take other forms of property or services in payment unless expressly authorized to do so.

Apparent Authority. Even though the principal did not actually give the alleged agent the express or implied authority to do the acts in question, the principal may be held liable nonetheless if he or she has created the "appearance" of authority. That is, if the principal has created a situation where it appears to a reasonable third party that the agent was authorized to do what he or she did, the principal is estopped to deny that an agency relationship existed once the third party has changed legal position in reliance on the appearances. This may also be called agency by *estoppel.*

Estoppel to deny agency

Apparent authority may arise where secret instructions or limitations of authority are communicated to the agent but not to third parties. Or it may arise where actual authority was terminated (as where the agent was fired) but third parties were not notified of the termination. Apparent authority may also arise from some other business relationship between the "principal" and the "agent" and even in a situation where there is no business relationship between them at all. These points are illustrated by the *Carl Wagner* case and by Problem 5 at the end of this chapter.

CARL WAGNER AND SONS v. APPENDAGEZ, INC.

485 F.Supp. 762 (New York, 1980)

FACTS

Plaintiffs operate four retail clothing stores in the greater New York City area. Defendant Appendagez, Inc. is a Massachusetts corporation which, in 1976, manufactured and sold wholesale a line of jeans, tops, and sweaters under the brand name "Faded Glory." Plaintiffs commenced this action in New York State Supreme Court, New York County, to recover compensatory and punitive damages arising out of defendant's alleged failure to fill and ship orders submitted by plaintiffs. Plaintiffs also asserted that defendant's failure to ship the goods ordered resulted from plaintiffs' refusal to sell at a fixed price as demanded by defendant, in violation of New York State's antitrust statute, referred to as the Donnelly Act. On this aspect of the case, plaintiffs claim treble damages.

Defendant removed the case to the U.S. District Court on the basis of diversity of citizenship. The parties waived a jury.

During 1976 the plaintiffs submitted a series of orders to Appendagez. Some of those orders were filled and the goods shipped; other orders were not filled. Appendagez received orders from the four plaintiffs totalling $25,089; filled orders totalling $5,484.50, the goods called for by such orders being shipped to plaintiffs; and refused to fill orders totalling the balance of $19,604.50.

The Wagner brothers first became aware of Appendagez's "Faded Glory" line when they observed it in early 1976 on display at one of the numerous trade shows in New York City organized by the industry. They placed orders then and there. Aaron Wagner spoke to an Appendagez representative from New England, who waited on him because he was free at the time. Ordinarily, orders are placed with salesmen who cover the particular geographic area. The initial orders were written for the Myrtle Avenue store in the name of a salesman, a Mr. Segal, who was the salesman for the Brooklyn territory at that time. Segal's initial orders for the Myrtle Avenue store were dated January 14, 1976. Those orders were filled.

Thereafter, plaintiffs planned the opening of the new store in Cedarhurst (which in point of fact opened in early April of 1976). The Wagners wished to feature the "Faded Glory" line at their new Cedarhurst location, which was in a high-income, sophisticated area. Aaron Wagner telephoned the corporate offices of Appendagez and asked to be placed in communication with the Appendagez salesman covering that area. This inquiry produced a visit, at the Cedarhurst location, from one Alan Friedman, who identified himself to Aaron Wagner as the Long Island salesman for Appendagez. Upon hearing of the other three stores, Friedman advised that he would write orders for all four stores, billing them through the Wagner Bros. Haberdashery account in Cedarhurst, so that the Wagners could examine the entire line at one time and there would be only one billing address. The Wagners agreed to this procedure. A number of orders were placed with Appendagez, through Friedman, for the four stores. To the extent that those orders were unfilled, they form the subject matter of this action.

Orders were written up by Friedman on a printed order form prepared by Appendagez. There is no statement to the effect that orders are subject to acceptance by Appendagez at Norwood before they become binding upon the seller.

Friedman advised Aaron Wagner that the policy of Appendagez required plaintiffs to sell the "Faded Glory" line at "keystone" prices, an industry term meaning a 100 percent advance over the retailer's cost. The Cedarhurst store began to sell the line at keystone, but the Wagners observed that the line was being sold at discount elsewhere in the area. Concerned with the competitive effect upon their new venture, the Wagners began to sell "Faded Glory" items at a mark-up of only 80 percent over wholesale price. The Cedarhurst store featured the line, at discount prices, in its advertising and display windows. This produced a vehement objection from Friedman, who in the late spring came to the Cedarhurst store, photographed the windows in which "Faded Glory" items were displayed at discount, and then had a heated discussion with Albert Wagner and Robert Ernst, the assistant manager of the store. Friedman said that a number of other accounts had complained to Earl Nash, the northeast regional sales manager of Appendagez, about plaintiffs' discounting the "Faded Glory" line. Friedman stated that if plaintiffs did not sell the line at keystone, Appendagez would not fill their orders. Albert Wagner stressed the competitive necessity to discount. The discussion, described at trial by both Albert Wagner and Ernst, was heated. Jacob Wagner, who had seen his brother Albert, Ernst, and Friedman go into the store's office, could hear voices raised in anger through the closed door. At about the time of this incident, plaintiffs began to encounter delays in receiving shipments.

Plaintiffs retained counsel, who under date of May 27, 1976, wrote to Appendagez at Norwood to protest its decision "not to sell your merchandise to any and all of my clients' stores for the reason my client will not sell at your fixed price. . . ."

ISSUE   Was there a contract executed between plaintiff and defendant's salesman? Also, was there a violation of the New York State Antitrust law?

DECISION   Yes, a contract was executed as the salesman had apparent authority to execute a contract. Yes, there was a violation of the New York antitrust law and the District Court judge awarded treble damages.

REASONS   District Court Judge Haight heard the testimony and gave the following opinion: "Appendagez's threshold contention is that the purchase orders did not give rise to binding contracts until they were accepted for shipment at the Appendagez offices in

Norwood. If no contractual obligations came into existence unless and until Appendagez accepted the purchase orders generated by salesmen, such as Friedman, then of course the case is at an end, since the purchase orders were not accepted by Appendagez, shipments were not made, and no contractual relationships came into existence.

"The rights and obligations of the parties are governed by the Uniform Commercial Code, as enacted in the State of New York. . . . In the case at bar, the issue is whether the purchase orders, prepared and signed by Friedman, constitute writings signed by an 'authorized agent' of Appendagez.

"Appendagez argues that this question must be answered in the negative, since the company did not endow its salesmen with authority to accept orders in the field. I accept this proposition, as a matter of Appendagez's internal policies. But the argument overlooks the familiar principle of apparent authority, defined by the Restatement of the Law of Agency, Second at Section 8 as:

> [T]he power to affect the legal relations of another person by transactions with third persons, professedly as agent for the other, arising from and in accordance with other's manifestations to such third persons.

In the case at bar, the Wagners wished to make further purchases from Appendagez. Aaron Wagner telephoned the offices of the company, made that desire known, and asked that the appropriate salesman call upon him. That produced Alan Friedman, complete with order forms, which were completed, Friedman returning to the plaintiffs what was designated as a 'confirmation copy.' No notice was given to plaintiffs, either orally or in writing on the order form or elsewhere, that the salesman's authority was limited, and that Appendagez did not consider itself bound by the orders until approved at the home office. In these circumstances, Friedman arrived at plaintiff's premises clothed in the apparent authority to accept orders from plaintiffs binding upon Appendagez; and there were no contrary, outward manifestations in respect of that authority.

"The internal limitations which Appendagez placed upon the authority of its salesmen are irrelevant because such limitations were not communicated to the plaintiffs. . . . This principle is illustrated by a wide variety of New York decisions. . . . I am mindful of Appendagez's contention that acceptance of a salesman's orders at the home office, as a condition precedent to a binding contract, is so well known in the industry that plaintiff must have known of it. To be sure, the terms of an agreement 'may be explained or supplemented by . . . usage of trade,' UCC Section 2–202(a). The 'usage of trade' concept is defined by UCC Section 1–205(2). . . . In the case at bar, Appendagez, seeking by trade usage to avoid contractual obligations which would otherwise arise from the writings and attendant circumstances, bears the burden of proving the 'existence and scope of such a usage.' It has failed to do so. The only witness giving evidence on the point was Nash. While he testified that in his experience with several clothing companies, including Appendagez, comparable order forms were not regarded as binding until approved by the home office, he also acknowledged on cross-examination that other companies specifically provided in their order forms that the orders were 'subject to acceptance at home office.' That concession is fatal to defendant's contention that everyone in the industry should have known that home office acceptance was a condition precedent to a binding contract, even if neither the salesman nor the order form gave notice of the condition to purchasers. . . .

"For comparable reasons, Appendagez's internal credit limitations placed upon plaintiffs' account is not of legal significance. Not only did Appendagez fail to advise plaintiffs of that credit limitation, their salesman cheerfully wrote up orders which substantially exceeded it. If Appendagez had advised plaintiffs of the credit limitations and given them an opportunity to meet the situation by further economic arrangements, the case would be different. In point of fact, Appendagez did neither; and in the circumstances of the case cannot plead its internal, uncommunicated credit limitation as justification for a refusal to recognize contractual obligations.

"I have found that Appendagez refused to fill plaintiffs' orders because plaintiffs refused to agree that they would sell the 'Faded Glory' line at keystone prices. Appendagez could not legally implement that policy in view of the New York fair trade law. . . .

"For the foregoing reasons, plaintiffs are entitled to recover on their causes of action for damages resulting from defendant's failure to ship goods which plaintiffs had ordered. . . .

"Defendant's failure to ship the goods covered by the purchase orders constituted action which is forbidden by the Donnelly Act, N.Y. General Business Law Section 340, and accordingly plaintiffs are entitled to recover treble damages. Plaintiffs are not entitled to recover punitive damages in addition to treble damages."

Ratification. Finally, the principal may be held liable for an agent's actions on the basis of ratification. Where the agent acted without authority but the principal wishes to accept the results of the agent's action anyway, the principal has the power to do so. In most states the principal must act to ratify before the third party discovers the agent's lack of authority and decides to repudiate the contract. If the principal does so, the third party ends up with exactly the contract he thought he was making and should have no basis for complaint.

Principal's choice

Ratification may be express ("I agree to be bound on this contract"), or it may be implied from the principal's retention of the benefits of the unauthorized transaction or from other conduct of the principal which indicates an intent to be bound to the contract. Obviously, the principal must have knowledge of the transaction when it speaks or acts to ratify; the principal generally will not be held to have ratified something it did not know about. Equally obvious, the principal has to ratify the entire transaction; the principal can't just accept the benefits and refuse to assume the reciprocal obligations. Generally, when the principal does ratify an unauthorized contract, the courts say that the principal has also agreed to accept responsibility for whatever conduct of the agent produced the contract, including false warranties and fraud.

Method of ratification

Ratification, like any of the other cases against the alleged principal, must be proved by evidence; agency is not necessarily assumed just because some other relationship exists. Generally, to be ratifiable, the act must be one which the principal could have authorized when it was done and when it is ratified.

■ UNDISCLOSED PRINCIPAL

A principal is "undisclosed" when the third party is unaware of the principal's existence or identity; that is, the third party either doesn't know that an agent is being dealt with or knows that an agent is being dealt with but doesn't know whom the agent represents. In most cases it probably makes no difference to the third party who is being dealt with, as long as the third party gets the contracted return performance. An undisclosed principal is given substantially the same rights to enforce the contract as is a disclosed principal.

Limits on enforcement by UDP

Because in certain circumstances it would be unfair to force the third party to do business with an undisclosed principal, the courts have worked out some limitations. These limitations are much the same as the limitations covering the assignment of contract rights. For instance, a third party cannot be forced to perform personal services for an undisclosed principal, or to loan an undisclosed principal money, or to sell to an undisclosed principal on credit. In such cases the third party's rights might be prejudiced by being forced to do business with someone other than the party believed to have been contracted with—the agent. A court may also refuse to force the third party to perform for an undisclosed principal where both the principal and the agent were aware that the third party would have refused to make the contract if the principal's identity had been disclosed.

Third party's choice

To make sure that the third party's rights are fully protected, the third party is given the choice of holding *either* the agent *or* the undisclosed principal liable for the promised return performance, once the third party discovers the principal's identity. This election may be made either expressly or impliedly, after the principal becomes known. The undisclosed principal is not liable to the third party under such an election where the third party has already received full performance under the contract, where the principal has already settled accounts with the agent on the basis of conduct by the third party, or where the principal's name does not appear on a negotiable instrument (because of the special liability rules for negotiable instruments).

■ PRINCIPAL'S LIABILITY FOR AGENT'S TORTS

When a person conducts affairs through agents or employees, the doctrine of *respondeat superior* holds the person liable for any wrongs they commit in trying to accomplish that person's business. Agents or employees are, of course, always liable for their own torts. The only question is whether the torts were committed within the "scope of employment" or the "scope of authority," so that the principal/employer is also liable. This is a form of vicarious liability—that is, liability for the wrongful acts of another, not for one's own conduct.

Agent's violation of instructions

The main question to be decided in such cases is one of fact: Was the tort committed by the agent or employee within the scope of employment? If the answer is yes, both the principal/employer and the agent/employee are liable for the tort; if the answer is no, the agent/employee is liable but the principal/employer is not. An agent/employee may have been within the "scope of employment" even where that person violated direct instructions, so long as the trier of fact feels that the agent or employee was attempting to accomplish the

Agent's frolic

assigned job. On the other hand, if agents are "off on a frolic of their own," or "doing their own thing," the principal is not liable for their actions. The "frolic" rule, however, may be subject to special motor vehicle statutory liabilities.

Agent's personal motives

Two other important variables in deciding the scope of authority question are the character and the location of the tort. If the tort was intentionally committed, rather than just negligence, the agent/employee may have been motivated by personal reasons rather than the employer's needs; if the intentional tort was so motivated, the employer ought not be held liable. The place where the tort occurred may be important in proving its connection with the principal/employer's business. However, acts on the "premises" may not be within the scope of employment. These fact issues are discussed in the following case.

MARBURY MANAGEMENT, INC. v. KOHN

629 F.2d 705 (U.S. Second Circuit, 1980)

FACTS

Marbury Management, Inc. and Harry Bader sued Alfred Kohn and Wood, Walker & Co., the brokerage house that employed Kohn, for losses incurred on securities purchased through Wood, Walker allegedly on the faith of Kohn's representations that he was a "lawfully licensed registered representative," authorized to transact buy and sell orders on behalf of Wood, Walker. After a nonjury trial before the Honorable Lee P. Gagliardi, District Judge, the court found that Kohn was employed by Wood, Walker as a trainee and that his repeated statements that he was a stockbroker and his use of a business card stating that he was a "portfolio management specialist" were undeniably false; the court found further that Kohn made the statements with intent to deceive, manipulate, or defraud in making them and that his misstatements were material. The court found that Kohn's misrepresentations about his employment status caused Marbury and Bader to purchase securities from Kohn between summer 1967 and April 1969. The District Court also found that the predictive statements Kohn made about various securities were not fraudulently made, and that there was no evidence that they were made without a firm basis.

Judge Gagliardi dismissed the plaintiffs' claims against Wood, Walker on the grounds of plaintiffs' failure to prove that Wood, Walker participated in the fraudulent manipulation or intended to deceive plaintiffs. Treating plaintiffs as basing their claims against Wood, Walker solely on the theory that the firm aided and abetted Kohn's fraud, the court found that the evidence supported neither a finding of conscious wrongful participation by the firm nor a legally equivalent recklessness but at best a finding of negligence in supervision. Plaintiffs appealed.

ISSUE

Was Wood, Walker and Co., the employer of Mr. Kohn, liable for Mr. Kohn's actions when he falsely held himself out to be a "lawfully licensed registered representative," when in fact he was not?

DECISION

Yes. Judgment of trial court is reversed and a new trial is granted.

REASONS

Judge Dooling, speaking for the court, said:

"The court did not consider Wood, Walker's possible liability under the *respondeat superior* theory, or as a 'controlling person' under Section 20(a) of the Securities Act of 1934. . . . It is concluded on this branch of the case, that the court's disposition of the 'aider and abettor' issues was correct, but that it was error, on the record before the court, not to consider and determine whether Wood, Walker was liable as a controlling person or as Kohn's employer. . . .

"There was evidence of Kohn's hiring, his compensation, his authority to accept orders over the telephone at the firm's Bronx office, the execution by Wood, Walker of the orders Kohn obtained from plaintiffs, the fact that Wood, Walker received the brokerage commission on all the transactions, the extent to which and the circumstances in which Kohn was authorized to recommend securities to the firm's customers, the uncertain provenance of Kohn's Wood, Walker business card, and the relation of the Bronx office of Wood, Walker to its main office. . . .

"While the precise standard of supervision required of broker-dealers to make good the good faith defense of Section 20(a) is uncertain, where, as in the present case, the erring salesman completes the transactions through the employing brokerage house and the brokerage house receives a commission on the transactions, the burden of proving good faith is shifted to the brokerage house . . . and requires it to show at least that it has not been negligent in supervision . . . and that it has maintained and enforced a reasonable and proper system of supervision and internal control over sales personnel. . . . That Wood, Walker has successfully met the charge that it aided and abetted Kohn does not establish that it has borne the burden of proving 'good faith' under the last clause of Section 20(a). . . .

"Different considerations control the application of *respondeat superior* principles. Here the concern is simply with scope or course of employment and whether the acts of the employee Kohn can fairly be considered to be within the scope of his employment. . . . The evidence of record in the present case presents substantial issues of credibility and interpretation, but it indicates, if taken at face value, that Kohn at all times acted as an employee of Wood, Walker and accounted to Wood, Walker for the transactions. The evidence contains no indication that he profited by any of the transactions other than by reason of his compensation from Wood, Walker as one of its employees. Whatever the specific limitations on his authority as between him and his employer, the evidence, again, indicates, although with some uncertainty, that it was his function as a trainee to be an intermediary in the making of transactions in securities, but that there were certain limitations on the manner in which he was to carry on his activities. Kohn's deviant conduct, while it may have induced the purchase of securities that would not otherwise have been purchased, did not appear, on the record made at the trial, to mark a deviation from Kohn's services to his employer. Arguably, what he did was done in Wood, Walker's service, though it was done badly and contrary to the practices of the industry and the standing instructions of the firm. The record on the *respondeat superior* issue more than sufficed to require the trier of the fact to dispose of the issue on the merits.

"The judgment against defendant Kohn is affirmed and the judgment in favor of Wood, Walker & Co. is reversed, and a new trial of the claims of Marbury Management and Harry Bader against Wood, Walker & Co. is granted."

▪ TERMINATION OF THE AGENCY RELATIONSHIP

Power to terminate

Right to terminate

In discussing the termination of the agency relationship, we must first distinguish between the principal's *power* to terminate and the principal's *right* to do so. As a rule, the principal has the power to terminate the agency at any time by revocation, provided the principal gives proper notice of termination to the agent and to third parties. Whether the principal also has the right to do so depends on the principal's arrangement with the agent. If there is a contract between them, the principal's wrongful termination may make the principal liable to the agent for breach, even though the agent's power to make contracts with third parties has been effectively terminated. The same distinction applies to the agent; the agent can effectively terminate the relationship at any time by simply refusing to continue as agent but may be liable to the principal for breach of contract.

The agency relationship may also be terminated, without liability for breach, by mutual agreement between the principal and the agent, by fulfillment of the purpose of the agency, or by expiration of an agreed duration. An agency may also be terminated without liability by the same sort of "impossibility" excuses as apply to contracts generally: the death, insanity, or bankruptcy of either party; the subsequent illegality of the agency's purpose; the destruction of the subject matter of the agency; a substantial change in business conditions; or war.

Notice of Termination. Generally, where termination has occurred by the act of either the principal or the agent, or by their mutual agreement, notice of the termination must be given to third parties. Otherwise, the agent may still have apparent authority to continue business as usual. Any third party who has actually dealt with the agent as an agent in the past must be given actual notice, either orally or in writing. A newspaper ad or similar "constructive notice" is sufficient for all other third parties, whether or not they ever read the ad or have it called to their attention. Where the termination of an agency occurs by "operation of law," no notice at all need be given to third parties, except that an insane principal is bound on contracts made by third parties in good faith before that person is judicially declared incompetent or before the third parties receive other notice of the principal's incapacity.

Agency Coupled with an Interest. As an exception to the general rule which gives the principal the power to revoke an agency at any time, the principal cannot revoke an agency in which the agent has a personal interest in the subject matter—an *agency coupled with an interest.* This phrase describes the cases where the agent is more than just a hired hand, where there is some other underlying relationship between the parties—most typically, a debtor-creditor relationship. The agency power has been given to the agent as the creditor of the principal, to try to make sure that the agent gets paid. In such cases, the principal cannot revoke the agent's power and the agent's power is not terminated by the subsequent incapacity of either party.

Most courts have held that the agent's power is terminated by the principal's death unless the principal has also transferred some sort of ownership interest in the subject matter to the agent. In other words, if the principal had merely authorized the agent to sell a specific piece of property to pay the principal's debt to the agent, the principal's death would terminate the power to sell; if the principal had given the agent a mortgage on the property (an "interest") plus the power to sell, the principal's death would not terminate that power.

Since the intent of the parties is basically the same in both cases, some modern decisions do not follow this distinction and hold that either a power given as security or a power "coupled with an interest" would survive the principal's death.

Such powers to sell collateral in the event of default would be terminated by the principal's bankruptcy, unless a proper filing of the security agreement or a financing statement has been made or other steps have been taken in accordance with bankruptcy law to establish priority over other creditors.

▪ SIGNIFICANCE OF THIS CHAPTER

Many business activities are carried on through other persons. Each of us, living in a complex society, needs to be aware of the basic rules for determining when one person is responsible for the actions of another. An important distinction exists between principals who employ agents and persons who employ independent contractors. Likewise, there are different rules for determining contract and tort liability for the actions of agents. Since we will all be dealing with and through agents on many occasions, we need to know how these basic rules work.

DISCUSSION CASE

HANSON v. KYNAST
494 N.E.2d 1091 (Ohio, 1986)

FACTS: On May 1, 1982, appellee, Brian K. Hanson, sustained a paralyzing injury while playing in a lacrosse game between Ohio State University and Ashland University, Inc. at the Ashland lacrosse field. During the game Roger Allen, an OSU player, intercepted an Ashland player's pass and scored a goal. As Allen was scoring the goal, he was body-checked from behind by Ashland defender William D. Kynast. Allen fell and Kynast allegedly stood over Allen taunting him. Brian Hanson saw the contact and Kynast's subsequent behavior. Concerned for Allen's welfare, Hanson grabbed Kynast from the side or back and held him in a bear hug. Kynast immediately twisted and threw Hanson off his back. Hanson's head struck the ground, and he sustained serious injuries.

The trainers for both teams came onto the field to attend Hanson. After discovering the seriousness of his injury (Hanson was numb and could not move), an assistant trainer for Ashland was sent to telephone the fire department for an ambulance.

Upon arriving on the scene, the ambulance driver discovered that the main entrance to the playing field was blocked by an illegally parked automobile. As a result, the ambulance driver had to find another entrance.

After immobilizing Hanson, the attendants transported him to Ashland Samaritan Hospital where he remained for almost an hour. He was then transferred to Mansfield General Hospital for surgery. The operation took place at approximately 11 P.M., more than five hours after he was taken from the first hospital. The surgery successfully relieved vascular compression thus preventing possible brain damage. Hanson, however, had sustained a serious spinal cord injury on impact. It was determined that he had suffered a compression fracture of his sixth vertebra and, as a result, Hanson is now an incomplete quadriplegic.

On December 13, 1983, Brian Hanson filed an amended complaint in the Court of Common Pleas of Ashland County against William Kynast and Ashland University, Inc. On April 11, 1984, Ashland filed a motion for summary judgment. The trial court granted Ashland's motion. In a split decision, the Court of Appeals reversed the trial court's judgment, holding that genuine issues of fact existed on the question of agency and upon Ashland's duty to provide medical personnel at the game.

■

Justice Parrino:

The first issue to be decided is whether the relationship of principal and agent existed between Kynast and Ashland. Because of the absence of proof as to the existence of a principal-agent relationship, the trial court essentially found as a matter of law that Ashland was not bound by Kynast's conduct under the doctrine of *respondeat superior*. We agree.

This court has held that the relationship of principal and agent or master and servant exists only when one party exercises the right of control over the actions of another, and those actions are directed toward the attainment of an objective which the former seeks. . . . Therefore, a principal-agent relationship can be found in the instant case only if Kynast were under the control of Ashland, and if he took some action directed toward the attainment of Ashland's objective.

In order to make this determination we must examine the relevant documentary evidence produced before the trial court. A review of the evidence reveals that William Kynast expressed an interest in Ashland when he was in high school. He requested and received written information from the university, and he spoke with Ashland lacrosse coach Dick Fahrney. In his deposition Kynast testified that he chose Ashland because it had a good business school, he could live away from home, and he would be able to play lacrosse. He also testified that no promises were made to him by any Ashland official to induce him to attend the university.

Kynast attended Ashland for three semesters, starting in August 1981. He financed his education through bank loans and with the assistance of his parents. While at Ashland, Kynast decided to play lacrosse; however, he was never obligated to play lacrosse for the university. In addition, Kynast did not receive a scholarship, he used his own equipment while playing, and he was not compensated for his participation.

Lacrosse was instituted at Ashland in an effort to meet the needs of students, especially those coming from the East Coast where lacrosse is a popular sport. Ashland provides a coach and the players are each given a game shirt which displays the university's name. The players also received free transportation to games at other schools, and on one occasion while Kynast played for Ashland, they received overnight lodging on a road trip. No admission fee is charged at the home games.

This court is of the opinion that this relationship between Kynast and Ashland is a relationship common to many students attending universities. A university offers a diversified educational experience which includes classroom instruction in a great variety of subjects as well as optional participation in events such as school clubs and intramural and intercollegiate sports. All of these offerings are designed to expand and enrich a student's overall educational experience. Students evaluate and determine which university best meets their needs and then pay a fee to attend that university. The relationship formed under these conditions has previously been characterized as contractual. . . . The student pays a fee and agrees to abide by the university rules. In exchange, the university provides the student with a worthwhile education.

This relationship does not constitute a principal-agent relationship. The student is a buyer of education rather than an agent. *Restatement of the Law of Agency, Second,* (1958) 73, Section 14J, states that a buyer retains goods primarily for his own benefit, while an agent is one who retains goods primarily for the benefit of the one who delivers those goods. In the instant case, the "goods" to be delivered is an education, and the university delivers that education to the student for a fee. It is clear that a student retains the benefit of that education for himself rather than for the university. . . .

In summary, the relationship discussed above constitutes a contractual one between the student and his university. The university is selling and the student is buying an education, and the formation of a principal-agent relationship was not intended, nor was one established, between the parties.

The appellee, however, maintains that Kynast's participation in lacrosse converted his status from the usual university-student relationship to that of principal-agent due to the control exercised by the lacrosse coach over Kynast and because his participation in lacrosse resulted in beneficial publicity of Ashland. We disagree. In applying the law of agency to the facts of this case, we must conclude that Kynast was not controlled by Ashland and that he was not playing the game for the school's benefit.

The degree of control necessary to establish agency has not been clearly defined. . . . Instead, courts have generally examined various factors in determining whether the requisite amount of control exists. One such factor is whether the individual is performing in the course of the principal's business rather than in some ancillary capacity. . . . In the case at bar, Kynast was not performing in the course of the principal's business: he was not educating students. On the contrary, he was participating in one of the educationally related opportunities offered by the university. Another factor to be considered is whether the individual was receiving any compensation from the principal. . . . It is undisputed that Kynast was never compensated for playing on the Ashland lacrosse team. A third factor is whether the principal supplied the tools and the place of work in the normal course of the relationship. . . . Kynast supplied his own equipment in order to play lacrosse. The university did, however, provide the playing field.

A review of these factors clearly shows that Kynast was not controlled by Ashland for the purpose of establishing an agency relationship. The control exerted over Kynast by the university—the Ashland coach running the lacrosse team—was merely incidental to the educational opportunity in which Kynast *voluntarily* participated. A limited amount of control is necessary to assure that each student is afforded a fair opportunity to benefit from the activity. The athletic guidance that was exercised by Ashland in this case does not satisfy the control element required to establish agency.

Further, the documentary evidence considered in determining appellee's motion for summary judgment clearly establishes that Kynast's activity was not directed toward the attainment of an objective by Ashland. Lacrosse at Ashland is not an income-producing sport. In fact, as previously noted, an admission fee is not charged to attend the games. The evidence established that Ashland initiated lacrosse for the benefit of the students wishing to play that game; it is simply one of the many educational opportunities offered to any Ashland student.

The appellee's claim that Ashland derived a benefit through the publicity the team gathered is not persuasive. . . . In the instant case, there is no evidence that Ashland derived a benefit from publicity; nor is there evidence that Kynast participated in lacrosse so that Ashland could benefit from publicity. Kynast engaged in lacrosse voluntarily, and for *his own* enjoyment. Under such a circumstance no agency relationship is created.

To summarize, we conclude that a student who attends a university of his choice, receives no scholarship or compensation, voluntarily becomes a member of the university lacrosse team that engages in intercollegiate contests with other universities for which games no attendance fee is charged, who purchases his own equipment and who receives instructions from a coach while preparing for and playing such games, but is not otherwise controlled by the coach, and who participates in the game as part of his total educational experience while attending school, is not the agent of the university at the time he is playing the game of lacrosse. Thus, appellee's claim that Ashland was liable for Kynast's wrongful acts through the doctrine of *respondeat superior* was properly rejected, and the trial court properly entered summary judgment for appellant on this issue.

The second and final issue to be resolved is whether the trial court properly entered summary judgment for Ashland upon Hanson's claims that Ashland was negligent for failing to have an ambulance and medical personnel at the game and for permitting an illegally parked car to block the playing field's entrance. The appellee maintains that such negligence resulted in the delay of his treatment.

In order to successfully establish negligence, the appellee must prove the existence of the following elements: (1) a duty owed by Ashland to Hanson, (2) a breach of this duty by Ashland, and (3) that Hanson's injuries were a proximate result of Ashland's conduct. . . . It is unnecessary at this time to consider whether genuine issues of fact existed as to the first two elements of negligence for the reason that the uncontradicted evidence submitted by Ashland established that no damages proximately resulted from Ashland's alleged wrongdoing.

Submitted in support of Ashland's motion for summary judgment was an affidavit from Dr. Thomas L. Strachan stating that Hanson's injury was sustained at the moment his head hit the ground. Dr. Strachan further stated that there was no evidence of neurological deterioration subsequent to impact; in other words, Hanson did not suffer additional injury as a proximate result of any delay in treatment. The trial court granted Hanson a continuance of 90 days for the purpose of conducting additional discovery. This gave [Hanson] the opportunity to find and offer expert testimony refuting Dr. Strachan's opinion. Hanson did not produce that evidence; hence, Dr. Strachan's opinion is unrebutted.

One of the elements necessary to establish negligence was not present; therefore, as a matter of law, the trial court properly granted Ashland's motion for summary judgment on Hanson's claims of negligence.

Accordingly, the judgment of the Court of Appeals is reversed.

■ IMPORTANT TERMS AND CONCEPTS

agency
independent contractor
agency relationship
franchisees as independent contractors
nondelegable duties
express authority
apparent authority
estoppel
undisclosed principal
termination of agency relationship
principal/agent
employee
employer-employee relationship
extra hazardous activities
power of attorney
implied authority
ratification
principal's liability for agent's torts
notice requirement
agency coupled with an interest

■ QUESTIONS AND PROBLEMS FOR DISCUSSION

1. How is an agency relationship created? How can an agency relationship be terminated?
2. If you purchase a McDonald's hamburger franchise to operate a McDonald's restaurant in Home Town, USA, will you be considered an independent contractor or an agent of the franchisor? What factors would be important to consider before answering this question?
3. You hire me to manage 20 apartment rental units which you own. I get a free apartment to live in and a small monthly salary. You didn't specify what authority I have; you just told me to collect the rents and manage the property. What implied authority do I have?
4. Generally speaking, an employer is responsible for torts committed by his or her agent or employee provided the agent or employee was acting in the scope of the employment. Are there any exceptions to this general rule? Explain.
5. On December 23, Mr. Kanelles entered the Hotel Ohio, operated by Mrs. Ida Locke, in downtown Cleveland. The one man who was in the lobby (it was 1 A.M.) got up out of his chair, came over to the registration desk, had Kanelles register, got a room key, and gave it to him. Kanelles then said he wanted to leave his valuables in the hotel safe, so he gave the man a diamond pin, two $5 checks, and $484 in cash. The man gave him a receipt signed: "Mrs. Locke—Hotel Ohio. J. C. Clemens." The man (Clemens) was merely a roomer in the hotel, and he left during the night with Kanelles' valuables. When Mrs. Locke failed to make good the loss, Kanelles sued her. How should this case be decided? Explain.
6. Cloris James opened a Servu Revolving Charge Account at the local Servu Store. She signed the application "Mrs. Ralph James." Cloris made over $600

worth of credit purchases on the account before Servu terminated her charging privileges because of nonpayment. Cloris has no separate job and no available personal assets. Servu sued her husband, Ralph, for the balance due on the account. There is no indication that Ralph ever used the charge account or that he ever made any of the payments credited on it. What is the result, and why?

7. Lucious, the sales manager, left his home one evening, supposedly to meet a client of his construction firm employer at a local restaurant. Lucious told his wife and the maid where he was going. When the maid asked when she could get her paycheck for the week, Lucious told her that he'd be back in a little while and write out her paycheck then. Less than an hour later, Lucious was shot and killed by an unknown person. When his wife filed for death benefits under workers' compensation, her claim was opposed by the employer. There was no record at Lucious' office of any such business appointment, nor did anyone at the construction firm know anything about it. (Workers' compensation, of course, covers only on-the-job injuries to employees.) Should Lucious' widow collect death benefits? Why or why not? Would it make any difference if he had been killed at the restaurant where he said he was going to be? Why?

8. Dewey owned an ice-cream parlor. He bought his ice cream from Dairy Products, Inc. The ice cream was delivered twice a week, as ordered by Dewey, by a Dairy truck driver who had instructions to collect the price when he left the ice cream. One hot July day, Dewey refused to accept a delivery of ice cream, saying it was "soft." Bonzo, the truck driver, said Dewey could do as he wished with the ice cream but that the price had to be paid. Dewey refused to pay, so Bonzo moved toward the cash register. Dewey was quicker and locked the cash register before Bonzo could take out any money. Bonzo then picked up the cash register and started to walk out with it. Dewey grabbed him, and they started to fight. Bonzo yelled for Herman, his assistant, who had been waiting on the truck, and the two of them beat Dewey severely. Dewey sues Dairy for damages. What is the result, and why?

40

Agency—Other
Legal Relationships

CHAPTER OBJECTIVES
THIS CHAPTER WILL:

- Discuss the duties and liabilities a principal has to the agent.
- Discuss the duties and liabilities an agent has to the principal.
- Discuss the liability an agent may have to a third party.
- Discuss the liability a third party may have to an agent.

▪ DUTIES AND LIABILITIES OF PRINCIPAL TO AGENT

Principal's Duty to Compensate Agent. Many of the cases in which an agent is suing a principal involve the principal's duty to compensate the agent. Based on their contract, the principal owes the agent whatever salary or commission was agreed on for doing the acts required. It is assumed that the principal should reimburse the agent for any expenses which the agent reasonably and necessarily incurred in carrying out the principal's instructions. If the agent is to pay expenses, this should be stated in the contract. In the absence of any specific agreement, it is also assumed that the agent should be reimbursed for any personal loss or damage sustained as a result of following the principal's instructions.

Compensation of real estate brokers

Special compensation rules apply to real estate brokers. Usually the broker does not actually have the power to sell the listed property but only to conduct negotiations with prospective buyers. The broker, therefore, has normally earned the commission by "bringing in a deal," that is, when the broker produces a buyer who is ready, willing, and able to meet the purchase terms specified by the seller in the listing agreement. The following case shows the significance of these special rules for brokers.

HECHT v. MELLER

244 N.E.2d 77 (New York, 1968)

FACTS

Helen Hecht, the plaintiff, a real estate broker, entered into a written contract with Herbert and Joyce Meller, the defendants, by which she became the exclusive selling agent for the sale of their residence. Through the plaintiff's efforts suitable buyers were introduced to the Mellers, and on May 30, 1963, a contract for the sale of the property was signed which acknowledged that Hecht had brought the parties together, established a sale price of $60,000, and set August 1 as the closing date.

On July 20, without fault of either party, the dwelling house on the property was substantially destroyed by fire. The buyers elected to rescind the contract, as provided for by New York State statutory law. The Mellers returned the buyers' down payment. The present action was commenced by the real estate broker when the sellers refused to pay the $3,600 commission allegedly earned by the broker in bringing the parties together. The lower court found for the plaintiff. The Appellate Division reversed the lower court. The plaintiff then appealed that decision to the Court of Appeals of New York.

ISSUE

Is a real estate agent entitled to a commission on the sale of real estate if the contract was rescinded because the residence burned down before closing?

DECISION

Yes. Judgment of the Appellate Division is reversed. Judgment of the trial court is reinstated.

🏛 REASONS

Judge Keating gave the opinion of the court:

"This appeal presents a question of first impression: Is a real estate broker entitled to commissions on the sale of real property if the purchaser asserts a statutory privilege to rescind the contract of sale because the property has been substantially destroyed by fire after the contract was executed, but before the buyer took title or possession? . . .

"The statutory provision applicable to the realty contract under consideration provides that any contract for the purchase and sale of realty shall be interpreted, unless the contract expressly provides otherwise, as including an agreement that the vendor cannot enforce the contract of sale if the property is substantially destroyed and the vendee has taken neither the legal title nor possession of the property. This section was enacted to alter the common-law rule which, absent any agreement to the contrary, cast the risk of destruction of the property between the time the contract of sale was entered into and passing of title upon the vendee. . . . The force of the enactment, however, did not render realty contracts unenforceable, but rather, simply bestowed a privilege on vendees to rescind the contract.

"Examination of the legislative history of the Uniform Vendor and Purchaser Risk Act . . . discloses no evidence that the legislature intended to shift the risk of payment of earned brokerage commissions, because of the assertion of a vendee's privilege, from the seller to a business loss of the broker. Professor Williston, the author of the provision, proposed its promulgation to the Commissioners on Uniform Laws in order to abrogate the injustice caused by the common-law rule which required a vendee to fulfill his contractual obligations even though the property was substantially destroyed and he neither took title nor possession. The announced justification for proposing the provision was the fact that normally a vendee failed to perceive the necessity of insuring the property and thus bore the loss of its destruction. . . . Our legislature adopted the model act in 1936, with minor revision, after the New York Law Revision Commission recommended its enactment. The Law Revision Report stated that the act embodied a 'wise policy of having the party in possession of the property care for it at his own peril.' . . . Thus support cannot be gleaned from the section's legislative history to provide a basis for determining that the enactment was intended by the legislature to alter a seller's preexisting obligation to compensate his broker, who fully performed an independent brokerage agreement.

"This court has consistently stated that a real estate broker's right to commission attaches when he procures a buyer who meets the requirements established by the seller. . . . At the juncture that the broker produces an acceptable buyer he has fully performed his part of the agreement with the vendor and his right to commission becomes enforceable. The broker's ultimate right to compensation has never been held to be dependent upon the performance of the realty contract or the receipt by the seller of the selling price unless the brokerage agreement with the vendor specifically so conditioned payment. . . . As stated in *Gilder* v. *Davis.* . . .: 'If from a defect in the title of the vendor, or a refusal to consummate the contract on the part of the purchaser for any reason in no way attributable to the broker, the sale falls through, nevertheless the broker is entitled to his commissions, for the simple reason that he has performed his contract.' "

Principal's Liability for Breach of Agency Contract. If the principal wrongfully prevents the agent from carrying out their contract and thus earning the agreed compensation, the principal, like any other employer, is liable to the agent for breach. Some of these cases involve an unjustified discharge of the agent; others result from the principal's improper interference with the agent's conduct of the agency, such as failing to provide the agent with new price and product information or attempting to impose arbitrary and discriminatory paperwork requirements.

If the agent fails to meet duties under the contract, the principal may be justified in firing the agent. Generally, if the agency has not been set up for a specific period of time, and therefore is "at will," the agent may be fired at any time, with or without reason, and the agent will have no case for breach of contract. While the following case involves an agent/employee, it does show that there are some "outer limits" on the right to discharge an employee even where the term of employment is "at will." The courts in many states have recognized similar limitations on the ***at-will employment*** doctrine. Some of the state legislatures are considering legislation to prohibit arbitrary dismissals of "at-will" employees. The law on this point is changing very rapidly. Lawsuits may be filed claiming breach of express or implied contract, or under various tort theories, as seen in the *Patton* case.

At-will employment rules

PATTON v. J. C. PENNEY CO.

719 P.2d 854 (Oregon, 1986)

FACTS

David Patton filed suit against J. C. Penney Co. and two supervisors, McKay and Chapin, alleging both "wrongful discharge" from employment and "outrageous conduct." The trial court granted defendants' motion to dismiss for failure to state a claim on both counts.

Plaintiff then appealed to the Court of Appeals. That court affirmed the dismissal of the wrongful discharge claim, but reversed on the intentional infliction of severe emotional distress claim, sending it back for trial in the circuit court.

Defendant J. C. Penney Co. hired plaintiff in 1969. Plaintiff worked in Eugene until 1980 when he was transferred to Portland where he worked as a merchandising manager. In 1981 the store manager, defendant McKay, told plaintiff to break off a social relationship with a female coemployee. Plaintiff responded by telling McKay that he did not socialize with the coemployee at work and that he intended to continue seeing her on his own time. Apparently, the social relationship did not interfere with the plaintiff's performance at work, for during this time he earned several awards for "Merchant of the Month" and one for "Merchant of the Year."

McKay later, while interrogating other employees about whether plaintiff had broken off the relationship, made statements to the effect that if plaintiff wanted to keep working he had to discontinue the relationship. Although no written or unwritten policy, rule, or regulation proscribed socializing between employees, other employees told plaintiff that McKay disfavored plaintiff's fraternization with the female coemployee. Nevertheless, plaintiff continued seeing the coemployee. When McKay warned plaintiff in late 1981 that his job performance was unsatisfactory and that he would be fired if there was no improvement, plaintiff asked for a transfer to another department. McKay denied the request. In February, McKay terminated plaintiff's employment for unsatisfactory job performance. The district manager, defendant Chapin, approved the termination.

ISSUE

Since plaintiff was an employee at will, does he have a cause of action for wrongful discharge and intentional infliction of severe emotional distress?

DECISION

No. Judgment of the court of appeals is reversed as to the intentional infliction of severe emotional distress claim and affirmed as to the wrongful discharge claim.

REASONS

Judge Jones, speaking for the court, stated:

"Generally an employer may discharge an employee at any time and for any reason, absent a contractual, statutory, or constitutional requirement. . . . Termination of employment ordinarily does not create a tortious cause of action. . . . We have set forth exceptions to the general rule which are discussed in a series of cases. . . .

"An employer could be held liable for discharging an employee who refused to sign a false and potentially defamatory statement about a former coemployee. . . . Article I, Section 10, of the Oregon Constitution, recognizes an obligation on members of society not to defame others. . . .

"A wrongful discharge claim may also exist when an employee is fired for pursuing private statutory rights directly relating to the employee's status or role of an employee. . . . In *Holien,* the court found plaintiff's allegations that she was fired for resisting sexual harassment sufficient to state a claim because on-the-job sexual harassment by supervisors is forbidden by state and federal law. . . .

"We have rejected wrongful discharge claims under a third category where the law provides other remedies than a common-law remedy for wrongful discharge. For example, in *Walsh* v. *Consolidated Freightways,* . . . this court found that an additional tort remedy for wrongful discharge was unnecessary when an employee was discharged for complaining about a safety violation for which there were statutory remedies.

"Plaintiff does not allege that his discharge was for pursuing statutory rights related to his status as an employee. Nor does plaintiff allege interference with an interest of public importance equal or analogous to serving on a jury or avoiding false, defamatory remarks. Plaintiff claims that certain of his 'fundamental, inalienable human rights were compromised, put on the auction block, and made the subject of an illicit barter in that he was forced to forego these rights or to purchase them with his job.' He claims that the employer invaded his personal right of privacy and that the employer could not fire him for pursuing a private right. But these claims blur 'rights' against governmental infringement with 'rights' against a private employer. Plaintiff's acts were voluntary, and no state or federal law mandates or prohibits discrimination on that account. It may seem harsh that an employer can fire an employee because of dislike of the employee's personal lifestyle, but because the plaintiff cannot show that the actions fit under an exception to the general rule, plaintiff is subject to the traditional doctrine of 'fire at will.'

"The Court of Appeals is affirmed on this issue.

"Count II of plaintiff's allegations demonstrates that he is attempting to plead the emerging tort of intentional infliction of severe emotional distress, which consists of several elements. First, ordinarily a plaintiff must allege that a defendant intended to inflict severe mental or emotional distress. It is not enough that he intentionally acted in a way that causes such distress. Second, a defendant's act must in fact cause a plaintiff severe mental or emotional distress. Third, a defendant's actions must consist of 'some extraordinary transgression of the bounds of socially tolerable conduct' or the actions must exceed 'any reasonable limit of social toleration.' . . .

"In the case at bar, the alleged manner in which plaintiff was discharged does not reach the level of intolerable conduct described in the aforementioned cases. We agree with the Court of Appeals dissent that McKay's alleged behavior was 'rude, boorish, tyrannical, churlish and mean—and those are its best points,' but that it was not 'outrageous in the extreme,' and that the allegations do not support plaintiff's claim for intentional infliction of severe emotional distress. . . . The Court of Appeals is affirmed as to the wrongful discharge claim and reversed as to the intentional infliction of severe emotional harm claim."

Principal's Liability for Defamation. One way to avoid liability for wrongful or discriminatory discharge of an agent or employee is to show that there was cause for the discharge. To prove that the discharged person's job performance had been unsatisfactory, the principal/employer usually has to produce a written record of warnings and reprimands. Employers are thus motivated to document all wrongful or improper employee actions in each individual's personnel file, just in case. In doing so, however, the employer faces something of a dilemma, since liability can also arise when defamatory statements about the employee are communicated to a third person.

The problem arises in many cases when a former employer is asked for a reference on one of its former employees. In answering such requests, the former employer must make sure that any statements made are absolutely true, and can be verified if necessary. The supervisor in the *Stuempges* case forgot this rule, and liability resulted.

STUEMPGES v. PARKE, DAVIS & COMPANY

297 N.W.2d 252 (Minnesota, 1980)

FACTS   Parke Davis, a pharmaceutical manufacturer, employed Neil Stuempges as one of its Minneapolis sales representatives from 1958 until February 25, 1974, when it asked him to resign or be fired. During the first 15 years of his employment, Stuempges had never been disparaged for his lack of ability as a salesperson and had even received commendations over the years for his outstanding sales record.

In July 1973, Robert Jones became the new district manager of the Minneapolis area in which Stuempges' sales territory was located. From the beginning, they clashed in their approaches to a number of issues.

On February 25, 1974, at Jones's request, Stuempges met with him and Donald Burgett, Jones's immediate supervisor. At this meeting Stuempges was asked to resign and was promised a good recommendation if he did so. If he refused to resign, however, Jones told him that he would be "blackballed" in the industry. Shortly thereafter, Stuempges submitted his resignation.

On March 5, 1974, Stuempges sought assistance in finding another job through Sales Consultants, Inc., an employment agency specializing in sales personnel. He was interviewed by Robert Hammer, at which time he listed Parke Davis as his most recent employer and Jones as his most recent supervisor and gave him permission for Sales Consultants to check his references at Parke Davis. Hammer called Jones for a reference. Jones told Hammer that Stuempges was a poor salesman, not industrious, hard to motivate, could not sell, and that he had been fired and had not just resigned. Hammer refused to try to place Stuempges in a job as a result of this poor recommendation. Stuempges sued Parke Davis & Company alleging he had been defamed by Parke Davis employees. The jury gave Stuempges an award of $17,250 for actual pecuniary loss, $10,500 in compensatory damages, and $10,000 in punitive damages. Defendants appealed.

ISSUE   Is the defendant Parke Davis guilty of defamation as a result of the new manager's comments about Mr. Stuempges? Was the award of punitive damages proper in this case?

DECISION   Yes. Judgment of the trial court is affirmed as to defamation. Yes. Punitive damages were properly awarded to punish defendants for this type of unsanctioned behavior.

REASONS   Chief Justice Sheran, speaking for the court, found the following issues to be decided by this appeal. He listed the issues as follows:

"**1.** Were appellant's statements nondefamatory because they were true?

2. Were the statements qualifiedly privileged and thus not actionable?

3. Did the trial court correctly instruct the jury on the definition of malice?

4. Were the damage awards proper?

"1. The elements of a common law defamation action are well settled. In order for a statement to be considered defamatory it must be communicated to someone other than the plaintiff, it must be false, and it must tend to harm the plaintiff's reputation and to lower him in the estimation of the community. . . . Slanders affecting the plaintiff in his business, trade, profession, office, or calling are slanders per se and thus actionable without any proof of actual damages. . . . Truth, however, is a complete defense, and true statements, however disparaging, are not actionable.

"Although Jones's words to Hammer clearly related to Stuempges' reputation in his profession, Parke Davis contends that they were not slanderous because substantially true. . . . There are indications in the record that Jones himself acknowledged the falsity or at least distortion of his statements to Hammer. The jury accepted Stuempges' version and found the statements made by Jones to Hammer to be false. . . .

"2. Parke Davis also argues that Jones's statements to Hammer are not defamatory because they were conditionally privileged. Thus, even if the statements were slanders per se, by pleading and proving the existence of a conditional privilege, it has rebutted the presumption of common law malice. . . .

"We agree with Park Davis that an employer called upon to give information about a former employee should be protected so that he can give an accurate assessment of the employee's qualifications. It is certainly in the public interest that this kind of information be readily available to prospective employers, and we are concerned that, unless a significant privilege is recognized by the courts, employers will decline to evaluate honestly their former employees' work records. We believe, however, that the falsity of the statements made by Jones to Hammer, after he had on February 25 indicated that he had a favorable impression of Stuempges' capabilities as a salesperson and would give a good recommendation to prospective employers, takes this case out of the realm of privilege. Thus, Parke Davis cannot be relieved of responsibility on the basis of this theory. . . .

"Since the evidence supports a jury find that Jones acted with malice in making the statement to Hammer, it was reasonable for the jury to have determined that the conditional privilege of fair comment concerning the character of a past employee had been abused.

"4. Finally, Parke Davis attacks the jury's award of damages to Stuempges. . . .

"Since media self-censorship is not involved in this case and since 'the imposition of liability for private defamation does not abridge the freedom of public speech or any other freedom protected by the First Amendment,' . . . we are free to permit juries to award punitive damages to punish defendants for this type of unsanctioned behavior."

Employer's Liability under Workers' Compensation

As noted in Chapter 7, an employer may also be held liable for an employee's on-the-job injuries. The employer owes a duty to provide a reasonably safe workplace. This duty is now expressed in state workers' compensation statutes, under which the employer is presumed to be liable for any job-related injuries. These statutes, and the state courts' decisions interpreting them, are not completely uniform. Chronic, long-term conditions such as black lung disease, and asbestosis, and mental illness resulting from job pressures, may or may not be covered. In general, state courts have been quite liberal in applying statutory coverage.

■ DUTIES AND LIABILITIES OF AGENT TO PRINCIPAL

In General. The agency relationship is based upon the trust and confidence that the principal has placed in the agent by giving the agent the power to manage the principal's affairs. The agent is thus a fiduciary, owing to the principal a duty of honesty and fair dealing in their relationship. The following specific aspects of this fiduciary duty may be easier to remember if you recall the boy scout's pledge: "Trustworthy, Loyal, Helpful, Friendly, Courteous, Kind, Obedient, Cheerful, Thrifty, Brave, Clean, and Reverent." Nearly all of these desirable characteristics of a successful scout also apply to the agent.

Loyalty and Good Faith. Loyalty to the principal's interests and good faith in dealing with that person are the most basic parts of the agent's fiduciary duty. Under the rule that a person "cannot faithfully serve two masters," an agent is prohibited from representing two persons with opposing interests, such as the two parties of a business transaction, unless both of them know of the dual agency and agree to it. A principal who does not know of the dual agency can rescind the resulting transaction upon learning the truth. Likewise, the agent can neither buy from, or sell to, himself or herself nor derive any other secret benefit from conducting the principal's affairs. The receipt of secret bribes, payoffs, or presents by the agent from third parties will justify dismissal of the agent and may also involve civil or criminal penalties against the agent. The following case involved a dual agency where the agent acted for both parties in a real estate transaction without disclosing the fact of his dual agency to either party.

No dual agency unless disclosed

TABORSKY v. MATHEWS

121 So.2d 61 (Florida, 1960)

FACTS   Sellers sued to foreclose on a mortgage signed by the purchasers when they purchased certain real estate from the sellers. The real estate agent who acted for defendants was also the agent for the plaintiffs in this transaction. The agent received a commission from both parties, and defendants had no knowledge of the dual agency. Defendants counterclaimed to recover the portion of the purchase price which they paid and asked that the entire transaction be voided and canceled. The plaintiffs won in the lower court. Defendants appealed.

ISSUE   Have the purchasers the right, upon discovering a broker's dual agency, to avoid the sale and purchase-money mortgage?

DECISION   Yes. Judgment reversed.

REASONS   Judge Shannon speaking for the court stated:
"In our jurisprudence it is well established that an agent for one party to a transaction

cannot act for the other party without the consent of both principals. Where an agent assumes to act in such a dual capacity without such assent, the transaction is voidable as a matter of public policy. Perhaps the best statement of the law applicable to the inquiry at bar is that found in *Evans* v. *Brown* . . .: No principle is better settled than that a man cannot be the agent of both the seller and the buyer in the same transaction, without the intelligent consent of both. Loyalty to his trust is the most important duty which the agent owes to his principal. Reliance upon his integrity, fidelity, and ability is the main consideration in the selection of agents; and so careful is the law in guarding this fiduciary relation that it will not allow an agent to act for himself and his principal, nor to act for two principals on opposite sides in the same transaction. In such cases the amount of consideration, the absence of undue advantage, and other like features are wholly immaterial. Nothing will defeat the principal's right of remedy, except his own confirmation, after full knowledge of all the facts."

Who owns secrets?

A related problem, and one which arises with some frequency in a technological society, is the conflict between employer and employee over who owns patents developed by the employee and other "secret" information used by the employee on the job (for example, customer lists). Courts generally hold that the fiduciary duty does not end simply because employment is terminated, and thus the employee (or agent) does not have the right to use formulas, processes, customer lists, or other trade secrets in competition with a former employer. As to patented devices and processes which the employee developed on the job, the employee may become the owner by having them patented in his or her own name, but the employer has a "shop right" to make use of them in the employer's business without paying royalties. Specific language in the employment contract will probably head off most of these problems.

Employment contracts may also contain an agreement by the agent/employee not to compete with the principal/employer after the relationship is terminated. As noted in Chapter 15, such agreements are lawful and enforceable so long as the area and the duration of the restraint are both reasonable. If an unreasonable restraint is included, courts are split as to what should happen. Some courts refuse to enforce the unreasonable restraint at all; others are willing to rewrite it so as to make it reasonable. If the employer materially breaches the employment contract, as by wrongfully discharging the employee, a court could decide that such a restraint clause in the contract was no longer enforceable by the employer. In the absence of such an agreement, an employee (after termination) could go to work for a competitor, but would still not be able to use the former employer's trade secrets.

Care and Skill in a Calling. A person, after accepting appointment as an agent, has the duty to use that degree of care and skill possessed by a reasonably competent practitioner in that line of business. A salesperson, for example, would be required to have and to exercise the knowledge, training, and diligence of "average" salespersons in the field involved. The existence of this duty means that an agent can be held liable for **misfeasance** (not doing lawful acts in a proper manner), *malfeasance* (doing a wrongful act), or *nonfeasance* (not being diligent in performing the job).

Agent's improper performance

Personal Performance. A person is chosen as an agent of a principal, and placed in a position of trust and confidence, on the basis of his or her unique personal characteristics. It therefore follows logically that the agent owes a duty to the agent to use those personal qualities in performing the assigned job and that the agent should not be able to delegate to others the exercise of his or her discretionary powers as an agent. Absent any specific agreement, delegation by the agent is permitted only where the nature of the business requires it, or where a known and established custom permits it, or where the delegation involves purely ministerial or mechanical acts (such as answering the telephone or typing correspondence). Except in these situations, the principal will not be liable to third parties for the acts of such "subagents," and their appointment by the original agent would be a breach of his or her duty to the principal.

Obedience to Instructions and Good Conduct. Like the boy scout, a good agent is obedient. The agent must obey the principal's instructions, even if they seem stupid or unreasonable; this control over methods, remember, is the main distinction between the agent/employee and the independent contractor. In general, the agent's only excuses for not obeying instructions are that they require doing something illegal or that it has become impossible to comply with them. The law is not too clear on the degree to which agents must subject themselves to personal danger to comply with the principal's instructions, although the *Restatement of Agency* does indicate that agents can disregard such instructions to "protect the agent's own superior interests." It is clear that the agent will have to follow instructions that are merely "unreasonable," unless the relationship involves an agency coupled with an interest and the unreasonable instructions would interfere with the agent's rights in the subject matter of the agency.

As far as third parties are concerned, the agent is the principal. This holds true particularly for agents who represent business concerns. The image and reputation of a business are in large part determined by the way its agents and employees conduct themselves toward third parties. The agent, and some extent even the employee, therefore owes a duty of "good conduct." This requirement clearly covers on-the-job conduct, so things like dress codes can be enforced if they are reasonably and uniformly applied. The *Restatement of Agency* also indicates that this duty extends to off-the-job conduct that might affect the principal's business, such as the conduct of the bank teller who becomes known in the community as the "patron of the races." The exact degree to which agents can be legally required to surrender their personality to keep their jobs remains an open question.

Use of Principal's Property. The agent is liable for any misuse of property which the principal has entrusted to the agent or which comes into the agent's possession in the course of acting as agent. As part of this duty, the agent is not to commingle money or other property of the principal with personal money or other property, and the agent is required to provide the principal with correct and reasonably detailed statements of account.

The agent also has a duty to communicate to the principal any information that the agent possesses which might materially affect the agency.

Delegation O.K. in some situations

Agent's duty to obey instructions

Principal's Ratification of Agent's Unauthorized Act. Typically where the principal has a clear choice and ratifies with full knowledge that the agent's actions were unauthorized, the agent is excused of any further liability to the principal. The *Restatement* says that the agent will remain liable for breach of duty either where the principal "is obliged to affirm the act in order to protect his own interest" or where the principal is induced to ratify by the agent's fraud or duress.

■ LIABILITY OF AGENT TO THIRD PARTY

Agent guarantees authority

Agent Acts beyond Authority. In most states, when the agent in a disclosed agency transaction acts beyond the scope of his or her authority, so that the third party has no contract with the principal, the third party has no contract with the agent either. In these states the third party's remedy against the agent is a tort claim for fraud, provided the agent knowingly misrepresented his or her authority, or a case for breach by the agent of an "implied warranty of authority." As a rule, it is assumed that the agent makes such a warranty to the third party. There is no such warranty, however, if the third party knew that the agent was unauthorized, or if the agent in good faith disclosed to the third party all the facts regarding the extent of the authority, or if the contract contains a disclaimer of the agent's liability. In a minority of states the agent could also be sued directly on the contract which the agent was not authorized to make for the principal.

No corporation formed yet

Principal Nonexistent or Incompetent. The two most common examples of the "nonexistent" principal are the corporation which has not yet been formed and the unincorporated association, which is usually not recognized as a separate legal person. In these cases, the agent is personally liable on the contracts made with the third party, even if the third party knows of the "nonexistence," unless the contracts specifically exempt the agent from personal liability.

Principal lacks capacity

Where the principal totally lacks contractual capacity at the time the contract is made (for instance, a person who has been judicially declared insane), most courts will probably arrive at the same result as would be reached if the principal were "nonexistent." Also, the agent would clearly be liable if the agent fraudulently misrepresented or concealed the principal's lack of capacity. Where the principal has merely exercised an option to disaffirm the contract, however, the results are not so clear cut, but even in such cases many courts would hold the agent liable.

Agent as surety

Agent Pledges Personal Credit. An agent who has pledged his or her personal credit on the contract, as surety for the principal, is also clearly liable to the third party. This occurs very frequently where the agent is acting on behalf of a small, brand-new corporation that has not yet established its own credit standing; in such cases the third party will often demand that the agent-promoter-shareholder cosign the contract. If the agent does so, the agent is liable according to the terms of the contract.

Agent signs negotiable instrument

Because this situation is so common, the agent may also be held personally liable where the contract language or the signatures on the contract indicate such liability. If it appears that the agent was a party (or the other party) to the contract, the agent may be prevented by the parol evidence rule from proving otherwise. If the principal's name does not appear on a negotiable instrument, and the agent's does, the agent is liable on it and the principal is not. To avoid these unintended results, the agent should always sign "Peter Principal, by John Able, agent"—thus clearly indicating that he or she is signing in a representative capacity.

Although Phillips did avoid liability in the next case, he could have avoided the lawsuit entirely by properly signing the contract and the check.

HENDERSON v. PHILLIPS

195 A.2d 400 (District of Columbia, 1963)

FACTS   Phillips telephoned Henderson, a plumbing contractor, to request estimates on the cost of doing plumbing work on a particular house. He identified himself as the president of the firm that was constructing the house. Henderson prepared two written contracts addressed to "Design for Modern Living" and mailed them to the corporation. Each was accepted under the signature of "James O. Phillips" and remailed to Henderson in an envelope bearing in the upper left-hand corner the name "Designed for Living, Inc., 2814 Pennsylvania Avenue, N.W., Washington 7, D.C." Thereafter, payment on account was made by checks mailed in a similar envelope. Printed on the first check in the upper left-hand corner was "Metropolitan Designed for Living, Inc.," showing the Pennsylvania Avenue address. It was signed by two persons, one of whom was Phillips, under the printed name of the corporation, with no indication as to the capacity of either signor. A second check, similarly drawn, was not paid upon presentment. Henderson then sued both the corporation and Phillips.

The lower court found the corporation liable but found that Phillips was not individually liable for the balance due on the contracts. The plaintiff appealed.

ISSUE   Is Phillips, president of Metropolitan Designed for Living, Inc., personally liable under two contracts for plumbing services rendered by the appellant?

DECISION   No. Judgment affirmed.

REASONS   Judge Meyers, speaking for the court, felt that the facts revealed that Henderson knew he was dealing with a corporation of which Phillips was an agent. Judge Meyers stated:

"The prior dealing between appellant and Phillips was sufficient to impute notice of the agency relationship of Phillips. The checks in payment for the work performed by Henderson were definitely revealing as to the corporate identity of the builder. . . . It is true that he 'accepted' the written contracts without indicating his agency capacity, but he did the same when co-signing the corporation check in payment for both jobs by Henderson. Henderson recognized that he was dealing with a corporate entity when he addressed his contracts to 'Design for Modern Living.' It is also significant that Henderson never testified that he thought he was dealing only with Phillips and intended to rely upon him for payment and not upon the corporate builder. Neither contract contained any words expressly binding Phillips personally or indicating any intent by him to be responsible for payment in the event the corporation defaulted. The identity of the principal being known and the agency of Phillips being established at the time of the transaction, upon default of the disclosed principal, personal liability could not be imposed upon its agent."

———————————————

Agent Commits Tort against Third Party. As stated in the last chapter, an agent is personally liable for torts committed against third parties. Where the agent's tort was within the scope of authority, the third party can sue *both* the agent and the principal and they are both liable, although the third party cannot collect damages twice.

As a rule, the agent is not liable to third parties for breach of a duty which is owed only to the principal, at least if the breach involves only nonfeasance or misfeasance.

Third party's election

Undisclosed Principal. As also indicated in the last chapter, where the existence or identity of the principal is not disclosed at the time the contract is made, the third party has the option of holding the agent personally liable on the contract. The courts do not agree on when the third party must make an election to hold one to the exclusion of the other, although of course all do agree that no double recovery is permitted. The only way for an agent to avoid being held liable on this basis is to disclose the principal when the contract is made.

■ LIABILITY OF THIRD PARTY TO AGENT

Third party injures agent

Agent Suing on Own Behalf. There are only a few situations where the agent will sue the third party on his or her own behalf. If the agent was also made a party to the original contract, or if the agent owns the contract rights by assignment from the principal, the agent can sue the third party. The agent can also sue a third party for wrongful interference in the contract relationship between the agent and the principal or for any other tort which the third party commits against the agent. Finally, where the agent has delivered money or goods to the third party under circumstances where the third party would be unjustly enriched at the agent's expense (e.g., the agent by mistake pays the third party more than the principal owes the third party), the agent can sue in his or her own name to prevent such unjust enrichment.

Agent Suing for the Principal. Generally, an agent cannot sue in his or her own name to enforce a contract that the agent made on behalf of the principal; the principal has to sue the third party. If specifically authorized to do so, an agent may be able to bring suit as an agent for collection, and an assignment may be made to such an agent for the purpose of collection only. An agent can also sue on the principal's behalf to recover goods the agent delivered to the third party by mistake or for interference by the third party with the agent's possession of the principal's goods.

Thus, while the main agency is the third party's suit against the principal, based on an alleged contract or on the agent's tort, any of the three parties to this relationship may have a case against either of the other two.

■ SIGNIFICANCE OF THIS CHAPTER

Since many of us will be employed as agents and will also be employing agents of our own, we also need to know the rights and duties that exist between principal and agent. Whether we are acting as agents or are the third parties with whom the agents are dealing, we should be aware of the rights and duties involved in that relationship as well. Although the major litigation pattern is a suit by the third party against the principal, based on actions of the agent, any of the three parties involved may have grounds for a suit against either of the others.

■ IMPORTANT TERMS AND CONCEPTS

principal's duty to compensate agent
at-will employment rules
employer's liability under Workers' Compensation laws
obedience to instructions of principal by agent
agent acts beyond authority
misfeasance

principal's liability for breach of agency contract
principal's liability for defamation
loyalty and good faith duties of agent
personal performance requirements of agent
nonexistent or incompetent principal

■ QUESTIONS AND PROBLEMS FOR DISCUSSION

1. What does it mean to be an employee at will?
2. What duties does an agent owe to the principal? List each and discuss.
3. Where the existence of the principal is not revealed in negotiations between the agent and the third party, and later after a breach of the contract, the third party learns of the existence of the principal, whom can the third party sue? Why?
4. If an employee invents a new process or a new device while working for the employer, who has the right to patent this process or device? Who gets the royalties? Discuss.
5. Lynseed, a sales representative for ABM Computers, calls at the home office of Deuce Hardware to try to sell it a computer system for its business. The president of Deuce, Spiro Ragsnow, asked several questions about what guarantees and services came with the computer system and told Lynseed that he would not buy without assurances from ABM on these matters. At that point, to close the sale, Lynseed showed Spiro a letter, purporting to be written by the president of ABM, which stated that Lynseed had "full authority" to deal with ABM's customers. In fact,

Lynseed had written and signed the letter himself, for use in case potential customers questioned his authority. If Deuce sues to enforce statements made by Lynseed about the computer system sold to it, does it have any rights against either ABM or Lynseed? Discuss.
6. Mavis, the purchasing agent for Wirthles Corporation, was told that the company needed 30 new cars for its sales representatives. Mavis bought cars from a dealer who promised to give her a new car for half of the list price if she bought Wirthles's cars from him. Mavis then resold that car for the full list price, $8,000. What rights does Wirthles have when it discovers what Mavis has done? Discuss.
7. Popaye was employed by the Olyve Oil Company as a retail sales manager. His duties included calling the various independent service station owners in his assigned territory. His supervisor told him to threaten and cajole the owners to bring their prices into line with the prices "suggested" by Olyve. When Popaye refused to engage in these bullying tactics, his supervisor told him he could be fired anytime, and he soon was. Popaye sues for wrongful discharge. What is the result and why?
8. Huey was employed as a welder by Chair Glide, which manufactures elevator chairs for persons who cannot climb stairs. He was not hired to do any engineering or designing work. One day, he got an idea for a safety device. He brought some scrap material to his workbench and started to make a model of the device. His foreman told him not to do that on company time, so Huey waited until his lunch hour and then built his model. He did use the company's welder and cutting torch, as well as his own tools. When he showed his model to Danny, the company's general manager, Danny said he liked the idea. Chair Glide used the idea on its products, but did not pay Huey anything for it, claiming a shop right. Huey sues for compensation. What is the result and why?

41

Government Regulation of Employment Relationships

CHAPTER OBJECTIVES

THIS CHAPTER WILL:

- Introduce the sources of law regulating employment relationships.
- Discuss major problem areas of labor relations law.
- Review labor standards legislation.
- Discuss the laws governing occupational safety.
- Discuss antidiscrimination legislation.

We have already discussed the basic legal rules involved in the employer-employee relationship in Chapters 39 and 40. We assumed in that discussion that the employer was negotiating with each employee or prospective employee on an individual basis. Many employees, of course, are union members and rely on their unions to negotiate on their behalf for improved wages, hours, and conditions of employment. In order to promote peaceful collective bargaining, the national government regulates this process in some detail. While the states may not enact regulations that conflict with the national labor law system, they are free to regulate collective bargaining by state and local government employees and by any other persons whose activities do not affect interstate commerce.

National and state governments have also enacted a variety of laws which provide benefits and safety standards for employees. Minimum wage laws, the Social Security system, the Employee Retirement Income Security Act, the Occupational Safety and Health Act, and similar laws provide required standards for the employee-employer relationship. National and state governments have also enacted employment discrimination laws with which employers must comply.

■ SOURCES OF LABOR RELATIONS LAW

Where does the law of employer-employee relationships come from? Originally, the employment contract was treated by the common law in much the same way as other types of contracts; it required offer and acceptance, consideration, and the other elements of a valid contract. It was a two-party contract, with each party having the freedom to accept or reject the bargain offered by the other and with the parties being pretty much free to agree on any terms they chose. Specific legal rules also developed to cover this "master-servant" relationship, such as the employer's liability for torts committed by his or her servant within the scope of the employment and the employer's responsibility for furnishing a reasonably safe place in which to work. Much of the common law has now been displaced in this area, as both national and state governments have moved in aggressively to redefine this relationship.

Several broad, comprehensive national statutes exist in each of the two major divisions of labor law—*labor relations* and *labor standards*. There is also considerable state regulation of both areas, and the Fourteenth Amendment to the U.S. Constitution may be invoked if the state itself, or one of its agencies or instrumentalities, is directly involved in the relationship as the employer.

Wagner Act

In the area of labor relations, the basic piece of national legislation is the National Labor Relations Act of 1935, as amended. The NLRA (also known as the *Wagner Act*) laid the cornerstone of national labor policy: belief in the process of collective bargaining between the employer and a representative freely chosen by his or her employees. The original act set out a series of forbidden employer "unfair labor practices," so that employers would not interfere with the selection of the *bargaining representative* and would be required to bargain. The governmental interference here was limited to providing the employees with a freely chosen bargaining representative; it was then up to the union to work out the terms and conditions of employment by bargaining with the employer.

Taft-Hartley Act

Concern over excessive union power and abuses, coupled with a wave of strikes after World War II, led to the adoption of a series of comprehensive amendments in 1947—the **Taft-Hartley Act** (or Labor-Management Relations Act). Taft-Hartley set out a series of forbidden *union* unfair labor practices and attempted to ensure certain basic employer and employee rights—such as the employer's right to tell his or her side of the story to the employees and the employee's right to *refrain* from participating in union activity if he or she so chose. These amendments also permitted the several states to prohibit agreements between employer and union which required union membership as a condition of employment *(state right-to-work laws)*.

Landrum-Griffin Act

Further disenchantment with union operations and evidence of widespread corruption in the internal management of unions, provided by nationally tele-vised hearings of the McClellan subcommittee, resulted in 1959 in a second substantial revision of the NLRA. The Labor-Management Reporting and Dis-closure Act (LMRDA), or **Landrum-Griffin Act,** again attempted to protect employers, individual employees, and the public from certain union abuses, particularly the abuse of exerting indirect pressure on a recalcitrant employer by involving third parties in the bargaining dispute. The LMRDA also placed certain requirements on the internal management of unions and union funds and provided machinery for dealing with so-called national emergency strikes.

As a result of these two sets of amendments, a good deal of the spirit of the original Wagner Act ("Let the union do it") has been dissipated. The rather considerable limitations contained in Taft-Hartley and Landrum-Griffin are not fully consistent with the free collective bargaining envisaged by the Wagner Act, and the law of labor relations thus becomes susceptible to radically different interpretations at several important points.

Public employees not covered by NLRA

The National Labor Relations Act of 1935 as amended in 1947 and 1959 does not cover railroad employees or airline employees, as they are covered by the **Railway Labor Act,** passed by Congress in 1926. Also the National Labor Relations Law does not cover public employees on the national, state, or local level. Employees of our national government are covered by the Federal Service Labor-Management and Employee Relations Act of 1978, which gives them the right to organize and be represented by a union for collective bargaining, but denies them the right to strike. Many states have enacted statutes authorizing and regulating collective bargaining by public employees. These laws usually deny such employees the right to strike. Since a strike is not allowed, many of these statutes provide for compulsory arbitration of the dispute if the parties cannot resolve the dispute between themselves.

Labor standards legislation provides direct regulation of the terms and condi-tions of employment; in that sense, it limits the freedom of the employer and the union, as well as the individual employee, to set their own terms of association with each other. The Wagner Act represented a basic commitment of national labor policy to the collective bargaining process, but the commitment has never been complete or without qualification. The mandatory "social security" system is itself an important piece of labor standards legislation, since it provides a required arrangement for retirement, disability, and dependent benefits. Social security can be supplemented, but not displaced, through collective bargain-ing.

The main piece of national *wages and hours legislation* is the *Fair Labor Standards Act (FLSA)* of 1938, as amended. Once again, it sets boundaries to the parties' freedom of contract by specifying certain minimum wages and required overtime which must be paid (even if there are persons ready and willing to work for less). Also included in this general category are several national statutes requiring the payment of "prevailing minimum wages" in a particular industry, as determined by the secretary of labor. The two such acts with broadest scope are the Walsh-Healy Act, for manufacturers and dealers supplying the national government with supplies valued at $10,000 or more, and the Davis-Bacon Act, covering building contracts with the national government for more than $2,000. Similar provisions have been inserted in national grant-in-aid legislation for the construction of airports, highways, housing for defense personnel, and urban renewal projects.

What is potentially the most far-reaching (and therefore the most costly) piece of "labor standards" legislation ever enacted became law in 1970: the *Occupational Safety and Health Act (OSHA)*. This act is designed to "assure as far as possible every working man and woman in the nation safe and healthful working conditions," by giving the secretary of labor very broad powers to adopt "standards" which will in effect be mandatory health and safety practices. To ensure compliance, the employer's premises are subject to unannounced inspection by "the man from OSHA," either on employee complaint or by random selection. Injunctive relief and criminal penalties are provided for violations.

In 1974 Congress passed another important piece of labor legislation—the *Employment Retirement Income Security Act. ERISA* establishes a new government agency, financed by contributions from employers with pension plans, to guarantee payment of earned pension benefits. It does not require any employer to establish a pension plan, but when he or she does, the plan must meet certain standards for the funding and management of assets and for the vesting of benefits. ERISA is thus a significant new protection for the more than 30 million workers who are covered by its provisions.

Labor legislation in a particular state may include all of the above types plus some additions. Many states now have statutes regulating collective bargaining by public employees, some of which provide for compulsory arbitration of bargaining disputes which the parties are unable to resolve themselves. The states have also enacted workers' compensation laws, which provide a statutory scheme for compensating employees for virtually all job-related injuries. (A similar national statute, the Federal Employees' Compensation Act, covers U.S. government employees.) Finally, workers who have lost their jobs are provided with at least some temporary help though state systems of unemployment compensation.

■ **LABOR-RELATIONS LAW—MAJOR PROBLEM AREAS**

Multiple plants and different trades

Selection of a Bargaining Agent.   Assuming that a group of employees have indicated a desire for union representation and that they are subject to NLRA jurisdiction, the first step in the procedure for selecting a bargaining agent is to define the extent of the bargaining unit. In some cases, where there is only one business location and where there is a substantial identity of interests among all concerned employees, this is an easy job.

Multiple jobsites create some definitional problems. What if one plant votes "no union" but a majority for all plants operated by the company votes in favor of a union? Do we decide plant by plant or companywide? The NLRB has generally favored the companywide approach.

How about employees with substantially different skills, interests, and professional identification? Are they all to be lumped together as an amorphous mass ("one big union"), or are they somehow to be split up (so that some smaller craft unions or even "no union" might have a better chance of winning the separate elections)? Conflicting equities can make it difficult to arrive at a "fair" resolution of these questions. The Board's general approach has been "one big union," meaning that a group of employees wishing to be excluded from the employerwide unit must have some strong evidence of their "uniqueness."

The following case shows that state labor agencies take a similar approach.

AMERICAN ASSOCIATION OF UNIVERSITY PROFESSORS v. BOARD OF REGENTS OF THE UNIVERSITY OF NEBRASKA

279 N.W.2d 621 (Nebraska, 1979)

FACTS   The Regents appealed an order of the state's Court of Industrial Relations which established a collective bargaining unit at the University of Nebraska at Omaha. The Regents contended that (1) the CIR had no jurisdiction over them; (2) the bargaining unit was inappropriate because it included only employees of U/N at Omaha; (3) the bargaining unit was inappropriate because it should not have included department chairpersons, librarians, counselors, assistant instructors, or academic personnel holding special appointments. The U/N-O College of Business Administration Faculty Association also appealed from the dismissal of its petition for intervention, which had asked for the establishment of a separate bargaining unit. Intercollegiate athletic coaches and trainers were excluded from the bargaining unit.

ISSUES   Does the CIR have jurisdiction over the university? If so, was the CIR's determination of the bargaining unit correct?

DECISION   Yes. Yes. Judgment affirmed.

 REASONS   The largest section of Justice Boslaugh's opinion dealt with the third point raised by the Regents. He quickly disposed of the first two points by noting that the Supreme Court had earlier approved the CIR's similar determination of a separate bargaining unit for the faculty at U/N-Lincoln.

"The evidence here is that the department chairmen at UNO are faculty members who serve as chairmen at the pleasure of the dean of the college. . . . In performing their duties, the chairmen consult with the other members of the faculty and, generally, there is little or no disagreement between the chairmen and the faculty of the department concerning recommendations and other decisions which the chairmen make. The evidence sustains the finding of the CIR that chairmen of the department should be included within the faculty bargaining unit.

"Although the library at UNO is not a college, it is considered to be an academic unit in some respects. The librarians do not perform instructional duties, but their work is related to the teaching and research functions performed by the faculty. To that extent there is a community of interest between the faculty and the librarians.

. . . We think the record sustains the finding by the CIR that librarians should be included in the faculty bargaining unit. . . .

"Although assistant instructors are considered to have an interim position, they teach and do research in much the same manner as other members of the faculty. While there is a relatively high turnover rate among assistant instructors, the evidence indicates the assistant instructors are a necessary part of the instructional staff.

"There is little in the record concerning the exact nature of the duties performed by the counselors. There is nothing to indicate they are management or supervisory personnel. The title suggests that the counselors work with the students in academic matters, and might be presumed to have some community of interest with the faculty."

The court also dismissed the business faculty's petition since the 20 persons it listed were less than 10 percent of the members of the bargaining unit. The court did indicate that the issue could be raised in a new proceeding, but it noted a "strong policy against undue fragmentation of bargaining units in the public sector."

Election procedure

In addition to determining the appropriate bargaining unit, the Board's pre-election hearing also decides which employees are entitled to vote and which unions will appear on the ballot. The original union petitioning for the election is required to present evidence of 30 percent support, typically by means of signature cards from the requisite number of employees. Any other union wishing to appear on the ballot need only show substantial interest, and the "no union" choice will appear automatically. The election is by secret ballot. The winner need only receive a majority of the votes actually cast. If there is no majority, a runoff election is held between the two choices receiving the highest vote totals. While a secret ballot election is clearly the preferred method and the one normally used, the board does have the power to grant bargaining rights to a union presenting signature cards from a majority, where the cards clearly indicate such an intent, where there has been no union misrepresentation of the purpose of the cards to the individual employees, and where the possibility of holding a fair election is lessened by the employer's serious unfair labor practices.

Free speech in elections

Section 7 of the NLRA gives employees "the right to self-organization, to form, join, or assist labor organizations." Section 8(a)(1) then makes it an unfair labor practice for an employer to "interfere with, restrain, or coerce employees in the exercises of the rights guaranteed in Section 7." Labor history contains many cases where unscrupulous employers used puppet unions to forestall genuine representation and to exploit their workers still further. The Board is vigorous and vigilant, therefore, in protecting these important organizing rights, so that the employer's conduct during an organizing campaign must now be circumspect to avoid an unfair labor practice charge. Taft-Hartley guarantees the employer's (and others') right of "free speech," so long as the employer does not make any threat of reprisal or promise any benefit, but the Board has ruled that such conduct may be a basis for invalidating a no-union vote, thus requiring a new election.

Union Security and Membership. Once selected as the official bargaining agent, the union is then legally required to bargain for all employees in the unit, union and nonunion alike, as well as to process the grievances of all employees on an equal basis. Violation of this duty of equal and fair representation could lead to decertification of the union by the NLRB or to charges before the EEOC.

Because it is legally required to represent all, the union makes the superficially logical argument that all employees in the unit should be required to become union members in order to keep their jobs. This is the so-called *free rider argument:* No nonunion employee should get a free ride on union-won benefits at the expense of dues-paying fellow employees. The first answer to this argument is that the union not only agreed to accept this status; it aggressively sought it. And second, it should be possible to work up some fair compensation to the union for benefits actually conferred by it on nonunion employees, without forcing them to join and financially support an organization with which they may disagree violently—philosophically, politically, and economically.

From a union's standpoint, the best union-security arrangement is the *closed shop,* where only union members are hired and where employees must remain union members to keep their jobs. The closed shop has been outlawed for nearly all industries, but the legally permitted *union shop* is almost as good. Under a union shop, the employee has an initial period of time after hiring, typically 30 days, to decide whether or not to join the union to keep the job. An employee who decides not to join is fired at the end of the trial period. In addition to the union shop, the union will probably also negotiate a contract provision for automatic payroll deduction of union dues.

Section 14(b) of Taft-Hartley gave the states the authority to ban compulsory unionism if they wished to do so; there are 20 states with such right-to-work laws. Since Section 14(b) speaks of required "membership" in a union, some of these states permit the *agency shop,* under which an employee is not required to join the union but instead pays it a fee which supposedly represents the value of the union's services to him or her as a member of the bargaining unit. Other states in this group hold that the agency shop is illegal too, and in those states the original open shop prevails. With an *open shop,* each individual employee is legally free to decide whether or not to become, or remain, a union member, and the union leaders are thus responsible to the membership on a continuing basis. Labor's annual drive in Congress to repeal 14(b) has thus far been unsuccessful.

Scope of the Duty to Bargain. Section 8(a)(5) of the NLRA makes it an unfair labor practice for the employer to refuse to bargain collectively with the representative of his or her employees; Section 8(b)(3) contains a similar requirement for the chosen union representative. But the parties are *required* to bargain only as to items which are classified as *mandatory subjects* of collective bargaining. As to those items, not only is it a violation of the NLRA to refuse to bargain, but it is also legally permissible to insist on one's bargaining position as the price of an agreement. That is, where a mandatory subject is involved, either party can use all of the weapons at its command—strike, lockout, picketing, and so on—to enforce the bargaining demand.

What are these mandatory subjects? Generally, they comprise items designated as "wages, hours, and other terms and conditions of employment." Very few bargaining demands would not fall into this category. Pension, profit-sharing, and stock-purchase plans; bonuses and merit raises; seniority and retirement

Margin notes:

Closed shop versus union shop

State right-to-work laws

Agency shop

Required bargaining topics

rules; prices for meals and housing furnished by the company; and union security arrangements—all have been ruled mandatory subjects.

Management decisions

Permissive subjects of collective bargaining are those which the parties are free to discuss if they *both* wish to, but which neither can insist on as the price of an agreement. Such insistence and/or the use of bargaining weapons would be a violation of the Section 8 duty to bargain and would subject the wrongdoer to unfair labor practice charges. Nearly all demands held to be merely permissive have related to the mechanics of the bargaining process itself, such as the size of the bargaining teams, or the requirement of a secret employee vote on ratification of the employer's last offer prior to a strike, or a secret ballot vote on ratification of the new contract. Product selection, distribu-

Management prerogatives

tion, and pricing have likewise thus far been held to be *management prerogatives* and thus not mandatory subjects for collective bargaining. But the contracting out of work which was formerly performed by members of the bargaining unit *is* a mandatory subject, and the NLRB has ordered the resumption of maintenance operations which were so terminated by the company without prior bargaining.

There are a few provisions, such as closed shop and "hot cargo" agreements, which may not be lawfully included in the collective bargaining contract even if both parties so desire. The next case illustrates the general approach to mandatory subjects of bargaining.

FORD MOTOR COMPANY v. NATIONAL LABOR RELATIONS BOARD

441 U.S. 488 (1979)

FACTS
Ford provided in-plant cafeteria and vending machine food services. ARA Services, Inc., an independent caterer, managed these services, but Ford had the right to approve the quality, quantity, and prices for the food served. Ford notified the UAW that food prices in its stamping plant at Chicago Heights, Illinois, would be increased by unspecified amounts. UAW Local 588, representing the 3,600 hourly workers at the plant, asked for bargaining on the prices and services and for information relevant to Ford's involvement in the food services operation. Ford refused, and the UAW filed unfair labor practice charges with the NLRB, alleging a refusal to bargain over a mandatory subject. The board sustained the charges and ordered Ford to bargain. The U.S. Seventh Circuit Court of Appeals upheld the board, although it and three other circuit courts had previously refused to do so. Ford asked for certiorari.

ISSUE
Were the in-plant food prices and services a mandatory subject of collective bargaining?

DECISION
Yes. Judgment affirmed.

REASONS
Justice White first noted that the Board had consistently held to this position, even though the courts of appeal had been refusing to enforce its orders. He felt that the Board's judgment should be given "considerable deference."

"It is not suggested by petitioner that an employee should work a full eight-hour shift without stopping to eat. It reasonably follows that the availability of food during working hours and the conditions under which it is to be consumed are matters of deep concern to workers, and one need not strain to consider them to be among

those 'conditions' of employment that should be subject to the mutual duty to bargain.
. . . The terms and conditions under which food is available on the job are plainly
germane to the 'working environment.' . . . Furthermore, the company is not in the
business of selling food to its employees, and the establishment of in-plant food prices
is not among those 'managerial decisions, which lie at the heart of entrepreneurial
control.' . . . The Board is in no sense attempting to permit the Union to usurp
managerial decision making; nor is it seeking to regulate an area from which Congress
intended to exclude it.

"Including within S.8(d) the prices of in-plant supplied food and beverages would
also serve the ends of the National Labor Relations Act. . . . National labor policy
contemplates that areas of common dispute between employers and employees be funneled
into collective bargaining. The assumption is that this is preferable to allowing recurring
disputes to fester outside the negotiation process until strikes or other forms of economic
warfare occur.

"The trend of industrial practice supports this conclusion. In response to increasing
employee concern over this issue, many contracts now are being negotiated that contain
provisions concerning in-plant food services."

Bargaining process

The duty imposed by the NLRA means that the parties must bargain in
"good faith." This at least includes meeting with each other, listening to the
other side's proposals, and discussing them. In the case of the employer, the
duty to bargain also means providing the union with such relevant information
as is within its possession and reasonably available. The NLRA does not require
any party to agree to a proposal from the other side, or even to make any
concession. Despite these clearly stated rules, however, both the NLRB and
the U.S. Second Circuit Court of Appeals held that General Electric committed
the unfair labor practice of refusing to bargain by making its "last, best offer"
at the start of negotiations and indicating to the employees that that was the
best it could do.

Union Tactics and Unfair Labor Practices. The union's main weapons in
support of its bargaining demands are the strike, picketing, and the boycott.

Illegal union objectives

There are some significant legal limitations (as well as economic ones) on the
use of each. In general, both the objectives sought and the tactics used must
be lawful.

Both Taft-Hartley and Landrum-Griffin tried to restrict union conduct that
had the effect of dragging neutral employers, and their employees, into the
primary dispute. The main relevant section of the amended NLRA is Section
8(b)(4). Strikes, refusals to handle or work on certain ("hot") goods, or any
other union conduct that threatens, coerces, or restrains any person is illegal
if its objective is:

(*a*) To force any employer or self-employed person to enter a labor organization or to enter into a "hot cargo" agreement, illegal under 8(e).

(*b*) To force any person to cease doing business with any other person.

(*c*) To force any employer to bargain with one union where another union
has already been certified.

(*d*) To force an employer to assign particular work to one group of employees
rather than another.

Section 8(b)(7) further limits the permissible objectives of picketing. Picketing is unlawful where it is done to force an employer to recognize a union or to force his or her employees to accept it as their agent if:

(a) Another union has already been recognized and there is no legal question as to its status.

(b) A valid election has been held within the past 12 months.

(c) Such picketing has been conducted for a reasonable time (not to exceed 30 days) and the union has not filed a petition for an election.

Illegal union conduct

In addition to the above legal restrictions on the purposes for which union collective-action weapons may be used, any such concerted activities must themselves be conducted in a lawful manner. In general, this means that the union's tactics must be "peaceful." Violence or threats of violence directed against the employer, his or her premises, employees who choose to go to work, or customers or others who wish to continue to do business with the "target" employer would clearly be illegal. Access to and egress from the target premises must not be impeded. The laws of libel and slander presumably still apply to picket signs and other information media. And so on.

Illegality of the union's objectives or tactics not only subjects it to unfair labor practice charges; there may also be other consequences. The union itself may be liable for the damages caused and/or subject to an injunction to prohibit the unlawful conduct. Civil rights violations could conceivably be involved in the union's conduct. Employees engaging in an "unprotected" strike are subject to lawful dismissal by the employer, with no right to reinstatement when the strike ends. The 1947 and 1959 amendments, coupled with a more critical public attitude toward unions, now make it reasonably clear that union hooliganism will be punished. However, the public still shows a high tolerance level for illegal, but peaceful, union conduct, such as illegal boycotts and illegal public employee strikes. These issues remain unresolved.

Employer Tactics and Unfair Labor Practices. The employer's arsenal of weapons includes some that are roughly comparable to those used by the union, as well as some for which the union has no real equivalent. The counterpart of the union's denial of services through a strike is the employer's denial of access to the workplace (and therefore wages) by means of a *lockout.* In lieu of picketing, the employer advises employees, customers, and other members of the public of his or her side of the dispute by advertising, typically in a local newspaper. There is no real employer counterpart to the boycott. In addition to the above "corresponding" weapons, the employer also possesses the ultimate sanctions of *plant relocation* and termination of the business, though the use of either is severely limited by the Board and the courts. Management may also do some forward planning to cushion the effects of a strike, by stockpiling inventories, readjusting contract schedules, or transferring work from one plant to another. The employer may also attempt to restrict the scope of the union's collective action by means of a court injunction.

Temporary plant closings

A lockout designed to prevent unionization or to discourage union membership would be an unfair labor practice, but an employer may use the lockout to protect his or her own legitimate economic interests. Where there is a bargaining impasse, the employer may lock out in support of his or her bargaining position. Or, if the union calls or threatens to call a strike, the employer can

Permanent closings

lock out in retaliation, and also lock out to prevent "economic hardship" to the business.

An employer has an absolute right to go out of business at any time, for any reason, even if the employer's sole reason for doing so is his or her antiunion bias. Where an employer closes only part of an operation, however, the employer's motives must be economic ones and not a desire to "chill unionism" at his or her other locations. In general, the legality of a plant relocation *(runaway shop)* would be tested in the same manner as that of a partial closing. The next case illustrates a related problem: moving work from a unionized plant to a non-union plant with lower costs.

INTERNATIONAL UNION, UNITED AUTOWORKERS v. N.L.R.B.

765 F.2d 175 (District of Columbia Circuit, 1985)

FACTS
Illinois Coil Spring Company decided to move its assembly operations, formerly conducted at its Milwaukee Division, to its McHenry Division. The labor costs at Milwaukee were $8 an hour in wages and $2 an hour in fringe benefits; at McHenry, $4.50 in wages and $1.35 in fringes. A labor contract was in force at Milwaukee but not at McHenry. Illinois did bargain with its Milwaukee union about the change, by asking for wage concessions in order to keep the Milwaukee location viable. After the union rejected any concessions, Illinois did begin to relocate its assembly operations to McHenry.

The union filed unfair labor practice charges, alleging a violation of Section 8(d), 8(a)(1), 8(a)(3), and 8(a)(5). The Board initially found a violation of Section 8(d), since the employer had made a material change in terms and conditions, without the union's consent, while an agreement was in force. After the decision was appealed to the Seventh Circuit, the new Reagan majority on the Board asked the Seventh Circuit to remand the case to the Board for further study. The Reagan Board then held that there had been no violation. The UAW appealed, this time to the District of Columbia Circuit.

ISSUE
Can an employer move and relocate its assembly operations without the consent of the union representing the workers involved, during the term of the collective bargaining contract?

DECISION
Yes. The decision of the NLRB in favor of the employer is affirmed.

REASONS
Judge Edwards, speaking for the court, stated:

"This case presents the narrow question whether, during the term of a collective bargaining agreement, Section 8(d) of the National Labor Relations Act prohibits an employer from advising union bargaining agents that part of the company's operations might be relocated unless the union agrees to midterm contract concessions and from then deciding to relocate when those concessions are not received. The stipulated facts indicate that the employer acted without antiunion animus, that the relocation was prompted by purely economic considerations, and that the employer satisfied all contractual and legal obligations to bargain over the proposed relocation. The employer further asserts, without challenge from the union, that the relocation was fully consistent with the terms of the parties' collective bargaining agreement. We hold that, under these circumstances, Section 8(d) proscribes neither the announcement of a tentative intention to relocate nor the final decision to relocate, and we therefore affirm the decision of the National Labor Relations Board. . . .

"We think the Board correctly held there to be no Section 8(d) violation here. Milwaukee Spring apparently possessed the contractual right to make the relocation decision. As the union seems to concede on appeal, no provision of the collective bargaining agreement was modified by that decision. In addition, no antiunion animus tainted the company's decision. Under these circumstances, we can discover nothing in Section 8(d) that proscribes Milwaukee Spring's actions. Furthermore, we find no merit to the union's argument that the announcement of the tentative intention to relocate violated Section 8(d). The value of the company's contractual right to relocate would be undermined—not to mention the strain it would place on logic—if we were to hold that although Milwaukee Spring had the right to decide unilaterally to relocate, the act prohibited it from declaring in advance the intention to do so. . . .

"Given that Milwaukee Spring acted without antiunion animus for purely economic reasons and fulfilled any statutory obligation to bargain that it might have had, we hold that the company did not violate Section 8(d) of the act, either by offering to exchange its right to relocate for a midterm modification of the contract or by deciding to relocate when the union rejected its modification proposals."

Injunctions against unions

Throughout most of the early history of unionism, the courts were on the employer's side. The standard operating procedure when confronted with union collective action was to ask for a court injunction to restrict or terminate the union activities. Employers got an unexpected bonanza when the courts applied the *Sherman Antitrust Act* to union activities, thus further restricting employee collective action.

Congress attempted to limit the use of the courts in labor disputes by including Sections 6 and 20 in the *Clayton Act* of 1914. Unfortunately, from the union viewpoint, Section 20 said that an injunction could be issued if "necessary to prevent irreparable injury to property, or to a property right," and the courts were very liberal in construing this qualifying phrase. It took the *Norris-LeGuardia Act* of 1932 to substantially eliminate the labor injunction from the U.S. District Courts. (Many states copied this act.) It is still theoretically possible for an employer to get an injunction in a labor dispute, but the strict jurisdictional requirements make this very unlikely. The one exceptional case where the employer will be granted an injunction is where there is a strike in violation of a no-strike clause in an existing collective agreement. (An employer can also get a specific performance order to enforce an arbitration clause in an existing contract.) In addition, the Board and the Attorney General are not bound by Norris-LaGuardia and can get injunctions issued.

Conflict Resolution. As indicated previously, the government's basic approach to management-union disputes is merely to see to it that the parties meet their obligation to bargain with each other in good faith and then to let the economic chips fall where they may. In 1947, however, Congress opted for additional governmental participation in the bargaining process, with the creation of the *Federal Mediation and Conciliation Service (FMCS),* an independent administrative agency.

Mediation

The primary responsibility of bargaining out, and living with, their agreement is still left up to the parties. But the services of the FMCS are available at the request of either party or on its own initiative where the labor dispute involves the public safety and interest or where it threatens to have a substantial adverse impact on interstate commerce. If the parties want to submit their dispute to binding arbitration, the FMCS will also make available to them a list of qualified labor arbitrators from which to select.

Arbitration provides a more civilized method of settling disputes than strikes, lockouts, and the like. It is usually less formal, less complicated, and therefore less time-consuming and less expensive than a court trial. Nearly all arbitration is voluntarily agreed to by the parties, but some states have compulsory arbitration laws for public employees, particularly fire fighters and police officers, and the Taft-Hartley Act contains special procedures for compulsory government action in "national emergency strikes." Today the courts recognize and enforce awards made by third-party arbitrators on matters submitted to them by the parties, and as indicated previously, arbitration clauses in existing contracts are specifically enforceable, despite the Norris-LaGuardia Act.

Internal Union Management; Reporting and Disclosure Requirements. The Landrum-Griffin amendments to the NLRA ushered in a new era in union organization and administration. The Landrum-Griffin Act was passed following the sensational disclosures of the McClellan subcommittee on the extent of corruption and gangster control in the labor movement. The findings received widespread publicity because many of the hearings were televised and because of the popularity of *The Enemy Within,* a book written by subcommittee counsel Robert Kennedy. The result was the passage of the Landrum-Griffin Act, which set out a "bill of rights" for labor union members and imposed substantial reporting and disclosure requirements on unions.

The bill of rights is an attempt to provide guarantees of minimum participatory access to the union's decision-making process and to protect the individual member's status within the union. Subject to the union's "reasonable rules," all members are to have equal rights to attend and vote at meetings, to nominate candidates, to vote in elections, and to exercise their freedoms of speech and assembly. Dues increases must be voted by secret ballot at a special membership meeting or by referendum. Except for failure to pay dues, an individual union member cannot be disciplined by his or her union unless served with written, specific charges and given a reasonable time to prepare a defense and a full and fair hearing. If a grievance against the union or its officers or agents is not resolved by internal procedures within four months, the member can bring a civil suit in a U.S. District Court to enforce any rights under the act. The member can demand a copy of any collective contract which affects him or her, and the secretary of labor is directed to bring suit on the member's behalf if a copy is not provided.

The union itself is required to file two major types of reports with the secretary of labor—procedural and financial. Each union must adopt a constitution and bylaws, and both must be filed. Existing provisions covering such things as membership qualifications, initiation fees, selection and removal of officers, contract ratification, and strike authorization must also be filed if such matters are not covered in the constitution and bylaws. Yearly financial reports must be filed, covering such matters as assets and liabilities; receipts and their

Arbitration

Bill of rights for union members

Required union reports

sources; salaries, loans, and other payments to officers and employees; and loans to any business. Full, periodic reports must also be filed when the national union places a local under "trusteeship." To try to prevent conflicts of interest, union officers and employees must file personal financial reports covering transactions with companies which the union has organized or is trying to organize.

The Landrum-Griffin Act thus contains important new legal protections for the individual union member and for the public.

■ LABOR STANDARDS LEGISLATION

Minimum wage

Wage and Hour Regulations

Required overtime pay

Where it applies, the Fair Labor Standards Act places a floor under wage rates; it does *not* place a ceiling on hours of work, either per day or per week. It is almost inconceivable today, but the first national minimum wage so provided was *25 cents* per hour, with the objective of reaching *40 cents* an hour after the act had been in force for seven years. The 1974 Amendments extended coverage to most employees of public agencies and institutions and to "in-home" domestic workers and babysitters, but the U.S. Supreme Court ruled that Congress could not impose such limits on state and local governments.

Subject again to some exceptions, the FLSA also requires the employer to pay overtime at a rate of time and a half for all hours worked in excess of 40 in the employee's normal workweek. There is no provision for daily overtime; the "workweek" is any seven consecutive days. Overtime must be calculated for each successive seven-day period; the employer gets no "credit" if an employee works fewer than 40 hours in a given week. An hourly wage must be calculated for each employee, but the employer can exclude such things as gifts, discretionary bonuses, and employer payments to certain qualified savings and profit-sharing plans.

The employer is required to keep records of such wage and hour data for up to three years. For violations of the minimum wage and overtime provisions, the injured employee can bring suit personally or request in writing that the secretary of labor do so on his or her behalf. The secretary can also ask the U.S. District Court for an injunction to prevent further violations and/or for the removal of goods so produced from interstate commerce.

Child Labor Legislation

Restrictions on child labor

There are also extensive regulations promulgated by the secretary which pertain to the use of child labor; that is, the use of minors under age 18. Generally, the employment of children under age 14 is prohibited; between 14 and 16, some jobs are permitted, subject to strict limits on work hours; between 16 and 18, employment is prohibited only in those industries which the secretary has found to be "hazardous," such as coal and other mining, slaughterhouses and meat-packing plants, building demolition, and roofing and excavation work. Criminal penalties—up to six months in jail, a fine of up to $10,000, or both—and/or injunctions are possible enforcement measures. Goods produced through the use of illegal child labor are subject to removal from the stream of commerce, but innocent purchasers of the goods, for value, are protected against confiscation if they receive a written certificate of compliance stating that the goods were produced in accordance with FLSA standards.

The Equal Pay Act of 1963, and the Age Discrimination in Employment Act passed in 1967 and later amended in 1974, were amendments to the

FLSA; however, since they are concerned with discrimination in employment they will be discussed later in the chapter under employment discrimination laws.

Health and Safety Regulation

Each state has its own workers' compensation law. Workers' compensation laws are really an example of no-fault liability. Generally speaking, if a worker who is covered by the law is injured by accident while in the scope of employment or if the worker becomes ill as a result of an occupational disease, the worker is entitled to reasonable medical care for the injuries and for compensation for lost wages after a specific waiting period. This period will depend on the particular state law. The amount of compensation is only a percentage of the worker's average weekly wage, and again specific state law will set that percentage figure. There are also minimum and maximum weekly benefits which will be paid. If the worker suffers a permanent impairment, then a settlement based on that impairment will be paid. Most states require employers to carry workers' compensation insurance, or to show evidence of ability to pay if they wish to be considered self-insured. A few states have state-operated plans whereby employers pay a percentage of their payroll to the state, and the state acts as the insurance company.

Many states also have their own Occupational Safety and Health Act (OSHA) laws and commissions and offer their assistance to employers to help employers identify and correct health and safety hazards.

■ EMPLOYMENT DISCRIMINA-TION LAWS

Beginning in the early 1960s the Congress of the United States recognized the need for antidiscrimination legislation to eliminate discrimination in employment. Several antidiscrimination laws have been passed by Congress in the past two decades. The first of these laws, the *Equal Pay Act of 1963,* which was an amendment to the Fair Labor Standards Act of 1938 (FLSA), requires employers to pay equal pay to men and women for doing equal work. The next law was the *Civil Rights Act of 1964,* which was amended in 1972. Title VII of that act forbids discrimination by either an employer or a union against an applicant for employment, an employee, or an applicant for membership and/or benefits in a union if such discrimination is based on race, color, religion, sex, or national origin. Discrimination by an employment agency in the referral of applications is also prohibited. In 1967 the Congress added a prohibition of discrimination based on age when they passed the Age Discrimination in Employment Act of 1967. This law was an amendment to the FLSA, as was the Equal Pay Act. This law was amended in 1978 and it now prohibits employment discrimination against persons between the ages of 40 and 70. In 1973 Congress passed the *Vocational Rehabilitation Act.* This act extends protection to handicapped workers but it only applies to employees and prospective employees of employers who have federal contracts of $2,500 or more. In 1974 Congress passed the *Vietnam Veterans Readjustment Act.* This law requires certain federal contractors to develop an affirmative action plan to hire Vietnam veterans. In 1978 Congress passed the *Pregnancy Discrimination Act,* which amended Title VII of the Civil Rights Act of 1964. This law prohibits discrimination in employment based on pregnancy or pregnancy-related conditions.

In addition to these laws, Presidential Executive Order 11246 directs the secretary of labor to supervise the various federal contracting agencies to see that there is equal opportunity afforded to employees of certain federal contractors. The secretary of labor created the **Office of Federal Contract Compliance Program (OFCCP)** to supervise both the awards of federal contracts and their affirmative action regarding equal employment opportunity.

Equal Pay Act of 1963

Equal pay for equal work

The Equal Pay Act of 1963 prohibits pay differentials based solely on sex. As indicated previously, it was an amendment to the FLSA and applies only to those employees who are covered by the provisions of the FLSA. Union conduct which causes or attempts to cause such employer discrimination is likewise prohibited.

To show a violation, the government must prove that the jobs in question require equal skill, equal effort, and equal responsibility and are performed under similar working conditions, and that males and females are paid different wages for performing them. If the employer wishes to raise one of the exceptions permitted by the Equal Pay Act as a defense, namely seniority, merit, quality of production, and any other factor other than sex, the employer then has the burden of proving that the differential is based on the alleged exception. Equal does not mean identical, but minor, insignificant job differences will not justify wage discrimination.

Where a violation is shown to exist, the employer is prohibited from reducing anyone's wages to eliminate the differential; someone's wages must be raised. Aside from this provision, all the standard FLSA enforcement procedures apply to the Equal Pay provisions, including criminal penalties. Originally enforcement of this law was the responsibility of the secretary of labor; however, in 1978, as a result of a Presidential order, the enforcement of this law was transferred to the Equal Employment Opportunity Commission (EEOC).

Civil Rights Act of 1964

Prohibited discrimination

Title VII of the Civil Rights Act of 1964 as amended by the Equal Employment Opportunity Act of 1972 forbids discrimination by employers in hiring, promotion, discharge, and with regard to compensation, terms, conditions, and privileges of employment. This law also forbids discrimination by unions with regard to union membership and representation. In addition to the prohibitions against employers and unions, the law also extends its prohibition to discrimination by employment agencies. They must not discriminate in the referral of applicants for employment. Unlawful discrimination under Title VII is discrimination based on a person's race, color, religion, sex, or national origin.

There are, however, several statutory exceptions. Discriminatory hiring on the basis of religion, sex, or national origin is permitted where such limitations can be justified as a **bona fide occupational qualification** which is reasonably necessary to the normal operation of that particular business or enterprise. This is called a **BFOQ.**

An example of a religious BFOQ would be the requirement that the person hired as a minister for a specific church be a person who has the necessary religious training in the specific faith of that church. Also certain jobs may have a valid BFOQ which would require the employee to be of a specific sex. Other jobs may have a BFOQ requiring a specific national origin. It must be noted however that an employer may not legally use a BFOQ to discriminate against an applicant or employee because of the applicant's race or color.

In addition to the BFOQ exception there is a specific exemption for businesses located on or near an Indian reservation; such businesses are permitted to have employment practices that give "preferential treatment" to Indians. Similarly, the U.S. Bureau of Indian Affairs can conduct preferential hiring for Indians.

Not all employers are covered by Title VII provisions. Private sector employers who employ fewer than 15 employees are exempt from Title VII provisions; however many states have enacted their own civil rights laws that cover employers with fewer than 15 employees. Also, not all unions are covered by this law. Unions with fewer than 15 members are not subject to the provisions of Title VII unless they operate a hiring hall. Unions that operate hiring halls and employment agencies are subject to the provisions of Title VII regardless of the number of members in the union or the number of employees employed by the employment agency or the volume of their referrals. The Civil Rights Act of 1964 also exempted state and local employees; however, the amendments passed by Congress in 1972 extended the coverage of Title VII to most state and local employees.

The Civil Rights Act of 1964 set up the *Equal Employment Opportunity Commission (EEOC)*. The EEOC was granted authority by the 1964 act to investigate and conciliate grievances by individuals that allege discrimination based on race, color, religion, sex, or national origin. The amendments to the Civil Rights Act passed in 1972 gave the EEOC the added authority to not only investigate and conciliate but to file litigation on behalf of the complaining party or parties if they deemed it necessary and proper. If the EEOC investigation reveals that there is reasonable evidence to support the complainant's charge that unlawful discrimination has occurred and further that the party charged is not willing to negotiate and conciliate, then the EEOC attorneys may commence litigation in the U.S. District Court on behalf of the complainant, at the expense of the EEOC. If the EEOC attorneys decide not to litigate the case, the EEOC will issue a "right to sue letter," which authorizes the complainant to file suit, but the suit must be filed at the complainant's expense.

There is a statutory time limit for filing of a complaint by a person who feels he or she has been discriminated against. The complaint (referred to as a charge) must be filed with the EEOC within 180 days after the discriminatory act occurred. If there is a state or local civil rights agency and the local or state law requires that the complaining party file with the state or local agency first before filing with the EEOC, then the time period is extended to 300 days. There is also a time limit for the filing of a lawsuit in U.S. District Court by a complainant in the case where the EEOC decides not to pursue litigation but issues the right to sue letter. The complaining party only has 90 days to file his or her lawsuit after receiving a right to sue letter.

The District Courts that hear these Title VII actions are empowered to issue an injunction to stop an unlawful discriminatory practice if it is a continuing practice, and in certain cases they may also order affirmative action by the guilty party. Also the court may order the hiring or reinstatement of the persons who were discriminated against with or without back pay. The law does, however, limit back pay awards to a period of two years prior to the date the charge was filed.

The 1972 amendments to the Civil Rights Act of 1964 not only gave the EEOC the right to commence litigation on behalf of complainants at the government's expense, the amendments also gave the EEOC a new and very important power to combat discrimination. Prior to the 1972 amendments the EEOC was primarily concerned with individual grievances concerning alleged discrimination. With the passage of the 1972 amendments the EEOC was given the power to bring class actions to litigate allegations of "pattern or practice" of discrimination.

Age Discrimination in Employment Act
Age discrimination prohibited

In 1967 Congress enacted the Age Discrimination in Employment Act (ADEA). This act was passed as an amendment to the Fair Labor Standards Act of 1938. It prohibits discrimination against "older" workers; that is, those workers over 40 years of age. Amendments to the law passed in 1974 extended the act's protection to state and local governmental employees. The ADEA was originally enforced through FLSA procedures. However, in 1978 under a Presidential Reorganization Plan, the enforcement of this law was transferred from the labor department to the EEOC, effective July 1, 1979.

BFOQ versus RFOTA

As with religion, sex, and national origin under Title VII, there is a "bona fide occupational qualification" exception to the ADEA. In addition, the employer may differentiate on the basis of *reasonable factors other than age (RFOTA)*. For example, a 40-year-old professional football player who was no longer able to run, block, and tackle with the necessary vigor could presumably be fired on the basis of RFOTA even though age as such is not a BFOQ for a position on the team. The employer may also observe the terms of any bona fide seniority system or employee benefit plan, but he cannot use the benefit plan as an excuse for refusing to hire the older employee. Of course, an employer can still discharge or discipline an employee for good cause. Once again, this new act requires a reexamination of some once standard employment practices.

Vocational Rehabilitation Act of 1973

With the passage of the Vocational Rehabilitation Act of 1973 Congress provided protection from private sector discrimination against the handicapped; however, such protection is limited only to the private sector employers making a contract with the U.S. government for $2,500 or more. Even so, coverage extends to most major companies and perhaps half of all the businesses in the country. All such companies must have an affirmative action plan for hiring and promoting qualified handicapped persons at all levels, so in that sense that 1973 act requires more than Title VII of the 1964 act. All departments and agencies of the executive branch of the national government are likewise covered by the 1973 act.

Vietnam Veterans Readjustment Act of 1974

Congress passed the Vietnam Veterans Readjustment Act to give Vietnam veterans a special priority with regard to employment; however, only employers with government contracts of $10,000 or more are required to take affirmative action to employ and advance disabled and qualified veterans of the Vietnam era. No other employers are required by law to give such preference or priority to the veterans of the Vietnam era. All covered employers have an obligation to list all suitable job openings with the appropriate local employment service. Referral priority will then be given to Vietnam era veterans.

Pregnancy Discrimination Act of 1978

A recent major addition to the antidiscrimination laws is the Pregnancy Discrimination Act. This act prohibits discrimination in any aspect of the employment relationship because of a female employee's pregnancy. Health and disability plans for employees, in particular, must provide coverage of pregnancy and childbirth on the same basis as other medical conditions.

State Antidiscrimination Laws

Many states have passed civil rights laws that extend coverage to more employers than the national law. For example, the national Civil Rights Act only covers employers with 15 or more employees. Some states' civil rights laws cover those employers with six or more employees. Many states also have their own civil rights commissions to enforce these laws.

■ MAJOR PROBLEM AREAS—CIVIL RIGHTS LAWS

Preemployment and Employee Job Testing and Educational Requirements. Title VII of the Civil Rights Act of 1964, as amended in 1972, does not prohibit employers from testing applicants or current employees. Tests may be used to measure the applicant's or employee's ability to do the job, provided the test does not discriminate against minorities or women. For example, an employer wants to hire a typist. A typing test would be a legal test if it simply tested the accuracy and speed of typing that could be performed by the applicant. With regard to requiring a certain level of education before a person will be considered for employment, any such requirement must be shown to be job related.

In 1971 the U.S. Supreme Court decided the now famous *Griggs* v. *Duke Power* case. In that case the employer used preemployment tests and had a job requirement stating that all applicants had to have a high school diploma to be hired. Neither the tests nor the requirement of a high school diploma were found to be job related. In that case both the tests and educational requirement were clearly devices designed to discriminate against blacks.

Generally speaking, employers may use tests and may have educational requirements for certain jobs, but the burden is on the employer to prove that the tests and educational requirements are job related.

Sexual Harassment. Section 703 of Title VII of the Civil Rights Act of 1964 as amended prohibits sexual harassment. Sexual harassment has been defined as conduct involving unwelcome sexual advances, requests for sexual favors, and other verbal or physical conduct of a sexual nature. Typically, a supervisor makes such advances, in return for a promotion, raise, or other job-related benefit.

There is no question but that the person guilty of the sexual harassment, such as a supervisor who requests sexual favors as a condition for hiring an applicant, continued employment, a salary increase, or a promotion is guilty of violating the law. Recently the courts have also held the employer liable for civil damages if it can be shown that the employer knew or should have known of the illegal conduct.

In the following case the employer was found liable for the action of one of its supervisors.

MERITOR SAVINGS BANK, FSB v. VINSON

477 U.S. 57 (1986)

FACTS In 1974, plaintiff Mechelle Vinson met Sidney Taylor, a vice president of what is now petitioner Meritor Savings Bank (the bank) and manager of one of its branch offices. When plaintiff asked whether she might obtain employment at the bank, Mr. Taylor gave her an application, which she completed and returned the next day; later that same day Mr. Taylor called her to say that she had been hired. With Mr. Taylor as her supervisor, she started as a teller-trainee and thereafter was promoted to teller, head teller, and assistant branch manager. She worked at the same branch for four years, and it is undisputed that her advancement there was based on merit alone. In September 1978, Ms. Vinson notified Mr. Taylor that she was taking sick leave for an indefinite period. On November 1, 1978, the bank discharged her for excessive use of that leave.

Ms. Vinson brought this action against Mr. Taylor (her supervisor) and the bank, claiming that during her four years at the bank she had "constantly been subjected to sexual harassment" by Mr. Taylor in violation of Title VII. She sought compensatory and punitive damages against Mr. Taylor and the bank.

At the trial, the parties presented conflicting testimony about Mr. Taylor's behavior during Ms. Vinson's employment. Ms. Vinson testified that shortly after she was hired, Mr. Taylor, who was her supervisor, invited her out to dinner and, during the course of the meal, suggested that they go to a motel to have sexual relations. At first she refused, but out of what she described as fear of losing her job she eventually agreed. According to Ms. Vinson, Mr. Taylor thereafter made repeated demands upon her for sexual favors, usually at the branch, both during and after business hours; she estimated that over the next several years she had intercourse with him some 40 or 50 times. Ms. Vinson testified that because she was afraid of Taylor she never reported his harassment to any of his supervisors and never attempted to use the bank's complaint procedure.

Mr. Taylor denied Vinson's allegations of sexual activity. He contended instead that Ms. Vinson made her accusations in response to a business-related dispute. The bank also denied Ms. Vinson's allegations and asserted that any sexual harassment by Taylor was unknown to the bank and engaged in without its consent or approval.

The District Court denied relief to the plaintiff, and although it concluded that Ms. Vinson had not proved a violation of Title VII, the District Court nevertheless went on to address the bank's liability. After noting the bank's express policy against discrimination and finding that neither Ms. Vinson nor any other employee had ever lodged a complaint about sexual harassment by Taylor, the court ultimately concluded that "the bank was without notice and cannot be held liable for the alleged actions of Taylor." The Court of Appeals reversed the judgment of the District Court and remanded the case for further proceedings.

ISSUE Was there a hostile work environment? Is the employer liable to the employee even though the employer was not aware of the actions of its supervisor?

DECISION Yes. Yes. Judgment of the Court of Appeals is affirmed.

REASONS **Justice Rehnquist gave the opinion of the court:**

"Since the guidelines were issued, courts have uniformly held, and we agree, that a plaintiff may establish a violation of Title VII by proving that discrimination based on sex has created a hostile or abusive work environment. As the Court of Appeals for the Eleventh Circuit wrote in Henson v. Dundee . . . (1982):

> Sexual harassment which creates a hostile or offensive environment for members of one sex is every bit the arbitrary barrier to sexual equality at the workplace that racial harassment is to racial equality. Surely, a requirement that a man or woman run a gauntlet of sexual abuse in return for the privilege of being allowed to work and make a living can be as demeaning and disconcerting as the harshest of racial epithets. . . .

"Of course, as the courts recognized, not all workplace conduct that may be described as 'harassment' affects a 'term, condition, or privilege' of employment within the meaning of Title VII. . . . ('mere utterance of an ethnic or racial epithet which engenders offensive feelings in an employee' would not affect the conditions of employment to a sufficiently significant degree to violate Title VII); . . . for sexual harassment to be actionable, it must be sufficiently severe or pervasive 'to alter the conditions of [the victim's] employment and create an abusive working environment.' . . . Respondent's allegations in this case—which include not only pervasive harassment but also criminal conduct of the most serious nature—are plainly sufficient to state a claim for 'hostile environment' sexual harassment. . . .

"Although the District Court concluded that respondent had not proved a violation of Title VII, it nevertheless went on to consider the question of the bank's liability. Finding that 'the bank was without notice' of Taylor's alleged conduct, and that notice to Taylor was not the equivalent of notice to the bank, the court concluded that the bank therefore could not be held liable for Taylor's alleged actions. The Court of Appeals took the opposite view, holding that an employer is strictly liable for a hostile environment created by a supervisor's sexual advances, even though the employer neither knew nor reasonably could have known of the alleged misconduct. The court held that a supervisor, whether or not he possesses the authority to hire, fire, or promote, is necessarily an 'agent' of his employer for all Title VII purposes, since 'even the appearance' of such authority may enable him to impose himself on his subordinates. . . .

"The EEOC, in its brief as *amicus curiae,* contends that courts formulating employer liability rules should draw from traditional agency principles. Examination of those principles has led the EEOC to the view that where a supervisor exercises the authority actually delegated to him by his employer by making or threatening to make decisions affecting the employment status of his subordinates, such actions are properly imputed to the employer whose delegation of authority empowered the supervisor to undertake them. Thus, the courts have consistently held employers liable for the discriminatory discharges of employees by supervisory personnel, whether or not the employer knew, should have known, or approved of the supervisor's actions."

Antidiscrimination in Employer Benefit Plans. Most employers provide some type of medical payment plan for employees and their families and some type of retirement plan. These plans can be financed entirely by contributions by the employer, or their cost may be shared between employer and employee. The discrimination problems with regard to these plans have been primarily in the area of sex discrimination. One question that arose was: Does a medical plan have to provide coverage for pregnancy? The Supreme Court of the United States answered that question in the negative in 1976. Then the U.S. Congress stepped in and in 1978 enacted the Pregnancy Discrimination Act, which now makes it unlawful for an employer to exclude pregnancy-related disabilities from any medical, hospital, or disability benefits plan, or any company plan or program that allows sick leaves.

Pregnancy discrimination prohibited

In 1983 the U.S. Supreme Court further defined the required "neutrality" in its decision in *Newport News Shipbuilding and Dry Dock Co.* v. *EEOC.* In that case, the employer gave women employees paid leave time to give birth to a child, and the question was raised as to whether the granting of such benefits to females was discriminatory against males. The Supreme Court held that the employer must also give paid leave time to any male employee whose wife gives birth to a child.

Retirement discrimination prohibited

Statistically, women have had a longer life expectancy than men. Pension plans, insurance annuity plans, and other forms of retirement plans have traditionally based contribution rates on life expectancy. That is to say, since women statistically have a longer life expectancy after retirement than men, it can be expected that they will have to be paid more benefits than would be paid to men who have a shorter life expectancy. Insurance companies, to have adequate funding, either increased the contribution to be made by women to offset the fact that they may receive benefits for a longer time, or the companies charged the same contribution rate but then paid the retired women a lower monthly retirement benefit than retired men who had made similar contributions. These practices were based on the contention that the woman would live longer and thus there would be more monthly payments to be made in the case of a retired woman than to a retired man. The Supreme Court has declared both of these practices discriminatory under Title VII.

Thus, after these decisions any contributions by employees to a retirement plan must be *sex-neutral,* and any distribution to retired employees from such plans must also be calculated without regard to the sex of the party receiving the distribution benefits.

Comparable Worth Doctrine. We have previously discussed the Equal Pay Act of 1963. As previously stated, that law requires an employer to pay equal pay for equal work. In order for a claimant to collect back pay under that law it must be shown that one sex (usually the males) are being paid more than the opposite sex who are doing the same job. If the job performed by one sex is not substantially equal to the job performed by the opposite sex then there is no violation.

Recently the proponents of equal pay for the sexes came up with the concept of "comparable worth." This concept would make the employer not only pay equal pay to both sexes for doing substantially equal work but also for doing jobs which are of comparable worth or value to the company. In 1981 the

U.S. Supreme Court, in *County of Washington* v. *Gunther,* found that women who were *not* doing substantially the same job as their male counterparts could bring a lawsuit under Title VII for back wages based on alleged intentional sexual discrimination in payment of wages to women.

That case involved complaints by four female prison guards who were being paid less than male prison guards. However, the evidence showed the jobs of the female prison guards and the male prison guards were not substantially the same because the male guards supervised 10 times as many prisoners per guard as did the female guards, and also a substantial part of the female guards' job was spent doing clerical work. Thus the jobs were not substantially equal. The Supreme Court found that there was sexual discrimination with regard to the wages paid to the women and remanded the case to provide for payment of back wages but without basing their decision on the concept of comparable worth. The advocates of comparable worth felt that the case was a first step in the acceptance of the comparable worth doctrine even though the court did not specifically address the comparable worth issue.

The state legislature of the state of Washington was favorably impressed with the fairness of the comparable worth concept and passed a law in applying the doctrine of comparable worth to the state employees' jobs, effective in June 1983.

While this doctrine on its face seems to be a fair doctrine and certainly a doctrine that would promote the cause of reducing discrimination against women in the workplace, it has not been widely accepted. The primary reason, of course, is not only the difficulty of deciding comparable worth of the various jobs, but also the bottom line of the dollars and cents cost of making such adjustments. Obviously you could not reduce the pay of one job to the level of the comparative job so it would mean increasing the pay for the lower paying job. Thus the future of comparative worth is still uncertain at this time.

Affirmative Action Required by Government Contractors.   We have previously referred to the Rehabilitation Act of 1973 and the Vietnam Veterans Readjustment Act of 1974. Both of these acts are legislative enactments that specify that government contractors with contracts exceeding a specific amount must take affirmative action with regard to hiring the persons protected by those laws, namely, the handicapped and Vietnam veterans.

In 1965 President Johnson issued Executive Order No. 11246 and in 1967 he issued Executive Order 11375. These executive orders set up the *Office of Federal Contract Compliance Programs (OFCCP)*. They also require a contractor who accepts a U.S. government contract of $50,000 or more with 50 employees to file a written Affirmative Action Plan with the OFCCP. This plan involves a complete review of the contractor's workforce and a breakdown of the workforce into categories of race, color, sex, and national origin. The surrounding area from which employees are recruited is then reviewed with regard to the same categories. The contractor is then reviewed with regard to the same categories. The contractor is then required to prepare a plan to take affirmative action to increase the numbers of employees in these various categories so that the percentage of persons in the various categories in the workforce of the employer is comparable to the percentage of the available workers in such categories in the recruiting area. Contractors are not required to fire nonminority or male persons or to hire more persons than necessary, nor are they required to hire persons who are not qualified for the job.

In addition to the contractors who accept U.S. contracts of $50,000 or more and who have 50 or more employees, several other groups are affected by executive orders 11246 and 11375. Those groups are (1) contractors or subcontractors that provide the government with more than $10,000 worth of supplies, services or work; (2) contractors or subcontractors that have had more than $10,000 worth of government business in any 12-month period; (3) anyone who has government bills of lading in any amount; (4) any firm that serves as an issuing or paying agent of U.S. savings bonds and notes; (5) any firm that serves as a depository of U.S. funds in any amount; (6) all contractors and subcontractors that hold U.S. assisted contracts in excess of $10,000; (7) any construction contractor's or subcontractor's construction employees who are engaged in on-site construction including those construction employees who work on a nonfederal or nonfederally assisted construction site.

The theory of affirmative action is to seek out women and persons from the minority categories to fill new and vacant positions to thus increase the percentage of women and minority persons in the employment of the contractor. OFCCP will periodically review the plan and the progress made. Failure to comply with the plan may cause cancellation of the government contract and disbarment from future government contracts for a period of time.

One of the problems of most concern with regard to affirmative action plans is the problem of "reverse discrimination" primarily against white males. In the discussion case, *Firefighters Local 1784* v. *Stotts,* at the end of this chapter, the Supreme Court of the United States addresses the problem of reverse discrimination which is a result of an affirmative action plan.

■ SIGNIFICANCE OF THIS CHAPTER

The relationship between employer and employee is a significant area of government regulation. Prior to such regulation, we saw blatant discrimination with regard to employees' rights concerning unionism and considerable discrimination as to employees' civil rights. Every manager needs to have knowledge of at least the major laws which regulate the employer-employee relationship. This chapter gives the manager a basic knowledge of those laws.

DISCUSSION CASE

FIREFIGHTERS LOCAL 1784 v. STOTTS
467 U.S. 561 (1984)

FACTS: Captain Carl Stotts, a black person employed by the Memphis, Tennessee Fire Department, filed a class action in U.S. District Court in Tennessee alleging that the fire department, the local union, and certain city officials of Memphis, Tennessee were engaged in a pattern or practice of discrimination on the basis of race and color in violation of Title VII of the Civil Rights Act of 1964 as amended in 1972. Another member of the Memphis Fire Department, Private Fred Jones, filed an action alleging a violation of Title VII, and his action was consolidated with Captain Stott's case so that the two were tried together. Mr. Jones complained that he had been denied promotion because he was black. These cases were settled by consent of the parties, and a consent decree was entered by the court ordering the Fire Department to remedy the department's hiring and promotion practices with regard to black persons. The consent decree dated April 25, 1980, required the city to promote 13 individuals and to provide back pay to 81 employees of the fire department. It also required the city to adopt a long-term goal to increase the amount of minority representation in each job classification. Then in May 1981, the city announced a budget cut which would require layoffs throughout city government. Layoffs were to be on the "last hired, first fired" basis. The plaintiff Stotts went back to court and requested an injunction forbidding the layoffs of any black employees.

The District Court entered an order granting an injunction. The court found that the layoff policy was not adopted with an intent to discriminate. Nonetheless, concluding that the proposed layoffs would have a racially discriminatory effect the District Court ordered that the city "not apply the seniority policy insofar as it would decrease the percentage of black lieutenants, drivers, inspectors, and privates that are presently employed." A layoff plan, aimed at protecting black employees so as to comply with the court's order, was presented and approved. Layoffs pursuant to the modified plan were then carried out. In certain instances, to comply with the injunction, nonminority employees with more seniority than minority employees were laid off or demoted in rank.

On appeal, the Court of Appeals for the Sixth Circuit affirmed the District Court. The city and the union filed separate petitions for certiorari. The two petitions were granted and the cases were consolidated for oral argument. The U.S. Supreme Court granted certiorari.

■

Justice White:

The issue at the heart of this case is whether the District Court exceeded its powers in entering an injunction requiring white employees to be laid off, when the otherwise applicable seniority system would have called for the layoff of black employees with less seniority. We are convinced that the Court of Appeals erred in resolving this issue and in affirming the District Court. . . .

The Court of Appeals held that even if the injunction is not viewed as compelling compliance with the terms of the decree, it was still properly entered because the District Court had inherent authority to modify the decree when an economic crisis unexpectedly required layoffs

which, if carried out as the city proposed, would undermine the affirmative action outlined in the decree and impose an undue hardship on respondents. This was true, the court held, even though the modification conflicted with a bona fide seniority system adopted by the City. The Court of Appeals erred in reaching this conclusion.

Section 703(h) of Title VII provides that it is not an unlawful employment practice to apply different standards of compensation or different terms, conditions, or privileges of employment pursuant to a bona fide seniority system, provided that such differences are not the result of an intention to discriminate because of race. It is clear that the city had a seniority system, that its proposed layoff plan conformed to that system, and that in making the settlement the city had not agreed to award competitive seniority to any minority employee whom the city proposed to lay off. The District Court held that the city could not follow its seniority system in making its proposed layoffs because its proposal was discriminatory in effect and hence not a bona fide plan. Section 703(h), however, permits the routine application of a seniority system absent proof of an intention to discriminate. . . . Here, the District Court itself found that the layoff proposal was not adopted with the purpose or intent to discriminate on the basis of race. Nor had the city in agreeing to the decree admitted in any way that it had engaged in intentional discrimination. The Court of Appeals was therefore correct in disagreeing with District Court's holding that the layoff plan was not a bona fide application of the seniority system, and it would appear that the city could not be faulted for following the seniority plan expressed in its agreement with the union. The Court of Appeals nevertheless held that the injunction was proper even though it conflicted with the seniority system. This was error.

To support its position, the Court of Appeals first proposed a "settlement" theory, that is, the strong policy favoring voluntary settlement of Title VII actions permitted consent decrees that encroached on seniority systems. But at this stage in its opinion, the Court of Appeals was supporting the proposition that even if the injunction was not merely enforcing the agreed-upon terms of the decree, the District Court had the authority to modify the decree over the objection of one of the parties. The settlement theory, whatever its merits might otherwise be, has no application when there is no "settlement" with respect to the disputed issue. Here, the agreed-upon decree neither awarded competitive seniority to the minority employees nor purported in any way to depart from the seniority system.

A second ground advanced by the Court of Appeals in support of the conclusion that the injunction could be entered notwithstanding its conflict with the seniority system was the assertion that "[i]t would be incongruous to hold that the use of the preferred means of resolving an employment discrimination action decreases the power of a court to order relief which vindicates the policies embodied within Title VII, and 42 U.S.C. Sections 1981 and 1983." The court concluded that if the allegations in the complaint had been proved, the District Court could have entered an order overriding the seniority provisions. Therefore, the court reasoned, "[t]he trial court had the authority to override the Firefighter's Union seniority provisions to effectuate the purpose of the 1980 Decree.". . .

The difficulty with this approach is that it overstates the authority of the trial court to disregard a seniority system in fashioning a remedy after a plaintiff has successfully proved that an employer has followed a pattern or practice having a discriminatory effect on black applicants or employees. If individual members of a plaintiff class demonstrate that they have been actual victims of the discriminatory practice, they may be awarded competitive seniority and given their rightful place on the seniority roster. . . .

Teamsters, however, also made clear that mere membership in the disadvantaged class is insufficient to warrant a seniority award; each individual must prove that the discriminatory practice had an impact on him. . . . Even when an individual shows that the discriminatory practice has had an impact on him, he is not automatically entitled to have a nonminority employee laid off to make room for him. He may have to wait until a vacancy occurs, and if there are nonminority employees on layoff, the court must balance the equities in determining who is entitled to the job. . . . Here, there was no finding that any of the blacks protected from layoff had been a victim of discrimination and no award of competitive seniority to any of them. Nor had the parties in formulating the consent decree purported to identify any specific employee entitled to particular relief other than those listed in the exhibits attached to the decree. It therefore seems to us that in light of *Teamsters,* the Court of Appeals imposed on the parties as an adjunct of settlement something that could not have been ordered had the case gone to trial and the plaintiffs proved that a pattern or practice of discrimination existed.

Our ruling in *Teamsters* that a court can award competitive seniority only when the beneficiary of the award has actually been a victim of illegal discrimination is consistent with the policy behind Section 706(g) of Title VII, which affects the remedies available in Title VII litigation. That policy, which is to provide make-whole relief only to those who have been actual victims of illegal discrimination, was repeatedly expressed by the sponsors of the act during the congressional debates. Opponents of the legislation that became Title VII charged that if the bill were enacted, employers could be ordered to hire and promote persons in order to achieve a racially-balanced work force even though those persons had not been victims of illegal discrimination. Responding to these charges, Senator Humphrey explained the limits on a court's remedial powers as follows:

> No court order can require hiring, reinstatement, admission to membership, or payment of back pay for anyone who was not fired, refused employment or advancement or admission to a union by an act of discrimination forbidden by this title. This is stated expressly in the last sentence of Section 707(e) [enacted without relevant change as § 706(g)]. . . . Contrary to the allegations of some opponents of this title, there is nothing in it that will give any power to the Commission or to any court to require . . . firing . . . of employees in order to meet a racial "quota" or to achieve a certain racial balance. That bugaboo has been brought up a dozen times; but is nonexistent. . . .

The Court of Appeals holding that the District Court's order was permissible as a valid Title VII remedial order ignores not only our ruling in *Teamsters* but the policy behind Section 706(g) as well. Accordingly, that holding cannot serve as a basis for sustaining the District Court's order.

Finally, the Court of Appeals was of the view that the District Court ordered no more than that which the city unilaterally could have done by way of adopting an affirmative action program. Whether the city, a public employer, could have taken this course without violating the law is an issue we need not decide. The fact is that in this case the city took no such action and that the modification of the decree was imposed over its objection.

We thus are unable to agree either that the order entered by the District Court was a justifiable effort to enforce the terms of the decree to which the city had agreed or that it was a legitimate modification of the decree that could be imposed on the city without its consent. Accordingly, the judgment of the Court of Appeals is reversed.

■ IMPORTANT TERMS AND CONCEPTS

Fair Labor Standards Act of 1938 (FSLA)
Employee Retirement Income Security Act (ERISA)

Railway Labor Act
bargaining agent
state right to work laws
unfair labor practices
free rider argument

Section 14(b) of Taft-Hartley
mandatory subjects of bargaining
management perogatives
lockout
Sherman Antitrust Act

Norris LaGuardia Act
arbitration
Civil Rights Act of 1964
BFOQ
RFOTA
Vietnam Veterans Readjustment Act of 1974

state antidiscrimination laws
job testing
hostile work environment
comparable worth doctrine
OFCCP
Occupational Safety & Health Act (OSHA)
Wagner Act
Taft-Hartley Act
Landrum-Griffin Act
union security and membership
closed shop
agency shop
permissive subjects of bargaining

plant relocation
runaway shop
Clayton Act
Equal Pay Act of 1963
EEOC
Age Discrimination in Employment Act
Vocational Rehabilitation Act of 1973
Pregnancy Discrimination Act of 1978
antidiscrimination in employer benefit plans
sexual harassment
sex-neutral
affirmative action

▪ QUESTION AND PROBLEMS FOR DISCUSSION

1. How does the NLRB determine the scope of the appropriate bargaining unit?
2. What topics are mandatory subjects of collective bargaining?
3. What is the difference between a BFOQ and an RFOTA?
4. What is the OFCCP? What is its role?
5. The Brewers United Union engaged in a lawful economic strike against the Belcher Beer Company and set up picket lines around all its plants. Horatio Hornswogle, a Belcher employee who was a member of the BUU, said he thought the strike was "stupid" and crossed the picket line. For this, he was fined by the BUU, for "conduct unbecoming a union member." BUU sues in court to collect the fine. Horatio files charges with the NLRB, alleging that the union's fine is a violation of Section 8(b)(1)(A), since it was union conduct which restrained or coerced him in the exercise of his right to refrain from concerted activities. The BUU claims that its fine is authorized by the proviso to that section which says "this paragraph shall not impair the right of a labor organization to prescribe its own rules with respect to the acquisi-

tion or retention of membership therein." Who's right, and why?

6. The United Steelworkers of America International Union has a provision in its constitution that limits the eligibility of a member to run for an office in a local union to those members who have attended at least one-half of the local's regular meetings for the three-year period prior to the election. The secretary of labor filed an action in U.S. District Court to have the provision ruled invalid. At the time of the challenge of this provision 96.5 percent of the members of local 3489 were ineligible to hold office if this provision was found to be legal. The law clearly allows the union to impose "reasonable qualifications" on the right to hold office. You are the judge. How should the court rule? Why?

7. Blackhound Bus Company established a mandatory retirement age for their bus drivers. They required all bus drivers to retire commencing the first day of the year following their 60th birthday. They stated as their reason the fact that the Federal Aviation Administration (FAA) prohibits persons over 60 years of age from being a pilot on a commercial airline. Since bus drivers are also "pilots" of a commercial vehicle and are responsible for the lives and welfare of their passengers, the company felt it would be a good idea to use the same age requirement for bus drivers. This new mandatory retirement age affected 13 drivers already over age 60 and 129 drivers nearing the age of 60. All of these persons immediately complained to the EEOC alleging a violation of the Age Discrimination in Employment Act. Will they be successful? Make arguments pro and con.

8. Jonah Jinx had been arrested 15 times by the police, on various charges, but had never been convicted of anything. Jonah applied for a job at Fussy Foods, Inc. One of the questions on the job application asked whether the applicant had ever been arrested. Jonah answered that he had been. On the basis of that answer, Fussy's Personnel Department automatically rejected his application. Jonah brought a suit for illegal discrimination. At the trial, Jonah's lawyer offered proof that this particular question had a statistically disproportionate impact on blacks. Does Jonah have a valid case of racial discrimination? Why or why not?

42

Partnerships—Nature, Creation, and Termination

CHAPTER OBJECTIVES

THIS CHAPTER WILL:

- Define a partnership.
- Describe the creation of a partnership.
- Discuss the classifications of partnerships.
- Review the process of dissolution, winding up, and termination of a partnership.

The partnership is perhaps the oldest and most common form of business organization involving more than one person. The partnership form of organization dates as far back as the Middle Ages and perhaps even before that. Traditionally the partnership was a nonstatutory form of business organization, whose creation was comparatively simple, inexpensive and informal.

The body of law governing the partnership business organization was developed on a case-by-case basis throughout the court system over the years. Whenever law is developed by the case method, there are bound to be variations in decisions by judges, a lack of uniformity from state to state, and a lack of real clarity as to what the law is on a particular point. Thus, the National Conference of Commissioners on Uniform State Laws, which was referred to in an earlier chapter, drafted the **Uniform Partnership Act (UPA)** in 1914. The purpose of this act was to clarify and codify the maze of court decisions on partnership law into a workable statutory form. The great majority of the states have adopted the UPA. Thus, references will be made to the UPA throughout the chapters on partnership law.

■ PARTNERSHIP AS LEGAL ENTITY

Under the common law, a partnership was not considered a separate legal entity, or person, but merely a collection of persons who were doing business together. There was no separate "it," but merely "them." In contrast, a corporation is clearly a separate legal person, even though "it" has no actual physical existence. All a corporation's business affairs are conducted in its name, even though it must use agents.

Failure to recognize a partnership as a separate entity makes the conduct of its business unnecessarily cumbersome. At common law, for example, a partnership could not hold title to real estate in its firm name; it had to be held in the name of one or more partners. Suits by or against large partnerships can be terribly complex if the rules require each partner to be specifically named. And so on.

Recognizing these problems, the UPA's drafters reached a compromise. For certain purposes, but not completely, the partnership is now recognized as a separate entity. Its property is treated as separate from that of the individual partners (as discussed in the next chapter), and it can own real estate in the firm name if it wishes. It keeps separate books and records and prepares separate (informational) tax returns. It does not, however, pay a separate tax, as it would if it were a separate entity. Many states, with newer civil procedure rules, now also permit suits by or against a partnership in the firm name. Separate bankruptcy proceedings can also be instituted by or against a partnership.

■ DEFINITION OF A PARTNERSHIP

Section 6 of the UPA defines a *partnership* as follows: "a partnership is an association of two or more persons to carry on as co-owners, a business for profit." This definition contains several requirements which must be met before there can be a partnership. First, the partnership must be an association of two or more persons. The word *association* implies that an agreement has been made. Thus, we are talking about contract law with regard to whether or not a legal agreement exists. Second, the association must consist of two or more persons. A person can be a natural person or a legal entity such as a corporation. Third, persons must carry on a business as co-owners. A partnership is not simply two or more people working together; it must be two or more people, each of whom has some rights of ownership in the business. It is not required that all of these people have equal rights of ownership; however, each must be a co-owner. Finally, the business must be for profit. This rules out the many organizations which have been established for religious, charitable, educational, and other not-for-profit purposes.

It is interesting to note that for tax purposes the Internal Revenue Code, Section 761(a) defines a partnership as a "syndicate, group, pool, joint venture, or other unincorporated organization through . . . which any business . . . is carried on, and which is not . . . a corporation or a trust or estate." The IRS is not concerned about the rights and duties between partners or between partners and third persons; it is only trying to classify business organizations for taxing purposes.

A *joint venture* is similar to a partnership in that it also involves two or more persons who are engaged in some business activity. Joint ventures differ from partnerships mainly in purpose and duration. A partnership is created to carry on a business for profit for an indefinite period of time and is dissolved by the death or resignation of one of the partners. A joint venture, on the other hand, is created to conduct a specific business activity over a specific period of time. An example of a joint venture would be a situation where two persons purchased an apartment house as an investment for resale and hired a manager to run it until it was sold. The purpose of this venture is specific, and the duration is limited. No general agency is created between the parties; they are simply joint investors.

A *syndicate,* like a partnership, involves two or more persons who are involved in some business activity. However, a syndicate differs from a partnership in that, like a joint venture, it is formed for a specific business activity and a specific duration. The parties involved in a syndicate can be classified as investors rather than as persons carrying on a business as co-owners. A syndicate was defined in the case of *Hambleton* v. *Rhind,* 84 Md. 456, as "[A]n association of individuals, formed for the purpose of conducting and carrying out some particular business transaction, ordinarily of a financial character, in which the members are mutually interested."

The terms *group* and *pool* as used in Section 761(a) are really just Internal Revenue Code language used to describe a group of people who are participating in a business activity or a situation where people pool their money to conduct a business for profit.

■ QUALIFICA-TIONS OF PARTNERS

Part I, Section 2 of the Uniform Partnership Act states that the word *persons* includes individuals, partners, corporations, and other associations. This means that not only individuals but also corporations, partnerships, and other associations may be partners in a partnership. Since the individual states may have specific rules and regulations regarding participation in partnerships by corporations, other partnerships, and other associations, whether these can be partners depends on state law.

Any natural person having the capacity to contract can become a partner. In Part II, Contracts, we dealt with the question of what persons are competent to contract. Insane persons may not become partners. Minors do not have full contractual capacity; however, they may become partners in a partnership. But, as with simple contracts, minors have the right to disaffirm their partnership contracts at any time before they reach majority and for a reasonable time thereafter. By such disaffirmance, a minor may avoid certain liability to partnership creditors. Also, a minor who disaffirms the partnership agreement is generally entitled to get back his or her capital investment and share of the profits up to that time, provided that such a distribution will not adversely affect the interest of existing partnership creditors. In some states, the disaffirming minor may be able to withdraw capital *before* creditors are paid.

Since a partnership is a voluntary association, the general rule is that no one can be forced to become a partner with another; there must be an agreement to be partners. This rule is summed up in the Latin phrase: *delectus personae* (choice of persons). Each of us has the right to choose the persons with whom we will be partners, and we're not partners unless we agree to be partners. In contrast, the shares of stock in a corporation are presumed to be fully and freely transferable, so that a person could become involved in a corporate business with someone who was a total stranger, of unknown abilities and personality.

In cases involving alleged discrimination by large law firms or accounting firms the courts have tried to balance the partners' freedom to choose new associates with the individual's right to be free from discriminatory evaluations.

CLASSIFICATION OF PARTNERSHIPS

Partnerships may be classified as ***general partnerships*** or ***limited partnerships***. The general partnership is the more common form. It is a partnership in which all of the partners have unlimited liability for partnership debts. A limited partnership is a partnership in which one or more of the partners are general partners with unlimited liability. However, one or more of the other partners are limited partners, and their liabilities for partnership debts are limited to the extent of their investment in the partnership. Like persons who buy stock in a corporation, they cannot be liable for more than their investment in the business.

Partnerships may be further classified as ***trading*** or ***nontrading partnerships***. A trading partnership is engaged in the business of buying or selling goods or real estate for a profit. A nontrading partnership is a business which provides services, such as a law partnership or an accounting partnership.

The law of limited partnerships will be dealt with in detail in Chapter 44.

METHODS OF CREATING A GENERAL PARTNERSHIP

The "association" requirement in Section 6 of the UPA means that for a partnership to exist there must be some sort of agreement among the persons involved in it. As is true under general contract law, however, this agreement may be express—either oral or written—or implied. Most courts would refuse to enforce, at least as between the partners themselves, an oral partnership agreement that was to last longer than one year. The Statute of Frauds might also be applicable where the partnership agreement called for the transfer of land, goods over $500, or miscellaneous intangibles over $5,000.

Although the parties' intent is certainly important in creating a partnership, it is not conclusive. If the parties wanted to create a partnership but left out one of the required elements, they did not form a partnership. Likewise, if the parties did not intend to create a partnership but in fact voluntarily entered into a relationship which contained all of the elements of a partnership, they become partners. No state action is required to form a partnership, though most states do require some sort of registration of the firm, at least where it is using a fictitious name. Failure to register under such a statute does not preclude a firm's existence, though it may prevent the firm from suing.

Section 16 of the UPA provides that persons who are not actual partners as to each other may be held liable to third parties as if they were partners where they have held themselves out as partners or where they have consented to having another hold them out as partners and where the third party has relied on such representations in making a decision to extend credit to the firm. Where the representation of partnership has been made publicly, no specific proof of reliance is required; reliance is assumed. Section 16 calls this sort of situation a ***partnership by estoppel.***

■ CONTENTS OF A PARTNERSHIP AGREEMENT

A ***partnership agreement,*** also called *articles of partnership* or *articles of copartnership*, should contain the basic provisions required to form a contract, as a partnership agreement is in fact a contract. In addition to these basic provisions, there will usually be certain provisions which relate to the type of business and to special problems connected with the management of that particular business. For example, a considerable number of the provisions in the articles of partnership of a large law firm would not be found in the articles of partnership of a family manufacturing firm. Note how the Delaware court dealt with the parties' detailed partnership agreements in the *Chaiken* case, which follows.

CHAIKEN v. EMPLOYMENT SECURITY COMMISSION

274 A.2d 707 (Delaware, 1971)

FACTS   Pursuant to 19 Del.C. Section 3359, the Employment Security Commission levied an involuntary assessment against Richard K. Chaiken, for not filing his unemployment security assessment report. Pursuant to the same statutory section, a hearing was held and a determination made by the Commission that Chaiken was the employer of two barbers in his barber shop and that he should be assessed as an employer for his share of unemployment compensation contributions. Chaiken appealed the Commission's decision.

ISSUES   Was there a partnership between Mr. Chaiken and the other barbers or was he an employer and subject to an unemployment security tax assessment for the other barbers?

DECISION   No. There was no partnership. Judgment of the Commission is affirmed.

REASONS

Judge Storey in his opinion stated:

"Both in the administrative hearing and in his appeal brief Chaiken argues that he had entered into partnership agreements with each of his barbers and, therefore, was and is not subject to unemployment compensation assessment. . . .

"Chaiken contends that he and his 'partners':

1. Properly registered the partnership name and names of partners in the Prothonotary's office, in accordance with 6 Del. C. Section 3101,
2. Properly filed federal partnership information returns and paid federal taxes quarterly on an estimated basis, and
3. Duly executed partnership agreements.

"Of the three factors, the last is most important. Agreements of 'partnership' were executed between Chaiken and Mr. Strazella, a barber in the shop, and between Chaiken and Mr. Spitzer, similarly situated. The agreements were nearly identical. The first paragraph declared the creation of a partnership and the location of the business. The second provided that Chaiken would provide barber chair, supplies, and licenses, while the other partner would provide tools of the trade. The paragraph also declared that upon dissolution of the partnership, ownership of items would revert to the party providing them. The third paragraph declared that the income of the partnership would be divided 30 percent for Chaiken, 70 percent for Strazella; 20 percent for Chaiken and 80 percent for Spitzer. The fourth paragraph declared that all partnership policy would be decided by Chaiken, whose decision was final. The fifth paragraph forbade assignment of the agreement without permission of Chaiken. The sixth paragraph required Chaiken to hold and distribute all receipts. The final paragraph stated hours of work for Strazella and Spitzer and holidays.

"The mere existence of an agreement labelled 'partnership' agreement and the characterization of signatories as 'partners' do not conclusively prove the existence of a partnership. Rather, the intention of the parties, as explained by the wording of the agreement, is paramount. . . .

"Evaluating Chaiken's agreement in the light of the elements implicit in a partnership, no partnership intent can be found. The absence of the important right of decision making or the important duty to share liabilities upon dissolution individually may not be fatal to a partnership. But when both are absent, coupled with the absence of profit sharing, they become strong factors in discrediting the partnership argument. . . .

"In addition, the total circumstances of the case taken together indicate the employer-employee relationship between Chaiken and his barbers. The agreement set forth the hours of work and days off—unusual subjects for partnership agreements. The barbers brought into the relationship only the equipment required of all barber shop operators. And each barber had his own individual 'partnership' with Chaiken. Furthermore, Chaiken conducted all transactions with suppliers and purchased licenses, insurance, and the lease for the business property in his own name. Finally, the name 'Richard's Barber Shop' continued to be used after the execution of the so-called partnership agreements.

"It is the conclusion of the court that Chaiken did not carry the burden of proving the existence of partnerships with Spitzer and Strazella."

■ DISSOLUTION, WINDING UP, AND TERMINATION

A partnership is based on a contract, which may be superseded by the parties' later actions. The firm may be dissolved by agreement of the partners, by acts of the partners, by a decree of court, or by operation of law. In the case of a partnership with a specific time span, it is dissolved at the end of the stipulated period of time. The partnership contract does, however, differ from many other contracts in that it concerns not only the contractual relationship between the parties to the contract but also the contractual relationship between the partnership and its various creditors. Thus, even though the partners may decide to dissolve their contractual relationship between themselves, the partnership is not really terminated until all of its debts are paid and all of its assets are distributed. This procedure is commonly called "winding up." Once the winding-up process has been completed, the partnership is considered terminated. Thus we have a three-step process: dissolution, winding up, and termination.

Dissolution is defined by Section 29 of the Uniform Partnership Act as "the change in the relation of the partners caused by any partner ceasing to be associated in the carrying on as distinguished from the winding up of the business." This change in relation can be voluntary or involuntary. An example of voluntary dissolution would be one in which the partners simply decide to end their relationship and go their separate ways. An example of involuntary dissolution would be one which occurred because a partner died or became mentally or physically incapacitated.

The key legal point to remember is that dissolution in itself does not terminate the partnership entity. Dissolution may trigger the next step; namely, the winding-up process. During the winding-up process, the partnership agreement is still legally in force. However, the authority of each partner to act as an agent of the partnership has been legally terminated except as necessary to wind up partnership affairs.

Dissolution by Agreement of the Partners

The partners may decide to dissolve their partnership for various reasons. This decision must be unanimous unless the partnership agreement specifies otherwise. For example, the agreement could specify that only a majority vote of the partners is needed to dissolve the partnership. Remember, a partnership is a voluntary agreement.

Dissolution by Acts of the Partners

1. Withdrawal by a Partner.   If a partner withdraws from the business, that action causes a dissolution of the partnership. This does not necessarily mean that the business will have to be terminated. If the partnership agreement has been drawn with this problem in mind, it will contain provisions that give the remaining partners the right to buy the withdrawing partner's interest so that they can continue the business.

Although a partner has the power to withdraw from the partnership for any reason that he or she may choose, the withdrawing partner may still be liable to the remaining partners for breach of contract. After all, the partnership agreement is a contract, and if its breach causes damage to the other contracting parties, then the violating party should be liable for such damages. Here again, a well-drawn partnership agreement should anticipate and provide a solution for such problems.

2. Expulsion of a Partner. Section 31(1)(d) of the Uniform Partnership Act states that a partnership is dissolved "by the expulsion of any partner from the business bona fide in accordance with such a power conferred by the agreement between the partners." Thus, if the agreement provides for the expulsion of a member under certain circumstances and the remaining partners exercise that power for good and valid cause, then the partnership is dissolved.

3. Death of a Partner. The Uniform Partnership Act, Section 31(4), states that the death of any partner will cause dissolution. The issue in the *Girard Bank* case is whether Anna had already dissolved her partnership prior to death.

GIRARD BANK v. HALEY

332 A.2d 443 (Pennsylvania, 1975)

FACTS   Anna Reid began this action against Haley and her two other partners, alleging that she had dissolved the firm and asking for a distribution of assets. Reid died after the lawsuit was commenced, and her executors were substituted as plaintiffs. Reid had written a letter to her partners, which stated in part: "I hereby notify you that I am terminating the partnership. . . ." Meetings were held, but the partners were unable to agree on a plan for liquidation or on the respective rights of the partners. At that point, Reid started this lawsuit. The partnership agreement gave the surviving partners the right to purchase the interest of a deceased partner, but it contained no such provision in the event that a partner dropped out voluntarily. The chancellor held that Reid's letter did not dissolve the firm but that her death did. He also held that the other partners could exercise their buyout option by paying her estate $29,165.48 plus Reid's 70 percent of the income for 1971. Reid's executors appealed.

ISSUE   Did the decedent's letter terminate the partnership?

DECISION   Yes. Judgment reversed and case remanded.

REASONS   Justice Pomeroy felt that the chancellor had been somewhat confused as to what the applicable law was. He said that the chancellor appeared to be overly impressed with the fact that Reid had been a "strong-willed person" who dominated the firm and with the fact that she and her representatives had not "justified" her termination.

"In supposing that justification was necessary, the learned court below fell into error. Dissolution of a partnership is caused, under s.31 of the Act, . . . 'by the express will of any partner.' The expression of that will need not be supported by any justification. If no 'definite term or particular undertaking [is] specified in the partnership agreement,' such an at-will dissolution does not violate the agreement between the partners; indeed, an expression of a will to dissolve is effective as a dissolution even if in contravention of the agreement. . . .

"There is no doubt in our minds that Mrs. Reid's letter . . . effectively dissolved the partnership between her and her three partners. It was definite and unequivocal. . . . The effective termination date is therefore February 10, 1971, and Mrs. Reid's subsequent death after this litigation was in progress is an irrelevant factor in determining the rights of the parties. . . .

"In light of our conclusion that an inter-vivos dissolution took place, the provisions of the Act rather than the post-mortem provisions of the agreement, will govern the winding-up of the partnership affairs and the distribution of its assets."

---

4. Bankruptcy of a Partner. The Uniform Partnership Act, Section 31(5), states that the bankruptcy of any partner will cause dissolution.

5. Addition of a Partner. The addition of a partner dissolves the partnership, technically, but in few situations would there be a winding-up and termination.

6. Assignment of a Partner's Interest for the Benefit of Creditors. Under the old common-law rule the voluntary or involuntary sale or assignment of a partner's interest would have dissolved the partnership. Section 27 of the Uniform Partnership Act specifically provides that neither a voluntary nor an involuntary sale for the benefit of creditors automatically dissolves the partnership. The creditors will simply receive the profits which the partner would have received. If, however, a dissolution did occur, then the assignees would get the capital interest of the partner. A few states still follow the old common-law rule of automatic dissolution.

As a general rule of law, a partnership is dissolved whenever its membership changes. When informed of this rule of law, the layperson asks, "If this is true, then how do large law firm and accounting firm partnerships handle the problem, as they are constantly bringing in partners, retiring partners, and so forth?" The answer is that the partnership agreement of such firms specifies the procedure to be followed in case of expulsion, voluntary withdrawal, the addition, death, or retirement of a partner, or any other change in membership. In effect, the old partnership is technically dissolved and reorganized in accordance with the provisions of the agreement each time such a situation occurs.

Dissolution by Operation of Law

The Uniform Partnership Act, Section 31(3) states, "Dissolution is caused: By any event which makes it unlawful for the business of the partnership to be carried on or for the members to carry it on in the partnership." This simply means that if by either legislative enactment or a court decision the business that the partnership was carrying on is no longer legal, then the partnership is dissolved by operation of the law. To refer to Part II, Contracts, the partnership agreement is then an illegal bargain and therefore void. As an illustration, let's say that a partnership is operating a casino in Atlantic City and the gaming commission takes away its license or the gambling law is repealed, making gambling illegal. The partnership will then be dissolved by operation of law.

Dissolution by Court Decree

Often circumstances arise that require a court to determine whether or not a partnership should be dissolved. For example, if an affliction has caused a partner to be of unsound mind and incapable of handling the partnership's affairs, then a remaining partner may petition the court to order the dissolution of the partnership. A court determination might also be desirable if one of the partners has become a drunkard or a drug addict and no longer assumes his or her share of the work and responsibility but refuses to dissolve the partnership voluntarily. Or, if fewer than the number of partners required for voluntary dissolution under the agreement will agree to dissolution, then the partners requesting dissolution may request that the court review the situation.

Dissolution by Expiration

A partnership may be created for a specified period of time, such as 1, 5, or 10 years. When that period expires, the contract of partnership is dissolved.

Rights and Liabilities of the Partners after Dissolution

Dissolution does not change either the existing liability of the partnership or the existing liabilities of the individual partners. Dissolution may be likened to the death of an individual. The person dies, and then an administrator is appointed to settle the affairs of the deceased's estate. The administration of the deceased's estate is a process similar to the winding-up process previously referred to.

The rights of the partners may be likened to the rights of the heirs of a deceased person's estate. The partners have a right to an accounting to see that their interests are being handled properly, and after all the debts have been paid, whatever is left is distributed to them.

Rights of Creditors after Dissolution

All partnership creditors and all other persons who have any current relationship with the partnership should be notified of the dissolution immediately. If these persons are not notified and if they continue to deal with the business after dissolution, the partnership and the individual partners may be liable as if the transaction had occurred prior to dissolution. Thus, once the decision has been made to dissolve the partnership, or once an act of dissolution has occurred, or once a court decree of dissolution has been entered, the first step is to notify in writing everyone who could possibly be concerned with the dissolution and termination of the business.

As indicated by the *Ellingson* case, there are different liability rules for withdrawing and incoming partners. The withdrawing partner remains fully personally liable for all debts of the firm which were incurred prior to withdrawal. Even if there is an agreement that the continuing partners will pay off all existing liabilities without any further contribution from the withdrawing partner, the third-party creditors are not bound by such agreement. Third-party creditors of the firm can, if necessary, impose full personal liability on any person who was a member of the firm when the debt was incurred. To avoid such continuing liability, the withdrawing partner would have to get the agreement of the third-party creditors of the firm. Notice of dissolution, in other words, does not terminate *existing* liabilities; it merely avoids additional *future* liabilities.

The incoming partner will, of course, assume full personal liability for all debts of the firm incurred after becoming a member. As to preexisting debts of the firm, the incoming partner is liable only to the extent of any capital contribution. Here again, if the firm's creditors wanted to have the new partner assume full liability for preexisting debts, a specific agreement to that effect would be necessary.

ELLINGSON v. WALSH, O'CONNOR & BARNESON

104 P.2d 507 (California, 1940)

FACTS   Ellingson was the receiver of the landlord; the suit was to enforce a lease executed by a partnership. Barneson, one of the partners, disputed his personal liability on the lease because it was executed by the firm before he became a member. After Barneson became a general partner in the firm, it subleased the premises in question for a time, collected rent from the sublessee, and paid its own rent to the landlord. The firm owed $2,374.13 for the period from March 1, 1932, to January 25, 1933. The trial court judgment imposed full liability on Barneson along with the other general partners.

ISSUE   Is an incoming partner personally liable for rentals which become due after he joins the firm, where the lease was executed before he joined it?

DECISION   Yes. Judgment affirmed.

REASONS   Chief Justice Gibson said that Barneson's argument based on Section 17 of the UPA did not apply to a lease obligation.

"This contention would be sound if the only obligation of the partnership in this transaction was one which arose prior to appellant's admission to the firm. . . . But appellant's contention overlooks the fact that a tenant of real property is not liable for rent solely by reason of the contract of lease. Tenancies in property need not necessarily be created by valid leases. . . . Where there is a lease, the liability of the tenant arising by operation of law is not superseded by the contractual obligation. Both liabilities exist simultaneously. . . .

"This second partnership did not expressly assume the obligations of the lease, but it occupied the premises. Whether it was liable contractually on the lease is immaterial; it became liable for rent as a tenant. Strangers coming in with consent and occupying the premises would be liable; tenants would be liable even if there were no lease at all; and this second partnership and all its members were liable regardless of any lack of assumption of the obligations of the lease. . . .

"Under the general law the obligation of a tenant arising from occupation of the premises is a continuing one; that is, it arises and binds him continually throughout the period of his occupation. This obligation on the part of appellant first arose when the new partnership, of which he was a member, occupied the premises as a tenant. It follows that his obligation as a tenant arose after his admission to the partnership."

Process of Winding Up

Winding up, the second step in ending a partnership, is the process of liquidating the partnership assets, that is, selling the real and personal property the partnership owned, collecting any outstanding accounts, paying any outstanding debts, and closing out any loose ends of the business—canceling orders not yet delivered, canceling any lease or rental agreements, terminating any relationships that the partnership may have had with persons who were not partners, and so on.

After all the outstanding accounts have been collected, all the assets have been turned into cash, and all the outstanding bills and claims against the partnership have been paid and settled, then any cash remaining has to be divided among the partners. First, if any of the partners have loaned money to the partnership, those loans are repaid with whatever interest was agreed on. Next, the partners will be given back their initial investment. Finally, if there is still some cash left, it will be divided among the partners as profits, and the distribution will be in the same proportions as the distribution of profits in the past and in accordance with the proportions set out in the partnership agreement.

The preceding discussion of the dissolution assumes that the assets of the partnership exceed its outstanding debts. This, of course, is not always the situation of a dissolved partnership which is in the process of winding up. If the assets are insufficient to pay its debts, then the personal assets of the various partners may be called upon to pay them. It must be noted, however, that the personal creditors of an individual partner with personal debts may have priority over creditors who are attempting to collect partnership debts from that partner. If a bankruptcy proceeding is instituted, both groups of creditors will have equal priority against a partner's personal assets. This point is discussed more fully in the next chapter.

Control of the Winding Up

The Uniform Partnership Act, Section 35(1)(a), allows a partner to do "any act appropriate for winding up partnership affairs or completing transactions unfinished at dissolution." Thus, the winding up can be done by any of the partners, or by a partner whom the other partners designate as the winding-up partner, or by an outsider who is appointed as a receiver for the purpose of winding up the partnership and making the final distribution of its assets. Where one partner has wrongfully caused the dissolution, the other partners have the right to do the winding up.

Continuing Business after Dissolution

As indicated previously, the dissolution of a partnership does not automatically mean the termination of its business. Among the common situations that cause dissolution are the death or withdrawal of a partner. In such cases the remaining partners do not necessarily want to terminate the business. Winding up in such situations will simply be an internal process of buying out the interest of the deceased or withdrawing partner and of making appropriate bookkeeping changes for the reorganization and continued operation of the business. Creditors and persons dealing with the firm may not even know that any changes were made when a partnership has been legally dissolved by death of one of the partners. However, if a partner withdraws from the firm, it is wise to so notify all creditors and all persons and firms that deal with the partnership.

Remember, in a general partnership each partner is an agent of the partnership. While dissolution terminates that relationship as between the partners, people who have been doing business with the partnership will not know that the person who has withdrawn is no longer a partner. Until such third parties are notified otherwise, the partnership may be liable for certain acts and dealings of the former partner. Thus, even though the business is to continue after dissolution, it is still necessary to give proper notification of the dissolution to all creditors and all persons who might be dealing with the continuing business.

■ SIGNIFICANCE OF THIS CHAPTER

The partnership is still the most simple and most commonly used form of business organization for small businesses. It is, therefore, important for the future business person to know what a partnership is, how a partnership is created, and how it can be terminated, either by some intentional act of the partners or some unexpected event such as death of a partner.

In this chapter the nature, creation, and termination of partnerships has been discussed. In the next chapter we are concerned with the operation of the partnership and powers, duties, and liabilities of the partners.

DISCUSSION CASE

FARMERS GRAIN CO., INC. v. IRVING
401 N.W.2d 596 (Iowa, 1986)

FACTS: In the spring of 1982 Larry Foster set up a dairy-farming operation on land owned by Paul Irving. The parties' written agreement, which was captioned as a lease, provided that Irving would furnish the land, Foster would be responsible for day-to-day operations, each would furnish 50 percent of the cattle, each would pay 50 percent of the feed expenses and certain other operating expenses, and each would receive 50 percent of the gross income.

During 1982 and early 1983, Foster purchased feed and other farming supplies on open account from the Farmers Grain Company. Farmers Grain asserts it was unaware during most of this time that Irving owned the land in question or had any role in the farming operation. The farming operation was shortlived due to financial difficulties. In the spring of 1983, Foster stopped operating the farm, and in late 1983 or early 1984 he took personal bankruptcy.

Prior to Foster's bankruptcy, Farmers Grain filed the present suit against both Foster and Irving for the unpaid balance of over $27,000 owed on the open account. After Foster's liability was discharged in bankruptcy, Farmers Grain continued the suit against Irving. Farmers Grain contended that Irving was liable for the open account balance because he was a partner in the farming operation rather than a mere landlord. In the alternative, Farmers Grain contended that Irving and Foster were involved in a joint venture or that Irving and Foster were in the relationship of principal and agent.

After a hearing, the district court rejected all of Farmers Grain's theories for imposing liability on Irving for the open account balance. The district court therefore entered judgment against Farmers Grain. Farmers Grain has appealed.

■

Judge Donielson:

In determining whether a partnership exists in the present case, we must address two issues. First, we must examine the written agreement between Foster and Irving to establish whether the elements essential to the creation of a partnership are present. Second, we must examine the actual conduct of Foster and Irving to determine whether such conduct evidenced a partnership. . . .

Iowa courts have traditionally held that "it will not be presumed that the parties to [stock-share farm leases] intended a partnership, in the absence of stipulations or evidence clearly manifesting such a purpose.". . . It is thus quite evident that our courts have held that such stock-sale lease agreements, like the one involved in the present case, generally do not constitute partnerships in order to prevent the exposure of the parties to unwarranted and unexpected liability for conduct that he or she is ordinarily powerless to control.

Having noted the historical treatment of stock-sale leases, we next turn to an examination of the contract between Foster and Irving. . . .

The cardinal principle in the construction of written contracts is that the intent of the parties must control and that except in cases of ambiguity the intent is determined by the language of the contract. . . . The contract in the present case, written on a standardized form provided by the Iowa State University Extension Service, is on its face, a common stock-share lease. The elements of a landlord-tenant are all present. . . . We must, however, examine the contract to determine whether the following elements required to create a partnership are present: (1) an intent by the parties to associate as partners; (2) a business; (3) earning of profits; and (4) co-ownership of profits, property, and control. . . .

Under Iowa law, an intention to associate is the crucial test of a partnership. . . . In the present case, the contract recites an express intention to create a landlord-tenant relationship. Nowhere in the body of the contract do the words *partner, partnership, firm,* or any other term appear. The contract is specifically headed "Iowa Stock-Share Farm Lease-(Non-Partnership)." Irving is consistently referred to as the "landlord" and Foster as the "tenant," and they are identified in no other way. The landlord-tenant language as employed by the parties is therefore useful in discerning their intent. . . .

It is also clear from the contract that the parties contemplated a business purpose when entering into the contract, and that the purpose of such business was the earning of profits. Less clear, however, are the parties' intentions concerning the co-ownership of profits, property, and control.

The contract signed by Foster and Irving contains no provision for the sharing of profits. The contract provides that "[t]he tenant shall set aside and pay to the landlord as rent for the leased premises and as payment for the use of the landlord's share of the co-owned property an amount equal to 50 percent of the gross income from the leased premises. . . ." The contract also contained a requirement that Foster and Irving each assume individually certain expenses. No provision for the sharing of losses is provided for in the contract.

The plaintiff contends that because Irving undoubtedly received some portion of the gross income from the milk receipts, there was prima facie evidence of a partnership. . . . Iowa Code Section 544.7(3), however, specifically states that "[t]he sharing of gross returns does not of itself establish a partnership, whether or not the persons sharing them have a joint or common right of interest in any property from which the returns are derived." Furthermore, the statute cited by the plaintiff, Section 544.7(4), provides that the receipt of a share of profits shall not create an inference of a partnership where such profits were received in payment for rent to a landlord. Thus, the fact that Irving received some portion of the gross receipts does not in and of itself establish the existence of a partnership. We also note that the plaintiff concedes that the parties never discussed the sharing of losses, and therefore unless a partnership is established by other evidence, no agreement to share losses may be inferred. . . .

The contract between Foster and Irving does provide that all livestock except for a 4-H Club calf were to be jointly owned as tenants in common. While the language contained in the contract evidenced some intent to create a community of interest in the dairy cattle, this does not, of itself, establish a partnership. . . .

Finally, concerning the element of co-ownership of control, the key element in determining the existence of a partnership is whether there was contemplated between the parties a community of interest in the administration of the business. . . . Pursuant to section VII of the contract, titled "Farm Operation," Foster was placed in virtually total control of the day-to-day operations of the farm. Pursuant to the contract, Foster was to exclusively handle the hiring of farm help, maintain the upkeep of the buildings and fences, and provide such machinery and equipment as was reasonable. Under section VI of the contract, however, all matters involving the sale or encumbrance of jointly-owned property could not be authorized without the consent of either party. Such a limitation upon the right of each party to act as agent of the other with the operation of the business also denies partnership intent. . . .

Upon an examination of the contract, we agree with the trial court that the contract as signed by Foster and Irving did not envision a partnership as between the parties.

We are aware, however, that a written agreement is not conclusive as to the existence of a partnership. The conduct of the parties and the circumstances surrounding the transactions are also important to our analysis. . . .

The record reveals that both parties did not follow the terms of the written contract, but rather used it only as a guide to be followed as either party chose. The record reveals that at no time did Irving represent himself as a partner of Foster in the dairy operation. In fact, an employee of the plaintiff grain company, Ralph Westlund, testified that Foster intimated that he and his wife owned the dairy operation. Westlund did testify that once when he was visiting Foster concerning his overdue accounts, Foster mentioned that the man walking around the property, Irving, was his partner, but at no other time did Foster intimate to the plaintiff that he was a partner with anyone. Westlund testified that he only looked to Foster for payment of the feed account and that it was not until just before the receivership was established that Irving came to plaintiff's business and told Westlund that he, not Foster, was the owner of the dairy farm.

The record also reveals that no joint bank account was ever established as between Foster and Irving. Though Foster testified that both he and Irving had discussed opening up a joint account from which all expenses and receipts were to be paid and deposited, the evidence reveals that the only authorized signatures on the account were Foster and his wife under the name "Foster Jersey Operating Account." All feed purchases made by Foster were paid pursuant to checks drawn on this account, and all feed purchases made in Foster's own name. The only deposit made by Irving in this account was a single deposit of $4,000 to ensure there were funds to begin the dairy operation.

Concerning the day-to-day operations of the farm, Irving testified that while he did frequently give advice on how to manage the farm, Foster usually ignored such advice. Foster testified that he basically ran the entire farming operation as he saw fit. Though Irving did keep the ledger of the dairy operation and balanced the ledger with the receipts provided him by Foster, it was Foster who had virtual control over how much feed to buy and from whom to buy it. The record reveals that though Irving kept the books, this proved to be difficult because Foster was often several months late in sending the receipts and copies of bills to Irving. Foster also had full control over where and with whom he was going to sell the milk. Though all dairy receipts were to be deposited into the "Foster Jersey Farm Operating Account" and all common expenses were to be paid out of such account, Foster did not deposit all dairy checks into the account but rather assigned his half-interest in the checks to various creditors.

Though the contract signed by the parties contemplated co-ownership of the dairy cattle, in reality the parties' cattle were kept as separate assets through eartags and tattoos. The farm real estate was solely owned by Irving; whereas the farm machinery and dairy equipment were solely owned by Foster.

Based on the above facts, the trial court concluded that the conduct of Foster and Irving did not evidence an intent to create a partnership. We agree. . . .

The trial court additionally rejected plaintiff's argument that a principal-agent relationship existed as between Foster and Irving. We agree.

The burden of proving an agency relationship is upon the party asserting its existence. . . . Though the question of whether an agency relationship exists is ordinarily one of fact, there must be substantial evidence on the question

to generate a jury question; a scintilla is not enough. . . . An agency relationship is a fiduciary relationship resulting from the manifestation of consent by one person, the "principal," that another, the "agent," shall act on the former's behalf and subject to the former's control and from consent by the latter to so act. . . .

We believe that much of our discussion concerning plaintiff's partnership agreement is applicable here. The contract signed by Foster and Irving clearly does not contemplate an agency relationship. The contract gives Foster control over the day-to-day farming operations, except for the sale of jointly owned property. The contract specifically states that any property purchased by either party is to be purchased in either party's own name and on his or her own account, nor could either party enter into a contract on behalf of the other. Regarding the conduct of the parties, Foster testified that it was he who managed the farming operations, and Irving testified that Foster did in fact buy feed on behalf of himself and Irving, Foster paid for such feed on his farm operations account and not on behalf of Irving. Though Irving was to pay one half of the expenses, the Iowa Supreme Court has held that such written agreement is not a sufficient basis for a supplier's cause of action against a landlord. . . . Finally, the evidence reveals that Irving at no time held Foster out as having authority to act on his behalf—Foster, in fact, apparently attempted to intimate that he and his wife were the owners of the farm. We therefore hold that the trial court was correct in finding that no agency relationship existed.

The plaintiff finally contends that the trial court erred in failing to make findings of fact and conclusions of law regarding the issue of joint venture. . . .

Because the theory of joint venture is necessarily intertwined with the applicability of the laws of agency or partnership, the trial court's detailed findings of fact and conclusions of law that no partnership or agency existed decided facts necessary to support a rejection of the joint venture theory.

Affirmed.

■ IMPORTANT TERMS AND CONCEPTS

Uniform Partnership Act of 1914 (UPA)
joint venture
general partnership
trading partnership
partnership by estoppel
dissolution of partnership
termination of a
  partnership

legal entity
syndicate
limited partnership
nontrading partnership
partnership agreement
winding up of
  partnership

■ QUESTIONS AND PROBLEMS FOR DISCUSSION

1. How is a partnership defined by the UPA?
2. What is the difference between a joint venture and a partnership?
3. How may a partnership be dissolved?
4. What is the winding-up process?
5. Lemke had managed a hardware store for Crumley for several years, when Lemke got an offer from one of Crumley's competitors for employment at an in-

creased salary and with a profit-sharing plan. Lemke told Crumley that the offer was so good that he was probably going to accept it. Crumley then offered Lemke a partnership in the new store he was opening. Lemke accepted Crumley's offer, and the parties signed an agreement to form a partnership upon the purchase of the new store. Lemke turned down the competitor's offer. After the new store had been open about six months, Crumley sold it without consulting Lemke and terminated his employment as manager. Lemke sues for damages. What is the result, and why?

6. Rocco Rizzo, Sr., owned and operated a wastepaper business in Chicago, under the firm name of Rocco Rizzo & Co. Each of his four sons came to work in the business. None of the sons received wages, but they were given room and board and all of the profits from the business were divided equally. When Michael joined the business, the name was changed to Rocco Rizzo Son & Co., and later it was changed to Rocco Rizzo Sons & Co. Rocco, Sr., retired from the business in 1915 and deeded the business property to Michael in 1929. Rocco, Jr., died in 1931, survived by his widow (the plaintiff) and two minor sons. The plaintiff brought suit against Michael, Joseph and John, alleging that Rocco, Jr., had been a partner and that an accounting was due. How should the court rule? Explain.

7. Sam Wright and Tom Wright entered into an agreement to purchase a travel agency which was to be operated as a partnership. Tom rejected Sam's offer to purchase Tom's interest in the firm. Tom alleges that Sam, without Tom's knowledge, took exclusive control and possession of the business assets. Tom claimed that Sam used the profits for personal benefit, to the exclusion of Tom and denied Tom participation in the management of the business. No partnership certificate was ever filed. Does Tom have a case? Discuss.

8. Arthur Rehnberg filed an action for an accounting and for breach of an alleged joint venture contract. Rehnberg's complaint alleged that he first conceived of the idea of developing a particular tract of land and building homes on it, that he interested Gilbert C. Hamm and others in the project, that pursuant to his efforts the defendant corporation was formed, and that it entered into a contract with Hamm and him. The contract called for the corporation to take title to the land, for Hamm to build the houses for a building fee of $500 each plus 25 percent of the net profit to the corporation from the sale of the houses, and for Rehnberg to sell the houses for a fee of $150 per house plus 25 percent of the corporation's net profit. Rehnberg had received nothing for the sale of the first 26 homes he sold, and Hamm and the corporation were now building 46 more, which they had listed with another sales agent. Do these facts indicate a joint venture? Why or why not?

43

Partnerships—Operation, Powers, Duties, and Liabilities

CHAPTER OBJECTIVES

THIS CHAPTER WILL:

- Describe a partner's rights and duties to the other partners.
- Explain the relationship of partners to third persons.
- Review the liability of a partner for torts.
- Discuss possible criminal liability of partners.

In the previous chapter we discussed the creation, dissolution, and termination of the partnership. In this chapter we are concerned with the law which governs the day-to-day operation of the partnership. We shall examine the legal relationships between partners; that is, the rights and duties between partners, and also the relationship of partners to third persons. Third persons, of course, include the public and persons doing business with the partnership.

■ PARTNER'S RIGHTS AND DUTIES WITH REGARD TO OTHER PARTNERS

One partner, one vote

Right to Participate in Management Decisions. In a general partnership, unless there is a specific agreement to the contrary, each partner has the right to participate in the partnership's management activities and management decisions. Each partner also has an equal vote with the other partners in the management and decision making of the partnership. Here a partnership differs from a corporation, since in a corporation a stockholder will have votes for directors in proportion to ownership of stock, whereas in a partnership every partner has an equal voice and vote regardless of the amount of money or services the partner has contributed to the business.

Majority vote versus unanimous vote

With regard to day-to-day business decisions, it is not uncommon for partners to delegate certain decision-making authority to a ***managing partner***. This partner will act as a general manager of the business. In a large law or accounting firm, for example, it is not possible for the partners to get together daily to make decisions on business matters. Typically the partners will meet on a regular basis to make policy and general management decisions other than the day-to-day decisions which are delegated to the managing partner. Usually a simple ***majority vote*** is needed on such matters. Certain types of decisions, however, require ***unanimous action*** of the partners. These include decisions involving an amendment of the original articles of partnership, the addition of a new partner, major changes in the business activities of the partnership, and any changes in the division of profits. Again, we must emphasize that a partnership is a contractual arrangement and that the partners may, if they so desire, provide in the partnership agreement that certain changes shall require only a majority vote, a two-thirds vote, a unanimous vote, and so on. Again, we emphasize the desirability of having specific provisions in the partnership agreement to cover these kinds of matters. Especially where there are only two partners, provisions should be included for deciding issues on which the partners are evenly divided, as happened in the next case.

NATIONAL BISCUIT COMPANY, INC. v. STROUD

106 S.E.2d 692 (North Carolina, 1959)

FACTS

C. N. Stroud and Earl Freeman were equal partners in a grocery store business known as Stroud's Food Center. During 1953, 1954, and 1955 the plaintiff regularly sold bread to the store. Several months prior to February 1956, Stroud told one of the plaintiff's agents that he did not want any more of its bread in the store and that he would not be personally responsible for any more bread purchases from it. From February 6 through February 25, 1956, the plaintiff sold $171.04 worth of bread to the store through this agent. The partnership was dissolved, and Stroud took over the business and paid off all of its existing debts ($12,014.45) except for "his" half of the bread bill, $85.52. The plaintiff recovered a judgment for $171.04, and Stroud appealed.

ISSUE Can one partner's act within the normal scope of the business bind the firm where there is an equal division of opinion and where the third party has been so notified?

DECISION Yes. Judgment affirmed.

REASONS Judge Parker noted that the textbooks disagreed on this point. The problem was not handled in the UPA either, so each state's courts had to make up their own mind as to which was the better rule. (In the few cases that had been decided, the state courts were split too.) Judge Parker began with the idea that this contract was within the ordinary scope of the firm's business and that Freeman was an equal partner, with no limitations in the partnership agreement on his ability to represent the firm. He then cited UPA, Section 18(e). "All partners have equal rights in the management and conduct of the partnership business," and Section 18(h), "Any difference arising as to ordinary matters connected with the partnership business may be decided by a majority of the partners." Freeman thus had equal rights to manage the business.

"Stroud, his copartner, could not restrict the power and authority of Freeman to buy bread for the partnership as a going concern, for such a purchase was an 'ordinary matter connected with the partnership business,' for the purpose of its business and within its scope, because in the very nature of things Stroud was not, and could not be, a majority of the partners. Therefore, Freeman's purchases of bread from plaintiff for Stroud's Food Center as a going concern bound the partnership and his co-partner Stroud. . . .

"It would seem a fair inference from the agreed statement of facts that the partnership got the benefit of the bread sold and delivered by plaintiff to Stroud's Food Center, at Freeman's request, from 6 February 1956 to 25 February 1956. . . . But whether it did or not, Freeman's acts, as stated above, bound the partnership and Stroud."

Agreement controls

Right to Share Profits and Duty to Share Losses. Generally speaking, each partner has a right to share in the profits of the partnership and is liable for its losses. The problem to be resolved is how much each partner's share is. If there is no agreement with regard to the sharing of profits, then the partners would share equally. However, it is best to have an agreement specifying a formula for sharing profits. This formula can be based on the various partners' contributions of capital and/or services.

If there is no specific agreement on the sharing of losses, then the partners will share losses in the same ratio as they share profits. However, if there is a formula for sharing losses, then that formula will be followed as between the partners. A partner with a large income from other sources might be willing to accept a larger allocation of losses, since such losses would be set off against the other income for tax purposes.

Once determined, the profit-sharing ratio must be applied to all aspects of the firm's business.

Rights to Salary or Other Compensation. A partner is not, as a matter of right, entitled to a salary or to other compensation for services rendered to the partnership. Absent an agreement which provides for salaries to the various partners, it is assumed that the partners have agreed to share the profits. Obviously, salaries would reduce the total profits. Thus, if salaries or other forms of compensation are contemplated, then a special agreement should be made with regard to these items. It is not uncommon for partners to be paid regular salaries, with profits then being distributed at the end of the calendar or fiscal year.

No salary unless so agreed

Right to Inspect Partnership Books of Account. Each partner has the right to inspect the partnership books and to make copies of those books for his or her own records. The partnership books must be kept at the principal office of the partnership unless the partnership agreement specifies otherwise.

Rights in Partnership Property. Section 8 of the Uniform Partnership Act indicates that all property which is contributed when the partnership is formed and all property which the partnership later acquires by purchase or otherwise is considered partnership property and not the property of any individual partner. Whether a particular asset has been contributed to the firm is a question of fact. Partners may permit the firm to use their personal assets, as for example, space in a building or a vehicle or other piece of equipment. The name listed on the deed or other registration document is some evidence on this question, but certainly not conclusive, since firm assets are sometimes held in the name of one or more individual partners. The fact that the firm is paying taxes, insurance, and license fees on the asset is likewise not conclusive, since these are sometimes paid by the firm in place of a monthly rental to the partner-owner. If there is a specific agreement, either in the articles of partnership or elsewhere, that should nearly always control. In the absence of a specific agreement, the way the asset is treated in the firm's books is probably the best indicator of ownership.

Right to use for firm's business

Section 24 of the UPA says that a partner has three property rights in the firm: (1) rights as to specific pieces of the firm's property; (2) an "interest" in the firm; and (3) the right to participate in management. We have already discussed a partner's management rights. What about the other two of these "property rights"?

As to specific pieces of property owned by the firm, the partners are co-owners in a special form of joint ownership known as "tenancy in partnership." As defined in Section 25, this co-ownership gives each partner an equal right to possess and use the firm's assets for the firm's business. A partner has no right to make any personal use of the firm's assets for personal purposes. A partner would have to get the other partners' permission to take the firm's delivery truck on a camping trip, for instance. Further, this right to make business use of the firm's property is personal in each partner, and cannot be transferred to anyone else by an individual partner. Of course, the firm's rights of ownership of its assets can be sold to someone else by the firm. It's just that a single partner cannot *separately* transfer that person's individual right to use the asset as a partner. As a corollary to that rule, the personal creditor of

Specific firm assets versus interest in the partnership

an individual partner has no claim against any specific firm asset. Partnership assets, in other words, cannot be seized and sold to satisfy personal claims against individual partners. Partnership creditors can seize the firm's assets; creditors of the partners as individuals cannot do so.

When a partner dies, that partner's right in specific firm assets passes to the surviving partner or partners, for partnership purposes. As indicated in the last chapter, when such a dissolution occurs, the firm will either be terminated or continued. In either case, the firm's assets will stay in the firm. There may be a pay-out to the estate of the deceased partner by the firm, as part of the process of settling up accounts, but the firm's assets as such do not pass directly into the deceased partner's estate.

■ **EXHIBIT 43–1**
Partnership Property

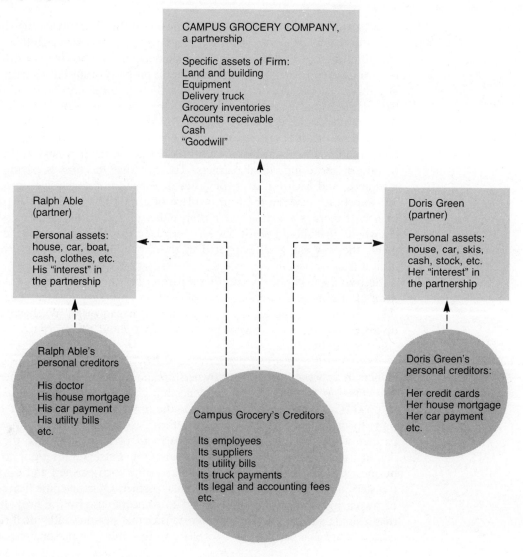

What is being paid over to the deceased partner's estate is actually the third thing mentioned in UPA Section 24: the partner's "interest in the partnership." This phrase has a very precise, technical meaning in the UPA. It means a partner's "share of the profits and surplus." This right to receive money from the firm (profits and surplus) is an item of property owned by each partner as an individual. This claim against the firm for money can thus be voluntarily transferred, or assigned, by each partner, without the consent of the other partners. Likewise, this claim for money can be garnisheed by the creditor of an individual partner. Neither a voluntary assignment nor a garnishment order ("charging order") automatically dissolves the firm. In either case, the firm is free to continue its business; one partner's share of the profits is simply being paid to someone else. That other person is not a partner, has no liability as a partner, and has no right to participate in management. An assignee is not even entitled to receive periodic information on the firm's business or to inspect the books. Further, the assignee can ask for an accounting, if the firm is dissolved, only back to the time of the assignment. Where a court has entered a charging order against a partner's interest, the court can require any information from the firm that is necessary to make sure its order is being obeyed. Where the partner's interest is transferred either voluntarily or involuntarily, the transferee may petition a court for a dissolution. Such a petition could be filed at any time if the partnership is one at will. If the partnership agreement specified a duration, the transferee could petition for dissolution at the end of that period. The trial judge in *Bohonus* apparently had not read the UPA.

BOHONUS v. AMERCO

602 P.2d 469 (Arizona, 1979)

FACTS

Amerco got a judgment against Jerry Bohonus, who was acting as his own attorney. The trial court ruled that his attempt to appeal from the summary judgment was not timely, and granted Amerco's request for a charging order against Bohonus's interest in a partnership. As part of that process, the trial court ordered a sale of Bohonus's interest in the assets of the partnership, which included a liquor license. The sheriff proceeded with the sale. Bohonus appeals.

ISSUE

May the trial court order the sale of partnership property to satisfy the individual debt of a partner?

DECISION

No. Judgment reversed, and case remanded.

REASONS

Speaking for the Arizona Supreme Court, Justice Hays first reviewed the facts and the applicable statutory provisions. The UPA was very clear: a partner's "interest" had a special and very precise meaning.

"With the foregoing statutes in mind, we note that it is only a partner's interest in the partnership which may be charged and, in some jurisdictions, sold. It cannot be overemphasized that 'interest in the partnership' has a special limited meaning in the context of the Uniform Partnership Act and hence in the Arizona statutes.

"The appellee urges that somehow A.R.S. § 29–228(A), *supra*, authorizes the sale of partnership assets and property. We note that the record reflects that pursuant to the provisions of the same statute a receiver was appointed in this case. The fact of the receivership provision enforces the conclusion that only the 'interest in the partnership' may be charged and we find no provision therein for sale of assets or property of the partnership.

"Appellee seeks aid and comfort in the language of A.R.S. § 29–232(B) which provides for dissolution of the partnership upon application of the purchaser of a partner's interest under §§ 29–227 or 29–228. No decree of dissolution however has been asked for here.

"We concur with appellee's position that the charged interest of a debtor-partner can be sold, but further enforcement of the creditor's rights must be pursuant to statute."

Right to Return of Capital Contributions. Section 18 of the Uniform Partnership Act provides that absent any agreement to the contrary among the partners, each partner shall be legally entitled to repayment of any capital contribution to the partnership. The repayment of capital contributions is considered a liability of the partnership. Unless otherwise agreed, a partner is not entitled to interest on a capital contribution. If, however, a partner contributes more than the required share, then the amount in excess of the required contribution will be treated as a loan, and interest will be paid on it.

No interest on capital unless so agreed

Right to Repayment of Expenses. Each partner has a right to be indemnified for payments which he or she makes and personal liabilities which he or she reasonably incurs in the ordinary and proper conduct of the partnership business or in order to preserve the partnership business or its property.

Right to Decide Who Will Be a Partner. No new partners may be admitted to a partnership without the consent of all present partners unless there is an agreed procedure to the contrary in the partnership agreement.

Duties of One Partner to the Other Partner. Each partner is an agent of the partnership and thus, in effect, an agent of every other partner in the partnership. As an agent, the partner has a *fiduciary* relationship with the partnership and with the other partners. This relationship carries with it a number of duties. Among these duties are the following:

Fiduciary duties

1. A partner must be loyal to the partnership and to his or her partners. A partner may not conduct business that will conflict with the partnership unless he or she has the other partner's permission to do so.

2. A partner has a duty to account to the other partners.

3. A partner must use reasonable care in conducting partnership business.

4. If the activities in which a partner engages or the information which a partner has acquired may affect the partnership, the partner has a duty to keep the other partners advised of them.

5. A partner has a legal duty to abide by the terms of the partnership agreement.

▪ PARTNERSHIP LIABILITIES

Liability for Contracts

Special limits on partner's authority

Unless there is a contrary agreement, every partner in a general partnership is an agent of the partnership for the purpose of conducting the partnership's business. It is not uncommon for articles of partnership to limit or to restrict the agency power of the various partners. This is an agreement between the partners, and such internal limitations or restrictions among the partners themselves would not relieve the partnership of liability to a third person who dealt with a partner who exceeded them unless that third person knew that the partner was limited in his or her authority. Since, generally speaking, each partner is an agent of the partnership, the basic law of agency is applicable to the relationship between partners and third persons.

It is a general rule of agency that third persons who deal with an agent have the duty to ascertain the nature and the extent of the alleged agent's authority. Third persons cannot simply rely on a person's statement that he or she is an agent and has certain authority. In the case of a partnership, if a third person verifies that a person is a partner, then the third person has a right to believe that the partner-agent has the normal authority of a partner unless he or she is told otherwise. In other words, if a partnership is going to restrict or limit a partner's authority, then the partnership is responsible for notifying all persons who might be dealing with the partner-agent that the partner-agent does not have the full authority that would ordinarily be expected of a person in that capacity.

The partnership is also a principal and the individual partner an agent with regard to any information that the individual partnership may secure which relates to the partnership's business affairs. If a partner acquires certain information, then the partnership as the principal is automatically charged with the same information. It is also a general rule of agency that statements and representations made by an agent will bind the principal even though the statements may be untrue, provided the statements were made in the course of the agent's business for the principal and provided the statements were within the normally expected authority of such an agent.

Limitations on a Partner's Authority by Law. Since each partner is an agent of the partnership, it would seem that as long as a partner's acts or transactions are within the scope of the partnership business, then the partnership would be liable for the contracts made by a partner on behalf of the partnership. However, there are a number of legal limitations on the authority of individual partners to act for the partnership.

The first such limitation concerns a partner's right to act as an agent with regard to the purchase and conveyance of real estate. Section 10 of the Uniform Partnership Act deals with the right to convey real property owned by the partnership. Where the partnership holds title to real property in the partnership name, any partner may convey the title to that property by a deed executed in the partnership name by that partner as agent. However, if the other partners have not authorized the partner to make such a conveyance, then the partnership can recover the property from the persons to whom it was conveyed. An exception would be made to this right of the partnership to recover the property where the person to whom the conveyance was made transferred the title to an innocent third person who had no knowledge of the situation. Then the innocent third person would prevail over the partnership, provided there was not fraud in the transaction. Another exception would be made where certain acts or past practices of the partnership had created the apparent authority of the particular agent to convey the real estate.

Partner's deed to real estate

The only safe way to purchase real estate from a partnership is to secure both a deed signed by one of the partners and a resolution signed by all of the partners which authorizes the sale of the real estate and also authorizes a specific partner to sign on behalf of the partnership.

Acts which require unanimous consent

Section 9(3) of the Uniform Partnership Act sets out these further restrictions:

> Unless authorized by the other partners or unless they have abandoned the business, one or more but less than all the partners have no authority to: *(a)* assign the partnership property in trust for creditors or on the assignee's promise to pay the debts of the partnership, *(b)* dispose of the good-will of the business, *(c)* do any other act which would make it impossible to carry on the ordinary business of a partnership, *(d)* confess a judgment, *(e)* submit a partnership claim or liability to arbitration or reference.

Section 9(4) of the UPA further confirms that no act of a partner in contravention of a restriction on the partner's authority shall bind the partnership to persons having knowledge of the restriction. Thus, as indicated previously, if there are so-called internal restrictions on the power and authority of a partnership's various agents and if those restrictions have been revealed to third persons, such third persons have no recourse against the partnership for the partner's unauthorized acts.

Authority to Hire and Fire Employees. Going back to the basic authority of the partner, as set out in Section 9 of the Uniform Partnership Act, every partner is an agent of the partnership for the purpose of its business. Every act of a partner, including the execution in the partnership name of any instrument apparently necessary for carrying on the business of the partnership in the usual way, binds the partnership unless the partner has no authority to act for the partnership in that particular matter and the person with whom he is dealing knows the lack of authority.

The articles of partnership could very well state that certain partners are charged with the duty of hiring and firing personnel and that the other partners have no direct authority to do so but have the right to be consulted on matters concerning the employment and tenure of personnel. For example, in a 50-partner law or accounting firm, you could not have each and every partner hiring and firing as he or she saw fit. In a two- or three-member partnership, on the other hand, each of the partners may be involved in the hiring and firing of personnel.

Partner's power to hire and fire

Absent an agreement to the contrary between partners, each partner would have the authority to hire persons whose services were reasonably necessary to carry on the partnership business and the further authority to bind the partnership for a reasonable salary for such persons. Each partner would also have the right to dismiss any employee whose services he or she felt were not reasonably necessary to carry on the partnership business. One can immediately see the problems that could arise if such authority were exercised in a firm with a large number of partners. This is why some internal agreement between the partners should specify which partner or partners have the authority to hire and fire personnel and should restrict the other partners accordingly.

Borrowing Money and Mortgaging the Partnership Property.   Going back to the general authority clause to which we referred briefly, any partner has the authority to borrow money and execute a mortgage on behalf of the partnership, provided this is done for the purpose of carrying on the partnership business in the usual way. The Uniform Partnership Act does not differentiate between the authority of an agent in a trading partnership and that of an agent in a nontrading partnership. However, in interpreting a partner's authority, courts in many jurisdictions have generally found that partners in a trading partnership which is engaged in buying and selling goods and property have greater implied and apparent authority to buy and sell property, to borrow in the partnership name, and to indorse or execute negotiable instruments in the partnership name if this is reasonably necessary to carry on the partnership business.

Trading versus nontrading partnerships

In partnerships that are considered to be engaged in a nontrading business, such as law firms or accounting firms, courts generally do not feel that individual partners should have the implied and apparent authority to borrow money or to execute or indorse negotiable instruments in the partnership name. Generally speaking, courts have held that the partners in nontrading partnerships do not have the authority to bind the partnership in such situations unless it was customary to do so in a given partnership or unless there was an actual necessity to do so. Thus trading partnerships are governed by standards different from the standards that govern partners in nontrading partnerships, insofar as their authority with relation to third parties is concerned.

Lawsuits Involving Partnerships.   Under the common law a partnership was not a legal entity, and therefore a partnership could not sue or be sued in the partnership name. If a third person wanted to sue a partnership, the complaint had to name all of the partners as individual defendants, and each partner had to be individually served with a summons. This could be accomplished without too much effort when dealing with simple father-son partnerships or three- or four-member partnerships. However, if it had to be done with a modern accounting firm having more than a hundred partners, not all of whom lived in the same jurisdiction, the chore could prove very frustrating. Many states have enacted statutes that allow a partnership to be sued as an entity by simply naming the partnership by its firm name. These statutes also allow a partnership to bring action as a legal entity against third persons. Most statutes, however, require that the partners be named as defendants and be served personally with process if this is at all possible. Most statutes also permit the petitioner to secure a judgment against the partnership if the petitioner served at least one of the partners even though several other partners were not served. In a case where the partnership entity was sued and at least one of the partners was named and served process, the judgment can be collected from the partnership assets. However, any judgment amount not collectible from the partnership assets cannot be collected from the individual partners unless the individual partners were sued, made a party to the lawsuit and properly served with a summons.

Lawsuit in firm name

Getting a judgment against a partnership is the first step. The next step is to collect it. Section 40(h) of the Uniform Partnership Act states: "When partnership property and the individual properties of the partners are in possession of a court for distribution, partnership creditors shall have priority on partnership property and separate creditors on individual property, saving the rights of lien or secured creditors as heretofore." In other words, lienholders and secured creditors come first; the partner's individual creditors for his or her individual bills come next; and then the balance can be taken for partnership debts. The new Bankruptcy Code which became law in October 1979 changes the law of distribution with regard to the assets of partners. It provides that in a case concerning the partnership, if the assets of the partnership are insufficient to satisfy the claims allowed, then the general partner in the partnership will be liable to the trustee in bankruptcy for the full amount of the deficiency. Thus, in the case of a bankrupt partnership the trustee in bankruptcy may now seek to recover the entire deficiency from any one of the general partners on a pro rata basis with the partner's personal creditors.

Liability for Torts
Torts within scope of business

Section 13 of the Uniform Partnership Act provides that when a partner is acting in the ordinary course of the business of the partnership or is acting with the authority of the co-partners of the partnership, then if that partner commits a tort, the partnership will be liable for damages to the same extent that the partner committing the tort was liable. If, however, the injured person was another partner in the partnership, then the partnership would not be liable for the claims of the injured partner.

What if the person who committed the tort was not a partner, but was an employee of the partnership? The UPA does not specifically state that the partnership is liable for the torts of its employees. However, Section 4(3) of the UPA states that the law of agency shall apply under this act. Thus, the partnership is the employer and is liable for the tortious acts of its employees, provided the employee was acting within the scope of employment.

Section 15 of the Uniform Partnership Act provides that all partners are liable not only jointly but severally for any liability chargeable to the partnership under Section 13 of the UPA. Thus, if there are insufficient funds in the partnership to pay the damages resulting from the tort, then the partners may jointly pay for the loss. Or, if the partnership has assets and one partner has personal assets and the others do not, that partner may be held severally liable for the entire loss. This should be a serious concern whenever you enter into a general partnership, as you could end up losing your personal assets, such as your home and your life savings, simply because of the negligence of some other person. This is one of the primary reasons that persons with individual assets over and above their investment in the business should consider being a limited partner in a limited partnership or forming a corporation. If there are unexpected tort losses, the most you as an investor will lose is your original investment, not your home and your life savings. It is, of course, recommended that the partnership carry liability insurance to cover tort losses. However, people sometimes forget to pay insurance policy premiums when due, and often the loss exceeds the policy limits. In the *Phillips* case Dan learned the hard way about his vicarious liability for Isadore's tort.

PHILLIPS v. COOK

210 A.2d 743 (Maryland, 1965)

FACTS   Daniel Phillips and Isadore Harris were equal partners in a business known as Dan's Used Cars. Neither of them owned a personal car. They had agreed that Harris would use the firm's cars for transportation to and from home. He could demonstrate and sell such cars, and they had "for sale" signs placed in them at various times. He could also use such cars to visit other dealerships and buy cars for the firm's inventory and to stop at the Department of Motor Vehicles so that necessary paperwork could be done for the firm's business. On January 7, 1960, while driving one of the firm's cars, Harris hit a car driven by Smith, which in turn hit a car driven by Dolores Cook. Harris was on his way home at the time. About a week later, the partnership was terminated. Dolores and her husband, Marshall, sued the partnership and received a judgment. Phillips appealed.

ISSUE   Did the accident occur within the scope of the firm's business?

DECISION   Yes. Judgment affirmed.

REASONS   Judge Marbury thought that the trial court had properly instructed the jury and that there was substantial evidence to support the jury's verdict.

"The test of the liability of the partnership and of its members for the torts of any one partner is whether the wrongful act was done within what may reasonably be found to be the scope of the business of the partnership and for its benefit. The extent of the authority of a partner is determined essentially by the same principles as those which measure the scope of an agent's authority. . . .

"In the past, we have held both in workmen's compensation cases and others that where an employer authorizes or furnishes the employee transportation to and from his work as an incident to his employment, or as a benefit to the employer, the employee is considered in the course of his employment when so traveling."

Judge Marbury then pointed out that the very car which Harris was driving was for sale and that Harris often returned to the dealership or called on customers at night. He also pointed to the specific agreement which permitted each partner to use the firm's cars. In addition, Maryland motor vehicle statutes provided a rebuttable presumption that a vehicle titled in the partnership name and being driven by a partner was being used for partnership business. Phillips had not overcome that presumption.

Liability for Crimes

As previously stated, under the common law a partnership was not viewed as a legal entity, and it could not sue or be sued. Any legal action had to be taken by or against the individual partners. Thus, if the partnership was not a legal entity, it could neither commit nor be charged with a crime. Again, most states have now enacted statutes which allow a partnership to be sued as a legal entity by simply naming the partnership by its firm name. Many states have gone further and found that a partnership can be a legal entity for criminal purposes and can be guilty of a crime. The criminal penalty is simply a fine to be paid by the partnership from partnership funds. The nonacting partners normally could not be jailed for a crime committed by the partnership,

Crimes by a partner

particularly if the crime requires proof of a specific wrongful intent. If the partners are to be punished, they must be separately charged and have separate trials.

An individual partner who commits a crime while in the course of activities on behalf of and in the scope of the partnership will be criminally liable. But neither the partnership as an entity nor any other partner will be criminally liable unless the other partner or partners and/or the partnership participated in the criminal actions. For example, Jerry Jones is a partner in Jones and Son Construction Co. Jerry is discussing a construction bid with a client, and they get into a heated argument. Jerry, an ex-professional boxer now weighing 275 pounds, strikes the client in the face, breaking his glasses injuring him. Jerry is arrested for criminal assault and battery. Neither the two other partners nor the partnership is guilty of any crime, although they could very likely be held liable in tort.

Let's change the facts. Say Jerry was hired as an "enforcer" to "convince" clients to accept the bids from Jones and Son Construction Co., and it was understood by the partners that Jerry would use force to get a desired result, a signed contract. In that case, the other partners would be found to be accessories to the criminal act and would be criminally liable.

Liability for Partner's Breach of Trust

Partner's misuse of another's property

As previously stated, each partner is an agent of the other partners. As such, each is responsible for the acts or omissions of the other partners, provided such acts or omissions are in the ordinary course of business of the partnership. If any partner acting in the course of the partnership business, or acting within the scope of apparent authority, receives money or property in its custody and such money or property is misapplied by one of the partners, then in both situations the partnership is liable and must make good the loss.

▪ SIGNIFICANCE OF THIS CHAPTER

Once a partnership is created and begins transacting business, many problems regarding day-to-day operation will arise. It becomes important to know what each partner's rights and duties are regarding the day-to-day business operation. This chapter sets out the partners' rights and duties to each other and also discusses the relationship of the partner to third persons.

DISCUSSION CASE

CLEMENT v. CLEMENT
260 A.2d 728 (Pennsylvania, 1970)

FACTS: Charles and L. W. Clement are brothers whose 40-year partnership has ended in acrimonious litigation. The essence of the conflict lies in Charles' contention that L. W. has over the years wrongfully taken for himself more than his share of the partnership's profits. Charles discovered these misdeeds during negotiations with L. W. over the sale of Charles' interest in the partnership in 1964. He then filed an action in equity, asking for dissolution of the partnership, appointment of a receiver, and an accounting. Dissolution was ordered and a receiver appointed. After lengthy hearings on the issue of the accounting the chancellor decided that L. W., who was the brighter of the two and who kept the partnership books, had diverted partnership funds. The chancellor awarded Charles a one-half interest in several pieces of property owned by L. W.; and in several insurance policies on L. W.'s life on the ground that these had been purchased with partnership assets.

The court en banc heard the case and reversed the chancellor's decree in several material respects. The reversal was grounded on two propositions: that Charles' recovery could only be premised on a showing of fraud and that this burden was not met, and that the doctrine of laches foreclosed Charles' right to complain about the bulk of the alleged misdeeds.

■

Justice Roberts gave the opinion for the court:

We disagree with the court en banc's statement of the applicable law and therefore reverse. Our theory is simple. There is a fiduciary relationship between partners. Where such a relationship exists, actual fraud need not be shown. There was ample evidence of self-dealing and diversion of partnership assets on the part of L. W.— more than enough to sustain the chancellor's conclusion that several substantial investments made by L. W. over the years were bankrolled with funds improperly withdrawn from the partnership. Further, we are of the opinion that the doctrine of laches is inapplicable because Charles' delay in asserting his rights was as much a product of L. W.'s concealment and misbehavior as of any negligence on his part. In all this we are strongly motivated by the fact that the chancellor saw and heard the various witnesses for exhausting periods of time and was in a much better position than we could ever hope to be to taste the flavor of the testimony. . . .

One should not have to deal with his partner as though he were the opposite party in an arm's-length transaction. One should be allowed to trust his partner, to expect that he is pursuing a common goal and not working at cross-purposes. This concept of the partnership entity was expressed most ably by Mr. Justice, then Judge, Cardozo. . . .

Joint adventurers, like copartners, owe to one another, while the enterprise continues, the duty of the finest loyalty. Many forms of conduct permissible in a workaday world for those acting at arm's length, are forbidden to those bound by fiduciary ties. A trustee is held to something stricter than the morals of the marketplace. Not honesty alone, but the punctilio of an honor the most sensitive, is then the standard of behavior. As to this there has developed a tradition that is unbending and inveterate. . . . Only thus has the level of conduct for fiduciaries been kept at a level higher than that trodden by the crowd. It will not consciously be lowered by any judgment of this court. . . .

It would be unduly harsh to require that one must prove actual fraud before he can recover for a partner's derelictions. Where one partner has so dealt with the partnership as to raise the probability of wrongdoing, it ought to be his responsibility to negate that inference. It has been held that "where a partner fails to keep a record of partnership transactions, and is unable to account for them, every presumption will be made against him.". . . Likewise, where a partner commingles partnership funds with his own and generally deals loosely with partnership assets he ought to have to shoulder the task of demonstrating the probity of his conduct.

In the instant case L. W. dealt loosely with partnership funds. At various times he made substantial investments in his own name. He was totally unable to explain where he got the funds to make these investments. The court en banc held that Charles had no claim on the fruits of these investments because he could not trace the money that was invested therein dollar for dollar from the partnership. Charles should not have had this burden. He did show that his brother diverted substantial sums from the partnership funds under his control. The inference that these funds provided L. W. with the wherewithal to make investments was a perfectly reasonable one for the chancellor to make, and his decision should have been allowed to stand.

The doctrine of laches has no role to play in the decision of this case. It is true that the transactions complained of cover a period of many years. However, we do not think that it can be said that Charles negligently slept on his rights to the detriment of his brother. L. W. actively concealed much of his wrongdoing. He cannot now rely upon the doctrine of laches—that defense was not intended to reward the successful wrongdoer.

The decree is vacated and the case remanded for further proceedings consistent with this opinion.

■ IMPORTANT TERMS AND CONCEPTS

managing partner
majority vote
right to share profits
partnership books of
accounts
return of capital contributions
mortgaging partnership
property
criminal liability of a partnership
liability of a partnership
for partner's breach of
trust

one partner, one vote
unanimous vote
duty to share losses
partnership property
fiduciary duties
lawsuits involving part-
nerships
liability of a partnership
for torts
liability for misuse of partnership funds by a
partner

■ QUESTIONS AND PROBLEMS
FOR DISCUSSION

1. What types of decisions require unanimous consent
of all the partners?
2. What are the presumptions as to the sharing of profits
and losses among partners?
3. What is the difference between a partner's rights in
specific firm assets and his or her "interest in the partnership"?
4. What authority does one partner have to make contracts for the firm?
5. Bennie and Beatrice Styles, husband and wife, operate
their farm as a partnership. Bennie had a serious accident with his camper-van while he was on a vacation
fishing trip. Huffy, the driver of the other car, got a
$40,000 judgment against Bennie, which judgment
has not been paid. In an attempt to collect the judgment, Huffy had the court issue a writ of execution
against all of Bennie's personal property. The sheriff
came out to the farm with this writ and seized and
sold 50 cows. Beatrice sues the sheriff and his bonding

company for conversion of partnership assets. Should
Beatrice win this lawsuit? Why or why not?
6. Harvey and Haviland formed a partnership for the
purpose of brewing and selling beer and ale. Without
Haviland's knowledge or consent, Harvey, in the firm's
name, negotiated the takeover of a lease on a brewery.
This lease still had seven years to run. Harvey, for
the firm, promised to take over the lease and to pay
the remaining rentals. The firm operated the brewery
for about seven months and then dissolved. The firm
sold the equipment and the lease to Dougherty, who
also went bankrupt. When the landlord sued for unpaid rentals, Haviland denied that he was liable in
any way. What is the result, and why?
7. Porks and Lozer agreed on a plan for the purchase
and resale of a particular tract of land. Lozer was to
buy the land, pay off the back taxes, and take title
in his own name. Porks was to look for buyers for
the property. Lozer bought the land for $45,000 and
paid off the back taxes of $3,500. Lozer also paid
off a $12,000 "claim" against the land, which was
presented to him. Lozer acted in good faith by paying
this claim, but if he had checked with Porks, Porks
would have told him that the claim was invalid and
not to pay it. Lozer then resold the land for $156,000.
Porks challenges the $12,000 payment as a proper
charge against the partnership profits. What is the
proper allocation of profits here? Explain.
8. J. T. Brewer and G. E. Padgett were partners in the
Alabama Cabinet Works, which was engaged in home
improvement and construction. Padgett bought certain building materials and supplies for the firm from
Benson Hardware and signed a promissory note in
the firm name for the contract price. Padgett's authority was limited by the partnership agreement, but
Benson didn't know of the limitation when he dealt
with Padgett. Brewer questioned Padgett's authority
to sign the note and argued that at least he should
not be held personally liable for the note. Who is
liable on this note? Explain.

44

Limited Partnerships and Other Forms of Business Organizations

CHAPTER OBJECTIVES

THIS CHAPTER WILL:

- Explain the differences between a limited partnership and a general partnership.
- Review the process of formation of a limited partnership.
- Discuss the changes under the Revised Uniform Limited Partnership Act of 1976.
- Discuss other forms of business organizations.

■ LIMITED PARTNERSHIPS

A limited partnership differs from a general partnership in two major respects. First, a limited partnership allows certain partners to have limited liability for the debts and other liabilities of the partnership. Second, a general partnership may be formed by an express oral or written agreement or by an implied agreement, whereas a limited partnership agreement must be in writing and must conform to the statutory requirements for the formation of such a partnership.

The National Conference of Commissioners on Uniform State Laws, after finding that limited partnership laws varied from state to state, recognized the need for uniformity. In 1916 the commissioners drafted the *Uniform Limited Partnership Act.* This act was adopted by every state except Louisiana, which has its own limited partnership law.

In 1976 the commissioners revised the Uniform Limited Partnership Act. Nearly all states have adopted the revised act, but it is still important to note what state is involved and whether the new act or the old act is the effective statutory law in that state. Our primary focus in this chapter will be the *Revised Uniform Limited Partnership Act (RULPA).*

Advantages of limited partnership

Limited partnerships have become a very popular form of business organization for persons who wish to invest but want limited liability, and who also wish to have their profits treated as partnership profits and not as corporate profits subject to the corporate income tax. There is no income tax on the profits of a limited partnership. The partners divide the profits in accordance with the partnership agreement. The partnership files with the Internal Revenue Service a partnership return which is merely an informational return. The individual partner's profit is then shown on his or her income tax return, and the individual pays tax on that profit along with the tax on his or her other income. The limited partnership form of business organization is found mostly in so-called tax shelter ventures, such as land development organizations, oil exploration ventures, and cattle feeding ventures.

Definition of a Limited Partnership

No voice in management

Section 101(7) of the Revised Uniform Limited Partnership Act (RULPA) defines a limited partnership as a "partnership formed by two or more persons . . . having as members one or more general partners and one or more limited partners." Thus, each limited partnership must have at least one general partner with unlimited liability for the business of the partnership and at least one partner with limited liability. The limited partner, like a stockholder in a corporation, cannot be liable for more than his or her investment. However, unlike the corporation stockholder, who has a voice in the control of the business through votes for directors based on the number of shares owned, the limited partner has no voice in the control of the business. In fact, a limited partner who does take a part in the management or control of the business may be held personally liable for the firm's debts, as seen in the *Holzman* case. Thus, if a limited partner wants to retain complete limited liability, he or she should not become involved in any way in the operation of the business.

Under RULPA, a limited partner who acts substantially like a general partner is liable as a general partner to all the firm's creditors. But if the limited partner merely participates in control, he or she has full liability only to those third parties with actual knowledge of that participation.

HOLZMAN v. DE ESCAMILLA

195 P.2d 833 (California, 1948)

FACTS   Ricardo de Escamilla was raising beans on a farm near Escondido when he organized Hacienda Farms, a limited partnership, with James Russell and H. W. Andrews. Russell and Andrews were the limited partners; Ricardo was the general partner. Hacienda Farms operated only from February to December 1943, when it went bankrupt. Holzman, Hacienda's trustee in bankruptcy, sought to hold Russell and Andrews personally liable for its debts, on the basis that they actively participated in the management of the farm. They appealed from a judgment imposing such liability.

ISSUE   Was the participation of these limited partners in management sufficient to impose liability as general partners on them?

DECISION   Yes. Judgment affirmed.

REASONS   Justice Marks, reviewing the facts, found that Russell and Andrews had participated substantially in the operation of Hacienda Farms. When asked whether he had had conversations with them prior to deciding to plant tomatoes, Ricardo said: "We also conferred and agreed as to what crops we would put in." He also said: "There . . . was never any crop that was planted or contemplated in planting that wasn't thoroughly discussed and agreed upon by the three of us; particularly Andrews and myself." In fact, Andrews and Russell overruled de Escamilla on the planting of peppers, watermelons, and eggplant. They also asked him to resign as manager of Hacienda and replaced him with Harry Miller. Russell and Andrews also seemed to have control of Hacienda's finances.

"The manner of withdrawing money from the bank accounts is particularly illuminating. The two men had absolute power to withdraw all the partnership funds in the banks without the knowledge or consent of the general partner. Either Russell or Andrews could take control of the business from de Escamilla by refusing to sign checks for bills contracted by him and thus limit his activities in the management of the business. They were active in dictating the crops to be planted, some of them against the wish of de Escamilla. This clearly shows they took part in the control of the business of the partnership and thus became liable as general partners."

Creation of a Limited Partnership

A *limited partnership certificate* must be prepared. This certificate must state the name of the limited partnership—for example, Wildcat Oil Exploration Associates, Ltd. If the Revised Uniform Limited Partnership Act of 1976 has been adopted by the state where the limited partnership is being formed, then the name of the limited partnership would have to be Wildcat Oil Exploration Associates, Limited Partnership. In other words the letters *Ltd.* are no longer allowed since many consumers do not know what *Ltd.* means. If the words *Limited Partnership* are written out in full, the public should be aware of the limited liability of some partners.

*Contents of certificate   Next, the certificate must state the purpose of the limited partnership. In this case the purpose would be to conduct oil explorations in the state of Texas. The principal place of business of the limited partnership, the names and addresses of each general and limited partner, the duration of the partnership, and the amount of the contribution that is to be received from each partner must also be stated. Other requirements include a statement as to whether the limited partners can be admitted to their partnership and whether the limited partners may sell and assign their interests to other persons. The limited partnership certificate must be filed and recorded in a designated office such as the office of the county recorder or the county clerk in the county where the principal office is located. The filing gives persons who deal with the limited partnership public notice as to the items of information that are provided on the certificate of limited partnership. In most states it is also necessary to file the limited partnership certificate with a state authority such as the secretary of state's office.

Once the limited partnership certificate has been filed and recorded, the limited partnership may proceed to do business. If the statutory requirements were properly adhered to, the limited partners should be free from liability beyond their investment. However, the partners may desire to draft more detailed articles of partnership in order to provide for matters not considered in the limited partnership certificate.

Defective Formation. What happens if the business associates fail to comply with the required procedures for becoming a limited partnership? Of course, any of them who are doing anything knowingly, with fraudulent intent, would be fully liable personally for all claims against the firm. But suppose one or more of the associates is acting in good faith, assuming that he or she is a limited partner, when in fact the statutory requirements have not been met. What happens to those good faith investors?

Potentially, each investor in the business would have full, unlimited personal liability for all the debts of the business. If they have failed to achieve the status of a limited partnership, they must then be general partners in a general partnership. They meet all the definitional elements as a partnership, so they will be held liable as general partners. Recognizing that this result is potentially unfair to an investor who acts in good faith, the old Uniform Limited Partnership Act (ULPA) included an "escape hatch" in Section 11. Such an investor is not held personally liable if he or she promptly renounces any interest in the profits of the business as soon as the mistake is discovered.

The Revised ULPA gives an investor a choice. When he discovers the mistake, he can either withdraw from future equity participation in the firm, *or* file a proper limited partnership certificate or an amendment, to correct the error. This rule is probably more fair to the investor, since it would permit the firm to proceed as planned once the correction was made. RULPA does provide, however, that such an investor continues to be fully personally liable to persons who thought the investor was a general partner before the correction was made.

General Partners' Rights and Duties

The general partner or partners have essentially the same rights and duties as any partner in a general partnership insofar as the partnership's day-to-day business operations are concerned. There is, however, one difference. Such partners cannot, on their own, take in other general partners or other limited partners unless this right has been granted to them in the limited partnership certificate.

Limited Partners' Rights and Duties

Protection for limited partner

Basically the limited partner has no specific duties. He or she is simply an investor. However, Section 305 of the Revised Uniform Limited Partnership Act gives the limited partner the right to inspect and copy the partnership certificate, list of partners, tax returns, and partnership agreement. The limited partner also has the right to demand full information on all matters affecting the partnership. Thus, the limited partner may not have a voice as such in the management of the limited partnership, but he or she need not stand by and watch as fraudulent or wasteful acts are being committed by the general partner. In addition, a limited partner may petition a court of proper jurisdiction to have a dissolution and winding up of the limited partnership. If that occurs, the limited partner is entitled to receive a share of the profits as income and may also be entitled to have his or her contribution returned in accordance with the limited partnership certificate, subject of course to any exceptions under local law. As an alternative to a lawsuit for dissolution, RULPA permits a limited partner to bring a derivative suit for damages on behalf of the firm. Such a suit might be brought against a general partner for injuries caused to the firm by a breach of fiduciary duty. Mrs. Allen is using this latter approach in the following case.

ALLEN v. STEINBERG

223 A.2d 240 (Maryland, 1966)

FACTS

Steinberg and his two general partners owned 84 acres of land in Baltimore County, which land they had encumbered with $365,000 worth of mortgages. To get operating capital, they solicited investments from persons who would become limited partners. The plaintiff's husband was one of those solicited. He said that he and his wife would not be interested in any construction project but that they would be interested in a land deal. Mrs. Allen sent a check for $10,000, after being assured that they were investing in land and that the building operation on that land would be separate. The partnership agreement which Mrs. Allen signed had been redrafted by her husband so that the definition of the firm's business was "the ownership and promotion for development of a tract of land" rather than "the ownership and development of a tract of land." Through various manipulations, the general partners had the firm assume $275,000 worth of utility installation costs and also mortgaged part of the tract for $140,000, all without the knowledge or consent of the limited partners. The firm's assets were lost, and Mrs. Allen sued the general partners for an accounting and for damages resulting from their mismanagement. She appealed from the trial court's dismissal of her suit.

ISSUE

Did the general partners act in contravention of the agreement, and/or possess the firm's property for other than the firm's purposes?

DECISION

Yes, if plaintiff's allegations are believed. Judgment reversed.

REASONS

Chief Judge Hammond felt that the case had to be tried, since Mrs. Allen had made out a prima facie case for recovery. Steinberg and the other defendants should be required to rebut her allegations with other evidence, if they had any.

"[T]he claims of appellant . . . might be paraphrased to be that she was a sheltered ewe, who, despite the guidance of a learned and experienced shepherd (her husband), was led by the general partners not to the slaughter but to the shearing area where she was fleeced of her investment and anticipated profits. . . .

"If the partnership agreement is looked to alone as the integration of the agreement of the parties, it would appear that the partnership purpose was to hold land and procure and facilitate its development by others. The phrase 'ownership and promotion for development of a tract of land' would seem to negate the conclusion that direct development of or direct participation in development by the partnership was intended. The wording of the partnership agreement might leave open exactly how far and to what extent 'promotion' might go, but it could hardly extend to subordinating ground rents to mortgages or making unsecured loans or mortgaging partnership land without receiving the proceeds of the mortgage. Any doubt as to the meaning intended by the phrase 'promotion for development' was removed, at least in the present posture of the case, by the extrinsic evidence which the chancellor received over objection by the appellee."

Dissolution, Winding Up, and Termination of a Limited Partnership

No dissolution if limited partners change

In Chapter 42 it was noted that the death, bankruptcy, or withdrawal of a partner were causes for dissolution of the partnership. These rules do not apply to a limited partnership. Since limited partners are simply limited liability investors, they have no voice in management, and are not liable for more than their investment. Thus, there is no specific loss to the limited partnership if a limited partner dies or becomes bankrupt. For these reasons, the substitution of a new limited partner for an old limited partner or the addition of a limited partner will not cause dissolution of a limited partnership. Only if all the limited partners have either died or withdrawn and no substitutions have been made would the death or withdrawal of limited partners necessitate the dissolution of a limited partnership. A limited partnership must have a minimum of one limited partner. Without the limited partner there is no limited partnership.

The death or withdrawal of a general partner from a limited partnership will cause the limited partnership to be dissolved unless there is a provision in the certificate to substitute another person for the deceased or withdrawing general partner.

Amendments to certificate

Thus, a limited partnership will normally not be dissolved until the general partners or their replacements decide to dissolve the partnership or until a specific term expires, if the limited partnership was created for a specified term.

Although the limited partnership need not be dissolved upon the death or withdrawal of a general partner if provisions were made for that partner's replacement, the limited partnership still has to file and record an amended limited partnership certificate to inform the public of the change. If a limited partner dies or withdraws and is not replaced, no amendments need be filed and recorded. However, if another person is substituted or added as a limited partner, then the certificate must be amended. Also, if a limited partnership decides to go into a different business or to make any other major changes in the business which concern matters covered in its certificate, it must file and record an amended certificate that gives the public full notice of these changes. Section 24 of the Uniform Limited Partnership Act specifies the various changes in the business that require an amended certificate be filed.

Under RULPA, amendments to the certificate must be filed within 30 days after (1) the admission of a new partner; (2) the withdrawal of a partner; (3) the continuation of the firm's operations after a judicial dissolution due to withdrawal of the last general partner; or (4) any change in a partner's contribution to the firm. Changes in the addresses of limited partners need only be filed once a year.

Changes under the Revised Uniform Limited Partnership Act of 1976

Definition of control under old ULPA

The Revised ULPA has now been adopted by nearly all states. A major reason for the revision of the Uniform Limited Partnership Act was to clarify the question of control. The 1916 ULPA states that a limited partner may not participate in the control of the limited partnership. A limited partner who does participate in the control of the business will be treated in the same way as a general partner and thus will lose limited liability. The problem is simply what is control. Can a limited partner make suggestions to the general partner? Can a limited partner have a vote? Conflicting court decisions have been reached in the various states as to what a limited partner may or may not do insofar as participation in the control of the business is concerned. Some states even amended their limited partnership statute to grant limited partners a right to vote on certain types of major business decisions.

Because of the concern over the growing nonuniformity of the Uniform Limited Partnership laws, the Revised ULPA was drafted. This act specifically allows the limited partner to do certain acts with the understanding that these acts do not constitute participation in the control of the business. The following acts are permitted by the Revised ULPA:

Permitted acts under revised ULPA

1. Being a contractor for, or an agent of, the partnership.
2. Consulting with and advising a partner with respect to the business.
3. Acting as a surety for the partnership.
4. Approving or disapproving of an amendment to the partnership agreement.
5. Voting on such matters as dissolution, winding up, the transfer of all or substantially all of the assets, the incurrence of debt other than in the ordinary course of business, a change in the nature of the business, and the removal of a general partner.

In addition to allowing the limited partner to do the above acts, the Revised ULPA also provides that if a limited partner does actively participate in the control of the partnership by doing acts other than those mentioned above, the limited partner will only be liable to those persons who did business with the partnership and who had knowledge of the limited partner's participation in its control. The Revised ULPA also makes some general changes in the filing requirements for limited partnerships. It requires that the certificate of limited partnership be filed in the office of the secretary of state in the state where the limited partnership is doing business, and it also requires that the limited partnership designate a resident in the state where it is doing business as the registered agent for the service of process for lawsuits which may be filed against it. These requirements are similar to the filing requirements for corporations.

Services OK under revised ULPA

The original ULPA restricted the limited partner's capital contribution to cash or other property. Under the Revised ULPA the limited partner may contribute services as a capital contribution as well as or in place of cash or other property. This is a very important change, since it means that the consulting expertise or other specialized talents of limited partners can now be contributed as a capital contribution to a limited partnership.

Another change in the Revised ULPA was previously referred to. That change requires that the full words *limited partnership* be used in the firm name rather than the abbreviation "Ltd.," which is allowed under the original ULPA.

■ OTHER ORGANI-ZATIONAL FORMS

Transferable shares

Joint Stock Company. The *joint stock company* is a form of business organization in which the management of the business is placed in the hands of trustees or directors. Shares represented by certificates are then issued to the members of the company, who are in effect, joint owners of the enterprise. These certificate holders then elect the board of directors or the board of trustees. Like the shares of a corporation, the shares or certificates are transferable, and their transfer does not cause dissolution, as it would in a partnership. Also the death of a shareholder does not dissolve the organization, as would be the case for a partnership. The joint stock company exists for the period of time stated in its bylaws. In reality, the joint stock company is a partnership; however, it has many of the advantages of the corporation. Its principle disadvantage is that there is still unlimited personal liability, as in a partnership. Depending on the state statute, the joint stock company may or may not be considered a legal entity for purposes of litigation.

One may wonder why the law recognizes a business organization such as the joint stock company. The joint stock company is a compromise between the partnership and the corporation. It has the partnership's tax advantages since it pays no separate corporation tax, and it has the corporation's advantages of transferability and duration, but it also has the partnership's disadvantage of unlimited liability. At one time, the joint stock company was a popular form of business. However, with the advent of the subchapter S corporation, it no longer has great appeal.

Business Trust. The **business trust,** or the **Massachusetts trust,** as it is often called, is a business organization where title to certain property is deeded over to a trustee or a board of trustees who manage and operate the business for the benefit of those parties who contributed property in the form of money or other assets to the trust. The people who contributed money or other assets to the trust are called **beneficiaries.** They no longer have any legal title to the trust corpus; however, they do have an equitable or beneficial interest in the trust. They are given trust certificates as evidence of their interest in it. As beneficiaries of the trust, the certificate holders will receive the profits from the operations and investments of the trust properties. However, the key factor is that the certificate holders do not have any right to control the enterprise. If, in fact, they do have a right to control the actions of the trustees, the courts will normally hold that the business is a partnership and not a trust.

The main purpose of the business trust is to ensure limited liability to the beneficiaries and yet avoid some of the statutory regulations and reporting procedures of a corporation.

This form of business organization, like the joint stock company, is not used extensively today.

Cooperative Association. One often hears of farm co-ops or student co-ops. A ***cooperative association*** is a union of individuals formed for the purpose of operating an enterprise to make profits or to provide benefits for its members. If it is a profit-making business, the legal rules governing it will be very similar to those that govern a partnership or a joint venture.

If a cooperative is nonprofit and unincorporated, the legal rules governing it are quite different, particularly those relating to the personal liability of the associates. Personal liability for the contract and tort debts of the organization is not automatically assumed on the basis of membership in a nonprofit cooperative. The liability of individual members must be based on proof of an agency relationship; that is, the members whom it is sought to hold personally liable must be shown to have authorized the liability-producing act. Such personal authorization may be proved by showing that the act in question is part of the organization's purposes, or that the act was specifically authorized by the persons sought to be held liable, or that those persons were active participants in the act. This kind of individual liability is at issue in the *Lyons* case.

LYONS v. AMERICAN LEGION POST NO. 650 REALTY CO.

175 N.E.2d 733 (Ohio, 1961)

FACTS   Plaintiff was injured by carbon monoxide fumes while attending a fish fry at Post 650. The petition alleges that the defendants, American Legion Post No. 650 Realty Co., Inc., and the individual members of the American Legion Post No. 650 "jointly and severally, conducted or caused to be conducted within said building a social affair known as a fish fry for which they charged each person attending the sum of one dollar ($1)," and that "defendants, each of them, were negligent in failing to provide a safe heating system in the building; in equipping and maintaining the building with a defective heating system; in failing to adequately inspect said heating system; in failing to provide proper ventilation in the building; and in failing to warn invitees in the building, including decedent, of the presence of carbon monoxide fumes therein."

The trial court dismissed the petition, and the Court of Appeals affirmed.

ISSUE   Are all of the individual members of a not-for-profit organization jointly and severally liable to a person who was injured on the premises of the organization?

DECISION   No. Only the members who were actively involved in the social affair resulting in plaintiff's decedent's injuries, would be liable.

REASONS   Judge Zimmerman, speaking for the court, stated:

"[A] recognized difference exists between an unincorporated association organized for the transaction of business and one organized for fraternal or social purposes. . . .

> In the case of a voluntary association formed for the purpose of engaging in business and making profits, its members are liable, as partners, to third persons upon contracts which are within its scope and are entered into with actual or apparent authority, and a joint judgment against them is justified. . . . But when, as here, the purpose of the association is not business

or profit, the liability, if any, of its members is not in its nature that of partners but that arising out of the relation of principal and agent, and only those members who authorize or subsequently ratify an obligation are liable on account of it.

"The same principle is recognized in relation to torts. . . .

"Such petition probably states causes of action good as against demurrer so that defendants should plead to conserve their interests, but on trial of the action to establish liability on the part of individual defendants evidence would have to be produced linking them as active participants in the affair resulting in plaintiff's decedent's alleged injuries, and, furthermore, that they knew or in the exercise of ordinary care should have known of the defective condition of the instrumentality claimed to have caused injury. And, of course, the other elements necessary to support recovery would have to be proved.

"The judgment of the Court of Appeals is reversed, and the cause is remanded to the trial court for further proceedings."

■ SIGNIFICANCE OF THIS CHAPTER

In the last few decades, limited partnerships have become a very important form of business organization, particularly for use in tax shelter business operations. It is therefore important for the businessperson to know what a limited partnership is, how it is formed, what the limited partners can and cannot do and still retain limited liability status, and also how a limited partnership can be terminated. While the limited partnership is certainly the most significant of these alternative forms of organization, there are several other possibilities. Since the rights and liabilities of the associates vary from one form to another, this chapter has also included a summary of the differences between the joint stock company, the business trust, the for-profit unincorporated association, and the nonprofit unincorporated association. Not only the associates, but also the third parties dealing with various organizations, need to know the basic rules for who can do what and who's liable for what.

DISCUSSION CASE

COURTS OF THE PHOENIX v. CHARTER OAK FIRE INSURANCE COMPANY
560 F.Supp. 858 (Illinois, 1983)

FACTS: This is an action by The Courts of the Phoenix, a partnership, and Lakeview Trust & Savings Bank, the legal title holder of the building operated by the partnership, against Charter Oak Fire Insurance Company on a fire insurance policy issued by Charter Oak. In May 1980, a fire occurred in the partnership's building, which housed several racquetball and handball courts. The Chicago Fire Department later determined that the fire had been intentionally set. Charter Oak denied the partnership's claim on the insurance policy on the basis that William Reich, the partnership's general partner, had set the fire or had arranged for it to be set in order to liquidate what Charter Oak claims was a failing investment. Charter Oak has raised other defenses to payment as well, including the alleged submission by the partnership of inflated damage claims and the partnership's failure to prevent the building from deteriorating.

Reich was the general partner of the partnership, and

the other named plaintiffs, with the exception of Lakeview Bank, were limited partners. None of the limited partners has greater than a 6 percent interest in the partnership. Reich had the majority interest (over 50 percent). Defendant has alleged that as a general partner, Reich had sole control over the operation and management of the racquet-ball-handball club. For the purpose of the present inquiry, because we are only determining the sufficiency of the arson defense, we will assume the validity of defendant's assertation.

■

Judge Marshall:

There are no Illinois cases that address the specific question at issue here: that is, whether a "limited partnership" can be denied recovery on a fire insurance policy where the partnership's sole general partner has procured the setting of the fire that gave rise to the claim on the policy. The parties agree that the Illinois case that states the general common-law rules applicable here is *D. I. Felsenthal Co.* v. *Northern Assurance Co., Ltd.*, 284 Ill. 343, . . . (1918). In *Felsenthal*, the plaintiff, a corporation, brought suit on a fire insurance policy issued by the defendant. The defendant responded by alleging that the fire had been set by or at the behest of a major stockholder in the corporation. . . . The court noted that in the circumstances presented, allowing the corporation to recover would be in effect indistinguishable from allowing an individual insured under a fire insurance policy to recover despite having set the fire, as Fox was the sole person who would benefit from the recovery demanded. . . . It stated: "[W]e cannot allow the corporation in this case to be used as a cloak to protect Fox and to aid him in his design to defraud the insurance company and at the same time to profit by his own wrong.". . .

A more recent Illinois case, *Economy Fire & Casualty Co.* v. *Warren*, 71 Ill.App.3d 625 . . . is, we think, also instructive. In *Economy Fire,* the insurer brought an action against two joint tenants of property covered by a fire insurance policy, seeking rescission of a settlement agreement and restitution of proceeds paid out under the policy. The evidence showed that one of the joint tenants had started the fire that had resulted in the claim. The other joint tenant contended that he was innocent of wrongdoing and therefore was entitled to half of the proceeds from the policy, regardless of the other joint tenant's conduct. The insurer argued that the arson of one joint tenant voided the entire policy.

In reaching its decision, the court in *Economy Fire* considered two divergent lines of authority from other jurisdictions, as the issue was one of first impression in Illinois. The first line of cases considered stood for the proposition

that the question whether the rights of obligees are joint and several is one which is to be determined by what a reasonable person in the position of the insured would have understood the words of the policy to mean. An ordinary person with an undivided interest in the property would naturally suppose that his individual interest was covered by a policy that named him as an insured and that his rights were not tied to those of the other joint tenant. . . . The second line of authority considered in *Economy Fire* held that the wrongdoing of one co-insured bars recovery as to all insureds, because the agreement of the insureds not to commit fraud is joint, with each promising that he and the other will not commit fraud. . . .

The court in *Economy Fire* sided with the innocent insured, holding that the fact that his joint tenant had committed arson should not bar him from recovery on the policy. It stated: "[W]e do not think that the reasonable person in the position of [defendant] would have supposed that the wrongdoing of his coinsured would be imputed to him. If the plaintiff intended such a result, it should have made the terms of the policy more express in that regard.". . . Thus, the court held that the innocent joint tenant was entitled to retain one-half of the proceeds from the insurance policy.

Economy Fire and *Felsenthal* represent the extent of Illinois common law doctrine directly pertinent to the issue of insurance law at hand. However, on the more general issue—whether the wrongful conduct of one partner may be imputed to another partner—both common law and statutory law exists. As a matter of Illinois law, the tortious or fraudulent wrongdoing of one partner, not within the scope of his authority or in furtherance of the partnership business, does not subject the other partners (or the partnership) to liability. . . . This doctrine is also embodied in an Illinois statute. [Section 13 of the Uniform Partnership Act]. . . . Section 15(a) of the act provides that all partners are jointly and severally liable for everything chargeable to the partnership under Section 13. . . . The act also provides that its provisions "shall apply to limited partnerships except in so far as the statutes relating to such partnerships are inconsistent."

Illinois' version of the Uniform Limited Partnership Act . . . [Section 44] provides that a limited partner shall not be personally bound—that is, for any amounts in excess of his or her contribution to capital—by the obligations of the partnership. Section 44 is inconsistent with Section 15(a) of the Uniform Partnership Act, and thus under Section 6(2), Section 44 controls where a limited partnership is concerned. However, there is nothing in the Limited Partnership Act, and therefore Section 13 applies to limited partnerships as well as to "ordinary" partnerships. While Section 13, taken literally, addressed only the liability of partnerships, we think that it provides persuasive authority for the proposition that the legislature intended that responsibility for the wrongful acts of one partner, even the general partner, is not to be attributed to other partners unless those acts are in the ordinary course of the partnership business or are undertaken with the express or implied authority of the other partners. . . . *Felsenthal* is not to the contrary, at least not in the present context. In that case, the court made it clear that its decision was based primarily on the fact that the wrongdoer would have been the sole beneficiary of the insurance policy, and thus of his own wrongdoing, if recovery were allowed. In the present case, there are, by contrast, many "innocent bystanders." We do not think that the holding in *Felsenthal* controls here.

Our determination that *Saiken* and Section 13 of the Uniform Partnership Act state the applicable rule raises two important questions. First, we must decide whether Reich's alleged acts were either within the course of business of the partnership or were done with the authority of the other partners. Second, if we determine that Reich's acts were outside of his authority and thus are not attributable to the limited partners, we must address the question whether the insurance contract here modified the common law and statutory rule.

We do not have before us the partnership agreement entered into among the limited partners and Reich. However, this does not prevent us from determining whether burning down the partnership's sole property was something that could be considered to have been done in the ordinary course of the partnership's business. Section 52 of the Uniform Limited Partnership Act provides that absent the written consent or subsequent ratification of all the limited partners, a general partner does not have the authority to "[d]o any which would make it impossible to carry on the ordinary business of the partnership" . . . . It is not alleged that there was any such consent here. Moreover, we would find it somewhat incongruous were the law to provide that an act taken to destroy a business' sole asset is an act "in the ordinary course of business." We are not so naive as to ignore the fact that the businesspeople, faced with a perceived need to liquidate a failing investment quickly, sometimes undertake unlawful acts such as arson in order to realize a return of their investment. However, we do not think that such an act may be considered to be within the ordinary course of their business, at least where one is concerned with the issue whether their conduct may be attributed to their innocent partners. . . .

The question becomes, therefore, whether the insurance contract here modified in any way the statutory and common-law doctrine that the wrongdoing of one partner not within the scope of his authority or in furtherance of the partnership's business is not attributable to the other partners. The insurance contract is attached to plaintiff's complaint. It provides that Charter Oak "insures against all risks of direct or physical loss or damages except as otherwise provided in this form and any other provisions of the policy which apply.". . . The most general exclusion of potential relevance here provides that

> [t]he Company shall not be liable for loss occurring while the hazard is increased by any means within the control or knowledge of the Insured unless the Company has received prior written notice. However, except as otherwise provided, permission is granted to make alterations and repairs. . . .

Other than this, we can find no provision specifically excluding coverage as to damage to the building due to the fraud or criminal acts of an insured. The same is true concerning the "business interruption" coverage. There is, however, a provision relating to personal property. It states:

> D. PERILS EXCLUDED OR SUBJECT TO LIMITATIONS—
> This firm does not insure against loss damage: . . .
> 3. TO PERSONAL PROPERTY . . .
> h. due to:
> (1) any fraudulent, dishonest or criminal act or omission done by or at the instigation of any Insured, partner or joint adventurer in or of any Insured, an officer, director, or trustee of any Insured. . . .

Under *Economy Fire,* only the provision relating to personal property is explicit enough to subject the limited partners to responsibility for the wrongful acts of the general partner. Therefore, the limited partners cannot be barred from recovery as to the "business interruption" and "building" claims, which amount to all but $50,000 of plaintiffs' $1.7 million-plus claim. If Charter Oak can demonstrate that any of the limited partners expressly or impliedly authorized Reich's conduct, however, any such partner may be barred from recovery as well. Reich will, of course, be barred from any recovery if Charter Oak can demonstrate by a preponderance of the evidence . . . that he set the fire or procured its setting.

The result we reach is that the total amount that would be due on the policy absent Reich's alleged arson is to be reduced by a percentage that equals the percentage of the partnership owned by the wrongdoers, if any. The innocent partners may recover the balance in proportion with their interest in the partnership. This result is permitted by *Economy Fire,* in which the total amount due under the policy was apportioned between the innocent joint tenant and the arsonist. It is also the result that we believe the Illinois Supreme Court would reach if faced with the issue.

■ IMPORTANT TERMS AND CONCEPTS

Uniform Limited Partnership Act of 1916 (ULPA)
defective formation
general partners' rights and duties
dissolution of limited partnership
termination of limited partnership
business trust (Massachusetts trust)
cooperative association

Revised Uniform Limited Partnership 1976 (RULPA)
certificate of limited partnership
limited partners' rights and duties
winding up of limited partnership
joint stock company
beneficiaries

■ QUESTIONS AND PROBLEMS FOR DISCUSSION

1. How does a limited partnership differ from a general partnership?
2. Why are limited partnerships a popular form of organization?
3. What are the disadvantages of the limited partnership?
4. What changes in the law are made by the Revised ULPA?
5. Wilma Banks, a 62-year-old widow, went to the Marble Motor Inn to attend a "free" meeting. At the meeting Verna Shill and Lucinda Sluggs made a presentation which involved mind reading and psychic fortune-telling. After reading Wilma's mind and telling her fortune, Verna and Lucinda asked her to become a limited partner in Papsh Films, Ltd., which was producing religious films for schools and was building a large amusement park. Wilma was an accountant, and Verna and Lucinda promised her that she could do all the film's bookwork at a generous salary. The three ladies filled out personal financial statements, borrowed $25,000 from the Octopus Bank, and cosigned a promissory note for the amount of the loan. Verna and Lucinda never filed any limited partnership articles with the State but simply took the $25,000 and skipped. Octopus sues Wilma. What is the result, and why?
6. Michael Halb was killed by Bernie Wells when Michael surprised Bernie in the process of robbing Michael's home. Michael's estate sued Bernie and his live-in lady friend, Lili Hamel, in a wrongful death action. Bernie and Lili had lived together for five years, during which time he frequently went out late at night, had no regular job, filed tax returns showing several hundred thousand dollars of income each year, and bought a million-dollar house and several expensive cars. Bernie told Lili he was in the "gold and silver business." He installed a metal smelting furnace in their garage. Lili handled the inventories, filed the tax returns which listed "cost of goods sold" although no invoices were ever received, and generally kept the books. When Bernie was caught, he had over three thousand stolen items in their basement. Lili says she's not a crook and didn't know what Bernie was doing. Is there any basis on which Lili can be held liable for Bernie's actions? Discuss.
7. Conn Company is the sole general partner in numerous limited partnerships, including ones formed to invest in Florida real estate, condominiums, and foreign film rights. A major inducement for investing in this exotic group of properties was the beneficial tax treatment that could be expected by a limited partner. However, at the end of the term some of the limited partners did not meet the financial requirements for tax "breaks." Limited partners sue Conn Company claiming fraud in the sale and promotion of these limited partnerships. Is Conn Company liable to these investors? Why or why not?
8. Texas requires that a certificate of limited partnership be filed with the secretary of state by limited partnerships. Koepke and Wood became limited partners in a limited partnership, and they were clearly named in the limited partnership agreement. In error the limited partnership agreement was not filed with the secretary of state of Texas. The partnership failed to pay certain debts, and one of the creditors sued Koepke and Wood, stating that since the limited partnership agreement was not filed, these persons are liable as general partners. The creditor knew he was dealing with a limited partnership when he gave credit to the partnership. He never dealt directly with either Koepke or Wood. Are they personally liable for this debt? Explain.

45

Corporations—Nature, Formation, and Powers

CHAPTER OBJECTIVES

THIS CHAPTER WILL:

- Describe the various classifications of corporations.
- Review the procedure for formation of a corporation.
- Discuss the problems which result from defective formation.
- Discuss "piercing the corporate veil" to hold corporate officers, directors, and stockholders liable for corporate actions.

A *corporation* is called a legal person or a **legal entity**. It may also be called a child of the state, since its birth, existence, and termination are regulated by statutory law. Upon the completion of certain requirements a state will grant a charter of incorporation which is in effect a birth certificate for the corporation. The corporation must abide by the specific statutory law during its existence, and if the corporation is to be terminated, then the termination must comply with the statutory law. Each state has specific statutes governing the creation, regulation, and termination of corporations and also regulating corporations created in other states but doing local business in that state.

CLASSIFICATIONS OF CORPORATIONS

The Private Corporation for Profit.   This is the most common type of corporation. Such a corporation is created for the purpose of conducting private, nongovernmental business.

Private corporations for profit may be further classified as *close corporations* or *publicly held corporations.* A close corporation is a corporation where the stock is owned by a small number of shareholders and the stock is not offered for sale to the general public. It is called a close corporation because it is closed to the general public. Its shares are not for sale on any stock exchange. A publicly held corporation is a corporation whose shares are offered for sale to the general public. These shares of stock are traded regularly on the various stock exchanges.

Publicly held corporations must comply with very strict rules and regulations as to their procedure in offering their shares of stock for sale to the public. These rules and regulations are made and enforced by the various State Securities Commissions as well as the national Securities Exchange Commission. These procedures and requirements will be discussed further in Chapter 48.

A subclassification of the close corporation is the *subchapter S corporation.*

Subchapter S corporations were mentioned briefly in Chapter 44. Subchapter S is simply a subdivision of the Internal Revenue Code which permits small close corporations to be exempt from payment of corporate income tax. The shareholders are allocated shares of the profits and then declare those profits as income. Also, if the corporation has losses, the shareholder can deduct his or her share of those losses from other personal income. The corporation files a corporate tax return, but it is simply an informational return similar to the return required to be filed by a general partnership. Thus, the shareholders gain the benefits of incorporation, such as limited liability, ease of transferability of their interest, and perpetual duration, but are not subjected to double taxation. There is no separate taxation of corporate income and a second tax when dividends are distributed as individual income.

No separate corporate income tax for subchapter S

Subchapter S status is a tax status granted by the Internal Revenue Service, upon application and IRS approval. There are several requirements which a corporation must meet before it will be granted subchapter S status by the Internal Revenue Service. The first requirement refers to the number of shareholders. A subchapter S corporation can have no more than 35 shareholders. Second, the corporation can have only one class of stock. Third, the corporation must be a U.S. corporation. And fourth, shareholders may not be nonresident aliens or nonhuman entities, such as other corporations. However, there is an

Subchapter S requirements

exception for estates and trusts, as they may be shareholders in a subchapter S corporation.

There are also limitations as to the percentage of non-U.S. income and investment income the corporation may receive and still retain subchapter S status. Another requirement is that all shareholders must join in the application for subchapter S status. However, if the shareholders decide to terminate the subchapter S status, they may do so. Only the consent of a majority of the stockholders is needed for revocation of subchapter S status.

Subchapter S status is advantageous only as long as it is in the best interests of the shareholders from a tax standpoint. For example, if the shareholders in a small corporation were three shareholders who all had other incomes that put them in the top tax bracket for their individual income taxes, then they would not want subchapter S status. Their preference would be to have the corporation profits taxed at corporation tax levels and then have the after-tax profits reinvested, rather than distributed as dividends. Then later, when they wanted to take their money out of the corporation, they could sell their stock and only have to pay capital gains taxes. However, if the corporation was sustaining losses, the three shareholders might want to use S status, so that they could offset the losses against their other income.

The Public Corporation. This is a corporation created for governmental purposes. An example of a public corporation would be a municipal corporation, a school corporation, and other corporations created by the state government or the national government for governmental purposes.

The Not-for-Profit Corporation. This is a corporation for a civic, charitable, or educational purpose. For example, a fraternity or sorority, if incorporated, would be incorporated as a not-for-profit corporation, since its purposes would be social and civic rather than the conduct of a profit-making business. Special tax considerations are given to not-for-profit corporations.

The Domestic Corporation. In the state where it was originally incorporated, a corporation is a domestic corporation. Acting in any other state, it is doing so as a "foreign" corporation.

The Foreign Corporation. This is a corporation which is incorporated in one state and is doing business in another state. Foreign corporations must file certain documents and pay certain fees before doing local business in states other than the state in which they are incorporated. This topic is discussed in more detail in Chapter 49.

The Professional Corporation. Many states now have specific incorporation laws which allow the incorporation of certain professionals; for example, a medical corporation. Such a corporation can be one doctor or many doctors. Dentists, veterinarians, architects, accountants, and lawyers may also incorporate their businesses under professional corporation statutes. Typically there are different requirements for incorporation and different provisions for regulation under the professional corporation statutes. The *Birt* case involves the interpretation of Indiana's P.C. statute.

BIRT v. ST. MARY MERCY HOSPITAL OF GARY, IND.

370 N.E.2d 379 (Indiana, 1978)

FACTS   Prior to March 17, 1972, Dr. Valencia and eight other medical doctors agreed to staff the emergency room at St. Mary's. On that date, the doctors executed articles of incorporation for Mercy Medical Associates, Inc. On April 6, the articles were approved by the secretary of state. Eugene Birt was treated by Dr. Valencia on May 13, at which time Birt claims malpractice occurred. On May 13 Associates had not received the required certificate of registration from the Board of Medical Registration and Examination, because they had not sent the board a copy of their corporate bylaws. When Birt sued for malpractice, he named the eight nontreating doctors along with Dr. Valencia, St. Mary's, and Associates. Birt appeals from a summary judgment for the eight doctors.

ISSUE   Are the other stockholder-employee members of a professional corporation personally liable for the malpractice of one member?

DECISION   No. Judgment affirmed.

REASONS   Judge Garrard, first decided that the corporation did exist, even though the Medical Board had not yet issued it a certificate. According to the statute, the organization of a professional corporation was governed by the general corporation law, which provided that the corporation came into existence when the secretary of state issued a certificate of incorporation. Although a certificate from the Medical Board was also required in order to do business, that was only to make sure that all persons involved were properly licensed to practice medicine.

The main issue was whether the limited liability concept from general corporation law was inconsistent with professional corporations.

"It is . . . apparent that our legislature intended that the IMPCA should not destroy the traditional relationship between a professional and his patient through the creation of a corporate shield. . . . It has been argued that such provisions must be construed to preserve more than the personal liability of a corporate employee for his own negligent tort existing under general corporations law. We agree. However, it does not necessarily follow that the statute imports the vicarious liability of the Uniform Partnership Act to apply to associating physicians. . . .

"Apprehension has also been expressed concerning the ability of an injured patient to collect a damage award without the existence of vicarious liability. Again, however, we believe the fear is overstated. Of course, the malpracticing physician is liable to the extent of his personal assets and such malpractice insurance as he, or the corporation may possess. In addition, it is beyond question that the corporate entity is liable for malpractice committed by one of its members. . . .

"The IMPCA manifests legislative intent that medical professional corporations be imbued with as many of the attributes of general corporations as may be, without destroying the traditional professional relationship between physician and patient. We conclude that neither the express language of the statute, nor the qualification purpose of maintaining strong professional relationships require importation of the partnership doctrine of vicarious liability into the professional corporate arena. Plainly general corporate concepts preclude it. Accordingly we hold that no vicarious liability arises solely from association under the IMPCA."

■ MODEL BUSINESS CORPORATION ACT

The *Model Business Corporation Act (MBCA)* was drafted by the Committee of Corporation Laws of the Section of Corporation Banking and Business Law of the American Bar Association in 1950 with the hope that the various states would pattern their state corporate statutes after the Model Act. The Model Act is similar to the Uniform Acts we have discussed earlier in the text in that they are not law until adopted by a specific state legislature. The Model Act has been reviewed and revised periodically, and in 1984 the committee completed a comprehensive revision of the Model Act.

■ RELATIONSHIP WITH STATE OF INCORPORA- TION

Formation of the Corporation

Incorporators.   Incorporators are the persons who actually apply to the state for the incorporation of a business. The incorporators sign a document, usually called *articles of incorporation,* and file it with the secretary of state of the state where they are requesting incorporation. Some states require the incorporators to be citizens of the incorporation state; others do not. The Model Business Corporation Act, which has been followed by many states, now allows a single incorporator to apply. Thus an individual may incorporate a business and may be the sole shareholder.

State action required

Procedure for Incorporation.   While each state has its own individual incorporation statute, the requirements for incorporation are similar in all states. Generally speaking, the incorporator or incorporators execute and sign articles of incorporation and file this document with the appropriate state official, usually the secretary of state. A filing fee is required, which, of course, varies from state to state. The corporation division of the secretary of state's office will review the articles, and if they comply with the applicable statute, the secretary of state's office will issue a certificate of incorporation which officially gives birth to the corporation. Many states require that a minimum amount of capital be paid into the corporation before it can legally commence business. Some states require that the articles of incorporation be filed in the recorder's office of any county where the corporation holds real estate, or where it has its home office.

Corporate name must include "Inc." or "Incorporated"

1. Name. The corporation, like a new baby, must be given a legal name. The incorporators are free to choose nearly any name, so long as it is not the same as or similar to the name of another corporation doing business in the state. Thus, before approving a name for the corporation, the state must run a check of all the corporations on file to find out whether this name is the same as or similar to the names of other corporations. Also, the name of the corporation must include the word *Incorporated* or the abbreviation *Inc.,* so that people will know that when they deal with this organization they are dealing with a limited liability organization.

2. The purpose for which the corporation is formed. The purpose for which the corporation is formed can be stated in general terms. In most states it is not necessary to state the specific business the corporation intends to participate in. For example, the purpose may be stated as follows: "to transact any and all lawful business for which a corporation may be incorporated" (under the specific state corporation act).

3. The address of the corporation's principal office and the name of its registered agent. The principal office, of course, will be the mailing address for all corporate correspondence, and the resident agent is the person who can officially accept service of process for lawsuits against the corporation.

4. The duration of the corporation. A corporation has perpetual existence unless its articles of incorporation provide otherwise.

5. Issuance of shares of stock. The incorporator or incorporators must here state the total number of shares of stock the corporation requests authority to issue, the number of shares of stock that are to have a par value, and the number of shares that are to have no par value. If there are to be different classes of stock, different series of stock, and different rights and preferences with regard to different classes of stock, then this information must also be provided. Some states require the name and addresses of the original subscribers to the capital stock and the amount of their subscriptions.

6. Directors and officers and qualifications of directors. Many states require the articles of incorporation to include the names of the members of the first board of directors, and often the names of the officers of the corporation are also required. Most states do not require their corporations' directors to be residents of that state.

7. Provisions for regulation of business and conduct of affairs of the corporation. Many states require specific statements as to the conduct and scheduling of annual and special meetings of shareholders and directors and as to other provisions concerning the conduct of the business.

8. Requirements prior to doing business. Many states have specific requirements that must be complied with prior to the commencement of business by the corporation. The most common requirement is the payment of a minimum amount of money, typically $1,000, by subscribers to the corporation before the corporation commences doing business.

Charter as a Contract

Contract with state

When the articles are approved or the ***corporate charter*** is issued by the state of incorporation, a "contract" is formed between the state and the corporation. As a contract, the corporate charter is protected by Article I, Section 10 of the U.S. Constitution, which prohibits a state from passing any law "impairing the obligation of contracts." In the days when each corporate charter was the result of a special statute, this decision barred much state regulation of corporations. Today, however, general corporation laws contain provisions that reserve to the state the power to amend or repeal the statute. The state's power to change the corporate rules thus becomes part of every contract formed with every corporation pursuant to the statute.

Contract with stockholders

The corporate charter also acts as a contract between the corporation and its stockholders, in the sense that it states the nature of the corporation's business. The bylaws adopted by the corporation also become part of this contract. To avoid unnecessary litigation, clear procedures for amending the corporate charter/articles and the corporate bylaws should be spelled out, and the power to amend should be specifically stated.

Other Obligations to the State of Incorporation

The obligations of the corporation to its home state do not end with the issuance of the charter. Typically annual reports to the state are required, and the corporation must pay an annual fee for the privilege of exercising its corporate powers. Corporation statutes usually provide for suspension or termination of the corporation's privileges for noncompliance with these annual requirements, at least where the default continues for an extended period of time.

Corporation as Person and Citizen

Due process protection

The corporation is, by definition, a legal person. As such, it enjoys the same constitutional protections as human persons. Under the Fifth Amendment, its life, liberty, and property cannot be taken, without due process of law, by the national government or any of its agencies. Under the Fourteenth Amendment, the same due process protection exists against the state governments. Likewise, states cannot deny corporate persons the equal protection of the law. (*Equal* here does not mean identical. It only means that distinctions must have a rational basis; arbitrary, invidious discrimination against corporations is prohibited.) These rules are discussed in the Bellotti case.

Corporations have no citizenship rights

Corporations are not considered citizens for the purpose of Fourteenth Amendment "privileges and immunities of citizenship." Most obviously, this means that corporations cannot vote in political elections, hold political office, or serve on juries. More important, as discussed in Chapter 49, corporations do not have a citizen's right to conduct business in states other than the domicile state. Corporations wishing to do local business in a second state must secure that state's permission to do so; human persons, as citizens, are exempt from this requirement.

Diversity of citizenship

To determine whether or not diversity of citizenship exists (so that an ordinary civil case may be brought into U.S. District Court), a corporation *is* considered to be a "citizen" of its state of incorporation. Courts have also recognized that a corporation may acquire a kind of "double citizenship" in the state where it has its principal place of business. If any of the opposing parties in a litigation were a citizen of either of those two states, there would not be complete diversity of citizenship, and the case could not be brought into the U.S. courts on that basis, no matter how large an amount was involved.

FIRST NATIONAL BANK OF BOSTON v. BELLOTTI

435 U.S. 765 (1978)

FACTS

In sustaining a state criminal statute that forbids certain expenditures by banks and business corporations for the purpose of influencing the vote on referendum proposals, the Massachusetts Supreme Judicial Court held that the First Amendment rights of a corporation are limited to issues that materially affect its business, property, or assets. The court rejected appellants' claim that the statute abridges freedom of speech in violation of the First and Fourteenth Amendments.

The statute at issue prohibits appellants, two national banking associations and three business corporations, from making contributions or expenditures "for the purpose of . . . influencing or affecting the vote on any question submitted to the voters, other than one materially affecting any of the property, business, or assets of the corporation." The statute further specifies that "[n]o question submitted to the voters solely concerning the taxation of the income, property or transactions of individuals shall be deemed materially to affect the property, business or assets of the corporation." A corporation that violates § 8 may receive a maximum fine of $50,000; a corporate officer, director, or agent who violates the section may receive a maximum fine of $10,000 or imprisonment for up to one year, or both.

Appellants wanted to spend money to publicize their views on a proposed constitutional amendment that was to be submitted to the voters as a ballot question at a general election on November 2, 1976. The amendment would have permitted the legislature to impose a graduated tax on the income of individuals. After appellee, the attorney general of Massachusetts, informed appellants that he intended to enforce § 8 against them, they brought this action seeking to have the statute declared unconstitutional.

ISSUE   Is the Massachusetts statute unconstitutional because it denies freedom of speech to corporations?

DECISION   Yes. Judgment of the Massachusetts Supreme Judicial Court is reversed.

REASONS   Justice Powell gave the opinion of the court:

"The court below framed the principal question in this case as whether and to what extent corporations have First Amendment rights. We believe that the court posed the wrong question. The Constitution often protects interests broader than those of the party seeking their vindication. The First Amendment, in particular, serves significant societal interests. The proper question therefore is not whether corporations 'have' First Amendment rights and, if so, whether they are coextensive with those of natural persons. Instead, the question must be whether § 8 abridges expression that the First Amendment was meant to protect. We hold that it does.

"The speech proposed by appellants is at the heart of the First Amendment's protection.

The freedom of speech and of the press guaranteed by the Constitution embraces at least the liberty to discuss publicly and truthfully all matters of public concern without previous restraint or fear of subsequent punishment. . . . Freedom of discussion, if it would fulfill its historic function in this nation, must embrace all issues about which information is needed or appropriate to enable the members of society to cope with the exigencies of their period. . . .

The referendum issue that appellants wish to address falls squarely within this description. In appellants' view, the enactment of a graduated personal income tax, as proposed to be authorized by constitutional amendment, would have a seriously adverse effect on the economy of the state. The importance of the referendum issue to the people and government of Massachusetts is not disputed. Its merits, however, are the subject of sharp disagreement.

"As the Court said in *Mills* v. *Alabama*, 'there is practically universal agreement that a major purpose of [the First] Amendment was to protect the free discussion of governmental affairs.' If the speakers here were not corporations, no one would suggest that the state could silence their proposed speech. It is the type of speech indispensable to decision making in a democracy, and this is no less true because the speech comes from a corporation rather than an individual. The inherent worth of the speech in terms of its capacity for informing the public does not depend upon the identity of its source, whether corporation, association, union, or individual. . . .

"We thus find no support in the First or Fourteenth Amendment, or in the decisions of this court, for the proposition that speech that otherwise would be within the protection of the First Amendment loses that protection simply because its source is a corporation that cannot prove, to the satisfaction of a court, a material effect on its business or property. The 'materially affecting' requirement is not an identification of the boundaries of corporate speech etched by the Constitution itself. Rather, it amounts to an impermissible legislative prohibition of speech based on the identity of the interests that spokesmen may represent in public debate over controversial issues and a requirement that the speaker have a sufficiently great interest in the subject to justify communication. . . .

"In the realm of protected speech, the legislature is constitutionally disqualified from dictating the subjects about which persons may speak and the speakers who may address a public issue. . . . If a legislature may direct business corporations to 'stick to business,' it also may limit other corporations—religious, charitable, or civic—to their respective 'business' when addressing the public. Such power in government to channel the expression of views is unacceptable under the First Amendment."

■ DEFECTIVE FORMATION

Mistakes are sometimes made during the incorporation process. Forms are filled out incorrectly, or some procedural step is omitted. The effect of such errors on the corporation's existence varies, depending on the seriousness of the mistake and on the intent of the human beings who were representing the corporation.

Substantial compliance

De Jure Corporation. Perfection is not required in order to attain full de jure corporate status. As long as any errors are minor, immaterial ones, the corporation's existence cannot be challenged by anyone, including the state of incorporation. Substantial compliance with all mandatory state requirements, in good faith, is all that is required. A mistake as to the last digit in the zip code on the corporation's mailing address would almost certainly be of this nature. If the corporation's name, street number, city, county, and state were correct, its mail would be delivered despite the (slightly) incorrect zip code.

Colorable compliance

De Facto Corporation. Even though the mandatory requirements of the corporation law have not been substantially complied with, so that the corporation has not attained de jure status, the corporation's de facto ("in fact") existence may nevertheless be recognized. Only very limited challenges against a de facto corporation are permitted. Subscribers cannot be forced to take and pay for stock in a de facto corporation; they are entitled to full de jure status. The state of incorporation, in a direct proceeding (usually called a *quo warranto*— "by whose authority") can force the suspension of a de facto corporation's business until the error is corrected. In order to attain de facto status, the promoters/incorporators must have made a good faith attempt to comply with a statute under which the corporation could be organized; they must be in at least "colorable" compliance with the statutory requirements (no mandatory step has been omitted); and the corporation must actually have used its powers. The stockholders of a de facto corporation have limited liability, and the de facto corporation can conduct its business free of third-party challenges.

Persons who claim to be incorporated cannot deny existence of corporation

Corporation by Estoppel. Courts sometimes apply the principle of estoppel against persons who have received benefits from a purported, but really nonexistent, corporation. The recipient of goods and services should have to pay for them, whether or not the provider was validly organized as a corporation. Similarly, insiders who were responsible for the defective organization but then dealt with it to their advantage should be prevented from asserting its defects.

The principle of estoppel can also be used to prevent persons who have held themselves out as a corporation from later trying to deny they were in fact a corporation. The *Bukacek* case illustrates these rules.

BUKACEK v. PELL CITY FARMS, INC.

237 So.2d 851 (Alabama, 1970)

FACTS

In 1965 ill health forced James Bukacek to sell his dairy business. His personal problems resulted in a divorce from his wife, Virginia. His financial affairs were also in bad shape. The sheriff was advertising his 300-acre farm for sale, to pay three judgments; he owed the state $15,000 for back taxes; and his mortgage payment was overdue. Bukacek was also unable to exercise the option which Virginia had given him on the 180 acres she owned. At this point, Bukacek went to see Burttram "about saving 'my farm.'" Together with Kelly and Wyatt, they agreed to organize Pell City Farms, Inc. Bukacek conveyed his 300 acres to Pell City, which also exercised the option on Virginia's 180 acres. Pell City (or its promoters) paid off all the back claims and personally assumed the old mortgage and executed a new one. When the deeds from James and Virginia were executed, Pell City's articles had not been filed with the local judge of probate, as required by Alabama law. James filed an action to quiet title to the land in himself, since Pell City was not incorporated and therefore could not take title. The trial court held for Pell City, and James appealed.

ISSUE

Can Bukacek avoid his deed by showing that Pell City was not properly incorporated?

DECISION

No. Judgment affirmed.

REASONS

After reviewing the facts, Justice Maddox first considered whether the failure to file the articles as required by statute meant that there was no corporation. He felt that most states would decide that there was no corporation, either *de jure* or *de facto,* until the required filing had occurred. But that did not end the inquiry in this case.

"[T]he incidents of corporate existence may exist as between the parties by virtue of an estoppel. Thus, besides corporations de jure and de facto, there can be a recognition of a third class known as 'Corporations by estoppel.' Corporations by estoppel are not based upon the same principles as corporations de facto. The doctrine de facto corporations has nothing to do with the principle of estoppel. In fact, a corporation de facto cannot be created by estoppel, the only effect of an estoppel being to prevent the raising of the question of the existence of a corporation.

"Bukacek was one of the incorporators; he dealt with the corporation as a corporation both before and after the Articles of Incorporation were filed. Under such facts, Bukacek is estopped to deny the existence of the corporation at the time he voluntarily executed a deed transferring property to the corporation even though the Articles of Incorporation had not been filed at that time.

"Our ruling is limited. It is based on equitable grounds which preclude the complainant here from denying corporate existence. . . . We hold, therefore, that Bukacek is estopped to deny the existence of Pell City Farms, Inc., even though it may have neither de facto nor de jure at the time he executed the deed making the corporation, *by its corporate name,* the grantee."

No corporation = Full personal liability

No Corporation; Partnership Liability.   Where the promoters acted in bad faith, or omitted a mandatory procedural step, or for any other reason failed to achieve at least de facto status for the corporation, the result is partnership liability for all the business associates. In such situations stockholders could be held fully liable personally for all the debts of the business. Persons trying to assert claims against the corporation would normally not be estopped from proving that it was not really a corporation and that all associates in the enterprise were personally liable for its torts and contracts.

■ SEPARATE CORPORATE ENTITY/ PIERCING THE CORPORATE VEIL

Valid organization = Separate person

Regulatory exceptions

Once a corporation has been successfully organized, it is recognized as a separate and distinct legal person or entity. It owns its own property, makes its own contracts, and pays its own taxes. So long as a corporation's separate identity is preserved by the persons who operate the corporation, that identity should be respected and upheld by the courts and other agencies of government. The fact that all of a corporation's stock is held by only a few persons is not, in itself, a basis for disregarding the separate corporate entity. A court should take this drastic step only where the corporation is being used to produce illegal or fraudulent results or where its human operators are themselves disregarding its existence. Severe under-capitalization of the new corporation may lead a court to infer fraud on the part of its organizers.

Some regulatory and taxation statutes permit enforcement agencies to impose liability on other persons for acts by a corporation. Although this is not quite the same as piercing the corporate veil, in effect the separate corporate entity is disregarded.

The argument in the following case is a bit different. The professional corporation is saying that, in "economic reality," it is really a partnership. Therefore, since Dr. Hyland was "really" a partner, he has no claim under the Age Discrimination in Employment Act.

HYLAND v. NEW HAVEN RADIOLOGY ASSOCIATES, P.C.

794 F.2d 793 (U.S. Second Circuit, 1986)

FACTS   Plaintiff-appellant, John Hyland, M.D., claiming a violation of the Age Discrimination in Employment Act (ADEA) alleges that he was forced to resign as an employee, officer, and director of defendant-appellee, New Haven Radiology Associates, P.C.

("NHRA") because he was 51 years of age. Following extensive discovery, NHRA, a professional corporation, moved for summary judgment, asserting that Hyland lacked the necessary standing to invoke the protections afforded by the ADEA. Applying an "economic realities" test, the District Court granted the motion, finding that NHRA "amounts to a partnership in all but name," and that Hyland was, in effect, a partner in the enterprise. According to the District Court, Hyland therefore was not an employee entitled to claim the benefits provided by the ADEA.

Appellant and four other radiologists organized NHRA in 1972 as a professional services corporation under the laws of the state of Connecticut to conduct the practice of radiology. Pursuant to the terms of a stockholder's agreement, each of the five founding members contributed the same amount of capital for equal shares in the corporation and an equal voice in management. Profits and losses were divided evenly among the members, all of whom served as corporate officers and directors. The stockholders agreed that stock could be held only by shareholder-members, who were required to be licensed physicians. Upon the death, withdrawal or termination of any member, the member or his estate was required to sell, and NHRA to purchase, that shareholder's stock at a price fixed in accordance with the valuation provisions of the agreement. No stock could be held in the corporation by a nonmember or nonemployee. The stockholders' agreement provided for the admission to membership of additional "Stockholder-Employees," who would enjoy the benefits of the corporation and participate in the management of its affairs equally with the other shareholders.

Each shareholder also signed a separate two-year renewable employment agreement with the corporation, and the terms of these agreements were substantially identical. All members were compensated at the rate of $60,000 annually, subject to withholding of applicable taxes. A further provision in each doctor's employment agreement allowed for the payment of bonuses to members in the sole discretion of the board of directors. Each physician was required to be "a full time employee of the company during the term of this agreement," with a duty to devote his best efforts in rendering services to NHRA's patients. He also was required to comply with all company policies and regulations, to turn over to the corporation all compensation earned from rendering professional services of any kind, and to maintain membership in medical societies as required by the board of directors. The agreement also entitled each member to a four-week paid vacation; disability payments from the corporation; leave to attend, and reimbursement for the cost of, educational programs; and certain payments upon termination of employment.

On July 22, 1980, upon the unanimous consent of all the other members, Hyland, then 51 years of age, was asked to resign his position as a member and employee of NHRA. Thereafter, appellant entered into an agreement with the corporation relating to the conditions of his termination as an employee, shareholder, director, and officer in the corporation. This agreement dealt with the repurchase of Hyland's stock, severance pay and the lump-sum withdrawal of a profit-sharing account balance, among other things. Dr. Hyland appeals.

ISSUE   Was Dr. Hyland an employee of a corporation and thus covered by the Age Discrimination law?

DECISION   Dr. Hyland was not a "partner," he was an officer, director, and employee and thus entitled to the protection of the Age Discrimination law. Judgment of the District Court is reversed and the case is remanded for further proceedings consistent with the court's opinion.

REASONS   **Circuit Judge Miner gave the opinion of the court:**
"Appellant advances his claim under Section 623(a)(1) of the ADEA. . . .
The act defines *employer* in general terms as 'a person engaged in an industry affecting

commerce who has twenty or more employees. . . .' *Person* is defined as 'one or more individuals, partnerships, associations, labor organizations, corporations, business trusts, legal representatives, or any organized groups of persons.' . . . The ADEA definition of *employee,* 'an individual employed by any employer,' . . . excludes only elected officials and their personal staff members. . . .

"It is generally accepted that the benefits of the antidiscrimination statutes . . . do not extend to those who properly are classified as partners. . . . It is by reason of their unique status as business owners and managers that true partners cannot be classified as employees. . . .

"The Equal Employment Opportunity Commission (EEOC) established the following standard for distinguishing between partners and employees: 'In determining whether the individual is a partner or an employee in a particular case, the Commission will consider relevant factors including, but not limited to the individual's ability to control and operate the business and to determine compensation and the administration of profits and losses.' . . .

"In only one reported case has the corporate form been disregarded in favor of a finding that the shareholders were in fact partners under the economic realities test. Without further analysis, the court in *E.E.O.C.* v. *Dowd & Dowd, Ltd.,* 736 F.2d 1177 . . . found that '[t]he role of the shareholder in a professional corporation is far more analogous to a partner in a partnership than it is to the shareholder of a general corporation,' and '[t]he economic reality of the professional corporation in Illinois is that the management, control and ownership of the corporation is much like the management, control and ownership of a partnership.' We disagree with the Seventh Circuit and hold that use of the corporate form precludes any examination designed to determine whether the entity is in fact a partnership.

"While it is true, as contended by NHRA, that shareholders of certain professional and other types of corporations have many of the attributes of partners, it also is true that partnerships frequently are organized in the manner of corporations. . . . The fact that certain modern partnerships and corporations are practically indistinguishable in structure and operation, however, is no reason for ignoring a form of business organization freely chosen and established. Concededly, the physician members of NHRA found that incorporation provided them with important tax advantages and employee benefits not available in any other type of business organization. Having made the election to incorporate, they should not now be heard to say that their corporation is 'essentially a medical partnership among co-equal radiologists.' . . .

"The status of Dr. Hyland is clear—not only was he an officer, director, and shareholder of NHRA, he also was specifically designated as an employee of the corporation in an employment agreement containing detailed provisions relating to the terms and conditions of his employment. There was nothing inconsistent between his proprietary interest (whether or not it was exactly equal to the interests of each of his associates) and the corporate employment relationship be held. An analysis of his status need proceed no further. His fellow shareholders, officers, and directors in NHRA simply are precluded from expelling him from the corporation on the statutorily disapproved basis of age discrimination."

CORPORATE POWERS

Powers given to all corporations

Since a corporation is a creature of the law, it possesses only those powers given to it by the law. It can only do those things it has been authorized to do. Authorization for particular acts of a corporation must be found either in its state's corporation statute or in its own charter. Powers that result from the corporation's existence as a legal person, such as the power to sue and be sued in its corporate name and the power to hold and convey property, are called *inherent powers.* These powers and others specifically stated in the corporation statute are also referred to as *statutory powers.* All corporations formed in the state have them.

Express powers are the powers specifically granted to a particular corporation by its charter. Many states permit such powers to be stated very broadly—for example, "to conduct any lawful business which may be conducted by corporations in this state." Corporations also have *implied powers;* that is, the powers that are necessary and appropriate to help carry out their express powers. Where a corporation has not used a very broad statement of its express powers, litigation may occur over whether a particular corporate activity is or is not within its implied powers.

Powers stated and implied

Problems have arisen, for example, over whether a corporation has the inherent or implied power to reacquire its own shares of stock, to be a partner in a partnership, to acquire shares of stock in other corporations not in the same line of business, and to make charitable contributions. Some state corporation statutes contain a long list of things that corporations formed thereunder are permitted to do. Section 302 of the MBCA contains such a list. If the corporation's powers/purpose clause has been stated as "any lawful business," there should be little chance of a successful court challenge to any of the above activities. While some state statutes are still rather restrictive, the modern tendency seems to be to take a liberal view of the corporation's powers. If specific investors/promoters wish to limit *their* corporation's operations, they would be free to do so by adopting a restrictive purpose clause and statement of powers.

Acts beyond powers given

Acts that do not fall within one of the above categories are said to be *ultra vires,* "outside" the corporation's powers. Courts have not agreed as to what should happen when a corporation engages in such unauthorized activity. The modern tendency is to severely limit such challenges to corporate acts. If a contract has been fully performed by both parties, neither party can raise the *ultra vires* claim so as to force rescission. If a contract is completely executory, neither party can sue for enforcement. Where only one party has performed, the courts disagree on what should happen; most courts permit the party that has performed to enforce the contract. In any case, the state should be able to enjoin the performance of unauthorized acts; a shareholder should be able to sue for an injunction and damages, and the corporation itself should be able to collect damages against the directors and officers who were responsible for the violation of the charter. Both the MCBA and the Revised MCBA follow this modern approach.

■ PROMOTERS

Organizers of corporation

Definition.   The classic definition of a *promoter* is found in the *Old Dominion* case: "those who undertake to form a corporation and to procure for it the rights, instrumentalities, and capital by which it is to carry out the purposes set forth in its charter and to establish it as fully able to do business." The promoters are the "idea people"; they conceive the idea of incorporation, and then they attempt to implement it. The incorporators, the persons who sign the documents specifically requesting the state of incorporation to recognize the corporation's existence, may or may not be promoters. Persons whose

■ EXHIBIT 45–1
Promoters Preincorporation
Contracts

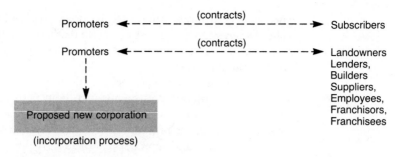

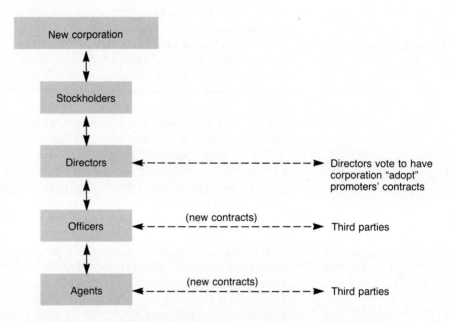

only function in the incorporation process is a professional one, such as lawyers, accountants, or engineers, are not necessarily promoters. The promoters are the driving force behind the corporation.

Liability Inter Se. As between themselves, promoters are in a sense partners, or at least joint venturers. Once agreement has been reached as to what will be done and how it will be done, they owe each other a fiduciary duty. This fiduciary duty does not arise, however, unless and until some agreement has been reached. A person who discloses a "good idea" to another person before any agreement has been reached therefore runs the risk that the other person will appropriate the idea without compensation.

Liability to the Corporation and/or Shareholders. Promoters also occupy a fiduciary relationship to their corporation and its subscribers/shareholders. Promoters should, of course, recover all reasonable expenses they have incurred during the incorporation process. They are not, however, entitled to retain *secret* profits which they have made during the incorporation process, for example, by reselling assets to the corporation for more than they paid for them. Full

Joint venture liability

No secret profits

disclosure of such proposed profits must be made. The question is: To whom? By the majority rule, disclosure to only the original promoters/subscribers is not sufficient, at least where there is a plan to sell more shares to the public. Full disclosure must be made to an independent (nonpromoters) board of directors, or to all subscribers, or to all shareholders, unless the promoters making the profits have themselves subscribed to all the shares to be issued.

Corporation's Liability on Promoter's Contracts. Since the corporation does not yet legally exist, the promoters cannot be its agents when they make preincorporation contracts. The promoters are thus personally liable on all preincorporation contracts (with suppliers, landlords, employees, and so on) unless and until the new corporation comes into existence and "adopts" these contracts as its own. If and when that happens, the states disagree on whether the promoter's liability on the contract is impliedly discharged. If the third party knew that the corporation had not yet been formed and did intend to deal with it through the promoter, and the corporation then comes into existence and adopts the contract, there would seem to be no reason to hold the promoter liable any further. Both parties got exactly the contract they intended and wanted. Some states so hold, but others do not. In this other group of states, the promoter is not discharged unless the third party agrees to a novation, either expressly or impliedly agreeing to accept the corporation in place of the promoter and to discharge the promoter. This second rule seems to give the third party more than he bargained for and more than the promoter originally agreed to. Because of these uncertainties, the preincorporation contract should be very carefully drafted, with a specific statement on when the promoter's liability ends.

Liable unless corporation adopts

■ SIGNIFICANCE OF THIS CHAPTER

The corporation is not only for big business. It is an organizational form that can be used by small family businesses, farmers, and professionals, such as doctors, accountants, lawyers, and architects. Nonprofit organizations also may have corporate status.

This chapter first discusses classifications of corporations, and then goes through a typical procedure to be followed in establishing a corporation. The chapter discusses what happens when a mistake is made, and who may be liable. Corporate powers also are discussed.

The focus of this chapter is the organization of corporations. The chapters that follow discuss corporate operating problems in more detail, including the rights and duties of the various parties involved.

DISCUSSION CASE

WHALER MOTOR INN, INC. v. PARSONS
339 N.E.2d 197 (Massachusetts, 1975)

FACTS: These two cases were tried together before a master and are here on the defendants' appeals from interlocutory and final decrees entered in the superior court in each case. Both cases arise out of complaints by Whaler Motor Inn, Inc. (corporation) against its promoters and certain of its stockholders other than the promoters.

In the first case the corporation sought the return for cancellation of capital stock which it issued to the defendants Richard Parsons (Parsons), Nathaniel Lipton (Lipton), and Lipton's wife, allegedly without payment. The trustees for the benefit of the creditors of the Liptons were also made defendants since Liptons' stock in the corporation had been transferred to those trustees. The corporation also sought an accounting against Lipton and Parsons, recovery of "secret profits" of Parsons arising from his sale of real estate to the corporation, the recovery of cash paid, and the cancellation of a promissory note of the corporation given to Parsons in connection with the repurchase by the corporation of certain shares of stock originally issued to him. In the second case the corporation sought the return for cancellation of capital stock issued to the defendants David and Louis Freedman, allegedly without payment.

Sometime in late 1965 or early 1966, at Lipton's behest, Lipton, Parsons, and the Freedmans met for the purpose of exploring the possibility of constructing a motel or motor inn in the New Bedford area. All four men had considerable experience in business. They met frequently to discuss the economic feasibility of the project, to exchange opinions, and to develop plans.

Having determined that site location was of paramount importance, they considered several sites in New Bedford and surrounding towns. They contracted for a feasibility study, which was completed on November 30, 1966. They selected a site owned by Parsons on Hathaway Road in New Bedford, close to Route 140 and Interstate Highway I-95. This site was superior to the other sites they had considered because of its location in the center of industrial, business, and recreation areas to which a motel would cater, its elevation, and its visibility and accessibility from major highways and roads.

Considerable amounts of time and money were spent by the defendants for site preparation, engineering services, legal fees and services, franchise fees, architectural fees, leasing of land, options, managers' services, and travel. Parsons and Lipton made expenditures for the benefit of the corporation in the amounts of $18,453.55 and

$31,433.82, respectively. In so doing the defendants were motivated by the intent and purpose of building a financially strong enterprise to insure themselves a sound investment and a reasonable profit. They did not enter into any formal agreement as to how they would be compensated.

In 1964, Parsons had acquired a small parcel of land for approximately $2,000 which eventually became part of the motel site. On July 20, 1966 he acquired an adjacent parcel for $35,000. That land had been acquired by him prior to the time of its selection as the motel site. Parsons had himself intended to build a motel on the site. The site was traversed by Rowe Street, a public way. In order to accommodate a motel at the site, Parsons had obtained from the city of New Bedford a discontinuance of Rowe Street, together with extensions of water mains and sewer lines to the property. Parsons had in turn granted the city an easement from Hathaway Road for the installation of the utility services which he had arranged. He had also acquired an option for the purchase of another parcel of land.

The promoters—Parsons, Lipton, and the Freedmans—caused the corporation to be formed and incorporated on February 14, 1967, with 1,000 shares of no-par stock authorized to be issued. Initially, the officers and directors of the corporation were members and employees of the law firm engaged to form the corporation. They resigned on October 18, 1967, and the four promoters, together with a fifth person, attorney Samuel Lipman, became the officers and directors. Parsons was the president, Lipton the treasurer, Lipman the clerk, David Freedman the vice president, and Louis Freedman the assistant treasurer. Those five constituted the board of directors.

Each of the promoters presented an offer to the board of directors to buy 130 shares of stock for $108,000. Lipman offered to buy 120 shares of stock for $100,000. On October 19, 1967, the directors voted to accept the offers and to issue the stock upon receipt of the purchase price by the corporation. The stock certificates were dated October 19, 1967, but were issued in April, 1968. Upon such issue the total holdings of the four promoters comprised 52 percent of the total authorized capital stock of the corporation. No cash was paid by the defendants for such stock. Lipman paid $100,000 in cash for the 120 shares issued to him. The per share value of no-par stock had previously been set at $833.

On October 28, 1967, Parsons conveyed the two parcels and assigned the option to the corporation for the total sum of $75,000. The transaction was neither embodied in a formal vote nor recorded in the records of the corporation. The value of the land for use as a motel was $25,000 per acre (or about $150,000 for the entire site).

The promoters spent considerable time and money conferring with banks and insurance companies seeking a commitment for construction and permanent financing and, as a result, obtained various proposals for such financing. The corporation decided to accept the proposal offered by a syndicate consisting of several participating banks. As a condition, the syndicate required the promoters to furnish individual financial statements and subjected them to credit checks. On March 25, 1968, the corporation executed and delivered its promissory vote in the amount of $1,130,000, payable to the lead bank of the syndicate and secured by mortgages of the corporation's property. Parsons, Lipton, and the Freedmans were required to and did endorse their individual guarantees upon the note. The guarantees were an important factor in the syndicate's decision to provide financing to the corporation. They were of value to the corporation; they also acted to impair the ability of the guarantors to borrow money. Those guarantees are still in force and effect.

The bank also required the corporation to deposit $300,000 with it and to pay from that amount the first $100,000 of construction bills. To raise that money the four promoters agreed to sell the remaining authorized but unissued stock at $833 a share. Most of that stock was then sold to 10 outside investors at that rate. Some of the investors were informed that the promoters had invested their money in the purchase of stock; none of the outside investors was informed that the promoters had not paid cash for the 520 shares of stock issued to them.

The construction of the motel began in the spring of 1968 and was substantially completed in early July of that year.

■

Chief Justice Hale:

The master found that Parsons' fellow promoters were aware of the price he had paid for the parcels and the option but that none of the outside investors was informed or was aware that the property had been acquired at that price. As a promoter, Parsons was a fiduciary in his dealings with the corporation and as such he would be liable for profits improperly made. . . .

The corporation argues that the proper measure of damages is, as the court ruled, the difference between the sales price and Parson's cost. . . . We think that, on the facts of this case, the use of that method of computing damages was incorrect.

We are of the opinion that the proper measure of damages here is the difference between the price paid by the corporation and the fair market value of the property at the time of the sale. The corporation recognizes that authority exists for such a position. . . . The property had been acquired by Parsons prior to the formation of the corporation and prior to its selection by the promoters as the site for the motel. It appears that the combined lots in their condition at the times of Parsons's acquisitions were unsuitable for the purposes of a motel. It was not until he, by his own efforts, had, among other things, obtained the discontinuance of a public way which ran through the property and secured extensions of water and sewer mains to service the property that the site was rendered suitable for such purpose. The amount of time and expense involved was not specifically found by the master. However, Parson's efforts resulted in a parcel of land which had a fair market value of about $150,000.

While we do not approve of the slipshod way in which the transaction was handled with respect to corporate votes concerning the acquisition of the property and the means by which Parsons received payment, it is nevertheless clear that the corporation received more than full value in return for the price it paid. While the outside investors were not informed of the details of the transaction, the master did not find, as the corporation contends, that Parsons actively misled the outside stockholders as to his cost or as to the sales price of the land to the corporation. The master did find that the deed from Parsons carried documentary stamps which indicated a sales price of $37,500. We do not agree with the corporation's assertion that such was necessarily an affirmative misrepresentation of the sales price, as there are other equally persuasive explanations for the presence on the deed of that amount of documentary stamps. Absent more specific findings we consider that any conclusion, based on the amount of such stamps, would be speculative. . . .

The application of our holding that Parsons is accountable to the corporation only for the difference between the price paid by the corporation for the property and its fair market value at the time of its transfer to the corporation would not result in any positive difference. Hence that part of the decree charging Parsons and Lipton $37,500 was error.

The final decrees in the cases ordered Parsons, the Lipton's trustees and the Freedmans to surrender for cancellation the stock certificates representing all the shares of stock initially issued to them. Parsons was ordered to deliver the certificate for the remaining 92 shares held by him, to deliver for cancellation the $71,000 note of the corporation dated November 8, 1969, and to repay to the corporation the $29,000 (less a small credit not involved in this appeal) paid by the corporation to him.

The corporation contends that the relief granted was correct for two reasons: (a) the defendants are liable to the corporation for secret profits realized in the form of stock because of the breach of the promoters' fiduciary duties as promoters, directors, and corporate officers; and (b) as the stock was accepted on condition of payment and as the defendants have failed to pay for it, they are liable to the corporation for breach of their subscription agreements.

The defendants do not contend that $108,000 in cash was paid for each block of 130 shares, nor do they make any contentions that the master did not properly determine the amount of the expenses incurred by each of the promoters. Their position is that the entrepreneurial services and the expenses of each promoter were the equivalent in value of that amount and that . . . the stock was properly issued for such services and expenses.

It is apparent that such was the posture in which the case was tried before the master. At least one of the means by which the defendants sought to establish that value was through the testimony of an expert. The expert's opinion was expressed on the basis of facts contained in a hypothetical question. His opinion of value was admitted in evidence. However, the master in his report stated that he placed no value on that testimony as the facts assumed by hypothesis had not been established. . . .

The master made no finding that there was any intention on the part of the promoters to deceive or defraud the outside investors, and we infer that there was none. Nonetheless, it was the duty of the promoters either to inform the investors that the stock had been issued for services and expenses and not for cash, or to obtain the ratification of such issuance at a later time upon a complete revelation of the facts to the outside stock-holders or to an independent board of directors. . . .

Moreover, the promoters and the corporation entered into a subscription contract by virtue of the board's acceptance of the promoters' offers on October 19, 1967. A failure on the part of the promoters to pay the agreed price would render them liable for the deficiency or for the return of that part of the stock for which no consideration was given. . . . The offers which were accepted by the corporation spoke of payment in terms of cash, not in terms of services or expenses. However, we are of the opinion that to limit credit on stock subscriptions to cash payments would amount to a rank injustice to the promoters. All of the extensive efforts of the promoters, which culminated in the issuance of a motel franchise and the transfer of the product of their labors to the corporation, accrued to the benefit of the corporation. All of these efforts were undertaken prior to the actual issuance of stock to the promoters. Depriving the promoters of credit for their contribution to the value of the corporation through services and expenses would preclude them from any participation in the corporation and would unjustly enrich the equity of the outside investors.

As the defendants' liability has been established under either theory advanced by the corporation, we hold on the facts of this case that the measure of damages for which the defendants are accountable to the corporation is the difference between the value of each block of shares at the time of issue and the fair value of the services rendered and expenses incurred by each promoter which benefited the corporation. . . .

The evidence to be taken on rehearing is to be limited to the determination of the value of the services of the several promoters. As those are matters of affirmative defense, the burden is upon each promoter to prove the amount of credit to which he may be entitled. . . .

■ IMPORTANT TERMS AND CONCEPTS

corporation	legal entity
private corporation for profit	publicly held corporation
close corporation	subchapter S corporation
public corporation	not-for-profit corporation
domestic corporation	foreign corporation
professional corporation	Model Business Corporation Act (MBCA)
incorporator	articles of incorporation
corporate charter	de jure corporation
de facto corporation	corporation by estoppel
inherent powers	statutory powers
express powers	*ultra vires*
promoter	liability *inter se*

■ QUESTIONS AND PROBLEMS FOR DISCUSSION

1. What is a "Subchapter S corporation"?
2. What is the difference between the incorporators and the promoters?
3. How can a corporation be a "citizen" for some purposes but not for others?
4. What is the difference between a *de jure* corporation and a *de facto* corporation?
5. Ferd was employed as a truck driver by Ace Delivery Company, Inc. Leon Crim was the president and principal stockholder of Ace. Ferd quit his job and sued for back wages and bonuses which he claimed were due. Ferd's suit named as defendant "Leon Crim

d/b/a Ace Delivery Company, Inc." Crim was served with process as an individual, not as Ace's president. Ace was never served with process. Throughout the trial, Crim denied that he personally was Ferd's employer, but Ferd insisted that he considered Crim and Ace to be "one and the same." The trial court entered judgment against Ace for $2,050 but entered no judgment against Crim. Crim appeals. What should the appeals court do to resolve this case? Explain.

6. Athos, Porthos, and Aramis subscribed for shares of common stock in Lille, Inc., a corporation that was being organized to develop, manufacture, and distribute high-technology medical products. Constance and Harry, the promoters, never filed the articles of incorporation. They nevertheless leased a factory building, bought the necessary equipment, hired several employees, and commenced business. After six months the business was bankrupt. The landlord, the equipment seller, the employees, and several other creditors had unpaid claims. Who may be held liable in this situation? Discuss.

7. David and Harry Felsenthal and their father, Isaac, owned all 150 shares of the capital stock of Felsenthal Company. When the company was unable to pay a bank loan of $20,000, David went to see an old family friend, Morris L. Fox. Fox paid off the bank loan and received 75 shares of stock, plus assignments of the other 75 shares. About two months prior to the fire which destroyed the premises, Morris and David went to Moe Rosenberg's saloon, had dinner, and discussed the burning out of the business. Moe directed them to Ben Fink, who was in the business of firing properties. They hired Ben, who burned the company's premises with 75 gallons of gasoline. Because of his loans to the company, Morris Fox would ultimately receive all of the insurance proceeds. The trial court and the appeals court found for the insurance company, and Felsenthal Company appealed. Should the court "pierce the corporate veil" here? Explain.

8. McDefendant, Inc. was in the beginning stages of becoming a nationwide chain of restaurants specializing in ½-pounders and Small Macs. McChiney, plaintiff, made an offer to McDefendant to invest in its restaurants in the form of an equipment lease to the subsidiary which owned the San Aglo restaurant. McChiney was the lessor. The restaurant was doing so poorly that it closed almost before it opened. McDefendant immediately transferred the equipment to a different restaurant, not the one in the lease. Plaintiff learned of the closing and demanded accelerated payments, which McDefendant refused. What is the result of a lawsuit against McDefendant, Inc., the parent corporation, and why?

46

Corporations— Stocks and Stockholders

CHAPTER OBJECTIVES

THIS CHAPTER WILL:

- Describe the classes of capital stock a corporation may be authorized to issue.
- Discuss the legal rules concerning subscriptions for shares of stock and the issuance of shares of corporate stock.
- Review the process of registration and transfer of shares.
- Discuss shareholders' rights.
- Discuss management rights.
- Describe the legal procedure that must be followed to expand or terminate a corporation.

The legal structure of a corporation differs substantially from that of a partnership. As discussed in Chapters 42 and 43, each partner is assumed to have an equal voice in managing the business, the right to an equal share of the profits, and the liability for an equal share of the losses. If necessary, any partner can be forced to pay the firm's debts in full. Each partner is assumed to be a general agent of the firm, with full authority to conduct all of its normal business operations. The partners' investments in the firm are governed by their own partnership agreement. These management and ownership rights and liabilities inhere in each partner individually, as the result of their partnership agreement. Partnership status cannot be transferred to someone else by the act of a single partner.

Nearly all these ownership and management rules are different for a corporation. The primary mechanism for corporation investment and control purposes is the share of stock. A corporation, as a separate legal person, can of course borrow money in much the same way as an individual or a partnership can. The equity investment in the corporation, however, is done by buying shares of stock. The investor agrees to buy a certain number of shares and receives a certificate indicating how many shares have been purchased. The investor, now a "stockholder" or "shareholder," has the right to vote the number of shares owned at stockholders' meetings. The investor also has the right to receive dividends, as earned and declared, based on the number of shares owned. While the stockholder is not considered an agent of the corporation, and generally has no authority to conduct its business operations, the shares of stock are assumed to be freely transferable. The shares can be sold to someone else without the consent of the other shareholders or of the corporation, and the transferee becomes a shareholder with the same rights as all other shareholders.

As a separate legal person, the corporation owns its own assets. Individual stockholders have no right to possess or use these assets just because they are stockholders. Their shares of stock simply make them the "owners" of proportionate parts of the corporation's net worth.

■ CLASSES OF STOCK

In some corporations there is normally only one type of stock. Typically all of the shares in a small corporation have the same value and all of the shareholders have the same rights. This is not true in large corporations where it is not uncommon to have several classes and series of stock. Some stock may have a par value, and other stock may have no-par value. Some stock may have voting rights, and other stock may not have voting rights. Some stock may be preferred, and other stock may be common.

Common Stock.   This is the basic class of stock issued by corporations. Typically a shareholder has one vote for each share of stock and the shareholder is

Right to vote, but last to be paid

entitled to receive a *pro rata* share of the corporation's profits in the form of dividends. The common stockholder is given no guarantees, no special preference. If the business succeeds, the common stockholders receive dividends and their share value will increase. If the business fails, the common stockholders get no return on their investment and they may lose the investment itself, as they share in the balance of the assets after creditors and preferred stockholders have been paid off.

Preferred Stock.   As the term indicates, this class of stockholders gets special preference. Typically the preferred stockholder receives a specific, guaranteed dividend before any dividends are paid to the persons owning the corporation's common stock. In case of dissolution of the corporation the preferred stockholders get their money back before any money is returned to the common stockholders. Usually, preferred stock is nonvoting.

First to be paid, but no vote

The preferred stockholder is not a creditor of the corporation, and normally the dividend on preferred stock does not have to be paid if the board of directors decides not to declare a dividend.

Cumulative Preferred Stock.   In some lean years the corporation may not have enough profits to declare a dividend for either the preferred stockholders or the common stockholder. This question then arises: Does the preferred stockholder lose out on the unpaid dividend for such years? Unless the articles of incorporation state otherwise, the unpaid dividends on preferred stock would accumulate. Thus, it is important that preferred stock be declared either noncumulative or cumulative. If the preferred stock is noncumulative, then, of course, if no dividends are declared by the board of directors during a given year, the preferred stockholders simply lose out for that year. If the stock is cumulative, then the next year they will get the past year's dividends plus the new year's dividends before any money is distributed to the common stockholders.

Required make-up for prior years

Participating Preferred Stock.   The preferred stockholder has the advantage of receiving dividends prior to the distribution of dividends to the common stockholder. Typically, however, the preferred stockholder is entitled to receive only a specific, guaranteed dividend, for example, 6 percent. If the corporation had a good year, the amount left to divide among the common stockholders might well exceed the percentage awarded to the preferred stockholders. However, if the preferred stockholder has participating preferred stock, then the preferred stockholder would share in the amount divided after the common stockholders received a dividend equal to the dividend paid to the preferred stockholders. Thus, if the preferred stockholders get 6 percent on their stock, then the common stockholders would get 6 percent on their stock and if there was extra money left over, it would be shared equally on a *pro rata* basis between the two classes of shared stock. This special feature would have to be expressly stated.

"Second helping" of dividends

In addition to the cumulative or noncumulative and participating or nonparticipating provisions of preferred stock, it is not uncommon to find ***redeemable*** or ***convertible*** provisions. Such provisions say, in effect, that at the election of the corporation or of the stockholder, preferred shares may be converted into another class of shares or may be redeemable by the corporation.

Par Value and No-Par-Value Stock.   A corporation may issue stock with or without a par value. The certificates for par value stock state an amount which must be paid per share for the stock by the subscriber. The amount paid per share of no-par-value stock is simply determined by the board of directors.

Par value ≠ Book value and ≠ Market value

The issuance of par value stock often creates misunderstanding. For example, if a new corporation issues 1,000 shares at a par value of $100 each and you buy 10 shares at $100 each, you will be given stock certificates that show a face value of $1,000. The corporation, however, proceeds to buy equipment and inventory and to pay the expenses of incorporation and other expenses of doing business, and thus the corporation no longer has a net worth of $100,000 or 1,000 times $100 per share of par value stock. As a result, even though your certificate of stock shows a par value of $100 per share, you could not necessarily sell the stock for $100 per share as the stock is now only worth $\frac{1}{1,000}$ of the net worth or book value of the corporation. The revised Model Business Corporation Act eliminates the concept of par value.

■ ISSUANCE OF SHARES

Number of shares that can be sold

Authorized Stock. This term describes the number of shares and the kind of stock that the corporation is authorized to issue. The original charter issued to the corporation by the state of its creation states the number of shares authorized and also the kind of shares authorized. If the corporation desires to increase its authority to issue more shares or different kinds of stock it must apply to the state of its creation. Such approval will be granted if the request complies with the requirements of the state's corporation laws. A minimal filing fee will be charged.

Unissued Stock. This term refers to the authorized stock that is not yet issued.

Issued Stock. This term refers to the shares of stock that have been sold and delivered to shareholders. It includes shares that have been reacquired by the corporation as treasury shares.

Outstanding Stock. This term describes that stock that has been issued and is currently owned by stockholders.

Treasury Stock. This term refers to stock that was issued to shareholders and was later repurchased by the corporation. Treasury stock must be paid for with the corporation's surplus funds; the corporation cannot use original capital funds to repurchase stock. Also, the shares of treasury stock, while they are held in the corporation's name, are not votable, and such shares cannot earn dividends. Treasury stock may be resold, held, or canceled. Canceling these shares reduces the number of shares issued, and the corporation can then issue new stock as long as it does not exceed the total number of shares authorized. The revised MBCA provides that such shares become authorized, unissued stock, unless their reissue is prohibited by the articles of incorporation.

■ SUBSCRIPTIONS FOR SHARES

Preincorporation offer to buy shares

One of the promoters' most important preincorporation functions is to make arrangements for acquiring the capital necessary to commence the firm's business. Persons making preincorporation offers to buy shares of the firm's stock are called *subscribers*. Since these offers are made to the corporation, they cannot be accepted until after incorporation. Unfortunately, in many cases proposed corporations fail before they ever commence business or after a very short period of operation. If there are unpaid creditors of the now insolvent corporation, it thus becomes very important to know exactly when subscribers become liable for their shares, and the extent of that liability.

Revocable Offer.   The general rule is that a stock subscription, like any offer, is revocable prior to acceptance. This rule creates problems for the promoters, since they can't count on having any set amount of capital until the corporation is formed and accepts the subscription offers. Some courts have found particular subscriptions to be irrevocable because the promoters' efforts provided consideration for an implied promise by the subscriber not to revoke. Some cases find mutual promise between the several subscribers not to revoke. Section 17 of the MBCA, which has been adopted in many states, makes the subscription offer irrevocable for six months without consideration. Of course, where fraud was committed against the subscriber, the offer can be revoked despite section 17 or the presence of consideration. The revised MBCA contains a similar provision.

MBCA rule: Irrevocable for six months

Implied Conditions Precedent.   For a subscriber to be held liable on a subscription contract, the courts have generally agreed that three conditions must be met. First, the corporation must be fully organized de jure. Second, it must be substantially like the one proposed to the subscriber. And finally, the shares subscribed for must be legally issuable by the corporation (in other words, must not be shares representing an oversubscription).

Express Conditions Precedent/Subscriptions on Special Terms.   Some potential subscribers may not be interested in investing in the proposed corporation unless certain return promises are made. These special promises could relate to the corporation's method of operation, the location of its place of business, or other matters. What happens when the corporation is organized, accepts the subscriptions, but goes into bankruptcy before it builds its main plant in Keokuk, as it promised one subscriber? Is that subscriber liable anyway, or was the "plant in Keokuk" an express condition precedent which has not been fulfilled? As between risk-taking investors and unpaid corporate creditors, the equities are all with the creditors. Courts will try as hard as possible to label these special deals as *subscriptions on special terms,* so as to hold the subscriber liable for the full price of the contracted shares. After paying in full, the subscriber then has a claim for damages, if any can be proved, for the corporation's breach of its promise to build the plant. If the parties' intent and the "no contract if no plant" results are spelled out clearly enough in the subscription, the subscriber may avoid liability.

Special promises to subscribers

Subscription versus Contract to Purchase Shares.   Particularly in cases where the stock is being paid for in installments, it may also be important to distinguish between a subscription and a contract to purchase shares. A subscriber becomes liable for the full price of the shares when the subscription offer is effectively accepted by the corporation. A purchaser does not become a shareholder (and thus become liable for the price of the shares) until a certificate is delivered or tendered. Where corporations have gone into bankruptcy before

When does liability arise?

issuance of the certificates, many courts have held that the purchasers were excused from further liability because they would never receive their certificates. Subscribers in such a case would be bound to pay any balance due on their shares.

Once again, in figuring out which is which, it's a question of the parties' intent and of some legal presumptions and rules. Prior to incorporation, the transaction can only be a subscription, not a purchase. After incorporation, the agreement to buy original, unissued shares may be either. Generally, a purchase is an individual agreement, whereas a subscription may involve several purchasers. If there is any ambiguity at all, most courts will try to impose full liability by classifying the transaction as a subscription. The revised MBCA makes all postincorporation agreements "contracts to purchase."

Minimum Liability Equals Full Par Value. In some instances subscribers may not be willing to pay the full par value per share, and the promoters may agree to sell shares at a discount. This is a dangerous practice at best, since all states agree, on one theory or another, that every subscriber must pay at least the full par value for each share taken. One early case held that the corporation's capital was sort of a "trust fund" for the benefit of its creditors. A few states analyze the discount to subscribers as a fraud on the firm's creditors. The most sensible analysis simply says that payment of at least full par is the price the state demands for the privilege of doing business in the corporate form with limited personal liability.

Required minimum payment for shares

Under any of these theories, creditors can force payment of the difference between the discounted contract price and the full par value. Creditors who knew about the discount when they extended credit, however, might have some difficulty in recovering in a fraud theory state. Stockholders who have paid full par for their shares might also sue to force the discounter to pay up. In some cases the corporation itself or the state of incorporation may bring the suit.

Liability of transferees and directors

In addition to the original subscriber who bought at a discount (whether or not still a stockholder), possible defendants include knowing transferees of the discounted shares, the directors who approved the sale, and the promoters. As states adopt the revised MBCA, these lawsuits will be almost completely eliminated, since there will be no "par value" for shares.

The *Bing Crosby* case indicates that creditors in a fraud theory state must also prove that they "relied" on some misrepresentation of the amount of the debtor corporation's capital.

BING CROSBY MINUTE MAID CORPORATION v. EATON

297 P.2d 5 (California, 1956)

FACTS

Wallazz Eaton owned and operated a frozen foods business. He organized a corporation and transferred the business to it in return for 4,500 shares of $10 par stock. The corporations commissioner required that 1,022 shares of the stock be placed in escrow and not transferred without his written consent; 1,022 shares were put in escrow in

Eaton's name, and the other 3,478 shares were issued directly to him. The plaintiff had a judgment against the corporation for $21,246.42, of which some $15,000 was still unpaid. The corporation was insolvent. The trial court found that the value of the transferred business was $34,780.83 and gave the plaintiff a judgment against Eaton for $10,219.17. Because it had failed to make a finding that the plaintiff relied on some misrepresentation in connection with the watered stock, the trial court granted Eaton a new trial. The plaintiff appealed the order granting a new trial.

ISSUE

Must a corporate creditor prove reliance on a misrepresentation in order to recover against the holder of watered stock?

DECISION

Yes. Order for new trial affirmed.

REASONS

After reciting the facts, Justice Shenk started with the proposition that stockholders were not personally liable for the debts of their corporation unless they had not paid what they promised for their stock or unless they held watered stock. The first exception didn't apply here because there was no proof that Eaton had in fact promised to pay full par for his shares. Justice Shenk did not think that the escrow arrangement made any difference, since Eaton could vote those shares and receive dividends on them. For statutory purposes, Eaton owned them. The real issue was what the plaintiff had to prove to recover.

"In his answer the defendant alleged that in extending credit to the corporation the plaintiff did not rely on the par value of the shares issued, but only on independent investigation and reports as to the corporation's current cash position, its physical assets, and its business experience. . . . Plaintiff's . . . admissions would be sufficient to support a finding that the plaintiff did not rely on any misrepresentation arising out of the issuance of watered stock. The court made no finding on the issue of reliance. If the misrepresentation theory prevails in California, that issue was material and the defendant was entitled to a finding thereon. . . .

"It is therefore necessary to determine which theory prevails in this state. The plaintiff concedes that before the enactment of section 1110 of the Corporations Code . . . in 1931, the misrepresentation theory was the only one available to creditors seeking to recover from holders of watered stock. . . . However, he contends that the enactment of that section reflected a legislative intent to impose on the holders of watered stock a statutory obligation to creditors to make good the 'water.' . . . The statute does not expressly impose an obligation to creditors. Most jurisdictions having similar statutes have applied the misrepresentation theory obviously on the ground that creditors are sufficiently protected against stock watering schemes under that theory. . . . In view of the cases in this state prior to 1931 adopting the misrepresentation theory, it is reasonable to assume that the Legislature would have used clear language expressing an intent to broaden the basis of liability of holders of watered stock had it entertained such an intention. In this state the liability of a holder of watered stock may only be based on the misrepresentation theory."

Validity of noncash payments

Payment in Property or Services.   Another potential area of liability arises when shares are paid for with noncash items. Property or services, to be valid payment for shares, must be usable by the corporation in operating its business. Generally, promises to perform services or to deliver property in the future do not constitute proper payment for shares, and subscribers who receive shares in exchange for such promises could be sued for the full par value of the shares they receive. The revised MBCA permits payment with promissory notes and with promises to perform services.

Complications arise not only from questions as to whether or not the corporation was authorized to receive the noncash items but also as to the valuation of those items. States use two very different rules in determining whether at least full par has been paid. The Model Act and most of the newer corporation statutes have adopted the *good faith rule:* the valuation of the board of directors is conclusive. Whatever the board says the property or services were worth binds the corporation and all its creditors, unless the board was acting fraudulently or was grossly negligent. Some of the states still follow the older *true value rule,* which holds that any such noncash item had a true market value when it was transferred to the firm in payment for shares, that such value presents a question of fact, and that a jury can thus determine the true value of the noncash item. The result of this rule is that jurors are second-guessing the parties, sometimes after a lapse of several years, on the basis of less than perfect information.

No-Par Shares. As noted above, no-par stock does not have any specific dollar figure indicated on the share certificate. Thus, most "valuation" problems are avoided when no-par stock is exchanged for a noncash item. Most statutes permit no-par shares to be issued for such consideration as is agreed to by the directors (or the existing stockholders). The no-par's price is thus permitted to fluctuate with market conditions, and the no-par stockholders would not be held liable for any "discount." No-par shares cannot, however, be issued as a gift. Moreover, there is case law that indicates that after the initial issue, if the price paid for no-par is not "fair" to the existing stockholders, they can bring suit to enjoin the dilution of their interest in the firm's net assets. Again, this difference in treatment will be eliminated under the revised MBCA, which eliminates the idea of par value.

Treasury Shares. Treasury shares (which were issued but then reacquired by the corporation) generally may be resold for any consideration fixed by the board of directors. Once again, there should be no "valuation" problem or "discount" liability as long as the directors were acting in good faith. The revised MBCA simply makes such stock additional authorized but unissued shares.

Shares Issued by Going Concern. What if the corporation needs additional capital after it has been in operation for some period of time? If it still has original, unissued par stock, can it sell that stock to investors at the market price, or is it still bound to receive at least par value per share? Only in a few states do the corporation statutes recognize this problem and specifically permit the directors, in this case, to sell par stock at the going market price. This problem, too, should be solved by the adoption of the revised MBCA.

Repurchase of Shares. Having required the payment of at least par value per share by subscribers/investors, courts do not want these risktakers to be able to escape easily if the firm gets into financial difficulties. Creditors should

Valuation of noncash items

Promised payment given = No-par share paid in full

Requirements for repurchase

be paid in full before stockholders recover any part of their investment. Thus, a contract for the repurchase of shares is valid only if the corporation has earned surplus when the contract is made, and for such a contract to be enforceable in court by the shareholder, the corporation must also have earned surplus when payment is to be made to the shareholder. At both points in time, the earned surplus shown on the books must be sufficient to cover the repurchase.

■ REGISTRATION AND TRANSFER OF SHARES

Registration with SEC

Registration.   Many securities issues must be registered with either the Securities and Exchange Commission, a similar state agency, or both. This is a very complex area of the law. Chapter 48 discusses the nature of these registration requirements and the potential liabilities involved.

Mechanics of Transfer.   Article 8 of the UCC contains many of the rules covering the transfer of corporate securities (both stocks and bonds). Many customary practices are also involved—stockbrokers' rules for dealing with each other and their customers, regulations adopted by the stock exchanges, and administrative rulings from the SEC. Large corporations usually appoint a bank or trust company to act as their *transfer agent;* that is, to record transfer of their securities and to issue new certificates in the new owner's names. Securities, particularly bonds, may also be issued in bearer form, in which case ownership transfers are not registered with the corporation. *Bearer bonds* are often called *coupon bonds,* since interest coupons attached to such bonds must be clipped and sent in by the bondholder in order to receive the interest due on the bonds.

Registration of ownership with corporation

The revised MBCA does not require that a corporation issue paper certificates as evidence of ownership of its shares. Most corporations have done so, and continue to do so, but computerized share transfers may become more popular in the near future. If used, share certificates provide proof of ownership of the shares they represent and furnish a handy means of dealing with the shares. When shares are sold, the certificate is indorsed over to the buyer or simply indorsed in blank. When shares are used as collateral in a credit transaction, the certificate is usually left with the creditor.

As discussed in Chapter 12, every contract for the sale of investment securities is subject to the Statute of Frauds rules in UCC 8–319. The contract is not enforceable unless the party against whom enforcement is sought (or an authorized agent) has signed a writing containing the quantity of the particular security being bought and sold and a statement of the price or a means of ascertaining the price. As an alternative, either party may send the other a writing in confirmation of their oral contract. If the confirmation is sufficient against the sender and if the receiver does not send back written notice of objection to its contents within 10 days after receipt, the confirmation does satisfy the writing requirement against the receiver as well as against the sender. Where a payment for the securities has been accepted or securities have been delivered to the buyer, the oral contract is enforceable by the person who has given the partial performance to the same extent that performance has been accepted. Finally, an oral contract for the sale of securities is enforceable to the extent that it is admitted in court.

Someone who transfers a certificate for value warrants to the purchaser that (1) the transfer is effective and rightful; (2) the certificate is genuine and has not been materially altered; and (3) the transferor knows of no fact that would impair the validity of the certificate. However, if the transfer is made by an intermediary, that person warrants only that the transfer is authorized and is made in good faith.

Registration of Transfer. Where securities have been issued in registered form, the corporation may continue to treat as owner the person whom they have registered as owner. That registered owner would, for instance, continue to receive dividends on the shares. A buyer of registered shares, therefore, may wish to have the transfer of ownership registered on the corporation's books. The corporation has a duty to do so if (1) the certificate has been properly indorsed; (2) reasonable assurance is given that the indorsement is valid; (3) no adverse ownership claims to the shares have been presented to the corporation and are still pending; (4) all applicable tax laws have been satisfied; and (5) the transfer was in fact rightful or was made to a bona fide purchaser who received the certificate free of adverse claims. A bona fide purchaser (BFP) of the certificate is a person who took it for value, in good faith, and without notice of any adverse claims. In order for the transferee to receive this BFP protection, the certificate must have been issued in bearer form or have been properly indorsed.

Lost or Stolen Securities. Where the missing securities were in bearer form or had been properly indorsed by the former registered owner, a good faith purchaser from the thief or finder owns the securities. If registered securities are involved, the *bona fide* purchaser (BFP) is entitled to be registered on the corporation's books as the new owner.

Protections for BFP

Where the securities were in registered form but the thief or finder forged the indorsement/assignment of the owner, the BFP does not own the certificates and must return them. If the BFP sends in an old certificate to the transfer agent, however, and the old certificate is canceled and a new one issued to the BFP, the BFP does own the new certificate. In this last situation the former owner has a claim against the corporation and its transfer agent for not catching the forgery. Because of the potential liabilities resulting from such a "double issuance" of a new certificate, corporations will uniformly require that persons who claim that their certificates have been lost or stolen post bonds protecting the corporation against the "reappearance" of the missing securities.

Restrictions. Corporate securities are generally freely transferable by the owner. In special situations, however, the persons operating the firm may wish to place limitations on the retransfer of its stock. In a small closely held corporation, for example, the stockholders might want to give the corporation itself or the other stockholders a right of first refusal before any stock is resold to outsiders. Similarly, there might be a requirement that shares issued to key employees be resold to the firm rather than to outsiders when the employment ends. For such restrictions to be effective against buyers who don't know about them, they must be noted conspicuously on the certificate.

■ SHAREHOLDER RIGHTS

Vested Rights. As noted in Chapter 45, the charter of the corporation is a contract. This means that the shareholders' rights the charter establishes cannot be changed without their consent. Where the power to amend the articles and the bylaws has been reserved, however, and the amendment procedure is followed, changes can be made in the respective rights and liabilities of the stockholders.

Right to subscribe to new issues

Preemptive Rights. One right recognized in many older cases is the right to maintain one's proportionate investment in the corporation. The original stock issue gave each stockholder a certain percentage of the votes and of any dividends declared. To protect this relationship among the stockholders, courts required that existing stockholders be given a right of first refusal for a proportionate part of any new issue. That is, the new stock had to be offered to existing stockholders first, before it could be sold to others. Courts did not agree as to whether this "preemptive right" also applied to originally authorized but unissued stock.

Insistence on such preemptive rights makes it very difficult for a firm to authorize a new stock issue for executive bonuses, acquisition of assets, mergers with other firms, or other possible business needs. The modern tendency is to limit or eliminate such preemptive rights unless they are specifically provided for in the articles or by agreement among the stockholders.

Shareholders: Voting Control Mechanisms

One share, one vote

Voting Rights. Except perhaps in Illinois, corporations are permitted to issue both voting and nonvoting stock. As previously noted, typically common stock has the right to vote, while preferred stock does not. Unlike partnerships, where each *partner* is presumed to have one vote regardless of the amount invested, in corporations each *share* is entitled to one vote.

Cumulative voting for directors

To facilitate minority representation on the board of directors, some corporations provide for cumulative voting. (In some states, in fact, cumulative voting for directors is required by law.) Under this voting system, all directors' vacancies that are to be filled in a given year are voted for at the same time, with each share having as many votes as there are directors to be elected. The idea is that by massing their votes for only one (or a few) candidates, minority stockholders may be able to get at least some representation on the board. A seat on the board enables the minority to obtain information and to present alternative proposals and views. To find out how many shares they need to assemble to be assured of electing their candidates, minority stockholders can use the following formula:

$$X = \frac{a \times c + 1}{b + 1}$$

Formula for guaranteed representation

where X equals the number of shares needed, a equals the number of shares voting in the election, b equals the number of directors to be elected, and c equals the number of directors the minority want to elect.

Assembling the needed votes

To assemble the number of shares needed to obtain board representation or to gain or maintain control, shareholder groups can use one of three devices: the proxy, the voting control agreement, or the voting trust. A *proxy* is merely

■ **EXHIBIT 46–1**
Shareholders: Voting
Control Mechanisms

1. Voting by proxy

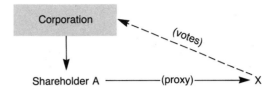

2. Voting control agreement

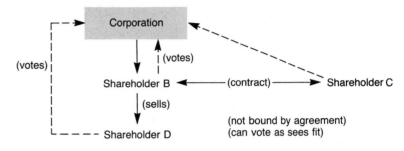

3. Voting trust

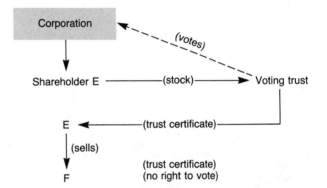

a revocable agency authority to vote shares. Changing conditions or new information could lead stockholders to withdraw their proxies or to give later proxies to the opposing side. Proxies thus do not provide a very stable coalition.

Some or all of the stockholders, particularly in closely held corporations, may enter into *voting control agreements*. Such agreements usually provide for reciprocal voting for the board of directors; A, B, and C agree to vote for each other, so that each retains a seat on the board. Such agreements are permitted in most states, at least for a limited period of time. They are not, however, binding on the corporation or on unknowing transferees of stock. A stockholder wishing to break up such an agreement could simply transfer shares to a BFP, who would then be free to vote them as he or she pleased.

The *voting trust* is the most durable arrangement for accumulating the votes necessary to maintain control of a corporation. Stockholders, the corporation itself, and transferees are all bound by the voting trust, since shares of stock are actually turned over to the voting trustees, who are registered as the owners of the shares on the corporation's books. In return for their shares, the (former) stockholders receive voting trust certificates, which give them all the rights of stockholders *except* the right to vote. Many voting trusts are set up by demand of the firm's creditors, as a condition to the extension of further credit. The creditors want to assure continuity of management, and a voting trust is a good way to do so.

Shareholders: Dividend Rights

Requirements for declaring

Many persons who invest in corporate stock are mainly motivated by the expectation of dividends. The firm's directors generally determine the timing and amount of dividends, subject to the requirements of the particular state. Most states require that there be earned surplus before dividends may be lawfully declared and paid, but a few states permit the payment of dividends from current earnings even though prior years' losses have not been made up. Once declared, cash dividends become debts of the corporation. If a dividend has been illegally declared, the directors who voted in favor are jointly and severally liable for the entire amount of the dividend. All of the states agree that shareholders

■ **EXHIBIT 46–2**
Proxy Statement

FOLD   **FOLD**

PROXY   **SOLICITED BY THE COMMITTEE OF SEPARATE ACCOUNT II**

**SEPARATE ACCOUNT II OF
EQUITABLE VARIABLE LIFE INSURANCE COMPANY**
Annual Meeting of Policyholders—April 25, 1984

The undersigned Owner of a Policy supported by assets of Separate Account II of Equitable Life Insurance Company ("Separate Account II") hereby appoints Donald J. Mooney, James W. Mason and Kevin Keefe, and each of them to act with full power without the others and with power of substitution, the attorneys and proxies of the undersigned, for and in the name of the undersigned, to exercise all the voting rights which the undersigned would be entitled to exercise if personally present at the Annual Meeting of Policyowners of Separate Account II to be held at 1285 Avenue of the Americas, New York, New York, on April 25, 1984 at 11:15 A.M., and any adjournments thereof, hereby ratifying and confirming all that each of said attorneys and proxies, or any subsite, shall lawfully do or cause to be done by virtue hereof, with respect to the following matters:

1. **ELECTION OF MEMBERS OF THE COMMITTEE OF SEPARATE ACCOUNT II:**

   FOR all nominees listed below   **WITHHOLD AUTHORITY**
   (except as marked to the contrary below) ☐   to vote for all nominees listed below ☐

   (INSTRUCTION: To withhold authority to vote for any individual nominee strike a line through the nominee's name in the list below.)

   Howard E. Hassler, Walter C. Kronke, Donald R. Kurtz, Gordon W. McKinley, and Donald J. Mooney

2. **PROPOSAL TO RATIFY THE SELECTION OF DELOITTE HASKINS & SELLS** as the independent auditors of Separate Account II for the year 1984:

   ☐ **FOR**   ☐ **AGAINST**   ☐ **ABSTAIN**

3. **PROPOSAL TO APPROVE THE INVESTMENT ADVISORY AGREEMENT** od Separate Account II as described in the accompanying Proxy Statement.

   ☐ **FOR**   ☐ **AGAINST**   ☐ **ABSTAIN**

4. In their descretion, the Proxies are authorized to vote upon such other matters as may properly come before the meeting or any adjournments thereof.

This proxy when properly executed will be voted in the manner directed herein by the undersigned. If no direction is made, this Proxy will be voted for Proposals 1, 2 and 3.
Receipt of the Notice of Meeting and Proxy Statement accompanying this Proxy is acknowledged by the undersigned.

Dated: . . . ., 1984

. . . .
Signature

The Policyholder should enter date, sign his/her name and return the signed Proxy in the enclosed envelope.

who know that a dividend was illegal can be forced to return it, but there is disagreement as to whether innocent stockholders can also be forced to return an illegal dividend.

Stock dividends are not debts of the corporation, and they may be rescinded by the board before the new shares are issued.

The *Dodge* presents an unusual claim: the directors are accused of being too stingy, rather than too generous, in declaring dividends.

DODGE v. FORD MOTOR CO.

170 N.W. 668 (Michigan, 1919)

FACTS   Minority stockholders sued to force the directors to declare an additional special dividend. Horace and John Dodge, the plaintiffs, were two of the original stockholders in Ford Motor Company, along with Horace Rackham, James Couzens, and Henry Ford himself. On the capitalization of $2 million, Ford Motor had been paying a quarterly dividend equal to 60 percent per year; it had also paid out a total of $41 million in special dividends. Ford Motor still had a capital surplus of nearly $112 million, however, and sales and profits were up. Henry now proposed a massive capital expansion to produce iron and steel (the Rouge plant) as well as a lowering of the price of the Model T from $440 to $360. At one point, Henry was quoted as saying: "My ambition is to employ still more men, to spread the benefits of this industrial system to the greatest possible number, to help them build up their lives and their homes. To do this, we are putting the greatest share of our profits back in the business." Ford Motor appealed from the trial court's decision ordering payment of a special dividend and enjoining the building of the Rouge plant.

ISSUE   Did the directors abuse their discretion in refusing to grant a dividend?

DECISION   Yes. Judgment affirmed as to dividends, reversed as to injunction.

REASONS   Chief Justice Ostrander first disposed of the claims that Ford Motor's activities had in some way violated its corporate charter. No statutory limits were intended on the size to which corporations might grow, and the Rouge smelter plant seemed closely enough connected with the company's main business so as not to be *ultra vires*. Likewise, there had been no violation of the antitrust laws. The court also cited several authorities which stated the general rule for the declaration of dividends: "The discretion of the directors will not be interfered with by the courts, unless there has been bad faith, willful neglect, or abuse of discretion." Despite this strong general rule, the court here felt that there had been an abuse of the directors' discretion, due to Ford's personal feelings.

"He had made up his mind in the summer of 1916 that no dividends other than the regular dividends should be paid, 'for the present.'. . .

"The record, and especially the testimony of Mr. Ford, convinces that he has to some extent the attitude towards shareholders of one who has dispensed and distributed to them large gains and that they should be content to take what he chooses to give. His testimony creates the impression, also, that he thinks the Ford Motor Company has made too much money, has had too large profits, and that, although large profits might still be earned, a sharing of them with the public, by reducing the price of the output of the company, ought to be undertaken. We have no doubt that certain sentiments, philanthropic and altruistic, creditable to Mr. Ford, had large influence in determining the policy to be pursued by the Ford Motor Company—the policy which has been herein referred to. . . .

"We are not, however, persuaded that we should interfere with the proposed expansion of the business of the Ford Motor Company. . . . The judges are not business experts. . . . The experience of the Ford Motor Company is evidence of capable management of its affairs."

Right of Access to Information. Stockholders have the right to receive information regarding the operation of "their" corporation. This right, however, is not unlimited. All of the states agree that financial information, such as the firm's annual balance sheet and its profit and loss statement should be available to the stockholders. There is some disagreement as to when an individual stockholder should have access to other information, particularly the firm's general books and business records. With unlimited rights of access, minority stockholders might be able to disrupt normal business operations. Competitors could simply buy one share of a firm's stock and then demand access to all of its trade secrets, formulas, and customer lists. "Junk mailers" of various sorts could buy one share and ask for lists of stockholders. For these reasons, courts have generally required that a stockholder must have a "proper purpose" in asking for access to corporate books and records. Some states require ownership of a certain percentage of a class of stock, and some also require that the stock have been owned for some minimum period of time (such as six months) prior to the demand for information. Where the demand is proper and the officers refuse to provide the information, some statutes make them liable for 10 percent of the value of the stock owned, in addition to any other appropriate remedy to which the stockholder may be entitled. The revised MBCA makes the corporation liable for the stockholder's legal fees in getting a court order for inspection, unless the corporation had a good faith doubt about the stockholder's right to inspect.

The *Pillsbury* case defines a "proper purpose."

Reasons for limited access

STATE EX REL. PILLSBURY v. HONEYWELL, INC.

191 N.W.2d 408 (Minnesota, 1971)

FACTS

On July 3, 1969, Pillsbury attended a meeting of a group involved in a so-called Honeywell Project. He had long opposed the Vietnam War, but it was at this meeting that he first learned of Honeywell's involvement as a manufacturer of antipersonnel fragmentation bombs. "Upset" and "shocked" by this information, he determined to stop Honeywell's munitions production. On July 14, he told his fiscal agent to buy 100 shares of Honeywell. The agent, not knowing that Pillsbury wanted the shares in his own name, put them in the name of Quad & Co., a family holding company, as he always did. Upon learning that the 100 shares had not been registered in his name, Pillsbury bought one share in his own name. Meanwhile, he learned that his grandmother's trust, of which he was a beneficiary, owned 242 Honeywell shares. He then made a written demand that Honeywell give him its original shareholder ledger, its current shareholder ledger, and "all corporate records dealing with weapons and munitions manufacture." Honeywell refused, and Pillsbury filed a petition to order disclosure. He appealed from the trial court's denial of his petition.

ISSUE   Does plaintiff have a right to the corporate records he requested?

DECISION   No. Judgment affirmed.

REASONS   Justice Kelly said that a few states held that a desire to communicate with other shareholders was per se a proper purpose for inspection of corporate books and records.

"We believe that a better rule would allow inspection only if the shareholder has a proper purpose for such communication. . . .

"The act of inspecting a corporation's shareholder ledger and business records must be viewed in its proper perspective. In terms of the corporate norm, inspection is merely the act of the concerned owner checking on what is in part his property. In the context of the large firm, inspection can be more akin to a weapon in corporate warfare. The effectiveness of the weapon is considerable. . . .

"Petitioner's standing as a shareholder is quite tenuous. He owns only one share in his own name, bought for the purposes of this suit. He had previously ordered his agent to buy 100 shares, but there is no showing of investment intent. . . . [P]etitioner made no attempt to determine whether Honeywell was a good investment or whether more profitable shares would have to be sold to finance the Honeywell purchase. Furthermore, petitioner's agent had the power to sell the Honeywell shares without his consent. Petitioner also had a contingent beneficial interest in 242 shares. . . . Indicative of petitioner's concern regarding his equitable holdings is the fact that he was unaware of them until he had decided to bring this suit.

"Petitioner had utterly no interest in the affairs of Honeywell before he learned of Honeywell's production of fragmentation bombs. Immediately after obtaining this knowledge, he purchased stock in Honeywell for the sole purpose of asserting ownership privileges in an effort to force Honeywell to cease such production. . . . But for his opposition to Honeywell's policy, petititoner probably would not have bought Honeywell stock, would not be interested in Honeywell's profits, and would not desire to communicate with Honeywell's shareholders. His avowed purpose in buying Honeywell stock was to place himself in a position to try to impress his opinions favoring a reordering of priorities upon Honeywell management and its other shareholders. Such a motivation can hardly be deemed a proper purpose germane to his economic interest as a shareholder. . . .

"His sole motivation was to change Honeywell's course of business because that course was incompatible with his political views. If unsuccessful, petitioner indicated that he would sell the Honeywell stock."

Shareholder Lawsuits

Individual shareholders can of course bring lawsuits, as individuals, to enforce their rights as shareholders. They may sue to enforce their right to dividends, to vote, to subscribe stockholder rights. A group of shareholders together may file a class action lawsuit if they meet the test outlined in Chapter 2. Such lawsuits by one or more shareholders are directed against the corporation, and any remedies given are directed against the corporation and for the benefit of the stockholders as individuals.

Derivative Suits. In certain extraordinary situations, individual stockholders may be able to bring lawsuits on behalf of their corporation. In these cases, they are suing for their own benefit only indirectly; the real plaintiff is the corporation. Any remedies given are for the corporation and against the third parties who are defendants—directors, officers, majority shareholders, or outsiders. Any benefits received by the corporation as plaintiff will indirectly benefit the shareholders who brought the case, but the primary purpose of the lawsuit is to protect the corporation.

Normally, of course, the shareholders have no right as such to manage the corporation directly. That rule would include the lack of stockholder authority to decide to bring a lawsuit on behalf of the corporation. What then are the "extraordinary circumstances" that justify a derivative suit? Typically, the wrongdoers are officers, directors, or majority stockholders. Because they control the corporation's decision-making process, the corporation is unlikely to sue. If there is an independent board of directors which could take action to correct the problem (as by firing the officer), the stockholder must make a demand to the board that it act. If such a demand would be "futile," because the wrongdoers also control the board, the stockholder can proceed to file the derivative lawsuit without making any demand. If a demand is made and the board decides that the corporation should sue, the complaining stockholders could not bring a second lawsuit in the name of the corporation. If a demand is made and the board decides that the corporation should not sue, that decision would also prevent the complaining stockholders from bringing a derivative suit. If the board is acting in good faith, its business judgment in deciding that the corporation should not sue would be upheld by the courts. Of course, if the board is the alleged wrongdoer, its decision that the corporation should not sue would not prevent the complaining shareholders from bringing the derivative suit against the board itself.

Some corporations have attempted to use a special board committee—the "stockholder litigation committee"—to convince the courts that it acted in good faith. Use of such a separate committee will not necessarily prevent a court from second-guessing the board's decision not to sue. Where a derivative lawsuit is successful, the corporation will probably be ordered to reimburse the complaining stockholders for any reasonable litigation expenses, including attorneys' fees. On the other hand, where the lawsuit is unsuccessful and has been brought without "reasonable cause," many corporation statutes require the complaining stockholders to pay the *defendants'* litigation expenses, including attorneys' fees.

Management Rights. In small, closely held corporations, where the stockholders are also the directors, officers, and managers, the stockholders may participate in the daily operations of the business. With large corporations like IBM or GM, however, stockholders will usually have only one annual meeting to attend. Special meetings other than the regular annual meeting may be called, but only after proper notice has been sent to all of the stockholders so that they all have a chance to attend. The Model Act specifies that a quorum at a stockholders' meeting is a majority of the voting shares (represented in person or by

Quorum for stockholders' meeting

proxy), unless the articles of the particular firm specify a lower percentage. Some of the newer statutes permit the stockholders to transact business if any shares are represented, as long as proper notice has been sent. Once a quorum has been established, stockholders cannot prevent the transaction of business by leaving the meeting and then having someone make another quorum call.

Election of directors

The main item of business to be transacted at the stockholders' meeting is the election of directors. As noted above, the cumulative voting system may be used. In most cases the slate of candidates proposed by management is elected without much, if any, opposition. Where a firm has had bad financial results, dissident stockholders may propose their own slate of directors and try to take control of the firm. Each side will solicit support from the rest of the stockholders through personal letters, ads in *The Wall Street Journal,* and other methods. The SEC has extensive regulations on the solicitation and use of proxies in such control battles.

No voting on ordinary business decisions

The stockholders generally have no say in making ordinary business decisions for "their" company. By custom and statute, the responsibility for day-to-day management is vested in the board of directors, which in turn delegates much of this authority to the officers. The directors and officers are usually called on to report to the stockholders at the annual meeting, and the stockholders can question them at that time about the decisions made during the year. The stockholders will also usually vote on the selection of the corporation's outside auditors. The independent CPA firm auditing the corporation's books provides another source of information to the stockholders and another method of checking on the directors' and officers' conduct of the firm's business. If changes in a corporation's bylaws are proposed, those will also have to be voted on by the stockholders. Extraordinary business decisions, such as amending the articles to change the nature of the firm's business or voluntary dissolution of the corporation, or merger or consolidation with another company, must also be presented for stockholder vote. While the Model Act now requires only a majority vote on such extraordinary decisions, many states still require a two-thirds or even a three-fourths favorable vote.

Fiduciary position of majority

Generally, the majority stockholders have the right to determine corporate policy as they see fit, through the directors they elect and through the officers those directors appoint. The majority control group, however, must act within the limits set by the charter and must act in good faith as far as the rights of the minority stockholders are concerned. Several cases, like Wilkes', have held that the majority control group occupies a fiduciary position with respect to the minority and that its acts can be challenged where it is abusing its control powers.

WILKES v. SPRINGSIDE NURSING HOME, INC.

353 N.E.2d, 657 (Massachusetts, 1976)

FACTS

On August 5, 1971, the plaintiff (Wilkes) filed a bill in equity for declaratory judgment in the Probate Court for Berkshire County, naming as defendants T. Edward Quinn (Quinn), Leon L. Riche (Riche), the First Agricultural Bank of Berkshire County, and Frank Sutherland MacShane as executors under the will of Lawrence R. Connor (Connor), and the Springside Nursing Home, Inc. (Springside or the corporation). Wilkes alleged that he, Quinn, Riche, and Dr. Hubert A. Pipkin (Pipkin) entered into a partnership agreement in 1951, prior to the incorporation of Springside, which agreement was breached in 1967 when Wilkes's salary was terminated and he was voted out as an officer and director of the corporation. Wilkes sought, among other forms of relief, damages in the amount of the salary he would have received had he continued as a director and officer of Springside subsequent to March 1967.

A judge of the probate court referred the suit to a master, who, after a lengthy hearing, issued his final report in late 1973. Wilkes's objections to the master's report were overruled after a hearing, and the master's report was confirmed in late 1974. A judgment was entered dismissing Wilkes's action on the merits. The state supreme court granted direct appellate review.

ISSUE

Can the majority stockholders in a close corporation "freeze out" a minority shareholder when no legitimate business purpose is shown or served?

DECISION

No. Judgment of the trial court is reversed and judgment entered in favor of Mr. Wilkes.

REASONS

Chief Justice Hennessey, speaking for the state supreme court, expressed the concern of the court for protection of the minority shareholder in a close corporation.
"[W]e reverse so much of the judgment as dismisses Wilkes's complaint and order the entry of a judgment substantially granting the relief sought by Wilkes.

"Each of the four men invested $1,000 and subscribed to 10 shares of $100 par value stock in Springside. At the time of incorporation it was understood by all of the parties that each would be a director of Springside and each would participate actively in the management and decision making involved in operating the corporation. It was, further, the understanding and intention of all the parties that, corporate resources permitting, each would receive money from the corporation in equal amounts as long as each assumed an active and ongoing responsibility for carrying a portion of the burdens necessary to operate the business.

"In *Donahue*, we held that 'stockholders in the close corporation owe one another substantially the same fiduciary duty in the operation of the enterprise that partners owe to one another.'. . .

"Therefore, when minority stockholders in a close corporation bring suit against the majority alleging a breach of the strict good faith duty owed to them by the majority, we must carefully analyze the action taken by the controlling stockholders in the individual case. It must be asked whether the controlling group can demonstrate a legitimate business purpose for its action. . . . In asking this question, we acknowledge the fact that the controlling group in a close corporation must have some room to maneuver in establishing the business policy of the corporation. It must have a large measure of discretion, for example, in declaring or withholding dividends, deciding whether to merge or consolidate, establishing the salaries of corporate officers, dismissing directors with or without cause, and hiring and firing corporate employees. . . .

"Applying this approach to the instant case, it is apparent that the majority stockholders in Springside have not shown a legitimate business purpose for severing Wilkes from the payroll of the corporation or for refusing to reelect him as a salaried officer and director. . . . There was no showing of misconduct on Wilkes's part as a director, officer, or employee of the corporation which would lead us to approve the majority action as a legitimate response to the disruptive nature of an undesirable individual bent on injuring or destroying the corporation. On the contrary, it appears that Wilkes had always accomplished his assigned share of the duties competently and that he had never indicated an unwillingness to continue to do so.

"It is an inescapable conclusion from all the evidence that the action of the majority stockholders here was a designed 'freeze out' for which no legitimate business purpose has been suggested. Furthermore, we may infer that a design to pressure Wilkes into selling his shares to the corporation at a price below their value well may have been at the heart of the majority's plan."

■ EXTRAORDINARY BUSINESS DECISIONS

Substantial changes in economic circumstances or regulatory policies may indicate the need for a firm to expand or to terminate its business. The Model Act and most state statutes contain fairly detailed procedures to cover each of these special situations and the stockholders' role in deciding how to deal with them.

Methods of Expansion. In addition to growing gradually by selling more of its product or service year by year, a corporation may wish to expand rapidly by entering into various sorts of combinations with other firms. It may wish to buy or lease all the assets of a second firm. It may wish to merge or consolidate with one or more other firms. Or it may wish to simply buy a controlling stock interest in other firms.

Possible antitrust problems

In general, the legality of any of the above sorts of combinations would be tested under the national antitrust laws if the firm is engaged in interstate commerce or if its activities have a substantial impact on interstate commerce. Even if a combination met all of the state procedural requirements, the Federal Trade Commission or the U.S. attorney general could still prevent the combination if it would have substantial anticompetitive effects. Antitrust law is discussed more thoroughly in Chapter 5.

Purchase or Lease of Assets. Where one corporation buys or leases all the existing assets of another, there is no change in the corporate identity of either; they both continue to exist as before. The seller or lessor firm has simply decided to liquidate its operations in one line of business and to reinvest in funds and efforts elsewhere. A TV manufacturer, for example, feels that the present and future competition is too tough, so it sells its TV manufacturing assets and starts making business machines. The stockholders of the seller or lessor firm must approve this extraordinary transaction by majority vote, after recommendation and proper notice of the special meeting from the board of directors. Once shareholder authorization has been given, however, the board may cancel the sale or lease, if conditions change, without further shareholder action. Assuming that all actions have been taken in good faith, the creditors of the seller or lessor firm would have no basis for objecting to the transaction. Since the buyer or lessee is paying fair value for the assets, it should own them free and clear of the seller/lessor's creditors.

Two firms still exist, but seller's stockholders must approve

Merger and Consolidation. Two or more firms may decide to combine by means of a merger or a consolidation. In a ***merger,*** one of the original firms survives and the others end. In a ***consolidation,*** all of the original firms end; a new corporation is formed, and the original ones all become parts of it. In

Majority of each class of stock must approve

either case, all assets and all liabilities are turned over to the surviving firm. In each case, the Model Act requires approval by the board and by a majority of each class of stock entitled to vote as a class. Since all liabilities are being assumed by the survivor firm, consent of the creditors of the original firms would generally not be required.

Purchase of Controlling Stock Interest.   Where the directors of X Corporation decide to have X buy a controlling stock interest in Y Corporation, both firms continue to exist as before. X Corporation offers to buy shares from Y's stockholders. This is a *tender offer* and is subject to extensive regulation by the SEC and the states. See Chapter 48 for further discussion of this concept.

Rights of Dissenting Shareholders.   The Model Act requires approval by majority stockholder vote in the case of sale or lease of all the firm's assets, merger, or consolidation. In the tender offer, each stockholder makes an individual decision as to whether to sell at the price offered. Generally, consent of the firm's creditors is not required. But what about the minority shareholders who object to this drastic change in their firm's operations?

Protection for minority

The revised Model Act tries to protect the minority by providing a mandatory buy-out procedure. Prior to attendance at the special stockholders' meeting, the dissenter must file written notice of objection to the proposed action. At the meeting, of course, the dissenter must not vote for the proposal. If the proposal is passed by the necessary majority vote, the dissenter may then file a written demand with the firm for payment of the fair value of his or her shares as of the day prior to the vote, "excluding any appreciation or depreciation in anticipation of such corporate action." This demand for payment must be made within the time period specified in the notice sent by the corporation to the dissenters. The theory of this procedure is that the individual should not be forced to maintain an investment in a substantially different firm.

Dissolution.   Assuming that it retained the power to amend, the legislature of the state of incorporation would presumably have the power to terminate the existence of that state's corporations. The state's attorney general or corporation commissioner could ask a court to decree dissolution where a corporation was in continuing default on its duties to file reports and to pay taxes and fees. In those rare cases where the articles did not provide for perpetual existence, the end of the specified time period or the occurrence of the specified event would cause a dissolution of the firm. The shareholders may act voluntarily to terminate their corporation, either by unanimous action or by majority vote, after a recommendation from the board of directors. Normally courts will not interfere with the shareholders' decision.

Majority of stockholders must approve dissolutions

Winding up corporation's business

Modern corporation law treats a dissolved corporation in much the same way as a dissolved partnership. That is, the corporation continues to operate for the limited purpose of winding up its affairs—collecting money owed to it, selling off its assets, and paying off its creditors. After the creditors have been paid in full, the preferred stockholders have the first claim on any assets remaining and then, finally, the common stockholders are paid.

Reorganization. Financial reorganizations under the Bankruptcy Act are covered in Chapter 23. An attempt may be made to save the firm by adjusting its debts, or the firm may be dissolved and its assets used to pay off as many claims as possible, according to bankruptcy priorities.

| ■ **SIGNIFICANCE OF THIS CHAPTER** | This chapter defines and discusses the various kinds of stock that corporations may issue, the process of subscribing to purchase shares, the issuance and transfer of such shares, and shareholders' rights. Thus, this chapter provides an overview of the methods by which stockholders own and control a corporation.

Corporations also have financial difficulties and often must be dissolved or perhaps reorganized under bankruptcy law, and procedures are needed for these changes. Also, corporations often desire to expand by purchasing other corporations and merging them within the parent corporation. This chapter also reviews these procedures and the rights of the stockholders in these matters. |

DISCUSSION CASE

FISH v. AMSTED INDUSTRIES, INC.

376 N.W.2d 820 (Wisconsin, 1985)

FACTS: This is an appeal from an order of the circuit court granting the defendants', Amsted Industries, Inc. (Amsted) and South Bend Lathe, Inc. (South Bend II), motion for summary judgment on Emily and Rodney Fish's (plaintiffs) claim of corporate successor liability.

On October 8, 1979, Emily Fish was severely injured while operating a power press, known as the "Johnson Mechanical Press," while on the premises of Hamilton Industries, her employer. The press involved here was manufactured by Bontrager Construction Company (Bontrager) in 1957, and was sold to Hamilton Industries by Interstate Machinery Co., Inc., a distributor of the presses.

Johnson Mechanical Presses were originally manufactured by the Johnson Machine and Press Company (Johnson) in Elkhart, Indiana. In 1956, Johnson transferred all of its assets and liabilities to Bontrager. Johnson continued to exist as a wholly owned subsidiary of Bontrager, but it no longer manufactured the presses. The sole share of outstanding stock in the Johnson Corporation was transferred to Bontrager in order to assign to Bontrager all rights to the Johnson trade name. Bontrager began manufacturing the Johnson press line at the Elkhart plant.

In 1962, Amsted acquired all the assets of Bontrager, including all the assets of Johnson (use of the Johnson

trade name) via a cash transfer. Bontrager agreed to use its "best efforts" to make its present employees available to Amsted. Amsted agreed to assume only those liabilities of Bontrager that were necessary for uninterrupted business, and it refused to assume Bontrager's tort liabilities arising out of defects in products manufactured by Johnson or Bontrager. None of the officers or directors of Amsted were ever an officer or director of Bontrager or Johnson. However, a Bontrager vice president was employed by Amsted as a plant manager at the Elkhart plant for approximately four years following the transfer.

Amsted manufactured the Johnson press line through its wholly owned subsidiary, South Bend Lathe, Inc. (South Bend I) at the Elkhart plant, using substantially the same manufacturing facilities and equipment that were used by Bontrager and Johnson. However, South Bend I did implement its own general manufacturing policy, planning procedures and standards, and marketing procedures.

On July 29, 1964, Bontrager was dissolved, and all of its assets were distributed to its shareholders. On August 2, 1965, Johnson was dissolved by Amsted, and its sole asset, the Johnson stock, was distributed to Amsted. On September 29, 1965, Amsted dissolved its subsidiary, South Bend I, but continued to operate it as an unincorporated division under the name South Bend Lathe. South Bend Lathe continued to manufacture the Johnson press. In 1966, Amsted sold the Elkhart plant and transferred its manufacturing operations to the South Bend, Indiana plant of South Bend Lathe.

In 1975, Amsted sold the Johnson press line business to LWE, Inc., an Indiana corporation, which subsequently changed its corporate name to South Bend Lathe, Inc. (South Bend II). Amsted agreed to indemnify South Bend II for any liability claims arising out of defects in the Johnson press line.

Amsted is no longer involved in the manufacturing of the Johnson press line. South Bend II (an entirely different entity from the South Bend Lathe subsidiary and division of Amsted) continues to manufacture the Johnson press line.

The plaintiffs brought a products liability claim against Amsted and South Bend II sounding in negligence and strict liability. The complaint alleges that as successor corporations Amsted and South Bend II are liable to the plaintiffs for the acts of their predecessor corporation, Bontrager, in manufacturing an allegedly defective press.

The circuit court denied plaintiffs' summary judgment motion asking the court to find, as a matter of law, that Amsted and South Bend II were responsible as successor corporations for the acts of a predecessor corporation. Based on its uncertainty as to the meaning of the term *identity* as a basis for imposing liability on successor corporations, the circuit court granted Amsted's and South Bend II's motion for summary judgment, holding that they could not be liable for claims of corporate successor liability.

The Court of Appeals sent the appeal directly to the state supreme court.

■

Justice Day:

As a general rule, "a corporation which purchases the assets of another corporation does not succeed to the liabilities of the selling corporation.". . . There are four well recognized exceptions to this general rule:

(1) when the purchasing corporation expressly or impliedly agreed to assume the selling corporation's liability; (2) when the transaction amounts to a consolidation or merger of the purchaser and seller corporations; (3) when the purchaser corporation is merely a continuation of the seller corporation; or (4) when the transaction is entered into fraudulently to escape liability for such obligations. . . .

Both the plaintiffs and the defendants (Amsted and South Bend II) agree that the traditional exceptions to the general rule of nonliability do not apply to the succes-

sion in this case. It is the plaintiffs' contention that the *Tift* decision expanded the second and third exceptions by setting forth the concept of "identity.". . .

We agree with the arguments advanced by the defendant and hold that the plaintiffs are in error in alleging that the *Tift* decision has expanded the exceptions to the rule of nonliability. This court expressly stated that it was applying existing corporate rules to the factual situation in *Tift*.

A court merely need determine that the defendant, despite business transformations, is substantially the same as the original manufacturer. This is the *application of existing corporate law; and such law governs the decision in this case,* because it is clear that there is identity between the original manufacturer and the present Forage King Industries, Inc. (Emphasis added.)

Identity refers to identity of ownership, not identity of product line. Since this court applied existing corporate rules in *Tift* to reverse the summary judgment, there was no need to determine whether or not this court should adopt the product line exception. In his dissent, Justice Callow analyzed this exception and stated that he would refuse to recognize it as a means of imposing liability on a successor corporation. . . .

In *Tift,* this court was confronted with a situation in which the predecessor was not a corporation, but rather a sole proprietorship. However, this court held that this factor was irrelevant and applied the corporate rules. Direct application of exceptions two or three is impossible when a sole proprietorship is involved because this form of ownership does not have officers, directors, and shareholders. The key element in determining whether a merger or de facto merger has occurred is that the transfer of ownership was for stock in the successor corporation rather than cash. . . . In determining if the successor is the "continuation" of the seller corporation, the key element "is a common identity of the officers, directors and stockholders in the selling and purchasing corporations.". . .

Thus, this court considered whether the successor was the same business organization as the predecessor and concluded that Forage King Industries, Inc. was "the continuation of the *same entity* as that operated as a sole proprietorship by Wiberg.". . . (Emphasis added.) There was identity of management and control throughout the transformation from sole proprietorship to partnership to corporation. Only the form of the business changed; in substance, the identical organization continued to manufacture the same product. This court refused to allow the successor corporation to escape liability when in substance the successor corporation was the same entity as the predecessor sole proprietorship.

In *Cody, Tift's* companion case, this court concluded

that there was no identity of business organizations between the predecessor and successor corporations. Though the successor shared the predecessor's name and place of business, the successor corporation was an entirely different corporation. It was a repair and job shop, rather than a manufacturer of drum sanders. There was no identity of management and control throughout the transfers of ownership. Unlike *Tift,* both parties were corporations, and there was "no common identity of officers, directors, and stockholders between the two companies.". . . When confronted with a factual situation in which both the predecessor and successor were corporations, this court refused to hold that "identity" exists when exceptions two and three were inapplicable. Since none of the corporate exceptions were applicable, Sheboygan III could not be liable as a successor corporation.

This court continues to apply the existing corporate law to product liability cases. Since it is undisputed that the succession in this case does not meet any of the existing exceptions to nonliability, the circuit court was correct in granting the defendants' motion for summary judgment.

Alternatively, the plaintiffs argue that this court should adopt the "product line" exception . . . for holding the defendants liable in this products liability action. During oral arguments, both parties agreed that this issue was properly before this court.

The traditional rule of nonliability of successor corporations and its exceptions were developed prior to the adoption of strict products liability law. . . .

> Courts have come to recognize that the traditional rule of nonliability was developed not in response to the interests of parties to products liability actions, but rather to protect the rights of commercial creditors and dissenting shareholders following corporate acquisitions, as well as to determine successor corporation liability for tax assessments and contractual obligations of the predecessor.

Some states, California, New Jersey, Pennsylvania, and Washington, have found the general rule and its exceptions to be too narrow when confronted with a strict products liability action. The purpose of strict products liability is to insure that the costs of any injuries resulting from the use of a defective product are borne by the manufacturer who placed the defective product on the market, rather than by the injured person. . . . Therefore, these states have adopted the product line exception to nonliability, which has developed to protect the interests of parties involved in a products liability action. . . .

After considering the arguments for and against adoption of the product line exception, we are in agreement with the arguments raised in opposition to the exception. Although strict products liability is a "no-fault" theory of liability, it imposes liability on manufacturers who are responsible for placing the defective product that caused the injury into the stream of commerce. This is not the case with a successor corporation. The successor did not manufacture nor did it place on the market the product that caused the injury. . . .

We conclude that the legislature is in a better position to make broad public policy decisions in actions based on products liability law. . . . The questions concerning the effect on the manufacturing business, the potential size and economic strength of successor corporations, the availability of commercial insurance, and the cost of such insurance are all questions that we cannot answer. These are the type of questions that the legislature is in a better position to ascertain. If such a basic change in corporate law is to be made it would seem reasonable for the change to come about through legislation rather than by court decision. . . .

> Courts are ill-equipped, however, to balance equities among future plaintiffs and defendants. Such forays can result in wide-ranging ramifications on society, the contemplation of which is precluded by the exigencies of deciding a particular case presented on a limited record developed by present parties. . . . As the Wisconsin Supreme Court has recognized, such broad policy issues are best handled by legislatures with their comprehensive machinery for public input and debate.

If the liability of successor corporations is to be expanded, we conclude that such changes should be promulgated by the legislature.

We decline to adopt the "expanded continuation" exception to nonliability for the same reasons that we declined to adopt the product line exception.

The decision of the circuit court is affirmed.

■ IMPORTANT TERMS AND CONCEPTS

common stock
cumulative preferred stock
par value stock
authorized stock

issued stock
treasury stock
preemptive rights
proxy

dividend rights
preferred stock
participating preferred stock
no par value stock
unissued stock
outstanding stock

registration and transfer
  of shares
cumulative voting
voting trust
derivative suits

■ QUESTIONS AND PROBLEMS FOR DISCUSSION

1. What is the difference between common stock and preferred stock?
2. What is the difference between cumulative preferred stock and participating preferred stock?
3. What is the difference between par and no-par stock?
4. What is treasury stock?
5. Carbor Oil Co. was dissolved by its state of incorporation due to failure to pay taxes. It owned 80 acres of land. All members of its last board of directors are now deceased; the last to die was E. Z. Froth. Froth's widow, Liza, has a certificate for 10 shares of Carbor stock. No other stockholders or officers can be found. What should happen to the 80 acres Carbor owned when it was dissolved, and why?
6. Mrs. Gertrude Weller, an elderly widow, owned 500 shares of stock in the American Telephone & Telegraph Company and 200 shares in the General Electric Company. Mrs. Weller, because of her advanced age, could not live alone, and she was invited to live at a friend's residence. While living there, her friend stole the stock certificates, forged Mrs. Weller's name to the certificates, and sold them in the open market. Later Mrs. Weller learned of the theft and reported it to the companies. She asked each company to reissue the stolen shares to her. They refused. She sues. Who wins? Why?
7. Danny Donaho owned 25 percent of the stock in Loyalty Electric Corporation and was its vice presi-

dent, but he was not on the board of directors. The other 75 percent of the stock was owned by Larry Hoddy, who was president and chairman of the board. In 1974 Larry put his sons, Kenny and Lennie, who worked for Loyalty, on the board and gave them each 25 shares. The board then voted to buy Larry's remaining 25 shares for $1,000 a share. At a special stockholders' meeting, Danny learned of the repurchase for the first time and voted against a resolution approving it. Danny then offered his 25 shares to Loyalty for $1,000 a share. Loyalty refused to buy Danny's shares. Danny died, and his widow, Ufemia, brings a lawsuit challenging the validity of this repurchase of Larry's shares. What is the result, and why?

8. Uriah Grant sues the Peppy Pickle Company, challenging the validity of an amendment to Peppy's articles of incorporation. Grant owned 3,000 shares of $1 par preferred 8 percent cumulative stock in Peppy. Dividends had not been declared (or paid) on Peppy's preferred stock for 10 years. Peppy's articles had expressly reserved the power to amend. Pursuant to the amendment procedure, a majority of Peppy's stockholders voted to cancel the old preferred shares and to issue one new preferred share of 10 percent cumulative preferred for each two old shares. The amendment also canceled the accumulated but undeclared dividends for the 10 years. Grant says that it would be unconstitutional to interpret this amendment so as to deprive him of accrued property rights. What is the result, and why?

47

Corporations— Management Duties

CHAPTER OBJECTIVES

THIS CHAPTER WILL:

- Explain the duties and responsibilities of corporate directors.
- Explain the duties and responsibilities of corporate officers.
- Discuss the liabilities of directors and officers.
- Introduce the Foreign Corrupt Practices Act.

▪ DIRECTORS

Authority and Qualifications. The directors are given management control of the normal business operations of the corporation. They are more than just agents for the shareholders, since a large part of their authority and duties flows from the state's corporation statute. Shareholders may try to influence or replace the directors, but shareholders as such have no right to participate in corporate management. So long as the directors are acting in good faith and within the statute, articles, and bylaws, they have exclusive control of the corporation's ordinary business decisions.

Number required

Older statutes required three or more directors. Recognizing the reality of the "one-person" corporation, modern corporation codes require only one director. Some states still require directors to be shareholders and/or residents of the state of incorporation. Again, the modern tendency, as seen in Section 8.02 of the revised *MBCA,* is to require neither unless the articles or bylaws of the particular corporation so specify. In other words, let each corporation decide for itself what qualifications its directors must have.

Selection and Removal. As noted in the last chapter, selection of the board of directors is the shareholders' most important management function. While some states require cumulative voting, most statutes permit it but do not require it. Most states also permit corporations to provide for staggered terms for directors, similar to those of U.S. senators. Electing only part of the board each year provides continuity of management and also prevents an outside group from taking over the board all at once, in one election.

Removal with or without cause

The rule in most states is that directors may be removed by the shareholders at any time, with or without cause. Directors, in other words, serve at the pleasure of the shareholders. In this sense, they are like agents. In a few states, such as New York, directors can be removed only if good cause is shown. In any corporation where cumulative voting is in force, a director could not be removed unless he or she failed to get enough votes to win a seat under the cumulative voting system.

Nearly all statutes provide for the replacement of directors by the remaining board members, where vacancies occur, at least until the next shareholders' meeting at which directors are elected. These procedural steps must be followed exactly.

Election rules are at issue in the *Grossman* case.

GROSSMAN v. LIBERTY LEASING CO., INC.

295 A.2d 749 (Delaware, 1972)

FACTS

Liberty was a Delaware corporation, with its main operations in Chicago. The plaintiffs and their families owned about 20 percent of Liberty's stock. Grossman was president and treasurer; Gross, executive vice president and secretary. They were directors, along with Sachnoff and Myers. Liberty's bylaws called for five directors and permitted the directors to amend the bylaws and fill vacancies on the board. The four were unable to agree on a candidate for the single vacancy, but they agreed to amend the bylaws to increase the number of directors to seven and to elect Malkin, Haas, and Roland to fill the three vacancies. The next day Grossman and Gross said that they wanted to rescind the board actions, but Sachnoff (an attorney) told them that this could not be done. At a later board meeting, Grossman and Gross were dismissed as officers and Malkin, Roland, and Haas were elected to the main offices. Grossman and Gross brought suit to declare that both the election of the three new directors and all subsequent board actions were invalid. The new directors moved to dismiss since they had not been personally served in Delaware.

ISSUES   Can the Delaware court determine the validity of directors' elections? Were the three new directors validly elected?

DECISION   Yes. Yes. Defendant's motion to dismiss denied; plaintiffs' motion for injunction denied.

REASONS   **Chancellor Duffy first decided that he did have jurisdiction over the defendants since Delaware law governed the validity of directors' election in Delaware corporations. Personal service of process in Delaware was not required.**

"We are here concerned not with a personal judgment against the individual defendants but only with their respective rights to hold office in a Delaware corporation over which this Court clearly has jurisdiction. That is the contest. In short, defendants' positions, not their pocketbooks, are in jeopardy in this suit."

Chancellor Duffy then proceeded to the merits of the plaintiff's claim for injunctive relief.

"Plaintiffs say that there was not [a vacancy] because the stockholders had deliberately left the position unfilled at two successive annual meetings called to elect directors. . . .

"It seems to me that under the circumstances of this case there was indeed a prior incumbency. . . . Nothing . . . requires an 'incumbency' since the last annual meeting of stockholders. . . . The key requirement is not when the office was last filled, but how it was created in the first place. . . .

"[W]hat was once regarded as the prerogative solely of stockholders is now permissible action under S.223. . . . [T]he significant amendment was made in 1949, . . . when directors in office were authorized to fill 'newly created directorships resulting from any increase in the authorized number of directors.'. . .

"Under S.223 directors in office now may fill vacancies in their membership if stockholders do not do so and if other requirements of the statute are met."

Meetings of the Board.   The general rule is that the directors must meet as a board to take official action for the corporation. Proxy voting is not permitted. Most states today permit the directors to meet outside the state of incorporation; this allows the board to select the most convenient location. Some modern statutes are even more flexible; they permit the directors to have a "meeting" by means of a conference telephone call. Some statutes also permit the directors to take official action by means of a signed document: if they all read and sign the same document, why require them to waste transportation facilities to come together in a meeting room?

No proxy voting

Section 8.25 of the revised MBCA and the laws in some states permit the directors to designate some board members as an executive committee and to delegate some decision-making authority to the smaller committee. Other similar committees may also be created. The modern tendency is toward flexible management.

Executive committee

If a director wishes to dissent from a decision of the board, the normal rule is that the dissent must be officially entered in the minutes of the board. Otherwise, concurrence with the majority decision is presumed. This rule is significant where a later lawsuit challenges board actions.

Powers and Duties. As noted previously, some extraordinary business decisions are left to the shareholders, but the directors have exclusive control of the ordinary business of the firm. In making these ordinary business decisions, the directors are given the widest possible discretion as long as they are acting in good faith. The individual directors are selected for their business skill and judgment, and courts do not feel that they should second-guess the directors when the directors exercise that judgment. There is, therefore, a very strong presumption in favor of the directors' decisions unless some abuse is shown.

Directors' business judgment

This principle of nonintervention in corporate affairs is summarized as the ***business judgment rule.*** The business decisions of the directors cannot be challenged in court so long as the directors are acting in good faith and with reasonable care. They cannot guarantee satisfactory results for the corporation in every case; there are too many uncertainties and factors beyond their control. All that can be required of directors is that they are honest and diligent. If they are, but nevertheless make a bad decision, they should not be held liable for the unfavorable results. The business judgment rule underlies the decision in the *Shlensky* case in Chapter 50.

Business judgment rule

On the other hand, where there is evidence that the directors are acting in a totally arbitrary and capricious way, to the corporation's detriment, their actions may be overturned. Henry Ford's arbitrary policy on dividends was successfully challenged by the stockholders in the *Dodge* case in the last chapter.

The following case looks at the business judgment rule in the context of a ***hostile takeover*** attempt. The directors' defensive tactics are being questioned.

UNOCAL CORP. v. MESA PETROLEUM CO.

493 A.2d 946 (Delaware, 1985)

FACTS

The court of chancery granted a preliminary injunction to the plaintiffs (collectively "Mesa"), enjoining an exchange offer of the defendant, Unocal Corporation, for its own stock. The trial court concluded that a selective exchange offer, excluding Mesa, was legally impermissible. The factual findings of the vice chancellor establish that Unocal's board, consisting of a majority of independent directors, acted in good faith, and after reasonable investigation found that Mesa's tender offer was both inadequate and coercive.

On April 8, 1985, Mesa, the owner of approximately 13 percent of Unocal's stock, commenced a two-tier "front loaded" cash tender offer for 64 million shares, or approximately 37 percent, of Unocal's outstanding stock at a price of $54 per share. The "back-end" was designed to eliminate the remaining publicly held shares by an exchange of securities purportedly worth $54 per share. However, pursuant to an order entered by the United States District Court for the Central District of California on April 26, 1985, Mesa issued a supplemental proxy statement to Unocal's stockholders disclosing that the securities offered in the second-step merger would be highly subordinated and that Unocal's capitalization would differ significantly from its present structure. Unocal has rather aptly termed such securities "junk bonds."

ISSUE
Can a corporation legally make a self tender for its own shares which excludes from participation a stockholder (Mesa) which is making a hostile tender offer for the company's stock?

DECISION
Yes. Judgment of the trial court is reversed and the preliminary injunction against Unocal is vacated.

REASONS
Justice Moore noted that the issue before the court was an issue not before adjudicated by the Delaware court. He stated:

"The issues we address involve these fundamental questions: Did the Unocal board have the power and duty to oppose a takeover threat it reasonably perceived to be harmful to the corporate enterprise, and if so, is its action here entitled to the protection of the business judgment rule? . . .

"We begin with the basic issue of the power of a board of directors of a Delaware corporation to adopt a defensive measure of this type. Absent such authority, all other questions are moot. Neither issues of fairness nor business judgment are pertinent without the basic underpinning of a board's legal power to act.

"The board has a larger reservoir of authority upon which to draw. Its duties and responsibilities proceed from the inherent powers conferred by 8 Del.C. Section 141(a), respecting management of the corporation's 'business and affairs.' Additionally, the powers here being exercised derive from 8 Del.C. Section 160(a), conferring broad authority upon a corporation to deal in its own stock. From this it is now well established that in the acquisition of its shares a Delaware corporation may deal selectively with its stockholders, provided the directors have not acted out of a sole or primary purpose to entrench themselves in office. . . .

"Finally, the board's power to act derives from its fundamental duty and obligation to protect the corporate enterprise, which includes stockholders, from harm reasonably perceived, irrespective of its source. . . . Thus, we are satisfied that in the broad context of corporate governance, including issues of fundamental corporate change, a board of directors is not a passive instrumentality.

"Given the foregoing principles, we turn to the standards by which director action is to be measured. . . . The business judgment rule, including the standards by which director conduct is judged, is applicable in the context of a takeover. . . . The business judgment rule is a 'presumption that in making a business decision the directors of a corporation acted on an informed basis, in good faith and in the honest belief that the action taken was in the best interests of the company.' . . . A hallmark of the business judgment rule is that a court will not substitute its judgment for that of the board if the latter's decision can be 'attributed to any rational business purpose.' . . .

"In the board's exercise of corporate power to forestall a takeover bid our analysis begins with the basic principle that corporate directors have a fiduciary duty to act in the best interests of the corporation's stockholders. . . . As we have noted, their duty of care extends to protecting the corporation and its owners from perceived harm whether a threat originates from third parties or other shareholders. But such powers are not absolute. . . .

"In adopting the selective exchange offer, the board states that its objective was either to defeat the inadequate Mesa offer or, should the offer still succeed, provide the 49 percent of its stockholders, who would otherwise be forced to accept junk bonds, with $72 worth of senior debt. We find that both purposes are valid.

"However, such efforts would have been thwarted by Mesa's participation in the exchange offer. First, if Mesa could tender its shares, Unocal would effectively be subsidizing the former's continuing effort to buy Unocal stock at $54 per share. Second, Mesa could not, by definition, fit within the class of shareholders being protected from its own coercive and inadequate tender offer.

"Thus, we are satisfied that the selective exchange offer is reasonably related to the threats posed. It is consistent with the principle that 'the minority stockholder shall receive the substantial equivalent in value of what he had before.' . . .

"[W]e cannot say that the Unocal directors have acted in such a manner as to have passed an unintelligent and unadvised judgment. The decision of the court of chancery is therefore reversed, and the preliminary injunction is vacated."

Directors' Fiduciary Duties.   The directors are fiduciaries, and as such, they owe their corporation and its stockholders responsibility and loyalty. Responsibility means that the directors must be more than just personally honest; they must "direct." They must be diligent and careful in managing the firm's business. They are responsible for knowing what's going on, and they may be held personally liable if they don't know but should.

A fiduciary must also be loyal. This means at least that the director cannot use his or her position for personal gain at the expense of the corporation. Most states today permit the directors to set their own compensation, but courts would be willing to review such arrangements to make sure there was no abuse of discretion. In any case where the director is dealing with the corporation and receiving a personal benefit, the transaction would be subject to very close judicial review.

The corporate opportunity rule   One specific aspect of the duty of loyalty owed by directors and officers is described as the ***corporate opportunity*** rule. A director or officer may not take, for personal benefit, a business opportunity which should rightfully belong to the corporation. If the director or officer does so, a court will order any profits from the "opportunity" turned over to the corporation. In deciding whether the opportunity rightfully belongs to the corporation, the courts will examine whether (1) it is within the scope of the corporation's business; (2) the director or officer learned of the opportunity while acting as such; or (3) corporate funds, equipment, or personnel were used to develop the opportunity. Under the strictest application of the rule, if any of these three conditions exist, the opportunity belongs to the corporation.

■ OFFICERS

Authority.   To a more limited extent, the firm's officers may also get some of their authority from the state's corporation statute. For the most part, the officers derive their authority from the corporation's articles and bylaws and from specific board resolutions. The states do not agree on the amount of power which is given to the corporation's president merely by appointment as such. In some states, the president is presumed to be a kind of "general manager," with automatic authority to make all contracts which are within the scope of the firm's normal business. In other states, the corporation president is only a "figurehead," unless specific powers have been given to the officeholder by articles, bylaws, or resolution. Third parties need to check carefully on whether the individual with whom they are negotiating has authority to bind the corporation. In no state would the president have the authority to execute unusual or extraordinary contracts without specific resolutions. The *Audit Services* case involves the question of authority to sign agreements.

AUDIT SERVICES, INC. v. ELMO ROAD CORP.

575 P.2d 77 (Montana, 1978)

FACTS Audit Services, a collection agency, sued on behalf of three union trust funds for monies owing pursuant to certain collective bargaining agreements and declarations of trust. Roy Winslow, Elmo Road's general manager, signed the collective agreements for the corporation, which was then obligated to make certain payments to the pension and welfare trusts for its employees' benefit. Elmo Road made these payments from April to October 1972, and then stopped. When further payments were refused, the trust funds assigned their claims to the plaintiff, which sued for $31,842.53 due, plus $1,802.02 attorney fees. The trial court gave judgment for Elmo Road, holding that Winslow had no express, implied, or apparent authority to sign for the corporation. Plaintiff appealed.

ISSUES Did Winslow have authority to sign the agreements? Did Elmo Road ratify his action by making the payments required by the contract? Were the agreements invalid because these unions had not been elected as exclusive employee representatives under NLRA procedures?

DECISION Yes. Yes. No. (State courts have no jurisdiction to decide this third issue anyway.) Judgment reversed, and $1,250 additional attorney fees awarded.

REASONS Justice Haswell first stated the general rule, "The general manager of a corporation can have either actual, implied, or ostensible authority to enter into contracts on behalf of the corporation." Applying this rule to the facts, Justice Haswell agreed that Winslow did not have express authority to sign the agreements. However, Justice Haswell disagreed with the trial court's conclusions as to Winslow's implied authority and apparent authority.

"We believe Winslow did have implied authority to sign the compliance agreements and the finding of the District Court on this issue cannot be upheld. The court found that one of Winslow's responsibilities was to procure work for the corporation. This finding is supported by the evidence. In order to procure work on the Polson school job, the evidence shows that he had to sign the compliance agreements. Thus, his signing of those agreements was proper, usual and necessary in the transaction of defendant's business. Winslow had the implied authority to sign the agreements. . . .

"Plaintiff also contends Winslow had ostensible authority. . . .

"This Court has previously held that ostensible authority arises from the facts of the particular case and the test is found in a determination of the exact extent to which the principal held the agent out or permitted him to hold himself out as authorized, and what a prudent person acting in good faith under the circumstances would reasonably believe the agent's authority to be. . . . Applying that standard here, we find Roy Winslow had ostensible authority to sign the compliance agreements and bind the defendant to them. He was held out to be the general manager of the corporation and the union representatives, unaware of any restrictions in his authority, could reasonably believe Winslow had the authority to sign the agreements."

Selection, Compensation, and Removal. Corporate officers are selected by the board of directors unless the articles provide otherwise. Officers are usually appointed for one-year, renewable terms, but they continue to serve at the will of the board. In other words, the general rule is that the board can remove

Removal by board, with or without cause

an officer at any time, with or without cause. If an officer is removed without good cause, any employment contract with the firm would probably require compensation for the remainder of the appointment period, but that person would no longer be permitted to function as a corporate officer. Most modern corporation statutes do not require more than one officer, though there may be requirements that more than one person sign certain documents for the corporation (deeds to land, for example).

Specific board of directors' action on all major personnel decisions might avoid lawsuits like the *Morton* case.

MORTON v. E-Z RAKE, INC.

397 N.E.2d 609 (Indiana, 1979)

FACTS On February 15, 1975 Bob Good, the vice president and secretary of E-Z Rake, fired Stanley Morton and Martin Paligraf. Both sued for benefits allegedly due, and Paligraf also claimed he had been wrongfully discharged. Paligraf had been hired June 1, 1971, as "executive vice president," for a period of five years, under a written contract which promised him $2,000 per month and 10 percent of the corporation's annual before-tax net profits. Paligraf really functioned as a general manager, and in that capacity, hired Morton in 1972 as "plant manager." Morton had no written employment contract. Two plant employees filed grievances with the union in January 1975. Malcolm Dick was not paid for a 15-minute break, and Joe Hasty was not paid for 33 minutes when he had to take his sick wife home. After Morton had denied both claims, Good wrote him a letter telling him to pay both employees' claims. Morton wrote back, refusing to pay either claim. Good talked to both Morton and Paligraf on the telephone and told them to pay the claims—or else. When they again refused, he told them they were both fired. E-Z Rake's board then appointed a new general manager and a new plant manager. The trial court held for E-Z Rake.

ISSUES Did Good have the authority to fire these employees? Were the discharges made for good cause?

DECISION Yes. Yes. Judgment for E-Z Rake affirmed.

REASONS After reviewing the facts, Judge Miller got right to the heart of the plaintiff's case.

"Morton and Paligraf contend Good did not have the authority to discharge them claiming such was a non-delegable duty of the Board of Directors. . . .

"We disagree.

"Although a board of directors may be charged with the control and management of the corporate business, it may nonetheless invest its officers with authority to act for the corporation by resolution, course of dealing, acquiescence, or ratification. . . .

"Even if Good did not have the authority to fire Morton and Paligraf on February 14, 1975, there is evidence in the record which supports a conclusion that the Board of Directors ratified Good's actions. This determination is a question of fact to be determined by the trial court and can be inferred from acts, words and the ordinary course of dealing. . . .

"The Board's February 23, 1975, minutes show the directors unanimously confirmed the appointments of Morton and Paligraf's successors. This is sufficient evidence to support the trial court's judgment in this regard."

Officer's compensation is determined by the board of directors, and their decision will generally not be second-guessed by a court. A director who is also an officer should not be present when the directors set the salary for that office. As with any other decision where the board's business judgment is involved, there are limits to the discretion that is given to the board with regard to officers' compensation.

Liabilities of Directors and Officers.   Most of the specific sources of directors' and officers' liability have already been discussed, in this and previous chapters. Directors are liable for the issuance of watered stock and for the declaration of illegal dividends. They may be held liable for refusing a stockholder's justified demand for corporate information or for breaching their fiduciary duty by self-dealing or by stealing a corporate opportunity. Directors and officers may also incur liability under state regulatory statutes for failure to file required reports and income statements. Under the national securities laws (see Chapter 49), such corporate insiders as directors and officers may be held liable for making personal profits at the expense of the corporation or its shareholders. And directors and officers may be held liable to their firm and its shareholders for failing to take reasonable care in the operation of its business.

In recent years, directors and officers have also been subjected to an increasing criminal liability exposure. Criminal prosecutions against the directors and officers responsible for antitrust and other regulatory violations have been becoming more common, as have prison terms for persons convicted of willful violations. (See the *Park* case in Chapter 6).

Wrongful payments, self-dealing, regulatory violations, lack of care

Foreign Corrupt Practices Act.   After SEC investigations disclosed that over 300 U.S. firms had made various kinds of payments and gifts to foreign officials to get contracts or favorable regulations, Congress passed the FCPA in 1977. The FCPA amends the 1934 Securities Exchange Act in three main areas: a U.S. firm, whether or not subject to the 1934 Act's registration and disclosure requirements, is prohibited from bribing foreign officials to misuse their official position to benefit the firm; a firm subject to the 1934 Act must maintain books and records which, in reasonable detail, accurately and fairly reflect the firm's transactions, and must also maintain a system of internal accounting controls which reasonably ensures that transactions are properly executed and recorded and that corporate assets are protected; new criminal penalties of up to $1 million for the firm and of up to $10,000 and five years' imprisonment for the individuals involved may be imposed for willful violations. This is a very important new area of potential liability for both corporate and noncorporate managers, but its exact dimensions will not be known until there have been more court interpretations of the FCPA.

Foreign bribes prohibited
Record-keeping requirements

■ SIGNIFICANCE OF THIS CHAPTER

The corporation is simply a legal entity, a piece of paper, a charter from the state. Thus, it must be managed by people. This chapter identifies those people as directors and officers, and reviews the process of their selection and removal, and their powers, duties, authority, compensation, and possible personal liability.

DISCUSSION CASE

RARE EARTH, INC. v. HOORELBEKE
401 F.Supp. 26 (New York, 1975)

FACTS: "Rare Earth" is a rock and roll performing group which has recorded several record albums and which enjoys national prominence in rock music circles. The group was organized in the late 1960s and originally consisted of five performers. A sixth member, Edward Guzman, later joined the band.

As the Rare Earth group gained national exposure and the revenues it derived from concerts and recordings increased, the "Rare Earth" name became a valuable asset. As a result, counsel, Henry Baskin, suggested that a corporation be formed. In July 1970 the plaintiff, Rare Earth, Inc., was incorporated under Michigan law. Fifty thousand shares of capital stock were authorized in the articles of incorporation, and 1,200 shares were subscribed to by the band members. As to 1,000 of these shares, it is conceded that the five original band members each received 200 shares. As to the remaining 200 shares, the parties vigorously dispute whether Edward Guzman ever became their lawful owner.

As time passed, three of the original members departed from the Rare Earth group and three new performers were engaged to replace them. It is not disputed that two of the departing members severed all ties with the group and transferred their stock back to the corporation. However, the litigants disagree dramatically concerning the present status in the corporation of the third, Kenneth Folcik.

In a nutshell, both factions concede that Bridges and Hoorelbeke each owns 200 shares of Rare Earth, Inc. In dispute between them is whether Guzman and Folcik are presently shareholders. The Bridges-Guzman faction asserts that Guzman owns 200 shares of Rare Earth, Inc., and that Folcik does not; thus they claim control of 400 to 600 outstanding shares of the corporation. Hoorelbeke, on the other hand, claims that Folcik remains a shareholder and that he, Hoorelbeke, is the voting trustee for the Folcik shares. This claim, when coupled with Hoorelbeke's assertion that Guzman is not a stockholder, allegedly placed working corporate control in his grasp.

■

Judge Canella gave the opinion for the court:

Rare Earth, Inc., is not, as one might surmise, an organization dedicated to environmental activism or the preservation of our natural resources. Rather, it is the corporate entity formed by a group of rock and roll musicians who publicly perform as "Rare Earth." From this group "comes the dissonant chord" of an intracorporate battle for control resulting from a schism among the band members in July, 1974. . . .

The plaintiff's complaint must be dismissed, albeit without prejudice. . . . [T]he defendants assert that "Neither a majority of the directors nor of the shareholders of Rare Earth, Inc., voting as a duly constituted meeting, authorized counsel to be retained or to initiate suit." . . . Although not for the precise reasons advanced, we find this position well founded in law and fact. . . .

Prior to the dissension which emerged in July 1974 between the members of the Rare Earth group, it is undisputed that Peter Hoorelbeke served as a director and president, as well as a 200 share owner of Rare Earth, Inc. However, in mid-July the Bridges faction became aware (through the musical "grapevine") of Hoorelbeke's purported resignation as a band member and as an officer and director of the corporation. . . .

There is no evidence at bar of a written resignation transmitted by Hoorelbeke to the corporation and thus, as of the July 12th meeting, he remained a director, officer, and shareholder of Rare Earth, Inc. This being so, the failure to notify Hoorelbeke of the meeting and his absence therefrom renders all actions taken by those present invalid and without effect.

With regard to directors' meetings, Michigan law requires that a "special meeting shall be held upon notice as prescribed in the bylaws" . . . and that a "director is entitled to a notice which will give him ample time to attend the meeting." . . . The statutory requirement that the meeting be convened "upon notice" clearly was not met in the present case, as Hoorelbeke received no notice whatsoever. Thus, it is a settled matter of Michigan law that "where a written notice of the meeting of the board of directors is not given although required by either a statute or the corporate bylaws, and action taken by the meeting at which all the directors are not present is void." . . . The import of the foregoing discussion is plain: the failure to notify Director Hoorelbeke of the July 12th meeting and his absence therefrom renders all actions taken threat invalid, including such action as was required to commence this suit either directly or through the appointment of Bridges as President. . . .

If the July 12th meeting is deemed a shareholders' meeting, the actions taken thereat similarly must fail for noncompliance with the notice requirements contained in Mich. Comp. Laws Ann. § 450.1404(1) or with the consent provisions contained in § 450.1407. . . .

The improper commencement of the main action on behalf of Rare Earth, Inc., and its dismissal by this Court does not conclude the matter. . . . Although the counterclaim is properly perceived as one which is compulsory under Fed.R.Civ.P. 13(a), it is nonetheless properly before the Court at this time because it is predicated upon federal jurisdiction independent of the complaint. . . .

We find that the receipt of Folcik's certificate by Baskin and, later, by Rosefielde (a corporate functionary who knew not Folcik) satisfied that aspect of delivery specified by § 440.8313(1)(a) and constitutes an acquisition of actual possession of the stock by an appropriate person on behalf of Rare Earth, Inc. The simultaneous issuance of a $5,000 corporate check to Folcik as (at least) partial payment for the stock, the notation which appears in the corporate check book that such check was "for closing" as well as the failure of the corporation to subsequently list Folcik as a shareholder on Rare Earth, Inc., tax returns both individually and collectively evidence that the corporation considered itself to be in receipt of the shares and the owner thereof. . . .

Two separate events in the corporate life of Rare Earth, Inc., cause us to conclude that Guzman has fully paid for his shares and is, therefore, a stockholder. The $5,000 check which Guzman tendered to the Corporation in April 1971 is well perceived as full payment of that portion of his indebtedness to Rare Earth, Inc., which arose on incorporation: $200 for his stock and $4,800 as a loan; as contrasted with his antecedent obligation to the Rare Earth group. . . . If, however, it is assumed arguendo that the April 1971 check served as payment for his earlier obligation, then the subsequent events of September 1971 (the corporation's payment of $7,530 to Bridges, Hoorelbeke, and Persh) served to discharge the remainder of Guzman's indebtedness to the corporation, including that which was attributable to the subscription contract. . . .

This being so, we conclude that of the 600 shares of Rare Earth, Inc., stock which are presently outstanding, the Bridges-Guzman faction controls 400 shares and represents a two-thirds majority of all shareholders. Thus, it is possessed of working corporate control, which, if necessity, permits it to determine who may use the "Rare Earth" name and mark in connection with musical performances, recordings, and the like. . . .

In the year which has elapsed since the ill-conceived directors' meeting of Rare Earth, Inc., at Los Angeles, the young musicians who once formed "Rare Earth" have expended substantial time, effort, and funds toward the resolution of the controversy which exists between them. Now, we are at the end of the road, at least insofar as the present litigation is concerned. This is not to suggest that we are entirely convinced that this opinion will stand to quell the raging battle. . . .

The present, somewhat discursive endeavor is well concluded with the following words of the modern poet and popular singer Bob Dylan:

> . . . goodbye's too good a word, gal
> So I'll just say a fare thee well
> I ain't sayin' you treated me unkind
> You could have done better but I don't mind
> You just kinda wasted my precious time
> But don't think twice, it's all right.

■ IMPORTANT TERMS AND CONCEPTS

directors
business judgment rule
directors' fiduciary duties
corporate officers
MCBA

hostile takeover
corporate opportunity rule
Foreign Corrupt Practices Act

■ QUESTIONS AND PROBLEMS FOR DISCUSSION

1. What management authority do directors have?
2. What management authority do officers have?
3. Why can't directors vote by proxy, the way stockholders do?
4. What is the business judgment rule?
5. The bylaws of Ozone Onion Farms, Inc. specify a maximum of 11 directors; there is no indication of any minimum number. Handel, Bach, Mozart, and eight other persons were serving on the board of directors when a special stockholders' meeting was called. Mozart owned 1,400 of the 2,700 shares of stock outstanding. The vote was 1,400 to 1,300 to remove all 11 directors. Mozart, his wife, and Lemming were then elected as directors. The state's statute provided that a corporation must have at least three directors and that the term of a director could not be shortened by amending the bylaws to decrease the number of directors. Handel and Bach file suit, challenging the removal and election. What is the result, and why?

6. Harry Smith, a minority stockholder in Alabama Dry Docks and Shipbuilding Company, Inc., brought a stockholder's derivative suit to recover for the corporation allegedly excessive salaries and bonuses paid to four of its director-officers. Smith tried to get the other directors and stockholders to take action on this matter, but they refused to do so. He then brought this derivative suit on behalf of the corporation. He appealed from the trial court's dismissal of the suit on demurrer. Did the complaint state a valid cause of action against the directors and officers? Discuss.

7. Tarnish Rentals, Inc. sues to collect $38,000 in unpaid rent from Yankem Associates, Inc., a professional dental corporation. Yancy Yankem was the sole stockholder, a director, and the president of Tarnish. He had originally formed Yankem, Inc. to operate his dental office, and had been its sole stockholder, a director, and the president. The lease had been executed between Tarnish and Yankem, Inc., while Yancy served on both boards. Sometime later, Yankem, Inc. had been merged into Yankem Associates, Inc., when Tess Trueblud came into the office as another dentist. Yancy and Tess each owned 50 percent of Yankem

Associates, Inc. The former tenant had paid $420 per month for the building. Tarnish did about $25,000 worth of remodeling and then leased the building to Yankem, Inc. for $880 per month, for five years. Yankem Associates took over this lease but now claims that it is unfair. How should the court try to resolve this dispute? Explain.

8. Nanna Nelish, representing her husband Ned's estate, sues the Govel Company, Inc., in which he had been a 45 percent stockholder, and Greg Govel, who also owned 45 percent of the company. Ned and Greg had originally each owned half of the stock but had been forced to sell some additional shares to outsiders to raise more capital. Ned had been president and general manager, and Greg had been corporate counsel. When Ned died, Greg became president. When Greg learned that the 10 percent minority shares were for sale, he bought them himself. Nanna sues to have these shares declared assets of the company or, in the alternative, to be allowed to buy half of them so as to maintain an equal voice in the company. Does she have a valid claim? Discuss.

48

Foreign Corporations

CHAPTER OBJECTIVES
THIS CHAPTER WILL:

- Define a foreign corporation.
- Review the requirements for filing as a foreign corporation.
- Explain the states' jurisdiction to tax and regulate foreign corporations.
- Discuss procedures for filing as a foreign corporation and penalties for failure to file.

DEFINITION OF A FOREIGN CORPORATION

Foreign versus alien corporations

When we see the term *foreign corporation* we normally think of a corporation from some country other than the United States. Actually any corporation for profit, organized and created in one state and doing business in another state, is a foreign corporation. For example, a corporation organized and created in Illinois is a foreign corporation when it is transacting intrastate business in Wisconsin or Iowa. Corporations organized in foreign countries and doing business in a state of the United States would technically be classified as *alien corporations* but are also usually regulated as foreign corporations. Simply stated, any corporation not organized in the specific state in which it is doing local business or requesting to do local business is a foreign corporation insofar as that state's law is concerned. A corporation organized and doing business in the state in which it is organized is termed a *domestic corporation*. Thus, a corporation can be both a domestic corporation and a foreign corporation, depending upon where it is doing business.

Oklahoma's severe restrictions on alien land ownership are challenged in the following case.

STATE, ETC. v. HILLCREST INVESTMENTS, LTD.

630 P.2d 1253 (Oklahoma, 1981)

FACTS

The attorney general of the state of Oklahoma, Jan Eric Cartwright, instituted a suit in behalf of the state of Oklahoma, praying for the escheat of several parcels of land which the attorney general had reason to believe were being held by an alien in contravention of Article 22, Section 1, of the Oklahoma Constitution, and the provisions of 60 O.S. 1971 Section 121 et seq. The defendant, Hillcrest Investments, Ltd. filed an answer admitting that it did own some of the land described in the petition, but denied ownership of other parcels, claiming to have conveyed such land prior to the commencement of the escheat action. Hillcrest admitted that it was a corporation formed under the laws of Alberta, Canada, in 1968, and that on October 14, 1977, it filed articles of domestication with the secretary of state of Oklahoma, and that on that same date it received a certificate of authority to transact business in the state of Oklahoma. Additionally, Hillcrest pled three defenses: (1) that under the provisions of Article 22, Section 2, of the Constitution of the State of Oklahoma, it was lawfully entitled to own the land and property described in the petition; (2) that the state was acting to selectively enforce, in an unlawful manner, the laws of the state of Oklahoma, in a manner prejudicial to Hillcrest; (3) that the provisions of Article 22 of the Constitution of the State of Oklahoma violate the defendant's rights under the Constitution of the State of Oklahoma, the Constitution of the United States of America, and treaties properly entered into by the United States of America.

After evidence was presented and argument of counsel was heard, the trial court issued a final order entering judgment for Hillcrest. The court found that the restriction on alien ownership contained in Article 22, Section 1, of the Oklahoma Constitution, applied only to natural persons and not to corporations. The court also determined that under the provisions of Article 22, Section 2, and various provisions of the Oklahoma Statutes, an alien corporation could own urban land within the state of Oklahoma, once it became domesticated.

ISSUE   Do the restrictions on alien land ownership in Article 22, Section 1, of the Oklahoma Constitution apply to a foreign corporation which has applied for and has been granted domestic status in Oklahoma?

DECISION   No. Judgment of trial court is affirmed.

REASONS   Justice Barnes first reviewed the history of alien ownership of land and noted that the U.S. Supreme Court in 1879, in *Havensteen* v. *Lynham,* 100 U.S. 483, held that the right to control alien ownership of land was a right to be exercised by the individual states. Thus he found Oklahoma did have the right to regulate ownership of land by aliens. Then Justice Barnes went on to decide the question as to whether the provision in the constitution applied to foreign corporations as well as foreign natural persons and further, could an alien who was a resident of the state own property or was that the provision aimed at only nonresident aliens. Justice Barnes answered these questions as follows:

"After an examination of the territorial statutory law which existed at the time the Constitution was adopted, and the propositions introduced at the Constitutional Convention, we conclude that the drafters of our constitution did intend to include corporations within the terms *person* and *alien,* as they were used in Section 1 of Article 22 of the Oklahoma Constitution. . . .

"Having determined that the restrictions on alien land ownership provided by Article 22, Section 1, of the Oklahoma Constitution apply to corporations, as well as natural persons, we must now determine whether the defendant corporation comes within the restrictions of that constitutional provision. A resolution of this issue requires this court to answer two questions: first, whether defendant corporation is an alien corporation, and, second, whether the defendant corporation is a *nonresident.*

"An answer to the first inquiry is easily ascertained. The defendant admitted in its answer that it was a corporation which was formed under the laws of Alberta, Canada, and which exists by virtue of the laws of that country. It is well settled that corporations formed under the laws of foreign nations are alien corporations. . . .

"Because the defendant is an alien corporation and because the restrictions of Article 22, Section 1, apply to alien corporations which are nonresidents, the determinative question then becomes whether the defendant corporation, for the purposes of restriction on alien land ownership, is a resident. If the defendant is a resident, the restrictions on alien ownership are not applicable, as the provisions of Article 22, Section 1 specifically provide that the restrictions do not apply to aliens or persons who become bona fide residents of this state. . . .

"After examining the constitutional and statutory provisions dealing with the treatment of domesticated corporations, we conclude that a foreign corporation, once it has complied with the domestication procedures established under Oklahoma law, is for the purposes of restrictions on alien land ownership a resident of the state—and thus no longer subject to the restrictions of Article 22, Section 1, of the Oklahoma Constitution. . . .

"For the above stated reasons, we hold that the trial court was correct in ruling that the defendant below, Hillcrest Investments, Ltd., could, by virtue of its domestication, own real property within the state of Oklahoma, located within an incorporated town or city."

■ DEGREES OF "DOING BUSINESS"

A foreign corporation may be subject to the jurisdiction of a state other than its state of incorporation for litigation, for taxation, or for regulation, on the basis of having done business in the second state. The degree of "doing business" necessary to sustain jurisdiction is not the same, however, in the three cases. One transaction may be sufficient to provide jurisdiction for litigation relating to that transaction. For taxation, the event or relationship being taxed must have occurred within the taxing state. For a corporation to be subject to a second state's regulatory system for foreign corporations, it must conduct some more substantial amount of local business in that state.

■ JURISDICTION FOR LITIGATION

If a foreign corporation has been granted a certificate of authority and it does business within a state, then the foreign corporation must designate a person or another corporation as a resident agent for service of process. Thus, there is no problem in securing service of process against a foreign corporation that is admitted and qualified to do business in the state.

A problem arises when a foreign corporation is doing business within a state but has not secured a certificate of authority and does not have an office nor any employees or agents within the state boundaries. In Chapter 2 we indicated that most states now have long arm civil procedure statutes. These statutes allow service of process upon foreign corporations even though they have not registered and have not appointed an agent to receive service of process within the state. Some statutes provide for service of process to the litigation state's secretary of state (who will then forward the notice to the defendant foreign corporation). Other statutes require the plaintiff to send copies of the summons and complaint directly to the out-of-state corporate defendant, by registered or certified mail. In any event, for the long arm process to be constitutionally valid, the defendant foreign corporation must have had some ***minimum contact*** with persons or property in the plaintiff's state. Exactly how minimal these contacts can be is not yet completely clear. (See the *Wiles* case in Chapter 2, as well as the next case.)

State long arm statutes

Minimum contact required

INPACO, INC. v. McDONALD'S CORP.

413 F.Supp. 415 (Pennsylvania, 1976)

FACTS

McDonald's Corporation is incorporated under the laws of Delaware and has its executive offices and principal place of business in Oak Brook, Illinois. Inasmuch as McDonald's Corporation is not licensed or qualified to do business in Pennsylvania, service of process in this action was carried out pursuant to the commonwealth's long arm statute. Section 8302 provides that a nonqualifying foreign corporation which does any business in Pennsylvania is conclusively presumed to have designated the Department of State as its agent for accepting service of process in any action arising in this commonwealth. For a definition of the conduct which constitutes doing business under Section 8302 reference must be made to Section 8309. The latter section, in pertinent part, provides:

Section 8309. Acts affecting jurisdiction

(a) *General rule.*—Any of the following shall constitute "doing business" for the purposes of this chapter:

(1) The doing by any person in this Commonwealth of a series of similar acts for the purpose of thereby realizing pecuniary benefit or otherwise accomplishing an object.

(2) The doing of a single act in this Commonwealth for the purpose of thereby realizing pecuniary benefit or otherwise accomplishing an object with the intention of initiating a series of such acts.

(3) The shipping of merchandise directly or indirectly into or through this Commonwealth.

(4) The engaging in any business or profession within this Commonwealth, whether or not such business requires license or approval by the Commonwealth or any of its agencies.

(5) The ownership, use or possession of any real property situate within this Commonwealth.

(b) *Exercise of full constitutional power over foreign corporations.*—In addition to the provisions of subsection (a) of this section the jurisdiction and venue of courts of the Commonwealth shall extend to all foreign corporations and the powers exercised by them to the fullest extent allowed under the Constitution of the United States.

The defendant conducts most of its extensive business in Pennsylvania through its two wholly owned subsidiaries, McDonald's Systems, Inc. and Franchise Realty Interstate Corp. The alleged contract which is the subject of this litigation was entered into by the parties on March 27, 1972. The record contains no indication of where the contract was made, but it called for the plaintiff, whose principal place of business is Allentown, Pennsylvania, to develop and produce a system of dispensing food sauces which would be suitable for use by a fast-food restaurant chain. Thus, the parties must have envisioned that at least a substantial portion of the contract would be performed in Pennsylvania. In fact, the affidavit of William C. Christine, president of plaintiff, states that the agreement provided that all the work other than on-site testing was to be accomplished at plaintiff's plant in Allentown. The Christine affidavit also states that there was considerable correspondence between the representatives of the defendant in Oak Brook, Illinois, and Christine in Allentown concerning the agreement and its performance in Allentown. The defendants have not controverted any of these allegations. In addition, it is undisputed that after the formation of the contract on at least two occasions, January 11, 1973, and February 1, 1973, a representative of the defendant met with representatives of the plaintiff in Allentown. Finally, representatives of the defendant have made certain "minimal" business trips into Pennsylvania and have had certain "minimal" contacts in Pennsylvania with a Philadelphia meat supplier, although none of these activities had any connection with the contract involved in the instant suit. Defendant filed a motion to dismiss this law suit.

ISSUE

Does McDonald's Corporation have sufficient contacts within the State of Pennsylvania to subject it to the provisions of the Pennsylvania long arm statute?

DECISION

Yes. The motion to dismiss is denied. The case will go to trial on its merits.

REASONS

District Judge Ditter reviewed the contacts which McDonald's had in Pennsylvania, and then stated:

"I am satisfied that defendant's contacts with Pennsylvania are sufficient to satisfy the requirements of Pennsylvania's long arm statute. In *Proctor & Schwartz, Inc.* v. *Cleveland Lumber Co.,* . . . it was held that Section 8309(b) gave Pennsylvania courts jurisdiction over a Georgia corporation whose sole contact with the commonwealth was a contract that it had made with a Pennsylvania corporation. After tracing the evolution of Pennsylvania's long arm statute, the court explained the effect of Section 8309(b) of the 1972 amendments on the 'doing business' test of the present and past versions of the statute.

Although the statute retains the requirement of 'doing business' as a jurisdictional trigger, the addition of the new section 8309(b), quoted supra, is clearly intended to liberalize Pennsylvania's position. Under this section those contacts sufficient to satisfy the constitutional requirements of due process are also sufficient to satisfy the 'doing business' requirements of Pennsylvania law. Thus, for purposes of in personam jurisdiction over unregistered foreign corporations the evolution of the Pennsylvania 'long arm' statute has now become coexistent with the evolution of substantive jurisdictional due process as expressed by the United States Supreme Court. . . .

"Since *Proctor* makes it clear that whatever contacts are sufficient to satisfy due process under Section 8309(b) also constitute 'doing business' in Pennsylvania under Section 8309(a), it is unnecessary to analyze the defendant's activities separately with respect to each of these two sections of the statute. Section 8309(b) also eliminates the need to engage in the type of dual-tiered analysis which has typically been used in deciding questions of personal jurisdiction. Instead of first determining whether a foreign corporation's contacts with the forum fall within the terms of the applicable statute, and, if so, then determining if the statute as so applied comports with due process, courts in Pennsylvania may now proceed directly to the constitutional issue. . . .

"In order to exercise in personam jurisdiction over a foreign corporation due process requires that it have sufficient contacts with the forum state that requiring it to defend a suit there 'does not offend traditional notions of fair play and substantial justice.' . . . Whether or not such contacts exist in a particular case must be determined on an *ad hoc* basis by a factual evaluation of the nature and quality of the foreign corporation's activities. . . .

"Bearing in mind that 'the due process clause defines a rather low threshold of state interest sufficient to justify exercise of the state's sovereign decisional authority with respect to a given transaction,' . . . I have no difficulty in holding that subjecting defendant to in personam jurisdiction in Pennsylvania is fully consistent with due process requirements. The defendant's contacts with Pennsylvania in this case are, in fact, more extensive than those of the defendant in *Proctor* and other cases which have upheld the exercise of in personam jurisdiction over foreign corporations. . . . In the case at bar not only did McDonald's Corporation voluntarily enter into a transaction with a Pennsylvania corporation, which is the equivalent of the situations presented in *Proctor,* . . . but it also had certain other business contacts with the commonwealth. Accepting defendant's contention that these other contacts were minimal, they nonetheless make a stronger case for exercising in personam jurisdiction than was present in the cases just cited.

"For the reasons stated above the motion to dismiss must be denied."

■ JURISDICTION FOR TAXATION

To tax a foreign corporation, the taxing state must show that the corporation has entered into the relationship, within the state, which the tax is designed to reach. Further, if challenged on constitutional grounds, the taxing state must show that the tax does not unfairly discriminate against interstate commerce. Where multistate relationships are involved, some rational apportionment formula must be used to allocate appropriate taxable shares to each state.

Taxing nexus required

With real estate that a foreign corporation owns in the taxing state, the relationship, or *nexus,* is clear. The foreign corporation, like any other landowner, will have to pay the assessed real estate taxes. Where personal property of a foreign corporation is being taxed, conflicts may arise if the property is being used in more than one state. For example, trucking companies, airlines, and railroads all have equipment that simply cannot stay in one place all year long. How much of their equipment can be taxed by each of the states where the equipment lands or travels? No uniform or standardized formula for taxing personal property is used in all states. The threat of multiple taxation continues to be a problem for corporations using property in more than one state.

Many difficulties also exist in the area of income taxation. Each state of course wants to tax as much of the foreign corporation's income as possible. In a landmark case the U.S. Supreme Court upheld the state of Minnesota in its taxation of income that the Northwestern States Portland Cement Company derived from sales in interstate commerce rather than intrastate business. After the decision in that case Congress enacted the interstate income law, which provides that a tax cannot be imposed on net income of a person or a corporation engaged in interstate business where the only activity of the person or the corporation is to solicit orders for the sale of tangible personal property, the orders are sent outside the state for approval or rejection, and approved orders are shipped or delivered from a point outside the state. The law also exempts income that a foreign corporation derives from selling or soliciting sales through independent contractors, even though the independent contractor may have an office within the state. There will continue to be many litigations in this area, since the revenue needs of the taxing state must be balanced against the discriminatory effect of the tax on interstate commerce and since the tax statute must provide a rational apportionment formula for multistate income.

Apportionment required

The *Mobil Oil* case is one of the key precedents on taxation of multinational corporations.

MOBIL OIL CORPORATION v. COMMISSIONER OF TAXES OF VERMONT

445 U.S. 425 (1980)

FACTS

Appellant Mobil Oil Corporation is a corporation organized under the laws of the state of New York. It has its principal place of business and its "commercial domicile" in New York City. It is authorized to do business in Vermont.

Mobile engages in an integrated petroleum business, ranging from exploration for petroleum reserves to production, refining, transportation, and distribution and sale of petroleum and petroleum products. It also engages in related chemical and mining enterprises. It does business in over 40 of our states and in the District of Columbia as well as in a number of foreign countries.

Much of appellant's business abroad is conducted through wholly and partly owned subsidiaries and affiliates. Many of these are corporations organized under the laws of foreign nations; a number, however, are domestically incorporated in states other than Vermont. None of appellant's subsidiaries or affiliates conducts business in Vermont, and appellant's shareholdings in those corporations are controlled and managed elsewhere, presumably from the headquarters in New York City.

In Vermont, appellant's business activities are confined to wholesale and retail marketing of petroleum and related products. Mobil has no oil or gas production or refineries within the state. Although appellant's business activity in Vermont is by no means insignificant, it forms but a small part of the corporation's worldwide enterprise.

Vermont imposes an annual net income tax on every corporation doing business within the state. Under its scheme, net income is defined as the taxable income of the taxpayer "under the laws of the United States." If a taxpayer corporation does business both within and without Vermont, the state taxes only that portion of the net income attributable to it under a three-factor apportionment formula. In order to determine that portion, net income is multiplied by a fraction representing the arithmetic average of the ratios of sales, payroll, and property values within Vermont to those of the corporation as a whole.

The Supreme Court of Vermont held Mobil Oil liable to pay an annual net income tax under their state apportionment formula. Mobil Oil appealed the decision to the U.S. Supreme Court.

ISSUE

Is the Vermont net income tax formula which allows taxation of income earned outside the state constitutional?

DECISION

Yes. Judgment of the Supreme Court of Vermont is affirmed.

REASONS

Justice Blackmun, giving the opinion of the Court, stated:

"In this case we are called upon to consider constitutional limits on a nondomiciliary state's taxation of income received by a domestic corporation in the form of dividends from subsidiaries and affiliates doing business abroad. The state of Vermont imposed a tax, calculated by means of an apportionment formula, upon appellant's so-called foreign source dividend income for the taxable years 1970, 1971, and 1972. The Supreme Court of Vermont sustained that tax. . . .

"It long has been established that the income of a business operating in interstate commerce is not immune from fairly apportioned state taxation. . . . For a state to tax income generated in interstate commerce, the due process clause of the Fourteenth Amendment imposes two requirements: a 'minimal connection' between the interstate activities and the taxing state, and a rational relationship between the income attributed to the state and the intrastate values of the enterprise. . . . The requisite 'nexus' is supplied if the corporation avails itself of the 'substantial privilege of carrying on business' within the state; and '[t]he fact that a tax is contingent upon events brought to pass without a state does not destroy the nexus between such a tax and transactions within a state for which the tax is an exaction.' . . .

"[T]he linchpin of apportionability in the field of state income taxation is the unitary business principle. In accord with this principle, what appellant must show in order to establish that its dividend income is not subject to an apportioned tax in Vermont is that the income was earned in the course of activities unrelated to the sale of petroleum products in that state. . . . [A]ppellant has made no effort to demonstrate that the foreign operations of its subsidiaries and affiliates are distinct in any business or economic sense from its petroleum sales activities in Vermont. Indeed, all indications in the record are to the contrary, since it appears that these foreign activities are part of appellant's integrated petroleum enterprise. In the absence of any proof of discrete business enterprise, Vermont was entitled to conclude that the dividend income's foreign source did not destroy the requisite nexus with in-state activities. . . . Since Vermont seeks to tax income, not ownership, we hold that its interest in taxing a proportionate share of appellant's dividend income is not overridden by any interest of the state of commercial domicile. . . .

"In sum, appellant has failed to demonstrate any sound basis, under either the due process clause or the Commerce Clause, for establishing a constitutional preference for allocation of its foreign source dividend income to the state of commercial domicile. Because the issue has not been presented, we need not, and do not, decide what the constituent elements of a fair apportionment formula applicable to such income would be. We do hold, however, that Vermont is not precluded from taxing its proportionate share."

▪ JURISDICTION FOR REGULATION

Local business = Registration required

MBCA list of acts permitted without registration

Since a foreign corporation is not a "citizen" under the Fourteenth Amendment, it has no right to transact intrastate business in states other than the state of its creation. However, all of the states have provisions in their corporation laws which allow foreign corporations to do intrastate business upon compliance with certain filing and licensing requirements. Moreover, a foreign corporation may transact interstate business across a state's borders without being required to file and comply with the state's requirements for foreign corporations.

Interstate commerce, that is, commerce among the states, is regulated by the national government under the authority of the Interstate Commerce Clause of the U.S. Constitution (Article I, Section 8). The individual states may not interfere with, burden, or discriminate against interstate commerce by their laws or regulations. The question which then arises is: What is interstate commerce, and what is intrastate commerce? The Model Business Corporation Act set out some general guidelines as to the activities of foreign corporations which will not be regarded as doing business in a state and will not require filing as a foreign corporation. These activities include selling goods through an independent contractor in another state, soliciting or procuring by mail orders which will be accepted in a home state rather than in the state where they are solicited; conducting isolated transactions; maintaining a bank account; maintaining an office or agency for the transfer, exchange, and registration of the corporation's securities; holding meetings of directors or shareholders; maintaining or defending a lawsuit; or taking out loans or mortgages.

The common element in all of these examples is that the foreign corporation is not intending to conduct a long-term business in the state; does not have employees, agents, or property within the state; and thus is dealing in interstate commerce only. Section 15.01 of the revised MCBA specifically states that the list it sets out is not exclusive. There is no clear rule of thumb as to what is and what is not interstate commerce. Thus, each case is going to have to review separately the amount of business conducted, the type of business conducted, the time span, and so on. These fact questions are discussed in the following case.

ROCHESTER CAPITAL LEASING CORP. v. SCHILLING

448 S.W.2d 64 (Tennessee, 1969)

FACTS

The plaintiff, a New York corporation with its principal place of business in Rochester, New York, was in the business of leasing machines and equipment. Schilling had leased 25 postage stamp vending machines at $55.35 a month for five years. The machines were delivered, but Schilling claimed that he had been defrauded by the salesman of a Florida company which had initially arranged the lease contract. Schilling refused to pay, and Rochester sued. Rochester was not registered to do business as a foreign corporation in Tennessee. It had no agents or employees there, and all dealings with it in this case had been by mail. The lease contract had been approved by Rochester at its New York office and had provided that all payments should be made there. The trial court dismissed the suit because Rochester was not registered to do business; the court of appeals affirmed; and Rochester then appealed to the Supreme Court.

ISSUE   Was Rochester "doing business" in Tennessee so as to require registration?

DECISION   No. Judgment reversed and case remanded for a new trial.

REASONS   Justice McCanless compared the facts of this case with those of two precedents. In one, where all negotiations were by mail and where the loan contract was made in New York and was to be paid there, a New York corporation which made a loan to a Tennessee resident and used Tennessee land as collateral had been held to be exempt from the registration requirement. In the other, where United Artists rented a local studio in Tennessee, hired an operator there, showed films there to theater owners and the board of censors, and then made contracts with exhibitors, United Artists had been held to be doing local business and had been required to register. Clearly, Justice McCanless felt, Rochester was more like the loan company than like United Artists.

"In this case the plaintiff had no agents in the State, and its only activity that was related to this State was to enter into a contract in the State of New York for the leasing of personal property located in Tennessee in consideration of monthly rent to be paid it at its office in the State of New York. . . .

"Rochester . . . was a mere property owner and investor; it invested in a lease contract providing for the payment to it periodically of a fixed amount of money. Its investment was comparable to the holder of a promissory note of a Tennessee citizen payable to a nonresident payee.

"We conclude that the plaintiff's acts did not constitute doing business in Tennessee within the meaning of Section 48–902, Tennessee Code Annotated, and that it was error for the court to dismiss its suit on that ground."

Procedure for Admission

Disclosures required for certificate of authority

Chapter 15 of the revised MBCA sets out procedures for the admission of foreign corporations and regulations concerning the doing of local business in a particular state. Similar provisions have been adopted by most of the states. However, it must be remembered that this was a "model" act and that not all states adopted it verbatim. Many states have made specific changes to take care of specific problems.

Generally speaking, a foreign corporation doing local business within a state must apply for a *certificate of authority.* Such an application will normally require the name of the corporation, when and where it was incorporated, the names and addresses of the directors and corporate officers, a breakdown of the number and types of shares issued, and authorization the corporation has regarding the further issuance of stock. The corporation will also be required to estimate the value of the property, both real and personal, that it intends to own within the state and the gross amount of the business that it will transact within the state in the coming year. In addition, it will have to designate some person within the state to be the *registered agent* upon whom service of process for lawsuits can be made and it will have to maintain a registered office within the state. A license fee must accompany the application. This license fee will differ from state to state. A *franchise tax* may be assessed annually, based on the corporation's property within the state and the business it conducts there. The foreign corporation must file an annual report similar to the annual reports filed by domestic corporations.

Doing Business without Authority

Noncompliance = No right to bring lawsuits

The Model Business Corporation Act states that a foreign corporation which transacts business within a state without first obtaining a certificate of authority will not be permitted to bring any lawsuit in a court of that state until it has obtained a certificate of authority. The compliance with the requirements for the certificate of authority can be retroactive, thus allowing the corporation to sue on transactions that were consummated prior to the granting of the certificate of authority.

Contracts still valid

The Model Act goes on to state that the failure of a foreign corporation to obtain a certificate of authority to transact business in a state will not impair the validity of any contracts or acts of the corporation and will not prevent the corporation from defending any action brought against it in a court in the state. Thus, a corporation does not have the right to bring action as a plaintiff in the courts in a state where it is not authorized to do business; however, it does have the right to defend itself.

Different states have different penalties

The foreign corporation will, of course, be liable for all fees and franchise taxes which it would have paid had it duly applied for a certificate of authority and received it. Also, many states have statutory penalties for doing business without first obtaining permission. These penalties may be fines imposed upon the corporation or its individual officers, directors, or resident agents. Another penalty imposed by some states is to make the officers, the directors, and any agents involved in contracts personally liable on the contracts, in effect taking away the corporate shield against liability. Again, it must be noted that not all states adopted the earlier MBCA in its entirety, and thus there are still differences in the treatment of foreign corporations which fail to comply with the requirements of a particular state. Before doing business in a state, a foreign corporation should check out the state's law carefully.

■ SIGNIFICANCE OF THIS CHAPTER

Nearly all large corporations do business in more than one state, and thus are foreign corporations when they do business in states other than the state that granted their charter. This chapter defines what a foreign corporation is, reviews the filing procedures for registration as a foreign corporation, discusses the rights and duties a foreign corporation has, and reviews the penalty for failure of a foreign corporation to comply with the registration and filing procedures.

Any corporation operating across state lines needs to be aware of these rules, since the consequences of noncompliance can be very serious. Not being licensed as required can result in the invalidation of contracts made in the other state. Failure to pay properly assessed taxes can result in large fines. Failure to defend a properly filed lawsuit can result in a default judgment, which can then be brought to the corporation's home state and enforced. For some of these violations, the human beings representing the foreign corporation may be subject to fines and/or imprisonment. Foreign corporation rules should definitely be factored into the decision to do business in another state.

DISCUSSION CASE

COMMONWEALTH EDISON CO. v. MONTANA

453 U.S. 609 (1981)

FACTS: Buried beneath Montana are large deposits of low sulfur coal, most of it on U.S.-owned land. Since 1921, Montana has imposed a severance tax on the output of Montana coal mines, including coal mined on U.S. land. After commissioning a study of coal production taxes in 1974 and 1975, the Montana legislature enacted the tax schedule at issue in this case. The tax is levied at varying rates depending on the value, energy content, and method of extraction of the coal and may equal, at a maximum, 30 percent of the contract sales price. Under the terms of a 1976 amendment to the Montana Constitution, after December 31, 1979, at least 50 percent of the revenues generated by the tax must be paid into a permanent trust fund, the principal of which may be appropriated only by a vote of three fourths of the members of each house of the legislature.

Appellants, 4 Montana coal producers and 11 of their out-of-state utility company customers, filed these suits in Montana state court in 1978. They sought refunds of over $5.4 million in severance taxes paid under protest, a declaration that the tax is invalid under the Supremacy and Commerce Clauses, and an injunction against further collection of the tax. Without receiving any evidence the court upheld the tax and dismissed the complaints.

On appeal, the Montana Supreme Court affirmed the judgment of the trial court.

■

Justice Marshall:

The court has . . . long since rejected any suggestion that a state tax or regulation affecting interstate commerce is immune from Commerce Clause scrutiny because it attaches only to a "local" or intrastate activity. . . . Correspondingly, the court has rejected the notion that state taxes levied on interstate commerce are *per se* invalid. . . . In reviewing Commerce Clause challenges to state taxes, our goal has instead been to "establish a consistent and rational method of inquiry" focusing on "the practical effect of a challenged tax.". . . We conclude that the same "practical" analysis should apply in reviewing Commerce Clause challenges to state severance taxes.

In the first place, there is no real distinction—in terms of economic effects—between severance taxes and other types of state taxes that have been subjected to Commerce Clause scrutiny. . . . Second, this court has acknowledged that "a State has a significant interest in exacting from interstate commerce its fair share of the cost of state government.". . .

We therefore hold that a state severance tax is not immunized from Commerce Clause scrutiny by a claim that the tax is imposed on goods prior to their entry into the stream of interstate commerce. Any contrary statements in *Heisler* and its progeny are disapproved. We agree with appellants that Montana tax must be evaluated under *Complete Auto Transit's* four-part test. Under that test, a state tax does not offend the Commerce Clause if it "is applied to an activity with a substantial nexus with the taxing State, is fairly apportioned, does not discriminate against interstate commerce, and is fairly related to services provided by the State.". . .

Appellants do not dispute that the Montana tax satisfies the first two prongs of the *Complete Auto Transit* test. . . .

Instead, the gravamen of appellants' claim is that a state tax must be considered discriminatory for purposes of the Commerce Clause if the tax burden is borne primarily by out-of-state consumers. Appellants do not suggest that this assertion is based on any of this court's prior discriminatory tax cases. In fact, a similar claim was considered and rejected in *Heisler*. . . . We share the *Heisler* court's misgivings about judging the validity of a state tax by assessing the state's "monopoly" position or its "exportation" of the tax burden out of state. . . .

In any event, appellants' discrimination theory ultimately collapses into their claim that the Montana tax is invalid under the fourth prong of the *Complete Auto Transit* test: that the tax is not "fairly related to the services provided by the State.". . . Because appellants concede that Montana may impose *some* severance tax on coal mined in the state, the only remaining foundation for their discrimination theory is a claim that the tax burden borne by the out-of-state consumers of Montana coal is excessive. This is, of course, merely a variant of appellants' assertion that the Montana tax does not satisfy the "fairly related" prong of the *Complete Auto Transit* test, and it is to this contention that we now turn.

Appellants argue that they are entitled to an opportunity to prove that the amount collected under the Montana tax is not fairly related to the additional costs the state incurs because of coal mining. Thus, appellants' objection is to the *rate* of the Montana tax, and even then, their only complaint is that the *amount* the state receives in taxes far exceeds the *value* of the services provided to the coal mining industry. In objecting to the tax on this ground, appellants may be assuming that the Montana tax is, in fact, intended to reimburse the state for the cost of specific services furnished to the coal mining industry. Alternatively, appellants could be arguing that a state's power to tax an activity connected to interstate commerce cannot exceed the value of the services specifically provided to the activity. Either way, the premise of appellants' argument have completely misunderstood the nature of the inquiry under the fourth prong of the *Complete Auto Transit* test.

The Montana Supreme Court held that the coal severance tax is "imposed for the general support of the government" . . . and we have no reason to question this characterization of the Montana tax as a general revenue tax. . . .

This court has indicated that states have considerable latitude in imposing general revenue taxes. The court has, for example, consistently rejected claims that the due process clause of the Fourteenth Amendment stands as a barrier against taxes that are "unreasonable" or "unduly burdensome." . . . Moreover, there is no requirement under the due process clause that the amount of general revenue taxes collected from a particular activity must be reasonably related to the value of the services provided to the activity. Instead, our consistent rule has been:

> Nothing is more familiar in taxation than the imposition of a tax upon a class or upon individuals who enjoy no direct benefit from its expenditure, and who are not responsible for the condition to be remedied.
>
> A tax is not an assessment of benefits. It is, as we have said, a means of distributing the burden of the cost of government. The only benefit to which the taxpayer is constitutionally entitled is that derived from his enjoyment of the privileges of living in an organized society, established and safeguarded by the devotion of taxes to public purposes.

There is no reason to suppose that this latitude afforded the states under the due process clause is somehow divested by the Commerce Clause merely because the taxed activity has some connection to interstate commerce; particularly when the tax is levied on an activity conducted with the state. . . .

Furthermore, there can be no question that Montana may constitutionally raise general revenue by imposing a severance tax on coal mined in the state. The entire value of the coal, before transportation, originates in the state, and mining of the coal depletes the resource base and wealth of the state, thereby diminishing a future source of taxes and economic activity. . . .

The relevant inquiry under the fourth prong of the *Complete Auto Transit* test is not as appellants suggest, the *amount* of the tax or the *value* of the benefits allegedly bestowed as measured by the costs the state incurs on account of the taxpayer's activities. Rather, the test is closely connected to the first prong of the *Complete Auto Transit* test. Under this threshold test, the interstate business must have a substantial nexus with the state before any tax may be levied on it. . . . Beyond the threshold requirement, the fourth prong of the *Complete Auto Transit* test imposes the additional limitation that the *measure* of the tax must be reasonably related to the extent of the contact, since it is the activities or presence of the taxpayer in the state that may properly be made to bear a "just share of state tax burden." . . .

Against this background, we have little difficulty concluding that the Montana tax satisfies the fourth prong of the *Complete Auto Transit* test. The "operating incidence" of the tax . . . is on the mining of coal within Montana. Because it is measured as a percentage of the value of the coal taken, the Montana tax is in "proper proportion" to appellants' activities within the state, and, therefore, to their "consequent enjoyment of the opportunities and protections which the State has afforded" in connection with those activities. . . .

Appellants argue, however, that the fourth prong of the *Complete Auto Transit* test must be construed as requiring a factual inquiry into the relationship between the revenues generated by a tax and costs incurred on account of the taxed activity in order to provide a mechanism for judicial disapproval under the Commerce Clause of state taxes that are excessive. This assertion reveals that appellants labor under a misconception about a court's role in cases such as this. The simple fact is that the appropriate level or rate of taxation is essentially a matter for legislative, and not judicial, resolution. . . . In essence, appellants ask this court to prescribe a test for the validity of state taxes that would require state and federal courts, as a matter of federal constitutional law, to calculate acceptable rates or levels of taxation of activities that are conceded to be legitimate subjects of taxation. This we decline to do.

In the first place, it is doubtful whether any legal test could adequately reflect the numerous and competing economic, geographic, demographic, social, and political considerations that must inform a decision about an acceptable rate or level of state taxation, and yet be reasonably capable of application in a wide variety of individual cases. But even apart from the difficulty of the judicial undertaking, the nature of the fact-finding and judgment that would be required of the courts merely reinforces the conclusion that questions about the appropriate level of state taxes must be resolved through the political process. Under our federal system, the determination is to be made by state legislatures in the first instance and, if necessary, by Congress, when particular state taxes are thought to be contrary to federal interests. . . .

In sum, we conclude that appellants have failed to demonstrate either that the Montana tax suffers from any of the constitutional defects alleged in their complaints, or that a trial is necessary to resolve the issue of the constitutionality of the tax. Consequently, the judgment of the Supreme Court of Montana is affirmed.

■ IMPORTANT TERMS AND CONCEPTS

foreign corporation	alien corporation
degree of "doing business"	registered agent
taxing nexus	minimum contacts
franchise tax	certificate of authority

■ QUESTIONS AND PROBLEMS FOR DISCUSSION

1. What is a "foreign" corporation?

2. When can a corporation be sued in a state other than its state of incorporation?

3. When can a corporation be taxed in a state other than its state of incorporation?

4. What are the penalties for doing local business in a second state, as a corporation, without having qualified to do so?

5. Tess Tribble entered into a sales commission contract as a representative for Vermin Company. Vermin made cash advances to her, from which she could deduct her selling expenses and the commissions she earned by making sales. When Tess quit, she still owned Vermin $1818.18. When she refused to pay this balance, Vermin sued. Tess moved to dismiss the complaint because Vermin had not registered as a foreign corporation in her state. How should the court decide, and why?

6. Michael Witteck, a minor and a novice rider, was given a horse to ride at Bill Cody's Ranch in Montana. Michael was thrown off the horse, but was immediately put back on the same horse by Ben Brite, the ranch manager. Michael was thrown off a second time, this time breaking his arm. Michael, from the state of Lohio, had read about the ranch in an advertisement published in Lohio. The ranch had no offices or agents in Lohio, but did send direct mail ads into Lohio and did accept telephone reservations from Lohio residents. Michael filed a lawsuit in Lohio for his injuries. The ranch moved to dismiss the complaint for lack of jurisdiction. Is the ranch subject to suit in Lohio? Explain.

7. Volksgeist Motor Corporation, a manufacturer of cars and trucks, challenges the validity of a tax imposed by Texas on the privilege of doing business within that state. The tax was measured by the gross wholesale sales of all motor vehicles, parts, and accessories delivered in the state. These products were all manufactured in other states and countries, but VMC did maintain a branch office in the state. The VMC manager at the branch office called on each of its dealers in the state at least once a month and helped train and motivate dealer personnel. VMC claims that the tax is discriminatory and burdensome to interstate commerce and that it is in effect a tax on the privilege of engaging in interstate commerce and thus unconstitutional. What is the result, and why?

8. Duane Hapless bought a "professional" electric razor as a graduation present for his son Harvey. Duane bought the razor from his barber in Little Rock, Arkansas. Harvey took the razor with him when he went to college at Ardmore, Oklahoma. This particular brand of electric razor was manufactured in Italy by Cantare, Inc., an Italian corporation, and distributed in the United States by a New York corporation, Zapper Products, Inc. Harvey received a severe electric shock when the razor fell apart. Can he sue some or all of these persons in Oklahoma? In Arkansas? Explain.

49

Securities Law

CHAPTER OBJECTIVES
THIS CHAPTER WILL:

- Explain the regulation of securities by the states.
- Explain the national regulation of securities.
- Discuss the provisions of the 1933 Securities Act.
- Discuss the provisions of the 1934 Securities and Exchange Act.

The securities industry is one of the most heavily regulated areas of business. With certain exemptions, both the original issue of securities and subsequent trading are subject to detailed and complicated regulations at both the national and state levels. These regulations impose duties and liabilities not only on buyers and sellers of securities but also on the corporate issuer, its officers and directors, and its attorneys, accountants, and other experts. Noncompliance may result in serious civil and criminal penalties as well as the loss of millions of dollars of value.

■ STATE REGULATION OF SECURITIES

State blue-sky laws

The great surge of economic development during the late 1800s and early 1900s and the greatly increased use of the corporate form of business organization brought with them many abuses. Promoters of dubious background and resources sold investments to a gullible public in all sort of "speculative schemes which have no more basis than as many feet of blue sky," as one judge put it. To deal with these abuses, the states passed *blue-sky laws,* regulating transactions in securities. Standing alone, the state laws were not very effective. Some states had no such law; others did not enforce their statute very effectively. The simplest method for the fraudulent promoter was to operate across state lines from a "friendly" state, beyond the reach of state officials who were trying to enforce their statute. Moreover, the early state laws had many exemptions and were thus relatively easy to evade. Finally, since enforcement depended primarily on the victims' willingness to pursue a lawsuit, the promoters who did get "caught" could escape simply by reaching a financial settlement with the plaintiffs in the lawsuit.

Uniform Securities Act

Since the national securities laws specifically permit concurrent regulation by the several states, blue-sky statutes are on the books in nearly all states. The effectiveness with which these statutes are enforced still varies. About half the states have adopted the *Uniform Securities Act.* It attempts to combine three types of state regulation:

1. *Antifraud provisions,* which prohibit fraud in the sale of securities and provide for injunctions and criminal penalties.
2. *Full-disclosure provisions,* similar to those in the national act, which require the disclosure of all material information to prospective purchasers of the security.
3. *Broker-licensing provisions,* which require registration and licensing for persons marketing securities.

Most of the states that have not adopted the Uniform Securities Act have at least adopted a full-disclosure statute. Even with the Uniform Act in force, an individual state would have difficulty in preventing securities frauds without the cooperation of other states.

State tender offer statutes

As business merged, reorganized, and relocated, many states became concerned with the possibility of the loss of jobs. The older industrial states of the Northeast and Midwest were particularly unhappy about the movement of factories to the South and Southwest. Several states tried to protect their businesses from being taken over by outside companies by passing *state tender offer statutes* which imposed certain requirements which the offeror company had to meet before the buy-out could occur. The validity of the Indiana antitakeover statute is at issue in the following case.

CTS CORP. v. DYNAMICS CORP. OF AMERICA

107 S.Ct. 1637 (1987)

FACTS   On March 4, 1986, the Governor of Indiana signed a revised Indiana Business Corporation Law. That law included the Control Share Acquisitions Chapter (Indiana Act or Act). Beginning on August 1, 1987, the Act will apply to any corporation incorporated in Indiana unless the corporation amends its articles of incorporation or bylaws to opt out the Act. Before that date, any Indiana corporation can opt into the Act by resolution of its board of directors. The Act applies only to "issuing public corporations." The term *corporation* includes only businesses incorporated in Indiana. An *issuing public corporation* is defined as: a corporation that has:

(1) one hundred (100) or more shareholders;
(2) its principal place of business, its principal office, or substantial assets within Indiana; and
(3) either:
    (a) more than ten percent (10%) of its shareholders resident in Indiana;
    (b) more than ten percent (10%) of its shares owned by Indiana residents; or
    (c) ten thousand (10,000) shareholders resident in Indiana.

The Act focuses on the acquisition of "control shares" in an issuing public corporation. Under the Act, an entity acquires "control shares" whenever it acquires shares that, but for the operation of the Act, would bring its voting power in the corporation to or above any of three thresholds: 20 percent, 33⅓ percent, or 50 percent. An entity that acquires control shares does not necessarily acquire voting rights. Rather, it gains those rights only "to the extent granted by resolution approved by the shareholders of the issuing public corporation." Section 99 requires a majority vote of all disinterested shareholders holding each class of stock for passage of such a resolution. The practical effect of this requirement is to condition acquisition of control of a corporation on approval of majority of the preexisting disinterested shareholders.

The shareholders decide whether to confer rights on the control shares at the next regularly scheduled meeting of the shareholders or at a specially scheduled meeting. The acquiror can require management of the corporation to hold such a special meeting within 50 days if it files an "acquiring person statement," requests the meeting, and agrees to pay the expenses of the meeting. If the shareholders do not vote to restore voting rights to the shares, the corporation may redeem the control shares from the acquiror at fair market value, but it is not required to do so. Similarly, if the acquiror does not file an acquiring person statement with the corporation, the corporation may, if its bylaws or articles of incorporation so provide, redeem the shares at any time after 60 days after the acquiror's last acquisition.

On March 10, 1986, appellee Dynamics Corporation of America (Dynamics) owned 9.6 percent of the common stock of appellant CTS Corporation, an Indiana corporation. On that day, six days after the Act went into effect, Dynamics announced a tender offer for another million shares in CTS; purchase of those shares would have brought Dynamics' ownership interest in CTS to 27.5 percent. Also on March 10, Dynamics filed suit in the United States District Court for the Northern District of Illinois, alleging that CTS had violated the national securities laws in a number of respects no longer relevant to these proceedings. On March 27, the board of directors of CTS, an Indiana corporation, elected to be governed by the provisions of the Act.

Four days later, on March 31, Dynamics moved for leave to amend its complaint to allege that the Act is preempted by the Williams Act and violates the Commerce Clause. Dynamics sought a temporary restraining order, a preliminary injunction, and declaratory relief against CTS's use of the Act. On April 9, the District Court ruled that the Williams Act preempts the Indiana Act and granted Dynamics' motion for declaratory relief.

CTS appealed the District Court's holdings on these claims to the Court of Appeals for the Seventh Circuit, which affirmed.

ISSUE

Is the new Indiana Control Share Acquisitions law preempted by the Williams Act, which is national legislation that sets out rules to govern tender offers? Does the Indiana law violate the Interstate Commerce Clause?

DECISION

No. No. Judgment of the Court of Appeals is reversed.

REASONS

Justice Powell, speaking for the Supreme Court, noted that in the passage of the Williams Act there was no explicit indication by Congress of an intent to preempt state laws like the Indiana law. Absent such an explicit indication of preemption, a state statute is preempted only where it is a physical impossibility to comply with both the state and national statutes, or if the state law is an obstacle to accomplishment of the full purposes and objectives of Congress. In this case, it is possible for corporations to comply with both the national and state statutes; thus the Indiana statute preempted only if it frustrates the purposes of the Williams Act. Justice Powell then proceeded to discuss the two statutes.

"Our discussion begins with a brief summary of the structure and purposes of the Williams Act. Congress passed the Williams Act in 1968 in response to the increasing number of hostile tender offers. Before its passage, these transactions were not covered by the disclosure requirements of the federal securities laws. . . . The Williams Act, backed by regulations of the Securities and Exchange Commission (SEC), imposes requirements in two basic areas. First, it requires the offeror to file a statement disclosing information about the offer, including: the offeror's background and identity; the source and amount of the funds to be used in making the purchase; the purpose of the purchase, including any plans to liquidate the company or make major changes in its corporate structure; and the extent of the offeror's holdings in the target company. . . .

"Second, the Williams Act and the regulations that accompany it establish procedural rules to govern tender offers. For example, stockholders who tender their shares may withdraw them during the first 15 business days of the tender offer and, if the offeror has not purchased their shares, any time after 60 days from commencement of the offer. . . . The offer must remain open for at least 20 business days. . . . If more shares are tendered than the offeror sought to purchase, purchases must be made on a pro rate basis from each tendering shareholder. . . . Finally, the offeror must pay the same price for all purchases; if the offering price is increased before the end of the offer, those who already have tendered must receive the benefit of the increased price. . . .

"The Indiana Act operates on the assumption, implicit in the Williams Act, that independent shareholders faced with tender offers often are at a disadvantage. By allowing such shareholders to vote as a group, the Act protects them from the coercive aspects of some tender offers. If, for example, shareholders believe that a successful tender offer will be followed by a purchase of nontendering shares at a depressed price, individual shareholders may tender their shares—even if they doubt the tender offer is in the corporation's best interest—to protect themselves from being forced to sell their shares at a depressed price. As the SEC explains: 'The alternative of not accepting the tender offer is virtual assurance that, if the offer is successful, the shares will have to be sold in the lower priced, second step.' . . . In such a situation under the Indiana Act, the shareholders as a group, acting in the corporation's best interest, could reject the offer, although individual shareholders might be inclined to accept it. The desire of the Indiana legislature to protect shareholders of Indiana corporations from this type of coercive offer does not conflict with the Williams Act. Rather, it furthers the federal policy of investor protection. . . .

"In our view, the possibility that the Indiana Act will delay some tender offers is insufficient to require a conclusion that the Williams Act preempts the Act. The longstanding prevalence of state regulation in this area suggests that, if Congress had intended to preempt all state laws that delay the acquisition of voting control following a tender offer, it would have said so explicitly. The regulatory conditions that the Act places on tender offers are consistent with the text and the purposes of the Williams Act. Accordingly, we hold that the Williams Act does not preempt the Indiana Act. . . .

"The principal objects of dormant Commerce Clause scrutiny are statutes that discriminate against interstate commerce. . . . The Indiana Act is not such a statute. It has the same effects on tender offers whether or not the offeror is a domiciliary or resident of Indiana. Thus, it 'visits its effects equally upon both interstate and local business.'. . .

"On its face, the Indiana Control Share Acquisitions Chapter evenhandedly determines the voting rights of shares of Indiana corporations. The Act does not conflict with the provisions or purposes of the Williams Act. To the limited extent that the Act affects interstate commerce, this is justified by the state's interests in defining the attributes of shares in its corporations and in protecting shareholders. Congress has never questioned the need for state regulation of these matters. Nor do we think such regulation offends the Constitution."

NATIONAL REGULATION OF SECURITIES

U.S. securities statutes

The fantastic boom times of the 1920s turned into the depression of the 1930s. Many an investment bubble was punctured by the great stock market crash of 1929. The 1929 crash exposed to the public for the first time the widespread price manipulations and credit abuses which had characterized the stock market of the 1920s. The first New Deal Congress passed the two main pieces of national securities legislation—the *Securities Act of 1933* and the *Securities Exchange Act of 1934*. Other legislation followed, such as the Public Utility Holding Company Act of 1935, the Trust Indenture Act of 1939, the Investment Company Act of 1940, and the Investment Advisors Act of 1940. More recently, Congress passed the Securities Investor Protection Act of 1970 (designed to protect investors against the insolvency of their stockbroker) and the 1975 Amendments to the 1933 Act, which extend the antifraud provisions of the act to dealers in municipal securities.

The SEC. The Securities Act of 1933 entrusted enforcement to the Federal Trade Commission, but Congress decided by the next year that this specialized area needed its own specialized regulatory body. The Securities Exchange Act of 1934 thus created the Securities and Exchange Commission and gave it the responsibility for enforcing both acts. Over the years the SEC has accumu-

SEC organization

lated jurisdiction under the various other new securities laws, and it also exercises important functions in corporate reorganizations in bankruptcy proceedings.

The SEC is headed by five commissioners, appointed for staggered five-year terms by the President with the advice and consent of the Senate. No more than three commissioners may be members of the same political party, but the President does have the power to name the Commission's chairperson. The SEC's headquarters is in Washington, but it has regional offices throughout the country, particularly in the large cities where corporate financing operations are concentrated. The commissioners are assisted by a large organizational staff of lawyers, accountants, economists, securities analysts, and other experts.

■ GOING PUBLIC: THE 1933 SECURITIES ACT

Basic Purposes. The 1933 Act was aimed solely at the first offering of a securities issue, not at later trading on the stock exchanges or over-the-counter. Its primary objective was *truth in securities:* to provide the potential investor with all the information needed to make a rational decision when purchasing a security. The 1933 Act did not provide for governmental "approval" of securities, in the sense of deciding whether they were good or bad investments. Its main objective was to require full disclosure by the offering company, so that the potential investor could make an informed decision. Only secondarily did the 1933 Act prohibit fraud and deceit in securities transactions generally.

Full disclosure required

Even this somewhat limited approach was a big change from the common-law rules. You will recall from Chapter 14 that mere nondisclosure was not usually regarded as a fraudulent misrepresentation unless some special facts were present in the case. The 1933 act imposed on the offering corporation a positive legal duty to speak out and tell the truth, and the whole truth, about the offered security.

Definition of "Security." The costs of complying with the full-disclosure requirement can be very high. When paying lawyers, accountants, experts, printers, and others, a quarter of a million dollars doesn't go very far. Since these costs have to be deducted from profits, promoters are always looking for "moneymaking" schemes that don't have to comply with the requirements of the 1933 Act.

Coverage of 1933 Act

Only *"securities"* are covered by the 1933 Act, but the courts have given that term a very broad definition. So does the act:

> The term "security" means any note, stock, treasury stock, bond, debenture, evidence of indebtedness, certificate of interest or participation in any profitsharing agreement, collateral-trust certificate, preorganization certificate or subscription, transferable share, investment contract, voting-trust certificate, certificate of deposit for a security, fractional undivided interest in oil, gas, or other mineral rights, or, in general, any interest or instrument commonly known as a "security," or any certificate of interest or participation in, temporary or interim certificate for, receipt for, guarantee of, or warrant or right to subscribe to or purchase, any of the foregoing. . . .

With that definition, it's hard to imagine any investment that's not a "security," but promoters keep trying, as the following case shows.

SECURITIES AND EXCHANGE COMMISSION v. KOSCOT INTERPLANETARY, INC.

497 F.2d 473 (U.S. Fifth Circuit, 1974)

FACTS

The SEC asked for an injunction to stop the sale of unregistered "securities" and to prohibit fradulent practices in connection with their sale. The U.S. District Court denied the injunction, and the SEC appealed.

Koscot was one of the subsidiaries of Glen W. Turner Enterprises; it was organized as a multilevel network of distributors for a line of cosmetics. Distributors received cash bonuses ranging up to $3,000 for each new person who was brought into the plan and advanced up the distribution chain. Prospective distributors were introduced to the plan at "Opportunity Meetings," which were to be run exactly according to a company-prepared script. Distributors were told to dress and live as if they had a very large income, so as to impress the prospects. At the Opportunity Meetings, films were shown, speeches were made, and high-pressure sales tactics were used to try to get the prospects to "make a decision."

ISSUE

Were these franchised distributorships "securities"?

DECISION

Yes. Judgment reversed and case remanded (for injunction).

REASONS

The distributorships were certainly not "commonly known as a security," so the Court of Appeals had to look for other authority. Its problem was that the leading U.S. Supreme Court precedent, the *Howey* case, said that a security was "a contract, transaction or scheme whereby a person invests his money in a common enterprise and is led to expect profits solely from the efforts of the promoter or a third party." In the Koscot scheme, there was clearly an investment of money. But since each investor owned a separate distributorship, and since the investors each earned more or less money as *they* sold the products and recruited new distributors, the *Howey* definition didn't seem to fit too well.

The Court of Appeals, however, worked its way around the *Howey* case: "The critical factor is not the similitude or coincidence of investor input, but rather the uniformity of impact of the promoter's efforts.

". . . [T]he fact that an investor's return is independent of that of other investors in the scheme is not decisive. Rather, the requisite commonality is evidenced by the fact that the fortunes of all investors are inextricably tied to the efficacy of the Koscot meetings and guidelines on recruiting prospects and consummating a sale.

"[T]he critical issue in this case is whether a literal or functional approach to the 'solely from the efforts of others' test should be adopted, i.e., whether the exertion of some effort by an investor is inimical to the holding that an investment scheme falls within the definition."

The court then said that the proper test was one adopted by the Ninth Circuit in an earlier case against Glen Turner Enterprises: "whether the efforts made by those other than the investor are the undeniably significant ones, those essential managerial efforts which affect the success or failure of the enterprise." Since the presentations at the Opportunity Meetings were run from a company script, the court said that "the role of investors at these meetings can be characterized as little more than a perfunctory one"; that the closing of a sale to a new investor "is essentially a ministerial not managerial one"; that following the script was merely a "nominal" function; and that "the critical determinant of the success of the Koscot Enterprise lies with the luring effect of the opportunity meetings." In sum, said the court, "the Koscot scheme does not qualify as a conventional franchising arrangement"; it is a security and must be registered under the 1933 Act.

━━━━━━━━━━━━━━━━━━━━━━━━━━━

As a result of this and many other cases filed by state attorneys general, Koscot and similar organizations were virtually run out of business. But new "multilevel" schemes have continued to arise. Many states now have statutes regulating franchise investments which prohibit or strictly limit the use of such multilevel plans. Given the ingenuity of promoters, the definition of a security has to be flexible.

Exemptions. Not every offering of securities is subject to the 1933 Act. Some *types* of securities and some *transactions* in securities are exempted. These exemptions only eliminate the need to register the security through SEC procedures; the antifraud (and other) provisions still apply.

Short-term commercial paper, ordinarily bought by banks rather than being issued to the general public, is exempt from SEC registration. Securities issued by governmental agencies and nonprofit organizations, such as churches and schools, are exempt. Transactions which involve only a private offering or which are exclusively intrastate in nature are exempt; in both of these cases the process of qualifying the securities for the exemption requires expert advice. Most individual sales of securities are exempt; the 1933 Act is aimed at the issuer, underwriter, and broker making the initial offering. The SEC is authorized by statute to provide a simplified registration procedure for issues which do not involve more than a minimal amount, currently set at $1,500,000.

Contents of registration statement

Registration Statement and Prospectus. The corporation issuing nonexempt securities must file multiple copies of a *registration statement* with the SEC, *before* offering the securities for sale to investors. The registration statement is the basic document for making "full disclosure." It must include such information as the company's business, organizational structure, and financial structure and condition; how the proceeds of the new issue are to be used; agreements for the distribution of the new issue; and extraordinary business contracts. The registration statement must be signed by the issuing company, its principal officers, at least a majority of the board of directors, and any expert named as having prepared or certified part of the statement. Certified financial statements for the current year and the last two years must also be filed.

Registration procedure

The registration statement becomes effective 20 days after filing unless the SEC advances the effective date or requires further data, in which case the 20 days starts again when the supplement is filed. Technically, the SEC doesn't have the power to "disapprove" a security because it's a bad investment, but by delaying and by requiring many negative disclosure statements, the SEC can certainly try to discourage the issuer. Where there are any delays in the final effective date, all materials in the registration statement must be reviewed to make sure they are still completely accurate.

The *prospectus* contains most of the information noted above, but not necessarily all of the exhibits or all of the details on how the securities are to be distributed. The prospectus is the document given directly to offeree-buyers.

Like the registration statement, it must be accurate *and* complete; literally true information, which is misleading in the context in which it is stated, is a violation.

Antifraud Provisions.   In addition to its disclosure requirements, the 1933 Act also contains a very broad prohibition in Section 17 against securities fraud. This section covers "any device, scheme, or artifice to defraud" and "any transaction, practice, or course of business which operates or would operate as a fraud or deceit upon the purchaser." It includes both false statements and material omissions which make otherwise true statements misleading. Securities which are exempt from registration are *not* exempt from these antifraud provisions.

Material omission = Violation

BEING PUBLIC: THE 1934 SECURITIES EXCHANGE ACT

Applicability of 1934 Act

Basic Purposes.   While the 1933 Act dealt primarily with the initial offering a securities issue, the 1934 Act attempted to deal with the abuses and manipulations which occurred once the stock got into the market. The original basis for regulation was that the security was traded on one of the national stock exchanges and was clearly "interstate commerce." More recent amendments require registration where the corporation has total assets of $1 million or more and a class of equity securities held by 500 or more persons. (Bonds are not *equity* securities; bondholders are creditors, so a company could have a class of bonds held by more than 500 persons and not have to register under the 1934 Act.) Once these minimum standards apply, the corporation and its stockholders become subject to all sorts of burdensome and costly regulations. For this reason, there has been a considerable movement in recent years to "go private"; that is, to buy back enough shares to reduce the number of stockholders below 500 and "deregister" the stock.

If the 1934 Act applies, the stock must be registered with the SEC, and if the stock is traded on an exchange, it must be registered with the exchange as well. These registration requirements are similar to those under the 1933 Act. In addition, certified annual reports must be filed each year, disclosing such matters as management changes, important legal proceedings, significant asset changes, and other material business events.

Disclosure of ownership required

Ownership and Proxy Regulations.   The SEC has adopted extensive regulations to prevent injury to the corporation or its shareholders by a few dominant "insiders" or by an outside group trying to take control. Within 10 days after becoming the *beneficial owner* of more than 5 percent of a registered equity security, the owner must file a disclosure statement with the SEC and send copies to the issuing corporation and to any stock exchange on which the shares are traded. The owner's identity must be disclosed as well as why he or she bought the shares, how many shares are owned, and where the funds came from to buy them. Updated reports must be filed 10 days after the end of any month in which the owner has changed the amount of holdings.

Short-swing insider profits must be paid over to corporation

Such beneficial owners must turn over to the corporation any *short-swing profits* if the owner holds more than 10 percent of the stock. Short-swing profits result from the purchase and sale of their company's shares within a six-month period. A stockholder with only 9 percent ownership could keep the profits. The corporation's directors and officers are also covered by this rule (Section 16 of the 1934 Act). If the buying and selling transactions extend beyond six months, all of these persons (directors, officers, 10 percent owners) could keep their profits. The reason for this short-swing rule is that insiders should not be allowed to take financial advantage of inside corporate information until there is a fair chance for it to be circulated to all investors.

In recent years there have been many criminal prosecutions of persons who used insider information to make a profit in the stock market. The question arises as to just who is an "insider." The following case discusses that issue.

CHIARELLA v. UNITED STATES

445 U.S. 222 (1980)

FACTS

Chiarella was a printer by trade. In 1975 and 1976, he worked as a "markup man" in the New York composing room of Pandick Press, a financial printer. Among documents that Chiarella handled were five announcements of corporate takeover bids. When these documents were delivered to the printer, the identities of the acquiring and target corporations were concealed by blank spaces or false names. The true names were sent to the printer on the night of the final printing.

Chiarella, however, was able to deduce the names of the target companies before the final printing from other information contained in the documents. Without disclosing his knowledge, he purchased stock in the target companies and sold shares immediately after the takeover attempts were made public. By this method, he realized a gain of slightly more than $30,000 in the course of 14 months. Subsequently, the SEC began an investigation of his trading activities. In May 1977, Chiarella entered into a consent decree with the Commission in which he agreed to return his profits to the sellers of the shares. On the same day, he was discharged by Pandick Press.

In January 1978, Chiarella was indicted on 17 counts of violating Section 10(b) of the Securities Exchange Act of 1934 (1934 Act) and SEC Rule 10b-5. After petitioner unsuccessfully moved to dismiss the indictment he was brought to trial and convicted on all counts. The Court of Appeals for the Second Circuit affirmed petitioner's conviction.

ISSUE

Was Mr. Chiarella an "insider" and thus in violation of the 1934 SEC Act and SEC Rule 10b-5?

DECISION

No. Judgment of the Court of Appeals is reversed.

REASONS

Justice Powell did not feel that Mr. Chiarella was an "insider" as contemplated by the law. He also did not find he had a duty to disclose the information which he learned from working with the documents.

"The federal courts have found violations of Section 10(b) where corporate insiders used undisclosed information for their own benefit. . . . The cases also have emphasized, in accordance with the common-law rule, that '[t]he party charged with failing to disclose market information must be under a duty to disclose it.' . . . Accordingly, a purchaser of stock who has no duty to a prospective seller because he is neither an insider nor a fiduciary has been held to have no obligation to reveal material facts. . . . [N]ot every instance of financial unfairness constitutes fraudulent activity under Section 10(b). . . . Second, the element required to make silence fraudulent—a duty to disclose—is absent in this case. No duty could arise from petitioner's relationship with the sellers of the target company's securities, for petitioner had no prior dealings with them. He was not their agent, he was not a fiduciary, he was not a person in whom the sellers had placed their trust and confidence. He was, in fact, a complete stranger who dealt with the sellers only through impersonal market transactions.

"We cannot affirm petitioner's conviction without recognizing a general duty between all participants in market transactions to forego actions based on material, nonpublic information. Formulation of such a broad duty, which departs radically from the established doctrine that duty arises from a specific relationship between two parties, . . . should not be undertaken absent some explicit evidence of congressional intent."

Proxy solicitation rules

Whether they are the existing management insiders or a group of outsiders seeking to gain control, persons soliciting proxies from stockholders must file an extensive disclosure statement with the SEC. This information must also be available to the stockholders being solicited. Since the 1968 Amendments to the 1934 Act, similar disclosures must be made in connection with a cash offer to the stockholders to buy all or part of a class of shares. The SEC's proxy rules also attempt to promote "shareholder democracy" by requiring management to include most shareholder proposals in the company's proxy statement and to provide shareholder lists or send out supporting material for the sponsors of such proposals.

Wide applicability of SEC Rule 10b-5

Antifraud Provisions. While all of the foregoing rules are important and have probably contributed to better corporate management, the most sweeping and revolutionary section of the 1934 Act is 10(b), the antifraud section. Together with the SEC's *Rule 10b-5,* as interpreted by the courts, this section potentially covers nearly any aspect of the securities markets one can imagine. It applies not only to the actual buyers and sellers of securities but to all other involved parties as well. It applies not only to the actual purchase and sale of securities but to *any* transaction *in connection with* their purchase and sale. It includes transactions in any securities, whether or not they are required to be listed and whether or not they are traded on an exchange. It covers much more than just common-law fraud, including such things as failure to comply with other securities law requirements, arbitrary withholding of dividends, breaches of fiduciary duty, and disclosure of too much or too little information.

In Chapter 7, Liability of Accountants and Other Professionals, we reviewed the antifraud provisions of the 1934 Act as they apply to accountants.

In the following case minority shareholders allege that Transamerica Corporation deceived them into selling their shares for less than their value and allege that such deception was a violation of the SEC's rule 10b-5 which reads as follows:

> It shall be unlawful for any person, directly or indirectly, by the use of any means or instrumentality of interstate commerce, or of the mails, or of any facility of any national securities exchange.
>
> *(a)* to employ any device, scheme, or artifice to defraud.
> *(b)* to make any untrue statement of a material fact or to omit to state a material fact necessary in order to make the statements made, in the light of the circumstances under which they were made, not misleading, or

(*c*) to engage in any act, practice, or course of business which operates or would operate as a fraud or deceit upon any person, in connection with the purchase or sale of any security.

SPEED ET AL. v. TRANSAMERICA CORP.

99 F. Supp. 808 (Delaware, 1951)

FACTS

Plaintiffs have sued defendant, Transamerica Corporation, for having purchased from them Class A and Class B stock of the Axton-Fisher Tobacco company at $40 and $12 per share, respectively, pursuant to a written offer dated November 12, 1942, which Transamerica made to all minority stockholders. The complaint alleges that at the time of the sale the true value of the Class A stock was more than $200 per share and such value of the Class B stock was in excess of $100 per share. Plaintiffs allege Transamerica deceived them into selling their shares in the manner hereinafter stated. Plaintiffs seek judgment in an amount equal to the difference between the sales price and the alleged true value. The action purports to be a class action on behalf of all Class A and Class B stockholders who accepted the offer.

The complaint alleges that in accepting Transamerica's offer, plaintiffs determined the value of their shares in reliance upon the Axton-Fisher annual report for 1941 and its accompanying letter, which Transamerica had caused to be mailed to the Axton-Fisher stockholders. The 1941 report showed the average cost of Axton-Fisher tobacco inventory to be $7,516,970, and the accompanying letter showed a decline in sales and net income since 1938; whereas, the complaint alleges, at the time when plaintiffs sold their stock the Axton-Fisher tobacco inventory had a real value in excess of $17 million and its earnings were improving.

The complaint further alleges that prior to the time when Transamerica made its offer, it had determined to purchase as many Class A and Class B shares as possible and thereafter to convert its Class A stock into Class B stock, to redeem the remaining Class A stock, and as a final step, to merge or dissolve Axton-Fisher, to the end it might capture for itself the increased but undisclosed value of the Axton-Fisher inventory, all of which Transamerica did. Under these circumstances, the complaint alleges, Transamerica was under a fiduciary duty as a majority stockholder to inform the minority stockholders that the real value of the Axton-Fisher inventory was in excess of $17,000,000; that its earnings were improving; and that Transamerica had determined upon a plan which had as its ultimate objective the merger or dissolution of Axton-Fisher; and that if Transamerica had made known these facts to plaintiffs, they would not have sold their stock.

The complaint contains four counts. The first count alleges a common law action of fraud and deceit. The last three counts allege violations of the three subparagraphs of Rule X-10B-5 of the Securities and Exchange Commission.

ISSUE

Did Transamerica intend, prior to November 12, 1942, to merge, dissolve, or liquidate Axton-Fisher?

DECISION

Yes. Judgment rendered against defendant. Defendant must respond in damages.

REASONS

Chief Judge Leahy reviewed the testimony to determine whether or not there was a preexisting plan to merge, dissolve or liquidate Axton-Fisher prior to November 12, 1942, when the written offer to purchase shares was made. Judge Leahy stated:

"From the testimony as a whole, it is palpable so far as decisions were concerned, Transamerica as well as Axton-Fisher were dominated by Giannini. When an important matter arose affecting Axton-Fisher and Transamerica, both Robbins and Cullman did not go to either board of directors but discussed the matter personally and privately with Giannini, *at Giannini's home*. Plaintiffs succeeded in proving . . . that Giannini planned to liquidate Axton-Fisher to capture the inventory profits before November 12, 1942; and this leaves me with the only realistic inference that can be drawn—that Transamerica had a similar intent. . . .

"I shall now consider more specifically the letter of November 12, 1942. It will be observed no information relative to the operations of Axton-Fisher was given the minority stockholders. The letter did provide: 'Any inquiries regarding the offer may be addressed to us.' Concededly, at the time the letter was mailed, the operating position of Axton-Fisher had vastly improved. This fact was well known to the directors of the company and consequently to Transamerica. But, if Transamerica did not at that time intend to liquidate etc., Axton-Fisher and capture the inventory profit, I think it would specifically have advised the stockholders as fully as possible. It would not have sought to make the stockholders 'dig' the information for themselves by making additional inquiries. A radical improvement in the operating position of the company was obviously a matter which every stockholder would be interested in. Transamerica knew this, and consequently the intentional imposition of this burden on the individual stockholder helps to persuade me that Transamerica planned to liquidate etc., Axton-Fisher at the time it mailed the letter. . . .

"Indeed, the price offered was so generous as to indicate there was, in fact, a preexisting intent to liquidate, etc., and that Transamerica wanted to get the stock and rid itself of other stockholders at a price which would be a bargain, when Transamerica decided the time was ripe to capture the inventory appreciation. I think this circumstance is of paramount importance because it is an indication that in this respect, at least, Transamerica overplayed its hand. . . .

"Since I find the existence of such a plan to be a fact, it follows defendant must respond in damages."

Remedies, Liabilities, and Penalties. The SEC uses a variety of court and administrative remedies to enforce the securities laws. It may seek an injunction to halt the sale of unregistered securities. It may ask a court to order the return of illegally received profits. Administratively, it may try to prevent employment of known violaters by securities firms. The SEC enters into many voluntary settlements ("consent decrees") with firms and individuals accused of violations. The accused does not admit guilt but agrees to refrain from certain specified practices, or to do certain things, in the future. Sometimes a penalty is accepted as part of the consent decree; sometimes not. Since the courts are usually quite lenient with securities law violators, the SEC feels these consent decrees are justified in many cases.

Consent decree settlements

Under Rule 2(e) of its rules of practice, the SEC may also bring disciplinary proceedings against professionals, such as accountants and attorneys, who are involved in securities transactions under the Commission's jurisdiction. The SEC, after giving the accused offender the opportunity for a hearing on the charges, may revoke the privilege of practicing before the Commission. Persons who lack the qualifications to represent others, or who have engaged in unethical professional conduct or otherwise lack character or integrity, or who have

Disciplinary proceedings against professionals

willfully violated or aided and abetted violations of the securities laws, may be prohibited from appearing before the Commission. Rule 2(e) also provides for automatic suspension of any attorney who has been suspended or disbarred, and any person whose state license has been suspended or revoked, and any person who has been convicted of a felony or of a misdemeanor involving moral turpitude. Temporary suspension may also occur where a professional has been subjected to an injunction against further violations of the securities laws. Commencing in 1975, the SEC has used this rule against corporate officers who also happened to be accountants or attorneys. In such a case, the corporate officer who could not practice before the SEC would be unable to sign the required filing documents for his company, and would thus be prevented from continuing to serve as the officer required to sign those documents. Since the Rule states that it applies to "any person," the SEC could conceivably try to apply it to officers who were neither accountants nor attorneys. Further litigation on the validity and scope of this Rule seems inevitable.

Investor lawsuits   Individual investors who have been damaged financially as a result of violations of the securities laws may bring their own lawsuits against those responsible. The problem of suing for individual relief is the same here as in any other case—legal fees. It will undoubtedly cost several thousand dollars to get a securities case instituted, and perhaps as much as $50,000 to see it through all the possible appeals and rehearings. Class action lawsuits are still possible, although the U.S. Supreme Court ruled in 1974 that each member of a "class" of potential plaintiffs has to be notified personally of the lawsuit, so that he or she can decide whether to join in as a plaintiff. Where such a class action is brought, with thousands of plaintiffs, including large institutional investors, damages can add up to millions of dollars very quickly.

Criminal penalities   Both the 1933 Act and the 1934 Act provide for criminal penalities—up to five years in prison and fines of up to $10,000 for most violations. Failure to file any report under the 1934 Act makes the issuing corporation liable for a fine of $100 per day until the required filing occurs. (A corporation can't be imprisoned, of course, but it can certainly be fined and enjoined.) Criminal cases are brought for the SEC by the U.S. Justice Department, so these two agencies must work together to prepare and present an effective criminal case. The *United States* v. *Natelli* case (presented in Chapter 6) is one of the rare criminal cases that have been brought against accountants for securities law violations.

Defenses to Civil Liability.   There are several possible defenses which may be used to avoid liability under the securities laws. First, the 1933 Act has a
Statute of limitations   relatively short statute of limitations: Suit must be brought within one year from the discovery of the violation or from the date when it would have been discovered using reasonable diligence; in no case, however, can suit be brought more than three years after the sale. With many analysts constantly studying the markets, most large frauds would probably be discovered within that time, but in the *Hochfelder* case (presented in Chapter 8) Nay defrauded people for some 25 years and was "discovered" only when he committed suicide.

It's at least theoretically possible for the courts to hold that a particular misstatement or omission was not material, but that is unlikely if investors have in fact sustained damage. The definition of *materiality* used in *Escott* (presented in Chapter 8) and similar cases is quite liberal: "any fact which *might* reasonably affect the value of the security."

While plaintiffs in securities cases don't have to prove that they specifically relied on a misstatement (as they would in a common-law fraud case), they can't recover if the defendant can prove that they knew when they entered into the securities transaction that the statement was false.

Due diligence defense

Probably the most important defense, and the one most open to interpretation, is the "due diligence" defense. This defense may be proved by any person other than the issuing corporation. As to parts of a registration statement not based on an expert's authority, the defendant is not liable if he or she can show that he or she "had, after reasonable investigation, reasonable ground to believe and did believe, at the time such part of the registration statement became effective, that the statements therein were true" (and not misleading). The standard of reasonableness specified is "that required of a prudent person in the management of his or her own property." As to the "expertised" sections of the registration statement (those certified by CPAs, engineers, or appraisers, for example), the defendant is not liable if he or she "had no reasonable ground to believe, and did not believe," that the statements were untrue or misleading. In other words, the statements made by experts can be relied on unless the defendant knew or reasonably should have known that the statements were false or misleading. However, lawyers are not necessarily "experts" on everything, under this definition. The court in the *Escott* case rejected the defendants' claim that they could rely on everything in the registration statement because it had been prepared by lawyers. Under this definition, lawyers would only be experts as to specifically legal questions; for example, the nature of the company's contingent liabilities.

Lawyers ≠ Experts under 1933 Act

■ SIGNIFICANCE OF THIS CHAPTER

Regulation of the issuance and sale of securities is a very important phase of government regulation on both the state and national level. It is not only the very rich, who obviously have access to excellent legal advice and valuable market information, who invest in securities. Investors include people from all walks of life and from all income levels. They must be protected from persons who would defraud them or take their money by deceptive practices. Also, the public buyer should be protected against the "insider" who because of special knowledge would get an unfair advantage as to new stock issues, stock splits, and similar material developments.

From the issuing company's standpoint, compliance with the securities law is burdensome in time, effort, and money. There are no easy shortcuts. But full and accurate compliance is clearly in the company's best interests. For all responsible individuals, the company's compliance should be checked and rechecked to avoid the possibility of ruinous damage suits by angry investors.

DISCUSSION CASE

DIRKS v. SECURITIES AND EXCHANGE COMMISSION

463 U.S. 653 (1983)

FACTS: In 1973, Dirks was an officer of a New York broker-dealer firm who specialized in providing investment analysis of insurance company securities to institutional investors. On March 6, 1973 Dirks received information from Ronald Secrist, a former officer of Equity Funding of America. Secrist alleged that the assets of Equity Funding, a diversified corporation primarily engaged in selling life insurance and mutual funds, were vastly overstated as the result of fraudulent corporate practices. Secrist also stated that various regulatory agencies had failed to act on similar charges made by Equity Funding employees. He urged Dirks to verify the fraud and disclose it publicly.

Dirks decided to investigate the allegations. He visited Equity Funding's headquarters in Los Angeles and interviewed several officers and employees of the corporation. The senior management denied any wrongdoing, but certain corporation employees corroborated the charges of fraud. Neither Dirks nor his firm owned or traded any Equity Funding stock, but throughout his investigation he openly discussed the information he had obtained with a number of clients and investors. Some of these persons sold their holdings of Equity Funding securities, including five investment advisers who liquidated holdings of more than $16 million.

While Dirks was in Los Angeles, he was in touch regularly with William Blundell, the Wall Street Journal's Los Angeles bureau chief. Dirks urged Blundell to write a story on the fraud allegations. Blundell did not believe, however, that such a massive fraud could go undetected and declined to write the story. He feared that publishing such damaging hearsay might be libelous.

During the 2-week period in which Dirks pursued his investigation and spread word of Secrist's charges, the price of Equity Funding stock fell from $26 per share to less than $15 per share. This led the New York Stock Exchange to halt trading on March 27. Shortly thereafter California insurance authorities impounded Equity Funding's records and uncovered evidence of the fraud. Only then did the Securities and Exchange Commission (SEC) file a complaint against Equity Funding and only then, on April 2, did the Wall Street Journal publish a front-page story based largely on information assembled by Dirks. Equity Funding immediately went into receivership.

The SEC began an investigation into Dirks' role in the exposure of the fraud. After a hearing by an Administrative Law Judge, the SEC found that Dirks had aided and abetted violations of the securities laws, by repeating the allegations of fraud to members of the investment community who later sold their Equity Funding stock. The SEC concluded: "Where 'tippees'—regardless of their motivation or occupation—come into possession of material 'corporate information that they know is confidential and know or should know came from a corporate insider,' they must either publicly disclose that information or refrain from trading."

Dirks sought review in the Court of Appeals for the District of Columbia Circuit. The court entered judgment against Dirks "for the reasons stated by the commission in its opinion."

In view of the importance to the SEC and to the securities industry of the question presented by this case, the Supreme Court granted a writ of certiorari.

■

Justice Powell delivered the opinion of the Court:

Petitioner Raymond Dirks received material nonpublic information from "insiders" of a corporation with which he had no connection. He disclosed this information to investors who relied on it in trading in the shares of the corporation. The question is whether Dirks violated the antifraud provisions of the federal securities laws by this disclosure.

In the seminal case of In re Cady, Roberts & Co., . . . (1961), the SEC recognized that the common law in some jurisdictions imposes on "corporate 'insiders,' particularly officers, directors, or controlling stockholders" an "affirmative duty of disclosure . . . when dealing in securities.". . . The SEC found that not only did breach of this common-law duty also establish the elements of a Rule 10b-5 violation, but that individuals other than corporate insiders could be obligated either to disclose material nonpublic information before trading or to abstain from trading altogether. . . . In Chiarella, we accepted the two elements set out in Cady, Roberts for establishing a Rule 10b-5 violation: "(i) the existence of a relationship affording access to inside information intended to be available only for a corporate purpose, and (ii) the unfairness of allowing a corporate insider to take advantage of that information by trading without disclosure.". . . In examining whether Chiarella had an obligation to disclose or abstain, the Court found that there is no general duty to disclose before trading on material nonpublic information, and held that "a duty to disclose under § 10(b) does not arise from the mere possession of nonpublic market information.". . .

We were explicit in Chiarella in saying that there can be no duty to disclose where the person who has traded on inside information "was not [the corporation's] agent, . . . was not a fiduciary, [or] was not a person in whom the sellers [of the securities] had placed their trust and confidence.". . .

[W]e find that there was no actionable violation by Dirks. It is undisputed that Dirks himself was a stranger to Equity Funding, with no pre-existing fiduciary duty to its shareholders. He took no action, directly or indirectly, that induced the shareholders or officers of Equity Funding to repose trust or confidence in him. There was no expectation by Dirks' sources that he would keep their information in confidence. Nor did Dirks misappropriate

or illegally obtain the information about Equity Funding. Unless the insiders breached their Cady, Roberts duty to shareholders in disclosing the nonpublic information to Dirks, he breached no duty when he passed it on to investors as well as to the Wall Street Journal.

It is clear that neither Secrist nor the other Equity Funding employees violated their Cady, Roberts duty to the corporation's shareholders by providing information to Dirks. The tippers received no monetary or personal benefit for revealing Equity Funding's secrets, nor was their purpose to make a gift of valuable information to Dirks. As the facts of this case clearly indicate, the tippers were motivated by a desire to expose the fraud. . . . In the absence of a breach of duty to shareholders by the insiders, there was no derivative breach by Dirks. . . . Dirks therefore could not have been "a participant after the fact in [an] insider's breach of a fiduciary duty." Chiarella, . . .

We conclude that Dirks, in the circumstances of this case, had no duty to abstain from use of the inside information that he obtained. The judgment of the Court of Appeals therefore is reversed.

■ IMPORTANT TERMS AND CONCEPTS

state blue-sky laws
state tender offer statutes
Securities Exchange
   Act of 1934
registration statement
antifraud provisions
beneficial owner
SEC Rule 10b-5
Uniform Securities Act

Securities Act of 1933
definition of a security
prospectus
ownership and proxy
   regulations
short-swing profits
SEC Act - 1934 Section
   10(b)

■ QUESTIONS AND PROBLEMS FOR DISCUSSION

1. What power do the states have to regulate securities transactions?
2. What is a "tender offer"? Why do states want to regulate it?
3. What is a "security" under the 1933 Act?
4. What is the difference between the 1933 Act and the 1934 Act?
5. Piano Company was a closely held South Carolina corporation. It had only four shareholders—Huey, Louis, Dewey, and Donald. From the time it was incorporated in 1976, it had been unprofitable. In

1984 Donald, who was the only shareholder actively involved in Piano's management, learned that certain market changes would make Piano very profitable. Donald persuaded the other three shareholders to sell their shares to him, without disclosing his new information. All of these representations and statements were made in person by Donald; he sent no letters, and he did not use the telephone. Do the other three shareholders have a case against Donald under Section 10(b) of the 1934 Act? Discuss.

6. Rake bought a large amount of Apco Corporation stock through a broker who used the facilities of the New York Stock Exchange, where Apco was listed. At the time of Rake's purchase, Apco's financial statements contained several serious misrepresentations, specifically, its assets and profits were grossly overstated. When these misrepresentations were disclosed, the price of Apco stock declined sharply and Rake and other investors lost money. Rake brings a class action against Apco's auditors, Beat, Airwick, & Richsell, for failure to use proper accounting techniques in preparing Apco's financial statements. BA&R says that it should not be held liable, since it engaged in no securities transactions and it made no profit on the information which was misrepresented. Should the auditors (BA&R) be held liable? Discuss.

7. Merry Lyncher, a stockbroker, developed what she thought was a surefire scheme for making money in the market. After study, she picked stocks she thought were sure to go down in price and placed "sell" orders with other brokers. She told them that she owned these shares; otherwise, they would have required a margin deposit or refused the orders altogether. Her plan was to buy the stocks when the price went down so that she'd have them by the time she was required to deliver them. Unfortunately, the stocks she selected rose sharply in price and she defaulted on her sales contracts. The other brokers were forced to buy in at the higher market prices to cover sales to their customers, and they now sue Merry for securities fraud. Merry contends that she is not liable, since Section 17(a)(1) of the 1933 Act only protects *investors,* not brokers. Has Merry violated the securities acts? Discuss.

8. Hoppe sold live silver foxes to about 100 persons at $970 a pair for "full silver" foxes and at $700 a pair for "three-quarter silver" foxes. Each buyer also entered into a "ranching agreement" with Hoppe, in which he agreed to care for the foxes at his ranch, to sell the offspring or their pelts, and to send all of the proceeds to each pair's owner. Hoppe promised to replace foxes lost through escape, theft, or death, and he guaranteed a minimum of three pups per pair in the first year following the purchase. Hoppe's ranching fee was $50 per pair per year. The SEC sued for injunction, alleging that Hoppe is violating the securities laws. What is the result, and why?

50

Business Ethics, Corporate Social Responsibility, and the Law

CHAPTER OBJECTIVES
THIS CHAPTER WILL:

- Review the history of business ethics and corporate social responsibility.
- Define ethical conduct.
- Review ethical issues in business.
- Discuss the social responsibility of corporations.
- Discuss the use of the corporate social audit.

Much has been said and written about business ethics and corporate social responsibility. Problems arise in defining ethical and unethical conduct, and the responsibilities of individuals and corporations to society. Obviously, individuals and corporations involved in business transactions must comply with the law. Individuals or corporations that clearly violate the law will be subject to prosecution and penalties.

Ethical problems arise when an individual's activity is in the so-called gray area, the area between activities which are clearly legal and activities which are clearly illegal. The same type of situation exists with regard to corporate social responsibility; the corporation clearly has legal duties and rights. As long as the corporation exercises the legal rights granted to it by its corporate charter and by the laws of the state in which it operates and as long as it does not violate the legal rights of others in such a manner as to cause either civil or criminal liability to itself, then, it is a *legally responsible,* but not necessarily a *socially responsible,* corporation. Another gray area exists where the ethically or socially responsible corporation could conduct or cease certain activities, even though it had no legal duty to do so, if such activity or nonactivity would be beneficial to society. This chapter will address these problems.

■ HISTORY OF BUSINESS ETHICS AND CORPORATE RESPONSIBILITY

Many businesspersons today complain about the consumer advocates who demand that businesses not only abide by the letter of the law but also make a reasonable attempt to produce a product which exceeds the bare safety standards, and which is designed to outlast the warranty.

Before judging and condemning those advocates as irresponsible and revolutionary, perhaps we should review the history of business ethics and business social responsibility in the Western world. In classical Greece 2,000 years ago, the businessperson was not highly regarded. In fact, they ranked no higher on the social ladder than slaves. In Greek society, business was allowed to exist only because it served the public and the community. Businesspersons were severely punished if found guilty of immoral business practices. Greek businesspersons were also subject to intense criticism from the upper classes if they failed to practice a standard of morality which exceeded that of common honesty. This ethical standard was considerably higher than the minimum required by law.

Ancient Greek view of business

The Greek society did not allow material gains from business to be used merely as the owner wished, without regard for the interest of the community. Greeks felt that since the businessperson realized profits from the community, those profits should be returned to the community in ways that benefit everyone, not just the businessperson. Thus, the merchant or producer of goods was not allowed to get rich, but only to make a living and live in the same manner as others of the same class. The level of business ethics and social responsibility expected of the businesspersons during the classical Greek period can be classified as most extreme.

Medieval view of business

The next historical period important to business ethics and social responsibility lasted from approximately 900 A.D. to 1500 A.D. and is often referred to as the Feudal or Medieval era. The Catholic church exercised a strong influence over the lives and activities of its members. The Catholic church distrusted both businesspersons and the business system in general. It viewed the profit motive as being anti-Christian, as reflected in the Roman motto: *Homo mercator vit aut numquam Deo placere potest ("the merchant seldom or never pleases God")*.

While the church mistrusted businesspersons and the business system, it understood that business had to exist. However, it recognized only the need for commerce that served the public interest. In the 13th century, St. Thomas Aquinas wrote that business could be justified only as long as it was operated for the good of the community, with honest motives and actions, just prices, living wages for employees, and a socially responsible use of profits. Fraud, dishonesty, and other such actions in business were punished severely during this period, and the ethical standards by which the businesspersons were expected to abide were still very high.

Calvinist view of business

The years between 1500 and 1800 were important to business ethics and social responsibility as well; this was a period of social and religious revolution. For the first time, business became a respectible occupation. The Catholic dogma, which so mistrusted business and the businessperson, began to crumble. In its place came the Calvinist doctrine which praised the industrious and thrifty businessperson. Businesspersons gained respectability and dignity in their communities. In both continental Europe and England, businesspersons were welcomed into the so-called upper class.

Calvinism encouraged business and trade; however, it still severely punished unethical and immoral business practices. Businesspersons were expected to tithe to the church and to give to charity in accordance with their profits and their means. Thus, the merchant who was previously looked down upon and treated with mistrust, both in the community and in the church, was now the leader of the community and a pillar of the church. They were persons of respect as long they followed the Christian doctrine to help the poor and the needy, paid a fair living wage to employees, and lived Christian lives.

Industrial Revolution

The next period of interest in the history of business ethics and social responsibility lasted from approximately 1800 to 1930. This was the period of the Industrial Revolution, and new attitudes toward business ethics and business social responsibility emerged. The businessperson finally replaced the aristocracy on the social ladder. Once viewed as lowly as the slave, the businessperson now had reached the top rung of the social ladder and had pushed aside the aristocracy. Employers became physically and morally separated from their employees. In previous centuries, the employer typically had only a few employees who were like family, often housed in the family home and cared for like children. With the changes in manufacturing processes came factories with large numbers of persons working for low wages, under poor working conditions, and for long, tedious hours at a time. The problem, of course, was that the employer was no longer working side by side with the employees.

Employers, now physically removed from the workplace, could no longer personally know and care for the large number of persons who worked for them. Thus, employees became only faces or numbers without close relationships to their employers. The pendulum had swung from a very high level of care and concern by employers for their employees, to a feeling that employees were no more than machines to whom the employer owed only a very minimal degree of care.

Corporations grew to gigantic proportions, and some had power nearly equal to that of government. Enormous, nearly unlimited, economic power became centered in the hands of only a few persons, who became a corporate ruling class. Many corporate leaders flagrantly violated the law, and the long-established ethics and morals of business. They seemed to view corporate social responsibility as the need to comply only with the very minimum requirements of the law and demonstrated the attitude that their economic power placed them beyond the reach of the law. The recognition and practice of good business ethics and social responsibility in business dropped to the lowest level in the history of the Western world during this period.

The period from approximately 1930 to the present brought the reenlightenment of business. Since the early 1930s, when the nation was regaining its strength after coming out of the Great Depression, a trend in both society and governmental regulation has been to reestablish the social obligations of business to the level that was expected before the Industrial Revolution.

New Deal regulation

The so-called New Deal administration of the 1930s brought about many radical changes in governmental regulation of business and established governmental benefits for workers. New legislation limited child labor abuses, gave workers the right to join unions, allowed workers to collectively bargain with their employers, and set minimum wages and hours. Various other laws were passed to restrain anticompetitive activities in interstate commerce. Also, since business would not accept their moral and ethical obligations in the areas of civil rights, safety in the workplace, environmental conservation and health, and employee pensions, specific laws had to be passed to force business to comply with at least minimum standards in those areas. Businesses must abide by the new laws; however, simply doing that is not an expression of business ethics or corporate social responsibility. Complying with the law is a requirement imposed on every individual in society.

Thus, we have seen business ethics and business social responsibility come from one extreme in the classical Greek period to another during the period of the Industrial Revolution. Now the pendulum is swinging between these two extremes.

■ DEFINITION OF ETHICAL CONDUCT

Ethical conduct can be generally defined that which complies with standards of right or proper conduct. *Nonethical* would be conduct which was contrary to or in violation of such standards.

We then must ask: "What are the standards, who makes them, to whom do they apply?" Also, what are the consequences if we do not choose to comply with them?

Social origin of ethical standards

First, let us address the question, "What standards?" As human beings living on this planet, we all have basic moral rights and duties to each other. Society adopts certain written and unwritten moral standards in an informal way. An example of such a standard is the *golden rule:* "Do unto others as you wish them to do unto you." Religious teachings add other standards, such as, "Thou shalt not steal," and "Turn the other cheek."

There is no hard-and-fast set of ethical standards for us to read, memorize, and obey. Also, these standards differ in different areas of the world. For example, commercial bribery has varying implications in many parts of the world. As a consequence the U.S. Congress passed the Foreign Corrupt Practices Act to force U.S. corporations to use the same standards in transactions in foreign countries that are used at home. Standards may change from time to time, and from generation to generation. Standards are created by and for society in a nonformal and nonlegislative manner. They apply to all of us as humans living in a society.

Unethical conduct = Social disapproval

Next, what are the consequences of violation of these moral standards? Generally speaking, no legal consequences will arise unless the action violates a criminal law, or unless a civil wrong has been committed. If a criminal law is violated, then criminal punishment shall follow; if a civil wrong is committed, civil damages may be assessed by a court. However, if the violation is in the "gray area" it is only punishable by public criticism, ostricism by the church or group to which the offender belongs, or fear of punishment after death.

Do those same moral standards by which we should abide as human beings apply when we are doing business for profit? The answer, of course, is obvious: We should still abide by basic ethical standards whether we are doing business or simply living our lives.

The next question to be addressed is: Are there specific standards of right or proper conduct with which persons in business must comply? Some of the professions have established ethical codes of conduct; however, business in general lacks such established codes. One example of the ethical standards of a profession is the Code of Professional Responsibility, published by the American Bar Association for practicing lawyers. Lawyers may refer to this code to determine how they should conduct themselves in a particular situation so that their activity will comply with both criminal and civil law and the recommended ethics of the profession.

Accounting, engineering, and other professions have also adopted codes of professional ethics, and thus have standards for making judgments about ethical or nonethical conduct.

It must be noted that standards, as set out in these codes, are not standards of conduct from a criminal law standpoint. They are ethical standards for the profession. Failure to adhere to them will not necessarily bring about criminal prosecution. However, such failure may bring disciplinary action by the professional organization, ranging from a warning to loss of the license to practice.

In this chapter we are primarily concerned about business ethics as it pertains to persons in sales, management, manufacturing, and consulting positions, and other persons not in a profession which is governed by a specific set of ethical standards.

Lack of a business code of conduct

One might ask: Why not have a code of professional ethics for business? The answer is: A code could be formulated, but how could the offenders be disciplined? In the legal profession a person can be disbarred, which ends the right to practice law in that jurisdiction. This is a very severe penalty that radically affects the person's livelihood, and is certainly a deterrent to violation and nonadherence to the standards. If a retailer, for example, sells inferior merchandise for an unreasonably high price, there is no way to impose sanctions unless the action is a criminal violation, because there are no standards other than the law and no governing body that can impose discipline. The only deterrent is that if the actions are too blatant, consumers will cease purchasing that person's goods. Thus, the marketplace may be said to be the ultimate judge, jury, and executioner for enforcement of ethics in business. The problem, however, is that this type of regulation is always after the fact. In other words, there must be injury to consumers, and usually injury to many consumers over a period of time, before any major action can occur. Today we are seeing the growth of consumer advocate groups which are acting as the conscience for business. They bring class actions and encourage newspapers to publish the unethical actions of businesses, in the hope that such action will convince businesspersons to adhere to a higher standard of morality in business.

The next case explores a crucial ethical-legal-moral question: should the law enforce any and every commercial bargain between consenting adults?

WHITEHEAD-GOULD v. STERN

542 A.2d 52 (New Jersey, 1988)

FACTS   This is the now-famous "Baby M" case. Mary Beth Whitehead agreed to bear a child for the Sterns in return for $10,000. She was artificially inseminated with Mr. Stern's sperm, and the child was born nine months later. Mrs. Whitehead during this period had changed her mind. She renounced the contract, and began a custody fight for the child. After a long and bitter struggle, the trial court awarded custody to the Sterns, and terminated Mrs. Whitehead's visitation and parental rights. Meanwhile, still married to Mr. Whitehead, she had become pregnant by Mr. Gould, whom she married after she divorced Mr. Whitehead. She appealed to the State Supreme Court.

ISSUE   Is the surrogacy contract made by Mrs. Whitehead-Gould to bear another persons' child for a fee a valid and enforceable contract?

DECISION   No. Mrs. Whitehead will be given visitation rights, to be determined by the court.

REASONS   Chief Justice Wilentz, speaking for the court, found the surrogacy contract in this case to be invalid. The Court then stated:

"Although in this case we grant custody to the natural father, the evidence having clearly proved such custody to be in the best interests of the infant, we void both the termination of the surrogate mother's parental rights and the adoption of the child by the wife/stepparent. We thus restore the 'surrogate' as the mother of the child. . . .

"We find no offense to our present laws where a woman voluntarily and without payment agrees to act as a 'surrogate' mother, provided that she is not subject to a binding agreement to surrender her child. Moreover, our holding today does not preclude the legislature from altering the current statutory scheme, within constitutional limits, so as to permit surrogacy contracts. Under current law, however, the surrogacy agreement before us is illegal and invalid. . . .

"We have found that our present laws do not permit the surrogacy contract used in this case. Nowhere, however, do we find any legal prohibition against surrogacy when the surrogate mother volunteers, without any payment, to act as a surrogate and is given the right to change her mind and to assert her parental rights. . . .

"We do not underestimate the difficulties of legislating on this subject. . . . Legislative consideration of surrogacy may also provide the opportunity to begin to focus on the overall implications of the new reproductive biotechnology—*in vitro* fertilization, preservation of sperm and eggs, embryo implantation, and the like. . . . The problem can be addressed only when society decides what its values and objectives are in this troubling, yet promising, area.

"The judgment is affirmed in part, reversed in part, and remanded for further proceedings consistent with this opinion."

ETHICAL ISSUES IN BUSINESS

Ethical conduct toward employees

The purpose of this chapter is not to prescribe ethical standards for business, nor to make value judgments on what business activity is ethical and what activity is unethical. Our purpose is simply to increase the student's awareness as to the issues in business which may be subject to ethical concerns.

Ethical Issues—Internal. Internal ethical issues primarily involve the relationship between the business and its employees. What ethical or moral responsibility does an employer have to employees? If the employer pays at least the legal minimum wage, pays overtime as legally required, provides a minimally safe place to work, does not violate the discrimination laws, what else can we expect?

When we look at the relationship between employer and employee we must consider the minimum requirements of the various laws governing that relationship and then ask, "Is that enough?" Is it ethically right to pay employees as low a wage as possible providing they receive at least the legal minimum wage? One might say that the employer should maximize profits and thus should not pay more for labor than is legally required. The counterargument is that the employer has an ethical (although not legal) obligation to pay a fair wage to employees. We will not attempt to answer the question for what is a fair wage and what is moral or immoral. Our purpose here is to heighten awareness of these issues, not to provide prescriptions.

Internal ethical issues arise in many areas of the employer-employee relationship. In the area of initial hiring, the laws that prohibit discrimination are fairly clear. However, they are hard to prosecute because the decision to hire is often based on intangible evidence, such as prejudices of the supervisor. What should the ethical manager or supervisor do? The laws that prohibit discrimination in employment are set out in Chapter 41. Is bare compliance with these laws enough? Internal ethical issues may also arise regarding basic wage issues, assignment of work, promotion, and tenure. Again there are labor laws that address these issues and that must be complied with.

The next area of employer-employee relations in which ethical issues are involved relates more to the environment of the workplace, that is, how the employee is treated on a day-to-day basis. Following are some of the most common corporate policies and/or actions that cause ethical problems: (1) unauthorized searches of the employee's locker, work station, or desk for drugs or stolen property, (2) a required drug-testing program, (3) the requirement that employees submit to a polygraph test, (4) the unauthorized disclosure of personal and private information about employees to a third party, (5) smoking rules to protect nonsmokers from smokers, (6) dress codes which are not based either on safety or the company's image to the public, (7) a corporate policy regarding employment of persons infected with AIDS, and (8) a corporate policy regarding sexual harassment.

There are of course many other policies and employer actions in the workplace which may give rise to ethical issues. With regard to the above policies or actions, the legal rights of the parties are not always clear or concise. Thus we are again faced with ethical decisions. Even though a certain action or policy may not be clearly illegal, is it ethical?

Another consideration is the economic effect of the above types of action or policy. Even though there may not be a national or state statute prohibiting such action, the actions of the employer could in some cases be grounds for a tort action. In the following case an employee sued K Mart, her employer, and the jury awarded a verdict of $8,000 actual damages and $100,000 in punitive damages for conducting an unauthorized search of her locker.

K MART CORP. STORE NO. 7441 v. TROTTI

677 S.W.2d 632 (Texas, 1984)

FACTS   On October 31, 1981, Ms. Trotti placed her purse in her locker when she arrived for work. She testified that she snapped the lock closed and then pulled on it to make sure it was locked. When she returned to her locker during her afternoon break, she discovered the lock hanging open. Searching through her locker, the appellee further discovered her personal items in her purse in considerable disorder. Nothing was missing from either the locker or the purse. The store manager testified that, in the company of three junior administrators at the store, he had that afternoon searched the lockers because of a suspicion raised by the appellants' security personnel that an unidentified employee, not the appellee, had stolen a watch. The manager and his assistants were also searching for missing price-marking guns. Ms. Trotti further testified that, as she left the employee's locker area after discovering her locker open, she heard the manager suggest to his assistants, "Let's get busy again." The manager testified that none of the parties searched through employees' personal effects.

Ms. Trotti approached the manager later that day and asked if he had searched employees' lockers and/or her purse. The manager initially denied either kind of search and maintained this denial for approximately one month. At that time, the manager then admitted having searched the employees' lockers and further mentioned that they had, in fact, searched the appellee's purse, later saying that he meant that they had searched only her locker and not her purse.

Ms. Trotti then sued her employer for an invasion of her privacy. The jury awarded $8,000 for actual damages and $100,000 for punitive damages. K Mart appealed.

ISSUE   Was the employer guilty of invasion of privacy? Was the award of punitive damages proper in this case?

DECISION   Yes. Yes. Verdict of the trial court jury is affirmed.

REASONS   Justice Bullock in his opinion affirming the jury's verdict, which included both actual and punitive damages, stated:

"The appellants intentionally intruded upon an area where the appellee had a legitimate expectation of privacy. The evidence supports a further finding that the appellants wrongfully intruded upon the appellee's personal property. The conduct of this inspection, and the appellants' subsequent denial and ultimate admission support the conclusion that they were aware that their actions constituted a covert intrusion. The appellants clearly made the wrongful intrusion with neither the appellee's permission nor justifiable suspicion that the appellee had stolen any store inventory. Sufficient factors exist to enable this court to conclude that the jury's award of exemplary damages was the result of proper motivations. We disagree with the appellant that any set ratio of exemplary to actual damages constitutes a ceiling beyond which a greater award would be excessive, and even were we to agree with appellants, we do not find that the exemplary damages in the instant case exceed that ceiling.

"The evidence supports the jury's award of exemplary damages from the factors cited. There is no evidence to support a conclusion that the jury acted as a result of passion or prejudice."

The last area of the employer-employee relationship that creates ethical issues is the discharge of an employee when there is no just cause. In recent years two types of discharge cases have drawn criticism from an ethical standpoint, and the questions of legality are not entirely clear.

First we have what is commonly referred to as "discriminate pricing." This occurs when a business discharges an older, more highly paid employee prior to retirement age, and replaces that employee with a younger, lower paid employee. The Age Discrimination in Employment Act prohibits discrimination for age with regard to persons aged 40 to 70 years of age, yet there is not a clear precedent that "discriminate pricing" is illegal. Is it ethical?

The second type of discharge that involves ethical considerations is what is termed a *wrongful discharge*. The question raised is what constitutes a wrongful discharge? The great majority of employees in the nation's work force are *employees-at-will*, which is generally held to mean their employer is legally free to terminate their employment at any time, even without just cause, as long as the discharge does not violate public policy or any specific law or regulation. One exception would be persons who are under contract for a specific term, such as school teachers or coaches. If these persons are terminated without just cause, the employer will still have to pay their salaries for the balance of the contract period or make some sort of a compromise settlement. Another exception would exist where a union contract guarantees the jobs of the union members except in the case of specific violations by a worker which might be interpreted by an arbitrator as just cause. A third exception would be where the employee is granted tenure.

Still, the great majority of workers are employees-at-will, and the question of what is a wrongful discharge remains. Does an employee who has served the employer faithfully for many years have any recourse if fired by the employer because he or she complained about some of the company's activities?

Many courts across the nation have begun looking beyond the historically narrow employment-at-will doctrine, and are asking: What is fair? What is ethical under the circumstances? However, most courts still want to tie their decision to a violation of some constitutional provision or statutory law which was passed to protect employees from unjustified discharge. For example, an employee was discharged because he refused to order the employees he supervised to work under hazardous conditions which the Occupational Safety and Health Administration (OSHA) had already found to be dangerous. The New Hampshire Supreme Court felt the employee was wrongfully discharged. The OSHA law was passed to make the workplace safe and reduce industrial injuries, and the court ruled that kind of discharge was against the public policy of the state of New Hampshire. The *Patton* case in Chapter 40 discussed another example of alleged wrongful discharge.

The problem still remains, regardless of how the courts interpret the employees' rights under an employment-at-will: What is ethical? What is right? What is the socially responsible decision? Do we have to have a law which applies to every type of decision which might be needed in business to guarantee that we make ethical decisions? What about the "golden rule"?

Internal ethical issues arise out of all phases of the employer-employee relationship. Many of these issues are still unregulated by law in many jurisdictions. Lacking legal standards, judgments in these situations remain ethical questions.

Ethical Issues—External. External ethical issues arise in the relationship between the business and its customers and between the business and the eventual consumer of the company's product or service. As in the case of internal ethical issues we will pose the question: What ethical or moral responsibility does a business have to customers and to the ultimate consumers of the company's product or service? If the business makes a product that passes governmental standards of safety, is that enough? If the government does not regulate the industry, what standards must the business follow? When must warnings be given to the consumer?

External ethical issues arise in many areas of the relationships between business and customer and business and consumer in addition to product safety standards. These areas include advertising, warranties, packaging and labeling, price-fixing, price discrimination, and unfair competitive practices. Specific national and state regulations apply to each of these areas, but the question is again posed: Is compliance with the minimum standards of the law enough, or should the businessperson do more than the law requires? Certainly there are arguments pro and con. Again, the purpose of this chapter is not to give value judgments but only to alert the student to potential ethical issues.

Another area of external ethical issues where conflict could occur involves the business and the public, more specifically, the local community. We will address these problems under the caption corporate social responsibility.

Ethical conduct toward customers

■ SOCIAL RESPONSIBILITY OF BUSINESS CORPORATIONS

Service beyond what's legally required

As we have stated, a corporation or any other legal entity conducting business must comply with the letter of the law or it will be subject to prosecution and punishment. However, a corporation or other legal entity that merely complies with the letter of the law may not be "socially responsible." *Corporate social responsibility* means going that extra mile, so to speak, doing more than is legally required. It means that the social impact of a business decision must be considered as well as the more immediate financial results.

In a sense, social responsibility means that a business must be concerned with the long term, as well as the short term. Closing a plant in a small town may produce favorable effects on this year's balance sheet and profit and loss statement. But what about the closing's devastating effects on the town? Will the closing promote employee loyalty, and thus productivity, at other plants? Will it promote brand loyalty among ex-employees, and their friends and relatives, toward the company's products?

The *Shlensky* case shows a corporation trying to justify a decision, at least in part, on "social responsibility" grounds.

SHLENSKY v. WRIGLEY

237 N.E.2d 776 (Illinois, 1968)

FACTS

Plaintiff is a minority stockholder of defendant corporation, Chicago National League Ball Club (Inc.), a Delaware corporation with its principal place of business in Chicago, Illinois. Defendant corporation owns and operates the major league professional baseball team known as the Chicago Cubs. The corporation also engages in the operation of Wrigley Field, the Cubs' home park, the concessionaire sales during Cubs' home games, television and radio broadcasts of Cubs' home games, the leasing of the field for football games and other events and receives its share, as visiting team, of admission moneys from games played in other National League stadia. The individual defendants are directors of the Cubs and have served for varying periods of years. Defendant Philip K. Wrigley is also president of the corporation and owner of approximately 80 percent of the stock therein.

Plaintiff alleges that since night baseball was first played in 1935, 19 of the 20 major league teams have scheduled night games. In 1966, out of a total of 1,620 games in the major leagues, 932 were played at night. Plaintiff alleges that every member of the major leagues, other than the Cubs, scheduled substantially all of its home games in 1966 at night, exclusive of opening days, Saturdays, Sundays, holidays, and days prohibited by league rules. Allegedly this has been done for the specific purpose of maximizing attendance and thereby maximizing revenue and income.

The Cubs, in the years 1961–65, sustained operating losses from its direct baseball operations. Plaintiff attributes those losses to inadequate attendance at Cubs' home games. He concludes that if the directors continue to refuse to install lights at Wrigley Field and schedule night baseball games, the Cubs will continue to sustain comparable losses and its financial condition will continue to deteriorate.

Plaintiff further alleges that defendant Wrigley has refused to install lights, not because of interest in the welfare of the corporation but because of his personal opinions "that baseball is a 'daytime sport' and that the installation of lights and night baseball games will have a deteriorating effect upon the surrounding neighborhood."

ISSUE

Does a minority stockholder have a cause of action against the directors for their decisions which stockholders do not agree with, if there is no fraud, illegality, or conflict of interest involved?

DECISION

No. The order of dismissal entered by the trial court is affirmed.

REASONS

Justice Sullivan found that there was no evidence that fraud, illegality, or conflict of interest was involved. The plaintiff, a minority stockholder, did not agree with the decision of the board of directors regarding the playing of night games in Wrigley field, and he felt that the failure to have night games was not in the best interest of the corporation. Judge Sullivan went on to state:

"Plaintiff in the instant case argues that the directors are acting for reasons unrelated to the financial interest and welfare of the Cubs. However, we are not satisfied that the motives assigned to Philip K. Wrigley, and through him to the other directors, are contrary to the best interests of the corporation and the stockholders. By these thoughts we do not mean to say that we have decided that the decision of the directors was a correct one. That is beyond our jurisdiction and ability. We are merely saying that the decision is one properly before directors, and motives alleged in the amended complaint showed no fraud, illegality, or conflict of interest in their making of that decision.

"While all the courts do not insist that one or more of the three elements must be present for a stockholder's derivative action to lie, nevertheless we feel that unless the conduct of the defendants at least borders on one of the elements, the courts should not interfere. . . .

"We feel that plaintiff's amended complaint was also defective in failing to allege damage to the corporation. . . .

"There is no allegation that the night games played by the other 19 teams enhanced their financial position or that the profits, if any, of those teams were directly related to the number of night games scheduled. . . .

"Finally, we do not agree with plaintiff's contention that failure to follow the example of the other major clubs in scheduling night games constituted negligence. Plaintiff made no allegation that these teams' night schedules were profitable or that the purpose for which night baseball had been undertaken was fulfilled. Furthermore, it cannot be said that directors, even those of corporations that are losing money, must follow the lead of the other corporations in the field. Directors are elected for their business capabilities and judgment, and the courts cannot require them to forego their judgment because of the decisions of directors of other companies. Courts may not decide these questions in the absence of a clear showing of dereliction of duty on the part of the specific directors, and mere failure to 'follow the crowd' is not such a dereliction.

"For the foregoing reasons the order of dismissal entered by the trial court is affirmed."

■ PROS AND CONS OF CORPORATE SOCIAL RESPONSIBILITY

Short-run profits versus long-term goodwill

One immediate response to pleas for corporate social responsibility is that it costs money and this cuts into profits. After all, a business's sole reason for existence is to make maximum profits for its investors, not to support the community. Also, if the business raises its prices to bring in extra revenue to support these "social responsibility costs," then the product becomes overpriced for the market and the "socially irresponsible" corporation will win in the marketplace because it can be more competitive, as it does not have to add the cost of social responsibility to its prices. With these convincing arguments, how can a business manager who has responsibility to corporate directors and shareholders ever be socially responsible?

The answer is clear. Socially responsible activities may reduce short-run profits; however, they can be justified by the belief that they will increase long-range profits. Social responsibility breeds goodwill; goodwill keeps business and brings in new business. Thus, in the long run social responsibility can be profitable. In our society, one cannot accept the classical Greeks' argument that all profits are bad. Today if a corporation or other business organization does not provide reasonable profits for its investor-owners, those investor-owners will take their funds elsewhere. Profit is and must remain a prime concern of managers. The problems are how much profit is needed before social responsibility expenditures can be justified, and what kinds of social activities the corporation should be concerned with.

Historically, individuals have felt a moral duty to serve their community and society by supporting charitable causes with contributions from their personal earnings, by giving their time to serve community needs, by helping those less fortunate in time of need, and in general giving not only money but also giving of themselves. Corporations are persons, true, but they are artificial rather than natural persons. Still, they take from the community and society, so why shouldn't they give back some of their wealth and expertise?

Another aspect of this problem is whether or not a corporate manager has a right to give away the stockholders' money for philanthropical or community purposes. The *Smith* v. *Barlow* case broke the ice and set a convenient precedent for other jurisdictions to follow. The U.S. Congress has also helped the cause of social responsibility by giving tax deductions for charitable contributions, which encourages companies to make charitable gifts.

A. P. SMITH MFG. CO. v. BARLOW

98 A.2d 581 (New Jersey, 1953)

FACTS

Smith Company made a contribution of $1,500 to Princeton University. Over the years, Smith had contributed to the local community chest, to Upsala College in East Orange, and to Newark University. Smith manufactured valves, fire hydrants, and special equipment for the water and gas industries. Barlow and other stockholders challenged the legality of the Princeton gift, since such gifts were neither expressly authorized nor (the stockholders claimed) impliedly authorized. Smith Co. filed a declaratory judgment action in the chancery division, which upheld the gift. The stockholders appealed.

ISSUE

Was this gift to a nonprofit educational institution within the corporation's implied powers?

DECISION

Yes. Judgment affirmed.

REASONS

Judge Jacobs noted that Smith's president thought that such contributions benefited the corporation by maintaining a favorable public climate for their business and by ensuring the "free flow of properly trained personnel for administrative and other corporate employment." The chairman of Standard Oil and the former chairman of U.S. Steel expressed similar feelings. Judge Jacobs then reviewed the history of corporate giving.

"In his discussion of the early history of business corporations Professor Williston refers to a 1702 publication where the author stated flatly that 'The general intent and end of all civil incorporations is for better government.' And he points out that the early corporate charters, particularly their recitals, furnish additional support for the notion that the corporate object was the public one of managing and ordering the trade as well as the private one of profit for the members. . . . However, with later economic and social developments and the free availability of the corporate device for all trades, the end of private profit became generally accepted as the controlling one in all businesses other than those classed broadly as public utilities. . . . The common-law rule developed that those who managed the corporation could not disburse any corporate funds for philanthropic or other worthy public cause unless the expenditure would benefit the corporation. . . .

"[C]ourts, while adhering to the terms of the common-law rule, have applied it very broadly to enable worthy corporate donations with indirect benefits to the corporations. . . .

"More and more [corporations] have come to recognize that their salvation rests upon sound economic and social environment which in turn rests in no insignificant part upon free and vigorous nongovernmental institutions of learning."

What social activity the firm will undertake or financially support is going to be an individual decision for each firm. No formula has been developed to determine just what role or what level of involvement is or should be expected of any firm.

■ CORPORATE SOCIAL AUDIT

How well are we meeting social needs?

In the 1988s we saw a process called *social auditing* emerge. Business managers who are concerned about corporate social responsibility seem convinced of the need for an accounting or audit procedure to determine just what is being done within their firm, whether the efforts are cost effective and aimed toward the proper goals for that particular firm, and whether the efforts are sufficient considering the resources involved.

The late 60s and 70s brought a great concern on the part of investors, consumers, and employees regarding the social activities of corporations. Management is beginning to realize that social responsibility can be profitable. Companies are becoming more concerned about their social image, and many have found that internal social audits give them information to use in their annual reports. Thus, favorable social audit results as well as favorable financial results are often shown in these annual reports.

How does a social audit differ from a financial audit? The answer is simple. In a financial audit there are standards of the profession and standards of law that must be adhered to; in a social audit, there are no standards of social responsibility, but there are basic legal standards regarding pollution, safety, and employment discrimination. However, as we have said before, social responsibility means performance beyond that which is legally required. The real purpose of the social audit is not to compare what you are doing to some standard of the profession. Rather, its purpose is to see what is presently being done in your firm in the area of social responsibility, then to serve as an aid in reviewing those findings, setting goals, and preparing long-range policies which can be implemented and reviewed in the future. Remember, corporate social responsibility is more than giving gifts to the United Way or to the local symphony group. It is real concern for employees, their needs, and their desires; it is better customer relations, a better product, and a better and more safe working environment, as well as many other areas of internal and external corporate activities previously commented on in this chapter.

A social audit is not required by law. It is simply a voluntary act of management. Management may take whatever action it pleases as a result of the audit. Of course, any violations of the law revealed by the audit must be corrected.

■ SIGNIFICANCE OF THIS CHAPTER

In this chapter we have reviewed the history of business ethics and corporate social responsibility, defined business ethics and corporate social responsibility, discussed the pros and cons of corporate social responsibility, and introduced a relatively new concept, the corporate social audit.

Since there is no enforceable code of business ethics or social responsibility, each manager has to develop a personal sense of moral consciousness to identify ethical issues that may be involved in the decision-making process. Managers need values that will help them consider the ethical issues as well as the traditional profit motives when making business decisions.

Businesspersons live in a very competitive environment, and it is often easy to justify wrongful actions, especially if the wrongful action produced a profit. Hopefully this chapter will show future business managers the need for the inclusion of ethical considerations as well as profit considerations in our business decision making. It is not true that ethical decisions are less profitable. In fact, corporations that have practiced corporate social responsibility in their daily decision making usually find their public image is much better than their less socially responsible competitors and, in the long run, the socially conscientious corporations usually come out ahead.

■ IMPORTANT TERMS AND CONCEPTS

ethical
internal ethical issues
employment at will
wrongful discharge
corporate social audit
golden rule

external ethical issues
age discrimination
corporate social
  responsibility
social auditing

■ QUESTIONS AND PROBLEMS FOR DISCUSSION

1. What is the difference between ethical conduct and lawful conduct?
2. What is employment at will? Explain and discuss the pros and cons of this doctrine.
3. What are the difficulties in establishing a code of ethics for business?
4. What is meant by the phrase "corporate social responsibility"?
5. Big Bucks Bakery Company makes cookies for various organizations to sell for fund-raising drives. After mixing a 1,000-pound batch of dough it was noted that a large box of rodent poison had been knocked over and got into the batter. One of the company chemists said the concentration would not be enough to cause a fatality, and it could not be detected by taste. People might get nauseated and possibly vomit, but the chemist didn't feel they would ever know where it came from. The problem is that the chemist tested the current batch, and that batch had no sign of the poison. The poisoned batch could have been made into cookies yesterday, last week, or any time in the last month. That was the last time anyone noticed the box of rodent poison being on the shelf and full. What do they do—close their eyes, or recall all the cookies baked in the last month?

6. Car Manufacturers, Inc. has designed a new model car. The only problem with the car is that the price is going to be noncompetitive, so the company officers and design engineers have to cut back on the cost of production. Many production cuts were made, but that was not enough. One last suggestion was to remove a protective steel bar and shield from the rear of the gas tank, thus saving several dollars. The counterargument was that if the car were struck from the rear end with considerable force, there is a good possibility that the unprotected gas tank could be ruptured and explode, killing the occupants. Should the company remove the protective shield and reduce the price of the car so it is competitive, even though they realize

that the car occupants could be killed because of this action, or should they keep the protective bar and shield and market the car based on safety features? Discuss.

7. Phil is the president of a large corporation, but he only owns relatively few shares. He was approached by several universities for corporate gifts. The board of directors authorized him to give gifts in the name of the company, not exceeding a total of $250,000 in that present fiscal year. They did not specify any specific universities to receive those gifts. On his own, Phil decided to give the entire amount to his alma mater rather than divide the sum between several universities. Is Phil in legal trouble? Did he act ethically?

8. During her senior year in the College of Business in Nebraska, Helen Senior was interviewed by the representatives of a number of business firms. A national accounting firm in New York City asked Helen to visit its head office for an interview during the Easter vacation. The company offered to pay all of her travel expenses. Helen lived in a suburb of New York City and found that three of her college friends were going back there. She would only have to pay one-fourth of the gas and oil. Shortly after returning home, Helen received a letter from the company asking for a statement of her expenses on the trip to New York. Although her travel had cost her only one-fourth of the gas and oil, Helen included in her account a charge of 22 cents per mile for automobile travel, reasoning that if she could arrange a less expensive ride to New York this was her business, a result of her own initiative, and that she had no obligation to pass this savings on to the company, especially since they did not need the money anyway. Was she right? Why or why not?

The Constitution of the United States

Preamble

We the People of the United States, in Order to form a more perfect Union, establish Justice, insure domestic Tranquility, provide for the common Defence, promote the general Welfare, and secure the Blessings of Liberty to ourselves and our Posterity, do ordain and establish this Constitution for the United States of America.

Article I

Section 1. All legislative Powers herein granted shall be vested in a Congress of the United States, which shall consist of a Senate and a House of Representatives.

Section 2. [1] The House of Representatives shall be composed of Members chosen every second Year by the People of the several States, and the Electors in each State shall have the Qualifications requisite for Electors of the most numerous Branch of the State Legislature.

[2] No Person shall be a Representative who shall not have attained to the Age of twenty five Years, and been seven Years a Citizen of the United States, and who shall not, when elected, be an Inhabitant of that State in which he shall be chosen.

[3] Representatives and direct Taxes shall be apportioned among the several States which may be included within this Union, according to their respective Numbers, which shall be determined by adding to the whole Number of free Persons, including those bound to Service for a Term of Years, and excluding Indians not taxed, three fifths of all other Persons. The actual Enumeration shall be made within three Years after the first Meeting of the Congress of the United States, and within every subsequent Term of ten Years, in such Manner as they shall by Law direct. The Number of Representatives shall not exceed one for every thirty Thousand, but each State shall have at Least one Representative; and until such enumeration shall be made, the State of New Hampshire shall

be entitled to chuse three, Massachusetts eight, Rhode Island and Providence Plantations one, Connecticut five, New York six, New Jersey four, Pennsylvania eight, Delaware one, Maryland six, Virginia ten, North Carolina five, South Carolina five, and Georgia three.

[4] When vacancies happen in the Representation from any State, the Executive Authority thereof shall issue Writs of Election to fill such Vacancies.

[5] The House of Representatives shall chuse their Speaker and other Officers; and shall have the sole Power of Impeachment.

Section 3. [1] The Senate of the United States shall be composed of two Senators from each State, chosen by the Legislature thereof, for six Years; and each Senator shall have one Vote.

[2] Immediately after they shall be assembled in Consequence of the first Election, they shall be divided as equally as may be into three Classes. The Seats of the Senators of the first Class shall be vacated at the Expiration of the Second Year, of the second Class at the Expiration of the fourth Year, and of the third Class at the Expiration of the sixth Year, so that one third may be chosen every second Year; and if Vacancies happen by Resignation, or otherwise, during the Recess of the Legislature of any State, the Executive thereof may make temporary Appointments until the next Meeting of the Legislature, which shall then fill such Vacancies.

[3] No Person shall be a Senator who shall not have attained to the Age of thirty Years, and been nine Years a Citizen of the United States, and who shall not, when elected, be an Inhabitant of that State for which he shall be chosen.

[4] The Vice President of the United States shall be President of the Senate, but shall have no Vote, unless they be equally divided.

[5] The Senate shall chuse their other Officers, and also a President pro tempore, in the Absence of the Vice

President, or when he shall exercise the Office of President of the United States.

[6] The Senate shall have the sole Power to try all Impeachments. When sitting for that Purpose, they shall be on Oath or Affirmation. When the President of the United States is tried, the Chief Justice shall preside: And no Person shall be convicted without the Concurrence of two thirds of the Members present.

[7] Judgment in Cases of Impeachment shall not extend further than to removal from Office, and disqualification to hold and enjoy any Office of Honor, Trust, or Profit under the United States: but the Party convicted shall nevertheless be liable and subject to Indictment, Trial, Judgment, and Punishment, according to Law.

Section 4. [1] The Times, Places and Manner of holding elections for Senators and Representatives, shall be prescribed in each State by the Legislature thereof; but the Congress may at any time by Law make or alter such Regulations, except as to the Places of chusing Senators.

[2] The Congress shall assemble at least once in every Year, and such Meeting shall be on the first Monday in December, unless they shall by Law appoint a different Day.

Section 5. [1] Each House shall be the Judge of the Elections, Returns, and Qualifications of its own Members, and a Majority of each shall constitute a Quorum to do Business; but a smaller Number may adjourn from day to day, and may be authorized to compel the Attendance of absent Members, in such Manner, and under such Penalties as each House may provide.

[2] Each House may determine the Rules of its Proceedings, punish its Members for disorderly Behavior, and, with the Concurrence of two thirds, expel a Member.

[3] Each House shall keep a Journal of its Proceedings, and from time to time publish the same, excepting such Parts as may in their Judgment require Secrecy; and the Yeas and Nays of the Members of either House on any question shall, at the Desire of one fifth of those Present, be entered on the Journal.

[4] Neither House, during the Session of Congress, shall, without the Consent of the other, adjourn for more than three days, nor to any other Place than that in which the two Houses shall be sitting.

Section 6. [1] The Senators and Representatives shall receive a Compensation for their Services, to be ascertained by Law, and paid out of the Treasury of the United States. They shall in all Cases, except Treason, Felony and Breach of the Peace, be privileged from Arrest during their Attendance at the Session of their respective Houses, and in going to and returning from the same; and for any Speech or Debate in either House, they shall not be questioned in any other Place.

[2] No Senator or Representative shall, during the Time for which he was elected, be appointed to any civil Office under the Authority of the United States, which shall have been created, or the Emoluments whereof shall have been increased during such time; and no Person holding any Office under the United States, shall be a Member of either House during his Continuance in Office.

Section 7. [1] All Bills for raising Revenue shall originate in the House of Representatives; but the Senate may propose or concur with Amendments as on other Bills.

[2] Every Bill which shall have passed the House of Representatives and the Senate, shall, before it becomes a Law, be presented to the President of the United States; If he approve he shall sign it, but if not he shall return it, with his Objections to the House in which it shall have originated, who shall enter the Objections at large on their Journal, and proceed to reconsider it. If after such Reconsideration two thirds of that House shall agree to pass the Bill, it shall be sent together with the Objections, to the other House, by which it shall likewise be reconsidered, and if approved by two thirds of that House, it shall become a Law. But in all such Cases the Votes of both Houses shall be determined by Yeas and Nays, and the Names of the Persons voting for and against the Bill shall be entered on the Journal of each House respectively. If any Bill shall not be returned by the President within ten Days (Sundays excepted) after it shall have been presented to him, the Same shall be a Law, in like Manner as if he had signed it, unless the Congress by their Adjournment prevent its Return in which Case it shall not be a Law.

[3] Every Order, Resolution, or Vote, to Which the Concurrence of the Senate and House of Representatives may be necessary (except on a question of Adjournment) shall be presented to the President of the United States; and before the Same shall take Effect, shall be approved by him, or being disapproved by him, shall be repassed by two thirds of the Senate and House of Representatives, according to the Rules and Limitations prescribed in the Case of a Bill.

Section 8. [1] The Congress shall have Power To lay and collect Taxes, Duties, Imposts and Excises, to pay the Debts and provide for the common Defence and general Welfare of the United States; but all Duties, Imposts and Excises shall be uniform throughout the United States;

[2] To borrow money on the credit of the United States;

[3] To regulate Commerce with foreign Nations, and among the several States, and with the Indian Tribes;

[4] To establish an Uniform Rule of Naturalization, and uniform Laws on the subject of Bankruptcies throughout the United States;

[5] To coin Money, regulate the Value thereof, and of foreign Coin, and fix the Standard of Weights and Measures;

[6] To provide for the Punishment of counterfeiting the Securities and current Coin of the United States;

[7] To Establish Post Offices and Post Roads;

[8] To promote the Progress of Science and useful Arts, by securing for limited Times to Authors and Inventors the exclusive Right to their respective Writings and Discoveries;

[9] To constitute Tribunals inferior to the supreme Court;

[10] To define and punish Piracies and Felonies committed on the high Seas, and Offenses against the Law of Nations;

[11] To declare War, grant Letters of Marque and Reprisal, and make Rules concerning Captures on Land and Water;

[12] To raise and support Armies, but no Appropriation of Money to that Use shall be for a longer Term than two Years;

[13] To provide and maintain a Navy;

[14] To make Rules for the Government and Regulation of the land and naval Forces;

[15] To provide for calling forth the Militia to execute the Laws of the Union, suppress Insurrections and repel Invasions;

[16] To provide for organizing, arming, and disciplining, the Militia, and for governing such Part of them as may be employed in the Service of the United States, reserving to the States respectively, the Appointment of the Officers, and the Authority of training the Militia according to the discipline prescribed by Congress;

[17] To exercise exclusive Legislation in all Cases whatsoever, over such District (not exceeding ten Miles square) as may, by Cession of particular States, and the Acceptance of Congress, become the Seat of the Government of the United States, and to exercise like Authority over all Places purchased by the Consent of the Legislature of the State in which the Same shall be, for the Erection of Forts, Magazines, Arsenals, dock-Yards and other needful Buildings;—And

[18] To make all Laws which shall be necessary and proper for carrying into Execution the foregoing Powers, and all other Powers vested by this Constitution in the Government of the United States, or in any Department or Officer thereof.

Section 9. [1] The Migration or Importation of Such Persons as any of the States now existing shall think proper to admit, shall not be prohibited by the Congress prior to the Year one thousand eight hundred and eight, but a Tax or duty may be imposed on such Importation, not exceeding ten dollars for each Person.

[2] The privilege of the Writ of Habeas Corpus shall not be suspended, unless when in Cases of Rebellion or Invasion the public Safety may require it.

[3] No Bill of Attainder or ex post facto Law shall be passed.

[4] No Capitation, or other direct, Tax shall be laid, unless in Proportion to the Census or Enumeration herein before directed to be taken.

[5] No Tax or Duty shall be laid on Articles exported from any State.

[6] No Preference shall be given by any Regulation of Commerce or Revenue to the Ports of one State over those of another: nor shall Vessels bound to, or from, one State be obliged to enter, clear, or pay Duties in another.

[7] No money shall be drawn from the Treasury, but in Consequence of Appropriations made by Law; and a regular Statement and Account of the Receipts and Expenditures of all public Money shall be published from time to time.

[8] No Title of Nobility shall be granted by the United States: And no Person holding any Office of Profit or Trust under them, shall, without the Consent of the Congress, accept of any present, Emolument, Office, or Title, of any kind whatever, from any King, Prince, or foreign State.

Section 10. [1] No State shall enter into any Treaty, Alliance, or Confederation; grant Letters of Marque and Reprisal; coin Money; emit Bills of Credit; make any Thing but gold and silver Coin a Tender in Payment of Debts; pass any Bill of Attainder, ex post facto Law, or Law impairing the Obligation of Contracts, or grant any Title of Nobility.

[2] No State shall, without the Consent of the Congress, lay any Imposts or Duties on Imports or Exports, except what may be absolutely necessary for executing its inspection Laws: and the net Produce of all Duties and Imposts, laid by any State on Imports or Exports, shall be for the Use of the Treasury of the United States; and all such Laws shall be subject to the Revision and Control of the Congress.

[3] No State shall, without the Consent of Congress, lay any Duty of Tonnage, keep Troops, or Ships of War in time of Peace, enter into any Agreement or Compact with another State, or with a foreign Power, or engage in War, unless actually invaded, or in such imminent Danger as will not admit of delay.

Article II

Section 1. [1] The executive Power shall be vested in a President of the United States of America. He shall hold his Office during the Term of four Years, and, together with the Vice President, chosen for the same Term, be elected, as follows:

[2] Each State shall appoint, in such Manner as the Legislature thereof may direct, a Number of Electors, equal to the whole Number of Senators and Representatives to which the State may be entitled in the Congress; but no Senator or Representative, or Person holding an Office of Trust or Profit under the United States, shall be appointed an Elector.

[3] The Electors shall meet in their respective States, and vote by Ballot for two Persons, of whom one at least shall not be an Inhabitant of the same State with themselves. And they shall make a List of all the Persons voted for, and of the Number of Votes for each; which List they shall sign and certify, and transmit sealed to the Seat of the Government of the United States, directed to the President of the Senate. The President of the Senate shall, in the Presence of the Senate and House of Representatives, open all the Certificates, and the Votes shall then be counted. The Person having the greatest Number of Votes shall be the President, if such Number be a Majority of the whole Number of Electors appointed; and if there be more than one who have such Majority, and have an equal Number of Votes, then the House of Representatives shall immediately chuse by Ballot one of them for President; and if no Person have a Majority, then from the five highest on the List the said House shall in like Manner chuse the President. But in chusing the President, the Votes shall be taken by States, the Representation from each State having one Vote; A quorum for this Purpose shall consist of a Member or Members from two thirds of the States, and a Majority of all the States shall be necessary to a Choice. In every Case, after the Choice of the President, the Person having the greater Number of Votes of the Electors shall be the Vice President. But if there shall remain two or more who have equal Votes, the Senate shall chuse from them by Ballot the Vice President.

[4] The Congress may determine the Time of chusing the Electors, and the Day on which they shall give their Votes; which Day shall be the same throughout the United States.

[5] No Person except a natural born Citizen, or a Citizen of the United States, at the time of the Adoption of this Constitution, shall be eligible to the Office of President; neither shall any Person be eligible to that Office who shall not have attained to the Age of thirty-five Years, and been fourteen Years a Resident within the United States.

[6] In Case of the Removal of the President from Office, or of his Death, Resignation, or Inability to discharge the Powers and Duties of the said Office, the Same shall devolve on the Vice President, and the Congress may by Law provide for the Case of Removal, Death, Resignation or Inability, both of the President and Vice President, declaring what Officer shall then act as President, and such Officer shall act accordingly, until the Disability be removed, or a President shall be elected.

[7] The President shall, at stated Times, receive for his Services, a Compensation, which shall neither be increased nor diminished during the Period for which he shall have been elected, and he shall not receive within that Period any other Emolument from the United States, or any of them.

[8] Before he enter on the Execution of his Office, he shall take the following Oath or Affirmation: "I do solemnly swear (or affirm) that I will faithfully execute the Office of President of the United States, and will to the best of my Ability, preserve, protect and defend the Constitution of the United States."

Section 2. [1] The President shall be Commander in Chief of the Army and Navy of the United States, and of the militia of the several States, when called into the actual Service of the United States; he may require the Opinion, in writing, of the principal Officer in each of the Executive Departments, upon any Subject relating to the Duties of their respective Offices, and he shall have Power to grant Reprieves and Pardons for Offenses against the United States, except in Cases of Impeachment.

[2] He shall have Power, by and with the Advice and Consent of the Senate to make Treaties, provided two thirds of the Senators present concur; and he shall nominate, and by and with the Advice and Consent of the Senate, shall appoint Ambassadors, other public Ministers and Consuls, Judges of the supreme Court, and all other Officers of the United States, whose Appointments are not herein otherwise provided for, and which shall be established by Law; but the Congress may by Law vest the Appointment of such inferior Officers, as they think proper, in the President alone, in the Courts of Law, or in the Heads of Departments.

[3] The President shall have Power to fill up all Vacancies that may happen during the Recess of the Senate, by granting Commissions which shall expire at the End of their next Session.

Section 3. He shall from time to time give to the Congress Information of the State of the Union, and recommend to their Consideration such Measures as he shall judge necessary and expendient; he may, on extraordinary Occasions, convene both Houses, or either of them, and in Case of Disagreement between them, with Respect to the Time of Adjournment, he may adjourn them to such Time as he shall think proper; he shall receive Ambassadors and other public Ministers; he shall take Care that the Laws be faithfully executed, and shall Commission all the Officers of the United States.

Section 4. The President, Vice President and all civil Officers of the United States, shall be removed from Office on Impeachment for, and Conviction of, Treason, Bribery, or other high Crimes and Misdemeanors.

Article III

Section 1. The judicial Power of the United States, shall be vested in one supreme Court, and in such inferior Courts as the Congress may from time to time ordain and establish. The Judges, both of the supreme and inferior Courts, shall hold their Offices during good Behaviour, and shall, at stated Times, receive for their Services a Compensation, which shall not be diminished during their Continuance in Office.

Section 2. [1] The judicial Power shall extend to all Cases, in Law and Equity, arising under this Constitution, the Laws of the United States, and Treaties made, or which shall be made, under their Authority;—to all Cases affecting Ambassadors, other public Ministers and Consuls;—to all Cases of admiralty and maritime Jurisdiction;—to Controversies to which the United States shall be a Party;—to Controversies between two or more States;—between a State and Citizens of another State;—between Citizens of different States;—between Citizens of the same State claiming Lands under the Grants of different States, and between a State, or the Citizens thereof, and foreign States, Citizens or Subjects.

[2] In all Cases affecting Ambassadors, other public Ministers and Consuls, and those in which a State shall be a Party, the supreme Court shall have original Jurisdiction. In all the other Cases before mentioned, the supreme Court shall have appellate Jurisdiction, both as to Law and Fact, with such Exceptions, and under such Regulations as the Congress shall make.

[3] The trial of all Crimes, except in Cases of Impeachment, shall be by Jury; and such Trial shall be held in the State where the said Crimes shall have been committed; but when not committed within any State, the Trial shall be at such Place or Places as the Congress may by Law have directed.

Section 3. [1] Treason against the United States, shall consist only in levying War against them, or, in adhering to their Enemies, giving them Aid and Comfort. No Person shall be convicted of Treason unless on the Testimony of two Witnesses to the same overt Act, or on Confession in open Court.

[2] The Congress shall have Power to declare the Punishment of Treason, but no Attainder of Treason shall work Corruption of Blood, or Forfeiture except during the Life of the Person attainted.

Article IV

Section 1. Full Faith and Credit shall be given in each State to the public Acts, Records, and judicial Proceedings of every other State. And the Congress may by general Laws prescribe the Manner in which such Acts, Records and Proceedings shall be proved, and the Effect thereof.

Section 2. [1] The Citizens of each State shall be entitled to all Privileges and Immunities of Citizens in the several States.

[2] A Person charged in any State with Treason, Felony, or other Crime, who shall flee from Justice, and be found in another State, shall on demand of the executive Authority of the State from which he fled, be delivered up, to be removed to the State having Jurisdiction of the Crime.

[3] No Person held to Service or Labour in one State, under the Laws thereof, escaping into another, shall, in Consequence of any Law or Regulation therein, be discharged from such Service or Labour, but shall be delivered up on Claim of the Party to whom such Service or Labour may be due.

Section 3. [1] New States may be admitted by the Congress into this Union; but no new State shall be formed or erected within the Jurisdiction of any other State; nor any State be formed by the Junction of two or more States, or Parts of States, without the Consent of the Legislatures of the States concerned as well as of the Congress.

[2] The Congress shall have Power to dispose of and make all needful Rules and Regulations respecting the Territory or other Property belonging to the United States; and nothing in this Constitution shall be so construed as to Prejudice any Claims of the United States, or of any particular State.

Section 4. The United States shall guarantee to every State in this Union a Republican Form of Government, and shall protect each of them against Invasion; and on Application of the Legislature, or of the Executive (when the Legislature cannot be convened) against domestic Violence.

Article V

The Congress, whenever two thirds of both Houses shall deem it necessary, shall propose Amendments to this Constitution, or, on the Application of the Legislatures of two thirds of the several States, shall call a Convention for proposing Amendments, which, in either case, shall be valid to all Intents and Purposes, as part of this Constitution, when ratified by the Legislatures of three fourths of the several States, or by Conventions in three fourths thereof, as the one or the other Mode of Ratification may be proposed by the Congress; Provided that no Amendment which may be made prior to the Year One thousand eight hundred and eight shall in any Manner affect the first and fourth Clauses in the Ninth Section of the first Article; and that no State, without its Consent, shall be deprived of its equal Suffrage in the Senate.

Article VI

[1] All Debts contracted and Engagements entered into, before the Adoption of this Constitution, shall be as valid against the United States under this Constitution, as under the Confederation.

[2] This Constitution, and the Laws of the United States which shall be made in Pursuance thereof; and all Treaties made, or which shall be made, under the Authority of the United States, shall be the supreme Law of the Land; and the Judges in every State shall be bound thereby, any Thing in the Constitution or Laws of any State to the Contrary notwithstanding.

[3] The Senators and Representatives before mentioned, and the Members of the several State Legislatures, and all executive and judicial Officers, both of the United States and of the several States, shall be bound by Oath or Affirmation, to support this Constitution; but no religious Test shall ever be required as a Qualification to any Office or public Trust under the United States.

Article VII

The Ratification of the Conventions of nine States shall be sufficient for the Establishment of this Constitution between the States so ratifying the Same.

Articles in addition to, and amendment of, the Constitution of the United States of America, proposed by Congress, and ratified by the Legislatures of the several States pursuant to the Fifth Article of the original Constitution.

Amendment I [1791]

Congress shall make no law respecting an establishment of religion, or prohibiting the free exercise thereof; or abridging the freedom of speech, or of the press; or the right of the people peaceably to assemble, and to petition the Government for a redress of grievances.

Amendment II [1791]

A well regulated Militia, being necessary to the security of a free State, the right of the people to keep and bear Arms, shall not be infringed.

Amendment III [1791]

No Soldier shall, in time of peace be quartered in any house, without the consent of the Owner, nor in time of war, but in a manner to be prescribed by law.

Amendment IV [1791]

The right of the people to be secure in their persons, houses, papers, and effects, against unreasonable searches and seizures, shall not be violated, and no Warrants shall issue, but upon probable cause, supported by Oath or affirmation, and particularly describing the place to be searched, and the persons or things to be seized.

Amendment V [1791]

No person shall be held to answer for a capital, or otherwise infamous crime, unless on a presentment or indictment of a Grand Jury, except in cases arising in the land or naval forces, or in the Militia, when in actual service in time of War or public danger; nor shall any person be subject for the same offence to be twice put in jeopardy of life or limb; nor shall be compelled in any criminal case to be a witness against himself, nor be deprived of life, liberty, or property, without due process of law; nor shall private property be taken for public use, without just compensation.

Amendment VI [1791]

In all criminal prosecutions, the accused shall enjoy the right to a speedy and public trial, by an impartial jury of the State and district wherein the crime shall have been committed, which district shall have been previously ascertained by law, and to be informed of the nature and cause of the accusation; to be confronted with the witnesses against him; to have compulsory process for obtaining witnesses in his favor, and to have the Assistance of Counsel for his defence.

Amendment VII [1791]

In Suits at common law, where the value in controversy shall exceed twenty dollars, the right of trial by jury shall be preserved, and no fact tried by jury, shall be otherwise reexamined in any Court of the United States, than according to the rules of common law.

Amendment VIII [1791]

Excessive bail shall not be required, nor excessive fines imposed, nor cruel and unusual punishments inflicted.

Amendment IX [1791]

The enumeration in the Constitution, of certain rights, shall not be construed to deny or disparage others retained by the people.

Amendment X [1791]

The powers not delegated to the United States by the Constitution, nor prohibited by it to the States, are reserved to the States respectively, or to the people.

Amendment XI [1798]

The Judicial power in the United States shall not be construed to extend to any suit in law or equity, commenced or prosecuted against one of the United States by Citizens of another State, or by Citizens or Subjects of any Foreign State.

Amendment XII [1804]

The Electors shall meet in their respective states and vote by ballot for President and Vice-President, one of whom, at least, shall not be an inhabitant of the same state with themselves; they shall name in their ballots the person voted for as President, and in distinct ballots the person voted for as Vice-President, and they shall make distinct lists of all persons voted for as President, and of all persons voted for as Vice-President, and of the number of votes for each, which lists they shall sign and certify, and transmit sealed to the seat of the government of the United States, directed to the President of the Senate;—The President

of the Senate shall, in the presence of the Senate and House of Representatives, open all the certificates and the votes shall then be counted;—The person having the greatest number of votes for President, shall be the President, if such number be a majority of the whole number of Electors appointed; and if no person have such majority, then from the persons having the highest numbers not exceeding three on the list of those voted for as President, the House of Representatives shall choose immediately, by ballot, the President. But in choosing the President, the votes shall be taken by states, the representation from each state having one vote; a quorum for this purpose shall consist of a member or members from two-thirds of the states, and a majority of all states shall be necessary to a choice. And if the House of Representatives shall not choose a President whenever the right of choice shall devolve upon them before the fourth day of March next following, then the Vice-President shall act as President, as in the case of the death or other constitutional disability of the President.—The person having the greatest number of votes as Vice-President, shall be the Vice-President, if such number be a majority of the whole number of Electors appointed, and if no person have a majority, then from the two highest numbers on the list, the Senate shall choose the Vice-President; a quorum for the purpose shall consist of two-thirds of the whole number of Senators, and a majority of the whole number shall be necessary to a choice. But no person constitutionally ineligible to the office of President shall be eligible to that of Vice-President of the United States.

Amendment XIII [1865]

Section 1. Neither slavery nor involuntary servitude, except as a punishment for crime whereof the party shall have been duly convicted, shall exist within the United States, or any place subject to their jurisdiction.

Section 2. Congress shall have power to enforce this article by appropriate legislation.

Amendment XIV [1868]

Section 1. All persons born or naturalized in the United States, and subject to the jurisdiction thereof, are citizens of the United States and of the State wherein they reside. No State shall make or enforce any law which shall abridge the privileges or immunities of citizens of the United States; nor shall any State deprive any person of life, liberty, or property, without due process of law; nor deny to any person within its jurisdiction the equal protection of the laws.

Section 2. Representatives shall be apportioned among the several States according to their respective numbers, counting the whole number of persons in each State, excluding Indians not taxed. But when the right to vote at any election for the choice of electors for President and Vice President of the United States, Representatives in Congress, the Executive and Judicial officers of a State, or the members of the Legislature thereof, is denied to any of the male inhabitants of such State, being twenty-one years of age, and citizens of the United States, or in any way abridged, except for participation in rebellion, or other crime, the basis of representation therein shall be reduced in the proportion which the number of such male citizens shall bear to the whole number of male citizens twenty-one years of age in such State.

Section 3. No person shall be a Senator or Representative in Congress, or elector of President and Vice President, or hold any office, civil or military, under the United States, or under any State, who having previously taken an oath, as a member of Congress, or as an officer of the United States, or as a member of any State legislature, or as an executive or judicial officer of any State, to support the Constitution of the United States, shall have engaged in insurrection or rebellion against the same, or given aid or comfort to the enemies thereof. But Congress may by a vote of two-thirds of each House, remove such disability.

Section 4. The validity of the public debt of the United States, authorized by law, including debts incurred for payment of pensions and bounties for services in suppressing insurrection or rebellion, shall not be questioned. But neither the United States nor any State shall assume or pay any debt or obligation incurred in aid of insurrection or rebellion against the United States, or any claim for the loss or emancipation of any slave; but all such debts, obligations and claims shall be held illegal and void.

Section 5. The Congress shall have power to enforce, by appropriate legislation, the provisions of this article.

Amendment XV [1870]

Section 1. The right of citizens of the United States to vote shall not be denied or abridged by the United States or by any State on account of race, color, or previous condition of servitude.

Section 2. The Congress shall have power to enforce this article by appropriate legislation.

Amendment XVI [1913]

The Congress shall have power to lay and collect taxes on incomes, from whatever source derived, without apportionment among the several States, and without regard to any census or enumeration.

Amendment XVII [1913]

[1] The Senate of the United States shall be composed of two Senators from each State, elected by the people thereof, for six years; and each Senator shall have one vote. The electors in each State shall have the qualifications requisite for electors of the most numerous branch of the State legislature.

[2] When vacancies happen in the representation of any State in the Senate, the executive authority of such State shall issue writs of election to fill such vacancies: *Provided,* That the legislature of any State may empower the executive thereof to make temporary appointments until the people fill the vacancies by election as the legislature may direct.

[3] This amendment shall not be so construed as to affect the election or term of any Senator chosen before it becomes valid as part of the Constitution.

Amendment XVIII [1919]

Section 1. After one year from the ratification of this article the manufacture, sale, or transportation of intoxicating liquors within, the importation thereof into, or the exportation thereof from the United States and all territory subject to the jurisdiction thereof for beverage purposes is hereby prohibited.

Section 2. The Congress and the several States shall have concurrent power to enforce this article by appropriate legislation.

Section 3. This article shall be inoperative unless it shall have been ratified as an amendment to the Constitution by the legislatures of the several States, as provided in the Constitution, within seven years from the date of the submission hereof to the States by the Congress.

Amendment XIX [1920]

[1] The right of citizens of the United States to vote shall not be denied or abridged by the United States or by any State on account of sex.

[2] Congress shall have power to enforce this article by appropriate legislation.

Amendment XX [1933]

Section 1. The terms of the President and Vice President shall end at noon on the 20th day of January, and the terms of Senators and Representatives at noon on the 3d day of January, of the years in which such terms would have ended if this article had not been ratified; and the terms of their successors shall then begin.

Section 2. The Congress shall assemble at least once in every year, and such meeting shall begin at noon on the 3d day of January, unless they shall by law appoint a different day.

Section 3. If, at the time fixed for the beginning of the term of the President, the President elect shall have died, the Vice President elect shall become President. If the President shall not have been chosen before the time fixed for the beginning of his term, or if the President elect shall have failed to qualify, then the Vice President elect shall act as President until a President shall have qualified; and the Congress may by law provide for the case wherein neither a President elect nor a Vice President elect shall have qualified, declaring who shall then act as President, or the manner in which one who is to act shall be selected, and such person shall act accordingly until a President or Vice President shall have qualified.

Section 4. The Congress may by law provide for the case of the death of any of the persons from whom the House of Representatives may choose a President whenever the right of choice shall have devolved upon them, and for the case of the death of any of the persons from whom the Senate may choose a Vice President whenever the right of choice shall have devolved upon them.

Section 5. Sections 1 and 2 shall take effect on the 15th day of October following the ratification of this article.

Section 6. This article shall be inoperative unless it shall have been ratified as an amendment to the Constitution by the legislatures of three-fourths of the several States within seven years from the date of its submission.

Amendment XXI [1933]

Section 1. The eighteenth article of amendment to the Constitution of the United States is hereby repealed.

Section 2. The transportation or importation into any State, Territory, or possession of the United States for delivery or use therein of intoxicating liquors, in violation of the laws thereof, is hereby prohibited.

Section 3. This article shall be inoperative unless it shall have been ratified as an amendment to the Constitution by conventions in the several States, as provided in the Constitution, within seven years from the date of the submission hereof to the States by the Congress.

Amendment XXII [1951]

Section 1. No person shall be elected to the office of the President more than twice, and no person who has held the office of President, or acted as President, for more than two years of a term to which some other person was elected President shall be elected to the office of President more than once. But this Article shall not apply to any person holding the office of President when this Article was proposed by the Congress, and shall not prevent any person who may be holding the office of President, or acting as President, during the term within which this Article becomes operative from holding the office of President or acting as President during the remainder of such term.

Section 2. This article shall be inoperative unless it shall have been ratified as an amendment to the Constitution by the legislatures of three-fourths of the several States within seven years from the date of its submission to the States by the Congress.

Amendment XXIII [1961]

Section 1. The District constituting the seat of Government of the United States shall appoint in such manner as the Congress may direct:

A number of electors of President and Vice President equal to the whole number of Senators and Representatives in Congress to which the District would be entitled if it were a State, but in no event more than the least populous state; they shall be in addition to those appointed by the states, but they shall be considered, for the purposes of the election of President and Vice President, to be electors appointed by a state; and they shall meet in the District and perform such duties as provided by the twelfth article of amendment.

Section 2. The Congress shall have power to enforce this article by appropriate legislation.

Amendment XXIV [1964]

Section 1. The right of citizens of the United States to vote in any primary or other election for President or Vice President, for electors for President or Vice President or for Senator or Representative in Congress, shall not be denied or abridged by the United States, or any State by reason of failure to pay any poll tax or other tax.

Section 2. The Congress shall have power to enforce this article by appropriate legislation.

Amendment XXV [1967]

Section 1. In case of the removal of the President from office or of his death or resignation, the Vice President shall become President.

Section 2. Whenever there is a vacancy in the office of the Vice President, the President shall nominate a Vice

President who shall take office upon confirmation by a majority vote of both Houses of Congress.

Section 3. Whenever the President transmits to the President pro tempore of the Senate and the Speaker of the House of Representatives his written declaration that he is unable to discharge the powers and duties of his office, and until he transmits to them a written declaration to the contrary, such powers and duties shall be discharged by the Vice President as Acting President.

Section 4. Whenever the Vice President and a majority of either the principal officers of the executive departments or of such other body as Congress may by law provide, transmit to the President pro tempore of the Senate and the Speaker of the House of Representatives their written declaration that the President is unable to discharge the powers and duties of his office, the Vice President shall immediately assume the powers and duties of the office as Acting President.

Thereafter, when the President transmits to the President pro tempore of the Senate and the Speaker of the House of Representatives his written declaration that no inability exists, he shall resume the powers and duties of his office unless the Vice President and a majority of either the principal officers of the executive department or of such other body as Congress may by law provide, transmit within four days to the President pro tempore of the Senate and the Speaker of the House of Representatives their written declaration and the President is unable to discharge the powers and duties of his office. Thereupon Congress shall decide the issue, assembling within forty-eight hours for that purpose if not in session. If the Congress, within twenty-one days after receipt of the latter written declaration, or, if Congress is not in session, within twenty-one days after Congress is required to assemble, determines by two-thirds vote of both Houses that the President is unable to discharge the powers and duties of his office, the Vice President shall continue to discharge the same as Acting President; otherwise, the President shall resume the powers and duties of his office.

Amendment XXVI [1971]

Section 1. The right of citizens of the United States, who are eighteen years of age or older, to vote shall not be denied or abridged by the United States or by any State on account of age.

Section 2. The Congress shall have power to enforce this article by appropriate legislation.

APPENDIX B

Uniform Commercial Code (1978 Text with 1987 Amendments)*

TITLE

An Act
To be known as the Uniform Commercial Code, Relating to Certain Commercial Transactions in or regarding Personal Property and Contracts and other Documents concerning them, including Sales, Commercial Paper, Bank Deposits and Collections, Letters of Credit, Bulk Transfers, Warehouse Receipts, Bills of Lading, other Documents of Title, Investment Securities, and Secured Transactions, including certain Sales of Accounts, Chattel Paper, and Contract Rights; Providing for Public Notice to Third Parties in Certain Circumstances; Regulating Procedure, Evidence and Damages in Certain Court Actions Involving such Transactions, Contracts or Documents; to Make Uniform the Law with Respect Thereto; and Repealing Inconsistent Legislation.

Article 1 General Provisions

Part 1 Short Title, Construction, Application and Subject Matter of the Act

Section 1–101. Short Title

This Act shall be known and may be cited as Uniform Commercial Code.

Section 1–102. Purposes; Rules of Construction; Variation by Agreement

(1) This Act shall be liberally construed and applied to promote its underlying purposes and policies.

(2) Underlying purposes and policies of this Act are

    (a) to simplify, clarify and modernize the law governing commercial transactions;

    (b) to permit the continued expansion of commercial practices through custom, usage and agreement of the parties;

    (c) to make uniform the law among the various jurisdictions.

(3) The effect of provisions of this Act may be varied by agreement, except as otherwise provided in this Act and except that the obligations of good faith, diligence, reasonableness and care prescribed by this Act may not be disclaimed by agreement but the parties may by agreement determine the standards by which the performance of such obligations is to be measured if such standards are not manifestly unreasonable.

(4) The presence in certain provisions of this Act of the word "unless otherwise agreed" or words of similar import does not imply that the effect of other provisions may not be varied by agreement under subsection (3).

(5) In this Act unless the context otherwise requires

    (a) words in the singular number include the plural, and in the plural include the singular;

    (b) words of the masculine gender include the feminine and the neuter, and when the sense so indicates words of the neuter gender may refer to any gender.

Section 1–103. Supplementary General Principles of Law Applicable

Unless displaced by the particular provisions of this Act, the principles of law and equity, including the law merchant and the law relative to capacity to contract, principal and agent, estoppel, fraud, misrepresentation, duress, coercion, mistake, bankruptcy, or other validating or invalidating cause shall supplement its provisions.

Section 1–104. Construction Against Implicit Repeal

This Act being a general act intended as a unified coverage of its subject matter, no part of it shall be deemed to be

---

impliedly repealed by subsequent legislation if such construction can reasonably be avoided.

Section 1–105. Territorial Application of the Act; Parties' Power to Choose Applicable Law (Text omitted)

Section 1–106. Remedies to Be Liberally Administered (Text omitted)

Section 1–107. Waiver or Renunciation of Claim or Right After Breach (Text omitted)

Section 1–108. Severability

If any provision or clause of this Act or application thereof to any person or circumstances is held invalid, such invalidity shall not affect other provisions or applications of the Act which can be given effect without the invalid provision or application, and to this end the provisions of this Act are declared to be severable.

Section 1–109. Section Captions

Section captions are parts of this Act.

Part 2 General Definitions and Principles of Interpretation

Section 1–201. General Definitions

Subject to additional definitions contained in the subsequent Articles of this Act which are applicable to specific Articles or Parts thereof, and unless the context otherwise requires, in this Act:

(1) "Action" in the sense of a judicial proceeding includes recoupment, counterclaim, set-off, suit in equity and any other proceedings in which rights are determined.

(2) "Aggrieved party" means a party entitled to resort to a remedy.

(3) "Agreement" means the bargain of the parties in fact as found in their language or by implication from other circumstances including course of dealing or usage of trade or course of performance as provided in this Act (Sections 1–205 and 2–208). Whether an agreement has legal consequences is determined by the provisions of this Act, if applicable; otherwise by the law of contracts (Section 1–103). (Compare "Contract.")

(4) "Bank" means any person engaged in the business of banking.

(5) "Bearer" means the person in possession of an instrument, document of title, or certificated security payable to bearer or indorsed in blank.

(6) "Bill of lading" means a document evidencing the receipt of goods for shipment issued by a person engaged in the business of transporting or forwarding goods, and includes an airbill. "Airbill" means a document serving for air transportation as a bill of lading does for marine or rail transportation, and includes an air consignment note or air waybill.

(7) "Branch" includes a separately incorporated foreign branch of a bank.

(8) "Burden of establishing" a fact means the burden of persuading the triers of fact that the existence of the fact is more probable than its non-existence.

(9) "Buyer in ordinary course of business" means a person who in good faith and without knowledge that the sale to him is in violation of the ownership rights or security interest of a third party in the goods buys in ordinary course from a person in the business of selling goods of that kind but does not include a pawnbroker. All persons who sell minerals or the like (including oil and gas) at wellhead or minehead shall be deemed to be persons in the business of selling goods of that kind. "Buying" may be for cash or by exchange of other property or on secured or unsecured credit and includes receiving goods or documents of title under a pre-existing contract for sale but does not include a transfer in bulk or as security for or in total or partial satisfaction of a money debt.

(10) "Conspicuous": A term or clause is conspicuous when it is so written that a reasonable person against whom it is to operate ought to have noticed it. A printed heading in capitals (as: Non-Negotiable Bill of Lading) is conspicuous. Language in the body of a form is "conspicuous" if it is in larger or other contrasting type or color. But in a telegram any stated term is "conspicuous." Whether a term or clause is "conspicuous" or not is for decision by the court.

(11) "Contract" means the total legal obligation which results from the parties' agreement as affected by this Act and any other applicable rules of law. (Compare "Agreement.")

(12) "Creditor" includes a general creditor, a secured creditor, a lien creditor and any representative of creditors, including an assignee for the benefit of creditors, a trustee in bankruptcy, a receiver in equity and an executor or administrator of an insolvent debtor's or assignor's estate.

(13) "Defendant" includes a person in the position of defendant in a cross-section or counterclaim.

(14) "Delivery" with respect to instruments, documents of title, chattel paper, or certificated securities means voluntary transfer of possession.

(15) "Document of title" includes bill of lading, dock warrant, dock receipt, warehouse receipt or order for the delivery of goods, and also any other document which in the regular course of business or financing is treated as adequately evidencing that the person in possession

of it is entitled to receive, hold and dispose of the document and the goods it covers. To be a document of title a document must purport to be issued by or addressed to a bailee and purport to cover goods in the bailee's possession which are either identified or are fungible portions of an identified mass.

(16) "Fault" means wrongful act, omission or breach.

(17) "Fungible" with respect to goods or securities means goods or securities of which any unit is, by nature or usage of trade, the equivalent of any other like unit. Goods which are not fungible shall be deemed fungible for the purposes of this Act to the extent that under a particular agreement or document unlike units are treated as equivalents.

(18) "Genuine" means free of forgery or counterfeiting.

(19) "Good faith" means honesty in fact in the conduct or transaction concerned.

(20) "Holder" means a person who is in possession of a document of title or an instrument or a certificated investment security drawn, issued, or indorsed to him or his order or to bearer or in blank.

(21) To "honor" is to pay or to accept and pay, or where a credit so engages to purchase or discount a draft complying with the terms of the credit.

(22) "Insolvency proceedings" includes any assignment for the benefit of creditors or other proceedings intended to liquidate or rehabilitate the estate of the person involved.

(23) A person is "insolvent" who either has ceased to pay his debts in the ordinary course of business or cannot pay his debts as they become due or is insolvent within the meaning of the federal bankruptcy law.

(24) "Money" means a medium of exchange authorized or adopted by a domestic or foreign government as part of its currency.

(25) A person has "notice" of a fact when

   (a) he has actual knowledge of it; or

   (b) he has received a notice or notification of it; or

   (c) from all the facts and circumstances known to him at the time in question he has reason to know that it exists.

A person "knows" or has "knowledge" of a fact when he has actual knowledge of it. "Discover" or "learn" or a word or phrase of similar import refers to knowledge rather than to reason to know. The time and circumstances under which a notice or notification may cease to be effective are not determined by this Act.

(26) A person "notifies" or "gives" a notice or notification to another by taking such steps as may be reasonably required to inform the other in ordinary course whether or not such other actually comes to know of it. A person "receives" a notice or notification when

   (a) it comes to his attention; or

   (b) it is duly delivered at the place of business through which the contract was made or at any other place held out by him as the place for receipt of such communications.

(27) Notice, knowledge or a notice or notification received by an organization is effective for a particular transaction from the time when it is brought to the attention of the individual conducting that transaction, and in any event from the time when it would have been brought to his attention if the organization had exercised due diligence. An organization exercises due diligence if it maintains reasonable routines for communicating significant information to the person conducting the transaction and there is reasonable compliance with the routines. Due diligence does not require an individual acting for the organization to communicate information unless such communication is part of his regular duties or unless he has reason to know of the transaction and that the transaction would be materially affected by the information.

(28) "Organization" includes a corporation, government or governmental subdivision or agency, business trust, estate, trust, partnership or association, two or more persons having a joint or common interest, or any other legal or commercial entity.

(29) "Party," as distinct from "third party," means a person who has engaged in a transaction or made an agreement within this Act.

(30) "Person" includes an individual or an organization (See Section 1–102):

(31) "Presumption" or "presumed" means that the trier of fact must find the existence of the fact presumed unless and until evidence is introduced which would support a finding of its nonexistence.

(32) "Purchase" includes taking by sale, discount, negotiation, mortgage, pledge, lien, issue or re-issue, gift or any other voluntary transaction creating an interest in property.

(33) "Purchaser" means a person who takes by purchase.

(34) "Remedy" means any remedial right to which an aggrieved party is entitled with or without resort to a tribunal.

(35) "Representative" includes an agent, an officer of a corporation or association, and a trustee, executor or administrator of an estate, or any other person empowered to act for another.

(36) "Rights" includes remedies.

(37) "Security interest" means an interest in personal property or fixtures which secures payment or performance of an obligation. The retention or reservation of title by a seller of goods notwithstanding shipment or delivery to the buyer (Section 2–401) is limited in effect to a reservation of a "security interest." The term also includes any interest of a buyer of accounts or chattel paper which is subject to Article 9. The special property interest of a buyer of goods on identification of those goods to a contract for sale under Section 2–401 is not a "security interest" but a buyer may also acquire a "security interest" by complying with Article 9. Unless a lease or consignment is intended as security, reservation of title thereunder is not a "security interest" but a consignment is in any event subject to the provisions on consignment sales (Section 2–326).

Whether a transaction creates a lease or security interest is determined by the facts of each case; however, a transaction creates a security interest if the consideration the lessee is to pay the lessor for the right to possession and use of the goods is an obligation for the term of the lease not subject to termination by the lessee, and

(a) the original term of the lease is equal to or greater than the remaining economic life of the goods,

(b) the lessee is bound to renew the lease for the remaining economic life of the goods or is bound to become the owner of the goods,

(c) the lessee has an option to renew the lease for the remaining economic life of the goods for no additional consideration or nominal additional consideration upon compliance with the lease agreement, or

(d) the lessee has an option to become the owner of the goods for no additional consideration or nominal additional consideration upon compliance with the lease agreement.

A transaction does not create a security interest merely because it provides that

(a) the present value of the consideration the lessee is obligated to pay the lessor for the right to possession and use of the goods is substantially equal to or is greater than the fair market value of the goods at the time the lease is entered into,

(b) the lessee assumes risk of loss of the goods, or agrees to pay taxes, insurance, filing, recording, or registration fees, or service or maintenance costs with respect to the goods,

(c) the lessee has an option to renew the lease or to become the owner of the goods,

(d) the lessee has an option to renew the lease for a fixed rent that is equal to or greater than the reasonably predictable fair market rent for the use of the goods for the term of the renewal at the time the option is to be performed, or

(e) the lessee has an option to become the owner of the goods for a fixed price that is equal to or greater than the reasonably predictable fair market value of the goods at the time the option is to be performed.

For purposes of this subsection (37):

(x) Additional consideration is not nominal if (i) when the option to renew the lease is granted to the lessee the rent is stated to be the fair market rent for the use of the goods for the term of the renewal determined at the time the option is to be performed, or (ii) when the option to become the owner of the goods is granted to the lessee the price is stated to be the fair market value of the goods determined at the time the option is to be performed. Additional consideration is nominal if it is less than the lessee's reasonably predictable cost of performing under the lease agreement if the option is not exercised;

(y) "Reasonably predictable" and "remaining economic life of the goods" are to be determined with reference to the facts and circumstances at the time the transaction is entered into; and

(z) "Present value" means the amount as of a date certain of one or more sums payable in the future, discounted to the date certain. The discount is determined by the interest rate specified by the parties if the rate is not manifestly unreasonable at the time the transaction is entered into; otherwise, the discount is determined by a commercially reasonable rate that takes into account the facts and circumstances of each case at the time the transaction was entered into.

(38) "Send" in connection with any writing or notice means to deposit in the mail or deliver for transmission by any other usual means of communication with postage or cost of transmission provided for and properly addressed and in the case of an instrument to an address specified thereon or otherwise agreed, or if there be none to any address reasonable under the circumstances. The receipt of any writing or notice within the time at which it would have arrived if properly sent has the effect of a proper sending.

(39) "Signed" includes any symbol executed or adopted by a party with present intention to authenticate a writing.

(40) "Surety" includes guarantor.

(41) "Telegram" includes a message transmitted by radio, teletype, cable, any mechanical method of transmission, or the like.

(42) "Term" means that portion of an agreement which relates to a particular matter.

(43) "Unauthorized" signature or indorsement means one made without actual, implied or apparent authority and includes a forgery.

(44) "Value." Except as otherwise provided with respect to negotiable instruments and bank collections (Sections 3–303, 4–208 and 4–209) a person gives "value" for rights if he acquires them

    (a) in return for a binding commitment to extend credit or for the extension of immediately available credit whether or not drawn upon and whether or not a chargeback is provided for in the event of difficulties in collection; or

    (b) as security for or in total or partial satisfaction of a pre-existing claim; or

    (c) by accepting delivery pursuant to a pre-existing contract purchase; or

    (d) generally, in return for any consideration sufficient to support a simple contract.

(45) "Warehouse receipt" means a receipt issued by a person engaged in the business of storing goods for hire.

(46) "Written" or "writing" includes printing, typewriting or any other intentional reduction to tangible form.

Section 1–202. Prima Facie Evidence by Third Party Documents

A document in due form purporting to be a bill of lading, policy or certificate of insurance, official weigher's or inspector's certificate, consular invoice, or any other document authorized or required by the contract to be issued by a third party shall be prima facie evidence of its own authenticity and genuineness and of the facts stated in the document by the third party.

Section 1–203. Obligation of Good Faith

Every contract or duty within this Act imposes an obligation of good faith in its performance or enforcement.

Section 1–204. Time; Reasonable Time; "Seasonably"

(1) Whenever this Act requires any action to be taken within a reasonable time, any time which is not manifestly unreasonable may be fixed by agreement.

(2) What is a reasonable time for taking any action depends on the nature, purpose and circumstance of such action.

(3) An action is taken "seasonably" when it is taken at or within the time agreed or if no time is agreed at or within a reasonable time.

Section 1–205. Course of Dealing and Usage of Trade

(1) A course of dealing is a sequence of previous conduct between the parties to a particular transaction which is fairly to be regarded as establishing a common basis of understanding for interpreting their expressions and other conduct.

(2) A usage of trade is any practice or method of dealing having such regularity of observance in a place, vocation or trade as to justify an expectation that it will be observed with respect to the transaction in question. The existence and scope of such a usage are to be proved as facts. If it is established that such a usage is embodied in a written trade code or similar writing the interpretation of the writing is for the court.

(3) A course of dealing between parties and any usage of trade in the vocation or trade in which they are engaged or of which they are or should be aware give particular meaning to and supplement or qualify terms of an agreement.

(4) The express terms of an agreement and an applicable course of dealing or usage of trade shall be construed wherever reasonable as consistent with each other; but when such construction is unreasonable express terms control both course of dealing and usage of trade and course of dealing controls usage of trade.

(5) An applicable usage of trade in the place where any part of performance is to occur shall be used in interpreting the agreement as to that part of the performance.

(6) Evidence of a relevant usage of trade offered by one party is not admissible unless and until he has given the other party such notice as the court finds sufficient to prevent unfair surprise to the latter.

Section 1–206. Statute of Frauds for Kinds of Personal Property Not Otherwise Covered

(1) Except in the cases described in subsection (2) of this section a contract for the sale of personal property is not enforceable by way of action or defense beyond five thousand dollars in amount or value of remedy unless there is some writing which indicates that a contract for sale has been made between the parties at a defined or stated price, reasonably identifies the subject matter, and is signed by the party against whom enforcement is sought or by his authorized agent.

(2) Subsection (1) of this section does not apply to contracts for the sale of goods (Section 2–201) nor of securi-

ties (Section 8–319) nor to security agreements (Section 9–203).

Section 1–207. Performance or Acceptance Under Reservation of Rights

A party who with explicit reservation of rights performs or promises performance or assents to performance in a manner demanded or offered by the other party does not thereby prejudice the rights reserved. Such words as "without prejudice," "under protest" or the like are sufficient.

Section 1–208. Option to Accelerate at Will

A term providing that one party or his successor in interest may accelerate payment or performance or require collateral or additional collateral "at will" or "when he deems himself insecure" or in words of similar import shall be construed to mean that he shall have power to do so only if he in good faith believes that the prospect of payment or performance is impaired. The burden of establishing lack of good faith is on the party against whom the power had been exercised.

Section 1–209. Subordinated Obligations

An obligation may be issued as subordinated to payment of another obligation of the person obligated, or a creditor may subordinate his right to payment of an obligation by agreement with either the person obligated or another creditor of the person obligated. Such a subordination does not create a security interest as against either the common debtor or a subordinated creditor. This section shall be construed as declaring the law as it existed prior to the enactment of this section and not as modifying it.

Note: *The new section is proposed as an optional provision to make it clear that a subordination agreement does not create a security interest unless so intended.*

ARTICLE 2 SALES

Part 1 Short Title, General Construction and Subject Matter

Section 2–101. Short Title

This Article shall be known and may be cited as Uniform Commercial Code—Sales.

Section 2–102. Scope; Certain Security and Other Transactions Excluded From This Article

Unless the context otherwise requires, this Article applies to transactions in goods; it does not apply to any transac-tion which although in the form of an unconditional con-tract to sell or present sale is intended to operate only as a security transaction nor does this Article impair or repeal any statute regulating sales to consumers, farmers or other specified classes of buyers.

Section 2–103. Definitions and Index of Definitions

(1) In this Article unless the context otherwise requires

    (a) "Buyer" means a person who buys or contracts to buy goods.

    (b) "Good faith" in the case of a merchant means honesty in fact and the observance of reasonable commercial standards of fair dealing in the trade.

    (c) "Receipt" of goods means taking physical posses-sion of them.

    (d) "Seller" means a person who sells or contracts to sell goods.

(2) Other definitions applying to this Article or to specific Parts thereof, and the sections in which they appear are:

    "Acceptance." Section 2–606.

    "Banker's credit." Section 2–325.

    "Between merchants." Section 2–104.

    "Cancellation." Section 2–106(4).

    "Commercial unit." Section 2–105.

    "Confirmed credit." Section 2–325.

    "Conforming to contract." Section 2–106.

    "Contract for sale." Section 2–106.

    "Cover." Section 2–712.

    "Entrusting." Section 2–403.

    "Financing agency." Section 2–104.

    "Future goods." Section 2–105.

    "Goods." Section 2–105.

    "Identification." Section 2–501.

    "Installment contract." Section 2–612.

    "Letter of Credit." Section 2–325.

    "Lot." Section 2–105.

    "Merchant." Section 2–104.

    "Overseas." Section 2–323.

    "Person in position of seller." Section 2–707.

    "Present sale." Section 2–106.

    "Sale." Section 2–106.

    "Sale on approval." Section 2–326.

    "Sale or return." Section 2–326.

    "Termination." Section 2–106.

(3) The following definitions in other Articles apply to this Article:

"Check." Section 3–104.

"Consignee." Section 7–102.

"Consignor." Section 7–102.

"Consumer goods." Section 9–109.

"Dishonor." Section 3–507.

"Draft." Section 3–104.

(4) In addition Article I contains general definitions and principles of construction and interpretation applicable throughout this Article.

Section 2–104. Definitions: "Merchant"; "Between Merchants"; "Financing Agency"

(1) "Merchant" means a person who deals in goods of the kind or otherwise by his occupation holds himself out as having knowledge or skill peculiar to the practices or goods involved in the transaction or to whom such knowledge or skill may be attributed by his employment of an agent or broker or other intermediary who by his occupation holds himself out as having such knowledge or skill.

(2) "Financing agency" means a bank, finance company or other person who in the ordinary course of business makes advances against goods or documents of title or who by arrangement with either the seller or the buyer intervenes in ordinary course to make or collect payment due or claimed under the contract for sale, as by purchasing or paying the seller's draft or making advances against it or by merely taking it for collection whether or not documents of title accompany the draft. "Financing agency" includes also a bank or other person who similarly intervenes between persons who are in the position of seller and buyer in respect to the goods (Section 2–707).

(3) "Between merchants" means in any transaction with respect to which both parties are chargeable with the knowledge or skill of merchants.

Section 2–105. Definitions: Transferability; "Goods"; "Future" Goods; "Lot"; "Commercial Unit"

(1) "Goods" means all things (including specially manufactured goods) which are movable at the time of identification to the contract for sale other than the money in which the price is to be paid, investment securities (Article 8) and things in action. "Goods" also includes the unborn young of animals and growing crops and other identified things attached to realty as described in the section on goods to be severed from realty (Section 2–107).

(2) Goods must be both existing and identified before any interest in them can pass. Goods which are not both existing and identified are "future" goods. A purported present sale of future goods or of any interest therein operates as a contract to sell.

(3) There may be a sale of a part interest in existing identified goods.

(4) An undivided share in an identified bulk of fungible goods is sufficiently identified to be sold although the quantity of the bulk is not determined. Any agreed proportion of such a bulk or any quantity thereof agreed upon by number, weight or other measure may to the extent of the seller's interest in the bulk be sold to the buyer who then becomes an owner in common.

(5) "Lot" means a parcel or a single article which is the subject matter of a separate sale or delivery, whether or not it is sufficient to perform the contract.

(6) "Commercial unit" means such a unit of goods as by commercial usage is a single whole for purposes of sale and division of which materially impairs its character or value on the market or in use. A commercial unit may be a single article (as a machine) or a set of articles (as a suite of furniture or an assortment of sizes) or a quantity (as a bale, gross, or carload) or any other unit treated in use or in the relevant market as a single whole.

Section 2–106. Definitions: "Contract"; "Agreement"; "Contract for Sale"; "Sale"; "Present Sale"; "Conforming" to Contract; "Termination"; "Cancellation"

(1) In this Article unless the context otherwise requires "contract" and "agreement" are limited to those relating to the present or future sale of goods. "Contract for sale" includes both a present sale of goods and a contract to sell goods at a future time. A "sale" consists in the passing of title from the seller to the buyer for a price (Section 2–401). A "present sale" means a sale which is accomplished by the making of the contract.

(2) Goods or conduct including any part of a performance are "conforming" or conform to the contract when they are in accordance with the obligations under the contract.

(3) "Termination" occurs when either party pursuant to a power created by agreement or law puts an end to the contract otherwise than for its breach. On "termination" all obligations which are still executory on both sides are discharged but any right based on prior breach or performance survives.

(4) "Cancellation" occurs when either party puts an end to the contract for breach by the other and its effect is the same as that of "termination" except that the cancelling party also retains any remedy for breach of the whole contract or any unperformed balance.

Section 2–107. Goods to Be Severed From Realty: Recording

(1) A contract for the sale of minerals or the like (including oil and gas) or a structure or its materials to be removed from realty is a contract for the sale of goods within this Article if they are to be severed by the seller but until severance a purported present sale thereof which is not effective as a transfer of an interest in land is effective only as a contract to sell.

(2) A contract for the sale apart from the land of growing crops or other things attached to realty and capable of severance without material harm thereto but not described in subsection (1) or of timber to be cut is a contract for the sale of goods within this Article whether the subject matter is to be severed by the buyer or by the seller even though it forms part of the realty at the time of contracting, and the parties can by identification effect a present sale before severance.

(3) The provisions of this section are subject to any third party rights provided by the law relating to realty records, and the contract for sale may be executed and recorded as a document transferring an interest in land and shall then constitute notice to third parties of the buyer's rights under the contract for sale.

Part 2 Form, Formation and Readjustment of Contract

Section 2–201. Formal Requirements; Statute of Frauds

(1) Except as otherwise provided in this section a contract for the sale of goods for the price of $500 or more is not enforceable by way of action or defense unless there is some writing sufficient to indicate that a contract for sale has been made between the parties and signed by the party against whom enforcement is sought or by his authorized agent or broker. A writing is not insufficient because it omits or incorrectly states a term agreed upon but the contract is not enforceable under this paragraph beyond the quantity of goods shown in such writing.

(2) Between merchants if within a reasonable time a writing in confirmation of the contract and sufficient against the sender is received and the party receiving it has reason to know its contents, it satisfies the requirements of subsection (1) against such party unless written notice of objection to its contents is given within 10 days after it is received.

(3) A contract which does not satisfy the requirements of subsection (1) but which is valid in other respects is enforceable

(a) if the goods are to be specially manufactured for the buyer and are not suitable for sale to others in the ordinary course of the seller's business and the seller, before notice of repudiation is received and under circumstances which reasonably indicate that the goods are for the buyer, has made either a substantial beginning of their manufacture or commitments for their procurement; or

(b) if the party against whom enforcement is sought admits in his pleading, testimony or otherwise in court that a contract for sale was made, but the contract is not enforceable under this provision beyond the quantity of goods admitted; or

(c) with respect to goods for which payment has been made and accepted or which have been received and accepted (Sec. 2–606).

Section 2–202. Final Written Expression: Parol or Extrinsic Evidence

Terms with respect to which the confirmatory memoranda of the parties agree or which are otherwise set forth in a writing intended by the parties as a final expression of their agreement with respect to such terms as are included therein may not be contradicted by evidence of any prior agreement or of a contemporaneous oral agreement but may be explained or supplemented

(a) by course of dealing or usage of trade (Section 1–205) or by course of performance (Section 2–208); and

(b) by evidence of consistent additional terms unless the court finds the writing to have been intended also as a complete and exclusive statement of the terms of the agreement.

Section 2–203. Seals Inoperative

The affixing of a seal to a writing evidencing a contract for sale or an offer to buy or sell goods does not constitute the writing a sealed instrument and the law with respect to sealed instruments does not apply to such a contract or offer.

Section 2–204. Formation in General

(1) A contract for sale of goods may be made in any manner sufficient to show agreement, including conduct by both parties which recognizes the existence of such a contract.

(2) An agreement sufficient to constitute a contract for sale may be found even though the moment of its making is undetermined.

(3) Even though one or more terms are left open a contract for sale does not fail for indefiniteness if the parties have intended to make a contract and there is a reasonably certain basis for giving an appropriate remedy.

Section 2–205. Firm Offers

An offer by a merchant to buy or sell goods in a signed writing which by its terms gives assurance that it will be held open is not revocable, for lack of consideration, during the time stated or if no time is stated for a reasonable time, but in no event may such period of irrevocability exceed three months; but any such term of assurance on a form supplied by the offeree must be separately signed by the offeror.

Section 2–206. Offer and Acceptance in Formation of Contract

(1) Unless otherwise unambiguously indicated by the language or circumstances

    (a) an offer to make a contract shall be construed as inviting acceptance in any manner and by any medium reasonable in the circumstances;

    (b) an order or other offer to buy goods for prompt or current shipment shall be construed as inviting acceptance either by a prompt promise to ship or by the prompt or current shipment of conforming or nonconforming goods, but such a shipment of non-conforming goods does not constitute an acceptance if the seller seasonably notifies the buyer that the shipment is offered only as an accommodation to the buyer.

(2) Where the beginning of a requested performance is a reasonable mode of acceptance an offeror who is not notified of acceptance within a reasonable time may treat the offer as having lapsed before acceptance.

Section 2–207. Additional Terms in Acceptance or Confirmation

(1) A definite and seasonable expression of acceptance or a written confirmation which is sent within a reasonable time operates as an acceptance even though it states terms additional to or different from those offered or agreed upon, unless acceptance is expressly made conditional on assent to the additional or different terms.

(2) The additional terms are to be construed as proposals for addition to the contract. Between merchants such terms become part of the contract unless:

    (a) the offer expressly limits acceptance to the terms of the offer;

    (b) they materially alter it; or

    (c) notification of objection to them has already been given or is given within a reasonable time after notice of them is received.

(3) Conduct by both parties which recognizes the existence of a contract is sufficient to establish a contract for sale although the writings of the parties do not otherwise establish a contract. In such case the terms of the particular contract consist of those terms on which the writings of the parties agree, together with any supplementary terms incorporated under any other provisions of this Act.

Section 2–208. Course of Performance or Practical Construction

(1) Where the contract for sale involves repeated occasions for performance by either party with knowledge of the nature of the performance and opportunity for objection to it by the other, any course of performance accepted or acquiesced in without objection shall be relevant to determine the meaning of the agreement.

(2) The express terms of the agreement and any such course of performance, as well as any course of dealing and usage of trade, shall be construed whenever reasonable as consistent with each other, but when such construction is unreasonable, express terms shall control course of performance and course of performance shall control both course of dealing and usage of trade (Section 1–205).

(3) Subject to the provisions of the next section on modification and waiver, such course of performance shall be relevant to show a waiver or modification of any term inconsistent with such course of performance.

Section 2–209. Modification, Rescission and Waiver

(1) An agreement modifying a contract within this Article needs no consideration to be binding.

(2) A signed agreement which excludes modification or rescission except by a signed writing cannot be otherwise modified or rescinded, but except as between merchants such a requirement on a form supplied by the merchant must be separately signed by the other party.

(3) The requirements of the statute of frauds section of this Article (Section 2–201) must be satisfied if the contract as modified is within its provisions.

(4) Although an attempt at modification or rescission does not satisfy the requirements of subsection (2) or (3) it can operate as a waiver.

(5) A party who has made a waiver affecting an executory portion of the contract may retract the waiver by reasonable notification received by the other party that strict performance will be required of any term waived, unless

the retraction would be unjust in view of a material change of position in reliance on the waiver.

Section 2–210. Delegation of Performance; Assignment of Rights

(1) A party may perform his duty through a delegate unless otherwise agreed or unless the other party has a substantial interest in having his original promisor perform or control the acts required by the contract. No delegation of performance relieves the party delegating of any duty to perform or any liability for breach.

(2) Unless otherwise agreed all rights of either seller or buyer can be assigned except where the assignment would materially change the duty of the other party, or increase materially the burden or risk imposed on him by his contract, or impair materially his chance of obtaining return performance. A right to damages for breach of the whole contract or a right arising out of the assignor's due performance of his entire obligation can be assigned despite agreement otherwise.

(3) Unless the circumstances indicate the contrary a prohibition of assignment of "the contract" is to be construed as barring only the delegation to the assignee of the assignor's performance.

(4) An assignment of "the contract" or of "all my rights under the contract" or an assignment in similar general terms is an assignment of rights and unless the language or the circumstances (as in an assignment for security) indicate the contrary, it is a delegation of performance of the duties of the assignor and its acceptance by the assignee constitutes a promise by him to perform those duties. This promise is enforceable by either the assignor or the other party to the original contract.

(5) The other party may treat any assignment which delegates performance as creating reasonable grounds for insecurity and may without prejudice to his rights against the assignor demand assurances from the assignee (Section 2–609).

Part 3 General Obligations and Construction of Contract

Section 2–301. General Obligations of Parties

The obligation of the seller is to transfer and deliver and that of the buyer is to accept and pay in accordance with the contract.

Section 2–302. Unconscionable Contract or Clause

(1) If the court as a matter of law finds the contract or any clause of the contract to have been unconscionable at the time it was made the court may refuse to enforce the contract, or it may enforce the remainder of the contract without the unconscionable clause, or it may so limit the application of any unconscionable clause as to avoid any unconscionable result.

(2) When it is claimed or appears to the court that the contract or any clause thereof may be unconscionable the parties shall be afforded a reasonable opportunity to present evidence as to its commercial setting, purpose and effect to aid the court in making the determination.

Section 2–303. Allocation or Division of Risks

Where this Article allocates a risk or a burden as between the parties "unless otherwise agreed," the agreement may not only shift the allocation but may also divide the risk or burden.

Section 2–304. Price Payable in Money, Goods, Realty, or Otherwise

(1) The price can be made payable in money or otherwise. If it is payable in whole or in part in goods each party is a seller of the goods which he is to transfer.

(2) Even though all or part of the price is payable in an interest in realty the transfer of the goods and the seller's obligations with reference to them are subject to this Article, but not the transfer of the interest in realty or the transferor's obligations in connection therewith.

Section 2–305. Open Price Term

(1) The parties if they so intend can conclude a contract for sale even though the price is not settled. In such a case the price is a reasonable price at the time for delivery if

(a) nothing is said as to price; or

(b) the price is left to be agreed by the parties and they fail to agree; or

(c) the price is to be fixed in terms of some agreed market or other standard as set or recorded by a third person or agency and it is not so set or recorded.

(2) A price to be fixed by the seller or by the buyer means a price for him to fix in good faith.

(3) When a price left to be fixed otherwise than by agreement of the parties fails to be fixed through fault of one party the other may at his option treat the contract as cancelled or himself fix a reasonable price.

(4) Where, however, the parties intend not to be bound unless the price be fixed or agreed and it is not fixed or agreed there is no contract. In such a case the buyer must return any goods already received or if unable so to do must pay their reasonable value at the time of delivery

and the seller must return any portion of the price paid on account.

Section 2–306. Output, Requirements and Exclusive Dealings

(1) A term which measures the quantity by the output of the seller or the requirements of the buyer means such actual output or requirements as may occur in good faith, except that no quantity unreasonably disproportionate to any stated estimate or in the absence of a stated estimate to any normal or otherwise comparable prior output or requirements may be tendered or demanded.

(2) A lawful agreement by either the seller or the buyer for exclusive dealing in the kind of goods concerned imposes unless otherwise agreed an obligation by the seller to use best efforts to supply the goods and by the buyer to use best efforts to promote the sale.

Section 2–307. Delivery in Single Lot or Several Lots

Unless otherwise agreed all goods called for by a contract for sale must be tendered in a single delivery and payment is due only on such tender but where the circumstances give either party the right to make or demand delivery in lots the price if it can be apportioned may be demanded for each lot.

Section 2–308. Absence of Specified Place for Delivery

Unless otherwise agreed

(a) the place for delivery of goods is the seller's place of business or if he has none his residence; but

(b) in a contract for sale of identified goods which to the knowledge of the parties at the time of contracting are in some other place, that place is the place for their delivery; and

(c) documents of title may be delivered through customary banking channels.

Section 2–309. Absence of Specific Time Provisions; Notice of Termination

(1) The time for shipment or delivery or any other action under a contract if not provided in this Article or agreed upon shall be a reasonable time.

(2) Where the contract provides for successive performances but is indefinite in duration it is valid for a reasonable time but unless otherwise agreed may be terminated at any time by either party.

(3) Termination of a contract by one party except on the happening of an agreed event requires that reasonable notification be received by the other party and an agreement dispensing with notification is invalid if its operation would be unconscionable.

Section 2–310. Open Time for Payment or Running of Credit: Authority to Ship Under Reservation

Unless otherwise agreed

(a) payment is due at the time and place at which the buyer is to receive the goods even though the place of shipment is the place of delivery; and

(b) if the seller is authorized to send the goods he may ship them under reservation, and may tender the documents of title, but the buyer may inspect the goods after their arrival before payment is due unless such inspection is inconsistent with the terms of the contract (Section 2–513); and

(c) if delivery is authorized and made by way of documents of title otherwise than by subsection (b) then payment is due at the time and place at which the buyer is to receive the documents regardless of where the goods are to be received; and

(d) where the seller is required or authorized to ship the goods on credit the credit period runs from the time of shipment but postdating the invoice or delaying its dispatch will correspondingly delay the starting of the credit period.

Section 2–311. Options and Cooperation Respecting Performance

(1) An agreement for sale which is otherwise sufficiently definite (subsection (3) of Section 2–204) to be a contract is not made invalid by the fact that it leaves particulars of performance to be specified by one of the parties. Any such specification must be made in good faith and within limits set by commercial reasonableness.

(2) Unless otherwise agreed specifications relating to assortment of the goods are at the buyer's option and except as otherwise provided in subsections (1) (c) and (3) of Section 2–319 specifications or arrangements relating to shipment are at the seller's option.

(3) Where such specification would materially affect the other party's performance but is not seasonably made or where one party's cooperation is necessary to the agreed performance of the other but is not seasonably forthcoming, the other party in addition to all other remedies

(a) is excused for any resulting delay in his own performance; and

(b) may also either proceed to perform in any reasonable manner or after the time for a material part of his own performance treat the failure to specify or to cooperate as a breach by failure to deliver or accept the goods.

Section 2–312. Warranty of Title and Against Infringement; Buyer's Obligation Against Infringement

(1) Subject to subsection (2) there is in a contract for sale a warranty by the seller that

    (a) the title conveyed shall be good, and its transfer rightful; and

    (b) the goods shall be delivered free from any security interest or other lien or encumbrance of which the buyer at the time of contracting has no knowledge.

(2) A warranty under subsection (1) will be excluded or modified only by specific language or by circumstances which give the buyer reason to know that the person selling does not claim title in himself or that he is purporting to sell only such right or title as he or a third person may have.

(3) Unless otherwise agreed a seller who is a merchant regularly dealing in goods of the kind warrants that the goods shall be delivered free of the rightful claim of any third person by way of infringement or the like but a buyer who furnishes specifications to the seller must hold the seller harmless against any such claim which arises out of compliance with the specifications.

Section 2–313. Express Warranties by Affirmation, Promise, Description, Sample

(1) Express warranties by the seller are created as follows:

    (a) Any affirmation of fact or promise made by the seller to the buyer which relates to the goods and becomes part of the basis of the bargain creates an express warranty that the goods shall conform to the affirmation or promise.

    (b) Any description of the goods which is made part of the basis of the bargain creates an express warranty that the goods shall conform to the description.

    (c) Any sample or model which is made part of the basis of the bargain creates an express warranty that the whole of the goods shall conform to the sample or model.

(2) It is not necessary to the creation of an express warranty that the seller use formal words such as "warrant" or "guarantee" or that he have a specific intention to make a warranty, but an affirmation merely of the value of the goods or a statement purporting to be merely the seller's opinion or commendation of the goods does not create a warranty.

Section 2–314. Implied Warranty: Merchantability; Usage of Trade

(1) Unless excluded or modified (Section 2–316), a warranty that the goods shall be merchantable is implied in a contract for their sale if the seller is a merchant with respect to goods of that kind. Under this section the serving for value of food or drink to be consumed either on the premises or elsewhere is a sale.

(2) Goods to be merchantable must be at least such as

    (a) pass without objection in the trade under the contract description; and

    (b) in the case of fungible goods, are of fair average quality within the description; and

    (c) are fit for the ordinary purposes for which such goods are used; and

    (d) run, within the variations permitted by the agreement, of even kind, quality and quantity within each unit and among all units involved; and

    (e) are adequately contained, packaged, and labeled as the agreement may require; and

    (f) conform to the promises or affirmations of fact made on the container or label if any.

(3) Unless excluded or modified (Section 2–316) other implied warranties may arise from course of dealing or usage of trade.

Section 2–315. Implied Warranty: Fitness for Particular Purpose

Where the seller at the time of contracting has reason to know any particular purpose for which the goods are required and that the buyer is relying on the seller's skill or judgment to select or furnish suitable goods, there is unless excluded or modified under the next section an implied warranty that the goods shall be fit for such purpose.

Section 2–316. Exclusion or Modification of Warranties

(1) Words or conduct relevant to the creation of an express warranty and words or conduct tending to negate or limit warranty shall be construed wherever reasonable as consistent with each other; but subject to the provisions of this Article on parol or extrinsic evidence (Section 2–202) negation or limitation is inoperative to the extent that such construction is unreasonable.

(2) Subject to subsection (3), to exclude or modify the implied warranty or merchantability or any part of it the language must mention merchantability and in case of a writing must be conspicuous, and to exclude or modify any implied warranty of fitness the exclusion must be by

a writing and conspicuous. Language to exclude all implied warranties of fitness is sufficient if it states, for example, that "There are no warranties which extend beyond the description on the face hereof."

(3) Notwithstanding subsection (2)

(a) unless the circumstances indicate otherwise, all implied warranties are excluded by expressions like "as is," "with all faults" or other language which in common understanding calls the buyer's attention to the exclusion of warranties and makes plain that there is no implied warranty; and

(b) when the buyer before entering into the contract has examined the goods or the sample or model as fully as he desired or has refused to examine the goods there is no implied warranty with regard to defects which an examination ought in the circumstances to have revealed to him; and

(c) an implied warranty can also be excluded or modified by course of dealing or course of performance or usage of trade.

(d) Remedies for breach of warranty can be limited in accordance with the provisions of this Article on liquidation or limitation of damages and on contractual modification of remedy (Sections 2–718 and 2–719).

Section 2–317. Cumulation and Conflict of Warranties Express or Implied

Warranties whether express or implied shall be construed as consistent with each other and as cumulative, but if such construction is unreasonable the intention of the parties shall determine which warranty is dominant. In ascertaining that intention the following rules apply:

(a) Exact or technical specifications displace an inconsistent sample or model or general language of description.

(b) A sample from an existing bulk displaces inconsistent general language of description.

(c) Express warranties displace inconsistent implied warranties other than an implied warranty of fitness for a particular purpose.

Section 2–318. Third Party Beneficiaries of Warranties Express or Implied

Note: *If this Act is introduced in the Congress of the United States this section should be omitted. (States to select one alternative.)*

Alternative A

A seller's warranty whether express or implied extends to any natural person who is in the family or household of his buyer or who is a guest in his home if it is reasonable to expect that such person may use, consume or be affected by the goods and who is injured in person by breach of the warranty. A seller may not exclude or limit the operation of this section.

Alternative B

A seller's warranty whether express or implied extends to any natural person who may reasonably be expected to use, consume or be affected by the goods and who is injured in person by breach of the warranty. A seller may not exclude or limit the operation of this section.

Alternative C

A seller's warranty whether express or implied extends to any person who may reasonably be expected to use, consume or be affected by the goods and who is injured by breach of the warranty. A seller may not exclude or limit the operation of this section with respect to injury to the person of an individual to whom the warranty extends.

Section 2–319. F.O.B. and F.A.S. Terms

(1) Unless otherwise agreed the term F.O.B. (which means "free on board") at a named place, even though used only in connection with the stated price, is a delivery term under which

(a) when the term is F.O.B. the place of shipment, the seller must at that place ship the goods in the manner provided in this Article (Section 2–504) and bear the expense and risk of putting them into the possession of the carrier; or

(b) when the term is F.O.B. the place of destination, the seller must at his own expense and risk transport the goods to that place and there tender delivery of them in the manner provided in this Article (Section 2–503);

(c) when under either (a) or (b) the term is also F.O.B. vessel, car or other vehicle, the seller must in addition at his own expense and risk load the goods on board. If the term is F.O.B. vessel the buyer must name the vessel and in an appropriate case the seller must comply with the provisions of this Article on the form of bill of lading (Section 2–323).

(2) Unless otherwise agreed the term F.A.S. vessel (which means "free alongside") at a named port, even though used only in connection with the stated price, is a delivery term under which the seller must

(a) at his own expense and risk deliver the goods alongside the vessel in the manner usual in that port or on a dock designated and provided by the buyer; and

(b) obtain and tender a receipt for the goods in exchange for which the carrier is under a duty to issue a bill of lading.

(3) Unless otherwise agreed in any case falling within subsection (1) (a) or (c) or subsection (2) the buyer must seasonably give any needed instructions for making delivery, including when the term is F.A.S. or F.O.B. the loading berth of the vessel and in an appropriate case its name and sailing date. The seller may treat the failure of needed instructions as a failure of cooperation under this Article (Section 2–311). He may also at his option move the goods in any reasonable manner preparatory to delivery or shipment.

(4) Under the term F.O.B. vessel or F.A.S. unless otherwise agreed the buyer must make payment against tender of the required documents and the seller may not tender nor the buyer demand delivery of the goods in substitution for the documents.

Section 2–320. C.I.F. And C. & F. Terms

(1) The term C.I.F. means that the price includes in a lump sum the cost of the goods and the insurance and freight to the named destination. The term C. & F. or C.F. means that the price so includes cost and freight to the named destination.

(2) Unless otherwise agreed and even though used only in connection with the stated price and destination, the term C.I.F. destination or its equivalent requires the seller at his own expense and risk to

(a) put the goods into the possession of a carrier at the port for shipment and obtain a negotiable bill or bills of lading covering the entire transportation to the named destination; and

(b) load the goods and obtain a receipt from the carrier (which may be contained in the bill of lading) showing that the freight has been paid or provided for; and

(c) obtain a policy or certificate of insurance, including any war risk insurance, of a kind and on terms then current at the port of shipment in the usual amount, in the currency of the contract, shown to cover the same goods covered by the bill of lading and providing for payment of loss to the order of the buyer or for the account of whom it may concern; but the seller may add to the price the amount of the premium for any such war risk insurance; and

(d) prepare an invoice of the goods and procure any other documents required to effect shipment or to comply with the contract; and

(e) forward and tender with commercial promptness all the documents in due form and with any indorsement necessary to perfect the buyer's rights.

(3) Unless otherwise agreed the term C. & F. or its equivalent has the same effect and imposes upon the seller the same obligations and risks as a C.I.F. term except the obligation as to insurance.

(4) Under the term C.I.F. or C. & F. unless otherwise agreed the buyer must make payment against tender of the required documents and the seller may not tender nor the buyer demand delivery of the goods in substitution for the documents.

Section 2–321. C.I.F. or C. & F.: "Net Landed Weights"; "Payment on Arrival"; Warranty of Condition on Arrival

Under a contract containing a term C.I.F. or C. & F.

(1) Where the price is based on or is to be adjusted according to "net landed weights," "delivered weights," "out turn" quantity or quality or the like, unless otherwise agreed the seller must reasonably estimate the price. The payment due on tender of the documents called for by the contract is the amount so estimated, but after final adjustment of the price a settlement must be made with commercial promptness.

(2) An agreement described in subsection (1) or any warranty of quality or condition of the goods on arrival places upon the seller the risk of ordinary deterioration, shrinkage and the like in transportation but has no effect on the place or time of identification to the contract for sale or delivery or on the passing of the risk of loss.

(3) Unless otherwise agreed where the contract provides for payment on or after arrival of the goods the seller must before payment allow such preliminary inspection as is feasible; but if the goods are lost delivery of the documents and payment are due when the goods should have arrived.

Section 2–322. Delivery "Ex-Ship"

(1) Unless otherwise agreed a term for delivery of goods "ex-ship" (which means from the carrying vessel) or in equivalent language is not restricted to a particular ship and requires delivery from a ship which has reached a place at the named port of destination where goods of the kind are usually discharged.

(2) Under such a term unless otherwise agreed

(a) the seller must discharge all liens arising out of the carriage and furnish the buyer with a direction which puts the carrier under a duty to deliver the goods; and

(b) the risk of loss does not pass to the buyer until the goods leave the ship's tackle or are otherwise properly unloaded.

Section 2–323. Form of Bill of Lading Required in Overseas Shipment; "Overseas"

(1) Where the contract contemplates overseas shipment and contains a term C.I.F. or C. & F. or F.O.B. vessel, the seller unless otherwise agreed must obtain a negotiable bill of lading stating that the goods have been loaded on board or, in the case of a term C.I.F. or C. & F., received for shipment.

(2) Where in a case within subsection (1) a bill of lading has been issued in a set of parts, unless otherwise agreed if the documents are not to be sent from abroad the buyer may demand tender of the full set; otherwise only one part of the bill of lading need be tendered. Even if the agreement expressly requires a full set

(a) due tender of a single part is acceptable within the provisions of this Article on cure of improper delivery (subsection (1) of Section 2–508); and

(b) even though the full set is demanded, if the documents are sent from abroad the person tendering an incomplete set may nevertheless require payment upon furnishing an indemnity which the buyer in good faith deems adequate.

(3) A shipment by water or by air or a contract contemplating such shipment is "overseas" insofar as by usage of trade or agreement it is subject to the commercial, financing or shipping practices characteristic of international deep water commerce.

Section 2–324. "No Arrival, No Sale" Term

Under a term "no arrival, no sale" or terms of like meaning, unless otherwise agreed,

(a) the seller must properly ship conforming goods and if they arrive by any means he must tender them on arrival but he assumes no obligation that the goods will arrive unless he has caused the non-arrival; and

(b) where without fault of the seller the goods are in part lost or have so deteriorated as no longer to conform to the contract or arrive after the contract time, the buyer may proceed as if there had been casualty to identified goods (Section 2–613).

Section 2–325. "Letter of Credit" Term; "Confirmed Credit"

(1) Failure of the buyer seasonably to furnish an agreed letter of credit is a breach of the contract for sale.

(2) The delivery to seller of a proper letter of credit suspends the buyer's obligation to pay. If the letter of credit is dishonored, the seller may on seasonable notification to the buyer require payment directly from him.

(3) Unless otherwise agreed the term "letter of credit" or "banker's credit" in a contract for sale means an irrevocable credit issued by a financing agency of good repute and, where the shipment is overseas, of good international repute. The term "confirmed credit" means that the credit must also carry the direct obligation of such as agency which does business in the seller's financial market.

Section 2–326. Sale on Approval and Sale or Return; Consignment Sales and Rights of Creditors

(1) Unless otherwise agreed, if delivered goods may be returned by the buyer even though they conform to the contract, the transaction is

(a) a "sale on approval" if the goods are delivered primarily for use, and

(b) a "sale or return" if the goods are delivered primarily for resale.

(2) Except as provided in subsection (3), goods held on approval are not subject to the claims of the buyer's creditors until acceptance; goods held on sale or return are subject to such claims while in the buyer's possession.

(3) Where goods are delivered to a person for sale and such person maintains a place of business at which he deals in goods of the kind involved, under a name other than the name of the person making delivery, then with respect to claims of creditors of the person conducting the business the goods are deemed to be on sale or return. The provisions of this subsection are applicable even though an agreement purports to reserve title to the person making delivery until payment or resale or uses such words as "on consignment" or "on memorandum." However, this subsection is not applicable if the person making delivery

(a) complies with an applicable law providing for a consignor's interest or the like to be evidenced by a sign, or

(b) establishes that the person conducting the business is generally known by his creditors to be substantially engaged in selling the goods of others, or

(c) complies with the filing provisions of the Article on Secured Transactions (Article 9).

(4) Any "or return" term of a contract for sale is to be treated as a separate contract for sale within the statute of frauds section of this Article (Section 2–201) and as contradicting the sale aspect of the contract within the

provisions of this Article or parol or extrinsic evidence (Section 2–202).

Section 2–327. Special Incidents of Sale on Approval and Sale or Return

(1) Under a sale on approval unless otherwise agreed

   (a) although the goods are identified to the contract the risk of loss and the title do not pass to the buyer until acceptance; and

   (b) use of the goods consistent with the purpose of trial is not acceptance but failure seasonably to notify the seller of election to return the goods is acceptance, and if the goods conform to the contract acceptance of any part is acceptance of the whole; and

   (c) after due notification of election to return, the return is at the seller's risk and expense but a merchant buyer must follow any reasonable instructions.

(2) Under a sale or return unless otherwise agreed

   (a) the option to return extends to the whole or any commercial unit of the goods while in substantially their original condition, but must be exercised seasonably; and

   (b) the return is at the buyer's risk and expense.

Section 2–328. Sale by Auction

(1) In a sale by auction if goods are put up in lots each lot is the subject of a separate sale.

(2) A sale by auction is complete when the auctioneer so announces by the fall of the hammer or in other customary manner. Where a bid is made while the hammer is falling in acceptance of a prior bid the auctioneer may in his discretion reopen the bidding or declare the goods sold under the bid on which the hammer was falling.

(3) Such a sale is with reserve unless the goods are in explicit terms put up without reserve. In an auction with reserve the auctioneer may withdraw the goods at any time until he announces completion of the sale. In an auction without reserve, after the auctioneer calls for bids on an article or lot, that article or lot cannot be withdrawn unless no bid is made within a reasonable time. In either case a bidder may retract his bid until the auctioneer's announcement of completion of sale, but a bidder's retraction does not revive any previous bid.

(4) If the auctioneer knowingly receives a bid on the seller's behalf or the seller makes or procures such a bid, and notice has not been given that liberty for such bidding is reserved, the buyer may at his option avoid the sale or take the goods at the price of the last good faith bid prior to the completion of the sale. This subsection shall not apply to any bid at a forced sale.

Part 4 Title, Creditors and Good Faith Purchasers

Section 2–401. Passing of Title; Reservation for Security; Limited Application of This Section

Each provision of this Article with regard to the rights, obligations and remedies of the seller, the buyer, purchasers or other third parties applies irrespective of title to the goods except where the provision refers to such title. Insofar as situations are not covered by the other provisions of this Article and matters concerning title become material the following rules apply:

(1) Title to goods cannot pass under a contract for sale prior to their identification to the contract (Section 2–501), and unless otherwise explicitly agreed the buyer acquires by their identification a special property as limited by this Act. Any retention or reservation by the seller of the title (property) in goods shipped or delivered to the buyer is limited in effect to a reservation of a security interest. Subject to these provisions and to the provisions of the Article on Secured Transactions (Article 9), title to goods passes from the seller to the buyer in any manner and on any conditions explicitly agreed on by the parties.

(2) Unless otherwise explicitly agreed title passes to the buyer at the time and place at which the seller completes his performance with reference to the physical delivery of the goods, despite any reservation of a security interest and even though a document of title is to be delivered at a different time or place; and in particular and despite any reservation of a security interest by the bill of lading

   (a) if the contract requires or authorizes the seller to send the goods to the buyer but does not require him to deliver them at destination, title passes to the buyer at the time and place of shipment; but

   (b) if the contract requires delivery at destination, title passes on tender there.

(3) Unless otherwise explicitly agreed where delivery is to be made without moving the goods,

   (a) if the seller is to deliver a document of title, title passes at the time when and the place where he delivers such documents; or

   (b) if the goods are at the time of contracting already identified and no documents are to be delivered, title passes at the time and place of contracting.

(4) A rejection or other refusal by the buyer to receive or retain the goods, whether or not justified, or a justified revocation of acceptance revests title to the goods in the

seller. Such revesting occurs by operation of law and is not a "sale."

Section 2–402. Rights of Seller's Creditors Against Sold Goods

(1) Except as provided in subsections (2) and (3), rights of unsecured creditors of the seller with respect to goods which have been identified to a contract for sale are subject to the buyer's rights to recover the goods under this Article (Sections 2–502 and 2–716).

(2) A creditor of the seller may treat a sale or an identification of goods to a contract for sale as void if as against him a retention of possession by the seller is fraudulent under any rule of law of the state where the goods are situated, except that retention of possession in good faith and current course of trade by a merchant-seller for a commercially reasonable time after a sale or identification is not fraudulent.

(3) Nothing in this Article shall be deemed to impair the rights of creditors of the seller

  (a) under the provision of the Article on Secured Transactions (Article 9); or

  (b) where identification to the contract or delivery is made not in current course of trade but in satisfaction of or as security for a pre-existing claim for money, security or the like and is made under circumstances which under any rule of law of the state where the goods are situated would apart from this Article constitute the transaction a fraudulent transfer or voidable preference.

Section 2–403. Power to Transfer; Good Faith Purchase of Goods; "Entrusting"

(1) A purchaser of goods acquires all title which his transferor had or had power to transfer except that a purchaser of a limited interest acquires rights only to the extent of the interest purchased. A person with voidable title has power to transfer a good title to a good faith purchaser for value. When goods have been delivered under a transaction of purchase the purchaser has such power even though

  (a) the transferor was deceived as to the identity of the purchaser, or

  (b) the delivery was in exchange for a check which is later dishonored, or

  (c) it was agreed that the transaction was to be a "cash sale," or

  (d) the delivery was procured through fraud punishable as larcenous under the criminal law.

(2) Any entrusting of possession of goods to a merchant who deals in goods of that kind gives him power to transfer all rights of the entruster to a buyer in ordinary course of business.

(3) "Entrusting" includes any delivery and any acquiescence in retention of possession regardless of any condition expressed between the parties to the delivery or acquiescence and regardless of whether the procurement of the entrusting or the possessor's disposition of the goods have been such as to be larcenous under the criminal law.

(4) The rights of other purchasers of goods and of lien creditors are governed by the Articles on Secured Transactions (Article 9), Bulk Transfers (Article 6) and Documents of Title (Article 7).

Part 5 Performance

Section 2–501. Insurable Interest in Goods; Manner of Identification of Goods

(1) The buyer obtains a special property and an insurable interest in goods by identification of existing goods as goods to which the contract refers even though the goods so identified are nonconforming and he has an option to return or reject them. Such identification can be made at any time and in any manner explicitly agreed to by the parties. In the absence of explicit agreement identification occurs

  (a) when the contract is made if it is for the sale of goods already existing and identified;

  (b) if the contract is for the sale of future goods other than those described in paragraph (c), when goods are shipped, marked or otherwise designated by the seller as goods to which the contract refers;

  (c) when the crops are planted or otherwise become growing crops or the young are conceived if the contract is for the sale of unborn young to be born within twelve months after contracting or for the sale of crops to be harvested within twelve months or the next normal harvest season after contracting whichever is longer.

(2) The seller retains an insurable interest in goods so long as title to or any security interest in the goods remains in him and where the identification is by the seller alone he may until default or insolvency or notification to the buyer that the identification is final substitute other goods for those identified.

(3) Nothing in this section impairs any insurable interest recognized under any other statute or rule of law.

Section 2–502. Buyer's Right to Goods on Seller's Insolvency

(1) Subject to subsection (2) and even though the goods have not been shipped a buyer who has paid a part or

all of the price of goods in which he has a special property under the provisions of the immediately preceding section may on making and keeping good a tender of any unpaid portion of their price recover them from the seller if the seller becomes insolvent within ten days after receipt of the first installment on their price.

(2) If the identification creating his special property has been made by the buyer he acquires the right to recover the goods only if they conform to the contract for sale.

Section 2–503. Manner of Seller's Tender of Delivery

(1) Tender of delivery requires that the seller put and hold conforming goods at the buyer's disposition and give the buyer any notification reasonably necessary to enable him to take delivery. The manner, time and place for tender are determined by the agreement and this Article, and in particular

    (a) tender must be at a reasonable hour, and if it is of goods they must be kept available for the period reasonably necessary to enable the buyer to take possession; but

    (b) unless otherwise agreed the buyer must furnish facilities reasonably suited to the receipt of the goods.

(2) Where the case is within the next section respecting shipment tender requires that the seller comply with its provisions.

(3) Where the seller is required to deliver at a particular destination tender requires that he comply with subsection (1) and also in any appropriate case tender documents as described in subsections (4) and (5) of this section.

(4) Where goods are in the possession of a bailee and are to be delivered without being moved

    (a) tender requires that the seller either tender a negotiable document of title covering such goods or procure acknowledgement by the bailee of the buyer's right to possession of the goods; but

    (b) tender to the buyer of a non-negotiable document of title or of a written direction to the bailee to deliver is sufficient tender unless the buyer seasonably objects, and receipt by the bailee of notification of the buyer's rights fixes those rights as against the bailee and all third persons; but risk of loss of the goods and of any failure by the bailee to honor the nonnegotiable document of title or to obey the direction remains on the seller until the buyer has had a reasonable time to present the document or direction, and a refusal by the bailee to honor the document or to obey the direction defeats the tender.

(5) Where the contract requires the seller to deliver documents

    (a) he must tender all such documents in correct form, except as provided in this Article with respect to bills of lading in a set (subsection (2) of Section 2–323); and

    (b) tender through customary banking channels is sufficient and dishonor of a draft accompanying the documents constitutes nonacceptance or rejection.

Section 2–504. Shipment by Seller

Where the seller is required or authorized to send the goods to the buyer and the contract does not require him to deliver them at a particular destination, then unless otherwise agreed he must

    (a) put the goods in the possession of such a carrier and make such a contract for their transportation as may be reasonable having regard to the nature of the goods and other circumstances of the case; and

    (b) obtain and promptly deliver or tender in due form any document necessary to enable the buyer to obtain possession of the goods or otherwise required by the agreement or by usage of trade; and

    (c) promptly notify the buyer of the shipment.

Failure to notify the buyer under paragraph (c) or to make a proper contract under paragraph (a) is a ground for rejection only if material delay or loss ensues.

Section 2–505. Seller's Shipment Under Reservation

(1) Where the seller has identified goods to the contract by or before shipment:

    (a) his procurement of a negotiable bill of lading to his own order or otherwise reserves in him a security interest in the goods. His procurement of the bill to the order of a financing agency or of the buyer indicates in addition only the seller's expectation of transferring that interest to the person named.

    (b) a non-negotiable bill of lading to himself or his nominee reserves possession of the goods as security but except in a case of conditional delivery (subsection (2) of Section 2–507) a non-negotiable bill of lading naming the buyer as consignee reserves no security interest even though the seller retains possession of the bill of lading.

(2) When shipment by the seller with reservation of a security interest is in violation of the contract for sale it constitutes an improper contract for transportation within

the preceding section but impairs neither the rights given to the buyer by shipment and identification of the goods to the contract nor the seller's powers as a holder of a negotiable document.

Section 2–506. Rights of Financing Agency

(1) A financing agency by paying or purchasing for value a draft which relates to a shipment of goods acquires to the extent of the payment or purchase and in addition to its own rights under the draft and any document of title securing it any rights of the shipper in the goods including the right to stop delivery and the shipper's right to have the draft honored by the buyer.

(2) The right to reimbursement of a financing agency which has in good faith honored or purchased the draft under commitment to or authority from the buyer is not impaired by subsequent discovery of defects with reference to any relevant document which was apparently regular on its face.

Section 2–507. Effect of Seller's Tender; Delivery on Condition

(1) Tender of delivery is a condition to the buyer's duty to accept the goods and, unless otherwise agreed, to his duty to pay for them. Tender entitles the seller to acceptance of the goods and to payment according to the contract.

(2) Where payment is due and demanded on the delivery to the buyer of goods or documents of title, his right as against the seller to retain or dispose of them is conditional upon his making the payment due.

Section 2–508. Cure by Seller of Improper Tender or Delivery; Replacement

(1) Where any tender or delivery by the seller is rejected because non-conforming and the time for performance has not yet expired, the seller may seasonably notify the buyer of his intention to cure and may then within the contract time make a conforming delivery.

(2) Where the buyer rejects a non-conforming tender which the seller had reasonable grounds to believe would be acceptable with or without money allowance the seller may if he seasonably notifies the buyer have a further reasonable time to substitute a conforming tender.

Section 2–509. Risk of Loss in the Absence of Breach

(1) Where the contract requires or authorizes the seller to ship the goods by carrier

  (a) if it does not require him to deliver them at a particular destination, the risk of loss passes to the buyer when the goods are duly delivered to the carrier even though the shipment is under reservation (Section 2–505); but

  (b) if it does require him to deliver them at a particular destination and the goods are there duly tendered while in the possession of the carrier, the risk of loss passes to the buyer when the goods are there duly so tendered as to enable the buyer to take delivery.

(2) Where the goods are held by a bailee to be delivered without being moved, the risk of loss passes to the buyer

  (a) on his receipt of a negotiable document of title covering the goods; or

  (b) on acknowledgment by the bailee of the buyer's right to possession of the goods; or

  (c) after his receipt of a non-negotiable document of title or other written direction to deliver, as provided in subsection (4) (b) of Section 2–503.

(3) In any case not within subsection (1) or (2), the risk of loss passes to the buyer on his receipt of the goods if the seller is a merchant; otherwise the risk passes to the buyer on tender of delivery.

(4) The provisions of this section are subject to contrary agreement of the parties and to the provisions of this Article on sale on approval (Section 2–327) and on effect of breach on risk of loss (Section 2–510).

Section 2–510. Effect of Breach on Risk of Loss

(1) Where a tender or delivery of goods so fails to conform to the contract as to give a right of rejection the risk of their loss remains on the seller until cure or acceptance.

(2) Where the buyer rightfully revokes acceptance he may to the extent of any deficiency in his effective insurance coverage treat the risk of loss as having rested on the seller from the beginning.

(3) Where the buyer as to conforming goods already identified to the contract for sale repudiates or is otherwise in breach before risk of their loss has passed to him, the seller may to the extent of any deficiency in his effective insurance coverage treat the risk of loss as resting on the buyer for a commercially reasonable time.

Section 2–511. Tender of Payment of Buyer; Payment of Check

(1) Unless otherwise agreed tender of payment is a condition to the seller's duty to tender and complete any delivery.

(2) Tender of payment is sufficient when made by any means or in any manner current in the ordinary course of business unless the seller demands payment in legal tender and gives any extension of time reasonably necessary to procure it.

(3) Subject to the provisions of this Act on the effect of an instrument on an obligation (Section 3–802), pay-

ment by check is conditional and is defeated as between the parties by dishonor of the check on due presentment.

Section 2–512. Payment by Buyer Before Inspection

(1) Where the contract requires payment before inspection non-conformity of the goods does not excuse the buyer from so making payment unless

    (a) the non-conformity appears without inspection; or

    (b) despite tender of the required documents the circumstances would justify injunction against honor under the provisions of this Act (Section 5–114).

(2) Payment pursuant to subsection (1) does not constitute an acceptance of goods or impair the buyer's right to inspect or any of his remedies.

Section 2–513. Buyer's Right to Inspection of Goods

(1) Unless otherwise agreed and subject to subsection (3), where goods are tendered or delivered or identified to the contract for sale, the buyer has a right before payment or acceptance to inspect them at any reasonable place and time and in any reasonable manner. When the seller is required or authorized to send the goods to the buyer, the inspection may be after their arrival.

(2) Expenses of inspection must be borne by the buyer but may be recovered from the seller if the goods do not conform and are rejected.

(3) Unless otherwise agreed and subject to the provisions of this Article on C.I.F. contracts (subsection (3) of Section 2–321), the buyer is not entitled to inspect the goods before payment of the price when the contract provides

    (a) for delivery "C.O.D." or on other like terms; or

    (b) for payment against documents of title, except where such payment is due only after the goods are to become available for inspection.

(4) A place or method of inspection fixed by the parties is presumed to be exclusive but unless otherwise expressly agreed it does not postpone identification or shift the place for delivery or for passing the risk of loss. If compliance becomes impossible, inspection shall be as provided in this section unless the place or method fixed was clearly intended as an indispensable condition failure of which avoids the contract.

Section 2–514. When Documents Deliverable on Acceptance; When on Payment

Unless otherwise agreed documents against which a draft is drawn are to be delivered to the drawee on acceptance of the draft if it is payable more than three days after presentment; otherwise, only on payment.

Section 2–515. Preserving Evidence of Goods in Dispute

In furtherance of the adjustment of any claim or dispute

    (a) either party on reasonable notification to the other and for the purpose of ascertaining the facts and preserving evidence has the right to inspect, test and sample the goods including such of them as may be in the possession or control of the other; and

    (b) the parties may agree to a third party inspection or survey to determine the conformity or condition of the goods and may agree that the findings shall be binding upon them in any subsequent litigation or adjustment.

Part 6 Breach, Repudiation and Excuse

Section 2–601. Buyer's Rights on Improper Delivery

Subject to the provisions of this Article on breach in installment contracts (Section 2–612) and unless otherwise agreed under the sections on contractual limitations of remedy (Sections 2–718 and 2–719), if the goods or the tender of delivery fail in any respect to conform to the contract, the buyer may

    (a) reject the whole; or

    (b) accept the whole; or

    (c) accept any commercial unit or units and reject the rest.

Section 2–602. Manner and Effect of Rightful Rejection

(1) Rejection of goods must be within a reasonable time after their delivery or tender. It is ineffective unless the buyer seasonably notifies the seller.

(2) Subject to the provisions of the two following sections on rejected goods (Sections 2–603 and 2–604).

    (a) after rejection any exercise of ownership by the buyer with respect to any commercial unit is wrongful as against the seller; and

    (b) if the buyer has before rejection taken physical possession of goods in which he does not have a security interest under the provisions of this Article (subsection (3) of Section 2–711), he is under a duty after rejection to hold them with reasonable care at the seller's disposition for a time sufficient to permit the seller to remove them; but

    (c) the buyer has no further obligations with regard to goods rightfully rejected.

(3) The seller's rights with respect to goods wrongfully rejected are governed by the provisions of this Article on Seller's remedies in general (Section 2–703).

Section 2–603. Merchant Buyer's Duties as to Rightfully Rejected Goods

(1) Subject to any security interest in the buyer (subsection (3) of Section 2–711), when the seller has no agent or place of business at the market of rejection a merchant buyer is under a duty after rejection of goods in his possession or control to follow any reasonable instructions received from the seller with respect to the goods and in the absence of such instructions to make reasonable efforts to sell them for the seller's account if they are perishable or threaten to decline in value speedily. Instructions are not reasonable if on demand indemnity for expenses is not forthcoming.

(2) When the buyer sells goods under subsection (1), he is entitled to reimbursement from the seller or out of the proceeds for reasonable expenses of caring for and selling them, and if the expenses include no selling commission then to such commission as is usual in the trade or if there is none to a reasonable sum not exceeding ten per cent on the gross proceeds.

(3) In complying with this section the buyer is held only to good faith and good faith conduct hereunder is neither acceptance nor conversion nor the basis of an action for damages.

Section 2–604. Buyer's Options as to Salvage of Rightfully Rejected Goods

Subject to the provisions of the immediately preceding section on perishables if the seller gives no instructions within a reasonable time after notification of rejection the buyer may store the rejected goods for the seller's account or reship them to him or resell them for the seller's account with reimbursement as provided in the preceding section. Such action is not acceptance or conversion.

Section 2–605. Waiver of Buyer's Objections by Failure to Particularize

(1) The buyer's failure to state in connection with rejection a particular defect which is ascertainable by reasonable inspection precludes him from relying on the unstated defect to justify rejection or to establish breach

(a) where the seller could have cured it if stated seasonably; or

(b) between merchants when the seller has after rejection made a request in writing for a full and final written statement of all defects on which the buyer proposes to rely.

(2) Payment against documents made without reservation of rights precludes recovery of the payment for defects apparent on the face of the documents.

Section 2–606. What Constitutes Acceptance of Goods

(1) Acceptance of goods occurs when the buyer

(a) after a reasonable opportunity to inspect the goods signifies to the seller that the goods are conforming or that he will take or retain them in spite of their non-conformity; or

(b) fails to make an effective rejection (subsection (1) of Section 2–602), but such acceptance does not occur until the buyer has had a reasonable opportunity to inspect them; or

(c) does any act inconsistent with the seller's ownership; but if such act is wrongful as against the seller it is an acceptance only if ratified by him.

(2) Acceptance of a part of any commercial unit is acceptance of that entire unit.

Section 2–607. Effect of Acceptance; Notice of Breach; Burden of Establishing Breach After Acceptance; Notice of Claim or Litigation to Person Answerable Over

(1) The buyer must pay at the contract rate for any goods accepted.

(2) Acceptance of goods by the buyer precludes rejection of the goods accepted and if made with knowledge of a non-conformity cannot be revoked because of it unless the acceptance was on the reasonable assumption that the non-conformity would be seasonably cured but acceptance does not of itself impair any other remedy provided by this Article for non-conformity.

(3) Where a tender has been accepted

(a) the buyer must within a reasonable time after he discovers or should have discovered any breach notify the seller of breach or be barred from any remedy; and

(b) if the claim is one for infringement or the like (subsection (3) of Section 2–312) and the buyer is sued as a result of such a breach he must so notify the seller within a reasonable time after he receives notice of the litigation or be barred from any remedy over for liability established by the litigation.

(4) The burden is on the buyer to establish any breach with respect to the goods accepted.

(5) Where the buyer is sued for breach of a warranty or other obligation for which his seller is answerable over

(a) he may give his seller written notice of the litigation. If the notice states that the seller may come in and defend and that if the seller does not do so he will be bound in any action against him by his buyer by any determination of fact common to the two litigations, then unless the seller after seasonable receipt of the notice does come in and defend he is so bound.

(b) if the claim is one for infringement or the like (subsection (3) of Section 2–312) the original seller may demand in writing that his buyer turn over to him control of the litigation including settlement or else be barred from any remedy over and if he also agrees to bear all expense and to satisfy any adverse judgment, then unless the buyer after seasonable receipt of the demand does turn over control the buyer is so barred.

(6) The provisions of subsections (3), (4) and (5) apply to any obligation of a buyer to hold the seller harmless against infringement or the like (subsection (3) of Section 2–312).

Section 2–608. Revocation of Acceptance in Whole or in Part

(1) The buyer may revoke his acceptance of a lot or commercial unit whose non-conformity substantially impairs its value to him if he has accepted it

(a) on the reasonable assumption that its nonconformity would be cured and it has not been seasonably cured; or

(b) without discovery of such non-conformity if his acceptance was reasonably induced either by the difficulty of discovery before acceptance or by the seller's assurances.

(2) Revocation of acceptance must occur within a reasonable time after the buyer discovers or should have discovered the ground for it and before any substantial change in conditions of the goods which is not caused by their own defects. It is not effective until the buyer notifies the seller of it.

(3) A buyer who so revokes has the same rights and duties with regard to the goods involved as if he had rejected them.

Section 2–609. Right to Adequate Assurance of Performance

(1) A contract for sale imposes an obligation on each party that the other's expectation of receiving due performance will not be impaired. When reasonable grounds for insecurity arise with respect to the performance of either party the other may in writing demand adequate assurance of due performance and until he received such assurance may if commercially reasonable suspend any performance for which he has not already received the agreed return.

(2) Between merchants the reasonableness of grounds for insecurity and the adequacy of any assurance offered shall be determined according to commercial standards.

(3) Acceptance of any improper delivery or payment does not prejudice the aggrieved party's right to demand adequate assurance of future performance.

(4) After receipt of a justified demand failure to provide within a reasonable time not exceeding thirty days such assurance of due performance as is adequate under the circumstances of the particular case is a repudiation of the contract.

Section 2–610. Anticipatory Repudiation

When either party repudiates the contract with respect to a performance not yet due the loss of which will substantially impair the value of the contract to the other, the aggrieved party may

(a) for a commercially reasonable time await performance by the repudiating party; or

(b) resort to any remedy for breach (Section 2–703 or Section 2–711), even though he has notified the repudiating party that he would await the latter's performance and has urged retraction; and

(c) in either case suspend his own performance or proceed in accordance with the provisions of this Article on the seller's right to identify goods to the contract notwithstanding breach or to salvage unfinished goods (Section 2–704).

Section 2–611. Retraction of Anticipatory Repudiation

(1) Until the repudiating party's next performance is due he can retract his repudiation unless the aggrieved party has since the repudiation cancelled or materially changed his position or otherwise indicated that he considers the repudiation final.

(2) Retraction may be by any method which clearly indicates to the aggrieved party that the repudiating party intends to perform, but must include any assurance justifiably demanded under the provisions of this Article (Section 2–609).

(3) Retraction reinstates the repudiating party's rights under the contract with due excuse and allowance to the aggrieved party for any delay occasioned by the repudiation.

Section 2–612. "Installment Contract"; Breach

(1) An "installment contract" is one which requires or authorizes the delivery of goods in separate lots to be

separately accepted, even though the contract contains a clause "each delivery is a separate contract" or its equivalent.

(2) The buyer may reject any installment which is nonconforming if the non-conformity substantially impairs the value of that installment and cannot be cured or if the non-conformity is a defect in the required documents; but if the nonconformity does not fall within subsection (3) and the seller gives adequate assurance of its cure the buyer must accept that installment.

(3) Whenever non-conformity or default with respect to one or more installments substantially impairs the value of the whole contract there is a breach of the whole. But the aggrieved party reinstates the contract if he accepts a non-conforming installment without seasonably notifying of cancellation or if he brings an action with respect only to past installments or demands performance as to future installments.

Section 2–613. Casualty to Identified Goods

Where the contract requires for its performance goods identified when the contract is made, and the goods suffer casualty without fault of either party before the risk of loss passes to the buyer, or in a proper case under a "no arrival, no sale" term (Section 2–324) then

(a) if the loss is total the contract is avoided; and

(b) if the loss is partial or the goods have so deteriorated as no longer to conform to the contract the buyer may nevertheless demand inspection and at his option either treat the contract as avoided or accept the goods with due allowance from the contract price for the deterioration or the deficiency in quantity but without further right against the seller.

Section 2–614. Substituted Performance

(1) Where without fault of either party the agreed berthing, loading, or unloading facilities fail or an agreed type of carrier becomes unavailable or the agreed manner of delivery otherwise becomes commercially impracticable but a commercially reasonable substitute is available, such substitute performance must be tendered and accepted.

(2) If the agreed means or manner of payment fails because of domestic or foreign governmental regulation, the seller may withhold or stop delivery unless the buyer provides a means or manner of payment which is commercially a substantial equivalent. If delivery has already been taken, payment by the means or in the manner provided by the regulation discharges the buyer's obligation unless the regulation is discriminatory, oppressive or predatory.

Section 2–615. Excuse by Failure of Presupposed Conditions

Except so far as a seller may have assumed a greater obligation and subject to the preceding section on substitute performance:

(a) Delay in delivery or non-delivery in whole or in part by a seller who complies with paragraphs (b) and (c) is not a breach of his duty under a contract for sale if performance as agreed has been made impracticable by the occurrence of a contingency the nonoccurrence of which was a basic assumption on which the contract was made or by compliance in good faith with any applicable foreign or domestic governmental regulation or order whether or not it later proves to be invalid.

(b) Where the causes mentioned in paragraph (a) affect only a part of the seller's capacity to perform, he must allocate production and deliveries among his customers but may at his option include regular customers not then under contract as well as his own requirements for further manufacture. He may so allocate in any manner which is fair and reasonable.

(c) The seller must notify the buyer seasonably that there will be delay or non-delivery and, when allocation is required under paragraph (b), of the estimated quota thus made available for the buyer.

Section 2–616. Procedure on Notice Claiming Excuse

(1) Where the buyer receives notification of a material or indefinite delay or an allocation justified under the preceding section he may by written notification to the seller as to any delivery concerned, and where the prospective deficiency substantially impairs the value of the whole contract under the provisions of this Article relating to breach of installment contracts (Section 2–612), then also as to the whole,

(a) terminate and thereby discharge any unexecuted portion of the contract; or

(b) modify the contract by agreeing to take his available quota in substitution.

(2) If after receipt of such notification from the seller the buyer fails so to modify the contract within a reasonable time not exceeding thirty days the contract lapses with respect to any deliveries affected.

(3) The provisions of this section may not be negated by agreement except in so far as the seller has assumed a greater obligation under the preceding section.

Part 7 Remedies

Section 2–701. Remedies for Breach of Collateral Contracts Not Impaired

Remedies for breach of any obligation or promise collateral or ancillary to a contract for sale are not impaired by the provisions of this Article.

Section 2–702. Seller's Remedies on Discovery of Buyer's Insolvency

(1) Where the seller discovers the buyer to be insolvent he may refuse delivery except for cash including payment for all goods theretofore delivered under the contract, and stop delivery under this Article (Section 2–705).

(2) Where the seller discovers that the buyer has received goods on credit while insolvent he may reclaim the goods upon demand made within ten days after the receipt, but if misrepresentation of solvency has been made to the particular seller in writing within three months before delivery the ten-day limitation does not apply. Except as provided in this subsection the seller may not base a right to reclaim goods on the buyer's fraudulent or innocent misrepresentation of solvency or of intent to pay.

(3) The seller's right to reclaim under subsection (2) is subject to the rights of a buyer in ordinary course or other good faith purchaser under this Article (Section 2–403). Successful reclamation of goods excludes all other remedies with respect to them.

Section 2–703. Seller's Remedies in General

Where the buyer wrongfully rejects or revokes acceptance of goods or fails to make a payment due on or before delivery or repudiates with respect to a part or the whole, then with respect to any goods directly affected and, if the breach is of the whole contract (Section 2–612), then also with respect to the whole undelivered balance, the aggrieved seller may

(a) withhold delivery of such goods;

(b) stop delivery by any bailee as hereafter provided (Section 2–705);

(c) proceed under the next section respecting goods still unidentified to the contract;

(d) resell and recover damages as hereafter provided (Section 2–706);

(e) recover damages for non-acceptance (Section 2–708) or in a proper case the price (Section 2–709);

(f) cancel.

Section 2–704. Seller's Right to Identify Goods to the Contract Notwithstanding Breach or to Salvage Unfinished Goods

(1) An aggrieved seller under the preceding section may

(a) identify to the contract conforming goods not already identified if at the time he learned of the breach they are in his possession or control;

(b) treat as the subject of resale goods which have demonstrably been intended for the particular contract even though those goods are unfinished.

(2) Where the goods are unfinished an aggrieved seller may in the exeircse of reasonable commercial judgment for the purposes of avoiding loss and of effective realization either complete the manufacture and wholly identify the goods to the contract or cease manufacture and resell for scrap or salvage value or proceed in any other reasonable manner.

Section 2–705. Seller's Stoppage of Delivery in Transit or Otherwise

(1) The seller may stop delivery of goods in the possession of a carrier or other bailee when he discovers the buyer to be insolvent (Section 2–702) and may stop delivery of carload, truckload, planeload or larger shipments of express or freight when the buyer repudiates or fails to make a payment due before delivery or if for any other reason the seller has a right to withhold or reclaim the goods.

(2) As against such buyer the seller may stop delivery until

(a) receipt of the goods by the buyer; or

(b) acknowledgment to the buyer by any bailee of the goods except a carrier that the bailee holds the goods for the buyer; or

(c) such acknowledgment to the buyer by a carrier by reshipment or as warehouseman; or

(d) negotiation to the buyer of any negotiable document of title covering the goods.

(3) (a) To stop delivery the seller must so notify as to enable the bailee by reasonable diligence to prevent delivery of the goods.

(b) After such notification the bailee must hold and deliver the goods according to the directions of the seller but the seller is liable to the bailee for any ensuing charges or damages.

(c) If a negotiable document of title has been issued for goods the bailee is not obliged to obey a notification to stop until surrender of the document.

(d) A carrier who has issued a non-negotiable bill of lading is not obliged to obey a notification to stop received from a person other than the consignor.

Section 2–706. Seller's Resale Including Contract for Resale

(1) Under the conditions stated in Section 2–703 on seller's remedies, the seller may resell the goods concerned or the undelivered balance thereof. Where the resale is made in good faith and in a commercially reasonable manner the seller may recover the difference between the resale price and the contract price together with any incidental damages allowed under the provisions of this Article (Section 2–710), but less expenses saved in consequence of the buyer's breach.

(2) Except as otherwise provided in subsection (3) or unless otherwise agreed resale may be at public or private sale including sale by way of one or more contracts to sell or of identification to an existing contract of the seller. Sale may be as a unit or in parcels and at any time and place and on any terms but every aspect of the sale including the method, manner, time, place and terms must be commercially reasonable. The resale must be reasonably identified as referring to the broken contract, but it is not necessary that the goods be in existence or that any or all of them have been identified to the contract before the breach.

(3) Where the resale is at private sale the seller must give the buyer reasonable notification of his intention to resell.

(4) Where the resale is at public sale

(a) only identified goods can be sold except where there is a recognized market for a public sale of futures in goods of the kind; and

(b) it must be made at a usual place or market for public sale if one is reasonably available and except in the case of goods which are perishable or threaten to decline in value speedily the seller must give the buyer reasonable notice of the time and place of the resale; and

(c) if the goods are not to be within the view of those attending the sale the notification of sale must state the place where the goods are located and provide for their reasonable inspection by prospective bidders; and

(d) the seller may buy.

(5) A purchaser who buys in good faith at a resale takes the goods free of any rights of the original buyer even though the seller fails to comply with one or more of the requirements of this section.

(6) The seller is not accountable to the buyer for any profit made on any resale. A person in the position of a seller (Section 2–707) or a buyer who has rightfully rejected or justifiably revoked acceptance must account for any excess over the amount of his security interest, as hereinafter defined (subsection (3) of Section 2–711).

Section 2–707. "Person in the Position of a Seller"

(1) A "person in the position of a seller" includes as against a principal an agent who has paid or become responsible for the price of goods on behalf of his principal or anyone who otherwise holds a security interest or other right in goods similar to that of a seller.

(2) A person in the position of a seller may as provided in this Article withhold or stop delivery (Section 2–705) and resell (Section 2–706) and recover incidental damages (Section 2–710).

Section 2–708. Seller's Damages for Non-Acceptance or Repudiation

(1) Subject to subsection (2) and to the provisions of this Article with respect to proof of market price (Section 2–723), the measure of damages for non-acceptance or repudiation by the buyer is the difference between the market price at the time and place for tender and the unpaid contract price together with any incidental damages provided in this Article (Section 2–710), but less expenses saved in consequence of the buyer's breach.

(2) If the measure of damages provided in subsection (1) is inadequate to put the seller in as good a position as performance would have done then the measure of damages is the profit (including reasonable overhead) which the seller would have made from full performance by the buyer, together with any incidental damages provided in this Article (Section 2–710), due allowance for costs reasonably incurred and due credit for payments or proceeds of resale.

Section 2–709. Action for the Price

(1) When the buyer fails to pay the price as it becomes due the seller may recover, together with any incidental damages under the next section, the price

(a) of goods accepted or of conforming goods lost or damaged within a commercially reasonable time after risk of their loss has passed to the buyer; and

(b) of goods identified to the contract if the seller is unable after reasonable effort to resell them at a reasonable price or the circumstances reasonably indicate that such effort will be unavailing.

(2) Where the seller sues for the price he must hold for the buyer any goods which have been identified to the contract and are still in his control except that if resale becomes possible he may resell them at any time prior to the collection of the judgment. The net proceeds of any such resale must be credited to the buyer and payment of the judgment entitles him to any goods not resold.

(3) After the buyer has wrongfully rejected or revoked acceptance of the goods or has failed to make a payment due or has repudiated (Section 2–610), a seller who is held not entitled to the price under this section shall nevertheless be awarded damages for non-acceptance under the preceding section.

Section 2–710. Seller's Incidental Damages

Incidental damages to an aggrieved seller include any commercially reasonable charges, expenses or commissions incurred in stopping delivery, in the transportation, care and custody of goods after the buyer's breach, in connection with return or resale of the goods or otherwise resulting from the breach.

Section 2–711. Buyer's Remedies in General; Buyer's Security Interest in Rejected Goods

(1) Where the seller fails to make delivery or repudiates or the buyer rightfully rejects or justifiably revokes acceptance then with respect to any goods involved, and with respect to the whole if the breach goes to the whole contract (Section 2–612), the buyer may cancel and whether or not he has done so may in addition to recovering so much of the price as has been paid

(a) "cover" and have damages under the next section as to all the goods affected whether or not they have been identified to the contract; or

(b) recover damages for non-delivery as provided in this Article (Section 2–713).

(2) Where the seller fails to deliver or repudiates the buyer may also

(a) if the goods have been identified recover them as provided in this Article (Section 2–502); or

(b) in a proper case obtain specific performance or replevy the goods as provided in this Article (Section 2–716).

(3) On rightful rejection or justifiable revocation of acceptance a buyer has a security interest in goods in his possession or control for any payments made on their price and any expenses reasonably incurred in their inspection, receipt, transportation, care and custody and may hold

such goods and resell them in like manner as an aggrieved seller (Section 2–706).

Section 2–712. "Cover"; Buyer's Procurement of Substitute Goods

(1) After a breach within the preceding section the buyer may "cover" by making in good faith and without unreasonable delay any reasonable purchase of or contract to purchase goods in substitution for those due from the seller.

(2) The buyer may recover from the seller as damages the difference between the cost of cover and the contract price together with any incidental or consequential damages as hereinafter defined (Section 2–715), but less expenses saved in consequence of the seller's breach.

(3) Failure of the buyer to effect cover within this section does not bar him from any other remedy.

Section 2–713. Buyer's Damages for Non-Delivery or Repudiation

(1) Subject to the provisions of this Article with respect to proof of market price (Section 2–723), the measure of damages for non-delivery or repudiation by the seller is the difference between the market price at the time when the buyer learned of the breach and the contract price together with any incidental and consequential damages provided in this Article (Section 2–715), but less expenses saved in consequence of the seller's breach.

(2) Market price is to be determined as of the place for tender or, in cases of rejection after arrival or revocation of acceptance, as of the place of arrival.

Section 2–714. Buyer's Damages for Breach in Regard to Accepted Goods

(1) Where the buyer has accepted goods and given notification (subsection (3) of Section 2–607) he may recover as damages for any nonconformity of tender the loss resulting in the ordinary course of events from the seller's breach as determined in any manner which is reasonable.

(2) The measure of damages for breach of warranty is the difference at the time and place of acceptance between the value of the goods accepted and the value they would have had if they had been warranted, unless special circumstances show proximate damages of a different amount.

(3) In a proper case any incidental and consequential damages under the next section may also be recovered.

Section 2–715. Buyer's Incidental and Consequential Damages

(1) Incidental damages resulting from the seller's breach include expenses reasonably incurred in inspection, re-

ceipt, transportation and care and custody of goods rightfully rejected, any commercially reasonable charges, expenses or commissions in connection with effecting cover and any other reasonable expense incident to the delay or other breach.

(2) Consequential damages resulting from the seller's breach include

(a) any loss resulting from general or particular requirements and needs of which the seller at the time of contracting had reason to know and which could not reasonably be prevented by cover or otherwise; and

(b) injury to person or property proximately resulting from any breach of warranty.

Section 2–716. Buyer's Right to Specific Performance or Replevin

(1) Specific performance may be decreed where the goods are unique or in other proper circumstances.

(2) The decree for specific performance may include such terms and conditions as to payment of the price, damages, or other relief as the court may deem just.

(3) The buyer has a right of replevin for goods identified to the contract if after reasonable effort he is unable to effect cover for such goods or the circumstances reasonably indicate that such effort will be unavailing or if the goods have been shipped under reservation and satisfaction of the security interest in them has been made or tendered.

Section 2–717. Deduction of Damages From the Price

The buyer on notifying the seller of his intention to do so may deduct all or any part of the damages resulting from any breach of the contract from any part of the price still due under the same contract.

Section 2–718. Liquidation or Limitation of Damages; Deposits

(1) Damages for breach by either party may be liquidated in the agreement but only at an amount which is reasonable in the light of the anticipated or actual harm caused by the breach, the difficulties of proof of loss, and the inconvenience or nonfeasibility of otherwise obtaining an adequate remedy. A term fixing unreasonably large liquidated damages is void as a penalty.

(2) Where the seller justifiably withholds delivery of goods because of the buyer's breach, the buyer is entitled to restitution of any amount by which the sum of his payments exceeds

(a) the amount to which the seller is entitled by virtue of terms liquidating the seller's damages in accordance with subsection (1), or

(b) in the absence of such terms, twenty per cent of the value of the total performance for which the buyer is obligated under the contract or $500, whichever is smaller.

(3) The buyer's right to restitution under subsection (2) is subject to offset to the extent that the seller establishes

(a) a right to recover damages under the provisions of this Article other than subsection (1), and

(b) the amount or value of any benefits received by the buyer directly or indirectly by reason of the contract.

(4) Where a seller has received payment in goods their reasonable value or the proceeds of their resale shall be treated as payments for the purposes of subsection (2); but if the seller has notice of the buyer's breach before reselling goods received in part performance, his resale is subject to the conditions laid down in this Article on resale by an aggrieved seller (Section 2–706).

Section 2–719. Contractual Modification or Limitation of Remedy

(1) Subject to the provisions of subsections (2) and (3) of this section and of the preceding section on liquidation and limitation of damages,

(a) the agreement may provide the remedies in addition to or in substitution for those provided in this Article and may limit or alter the measure of damages recoverable under this Article, as by limiting the buyer's remedies to return of the goods and repayment of the price or to repair and replacement of nonconforming goods or parts; and

(b) resort to a remedy as provided is optional unless the remedy is expressly agreed to be exclusive, in which case it is the sole remedy.

(2) Where circumstances cause an exclusive or limited remedy to fail of its essential purpose, remedy may be had as provided in this Act.

(3) Consequential damages may be limited or excluded unless the limitation or exclusion is unconscionable. Limitation of consequential damages for injury to the person in the case of consumer goods is prima facie unconscionable but limitation of damages where the loss is commercial is not.

Section 2–720. Effect of "Cancellation" or "Rescission" on Claims for Antecedent Breach

Unless the contrary intention clearly appears, expressions of "cancellation" or "rescission" of the contract or the like shall not be construed as a renunciation or discharge or any claim in damages for an antecedent breach.

Section 2–721. Remedies for Fraud

Remedies for material misrepresentation or fraud include all remedies available under this Article for non-fraudulent breach. Neither rescission or a claim for rescission of the contract for sale nor rejection or return of the goods shall bar or be deemed inconsistent with a claim for damages or other remedy.

Section 2–722. Who Can Sue Third Parties for Injury to Goods

Where a third party so deals with goods which have been identified to a contract for sale as to cause actionable injury to a party to that contract

(a) a right of action against the third party is in either party to the contract for sale who has title to or a security interest or a special property or an insurable interest in the goods; and if the goods have been destroyed or converted a right of action is also in the party who either bore the risk of loss under the contract for sale or has since the injury assumed that risk as against the other;

(b) if at the time of the injury the party plaintiff did not bear the risk of loss as against the other party to the contract for sale and there is no arrangement between them for disposition of the recovery, his suit or settlement is, subject to his own interest, as a fiduciary for the other party to the contract;

(c) either party may with the consent of the other sue for the benefit of whom it may concern.

Section 2–723. Proof of Market Price: Time and Place

(1) If an action based on anticipatory repudiation comes to trial before the time for performance with respect to some or all of the goods, any damages based on market price (Section 2–708 or Section 2–713) shall be determined according to the price of such goods prevailing at the time when the aggrieved party learned of the repudiation.

(2) If evidence of a price prevailing at the times or places described in this Article is not readily available the price prevailing within any reasonable time before or after the time described or at any other place which in commercial judgment or under usage of trade would serve as a reasonable substitute for the one described may be used, making any proper allowance for the cost of transporting the goods to or from such other place.

(3) Evidence of a relevant price prevailing at a time or place other than the one described in this Article offered by one party is not admissible unless and until he has given the other party such notice as the court finds sufficient to prevent unfair surprise.

Section 2–724. Admissibility of Market Quotations

Whenever the prevailing price or value of any goods regularly bought and sold in any established commodity market is in issue, reports in official publications or trade journals or in newspapers or periodicals of general circulation published as the reports of such market shall be admissible in evidence. The circumstances of the preparation of such a report may be shown to affect its weight but not its admissibility.

Section 2–725. Statute of Limitations in Contracts for Sale

(1) An action for breach of any contract for sale must be commenced within four years after the cause of action has accrued. By the original agreement the parties may reduce the period of limitation to not less than one year but may not extend it.

(2) A cause of action accrues when the breach occurs, regardless of the aggrieved party's lack of knowledge of the breach. A breach of warranty occurs when tender of delivery is made, except that where a warranty explicitly extends to future performance of the goods and discovery of the breach must await the time of such performance the cause of action accrues when the breach is or should have been discovered.

(3) Where an action commenced within the time limited by subsection (1) is so terminated as to leave available a remedy by another action for the same breach such other action may be commenced after the expiration of the time limited and within six months after the termination of the first action unless the termination resulted from voluntary discontinuance or from dismissal for failure or neglect to prosecute.

(4) This section does not alter the law on tolling of the statute of limitations nor does it apply to causes of action which have accrued before this Act becomes effective.

ARTICLE 2A. LEASES

Part 1 General Provisions

Section 2A–101. Short Title

This Article shall be known and may be cited as the Uniform Commercial Code—Leases.

Section 2A–102. Scope

This Article applies to any transaction, regardless of form, that creates a lease.

Section 2A–103. Definitions and Index of Definitions

(1) In this Article unless the context otherwise requires:

(a) "Buyer in ordinary course of business" means a person who in good faith and without knowledge that the sale to him [or her] is in violation of the ownership rights or security interest or leasehold interest of a third party in the goods buys in ordinary course from a person in the business of selling goods of that kind but does not include a pawnbroker. "Buying" may be for cash or by exchange of other property or on secured or unsecured credit and includes receiving goods or documents of title under a pre-existing contract for sale but does not include a transfer in bulk or as security for or in total or partial satisfaction of a money debt.

(b) "Cancellation" occurs when either party puts an end to the lease contract for default by the other party.

(c) "Commercial unit" means such a unit of goods as by commercial usage is a single whole for purposes of lease and division of which materially impairs its character or value on the market or in use. A commercial unit may be a single article, as a machine, or a set of articles, as a suite of furniture or a line of machinery, or a quantity, as a gross or carload, or any other unit treated in use or in the relevant market as a single whole.

(d) "Conforming" goods or performance under a lease contract means goods or performance that are in accordance with the obligations under the lease contract.

(e) "Consumer lease" means a lease that a lessor regularly engaged in the business of leasing or selling makes to a lessee, except an organization, who takes under the lease primarily for a personal, family, or household purpose, if the total payments to be made under the lease contract, excluding payments for options to renew or buy, do not exceed $25,000.

(f) "Fault" means wrongful act, omission, breach, or default.

(g) "Finance lease" means a lease in which (i) the lessor does not select, manufacture or supply the goods, (ii) the lessor acquires the goods or the right to possession and use of the goods in connection with the lease, and (iii) either the lessee receives a copy of the contract evidencing the lessor's purchase of the goods on or before signing the lease contract, or the lessee's approval of the contract evidencing the lessor's purchase of the goods is a condition to effectiveness of the lease contract.

(h) "Goods" means all things that are movable at the time of identification to the lease contract, or are fixtures (Section 2A–309), but the term does not include money, documents, instruments, accounts, chattel paper, general intangibles, or minerals or the like, including oil and gas, before extraction. The term also includes the unborn young of animals.

(i) "Installment lease contract" means a lease contract that authorizes or requires the delivery of goods in separate lots to be separately accepted, even though the lease contract contains a clause "each delivery is a separate lease" or its equivalent.

(j) "Lease" means a transfer of the right to possession and use of goods for a term in return for consideration, but a sale, including a sale on approval or a sale or return, or retention or creation of a security interest is not a lease. Unless the context clearly indicates otherwise, the term includes a sublease.

(k) "Lease agreement" means the bargain, with respect to the lease, of the lessor and the lessee in fact as found in their language or by implication from other circumstances including course of dealing or usage of trade or course of performance as provided in this Article. Unless the context clearly indicates otherwise, the term includes a sublease agreement.

(1) "Lease contract" means the total legal obligation that results from the lease agreement as affected by this Article and any other applicable rules of law. Unless the context clearly indicates otherwise, the term includes a sublease contract.

(m) "Leasehold interest" means the interest of the lessor or the lessee under a lease contract.

(n) "Lessee" means a person who acquires the right to possession and use of goods under a lease. Unless the context clearly indicates otherwise, the term includes a sublessee.

(o) "Lessee in ordinary course of business" means a person who in good faith and without knowledge that the lease to him [or her] is in violation of the ownership rights or security interest or leasehold interest of a third party in the goods, leases in ordinary course from a person in the business of selling or leasing goods of that kind but does not include a pawnbroker. "Leasing" may be for cash or by exchange of other property or on secured or unsecured credit and includes receiving goods or documents of title under a pre-existing lease contract but does not include a transfer in bulk or as security for or in total or partial satisfaction of a money debt.

(p) "Lessor" means a person who transfers the right to possession and use of goods under a lease. Unless the context clearly indicates otherwise, the term includes a sublessor.

(q) "Lessor's residual interest" means the lessor's interest in the goods after expiration, termination, or cancellation of the lease contract.

(r) "Lien" means a charge against or interest in goods to secure payment of a debt or performance of an obligation, but the term does not include a security interest.

(s) "Lot" means a parcel or a single article that is the subject matter of a separate lease or delivery, whether or not it is sufficient to perform the lease contract.

(t) "Merchant lessee" means a lessee that is a merchant with respect to goods of the kind subject to the lease.

(u) "Present value" means the amount as of a date certain of one or more sums payable in the future, discounted to the date certain. The discount is determined by the interest rate specified by the parties if the rate was not manifestly unreasonable at the time the transaction was entered into; otherwise, the discount is determined by a commercially reasonable rate that takes into account the facts and circumstances of each case at the time the transaction was entered into.

(v) "Purchase" includes taking by sale, lease, mortgage, security interest, pledge, gift, or any other voluntary transaction creating an interest in goods.

(w) "Sublease" means a lease of goods the right to possession and use of which was acquired by the lessor as a lessee under an existing lease.

(x) "Supplier" means a person from whom a lessor buys or leases goods to be leased under a finance lease.

(y) "Supply contract" means a contract under which a lessor buys or leases goods to be leased.

(z) "Termination" occurs when either party pursuant to a power created by agreement or law puts an end to the lease contract otherwise than for default.

(2) Other definitions applying to this Article and the sections in which they appear are:

"Accessions." Section 2A–310(1).

"Construction mortgage." Section 2A–309(1)(d).

"Encumbrance." Section 2A–309(1)(e).

"Fixtures." Section 2A–309(1)(a).

"Fixture filing." Section 2A–309(1)(b).

"Purchase money lease." Section 2A–309(1)(c).

(3) The following definitions in other articles apply to this Article:

"Accounts." Section 9–106.

"Between merchants." Section 2–104(3).

"Buyer." Section 2–103(1)(a).

"Chattel paper." Section 9–105(1)(b).

"Consumer goods." Section 9–109(1).

"Documents." Section 9–105(1)(f).

"Entrusting." Section 2–403(3).

"General intangibles." Section 9–106.

"Good faith." Section 2–103(1)(b).

"Instruments." Section 9–105(1)(i).

"Merchant." Section 2–104(1).

"Mortgage." Section 9–105(1)(j).

"Pursuant to commitment." Section 9–105(1)(k).

"Receipt." Section 2–103(1)(c).

"Sale." Section 2–106(1).

"Sale on approval." Section 2–326.

"Sale or return." Section 2–326.

"Seller." Section 2–103(1)(d).

(4) In addition Article 1 contains general definitions and principles of construction and interpretation applicable throughout this Article.

Section 2A–104. Leases Subject to Other Statutes.

(1) A lease, although subject to this Article, is also subject to any applicable:

(a) statute of the United States;

(b) certificate of title statute of this State: (list any certificate of title statutes covering automobiles, trailers, mobile homes, boats, farm tractors, and the like);

(c) certificate of title statute of another jurisdiction (Section 2A–105); or

(d) consumer protection statute of this State.

(2) In case of conflict between the provisions of this Article, other than Sections 2A–105, 2A–304(3) and 2A–305(3), and any statute referred to in subsection (1), the provisions of that statute control.

(3) Failure to comply with any applicable statute has only the effect specified therein.

Section 2A–105. Territorial Application of Article to Goods Covered by Certificate of Title.

Subject to the provisions of Sections 2A–304(3) and 2A–305(3), with respect to goods covered by a certificate of title issued under a statute of this State or of another jurisdiction, compliance and the effect of compliance or noncompliance with a certificate of title statute are governed by the law (including the conflict of laws rules) of the jurisdiction issuing the certificate until the earlier of (a) surrender of the certificate, or (b) four months after the goods are removed from that jurisdiction and thereafter until a new certificate of title is issued by another jurisdiction.

Section 2A–106. Limitation on Power of Parties to Consumer Lease to Choose Applicable Law and Judicial Forum.

(1) If the law chosen by the parties to a consumer lease is that of a jurisdiction other than a jurisdiction in which the lessee resides at the time the lease agreement becomes enforceable or within 30 days thereafter or in which the goods are to be used, the choice is not enforceable.

(2) If the judicial forum chosen by the parties to a consumer lease is a forum that would not otherwise have jurisdiction over the lessee, the choice is not enforceable.

Section 2A–107. Waiver or Renunciation of Claim or Right After Default.

Any claim or right arising out of an alleged default or breach of warranty may be discharged in whole or in part without consideration by a written waiver or renunciation signed and delivered by the aggrieved party.

Section 2A–108. Unconscionability.

(1) If the court as a matter of law finds a lease contract or any clause of a lease contract to have been unconscionable at the time it was made the court may refuse to enforce the lease contract, or it may enforce the remainder of the lease contract without the unconscionable clause, or it may so limit the application of any unconscionable clause as to avoid any unconscionable result.

(2) With respect to a consumer lease, if the court as a matter of law finds that a lease contract or any clause of a lease contract has been induced by unconscionable conduct or that unconscionable conduct has occurred in the collection of a claim arising from a lease contract, the court may grant appropriate relief.

(3) Before making a finding of unconscionability under subsection (1) or (2), the court, on its own motion or that of a party, shall afford the parties a reasonable opportunity to present evidence as to the setting, purpose, and effect of the lease contract or clause thereof, or of the conduct.

(4) In an action in which the lessee claims unconscionability with respect to a consumer lease:

    (a) If the court finds unconscionability under subsection (1) or (2), the court shall award reasonable attorney's fees to the lessee.

    (b) If the court does not find unconscionability and the lessee claiming unconscionability has brought or maintained an action he [or she] knew to be groundless, the court shall award reasonable attorney's fees to the party against whom the claim is made.

    (c) In determining attorney's fees, the amount of the recovery on behalf of the claimant under subsections (1) and (2) is not controlling.

Section 2A–109. Option to Accelerate at Will.

(1) A term providing that one party or his [or her] successor in interest may accelerate payment or performance or require collateral or additional collateral "at will" or "when he [or she] deems himself [or herself] insecure" or in words of similar import must be construed to mean that he [or she] has power to do so only if he [or she] in good faith believes that the prospect of payment or performance is impaired.

(2) With respect to a consumer lease, the burden of establishing good faith under subsection (1) is on the party who exercised the power; otherwise the burden of establishing lack of good faith is on the party against whom the power has been exercised.

Part 2 Formation and Construction of Lease Contract

Section 2A–201. Statute of Frauds.

(1) A lease contract is not enforceable by way of action or defense unless:

    (a) the total payments to be made under the lease contract, excluding payments for options to renew or buy, are less than $1,000; or

    (b) there is a writing, signed by the party against whom enforcement is sought or by that party's authorized agent, sufficient to indicate that a lease contract has been made between the parties and to describe the goods leased and the lease term.

(2) Any description of leased goods or of the lease term is sufficient and satisfies subsection (1)(b), whether or not it is specific, if it reasonably identifies what is described.

(3) A writing is not insufficient because it omits or incorrectly states a term agreed upon, but the lease contract is not enforceable under subsection (1)(b) beyond the lease term and the quantity of goods shown in the writing.

(4) A lease contract that does not satisfy the requirements of subsection (1), but which is valid in other respects, is enforceable:

(a) if the goods are to be specially manufactured or obtained for the lessee and are not suitable for lease or sale to others in the ordinary course of the lessor's business, and the lessor, before notice of repudiation is received and under circumstances that reasonably indicate that the goods are for the lessee, has made either a substantial beginning of their manufacture or commitments for their procurement;

(b) if the party against whom enforcement is sought admits in that party's pleading, testimony or otherwise in court that a lease contract was made, but the lease contract is not enforceable under this provision beyond the quantity of goods admitted; or

(c) with respect to goods that have been received and accepted by the lessee.

(5) The lease term under a lease contract referred to in subsection (4) is:

(a) if there is a writing signed by the party against whom enforcement is sought or by that party's authorized agent specifying the lease term, the term so specified;

(b) if the party against whom enforcement is sought admits in that party's pleading, testimony, or otherwise in court a lease term, the term so admitted; or

(c) a reasonable lease term.

Section 2A–202. Final Written Expression: Parol or Extrinsic Evidence.

Terms with respect to which the confirmatory memoranda of the parties agree or which are otherwise set forth in a writing intended by the parties as a final expression of their agreement with respect to such terms as are included therein may not be contradicted by evidence of any prior agreement or of a contemporaneous oral agreement but may be explained or supplemented:

(a) by course of dealing or usage of trade or by course of performance; and

(b) by evidence of consistent additional terms unless the court finds the writing to have been intended also as a complete and exclusive statement of the terms of the agreement.

Section 2A–203. Seals Inoperative.

The affixing of a seal to a writing evidencing a lease contract or an offer to enter into a lease contract does not render the writing a sealed instrument and the law with respect to sealed instruments does not apply to the lease contract or offer.

Section 2A–204. Formation in General.

(1) A lease contract may be made in any manner sufficient to show agreement, including conduct by both parties which recognizes the existence of a lease contract.

(2) An agreement sufficient to constitute a lease contract may be found although the moment of its making is undetermined.

(3) Although one or more terms are left open, a lease contract does not fail for indefiniteness if the parties have intended to make a lease contract and there is a reasonably certain basis for giving an appropriate remedy.

Section 2A–205. Firm Offers.

An offer by a merchant to lease goods to or from another person in a signed writing that by its terms gives assurance it will be held open is not revocable, for lack of consideration, during the time stated or, if no time is stated, for a reasonable time, but in no event may the period of irrevocability exceed 3 months. Any such term of assurance on a form supplied by the offeree must be separately signed by the offeror.

Section 2A–206. Offer and Acceptance in Formation of Lease Contract.

(1) Unless otherwise unambiguously indicated by the language or circumstances, an offer to make a lease contract must be construed as inviting acceptance in any manner and by any medium reasonable in the circumstances.

(2) If the beginning of a requested performance is a reasonable mode of acceptance, an offeror who is not notified of acceptance within a reasonable time may treat the offer as having lapsed before acceptance.

Section 2A–207. Course of Performance or Practical Construction.

(1) If a lease contract involves repeated occasions for performance by either party with knowledge of the nature of the performance and opportunity for objection to it by the other, any course of performance accepted or acquiesced in without objection is relevant to determine the meaning of the lease agreement.

(2) The express terms of a lease agreement and any course of performance, as well as any course of dealing and usage of trade, must be construed whenever reasonable as consistent with each other; but if that construction is unreasonable, express terms control course of performance, course

of performance controls both course of dealing and usage of trade, and course of dealing controls usage of trade.

(3) Subject to the provisions of Section 2A–208 on modification and waiver, course of performance is relevant to show a waiver or modification of any term inconsistent with the course of performance.

Section 2A–208. Modification, Rescission and Waiver.

(1) An agreement modifying a lease contract needs no consideration to be binding.

(2) A signed lease agreement that excludes modification or rescission except by a signed writing may not be otherwise modified or rescinded, but, except as between merchants, such a requirement on a form supplied by a merchant must be separately signed by the other party.

(3) Although an attempt at modification or rescission does not satisfy the requirements of subsection (2), it may operate as a waiver.

(4) A party who has made a waiver affecting an executory portion of a lease contract may retract the waiver by reasonable notification received by the other party that strict performance will be required of any term waived, unless the retraction would be unjust in view of a material change of position in reliance on the waiver.

Section 2A–209. Lessee Under Finance Lease as Beneficiary of Supply Contract

(1) The benefit of the supplier's promises to the lessor under the supply contract and of all warranties, whether express or implied, under the supply contract, extends to the lessee to the extent of the lessee's leasehold interest under a finance lease related to the supply contract, but subject to the terms of the supply contract and all of the supplier's defenses or claims arising therefrom.

(2) The extension of the benefit of the supplier's promises and warranties to the lessee (Section 2A–209(1)) does not: (a) modify the rights and obligations of the parties to the supply contract, whether arising therefrom or otherwise, or (b) impose any duty or liability under the supply contract on the lessee.

(3) Any modification or rescission of the supply contract by the supplier and the lessor is effective against the lessee unless, prior to the modification or rescission, the supplier has received notice that the lessee has entered into a finance lease related to the supply contract. If the supply contract is modified or rescinded after the lessee enters the finance lease, the lessee has a cause of action against the lessor, and against the supplier if the supplier has notice of the lessee's entering the finance lease when the supply contract is modified or rescinded. The lessee's recovery from such action shall put the lessee in as good a position as if the modification or rescission had not occurred.

Section 2A–210. Express Warranties

(1) Express warranties by the lessor are created as follows:

    (a) Any affirmation of fact or promise made by the lessor to the lessee which relates to the goods and becomes part of the basis of the bargain creates an express warranty that the goods will conform to the affirmation or promise.

    (b) Any description of the goods which is made part of the basis of the bargain creates an express warranty that the goods will conform to the description.

    (c) Any sample or model that is made part of the basis of the bargain creates an express warranty that the whole of the goods will conform to the sample or model.

(2) It is not necessary to the creation of an express warranty that the lessor use formal words, such as "warrant" or "guarantee," or that the lessor have a specific intention to make a warranty, but an affirmation merely of the value of the goods or a statement purporting to be merely the lessor's opinion or commendation of the goods does not create a warranty.

Section 2A–211. Warranties Against Interference and Against Infringement: Lessee's Obligation Against Infringement

(1) There is in a lease contract a warranty that for the lease term no person holds a claim to or interest in the goods that arose from an act or omission of the lessor, other than a claim by way of infringement or the like, which will interfere with the lessee's enjoyment of its leasehold interest.

(2) Except in a finance lease there is in a lease contract by a lessor who is a merchant regularly dealing in goods of the kind a warranty that the goods are delivered free of the rightful claim of any person by way of infringement or the like.

(3) A lessee who furnishes specifications to a lessor a supplier shall hold the lessor and the supplier harmless against any claim by way of infringement or the like that arises out of compliance with the specifications.

Section 2A–212. Implied Warranty of Merchantability

(1) Except in a finance lease, a warranty that the goods will be merchantable is implied in a lease contract if the lessor is a merchant with respect to goods of that kind.

(2) Goods to be merchantable must be at least such as

    (a) pass without objection in the trade under the description in the lease agreement;

    (b) in the case of fungible goods, are of fair average quality within the description;

(c) are fit for the ordinary purpose for which goods of that type are used;

(d) run, within the variation permitted by the lease agreement, of even kind, quality, and quantity within each unit and among all units involved;

(e) are adequately contained, packaged, and labeled as the lease agreement may require; and

(f) conform to any promises or affirmations of fact made on the container or label.

(3) Other implied warranties may arise from course of dealing or usage of trade.

Section 2A–213. Implied Warranty of Fitness for Particular Purpose

Except in a finance lease, if the lessor at the time the lease contract is made has reason to know of any particular purpose for which the goods are required and that the lessee is relying on the lessor's skill or judgment to select or furnish suitable goods, there is in the lease contract an implied warranty that the goods will be fit for that purpose.

Section 2A–214. Exclusion or Modification of Warranties

(1) Words or conduct relevant to the creation of an express warranty and words or conduct tending to negate or limit a warranty must be construed wherever reasonable as consistent with each other; but, subject to the provisions of Section 2A–202 on parol or extrinsic evidence, negation or limitation is inoperative to the extent that the construction is unreasonable.

(2) Subject to subsection (3), to exclude or modify the implied warranty of merchantability or any part of it the language must mention "merchantability," be by a writing, and be conspicuous. Subject to subsection (3), to exclude or modify any implied warranty of fitness the exclusion must be by a writing and be conspicuous. Language to exclude all implied warranties of fitness is sufficient if it is in writing, is conspicuous and states, for example, "There is no warranty that the goods will be fit for a particular purpose."

(3) Notwithstanding subsection (2), but subject to subsection (4),

(a) unless the circumstances indicate otherwise, all implied warranties are excluded by expressions like "as is," or "with all faults," or by other language that in common understanding calls the lessee's attention to the exclusion of warranties and makes plain that there is no implied warranty, if in writing and conspicuous;

(b) if the lessee before entering into the lease contract has examined the goods or the sample or model

as fully as desired or has refused to examine the goods, there is no implied warranty with regard to defects that an examination ought in the circumstances to have revealed; and

(c) an implied warranty may also be excluded or modified by course of dealing, course of performance, or usage of trade.

(4) To exclude or modify a warranty against interference or against infringement (Section 2A–211) or any part of it, the language must be specific, be by a writing, and be conspicuous, unless the circumstances, including course of performance, course of dealing, or usage of trade, give the lessee reason to know that the goods are being leased subject to a claim or interest of any person.

Section 2A–215. Cumulation and Conflict of Warranties Express or Implied

Warranties, whether express or implied, must be construed as consistent with each other and as cumulative, but if that construction is unreasonable, the intention of the parties determines which warranty is dominant. In ascertaining that intention the following rules apply:

(a) Exact or technical specifications displace an inconsistent sample or model or general language of description.

(b) A sample from an existing bulk displaces inconsistent general language of description.

(c) Express warranties displace inconsistent implied warranties other than an implied warranty of fitness for a particular purpose.

Section 2A–216. Third-Party Beneficiaries of Express and Implied Warranties

Alternative A

A warranty to or for the benefit of a lessee under this Article, whether express or implied, extends to any natural person who is in the family or household of the lessee or who is a guest in the lessee's home if it is reasonable to expect that such person may use, consume, or be affected by the goods and who is injured in person by breach of the warranty. This section does not displace principles of law and equity that extend a warranty to or for the benefit of a lessee to other persons. The operation of this section may not be excluded, modified, or limited, but an exclusion, modification, or limitation of the warranty, including any with respect to rights and remedies, effective against the lessee is also effective against any beneficiary designated under this section.

Alternative B

A warranty to or for the benefit of a lessee under this Article, whether express or implied, extends to any natural person who may reasonably be expected to use, consume, or be affected by the goods and who is injured in person by breach of the warranty. This section does not displace principles of law and equity that extend a warranty to or for the benefit of a lessee to other persons. The operation of this section may not be excluded, modified, or limited, but an exclusion, modification, or limitation of the warranty, including any with respect to rights and remedies, effective against the lessee is also effective against the beneficiary designated under this section.

Alternative C

A warranty to or for the benefit of a lessee under this Article, whether express or implied, extends to any person who may reasonably be expected to use, consume, or be affected by the goods and who is injured by breach of the warranty. The operation of this section may not be excluded, modified, or limited with respect to injury to the person of an individual to whom the warranty extends, but an exclusion, modification, or limitation of the warranty, including any with respect to rights and remedies, effective against the lessee is also effective against the beneficiary designated under this section.

Section 2A–217. Identification

Identification of goods as goods to which a lease contract refers may be made at any time and in any manner explicitly agreed to by the parties. In the absence of explicit agreement, identification occurs:

(a) when the lease contract is made if the lease contract is for a lease of goods that are existing and identified:

(b) when the goods are shipped, marked, or otherwise designated by the lessor as goods to which the lease contract refers, if the lease contract is for a lease of goods that are not existing and identified; or

(c) when the young are conceived, if the lease contract is for a lease of unborn young of animals.

Section 2A–218. Insurance and Proceeds

(1) A lessee obtains an insurable interest when existing goods are identified to the lease contract even though the goods identified are nonconforming and the lessee has an option to reject them.

(2) If a lessee has an insurable interest only by reason of the lessor's identification of the goods, the lessor, until default or insolvency or notification to the lessee that identification is final, may substitute other goods for those identified.

(3) Notwithstanding a lessee's insurable interest under subsections (1) and (2), the lessor retains an insurable interest until an option to buy has been exercised by the lessee and risk of loss has passed to the lessee.

(4) Nothing in this section impairs any insurable interest recognized under any other statute or rule of law.

(5) The parties by agreement may determine that one or more parties have an obligation to obtain and pay for insurance covering the goods and by agreement may determine the beneficiary of the proceeds of the insurance.

Section 2A–219. Risk of Loss

(1) Except in the case of a finance lease, risk of loss is retained by the lessor and does not pass to the lessee. In the case of a finance lease, risk of loss passes to the lessee.

(2) Subject to the provisions of this Article on the effect of default on risk of loss (Section 2A–220), if risk of loss is to pass to the lessee and the time of passage is not stated, the following rules apply:

(a) If the lease contract requires or authorizes the goods to be shipped by carrier

(i) and it does not require delivery at a particular destination, the risk of loss passes to the lessee when the goods are duly delivered to the carrier; but

(ii) if it does require delivery at a particular destination and the goods are there duly tendered while in the possession of the carrier, the risk of loss passes to the lessee when the goods are there duly so tendered as to enable the lessee to take delivery.

(b) If the goods are held by a bailee to be delivered without being moved, the risk of loss passes to the lessee on acknowledgment by the bailee of the lessee's right to possession of the goods.

(c) In any case not within subsection (a) or (b), the risk of loss passes to the lessee on the lessee's receipt of the goods if the lessor, or, in the case of a finance lease, the supplier, is a merchant; otherwise the risk passes to the lessee on tender of delivery.

Section 2A–220. Effect of Default on Risk of Loss

(1) Where risk of loss is to pass to the lessee and the time of passage is not stated:

(a) If a tender or delivery of goods so fails to conform to the lease contract as to give a right of rejection, the risk of their loss remains with the lessor, or, in the case of a finance lease, the supplier, until cure or acceptance.

(b) If the lessee rightfully revokes acceptance, he [or she], to the extent of any deficiency in his [or her] effective insurance coverage, may treat the risk of loss as having remained with the lessor from the beginning.

(2) Whether or not risk of loss is to pass to the lessee, if the lessee as to conforming goods already identified to a lease contract repudiates or is otherwise in default under the lease contract, the lessor, or, in the case of a finance lease, the supplier, to the extent of any deficiency in his [or her] effective insurance coverage may treat the risk of loss as resting on the lessee for a commercially reasonable time.

Section 2A–221. Casualty to Identified Goods

If a lease contract requires goods identified when the lease contract is made, and the goods suffer casualty without fault of the lessee, the lessor or the supplier before delivery, or the goods suffer casualty before risk of loss passes to the lessee pursuant to the lease agreement or Section 2A–219, then:

(a) if the loss is total, the lease contract is avoided; and

(b) if the loss is partial or the goods have so deteriorated as to no longer conform to the lease contract, the lessee may nevertheless demand inspection and at his [or her] option either treat the lease contract as avoided or, except in a finance lease that is not a consumer lease, accept the goods with due allowance from the rent payable for the balance of the lease term for the deterioration or the deficiency in quantity but without further right against the lessor.

Part 3 Effect of Lease Contract

Section 2A–301. Enforceability of Lease Contract

Except as otherwise provided in this Article, a lease contract is effective and enforceable according to its terms between the parties, against purchasers of the goods and against creditors of the parties.

Section 2A–302. Title to and Possession of Goods

Except as otherwise provided in this Article, each provision of this Article applies whether the lessor or a third party has title to the goods, and whether the lessor, the lessee, or a third party has possession of the goods, notwithstanding any statute or rule of law that possession or the absence of possession is fraudulent.

Section 2A–303. Alienability of Party's Interest Under Lease Contract or of Lessor's Residual Interest in Goods; Delegation of Performance; Assignment of Rights

(1) Any interest of a party under a lease contract and the lessor's residual interest in the goods may be transferred unless

(a) the transfer is voluntary and the lease contract prohibits the transfer; or

(b) the transfer materially changes the duty of or materially increases the burden or risk imposed on the other party to the lease contract, and within a reasonable time after notice of the transfer the other party demands that the transferee comply with subsection (2) and the transferee fails to comply.

(2) Within a reasonable time after demand pursuant to subsection (1)(b), the transferee shall:

(a) cure or provide adequate assurance that he [or she] will promptly cure any default other than one arising from the transfer;

(b) compensate or provide adequate assurance that he [or she] will promptly compensate the other party to the lease contract and any other person holding an interest in the lease contract, except the party whose interest is being transferred, for any loss to that party resulting from the transfer;

(c) provide adequate assurance of future due performance under the lease contract; and

(d) assume the lease contract.

(3) Demand pursuant to subsection (1)(b) is without prejudice to the other party's rights against the transferee and the party whose interest is transferred.

(4) An assignment of "the lease" or of "all my rights under the lease" or an assignment in similar general terms is a transfer of rights, and unless the language or the circumstances, as in an assignment for security, indicate the contrary, the assignment is a delegation of duties by the assignor to the assignee and acceptance by the assignee constitutes a promise by him [or her] to perform those duties. This promise is enforceable by either the assignor or the other party to the lease contract.

(5) Unless otherwise agreed by the lessor and the lessee, no delegation of performance relieves the assignor as against the other party of any duty to perform or any liability for default.

(6) A right to damages for default with respect to the whole lease contract or a right arising out of the assignor's due performance of his [or her] entire obligation can be assigned despite agreement otherwise.

(7) To prohibit the transfer of an interest of a party under a lease contract, the language of prohibition must be specific, by a writing, and conspicuous.

Section 2A–304. Subsequent Lease of Goods by Lessor

(1) Subject to the provisions of Section 2A–303, a subsequent lessee from a lessor of goods under an existing lease contract obtains, to the extent of the leasehold interest transferred, the leasehold interest in the goods that the

lessor had or had power to transfer, and except as provided in subsection (2) and Section 2A–527(4), takes subject to the existing lease contract. A lessor with voidable title has power to transfer a good leasehold interest to a good faith subsequent lessee for value, but only to the extent set forth in the preceding sentence. When goods have been delivered under a transaction of purchase the lessor has that power even though:

(a) the lessor's transferor was deceived as to the identity of the lessor;

(b) the delivery was in exchange for a check which is later dishonored;

(c) it was agreed that the transaction was to be a "cash sale;" or

(d) the delivery was procured through fraud punishable as larcenous under the criminal law.

(2) A subsequent lessee in the ordinary course of business from a lessor who is a merchant dealing in goods of that kind to whom the goods were entrusted by the existing lessee before the interest of the subsequent lessee became enforceable against the lessor obtains, to the extent of the leasehold interest transferred, all of the lessor's and the existing lessee's rights to the goods, and takes free of the existing lease contract.

(3) A subsequent lessee from the lessor of goods that are subject to an existing lease contract and are covered by a certificate of title issued under a statute of this State or of another jurisdiction takes no greater rights than those provided both by this section and by the certificate of title statute.

Section 2A–305. Sale or Sublease of Goods by Lessee

(1) Subject to the provisions of Section 2A–303, a buyer or sublessee from the lessee of goods under an existing lease contract obtains, to the extent of the interest transferred, the leasehold interest in the goods that the lessee had or had power to transfer, and except as provided in subsection (2) and Section 2A–511(4), takes subject to the existing lease contract. A lessee with a voidable leasehold interest has power to transfer a good leasehold interest to a good faith buyer for value or a good faith sublessee for value, but only to the extent set forth in the preceding sentence. When goods have been delivered under a transaction of lease the lessee has that power even though:

(a) the lessor was deceived as to the identity of the lessee;

(b) the delivery was in exchange for a check which is later dishonored; or

(c) the delivery was procured through fraud punishable as larcenous under the criminal law.

(2) A buyer in the ordinary course of business or a sublessee in the ordinary course of business from a lessee who is a merchant dealing in goods of that kind to whom the goods were entrusted by the lessor obtains, to the extent of the interest transferred, all of the lessor's and lessee's rights to the goods, and takes free of the existing lease contract.

(3) A buyer or sublessee from the lessee of goods that are subject to an existing lease contract and are covered by a certificate of title issued under a statute of this State or of another jurisdiction takes no greater rights than those provided both by this section and by the certificate of title statute.

Section 2A–306. Priority of Certain Liens Arising by Operation of Law

If a person in the ordinary course of his [or her] business furnishes services or materials with respect to goods subject to a lease contract, a lien upon those goods in the possession of that person given by statute or rule of law for those materials or services takes priority over any interest of the lessor or lessee under the lease contract or this Article unless the lien is created by statute and the statute provides otherwise or unless the lien is created by rule of law and the rule of law provides otherwise.

Section 2A–307. Priority of Liens Arising by Attachment or Levy on, Security Interests in, and Other Claims to Goods

(1) Except as otherwise provided in Section 2A–306, a creditor of a lessee takes subject to the lease contract.

(2) Except as otherwise provided in subsections (3) and (4) of this section and in Sections 2A–306 and 2A–308, a creditor of a lessor takes subject to the lease contract:

(a) unless the creditor holds a lien that attached to the goods before the lease contract became enforceable, or

(b) unless the creditor holds a security interest in the goods that under the Article on Secured Transactions (Article 9) would have priority over any other security interest in the goods perfected by a filing covering the goods and made at the time the lease contract became enforceable, whether or not any other security interest existed.

(3) A lessee in the ordinary course of business takes the leasehold interest free of a security interest in the goods created by the lessor even though the security interest is perfected and the lessee knows of its existence.

(4) A lessee other than a lessee in the ordinary course of business takes the leasehold interest free of a security interest to the extent that it secures future advances made after the secured party acquires knowledge of the lease or more than 45 days after the lease contract becomes enforceable, whichever first occurs, unless the future advances are made pursuant to a commitment entered into

without knowledge of the lease and before the expiration of the 45-day period.

Section 2A–308. Special Rights of Creditors

(1) A creditor of a lessor in possession of goods subject to a lease contract may treat the lease contract as void if as against the creditor retention of possession by the lessor is fraudulent under any statute or rule of law, but retention of possession in good faith and current course of trade by the lessor for a commercially reasonable time after the lease contract becomes enforceable is not fraudulent.

(2) Nothing in this Article impairs the rights of creditors of a lessor if the lease contract (a) becomes enforceable, not in current course of trade but in satisfaction of or as security for a pre-existing claim for money, security, or the like, and (b) is made under circumstances which under any statute or rule of law apart from this Article would constitute the transaction a fraudulent transfer or voidable preference.

(3) A creditor of a seller may treat a sale or an identification of goods to a contract for sale as void if as against the creditor retention of possession by the seller is fraudulent under any statute or rule of law, but retention of possession of the goods pursuant to a lease contract entered into by the seller as lessee and the buyer as lessor in connection with the sale or identification of the goods is not fraudulent if the buyer bought for value and in good faith.

Section 2A–309. Lessor's and Lessee's Rights When Goods Become Fixtures

(1) In this section:

    (a) goods are "fixtures" when they become so related to particular real estate that an interest in them arises under real estate law;

    (b) a "fixture filing" is the filing, in the office where a mortgage on the real estate would be recorded or registered, of a financing statement concerning goods that are or are to become fixtures and conforming to the requirements of subsection (5) of Section 9–402;

    (c) a lease is a "purchase money lease" unless the lessee has possession or use of the goods or the right to possession or use of the goods before the lease agreement is enforceable;

    (d) a mortgage is a "construction mortgage" to the extent it secures an obligation incurred for the construction of an improvement on land including the acquisition cost of the land, if the recorded writing so indicates; and

    (e) "encumbrance" includes real estate mortgages and other liens on real estate and all other rights in real estate that are not ownership interests.

(2) Under this Article a lease may be of goods that are fixtures or may continue in goods that become fixtures, but no lease exists under this Article of ordinary building materials incorporated into an improvement on land.

(3) This Article does not prevent creation of a lease of fixtures pursuant to real estate law.

(4) The perfected interest of a lessor of fixtures has priority over a conflicting interest of an encumbrancer or owner of the real estate if:

    (a) the lease is a purchase money lease, the conflicting interest of the encumbrancer or owner arises before the goods become fixtures, the interest of the lessor is perfected by a fixture filing before the goods become fixtures or within ten days thereafter, and the lessee has an interest of record in the real estate or is in possession of the real estate; or

    (b) the interest of the lessor is perfected by a fixture filing before the interest of the encumbrancer or owner is of record, the lessor's interest has priority over any conflicting interest of a predecessor in title of the encumbrancer or owner, and the lessee has an interest of record in the real estate or is in possession of the real estate.

(5) The interest of a lessor of fixtures, whether or not perfected, has priority over the conflicting interest of an encumbrancer or owner of the real estate if:

    (a) the fixtures are readily removable factory or office machines, readily removable equipment that is not primarily used or leased for use in the operation of the real estate, or readily removable replacements of domestic appliances that are goods subject to a consumer lease, and before the goods become fixtures the lease contract is enforceable; or

    (b) the conflicting interest is a lien on the real estate obtained by legal or equitable proceedings after the lease contract is enforceable; or

    (c) the encumbrancer or owner has consented in writing to the lease or has disclaimed an interest in the goods as fixtures; or

    (d) the lessee has a right to remove the goods as against the encumbrancer or owner. If the lessee's right to remove terminates, the priority of the interest of the lessor continues for a reasonable time.

(6) Notwithstanding paragraph (a) of subsection (4) but otherwise subject to subsections (4) and (5), the interest of a lessor of fixtures is subordinate to the conflicting interest of an encumbrancer of the real estate under a construction mortgage recorded before the goods become fixtures if the goods become fixtures before the completion

of the construction. To the extent given to refinance a construction mortgage, the conflicting interest of an encumbrancer of the real estate under a mortgage has this priority to the same extent as the encumbrancer of the real estate under the construction mortgage.

(7) In cases not within the preceding subsections, priority between the interest of a lessor of fixtures and the conflicting interest of an encumbrancer or owner of the real estate who is not the lessee is determined by the priority rules governing conflicting interests in real estate.

(8) If the interest of a lessor has priority over all conflicting interests of all owners and encumbrancers of the real estate, the lessor or the lessee may (a) on default, expiration, termination, or cancellation of the lease agreement by the other party but subject to the provisions of the lease agreement and this Article, or (b) if necessary to enforce his [or her] other rights and remedies under this Article, remove the goods from the real estate, free and clear of all conflicting interests of all owners and encumbrancers of the real estate, but he [or she] must reimburse any encumbrancer or owner of the real estate who is not the lessee and who has not otherwise agreed for the cost of repair of any physical injury, but not for any diminution in value of the real estate caused by the absence of the goods removed or by any necessity of replacing them. A person entitled to reimbursement may refuse permission to remove until the party seeking removal gives adequate security for the performance of this obligation.

(9) Even though the lease agreement does not create a security interest, the interest of a lessor of fixtures is perfected by filing a financing statement as a fixture filing for leased goods that are or are to become fixtures in accordance with the relevant provisions of the Article on Secured Transactions (Article 9).

Section 2A–310. Lessor's and Lessee's Rights When Goods Become Accessions

(1) Goods are "accessions" when they are installed in or affixed to other goods.

(2) The interest of a lessor or a lessee under a lease contract entered into before the goods became accessions is superior to all interests in the whole except as stated in subsection (4).

(3) The interest of a lessor or a lessee under a lease contract entered into at the time or after the goods became accessions is superior to all subsequently acquired interests in the whole except as stated in subsection (4) but is subordinate to interests in the whole existing at the time the lease contract was made unless the holders of such interests in the whole have in writing consented to the lease or disclaimed an interest in the goods as part of the whole.

(4) The interest of a lessor or a lessee under a lease contract

described in subsection (2) or (3) is subordinate to the interest of

(a) a buyer in the ordinary course of business or a lessee in the ordinary course of business of any interest in the whole acquired after the goods became accessions; or

(b) a creditor with a security interest in the whole perfected before the lease contract was made to the extent that the creditor makes subsequent advances without knowledge of the lease contract.

(5) When under subsections (2) or (3) and (4) a lessor or a lessee of accessions holds an interest that is superior to all interests in the whole, the lessor or the lessee may (a) on default, expiration, termination, or cancellation of the lease contract by the other party but subject to the provisions of the lease contract and this Article, or (b) if necessary to enforce his [or her] other rights and remedies under this Article, remove the goods from the whole, free and clear of all interests in the whole, but he [or she] must reimburse any holder of an interest in the whole who is not the lessee and who has not otherwise agreed for the cost of repair of any physical injury but not for any diminution in value of the whole caused by the absence of the goods removed or by any necessity for replacing them. A person entitled to reimbursement may refuse permission to remove until the party seeking removal gives adequate security for the performance of this obligation.

Part 4 Performance of Lease Contract: Repudiated, Substituted and Excused

Section 2A–401. Insecurity: Adequate Assurance of Performance

(1) A lease contract imposes an obligation on each party that the other's expectation of receiving due performance will not be impaired.

(2) If reasonable grounds for insecurity arise with respect to the performance of either party, the insecure party may demand in writing adequate assurance of due performance. Until the insecure party receives that assurance, if commercially reasonable the insecure party may suspend any performance for which he [or she] has not already received the agreed return.

(3) A repudiation of the lease contract occurs if assurance of due performance adequate under the circumstances of the particular case is not provided to the insecure party within a reasonable time, not to exceed 30 days after receipt of a demand by the other party.

(4) Between merchants, the reasonableness of grounds for insecurity and the adequacy of any assurance offered must be determined according to commercial standards.

(5) Acceptance of any nonconforming delivery or payment does not prejudice the aggrieved party's right to demand adequate assurance of future performance.

Section 2A–402. Anticipatory Repudiation

If either party repudiates a lease contract with respect to a performance not yet due under the lease contract, the loss of which performance will substantially impair the value of the lease contract to the other, the aggrieved party may:

(a) for a commercially reasonable time, await retraction of repudiation and performance by the repudiating party;

(b) make demand pursuant to Section 2A–401 and await assurance of future performance adequate under the circumstances of the particular case; or

(c) resort to any right or remedy upon default under the lease contract or this Article, even though the aggrieved party has notified the repudiating party that the aggrieved party would await the repudiating party's performance and assurance and has urged retraction. In addition, whether or not the aggrieved party is pursuing one of the foregoing remedies, the aggrieved party may suspend performance or, if the aggrieved party is the lessor, proceed in accordance with the provisions of this Article on the lessor's right to identify goods to the lease contract notwithstanding default or to salvage unfinished goods (Section 2A–524).

Section 2A–403. Retraction of Anticipatory Repudiation

(1) Until the repudiating party's next performance is due, the repudiating party can retract the repudiation unless, since the repudiation, the aggrieved party has cancelled the lease contract or materially changed the aggrieved party's position or otherwise indicated that the aggrieved party considers the repudiation final.

(2) Retraction may be by any method that clearly indicates to the aggrieved party that the repudiating party intends to perform under the lease contract and includes any assurance demanded under Section 2A–401.

(3) Retraction reinstates a repudiating party's rights under a lease contract with due excuse and allowance to the aggrieved party for any delay occasioned by the repudiation.

Section 2A–404. Substituted Performance

(1) If without fault of the lessee, the lessor and the supplier, the agreed berthing, loading, or unloading facilities fail or the agreed type of carrier becomes unavailable or the agreed manner of delivery otherwise becomes commercially impracticable, but a commercially reasonable substitute is available, the substitute performance must be tendered and accepted.

(2) If the agreed means or manner of payment fails because of domestic or foreign governmental regulation:

(a) the lessor may withhold or stop delivery or cause the supplier to withhold or stop delivery unless the lessee provides a means or manner of payment that is commercially a substantial equivalent; and

(b) if delivery has already been taken, payment by the means or in the manner provided by the regulation discharges the lessee's obligation unless the regulation is discriminatory, oppressive, or predatory.

Section 2A–405. Excused Performance

Subject to Section 2A–404 on substituted performance, the following rules apply:

(a) Delay in delivery or nondelivery in whole or in part by a lessor or a supplier who complies with paragraphs (b) and (c) is not a default under the lease contract if performance as agreed has been made impracticable by the occurrence of a contingency the nonoccurrence of which was a basic assumption on which the lease contract was made or by compliance in good faith with any applicable foreign or domestic governmental regulation or order, whether or not the regulation or order later proves to be invalid.

(b) If the causes mentioned in paragraph (a) affect only part of the lessor's or the supplier's capacity to perform, he [or she] shall allocate production and deliveries among his [or her] customers but at his [or her] option may include regular customers not then under contract for sale or lease as well as his [or her] own requirements for further manufacture. He [or she] may so allocate in any manner that is fair and reasonable.

(c) The lessor seasonably shall notify the lessee and in the case of a finance lease the supplier seasonably shall notify the lessor and the lessee, if known, that there will be delay or nondelivery and, if allocation is required under paragraph (b), of the estimated quota thus made available for the lessee.

Section 2A–406. Procedure on Excused Performance

(1) If the lessee receives notification of a material or indefinite delay or an allocation justified under Section 2A–405, the lessee may by written notification to the lessor

as to any goods involved, and with respect to all of the goods if under an installment lease contract the value of the whole lease contract is substantially impaired (Section 2A–510):

(a) terminate the lease contract (Section 2A–505(2); or

(b) except in a finance lease that is not a consumer lease, modify the lease contract by accepting the available quota in substitution, with due allowance from the rent payable for the balance of the lease term for the deficiency but without further right against the lessor.

(2) If, after receipt of a notification from the lessor under Section 2A–405, the lessee fails so to modify the lease agreement within a reasonable time not exceeding 30 days, the lease contract lapses with respect to any deliveries affected.

Section 2A–407. Irrevocable Promises: Finance Leases

(1) In the case of a finance lease that is not a consumer lease the lessee's promises under the lease contract become irrevocable and independent upon the lessee's acceptance of the goods.

(2) A promise that has become irrevocable and independent under subsection (1):

(a) is effective and enforceable between the parties, and by or against third parties including assignees of the parties, and

(b) is not subject to cancellation, termination, modification, repudiation, excuse, or substitution without the consent of the party to whom the promise runs.

Part 5 Default

A. In General

Section 2A–501. Default: Procedure

(1) Whether the lessor or the lessee is in default under a lease contract is determined by the lease agreement and this Article.

(2) If the lessor or the lessee is in default under the lease contract, the party seeking enforcement has rights and remedies as provided in this Article and, except as limited by this Article, as provided in the lease agreement.

(3) If the lessor or the lessee is in default under the lease contract, the party seeking enforcement may reduce the party's claim to judgment, or otherwise enforce the lease contract by self-help or any available judicial procedure or nonjudicial procedure, including administrative proceeding, arbitration, or the like, in accordance with this Article.

(4) Except as otherwise provided in this Article or the lease agreement, the rights and remedies referred to in subsections (2) and (3) are cumulative.

(5) If the lease agreement covers both real property and goods, the party seeking enforcement may proceed under this Part as to the goods, or under other applicable law as to both the real property and the goods in accordance with his [or her] rights and remedies in respect of the real property, in which case this Part does not apply.

Section 2A–502. Notice After Default

Except as otherwise provided in this Article or the lease agreement, the lessor or lessee in default under the lease contract is not entitled to notice of default or notice of enforcement from the other party to the lease agreement.

Section 2A–503. Modification or Impairment of Rights and Remedies

(1) Except as otherwise provided in this Article, the lease agreement may include rights and remedies for default in addition to or in substitution for those provided in this Article and may limit or alter the measure of damages recoverable under this Article.

(2) Resort to a remedy provided under this Article or in the lease agreement is optional unless the remedy is expressly agreed to be exclusive. If circumstances cause an exclusive or limited remedy to fail of its essential purpose, or provision for an exclusive remedy is unconscionable, remedy may be had as provided in this Article.

(3) Consequential damages may be liquidated under Section 2A–504, or may otherwise be limited, altered, or excluded unless the limitation, alteration, or exclusion is unconscionable. Limitation of consequential damages for injury to the person in the case of consumer goods is prima facie unconscionable but limitation of damages where the loss is commercial is not.

(4) Rights and remedies on default by the lessor or the lessee with respect to any obligation or promise collateral or ancillary to the lease contract are not impaired by this Article.

Section 2A–504. Liquidation of Damages

(1) Damages payable by either party for default, or any other act or omission, including indemnity for loss or diminution of anticipated tax benefits or loss or damage to lessor's residual interest, may be liquidated in the lease agreement but only at an amount or by a formula that is reasonable in light of the then anticipated harm caused by the default or other act or omission.

(2) If the lease agreement provides for liquidation of damages, and such provision does not comply with subsection (1), or such provision is an exclusive or limited remedy

that circumstances cause to fail of its essential purpose, remedy may be had as provided in this Article.

(3) If the lessor justifiably withholds or stops delivery of goods because of the lessee's default or insolvency (Section 2A–525 or 2A–526), the lessee is entitled to restitution of any amount by which the sum of his [or her] payments exceeds:

(a) the amount to which the lessor is entitled by virtue of terms liquidating the lessor's damages in accordance with subsection (1); or

(b) in the absence of those terms, 20 percent of the then present value of the total rent the lessee was obligated to pay for the balance of the lease term, or, in the case of a consumer lease, the lesser of such amount or $500.

(4) A lessee's right to restitution under subsection (3) is subject to offset to the extent the lessor establishes:

(a) a right to recover damages under the provisions of this Article other than subsection (1); and

(b) the amount or value of any benefits received by the lessee directly or indirectly by reason of the lease contract.

Section 2A–505. Cancellation and Termination and Effect of Cancellation, Termination, Rescission, or Fraud on Rights and Remedies

(1) On cancellation of the lease contract, all obligations that are still executory on both sides are discharged, but any right based on prior default or performance survives, and the cancelling party also retains any remedy for default of the whole lease contract or any unperformed balance.

(2) On termination of the lease contract, all obligations that are still executory on both sides are discharged but any right based on prior default or performance survives.

(3) Unless the contrary intention clearly appears, expressions of "cancellation," "rescission," or the like of the lease contract may not be construed as a renunciation or discharge of any claim in damages for an antecedent default.

(4) Rights and remedies for material misrepresentation or fraud include all rights and remedies available under this Article for default.

(5) Neither rescission nor a claim for rescission of the lease contract nor rejection or return of the goods may bar or be deemed inconsistent with a claim for damages or other right or remedy.

Section 2A–506. Statute of Limitations

(1) An action for default under a lease contract, including breach of warranty or indemnity, must be commenced within 4 years after the cause of action accrued. By the original lease contract the parties may reduce the period of limitation to not less than one year.

(2) A cause of action for default accrues when the act or omission on which the default or breach of warranty is based is or should have been discovered by the aggrieved party, or when the default occurs, whichever is later. A cause of action for indemnity accrues when the act or omission on which the claim for indemnity is based is or should have been discovered by the indemnified party, whichever is later.

(3) If an action commenced within the time limited by subsection (1) is so terminated as to leave available a remedy by another action for the same default or breach of warranty or indemnity, the other action may be commenced after the expiration of the time limited and within 6 months after the termination of the first action unless the termination resulted from voluntary discontinuance or from dismissal for failure or neglect to prosecute.

(4) This section does not alter the law on tolling of the statute of limitations nor does it apply to causes of action that have accrued before this Article becomes effective.

Section 2A–507. Proof of Market Rent: Time and Place

(1) Damages based on market rent (Section 2A–519 or 2A–528) are determined according to the rent for the use of the goods concerned for a lease term identical to the remaining lease term of the original lease agreement and prevailing at the time of the default.

(2) If evidence of rent for the use of the goods concerned for a lease term identical to the remaining lease term of the original lease agreement and prevailing at the times or places described in this Article is not readily available, the rent prevailing within any reasonable time before or after the time described or at any other place or for a different lease term which in commercial judgment or under usage of trade would serve as a reasonable substitute for the one described may be used, making any proper allowance for the difference, including the cost of transporting the goods to or from the other place.

(3) Evidence of a relevant rent prevailing at a time or place or for a lease term other than the one described in this Article offered by one party is not admissible unless and until he [or she] has given the other party notice the court finds sufficient to prevent unfair surprise.

(4) If the prevailing rent or value of any goods regularly leased in any established market is in issue, reports in official publications or trade journals or in newspapers or periodicals of general circulation published as the reports of that market are admissible in evidence. The circumstances of the preparation of the report may be shown to affect its weight but not its admissibility.

B. Default by Lessor

Section 2A–508. Lessee's Remedies

(1) If a lessor fails to deliver the goods in conformity to the lease contract (Section 2A–509) or repudiates the lease contract (Section 2A–402), or a lessee rightfully rejects the goods (Section 2A–509) or justifiably revokes acceptance of the goods (Section 2A–517), then with respect to any goods involved, and with respect to all of the goods if under an installment lease contract the value of the whole lease contract is substantially impaired (Section 2A–510), the lessor is in default under the lease contract and the lessee may:

    (a) cancel the lease contract (Section 2A–505(1));

    (b) recover so much of the rent and security as has been paid, but in the case of an installment lease contract the recovery is that which is just under the circumstances;

    (c) cover and recover damages as to all goods affected whether or not they have been identified to the lease contract (Sections 2A–518 and 2A–520), or recover damages for nondelivery (Sections 2A–519 and 2A–520).

(2) If a lessor fails to deliver the goods in conformity to the lease contract or repudiates the lease contract, the lessee may also:

    (a) if the goods have been identified, recover them (Section 2A–522); or

    (b) in a proper case, obtain specific performance or replevy the goods (Section 2A–521).

(3) If a lessor is otherwise in default under a lease contract, the lessee may exercise the rights and remedies provided in the lease contract and this Article.

(4) If a lessor has breached a warranty, whether express or implied, the lessee may recover damages (Section 2A–519(4)).

(5) On rightful rejection or justifiable revocation of acceptance, a lessee has a security interest in goods in the lessee's possession or control for any rent and security that has been paid and any expenses reasonably incurred in their inspection, receipt, transportation, and care and custody and may hold those goods and dispose of them in good faith and in a commercially reasonable manner, subject to the provisions of Section 2A–527(5).

(6) Subject to the provisions of Section 2A–407, a lessee, on notifying the lessor of the lessee's intention to do so, may deduct all or any part of the damages resulting from any default under the lease contract from any part of the rent still due under the same lease contract.

Section 2A–509. Lessee's Rights on Improper Delivery; Rightful Rejection

(1) Subject to the provisions of Section 2A–510 on default in installment lease contracts, if the goods or the tender or delivery fail in any respect to conform to the lease contract, the lessee may reject or accept the goods or accept any commercial unit or units and reject the rest of the goods.

(2) Rejection of goods is ineffective unless it is within a reasonable time after tender or delivery of the goods and the lessee seasonably notifies the lessor.

Section 2A–510. Installment Lease Contracts: Rejection and Default

(1) Under an installment lease contract a lessee may reject any delivery that is nonconforming if the nonconformity substantially impairs the value of that delivery and cannot be cured or the nonconformity is a defect in the required documents; but if the nonconformity does not fall within subsection (2) and the lessor or the supplier gives adequate assurance of its cure, the lessee must accept that delivery.

(2) Whenever nonconformity or default with respect to one or more deliveries substantially impairs the value of the installment lease contract as a whole there is a default with respect to the whole. But, the aggrieved party reinstates the installment lease contract as a whole if the aggrieved party accepts a nonconforming delivery without seasonably notifying of cancellation or brings an action with respect only to past deliveries or demands performance as to future deliveries.

Section 2A–511. Merchant Lessee's Duties as to Rightfully Rejected Goods

(1) Subject to any security interest of a lessee (Section 2A–508(5)), if a lessor or a supplier has no agent or place of business at the market of rejection, a merchant lessee, after rejection of goods in his [or her] possession or control, shall follow any reasonable instructions received from the lessor or the supplier with respect to the goods. In the absence of those instructions, a merchant lessee shall make reasonable efforts to sell, lease, or otherwise dispose of the goods for the lessor's account if they threaten to decline in value speedily. Instructions are not reasonable if on demand indemnity for expenses is not forthcoming.

(2) If a merchant lessee (subsection (1)) or any other lessee (Section 2A–512) disposes of goods, he [or she] is entitled to reimbursement either from the lessor or the supplier or out of the proceeds for reasonable expenses of caring for and disposing of the goods and, if the expenses include no disposition commission, to such com-

mission as is usual in the trade, or if there is none, to a reasonable sum not exceeding 10 percent of the gross proceeds.

(3) In complying with this section of Section 2A–512, the lessee is held only to good faith. Good faith conduct hereunder is neither acceptance or conversion nor the basis of an action for damages.

(4) A purchaser who purchases in good faith from a lessee pursuant to this section or Section 2A–512 takes the goods free of any rights of the lessor and the supplier even though the lessee fails to comply with one or more of the requirements of this Article.

Section 2A–512. Lessee's Duties as to Rightfully Rejected Goods

(1) Except as otherwise provided with respect to goods that threaten to decline in value speedily (Section 2A–511) and subject to any security interest of a lessee (Section 2A–508(5)):

(a) the lessee, after rejection of goods in the lessee's possession, shall hold them with reasonable care at the lessor's or the supplier's disposition for a reasonable time after the lessee's seasonable notification of rejection;

(b) if the lessor or the supplier gives no instructions within a reasonable time after notification of rejection, the lessee may store the rejected goods for the lessor's or the supplier's account or ship them to the lessor or the supplier or dispose of them for the lessor's or the supplier's account with reimbursement in the manner provided in Section 2A–511; but

(c) the lessee has no further obligations with regard to goods rightfully rejected.

(2) Action by the lessee pursuant to subsection (1) is not acceptance or conversion.

Section 2A–513. Cure by Lessor of Improper Tender or Delivery; Replacement

(1) If any tender or delivery by the lessor or the supplier is rejected because nonconforming and the time for performance has not yet expired, the lessor or the supplier may seasonably notify the lessee of the lessor's or the supplier's intention to cure and may then make a conforming delivery within the time provided in the lease contract.

(2) If the lessee rejects a nonconforming tender that the lessor or the supplier had reasonable grounds to believe would be acceptable with or without money allowance, the lessor or the supplier may have a further reasonable time to substitute a conforming tender if he [or she] seasonably notifies the lessee.

Section 2A–514. Waiver of Lessee's Objections

(1) In rejecting goods, a lessee's failure to state a particular defect that is ascertainable by reasonable inspection precludes the lessee from relying on the defect to justify rejection or to establish default:

(a) if, stated seasonably, the lessor or the supplier could have cured it (Section 2A–513); or

(b) between merchants if the lessor or the supplier after rejection has made a request in writing for a full and final written statement of all defects on which the lessee proposes to rely.

(2) A lessee's failure to reserve rights when paying rent or other consideration against documents precludes recovery of the payment for defects apparent on the face of the documents.

Section 2A–515. Acceptance of Goods

(1) Acceptance of goods occurs after the lessee has had a reasonable opportunity to inspect the goods and

(a) the lessee signifies or acts with respect to the goods in a manner that signifies to the lessor or the supplier that the goods are conforming or that the lessee will take or retain them in spite of their nonconformity; or

(b) the lessee fails to make an effective rejection of the goods (Section 2A–509(2)).

(2) Acceptance of a part of any commercial unit is acceptance of that entire unit.

Section 2A–516. Effect of Acceptance of Goods; Notice of Default; Burden of Establishing Default After Acceptance; Notice of Claim or Litigation to Person Answerable Over

(1) A lessee must pay rent for any goods accepted in accordance with the lease contract, with due allowance for goods rightfully rejected or not delivered.

(2) A lessee's acceptance of goods precludes rejection of the goods accepted. In the case of a finance lease, if made with knowledge of a nonconformity, acceptance cannot be revoked because of it. In any other case, if made with knowledge of a nonconformity, acceptance cannot be revoked because of it unless the acceptance was on the reasonable assumption that the nonconformity would be seasonably cured. Acceptance does not of itself impair any other remedy provided by this Article or the lease agreement for nonconformity.

(3) If a tender has been accepted:

(a) within a reasonable time after the lessee discovers or should have discovered any default, the lessee shall notify the lessor and the supplier, or be barred from any remedy;

APPENDIX B   B–55

Uniform Commercial Code

(b) except in the case of a consumer lease, within a reasonable time after the lessee receives notice of litigation for infringement or the like (Section 2A–211) the lessee shall notify the lessor or be barred from any remedy over for liability established by the litigation; and

(c) the burden is on the lessee to establish any default.

(4) If a lessee is sued for breach of a warranty or other obligation for which a lessor or a supplier is answerable over:

(a) The lessee may give the lessor or the supplier written notice of the litigation. If the notice states that the lessor or the supplier may come in and defend and that if the lessor or the supplier does not do so he [or she] will be bound in any action against him [or her] by the lessee by any determination of fact common to the two litigations, then unless the lessor or the supplier after seasonable receipt of the notice does come in and defend he [or she] is so bound.

(b) The lessor or the supplier may demand in writing that the lessee turn over control of the litigation including settlement if the claim is one for infringement or the like (Section 2A–211) or else be barred from any remedy over. If the demand states that the lessor or the supplier agrees to bear all expense and to satisfy any adverse judgment, then unless the lessee after seasonable receipt of the demand does turn over control the lessee is so barred.

(5) The provisions of subsections (3) and (4) apply to any obligation of a lessee to hold the lessor or the supplier harmless against infringement or the like (Section 2A–211).

Section 2A–517. Revocation of Acceptance of Goods

(1) A lessee may revoke acceptance of a lot or commercial unit whose nonconformity substantially impairs its value to the lessee if he [or she] has accepted it:

(a) except in the case of a finance lease, on the reasonable assumption that its nonconformity would be cured and it has not been seasonably cured; or

(b) without discovery of the nonconformity if the lessee's acceptance was reasonably induced either by the lessor's assurances or, except in the case of a finance lease, by the difficulty of discovery before acceptance.

(2) Revocation of acceptance must occur within a reasonable time after the lessee discovers or should have discovered the ground for it and before any substantial change in condition of the goods which is not caused by the nonconformity. Revocation is not effective until the lessee notifies the lessor.

(3) A lessee who so revokes has the same rights and duties with regard to the goods involved as if the lessee had rejected them.

Section 2A–518. Cover; Substitute Good

(1) After default by a lessor under the lease contract (Section 2A–508(1)), the lessee may cover by making any purchase or lease of or contract to purchase or lease goods in substitution for those due from the lessor.

(2) Except as otherwise provided with respect to damages liquidated in the lease agreement (Section 2A–504) or determined by agreement of the parties (Section 1–102(3)), if a lessee's cover is by lease agreement substantially similar to the original lease agreement and the lease agreement is made in good faith and in a commercially reasonable manner, the lessee may recover from the lessor as damages (a) the present value, as of the date of default, of the difference between the total rent for the lease term of the new lease agreement and the total rent for the remaining lease term of the original lease agreement and (b) any incidental or consequential damages less expenses saved in consequence of the lessor's default.

(3) If a lessee's cover is by lease agreement that for any reason does not qualify for treatment under subsection (2), or is by purchase or otherwise, the lessee may recover from the lessor as if the lessee had elected not to cover and Section 2A–519 governs.

Section 2A–519. Lessee's Damages for Nondelivery, Repudiation, Default and Breach of Warranty in Regard to Accepted Goods

(1) Except as otherwise provided with respect to damages liquidated in the lease agreement (Section 2A–504) or determined by agreement of the parties (Section 1–102(3)), if a lessee elects not to cover or a lessee elects to cover and the cover is by lease agreement that for any reason does not qualify for treatment under Section 2A–518(2), or is by purchase or otherwise, the measure of damages for nondelivery or repudiation by the lessor or for rejection or revocation of acceptance by the lessee is the present value as of the date of the default of the difference between the then market rent and the original rent, computed for the remaining lease term of the original lease agreement together with incidental and consequential damages, less expenses saved in consequence of the lessor's default.

(2) Market rent is to be determined as of the place for tender or, in cases of rejection after arrival or revocation of acceptance, as of the place of arrival.

(3) If the lessee has accepted goods and given notification (Section 2A–516(3)), the measure of damages for non-

conforming tender or delivery by a lessor is the loss resulting in the ordinary course of events from the lessor's default as determined in any manner that is reasonable together with incidental and consequential damages, less expenses saved in consequence of the lessor's default.

(4) The measure of damages for breach of warranty is the present value at the time and place of acceptance of the difference between the value of the use of the goods accepted and the value if they had been as warranted for the lease term, unless special circumstances show proximate damages of a different amount, together with incidental and consequential damages, less expenses saved in consequence of the lessor's default or breach of warranty.

Section 2A–520. Lessee's Incidental and Consequential Damages

(1) Incidental damages resulting from a lessor's default include expenses reasonably incurred in inspection, receipt, transportation, and care and custody of goods rightfully rejected or goods the acceptance of which is justifiably revoked, any commercially reasonable charges, expenses or commissions in connection with effecting cover, and any other reasonable expense incident to the default.

(2) Consequential damages resulting from a lessor's default include:

    (a) any loss resulting from general or particular requirements and needs of which the lessor at the time of contracting had reason to know and which could not reasonably be prevented by cover or otherwise; and

    (b) injury to person or property proximately resulting from any breach of warranty.

Section 2A–521. Lessee's Right to Specific Performance or Replevin

(1) Specific performance may be decreed if the goods are unique or in other proper circumstances.

(2) A decree for specific performance may include any terms and conditions as to payment of the rent, damages, or other relief that the court deems just.

(3) A lessee has a right to replevin, detinue, sequestration, claim and delivery, or the like for goods identified to the lease contract if after reasonable effort the lessee is unable to effect cover for those goods or the circumstances reasonably indicate that the effort will be unavailing.

Section 2A–522. Lessee's Right to Goods on Lessor's Insolvency

(1) Subject to subsection (2) and even though the goods have not been shipped, a lessee who has paid a part or all of the rent and security for goods identified to a lease contract (Section 2A–217) on making and keeping good a tender of any unpaid portion of the rent and security due under the lease contract may recover the goods identified from the lessor becomes insolvent within 10 days after receipt of the first installment of rent and security.

(2) A lessee acquires the right to recover goods identified to a lease contract only if they conform to the lease contract.

C. Default by Lessee

Section 2A–523. Lessor's Remedies

(1) If a lessee wrongfully rejects or revokes acceptance of goods or fails to make a payment when due or repudiates with respect to a part or the whole, then, with respect to any goods involved, and with respect to all of the goods if under an installment lease contract the value of the whole lease contract is substantially impaired (Section 2A–510), the lessee is in default under the lease contract and the lessor may:

    (a) cancel the lease contract (Section 2A–505(1));

    (b) proceed respecting goods not identified to the lease contract (Section 2A–524);

    (c) withhold delivery of the goods and take possession of goods previously delivered (Section 2A–525);

    (d) stop delivery of the goods by any bailee (Section 2A–526);

    (e) dispose of the goods and recover damages (Section 2A–527), or retain the goods and recover damages (Section 2A–528), or in a proper case recover rent (Section 2A–529).

(2) If a lessee is otherwise in default under a lease contract, the lessor may exercise the rights and remedies provided in the lease contract and this Article.

Section 2A–524. Lessor's Right to Identify Goods to Lease Contract

(1) A lessor aggrieved under Section 2A–523(1) may:

    (a) identify to the lease contract conforming goods not already identified if at the time the lessor learned of the default they were in the lessor's or the supplier's possession or control; and

    (b) dispose of goods (Section 2A–527(1)) that demonstrably have been intended for the particular lease contract even though those goods are unfinished.

(2) If the goods are unfinished, in the exercise of reasonable commercial judgment for the purposes of avoiding loss and of effective realization, an aggrieved lessor or the supplier may either complete manufacture and wholly identify the goods to the lease contract or cease manufac-

ture and lease, sell, or otherwise dispose of the goods for scrap or salvage value or proceed in any other reasonable manner.

Section 2A–525. Lessor's Right to Possession of Goods

(1) If a lessor discovers the lessee to be insolvent, the lessor may refuse to deliver the goods.

(2) The lessor has on default by the lessee under the lease contract the right to take possession of the goods. If the lease contract so provides, the lessor may require the lessee to assemble the goods and make them available to the lessor at a place to be designated by the lessor which is reasonably convenient to both parties. Without removal, the lessor may render unusable any goods employed in trade or business, and may dispose of goods on the lessee's premises (Section 2A–527).

(3) The lessor may proceed under subsection (2) without judicial process if that can be done without breach of the peace or the lessor may proceed by action.

Section 2A–526. Lessor's Stoppage of Delivery in Transit or Otherwise

(1) A lessor may stop delivery of goods in the possession of a carrier or other bailee if the lessor discovers the lessee to be insolvent and may stop delivery of carload, truckload, planeload, or larger shipments of express or freight if the lessee repudiates or fails to make a payment due before delivery, whether for rent, security or otherwise under the lease contract, or for any other reason the lessor has a right to withhold or take possession of the goods.

(2) In pursuing its remedies under subsection (1), the lessor may stop delivery until

    (a) receipt of the goods by the lessee;

    (b) acknowledgment to the lessee by any bailee of the goods, except a carrier, that the bailee holds the goods for the lessee; or

    (c) such an acknowledgment to the lessee by a carrier via reshipment or as warehouseman.

(3) (a) To stop delivery, a lessor shall so notify as to enable the bailee by reasonable diligence to prevent delivery of the goods.

    (b) After notification, the bailee shall hold and deliver the goods according to the directions of the lessor, but the lessor is liable to the bailee for any ensuing charges or damages.

    (c) A carrier who has issued a nonnegotiable bill of lading is not obliged to obey a notification to stop received from a person other than the consignor.

Section 2A–527. Lessor's Rights to Dispose of Goods

(1) After a default by a lessee under the lease contract (Section 2A–523(1)) or after the lessor refuses to deliver or takes possession of goods (Section 2A–525 or 2A–526), the lessor may dispose of the goods concerned or the undelivered balance thereof by lease, sale or otherwise.

(2) Except as otherwise provided with respect to damages liquidated in the lease agreement (Section 2A–504) or determined by agreement of the parties (Section 1–102(3)), if the disposition is by lease agreement substantially similar to the original lease agreement and the lease agreement is made in good faith and in a commercially reasonable manner, the lessor may recover from the lessee as damages (a) accrued and unpaid rent as of the date of default, (b) the present value as of the date of default of the difference between the total rent for the remaining lease term of the original lease agreement and the total rent for the lease term of the new lease agreement, and (c) any incidental damages allowed under Section 2A–530, less expenses saved in consequence of the lessee's default.

(3) If the lessor's disposition is by lease agreement that for any reason does not qualify for treatment under subsection (2), or is by sale or otherwise, the lessor may recover from the lessee as if the lessor had elected not to dispose of the goods and Section 2A–528 governs.

(4) A subsequent buyer or lessee who buys or leases from the lessor in good faith for value as a result of a disposition under this section takes the goods free of the original lease contract and any rights of the original lessee even though the lessor fails to comply with one or more of the requirements of this Article.

(5) The lessor is not accountable to the lessee for any profit made on any disposition. A lessee who has rightfully rejected or justifiably revoked acceptance shall account to the lessor for any excess over the amount of the lessee's security interest (Section 2A–508(5)).

Section 2A–528. Lessor's Damages for Non-Acceptance or Repudiation

(1) Except as otherwise provided with respect to damages liquidated in the lease agreement (Section 2A–504) or determined by agreement of the parties (Section 1–102(3)), if a lessor elects to retain the goods or a lessor elects to dispose of the goods and disposition is by lease agreement that for any reason does not qualify for treatment under Section 2A–527(2), or is by sale or otherwise, the lessor may recover from the lessee as damages for non-acceptance or repudiation by the lessee (a) accrued and unpaid rent as of the date of default, (b) the present value as of the date of default of the difference between the total rent for the remaining lease term of the original

lease agreement and the market rent at the time and place for tender computed for the same lease term, and (c) any incidental damages allowed under Section 2A–530, less expenses saved in consequence of the lessee's default.

(2) If the measure of damages provided in subsection (1) is inadequate to put a lessor in as good a position as performance would have, the measure of damages is the profit, including reasonable overhead, the lessor would have made from full performance by the lessee, together with any incidental damages allowed under Section 2A–530, due allowance for costs reasonably incurred and due credit for payments or proceeds of disposition.

Section 2A–529. Lessor's Action for the Rent

(1) After default by the lessee under the lease contract (Section 2A–523(1)), if the lessor complies with subsection (2), the lessor may recover from the lessee as damages:

   (a) for goods accepted by the lessee and for conforming goods lost or damaged within a commercially reasonable time after risk of loss passes to the lessee (Section 2A–219), (i) accrued and unpaid rent as of the date of default, (ii) the present value as of the date of default of the rent for the remaining lease term of the lease agreement, and (iii) any incidental damages allowed under Section 2A–530, less expenses saved in consequence of the lessee's default; and

   (b) for goods identified to the lease contract if the lessor is unable after reasonable effort to dispose of them at a reasonable price or the circumstances reasonably indicate that effort will be unavailing, (i) accrued and unpaid rent as of the date of default, (ii) the present value as of the date of default of the rent for the remaining lease term of the lease agreement, and (iii) any incidental damages allowed under Section 2A–530, less expenses saved in consequence of the lessee's default.

(2) Except as provided in subsection (3), the lessor shall hold for the lessee for the remaining lease term of the lease agreement any goods that have been identified to the lease contract and are in the lessor's control.

(3) The lessor may dispose of the goods at any time before collection of the judgment for damages obtained pursuant to subsection (1). If the disposition is before the end of the remaining lease term of the lease agreement, the lessor's recovery against the lessee for damages will be governed by Section 2A–527 or Section 2A–528.

(4) Payment of the judgment for damages obtained pursuant to subsection (1) entitles the lessee to use and possession of the goods not then disposed of for the remaining lease term of the lease agreement.

(5) After a lessee has wrongfully rejected or revoked acceptance of goods, has failed to pay rent then due, or has repudiated (Section 2A–402), a lessor who is held not entitled to rent under this section must nevertheless be awarded damages for non-acceptance under Sections 2A–527 and 2A–528.

Section 2A–530. Lessor's Incidental Damages

Incidental damages to an aggrieved lessor include any commercially reasonable charges, expenses, or commissions incurred in stopping delivery, in the transportation, care and custody of goods after the lessee's default, in connection with return or disposition of the goods, or otherwise resulting from the default.

Section 2A–531. Standing to Sue Third Parties for Injury to Goods

(1) If a third party so deals with goods that have been identified to a lease contract as to cause actionable injury to a party to the lease contract (a) the lessor has a right of action against the third party, and (b) the lessee also has a right of action against the third party if the lessee:

   (i) has a security interest in the goods:

   (ii) has an insurable interest in the goods; or

   (iii) bears the risk of loss under the lease contract or has since the injury assumed that risk as against the lessor and the goods have been converted or destroyed.

(2) If at the time of the injury the party plaintiff did not bear the risk of loss as against the other party to the lease contract and there is no arrangement between them for disposition of the recovery, his [or her] suit or settlement, subject to his [or her] own interest, is as a fiduciary for the other party to the lease contract.

(3) Either party with the consent of the other may sue for the benefit of whom it may concern.

ARTICLE 3 COMMERCIAL PAPER

Part 1 Short Title, Form and Interpretation

Section 3–101. Short Title

This Article shall be known and may be cited as Uniform Commercial Code—Commercial Paper.

Section 3–102. Definitions and Index of Definitions

(1) In this Article unless the context otherwise requires

   (a) "Issue" means the first delivery of an instrument to a holder or a remitter.

   (b) An "order" is a direction to pay and must be more than an authorization or request. It must identify the person to pay with reasonable certainty. It may be addressed to one or more such persons jointly or in the alternative but not in succession.

(c) A "promise" is an undertaking to pay and must be more than an acknowledgment of an obligation.

(d) "Secondary party" means a drawer or endorser.

(e) "Instrument" means a negotiable instrument.

(2) Other definitions applying to this Article and the sections in which they appear are:

"Acceptance." Section 3–410.

"Accommodation party." Section 3–415.

"Alteration." Section 3–407.

"Certificate of deposit." Section 3–104.

"Certification." Section 3–411.

"Check." Section 3–104.

"Definite time." Section 3–109.

"Dishonor." Section 3–507.

"Draft." Section 3–104.

"Holder in due course." Section 3–302.

"Negotiation." Section 3–202.

"Note." Section 3–104.

"Notice of dishonor." Section 3–508.

"On demand." Section 3–108.

"Presentment." Section 3–504.

"Protest." Section 3–509.

"Restrictive Indorsement." Section 3–205.

"Signature." Section 3–401.

(3) The following definitions in other Articles apply to this Article:

"Account." Section 4–104.

"Banking Day." Section 4–104.

"Clearing house." Section 4–104.

"Collecting bank." Section 4–105.

"Customer." Section 4–104.

"Depositary Bank." Section 4–105.

"Documentary Draft." Section 4–104.

"Intermediary Bank." Section 4–105.

"Item." Section 4–104.

"Midnight deadline." Section 4–104.

"Payor bank." Section 4–105.

(4) In addition Article 1 contains general definitions and principles of construction and interpretation applicable throughout this Article.

Section 3–103. Limitations on Scope of Article

(1) This Article does not apply to money, documents of title or investment securities.

(2) The provisions of this Article are subject to the provisions of the Article on Bank Deposits and Collections (Article 4) and Secured Transactions (Article 9).

Section 3–104. Form of Negotiable Instruments; "Draft"; "Check"; "Certificate of Deposit"; "Note"

(1) Any writing to be a negotiable instrument within this Article must

(a) be signed by the maker or drawer; and

(b) contain an unconditional promise or order to pay a sum certain in money and no other promise, order, obligation or power given by the maker or drawer except as authorized by this Article; and

(c) be payable on demand or at a definite time; and

(d) be payable to order or to bearer.

(2) A writing which complies with the requirements of this section is

(a) a "draft" ("bill of exchange") if it is an order;

(b) a "check" if it is a draft drawn on a bank and payable on demand;

(c) a "certificate of deposit" if it is an acknowledgment by a bank of receipt of money with an engagement to repay it;

(d) a "note" if it is a promise other than a certificate of deposit.

(3) As used in other Articles of this Act, and as the context may require, the terms "draft," "check," "certificate of deposit" and "note" may refer to instruments which are not negotiable within this Article as well as to instruments which are so negotiable.

Section 3–105. When Promise or Order Unconditional

(1) A promise or order otherwise unconditional is not made conditional by the fact that the instrument

(a) is subject to implied or constructive conditions; or

(b) states its consideration, whether performed or promised, or the transaction which gave rise to the instrument, or that the promise or order is made or the instrument matures in accordance with or "as per" such transaction; or

(c) refers to or states that it arises out of a separate agreement or refers to a separate agreement for rights as to repayment or acceleration; or

(d) states that it is drawn under a letter of credit; or

(e) states that it is secured, whether by mortgage, reservation of title or otherwise; or

(f) indicates a particular account to be debited or any other fund or source from which reimbursement is expected; or

(g) is limited to payment out of a particular fund or the proceeds of a particular source, if the instrument is issued by a government or governmental agency or unit; or

(h) is limited to payment out of the entire assets of a partnership, unincorporated association, trust or estate by or on behalf of which the instrument is issued.

(2) A promise or order is not unconditional if the instrument

(a) states that it is subject to or governed by any other agreement; or

(b) states that it is to be paid only out of a particular fund or source except as provided in this section.

Section 3–106. Sum Certain

(1) The sum payable is a sum certain even though it is to be paid

(a) with stated interest or by stated installments; or

(b) with stated different rates of interest before and after default or a specified date; or

(c) with a stated discount or addition if paid before or after the date fixed for payment; or

(d) with exchange or less exchange, whether at a fixed rate or at the current rate; or

(e) with costs of collection or an attorney's fee or both upon default.

(2) Nothing in this section shall validate any term which is otherwise illegal.

Section 3–107. Money

(1) An instrument is payable in money if the medium of exchange in which it is payable is money at the time the instrument is made. An instrument payable in "currency" or "current funds" is payable in money.

(2) A promise or order to pay a sum stated in a foreign currency is for a sum certain in money and, unless a different medium of payment is specified in the instrument, may be satisfied by payment of that number of dollars which the stated foreign currency will purchase at the buying sight rate for that currency on the day on which the instrument is payable or, if payable on demand, on the day of demand. If such an instrument specifies a foreign currency as the medium of payment the instrument is payable in that currency.

Section 3–108. Payable on Demand

Instruments payable on demand include those payable at sight or on presentation and those in which no time for payment is stated.

Section 3–109. Definite Time

(1) An instrument is payable at a definite time if by its terms it is payable

(a) on or before a stated date or at a fixed period after a stated date; or

(b) at a fixed period after sight; or

(c) at a definite time subject to any acceleration; or

(d) at a definite time subject to extension at the option of the holder, or to extension to a further definite time at the option of the maker or acceptor or automatically upon or after a specified act or event.

(2) An instrument which by its terms is otherwise payable only upon an act or event uncertain as to time of occurrence is not payable at a definite time even though the act or event has occurred.

Section 3–110. Payable to Order

(1) An instrument is payable to order when by its terms it is payable to the order or assigns of any person therein specified with reasonable certainty, or to him or his order, or when it is conspicuously designated on its face as "exchange" or the like and names a payee. It may be payable to the order of

(a) the maker or drawer; or

(b) the drawee; or

(c) a payee who is not maker, drawer or drawee; or

(d) two or more payees together or in the alternative; or

(e) an estate, trust or fund, in which case it is payable to the order of the representative of such estate, trust or fund or his successors; or

(f) an office, or an officer by his title as such in which case it is payable to the principal but the incumbent of the office or his successors may act as if he or they were the holder; or

(g) a partnership or unincorporated association, in which case it is payable to the partnership or association and may be indorsed or transferred by any person thereto authorized.

(2) An instrument not payable to order is not made so payable by such words as "payable upon return of this instrument properly indorsed."

(3) An instrument made payable both to order and to bearer is payable to order unless the bearer words are handwritten or typewritten.

Section 3–111. Payable to Bearer

An instrument is payable to bearer when by its terms it is payable to

(a) a bearer or the order of bearer; or

(b) a specified person or bearer; or

(c) "cash" or the order of "cash" or any other indication which does not purport to designate a specific payee.

Section 3–112. Terms and Omissions Not Affecting Negotiability

(1) The negotiability of an instrument is not affected by

(a) the omission of a statement of any consideration or of the place where the instrument is drawn or payable; or

(b) a statement that collateral has been given to secure obligations either on the instrument or otherwise of an obligor on the instrument or that in case of default on those obligations the holder may realize on or dispose of the collateral; or

(c) a promise or power to maintain or protect collateral or to give additional collateral; or

(d) a term authorizing a confession of judgment on the instrument if it is not paid when due; or

(e) a term purporting to waive the benefit of any law intended for the advantage or protection of any obligor; or

(f) a term in a draft providing that the payee by indorsing or cashing it acknowledges full satisfaction of an obligation of the drawer; or

(g) a statement in a draft drawn in a set of parts (Section 3–801) to the effect that the order is effective only if no other part has been honored.

(2) Nothing in this section shall validate any term which is otherwise illegal.

Section 3–113. Seal

An instrument otherwise negotiable is within this Article even though it is under a seal.

Section 3–114. Date, Antedating, Postdating

(1) The negotiability of an instrument is not affected by the fact that it is undated, antedated or postdated.

(2) Where an instrument is antedated or postdated the time when it is payable is determined by the stated date if the instrument is payable on demand or at a fixed period after date.

(3) Where the instrument or any signature thereon is dated, the date is presumed to be correct.

Section 3–115. Incomplete Instruments

(1) When a paper whose contents at the time of signing show that it is intended to become an instrument is signed while still incomplete in any necessary respect it cannot be enforced until completed, but when it is completed in accordance with authority given it is effective as completed.

(2) If the completion is unauthorized the rules as to material alteration apply (Section 3–407), even though the paper was not delivered by the maker or drawer; but the burden of establishing that any completion is unauthorized is on the party so asserting.

Section 3–116. Instruments Payable to Two or More Persons

An instrument payable to the order of two or more persons

(a) if in the alternative is payable to any one of them and may be negotiated, discharged or enforced by any of them who has possession of it;

(b) if not in the alternative is payable to all of them and may be negotiated, discharged or enforced only by all of them.

Section 3–117. Instruments Payable With Words of Description

An instrument made payable to a named person with the addition of words describing him

(a) as agent or officer of a specified person is payable to his principal but the agent or officer may act as if he were the holder;

(b) as any other fiduciary for a specified person or purpose is payable to the payee and may be negotiated, discharged or enforced by him;

(c) in any other manner is payable to the payee unconditionally and the additional words are without effect on subsequent parties.

Section 3–118. Ambiguous Terms and Rules of Construction

The following rules apply to every instrument:

(a) Where there is doubt whether the instrument is a draft or a note that holder may treat it as either. A draft drawn on the drawer is effective as a note.

(b) Handwritten terms control typewritten and printed terms, and typewritten control printed.

(c) Words control figures except that if the words are ambiguous figures control.

(d) Unless otherwise specified a provision for interest means interest at the judgment rate at the place of payment from the date of the instrument, or if it is undated from the date of issue.

(e) Unless the instrument otherwise specifies two or more persons who sign as maker, acceptor or drawer or indorser and as a part of the same transaction are jointly and severally liable even though the instrument contains such words as "I promise to pay."

(f) Unless otherwise specified consent to extension authorizes a single extension for not longer than the original period. A consent to extension, expressed in the instrument, is binding on secondary parties and accommodation makers. A holder may not exercise his option to extend an instrument over the objection of a maker or acceptor or other party who in accordance with Section 3–604 tenders full payment when the instrument is due.

Section 3–119. Other Writings Affecting Instrument

(1) As between the obligor and his immediate obligee or any transferee the terms of an instrument may be modified or affected by any other written agreement executed as a part of the same transaction, except that a holder in due course is not affected by any limitation of his rights arising out of the separate written agreement if he had no notice of the limitation when he took the instrument.

(2) A separate agreement does not affect the negotiability of an instrument.

Section 3–120. Instruments "Payable Through" Bank

An instrument which states that it is "payable through" a bank or the like designates that bank as a collecting bank to make presentment but does not of itself authorize the bank to pay the instrument.

Section 3–121. Instruments Payable at Bank

Note: *If this Act is introduced in the Congress of the United States this section should be omitted. (States to select either alternative.)*

Alternative A

A note or acceptance which states that it is payable at a bank is the equivalent of a draft drawn on the bank payable when it falls due out of any funds of the maker or acceptor in current account or otherwise available for such payment.

Alternative B

A note or acceptance which states that it is payable at a bank is not of itself an order or authorization to the bank to pay it.

Section 3–122. Accrual of Cause of Action

(1) A cause of action against a maker or an acceptor accrues

(a) in the case of a time instrument on the day after maturity;

(b) in the case of a demand instrument upon its date or, if no date is stated, on the date of issue.

(2) A cause of action against the obligor of a demand or time certificate of deposit accrues upon demand, but demand on a time certificate may not be made until on or after the date of maturity.

(3) A cause of action against a drawer of a draft or an indorser of any instrument accrues upon demand following dishonor of the instrument. Notice of dishonor is a demand.

(4) Unless an instrument provides otherwise, interest runs at the rate provided by law for a judgment

(a) in the case of a maker, acceptor or other primary obligor of a demand instrument, from the date of demand;

(b) in all other cases from the date of accrual of the cause of action.

Part 2 Transfer and Negotiation

Section 3–201. Transfer: Right to Indorsement

(1) Transfer of an instrument vests in the transferee such rights as the transferor has therein, except that a transferee who has himself been a party to any fraud or illegality affecting the instrument or who as a prior holder had notice of a defense or claim against it cannot improve his position by taking from a later holder in due course.

(2) A transfer of a security interest in an instrument vests the foregoing rights in the transferee to the extent of the interest transferred.

(3) Unless otherwise agreed any transfer for value of an instrument not then payable to bearer gives the transferee the specifically enforceable right to have the unqualified indorsement of the transferor. Negotiation takes effect only when the indorsement is made and until that time there is no presumption that the transferee is the owner.

Section 3–202. Negotiation

(1) Negotiation is the transfer of an instrument in such form that the transferee becomes a holder. If the instrument is payable to order it is negotiated by delivery with any necessary indorsement; if payable to bearer it is negotiated by delivery.

(2) An indorsement must be written by or on behalf of the holder and on the instrument or on a paper so firmly affixed thereto as to become a part thereof.

(3) An indorsement is effective for negotiation only when it conveys the entire instrument or any unpaid residue. If it purports to be of less it operates only as a partial assignment.

(4) Words of assignment, condition, waiver, guaranty, limitation or disclaimer of liability and the like accompanying an indorsement do not affect its character as an indorsement.

Section 3–203. Wrong or Misspelled Name

Where an instrument is made payable to a person under a misspelled name or one other than his own he may indorse in that name or his own or both; but signature in both names may be required by a person paying or giving value for the instrument.

Section 3–204. Special Indorsement; Blank Indorsement

(1) A special indorsement specifies the person to whom or to whose order it makes the instrument payable. Any instrument specially indorsed becomes payable to the order of the special indorsee and may be further negotiated by his indorsement.

(2) An indorsement in blank specifies no particular indorsee and may consist of a mere signature. An instrument payable to order and indorsed in blank becomes payable to bearer and may be negotiated by delivery alone until specially indorsed.

(3) The holder may convert a blank indorsement into a special indorsement by writing over the signature of the indorser in blank any contract consistent with the character of the indorsement.

Section 3–205. Restrictive Indorsements

An indorsement is restrictive which either

    (a) is conditional; or

    (b) purports to prohibit further transfer of the instrument; or

    (c) includes the words "for collection," "for deposit," "pay any bank," or like terms signifying a purpose of deposit or collection; or

    (d) otherwise states that it is for the benefit or use of the indorser or of another person.

Section 3–206. Effect of Restrictive Indorsement

(1) No restrictive indorsement prevents further transfer or negotiation of the instrument.

(2) An intermediary bank, or a payor bank which is not the depositary bank, is neither given notice nor otherwise affected by a restrictive indorsement of any person except the bank's immediate transferor or the person presenting for payment.

(3) Except for an intermediary bank, any transferee under an indorsement which is conditional or includes the words "for collection," "for deposit," "pay any bank," or like terms (subparagraphs (a) and (c) of Section 3–205) must pay or apply any value given by him for or on security of the instrument consistently with the indorsement and to the extent that he does so he becomes a holder for value. In addition such transferee is a holder in due course if he otherwise complies with the requirements of Section 3–302 on what constitutes a holder in due course.

(4) The first taker under an indorsement for the benefit of the indorser or another person (subparagraph (d) of Section 3–205) must pay or apply any value given by him for or on the security of the instrument consistently with the indorsement and to the extent that he does so he becomes a holder for value. In addition such taker is a holder in due course if he otherwise complies with the requirements of Section 3–302 on what constitutes a holder in due course. A later holder for value is neither given notice nor otherwise affected by such restrictive indorsement unless he has knowledge that a fiduciary or other person has negotiated the instrument in any transaction for his own benefit or otherwise in breach of duty (subsection (2) of Section 3–304).

Section 3–207. Negotiation Effective Although It May Be Rescinded

(1) Negotiation is effective to transfer the instrument although the negotiation is

    (a) made by an infant, a corporation exceeding its powers, or any other person without capacity; or

(b) obtained by fraud, duress or mistake of any kind; or

(c) part of an illegal transaction; or

(d) made in breach of duty.

(2) Except as against a subsequent holder in due course such negotiation is in an appropriate case subject to rescission, the declaration of a constructive trust or any other remedy permitted by law.

Section 3–208. Reacquisition

Where an instrument is returned to or reacquired by a prior party he may cancel any indorsement which is not necessary to his title and reissue or further negotiate the instrument, but any intervening party is discharged as against the reacquiring party and subsequent holders not in due course and if his indorsement has been cancelled is discharged as against subsequent holders in due course as well.

Part 3 Rights of a Holder

Section 3–301. Rights of a Holder

The holder of an instrument whether or not he is the owner may transfer or negotiate it and, except as otherwise provided in Section 3–603 on payment or satisfaction, discharge it or enforce payment in his own name.

Section 3–302. Holder in Due Course

(1) A holder in due course is a holder who takes the instrument

(a) for value, and

(b) in good faith; and

(c) without notice that it is overdue or has been dishonored or of any defense against or claim to it on the part of any person.

(2) A payee may be a holder in due course.

(3) A holder does not become a holder in due course of an instrument:

(a) by purchase of it at judicial sale or by taking it under legal process; or

(b) by acquiring it in taking over an estate; or

(c) by purchasing it as part of a bulk transaction not in regular course of business of the transferor.

(4) A purchaser of a limited interest can be a holder in due course only to the extent of the interest purchased.

Section 3–303. Taking for Value

A holder takes the instrument for value

(a) to the extent that the agreed consideration has been performed or that he acquires a security

interest in or a lien on the instrument otherwise than by legal process; or

(b) when he takes the instrument in payment of or as security for an antecedent claim against any person whether or not the claim is due; or

(c) when he gives a negotiable instrument for it or makes an irrevocable commitment to a third person.

Section 3–304. Notice to Purchaser

(1) The purchaser has notice of a claim or defense if

(a) the instrument is so incomplete, bears such visible evidence of forgery or alteration, or is otherwise so irregular as to call into question its validity, terms or ownership or to create an ambiguity as to the party to pay; or

(b) the purchaser has notice that the obligation of any party is voidable in whole or in part, or that all parties have been discharged.

(2) The purchaser has notice of a claim against the instrument when he has knowledge that a fiduciary has negotiated the instrument in payment of or as security for his own debt or in any transaction for his own benefit or otherwise in breach of duty.

(3) The purchaser has notice that an instrument is overdue if he has reason to know

(a) that any part of the principal amount is overdue or that there is an uncured default in payment of another instrument of the same series; or

(b) that acceleration of the instrument has been made; or

(c) that he is taking a demand instrument after demand has been made or more than a reasonable length of time after its issue. A reasonable time for a check drawn and payable within the states and territories of the United States and the District of Columbia is presumed to be thirty days.

(4) Knowledge of the following facts does not of itself give the purchaser notice of a defense or claim

(a) that the instrument is antedated or postdated;

(b) that it was issued or negotiated in return for an executory promise or accompanied by a separate agreement, unless the purchaser has notice that a defense or claim has arisen from the terms thereof;

(c) that any party has signed for accommodation;

(d) that an incomplete instrument has been completed, unless the purchaser has notice of any improper completion;

(e) that any person negotiating the instrument is or was a fiduciary;

(f) that there has been default in payment of interest on the instrument or in payment of any other instrument, except one of the same series.

(5) The filing or recording of a document does not of itself constitute notice within the provisions of this Article to a person who would otherwise be a holder in due course.

(6) To be effective notice must be received at such time and in such manner as to give a reasonable opportunity to act on it.

Section 3–305. Rights of a Holder in Due Course

To the extent that a holder is a holder in due course he takes the instrument free from

(1) all claims to it on the part of any person; and

(2) all defenses of any party to the instrument with whom the holder has not dealt except

(a) infancy, to the extent that it is a defense to a simple contract; and

(b) such other incapacity, or duress, or illegality or the transaction, as renders the obligation of the party a nullity; and

(c) such misrepresentation as has induced the party to sign the instrument with neither knowledge nor reasonable opportunity to obtain knowledge of its character or its essential terms; and

(d) discharge in insolvency proceedings; and

(e) any other discharge of which the holder has notice when he takes the instrument.

Section 3–306. Rights of One Not Holder in Due Course

Unless he has the rights of a holder in due course any person takes the instrument subject to

(a) all valid claims to it on the part of any person; and

(b) all defenses of any party which would be available in an action on a simple contract; and

(c) the defenses of want or failure of consideration, non-performance of any condition precedent, non-delivery, or delivery for a special purpose (Section 3–408); and

(d) the defense that he or a person through whom he holds the instrument acquired it by theft, or that payment or satisfaction to such holder would be inconsistent with the terms of a restrictive indorsement. The claim of any third person to the instrument is not otherwise available as a defense to any party liable thereon unless the third person himself defends the action for such party.

Section 3–307. Burden of Establishing Signatures, Defenses and Due Course

(1) Unless specifically denied in the pleadings each signature on an instrument is admitted. When the effectiveness of a signature is put in issue

(a) the burden of establishing it is on the party claiming under the signature; but

(b) the signature is presumed to be genuine or authorized except where the action is to enforce the obligation of a purported signer who had died or become incompetent before proof is required.

(2) When signatures are admitted or established, production of the instrument entitles a holder to recover on it unless the defendant establishes a defense.

(3) After it is shown that a defense exists a person claiming the rights of a holder in due course has the burden of establishing that he or some person under whom he claims is in all respects a holder in due course.

Part 4 Liability of Parties

Section 3–401. Signature

(1) No person is liable on an instrument unless his signature appears thereon.

(2) A signature is made by use of any name, including any trade or assumed name, upon an instrument, or by any word or mark used in lieu of a written signature.

Section 3–402. Signature in Ambiguous Capacity

Unless the instrument clearly indicates that a signature is made in some other capacity it is an indorsement.

Section 3–403. Signature by Authorized Representative

(1) A signature may be made by an agent or other representative, and his authority to make it may be established as in other cases of representation. No particular form of appointment is necessary to establish such authority.

(2) An authorized representative who signs his own name to an instrument

(a) is personally obligated if the instrument neither names the person represented nor shows that the representative signed in a representative capacity;

(b) except as otherwise established between the immediate parties, is personally obligated if the instrument names the person represented but does not show that the representative signed in a representative capacity, or if the instrument does not name the person represented but does show that the representative signed in a representative capacity.

(3) Except as otherwise established the name of an organization preceded or followed by the name and office of an authorized individual is a signature made in a representative capacity.

Section 3–404. Unauthorized Signatures

(1) Any unauthorized signature is wholly inoperative as that of the person whose name is signed unless he ratifies it or is precluded from denying it; but it operates as the signature of the unauthorized signer in favor of any person who in good faith pays the instrument or takes it for value.

(2) Any unauthorized signature may be ratified for all purposes of this Article. Such ratification does not of itself affect any rights of the person ratifying against the actual signer.

Section 3–405. Impostors; Signature in Name of Payee

(1) An indorsement by any person in the name of a named payee is effective if

(a) an impostor by use of the mails or otherwise has induced the maker or drawer to issue the instrument to him or his confederate in the name of the payee; or

(b) a person signing as or on behalf of a maker or drawer intends the payee to have no interest in the instrument; or

(c) an agent or employee of the maker or drawer has supplied him with the name of the payee intending the latter to have no such interest.

(2) Nothing in this section shall affect the criminal or civil liability of the person so indorsing.

Section 3–406. Negligence Contributing to Alteration or Unauthorized Signature

Any person who by his negligence substantially contributes to a material alteration of the instrument or to the making of an unauthorized signature is precluded from asserting the alteration or lack of authority against a holder in due course or against a drawee or other payor who pays the instrument in good faith and in accordance with the reasonable commercial standards of the drawee's or payor's business.

Section 3–407. Alteration

(1) Any alteration of an instrument is material which changes the contract of any party thereto in any respect, including any such change in

(a) the number or relations of the parties; or

(b) an incomplete instrument, by completing it otherwise than as authorized; or

(c) the writing as signed, by adding to it or by removing any part of it.

(2) As against any person other than a subsequent holder in due course.

(a) alteration by the holder which is both fraudulent and material discharges any party whose contract is thereby changed unless that party assents or is precluded from asserting the defense.

(b) no other alteration discharges any party and the instrument may be enforced according to its original tenor, or as to incomplete instruments according to the authority given.

(3) A subsequent holder in due course may in all cases enforce the instrument according to its original tenor, and when an incomplete instrument has been completed, he may enforce it as completed.

Section 3–408. Consideration

Want or failure of consideration is a defense as against any person not having the rights of a holder in due course (Section 3–305), except that no consideration is necessary for an instrument or obligation thereon given in payment of or as security for an antecedent obligation of any kind. Nothing in this section shall be taken to displace any statute outside this Act under which a promise is enforceable notwithstanding lack or failure of consideration. Partial failure of consideration is a defense pro tanto whether or not the failure is in an ascertained or liquidated amount.

Section 3–409. Draft Not an Assignment

(1) A check or other draft does not of itself operate as an assignment of any funds in the hands of the drawee available for its payment, and the drawee is not liable on the instrument until he accepts it.

(2) Nothing in this section shall affect any liability in contract, tort or otherwise arising from any letter of credit or other obligation or representation which is not an acceptance.

Section 3–410. Definition and Operation of Acceptance

(1) Acceptance is the drawee's signed engagement to honor the draft as presented. It must be written on the

draft, and may consist of his signature alone. It becomes operative when completed by delivery or notification.

(2) A draft may be accepted although it has not been signed by the drawer or is otherwise incomplete or is overdue or has been dishonored.

(3) Where the draft is payable at a fixed period after sight and the acceptor fails to date his acceptance the holder may complete it by supplying a date in good faith.

Section 3–411. Certification of a Check

(1) Certification of a check is acceptance. Where a holder procures certification the drawer and all prior indorsers are discharged.

(2) Unless otherwise agreed a bank has no obligation to certify a check.

(3) A bank may certify a check before returning it for lack of proper indorsement. If it does so the drawer is discharged.

Section 3–412. Acceptance Varying Draft

(1) Where the drawee's proffered acceptance in any manner varies the draft as presented the holder may refuse the acceptance and treat the draft as dishonored in which case the drawee is entitled to have his acceptance cancelled.

(2) The terms of the draft are not varied by an acceptance to pay at any particular bank or place in the United States, unless the acceptance states that the draft is to be paid only at such bank or place.

(3) Where the holder assents to an acceptance varying the terms of the draft each drawer and indorser who does not affirmatively assent is discharged.

Section 3–413. Contract of Maker, Drawer and Acceptor

(1) The maker or acceptor engages that he will pay the instrument according to its tenor at the time of his engagement or as completed pursuant to Section 3–115 on incomplete instruments.

(2) The drawer engages that upon dishonor of the draft and any necessary notice of dishonor or protest he will pay the amount of the draft to the holder or to any indorser who takes it up. The drawer may disclaim this liability by drawing without recourse.

(3) By making, drawing or accepting the party admits as against all subsequent parties including the drawee the existence of the payee and his then capacity to indorse.

Section 3–414. Contract of Indorser; Order of Liability

(1) Unless the indorsement otherwise specifies (as by such words as "without recourse") every indorser engages that upon dishonor and any necessary notice of dishonor and protest he will pay the instrument according to its tenor at the time of his indorsement to the holder or to any subsequent indorser who takes it up, even though the indorser who takes it up was not obligated to do so.

(2) Unless they otherwise agree indorsers are liable to one another in the order in which they indorse, which is presumed to be the order in which their signatures appear on the instrument.

Section 3–415. Contract of Accommodation Party

(1) An accommodation party is one who signs the instrument in any capacity for the purpose of lending his name to another party to it.

(2) When the instrument has been taken for value before it is due the accommodation party is liable in the capacity in which he has signed even though the taker knows of the accommodation.

(3) As against a holder in due course and without notice of the accommodation oral proof of the accommodation is not admissible to give the accommodation party the benefit of discharges dependent on his character as such. In other cases the accommodation character may be shown by oral proof.

(4) An indorsement which shows that it is not in the chain of title is notice of its accommodation character.

(5) An accommodation party is not liable to the party accommodated, and if he pays the instrument has a right of recourse on the instrument against such party.

Section 3–416. Contract of Guarantor

(1) "Payment guaranteed" or equivalent words added to a signature mean that the signer engages that if the instrument is not paid when due he will pay it according to its tenor without resort by the holder to any other party.

(2) "Collection guaranteed" or equivalent words added to a signature mean that the signer engages that if the instrument is not paid when due he will pay it according to its tenor, but only after the holder has reduced his claim against the maker or acceptor to judgment and execution has been returned unsatisfied, or after the maker or acceptor has become insolvent or it is otherwise apparent that it is useless to proceed against him.

(3) Words of guaranty which do not otherwise specify guarantee payment.

(4) No words of guaranty added to the signature of a sole maker or acceptor affect his liability on the instrument. Such words added to the signature of one of two or more makers or acceptors create a presumption that the signature is for the accommodation of the others.

(5) When words of guaranty are used presentment, notice of dishonor and protest are not necessary to charge the user.

(6) Any guaranty written on the instrument is enforceable notwithstanding any statute of frauds.

Section 3–417. Warranties on Presentment and Transfer

(1) Any person who obtains payment or acceptance and any prior transferor warrants to a person who in good faith pays or accepts that

(a) he has a good title to the instrument or is authorized to obtain payment or acceptance on behalf of one who has a good title; and

(b) he has no knowledge that the signature of the maker or drawer is unauthorized, except that this warranty is not given by a holder in due course acting in good faith

(i) to a maker with respect to the maker's own signature; or

(ii) to a drawer with respect to the drawer's own signature, whether or not the drawer is also the drawee; or

(iii) to an acceptor of a draft if the holder in due course took the draft after the acceptance or obtained the acceptance without knowledge that the drawer's signature was unauthorized; and

(c) the instrument has not been materially altered, except that this warranty is not given by a holder in due course acting in good faith

(i) to the maker of a note; or

(ii) to the drawer of a draft whether or not the drawer is also the drawee; or

(iii) to the acceptor of a draft with respect to an alteration made prior to the acceptance if the holder in due course took the draft after the acceptance, even though the acceptance provided "payable as originally drawn" or equivalent terms; or

(iv) to the acceptor of a draft with respect to an alteration made after the acceptance.

(2) Any person who transfers an instrument and receives consideration warrants to his transferee and if the transfer is by indorsement to any subsequent holder who takes the instrument in good faith that

(a) he has a good title to the instrument or is authorized to obtain payment or acceptance on behalf of one who has a good title and the transfer is otherwise rightful; and

(b) all signatures are genuine or authorized; and

(c) the instrument has not been materially altered; and

(d) no defense of any party in good against him; and

(e) he has no knowledge of any insolvency proceeding instituted with respect to the maker or acceptor or the drawer of an unaccepted instrument.

(3) By transferring "without recourse" the transferor limits the obligation stated in subsection (2) (d) to a warranty that he has no knowledge of such a defense.

(4) A selling agent or broker who does not disclose the fact that he is acting only as such gives the warranties provided in this section, but if he makes such disclosure warrants only his good faith and authority.

Section 3–418. Finality of Payment or Acceptance

Except for recovery of bank payments as provided in the Article on Bank Deposits and Collections (Article 4) and except for liability for breach of warranty on presentment under the preceding section, payment or acceptance of any instrument is final in favor of a holder in due course, or a person who has in good faith changed his position in reliance on the payment.

Section 3–419. Conversion of Instrument; Innocent Representative

(1) An instrument is converted when

(a) a drawee to whom it is delivered for acceptance refuses to return it on demand; or

(b) any person to whom it is delivered for payment refuses on demand either to pay or to return it; or

(c) it is paid on a forged indorsement.

(2) In an action against a drawee under subsection (1) the measure of the drawee's liability is the face amount of the instrument. In any other action under subsection (1) the measure of liability is presumed to be the face amount of the instrument.

(3) Subject to the provisions of this Act concerning restrictive indorsements a representative, including a depositary or collecting bank, who has in good faith and in accordance with the reasonable commercial standards applicable to the business of such representative dealt with an instrument or its proceeds on behalf of one who was not the true owner is not liable in conversion or otherwise to the true owner beyond the amount of any proceeds remaining in his hands.

(4) An intermediary bank or payor bank which is not a depositary bank is not liable in conversion solely by reason of the fact that proceeds of an item indorsed restrictively

(Sections 3–205 and 3–206) are not paid or applied consistently with the restrictive indorsement of an indorser other than its immediate transferor.

Part 5 Presentment, Notice of Dishonor and Protest

Section 3–501. When Presentment, Notice of Dishonor, and Protest Necessary or Permissible

(1) Unless excused (Section 3–511) presentment is necessary to charge secondary parties as follows:

(a) presentment for acceptance is necessary to charge the drawer and indorsers of a draft where the draft so provides, or is payable elsewhere than at the residence or place of business of the drawee, or its date of payment depends upon such presentment. The holder may at his option present for acceptance any other draft payable at a stated date:

(b) presentment for payment is necessary to charge any indorser;

(c) in the case of any drawer, the acceptor of a draft payable at a bank or the maker of a note payable at a bank, presentment for payment is necessary, but failure to make presentment discharges such drawer, acceptor or maker only as stated in Section 3–502(1)(b).

(2) Unless excused (Section 3–511)

(a) notice of any dishonor is necessary to charge any indorser:

(b) in the case of any drawer, the acceptor of a draft payable at a bank or the maker of a note payable at a bank, notice of any dishonor is necessary, but failure to give such notice discharges such drawer, acceptor or maker only as stated in Section 3–502(1)(b).

(3) Unless excused (Section 3–511) protest of any dishonor is necessary to charge the drawer and indorsers of any draft which on its face appears to be drawn or payable outside of the states, territories, dependencies and possessions of the United States, the District of Columbia and the Commonwealth of Puerto Rico. The holder may at his option make protest of any dishonor of any other instrument and in the case of a foreign draft may on insolvency of the acceptor before maturity make protest for better security.

(4) Notwithstanding any provision of this section, neither presentment nor notice of dishonor nor protest is necessary to charge an indorser who has indorsed an instrument after maturity.

Section 3–502. Unexcused Delay; Discharge

(1) Where without excuse any necessary presentment or notice of dishonor is delayed beyond the time when it is due

(a) any indorser is discharged; and

(b) any drawer or the acceptor of a draft payable at a bank or the maker of a note payable at a bank who because the drawee or payor bank becomes insolvent during the delay is deprived of funds maintained with the drawee or payor bank to cover the instrument may discharge his liability by written assignment to the holder of his rights against the drawee or payor bank in respect of such funds, but such drawer, acceptor or maker is not otherwise discharged.

(2) Where without excuse a necessary protest is delayed beyond the time when it is due any drawer or indorser is discharged.

Section 3–503. Time of Presentment

(1) Unless a different time is expressed in the instrument the time for any presentment is determined as follows:

(a) where an instrument is payable at or a fixed period after a stated date any presentment for acceptance must be made on or before the date it is payable;

(b) where an instrument is payable after sight it must either be presented for acceptance or negotiated within a reasonable time after date or issue whichever is later;

(c) where an instrument shows the date on which it is payable presentment for payment is due on that date;

(d) where an instrument is accelerated presentment for payment is due within a reasonable time after the acceleration;

(e) with respect to the liability of any secondary party presentment for acceptance or payment of any other instrument is due within a reasonable time after such party becomes liable thereon.

(2) A reasonable time for presentment is determined by the nature of the instrument, any usage of banking or trade and the facts of the particular case. In the case of an uncertified check which is drawn and payable within the United States and which is not a draft drawn by a bank the following are presumed to be reasonable periods within which to present for payment or to initiate bank collection:

(a) with respect to the liability of the drawer, thirty days after date or issue whichever is later; and

(b) with respect to the liability of an indorser, seven days after his indorsement.

(3) Where any presentment is due on a day which is not a full business day for either the person making presentment or the party to pay or accept, presentment is due on the next following day which is a full business day for both parties.

(4) Presentment to be sufficient must be made at a reasonable hour and if at a bank during its banking day.

Section 3–504. How Presentment Made

(1) Presentment is a demand for acceptance or payment made upon the maker, acceptor, drawee or other payor by or on behalf of the holder.

(2) Presentment may be made

(a) by mail, in which event the time of presentment is determined by the time of receipt of the mail; or

(b) through a clearing house; or

(c) at the place of acceptance or payment specified in the instrument or if there be none at the place of business or residence of the party to accept or pay. If neither the party to accept or pay nor anyone authorized to act for him is present or accessible at such place presentment is excused.

(3) It may be made

(a) to any one of two or more makers, acceptors, drawees or other payors; or

(b) to any person who has authority to make or refuse the acceptance or payment.

(4) A draft accepted or a note made payable at a bank in the United States must be presented at such bank.

(5) In the case described in Section 4–210 presentment may be made in the manner and with the result stated in that section.

Section 3–505. Rights of Party to Whom Presentment Is Made

(1) The party to whom presentment is made may without dishonor require

(a) exhibition of the instrument; and

(b) reasonable identification of the person making presentment and evidence of his authority to make it if made for another; and

(c) that the instrument be produced for acceptance or payment at a place specified in it, or if there be none at any place reasonable in the circumstances; and

(d) a signed receipt on the instrument for any partial or full payment and its surrender upon full payment.

(2) Failure to comply with any such requirement invalidates the presentment but the person presenting has a reasonable time in which to comply and the time for acceptance or payment runs from the time of compliance.

Section 3–506. Time Allowed for Acceptance of Payment

(1) Acceptance may be deferred without dishonor until the close of the next business day following presentment. The holder may also in a good faith effort to obtain acceptance and without either dishonor of the instrument or discharge of secondary parties allow postponement of acceptance for an additional business day.

(2) Except as a longer time is allowed in the case of documentary drafts drawn under a letter of credit, and unless an earlier time is agreed to by the party to pay, payment of an instrument may be deferred without dishonor pending reasonable examination to determine whether it is properly payable, but payment must be made in any event before the close of business on the day of presentment.

Section 3–507. Dishonor; Holder's Right of Recourse; Term Allowing Re-Presentment

(1) An instrument is dishonored when

(a) a necessary or optional presentment is duly made and due acceptance or payment is refused or cannot be obtained within the prescribed time or in case of bank collections the instrument is seasonably returned by the midnight deadline (Section 4–301); or

(b) presentment is excused and the instrument is not duly accepted or paid.

(2) Subject to any necessary notice of dishonor and protest, the holder has upon dishonor an immediate right of recourse against the drawers and indorsers.

(3) Return of an instrument for lack of proper indorsement is not dishonor.

(4) A term in a draft or an indorsement thereof allowing a stated time for re-presentment in the event of any dishonor of the draft by nonacceptance if a time draft or by nonpayment if a sight draft gives the holder as against any secondary party bound by the term an option to waive the dishonor without affecting liability of the secondary party and he may present again up to the end of the stated time.

Section 3–508. Notice of Dishonor

(1) Notice of dishonor may be given to any person who may be liable on the instrument by or on behalf of the holder or any party who has himself received notice, or any other party who can be compelled to pay the instrument. In addition an agent or bank in whose hands the instrument is dishonored may give notice to his principal or customer or to another agent or bank from which the instrument was received.

(2) Any necessary notice must be given by a bank before its midnight deadline and by any other person before midnight of the third business day after dishonor or receipt of notice of dishonor.

(3) Notice may be given in any reasonable manner. It may be oral or written and in any terms which identify the instrument and state that it has been dishonored. A misdescription which does not mislead the party notified does not vitiate the notice. Sending the instrument bearing a stamp, ticket or writing stating that acceptance or payment has been refused or sending a notice of debit with respect to the instrument is sufficient.

(4) Written notice is given when sent although it is not received.

(5) Notice to one partner is notice to each although the firm has been dissolved.

(6) When any party is in insolvency proceedings instituted after the issue of the instrument notice may be given either to the party or to the representative of his estate.

(7) When any party is dead or incompetent notice may be sent to his last known address or given to his personal representative.

(8) Notice operates for the benefit of all parties who have rights on the instrument against the party notified.

Section 3–509. Protest; Noting for Protest

(1) A protest is a certificate of dishonor made under the hand and seal of a United States consul or vice consul or a notary public or other person authorized to certify dishonor by the law of the place where dishonor occurs. It may be made upon information satisfactory to such person.

(2) The protest must identify the instrument and certify either that due presentment has been made or the reason why it is excused and that the instrument has been dishonored by nonacceptance or nonpayment.

(3) The protest may also certify that notice of dishonor has been given to all parties or to specified parties.

(4) Subject to subsection (5) any necessary protest is due by the time that notice of dishonor is due.

(5) If, before protest is due, an instrument has been noted for protest by the officer to make protest, the protest may be made at any time thereafter as of the date of the noting.

Section 3–510. Evidence of Dishonor and Notice of Dishonor

The following are admissible as evidence and create a presumption of dishonor and of any notice of dishonor therein shown:

(a) a document regular in form as provided in the preceding section which purports to be a protest;

(b) the purported stamp or writing of the drawee, payor bank or presenting bank on the instrument or accompanying it stating that acceptance or payment has been refused for reasons consistent with dishonor;

(c) any book or record of the drawee, payor bank, or any collecting bank kept in the usual course of business which shows dishonor, even though there is no evidence of who made the entry.

Section 3–511. Waived or Excused Presentment, Protest or Notice of Dishonor or Delay Therein

(1) Delay in presentment, protest or notice of dishonor is excused when the party is without notice that it is due or when the delay is caused by circumstances beyond his control and he exercises reasonable diligence after the cause of the delay ceases to operate.

(2) Presentment or notice or protest as the case may be is entirely excused when

(a) the party to be charged has waived it expressly or by implication either before or after it is due; or

(b) such party has himself dishonored the instrument or has countermanded payment or otherwise has no reason to expect or right to require that the instrument be accepted or paid; or

(c) by reasonable diligence the presentment or protest cannot be made or the notice given.

(3) Presentment is also entirely excused when

(a) the maker, acceptor, or drawee of any instrument except a documentary draft is dead or in insolvency proceedings instituted after the issue of the instrument; or

(b) acceptance or payment is refused but not for want of proper presentment.

(4) Where a draft has been dishonored by nonacceptance a later presentment for payment and any notice of dishonor

and protest for nonpayment are excused unless in the meantime the instrument has been accepted.

(5) A waiver of protest is also a waiver of presentment and of notice of dishonor even though protest is not required.

(6) Where a waiver of presentment or notice or protest is embodied in the instrument itself it is binding upon all parties; but where it is written above the signature of an indorser it binds him only.

Part 6 Discharge

Section 3–601. Discharge of Parties

(1) The extent of the discharge of any party from liability on an instrument is governed by the sections on

   (a) payment or satisfaction (Section 3–603); or

   (b) tender of payment (Section 3–604); or

   (c) cancellation or renunciation (Section 3–605); or

   (d) impairment of right of recourse or of collateral (Section 3–606); or

   (e) reacquisition of the instrument by a prior party (Section 3–208); or

   (f) fraudulent and material alteration (Section 3–407); or

   (g) certification of a check (Section 3–411); or

   (h) acceptance varying a draft (Section 3–412); or

   (i) unexcused delay in presentment or notice of dishonor or protest (Section 3–502).

(2) Any party is also discharged from his liability on an instrument to another party by any other act or agreement with such party which would discharge his simple contract for the payment of money.

(3) The liability of all parties is discharged when any party who has himself no right of action or recourse on the instrument

   (a) reacquires the instrument in his own right; or

   (b) is discharged under any provision of this Article, except as otherwise provided with respect to discharge for impairment of recourse or of collateral (Section 3–606).

Section 3–602. Effect of Discharge Against Holder in Due Course

No discharge of any party provided by this Article is effective against a subsequent holder in due course unless he has notice thereof when he takes the instrument.

Section 3–603. Payment or Satisfaction

(1) The liability of any party is discharged to the extent of his payment or satisfaction to the holder even though it is made with knowledge of a claim of another person to the instrument unless prior to such payment or satisfaction the person making the claim either supplies indemnity deemed adequate by the party seeking the discharge or enjoins payment or satisfaction by order of a court of competent jurisdiction in an action in which the adverse claimant and the holder are parties. This subsection does not, however, result in the discharge of the liability

   (a) of a party who in bad faith pays or satisfies a holder who acquired the instrument by theft or who (unless having the rights of a holder in due course) holds through one who so acquired it; or

   (b) of a party (other than an intermediary bank or a payor bank which is not a depositary bank) who pays or satisfies the holder of an instrument which has been restrictively indorsed in a manner not consistent with the terms of such restrictive indorsement.

(2) Payment or satisfaction may be made with the consent of the holder by any person including a stranger to the instrument. Surrender of the instrument to such a person gives him the rights of a transferee (Section 3–201).

Section 3–604. Tender of Payment

(1) Any party making tender of full payment to a holder when or after it is due is discharged to the extent of all subsequent liability for interest, costs and attorney's fees.

(2) The holder's refusal of such tender wholly discharges any party who has a right of recourse against the party making the tender.

(3) Where the maker or acceptor of an instrument payable otherwise than on demand is able and ready to pay at every place of payment specified in the instrument when it is due, it is equivalent to tender.

Section 3–605. Cancellation and Renunciation

(1) The holder of an instrument may even without consideration discharge any party

   (a) in any manner apparent on the face of the instrument or the indorsement, as by intentionally cancelling the instrument or the party's signature by destruction or mutilation, or by striking out the party's signature; or

   (b) by renouncing his rights by a writing signed and delivered or by surrender of the instrument to the party to be discharged.

(2) Neither cancellation nor renunciation without surrender of the instrument affects the title thereto.

Section 3–606. Impairment of Recourse or of Collateral

(1) The holder discharges any party to the instrument to the extent that without such party's consent the holder

(a) without express reservation of rights releases or agrees not to sue any person against whom the party has to the knowledge of the holder a right of recourse or agrees to suspend the right to enforce against such person the instrument or collateral or otherwise discharges such person, except that failure or delay in effecting any required presentment, protest or notice of dishonor with respect to any such person does not discharge any party as to whom presentment, protest or notice of dishonor is effective or unnecessary; or

(b) unjustifiably impairs any collateral for the instrument given by or on behalf of the party or any person against whom he has a right of recourse.

(2) By express reservation of rights against a party with a right of recourse the holder preserves

(a) all his rights against such party as of the time when the instrument was originally due; and

(b) the right of the party to pay the instrument as of that time; and

(c) all rights of such party to recourse against others.

Part 7 Advice of International Sight Draft

Section 3–701. Letter of Advice of International Sight Draft

(1) A "letter of advice" is a drawer's communication to the drawee that a described draft has been drawn.

(2) Unless otherwise agreed when a bank receives from another bank a letter of advice of an international sight draft the drawee bank may immediately debit the drawer's account and stop the running of interest pro tanto. Such a debit and any resulting credit to any account covering outstanding drafts leaves in the drawer full power to stop payment or otherwise dispose of the amount and creates no trust or interest in favor of the holder.

(3) Unless otherwise agreed and except where a draft is drawn under a credit issued by the drawee, the drawee of an international sight draft owes the drawer no duty to pay an unadvised draft but if it does so and the draft is genuine, may appropriately debit the drawer's account.

Part 8 Miscellaneous

Section 3–801. Drafts in a Set

(1) Where a draft is drawn in a set of parts, each of which is numbered and expressed to be an order only if no other part has been honored, the whole of the parts constitutes one draft but a taker of any part may become a holder in due course of the draft.

(2) Any person who negotiates, indorses or accepts a single part of a draft drawn in a set thereby becomes liable to any holder in due course of that part as if it were the whole set, but as between different holders in due course to whom different parts have been negotiated the holder whose title first accrues has all rights to the draft and its proceeds.

(3) As against the drawee the first presented part of a draft drawn in a set is the part entitled to payment, or if a time draft to acceptance and payment. Acceptance of any subsequently presented part renders the drawee liable thereon under subsection (2). With respect both to a holder and to the drawer payment of a subsequently presented part of a draft payable at sight has the same effect as payment of a check notwithstanding an effective stop order (Section 4–407).

(4) Except as otherwise provided in this section, where any part of a draft in a set is discharged by payment or otherwise the whole draft is discharged.

Section 3–802. Effect of Instrument on Obligation for Which It Is Given

(1) Unless otherwise agreed where an instrument is taken for an underlying obligation

(a) the obligation is pro tanto discharged if a bank is drawer, maker or acceptor of the instrument and there is no recourse on the instrument against the underlying obligor; and

(b) in any other case the obligation is suspended pro tanto until the instrument is due or if it is payable on demand until its presentment. If the instrument is dishonored action may be maintained on either the instrument or the obligation; discharge of the underlying obligor on the instrument also discharges him on the obligation.

(2) The taking in good faith of a check which is not postdated does not of itself so extend the time on the original obligation as to discharge a surety.

Section 3–803. Notice to Third Party

Where a defendant is sued for breach of an obligation for which a third person is answerable over under this

Article he may give the third person written notice of the litigation, and the person notified may then give similar notice to any other person who is answerable over to him under this Article. If the notice states that the person notified may come in and defend and that if the person notified does not do so he will in any action against him by the person giving the notice be bound by any determination of fact common to the two litigations, then unless after seasonable receipt of the notice the person notified does come in and defend he is so bound.

Section 3–804. Lost, Destroyed or Stolen Instruments

The owner of an instrument which is lost, whether by destruction, theft or otherwise, may maintain an action in his own name and recover from any party liable thereon upon due proof of his ownership, the facts which prevent his production of the instrument and its terms. The court may require security indemnifying the defendant against loss by reason of further claims on the instrument.

Section 3–805. Instruments Not Payable to Order or to Bearer

This Article applies to any instrument whose terms do not preclude transfer and which is otherwise negotiable within this Article but which is not payable to order or to bearer, except that there can be no holder in due course of such an instrument.

ARTICLE 4 BANK DEPOSITS AND COLLECTIONS

Part 1 General Provisions and Definitions

Section 4–101. Short Title

This Article shall be known and may be cited as Uniform Commercial Code—Bank Deposits and Collections.

Section 4–102. Applicability

(1) To the extent that items within this Article are also within the scope of Articles 3 and 8, they are subject to the provisions of those Articles. In the event of conflict the provisions of this Article govern those of Article 3 but the provisions of Article 8 govern those of this Article.

(2) The liability of a bank for action or nonaction with respect to any item handled by it for purposes of presentment, payment or collection is governed by the law of the place where the bank is located. In the case of action or non-action by or at a branch or separate office of a bank, its liability is governed by the law of the place where the branch or separate office is located.

Section 4–103. Variation by Agreement; Measure of Damages; Certain Action Constituting Ordinary Care

(1) The effect of the provisions of this Article may be varied by agreement except that no agreement can disclaim a bank's responsibility for its own lack of good faith or failure to exercise ordinary care or can limit the measure of damages for such lack of failure; but the parties may by agreement determine the standards by which such responsibility is to be measured if such standards are not manifestly unreasonable.

(2) Federal Reserve regulations and operating letters, clearing house rules, and the like, have the effect of agreements under subsection (1), whether or not specifically assented to by all parties interested in items handled.

(3) Action or non-action approved by this Article or pursuant to Federal Reserve regulations or operating letters constitutes the exercise of ordinary care and, in the absence of special instructions, action or non-action consistent with clearing house rules and the like or with a general banking usage not disapproved by this Article, prima facie constitutes the exercise of ordinary care.

(4) The specification or approval of certain procedures by this Article does not constitute disapproval of other procedures which may be reasonable under the circumstances.

(5) The measure of damages for failure to exercise ordinary care in handling an item is the amount of the item reduced by an amount which could not have been realized by the use of ordinary care, and where there is bad faith it includes other damages, if any, suffered by the party as a proximate consequence.

Section 4–104. Definitions and Index of Definitions

(1) In this Article unless the context otherwise requires

(a) "Account" means any account with a bank and includes a checking, time, interest or savings account;

(b) "Afternoon" means the period of a day between noon and midnight;

(c) "Banking day" means that part of any day on which a bank is open to the public for carrying on substantially all of its banking functions;

(d) "Clearing house" means any association of banks or other payor regularly clearing items;

(e) "Customer" means any person having an account with a bank or for whom a bank has agreed to collect items and includes a bank carrying an account with another bank;

(f) "Documentary draft" means any negotiable or non-negotiable draft with accompanying documents, securities or other papers to be delivered against honor of the draft;

(g) "Item" means any instrument for the payment of money even though it is not negotiable but does not include money;

(h) "Midnight deadline" with respect to a bank is midnight on its next banking day following the banking day on which it receives the relevant item or notice or from which the time for taking action commences to run, whichever is later;

(i) "Properly payable" includes the availability of funds for payment at the time of decision to pay or dishonor;

(j) "Settle" means to pay in cash, by clearing house settlement, in a charge or credit or by remittance, or otherwise as instructed. A settlement may be either provisional or final;

(k) "Suspends payments" with respect to a bank means that it has been closed by order of the supervisory authorities, that a public officer has been appointed to take it over or that it ceases or refuses to make payments in the ordinary course of business.

(2) Other definitions applying to this Article and the sections in which they appear are:

"Collecting bank." Section 4–105.

"Depositary bank." Section 4–105.

"Intermediary bank." Section 4–105.

"Payor bank." Section 4–105.

"Presenting bank." Section 4–105.

"Remitting bank." Section 4–105.

(3) The following definitions in other Articles apply to this Article:

"Acceptance." Section 3–410.

"Certificate of deposit." Section 3–104.

"Certification." Section 3–411.

"Check." Section 3–104.

"Draft." Section 3–104.

"Holder in due course." Section 3–302.

"Notice of dishonor." Section 3–508.

"Presentment." Section 3–504.

"Protest." Section 3–509.

"Secondary party." Section 3–102.

(4) In addition Article 1 contains general definitions and principles of construction and interpretation applicable throughout this Article.

Section 4–105. "Depository Bank"; "Intermediary Bank"; "Collecting Bank"; "Payor Bank"; "Presenting Bank"; "Remitting Bank"

In this Article unless the context otherwise requires:

(a) "Depositary bank" means the first bank to which an item is transferred for collection even though it is also the payor bank;

(b) "Payor bank" means a bank by which an item is payable as drawn or accepted;

(c) "Intermediary bank" means any bank to which an item is transferred in course of collection except the depositary or payor bank;

(d) "Collecting bank" means any bank handling the item for collection except the payor bank;

(e) "Presenting bank" means any bank presenting an item except a payor bank;

(f) "Remitting bank" means any payor or intermediary bank remitting for an item.

Section 4–106. Separate Office of a Bank

A branch or separate office of a bank [maintaining its own deposit ledgers] is a separate bank for the purpose of computing the time within which and determining the place at or to which action may be taken or notices or orders shall be given under this Article and under Article 3.

Note: *The brackets are to make it optional with the several states whether to require a branch to maintain its own deposit ledgers in order to be considered to be a separate bank for certain purposes under Article 4. In some states "maintaining its own deposit ledgers" is a satisfactory test. In others branch banking practices are such that this test would not be suitable.*

Section 4–107. Time of Receipt of Items

(1) For the purpose of allowing time to process items, prove balances and make the necessary entries on its books to determine its position for the day, a bank may fix an afternoon hour of 2 P.M. or later as a cut-off hour for the handling of money and items and the making of entries on its books.

(2) Any item or deposit of money received on any day after a cut-off hour so fixed or after the close of the banking day may be treated as being received at the opening of the next banking day.

Section 4–108. Delays

(1) Unless otherwise instructed, a collecting bank in a good faith effort to secure payment may, in the case of specific items and with or without the approval of any person involved, waive, modify or extend time limits im-

posed or permitted by this Act for a period not in excess of an additional banking day without discharge of secondary parties and without liability to its transferor or any prior party.

(2) Delay by a collecting bank or payor bank beyond time limits prescribed or permitted by this Act or by instructions is excused if caused by interruption of communication facilities, suspension of payments by another bank, war, emergency conditions or other circumstances beyond the control of the bank provided it exercises such diligence as the circumstances require.

Section 4–109. Process of Posting

The "process of posting" means the usual procedure followed by a payor bank in determining to pay an item and in recording the payment including one or more of the following or other steps as determined by the bank:

(a) verification of any signature;

(b) ascertaining that sufficient funds are available;

(c) affixing a "paid" or other stamp

(d) entering a charge or entry to a customer's account;

(e) correcting or reversing an entry or erroneous action with respect to the item.

Part 2 Collection of Items: Depositary and Collecting Banks

Section 4–201. Presumption and Duration of Agency Status of Collecting Banks and Provisional Status of Credits; Applicability of Article; Item Indorsed "Pay Any Bank"

(1) Unless a contrary intent clearly appears and prior to the time that a settlement given by a collecting bank for an item is or becomes final (subsection (3) of Section 4–211 and Sections 4–212 and 4–213) the bank is an agent or sub-agent of the owner of the item and any settlement given for the item is provisional. This provision applies regardless of the form of indorsement or lack of indorsement and even though credit given for the item is subject to immediate withdrawal as of right or is in fact withdrawn; but the continuance of ownership of an item by its owner and any rights of the owner to proceeds of the item are subject to rights of a collecting bank such as those resulting from outstanding advances on the item and valid rights of set-off. When an item is handled by banks for purposes of presentment, payment and collection, the relevant provisions of this Article apply even though action of parties clearly establishes that a particular bank has purchased the item and is the owner of it.

(2) After an item has been indorsed with the words "pay any bank" or the like, only a bank may acquire the rights of a holder

(a) until the item has been returned to the customer initiating collection; or

(b) until the item has been specially indorsed by a bank to a person who is not a bank.

Section 4–202. Responsibility for Collection; When Action Seasonable

(1) A collecting bank must use ordinary care in

(a) presenting an item or sending it for presentment; and

(b) sending notice of dishonor or non-payment or returning an item other than a documentary draft to the bank's transferor [or directly to the depositary bank under subsection (2) of Section 4–212] *(See note to Section 4–212)* after learning that the item has not been paid or accepted, as the case may be; and

(c) settling for an item when the bank receives final settlement; and

(d) making or providing for any necessary protest; and

(e) notifying its transferor of any loss or delay in transit within a reasonable time after discovery thereof.

(2) A collecting bank taking proper action before its midnight deadline following receipt of an item, notice or payment acts seasonably; taking proper action within a reasonably longer time may be seasonable but the bank has the burden of so establishing.

(3) Subject to subsection (1) (a), a bank is not liable for the insolvency, neglect, misconduct, mistake or default of another bank or person or for loss or destruction of an item in transit or in the possession of others.

Section 4–203. Effect of Instructions

Subject to the provisions of Article 3 concerning conversion of instruments (Section 3–419) and the provisions of both Article 3 and this Article concerning restrictive indorsements only a collecting bank's transferor can give instructions which affect the bank or constitute notice to it and a collecting bank is not liable to prior parties for any action taken pursuant to such instructions or in accordance with any agreement with its transferor.

Section 4–204. Methods of Sending and Presenting; Sending Direct to Payor Bank

(1) A collecting bank must send items by reasonably prompt method taking into consideration any relevant instructions, the nature of the item, the number of such items on hand, and the cost of collection involved and the method generally used by it or others to present such items.

(2) A collecting bank may send

   (a) any item direct to the payor bank;

   (b) any item to any non-bank payor, if authorized by its transferor; and

   (c) any item other than documentary drafts to any non-bank payor, if authorized by Federal Reserve regulation or operating letter, clearing house rule or the like.

(3) Presentment may be made by a presenting bank at a place where the payor bank has requested that presentment be made.

Section 4–205. Supplying Missing Indorsement; No Notice from Prior Indorsement

(1) A depositary bank which has taken an item for collection may supply any indorsement of the customer which is necessary to title unless the item contains the words "payee's indorsement required" or the like. In the absence of such a requirement a statement placed on the item by the depositary bank to the effect that the item was deposited by a customer or credited to his account is effective as the customer's indorsement.

(2) An intermediatry bank, or payor bank which is not a depositary bank, is neither given notice nor otherwise affected by a restrictive indorsement of any person except the bank's immediate transferor.

Section 4–206. Transfer Between Banks

Any agreed method which identifies the transferor bank is sufficient for the item's further transfer to another bank.

Section 4–207. Warranties of Customer and Collecting Bank on Transfer or Presentment of Items; Time for Claims

(1) Each customer or collecting bank who obtains payment or acceptance of an item and each prior customer and collecting bank warrants to the payor bank or other payor who in good faith pays or accepts the item that

   (a) he has a good title to the item or is authorized to obtain payment or acceptance on behalf of one who has a good title; and

   (b) he had no knowledge that the signature of the maker or drawer is unauthorized, except that this warranty is not given by any customer or collecting bank that is a holder in due course and acts in good faith

      (i) to a maker with respect to the maker's own signature; or

      (ii) to a drawer with respect to the drawer's own signature, whether or not the drawer is also the drawee; or

      (iii) to an acceptor of an item if the holder in due course took the item after the acceptance or obtained the acceptance without knowledge that the drawer's signature was unauthorized; and

   (c) the item has not been materially altered, except that this warranty is not given by any customer or collecting bank that is a holder in due course and acts in good faith

      (i) to the maker of a note; or

      (ii) to the drawer of a draft whether or not the drawer is also the drawee; or

      (iii) to the acceptor of an item with respect to an alteration made prior to the acceptance if the holder in due course took the item after the acceptance, even though the acceptance provided "payable as originally drawn" or equivalent terms; or

      (iv) to the acceptor of an item with respect to an alteration made after the acceptance.

(2) Each customer and collecting bank who transfers an item and receives a settlement or other consideration for it warrants to his transferee and to any subsequent collecting bank who takes the item in good faith that

   (a) he has a good title to the item or is authorized to obtain payment or acceptance on behalf of one who has a good title and the transfer is otherwise rightful; and

   (b) all signatures are genuine or authorized; and

   (c) the item has not been materially altered; and

   (d) no defense of any party is good against him; and

   (e) he has no knowledge of any insolvency proceeding instituted with respect to the maker or acceptor or the drawer of an unaccepted item.

In addition each customer and collecting bank so transferring an item and receiving a settlement or other consideration engages that upon dishonor and any necessary notice of dishonor and protest he will take up the item.

(3) The warranties and the engagement to honor set forth in the two preceding subsections arise notwithstanding the absence of indorsement or words of guaranty or warranty in the transfer or presentment and a collecting bank remains liable for their breach despite remittance to its transferor. Damages for breach of such warranties or engagement to honor shall not exceed the consideration received by the customer or collecting bank responsible plus finance charges and expenses related to the item, if any.

(4) Unless a claim for breach of warranty under this section is made within a reasonable time after the person claiming learns of the breach, the person liable is discharged to the extent of any loss caused by the delay in making claim.

Section 4–208. Security Interest of Collecting Bank in Items, Accompanying Documents and Proceeds

(1) A bank has a security interest in an item and any accompanying documents or the proceeds of either

- (a) in case of an item deposited in an account to the extent to which credit given for the item has been withdrawn or applied;

- (b) in case of an item for which it has given credit available for withdrawal as of right, to the extent of the credit given whether or not the credit is drawn upon and whether or not there is a right of charge-back; or

- (c) if it makes an advance on or against the item.

(2) When credit which has been given for several items received at one time or pursuant to a single agreement is withdrawn or applied in part the security interest remains upon all the items, any accompanying documents or the proceeds of either. For the purpose of this section, credits first given are first withdrawn.

(3) Receipt by a collecting bank of a final settlement for an item is a realization on its security interest in the item, accompanying documents and proceeds. To the extent and so long as the bank does not receive final settlement for the item or give up possession of the item or accompanying documents for purposes other than collection, the security interest continues and is subject to the provisions of Article 9 except that

- (a) no security agreement is necessary to make the security interest enforceable (subsection (1) (a) of Section 9–203); and

- (b) no filing is required to perfect the security interest; and

- (c) the security interest has priority over conflicting perfected security interests in the item, accompanying documents or proceeds.

Section 4–209. When Bank Gives Value for Purposes of Holder in Due Course

For purposes of determining its status as a holder in due course, the bank has given value to the extent that it has a security interest in an item provided that the bank otherwise complies with the requirements of Section 3–302 on what constitutes a holder in due course.

Section 4–210. Presentment by Notice of Item Not Payable by, Through or at a Bank; Liability of Secondary Parties

(1) Unless otherwise instructed, a collecting bank may present an item not payable by, through or at a bank by sending to the party to accept or pay a written notice that the bank holds the item for acceptance or payment. The notice must be sent in time to be received on or before the day when presentment is due and the bank must meet any requirement of the party to accept or pay under Section 3–505 by the close of the bank's next banking day after it knows of the requirement.

(2) Where presentment is made by notice and neither honor nor request for compliance with a requirement under Section 3–505 is received by the close of business on the day after maturity or in the case of demand items by the close of business on the third banking day after notice was sent, the presenting bank may treat the item as dishonored and charge any secondary party by sending him notice of the facts.

Section 4–211. Media of Remittance; Provisional and Final Settlement in Remittance Cases

(1) A collecting bank may take in settlement of an item

- (a) a check of the remitting bank or of another bank on any bank except the remitting bank; or

- (b) a cashier's check or similar primary obligation of a remitting bank which is a member of or clears through a member of the same clearing house or group as the collecting bank; or

- (c) appropriate authority to charge an account of the remitting bank or of another bank with the collecting bank; or

- (d) if the item is drawn upon or payable by a person other than a bank, a cashier's check, certified check or other bank check or obligation.

(2) If before its midnight deadline the collecting bank properly dishonors a remittance check or authorization to charge on itself or presents or forwards for collection a remittance instrument of or on another bank which is of a kind approved by subsection (1) or has not been authorized by it, the collecting bank is not liable to prior parties in the event of the dishonor of such check, instrument or authorization.

(3) A settlement for an item by means of a remittance instrument or authorization to charge is or becomes a final settlement as to both the person making and the person receiving the settlement

- (a) if the remittance instrument or authorization to charge is of a kind approved by subsection (1) or has not been authorized by the person receiving the settlement and in either case the person receiving the settlement acts seasonably before its midnight deadline in presenting, forwarding for collection or paying the instrument or authorization,—at the time the remittance instrument or authorization is finally paid by the payor by which it is payable;

(b) if the person receiving the settlement has authorized remittance by a non-bank check or obligation or by a cashier's check or similar primary obligation of or a check upon the payor or other remitting bank which is not of a kind approved by subsection (1)(b),—at the time of the receipt of such remittance check or obligation; or

(c) if in a case not covered by sub-paragraphs (a) or (b) the person receiving the settlement fails to seasonably present, forward for collection, pay or return a remittance instrument or authorization to it to charge before its midnight deadline,—at such midnight deadline.

Section 4–212. Right of Charge-Back or Refund

(1) If a collecting bank has made provisional settlement with its customer for an item and itself fails by reason of dishonor, suspension of payments by a bank or otherwise to receive a settlement for the item which is or becomes final, the bank may revoke the settlement given by it, charge back the amount of any credit given for the item to its customers' account or obtain refund from its customer whether or not it is able to return the items if by its midnight deadline or within a longer reasonable time after it learns the facts it returns the items or sends notification of the facts. These rights to revoke, charge-back and obtain refund terminate if and when a settlement for the item received by the bank is or becomes final (subsection (3) of Section 4–211 and subsections (2) and (3) of Section 4–213).

[(2) Within the time and manner prescribed by this section and Section 4–301, an intermediary or payor bank, as the case may be, may return an unpaid item directly to the depositary bank and may send for collection a draft on the depositary bank and obtain reimbursement. In such case, if the depositary bank has received provisional settlement for the item, it must reimburse the bank drawing the draft and any provisional credits for the item between banks shall become and remain final.]

Note: *Direct return is recognized as an innovation that is not yet established bank practice, and therefore, Paragraph 2 has been bracketed. Some lawyers have doubts whether it should be included in legislation or left to development by agreement.*

(3) A depositary bank which is also the payor may charge-back the amount of an item to its customer's account or obtain refund in accordance with the section governing return of an item received by a payor bank for credit on its books (Section 4–301).

(4) The right to charge-back is not affected by

(a) prior use of the credit given for the item; or

(b) failure by any bank to exercise ordinary care with respect to the item but any bank so failing remains liable.

(5) A failure to charge-back or claim refund does not affect other rights of the bank against the customer or any other party.

(6) If credit is given in dollars as the equivalent of the value of an item payable in a foreign currency the dollar amount of any charge-back or refund shall be calculated on the basis of the buying sight rate for the foreign currency prevailing on the day when the person entitled to the charge-back or refund learns that it will not receive payment in ordinary course.

Section 4–213. Final Payment of Item by Payor Bank; When Provisional Debits and Credits Become Final; When Certain Credits Become Available for Withdrawal

(1) An item is finally paid by the payor bank when the bank has done any of the following, whichever happens first:

(a) paid the item in cash; or

(b) settled for the item without reserving a right to revoke the settlement and without having such right under statute, clearing house rule or agreement; or

(c) completed the process of posting the item to the indicated account of the drawer, maker or other person to be charged therewith; or

(d) made a provisional settlement for the item and failed to revoke the settlement in the time and manner permitted by statute, clearing house rule or agreement.

Upon a final payment under subparagraphs (b), (c) or (d) the payor bank shall be accountable for the amount of the item.

(2) If provisional settlement for an item between the presenting and payor banks is made through a clearing house or by debits or credits in an account between them, then to the extent that provisional debits or credits for the item are entered in accounts between the presenting and payor banks or between the presenting and successive prior collecting banks seriatim, they become final upon final payment of the item by the payor bank.

(3) If a collecting bank receives a settlement for an item which is or becomes final (subsection (3) of Section 4–211, subsection (2) of Section 4–213) the bank is accountable to its customer for the amount of the item and any provisional credit given for the item in an account with its customer becomes final.

(4) Subject to any right of the bank to apply the credit to an obligation of the customer, credit given by a bank for an item in an account with its customer becomes available for withdrawal as of right

    (a) in any case where the bank has received a provisional settlement for the item,—when such settlement becomes final and the bank has had a reasonable time to learn that the settlement is final.

    (b) in any case where the bank is both a depositary bank and a payor bank and the item is finally paid,—at the opening of the bank's second banking day following receipt of the item.

(5) A deposit of money in a bank is final when made but, subject to any right of the bank to apply the deposit to an obligation of the customer, the deposit becomes available for withdrawal as of right at the opening of the bank's next banking day following receipt of the deposit.

Section 4–214. Insolvency and Preference

(1) Any item in or coming into the possession of a payor or collecting bank which suspends payment and which item is not finally paid shall be returned by the receiver, trustee or agent in charge of the closed bank to the presenting bank or the closed bank's customer.

(2) If a payor bank finally pays an item and suspends payments without making a settlement for the item with its customer or the presenting bank which settlement is or becomes final, the owner of the item has a preferred claim against the payor bank.

(3) If a payor bank gives or a collecting bank gives or receives a provisional settlement for an item and thereafter suspends payments, the suspension does not prevent or interfere with the settlement becoming final if such finality occurs automatically upon the lapse of certain time or the happening of certain events (subsection (3) of Section 4–211, subsections (1)(d), (2) and (3) of Section 4–213).

(4) If a collecting bank receives from subsequent parties settlement for an item which settlement is or becomes final and suspends payments without making a settlement for the item with its customer which is or becomes final, the owner of the item has a preferred claim against such collecting bank.

Part 3 Collection of Items; Payor Banks

Section 4–301. Deferred Posting; Recovery of Payment by Return of Items; Time of Dishonor

(1) Where an authorized settlement for a demand item (other than a documentary draft) received by a payor bank otherwise than for immediate payment over the counter has been made before midnight of the banking day of receipt the payor bank may revoke the settlement and recover any payment if before it has made final payment (subsection (1) of Section 4–213) and before its midnight deadline it

    (a) returns the item; or

    (b) sends written notice of dishonor or nonpayment if the item is held for protest or is otherwise unavailable for return.

(2) If a demand item is received by a payor bank for credit on its books it may return such item or send notice of dishonor and may revoke any credit given or recover the amount thereof withdrawn by its customer, if it acts within the time limit and in the manner specified in the preceding subsection.

(3) Unless previous notice of dishonor has been sent an item is dishonored at the time when for purposes of dishonor it is returned or notice sent in accordance with this section.

(4) An item is returned:

    (a) as to an item received through a clearing house, when it is delivered to the presenting or last collecting bank or to the clearing house or is sent or delivered in accordance with its rules; or

    (b) in all other cases, when it is sent or delivered to the bank's customer or transferor or pursuant to his instructions.

Section 4–302. Payor Banks' Responsibility for Late Return of Item

In the absence of a valid defense such as breach of a presentment warranty (subsection (1) of Section 4–207), settlement effected or the like, if an item is presented on and received by a payor bank the bank is accountable for the amount of

    (a) a demand item other than a documentary draft whether properly payable or not if the bank, in any case where it is not also the depositary bank, retains the item beyond midnight of the banking day of receipt without settling for it or, regardless of whether it is also the depositary bank, does not pay or return the item or send notice of dishonor until after its midnight deadline, or

(b) any other properly payable item unless within the time allowed for acceptance or payment of that item the bank either accepts or pays the item or returns it and accompanying documents.

Section 4–303. When Items Subject to Notice, Stop-Order, Legal Process or Setoff; Order in Which Items May Be Charged or Certified

(1) Any knowledge, notice or stop-order received by, legal process served upon or setoff exercised by a payor bank, whether or not effective under other rules of law to terminate, suspend or modify the bank's right or duty to pay an item or to charge its customer's account for the item, comes too late to so terminate, suspend or modify such right or duty if the knowledge, notice, stop-order or legal process is received or served and a reasonable time for the bank to act thereon expires or the setoff is exercised after the bank has done any of the following:

(a) accepted or certified the item;

(b) paid the item in cash;

(c) settled for the item without reserving a right to revoke the settlement and without having such right under statute, clearing house rule or agreement;

(d) completed the process of posting the item to the indicated account of the drawer, maker or other person to be charged therewith or otherwise has evidenced by examination of such indicated account and by action its decision to pay the item; or

(e) become accountable for the amount of the item under subsection (1) (d) of Section 4–213 and Section 4–302 dealing with the payor bank's responsibility for late return of items.

(2) Subject to the provisions of subsection (1) items may be accepted, paid, certified or charged to the indicated account of its customer in any order convenient to the bank.

Part 4 Relationship Between Payor Bank and Its Customers

Section 4–401. When Bank May Charge Customer's Account

(1) As against its customer, a bank may charge against his account any item which is otherwise properly payable from that account even though the charge creates an overdraft.

(2) A bank which in good faith makes payment to a holder may charge the indicated account of its customer according to

(a) the original tenor of his altered item; or

(b) the tenor of his completed item, even though the bank knows the item has been completed unless the bank has notice that the completion was improper.

Section 4–402. Bank's Liability to Customer for Wrongful Dishonor

A payor bank is liable to its customer for damages proximately caused by the wrongful dishonor of an item. When the dishonor occurs through mistake liability is limited to actual damages proved. If so proximately caused and proved damages may include damages for an arrest or prosecution of the customer or other consequential damages. Whether any consequential damages are proximately caused by the wrongful dishonor is a question of fact to be determined in each case.

Section 4–403. Customer's Right to Stop Payment; Burden of Proof of Loss

(1) A customer may by order to his bank stop payment of any item payable for his account but the order must be received at such time and in such manner as to afford the bank a reasonable opportunity to act on it prior to any action by the bank with respect to the item described in Section 4–303.

(2) An oral order is binding upon the bank only for fourteen calendar days unless confirmed in writing within that period. A written order is effective for only six months unless renewed in writing.

(3) The burden of establishing the fact and amount of loss resulting from the payment of an item contrary to a binding stop payment order is on the customer.

Section 4–404. Bank Not Obligated to Pay Check More Than Six Months Old

A bank is under no obligation to a customer having a checking account to pay a check, other than a certified check, which is presented more than six months after its date, but it may charge its customer's account for a payment made thereafter in good faith.

Section 4–405. Death or Incompetence of Customer

(1) A payor collecting bank's authority to accept, pay or collect an item or to account for proceeds of its collection if otherwise effective is not rendered ineffective by incompetence of a customer of either bank existing at the time the item is issued or its collection is undertaken if the bank does not know of an adjudication of incompetence. Neither death nor incompetence of a customer revokes such authority to accept, pay, collect or account until the bank knows of the fact of death or of an adjudica-

tion of incompetence and has reasonable opportunity to act on it.

(2) Even with knowledge a bank may for 10 days after the date of death pay or certify checks drawn on or prior to that date unless ordered to stop payment by a person claiming an interest in the account.

Section 4–406. Customer's Duty to Discover and Report Unauthorized Signature or Alteration

(1) When a bank sends to its customer a statement of account accompanied by items paid in good faith in support of the debit entries or holds the statement and items pursuant to a request or instructions of its customer or otherwise in a reasonable manner makes the statement and items available to the customer, the customer must exercise reasonable care and promptness to examine the statement and items to discover his unauthorized signature or any alteration on an item and must notify the bank promptly after discovery thereof.

(2) If the bank establishes that the customer failed with respect to an item to comply with the duties imposed on the customer by subsection (1) the customer is precluded from asserting against the bank

    (a) his unauthorized signature or any alteration on the item if the bank also establishes that it suffered a loss by reason of such failure; and

    (b) an unauthorized signature or alteration by the same wrongdoer or any other item paid in good faith by the bank after the first item and statement was available to the customer for a reasonable period not exceeding fourteen calendar days and before the bank receives notification from the customer of any such unauthorized signature or alteration.

(3) The preclusion under subsection (2) does not apply if the customer establishes lack of ordinary care on the part of the bank in paying the item(s).

(4) Without regard to care or lack of care of either the customer or the bank a customer who does not within one year from the time the statement and items are made available to the customer (subsection (1)) discover and report his unauthorized signature or any alteration on the face or back of the item or does not within 3 years from that time discover and report any unauthorized indorsement is precluded from asserting against the bank such unauthorized signature or indorsement or such alteration.

(5) If under this section a payor bank has a valid defense against a claim of a customer upon or resulting from payment of an item and waives or fails upon request to assert the defense the bank may not assert against any collecting bank or other prior party presenting or transferring the item a claim based upon the unauthorized signature or alteration giving rise to the customer's claim.

Section 4–407. Payor Bank's Right to Subrogation on Improper Payment

If a payor bank has paid an item over the stop payment order of the drawer or maker or otherwise under circumstances giving a basis for objection by the drawer or maker, to prevent unjust enrichment and only to the extent necessary to prevent loss to the bank by reason of its payment of the item, the payor bank shall be subrogated to the rights

    (a) of any holder in due course on the item against the drawer or maker; and

    (b) of the payee or any other holder of the item against the drawer or maker either on the item or under the transaction out of which the item arose; and

    (c) of the drawer or maker against the payee or any other holder of the item with respect to the transaction out of which the item arose.

Part 5 Collection of Documentary Drafts

Section 4–501. Handling of Documentary Drafts; Duty to Send for Presentment and to Notify Customer of Dishonor

A bank which takes a documentary draft for collection must present or send the draft and accompanying documents for presentment and upon learning that the draft has not been paid or accepted in due course must seasonably notify its customer of such fact even though it may have discounted or bought the draft or extended credit available for withdrawal as of right.

Section 4–502. Presentment of "On Arrival" Drafts

When a draft or the relevant instructions require presentment "on arrival," "when goods arrive" or the like, the collecting bank need not present until in its judgment a reasonable time for arrival of the goods has expired. Refusal to pay or accept because the goods have not arrived is not dishonor; the bank must notify its transferor of such refusal but need not present the draft again until it is instructed to do so or learns of the arrival of the goods.

Section 4–503. Responsibility of Presenting Bank for Documents and Goods; Report of Reasons for Dishonor; Referee in Case of Need

Unless otherwise instructed and except as provided in Article 5 a bank presenting a documentary draft

(a) must deliver the documents to the drawee on acceptance of the draft if it is payable more than three days after presentment; otherwise, only on payment; and

(b) upon dishonor, either in the case of presentment for acceptance or presentment for payment, may seek and follow instructions from any referee in case of need designated in the draft or if the presenting bank does not choose to utilize his services it must use diligence and good faith to ascertain the reason for dishonor, must notify its transferor of the dishonor and of the results of its effort to ascertain the reasons therefor and must request instructions.

But the presenting bank is under no obligation with respect to goods represented by the documents except to follow any reasonable instructions seasonably received; it has a right to reimbursement for any expense incurred in following instructions and to prepayment of or indemnity for such expenses.

Section 4–504. Privilege of Presenting Bank to Deal With Goods; Security Interest for Expenses

(1) A presenting bank which, following the dishonor of a documentary draft, has seasonably requested instructions but does not receive them within a reasonable time may store, sell, or otherwise deal with the goods in any reasonable manner.

(2) For its reasonable expenses incurred by action under subsection (1) the presenting bank has a lien upon the goods or their proceeds, which may be foreclosed in the same manner as an unpaid seller's lien.

ARTICLE 5 LETTERS OF CREDIT

(Text omitted.)

ARTICLE 6 BULK TRANSFERS

(Text omitted.)

ARTICLE 7 WAREHOUSE RECEIPTS, BILLS OF LADING AND OTHER DOCUMENTS OF TITLE

(Text omitted.)

ARTICLE 8 INVESTMENT SECURITIES

(Text omitted.)

ARTICLE 9 SECURED TRANSACTIONS; SALES OF ACCOUNTS AND CHATTEL PAPER

Part 1 Short Title, Applicability and Definitions

Section 9–101. Short Title

This Article shall be known and may be cited as Uniform Commercial Code—Secured Transactions.

Section 9–102. Policy and Subject Matter of Article

(1) Except as otherwise provided in Section 9–104 on excluded transactions, this Article applies

(a) to any transaction (regardless of its form) which is intended to create a security interest in personal property or fixtures including goods, documents, instruments, general intangibles, chattel paper or accounts; and also

(b) to any sale of accounts or chattel paper.

(2) This Article applies to security interests created by contract including pledge, assignment, chattel mortgage, chattel trust, trust deed, factor's lien, equipment trust, conditional sale, trust receipt, other lien or title retention contract and lease or consignment intended as security. This Article does not apply to statutory liens except as provided in Section 9–310.

(3) The application of this Article to a security interest in a secured obligation is not affected by the fact that the obligation is itself secured by a transaction or interest to which this Article does not apply.

Note: *The adoption of this Article should be accompanied by the repeal of existing statutes dealing with conditional sales, trust receipts, factor's liens where the factor is given a nonpossessory lien, chattel mortgages, crop mortgages, mortgages on railroad equipment, assignment of accounts and generally statutes regulating security interests in personal property.*

Where the state has a retail installment selling act or small loan act, that legislation should be carefully examined to determine what changes in those acts are needed to conform them to this Article. This Article primarily sets out rules defining rights of a secured party against persons dealing with the debtor; it does not prescribe regulations and controls which may be necessary to curb abuses arising in the small loan business or in the financing of consumer purchases on credit. Accordingly there is no intention to repeal existing regulatory acts in those fields by enactment or reenactment of Article 9. See Section 9–203(4) and the Note thereto.

Section 9–103. Perfection of Security Interest in Multiple State Transactions

(1) Documents, instruments and ordinary goods.

(a) This subsection applies to documents and instruments and to goods other than those covered by a certificate of title described in subsection (2), mobile goods described in subsection (3), and minerals described in subsection (5).

(b) Except as otherwise provided in this subsection, perfection and the effect of perfection or non-perfection of a security interest in collateral are governed by the law of the jurisdiction where the collateral is when the last event occurs on which is based the assertion that the security interest is perfected or unperfected.

(c) If the parties to a transaction creating a purchase money security interest in goods in one jurisdiction understand at the time that the security interest attaches that the goods will be kept in another jurisdiction, then the law of the other jurisdiction governs the perfection and the effect of perfection or non-perfection of the security interest from the time it attaches until thirty days after the debtor receives possession of the goods and thereafter if the goods are taken to the other jurisdiction before the end of the thirty-day period.

(d) When collateral is brought into and kept in this state while subject to a security interest perfected under the law of the jurisdiction from which the collateral was removed, the security interest remains perfected, but if action is required by Part 3 of this Article to perfect the security interest,

    (i) if the action is not taken before the expiration of the period of perfection in the other jurisdiction or the end of four months after the collateral is brought into this state, whichever period first expires, the security interest becomes unperfected at the end of that period and is thereafter deemed to have been unperfected as against a person who became a purchaser after removal;

    (ii) if the action is taken before the expiration of the period specified in subparagraph (i), the security interest continues perfected thereafter;

    (iii) for the purpose of priority over a buyer of consumer goods (subsection (2) of Section 9–307), the period of the effectiveness of a filing in the jurisdiction from which the collateral is removed is governed by the rules with respect to perfection in subparagraphs (i) and (ii).

(2) Certificate of title.

(a) This subsection applies to goods covered by a certificate of title issued under a statute of this state or of another jurisdiction under the law of which indication of a security interest on the certificate is required as a condition of perfection.

(b) Except as otherwise provided in this subsection, perfection and the effect of perfection or non-perfection of the security interest are governed by the law (including the conflict of law rules) of the jurisdiction issuing the certificate until four months after the goods are removed from that jurisdiction and thereafter until the goods are registered in another jurisdiction, but in any event not beyond surrender of the certificate. After the expiration of that period, the goods are not covered by the certificate of title within the meaning of this section.

(c) Except with respect to the rights of a buyer described in the next paragraph, a security interest, perfected in another jurisdiction otherwise than by notation on a certificate of title, in goods brought into this state and thereafter covered by a certificate of title issued by this state is subject to the rules stated in paragraph (d) of subsection (1).

(d) If goods are brought into this state while a security interest therein is perfected in any manner under the law of the jurisdiction from which the goods are removed and a certificate of title is issued by this state and the certificate does not show that the goods are subject to the security interest or that they may be subject to security interests not shown on the certificate, the security interest is subordinate to the rights of a buyer of the goods who is not in the business of selling goods of that kind to the extent that he gives value and receives delivery of the goods after issuance of the certificate and without knowledge of the security interest.

(3) Accounts, general intangibles and mobile goods.

(a) This subsection applies to accounts (other than an account described in subsection (5) on minerals) and general intangibles (other than uncertificated securities) and to goods which are mobile and which are of a type normally used in more than one jurisdiction, such as motor vehicles, trailers, rolling stock, airplanes, shipping containers, road building and construction machinery and commercial harvesting machinery and the like, if the goods are equipment or are inventory leased or held for lease by the debtor to others, and are not covered by a certificate of title described in subsection (2).

(b) The law (including the conflict of laws rules) of the jurisdiction in which the debtor is located governs the perfection and the effect of perfection or nonperfection of the security interest.

(c) If, however, the debtor is located in a jurisdiction which is not a part of the United States, and which does not provide for perfection of the security interest by filing or recording in that jurisdiction, the law of the jurisdiction in the United States in which the debtor has its major executive office governs the perfection and the effect of perfection or non-perfection of the security interest through filing. In the alternative, if the debtor is located in a jurisdiction which is not a part of the United States or Canada and the collateral is accounts or general intangibles for money due or to become due, the security interest may be perfected by notification to the account debtor. As used in this paragraph, "United States" includes its territories and possessions and the Commonwealth of Puerto Rico.

(d) A debtor shall be deemed located at his place of business if he has one, at his chief executive office if he has more than one place of business, otherwise at his residence. If however, the debtor is a foreign air carrier under the Federal Aviation Act of 1958, as amended, it shall be deemed located at the designated office of the agent upon whom service of process may be made on behalf of the foreign air carrier.

(e) A security interest perfected under the law of the jurisdiction of the location of the debtor is perfected until the expiration of four months after a change of the debtor's location to another jurisdiction, or until perfection would have ceased by the law of the first jurisdiction, whichever period first expires. Unless perfected in the new jurisdiction before the end of that period, it becomes unperfected thereafter and is deemed to have been unperfected as against a person who became a purchaser after the change.

(4) Chattel paper. The rules stated for goods in subsection (1) apply to a possessory security interest in chattel paper. The rules stated for accounts in subsection (3) apply to a nonpossessory security interest in chattel paper, but the security interest may not be perfected by notification to the account debtor.

(5) Minerals. Perfection and the effect of perfection or non-perfection of a security interest which is created by a debtor who has an interest in minerals or the like (including oil and gas) before extraction and which attaches thereto as extracted, or which attaches to an account resulting from the sale thereof at the wellhead or minehead are governed by the law (including the conflict of laws rules) of the jurisdiction wherein the wellhead or minehead is located.

(6) Uncertificated securities. The law (including the conflict of laws rules) of the jurisdiction of organization of the issuer governs the perfection and the effect of perfection or nonperfection a security interest in uncertificated securities.

Section 9–104. Transactions Excluded From Article

This Article does not apply

(a) to a security interest subject to any statute of the United States, to the extent that such statute governs the rights of parties to and third parties affected by transactions in particular types of property; or

(b) to a landlord's lien; or

(c) to a lien given by statute or other rule of law for services or materials except as provided in Section 9–310 on priority of such liens; or

(d) to a transfer of a claim for wages, salary or other compensation of an employee; or

(e) to a transfer by a government or governmental subdivision or agency; or

(f) to a sale of accounts or chattel paper as part of a sale of the business out of which they arose, or an assignment of accounts or chattel paper which is for the purpose of collection only, or a transfer of a right to payment under a contract to an assignee who is also to do the performance under the contract or a transfer of a single account to an assignee in whole or partial satisfaction of a preexisting indebtedness; or

(g) to a transfer of an interest in or claim in or under any policy of insurance, except as provided with respect to proceeds (Section 9–306) and priorities in proceeds (Section 9–312); or

(h) to a right represented by a judgment (other than a judgment taken on a right to payment which was collateral); or

(i) to any right of set-off; or

(j) except to the extent that provision is made for fixtures in Section 9–313, to the creation or transfer of an interest in or lien on real estate, including a lease or rents thereunder; or

(k) to a transfer in whole or in part of any claim arising out of tort; or

(l) to a transfer of an interest in any deposit account (subsection (1) of Section 9–105), except as provided with respect to proceeds (Section 9–306) and priorities in proceeds (Section 9–312).

Section 9–105. Definitions and Index of Definitions

(1) In this Article unless the context otherwise requires:

(a) "Account debtor" means the person who is obligated on an account, chattel paper or general intangible;

(b) "Chattel paper" means a writing or writings which evidence both a monetary obligation and a security interest in or a lease of specific goods, but a charter or other contract involving the use of hire of a vessel is not chattel paper. When a transaction is evidenced both by such a security agreement or a lease and by an instrument or a series of instruments, the group of writings taken together constitutes chattel paper;

(c) "Collateral" means the property subject to a security interest, and includes accounts and chattel paper which have been sold;

(d) "Debtor" means the person who owes payment or other performance of the obligation secured, whether or not he owns or has rights in the collateral, and includes the seller of accounts or chattel paper. Where the debtor and the owner of the collateral are not the same person, the term "debtor" means the owner of the collateral in any provision of the Article dealing with the collateral, the obligor in any provision dealing with the obligation, and may include both where the context so requires;

(e) "Deposit account" means a demand, time, savings, passbook or like account maintained with a bank, savings and loan association, credit union or like organization, other than an account evidenced by a certificate of deposit;

(f) "Document" means document of title as defined in the general definitions of Article 1 (Section 1–201), and a receipt of the kind described in subsection (2) of Section 7–201;

(g) "Encumbrance" includes real estate mortgages and other liens on real estate and all other rights in real estate that are not ownership interests;

(h) "Goods" includes all things which are movable at the time the security interest attaches or which are fixtures (Section 9–313), but does not include money, documents, instruments, accounts, chattel paper, general intangibles, or minerals or the like (including oil and gas) before extraction. "Goods" also includes standing timber which is to be cut and removed under a conveyance or contract for sale, the unborn young of animals, and growing crops;

(i) "Instrument" means a negotiable instrument (defined in Section 3–104), or a certificated security (defined in Section 8–102) or any other writing which evidences a right to the payment of money and is not itself a security agreement or lease and is of a type which is in ordinary course of business transferred by delivery with any necessary indorsement or assignment;

(j) "Mortgage" means a consensual interest created by a real estate mortgage, a trust deed on real estate, or the like;

(k) An advance is made "pursuant to commitment" if the secured party has bound himself to make it, whether or not a subsequent event of default or other event not within his control has relieved or may relieve him from his obligation;

(l) "Security agreement" means an agreement which creates or provides for a security interest;

(m) "Secured party" means a lender, seller or other person in whose favor there is a security interest, including a person to whom accounts or chattel paper have been sold. When the holders of obligations issued under an indenture of trust, equipment trust agreement or the like are represented by a trustee or other person, the representative is the secured party;

(n) "Transmitting utility" means any person primarily engaged in the railroad, street railway or trolley bus business, the electric or electronics communications transmission business, the transmission of goods by pipeline, or the transmission or the production and transmission of electricity, steam, gas or water, or the provision of sewer service.

(2) Other definitions applying to this Article and the sections in which they appear are:

"Account." Section 9–106.

"Attach." Section 9–203.

"Construction mortgage." Section 9–313 (1).

"Consumer goods." Section 9–109 (1).

"Equipment." Section 9–109 (2).

"Farm products." Section 9–109 (3).

"Fixture." Section 9–313 (1).

"Fixture filing." Section 9–313 (1).

"General intangibles." Section 9–106.

"Inventory." Section 9–109 (4).

"Lien creditor." Section 9–301 (3).

"Proceeds." Section 9–306 (1).

"Purchase money security interest." Section 9–107.

"United States." Section 9–103.

(3) The following definitions in other Articles apply to this Article:

"Check." Section 3–104.

"Contract for sale." Section 2–106.

"Holder in due course." Section 3–302.

"Note." Section 3–104.

"Sale." Section 2–106.

(4) In addition Article 1 contains general definitions and principles of construction and interpretation applicable throughout this Article.

Section 9–106. Definitions: "Account"; "General Intangibles"

"Account" means any right to payment for goods sold or leased or for services rendered which is not evidenced by an instrument or chattel paper, whether or not it has been earned by performance. "General intangibles" means any personal property (including things in action) other than goods, accounts, chattel paper, documents, instruments, and money. All rights to payment earned or unearned under a charter or other contract involving the use or hire of a vessel and all rights incident to the charter or contract are accounts.

Section 9–107. Definitions: "Purchase Money Security Interest"

A security interest is a "purchase money security interest" to the extent that it is

(a) taken or retained by the seller of the collateral to secure all or part of its price; or

(b) taken by a person who by making advances or incurring an obligation gives value to enable the debtor to acquire rights in or the use of collateral if such value is in fact so used.

Section 9–108. When After-Acquired Collateral Not Security for Antecedent Debt

Where a secured party makes an advance, incurs an obligation, releases a perfected security interest, or otherwise gives new value which is to be secured in whole or in part by after-acquired collateral shall be deemed to be taken for new value and not as security for an antecedent debt if the debtor acquires his rights in such collateral either in the ordinary course of his business or under a contract of purchase made pursuant to the security agreement within a reasonable time after new value is given.

Section 9–109. Classification of Goods: "Consumer Goods"; "Equipment"; "Farm Products"; "Inventory"

Goods are

(1) "consumer goods" if they are used or bought for use primarily for personal, family or household purposes;

(2) "equipment" if they are used or bought for use primarily in business (including farming or a profession) or by a debtor who is a nonprofit organization or a governmental subdivision or agency or if the goods are not included in the definitions of inventory, farm products or consumer goods;

(3) "farm products" if they are crops or livestock or supplies used or produced in farming operations or if they are products of crops or livestock in their unmanufactured states (such as ginned cotton, wool-clip, maple syrup, milk and eggs), and if they are in the possession of a debtor engaged in raising, fattening, grazing or other farming operations. If goods are farm products they are neither equipment nor inventory;

(4) "inventory" if they are held by a person who holds them for sale or lease or to be furnished under contracts of service or if he has so furnished them, or if they are raw materials, work in process or materials used or consumed in a business. Inventory of a person is not to be classified as his equipment.

Section 9–110. Sufficiency of Description

For the purposes of this Article any description of personal property or real estate is sufficient whether or not it is specific if it reasonably identifies what is described.

Section 9–111. Applicability of Bulk Transfer Laws

The creation of a security interest is not a bulk transfer under Article 6 (see Section 6–103).

Section 9–112. Where Collateral Is Not Owned by Debtor

Unless otherwise agreed, when a secured party knows that collateral is owned by a person who is not the debtor, the owner of the collateral is entitled to receive from the secured party any surplus under Section 9–502 (2) or under Section 9–504 (1), and is not liable for the debt or for any deficiency after resale, and he has the same right as the debtor

(a) to receive statements under Section 9–208;

(b) to receive notice of and to object to a secured party's proposal to retain the collateral in satisfaction of the indebtedness under Section 9–505;

(c) to redeem the collateral under Section 9–506;

(d) to obtain injunctive or other relief under Section 9–507 (1); and

(e) to recover losses caused to him under Section 9–208 (2).

Section 9–113. Security Interests Arising Under Article on Sales or Under Article on Leases

A security interest arising solely under the Article on Sales (Article 2) or the Article on Leases (Article 2A) is subject to the provisions of this Article except that to the extent that and so long as the debtor does not have or does not lawfully obtain possession of the goods

(a) no security agreement is necessary to make the security interest enforceable; and

(b) no filing is required to perfect the security interest; and

(c) the rights of the secured party on default by the debtor are governed (i) by the Article on Sales (Article 2) in the case of a security interest arising solely under such Article or (ii) by the Article on Leases in the case of a security interest arising solely under such Article.

Section 9–114. Consignment

(1) A person who delivers goods under a consignment which is not a security interest and who would be required to file under this Article by paragraph (3) (c) of Section 2–326 has priority over a secured party who is or becomes a creditor of the consignee and who would have a perfected security interest in the goods if they were the property of the consignee, and also priority with respect to identifiable cash proceeds received on or before delivery of the goods to a buyer, if

(a) the consignor complies with the filing provision of the Articles on Sales with respect to consignments (paragraph (3) (c) of Section 2–326) before the consignee receives possession of the goods; and

(b) the consignor gives notification in writing to the holder of the security interest if the holder has filed a financing statement covering the same types of goods before the date of the filing made by the consignor; and

(c) the holder of the security interest receives the notification within five years before the consignee receives possession of the goods; and

(d) the notification states that the consignor expects to deliver goods on consignment to the consignee, describing the goods by item or type.

(2) In the case of a consignment which is not a security interest and in which the requirements of the preceding subsection have not been met, a person who delivers goods to another is subordinate to a person who would have a perfected security interest in the goods if they were the property of the debtor.

Part 2 Validity of Security Agreement and Rights of Parties Thereto

Section 9–201. General Validity of Security Agreement

Except as otherwise provided by this Act a security agreement is effective according to its terms between the parties, against purchasers of the collateral and against creditors. Nothing in this Article validates any charge or practice illegal under any statute or regulation thereunder governing usury, small loans, retail installment sales, or the like, or extends the application of any such statute or regulation to any transaction not otherwise subject thereto.

Section 9–202. Title to Collateral Immaterial

Each provision of this Article with regard to rights, obligations and remedies applies whether title to collateral is in the secured party or in the debtor.

Section 9–203. Attachment and Enforceability of Security Interest; Proceeds; Formal Requisites

(1) Subject to the provisions of Section 4–208 on the security interest of a collecting bank, Section 8–321 on security interests in securities and Section 9–113 on a security interest arising under the Article on Sales, a security interest is not enforceable against the debtor or third parties with respect to the collateral and does not attach unless:

(a) the collateral is in the possession of the secured party pursuant to agreement, or the debtor has signed a security agreement which contains a description of the collateral and in addition, when the security interest covers crops growing or to be grown or timber to be cut, a description of the land concerned;

(b) value has been given; and

(c) the debtor has rights in the collateral.

(2) A security interest attaches when it becomes enforceable against the debtor with respect to the collateral. Attachment occurs as soon as all of the events specified in subsection (1) have taken place unless explicit agreement postpones the time of attaching.

(3) Unless otherwise agreed a security agreement gives the secured party the rights to proceeds provided by Section 9–306.

(4) A transaction, although subject to this Article, is also subject to . . . .*, and in the case of conflict between the provisions of this Article and any such statute, the provisions of such statute control. Failure to comply with any applicable statute has only the effect which is specified therein.

Note: *At * in subsection (4) insert reference to any local statute regulating small loans, retail installment sales and the like.*

For foregoing subsection (4) is designed to make it clear that certain transactions, although subject to this Article, must also comply with other applicable legislation.

This Article is designed to regulate all the "security" aspects of transactions within its scope. There is, however, much regulatory legislation, particularly in the consumer field, which supplements this Article and should not be repealed by its enactment. Examples are small loan acts, retail installment selling acts and the like. Such acts may provide for licensing and rate regulation and may prescribe particular forms of contract. Such provisions should remain in force despite the enactment of this Article. On the other hand if a retail installment selling act contains provisions on filing, rights on default, etc., such provisions should be repealed as inconsistent with this Article except that inconsistent provisions as to deficiencies, penalties, etc., in the Uniform Consumer Credit Code and other recent related legislation should remain because those statutes were drafted after the substantial enactment of the Article and with the intention of modifying certain provisions of this Article as to consumer credit.

Section 9–204. After-Acquired Property; Future Advances

(1) Except as provided in subsection (2), a security agreement may provide that any or all obligations covered by the security agreement are to be secured by after-acquired collateral.

(2) No security interest attaches under an after-acquired property clause to consumer goods other than accessions (Section 9–314) when given as additional security unless the debtor acquires rights in them within ten days after the secured party gives value.

(3) Obligations covered by a security agreement may include future advances or other value whether or not the advances or value are given pursuant to commitment (subsection (1) of Section 9–105).

Section 9–205. Use or Disposition of Collateral Without Accounting Permissible

A security interest is not invalid or fraudulent against creditors by reason of liberty in the debtor to use, commingle or dispose of all or part of the collateral (including returned or repossessed goods) or to collect or compromise accounts or chattel paper, or to accept the return of goods or make repossessions, or to use, commingle or dispose of proceeds, or by reason of the failure of the secured party to require the debtor to account for proceeds or replace collateral. This section does not relax the requirements of possession where perfection of a security interest depends upon possession of the collateral by the secured party or by a bailee.

Section 9–206. Agreement Not to Assert Defenses Against Assignee; Modification of Sales Warranties Where Security Agreement Exists

(1) Subject to any statute or decision which establishes a different rule for buyers or lessees of consumer goods, an agreement by a buyer or lessee that he will not assert against an assignee any claim or defense which he may have against the seller or lessor is enforceable by an assignee who takes his assignment for value, in good faith and without notice of a claim or defense, except as to the defenses of a type which may be asserted against a holder in due course of a negotiable instrument under the Article on Commercial Paper (Article 3). A buyer who as part of one transaction signs both a negotiable instrument and a security agreement makes such an agreement.

(2) When a seller retains a purchase money security interest in goods the Article on Sales (Article 2) governs the sale and any disclaimer, limitation or modification of the seller's warranties.

Section 9–207. Rights and Duties When Collateral Is in Secured Party's Possession

(1) A secured party must use reasonable care in the custody and preservation of collateral in his possession. In the case of an instrument or chattel paper reasonable care includes taking necessary steps to preserve rights against prior parties unless otherwise agreed.

(2) Unless otherwise agreed, when collateral is in the secured party's possession

(a) reasonable expenses (including the cost of any insurance and payment of taxes or other charges) incurred in the custody, preservation, use or operation of the collateral are chargeable to the debtor and are secured by the collateral;

(b) the risk of accidental loss or damage is on the debtor to the extent of any deficiency in any effective insurance coverage;

(c) the secured party may hold as additional security any increase or profits (except money) received from the collateral, but money so received, unless remitted to the debtor, shall be applied in reduction of the secured obligation;

(d) the secured party must keep the collateral identifiable but fungible collateral may be commingled;

(e) the secured party may repledge the collateral upon terms which do not impair the debtor's right to redeem it.

(3) A secured party is liable for any loss caused by his failure to meet any obligation imposed by the preceding subsections but does not lose his security interest.

(4) A secured party may use or operate the collateral for the purpose of preserving the collateral or its value or pursuant to the order of a court of appropriate jurisdiction or, except in the case of consumer goods, in the manner and to the extent provided in the security agreement.

Section 9–208. Request for Statement of Account or List of Collateral

(1) A debtor may sign a statement indicating what he believes to be the aggregate amount of unpaid indebtedness as of a specified date and may send it to the secured party with a request that the statement be approved or corrected and returned to the debtor. When the security agreement or any other record kept by the secured party identifies the collateral a debtor may similarly request the secured party to approve or correct a list of the collateral.

(2) The secured party must comply with such a request within two weeks after receipt by sending a written correction or approval. If the secured party claims a security interest in all of a particular type of collateral owned by the debtor he may indicate that fact in his reply and need not approve or correct an itemized list of such collateral. If the secured party without reasonable excuse fails to comply he is liable for any loss caused to the debtor thereby; and if the debtor has properly included in his request a good faith statement of the obligation or a list of the collateral or both the secured party may claim a security interest only as shown in the statement against persons misled by his failure to comply. If he no longer has an interest in the obligation or collateral at the time the request is received he must disclose the name and address of any successor in interest known to him and he is liable for any loss caused to the debtor as a result of failure to disclose. A successor in interest is not subject to this section until a request is received by him.

(3) A debtor is entitled to such a statement once every six months without charge. The secured party may require payment of a charge not exceeding $10 for each additional statement furnished.

Part 3 Rights of Third Parties; Perfected and Unperfected Security Interests; Rules of Priority

Section 9–301. Persons Who Take Priority Over Unperfected Security Interests; Rights of "Lien Creditor"

(1) Except as otherwise provided in subsection (2), an unperfected security interest is subordinate to the rights of

(a) persons entitled to priority under Section 9–312;

(b) a person who becomes a lien creditor before the security interest is perfected;

(c) in the case of goods, instruments, documents, and chattel paper, a person who is not a secured party and who is a transferee in bulk or other buyer not in ordinary course of business or is a buyer of farm products in ordinary course of business, to the extent that he gives value and receives delivery of the collateral without knowledge of the security interest and before it is perfected;

(d) in the case of accounts and general intangibles, a person who is not a secured party and who is a transferee to the extent that he gives value without knowledge of the security interest and before it is perfected.

(2) If the secured party files with respect to a purchase money security interest before or within ten days after the debtor receives possession of the collateral, he takes priority over the rights of a transferee in bulk or of a lien creditor which arise between the time the security interest attaches and the time of filing.

(3) A "lien creditor" means a creditor who has acquired a lien on the property involved by attachment, levy or the like and includes an assignee for benefit of creditors from the time of assignment, and as trustee in bankruptcy from the date of the filing of the petition or a receiver in equity from the time of appointment.

(4) A person who becomes a lien creditor while a security interest is perfected takes subject to the security interest only to the extent that it secures advances made before he becomes a lien creditor or within 45 days thereafter or made without knowledge of the lien or pursuant to a commitment entered into without knowledge of the lien.

Section 9–302. When Filing Is Required to Perfect Security Interest; Security Interests to Which Filing Provisions of This Article Do Not Apply

(1) A financing statement must be filed to perfect all security interests except the following:

(a) a security interest in collateral in possession of the secured party under Section 9–305;

(b) a security interest temporarily perfected in instruments or documents without delivery under Section 9–304 or in proceeds for a 10 day period under Section 9–306;

(c) a security interest created by an assignment of a beneficial interest in a trust or a decedent's estate;

(d) a purchase money security interest in consumer goods; but filing is required for a motor vehicle required to be registered; and fixture filing is required for priority over conflicting interests in fixtures to the extent provided in Section 9–313;

(e) an assignment of accounts which does not alone or in conjunction with other assignments to the same assignee transfer a significant part of the outstanding accounts of the assignor;

(f) a security interest of a collecting bank (Section 4–208) or in securities (Section 8–321) or arising under the Article on Sales (see Section 9–113) or covered in subsection (3) of this section;

(g) an assignment for the benefit of all the creditors of the transferor, and subsequent transfers by the assignee thereunder.

(2) If a secured party assigns a perfected security interest, no filing under this Article is required in order to continue the perfected status of the security interest against creditors of the transferees from the original debtor.

(3) The filing of a financing statement otherwise required by this Article is not necessary or effective to perfect a security interest in property subject to

(a) a statute or treaty of the United States which provides for a national or international registration or a national or international certificate of title or which specifies a place of filing different from that specified in this Article for filing of the security interest; or

(b) the following statutes of this state: [list any certificate of title statute covering automobiles, trailers, mobile homes, boats, farm tractors, or the like, and any central filing statute.*]; but during any period in which collateral is inventory held for sale by a person who is in the business of selling goods of that kind, the filing provisions of this Article (Part 4) apply to a security interest in that collateral created by him as debtor; or

(c) a certificate of title statute of another jurisdiction under the law of which indication of a security interest on the certificate is required as a condition of perfection (subsection (2) of Section 9–103).

(4) Compliance with a statute or treaty described in subsection (3) is equivalent to the filing of a financing statement under this Article, and a security interest in property subject to the statute or treaty can be perfected only by compliance therewith except as provided in Section 9–103 on multiple state transactions. Duration and renewal of perfection of a security interest perfected by compliance with the statute or treaty are governed by the provisions of the statute or treaty; in other respects the security interest is subject to this Article.

*Note: *It is recommended that the provisions of certificate of title acts for perfection of security interests by notation on the certificates should be amended to exclude coverage of inventory held for sale.*

Section 9–303. When Security Interest Is Perfected; Continuity of Perfection

(1) A security interest is perfected when it has attached and when all of the applicable steps required for perfection have been taken. Such steps are specified in Sections 9–302, 9–304, 9–305 and 9–306. If such steps are taken before the security interest attaches, it is perfected at the time when it attaches.

(2) If a security interest is originally perfected in any way permitted under this Article and is subsequently perfected in some other way under this Article, without an intermediate period when it was unperfected, the security interest shall be deemed to be perfected continuously for the purposes of this Article.

Section 9–304. Perfection of Security Interest in Instruments, Documents, and Goods Covered by Documents; Perfection by Permissive Filing; Temporary Perfection Without Filing or Transfer of Possession

(1) A security interest in chattel paper or negotiable documents may be perfected by filing. A security interest in money or instruments (other than certificated securities or instruments which constitute part of chattel paper) can be perfected only by the secured party's taking possession, except as provided in subsections (4) and (5) of this section and subsections (2) and (3) of Section 9–306 on proceeds.

(2) During the period that goods are in the possession of the issuer of a negotiable document therefor, a security interest in the goods is perfected by perfecting a security interest in the document, and any security interest in the goods otherwise perfected during such period is subject thereto.

(3) A security interest in goods in the possession of a bailee other than one who has issued a negotiable document therefor is perfected by issuance of a document in the name of the secured party or by the bailee's receipt of notification of the secured party's interest or by filing as to the goods.

(4) A security interest in instruments (other than certificated securities) or negotiable documents is perfected without filing or the taking of possession for a period of 21 days from the time it attaches to the extent that it arises from new value given under a written security agreement.

(5) A security interest remains perfected for a period of 21 days without filing where a secured party having a perfected security interest in an instrument (other than a certificated security), a negotiable document or goods in possession of a bailee other than one who has issued a negotiable document therefor

    (a) makes available to the debtor the goods or documents representing the goods for the purpose of ultimate sale or exchange or for the purpose of loading, unloading, storing, shipping, transshipping, manufacturing, processing or otherwise dealing with them in a manner preliminary to their sale or exchange, but priority between conflicting security interests in the goods is subject to subsection (3) of Section 9–312; or

    (b) delivers the instrument to the debtor for the purpose of ultimate sale or exchange or of presentation, collection, renewal or registration of transfer.

(6) After the 21-day period in subsections (4) and (5) perfection depends upon compliance with applicable provisions of this Article.

Section 9–305. When Possession by Secured Party Perfects Security Interest Without Filing

A security interest in letters of credit and advices of credit (subsection (2) (a) of Section 5–116), goods, instruments (other than certificated securities), money, negotiable documents, or chattel paper may be perfected by the secured party's taking possession of the collateral. If such collateral other than goods covered by a negotiable document is held by a bailee, the secured party is deemed to have possession from the time the bailee receives notification of the secured party's interest. A security interest is perfected by possession from the time possession is taken without a relation back and continues only so long as possession is retained, unless otherwise specified in this Article. The security interest may be otherwise perfected as provided in this Article before or after the period of possession by the secured party.

Section 9–306. "Proceeds"; Secured Party's Rights on Disposition of Collateral

(1) "Proceeds" includes whatever is received upon the sale, exchange, collection or other disposition of collateral or proceeds. Insurance payable by reason of loss or damage to the collateral is proceeds, except to the extent that it is payable to a person other than a party to the security agreement. Money, checks, deposit accounts, and the like are "cash proceeds." All other proceeds are "non-cash proceeds."

(2) Except where this Article otherwise provides, a security interest continues in collateral notwithstanding sale, exchange or other disposition thereof unless the disposition was authorized by the secured party in the security agreement or otherwise, and also continues in any identifiable proceeds including collections received by the debtor.

(3) The security interest in proceeds is a continuously perfected security interest if the interest in the original collateral was perfected but it ceases to be a perfected security interest and becomes unperfected ten days after receipt of the proceeds by the debtor unless

    (a) a filed financing statement covers the original collateral and the proceeds are collateral in which a security interest may be perfected by filing in the office or offices where the financing statement has been filed and, if the proceeds are acquired with cash proceeds, the description of collateral in the financing statement indicates the types of property constituting the proceeds; or

    (b) a filed financing statement covers the original collateral and the proceeds are identifiable cash proceeds; or

    (c) the security interest in the proceeds is perfected before the expiration of the ten-day period.

Except as provided in this section, a security interest in proceeds can be perfected only by the methods or under the circumstances permitted in this Article for original collateral of the same type.

(4) In the event of insolvency proceedings instituted by or against a debtor, a secured party with a perfected security interest in proceeds has a perfected security interest only in the following proceeds:

    (a) in identifiable non-cash proceeds and in separate deposit accounts containing only proceeds;

    (b) in identifiable cash proceeds in the form of money which is neither commingled with other money nor deposited in a deposit account prior to the insolvency proceedings;

(c) in identifiable cash proceeds in the form of checks and the like which are not deposited in a deposit account prior to the insolvency proceedings; and

(d) in all cash and deposit accounts of the debtor in which proceeds have been commingled with other funds, but the perfected security interest under this paragraph (d) is

    (i) subject to any right to setoff; and

    (ii) limited to an amount not greater than the amount of any cash proceeds received by the debtor within ten days before the institution of the insolvency proceedings less than sum of (I) the payments to the secured party on account of cash proceeds received by the debtor during such period and (II) the cash proceeds received by the debtor during such period to which the secured party is entitled under paragraphs (a) through (c) of this subsection (4).

(5) If a sale of goods results in an account or chattel paper which is transferred by the seller to a secured party, and if the goods are returned to or are repossessed by the seller or the secured party, the following rules determine priorities:

(a) If the goods were collateral at the time of sale, for an indebtedness of the seller which is still unpaid, the original security interest attaches again to the goods and continues as a perfected security interest if it was perfected at the time when the goods were sold. If the security interest was originally perfected by a filing which is still effective, nothing further is required to continue the perfected status; in any other case, the secured party must take possession of the returned or repossessed goods or must file.

(b) An unpaid transferee of the chattel paper has a security interest in the goods against the transferor. Such security interest is prior to a security interest asserted under paragraph (a) to the extent that the transferee of the chattel paper was entitled to priority under Section 9–308.

(c) An unpaid transferee of the account has a security interest in the goods against the transferor. Such security interest is subordinate to a security interest asserted under paragraph (a).

(d) A security interest of an unpaid transferee asserted under paragraph (b) or (c) must be perfected for protection against creditors of the transferor and purchasers of the returned or repossessed goods.

Section 9–307. Protection of Buyers of Goods

(1) A buyer in ordinary course of business (subsection (9) of Section 1–201) other than a person buying farm products from a person engaged in farming operations takes free of a security interest created by his seller even though the security interest is perfected and even though the buyer knows of its existence.

(2) In the case of consumer goods, a buyer takes free of a security interest even though perfected if he buys without knowledge of the security interest, for value and for his own personal, family or household purposes unless prior to the purchase the secured party has filed a financing statement covering such goods.

(3) A buyer other than a buyer in ordinary course of business (subsection (1) of this section) takes free of a security interest to the extent that it secures future advances made after the secured party acquires knowledge of the purchase, or more than 45 days after the purchase, whichever first occurs, unless made pursuant to a commitment entered into without knowledge of the purchase and before the expiration of the 45-day period.

Section 9–308. Purchase of Chattel Paper and Instruments

A purchaser of chattel paper or an instrument who gives new value and takes possession of it in the ordinary course of his business has priority over a security interest in the chattel paper or instrument

(a) which is perfected under Section 9–304 (permissive filing and temporary perfection) or under Section 9–306 (perfection as to proceeds) if he acts without knowledge that the specific paper or instrument is subject to a security interest; or

(b) which is claimed merely as proceeds of inventory subject to a security interest (Section 9–306) even though he knows that the specific paper or instrument is subject to the security interest.

Section 9–309. Protection of Purchasers of Instruments, Documents and Securities

Nothing in this Article limits the rights of a holder in due course of a negotiable instrument (Section 3–302) or a holder to whom a negotiable document of title has been duly negotiated (Section 7–501) or a bona fide purchaser of a security (Section 8–302) and the holders or purchasers take priority over an earlier security interest even though perfected. Filing under this Article does not constitute notice of the security interest to such holders or purchasers.

Section 9–310. Priority of Certain Liens Arising by Operation of Law

When a person in the ordinary course of his business furnishes services or materials with respect to goods subject to a security interest, a lien upon goods in the possession of such person given by statute or rule of law for such materials or services takes priority over a perfected security interest unless the lien is statutory and the statute expressly provides otherwise.

Section 9–311. Alienability of Debtor's Rights: Judicial Process

The debtor's rights in collateral may be voluntarily or involuntarily transferred (by way of sale, creation of a security interest, attachment, levy, garnishment or other judicial process) notwithstanding a provision in the security agreement prohibiting any transfer or making the transfer constitute a default.

Section 9–312. Priorities Among Conflicting Security Interests in the Same Collateral

(1) The rules of priority stated in other sections of this Part and in the following sections shall govern when applicable: Section 4–208 with respect to the security interests of collecting banks in items being collected, accompanying documents and proceeds; Section 9–103 on security interests related to other jurisdictions; Section 9–114 on consignments.

(2) A perfected security interest in crops for new value given to enable the debtor to produce the crops during the production season and given not more than three months before the crops become growing crops by planting or otherwise takes priority over an earlier perfected security interest to the extent that such earlier interest secures obligations due more than six months before the crops become growing crops by planting or otherwise, even though the person giving new value had knowledge of the earlier security interest.

(3) A perfected purchase money security interest in inventory has priority over a conflicting security interest in the same inventory and also has priority in identifiable cash proceeds received on or before the delivery of the inventory to a buyer if

(a) the purchase money security interest is perfected at the time the debtor receives possession of the inventory; and

(b) the purchase money secured party gives notification in writing to the holder of the conflicting security interest if the holder had filed a financing statement covering the same types of inventory

(i) before the date of the filing made by the purchase money secured party, or (ii) before the beginning of the 21-day period where the purchase money security interest is temporarily perfected without filing or possession (subsection (5) of Section 9–304); and

(c) the holder of the conflicting security interest receives the notification within five years before the debtor receives possession of the inventory; and

(d) the notification states that the person giving the notice has or expects to acquire a purchase money security interest in inventory of the debtor, describing such inventory by item or type.

(4) A purchase money security interest in collateral other than inventory has priority over a conflicting security interest in the same collateral or its proceeds if the purchase money security interest is perfected at the time the debtor receives possession of the collateral or within ten days thereafter.

(5) In all cases not governed by other rules stated in this section (including cases of purchase money security interests which do not qualify for the special priorities set forth in subsections (3) and (4) of this section), priority between conflicting security interests in the same collateral shall be determined according to the following rules:

(a) Conflicting security interests rank according to priority in time of filing or perfection. Priority dates from the time a filing is first made covering the collateral or the time the security interest is first perfected, whichever is earlier, provided that there is no period thereafter when there is neither filing nor perfection.

(b) So long as conflicting security interests are unperfected, the first to attach has priority.

(6) For the purposes of subsection (5) a date of filing or perfection as to collateral is also a date of filing or perfection as to proceeds.

(7) If future advances are made while a security interest is perfected by filing, the taking of possession, or under Section 8–321 on securities, the security interest has the same priority for the purposes of subsection (5) with respect to the future advances as it does with respect to the first advance. If a commitment is made before or while the security interest is so perfected, the security interest has the same priority with respect to advances made pursuant thereto. In other cases a perfected security interest has priority from the date the advance is made.

Section 9–313. Priority of Security Interests in Fixtures

(1) In this section and in the provisions of Part 4 of this Article referring to fixture filing, unless the context otherwise requires

(a) goods are "fixtures" when they become so related to particular real estate that an interest in them arises under real estate law

(b) a "fixture filing" is the filing in the office where a mortgage on the real estate would be filed or recorded of a financing statement covering goods which are or are to become fixtures and conforming to the requirements of subsection (5) of Section 9–402

(c) a mortgage is a "construction mortgage" to the extent that it secures an obligation incurred for the construction of an improvement on land including the acquisition cost of the land, if the recorded writing so indicates.

(2) A security interest under this Article may be created in goods which are fixtures or may continue in goods which become fixtures, but no security interest exists under this Article in ordinary building materials incorporated into an improvement on land.

(3) This Article does not prevent creation of an encumbrance upon fixtures pursuant to real estate law.

(4) A perfected security interest in fixtures has priority over the conflicting interest of an encumbrancer or owner of the real estate where

(a) the security interest is a purchase money security interest, the interest of the encumbrancer or owner arises before the goods become fixtures, the security interest is perfected by a fixture filing before the goods become fixtures or within ten days thereafter, and the debtor has an interest of record in the real estate or is in possession of the real estate; or

(b) the security interest is perfected by a fixture filing before the interest of the encumbrancer or owner is of record, the security interest has priority over any conflicting interest of a predecessor in title of the encumbrancer or owner, and the debtor has an interest of record in the real estate or is in possession of the real estate; or

(c) the fixtures are readily removable factory or office machines or readily removable replacements of domestic appliances which are consumer goods, and before the goods become fixtures the security interest is perfected by any method permitted by this Article; or

(d) the conflicting interest is a lien on the real estate obtained by legal or equitable proceedings after the security interest was perfected by any method permitted by this Article.

(5) A security interest in fixtures, whether or not perfected, has priority over the conflicting interest of an encumbrancer or owner of the real estate where

(a) the encumbrancer or owner has consented in writing to the security interest or has disclaimed an interest in the goods as fixtures; or

(b) the debtor has a right to remove the goods as against the encumbrancer or owner. If the debtor's right terminates, the priority of the security interest continues for a reasonable time.

(6) Notwithstanding paragraph (a) of subsection (4) but otherwise subject to subsections (4) and (5), a security interest in fixtures is subordinate to a construction mortgage recorded before the goods become fixtures if the goods become fixtures before the completion of the construction. To the extent that it is given to refinance a construction mortgage, a mortgage has this priority to the same extent as the construction mortgage.

(7) In cases not within the preceding subsections, a security interest in fixtures is subordinate to the conflicting interest of an encumbrancer or owner of the related real estate who is not the debtor.

(8) When the secured party has priority over all owners and encumbrancers of the real estate, he may, on default, subject to the provisions of Part 5, remove his collateral from the real estate but he must reimburse any encumbrancer or owner of the real estate who is not the debtor and who has not otherwise agreed for the cost of repair of any physical injury, but not for any diminution in value of the real estate caused by the absence of the goods removed or by any necessity of replacing them. A person entitled to reimbursement may refuse permission to remove until the secured party gives adequate security for the performance of this obligation.

Section 9–314. Accessions

(1) A security interest in goods which attaches before they are installed in or affixed to other goods takes priority as to the goods installed or affixed (called in this section "accessions") over the claims of all persons to the whole except as stated in subsection (3) and subject to Section 9–315(1).

(2) A security interest which attaches to goods after they become part of a whole is valid against all persons subsequently acquiring interests in the whole except as stated in subsection (3) but is invalid against any person with an interest in the whole at the time the security interest

attaches to the goods who has not in writing consented to the security interest or disclaimed an interest in the goods as part of the whole.

(3) The security interests described in subsection (1) and (2) do not take priority over

   (a) a subsequent purchaser for value of any interest in the whole; or

   (b) a creditor with a lien on the whole subsequently obtained by judicial proceedings; or

   (c) a creditor with a prior perfected security interest in the whole to the extent that he makes subsequent advances

if the subsequent purchase is made, the lien by judicial proceedings obtained or the subsequent advance under the prior perfected security interest is made or contracted for without knowledge of the security interest and before it is perfected. A purchaser of the whole at a foreclosure sale other than the holder of a perfected security interest purchasing at his own foreclosure sale is a subsequent purchaser within this section.

(4) When under subsections (1) and (2) and (3) a secured party has an interest in accessions which has priority over the claims of all persons who have interests in the whole, he may on default subject to the provisions of Part 5 remove his collateral from the whole but he must reimburse any encumbrancer or owner of the whole who is not the debtor and who has not otherwise agreed for the cost of repair of any physical injury but not for any diminution in value of the whole caused by the absence of the goods removed or by any necessity for replacing them. A person entitled to reimbursement may refuse permission to remove until the secured party gives adequate security for the performance of this obligation.

Section 9–315. Priority When Goods Are Commingled or Processed

(1) If a security interest in goods was perfected and subsequently the goods or a part thereof have become part of a product or mass, the security interest continues in the product or mass if

   (a) the goods are so manufactured, processed, assembled or commingled that their identity is lost in the product or mass; or

   (b) a financing statement covering the original goods also covers the product into which the goods have been manufactured, processed or assembled.

In a case to which paragraph (b) applies, no separate security interest in that part of the original goods which have been manufactured, processed or assembled into the product may be claimed under Section 9–314.

(2) When under subsection (1) more than one security interest attaches to the product or mass, they rank equally according to the ratio that the cost of the goods to which each interest originally attached bears to the cost of the total product or mass.

Section 9–316. Priority Subject to Subordination

Nothing in this Article prevents subordination by agreement by any person entitled to priority.

Section 9–317. Secured Party Not Obligated on Contract of Debtor

The mere existence of a security interest or authority given to the debtor to dispose of or use collateral does not impose contract or tort liability upon the secured part for the debtor's acts or omissions.

Section 9–318. Defenses Against Assignee; Modification of Contract After Notification of Assignment; Term Prohibiting Assignment Ineffective; Identification and Proof of Assignment

(1) Unless an account debtor has made an enforceable agreement not to assert defenses or claims arising out of a sale as provided in Section 9–206 the rights of an assignee are subject to

   (a) all the terms of the contract between the account debtor and assignor and any defense or claim arising therefrom; and

   (b) any other defense or claim of the account debtor against the assignor which accrues before the account debtor receives notification of the assignment.

(2) So far as the right to payment or a part thereof under an assigned contract has not been fully earned by performance, and notwithstanding notification of the assignment, any modification of or substitution for the contract made in good faith and in accordance with reasonable commercial standards is effective against an assignee unless the account debtor has otherwise agreed but the assignee acquires corresponding rights under the modified or substituted contract. The assignment may provide that such modification or substitution is a breach by the assignor.

(3) The account debtor is authorized to pay the assignor until the account debtor receives notification that the amount due or to become due has been assigned and that payment is to be made to the assignee. A notification which does not reasonably identify the rights assigned is ineffective. If requested by the account debtor, the assignee must seasonably furnish reasonable proof that the assignment has been made and unless he does so the account debtor may pay the assignor.

(4) A term in any contract between an account debtor and an assignor is ineffective if it prohibits assignment of an account or prohibits creation of a security interest in a general intangible for money due or to become due or requires the account debtor's consent to such assignment or security interest.

Part 4 Filing

Section 9–401. Place of Filing; Erroneous Filing; Removal of Collateral

First Alternative Subsection (1)

(1) The proper place to file in order to perfect a security interest is as follows:

    (a) when the collateral is timber to be cut or is minerals or the like (including oil and gas) or accounts subject to subsection (5) of Section 9–103, or when the financing statement is filed as a fixture filing (Section 9–313) and the collateral is goods which are or are to become fixtures, then in the office where a mortgage on the real estate would be filed or recorded;

    (b) in all other cases, in the office of the [Secretary of State].

Second Alternative Subsection (1)

(1) The proper place to file in order to perfect a security interest is as follows:

    (a) when the collateral is equipment used in farming operations, or farm products, or accounts or general intangibles arising from or relating to the sale of farm products by a farmer, or consumer goods, then in the office of the . . . . in the county of the debtor's residence or if the debtor is not a resident of this state then in the office of the . . . . in the county where the goods are kept, and in addition when the collateral is crops growing or to be grown in the office of the . . . . in the county where the land is located;

    (b) when the collateral is timber to be cut or is minerals or the like (including oil and gas) or accounts subject to subsection (5) of Section 9–103, or when the financing statement is filed as a fixture filing (Section 9–313) and the collateral is goods which are or are to become fixtures, then in the office where a mortgage on the real estate would be filed or recorded;

    (c) in all other cases, in the office of the [Secretary of State].

Third Alternative Subsection (1)

(1) The proper place to file in order to perfect a security interest is as follows:

    (a) when the collateral is equipment used in farming operations, or farm products, or accounts or general intangibles arising from or relating to the sale of farm products by a farmer, or consumer goods, then in the office of the . . . . . . in the county of the debtor's residence or if the debtor is not a resident of this state then in the office of the . . . . in the county where the goods are kept, and in addition when the collateral is crops growing or to be grown in the office of the . . . . . . in the county where the land is located;

    (b) when the collateral is timber to be cut or is minerals or the like (including oil and gas) or accounts subject to subsection (5) of Section 9–103, or when the financing statement is filed as a fixture filing (Section 9–313) and the collateral is goods which are or are to become fixtures, then in the office where a mortgage on the real estate would be filed or recorded;

    (c) in all other cases, in the office of the [Secretary of State] and in addition, if the debtor has a place of business in only one county of this state, also in the office of . . . . . . of such county, or, if the debtor has no place of business in this state, but resides in the state, also in the office of . . . . . . of the county in which he resides.

Note: *One of the three alternatives should be selected as subsection (1).*

(2) A filing which is made in good faith in an improper place or not in all of the places required by this section is nevertheless effective with regard to any collateral as to which the filing complied with the requirements of this Article and is also effective with regard to collateral covered by the financing statement against any person who has knowledge of the contents of such financing statement.

(3) A filing which is made in the proper place in this state continues effective even though the debtor's residence or place of business or the location of the collateral or its use, whichever controlled the original filing, is thereafter changed.

[(3) A filing which is made in the proper county continues effective for four months after a change to another county of the debtor's residence or place of business or the location of the collateral, whichever controlled the original filing.

It becomes ineffective thereafter unless a copy of the financing statement signed by the secured party is filed in the new county within said period. The security interest may also be perfected in the new county after the expiration of the four-month period; in such case perfection dates from the time of perfection in the new county. A change in the use of the collateral does not impair the effectiveness of the original filing.]

(4) The rules stated in Section 9–103 determine whether filing is necessary in this state.

(5) Notwithstanding the preceding subsections, and subject to subsection (3) of Section 9–302, the proper place to file in order to perfect a security interest in collateral, including fixtures, of a transmitting utility is the office of the [Secretary of State]. This filing constitutes a fixture filing (Section 9–313) as to the collateral described therein which is or is to become fixtures.

(6) For the purposes of this section, the residence of an organization is its place of business if it has one or its chief executive office if it has more than one place of business.

Note: *Subsection (6) should be used only if the state chooses the Second or Third Alternative Subsection (1).*

Section 9–402. Formal Requisites of Financing Statement; Amendments; Mortgage as Financing Statement

(1) A financing statement is sufficient if it gives the names of the debtor and the secured party, is signed by the debtor, gives an address of the secured party from which information concerning the security interest may be obtained, gives a mailing address of the debtor and contains a statement indicating the types, or describing the items, of collateral. A financing statement may be filed before a security agreement is made or a security interest otherwise attaches. When the financing statement covers crops growing or to be grown, the statement must also contain a description of the real estate concerned. When the financing statement covers timber to be cut or covers minerals or the like (including oil and gas) or accounts subject to subsection (5) of Section 9–103, or when the financing statement is filed as a fixture filing (Section 9–313) and the collateral is goods which are or are to become fixtures, the statement must also comply with subsection (5). A copy of the security agreement is sufficient as a financing statement if it contains the above information and is signed by the debtor. A carbon, photographic or other reproduction of a security agreement or a financing statement is sufficient as a financing statement if the security agreement so provides or if the original has been filed in this state.

(2) A financing statement which otherwise complies with subsection (1) is sufficient when it is signed by the secured party instead of the debtor if it is filed to perfect a security interest in

(a) collateral already subject to a security interest in another jurisdiction when it is brought into this state, or when the debtor's location is changed to this state. Such a financing statement must state that the collateral was brought into his state or that the debtor's location was changed to this state under such circumstances; or

(b) proceeds under Section 9–306 if the security interest in the original collateral was perfected. Such a financing statement must describe the original collateral; or

(c) collateral as to which the filing has lapsed; or

(d) collateral acquired after a change of name, identity or corporate structure of the debtor (subsection (7)).

(3) A form substantially as follows is sufficient to comply with subsection (1):

Name of debtor (or assignor)

Address

Name of secured party (or assignee)

Address

1. This financing statement covers the following types (or type) of property:
(Describe)

2. (If collateral is crops) The above described crops are growing or are to be grown on:
(Describe Real Estate)

3. (If applicable) The above goods are to become fixtures on*
(Describe Real Estate)
and this financing statement is to be filed [for record] in the real estate records. (If the debtor does not have an interest of record) The name of a record owner is

4. (If products of collateral are claimed) Products of the collateral are also covered.

(use whichever is applicable)
Signature of Debtor (or Assignor)
Signature of Secured Party (or Assignee)

(4) A financial statement may be amended by filing a writing signed by both the debtor and the secured party.

---

* *Where appropriate substitute either "The above timber is standing on . . ." or "The above minerals or the like (including oil and gas) or accounts will be financed at the wellhead or minehead of the well or mine located on. . . ."*

An amendment does not extend the period of effectiveness of a financing statement. If any amendment adds collateral, it is effective as to the added collateral only from the filing date of the amendment. In this Article, unless the context otherwise requires, the term "financing statement" means the original financing statement and any amendments.

(5) A financing statement covering timber to be cut or covering minerals or the like (including oil and gas) or accounts subject to subsection (5) of Section 9–103, or a financing statement filed as a fixture filing (Section 9–313) where the debtor is not a transmitting utility, must show that it covers this type of collateral, must recite that it is to be filed [for record] in the real estate records, and the financing statement must contain a description of the real estate [sufficient if it were contained in a mortgage of the real estate to give constructive notice of the mortgage under the law of this state]. If the debtor does not have an interest of record in the real estate, the financing statement must show the name of a record owner.

(6) A mortgage is effective as a financing statement filed as a fixture filing from the date of its recording if

(a) the goods are described in the mortgage by item or type; and

(b) the goods are or are to become fixtures related to the real estate described in the mortgage; and

(c) the mortgage complies with the requirements for a financing statement in this section other than a recital that it is to be filed in the real estate records; and

(d) the mortgage is duly recorded.

No fee with reference to the financing statement is required other than the regular recording and satisfaction fees with respect to the mortgage.

(7) A financing statement sufficiently shows the name of the debtor if it gives the individual, partnership or corporate name of the debtor, whether or not it adds other trade names or names of partners. Where the debtor so changes his name or in the case of an organization its name, identity or corporate structure that a filed financing statement becomes seriously misleading, the filing is not effective to perfect a security interest in collateral acquired by the debtor more than four months after the change, unless a new appropriate financing statement is filed before the expiration of that time. A filed financing statement remains effective with respect to collateral transferred by the debtor even though the secured party knows of or consents to the transfer.

(8) A financing statement substantially complying with the requirements of this section is effective even though it contains minor errors which are not seriously misleading.

Note: *Language in brackets is optional.*

Note: *Where the state has any special recording system for real estate other than the usual grantor-grantee index (as, for instance, a tract system or a title registration or Torrens system) local adaptations of subsection (5) and Secton 9–403(7) may be necessary. See Mass. Gen. Laws Chapter 106, Section 9–409.*

Section 9–403. What Constitutes Filing; Duration of Filing; Effect of Lapsed Filing; Duties of Filing Officer

(1) Presentation for filing of a financing statement and tender of the filing fee or acceptance of the statement by the filing officer constitutes filing under this Article.

(2) Except as provided in subsection (6) a filed financing statement is effective for a period of five years from the date of filing. The effectiveness of a filed financing statement lapses on the expiration of the five-year period unless a continuation statement is filed prior to the lapse. If a security interest perfected by filing exists at the time insolvency proceedings are commenced by or against the debtor, the security interest remains perfected until termination of the insolvency proceedings and thereafter for a period of sixty days or until expiration of the five-year period, whichever occurs later. Upon lapse the security interest becomes unperfected, unless it is perfected without filing. If the security interest becomes unperfected upon lapse, it is deemed to have been unperfected as aganist a person who became a purchaser or lien creditor before lapse.

(3) A continuation statement may be filed by the secured party within six months prior to the expiration of the five-year period specified in subsection (2). Any such continuation statement must be signed by the secured party, identify the original statement by file number and state that the original statement is still effective. A continuation statement signed by a person other than the secured party of record must be accompanied by a separate written statement of assignment signed by the secured party of record and complying with subsection (2) of Section 9–405, including payment of the required fee. Upon timely filing of the continuation statement, the effectiveness of the original statement is continued for five years after the last date to which the filing was effective whereupon it lapses in the same manner as provided in subsection (2) unless another continuation statement is filed prior to such lapse. Succeeding continuation statements may be filed in the same manner to continue the effectiveness

of the original statement. Unless a statute on disposition of public records provides otherwise, the filing officer may remove a lapsed statement from the files and destroy it immediately if he has retained a microfilm or other photographic record, or in other cases after one year after the lapse. The filing officer shall so arrange matters by physical annexation of financing statements to continuation statements or other related filings, or by other means, that if he physically destroys the financing statements of a period more than five years past, those which have been continued by a continuation statement or which are still effective under subsection (6) shall be retained.

(4) Except as provided in subsection (7) a filing officer shall mark each statement with a file number and with the date and hour of filing and shall hold the statement or a microfilm or other photographic copy thereof for public inspection. In addition the filing officer shall index the statement according to the name of the debtor and shall note in the index the file number and the address of the debtor given in the statement.

(5) The uniform fee for filing and indexing and for stamping a copy furnished by the secured party to show the date and place of filing for an original financing statement or for a continuation statement shall be $. . . . . . . if the statement is in the standard form prescribed by the [Secretary of State] and otherwise shall be $. . . . . . , plus in each case, if the financing statement is subject to subsection (5) of Section 9–402, $. . . . . . . The uniform fee for each name more than one required to be indexed shall be $. . . . . . . The secured party may at his option show a trade name for any person and an extra uniform indexing fee of $. . . . . . . shall be paid with respect thereto.

(6) If the debtor is a transmitting utility (subsection (5) of Section 9–401) and a filed financing statement so states, it is effective until a termination statement is filed. A real estate mortgage which is effective as a fixture filing under subsection (6) of Section 9–402 remains effective as a fixture filing until the mortgage is released or satisfied of record or its effectiveness otherwise terminates as to the real estate.

(7) When a financing statement covers timber to be cut or covers minerals or the like (including oil and gas) or accounts subject to subsection (5) of Section 9–103, or is filed as a fixture filing, [it shall be filed for record and] the filing officer shall index it under the names of the debtor and any owner of record shown on the financing statement in the same fashion as if they were the mortgagors in a mortgage of the real estate described, and, to the extent that the law of this state provides for the indexing of mortgages under the name of the mortgagee, under

the name of the secured party as if he were the mortgagee thereunder, or where indexing is by description in the same fashion as if the financing statement were a mortgage of the real estate described.

Note: *In states in which writings will not appear in the real estate records and indices unless actually recorded the bracketed language in subsection (7) should be used.*

Section 9–404. Termination Statement

(1) If a financing statement covering consumer goods is filed on or after . . . . , then within one month or within ten days following written demand by the debtor after there is no outstanding secured obligation and no commitment to make advances, incur obligations or otherwise give value, the secured party must file with each filing officer with whom the financing statement was filed, a termination statement to the effect that he no longer claims a security interest under the financing statement, which shall be identified by file number. In other cases whenever there is no outstanding secured obligation and no commitment to make advances, incur obligations or otherwise give value, the secured party must on written demand by the debtor send the debtor, for each filing officer with whom the financing statement was filed, a termination statement to the effect that he no longer claims a security interest under the financing statement, which shall be identified by file number. A termination statement signed by a person other than the secured party of record must be accompanied by a separate written statement of assignment signed by the secured party of record complying with subsection (2) of Section 9–405, including payment of the required fee. If the affected secured party fails to file such a termination statement as required by this subsection, or to send such a termination statement within ten days after proper demand therefor, he shall be liable to the debtor for one hundred dollars, and in addition for any loss caused to the debtor by such failure.

(2) On presentation to the filing officer of such a termination statement he must note it in the index. If he has received the termination statement in duplicate, he shall return one copy of the termination statement to the secured party stamped to show the time of receipt thereof. If the filing officer has a microfilm or other photographic record of the financing statement, and of any related continuation statement, statement of assignment and statement of release, he may remove the originals from the files at any time after receipt of such termination statement, or if he has no such record, he may remove them from the files at any time after one year after receipt of the termination statement.

(3) If the termination statement is in the standard form prescribed by the [Secretary of State], the uniform fee

for filing and indexing the termination statement shall be $. . . . . . . , and otherwise shall be $. . . . . . . , plus in each case an additional fee of $. . . . . for each name more than one against which the termination statement is required to be indexed.

Note: *The date to be inserted should be the effective date of the revised Article 9.*

Section 9–405. Assignment of Security Interest; Duties of Filing Officer; Fees

(1) A financing statement may disclose an assignment of a security interest in the collateral described in the financing statement by indication in the financing statement of the name and address of the assignee or by an assignment itself or a copy thereof on the face or back of the statement. On presentation to the filing officer of such a financing statement the filing officer shall mark the same as provided in Section 9–403(4). The uniform fee for filing, indexing and furnishing filing date for a financing statement so indicating as assignment shall be $. . . . . . . if the statement is in the standard form prescribed by the [Secretary of State] and otherwise shall be $. . . . . . . , plus in each case an additional fee of $. . . . . . . for each name more than one against which the financing statement is required to be indexed.

(2) A secured party may assign of record all or part of his rights under a financing statement by the filing in the place where the original financing statement was filed of a separate written statement of assignment signed by the secured party of record and setting forth the name of the secured party of record and the debtor, the file number and the date of filing of the financing statement and the name and address of the assignee and containing a description of the collateral assigned. A copy of the assignment is sufficient as a separate statement if it complies with the preceding sentence. On presentation to the filing officer of such a separate statement, the filing officer shall mark such separate statement with the date and hour of the filing. He shall note the assignment on the index of the financing statement, or in the case of a fixture filing, or a filing covering timber to be cut, or covering minerals or the like (including oil and gas) or accounts subject to subsection (5) of Section 9–103, he shall index the assignment under the name of the assignor as grantor and, to the extent that the law of this state provides for indexing the assignment of a mortgage under the name of the assignee, he shall index the assignment of the financing statement under the name of the assignee. The uniform fee for filing, indexing and furnishing filing data about such a separate statement of assignment shall be $. . . . . . . if the statement is in the standard form prescribed by the [Secretary of State] and otherwise shall

be $. . . . . . . , plus in each case an additional fee of $. . . . . . . for each name more than one against which the statement of assignment is required to be indexed. Notwithstanding the provisions of this subsection, an assignment of record of a security interest in a fixture contained in a mortgage effective as a fixture filing (subsection (6) of Section 9–402) may be made only by an assignment of the mortgage in the manner provided by law of this state other than this Act.

(3) After the disclosure or filing of an assignment under this section, the assignee is the secured party of record.

Section 9–406. Release of Collateral; Duties of Filing Officer; Fees

A secured party of record may by his signed statement release all or a part of any collateral described in a filed financing statement. The statement of release is sufficient if it contains a description of the collateral being released, the name and address of the debtor, the name and address of the secured party, and the file number of the financing statement. A statement of release signed by a person other than the secured party of record must be accompanied by a separate written statement of assignment signed by the secured party of record and complying with subsection (2) of Section 9–405, including payment of the required fee. Upon presentation of such a statement of release to the filing officer he shall mark the statement with the hour and date of filing and shall note the same upon the margin of the index of the filing of the financing statement. The uniform fee for filing and noting such a statement of release shall be $. . . . . . . if the statement is in the standard form prescribed by the [Secretary of State] and otherwise shall be $. . . . . . . , plus in each case an additional fee of $. . . . . . . for each name more than one against which the statement of release is required to be indexed.

Section 9–407. Information From Filing Officer

[(1) If the person filing any financing statement, termination statement, statement of assignment, or statement of release, furnishes the filing officer a copy thereof, the filing officer shall upon request note upon the copy the file number and date and hour of the filing of the original and deliver or send the copy to such person.]

[(2) Upon request of any person, the filing officer shall issue his certificate showing whether there is on file on the date and hour stated therein, any presently effective financing statement naming a particular debtor and any statement of assignment thereof and if there is, giving the date and hour of filing of each such statement and the names and addresses of each secured party therein. The uniform fee for such a certificate shall be

$. . . . . . . if the request for the certificate is in the standard form prescribed by the [Secretary of State] and otherwise shall be $. . . . . Upon request the filing officer shall furnish a copy of any filed financing statement or statement of assignment for a uniform fee of $. . . . . . . per page.]

Note: *This section is proposed as an optional provision to require filing officers to furnish certificates. Local law and practices should be consulted with regard to the advisability of adoption.*

Section 9–408. Financing Statements Covering Consigned or Leased Goods

A consignor or lessor of goods may file a financing statement using the terms "consignor," "consignee," "lessor," "lessee" or the like instead of the terms specified in Section 9–402. The provisions of this Part shall apply as appropriate to such a financing statement but its filing shall not of itself be a factor in determining whether or not the consignment or lease is intended as security (Section 1–201(37)). However, if it is determined for other reasons that the consignment or lease is so intended, a security interest of the consignor or lessor which attaches to the consigned or leased goods is perfected by such filing.

Part 5 Default

Section 9–501. Default; Procedures When Security Agreement Covers Both Real and Personal Property

(1) When a debtor is in default under a security agreement, a secured party has the rights and remedies provided in this Part and except as limited by subsection (3) those provided in the security agreement. He may reduce his claim to judgment, foreclose or otherwise enforce the security interest by an available judicial procedure. If the collateral is documents the secured party may proceed either as to the documents or as to the goods covered thereby. A secured party in possession has the rights, remedies and duties provided in Section 9–207. The rights and remedies referred to in this subsection are cumulative.

(2) After default, the debtor has the rights and remedies provided in this Part, those provided in the security agreement and those provided in Section 9–207.

(3) To the extent that they give rights to the debtor and impose duties on the secured party, the rules stated in the subsections referred to below may not be waived or varied except as provided with respect to compulsory disposition of collateral (subsection (3) of Section 9–504 and Section 9–505) and with respect to redemption of collateral (Section 9–506) but the parties may by agreement determine the standards by which the fulfillment of these rights and duties is to be measured if such standards are not manifestly unreasonable:

- (a) subsection (2) of Section 9–502 and subsection (2) of Section 9–504 insofar as they require accounting for surplus proceeds of collateral;
- (b) subsection (3) of Section 9–504 and subsection (1) of Section 9–505 which deal with disposition of collateral;
- (c) subsection (2) of Section 9–505 which deals with acceptance of collateral as discharge of obligation;
- (d) Section 9–506 which deals with redemption of collateral; and
- (e) subsection (1) of Section 9–507 which deals with the secured party's liability for failure to comply with this Part.

(4) If the security agreement covers both real and personal property, the secured party may proceed under this Part as to the personal property or he may proceed as to both the real and the personal property in accordance with his rights and remedies in respect of the real property in which case the provisions of this Part do not apply.

(5) When a secured party has reduced his claim to judgment the lien of any levy which may be made upon his collateral by virtue of any execution based upon the judgment shall relate back to the date of the perfection of the security interest in such collateral. A judicial sale, pursuant to such execution, is a foreclosure of the security interest by judicial procedure within the meaning of this section, and the secured party may purchase at the sale and thereafter hold the collateral free of any other requirements of this Article.

Section 9–502. Collection Rights of Secured Party

(1) When so agreed and in any event on default the secured party is entitled to notify an account debtor or the obligor on an instrument to make payment to him whether or not the assignor was theretofore making collections on the collateral, and also to take control of any proceeds to which he is entitled under Section 9–306.

(2) A secured party who by agreement is entitled to charge back uncollected collateral or otherwise to full or limited recourse against the debtor and who undertakes to collect from the account debtors or obligors must proceed in a commercially reasonable manner and may deduct his reasonable expenses of realization from the collections. If the security agreement secures an indebtedness, the secured party must account to the debtor for any surplus, and unless otherwise agreed, the debtor is liable for any deficiency. But, if the underlying transaction was a sale of accounts or chattel paper, the debtor is entitled to any surplus or is liable for any deficiency only if the security agreement so provides.

Section 9–503. Secured Party's Right to Take Possession After Default

Unless otherwise agreed a secured party has on default the right to take possession of the collateral. In taking possession a secured party may proceed without judicial process if this can be done without breach of the peace or may proceed by action. If the security agreement so provides the secured party may require the debtor to assemble the collateral and make it available to the secured party at a place to be designated by the secured party which is reasonably convenient to both parties. Without removal a secured party may render equipment unusable, and may dispose of collateral on the debtor's premises under Section 9–504.

Section 9–504. Secured Party's Right to Dispose of Collateral After Default; Effect of Disposition

(1) A secured party after default may sell, or lease or otherwise dispose of any or all of the collateral in its then condition or following any commercially reasonable preparation or processing. Any sale of goods is subject to the Article on Sales (Article 2). The proceeds of disposition shall be applied in the order following to

  (a) the reasonable expenses of retaking, holding, preparing for sale or lease, selling, leasing and the like and, to the extent provided for in the agreement and not prohibited by law, the reasonable attorney's fees and legal expenses incurred by the secured party;

  (b) the satisfaction of indebtedness secured by the security interest under which the disposition is made;

  (c) the satisfaction of indebtedness secured by any subordinate security interest in the collateral if written notification of demand therefor is received before distribution of the proceeds is completed. If requested by the secured party, the holder of a subordinate security interest must seasonably furnish reasonable proof of his interest, and unless he does so, the secured party need not comply with his demand.

(2) If the security interest secures an indebtedness, the secured party must account to the debtor for any surplus, and, unless otherwise agreed, the debtor is liable for any deficiency. But if the underlying transaction was a sale of accounts or chattel paper, the debtor is entitled to any surplus or is liable for any deficiency only if the security agreement so provides.

(3) Disposition of the collateral may be by public or private proceedings and may be made by way of one or more contracts. Sale or other disposition may be as a unit or in parcels and at any time and place and on any terms but every aspect of the disposition including the method, manner, time, place and terms must be commercially reasonable. Unless collateral is perishable or threatens to decline speedily in value or is of a type customarily sold on a recognized market, reasonable notification of the time and place of any public sale or reasonable notification of the time after which any private sale or other intended disposition is to be made shall be sent by the secured party to the debtor, if he has not signed after default a statement renouncing or modifying his right to notification of sale. In the case of consumer goods no other notification need be sent. In other cases notification shall be sent to any other secured party from whom the secured party has received (before sending his notification to the debtor or before the debtor's renunciation of his rights) written notice of a claim of an interest in the collateral. The secured party may buy at any public sale and if the collateral is of a type customarily sold in a recognized market or is of a type which is the subject of widely distributed standard price quotations he may buy at private sale.

(4) When collateral is disposed of by a secured party after default, the disposition transfers to a purchaser for value of all the debtor's rights therein, discharges the security interest under which it is made and any security interest or lien subordinate thereto. The purchaser takes free of all such rights and interests even though the secured party fails to comply with the requirements of this Part or of any judicial proceedings

  (a) in the case of a public sale, if the purchaser has no knowledge of any defects in the sale and if he does not buy in collusion with the secured party, other bidders or the person conducting the sale; or

  (b) in any other case, if the purchaser acts in good faith.

(5) A person who is liable to a secured party under a guaranty, indorsement, repurchase agreement or the like and who receives a transfer of collateral from the secured party or is subrogated to his rights has thereafter the rights and duties of the secured party. Such a transfer of collateral is not a sale or disposition of the collateral under this Article.

Section 9–505. Compulsory Disposition of Collateral; Acceptance of the Collateral as Discharge of Obligation

(1) If the debtor has paid sixty per cent of the cash price in the case of a purchase money security interest in consumer goods or sixty per cent of the loan in the case of another security interest in consumer goods, and has not signed after default a statement renouncing or modifying

his rights under this Part a secured party who has taken possession of collateral must dispose of it under Section 9–504 and if he fails to do so within ninety days after he takes possession the debtor at his option may recover in conversion or under Section 9–507(1) on secured party's liability.

(2) In any other case involving consumer goods or any other collateral a secured party in possession may, after default, propose to retain the collateral in satisfaction of the obligation. Written notice of such proposal shall be sent to the debtor if he has not signed after default a statement renouncing or modifying his rights under this subsection. In the case of consumer goods no other notice need be given. In other cases notice shall be sent to any other secured party from whom the secured party has received (before sending his notice to the debtor or before the debtor's renunciation of his rights) written notice of a claim of an interest in the collateral. If the secured party receives objection in writing from a person entitled to receive notification within twenty-one days after the notice was sent, the secured party must dispose of the collateral under Section 9–504. In the absence of such written objection the secured party may retain the collateral in satisfaction of the debtor's obligation.

Section 9–506. Debtor's Right to Redeem Collateral

At any time before the secured party has disposed of collateral or entered into a contract for its disposition under Section 9–504 or before the obligation has been discharged under Section 9–505(2) the debtor or any other secured party may unless otherwise agreed in writing after default redeem the collateral by tendering fulfillment of all obligations secured by the collateral as well as the expenses reasonably incurred by the secured party in retaking, holding and preparing the collateral for disposition, in arranging for the sale, and to the extent provided in the agreement and not prohibited by law, his reasonable attorney's fees and legal expenses.

Section 9–507. Secured Party's Liability for Failure to Comply With This Part

(1) If it is established that the secured party is not proceeding in accordance with the provisions of this Part disposition may be ordered or restrained on appropriate terms and conditions. If the disposition has occurred the debtor or any person entitled to notification or whose security interest has been made known to the secured party prior to the disposition has a right to recover from the secured party any loss caused by a failure to comply with the provisions of this Part. If the collateral is consumer goods, the debtor has a right to recover in any event an amount not less than the credit service charge plus ten per cent of the principal amount of the debt or the time price differential plus 10 per cent of the cash price.

(2) The fact that a better price could have been obtained by a sale at a different time or in a different method from that selected by the secured party is not of itself sufficient to establish that the sale was not made in a commercially reasonable manner. If the secured party either sells the collateral in the usual manner in any recognized market therefor or if he sells at the price current in such market at the time of his sale or if he has otherwise sold in conformity with reasonable commercial practices among dealers in the type of property sold he has sold in a commercially reasonable manner. The principles stated in the two preceding sentences with respect to sales also apply as may be appropriate to other types of disposition. A disposition which has been approved in any judicial proceeding or by any bona fide creditors' committee or representative of creditors shall conclusively be deemed to the commercially reasonable, but this sentence does not indicate that any such approval must be obtained in any case nor does it indicate that any disposition not so approved is not commercially reasonable.

Author's note: *Articles 10 and 11 have been omitted as unnecessary for the purposes of this text.*

Glossary

Ab initio. From the beginning.

Abandonment. An owner's voluntary relinquishment of the possession of an item of personal property, with the owner exercising no further interest or control.

Acceleration clause. Provision in a contract that shortens the time for the performance of that contract.

Adverse possession. Gaining legal ownership of real property by openly, exclusively, and continuously occupying the land for a required amount of time.

Abstract of title. A historical record of the title to a parcel of land, including all changes in the chain of title and all liens and encumbrances recorded against the parcel.

Acceptance. An offeree's manifestation of assent to the terms of an offer made to him or her by an offeror. The acceptance is the act, the oral or written assent, or in certain instances the silence that creates contractual liabilities for both the offeror and the offeree.

Accession. The acquisition of title to something because it has been added to the property one owns. For example, a tenant plants shrubs and trees on the owner's land, and the owner thus acquires title by accession.

Accommodation party. A cosigner to a credit transaction who signs without receiving any payment or value therefor, merely to help a person get credit.

Accord. A new contract which replaces another contract.

Accord and satisfaction. Two persons agree that one of them has a right of action against the other, but they accept a substitute or different act or value as performance.

Account. Any right to payment for goods sold, leased, or delivered or for services performed. Also referred to as an account receivable.

Accretion. Adding to the boundaries of property naturally by gradual deposits of silt, sand, or other solid material. For example, a river deposits sand and silt and builds up the land on its sides.

Acknowledgment. A formally signed statement (usually before a notary public) denoting the execution of a particular legal document.

Act of God. In civil law, an unforeseen accident or casualty caused strictly by the forces of nature, such as flood, drought, and hurricane.

Action. Something that is done; conduct; behavior; in legal terms, a court proceeding for the enforcement of rights.

Ad valorem. According to value.

Adjudication. The pronouncement of a judgment or a decree; a final court determination. (In bankruptcy cases, the proclaiming that a debtor is a bankrupt.)

Administrator, administratrix. In probate law, a person appointed by the court to distribute the property and belongings of the deceased where there was no will. (Administrator refers to a man; administratrix refers to a woman.)

Affiant. A person who subscribes to or makes an affidavit.

Affidavit. A printed or written statement or declaration made under oath before an authorized public official, usually a notary public.

Agency. A relationship whereby the principal authorizes another (the agent) to act for and on behalf of the principal and to bind the principal in contract.

Air rights, airspace. Ascertainment of the ownership of the airspace (sky) above one's land.

Alien. Born in one country and residing in another country without being admitted to citizenship in that country.

Alimony. An allowance granted from the husband or wife to his or her spouse, who is living separately or legally divorced. (Laws regarding alimony differ among the states.)

Allegation. The statement or declaration made in a pleading in which a party points out the facts that the party intends to prove.

Amicus curiae. A Latin phrase which means "a friend of the court." An amicus curiae would be a person with a strong interest in the case and the legal principles involved who requests permission to file a legal brief giving his or her views to the court.

Amnesty. In international law, the act of absolution for past offensive acts ("burying the hatchet").

Annuity. In insurance policies, an amount paid periodically to the insured for a specified period or until the death of the insured.

Answer. The defendant's response to plaintiff's petition or complaint.

Anticipatory breach. Before the performance time on a contract is due, one party announces that he or she will not perform his or her part of the contract, thus giving the nonbreaching party an opportunity to seek a remedy in the courts.

Apparent authority. The assumed authority or permission, not actually granted, which a principal knowingly permits an agent to possess when dealing with a third person.

Appellant. The party appealing to a higher court to overrule a decision made by a lower court.

Appellee. The party against whom an appeal is made; the respondent.

Arbitration. To settle a dispute, an appointed arbitrator (third person) comes in to help the parties make an out-of-court decision. This saves the time and expense of litigation.

Arbitrator. A third person chosen to decide a dispute between two other persons.

Articles of incorporation. A legal document submitted to a designated officer of the state for permission to commence business as a corporation. The articles of incorporation or the corporate charter state the purpose, rights, and duties of the corporation and must comply with state corporation laws.

Articles of partnership. An agreement drawn up to govern a business to be operated by a partnership. The agreement need not be filed with any state official.

Artisan's lien. A possessory claim levied on goods owned by another because of improvements made or work done thereon by the artisan. An artisan is a skilled tradesperson, such as a carpenter or a plumber.

Assignee. The person to whom an assignment is made.

Assignment. A transfer of rights (usually contract rights) from an assignor to an assignee.

Assignor. The person who makes an assignment.

Attachment. The seizure through legal process by proper legal authority, usually the sheriff, of nonexempt property of the defendant, pending a lawsuit for the collection of a debt owed by the defendant to a creditor.

Attestation. The act of witnessing the signing of a legal document.

Attractive nuisance. Any dangerous object or condition on real property which is inviting to young children and tempts them to trespass.

Auction with reserve. A sale whereby the goods sold may be withdrawn before the actual bid is accepted by the owner.

Auction without reserve. An auction sale wherein goods are sold to the highest bidder with no chance of withdrawal by the owner after the goods are placed on the auction block.

Bailee. A person who receives personal property under contract of bailment.

Bailment. The temporary transfer of possession of personal property without a change of ownership for a specific purpose and with the intent that possession will revert to the owner at a later date. Example: Owner gives his or her car to a mechanic for repairs; owner will get the car back when it has been repaired.

Bailor. A person who entrusts or bails personal property to another under a bailment arrangement.

Bankrupt. An insolvent person, one who has been declared by the court to have more debts than assets.

Bankruptcy. When a person is bankrupt, the court proceeds to have that person's nonexempt assets distributed to his or her creditors and releases him or her from further payment of past debts.

Bearer. A person in possession of a security, instrument, or document of title payable to the bearer or indorsed in blank.

Beneficiary. A person receiving proceeds from a will, insurance policy, trust, or third-party beneficiary contract.

Bilateral contract. A contract formed by the mutual exchange of promises between an offeror and an offeree.

Bilateral mistake. Both parties to a contract are in error as to the terms of the contract or the performance expected.

Bill of exchange. A written command ordering the addressee to pay on demand or at a predetermined time, a certain sum of money to the holder of the bill.

Bill of lading. A formal document issued by a carrier of goods to a shipper of goods. This document identifies the goods and states the terms of the shipping agreement.

Bill of sale. A written statement by which a seller acknowledges transfer of personal property to another.

Binder. A guarantee of temporary insurance coverage while the policy is being issued.

Blue-sky laws. State regulatory and supervisory laws governing investment companies to avoid fraudulent sales to investors in get-rich-quick schemes.

Board of directors. A specific number of persons elected by a corporation's stockholders to manage and govern the corporation on their behalf.

Bona fide. With good faith or in good faith.

Bond. With regard to corporate financing, a legal instrument which is evidence of a corporation's debt to the bondholder. The instrument obligates the corporation to pay the bondholder a fixed rate of interest on the principal amount and to pay the principal to the bondholder at a fixed maturity date.

Broker. In real property law, a person who acts as an agent and representative of others to negotiate the purchase and sale of real estate.

Bulk transfer. A sale or transfer of all or the major portion of the total inventory of materials, supplies, or merchandise or other inventory not in the ordinary course of the transferor's business.

C&F. Cost plus freight.

Cause of action. The legal grounds needed to successfully pursue a lawsuit in court.

Caveat emptor. A Latin phrase which means "let the buyer beware."

Certiorari. A Latin term which means "to be informed of." It is a writ or certification by which an appellate court orders a review of a case from a lower court. The lower court must then send a certified record of the case to the appellate court.

Chancellor. The name given in some states to the presiding judge of a court of chancery (also called a court of equity).

Chancery court. A court of equity.

Charter. A grant or certification from a state to a corporation granting the corporation the right to operate its business. In maritime law, the leasing or hiring of a vessel.

Chattel. A term used to describe tangible and movable personal property.

Chattel mortgage. A mortgage showing that another person besides the title holder has an interest (lien) on the personal property.

Chattel paper. A writing which shows that there is both a monetary obligation and a security interest in specific goods.

Check. A signed document by which a depositor to a bank orders payment of a certain sum of money to a named payee.

Chose in action. A right to personal things of which the owner does not have possession but the owner does have a right of action for their possession.

CIF. Cost, insurance, and freight.

COD. Cash on delivery.

Codicil. An addition to, or modification of a will.

Collateral. Something of value, either real or personal property, which a creditor can convert into cash to pay off a debt if the debtor fails to pay the debt. For example, you borrow money from a bank, and the bank has you pledge your household furniture as collateral.

Common carrier. A carrier which holds itself out as being for hire to the general public for the transportation of goods and passengers for compensation.

Common law. Written or unwritten laws which have evolved through custom and usage (from English common law) without written legislation.

Common stock. A class of corporate stock which is usually the voting stock in a corporation. Common stockholders have a right to dividends and assets upon dissolution second only to that of preferred stockholders, if any.

Composition agreement. An agreement whereby an insolvent debtor pays each of the creditors a portion of what he or she owes them in return for a release from them for the whole debt.

Condition. A qualifying or limiting provision or clause in a contract which must be taken into consideration by all of the parties involved.

Conditional sales contract. A contract which covers the sale of goods or real estate wherein the seller retains title until the buyer makes the payment in full; however, the buyer has possession and use while he or she makes the payments.

Consignment. The transfer of personal property from one person to another for the purpose of transportation or sale. The owner retains ownership of the property.

Consumer goods. Products primarily purchased for home or private and family use.

Consumer Product Safety Act. This act established the Consumer Product Safety Commission, which oversees the safety of consumer-oriented products.

Contract carrier. A private carrier which transports goods for an individual but not for the general public.

Conveyance. A written instrument which transfers an interest in real property, ordinarily by the execution and delivery of a deed. Personal property can also be conveyed, and this is ordinarily done by a bill of sale.

Corporate express powers. Powers specifically set out in the corporation's articles of incorporation and in statutes.

Corporate implied powers. Those powers reasonable and necessary to carry out the corporation's express powers.

Corporation. A legal entity created by authority of statutory law upon application to a proper state authority. This legal entity is an artificial person with the right to sue or be sued in its own name and to purchase, own, and sell property, real and personal, tangible and intangible.

Counterclaim. In a civil suit, the claim the defendant makes in opposition to the plaintiff's claim.

Counteroffer. A counterproposal different from an offer which an offeree makes in response to the offer. In making a counteroffer, the offeree rejects the previous offer.

Course of dealing. When two parties have previously been involved in a contract matter, their past performance may be used as a basis for interpreting ambiguities, if any, in the present contract.

Covenant. A contractual promise contained in a deed, mortgage, lease, or contract.

Creditor. A person to whom money or performance is owed.

D/b/a. Doing business as.

Damages. Monetary harm or monetary loss caused by wrongdoing that the injured person may recover in court.

De facto. A Latin phrase which means "in fact." A de facto corporation has not "in fact" complied with the laws of a state, and therefore its existence can be challenged by the state.

De jure corporation. A de jure corporation is one which has been rightfully formed in full compliance with the laws of a state.

De novo. (Latin) Starting anew.

Debtor. One who owes payment or performance.

Deceit. Fraudulent misrepresentation of facts intended to mislead or trick another, which in turn causes financial loss or harm.

Deed. A legal instrument which transfers property ownership.

Defamation. The act of intentionally injuring the character or reputation of another person.

Default. The failure to perform a legal obligation or duty.

Defendant. The person who is being sued in a legal action.

Deficiency judgment. A personal judgment against a debtor in default, where the value of the secured property was not equal to the amount of the indebtedness.

Demurrer. This is a pleading which disputes the legal sufficiency of the other party's pleading. It is also referred to as a motion to dismiss for the failure to state a legal cause of action.

Deposition. Testimony which is taken under oath and subject to cross-examination in order to discover what the witness is going to say and to ensure the preservation of the witness's testimony should the witness die or disappear or forget before the trial.

Derivative suit. An action filed by one or more stockholders of a corporation under the corporation name to enforce a corporate cause of action.

Devise. To give a gift of property by will.

Directed verdict. A verdict that the jury returns as directed by the judge.

Discharge. The termination of a contractual obligation regarding the payment of money or the performance of an act.

Disclaimer. A repudiation or denial of a claim or obligation.

Dissolution. The process by which a corporation or partnership terminates its existence.

Dividend. The portion of corporate profits which is distributed periodically to stockholders.

Document of title. A warehouse receipt, a bill of lading, or any other paper which is evidence of the holder's right to have the goods it covers.

Domestic corporation. A corporation doing business in the state where its incorporation took place.

Donee. A person who receives a gift.

Donor. A person who gives a gift.

Draft. A legal instrument wherein one person orders another person to pay a third party a sum of money.

Duress. Coercion, threat, or force which causes a person to do something he or she would not have done otherwise.

Earnest money. Money advanced on a contract by a buyer to bind a seller to his or her obligations. This money is given as an indication of good faith by the buyer and usually will be forfeited if the buyer does not perform.

Easement. The right to use the land of another for a special purpose (such as an easement to lay power lines).

Emancipation. Setting free; release. This term is used with reference to the release of a child from the care and custody of his or her parents before the child reaches the age of majority.

Eminent domain. The government's right to take over private property for public use with just compensation.

Equity. This was a court system separate from the common-law system, originating in England. Fairness and justice in the particular case were the concern of the law and the court.

Escheat. The transfer of property to the state when no heirs can be found.

Estoppel. This is a rule of law which bars, prevents, and precludes a party from alleging or denying certain facts because of a previous allegation or denial or because of his or her previous conduct or admission.

Eviction. The legal process of removing a tenant from a landlord's property.

Ex contractu. A Latin phrase which means a right arising out of a contract.

Ex delicto. A Latin phrase which refers to a right arising out of a tort.

Ex post facto law. A law passed to punish wrongdoers, which is alleged to apply to acts committed before its passage. Such laws are unconstitutional. Criminal law may only apply to acts committed after their passage.

Executor, executrix. The person named in a last will and testament to administer the estate of the deceased. *Executor* is the term used if the person is a male, and *executrix* is the term used if the person is a female.

Express authority. The authority which a principal gives to an agent either in writing or orally.

Factor. A person or a legal entity that is employed as an agent to sell goods for a principal. Usually the factor is given possession of the goods for sale and sells them in his or her own name. The factor then receives a commission on the sale.

Fair market value. The price that a willing buyer is willing to pay and that a willing seller will accept for real or personal property.

FAS. An abbreviation of the phrase "free alongside" (a boat).

Fee simple. Absolute ownership of a specific tract of real estate. This gives the owner the unconditional power to dispose of the property during his or her lifetime and to pass the absolute ownership on to his or her heirs at death.

Felony. A statutory criminal offense which is more serious than a misdemeanor. Felonies are punishable by fine or imprisonment or both, and in some situations, by death.

Fiduciary. A person who handles another person's money or property in a capacity that involves a confidence or trust. Examples of fiduciaries are executors or guardians of the estates of minors or deceased persons.

Fixture. An article of personal property which has been affixed to real property with the intent that it become a permanent part of the real property.

FOB. An abbreviation of the phrase "free on board." This phrase means that the seller or consignor of goods will place them on board a carrier such as a train or truck at a designated place with instructions to ship them through to a designated destination. The expense of the shipping and insurance for the trip are to be paid by the buyer or consignee, and thus the shipping and insurance are free to the seller or consignor.

Foreclosure. The legal process used to enforce the payment of a debt secured by a mortgage whereby the secured property is sold to satisfy the debt.

Foreign corporation. A corporation doing business in a state other than the state in which it was incorporated. *Foreign* does not mean from outside the country, only from outside the particular state.

Forensic medicine. Medical jurisprudence; the science of applying medical knowedge to the law.

Forgery. Falsely making or materially altering with criminal intent a legal document such as a check, power of attorney, or deed.

Franchise. In the public sector, a franchise is a right to operate a certain essential business which a city, county, state, or national authority grants to a private entity. For example, a city grants a bus company a franchise to be the sole bus company that can operate within the city, or it grants an electric company a franchise to be the exclusive supplier of electricity to the city. In the private sector, a franchise is a means by which one person can grant another person the right to use his or her name and business expertise on a contract basis. Examples include the various fast-food franchises.

Fraud. An intentional concealment or misrepresentation of a material fact with the intent to deceive another person, which concealment or misrepresentation causes damage to the deceived person. Such deceived persons may then sue for their damages, provided they can show that they justifiably relied upon such misrepresentation or concealment and that such reliance caused the damage.

Fungible goods. Goods that if mixed cannot be individually identified, one unit of which is equivalent to any other unit. For example, the milk from five dairy farms is pumped into a storage tank. Each farmer owns the number of gallons taken from him or her but cannot identify the specific milk that he or she contributed once it is mixed with the rest.

Future advances clause. A clause found in security agreements which permits the collateral of the debtor, if sufficiently valuable, to be used to secure future loans.

Garnishment. A legal proceeding whereby a creditor can secure the payment of a judgment against a debtor by securing a court order which requires an employer or other person having funds belonging to the debtor to pay such funds directly to the creditor.

Gift causa mortis. (Latin) A gift which is given in contemplation of death, usually with the understanding that the gift will be returned if the donor survives.

Gift inter vivos. (Latin) An irrevocable gift which is given during the donor's lifetime.

Grantee. The person to whom a conveyance of real property is made.

Grantor. The person by whom a conveyance of real property is made.

Guaranty. A promise by one person to pay some or all of the debts of another person or to answer for the performance of some act or acts by another person.

Heirs. The person designated by the intestate law of a state to inherit the estate of a deceased where the deceased left no will.

Holder in due course. As defined by the Uniform Commercial Code, a holder who takes the instrument for value, in good faith and without notice that it is overdue or has been dishonored or of any defense against or any claim to it.

Illusory. Like an illusion; something that seems to be so but really isn't so. An illusory promise appears to be a binding promise but actually promises nothing, as the choice of performance or nonperformance is really left up to the promisor.

Indemnity contract. A contract whereby one party contracts to compensate another party in case of a loss. A fire insurance contract is an indemnity contract.

Independent contractor. A person who contracts to do a specific piece of work under his own direction and control for an employer.

Indictment. A formal accusation of a crime by a grand jury.

Indorsement. The signing of one's name on a negotiable instrument such as a check or draft fot the purpose of passing title to the instrument to another person. Usually the indorsement is on the back of the instrument.

Infant. A person who has not reached the legal age of majority.

Injunction. An order of a court of equity that tells a person to do or refrain from doing some act or acts.

In pari delicto. Equally at fault, equally guilty.

In re. A Latin phrase which means "in the matter of." The phrase precedes the name of the party involved in estate and guardian's matters and other nonadversary judicial proceedings. For example: In re Estate of John Jones, Deceased.

In rem. A Latin phrase which means "against the thing."

Insolvency. A party's inability to pay his debts as they come due.

Inter alia. A Latin phrase which means "among other things."

Intestate. A term which refers to a deceased person who died without leaving a will. If a person dies and had a will, he or she died testate; if the person had no will, he or she died intestate.

Ipso facto. A Latin phrase which means "by the fact itself."

Joint tenancy. An estate owned by two or more persons recognizing the right of survivorship.

Judgment. The final determination of a court in an action or proceeding instituted in that court.

Judgment n.o.v. Judgment notwithstanding the verdict.

Jurisdiction. The power of a specific court to hear and decide certain cases.

Lease. A contract whereby an owner of real property, the landlord, agrees to give possession to the tenant, the person requesting possession, for a specific period of time in return for the payment of money or service.

Legacy. A gift made by will.

Legal entity. Also referred to as an artificial person. Legal entities include corporations, which exist by legal creation and have the right to contract and the right to own and dispose of property as well as other rights and duties of natural persons.

Levy. To seize, assess, or collect property or money.

Libel. Written or visual defamation intentionally made to injure the reputation of another.

License. Formal personal authorization to perform some act.

Lien. A claim against property. A lien can be agreed upon under contract, or it can be imposed by law. A carpenter who works on your home will have a right to a lien on your home if you do not pay the reasonable cost of his or her services.

Life estate. An interest in property only for the duration of someone's life, not transferable to an heir.

Liquidated damages. The amount of money which, according to the contract, is to be forfeited or paid as a remedy for breach of the contract.

Long arm statute. A state enactment allowing service of process on out-of-state residents who own property in the state, had an automobile accident in the state, or do business in the state.

Malpractice. Failure of a professional person such as an accountant, physician, or lawyer, to provide reasonably competent services.

Mandamus. A Latin term which means "we command." A mandamus is an order commanding that some specific act be done which a court can issue to an inferior court, a person, or a corporation.

Mechanic's lien. A workman's claim by law against property (including the land upon which a building rests) until services and materials provided are paid for.

Mens rea. Guilty mind or wrongful intent.

Minor. A person who has not yet reached the age of majority. The common-law age of majority was 21. Most states now set the age of majority for contracts at 18 but still make 21 the age of majority with regard to the drinking of intoxicating beverages.

Misdemeanors. Minor criminal offenses that usually encompass all crimes not classified as felonies or treason.

Mortgage. An interest in property, given to another as security for payment of a debt.

Necessaries. This term refers to the needs of minors, such as food, reasonable clothing, reasonable lodging, and medical attention. The reasonableness of such items as food, clothing, and lodging depends on the minor's earning level and the mode of living of the minor's parents.

Negligence. The failure to exercise reasonable care, thereby causing harm to another or to property.

No-par stock. Corporate stock to which no "par" value is assigned. Before stock is issued, the directors fix a sale price per share, but that price is not stated on the stock certificate.

Nominal damages. An award given to a party whose rights have been violated but where no actual loss or damages have occurred.

Non obstante veredicto. A Latin phrase which means "notwithstanding the verdict." It is used to indicate that the court has entered a judgement contrary to the verdict of the jury. In essence, the judge has vetoed the jury's verdict.

Notary public. An appointed public officer who has the authority to administer oaths; to attest to and certify certain legal documents; and to take and certify acknowledgments of deeds, mortgages, and other such legal documents. A notary public is limited in jurisdiction to the state where he or she is appointed and in some instances to the county where he or she resides.

Novation.   The substitution of a new obligation for a previous one with the understanding that the previous obligation has been discharged and terminated.

Nuisance.   Any activity or use of land which is offensive, obstructs use of property, or is harmful to others.

Obiter dictum.   Remarks by the court said in passing that are unrelated to the decision of that case.

Obligee.   A person to whom an obligor owes an obligation.

Obligor.   A person who owes an obligation to an obligee.

Offer.   A proposal to make a contract. It is made orally, in writing, or by other conduct, and it must contain the terms legally necessary to create a contract. Acceptance of the proposal creates the contract.

Offeree.   A person to whom an offer is made.

Offeror.   A person who makes an offer.

Option contract.   A contract to hold open an offer to buy or sell something for a certain price within a specified period of time.

Ordinances.   The term used to identify the legislative enactments of a city or municipality.

Par stock.   Shares of corporate stock that have been assigned a fixed "par value" by the articles of incorporation. The par value of one share is printed on each stock certificate.

Pari delicto.   A Latin term which means "the parties are equally at fault."

Patent.   A title of land given to an individual by the government, or an exclusive right given to an inventor to manufacture and sell an invention for a certain period of time.

Pawn.   To pledge tangible personal property as a guarantee for payment of a debt within a certain period of time or the property will be sold.

Pecuniary.   Relating to money or financial matters.

Penal damages.   A monetary penalty agreed upon in a contractual clause not as compensation for actual losses but as punishment for possible nonperformance or late performance. If in fact the agreed damage amount is a penalty and not a reasonable compensation for loss, the court will not enforce the clause.

Per curiam.   A Latin term which means "by the court." The entire court wrote the opinion, not just one justice.

Per se.   A Latin term which means "in itself; taken alone; unconnected with other matters."

Plaintiff.   A person who files a lawsuit in court.

Pledge.   Pawning or giving up the possession of an item of personal property as security for a loan. You borrow $100 from the pawnshop and leave your gold pocket watch as security.

Possession.   Occupancy or control of personal property, land, or buildings.

Power of attorney.   A writing whereby one person appoints and authorizes another person to act on his or her behalf. This power can be limited or unlimited and can be for a specified time or for life.

Preferred stock.   A class of corporate stock, usually nonvoting stock, that has rights to dividends superior to those of common stock and in case of dissolution also has rights to the assets of the corporation superior to those of common stock.

Prima facie.   A Latin phrase which means "on the face of it." For example, a valid driver's license in your possession is prima facie evidence that you have a valid right to drive; however, this evidence could be disproved by evidence that there was a court judgment to pick up and suspend your license which had not yet been served upon you.

Principal.   A person who has given an agent authority to do some act or acts for him or her.

Privity.   A close mutual relationship, such as that between parties to a contract.

Pro rata.   A Latin phrase which means "proportionately." In other words, to share equally.

Pro tem.   A Latin phrase which means "temporarily." For example, a judge pro tem might be a judge who is sitting in temporarily for the regular judge while the regular judge is on vacation.

Probate.   The term describing the legal procedure followed in the administration of the estate of deceased persons and persons under guardianship.

Promisee.   A person to whom a contractual promise is made.

Promisor.   A person who makes a contractual promise.

Promisory estoppel.   A rule of law which is often called justifiable reliance. When the promisor makes a promise and the promisee justifiably relies on that promise to his or her detriment, the promisor is estopped from denying liability on the promise.

Promoters.   Person or persons who form and organize a corporation.

Proximate cause. The act or omission to act which, in a natural and continuous sequence, unbroken by an intervening cause, produces damage or injury.

Proxy. A document which authorizes another to vote for you. Stockholders who will be absent from stockholders' meetings often give their proxy to persons who will attend the meetings.

Punitive damages. Damages awarded against a person to punish him or her. These damages are in addition to compensatory damages, which pay the plaintiff for his or her actual losses. Punitive damages are often also referred to as exemplary damages because they are awarded not only to punish but to set an example for similar wrongdoers.

Qualified acceptance. A conditional acceptance that modifies the terms of an offer; it is usually a counteroffer.

Quantum meruit. "As much as he deserved." When seeking compensation under common law for services rendered, this term will be used; it also can be interpreted as meaning the reasonable value of the services rendered.

Quasi contract. The word *quasi* means resembling or somewhat like; thus a quasi contract is not a true contract. It resembles a contract but does not possess all the elements of a legally binding contract. The law does not allow unjust enrichment, and it provides a restitutory remedy (quasi contract) that allows the person with a claim for damages to recover the reasonable value of the goods or services which he or she provided to the other party. Quasi contract is often referred to as a contract implied in law.

Quitclaim deed. A deed which is intended to pass any title or interest which the grantor has in a certain tract of real estate, but does not warrant, profess, or guarantee that the grantor had any title or interest in the real estate or that his or her title was free and clear of liens.

Quo warranto. A Latin phrase which means "by what authority." It is a legal action which a government may commence to remove a person from a public office or to dissolve a corporation.

Quorum. Both incorporated and unincorporated organizations have a governing body, and a quorum is the minimum number of persons in the governing body that have to be present at a meeting to lawfully conduct the business of an organization. The usual requirement for a quorum is a majority of the persons who are eligible to vote, but a lesser number may be agreed upon in the organization's charter or bylaws.

Ratification. The present confirmation of a previous promise or act. In the case of a former minor, ratification is the confirmation by that person once he or she has reached the age of majority of the intention to be bound by a contract which he or she had entered into as a minor. In agency law, ratification is the confirmation by a principal of a promise or act made by his or her agent which was unauthorized at the time it was made. The ratification legalizes the previously unauthorized promise or act and creates a binding contract.

Receiver. A person or a bank or other fiduciary institution appointed by the court to receive and preserve property or funds in litigation. The receiver must have no interest in the litigation and will simply hold and manage the property or funds until directed to hand them over to whomever the court awards them.

Redemption. The repurchasing or buying back of property legally taken from a person and sold. In a mortgage foreclosure, a person's land is taken and sold by the sheriff to secure money to pay the person's debt. After the sale the owner has a limited time during which he or she can redeem the property.

Referee. In bankruptcy, this is the person who is in charge of the administration of the bankrupt's estate until the bankrupt has been discharged and the estate has been distributed among the bankrupt's creditors.

Reformation. The rewriting of a contract by the court to correct ambiguities and errors so that the contract reflects the agreement of the parties.

Release. The voluntary giving up of a claim for money or property from another person, usually for consideration.

Remedy. Action taken to enforce a right or to compensate a violation of rights.

Replevin. A legal action whereby the owner of goods can legally recover them from someone who is holding them unlawfully.

Res. A Latin word which means "the thing."

Res ipsa loquitur. A Latin phrase which means "the thing speaks for itself." For example, an airplane may explode in midair. In tort law, the heirs of the deceased passengers would normally have the burden of proving negligence on the defendant. However, it is obvious that planes do not explode unless there was negligence on someone's part. Thus the plaintiff sues and pleads res ipsa loquitur, and the defendants must prove that they were not negligent.

Res judicata.   A Latin phrase which means "the thing is settled"; that is, the case is finished.

Respondeat superior.   A Latin phrase which means "let the master answer." In other words, let the employer be liable for the acts of his or her employees for damages that the employees have caused to others.

Rider.   A provision added to an insurance policy to restrict or enlarge its coverage.

Riparian.   A term which refers to the bank of a river. A riparian owner is a person who owns land on the bank of a river.

Scienter.   The knowledge of a person making a representation that the representation he or she is making is false. In a tort action for deceit, scienter must be proved.

Security agreement.   An agreement which gives a security interest in certain property to a creditor. Such an agreement must be in writing to be enforced.

Security interest.   An interest in a specific item of personal property, such as possession of the item or its title, which a creditor retains to secure the payment of a debt.

Seal.   Under common law, an identification mark impressed in wax. Today the letters "l.s." or the word "seal" itself are used and accepted.

Setoff.   A claim which a defendant has against a plaintiff; similar to a counterclaim. For example, if the plaintiff sued the defendant for $100 but owed the defendant $50, the plaintiff's $50 debt to the defendant would be a setoff and the balance owed by the defendant to the plaintiff would be only $50.

Settlor.   The term used to describe the donor in a trust document.

Severable contract.   A contract divisible into separate parts; a default of one section does not invalidate the whole contract.

Shareholder.   A person who owns a portion of the capital stock of a corporation. The shareholder's interest in the corporation is evidenced by a stock certificate.

Shop right.   The employer's right to use, without paying royalties, any invention which an employee developed while using the employer's facilities or any invention which the employee conceived in the course of the employee's employment with the employer. An employee who is hired to do research and development agrees by contract that the employer will own the em-

ployee's inventions and discoveries as that is what such an employee would be getting paid for.

Situs.   The location of a thing. All tangible property has a situs.

Slander.   Defamatory statements orally made by one person which injure the reputation of another person.

Specific performance.   A remedy by which a court of equity orders a person to perform in accordance with the terms of his or her contract.

Spendthrift trust.   A trust set up to care for an immature, incompetent, or inexperienced beneficiary. Such a trust is also intended to keep money away from a beneficiary who might use it unwisely or foolishly.

Stare decisis.   A Latin phrase which means "to abide by." This phrase is also defined as "let the decision stand." Once a case has set a precedent, courts will follow that precedent wherever it is feasible to do so. However, law must change as technology and mores change; thus no precedent is cast in concrete.

Status quo.   A Latin phrase which means "the state of things at any given time."

Statute of limitations.   A statute which sets limits to the time in which a lawsuit may be filed in certain causes of action. For example, a tort lawsuit must be filed within two years from the day the wrongful act was committed, and if it was not filed by that time, the action is forever barred.

Subpoena.   A legal process from a court ordering a witness to appear and testify or ordering a witness to produce certain documents for the court's inspection.

Subrogation.   The act of substituting one person for another to prosecute a lawful claim. In insurance, the insurance company pays the collision loss to your automobile, and you give the company subrogation rights to sue and collect from the person who negligently damaged your automobile.

Substantive law.   The law that is concerned with the rights and duties of the parties, as contrasted with procedural law, which is concerned with the procedure to be followed in the litigation.

Sui generis.   One of a kind, unique.

Summons.   A writ to appear in court in defense of a civil action.

Surety.   A person who binds himself or herself with another person, called the principal, for the payment of money or the performance of some obligation. However, the principal is already bound to that payment or obligation and the surety serves as a backup person who is available in case the principal does not pay or perform properly.

Tangible property. Property which can be touched—a tract of land, a chair, a table, etc. Intangible property, on the other hand, is property which cannot be touched, such as the ownership of a patent right or of corporate stock and other such ownerships of rights, not things.

Tenancy. The leasing or renting of land or property, giving certain ownership rights to the tenant.

Tender. An offer to settle or perform an obligation in contract. If a party offers to perform his or her obligation under a contract, such an offer is called a tender. If the other party unjustifiably refuses to accept the performance offered, that party would be guilty of breach of contract.

Testimony. Witnesses' answers given under oath as evidence.

Testate. A deceased person who died leaving a will died testate; a deceased person who died without leaving a will died intestate.

Testator. A deceased person who left a will.

Third-party beneficiary. A person who was not a party to a contract but a party to whom the contracting parties intended benefits to be given.

Torrens system. A system of land registration which was developed by Sir Robert Torrens in Australia in 1858. This system has been adopted in some jurisdictions in the United States.

Tort. A civil wrong for which civil damages may be awarded, as contrasted with a criminal wrong for which punishment may be given. A wrongful act may be both a tort and a crime.

Trade fixtures. Personal property which has been attached to land or a building and is necessary for conducting a trade.

Trade name. A name under which a particular business operates.

Trademark. A distinctive mark or emblem which a manufacturer prints on or affixes to goods so that consumers can identify the manufacturer's goods in the marketplace.

Trespass. Although most commonly used to refer to a person's unauthorized entry onto another person's real property, in its broadest sense this term refers to any intentional injury or damage caused by force to either the person or the property of another.

Trust. A transfer of property or money to one party to be held for the benefit of another.

Ultra vires. A Latin phrase which means "beyond the powers of," or beyond the scope of authority. An *ultra vires* act is an act which is not within the powers of the person who does it.

Unconscionability. Conduct by a party to a contract which cannot be shown to be fraud and is not duress but is unjust and unfair and because of which the court will not enforce performance of the contract.

Undue influence. A condition which results from the use of unfair persuasion by one person in order to overcome the free will of another person and to influence that person to act in the manner in which he or she is directed to act.

Usury. The charging of an unlawful rate of interest.

Valid. Legally sufficient and binding.

Vest. To take effect. To vest a right is to give a right to a present or future benefit. The term *vest* is used in pension law. One's rights in a pension plan will be vested after certain minimum requirements have been met.

Verdict. A jury's decision given to the court.

Void. No legal effect; not binding. If an agreement is void, it is legally unenforceable.

Voidable. A term which means that a contract is not void but can be avoided by one or both of the parties at their will. A contract between a minor and an adult is voidable by the minor only; a contract between two minors can be avoided by either minor.

Waiver. The voluntary relinquishment by a person of a right which he or she has.

Warehouse receipt. A written acknowledgment of the receipt of goods by a person engaged in the business of storing goods for hire.

Warranty. In the sale of goods, a promise or guarantee by the seller that goods have certain qualities or that the seller has title to the goods. A warranty may be offered by the seller as a contractual term, or a warranty not stated in the contract may be imposed by law. The warranties imposed by law are the warranty of merchantability and the warranty of fitness for purpose. The warranty of merchantability warrants that the goods are of at least fair or average quality. The warranty of fitness for purpose warrants that the goods are fit for the particular purpose of the buyer.

Watered stock.   Par value stock which is issued by a corporation as fully paid-up stock when in fact the whole amount of the par value has not been paid in.

Will.   A person's declaration of how his or her property is to be distributed after his or her death.

Writ.   A written document issued by a court, directed to a sheriff or some other officer of the law, and ordering that person to carry out a command of the court. For example, a writ of attachment orders a sheriff to attach certain property and hold it for disposition by the court.

Zoning.   The process of separating the areas of a city or county by confining them to particular uses, such as residential use, industrial use, or business use.

Table of Cases*

---

* Cases in capital letters are discussion cases at the ends of chapters; the other cases are located within the chapters.

Index